Applied Mathematics in Ferroelectricity and Piezoelectricity

Applied Mathematics in Ferroelectricity and Piezoelectricity

Kenji Uchino

MDPI

Basel • Beijing • Wuhan • Barcelona • Belgrade • Novi Sad • Cluj • Manchester

Author
Kenji Uchino
Pennsylvania State University
State College, PA, USA

Editorial Office
MDPI
St. Alban-Anlage 66
4052 Basel, Switzerland

For citation purposes, cite as indicated below:

Lastname, Firstname, Firstname Lastname, and Firstname Lastname. Year. *Book Title*. Series Title (optional). Basel: MDPI, Page Range.

ISBN 978-3-0365-1320-1 (Hbk)
ISBN 978-3-0365-1319-5 (PDF)
doi.org/10.3390/books978-3-0365-1319-5

Cover image courtesy of Kenji Uchino.
This research was funded by the US Office of Naval Research (ONR) Code 332 during 1991–2021 without intermission through the grants N00014-91-J-4145, 92-J-1510, 96-1-1173, 99-1-0754, 08-1-0912, 12-1-1044, 17-1-2088, and 20-1-2309. The online publication charge was supported by the International Center for Actuators and Transducers, Pennsylvania State University.

Contents

List of Symbols

D	Electric displacement
E	Electric field
P	Dielectric polarization
P_S	Spontaneous polarization
α	Ionic polarizability
γ	Lorentz factor
μ	Dipole moment
ε_0	Dielectric permittivity of free space
ε	Dielectric permittivity
ε_r	Relative permittivity or dielectric constant (assumed for ferroelectrics: $\varepsilon \approx \chi = \varepsilon - 1$)
κ	Inverse dielectric constant
χ	Dielectric susceptibility
C	Curie–Weiss constant
T_0	Curie–Weiss temperature
T_C	Curie temperature (phase transition temperature)
G	Gibbs free energy
A	Helmholtz free energy
F	Landau free energy density
x	Strain
x_S	Spontaneous strain
X	Stress
s	Elastic compliance
c	Elastic stiffness
v	Sound velocity
d	Piezoelectric charge coefficient
h	Inverse piezoelectric charge coefficient
g	Piezoelectric voltage coefficient
M, Q	Electrostrictive coefficients
k	Electromechanical coupling factor
η	Energy transmission coefficient
Y	Young's modulus
μ	Friction constant (note the same symbol as dipole moment)
$\tan\delta$ ($\tan\delta'$)	Extensive (intensive) dielectric loss
$\tan\varphi$ ($\tan\varphi'$)	Extensive (intensive) elastic loss
$\tan\theta$ ($\tan\theta'$)	Extensive (intensive) piezoelectric loss
Q	Charge, total energy per mass

About the Author

Kenji Uchino, one of the pioneers in piezoelectric actuators and energy harvesting systems, is currently Academy Professor of Emeritus Academy, was the Director of the International Center for Actuators and Transducers (ICAT) and Professor of Electrical Engineering and Materials Science and Engineering, and a Distinguished Honors Faculty at Schreyer Honors College at the Pennsylvania State University. He has been a university professor for 48 years so far, including 18 years in Japanese universities. He has also been a company executive (president or vice president) for 21 years in four companies, most recently the Founder and Senior Vice President of Micromechatronics Inc., a spin-off company from the above ICAT, where he was working to commercialize the ICAT-invented piezo-actuators, transducers and energy harvesters. He was a government officer for 7 years in both Japan and the US, and recently a "Navy Ambassador to Japan" (2010–2014) for assisting the rescue program from the Big Northern Japan Earthquake. He was teaching "Ferroelectric Devices", "Micromechatronics", "FEM Application for Smart Materials", and "Entrepreneurship for Engineers" for the Engineering and Business School graduate students using the textbooks authored by himself and titled as the same.

After being awarded his Ph. D. degree from Tokyo Institute of Technology, Japan, Uchino became Research Associate/Assistant Professor in the Physical Electronics Department in 1976 at this university. Then, he joined Sophia University, Japan, as an Associate Professor in Physics in 1985. He was then recruited to Penn State in 1991 under a strong request from the US Navy community. He was also involved with the Space Shuttle Utilizing Committee in NASDA (current JAXA, equivalent to the US NASA), Japan, during 1986-1988, and was the Vice President of NF Electronic Instruments, USA, during 1992-1994. He has his additional Master's degree in Business and Administration from St. Francis University, PA. He has been consulting with more than 138 Japanese, US, and European industries to commercialize the piezoelectric actuators and electro-optic devices. He was the Chair of Smart Actuator/Sensor Study Committee partly sponsored by the Japanese Government, MITI (1987–2014). He was also the associate editor for *Journal of Materials Technology* (Matrice Technology) and the editorial board member for *Journal of Ferroelectrics* (Gordon & Breach) and *Journal of Electroceramics* (Kluwer Academic). He is currently Editor in Chief of *Insight-Material Science* (PiscoMed Publishing) and of *Actuators* (MDPI). He also served as an Administrative Committee member for IEEE, Ultrasonics, Ferroelectrics, Frequency Control Society (1998–2000), and Secretary of American Ceramic Society, Electronics Division (2002–2003).

His research interests are in solid state physics—especially dielectrics, ferroelectrics and piezoelectrics, including basic research on materials, device designing and fabrication processes, as well as development of solid-state actuators for precision positioners, ultrasonic motors, and energy harvesting systems. He has authored 584 papers, 84 books, and 33 patents in the piezoelectric actuator and optical device area. He is Life Fellow of American Ceramic Society from 1997, Life Fellow of IEEE since 2012, Senior Member of National Academy of Inventors since 2019, and also a recipient of 34 awards, including Japan Ceramics Award from Japanese Ceramics Society (2022), the Wilhelm R. Buessem Award from the Center for Dielectrics and Piezoelectrics, The Penn State University (2019), Distinguished Lecturer of the IEEE UFFC Society (2018), International Ceramic Award from Global Academy of Ceramics (2016), IEEE-UFFC Ferroelectrics Recognition Award (2013), Inventor Award from Center for Energy Harvesting Materials and Systems, Virginia Tech (2011), Premier Research Award from The Penn State Engineering Alumni Society (2011), the Japanese Society of Applied Electromagnetics and Mechanics Award (2008), the SPIE Smart Product Implementation Award (2007), R&D 100 Award (2007), ASME Adaptive Structures Prize (2005), Outstanding Research Award from Penn State Engineering Society (1996), and Best Paper Award from Japanese Society of Oil/Air Pressure Control (1987).

In addition to his academic carrier, Uchino is an honorary member of KERAMOS (National Professional Ceramic Engineering Fraternity) and obtained the Best Movie Memorial Award as the director/producer in the Japan Scientific Movie Festival (1989) on several educational video tapes on "Dynamical Optical Observation of Ferroelectric Domains" and "Ceramic Actuators".

Preface

The author has been teaching three graduate courses, "Ferroelectric Devices" (Materials science and engineering-oriented), "Micromechatronics" (Electrical and mechanical engineering-oriented), and "Application of Finite Element Method" (Design engineering with computer simulation) regularly over 46 years.

As ferroelectric device development is really an interdisciplinary area between physics, electrical, and mechanical engineering, my courses are open to any department students without setting particular "prerequisite courses" in the curriculum. However, in order to teach the course materials smoothly, I set a "Prerequisite Knowledge Check", which examines the students' basic physics knowledge (high school and freshmen-level), covering physics, electrical, and mechanical engineering. Refer to "Prerequisite Knowledge Check" on page xiv after List of Contents. This quiz (exactly the same over 30 years) is conducted on the first class-day, is evaluated, and the teaching level is changed every year. The figure below plotted the average score (among 10 in total) change with year on Prerequisite Knowledge Check for the "Micromechatronics" course. In the 1990s and early 2000s, the average score was constantly 70–80%. However, in the middle of the 2000s, the average score decreased year-by-year, and most recently, it is around only 30–40%; there was significant reduction of basic engineering knowledge during 2005–2015. Note that since the National Ranking of the Penn State University has not been dropped significantly in these 10 years, this may not be related to the student-quality degradation of the Penn State University. Rather, the author believes the basic knowledge degradation in the graduate students seems to be a general tendency due to the generation difference in the educational principle. The author points out that the "turning point" of the average score in the middle of 2000s coincides with the "Google Search Engine" starting time.

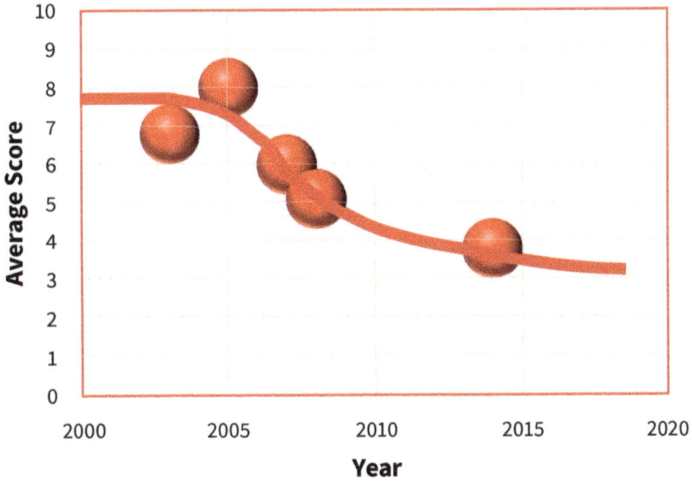

In the Pre-"Google" age, we analyzed and calculated the physical model by ourselves, and checked the correctness from the published papers (if any) in the library. After finishing the experiment and summarizing our results, we used to approach the published papers in order to find whether our result is reasonable, or is explainable by some theories. On the contrary, the "Google" generation takes a rather different approach. When the author indicates the need to research something new, many of my current Ph. D. graduate students take the following research steps: (1) searching the recent research papers on the indicated topics on "Google", (2) summarizing the results, picking up the unstudied parts by believing the published results are correct, (3) setting the research plan for himself/herself. Recently, even the reader's professor ("Google generation") may order you to "search the recent published papers on the indicated topics" as your first job task. Actually, the author's generation is disappointed with the current students' lack of skills or capabilities on various fundamental mathematical skills, such as linear differential equations, linear algebra (tensor/matrix), or even unit exchange of simple calculations between [cgs], [MKS], and [inch-pound] units. As there are many pieces of computer software available on these analyses and calculations, the students are reluctant to remember the basic knowledge and mathematical skills.

When the author started to write research papers on the "piezoelectric actuators" in the early 1980s, most of my papers cited the previous studies from my own publications, because I was one of the pioneers in this area, leading to less references to be cited, and my distrustful eyes on the other researchers' data and analyses. Thus, I usually received strong criticisms from the reviewers on this self-citation issue. On the contrary, many of the present publications include plenty of reference studies from the "Google" search engine ("more than a half of the citations should be from the other research groups" seems to be a sort of the journal "acceptance" criterion), and the author's argument seems to be based on the belief on the previous studies, seeking for "undone" research topics without repeating the same topic from a different angle to find different results. The "Google" generation seems to be intoxicated by big research data, including lots of "misleading" research content.

I have authored "Ferroelectric Devices 2nd Edition (2010)", "Micromechatronics 2nd Edition (2019)", "FEM and Micromechatronics with ATILA Software (2008)", all published by CRC Press, being used for my regular three teaching courses under the same course titles. However, in the last 10 years, due to the lack of "Prerequisite Knowledge", the students cannot digest the above textbooks completely. My purpose of authoring this textbook, "Applied Mathematics in Ferroelectricity and Piezoelectricity", is to provide the reader a solid mathematical background for studying ferroelectricity and piezoelectricity, in order to stop the above "Google

Syndrome" (i.e., just relying on the internet information), and to cultivate the reader's mathematical skills. This book is a sort of "open access supplemental" book to be used in parallel to the above textbooks, or to strengthen your analytical and theoretical skills in the field of ferroelectricity and piezoelectricity.

Let me introduce the contents. Chapter 1 introduces the "Background", including an "overview of ferroelectrics" for the reader, who is not familiar with ferroelectricity and piezoelectricity. The advanced reader can skip this fundamental explanation. Based on the Taylor expansion approach, Chapter 2, "Linear Coupling in Ferroelectrics", introduces piezothermal and electrothermal couplings, in addition to the piezoelectric coupling effect in detail. Most of the physical parameters in piezoelectrics, such as elastic constant and permittivity, are dependent on the constraint conditions (stress and electric constraint). Chapter 3, "Tensor/ Matrix Description in Piezoelectricity", describes how to generate a physical parameter tensor/matrix in a certain crystal symmetry using transformation matrix, an advanced technique in linear algebraic equations. Chapter 4, "Nonlinear Phenomenology", demonstrates Landau and Devonshire phase transition theories based on the higher-order Taylor expansion series, detailing the electromechanical coupling terms. The phenomenology of antiferroelectrics and of solid solution among ferro- and antiferroelectrics are also introduced, including how to integrate the sublattice coupling terms. "Time-dependent phenomenology" is discussed in Chapters 5, "Relaxation Phenomena", where the recovery speed to the equilibrium status is the focus. Dielectric relaxation models are also learned. Chapter 6 covers "Losses in Piezoelectrics", where we introduce a "complex number" for handling "viscous damping", in addition to "solid" and "Coulomb (friction) damping". "Bode plot" (gain, phase) is introduced from the engineering viewpoint. "Intensive and extensive loss" difference is also the key in understanding the piezoelectricity. Chapter 7, "AC Drive on Piezoelectrics", is one of this book's highlights, in which we discuss both electrical and mechanical drive methods on piezoelectric resonance and antiresonance modes, using the Fourier transform method. Various vibration modes are introduced, including k_{31}, k_{33}, disk, and bimorph design specimens. The vibration mode difference between the resonance (zero impedance), antiresonance (zero admittance), and the intermediate mode (under matched impedance) is also described. To the contrary, "Pulse Drive on Piezoelectrics" in Chapter 8 describes the Laplace transform method, which exhibits interesting triangular displacement vibrations. The difference of the vibration analysis is pointed out among a continuum piezoelectric specimen and a discrete mass-spring model (i.e., equivalent circuit). Based on the discussion in Chapter 7, "Equivalent Circuit" is introduced in Chapter 9. The piezoelectric performance can be simulated by using simple LCR circuit. Chapter 10, "Impedance Matching", discusses both electrical and mechanical impedance matching in order to enhance the efficiency in the system. Chapter 11, "Lattice Vibration", discusses linear "harmonic" lattice vibration in terms of linear differential equations in periodic phenomena. Specific heat can be derived from the harmonic model. Nonlinear atomic spring and anharmonic phonon are slightly introduced in the latter part, since ferroelectricity occurrence originates from the phonon–phonon interaction. Extending the phonon discussion, Chapter 12, "Heat Conduction", describes another category of linear differential equation, that is, the "diffusion equation". Secondary electrothermal coupling factor is introduced on this non-equilibrium phenomenon. Thermal analysis on DC- and AC-driven piezoelectric transducers is also detailed. Chapter 13 is devoted to "Electro-optic Effect", where the derivation processes of necessary complicated physical formulae are explained. This chapter provides the basic knowledge in understanding the optical beam control. Finally, Chapter 14, "Nonlinear Oscillatory System", considers the mechanism of piezoelectric inertial motors based on friction (i.e., stick–slick action) and chaotic oscillation under nonlinear recovery force. Though there are multiple computer software just for receiving the solutions, the author's intention is to provide the manual calculation methods for deep understanding. Additionally, further discussions on the lattice vibration under "anharmonic" potential, which leads to thermal expansion, electrostriction, and phonon transfer/heat conductivity, are made to supplement the contents in Chapters 11 and 12.

This textbook was written for undergraduates, graduate students, university researchers, and industry engineers studying or working in the fields of "ferroelectricity and piezoelectricity". Since this textbook is designed for self-learning by the reader by himself/herself, professors in other areas, such as piezo-MEMS or energy harvesting, who may not have strong physical and mathematical backgrounds in ferroelectrics and piezoelectrics, are also very welcome to learn the mathematical skills introduced in this book. Self-learning is possible, aided by the availability of:

- Chapter Essentials;
- Check Points [Quick Answer in this book Appendix];
- Example Problems ["Solution" provided successively];
- Chapter Problems ["Hint" available successively].

The author strongly desires that the reader will be released from the "Google" syndrome, and be a "Post-Google" generation, with your strong research philosophy based on the mathematical/physical fundament concepts. Since this is the first edition, critical review and content/typo corrections on this book are highly appreciated. Send the information to Kenji Uchino at The Pennsylvania State University, University Park, PA 16802-4800. E-mail: KenjiUchino@psu.edu.

I am indebted to the continuous research fund from the US Office of Naval Research Code 332 during 1991–2021 without intermission through the grants N00014-91-J-4145, 92-J-1510, 96-1-1173, 99-1-0754, 08-1-0912, 12-1-1044, 17-1-2088, and 20-1-2309. Finally, I would like to show appreciation for my former colleagues, Post Docs, Ph. D., and MS students over these last 46 years; in particular, my greatest appreciation goes to my wife, Michiko, who constantly encourages me in my activities.

Kenji Uchino

Kenji Uchino, MS, MBA, Ph. D.
March 2021 at State College, PA

(Photo taken 12/17/2020)

Acknowledgements

The author is indebted to the continuous research fund from the US Office of Naval Research, Code 332, without interuption from 1991 to 2021, via the grants N00014-91-J-4145, 92-J-1510, 96-1-1173, 99-1-0754, 08-1-0912, 12-1-1044, 17-1-2088, and 20-1-2309. I would also like to show appreciation for my former colleagues, including post doctorates, and Ph.D. and MS students over these last 46 years. Finally, I would particularly like to thank my wife, Michiko, who constantly encourages me in my activities.

Prerequisite Knowledge Check

Studying "ferroelectricity and piezoelectricity" assumes certain basic knowledge. Answer the following questions by yourself prior to referring to the answers on the next page.

Q1 Provide definitions for the *elastic stiffness*, c, and *elastic compliance*, s, using stress (X)—strain (x) equations.

Q2 Sketch a *shear stress* (X_4) by arrows and the corresponding *shear strain* (x_4)/*deformation* on the square material depicted below.

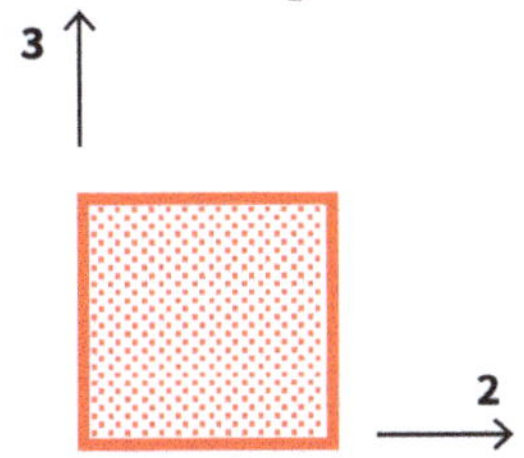

Q3 Describe an equation for the *velocity of sound*, v, in a material with mass density, ρ, and elastic compliance, s.

Q4 Given a rod of length, L, made of a material through which sound travels with a velocity, v, describe an equation for the *fundamental extensional resonance frequency*, f_R.

Q5 When two solid materials are brought into contact and moved along the contact plane, friction force is introduced. How do you describe the friction force F in terms of the force N normal to the contact plane and the friction constant μ?

Q6 Provide the capacitance, C, of a capacitor with area, A, and electrode gap, t, filled with a material of *relative permittivity*, ε_r.

Q7 Describe an equation for the *resonance frequency* of the circuit pictured below:

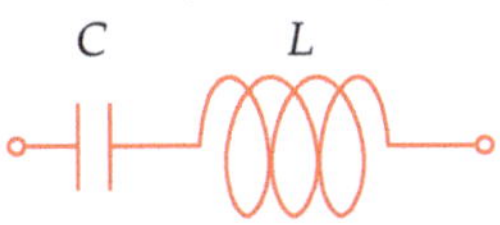

Q8 Given a power supply with an internal impedance, Z_0, what is the optimum circuit impedance, Z_1, required for maximum power transfer?

Q9 Calculate the polarization P of a material with dipole density N (m^{-3}) of the unit cell dipole moment $q \cdot u$ (C·m). Provide a correct unit for P.

Q10 Provide the polarization, P, induced in a *piezoelectric* with a piezoelectric strain coefficient, d, when it is subjected to an external stress, X.

Answers: [70% or better score is expected.]

Q1 $X = cx$, $x = sX$

[Note: c stands for "stiffness" and s stands for "compliance".]

Q2 $x_4 = 2x_{23} = 2\phi$

[Note: A pair of anti-parallel forces creates X_{23} or X_{32}. Radian measure is generally preferred for the angle ϕ unit or strain. This shear stress is not directly equivalent to the diagonal extensional stress.]

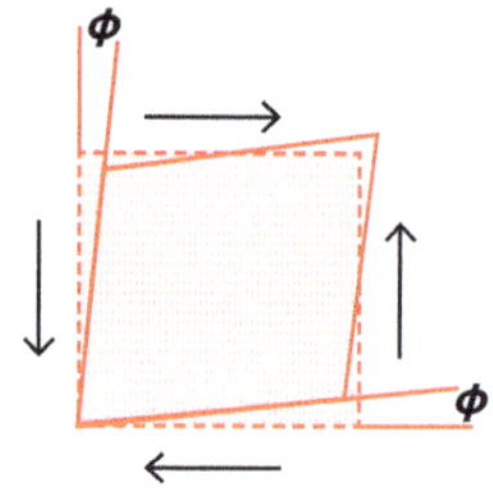

Q3 $v = \frac{1}{\sqrt{\rho s}}$

Q4 $f = v/2L$

Q5 $F = \mu \cdot N$

Q6 $C = \varepsilon_0 \varepsilon_r (A/t)$

Q7 $f = 1/2\pi\sqrt{LC}$

Q8 $Z_1 = Z_0$ or $Z_1 = Z_0^*$

[Note: The current and voltage associated with Z_1 are $V/(Z_0 + Z_1)$ and $[Z_1/(Z_0 + Z_1)]V$, respectively, the product of which yields the power. The maximum power transfer occurs when $Z_0/\sqrt{Z_1} = \sqrt{Z_1}$ when impedance is resistive. When the impedance is complex, $Z_1 = Z_0^*$].

Q9 $P = Nqu$ [C/m^2]

[Note: The unit of the polarization is given by C/m^2, equivalent to the charge density on the surface.]

Q10 $P = dX$

[Note: This is called the *direct piezoelectric effect*.]

1. Background

1.1. Background of This Book

This textbook, *Applied Mathematics in Ferroelectricity and Piezoelectricity*, was authored to provide the reader solid mathematical background for studying "ferroelectricity and piezoelectricity", as an open access supplement to my three course books: *Ferroelectric Devices 2nd Edition* (2010), *Micromechatronics 2nd Edition* (2019), and *FEM and Micromechatronics with ATILA Software* (2008), all published by CRC Press.

"Physics" prefers "simplicity"; converting a complicated phenomenon expressed by a function $f(x, y, \cdots)$ into a Taylor expansion form $f \approx f(0, 0, \cdots) + a_1 x + b_1 y + \cdots + a_2 x^2 + b_2 y^2 + c_2 xy + \cdots$ (nonlinear handling), or a 1D to 3D analytical extension with linear algebraic equations (tensor/matrix), is a typical model simplification. FEM (finite element method) computer software is popularly utilized to solve practical piezoelectric vibrations, but without simply adopting computer simulation, analytical formulae for a simplified model sometimes provide us with a much easier intuitive idea. Having a solid problem-solving mathematical skill renders the development of new devices significantly easier from the author's experience. The author attempted to cover most of the necessary "applied mathematics" for learning the areas of ferroelectricity and piezoelectricity much more deeply.

1.2. Overview of Ferroelectrics

We start with a brief overview of ferroelectrics for the reader who is not very familiar with ferroelectricity and piezoelectricity. You can refresh your current fundamental knowledge through this section.

Applications of "ferroelectrics" can be found in various devices such as high-permittivity dielectric capacitors, ferroelectric memories, pyroelectric sensors, piezoelectric devices, electro-optic devices, and PTCR (positive temperature coefficient of resistivity) components. However, historically, with the existence of competitive materials, ferroelectric devices often failed to be commercialized. In photo-sensors, for example, semiconductive materials are superior to ferroelectrics in terms of response speed and sensitivity. Magnetic devices and flash memories are much more popular in the memory field, and liquid crystals (LCD) and light-emitting diodes (LED) are typically used for optical displays. The commercialization failure was related to a lack of systematic and comprehensive accumulation of knowledge on ferroelectricity, though we can recognize recent success in specific areas such as pyroelectric cameras and ferroelectric memories.

This section covers the theoretical background of ferroelectric devices, before focusing on practical materials and typical applications, including (1) crystal structures and ferroelectricity, (2) the origin of spontaneous polarization, (3) the origin of field-induced strain, (4) piezoelectric constitutive equations, (5) ferroelectric materials, and (6) applications of ferroelectrics. This section is based on my textbook, *Ferroelectric Devices 2nd Edition* [1].

1.2.1. Smart Materials

Ferroelectrics belong to "smart materials". What is the definition of the "smartness" of a material? Various effects relating the input (electric field, magnetic field, stress, heat, and light) to the output (charge/current, magnetization, strain, temperature, and light) are summarized in Table 1.1. The input, voltage or stress, generates a current or strain output ("electrical conductor" and "elastic" materials, which are sometimes called "trivial" materials), relating to well-known phenomena such as Ohm's and Hooke's laws. On the other hand, "pyroelectric" and "piezoelectric" materials, which generate an electric field with the input of heat and stress (unexpected phenomena!), respectively, are called "smart" materials. These off-diagonal couplings have corresponding converse effects, namely, "electrocaloric" and "converse piezoelectric" effects, and both "sensing" and "actuating" functions can be realized in the same materials. Because ferroelectric materials exhibit most of these effects (with the exception of the magnetic phenomena), ferroelectrics are said to be very "smart" materials.

Table 1.1. Various effects in materials.

Input —>	Material Device	—> Output

Input	Output				
	Change Current	**Magnetization**	**Strain**	**Temperature**	**Light**
Electric Field	Permittivity Conductivity	Electric–magnetic effect	Converse piezo-effect	Electric caloric effect	Electro-optic effect
Magnetic Field	Magnetic–electric effect	Permeability	Magnetostriction	Magnetic caloric effect	Magneto-optic effect
Stress	Piezoelectric effect	Piezomagnetic effect	Elastic constant	Mechano-thermal effect	Photoelastic effect
Heat	Pyroelectric effect	Pyromagnetic effect	Thermal expansion	Specific heat	Thermal radiation
Light	Photovoltaic effect	Photomagnetic effect	Photostriction	Photothermal effect	Refractive index

Diagonal Coupling
Sensor
Actuator

Source: Table by author, adapted from [1].

1.2.2. Crystal Structure and Ferroelectricity

So-called "dielectric" materials are electrically resistive, the constituent atoms of which are considered to be ionized to a certain degree and are either positively or negatively charged. In such ionic (or covalent in polymers) crystals, when an electric field is applied, cations are attracted to the cathode direction and anions to the anode due to electrostatic interaction. The electron clouds also deform, causing "electric dipoles". This phenomenon is known as "electric polarization" of the dielectric, and the polarization is expressed quantitatively as the sum of the electric dipoles per unit volume [C/m^2]. Figure 1.1 schematically shows the origin of electric polarization. There are three primary contributions: "electronic", "ionic", and "dipole reorientation-related". The degree to which each mechanism contributes to the overall polarization of the material depends on the frequency of the applied field. "Electronic polarization" can follow alternating fields with frequencies up to THz–PHz (10^{12}–10^{15} cycles/second, higher than "visible light waves"), while "ionic polarization" responds up to GHz–THz (10^9–10^{12} cycles/second, microwave region). Thus, you should understand that the famous relation between the relative permittivity ε and refractive index n, i.e.,

$$\varepsilon = n^2, \tag{1.1}$$

is only valid when the applied electric field has a frequency on the order of THz or higher. On the contrary, "permanent dipole reorientation" can follow only up to MHz–GHz (10^6–10^9 cycles/second). Water is boiled by a 100 MHz microwave oven. This is why ferroelectric materials with permanent dipoles cannot be used as microwave dielectric materials; their permittivity, which is typically high at low frequencies (kHz), decreases drastically with an increasing applied electric field frequency. The frequency dependence of the total polarizability (or permittivity) is depicted in Figure 1.2.

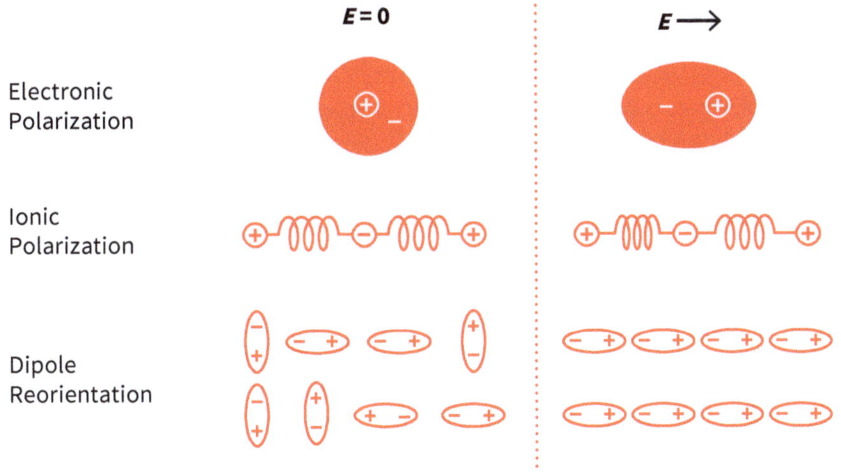

Figure 1.1. Microscopic origins of electric polarization. Source: [1] ©Uchino, K. *Ferroelectric Devices*, 2nd ed. CRC Press, 2010; p. 2. Reproduced by permission of Taylor & Francis Group.

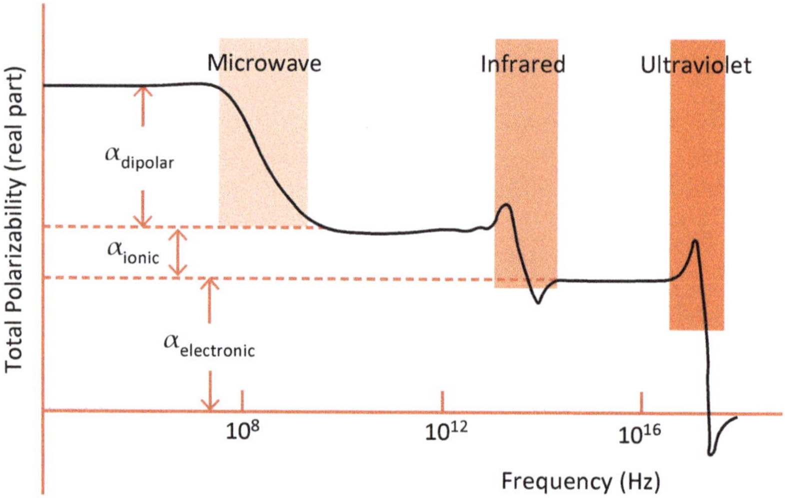

Figure 1.2. Frequency dependence of polarizability (or permittivity). Source: [1] ©Uchino, K. *Ferroelectric Devices*, 2nd ed. CRC Press, 2010; p. 3. Reproduced by permission of Taylor & Francis Group.

In comparison with air-filled capacitors, Figure 1.3 shows the charge storage mechanism in a dielectric capacitor, where there is a greater charge due to the dielectric polarization P. The physical quantity corresponding to the stored electric charge per unit area is called the "electric displacement" D and is related to the electric field E as follows:

$$D = \varepsilon_0 E + P = \varepsilon \varepsilon_0 E. \tag{1.2}$$

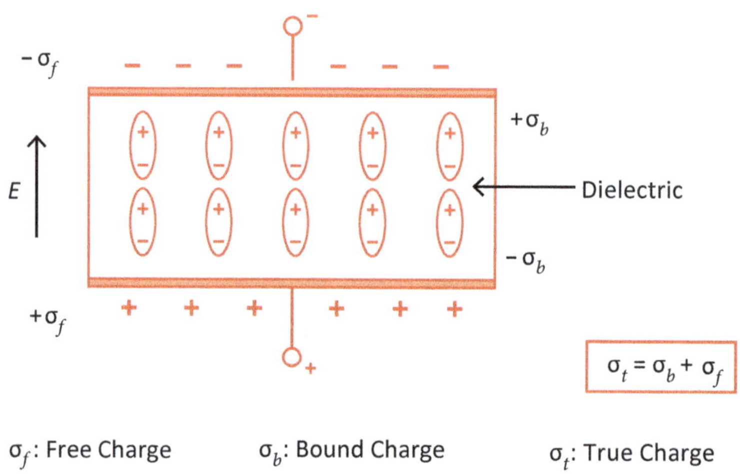

Figure 1.3. Charge accumulation in a dielectric capacitor. Source: [1] ©Uchino, K. *Ferroelectric Devices*, 2nd ed. CRC Press, 2010; p. 3. Reproduced by permission of Taylor & Francis Group.

Here, ε_0 is the vacuum permittivity (=8.854 $\times$ 10^{-12} F/m) and ε is the "relative permittivity" of the material (also simply called the permittivity or "dielectric constant", functioning as a tensor property) (discussed in Chapter 3).

Depending on the crystal structure, the centers of the positive and negative charges may not coincide, even without the application of an external electric field. We say such crystals possess a "spontaneous polarization" (or "pyroelectric"). When the spontaneous polarization of a dielectric can be reversed under an electric field, it is called a "ferroelectric".

Not every dielectric is a ferroelectric. Crystals can be classified into 32 "point groups" according to their crystallographic symmetry, and these point groups can be classified into two groups initially: one with a center of symmetry, and another without, as summarized in Table 1.2. There are 21-point groups which do not possess a center of symmetry. In crystals belonging to 20 of these point groups (the sole exception being point group (432)), positive and negative charges are generated on the crystal surfaces when appropriate stresses are applied. These materials are known as "piezoelectrics" (discussed in Chapter 2).

Table 1.2. Crystallographic classification according to crystal centrosymmetry and polarity.

Polarity	Symmetry	Crystal System										
		Cubic		Hexagonal		Tetragonal		Rhombohedral		Orthorhombic	Monoclinic	Triclinic
Nonpolar (22)	Centro (11)	$m3m$		$6/mmm$	$6/m$	$4/mmm$	$4/m$	$\bar{3}m$	$\bar{3}$	mmm	$2/m$	$\bar{1}$
	Noncentro (21)	432 $\bar{4}3m$	23	622 $\bar{6}m2$	$\bar{6}$	422 $\bar{4}2m$	$\bar{4}$	32		222		
Polar (Pyroelectric) (10)				$6mm$	6	$4mm$	4	$3m$	3	$mm2$	$2m$	1

Note: In the orange fields are piezoelectrics. Source: Table by author, adapted from [1].

"Pyroelectricity" is the phenomenon whereby, as the temperature of the crystal is changed, electric charges corresponding to the change in the spontaneous polarization with temperature appear on the surface of the crystal. Among pyroelectric crystals, if the spontaneous polarization can be reversed by an external electric field (not exceeding the breakdown limit of the crystal), they are called "ferroelectrics". Thus, there is some experimental ambiguity in this definition: in establishing "ferroelectricity", it is necessary to apply an electric field to a pyroelectric material and experimentally ascertain the polarization reversal.

1.2.3. Origin of Spontaneous Polarization

We consider a mechanism for why the polarization is generated spontaneously with a decreasing temperature from a high temperature-stable, nonpolar, symmetric crystal structure: that is, the spontaneous shifting of cations and anions. For simplicity, let us assume that dipole moments result from the displacement of one type of ion, A (electric charge q), relative to the crystal lattice. Consider the case in which the polarization is caused by all the A ions being displaced equally in a lattice. This type of ionic displacement can be expected through lattice vibrations at a finite temperature. Figure 1.4 depicts some of the possible "eigen lattice vibrations" in a perovskite-like crystal. The center solid black circles may correspond to B ions of ABO_3. Figure 1.4a shows an initial cubic (symmetrical) structure, Figure 1.4b shows a symmetrically elongated structure (i.e., no polarization is generated), Figure 1.4c shows coherently shifted center cations (i.e., rightward polarization), and Figure 1.4d exhibits a zig-zag (antipolarized) shift of the center cations (i.e., no net polarization). If one particular lattice vibration lowers the crystal energy, the ions will shift and stabilize the crystal structure so as to minimize the energy. Starting with the original cubic structure (a), if (b) is stabilized, only oxygen octahedra are distorted without generating dipole moments ("acoustic mode"). On the other hand, when (c) or (d) is stabilized, dipole moments are generated ("optical mode"). Since the light wave preferably interacts with these dipole vibrations, these vibration modes are called "optical modes". The final stabilized states (c) and (d) correspond to "polar/ferroelectric" and "antipolar/antiferroelectric" states, respectively. If these particular modes become stabilized, with a decreasing temperature, the vibration mode frequency decreases (i.e., "soft phonon mode"), and, finally, at a certain phase transition temperature, this frequency approaches zero. Refer to Section 11.2 for a detailed discussion.

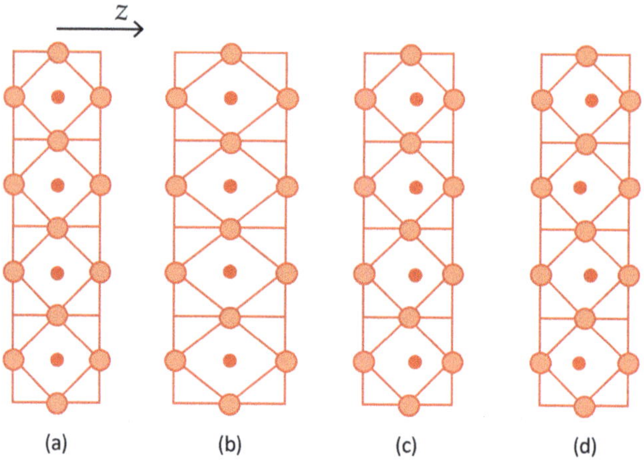

Figure 1.4. Some eigen lattice vibration modes in a perovskite: (**a**) initial cubic; (**b**) elongated structure with no polarization; (**c**) polar structure; (**d**) antipolar structure. Source: [1] ©Uchino, K. *Ferroelectric Devices*, 2nd ed. CRC Press, 2010; p. 4. Reproduced by permission of Taylor & Francis Group.

Further, what type of energy motivates the dipole generation in a crystal? It follows that, at any individual A ion site, there exists a local field from the surrounding polarization P, even if there is no external field. The concept of the "local field" is illustrated schematically in Figure 1.5. It can be found that

$$\boldsymbol{E}^{loc} = \boldsymbol{E}_0 + \sum_i [3(\boldsymbol{p}_i \cdot \boldsymbol{r}_i)\boldsymbol{r}_i - r_i^2 \boldsymbol{p}_i]/4\pi\varepsilon_0 r_i^5 = (\gamma/3\varepsilon_0)\boldsymbol{P}. \quad (1.3)$$

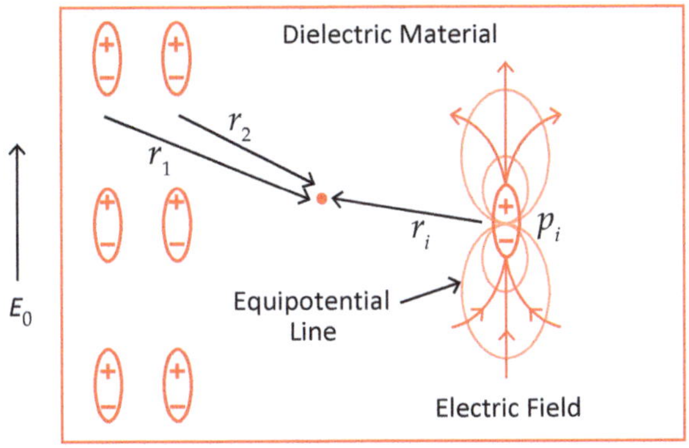

Figure 1.5. Concept of the local field. E^{loc} is given by $\boldsymbol{E}^{loc} = \boldsymbol{E}_0 + \sum_i [3(p_i \cdot r_i)\boldsymbol{r}_i - r_i^2 \boldsymbol{p}_i]/4\pi\varepsilon_0 {r_i}^5$. Source: Figure by author.

Example Problem 1.1 provides the derivation process of the above formula. This local field is the driving force for the ion shift. Here, γ is called the "Lorentz factor". For an isotropic cubic system, it is known that $\gamma = 1$, but in some crystals, $\gamma = 10$ (significantly large) [2]. Section 11.3.3 describes the γ derivation process. ε_0 is the vacuum permittivity and is equal to 8.854×10^{-12} F/m. Though the electric field from the dipole moment diminishes rather quickly with an increasing distance r ($\propto 1/r^3$), since there are so many dipoles in a condensed material as the Avogadro number is 6.022×10^{23} mol^{-1}, the local field E^{loc} is much larger than the externally applied field E_0, particularly in anisotropic crystal structures. If the "ionic polarizability" of ion A is α, then the dipole moment of the unit cell of this crystal is

$$\mu = (\alpha\gamma/3\varepsilon_0)\boldsymbol{P}. \tag{1.4}$$

The energy of this dipole moment ("dipole–dipole coupling") is given by

$$w_{dip} = -\mu \boldsymbol{E}^{loc} = -(\alpha\gamma^2/9{\varepsilon_0}^2)P^2. \tag{1.5}$$

We can understand that the mechanism seems to be a type of "positive feedback"; that is, once a small fluctuation in P occurs in a crystal, which enhances the local field E^{loc} by a factor of γ, the dipole–dipole coupling energy w_{dip} decreases by a factor of γ squared. In other words, the polarized state becomes stabilized with an increase in P. Defining N to be the number of atoms per unit volume, the dipole–dipole coupling energy per unit volume is expressed as

$$W_{dip} = N w_{dip} = -(N\alpha\gamma^2/9{\varepsilon_0}^2)\boldsymbol{P}^2. \tag{1.6}$$

On the other hand, when the A ions are displaced from their nonpolar equilibrium positions, the elastic energy also increases, which stops the cation–anion ionic separation. If the displacement is u, and the force constants are k and k', then the increase in the elastic energy per unit volume can be expressed as

$$W_{elas} = N[(k/2)\boldsymbol{u}^2 + (k'/4)\boldsymbol{u}^4]. \tag{1.7}$$

Here, k' (>0) is the higher-order force constant. It should be noted that in pyroelectrics (i.e., polar status), k' plays an important role in determining the magnitude of the dipole moment. Rewriting Equation (1.7) with

$$\boldsymbol{P} = Nq\boldsymbol{u}, \tag{1.8}$$

where q is the electric charge, and combining it with Equation (1.6), the total energy can be expressed as follows:

$$W_{tot} = W_{dip} + W_{elas} = [(k/2Nq^2) - (N\alpha\gamma^2/9\varepsilon_0{}^2)]\boldsymbol{P}^2 + [k'/4N^3q^4]\boldsymbol{P}^4. \tag{1.9}$$

See Figure 1.6. We can understand that if the coefficient of the harmonic term $(k/2Nq^2)$ of the elastic energy is equal to or greater than the coefficient of the dipole–dipole coupling $(N\alpha\gamma^2/9\varepsilon_0{}^2)$, then $P = 0$; the A ions are stable and remain at the nonpolar equilibrium positions. However, if $[(k/2Nq^2) - (N\alpha\gamma^2/9\varepsilon_0{}^2)] < 0$, a more stable state can be found with a shift from the equilibrium position (by solving $\frac{\partial W_{tot}}{\partial P} = 0$):

$$\boldsymbol{P}_S{}^2 = [(2N\alpha\gamma^2/9\varepsilon_0{}^2) - (k/Nq^2)]/[k'/N^3q^4]. \tag{1.10}$$

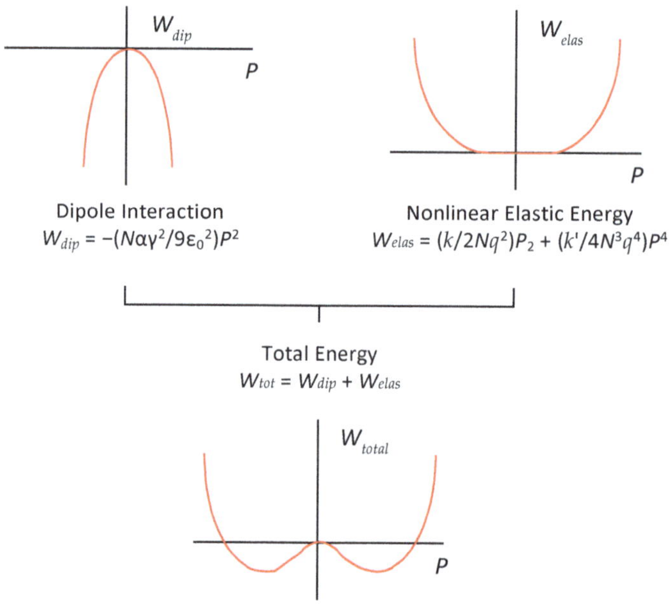

Figure 1.6. Energy explanation of the origin of spontaneous polarization. Source: Figure by author, adapted from [1].

Spontaneous polarization can occur more easily in the perovskite-type crystal structure (e.g., barium titanate) due to the higher value of the Lorentz factor γ (=10) [3] than found for other crystal structures, because the dipole–dipole coupling energy is 100 times higher than that of normal dielectrics (refer to Section 11.3.3). It is noteworthy that the polarizability is changed with the temperature (i.e., α increases with a decrease in the temperature in oxide perovskites), which leads to a phase transition. With an increase in the ionic polarizability α with a decreasing temperature, even if $[(k/2Nq^2) - (N\alpha\gamma^2/9\varepsilon_0{}^2)] > 0$ (paraelectric!) at a high temperature, this value may become negative, leading to a ferroelectric phase transition at a certain temperature. Considering a first approximation, namely, a linear relation between α and the temperature, we can derive the well-known Curie–Weiss law:

$$[(k/2Nq^2) - (N\alpha\gamma^2/9\varepsilon_0{}^2)] = (T - T_0)/\varepsilon_0 C. \tag{1.11}$$

Phenomenological approaches with the theories of Landau and Devonshire are introduced in Chapter 4.

The temperature dependence of the total energy W_{tot} curve is shown in 3D (temperature axis) in Figure 1.7. One potential minimum at a high temperature will split into two minimum branches at a low-temperature phase. This "Y"-shaped phase splitting is called "bifurcation". The critical point corresponds to the Curie temperature T_C (in this second-order transition case, also $T_C = T_0$). Because the total energy W_{tot} curve is symmetric with respect to the polarization P when the external field $E = 0$ (see Figure 1.7, bottom), the probability of the state $+P_S$ or $-P_S$ should be equal. Thus, with a decreasing temperature, passing through T_C, $+P_S$ domains and $-P_S$ domains may arise locally in a specimen with an equal volumetric ratio, leading to multidomain states. The total polarization should be zero because of the compensation between the $+P_S$ and $-P_S$ domains. This state is called the "depolarized/depoled" state. Refer to Section 14.2 to learn the domain structures.

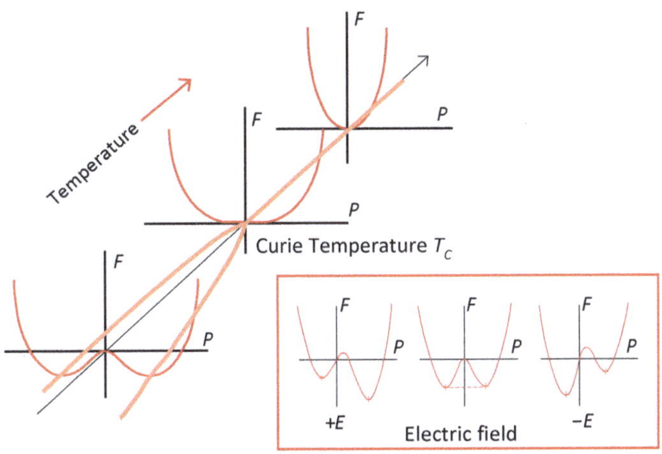

Figure 1.7. Temperature and electric field dependence of the Landau free energy curve. Source: Figure by author.

In order to generate ferroelectricity and piezoelectricity, we need the "poling" process; that is, by applying a reasonably large external electric field, the polarization direction is aligned in one direction ($+P_S$ or $-P_S$). The electric field dependence of the energy curve is shown in the inserted figure of Figure 1.7. Under the external electric field, the energy curve becomes asymmetric, which promotes polarization switching to one direction. When we apply $+E$, we expect the $+P_S$ polarized structure, which is called the "poling" process. Though we cannot expect a perfectly polarized state thermodynamically, a large portion of the ferroelectric specimen will be polarized.

Example Problem 1.1

The electric potential arising from a point charge q at a distance r from the charge is given by $V = \frac{1}{4\pi\varepsilon_0}\frac{q}{r}$, and the electric field is obtained as $\boldsymbol{E} = -grad(V) = \frac{1}{4\pi\varepsilon_0}\frac{q}{r^3}\boldsymbol{r}$, where $\boldsymbol{r}$ stands for the position vector along the radius direction. Now, calculate the electric field distribution surrounding a dipole (=$q{\cdot}\boldsymbol{u}$), that is, charges $+q$ and $-q$ are situated at a short distance u, as illustrated in Figure 1.8.

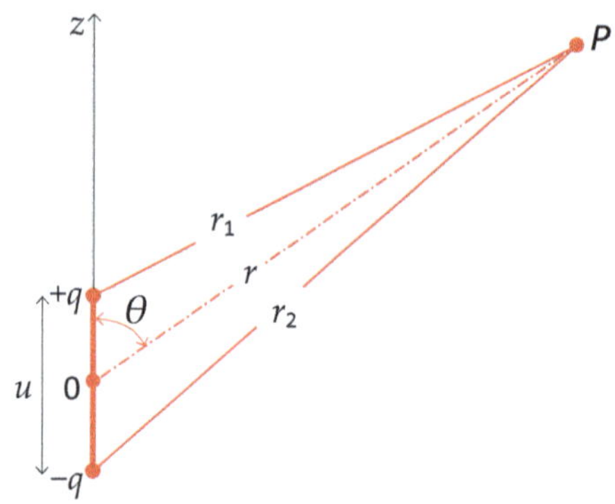

Figure 1.8. Electric potential calculation surrounding a dipole. Source: Figure by author.

Hint

The distance of $+q$ to point P, r_1, and the distance of $-q$ to point P, r_2, are expressed as

$$r_1 = \sqrt{r^2 + \tfrac{u^2}{4} - ru{\cdot}\cos\theta},\ r_2 = \sqrt{r^2 + \tfrac{u^2}{4} + ru{\cdot}\cos\theta}.$$

Solution

The electric potential at point P in Figure 1.8 is expressed by superposing the potential from $+q$ and $-q$ as

$$V = \frac{1}{4\pi\varepsilon_0}\frac{q}{r_1} - \frac{1}{4\pi\varepsilon_0}\frac{q}{r_2} = \frac{q}{4\pi\varepsilon_0}\left(\frac{1}{\sqrt{r^2 + \frac{u^2}{4} - ru{\cdot}\cos\theta}} - \frac{1}{\sqrt{r^2 + \frac{u^2}{4} + ru{\cdot}\cos\theta}}\right). \quad \text{(P1.1.1)}$$

Since we are interested in the case in which $r >> u$, we can rewrite Equation (P1.1.1) in the approximate form

$$V = q{\cdot}u{\cdot}\cos\theta/4\pi\varepsilon_0 r^2 = p{\cdot}\cos\theta/4\pi\varepsilon_0 r^2 = \boldsymbol{p}{\cdot}\boldsymbol{r}/4\pi\varepsilon_0 r^3. \quad \text{(P1.1.2)}$$

The quantity $\boldsymbol{p}$ here is the dipole moment (product of the charge q and small distance u) with the vector direction from $-q$ to $+q$. Then, the electric field is obtained as $\boldsymbol{E} = -grad(V)$, and knowing the gradient operator in the spherical coordinate is

$$grad(V) = \hat{\boldsymbol{r}}\frac{\partial V}{\partial r} + \hat{\boldsymbol{\theta}}\frac{1}{r}\frac{\partial V}{\partial \theta} + \hat{\boldsymbol{\varphi}}\frac{1}{r{\cdot}\sin\theta}\frac{\partial V}{\partial \varphi}, \tag{P1.1.3}$$

where $\hat{\boldsymbol{r}}$, $\hat{\boldsymbol{\theta}}$, $\hat{\boldsymbol{\varphi}}$ are unit vectors along the r, θ, and φ directions, we obtain the following:

$$\begin{aligned} \boldsymbol{E} = -grad(V) &= \hat{\boldsymbol{r}}\left(2p\tfrac{\cos\theta}{4\pi\varepsilon_0 r^3}\right) + \hat{\boldsymbol{\theta}}\tfrac{1}{r}\left(p\tfrac{\sin\theta}{4\pi\varepsilon_0 r^2}\right) \\ &= \tfrac{1}{4\pi\varepsilon_0 r^3}\left[\hat{\boldsymbol{r}}(2p{\cdot}\cos\theta) + \hat{\boldsymbol{\theta}}(p{\cdot}\sin\theta)\right] \\ &= \left[3(\boldsymbol{p}{\cdot}\boldsymbol{r})\boldsymbol{r} - r^2\boldsymbol{p}\right]/4\pi\varepsilon_0 r^5. \end{aligned} \tag{P1.1.4}$$

Above is the derivation process of Equation (1.3). The electric potential and field contour are illustrated in Figure 1.5, which looks like a "dumbbell" shape.

Example Problem 1.2

Perovskite-type barium titanate, $BaTiO_3$, exhibits a tetragonal symmetry at room temperature, and the ion shift is illustrated in Figure 1.9. The lattice constants are c = 4.036 (Å) and a = 3.992 (Å). Calculate the magnitude of the spontaneous polarization for barium titanate.

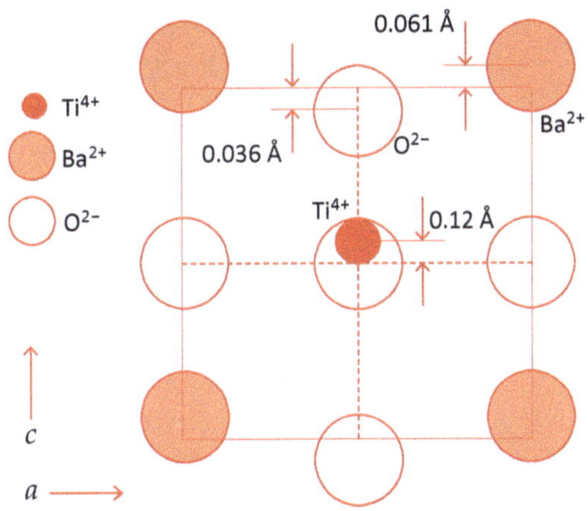

Figure 1.9. Ionic shifts in $BaTiO_3$ at room temperature. Source: Source: [1] ©Uchino, K. *Ferroelectric Devices*, 2nd ed. CRC Press, 2010; p. 7. Reproduced by permission of Taylor & Francis Group.

<u>Hint</u>

First calculate the dipole moment μ by the product of the ionic charge and the ionic displacement, and then the polarization $P = N\mu$ (N: number of dipole moments included in a unit volume). After calculating the dipole moment sum in a unit cell, divide it by the unit volume.

Solution

The dipole moment is defined as the product of the magnitude of the ion charge and its displacement. The total dipole moment in a unit cell is calculated by summing the contributions of all the Ba^{2+}-, Ti^{4+}-, and O^{2-}-related dipoles. Each corner Ba ion contributes 1/8, each O face ion contributes 1/2, and the center Ti contributes 1. Note that four O^{2-} ions of the oxygen octahedron do not shift (this position is taken as the origin), leading to zero contribution to the dipole moment.

$$\begin{aligned} P &= 8[2e/8][0.061 \times 10^{-10}\ (\mathrm{m})] + [4e][0.12 \times 10^{-10}\ (\mathrm{m})] \\ &\quad + 2[-2e/2][-0.036 \times 10^{-10}\ (\mathrm{m})] \\ &= e[0.674 \times 10^{-10}\ (\mathrm{m})] = 1.08 \times 10^{-29}\ (\mathrm{C{\cdot}m}), \end{aligned} \tag{P1.2.1}$$

where e is the fundamental charge: 1.602×10^{-19} (C).

Next, the unit cell volume is given by

$$v = a^2c = (3.992)^2(4.036) \times 10^{-30}\ (\mathrm{m}^3) = 64.3 \times 10^{-30}\ (\mathrm{m}^3). \tag{P1.2.2}$$

The spontaneous polarization represents the number of (spontaneous) electric dipoles p per unit volume:

$$P_S = P/v = 1.08 \times 10^{-29}\ (\mathrm{C{\cdot}m})/64.3 \times 10^{-30}\ (\mathrm{m}^3) = 0.17\ (\mathrm{C/m}^2). \tag{P1.2.3}$$

This theoretical value of P_S is in reasonable agreement with the experimental value of 0.25 ($\mathrm{C/m}^2$).

1.2.4. Origin of Field-Induced Strain

Solid materials, especially inorganic materials, are elastically stiff but still expand or contract depending on the change in the input parameters. The linear "strain" (defined as the "displacement" ΔL/initial length L) caused by a temperature change or stress is known as thermal expansion or elastic deformation, respectively. In insulating materials, the application of an electric field can also cause deformation. This is called "electric field-induced strain". We consider the microscopic origin in this section. The "piezoelectric constant" d and "electrostrictive coefficient" Q, M, are derived phenomenologically in Chapter 4, and the microscopic strain formula derivation is described in Section 14.3.3.

The word "electrostriction" is occasionally used, in a sense, to describe electric field-induced strain and, hence, frequently also implies the "converse piezoelectric effect". However, precisely speaking, the converse piezoelectric effect is defined as a "primary" electromechanical coupling effect, that is, the strain is directly proportional to the electric field, while electrostriction is a "secondary" coupling in which the strain is proportional to the square of the electric field. Thus, they should be distinguished theoretically. In practice, because the piezoelectricity of a ferroelectric which has a centrosymmetric prototype phase at high temperature is considered to originate from the "electrostrictive interaction", these two effects are occasionally observed as a combination (e.g., a high electric field induces a ferroelectric from a paraelectric phase). The above phenomena hold strictly under the assumptions that the object material is a mono-domain single crystal, and that its state does not change under the application of an electric field. In a practical piezoelectric ceramic, additional strains accompanied by the reorientation of ferroelectric domains are also important.

The origin of electric field-induced strain is explained in [4]. For simplicity, we consider an ionic crystal such as NaCl. Figure 1.10a,b show a 1D rigid-ion spring model of the crystal lattice. The springs equivalently represent the cohesive force resulting from the electrostatic Coulomb energy and the quantum mechanical repulsive energy (detailed discussion in Section 14.3.2). Figure 1.10b shows the centrosymmetric case, whereas Figure 1.10a shows the more general non-centrosymmetric case. The springs joining the ions are all the same in Figure 1.10b, whereas in Figure 1.10a, the springs joining the ions are different for the longer and shorter ionic distances; in other words, hard and soft springs are arranged alternately. When we consider the state of the crystal lattice in Figure 1.10a under an applied electric field, the cations are drawn in the direction of the electric field and the anions in the opposite direction, leading to a relative change in the inter-ionic distance. Note that the forces on the hard and soft springs should be equal. Depending on the direction of the electric field, the soft spring expands (or contracts) more than the contraction (or expansion) of the hard spring, the subtraction of which causes a strain x (a unit cell length change) in proportion to the electric field E. This is the "converse piezoelectric effect". When expressed as

$$x = dE, \tag{1.12}$$

the proportionality constant d is called the "piezoelectric constant".

On the other hand, in Figure 1.10b, the amounts of extension and contraction of the spring are usually the same, and the distance between the two cations (lattice parameter) remains the same; hence, there is no strain if the springs are ideally harmonic. However, more precisely, ions are not connected by such ideal springs called "harmonic springs", in which force (F) = spring constant (k) $\times$ displacement (Δ) holds. In most crystal lattice cases, the springs possess "anharmonicity" expressed by $F = k_1\Delta - k_2\Delta^2$; that is, they are somewhat easy to extend but hard to contract (a more precise model is discussed in Section 14.3.3). Such an intrinsic directional difference in the displacement causes a change in the lattice parameter, producing a strain which is independent of the direction of the applied electric field ($+E$ or $-E$) and, hence, is an even function of the electric field. Regardless of the electric field direction, extension always occurs in the unit cell size. This is called the "electrostrictive effect" and can be expressed as

$$x = ME^2, \tag{1.13}$$

where M is called the "electrostrictive constant".

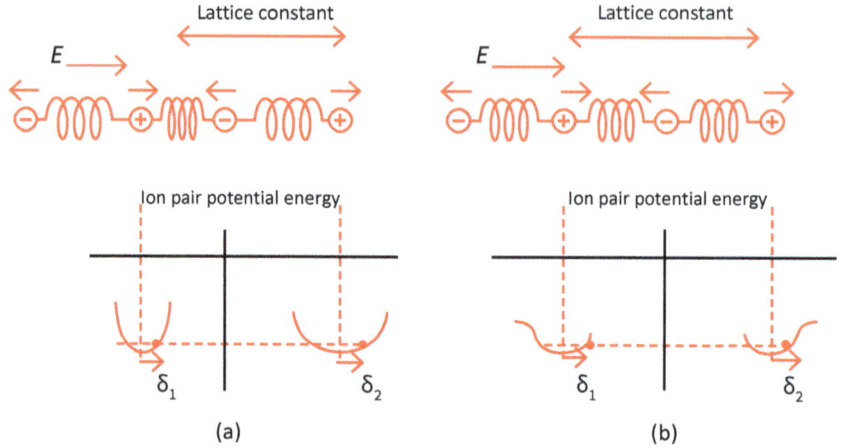

Figure 1.10. Microscopic explanation of piezoelectric strain (**a**) and electrostriction (**b**). Source: [1] ©Uchino, K. *Ferroelectric Devices*, 2nd ed. CRC Press, 2010; p. 8. Reproduced by permission of Taylor & Francis Group.

Note that the 1D asymmetric crystal pictured in Figure 1.10a also possesses a spontaneous bias of the electrical charge, or a spontaneous dipole moment. The total dipole moment per unit volume is called the "spontaneous polarization". When a large reverse bias electric field is applied to a crystal that has a positively aligned spontaneous polarization, another polarization status is formed which is another stable crystal state in which the relative positions of the ions are reversed. In terms of an untwinned single crystal, this is equivalent to rotating the crystal 180° about an axis perpendicular to its polar axis. This is also understood from the potential double minima in Figure 1.7. This transition, referred to as "polarization reversal", also causes a remarkable change in strain. This particular class of substances is referred to as "ferroelectrics", as mentioned in Section 1.2.2. Generally, what is actually observed to be a field-induced strain is a complicated combination of the three basic effects just described above.

A schematic of the polarization reorientation process or poling process in a polycrystalline specimen is visualized in Figure 1.11. First, the polycrystal is composed of many small single crystals (each is called a "grain") with random crystal orientations. Thus, complete alignment of the polarization is impossible. Further, due to this crystallographic misorientation, some residual stress exists in the specimen, which promotes a multidomain status even under a high electric field. We start from the initially negatively poled status "1". You can notice some domains in each grain. With an increasing electric field up to the "coercive" field E_C "2" (where the free energy at $-P_S$ reaches zero), the largest number of domains appears, and the total polarization becomes almost zero. When we further increase the field to "3", the domain rapidly disappears to become close to the mono-domain state in each grain. The slope of the strain vs. electric field around "3" corresponds to the piezoelectric constant. Now, if we decrease the field down to the coercive field "4", we may start to observe some domain generation in the grains; then, finally at the zero field "5", we observe similar domains in each grain to those in state "1", though the polarization directions are opposite to those of state "1".

Figure 1.12 shows typical strain curves for piezoelectric lead zirconate titanate (PZT)-based and electrostrictive lead magnesium niobate (PMN)-based ceramics [5]. The almost linear strain curve for PZT becomes distorted and shows large hysteresis with an increasing applied electric field level, which is due to the polarization reorientation. On the other hand, PMN does not exhibit hysteresis under the electric field cycle because no domain exists. However, the strain curve deviates from the quadratic relation (E^2), showing a saturation tendency at a high electric field level.

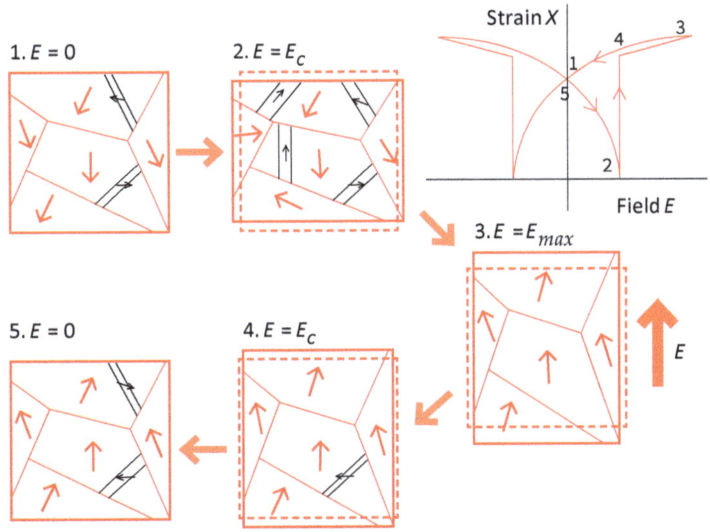

Figure 1.11. Domain structure change with the external electric field in polycrystalline ferroelectrics. Source: Figure by author.

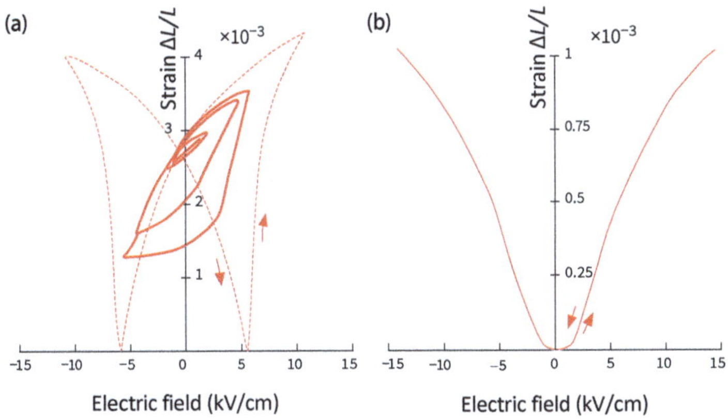

Figure 1.12. Typical strain curves for piezoelectric lead zirconate titanate (PZT)-based (**a**) and electrostrictive lead magnesium niobate (PMN)-based ceramics (**b**). Source: [1] ©Uchino, K. *Ferroelectric Devices*, 2nd ed. CRC Press, 2010; p. 9. Reproduced by permission of Taylor & Francis Group.

The converse piezoelectric effect is described above. Then, what about the "direct piezoelectric effect"? This is the phenomenon whereby a charge (i.e., polarization [C/m^2]) is generated under the application of an external stress (N/m^2). The piezoelectric equation can be described using the same piezoelectric coefficient d in Equation (1.12) for the converse effect:

$$P = dX. \tag{1.14}$$

1.2.5. Piezoelectric Constitutive Equations

When an electric field is applied on a piezoelectric material, displacement (ΔL) or strain ($\Delta L/L$) arises, as described in Section 1.2.4. When the applied electric field and the generated stress are not large, as the first-order approximation, the stress X and the dielectric displacement D can be represented by the following linear equations (derivation process is detailed in Chapter 2):

$$\begin{cases} x_i = s_{ij}^E X_j + d_{mi} E_m \\ D_m = d_{mi} X_i + \varepsilon_0 \varepsilon_{mk}^X E_k \end{cases} (i, j = 1, 2, \cdots, 6; m, k = 1, 2, 3). \tag{1.15a,b}$$

The above equations are referred to as "piezoelectric constitutive equations". For the reader's sake, the number of independent parameters for the lowest-symmetry trigonal crystal is 21 for $s_{ij}{}^E$, 18 for d_{mi}, and 6 for $\varepsilon_{mk}{}^X$. The number of independent parameters decreases with increasing crystallographic symmetry, as explained in Chapter 3. Concerning polycrystalline ceramics such as PZTs, the poled axis is usually denoted as the z-axis, and the ceramic is isotropic with respect to this z-axis (Curie group $C_{\infty v}$ (∞m)). The number of non-zero matrix elements in this case is 10 ($s_{11}{}^E$, $s_{12}{}^E$, $s_{13}{}^E$, $s_{33}{}^E$, and $s_{44}{}^E$; d_{31}, d_{33}, and d_{15}; $\varepsilon_{11}{}^X$ and $\varepsilon_{33}{}^X$).

The input electric energy is transduced to the output mechanical energy, or vice versa, in a piezoelectric. We introduce the concept of the "electromechanical coupling factor" k, which corresponds to the rate of electromechanical transduction. The internal energy U of a piezoelectric is given by the summation of the mechanical energy U_M (= $\int xdX$) and the electrical energy U_E (=$\int DdE$) in general. Then, U is calculated as follows, where the linear relations Equation (1.15a,b) are applicable:

$$\begin{aligned} U &= U_M + U_E \\ &= \left[(1/2)\textstyle\sum_{i,j} s_{ij}{}^E X_j X_i + (1/2)\sum_{m,i} d_{mi} E_m X_i\right] \\ &\quad + \left[(1/2)\textstyle\sum_{m,i} d_{mi} X_i E_m + (1/2)\sum_{k,m} \varepsilon_{mk}{}^X E_k E_m\right] \\ &= U_{MM} + 2U_{ME} + U_{EE} \\ &= (1/2)\textstyle\sum_{i,j} s_{ij}{}^E X_j X_i + 2(1/2)\sum_{m,i} d_{mi} E_m X_i + (1/2)\sum_{k,m} \varepsilon_{mk}{}^X E_k E_m. \end{aligned} \tag{1.16}$$

The s and ε terms represent purely mechanical and electrical energies (U_{MM} and U_{EE}), respectively, and the d term denotes the energy transduced from electrical to mechanical energy, or vice versa, through the piezoelectric effect (U_{ME}). The electromechanical coupling factor k is defined by

$$k = U_{ME} / \sqrt{U_{MM} \cdot U_{EE}}. \tag{1.17}$$

Note that this definition is equivalent to the definition provided as follows:

$$k^2 = U_{ME}/U_E = (\text{Stored mechanical energy}/\text{Input electrical energy}) \tag{1.18a}$$

or

$$k^2 = U_{ME}/U_M = (\text{Stored electrical energy}/\text{Input mechanical energy}). \quad (1.18b)$$

Let us obtain the coupling factor k in terms of physical properties (d, s, and ε). When electric energy is supplied to a piezoelectric sample and some part is transduced into mechanical energy, the square of the "electromechanical coupling factor" k^2 is defined by

$$\begin{aligned} k^2 &= (\text{Stored mechanical energy})/(\text{Input electrical energy}) \\ &= (1/2)(x^2/s)/(1/2)(\varepsilon_0\varepsilon E^2) = (1/2)((dE)^2/s)/(1/2)(\varepsilon_0\varepsilon E^2)\ [\text{from } x = dE] \\ &= d^2/s\varepsilon_0\varepsilon. \end{aligned} \quad (1.19)$$

The k is expressed in the form of $d/\sqrt{s\varepsilon_0\varepsilon}$ in general, which varies with the driving mode (even in the same ceramic sample), with either a positive or negative value. The $|k_{31}/k_{33}|$ ratio around 0.47 originates from the $|d_{31}/d_{33}|$ ratio around 0.4 (i.e., Poisson's ratio). The k value is primarily governed by the contributing piezoelectric d constant for that vibration mode. Note also that "k^2" has an actual physical meaning for representing the energy transduction ratio (no particular meaning in k itself).

When the field is alternating, mechanical vibration is generated in a piezoelectric device, and if the driving frequency is adjusted to the mechanical resonance frequency of the piezoelectric device, a large resonating strain is excited. This phenomenon can be understood as a strain amplification due to input energy accumulation with time (amplification in terms of time), which is called "piezoelectric resonance". The amplification factor is proportional to the mechanical quality factor Q_M (inversely proportional to the elastic loss). Piezoelectric resonance is very useful for realizing medical and underwater ultrasonic transducers, piezo-transformers, actuators, energy trap devices, etc. (detailed discussion in Chapter 7).

1.2.6. Electro-Optic Effect

Electro-optic devices have been widely commercialized as displays since the 1980s, initially exemplified by LCDs (i.e., liquid crystal displays); recently, they have been refocused for optical communication applications. Light is an alternating electromagnetic wave with electric and magnetic field vibration directions that are almost perpendicular to one another, where the electric field induces an electric polarization in a dielectric crystal, and the light itself is influenced by the crystal. Because the oscillating frequency of the light is so high (PHz = 10^{15} Hz) that only the "electronic polarization" can follow the electric field change (see Figure 1.2), the permittivity of an optically transparent crystal (even in a ferroelectric crystal) is small, not exceeding 10. The reader is reminded of the famous relation between the relative permittivity ε_r at this high frequency and the refractive index n:

$$\varepsilon_r = n^2 [\text{assuming magnetic permeability } \mu_r = 1]. \quad (1.20)$$

When an external electric field (much lower than PHz) is applied to the crystal, ion displacement is induced, deforming the shape of the electron cloud, and, consequently, the "refractive index" n is changed. The refractive index is directly related to the electron density in a material. This phenomenon is called the "electro-optic effect" [1]. Generally, the refractive index is treated as a symmetrical second-rank tensor quantity and is represented geometrically by the "optical indicatrix", which is described by

$$\frac{x^2}{{n_1}^2}+\frac{y^2}{{n_2}^2}+\frac{z^2}{{n_3}^2}=1, \tag{1.21}$$

where n_1, n_2, and n_3 are the principal refractive indices. Refer to Chapter 13 for the details. With the application of an electric field, the change in the inverse permittivity κ is given by a Taylor/Maclaurin expansion expression in terms of E:

$$\kappa(E)-\kappa(0)=rE+RE^2+\cdots. \tag{1.22}$$

Using $\kappa=1/\varepsilon=1/n^2$, we obtain

$$1/{n_{ij}}^2(E)-1/{n_{ij}}^2(0)=\Sigma r_{ijk}E_k+\Sigma R_{ijkl}E_kE_l. \tag{1.23}$$

Here, $n(E)$ and $n(0)$ ($=n_0$) are the refractive indices at the E and the zero field. The coefficient r_{ijk} is called the "primary electro-optic coefficient" ("Pockels effect"), and R_{ijkl} is the secondary coefficient ("Kerr effect"). Remember that the Maclaurin expansion is not based on n_{ij}, but on $1/{n_{ij}}^2$.

Considering the paraelectric phase of a perovskite crystal ($m3m$) as an example, the Kerr coefficients are represented in the following matrix:

$$\begin{pmatrix} R_{11} & R_{12} & R_{12} & 0 & 0 & 0 \\ R_{12} & R_{11} & R_{12} & 0 & 0 & 0 \\ R_{12} & R_{12} & R_{11} & 0 & 0 & 0 \\ 0 & 0 & 0 & R_{44} & 0 & 0 \\ 0 & 0 & 0 & 0 & R_{44} & 0 \\ 0 & 0 & 0 & 0 & 0 & R_{44} \end{pmatrix},$$

meaning that the refractive indicatrix under an electric field applied along the z direction is expressed as

$$\frac{x^2+y^2}{{n_0}^2\left[1-\left(\frac{{n_0}^2}{2}\right)R_{12}{E_z}^2\right]^2}+\frac{z^2}{{n_0}^2\left[1-\left(\frac{{n_0}^2}{2}\right)R_{11}{E_z}^2\right]^2}=1. \tag{1.24}$$

Let us consider the refractive index change under an external electric field intuitively with a visual figure (Figure 1.13a). A cubic perovskite crystal is elongated along the z-axis and contracted along both perpendicular x- and y-axes when an electric field E_z is applied, via the "electrostrictive effect". Consequently, the material's axial density or compactness will be decreased along the z-axis and densified along the x- and y-axes, leading to a decrease in the refractive index nz and an increase in the indices n_x and n_y, as shown in Figure 1.13b. That is, the initial sphere becomes a doughnut shape. Note that the refractive index is proportional to the electron density or ion compactness along the polarized light electric field direction, which is perpendicular to the light propagation direction. Taking into account the above description, R_{11} and R_{12} in Equation (1.24) are positive and negative, respectively, directly correlated with the electrostrictive coefficients M_{11} and M_{12}.

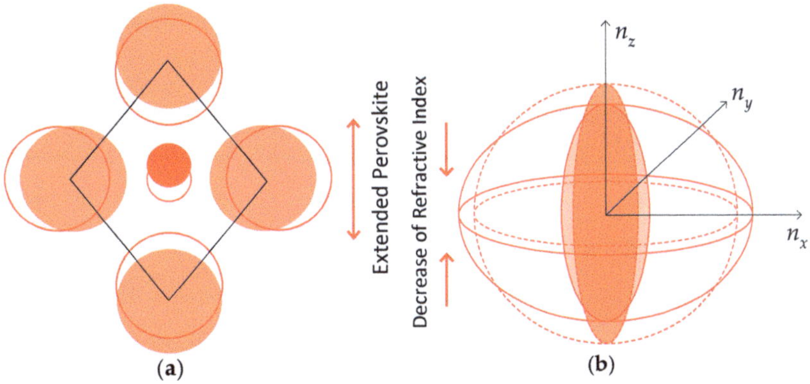

Figure 1.13. (**a**) Perovskite unit cell change with electric field. (**b**) Corresponding refractive indicatrix change of a cubic crystal with electric field (Kerr effect). The original sphere becomes a doughnut shape. Source: Figure by author, adapted from [1].

When light is transmitted along the y direction, the "phase retardation" Γ_y between the "ordinary" (polarized along the x orientation) and "extraordinary" waves (polarized along the electric field z orientation) can be expressed as

$$\Gamma_y = (2\pi/\lambda)(n_0{}^3/2)(R_{11} - R_{12})L(V_z/d)^2, \tag{1.25}$$

where d and L are the electrode gap and "optical path length", respectively. By placing the crystal between a pair of crossed polarizers arranged at +45° and −45° angles with respect to the z-axis, as in Figure 1.14, the output light intensity is modulated as a function of the applied voltage according to

$$I = I_0\sin^2(\Gamma_y/2) = (1/2)I_0(1 - \cos\Gamma_y). \tag{1.26}$$

The detailed derivation is described in Chapter 13.

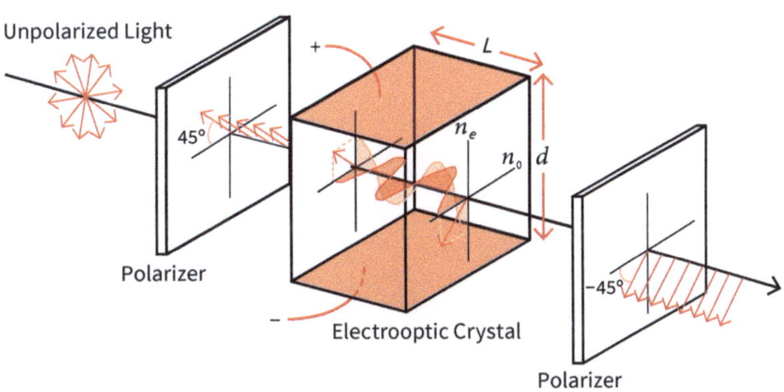

Figure 1.14. Optical phase retardation through an electro-optic crystal. Notice the crossed polarizer configuration. Source: [1] ©Uchino, K. *Ferroelectric Devices*, 2nd ed. CRC Press, 2010; p. 13. Reproduced by permission of Taylor & Francis Group.

The variation in the light intensity with the applied voltage is shown in Figure 1.15. The sinusoidal intensity modulation period (second and third peaks) shrinks with the voltage because the retardation Γ_y is proportional to the "square" of the applied voltage. This is the principle behind the operation of a "light shutter/valve", and the voltage required for the first intensity maximum (i.e., $\Gamma_y = \pi$) is an important characteristic called the "half-wave voltage", given by

$$V_z = d[\lambda / n_0{}^3(R_{11} - R_{12})L]^{1/2}. \quad (1.27)$$

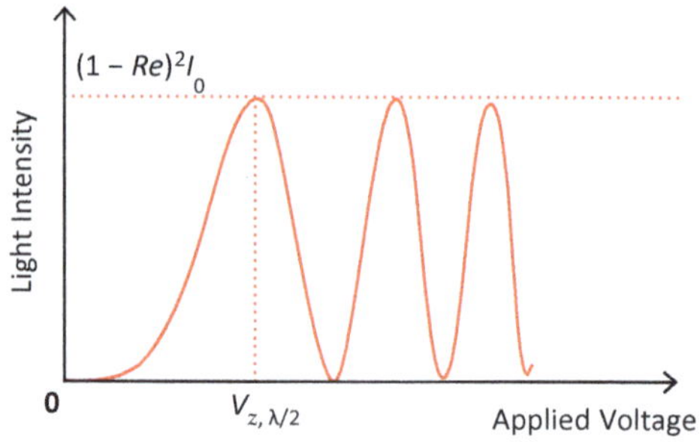

Figure 1.15. Light intensity change of a Kerr effect electro-optic shutter with the applied voltage. Source: Figure by author, adapted from [1].

Example Problem 1.3

PLZT 10/65/35, with a cubic symmetry, shows electro-optic coefficients $R_{11} = 0.83 \times 10^{-16}$ [m^2/V^2] and $R_{12} = -0.27 \times 10^{-16}$ [m^2/V^2], and $n_0 = 2.49$. Calculate the "half-wave electric field" for a sample with $L = 1$ mm, when $\lambda = 633$ nm light is transmitted perpendicularly to the electric field, as in Figure 1.14.

Hint

The half-wave voltage is calculated from

$$\Gamma_y = (\pi/\lambda) n_0{}^3 E_3{}^2 (R_{11} - R_{12}) L = \pi, \quad \text{(P1.3.1)}$$

where Γ_y is the phase retardation (see Equation (1.25)). Note also $R = (R_{11} - R_{12}) = 1.1 \times 10^{-16}$ [m^2/V^2].

Solution

$$E_3 = [\lambda / n_0^3 (R_{11} - R_{12}) L]^{1/2} = (633 \times 10^{-9}/2.49^3 \times 1.1 \times 10^{-16} \times 1 \times 10^{-3})^{1/2}$$
$$= 6.1 \times 10^5 [\mathrm{V/m}]. \quad \text{(P1.3.2)}$$

How much does the refractive index change in practice? From the formula $n_0\left[1-\left(\frac{n_0{}^2}{2}\right)R_{11}E_z{}^2\right]$,

$$\left(\frac{n_0{}^2}{2}\right)R_{11}E_z{}^2=\left(\frac{2.49^2}{2}\right)\times 0.83\times 10^{-16}\times\left(6.1\times 10^5\right)^2\approx 1\times 10^{-4}.$$

The refractive index n changes by only 0.01%, even under the half-wave voltage applied.

1.2.7. Ferroelectric Materials

Quartz (SiO_2) and zinc oxide (ZnO) are popular piezoelectric, but non-ferroelectric (nonpolar), materials. The "direct" piezoelectric effect was first discovered in quartz by Piere and Jacques Curie in 1880. Immediately after in 1881, the "converse piezoelectric effect" was discovered by Gabriel Lippmann. The application of piezoelectricity was motivated by the famous Titanic shipwreck and other shipwrecks from World War I in the undersea transducer and sonar area. Paul Langevin developed the so-called Langenvin-type transducer, which was originally composed of natural tiny quartz single crystals sandwiched by two metal blocks, in order to tune the transducer resonance frequency around 26 kHz, which was a desired range for underwater applications to detect German U-boats.

On the other hand, ferroelectricity was first discovered in Rochelle salt ($NaKC_4H_4O_6{\cdot}4H_2O$) in 1921. Though this material has been studied from an academic viewpoint, it has not been widely utilized in practice because it is water soluble (i.e., non-durable in seawater) and its Curie temperature is just above room temperature. KH_2PO_4 (KDP) was the second discovery in 1935, which is also water soluble, and its Curie temperature is −150 °C. We needed to wait until World War II for the third and most famous ceramic ferroelectric, i.e., barium titanate ($BaTiO_3$), which was actually first commercialized as a transducer material. In order to develop compact capacitors for portable "radar" systems to be used in the battlefields, TiO_2-based conventional "condenser materials" were widely researched by doping various ions such as CaO, SrO, BaO, MgO, and Fe_2O_3. Four groups in the US, Russia, Germany, and Japan discovered $BaTiO_3$ around almost the same time in World War II [6]. The discovery of isomorphous PZT (lead zirconate titanate) after WWII established the present wide and steady piezoelectric device market, which has been operating for more than 60 years.

Barium Titanate (BT)

The basic properties of ferroelectrics are reviewed, using barium titanate as an example. $BaTiO_3$ has a perovskite crystal structure, as shown in Figure 1.16. Refer to Figure 1.9 in Example Problem 1.2 for the accurate ionic displacements. The paraelectric phase (nonpolar phase) at high temperature possesses no spontaneous polarization with a cubic symmetry of O_h—$m3m$. Below the transition temperature T_C, called the "Curie temperature" (about 130 °C), spontaneous polarization arises, with a slightly elongated crystal structure, that is, tetragonal C_{4v}—$4mm$. The temperature dependence of the spontaneous polarization P_S, spontaneous strain x_S, and permittivity (dielectric constant) ε is illustrated in Figure 1.17 for a "first-order phase transition" ferroelectric such as BT. P_S decreases with an increasing temperature and vanishes suddenly at the Curie temperature, while ε tends to diverge near T_C. Additionally, the reciprocal (relative) permittivity 1/ε is known to be linear with respect to the temperature over a wide range in the paraelectric phase (so-called Curie–Weiss law),

$$\varepsilon = C/(T - T_0), \tag{1.28}$$

where C is the "Curie–Weiss constant", and T_0 is the "Curie–Weiss temperature", which is slightly lower than the exact transition temperature T_C. It is also known that the spontaneous polarization P_S and the spontaneous strain x_S follow the electrostrictive coupling relationship

$$x_S = QP_S{}^2, \tag{1.29}$$

and x_S decreases almost linearly with an increasing temperature. In the case of $BaTiO_3$ (BT), it exhibits the piezoelectric effect in the ferroelectric phase, while in the paraelectric phase, it is non-piezoelectric and exhibits only the electrostrictive effect (i.e., $x = ME^2$). The general descriptions above are almost consistent with the phenomenological approach for the "second-order" phase transition, except for jump or discontinuous phenomena at the Curie temperature T_C, in the first-order phase transition. Refer to Chapter 4.

The temperature dependence of the ferroelectric properties described above suggests materials' development strategies: capacitor materials are designed to have a Curie temperature around room temperature (RT) because of the maximum permittivity; memory materials should possess a T_C that is around 100 °C higher than RT for obtaining a reasonably large P_S; the T_C for pyro-sensors is just above RT because of the large $\left|\frac{\partial P_S}{\partial T}\right|$; piezoelectric transducer materials' T_C is set typically much higher than RT, and higher than 200 °C, in order to stabilize the P_S, even under a high-voltage drive with excessive heat generation; the T_C for electro-optic (Kerr effect) and electrostrictive devices is slightly lower than RT to use their paraelectric state. In other words, we design practical materials with their Curie points suitable for each application.

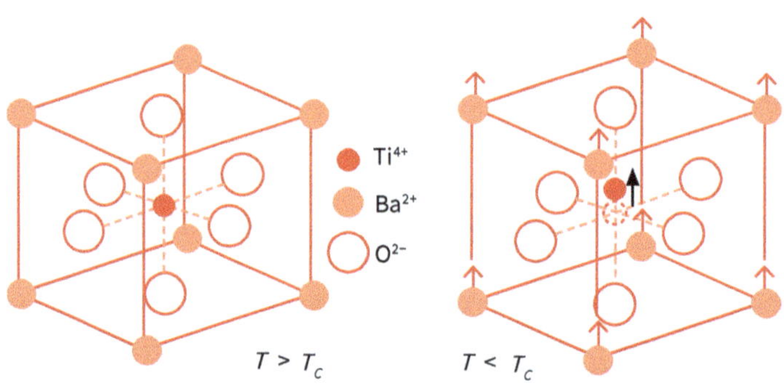

Figure 1.16. Crystal structures of $BaTiO_3$: higher (**left**) and lower (**right**) than T_C. Source: [1] ©Uchino, K. *Ferroelectric Devices*, 2nd ed. CRC Press, 2010; p. 17. Reproduced by permission of Taylor & Francis Group.

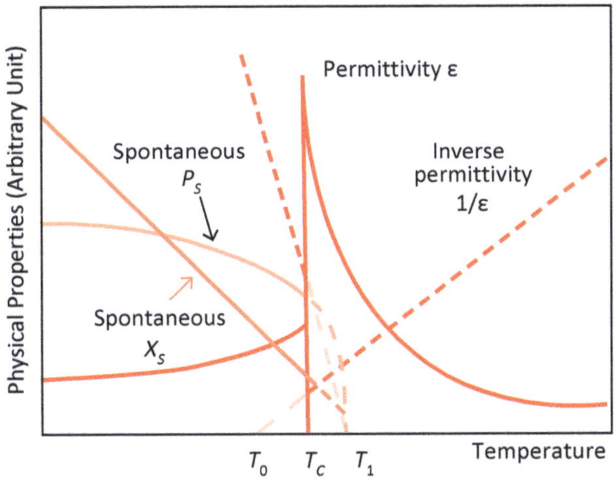

Figure 1.17. Temperature dependence of the spontaneous polarization, strain, and permittivity in a ferroelectric. Source: Figure by author, adapted from [1].

The situation of BT is very complicated in practice. With a decreasing temperature, BT undergoes three successive phase transitions from the cubic to the tetragonal phase at 130 °C, then from the tetragonal to the orthorhombic phase around 0 °C, and, finally, from the orthorhombic to the rhombohedral phase at −90 °C. Figure 1.18 shows the temperature dependence of the permittivity along the *c*- and *a*-axes of the tetragonal phase, according to these successive phase transitions. The polarization direction change is also inserted in the crystal structures of the cubic, tetragonal, orthorhombic, and rhombohedral phases [1].

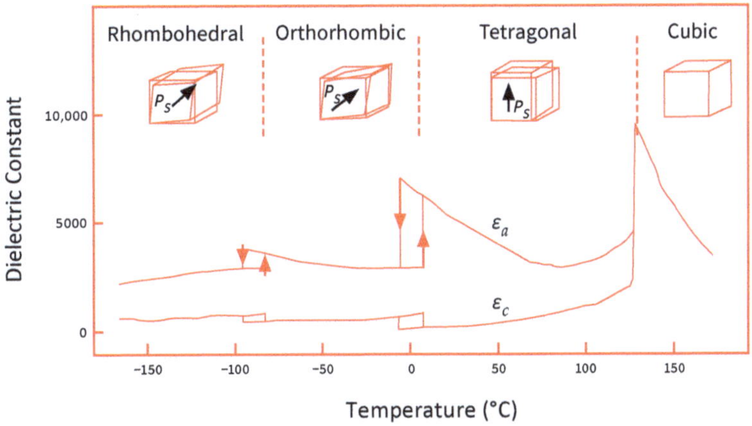

Figure 1.18. Various phase transitions in barium titanate (BT). Source: [1] ©Uchino, K. *Ferroelectric Devices*, 2nd ed. CRC Press, 2010; p. 19. Reproduced by permission of Taylor & Francis Group.

Example Problem 1.4

Barium titanate at room temperature (tetragonal *4mm* symmetry) has a crystallographic anisotropy in the dielectric constant, as shown in Figure 1.18. The permittivity along the spontaneous polarization direction ε_3 is much smaller than that perpendicular to the spontaneous polarization direction ε_1. Let us consider the electric poling of a uniformly oriented polycrystalline sample. Describe the change in the permittivity before and after poling.

Solution

Before poling, the polarization direction in micro-crystals (i.e., grains) is randomly oriented. Thus, the dielectric constant should have an average value between ε_a and ε_c, that is, $\varepsilon_{ave} = \left(\frac{1}{3}\right)(\varepsilon_c + 2\varepsilon_a)$. Since electric poling orients the polarization mostly along the *z*-axis (or *c*-axis), the permittivity approaches ε_c, leading to a decrease in the permittivity after poling. By measuring the permittivity decrease as a function of the poling field, we can find the saturation tendency, meaning that we can evaluate the minimum required electric field for the poling process. Statistical theory (Uchida–Ikeda model) [7] suggests that the saturated P_S value in a polycrystalline specimen should be 83% of that of the single crystal.

Lead Zirconate Titanate (PZT)

Lead zirconate titanate ($Pb(Zr,Ti)O_3$, PZT) solid solution systems were discovered in 1954 by Japanese researchers Shirane, Sawaguchi, and Takagi [8]. The phase diagram of the PZT system is shown in Figure 1.19, where the "morphotropic phase boundary" (MPB) between the tetragonal and rhombohedral phases exists around the 52 PZ–48 PT composition. The significant piezoelectric properties of the MPB composition were discovered by Jaffe [9] of the Clevite Corporation, and Clevite obtained the most important PZT patent for transducer applications. Because of this strong basic patent, Japanese piezo-ceramic companies were actually encouraged to develop ternary systems to overcome the performance of the binary system and, more importantly, to escape from Clevite's patent: that is, PZT + a complex perovskite such as $Pb(Mg_{1/3}Nb_{2/3})O_3$ (Matsushita Panasonic), $Pb(Ni_{1/3}Nb_{2/3})O_3$ (NEC), and $Pb(Zn_{1/3}Nb_{2/3})O_3$ (Toshiba), which is the basic composition at present. Figure 1.20 plots the dependence of several piezoelectric *d* constants on the composition near the MPB in the PZT system. Note that the maximum piezoelectric performance is obtained around the MPB composition in the pure PZT system.

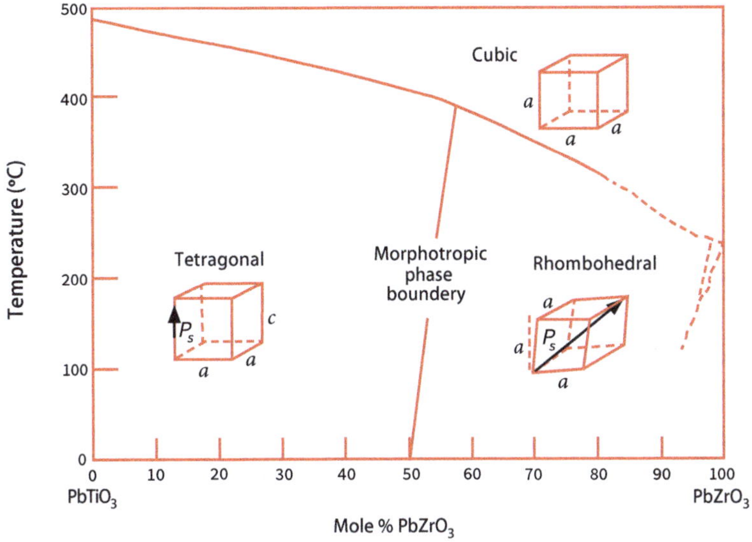

Figure 1.19. Phase diagram of lead zirconate titanate (PZT). Source: [1] ©Uchino, K. *Ferroelectric Devices*, 2nd ed. CRC Press, 2010; p. 169. Reproduced by permission of Taylor & Francis Group.

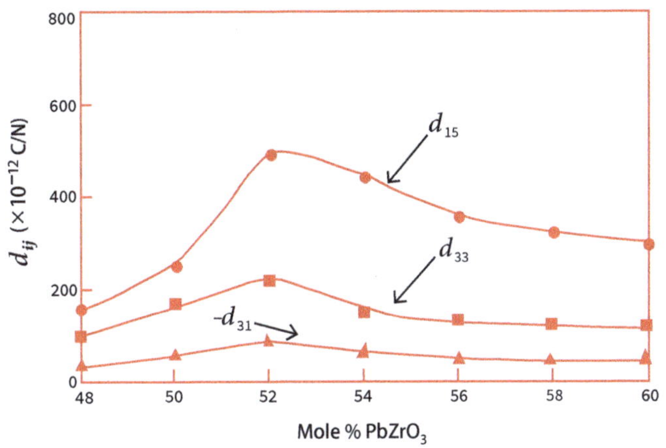

Figure 1.20. Dependence of several *d* constants on the composition near the morphotropic phase boundary in the PZT system. Source: [1] ©Uchino, K. *Ferroelectric Devices*, 2nd ed. CRC Press, 2010; p. 169. Reproduced by permission of Taylor & Francis Group.

Relaxor Ferroelectrics

Relaxor ferroelectrics, many of which are composed of a "complex perovskite" structure, can be prepared in either polycrystalline or single-crystal forms. Different from the previously mentioned normal ferroelectrics such as BT and PZT, the relaxor types are characterized by (1) a broad phase transition from the paraelectric to the ferroelectric state, (2) a significant frequency dependency of the dielectric constant (i.e., "dielectric relaxation"), and (3) a weak remanent polarization under $E = 0$. Relaxor ferroelectrics have complex "disordered perovskite" structures.

A binary system of relaxor-type $Pb(Mg_{1/3}Nb_{2/3})O_3$–$PbTiO_3$ (or PMN-PT) exhibits enormous electrostriction under an external electric field with almost zero hysteresis, which is highly suitable for positioner applications. This relaxor ferroelectric also exhibits an induced piezoelectric effect under a DC bias electric field. That is, the electromechanical coupling factor k_t varies with the external bias field. As the DC bias field increases, the coupling increases and saturates. Since this behavior is reproducible, these materials can be applied as ultrasonic transducers which are tunable by the bias field [10].

Relaxor ferroelectrics with the morphotropic phase boundary (MPB) composition can be synthesized in single-crystal form rather easily. The author's group discovered superior electromechanical coupling in these crystals by manipulating the crystal orientation in the late 1970s, which enhanced the performance for ultrasonic transducers and electromechanical actuators. $Pb(Zn_{1/3}Nb_{2/3})O_3$ (PZN)- and $Pb(Mg_{1/3}Nb_{2/3})O_3$ (PMN)-based binary systems with $PbTiO_3$ (PZN-PT and PMN-PT) were demonstrated to have extremely large electromechanical coupling factors [11,12]. Large coupling coefficients and large piezoelectric constants have been found for crystals with the MPB composition. PZN-8%PT single crystals with a rhombohedral symmetry were found to possess a high k_{33} value of 0.94 for the (001) crystal cuts (57° cant from the spontaneous polarization direction); this is very high compared to the k_{33} of conventional PZT ceramics of around 0.70~0.80.

PVDF

Thanks to Kawai's efforts, polyvinylidene difluoride (PVDF or PVF_2) was discovered in 1969 [13]. Though the piezoelectric d constant (actuator figure of merit) is not as high as that of piezo-ceramics, a high piezoelectric g constant (sensor figure of merit) due to a low permittivity is attractive from the sensor application viewpoint.

PVDF is a polymer with monomers of CH_2CF_2, where H and F are aligned in the opposite positions around the carbon chain, as shown in Figure 1.21. Because H and F have positive and negative ionization tendencies, the monomer itself possesses a dipole moment (upward dipole moment in the figure). Crystallization from the melt forms the nonpolar α-phase, which can be converted into the polar β-phase by a uniaxial or biaxial drawing operation; the resulting dipoles are then reoriented through electric poling.

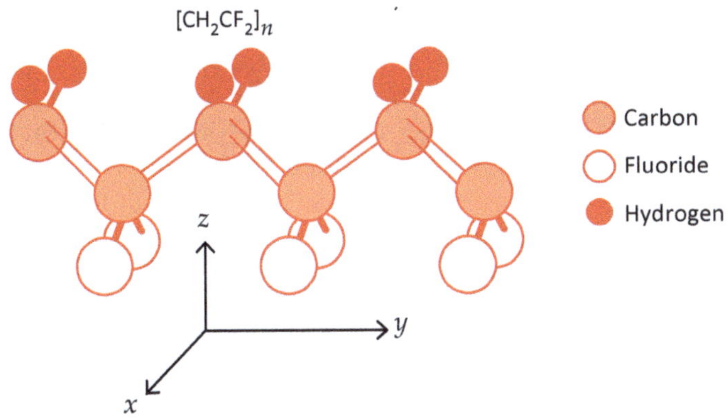

Figure 1.21. Molecular structure of polyvinylidene diflouride (PVDF). Source: [1] ©Uchino, K. *Ferroelectric Devices*, 2nd ed. CRC Press, 2010; p. 19. Reproduced by permission of Taylor & Francis Group.

Large sheets can be manufactured and thermally formed by a hot roller into complex shapes. Piezoelectric polymers have the following characteristics: (a) small piezoelectric *d* constants (for actuators), but large *g* constants (for sensors), (b) light weight and soft elasticity, leading to good "acoustic impedance matching" with water and the human body, (c) a low mechanical quality factor Q_m, allowing for a broad resonance bandwidth. On the other hand, for actuator applications, the PVDF polymer degrades the performance significantly under a large cyclical (AC) electric field because of heat generation via a large viscous damping or elastic loss factor. Even self-melting is observed in the worst scenario such as when it is operated at its resonance frequency. Slow operation for actuators and energy harvesting is definitely required.

Pb-Free Piezo-Ceramics

In 2006, the European community implemented the RoHS Directive (Restrictions of the Use of Certain Hazardous Substances), which explicitly limits the usage of lead (Pb) in electronic equipment. Basically, we may need to regulate the usage of lead zirconate titanate (PZT), the most famous current piezoelectric ceramic, in the future. The Japanese and European communities may experience governmental regulation on the usage of PZT in the next 10 years. Pb (lead)-free piezo-ceramics started to be developed after 1999. Pb-free materials include (1) $(K,Na)(Ta,Nb)O_3$-based, (2) $(Bi,Na)TiO_3$, and (3) $BaTiO_3$ materials, which were studied extensively in the 1960s–1970s; this reminds us that "history will repeat itself" (i.e., "Piezoelectric Renaissance") after one generation (~30 years).

1.2.8. Applications of Ferroelectrics

Ferroelectric materials, especially polycrystalline ceramics, are very promising for a variety of applications such as "high-permittivity capacitors", "ferroelectric memories", "pyroelectric sensors", "piezoelectric and electrostrictive transducers", "electro-optic devices", and "PTC thermistors". Refer to [1] for a detailed discussion.

Capacitor dielectrics utilize the peak dielectric constant around the transition (Curie) temperature, meaning that T_C should be adjusted around room temperature, while for memory applications, the material must be ferroelectric at room temperature (refer to Figure 1.17). Since a large temperature derivative of the spontaneous polarization is required for pyroelectric sensors, the T_C is set to be just above room temperature. The converse pyroelectric effect is called the "electrocaloric effect" (the electric field generates the temperature decrease), which is becoming a new refrigeration technique in this energy saving age. Piezoelectric materials are used for both sensors and actuators, where the T_C should be significantly above room temperature. Pressure and acceleration sensors are now commercially available in addition to conventional piezo-vibrators. Precision positioners and pulse drive linear motors have already been installed in precision lathe machines, semiconductor manufacturing apparatuses, and office equipment. Exciting developments can be found in ultrasonic motors, aiming at being "electromagnetic and sound noise free", and very compact motor applications. Recently, in parallel to the new energy source programs, piezoelectric energy harvesting systems have become popular. Waste mechanical energy such as machine noise vibration, wind, and human walking vibration can be converted into electrical energy for direct use in signal transmission or for charging up batteries for portable electronics. Its target is set on the elimination of batteries from portable electronic equipment that are hazardous to the world. Electro-optic materials have widely been commercialized in displays (such as liquid crystal displays) and will become key components in optical communication systems in the near future. Optical beam scanners, light valves, and switches are urgent necessities. For thermistor applications, semiconductive ferroelectric ceramics with a positive temperature coefficient of resistivity (PTCR) based on a junction effect have also been developed from barium titanate-based materials.

From the actual worldwide revenue viewpoint of ferroelectric and piezoelectric devices, "capacitors" share more than 50%, followed by "piezoelectric devices" with ~30%, and then "PTCR thermistors" with ~15%. Because "piezoelectricity" has a rather unique performance without finding strong competitors (electromagnetic counterpart motors/transformers are inferior in terms of efficiency in compact component domains smaller than 30 W), piezoelectric applications are currently expanding significantly. Though the electro-optic and pyroelectric/electrocaloric effects seem to be very intriguing personally, their revenue contributions are very small from the industrial viewpoints at present. Three examples commercialized recently with a high revenue amount (i.e., million-selling devices) are introduced below.

Piezoelectric Multilayer Actuators for Automobiles

Diesel engines are a better choice than regular gasoline cars from the energy conservation and global warming viewpoint. When we consider the total energy required for gasoline production, both "well-to-tank" and "tank-to-wheel" should be taken into account. The energy efficiency, measured by the energy required to realize the unit drive distance for a vehicle (MJ/km), is of course better for high-octane gasoline than diesel oil. However, since gasoline requires a huge amount of electrical energy for its purification, gasoline is inferior to diesel fuel from the total energy consumption viewpoint [14]. However, because conventional diesel engines generate toxic exhaust gases such as SO_x and NO_x due to insuffіcent burning of the fuel, new diesel injection valves have been required to solve this problem. Siemens, Bosch, and Toyota developed multi-injection-type diesel engines with piezoelectric multilayered actuators. Figure 1.22 shows such a common rail-type diesel injection valve with an ML piezo-actuator which produces high-pressure fuel and quick injection control. Owning to the large force and quick response of the PZT ML actuator, a very fine mist of diesel fuel can be injected in order to be burned effectively. ML piezo-actuators should possess the highest reliability at an elevated temperature (150 °C) for a long lifetime period (10 years) [15]. Piezoelectric actuators are namely the key to increasing burning efficiency and minimizing toxic exhaust gases. The success of this project seems to be attributed to the author's "pulse drive technique" for ML actuators without generating troublesome vibration ringing after the quick actuation, which will be discussed in Chapter 8. The current research target of this project includes Cu internal electrode usage for replacing the Ag-Pd electrode to reduce the manufacturing cost of piezo-MLs.

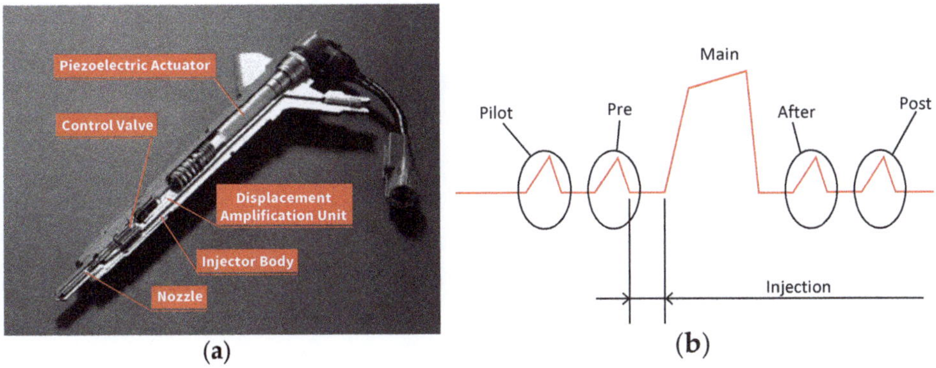

Figure 1.22. (**a**) Common rail-type diesel injection valve with a piezoelectric multilayer actuator (courtesy of Denso Corporation). (**b**) Diesel injection timing chart. Source: [16] ©Uchino, K. *Micromechatronics*, 2nd ed. CRC Press, 2019; pp. 460–461. Reproduced by permission of Taylor & Francis Group.

Ultrasonic Motors (USMs) for Camera Modules

Surface wave-type traveling wave ultrasonic motors were firstly installed in Canon EOS zoom/focus mechanisms in the 1990s. The necessity of camera modules for mobile phones in the early 2000s accelerated the development of micro motors at an inexpensive cost. The so-called "metal tube type" consisting of a hollow metal cylinder and two PZT rectangular plates was developed by Penn State University in the late 1990s (see Figure 1.23a). When one of the PZT plates, Plate X, is driven (single-phase drive), a bending resonant vibration is excited basically along the x'-axis. However, because of an asymmetrical mass (Plate Y), another hybridized bending mode is excited with some phase lag along the y'-axis, leading to an elliptical locus on this metal tube end in a clockwise direction, similar to a "hula-hoop" motion. The rotor of this motor is a cylindrical tube with a pair of stainless ferrules pressing down with a spring. The metal cylinder motor, 2.4 mm in diameter and 12 mm in length, was driven at 62.1 kHz in both rotation directions. A no-load speed of 1800 rpm and a maximum output torque of 1.8 mN·m were obtained for bi-directional rotation under an applied rms voltage of 80 V. The rather high maximum efficiency of about 28% for this small motor is a noteworthy feature [17,18]. Various modifications were made for the stator, including a type with four PZT plates, arranged symmetrically and driven by two-phase (sine and cosine) voltages (Chapter 7 handles the AC drive technique for piezoelectrics).

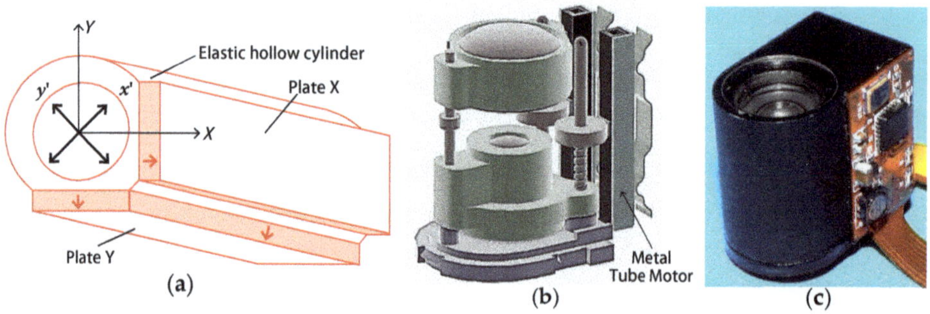

Figure 1.23. (**a**) A "metal tube" motor structure using a metal tube and two rectangular PZT plates. (**b**) Camera automatic zoom/focus mechanism with two metal tube USMs. (**c**) Photo of the camera module installed in a Samsung flip-type cellular phone in 2003. Source: [16] ©Uchino, K. *Micromechatronics*, 2nd ed. CRC Press, 2019; pp. 472–473. Reproduced by permission of Taylor & Francis Group.

Samsung Electromechanics, Korea, in collaboration with the author's group, developed a zoom and focus mechanism with two micro rotary motors in 2003. Two micro metal tube motors with a 2.4 mm diameter and 14 mm length were installed to control zooming and focusing lenses independently in conjunction with screw mechanisms, as illustrated in Figure 1.23b [19]. A screw is rotated through a pulley, which is then transferred to the lens up–down motion. The square chip (3×3 mm^2) on the camera module in Figure 1.23c is a high-frequency drive voltage supply. Newscale Technologies (Victor, NY) integrated a screw in the metal tube motor and commercialized "squiggle motors" worldwide for camera module applications, in partnership with ALPS, Tamron, and TDK-EPC [20]. Samsung Electromechanics is now utilizing much smaller micro-ML chip linear USMs for the Galaxy smartphone series' camera modules due to the thinner design necessity [21].

In parallel to the USM usage, Konica-Minolta, Japan, developed a smooth impact drive mechanism (SIDM) using a multilayer (ML) piezo-element [22]. The idea comes from the "stick and slick" condition of the ring object attached on a drive rod. By applying a sawtooth-shaped voltage to a multilayer actuator, alternating slow expansion and quick shrinkage are excited on the drive friction rod. A ring slider placed on the drive rod will "stick" on the rod due to friction during a slow expansion period, while it will "slick" during a quick shrinkage period, meaning that the slider moves from one end of the rod to the other. Example Problem 14.1 demonstrates how to simulate the slider motion via the "stick and slick" condition. The lens is attached to this slider. When the voltage saw shape is reversed, an opposite motion can be obtained. Piezo Tech, Korea, developed a similar SIDM motor, but using a bimorph, instead of an ML actuator, that suppressed the manufacturing cost significantly. For

TULAs (tiny ultrasonic linear actuators) [23], though a flexural bimorph is used, the driving frequency is much higher than 40 kHz (ultrasonic range) due to their small size (inertial motor principle is described in Chapter 14).

Piezoelectric Energy Harvesting Systems

One of the recent research interests is "piezoelectric energy harvesting". Cyclic electric energy generated in a piezoelectric component by environmental noise vibration can be accumulated into a rechargeable battery. Originally, in the 1980s, we consumed the converted electrical energy via Joule heat in order to rapidly damp the noise vibration [24]. After transitioning into the 1990s, we started to accumulate this energy in a rechargeable battery [25–27]. Because the generating power is limited up to the 100 W level, the development target is not to compete with MW~GW electric power projects with other renewable windmill/watermill or solar cell technologies, but to eliminate small single-use batteries that are hazardous to the world. There are three major phases/steps associated with piezoelectric energy harvesting: (i) mechanical–mechanical energy transfer, including "mechanical impedance matching" and the mechanical stability of piezoelectric transducers under large stresses (refer to Chapter 10), (ii) mechanical–electrical energy transduction, relating to the electromechanical coupling factor in composite transducer structures, and (iii) electrical–electrical energy transfer, including "electrical impedance matching" (refer to Chapter 10). A suitable DC–DC converter is required to accumulate the electrical energy from a high-impedance piezo-device into a rechargeable battery (low impedance) [28] (Chapters 7 and 8 discuss both pulse and AC mechanical drive techniques for receiving the maxium electric energy).

Our application target of the "cymbal" was set to hybridize vehicles with both an engine and an electromagnetic motor, in collaboration with Toyota Central Research Labs, reducing the engine vibration and harvested electrical energy (~1 W) in car batteries to increase the mileage. A cymbal with a 29 mm diameter and 1~2 mm thickness (0.3 mm-thick stainless steel endcaps), to be inserted below a 7 kg engine weight (70 N bias force), was shaken under an electromagnetic shaker (in an experiment) at 100 Hz, which generated 80 mW of electric power [25,26]. By parallely connecting nine cymbals embedded in rubber engine damping sheets, we succeeded in obtaining a total electric power level close to 1 W for a rechargeable battery.

Another development target of piezo-energy harvesting can be found in the small energy harvesting (mW) area for signal transfer applications, where the efficiency is not a primary objective because the use period is limited. These applications usually handle an impulse/snap action load to generate instantaneous electrical energy for transmitting signals for a short period (100 ms–10 s), without accumulating the electricity in a rechargeable battery. NEC-Tokin developed an LED traffic light array system driven by a piezoelectric windmill, which is operated by wind effectively generated by passing automobiles. Successful million-selling products in the commercial market belong mostly to this category at present, including the "Lightning Switch" [28] and the 25 mm caliber "programmable air-burst munition" [29]. The former, by PulseSwitch Systems, VA, is a remote switch for room lights, using a unimorph piezoelectric component (Figure 1.24a). In addition to living convenience, the Lightning Switch can reduce housing construction costs drastically, due to a significant reduction in the copper electric wire length and the labor of aligning it in the ceiling. On the contrary, the 25 mm caliber "programmable air-burst munition (PABM)" [29] is based on electricity generation with a multilayer piezo-actuator under shot impact to maneuver the bullet via an operational amplifier, developed by Micromechatronics Inc., PA, and ATK Integrated Weapon Systems, AZ, during the revenge war against Afghanistan (2003). The current bullet seems to be a micro missile with a programmable function (microcomputer for pin-point tageting). A piezo-energy harvesting device was installed because the original button battery (for operating microchips for 2–3 s to maneuver the bullet) decayed after only two months under the high-temperature atomosphere of the Afghanistan battlefield.

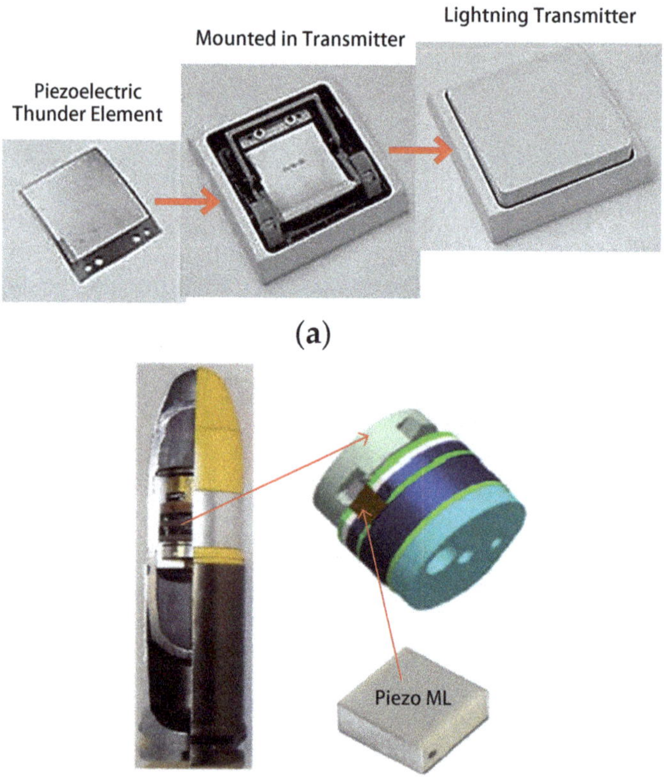

(a)

(b)

Figure 1.24. (**a**) Lightning Switch with a piezoelectric Thunder actuator (courtesy of Face Electronics). (**b**) Programmable air-burst munition (PABM, 25 mm caliber) developed by Micromechatonics. Source: Figure by author.

Though relatively large investments and research efforts are being devoted to MEMS/NEMS and "nano-harvesting" devices, a positive comment cannot be provided at the moment, except for the sensor applications [30]. Even for medical applications, the obtained/reported energy level of nW~μW from one MEMS component (this level practically refers to "sensors", not "energy harvestors", in engineering) is a useless level, which originates from the inevitable small volume of the used piezoelectric material (i.e., thin films). A minimum of 0.1 mm^3 PZT is required for generating a couple of megawatts (minimum level to be called "energy harvesting"), because the current high-power PZT ceramics can handle a maximum of 30 W/cm^3. In practice, at minimum, a 30 μm-thick PZT film is required for maintaining a small area less than 3×3 mm^2. A total of 90% of the current research papers do not satisfy this minimum requirement. Another solution is to invent a genius idea of how to combine thousands of these nano-devices in parallel and synchronously in phase. "Nano- or microgrid" research aimed at reaching a minimum 1 mW level by connecting thousands of nano-harvesting devices is highly encouraged, rather than merely the MEMS fabrication process from an academic viewpoint. Refer to [31].

Chapter Essentials

1. Ferroelectric and piezoelectric category:
   Dielectrics > Piezoelectrics > Pyroelectrics > Ferroelectrics
2. Ferroelectric materials are very promising for a variety of applications:
   - High-permittivity capacitors (high permittivity around T_C);
   - Ferroelectric memories (large spontaneous polarization);
   - Pyroelectric sensors, electrocaloric refrigeration (large temperature dependence of P_S);
   - Piezoelectric/electrostrictive transducers, piezoelectric energy harvesting (electromechanical k);
   - Electro-optic devices (refractive index control);
   - PTC thermistors (semiconductor junction effect).
3. Origin of spontaneous polarization: balancing the following two types of energy:
   - Dipole coupling with the local field—driving force of ionic displacement;
   - Elastic anharmonic term—impeding ionic displacement.
4. Field-induced strains:
   - Piezoelectric strain $-x = dE$ in an asymmetric crystal.
     - ✔ Difference in the harmonic term of the two equivalent springs.
   - Strain associated with polarization reorientations.
   - Electrostriction $-x = ME^2$ in a symmetric crystal.
     - ✔ Anharmonicity of the equivalent springs (slightly compliant for extension).
5. Electro-optic effect: Refractive index change with an external electric field. The secondary Kerr effect is frequently used. Devices making use of this effect require a pair of crossed polarizers arranged at a ±45° angle with respect to the electric field direction. Half-wave voltage: minimum voltage required for an electro-optic crystal to exhibit the first maximum light intensity.
6. Recent "million-selling" piezoelectric products:
   - Piezoelectric multilayer actuators for diesel injection valve control;
   - Ultrasonic motors (USMs and inertial type) for smartphone camera modules;

- Piezoelectric energy harvesting devices for "programmable air-burst munition"

Check Point

1. There are three microscopic origins of polarization: electronic polarization, ionic polarization, and (   ). Fill in the blank.
2. The local field is the driving force for spontaneous polarization. What is the positive feedback amplification factor "γ" called, which enhances the applied electric field E?
3. (T/F) Taking into account a famous relation between the relative permittivity ε and the refractive index n: $\varepsilon = n^2$, we can obtain $n = 4$ for a crystal with $\varepsilon = 16$ (at 1 kHz). Is this argument true or false?
4. Randomly oriented light passes through a polarizer. When we neglect the light absorption by the polarizer, what percentage of the light intensity can we obtain after the polarizer in comparison with the input intensity?
5. (T/F) The definition of the Pockels electro-optic coefficient r_{1jk} is given by an expansion expression: $1/n_{ij}(E) - 1/n_{ij}(0) = \Sigma r_{ijk} E_k$. True or false?
6. (T/F) The Curie temperature of a ferroelectric capacitor material should be around room temperature. True or false?
7. (T/F) The Curie temperature of a piezoelectric transducer material should be 100 °C lower than room temperature. True or false?
8. (T/F) The Curie temperature of a pyroelectric sensor material should be 200 °C higher than room temperature. True or false?
9. Provide the name of a representative polymer piezoelectric.
10. Provide the full expression of "PZT".

Chapter Problems

1.1 Ferroelectricity disappears in general with a decreasing particle size. In order to explain this phenomenon, we consider the energy fluctuation for a nano-size ferroelectric particle as follows: Consider a 1D finite chain of two types of ions, $+q$ and $-q$, arranged alternately with a distance of a (see Figure 1.25a). A nano-size crystal grows gradually, starting from a single positive ion, then adding a pair of negative or positive ions, thus maintaining a crystal size of $2na$ ($n = 1, 2, 3, \ldots$). With an increasing crystal size, the crystal Coulomb energy will be changed as follows:
$U_1 = (2/4\pi\varepsilon_0\varepsilon)\,[-(q^2/a)]$
$U_2 = (2/4\pi\varepsilon_0\varepsilon)\,[-(q^2/a) + (q^2/2a)]$
$U_3 = (2/4\pi\varepsilon_0\varepsilon)\,[-(q^2/a) + (q^2/2a) - (q^2/3a)]$
. . . .

(a) For the infinite (large) crystal, calculate the "Madelung constant" when the saturated energy is expressed by

$$U = (-M/4\pi\varepsilon_0\varepsilon)(q^2/a). \qquad \text{(CP1.1.1)}$$

(b) With an increasing crystal size layer by layer, how many layers are required to stabilize the energy fluctuation to less than $\pm 10\%$ around the Madelung energy?

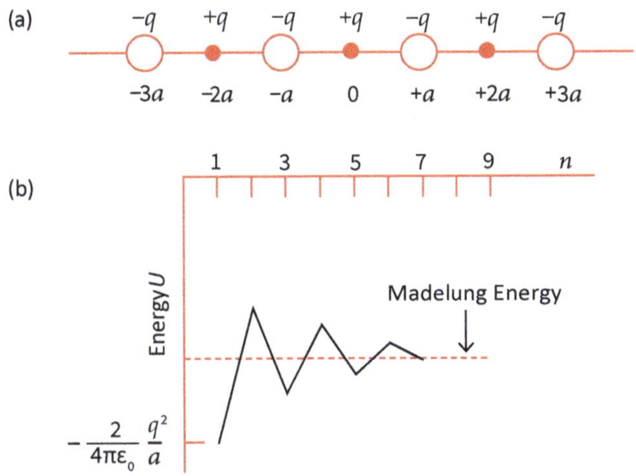

Figure 1.25. One-dimensional linear chain (**a**), and Madelung energy (**b**). Source: Figure by author.

<u>Hint</u>

Use the relation: $\ln(1+x) = x - \frac{x^2}{2} + \frac{x^3}{3} - \cdots$. The value 2ln2 = 1.386 is called the Madelung constant for a 1D chain.

(a) With an increasing crystal size, the crystal Coulomb energy will be changed as follows:

$$U_n = -\left(\frac{2}{4\pi\varepsilon_0\varepsilon}\right)\left(\frac{q^2}{a}\right)\left(1 - \frac{1}{2} + \frac{1}{3} - \frac{1}{4} + \cdots + \frac{1}{n}\right). \quad \text{(CP1.1.2)}$$

Knowing the relation: $\ln(1+1) = 1 - \frac{1}{2} + \frac{1}{3} - \frac{1}{4} + \cdots = \ln(2)$,

$$U_\infty = -\left(\frac{2}{4\pi\varepsilon_0\varepsilon}\right)\left(\frac{q^2}{a}\right)\ln(2). \quad \text{(CP1.1.3)}$$

Since the Madelung constant is defined by

$$U_\infty = -\left(\frac{M}{4\pi\varepsilon_0\varepsilon}\right)\left(\frac{q^2}{a}\right), M = 2\ln(2) = 1.386. \quad \text{(CP1.1.4)}$$

(b) The Coulomb potential change at the center point is shown in Figure 1.25b as a function of the crystal size n, with a final saturating value of the Madelung energy. When the energy fluctuation is so large, a small energy imbalance between the paraelectric and the ferroelectric state may not cause a phase transition. Suppose that the minimum crystal size ($2na$) is required to maintain the potential energy fluctuation at less than $\pm$10% at the center positive ion, even when adding or subtracting a pair of ions (i.e., $n + 1$ or $n - 1$). If the basic crystal Coulomb energy is not stabilized to less than this degree of fluctuation, we cannot expect the ferroelectric phase transition to occur as a cooperative phenomenon.

By equating $1/n = 10\%$, we obtain $n = 10$. If we use $a = 4$ Å, $2na = 80$ Å = 8 nm. According to the study on amorphous $PbTiO_3$, the soft phonon mode and the maximum permittivity indicate that the appearance of ferroelectricity starts to be observed around 100 Å, with an increasing crystalline size during the annealing process. This crystalline size is in the same range as the above theoretically estimated crystal size. The reader is requested to extend the theory to the 2D model (try Example Problem 14.4 for 2D Madelung constant calculation, which exhibits a much more stable idea than the 1D model).

1.2 Potassium tantalate niobate $K(Ta_{0.65}Nb_{0.35})O_3$ is cubic at room temperature. By applying an electric field E_z along a perovskite [100] axis, it exhibits an induced polarization P_3, electrostrictive strains $x_3 = Q_{11}P_3^2$ and $x_1 = Q_{12}P_3^2$, and refractive index changes $\Delta n_3 = -(1/2)n_0^3 g_{11}P_3^2$ and $\Delta n_1 = -(1/2)n_0^3 \times g_{12}P_3^2$. Experimental values of these are: $Q_{11} = 0.090$ m^{4}C^{-2}, and $Q_{12} = -0.035$ m^{4}C^{-2}; $g_{11} = 0.136$ m^{4}C^{-2}, and $g_{12} = -0.038$ m^{4}C^{-2}. Comparing the absolute values between Q and g and the ratios Q_{11}/Q_{12} and g_{11}/g_{12}, discuss similarities in terms of the crystal lattice compactness along and perpendicular to the electric field.

1.3 PZT 5H and PZT 8 have the following physical parameters:

Physical Parameters	PZT 5H	PZT 8
d_{33} (10^{-12} m/V)	593	225
$\varepsilon_{33}^X/\varepsilon_0$	3400	1000
s_{33}^E(10^{-12} m^2/N)	20.8	13.5

(a) Calculate the electromechanical coupling factor k_{33} for both PZT specimens.

(b) Which specimen, PZT5H or PZT8, is a "hard" PZT? Explain the reason for this judgement.

References

1. Uchino, K. *Ferroelectric Devices*, 2nd ed.; CRC Press: Boca Raton, FL, USA, 2010.
2. Kittel, C. *Introduction to Solid State Physics*, 6th ed.; John Wiley & Sons: New York, NY, USA, 1986; Chapter 13.
3. Kinase, W.; Uemura, Y.; Kikuchi, M. Correction of Dipole Field Due to Lattice Deformation of a Perovskite-Type Crystal. *J. Phys. Chem. Solids* **1969**, *30*, 441. [CrossRef]
4. Uchino, K.; Nomura, S.; Cross, L.E.; Newnham, R.E.; Jang, S.J. Electrostrictive Effect in Perovskites and Its Transducer Applications. *J. Mater. Sci.* **1981**, *16*, 569. [CrossRef]
5. Uchino, K. Electrostrictive Actuators: Materials and Applications. *Bull. Am. Ceram. Soc.* **1986**, *65*, 647.
6. Uchino, K. The development of piezoelectric materials and the new perspective. In *Advanced Piezoelectric Materials*, 2nd ed.; Kenji, U., Ed.; Woodhead Publishing/Elsevier: Cambridge, UK, 2017; Chapter 1.
7. Uchida, N.; Ikeda, T. Electrostriction in Perovskite-Type Ferroelectric Ceramics. *Jpn. J. Appl. Phys.* **1967**, *6*, 1079. [CrossRef]
8. Sawaguchi, E.; Shirane, G.; Takagi, Y. Phase Transition in Lead Zirconate. *J. Phys. Soc. Jpn.* **1951**, *6*, 333–339. [CrossRef]
9. Jaffe, B. Piezoelectric Transducers Using Lead Titanate and Lead Zirconate. U.S. Patent 2,708,244, 10 May 1955.

10. Takeuchi, H.; Masuzawa, H.; Nakaya, C.; Ito, Y. Relaxor Ferroelectric Transducers. In Proceedings of the IEEE 1990 Ultrasonics Symposium, Honolulu, HI, USA, 4–7 December 1990; p. 697.
11. Kuwata, J.; Uchino, K.; Nomura, S. Dielectric and Piezoelectric Properties of $0.91Pb(Zn_{1/3}Nb_{2/3})O_3$-$0.09PbTiO_3$ Single Crystals. *Jpn. J. Appl. Phys.* **1982**, *21*, 1298. [CrossRef]
12. Shrout, T.R.; Chang, Z.P.; Kim, N.; Markgraf, S. Dielectric Behavior of Single Crystals Near the $(1-X)$ $Pb(Mg_{1/3}Nb_{2/3})O_3$-(x) $PbTiO_3$ Morphotropic Phase Boundary. *Ferroelectr. Lett.* **1990**, *12*, 63. [CrossRef]
13. Kawai, H. The Piezoelectricity of Poly (vinylidene Fluorides). *Jpn. J. Appl. Phys.* **1969**, *8*, 975. [CrossRef]
14. Available online: www.marklines.com/ja/amreport/rep094_200208.jsp (accessed on 30 October 2005).
15. Fujii, A. Piezoelectric ML Actuators for Diesel Injection Valve Applications. In Proceedings of the JTTAS Meeting, Tokyo, Japan, 2 December 2005.
16. Uchino, K. *Micromechatronics*, 2nd ed.; CRC Press: Boca Raton, FL, USA, 2019.
17. Koc, B.; Cagatay, S.; Uchino, K. A Piezoelectric Motor Using Two Orthogonal Bending Modes of a Hollow Cylinder. *IEEE Ultrason. Ferroelectr. Freq. Control. Trans.* **2002**, *49*, 495–500. [CrossRef]
18. Cagatay, S.; Koc, B.; Uchino, K. A 1.6 mm Metal Tube Ultrasonic Motor. *IEEE Trans.-UFFC* **2003**, *50*, 782–786. [CrossRef]
19. Uchino, K. Piezoelectric Actuators 2004—Materials, Design, Drive/Control, Modeling and Applications. In Proceedings of the New Actuator 2004, Bremen, Germany, 14–16 June 2004; p. 127.
20. New Scale Technologies. Available online: https://www.newscaletech.com/about-us/ (accessed on 30 April 2005).
21. Koc, B.; Ryu, J.; Lee, D.; Kang, B.; Kang, B.H. Piezoelectric Ultrasonic Motors for Lens Positioning of Cellular Phone Camera Modules. In Proceedings of the New Actuator 2006, Bremen, Germany, 14–16 June 2006; p. 58.
22. Okamoto, Y.; Yoshida, R.; Sueyoshi, H. Development of Smooth Impact Drive Mechanism. *Konica Minolta Tech. Rep.* **2004**, *1*, 23.
23. Piezo-Electric Technology. Available online: http://www.piezo-tech.com/eng/product/ (accessed on 30 June 2004).
24. Uchino, K.; Ishii, T.J. Mechanical Damper Using Piezoelectric Ceramics. *Jpn. Ceram. Soc.* **1988**, *96*, 863–867. [CrossRef]
25. Kim, H.W.; Batra, A.; Priya, S.; Uchino, K.; Markley, D.; Newnham, R.E.; Hofmann, H.F. Energy Harvesting Using a Piezoelectric "Cymbal" Transducer in Dynamic Environment. *Jpn. J. Appl. Phys.* **2004**, *43*, 6178–6183. [CrossRef]
26. Kim, H.W.; Priya, S.; Uchino, K.; Newnham, R.E. Piezoelectric Energy Harvesting under High Pre-Stressed Cyclic Vibrations. *J. Electroceramics* **2005**, *15*, 27–34. [CrossRef]
27. Uchino, K. Energy Flow Analysis in Piezoelectric Harvesting Systems. In *Energy Harvesting with Piezoelectric and Pyroelectric Materials*; Nantakan, M., Ed.; Trans Tech Publications: Zuerich, Switzerland, 2011; Chapter 4.
28. Uchino, K. Piezoelectric Actuators—Piezoelectric Devices in the Sustainable Society. In Proceedings of the 12th Int'l Conf. New Actuators, A3.0, Bremen, Germany, 14–16 June 2010; Available online: http://www.lightningswitch.com/ (accessed on 30 June 2010).
29. ATK. Available online: http://www.atk.com/MediaCenter/mediacenter_%20videogallery.asp (accessed on 30 May 2005).
30. Uchino, K. Piezoelectric Actuator Renaissance. *J. Energy Harvest. Syst.* **2014**, *1*, 45–56. [CrossRef]

31. Uchino, K. *Essentials of Piezoelectric Energy Harvesting*; World Scientific Pub. Co.: Singapore, 2021.

2. Linear Coupling in Ferroelectrics—Taylor Expansion Series

2.1. Thermodynamical Functions

2.1.1. Various Energy Descriptions

A thermodynamic phenomenological theory is discussed basically in the form of expansion series of the "internal energy" U as a function of the physical properties; the free energy is composed of "thermal energy" dQ, "mechanical energy" Xdx (stress X, strain x), and "electrical energy" EdD (dielectric displacement D (almost equal to polarization P in high-permittivity materials), electric field E) in ferroelectrics. When a material is ferromagnetic, magnetic energy HdB is integrated. Further, thermal energy dQ is given by $dQ \leq TdS$, where temperature is T and entropy is S. Equality "=" is true for a reversible process, and "<" is true for an irreversible process. We can describe U as follows:

$$dU = dQ + Xdx + EdD \leq TdS + Xdx + EdD. \tag{2.1}$$

According to the combination possibilities among (T, S), (X, x), and (E, D), there are the following eight types of energy:

• Internal energy	$U = Q + W$	$dU = TdS + Xdx + EdD$	(2.2)
• Helmholtz free energy	$A = U - TS$	$dA = -SdT + Xdx + EdD$	(2.3)
• Enthalpy	$H = U - Xx - ED$	$dH = TdS - xdX - DdE$	(2.4)
• Elastic enthalpy	$H_1 = U - Xx$	$dH_1 = TdS - xdX + EdD$	(2.5)
• Electric enthalpy	$H_2 = U - ED$	$dH_2 = TdS + Xdx - DdE$	(2.6)
• Gibbs free energy	$G = U - TS - Xx - ED$	$dG = -SdT - xdX - DdE$	(2.7)
• Elastic Gibbs energy	$G_1 = U - TS - Xx$	$dG_1 = -SdT - xdX + EdD$	(2.8)
• Electric Gibbs energy	$G_2 = U - TS - ED$	$dG_2 = -SdT + Xdx - DdE$	(2.9)

According to the IUPAC (International Union of Pure and Applied Chemistry), an "extensive" parameter depends on the volume of the material (e.g., the length, charge, or entropy S is halved by cutting the material in half), while an "intensive" parameter is the ratio of two extensive parameters and, therefore, is independent of the volume of the material (e.g., the force, voltage, or temperature T does not change by cutting the material in half) [1]. Consequently, stress (X), the electric field (E), and temperature (T) are intensive parameters, which are externally controllable, while strain (x), electric displacement (D) (almost the same as polarization (P) in this textbook), and entropy (S) are extensive parameters, which are internally determined in a material. Internal energy U (per unit volume, [J/m^3]) is described in terms of "extensive" physical parameters (S, x, D). Since the phase transition and experiments are normally conducted under external parameter changes by keeping some constant such as T = constant (isothermal), $X = 0$ (stress free), or $E = 0$ (short circuit), the Gibbs free energy described in terms of "intensive" physical parameters (T, X, E) is the most popularly utilized type to analyze experimental data. On the other hand, the elastic Gibbs energy G_1 is most convenient for discussing the ferroelectric phase transition due to two merits: (1) by describing higher-order Taylor expansion terms of the "order parameter" D (or P), we can derive the spontaneous polarization; (2) external X can be controlled explicitly, and E is easily related to $(\frac{\partial G_1}{\partial P})_{T,X}$. We discuss Devonshire theory in Chapter 4.

2.1.2. Maxwell Relations

We can obtain some of the "Maxwell relationship" examples from Equations (2.2)–(2.9) as follows, taking the second partial derivative:

$$(\frac{\partial D}{\partial X})_{T,E} = (\frac{\partial}{\partial X}(-\frac{\partial G}{\partial E})_{T,X})_{T,E} = (\frac{\partial}{\partial E}(-\frac{\partial G}{\partial X})_{x,T})_{T,D} = (\frac{\partial x}{\partial E})_{T,X}, \tag{2.10a}$$

$$(\frac{\partial X}{\partial D})_{T,x} = (\frac{\partial}{\partial D}(\frac{\partial A}{\partial x})_{X,D})_{T,x} = (\frac{\partial}{\partial x}(\frac{\partial A}{\partial D})_{x,T})_{T,D} = (\frac{\partial E}{\partial x})_{T,D}, \tag{2.10b}$$

$$(\frac{\partial S}{\partial E})_{T,X} = (\frac{\partial}{\partial E}(-\frac{\partial G}{\partial T})_{X,E})_{T,X} = (\frac{\partial}{\partial T}(-\frac{\partial G}{\partial E})_{X,T})_{T,X} = (\frac{\partial D}{\partial T})_{X,E}. \tag{2.10c}$$

Equations (2.10a) and (2.10b) are for the piezoelectric d coefficients, discussed in Section 2.2.1, while Equation (2.10c) is used in the "pyroelectric coefficient" p derivation in Section 2.4.1.

Figure 2.1 shows a convenient memorization method for obtaining the Maxwell relations. The arrow from "S" to "T" stands for the following: "T" is obtained from the partial derivative of H_1 (D-constant) or H_2 (E-constant) in terms of "S", or "S" is obtained from the partial derivative of G_1 (D-constant) or G_2 (E-constant) in terms of "T" with a negative sign (arrow direction is opposite!). The other arrow from "E" to "$-D$" has similar meanings. Thus, we can obtain the following relations, leading to the right-hand side Maxwell relations:

$$\begin{array}{llll}
T = (\frac{\partial H_1}{\partial S})_D; & E = (\frac{\partial H_1}{\partial D})_S & \rightarrow & (\frac{\partial T}{\partial D})_S = (\frac{\partial E}{\partial S})_D \\
T = (\frac{\partial H_2}{\partial S})_E; & -D = (\frac{\partial H_2}{\partial E})_S & \rightarrow & (\frac{\partial T}{\partial E})_S = -(\frac{\partial D}{\partial S})_E \\
-S = (\frac{\partial G_2}{\partial T})_E; & -D = (\frac{\partial G_2}{\partial E})_T & \rightarrow & (\frac{\partial S}{\partial E})_T = (\frac{\partial D}{\partial T})_E \\
-S = (\frac{\partial G_1}{\partial T})_D; & E = (\frac{\partial G_1}{\partial D})_T & \rightarrow & (\frac{\partial S}{\partial D})_T = -(\frac{\partial E}{\partial T})_D
\end{array}$$

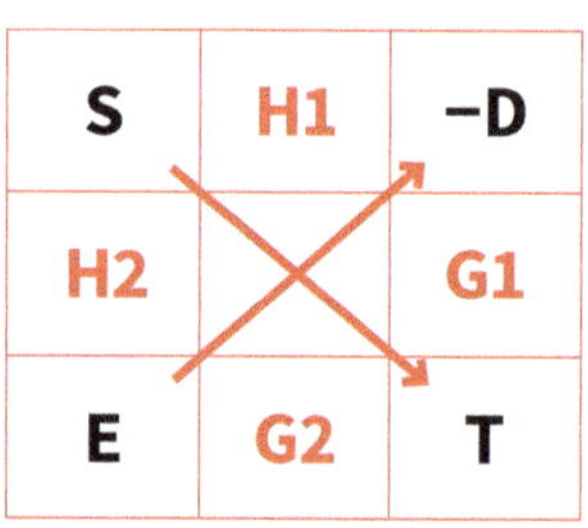

Figure 2.1. Maxwell relation derivation chart. Source: Figure by author.

2.1.3. *Linear Energy Handling*

We consider a practical formula of the Gibbs free energy $G(T, X, E)$ for the case of a small value change in temperature $\theta = T - T_R$ (room temperature), external X, and E (1D case). If the change in parameters is small, we may adopt the three-parameter Taylor expansion approximation up to the second derivatives in order to discuss just the linear relationships, based on the description by Mitsui et al. [2]:

$$\begin{aligned} G(T,X,E) = G_0 &+ \left(\tfrac{\partial G}{\partial T}\right)\theta + \left(\tfrac{\partial G}{\partial X}\right)X + \left(\tfrac{\partial G}{\partial E}\right)E + \tfrac{1}{2}\left(\tfrac{\partial^2 G}{\partial T^2}\right)\theta^2 + \tfrac{1}{2}\left(\tfrac{\partial^2 G}{\partial X^2}\right)X^2 \\ &+ \tfrac{1}{2}\left(\tfrac{\partial^2 G}{\partial E^2}\right)E^2 + \left(\tfrac{\partial^2 G}{\partial T \partial X}\right)\theta X + \left(\tfrac{\partial^2 G}{\partial T \partial E}\right)\theta E + \left(\tfrac{\partial^2 G}{\partial X \partial E}\right)XE. \end{aligned} \tag{2.11}$$

Taking into account $dG = -SdT - xdX - DdE$, we first obtain the relations $\left(\frac{\partial G}{\partial T}\right)_{\theta,X,E=0} = -S_0$, $\left(\frac{\partial G}{\partial X}\right)_{\theta,X,E=0} = -x_0$, and $\left(\frac{\partial G}{\partial E}\right)_{\theta,X,E=0} = -D_0$. Since S_0 is the entropy density at $\theta, X, E = 0$, we take this as the "origin" value and set it as $S_0 = 0$. The values x_0 and D_0 ($\approx P_0$) are considered to be spontaneous strain and spontaneous polarization in the ferroelectric phase of this material (refer to Chapter 4), and we set them as new "origins" in the discussion merely in the ferroelectric phase. Now, Equation (2.11) can be transformed as follows:

$$S = -\left(\frac{\partial G}{\partial T}\right) = -\left(\frac{\partial^2 G}{\partial T^2}\right)\theta - \left(\frac{\partial^2 G}{\partial T \partial X}\right)X - \left(\frac{\partial^2 G}{\partial T \partial E}\right)E, \tag{2.12a}$$

$$x = -\left(\frac{\partial G}{\partial X}\right) = -\left(\frac{\partial^2 G}{\partial T \partial X}\right)\theta - \left(\frac{\partial^2 G}{\partial X^2}\right)X - \left(\frac{\partial^2 G}{\partial X \partial E}\right)E, \tag{2.12b}$$

$$D = -\left(\frac{\partial G}{\partial E}\right) = -\left(\frac{\partial^2 G}{\partial T \partial E}\right)\theta - \left(\frac{\partial^2 G}{\partial X \partial E}\right)X - \left(\frac{\partial^2 G}{\partial E^2}\right)E. \tag{2.12c}$$

Based on the above linear relationships, we derive several types of "constitutive equations" in the following sections.

2.2. Isothermal Process—Piezoelectric Coupling

2.2.1. *Thermodynamical Meaning of Piezoelectric Constant*

When the temperature is constant (i.e., "isothermal"), $\theta = 0$ in Equations (1.12b) and (1.12c), we can obtain the "intensive" parameter-based piezoelectric constitutive equations

$$x = s^E X + dE, \tag{2.13a}$$

$$D = dX + \varepsilon_0 \varepsilon^X E, \tag{2.13b}$$

where the following denotations are used: s^E is the elastic compliance under a constant E, and $\varepsilon_0 \varepsilon^X$ is the dielectric permittivity under a stress-free condition:

$$\begin{cases} s^E = -\left(\frac{\partial^2 G}{\partial X^2}\right) \\ \varepsilon_0 \varepsilon^X = -\left(\frac{\partial^2 G}{\partial E^2}\right) \\ d = -\left(\frac{\partial^2 G}{\partial X \partial E}\right) \end{cases}. \tag{2.14}$$

The Maxwell relation, Equation (2.10a), $\left(\frac{\partial D}{\partial X}\right)_{T,E} = \left(\frac{\partial x}{\partial E}\right)_{T,X}$, verifies that the piezoelectric coefficients d in Equations (2.13a) and (2.13b) are thermodynamically the same.

When we start from the Helmholtz free energy A ($dA = -SdT + Xdx + EdD$), by taking a similar Taylor expansion approach, we obtain another set of piezoelectric constitutive equations in terms of "extensive" parameters, x and D:

$$X = c^D x - hD, \tag{2.15a}$$

$$E = -hx + \kappa_0 \kappa^x D, \tag{2.15b}$$

where c^D is the elastic stiffness under a constant D, and $\kappa_0\kappa^x$ is the inverse permittivity ($\kappa_0 = 1/\varepsilon_0$) under a strain-free condition, and these coefficients are expressed by

$$\begin{cases} c^D = \left(\frac{\partial^2 A}{\partial x^2}\right) \\ \kappa_0\kappa^x = \left(\frac{\partial^2 A}{\partial D^2}\right) \\ h = -\left(\frac{\partial^2 A}{\partial x \partial D}\right) \end{cases}. \tag{2.16}$$

The Maxwell relation $\left(\frac{\partial X}{\partial D}\right)_{T,x} = \left(\frac{\partial E}{\partial x}\right)_{T,D}$ in Equation (2.10b) verifies that the inverse piezoelectric coefficients h in Equations (2.15a) and (2.15b) are thermodynamically the same.

2.2.2. Electromechanical Coupling Factor

The term "electromechanical coupling factor" k is defined as the square value k^2 of the ratio of the converted energy over the input energy: when electric to mechanical,

$$k^2 = \text{(Stored mechanical energy/Input electrical energy)}, \tag{2.17a}$$

or when mechanical to electric,

$$k^2 = \text{(Stored electrical energy/Input mechanical energy)}. \tag{2.17b}$$

Let us derive Equation (2.17a) first practically, where an external electric field E_3 is applied to a piezoelectric material in a pseudo-static process. See Figure 2.2a, where we apply an electric field on the top and bottom electrodes under a stress-free condition ($X = 0$) [3]. The input electric energy must be equal to $(1/2)\cdot\varepsilon_0\varepsilon_3{}^X E_3{}^2$ from Equation (2.11) (under $X = 0$), and the output strain generated by E_3 should be $d_{33}E_3$ from Equation (2.13a). Since the converted/stored mechanical energy is obtained as $(1/2\cdot s_{33}{}^E)\cdot x_3{}^2$, we obtain

$$k_{33}{}^2 = [(1/2)(d_{33}E_3)^2/s_{33}{}^E]/[(1/2)\cdot\varepsilon_0\varepsilon_3{}^X E_3{}^2] = d_{33}{}^2/\varepsilon_0\varepsilon_3{}^X\cdot s_{33}{}^E. \tag{2.18a}$$

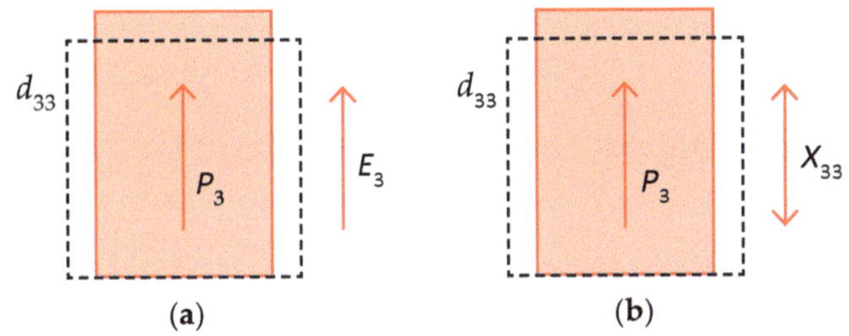

Figure 2.2. Calculation models of the electromechanical coupling factor k for (**a**) an electric input under a stress-free condition, and (**b**) a stress input under a short-circuit condition. Source: Figure by author, adapted from [4].

Let us now consider Equation (2.17b), where an external stress X_3 is applied to a piezoelectric material in a pseudo-static process. Refer to Figure 2.2b. Under a short-circuit condition ($E_3 = 0$), the input mechanical energy must be equal to $(1/2)\, s_{33}{}^E X_3{}^2$ from Equation (2.11), and the electric displacement D_3 (or polarization P_3) generated by X_3 should be equal to $d_{33}X_3$ from Equation (2.13b). This D_3 can be obtained by integrating the short-circuit current in terms of time through the electric lead. Since the converted/stored electric energy is obtained as $(1/2\ \varepsilon_0\varepsilon_3{}^X)$ $D_3{}^2$, we obtain

$$k_{33}{}^2 = [(1/2\varepsilon_0\varepsilon_3{}^X)(d_{33}X_3)^2]/[(1/2)\cdot s_3{}^E X_3{}^2] = d_{33}{}^2/\varepsilon_0\varepsilon_3{}^X\cdot s_{33}{}^E. \tag{2.18b}$$

It is essential to understand that the electromechanical coupling factor k (or k^2, which has a physical meaning of the energy transduction/conversion rate) can be exactly the same for both converse (2.18a) and direct (2.18b) piezoelectric effects. The conditions under constant X (stress free) or a constant E (short circuit) are considered to be non-constrained.

2.2.3. Constraint Physical Parameters—Permittivity and Elastic Compliance

It is important to consider the conditions under which a material will be operated when characterizing the dielectric constant and elastic compliance of that material [3]. When a constant electric field is applied to a piezoelectric sample, as illustrated in Figure 2.3, top, the total input electric energy (left) should be equal to a combination of the energies associated with two distinct mechanical conditions that may be applied to the material: (1) stored electric energy under the "mechanically clamped state", where a constant strain (zero strain) is maintained and the specimen cannot deform, and (2) converted mechanical energy under the "mechanically free state", in which the material is not constrained and is free to deform. This situation can be expressed by

$$\left(\tfrac{1}{2}\right)\varepsilon^X\varepsilon_0E_0^2 = \left(\tfrac{1}{2}\right)\varepsilon^x\varepsilon_0E_0^2 + \left(\tfrac{1}{2s^E}\right)x^2 = \left(\tfrac{1}{2}\right)\varepsilon^x\varepsilon_0E_0^2 + \left(\tfrac{1}{2s^E}\right)(dE_0)^2,$$

such that

$$\varepsilon^X\varepsilon_0 = \varepsilon^x\varepsilon_0 + \left(\frac{d^2}{s^E}\right) \text{ or } \varepsilon^x = \varepsilon^X\left(1-k^2\right)\ [k^2 = \frac{d^2}{\varepsilon^X\varepsilon_0\, s^E}]. \tag{2.19a}$$

When a constant stress is applied to the piezoelectric, as illustrated in Figure 2.3, bottom, the total input mechanical energy will be a combination of the energies associated with two distinct electrical conditions that may be applied to the material: (1) stored mechanical energy under the "open-circuit state", where a constant electric displacement is maintained, and (2) converted electric energy (i.e., "depolarization field") under the "short-circuit condition", in which the material is subject to a constant electric field. This can be expressed as

$$\left(\frac{1}{2}\right)s^E X_0^2 = \left(\frac{1}{2}\right)s^D X_0^2 + \left(\frac{1}{2}\right)\varepsilon^X \varepsilon_0 E^2 = \left(\frac{1}{2}\right)s^D X_0^2 + \left(\frac{1}{2}\right)\varepsilon^X \varepsilon_0 \left(d/\varepsilon_0 \varepsilon_3{}^X\right)^2 X_0^2,$$

which leads to

$$s^E = s^D + \left(\frac{d^2}{\varepsilon^X \varepsilon_0}\right) \text{ or } s^D = s^E(1-k^2)[k^2 = \frac{d^2}{\varepsilon^X \varepsilon_0\, s^E}]. \tag{2.19b}$$

In principle, if we measure the permittivity in a piezoelectric specimen under stress-free and completely clamped conditions, we can obtain ε^X and ε^x, respectively. However, in practice, ε^x cannot be measured because of the experimental difficulty of maintaining the ideal strain-free (clamped) condition for a long period. Similarly, if we measure the strain in a piezoelectric specimen as a function of the applied stress pseudo-statically, under short-circuit and open-circuit conditions, we can obtain s^E and s^D, respectively. However, in practice, s^D cannot be measured because of the induced bound charge (or polarization) "screening" by the migrating charge in the electrode, specimen, or surrounding atmosphere within a couple of minutes. Thus, the clamped permittivity ε^x or open-circuit D-constant s^D can only be measured with high-frequency dynamical methods, such as an impedance analyzer around the resonance/antiresonance frequencies. Constraint parameters are discussed again in Chapter 9.

In conclusion, we obtain the following equations:

$$\varepsilon^x/\varepsilon^X = (1-k^2), \tag{2.20a}$$

$$s^D/s^E = (1-k^2), \tag{2.20b}$$

where

$$k^2 = \frac{d^2}{s^E \varepsilon^X \varepsilon_0}. \tag{2.21a}$$

We can also write equations of a similar form for the corresponding reciprocal quantities:

$$\kappa^X/\kappa^x = (1-k^2), \tag{2.22a}$$

$$c^E/c^D = (1-k^2), \tag{2.22b}$$

where, in this context,

$$k^2 = \frac{h^2}{c^D(\kappa_0\, \kappa^x)}. \tag{2.21b}$$

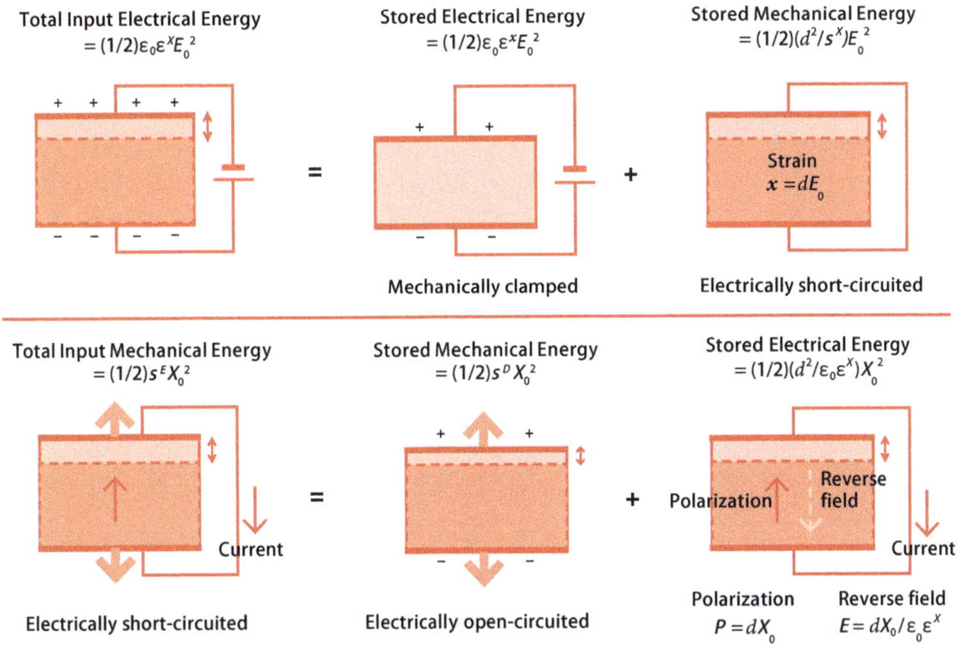

Figure 2.3. Schematic representation of the response of a piezoelectric material under (**top**) constant applied electric field and (**bottom**) constant applied stress conditions. Source: [4] ©Uchino, K. *Micromechatronics*, 2nd ed. CRC Press, 2019; p. 76. Reproduced by permission of Taylor & Francis Group.

This new parameter k in Equation (2.21b) is also the "electromechanical coupling factor" in the "extensive" parameter description and identical to the k in Equation (2.21a). Note the k expression derivation from the piezoelectric constitutive equations, Equations (2.13a), (2.13b), (2.15a), and (2.15b):

$$k^2 = \frac{(\text{Coupling factor})^2}{(\text{Product of the diagonal parameters})} = \frac{d^2}{s^E\varepsilon^X\varepsilon_0} = \frac{h^2}{c^D(\kappa_0\ \kappa^x)}\ [\kappa_0\ = 1/\varepsilon_0\ ].$$

Example Problem 2.1

(1) Verify the relationship

$$\frac{d^2}{s^E\varepsilon^X\varepsilon_0} = \frac{h^2}{c^D(\kappa_0\kappa^x)}. \tag{P2.1.1}$$

This value is defined as the square of an electromechanical coupling factor (k^2), which should be the same even for different energy description systems (i.e., intensive or extensive description).

(2) Derive the following relationships:

$$\varepsilon^X\varepsilon_0 = \frac{1}{(\kappa_0\kappa^x)[1 - \frac{h^2}{c^D(\kappa_0\kappa^x)}]} = \frac{1}{(\kappa_0\kappa^x)(1-k^2)}, \tag{P2.1.2}$$

$$s^E = \frac{1}{c^D[1 - \frac{h^2}{c^D(\kappa_0\kappa^x)}]} = \frac{1}{c^D(1-k^2)}, \tag{P2.1.3}$$

$$d = \frac{\frac{h^2}{c^D(\kappa_0\kappa^x)}}{h[1 - \frac{h^2}{c^D(\kappa_0\kappa^x)}]} = \frac{k^2}{h(1-k^2)}. \tag{P2.1.4}$$

Solution

(1) When Equations (2.13a) and (2.13b) are combined with Equations (2.15a) and (2.15b), we obtain

$$X = c^D(s^E X + dE) + h(dX + \varepsilon_0\varepsilon^X E), \tag{P2.1.5}$$

$$E = -h(s^E X + dE) + (\kappa_0\kappa^x)(dX + \varepsilon_0\varepsilon^X E), \tag{P2.1.6}$$

or upon rearranging,

$$(1 - c^D s^E + hd)X + (h\varepsilon_0\varepsilon^X - c^D d)E = 0, \tag{P2.1.7}$$

$$[hs^E - (\kappa_0\kappa^x)d]\, X + [1 - (\kappa_0\kappa^x)\varepsilon_0\varepsilon^X + hd]E = 0. \tag{P2.1.8}$$

Combining the last two equations yields

$$(1 - c^D s^E + hd)[1 - (\kappa_0\kappa^x)\varepsilon_0\varepsilon^X + hd] - (h\varepsilon_0\varepsilon^X - c^D d)[hs^E - (\kappa_0\kappa^x)d] = 0, \tag{P2.1.9}$$

which, when simplified, produces the desired relationship:

$$\frac{d^2}{s^E\varepsilon^X\varepsilon_0} = \frac{h^2}{c^D(\kappa^x\kappa_0)}. \tag{P2.1.10}$$

(2) From the two constitutive equations

$$\begin{bmatrix} x \\ D \end{bmatrix} = \begin{bmatrix} s^E & d \\ d & \varepsilon_0\varepsilon^X \end{bmatrix} \begin{bmatrix} X \\ E \end{bmatrix}, \text{ and} \begin{bmatrix} X \\ E \end{bmatrix} = \begin{bmatrix} c^D & -h \\ -h & \kappa_0\kappa^x \end{bmatrix} \begin{bmatrix} x \\ D \end{bmatrix}, \tag{P2.1.11}$$

we obtain

$$\begin{bmatrix} x \\ D \end{bmatrix} = \begin{bmatrix} s^E & d \\ d & \varepsilon_0\varepsilon^X \end{bmatrix} \begin{bmatrix} c^D & -h \\ -h & \kappa_0\kappa^x \end{bmatrix} \begin{bmatrix} x \\ D \end{bmatrix}. \tag{P2.1.12}$$

Thus, the following equation should be satisfied:

$$\begin{bmatrix} s^E & d \\ d & \varepsilon_0\varepsilon^X \end{bmatrix} \begin{bmatrix} c^D & -h \\ -h & \kappa_0\kappa^x \end{bmatrix} = \begin{bmatrix} 1 & 0 \\ 0 & 1 \end{bmatrix}. \tag{P2.1.13}$$

Accordingly, $s^E c^D - dh = 1$, $-s^E h + d\kappa_0\kappa^x = 0$, $dc^D - \varepsilon_0\varepsilon^X h = 0$, and $-dh + \varepsilon_0\varepsilon^X\kappa_0\kappa^x = 1$. Then, we obtain the relationships Equations (P2.1.2)–(P2.1.4), by expressing the intensive parameters $\varepsilon_0\varepsilon^X$, s^E, and d in terms of the extensive parameters $\kappa_0\kappa^x$, c^D, h, and k^2.

2.3. Adiabatic Process 1—Piezothermal Effect

2.3.1. Piezothermal Coupling Effect

When we discuss piezoelectric coupling phenomena, we assume the isothermic condition; that is, the specimen temperature is maintained constant, and even the energy conversion is conducted between the electrical and mechanical energy. We next consider the "adiabatic process"; that is, the specimen is isolated from the external heat source, and the temperature may be changed during the energy conversion process by the external input. When the electric field is constant, $E = 0$ in Equations (2.12a) and (2.12b), we can obtain the following equations:

$$S = -\left(\frac{\partial^2 G}{\partial T^2}\right)\theta - \left(\frac{\partial^2 G}{\partial T \partial X}\right)X, \tag{2.23a}$$

$$x = -\left(\frac{\partial^2 G}{\partial T \partial X}\right)\theta - \left(\frac{\partial^2 G}{\partial X^2}\right)X, \tag{2.23b}$$

or

$$S = \frac{C_p}{T}\theta + \alpha_L X, \tag{2.24a}$$

$$x = \alpha_L \theta + s^E X, \tag{2.24b}$$

where the following notations are used: C_p is the "heat capacitance per volume" under $X = 0$ and $E = 0$, and s^E is the elastic compliance under a constant E:

$$\begin{cases} C_p = -T\left(\frac{\partial^2 G}{\partial T^2}\right)_{X,E} \\ s^E = -\left(\frac{\partial^2 G}{\partial X^2}\right)_{E,T} \\ \alpha_L = -\left(\frac{\partial^2 G}{\partial T \partial X}\right)_E \end{cases}. \tag{2.25}$$

Let us discuss here the diagonal expansion coefficient $-\left(\frac{\partial^2 G}{\partial T^2}\right)$ in terms of the specific heat capacity. Recall the relation $dq = TdS$ in the "reversible" thermal process, where dq is the thermal energy flow per unit "volume", given by the total energy flow $dQ = Vdq$ (V: volume). The heat capacitance C_p is defined by

$$C_p = \frac{\partial q}{\partial T} = T\left(\frac{\partial S}{\partial T}\right)_{X,E} = -T\left(\frac{\partial^2 G}{\partial T^2}\right)_{X,E}. \tag{2.26}$$

Here, we used the relation $S = -\left(\frac{\partial G}{\partial T}\right)_{X,E}$. It is noteworthy that the "specific heat capacity" c_p, more popularly measured experimentally, is defined by the required thermal energy per unit "mass" to increase the unit temperature. Thus, the above C_p is related to the specific heat capacity with the mass density ρ:

$$C_p = \rho c_p \tag{2.27}$$

The "piezothermal coefficient" α_L is usually called the "linear thermal expansion coefficient", because $-\left(\frac{\partial^2 G}{\partial T \partial X}\right)_E = \left(\frac{\partial x}{\partial T}\right)$. The piezothermal coefficient α_L originates from a nonlinear elastic vibration or the anharmonic phonon interaction, which will be discussed in Chapter 11.

This piezothermal coefficient α_L contributes to the converse effect; that is, a temperature change under stress application. Considering an adiabatic condition, Equation (2.24a) gives $\frac{C_p}{T}\theta = -\alpha_L X$ or $\theta = -\frac{\alpha_L}{\left(\frac{C_p}{T}\right)} X$, which means that a sudden tensile stress generates a temperature decrease. The reader might have experienced in their elementary or middle school age the feeling of a "cool" temperature when they touched a thick rubber band on their lip immediately after expanding it (I liked this experiment, though I could not understand the principle correctly).

The "piezothermal coupling factor" k^{PT} can be defined from Equations (2.24a) and (2.24b) by

$$k^{PT^2} = \frac{(\text{Coupling factor})^2}{(\text{Product of the diagonal parameters})} = \frac{{\alpha_L}^2}{\left(\frac{C_p}{T}\right) s^E}. \tag{2.28}$$

2.3.2. *Constraint Physical Parameters—Heat Capacitance and Elastic Compliance*

We can derive the completely "clamped" (strain x free) heat capacitance and the "adiabatic" elastic compliance in terms of k^{PT^2} theoretically, as follows, though these may not be useful physical parameters.

Clamped Specific Heat Capacity

Under a strain-free condition ($x = 0$), we obtain $X = -\frac{\alpha_L}{s^E}\theta$ from Equation (2.24b). We experience this effect when a train rail track bends on a hot summer day, which occasionally causes derailment accidents. Since Equation (2.24a) gives
$S = \frac{C_p}{T}\theta + \alpha_L\left(-\frac{\alpha_L}{s^E}\theta\right) = \frac{C_p}{T}(1 - k^{PT^2})\theta$,
we finally obtain

$$C_p^x = C_p^X(1 - k^{PT^2}). \tag{2.29}$$

The heat capacitance becomes smaller under the mechanical clamping.

Adiabatic Elastic Compliance

Under an adiabatic condition ($S = 0$), we obtain $\theta = -\frac{T}{C_p}\alpha_L X$ from Equation (2.24a). The reader is reminded of the feeling of a "cool" temperature when you expanded (tensile stress) a rubber band quickly and touched it on their lip. Since Equation (2.24b) gives
$x = \alpha_L\left(-\frac{T}{C_p}\alpha_L X\right) + s^E X = s^E\left(1 - k^{PT^2}\right)X$,

we obtain

$$s_{adia}^{E,S} = s_{iso}^{E,T}\left(1 - k^{PT^2}\right). \tag{2.30}$$

2.4. Adiabatic Process 2—Electrothermal Effect

2.4.1. *Electrothermal Coupling Effect*

When the stress is constant, $X = 0$ in Equations (2.12a) and (2.12c), we can obtain the following equations:

$$S = -\left(\frac{\partial^2 G}{\partial T^2}\right)\theta - \left(\frac{\partial^2 G}{\partial T \partial E}\right)E, \tag{2.31a}$$

$$D = -\left(\frac{\partial^2 G}{\partial T \partial E}\right)\theta - \left(\frac{\partial^2 G}{\partial E^2}\right)E, \tag{2.31b}$$

or

$$S = \frac{C_p^E}{T}\theta - pE, \tag{2.32a}$$

$$D = -p\theta + \varepsilon_0 \varepsilon^X E, \tag{2.32b}$$

where the following denotations are used: C_p^E is the heat capacitance (per unit volume) under $X = 0$ and $E = 0$, and $\varepsilon_0\varepsilon^X$ is the permittivity under constant stress X:

$$\begin{cases} C_p^E = -T\left(\frac{\partial^2 G}{\partial T^2}\right)_{X,E} \\ \varepsilon_0\varepsilon^X = -\left(\frac{\partial^2 G}{\partial E^2}\right)_{T,X} \\ p = \left(\frac{\partial^2 G}{\partial T \partial E}\right)_X \end{cases}. \tag{2.33}$$

The primary electrothermal coupling coefficient p is usually called the "pyroelectric coefficient", defined by

$$p = \left(\frac{\partial^2 G}{\partial T \partial E}\right)_X = -\left(\frac{\partial P}{\partial T}\right)_X, \tag{2.34}$$

where we intentionally used the relation $\left(\frac{\partial G}{\partial E}\right)_X = D\ (\approx P)$, since the permittivity ε^X is large in ferroelectrics.

We can denote the primary "electrothermal coupling factor" k^{ET} from Equations (2.32a) and (2.32b) as

$$k^{ET^2} = \frac{(\text{Coupling factor})^2}{(\text{Product of the diagonal parameters})} = \frac{p^2}{\left(\frac{C_p^E}{T}\right)\varepsilon_0\varepsilon^X}. \tag{2.35}$$

2.4.2. *Constraint Specific Heat Capacity*

In Equation (2.33), we introduced the C_p^E heat capacitance (per unit volume) under $X = 0$ and $E = 0$; that is, under a short-circuit condition of a ferroelectric specimen's surface electrodes. We may consider a different heat capacitance under an open-circuit condition (i.e., D = constant or zero).

Taking the first derivative of Equation (2.32a) with respect to T by keeping $X = D = 0$,

$$(\frac{\partial S}{\partial T})_{X,D} = \frac{C_p^E}{T}(\frac{\partial \theta}{\partial T})_{X,D} - p(\frac{\partial E}{\partial T})_{X,D}. \quad (2.36)$$

From Equation (2.32b) at $D = 0$, we obtain

$$E = \frac{p}{\varepsilon_0 \varepsilon^X}\theta, \quad (2.37a)$$

$$(\frac{\partial E}{\partial T})_{X,D} = \frac{p}{\varepsilon_0 \varepsilon^X}. \quad (2.37b)$$

If we consider that $C_p^D = T(\frac{\partial S}{\partial T})_{X,D}$ and $(\frac{\partial \theta}{\partial T})_{X,D} = 1$, we can obtain

$$C_p^D = C_p^E - \frac{Tp^2}{\varepsilon_0 \varepsilon^X} = C_p^E[1 - \frac{p^2}{\left(\frac{C_p^E}{T}\right)\varepsilon_0 \varepsilon^X}] = C_p^E(1 - k^{ET^2}). \quad (2.38)$$

It is important to note that Equation (2.38) is analogous to Equation (2.20b) to correlate the D-constant and E-constant parameters in terms of the "coupling factors", k^{ET^2} and k^2.

2.4.3. Constraint (Adiabatic) Permittivity

Permittivity has been defined isothermally thus far. However, we may consider "adiabatic" permittivity theoretically when no heat flow is hypothesized, such as the case where a ferroelectric specimen is suspended in a vacuum chamber [2].

From Equation (2.32b), isothermal permittivity ($\theta = 0$) is given by

$$\varepsilon_0 \varepsilon^{X,T} = (\frac{\partial D}{\partial E})_{X,T}. \quad (2.39)$$

Under an adiabatic condition, by inserting $S = 0$ into Equation (2.32a), we obtain

$$\theta = \frac{pT}{C_p^E}E. \quad (2.40)$$

Inserting Equation (2.40) into Equation (2.32b),

$$D = -p\frac{pT}{C_p^E}E + \varepsilon_0 \varepsilon^{X,T}E = \varepsilon_0 \varepsilon^{X,T}\left[1 - \frac{Tp^2}{C_p^E \varepsilon_0 \varepsilon^X}\right]E. \quad (2.41)$$

Thus, "adiabatic (S = constant) permittivity" is related to "isothermal (T = constant) permittivity" again by using the primary electrothermal coupling factor k^{ET} as

$$\varepsilon_0 \varepsilon^{X,S} = \varepsilon_0 \varepsilon^{X,T}(1 - k^{ET^2}). \quad (2.42)$$

The permittivity is lower under the "adiabatic" condition, in comparison with that under the isothermal condition.

2.4.4. Electrocaloric Effect

Electrocaloric materials were initially the focus of significant application interest in the 1940s (during World War II). The US and Japan accelerated the research for developing air-cooling systems, particularly in submarines, without generating mechanical noise (such as air compressor-embedded refrigerators). Due to the confidential military research, not many publications have been disclosed on this research. The author personally learned this from his former advisor at university in the 1960s, when the research on this topic was fading out because the electrocaloric effect was insufficient then for practical applications. However, at the beginning of the 21st century, we restarted its development in parallel to the enthusiasm on new compact refrigeration techniques in the "sustainable" society. Our report on the giant response in $Pb(Zn_{1/3}Nb_{2/3})O_3$-$PbTiO_3$ (PZN-PT) bulk single crystals in 2003 [5], being 0.3 °C under an applied 1 kV/mm electric field, ignited the "renaissance of the electrocaloric effect". Successive reports on the high response, such as 12 °C under an applied electric field of 48 kV/mm in thin-film (or ribbon) lead zirconate-titanate (PZT) by Mischenko et al. in 2006 [6] (that is equivalent to 0.25 °C under 1 kV/mm, a lower performance than PZN-PT single crystals), and the demonstration of 12 °C of cooling near room temperature with a ferroelectric polymer by Neese et al. in 2008 [7], also accelerated the research boom in electrocaloric devices.

Equation (2.32a) gives the necessary formula for the electrocaloric effect. Consider an "adiabatic" condition, that is, $dQ = TdS = 0$, or a constant entropy $dS = 0$, and Equation (2.40), $\theta = \frac{pT}{C_p^E}E$. Here, C_p^E is the heat capacitance per unit volume (which is related to the "specific heat capacity" per unit mass as $c_p^E = C_p^E/\rho$) under $E = 0$, and p is the pyroelectric coefficient given by $p = -(\frac{\partial P}{\partial T})_X$. A material's development strategy should be a higher p and a lower C_p^E at room temperature (i.e., operation temperature of ~300 K). A decreasing temperature requires a large negative electric field. In order to escape from the electric depoling, we usually initially increase the electric field gradually (isothermally) and then make it short circuit suddenly (adiabatically).

2.4.5. Values of "Electrothermal Coupling Factor" k^{ET}

Let us obtain a practical number for the "electrothermal coupling factor" k^{ET} (Equation (2.35)) in PZTs at room temperature:

$$k^{ET^2} = \frac{p^2}{\left(\frac{\rho c^E}{T}\right)\varepsilon_0\varepsilon^X}.$$

- Pyroelectric coefficient p
  $Pb(Zr_{0.52}Ti_{0.48})O_3$—0.3–0.7 × 10^{-4} [C/m²·K] [8]
  PZT-5A—0.3–0.5 × 10^{-4} [C/m²·K] [9]
  $Pb(Zr_{0.74}Ti_{0.36})O_3$—2.7 × 10^{-4} [C/m²·K] [10]
- Specific heat capacity c_p^E
  PZT-APC841—340 [J/kg·K] [11]

PLZT(6/80/20)—[338 J/kg·K] [12]

The specific heat capacity is measured by differential scanning calorimetry (DSC), where endothermic and exothermic processes are monitored by keeping the input energy flow constant. Since the measuring time period is around 5–10 minutes, we cannot observe the difference between the short-circuited and open-circuited ferroelectric specimens, that is, c^E and c^D. This probably happens because the pyroelectrically induced charge is almost screened by the migrating free charge during a rather long measuring time (several minutes).

- Mass density ρ
  PZT-APC841—7600 [kg/m^3] [11]
- Permittivity ε^X
  PZT-APC841—1375 [13]

Finally, the electrothermal coupling factor is calculated as follows:

$$k^{ET^2} = \frac{p^2}{\left(\frac{\rho c^E}{T}\right)\varepsilon_0\varepsilon^X} = \frac{\left(0.5\times 10^{-4}\mathrm{C/m^2K}\right)^2}{\left(\frac{7600\ \mathrm{kg/m^3}\cdot 340\ \mathrm{J/kgK}}{300\ \mathrm{K}}\right)\left(8.854\times 10^{-12}\frac{\mathrm{F}}{\mathrm{m}}\right)\times 1375} = 1.11\times 10^{-6}, \tag{2.43a}$$

$$k^{ET} = 0.105\%. \tag{2.43b}$$

We can conclude that the electrothermal coupling factor k^{ET} in PZTs is two orders of magnitude smaller than the electromechanical coupling factor k of 30–70%. Though we discussed theoretical differences, the constraint condition difference between the E- and the D-constant or isothermal and adiabatic conditions does not provide a measurable difference in experimental values for the specific heat capacity and permittivity.

Example Problem 2.2

There is a PLZT (6/80/20) ceramic disk 1 cm^2 in area and 1 mm in thickness that is electrically poled along the thickness at room temperature (27 °C). For an external electric field of 1 kV applied to this sample anti-parallel to the polarization, calculate the temperature fall of the sample, using the following data: p = 76 nC·cm^{-2}K^{-1}, and C_p = 2.57 J·cm^{-3}K^{-1}. Note that C_p is the heat capacitance, not the specific heat capacity c_p, here.

Solution

The necessary equation is

$$(dT)_S = p\cdot(T/C_p)\cdot(dE)_S, \tag{P2.2.1}$$

where $p = 76 \times 10^{-5}$ C·m^{-2}K^{-1}, $C_p = 2.57 \times 10^6$ J·m^{-3}K^{-1}, $T = 300$ K, and $E = -10^6$ V/m. Then,

$$(dT)_S = [76 \times 10^{-5}\ \text{C·m}^{-2}\text{K}^{-1} \times 300\ \text{K} \times (-10^6\ \text{V/m})]/ \\ [2.57 \times 10^6\ \text{J·m}^{-3}\text{K}^{-1}] = -\ 0.089\ °\text{C}. \tag{P2.2.2}$$

The negative electric field generates the temperature decrease.

A negative electric field of 1 kV/mm is rather high, close to the coercive field of PZT ceramics. Thus, if we work on this specimen experimentally, significant performance decay is anticipated under a cyclical operation, due to the depoling. In practice, by increasing the field gradually (i.e., isothermally) up to $E = 10^6$ V/m, we suddenly (i.e., adiabatically) reduce the field to $E = 0$, meaning that we obtain a similar temperature decrease, without causing the "depoling problem" in the sample (under the supposition that an almost linear relation is sustained for both + and − electric fields).

2.5. Definitions of the Electromechanical Coupling Factor

Five different (but equivalent) definitions were introduced for the "electromechanical coupling factor" k, which corresponds to the rate of electromechanical transduction: the input electric energy to the output mechanical energy, and vice versa [4]. Notice the difference between the static k_v and the dynamic k_{vn}, which are used for "off-resonance" and "resonance" applications, respectively.

2.5.1. Mason's Definition

When we apply the electric field on a piezoelectric material or when we apply the mechanical force on the sample pseudo-statically or off-resonance ($\omega \to 0$), the electromechanical coupling factors are defined, respectively, by Mason [14] as follows:

$$k^2 = (\text{Stored mechanical energy/Input electrical energy}), \tag{2.44a}$$

$$k^2 = (\text{Stored electrical energy/Input mechanical energy}). \tag{2.44b}$$

Refer to Section 2.2.2 for the derivation process. Equations (2.18a) and (2.18b) indicate that both the above Equations (2.44a) and (2.44b) can be calculated exactly the same as

$$k^2 = d^2/\varepsilon_0\varepsilon^X \cdot s^E. \tag{2.45}$$

where d is the piezoelectric constant, $\varepsilon_0\varepsilon^X$ is the permittivity under constant stress, and s^E is the elastic compliance under a constant electric field condition. Recall Figure 2.2 for the derivation process.

2.5.2. Definition in Materials

Recall Equation (2.11) under an isothermal condition $\theta = 0$:

$$G(X, E) = G_0 + \frac{1}{2}\left(\frac{\partial^2 G}{\partial X^2}\right)X^2 + \frac{1}{2}\left(\frac{\partial^2 G}{\partial E^2}\right)E^2 + \left(\frac{\partial^2 G}{\partial X \partial E}\right)XE. \tag{2.46}$$

Denoting $\left(\frac{\partial^2 G}{\partial X^2}\right)$, $\left(\frac{\partial^2 G}{\partial E^2}\right)$, and $\left(\frac{\partial^2 G}{\partial X \partial E}\right)$ as s^E, $\varepsilon_0\varepsilon^X$, and d, respectively, the internal energy (per unit volume) U of a piezoelectric is given by the summation of the mechanical energy U_M (= $\int$ xdX) and the electrical energy U_E (= $\int$ DdE), as follows:

$$\begin{aligned} U = U_M + U_E = [(1/2)\textstyle\sum_{i,j} s_{ij}{}^E X_j X_i + (1/2)\sum_{m,i} d_{mi} E_m X_i] \\ +[(1/2)\textstyle\sum_{m,i} d_{mi} X_i E_m + (1/2) + \sum_{k,m} \varepsilon_0 \varepsilon_{mk}{}^X E_k E_m] = U_{EE} + 2\,U_{ME} + U_{EE} \\ = (1/2)\textstyle\sum_{i,j} s_{ij}{}^E X_j X_i + 2(1/2)\sum_{m,i} d_{mi} E_m X_i + (1/2)\sum_{k,m} \varepsilon_0 \varepsilon_{mk}{}^X E_k E_m. \end{aligned} \quad (2.47)$$

The above description includes the 3D tensor representation (refer to Chapter 3 for the details). The s and ε terms represent purely mechanical and electrical energies (U_{MM} and U_{EE}), respectively, and the d term denotes the energy transduced from the electrical to the mechanical energy or vice versa through the piezoelectric effect (U_{ME}). The electromechanical coupling factor k is defined by

$$k^2 = U_{ME^2}/U_{MM}U_{EE}, \text{or } k = U_{ME}/\sqrt{U_{MM}U_{EE}} \quad (2.48)$$

That is, k is the ratio of U_{ME} over the geometrical average of U_{MM} and U_{EE}.

Using the above energy terms (Equation (2.47)) with the s^E, $\varepsilon_0\varepsilon^X$, and d notations,

$$k^2 = \frac{\left(\frac{1}{2}dEX\right)^2}{\left(\frac{1}{2}s^E X^2\right)\left(\frac{1}{2}\varepsilon_0\varepsilon^X E^2\right)} = \frac{d^2}{s^E\varepsilon^X\varepsilon_0}. \quad (2.49)$$

2.5.3. Definition in Devices

Though the constitutive equations can be derived from the internal energy in Equations (2.13a) and (2.13b) in general, since the key equations are limited depending on the specimen geometry, there are several definitions according to the mode or specimen geometry in consideration:

$$\begin{bmatrix} x \\ D \end{bmatrix} = \begin{bmatrix} s^E & d \\ d & \varepsilon_0\varepsilon^X \end{bmatrix} \begin{bmatrix} X \\ E \end{bmatrix}, \quad (2.50)$$

and the electromechanical coupling factor is defined by

$$k^2 = \frac{(\text{Coupling factor})^2}{(\text{Product of the diagonal parameters})} = \frac{(d)^2}{(s^E\varepsilon_0\varepsilon^X)} \quad (2.51)$$

Table 2.1 summarizes the electromechanical coupling k_{ij} for typical piezoelectric resonators with different shapes and sizes.

Table 2.1. The characteristics of various piezoelectric resonators with different shapes and sizes.

	Factor	Boundary Conditions	Resonator Shape	Definition
(a)	k_{31}	$X_1 \neq 0, X_2 = X_3 = 0$ $x_1 \neq 0, x_2 \neq 0, x_3 \neq 0$	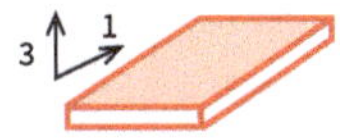	$\frac{d_{31}}{\sqrt{s_{11}^E \varepsilon_0 \varepsilon_{33}^X}}$
(b)	k_{33}	$X_1 = X_2 = 0, X_3 \neq 0$ $x_1 = x_2 \neq 0, x_3 \neq 0$	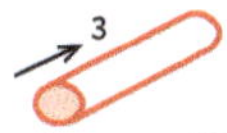 Fundamental Mode	$\frac{d_{33}}{\sqrt{s_{33}^E \varepsilon_0 \varepsilon_{33}^X}}$
(c)	k_p	$X_1 = X_2 \neq 0, X_3 = 0$ $x_1 = x_2 \neq 0, x_3 \neq 0$	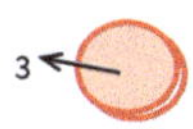 Planar/Radial Mode	$k_{31}\sqrt{\frac{2}{1-\sigma}}$
(d)	k_t	$X_1 = X_2 \neq 0, X_3 \neq 0$ $x_1 = x_2 = 0, x_3 \neq 0$	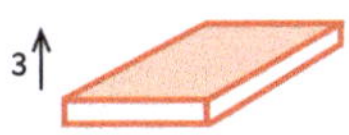 Thickness Mode	$k_{33}\sqrt{\frac{\varepsilon_0 \varepsilon_{33}^x}{c_{33}^D}}$
(e)	$k_{24} = k_{15}$	$X_1 = X_2 = X_3 = 0, X_4 \neq 0$ $x_1 = x_2 = x_3 = 0, x_5 \neq 0$	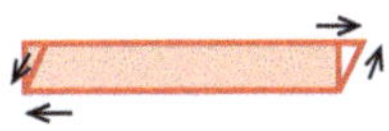 Shear Mode	$\frac{d_{15}}{\sqrt{s_{55}^E \varepsilon_0 \varepsilon_{11}^X}}$
(f)	k_{eff}	d_{31} Type Bimorph Bending	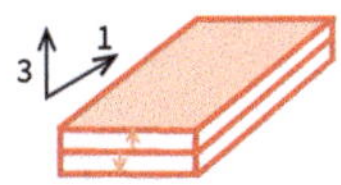	$\sqrt{\frac{3}{4}}k_{31}$

Source: Table by author.

Simple Piezo-Plate Configuration

When the vibration mode can be expressed directly by the same constitutive piezoelectric equations, the electromechanical coupling factor k of the resonator is equal to the material's electromechanical coupling factor, which are represented merely by the material's constants such as the piezoelectric constant, dielectric permittivity, and elastic compliance (and Poisson's ratio).

Examples can be found:

- k_{31} mode—$\begin{bmatrix} x_1 \\ D_3 \end{bmatrix} = \begin{bmatrix} s_{11}{}^E & d_{31} \\ d_{31} & \varepsilon_0 \varepsilon_{33}{}^X \end{bmatrix} \begin{bmatrix} X_1 \\ E_3 \end{bmatrix}$ provides $k_{31} = \frac{d_{31}}{\sqrt{s_{11}{}^E \varepsilon_0 \varepsilon_{33}{}^X}}$;
- k_{33} mode—$\begin{bmatrix} x_3 \\ D_3 \end{bmatrix} = \begin{bmatrix} s_{33}{}^E & d_{33} \\ d_{33} & \varepsilon_0 \varepsilon_{33}{}^X \end{bmatrix} \begin{bmatrix} X_3 \\ E_3 \end{bmatrix}$ provides $k_{33} = \frac{d_{33}}{\sqrt{s_{33}{}^E \varepsilon_0 \varepsilon_{33}{}^X}}$;
- k_p mode—$\begin{bmatrix} x_1 + x_2 \\ D_3 \end{bmatrix} = \begin{bmatrix} 2(s_{11}{}^E + s_{12}{}^E) & 2d_{31} \\ 2d_{31} & \varepsilon_0 \varepsilon_{33}{}^X \end{bmatrix} \begin{bmatrix} X_p \\ E_3 \end{bmatrix}$
  provides $k_p = k_{31}\sqrt{2/(1-\sigma)}$.

Because the piezoelectric Poisson ratio $|d_{31}/d_{33}| \approx 1/3$ in PZTs, supposing the difference in elastic compliances $s_{11}{}^E$ and $s_{33}{}^E$ is just around 10%, the reader can easily understand that $k_{33} >> k_{31}$ by a factor of three. You can conclude similarly that $k_p > k_{31}$ by a factor of $\sqrt{3}$ ($\sigma \approx 1/3$).

Example Problem 2.3

Piezoelectric, dielectric, and elastic properties of representative PZTs: soft PZT-5H, semi-hard PZT-4, and hard PZT-8, are summarized in Table 2.2. Using these data, answer the following questions, and learn the interrelations between these parameters.

(a) From the values of the piezoelectric d constant and permittivity ε, calculate the piezoelectric g constants, and compare these calculations with the values already provided in Table 2.2. Recall that g is a figure of merit for the "sensor" application.
(b) From the values of the piezoelectric d constant, permittivity ε, and elastic compliance s^E, calculate the electromechanical coupling factors k, and compare these calculations with the values in Table 2.2.
(c) Calculate the elastic Poisson ratio, $|s_{13}{}^E/s_{33}{}^E|$, and piezoelectric Poisson ratio, $|d_{31}/d_{33}|$, for the above three PZTs, then compare the similarity. The elastic Poisson ratio, $|s_{13}{}^E/s_{33}{}^E|$, is essential to calculate the disk vibration (i.e., k_p) (refer to Chapter 7).
(d) We apply 100 W of electric energy on a k_{33}-type PZT-4 rod. How much of that electric energy will be converted to mechanical energy stored in the PZT rod? Among that stored mechanical energy, how much, at most, can we spend on the outside work, taking into account the mechanical impedance matching?

Solution

(a) The example calculation for PZT-4 is performed with a k_{33}-type rod:
$g_{33} = d_{33}/\varepsilon_0\varepsilon_{33}{}^E = 285 \times 10^{-12}/8.854 \times 10^{-12} \times 1300 = 24.8 \times 10^{-3}$ [Vm/N]
Calculate this similarly for g_{31} and g_{15}, and for other PZTs.
(b) The example calculation for PZT-4 is performed with a k_{33}-type rod:
$k33 = d33/\sqrt{s_{33}{}^E\varepsilon_0\varepsilon_{33}{}^X} =$
$854 \times 10^{-12}/\sqrt{15.2 \times 10^{-12} \times 8.854 \times 10^{-12} \times 1300} = 0.68$
Calculate this similarly for k_{31} and k_{15}, and for other PZTs.
(c) PZT-5H: $|s_{13}{}^E/s_{33}{}^E| = 7.2 \times 10^{-12}/20.8 \times 10^{-12} = 0.35$
$|d_{31}/d_{33}| = 274 \times 10^{-12}/593 \times 10^{-12} = 0.46$
PZT-4: $|s_{13}{}^E/s_{33}{}^E| = 5.3 \times 10^{-12}/15.2 \times 10^{-12} = 0.35$
$|d_{31}/d_{33}| = 122 \times 10^{-12}/285 \times 10^{-12} = 0.42$
PZT-8: $|s_{13}{}^E/s_{33}{}^E| = 4.8 \times 10^{-12}/13.5 \times 10^{-12} = 0.36$
$|d_{31}/d_{33}| = 97 \times 10^{-12}/225 \times 10^{-12} = 0.43$
Both Poisson ratios are close in number, but $|d_{31}/d_{33}|$ seems to be a little larger than $|s_{13}{}^E/s_{33}{}^E|$.
(d) Mechanically converted and stored energy = 100 W $\times$ $k_{33}{}^2$ = 49 W. Among the stored mechanical energy, 1/3–1/4 is usually spent. The maximum output mechanical energy is 1/2 of the stored energy = 25 W, when we choose the external electrical load by exactly matching the internal impedance (=$1/\omega C$).

Table 2.2. Piezoelectric, dielectric, and elastic properties of typical PZTs.

Physical Parameter	Soft PZT-5H	Semi-Hard PZT-4	Hard PZT-8
EM Coupling Factor			
k_p	0.65	0.58	0.51
k_{31}	0.39	0.33	0.30
k_{33}	0.75	0.70	0.64
k_{15}	0.68	0.71	0.55
Piezoelectric Coefficient			
d_{31} (10^{-12} m/V)	−274	−122	−97
d_{33}	593	285	225
d_{15}	741	495	330
g_{31} (10^{-3} Vm/N)	−9.1	−10.6	−11.0
g_{33}	19.7	24.9	25.4
g_{15}	26.8	38.0	28.9
Permittivity			
$\varepsilon_{33}X/\varepsilon_0$	3400	1300	1000
$\varepsilon_{11}X/\varepsilon_0$	3130	1475	1290
Dielectric Loss (tanδ) (%)	2.00	0.40	0.40
Elastic Compliance			
s_{11}^E (10^{-12} m²/N)	16.4	12.2	11.5
s_{12}^E	−4.7	−4.1	−3.7
s_{13}^E	−7.2	−5.3	−4.8
s_{33}^E	20.8	15.2	13.5
s_{44}^E	43.5	38.5	32.3
Mechanical Q_M	65	500	1000
Density ρ (10^3 kg/m³)	7.5	7.5	7.6
Curie Temperature T_C (°C)	193	325	300

Source: Table by author, adapted from various company catalogues.

Complicated Piezo Component Configuration

When the structure of a vibrator is complicated, the electromechanical coupling factor k of the vibrator is dependent on the specimen geometry/size, in addition to the material's constants such as the piezoelectric constant, dielectric permittivity, and elastic compliance (and Poisson's ratio). An example can be found in bimorph structures, where k is dependent on the elastic shim material (metal) and thickness. Only for a pure piezo-plate bimorph without a shim is the electromechanical coupling factor irrelevant to the specimen size; that is, $k_{eff} = \sqrt{3/4}\cdot k_{31}$ for k_{31}-type bimorphs. Note that the bending or flexural mode exhibits a smaller electromechanical coupling factor in comparison with that of the base k_{31} plate.

2.5.4. Constraint Condition Method

From the relations between the E-constant, E-constant elastic compliances, s^E, s^D, stiffness c^E, c^D, stress-free and strain-free permittivity $\varepsilon_0\varepsilon^X$, $\varepsilon_0\varepsilon^x$, and inverse permittivity $\kappa_0\kappa^X$, $\kappa_0\kappa^x$ (refer to Equations (2.20a,b)–(2.22a,b)):

$$1 - k^2 = \frac{s^D}{s^E} = \frac{c^E}{c^D} = \frac{\varepsilon^x}{\varepsilon^X} = \frac{\kappa^X}{\kappa^x}. \quad (2.52)$$

2.5.5. Dynamic Definition

Though the details are discussed in Chapter 9, the k_{31}-type piezoelectric plate geometry and its four-terminal equivalent circuit are shown in Figure 2.4. In the four-terminal equivalent circuit, the electric terminal parameters, voltage V and current I, and the mechanical terminal parameters, force F and vibration velocity $\dot{u}$, at the plate end are related to each other as follows:

$$\begin{bmatrix} F \\ I \end{bmatrix} = \begin{bmatrix} Z_1 & -A \\ A & Y_1 \end{bmatrix} \begin{bmatrix} \dot{u} \\ V \end{bmatrix}. \tag{2.53}$$

The dynamic electromechanical coupling factor $k_v{}^2$ is defined by "(complex power in the mechanical branch)/(complex power in the electrical branch)" under a short-circuit condition of the mechanical terminal, or "(complex power in the electrical branch)/(complex power in the mechanical branch)" under a short-circuit condition of the electrical terminal, which leads to

$$k_v^2 = \left| \frac{\left(\frac{A^2}{Z_1 Y_1}\right)}{1 + \left(\frac{A^2}{Z_1 Y_1}\right)} \right|. \tag{2.54}$$

Since $Z_1 = jZ_0 \tan(\frac{\omega L}{2v})$, $Y_1 = j\omega C_d$, $A = \frac{2d_{31}w}{s_{11}^E}$, and $Z_0 = wb\rho v = \frac{wb}{v s_{11}^E}$ in the k_{31} mode, k_v^2 is ω dependent. By taking $\omega \to 0$, $k_v^2 \to k_{31}^2 = \frac{d_{31}^2}{s^E \varepsilon_0 \varepsilon^X}$. This dynamic k definition is particularly useful when considering/calculating a complex structured piezo-transducer, which is detailed in Chapters 7 and 9.

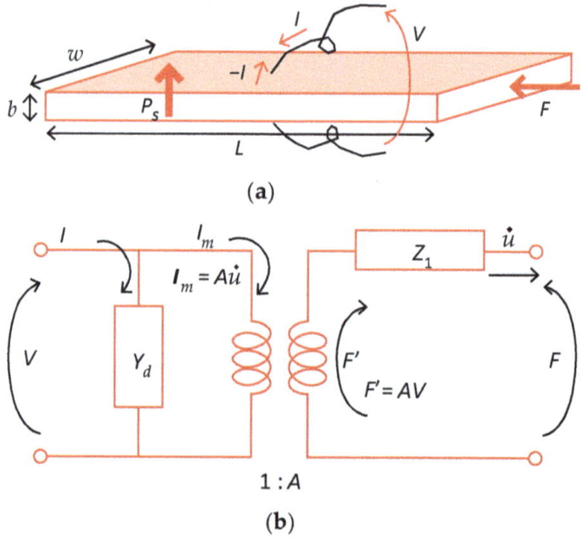

Figure 2.4. (**a**) k_{31}-type piezoelectric plate geometry; (**b**) four-terminal equivalent circuit for k_{31} piezo-plate. Source: Figure by author.

Chapter Essentials

1. Useful free energy expressions:
   - Internal energy $U = Q + W$ $dU = TdS + XdxEd$
   - Helmholtz free energy $A = U - TS$ $dA = -SdT + Xdx + EdD$
   For isothermal analysis of the material's properties.
   - Enthalpy $H = U - Xx - ED$ $dH = TdS - xdX - DdE$
   For adiabatic analysis under externally controllable parameters.
   - Gibbs free energy $G = U - TS - Xx - ED$ $dG = -SdT - xdX - DdE$
   For isothermal analysis under externally controllable parameters.
   - Elastic Gibbs energy $G_1 = U - TS - Xx$ $dG_1 = -SdT - xdX + EdD$
   For isothermal analysis of polarization under a stress-free condition.
2. Isothermal Process—Piezoelectric Coupling
   $$\begin{cases} x = s^E X + dE \\ D = dX + \varepsilon_0\varepsilon^X E \end{cases} \quad k^2 = \frac{d^2}{\varepsilon^X \varepsilon_0\, s^E}$$
   s^E: elastic compliance under constant E; $\varepsilon_0\varepsilon^X$: dielectric permittivity under stress free; d: piezoelectric constant
3. Adiabatic Process I—Piezothermal Coupling
   $$\begin{cases} S = \frac{C_p}{T}\theta + \alpha_L X \\ x = \alpha_L\theta + s^E X \end{cases} \quad k^{PT2} = \frac{\alpha_L{}^2}{\left(\frac{C_p}{T}\right) s^E}$$
   C_p : heat capacitance per volume under $X = 0$ and $E = 0$; s^E: elastic compliance under constant E; α_L: linear thermal expansion coefficient
4. Adiabatic Process II—Electrothermal Coupling
   $$\begin{cases} S = \frac{C_p^E}{T}\theta - pE \\ D = -p\theta + \varepsilon_0\varepsilon^X E \end{cases} \quad k^{ET2} = \frac{p^2}{\left(\frac{C_p^E}{T}\right)\varepsilon_0\varepsilon^X}$$
   C_p^E: heat capacitance (per unit volume) under $X = 0$ and $E = 0$; $\varepsilon_0\varepsilon^X$: permittivity under constant stress X; p: pyroelectric coefficient
5. Heat capacitance (per unit volume) C_p^E [J/Km^{-3}]; specific heat capacity (per unit mass) c_p^E [J/kg·K]
   $C_p^E = \rho c_p^E$.
6. Typical electrothermal coupling factor in PZTs: $k^{ET^2} = 1 \times 10^{-6}$ (much smaller than k^2).
7. Five definitions of the electromechanical coupling factor:

   (a) *Mason's definition:*

   k^2 = (Stored mechanical energy/Input electrical energy)= $\dfrac{(d)^2}{(s^E\varepsilon_0\varepsilon^X)}$

   or

   k^2 = (Stored electrical energy/Input mechanical energy)= $\dfrac{(d)^2}{(s^E\varepsilon_0\varepsilon^X)}$.

   (b) *Material definition* (under a static condition):
   $U = U_{MM} + 2U_{ME} + U_{EE}$
   $= (1/2)\sum_{i,j} s_{ij}{}^E X_j X_i + 2(1/2)\sum_{m,i} d_{mi} E_m X_i$

$$+ (1/2)\sum_{k,m} \varepsilon_0 \varepsilon_{mk}{}^X E_k E_m k^2 = U_{ME}{}^2 / U_{MM} U_{EE} = \frac{(d)^2}{(s^E \varepsilon_0 \varepsilon^X)}.$$

(c) *Device definition* (under a static condition):

When the primary constitutive equations are defined in a certain piezo component as

$$\begin{bmatrix} x \\ D \end{bmatrix} = \begin{bmatrix} s^E & d \\ d & \varepsilon_0 \varepsilon^X \end{bmatrix} \begin{bmatrix} X \\ E \end{bmatrix},$$

$$k^2 = \frac{(\text{Coupling factor})^2}{(\text{Product of the diagonal parameters})} = \frac{(d)^2}{(s^E \varepsilon_0 \varepsilon^X)}.$$

(d) *Constraint condition method*:

Between the *E*-constant, *E*-constant elastic compliances, s^E, s^D, stiffness c^E, c^D, stress-free and strain-free permittivity $\kappa_0 \kappa^X$, $\kappa_0 \kappa^x$, and inverse permittivity $\kappa_0 \kappa^X$, $\kappa_0 \kappa^x$:

$$1 - k^2 = \frac{s^D}{s^E} = \frac{c^E}{c^D} = \frac{\varepsilon^x}{\varepsilon^X} = \frac{\kappa^X}{\kappa^x}; k^2 = \frac{(d)^2}{(s^E \varepsilon_0 \varepsilon^X)} = \frac{h^2}{c^D (\kappa_0 \kappa^x)}.$$

(e) *Dynamic definition*: four-terminal equivalent circuit (Figure 2.4b):

Voltage V and current I, and mechanical terminal parameters force F and vibration velocity $\dot{u}$:

$$\begin{bmatrix} F \\ I \end{bmatrix} = \begin{bmatrix} Z_1 & -A \\ A & Y_1 \end{bmatrix} \begin{bmatrix} \dot{u} \\ V \end{bmatrix},$$

$$k_v^2 = \left| \frac{\left(\frac{A^2}{Z_1 Y_1}\right)}{1 + \left(\frac{A^2}{Z_1 Y_1}\right)} \right|.$$

$k_v = k$ for $\omega \to 0$;

$k_{v,n} = P_n k_v{}^2$: k for n-th resonance mode.

Check Point

1. (T/F) When we discuss the material's performance change with the external electric field E and stress X under an isothermal condition, the Gibbs free energy $dG = -SdT - xdX - DdE$ is most convenient. True or false?
2. (T/F) The Maxwell relation $(\frac{\partial D}{\partial X})_{T,E} = (\frac{\partial x}{\partial E})_{T,X}$ indicates that the piezoelectric constant d for the direct piezoelectric effect and converse piezoelectric effect should be exactly the same. True or false?
3. From the following piezoelectric constitutive equations, derive the electromechanical coupling factor k:
$$\begin{bmatrix} X \\ E \end{bmatrix} = \begin{bmatrix} c^D & -h \\ -h & \kappa_0 \kappa^x \end{bmatrix} \begin{bmatrix} x \\ D \end{bmatrix}.$$
4. (T/F) The elastic compliance of a piezoelectric material under a short-circuit condition (s^E) is smaller than that under an open-circuit condition (s^D). True or false?
5. Provide the relationship between the permittivity of a piezoelectric material under a completely clamped condition (ε^x) and that under a mechanically free condition (ε^X).

6. (T/F) The piezothermal effect indicates that the sudden tensile stress on a solid material usually exhibits a temperature decrease in this material. True or false?
7. What do you usually call the converse effect of the piezothermal effect mentioned above?
8. What do you usually call the converse electrocaloric effect?
9. (T/F) In a pyroelectric material, the spontaneous polarization increases with an increasing temperature. True or false?
10. Which is larger when $|d_{33}| > |d_{31}|$, $|k_{33}|$ or $|k_{31}|$?

Chapter Problems

2.1 We consider a more general effect in a ferroelectric without keeping any external parameters (temperature, stress, electric field) constant. Let us start from

$$S = \frac{C_p}{T}\theta + \alpha_L X - pE, \tag{CP2.1.1}$$

$$x = \alpha_L \theta + s^E X + dE, \tag{CP2.1.2}$$

$$D = -p\theta + dX + \varepsilon_0 \varepsilon^X E. \tag{CP2.1.3}$$

In comparison with the normal piezoelectric effect (constitutive equations), what modification is required?

Hint

When we consider a sudden external electric field E application, in addition to the normal piezoelectric effect, the electrothermal effect is superposed; that is, temperature modulation should be taken into account. On the contrary, when we consider a sudden stress X application, in addition to the normal piezoelectric effect, the piezothermal effect is superposed; that is, temperature modulation should be taken into account. Suppose that the "quick external parameter (E or X) application" is considered to be "adiabatic", $dS = 0$. From Equation (CP2.1.1),

$S = \frac{C_p}{T}\theta + \alpha_L X - pE = 0.$

Thus,

$$\theta = -(\alpha_L X - pE)/(\frac{C_p}{T}). \tag{CP2.1.4}$$

Equations (CP2.1.2) and (CP2.1.3) can be transformed as follows:

$x = -\alpha_L(\alpha_L X - pE)/(\frac{C_p}{T}) + s^E X + dE,$

$D = p(\alpha_L X - pE)/(\frac{C_p}{T}) + dX + \varepsilon_0 \varepsilon^X E.$

By introducing the piezothermal and electrothermal coupling coefficients as follows:

$$k^{PT2} = \frac{\alpha_L{}^2}{(\frac{C_p}{T})s^E},$$
$$k^{ET2} = \frac{p^2}{(\frac{C_p^E}{T})\varepsilon_0\varepsilon^X}$$

the above piezoelectric constitutive equations are re-transformed as follows:

$$x = s^E(1 - k^{PT2})X + (d + \alpha_L p/(\frac{C_p}{T}))E, \quad \text{(CP2.1.5)}$$

$$D = (d + \alpha_L p/(\frac{C_p}{T}))X + \varepsilon_0\varepsilon^X(1 - k^{ET2})E. \quad \text{(CP2.1.6)}$$

We can understand that, in addition to the pure piezothermal effect on s^E and the electrothermal effect on $\varepsilon_0\varepsilon^X$, the piezoelectric coefficient is also modified. If we define a new electromechanical coupling factor as

$$k^2 = \frac{(\text{Coupling factor})^2}{(\text{Product of the diagonal parameters})} = \frac{(d + \alpha_L p/(\frac{C_p}{T}))^2}{(s^E(1 - k^{PT2})\varepsilon_0\varepsilon^X(1 - k^{ET2})}, \quad \text{(CP2.1.7)}$$

the formula indicates an enhancement of the electromechanical coupling factor under an "adiabatic" condition. It is important to note the piezoelectric constant modulation:

$$(d + \alpha_L p/(\frac{C_p}{T})) = d[1 + \alpha_L p/d(\frac{C_p}{T})] = d(1 + \frac{k^{PT}k^{ET}}{k}). \quad \text{(CP2.1.8)}$$

The coupling coefficient d modification is a coupled description of three coupling factors, namely, the piezothermal k^{PT}, electrothermal k^{ET}, and electromechanical k coupling factors. Because k^{PT} and k^{ET} $<<$ k in PZTs, a measurable difference may not be anticipated in practice.

References

1. Tobergte, D.R.; Curtis, S. *Compendium of Chemical Terminology (The "Gold Book")*; IUPAC: Research Triangle Park, NC, USA, 2013; p. 53.
2. Mitsui, T.; Tatsuzaki, T.; Nakamura, E. *Ferroelectrics*; Maki Pub. Co.: Tokyo, Japan, 1969.
3. Uchino, K. *Ferroelectric Devices*, 2nd ed.; CRC Press: Boca Raton, FL, USA, 2010.
4. Uchino, K. *Micromechatronics*, 2nd ed.; CRC Press: Boca Raton, FL, USA, 2019.
5. Priya, S.; Uchino, K. Estimation of polarocaloric contribution to dielectric loss in oriented 0.92PZN-0.08PT single crystals. *Jpn. J. Appl. Phys.* **2003**, *42*, 5158–5164. [CrossRef]
6. Mischenko, A.S.; Zhang, Q.; Scott, J.F.; Whatmore, R.W.; Mathur, N.D. giant electrocaloric effect in thin-film PbZr0.95Ti0.05O3. *Science* **2006**, *311*, 1270–1271. [CrossRef] [PubMed]
7. Neese, B.; Chu, B.; Lu, S.-G.; Wang, Y.; Furman, E.; Zhang, Q.M. Large electrocaloric effect in ferroelectric polymers near room temperature. *Science* **2008**, *321*, 821–823. [CrossRef] [PubMed]
8. Cooks, W.R., Jr.; Berlincourt, D.A.; Scholz, F.J. Thermal expansion and pyroelectricity in lead titanate zirconate and barium titanate. *J. Appl. Phys.* **1963**, *34*, 1392–1398. [CrossRef]

9. Lang, S.B.; Shaw, S.A.; Rice, L.H.; Timmerhaus, K.D. Pyroelectric thermometer for use at low temperatures. *Rev. Sci. Instr.* **1969**, *40*, 274–284. [CrossRef]
10. Lane, R.; Luff, D.; Brown, K.R.; Marshallsay, H.J. The variation of the pyroelectric coefficient with composition and phase structure for lead zirconate titanate ceramics. *Trans. J. Br. Ceram. Soc.* **1973**, *72*, 39–42.
11. Shekhani, H.N.; Gurdal, E.A.; Ganapatibhotla, L.; Maranas, J.K.; Staut, R.; Uchino, K. Thermal conductivities of PZT piezoelectric ceramics under different electrical boundary conditions. *Insight-Mater. Sci.* **2020**, 3, 10–14. [CrossRef]
12. Lines, M.E.; Glass, A.M. *Principles and Applications of Ferroelectrics and Related Materials*; Clarendon Press: Oxford, UK, 1977.
13. Physical and Piezoelectric Properties of APC Materials. Available online: https://www.americanpiezo.com/apc-materials/physical-piezoelectric-properties.html (accessed on 30 May 2020).
14. Mason, W.P. *Physical Acoustics and the Properties of Solids*; Van Nostrand: New York, NY, USA, 1958.

3. Tensor/Matrix Description in Piezoelectricity—Linear Algebraic Equations

3.1. Tensor Representation

3.1.1. Fundamentals in Tensor

A physical property is a relationship between an input physical parameter and the corresponding output physical parameter. A physical parameter can be a "scalar", "vector", or "tensor". Some "intensive" and corresponding "extensive" parameters are summarized below:

		Thermal	**Electric**		Mechanical
Scalar	intensive	Temperature T	Voltage V		
	extensive	Entropy S	Charge Q		Mass M
Vector	intensive	$-grad(T)$	Electric field E_i		Force F_i
	extensive	Heat flux q_i	Electric displacement D_i	Current density J_i	Displacement L_i
Tensor	intensive				Stress X_{ij}
	extensive				Strain x_{ij}

Remember that the IUPAC defines "extensive" and "intensive" parameters according to the dependency on the material's volume, as introduced in Chapter 2. Examples of linear physical properties include the following: First, the relation between a scalar (zeroth-rank tensor) and a scalar (zeroth-rank tensor) is given by a scalar constant, exemplified by the electric capacitance C for the charge Q and voltage V relation $Q = CV$, or by the specific heat capacity c_p for a temperature change θ and the thermal energy per mass Q: $Q = c_p\theta$ (Do not confuse the same notation Q). Second, the relation between a vector (first-rank tensor) and a vector (first-rank tensor) is given by a second-rank (i.e., 1 + 1) tensor, exemplified by the permittivity tensor for electric displacement D_j and the E_i relation

$$\begin{pmatrix} D_1 \\ D_2 \\ D_3 \end{pmatrix} = \begin{pmatrix} \varepsilon_{11} & \varepsilon_{12} & \varepsilon_{13} \\ \varepsilon_{21} & \varepsilon_{22} & \varepsilon_{23} \\ \varepsilon_{31} & \varepsilon_{32} & \varepsilon_{33} \end{pmatrix} \begin{pmatrix} E_1 \\ E_2 \\ E_3 \end{pmatrix}.$$

Third, the relation between a second-rank tensor and a vector (first-rank tensor) is given by a third-rank (i.e., 2 + 1) tensor, exemplified by the piezoelectric constant tensor d_{ijk} for stress X_{jk} and the electric displacement D_i (or polarization P_i) relation

$$\begin{pmatrix} D_1 \\ D_2 \\ D_3 \end{pmatrix} = \left[\begin{pmatrix} d_{111} & d_{112} & d_{113} \\ d_{121} & d_{122} & d_{123} \\ d_{131} & d_{132} & d_{113} \end{pmatrix}, \begin{pmatrix} d_{211} & d_{212} & d_{213} \\ d_{221} & d_{222} & d_{223} \\ d_{231} & d_{232} & d_{213} \end{pmatrix}, \begin{pmatrix} d_{311} & d_{312} & d_{313} \\ d_{321} & d_{322} & d_{323} \\ d_{331} & d_{332} & d_{313} \end{pmatrix} \right] \begin{pmatrix} X_{11} & X_{12} & X_{13} \\ X_{21} & X_{22} & X_{23} \\ X_{31} & X_{32} & X_{33} \end{pmatrix}$$

Note that [(first layer matrix), (second layer matrix), (third layer matrix)] is used, because we cannot describe the 3D ($3 \times 3 \times 3$) tensor expression in a 2D paper.

In general, an input physical parameter X is correlated with an output parameter Y with a proportional parameter A in a linear relation approximation:

$$Y = AX. \tag{3.1}$$

If X and Y are p-rank and q-rank tensors, A is supposed to be expressed by using a (p + q)-rank tensor:

$$Y_{ij\ldots q} = \sum_{lm\ldots p} A_{ij\ldots qlm\ldots p} X_{lm\ldots p}. \tag{3.2}$$

A p-rank tensor $X_{lm\ldots p}$ is represented based on an (x, y, z) coordinate system.

3.1.2. Transformation Matrix

When a tensor described in an original (x, y, z) coordinate system is expressed by using a different (x', y', z') coordinate system, a new tensor X' can be represented as:

$$X'_{ij\ldots p} = \sum\nolimits_{lm\ldots p} a_{il} a_{jm} \ldots a_{pq} X_{lm\ldots q}, \tag{3.3}$$

where a_{ij} is called the "transformation matrix". The transformation matrix is a "unitary matrix" without an imaginary part, satisfying the following relation (inverse matrix $\equiv$ transposed matrix):

$$\begin{pmatrix} a_{11} & a_{12} & a_{13} \\ a_{21} & a_{22} & a_{23} \\ a_{31} & a_{32} & a_{33} \end{pmatrix}^{-1} = \begin{pmatrix} a_{11} & a_{21} & a_{31} \\ a_{12} & a_{22} & a_{32} \\ a_{13} & a_{23} & a_{33} \end{pmatrix}. \tag{3.4}$$

Try to familiarize yourself with the transformation matrix through Example Problem 3.1.

Example Problem 3.1

Provide the physical meaning of the following "transformation matrices":

(a) $\begin{pmatrix} -1 & 0 & 0 \\ 0 & -1 & 0 \\ 0 & 0 & -1 \end{pmatrix}$; (b) $\begin{pmatrix} -1 & 0 & 0 \\ 0 & 1 & 0 \\ 0 & 0 & 1 \end{pmatrix}$; (c) $\begin{pmatrix} -1 & 0 & 0 \\ 0 & -1 & 0 \\ 0 & 0 & 1 \end{pmatrix}$; (d) $\begin{pmatrix} 0 & 1 & 0 \\ -1 & 0 & 0 \\ 0 & 0 & 1 \end{pmatrix}$

Solution

(a) When we start from the transformation matrix definition,

$$\begin{pmatrix} x' \\ y' \\ z' \end{pmatrix} = \begin{pmatrix} -1 & 0 & 0 \\ 0 & -1 & 0 \\ 0 & 0 & -1 \end{pmatrix} \begin{pmatrix} x \\ y \\ z \end{pmatrix}. \quad \text{(P3.1.1)}$$

The above transformation can generate the point (x, y, z) movement of $x \to -x$, $y \to -y$, $z \to -z$, which is illustrated in Figure 3.1a. This corresponds to the centro-symmetrical transformation with respect to the origin (0,0,0).

(b) $\begin{pmatrix} -1 & 0 & 0 \\ 0 & 1 & 0 \\ 0 & 0 & 1 \end{pmatrix}$ generates the point movement $x \to -x$, $y \to y$, $z \to z$, which is illustrated in Figure 3.1b. This corresponds to a mirror (y-z plane) -symmetrical transformation.

(c) $\begin{pmatrix} -1 & 0 & 0 \\ 0 & -1 & 0 \\ 0 & 0 & 1 \end{pmatrix}$ generates the point movement $x \to -x$, $y \to -y$, $z \to z$, which is illustrated in Figure 3.1c. This corresponds to an axis (z-axis)-symmetrical transformation by 180°, or 2-fold symmetry.

(d) $\begin{pmatrix} 0 & 1 & 0 \\ -1 & 0 & 0 \\ 0 & 0 & 1 \end{pmatrix}$ realizes the point movement $x \to y$, $y \to -x$, $z \to z$, which is illustrated in Figure 3.1d. This corresponds to an axis (z-axis)-symmetrical transformation by 90° or 4-fold symmetry.

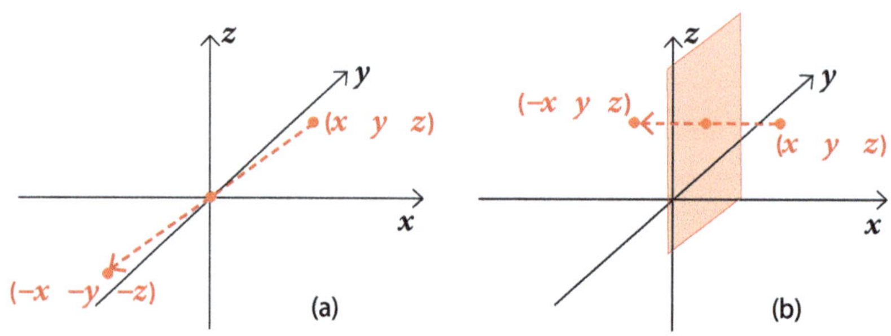

Figure 3.1. *Cont.*

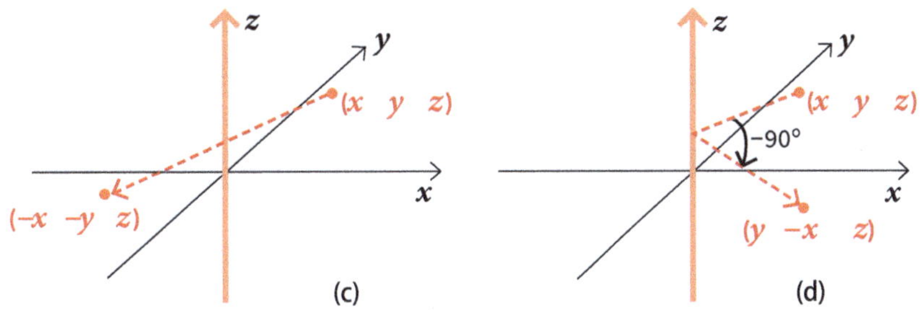

Figure 3.1. Rotation matrix examples: (**a**) center symmetry, (**b**) mirror symmetry, (**c**) 2-fold symmetry, and (**d**) 4-fold symmetry. Source: Figure by author.

The "rotation matrix" is one of the most important and useful transformation matrices, which the reader needs to use all the time. The axial rotation for a rotation angle θ about a principal z-axis is expressed by

$$\begin{pmatrix} \cos\theta & \sin\theta & 0 \\ -\sin\theta & \cos\theta & 0 \\ 0 & 0 & 1 \end{pmatrix}. \tag{3.5}$$

3.1.3. Crystal Symmetry

The symmetry of crystals is determined by three elements: centrosymmetry, mirror symmetry and axisymmetry. In centrosymmetry, there exists a point around which all faces or edges are translated to parallel pairs on opposite sides of the crystal. The plane of symmetry ("mirror plane") is a plane by which the crystal may be divided into two halves which are mirror images of each other. Axisymmetry possesses a line around which a crystal may be rotated $360°/n$ until it assumes a congruent position; n may equal 2, 3, 4, or 6. These correspond, respectively to 2-fold, 3-fold, 4-fold, and 6-fold axes. Based on these elements, all crystals can be classified into 32 "point groups" (that is, crystallographic symmetry), and these point groups can be divided into two classes, one with a center of symmetry and the other without, as indicated already in Table 1.2 in Chapter 1. There are 21 point groups which do not have a center of symmetry, among which 20 groups (point group (*432*) being the sole exception) exhibit positive and negative charges generated on the crystal surfaces when appropriate stresses are applied. These materials are known as "piezoelectrics". On the contrary, "pyroelectricity" is the phenomenon whereby, due to the temperature dependence of the spontaneous polarization, as the temperature of the crystal is changed, electric charges corresponding to the change in the spontaneous polarization appear on the surface of the crystal.

Let us consider three example symmetries, *4*, *4mm* and *32* for further clarification of these symbols. Figure 3.2 shows the symbolic expression of crystal symmetry: *4*, *4mm*, *32*. The crystal symmetry *4* possesses a 4-fold symmetry, which means that a 90° rotation around the axis (usually defined as the z-axis) does not change any part of the physical performance. The rotation matrix for this crystal is $\begin{pmatrix} 0 & -1 & 0 \\ 1 & 0 & 0 \\ 0 & 0 & 1 \end{pmatrix}$ around the z-axis. The crystal symmetry *4mm*, which is exemplified by tetragonal $BaTiO_3$, possesses two mirror symmetry, as well as a 4-fold symmetry, which means that a 90° rotation around the z-axis, and/or a mirror transformation with respect to the y-z and x-z planes, should not change any physical properties. The transformation matrices for this crystal are rotation $\begin{pmatrix} 0 & -1 & 0 \\ 1 & 0 & 0 \\ 0 & 0 & 1 \end{pmatrix}$ around the z-axis, and mirrors $\begin{pmatrix} -1 & 0 & 0 \\ 0 & 1 & 0 \\ 0 & 0 & 1 \end{pmatrix}$ and $\begin{pmatrix} 1 & 0 & 0 \\ 0 & -1 & 0 \\ 0 & 0 & 1 \end{pmatrix}$. The crystal symmetry *32*, exemplified by alpha quartz, possesses a 3-fold symmetry around the z-axis and a 2-fold symmetry around the x-axis, which means that a 120° rotation around the z-axis and a 180° rotation around the x-axis should not change any part of the physical performance. The rotation matrices for this crystal are $\begin{pmatrix} -1/2 & \sqrt{3}/2 & 0 \\ -\sqrt{3}/2 & -1/2 & 0 \\ 0 & 0 & 1 \end{pmatrix}$ around the z-axis, and $\begin{pmatrix} 1 & 0 & 0 \\ 0 & -1 & 0 \\ 0 & 0 & -1 \end{pmatrix}$ around the x-axis. Both are obtained from a general formula $\begin{pmatrix} \cos\theta & \sin\theta & 0 \\ -\sin\theta & \cos\theta & 0 \\ 0 & 0 & -1 \end{pmatrix}$.

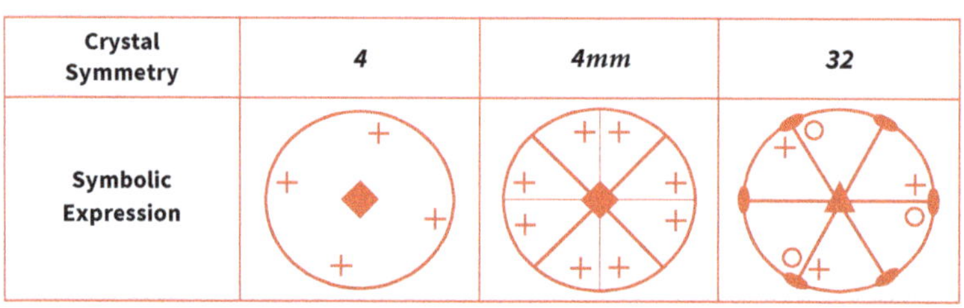

Figure 3.2. Symbolic expression of crystal symmetry: *4*, *4mm*, *32*. Source: Figure by author.

3.2. Tensor Component Reduction with Crystal Symmetry

3.2.1. Dielectric Permittivity

We consider the tensor component reduction scheme in this section. We first take the simplest tensor (i.e., matrix) for the dielectric permittivity, which is defined so as to correlate an applied electric field $\boldsymbol{E}$ (vector) with and the induced dielectric displacement $\boldsymbol{D}$ (or polarization $\boldsymbol{P}$, vector) as follows:

$$\boldsymbol{D} = \varepsilon_0 \varepsilon \boldsymbol{E}. \tag{3.6}$$

Since both the electric field and the dielectric displacement are first-rank tensor (that is, vector) quantities, the permittivity should have a second-rank tensor representation (that is, with two suffixes); this is described as

$$\begin{pmatrix} D_1 \\ D_2 \\ D_3 \end{pmatrix} = \varepsilon_0 \begin{pmatrix} \varepsilon_{11} & \varepsilon_{12} & \varepsilon_{13} \\ \varepsilon_{21} & \varepsilon_{22} & \varepsilon_{23} \\ \varepsilon_{31} & \varepsilon_{32} & \varepsilon_{33} \end{pmatrix} \begin{pmatrix} E_1 \\ E_2 \\ E_3 \end{pmatrix}, \tag{3.7a}$$

or

$$D_i = \sum_j \varepsilon_0 \varepsilon_{ij} E_j. \tag{3.7b}$$

A physical property measured along two different directions must be equal if these two directions are crystallographically equivalent. This consideration sometimes reduces the number of independent tensor components representing the above property.

If the dielectric displacement $\boldsymbol{D}$ in an (x, y, z) coordinate system is described in an (x', y', z') system as $\boldsymbol{D}'$, $\boldsymbol{D}$ and $\boldsymbol{D}'$ are related using a unitary transformation matrix as follows:

$$\begin{pmatrix} D_1' \\ D_2' \\ D_3' \end{pmatrix} = \begin{pmatrix} a_{11} & a_{12} & a_{13} \\ a_{21} & a_{22} & a_{23} \\ a_{31} & a_{32} & a_{33} \end{pmatrix} \begin{pmatrix} D_1 \\ D_2 \\ D_3 \end{pmatrix}. \tag{3.8}$$

The electric field is transformed in the same way:

$$\begin{pmatrix} E_1' \\ E_2' \\ E_3' \end{pmatrix} = \begin{pmatrix} a_{11} & a_{12} & a_{13} \\ a_{21} & a_{22} & a_{23} \\ a_{31} & a_{32} & a_{33} \end{pmatrix} \begin{pmatrix} E_1 \\ E_2 \\ E_3 \end{pmatrix}, \tag{3.9a}$$

or

$$E_i' = \sum_j a_{ij} E_j. \tag{3.9b}$$

Then, we can calculate the corresponding ε' tensor defined by

$$\begin{pmatrix} D_1' \\ D_2' \\ D_3' \end{pmatrix} = \varepsilon_0 \varepsilon' \begin{pmatrix} E_1' \\ E_2' \\ E_3' \end{pmatrix}. \tag{3.10}$$

Inserting Equations (3.8) and (3.9a) into Equation (3.10),

$$\begin{pmatrix} a_{11} & a_{12} & a_{13} \\ a_{21} & a_{22} & a_{23} \\ a_{31} & a_{32} & a_{33} \end{pmatrix} \begin{pmatrix} D_1 \\ D_2 \\ D_3 \end{pmatrix} = \varepsilon_0 \varepsilon' \begin{pmatrix} a_{11} & a_{12} & a_{13} \\ a_{21} & a_{22} & a_{23} \\ a_{31} & a_{32} & a_{33} \end{pmatrix} \begin{pmatrix} E_1 \\ E_2 \\ E_3 \end{pmatrix},$$

then

$$\begin{pmatrix} D_1 \\ D_2 \\ D_3 \end{pmatrix} = \begin{pmatrix} a_{11} & a_{12} & a_{13} \\ a_{21} & a_{22} & a_{23} \\ a_{31} & a_{32} & a_{33} \end{pmatrix}^{-1} \varepsilon_0 \varepsilon' \begin{pmatrix} a_{11} & a_{12} & a_{13} \\ a_{21} & a_{22} & a_{23} \\ a_{31} & a_{32} & a_{33} \end{pmatrix} \begin{pmatrix} E_1 \\ E_2 \\ E_3 \end{pmatrix}.$$

From the definition in Equation (3.7a),

$$\begin{aligned} &\begin{pmatrix} \varepsilon_{11}' & \varepsilon_{12}' & \varepsilon_{13}' \\ \varepsilon_{21}' & \varepsilon_{22}' & \varepsilon_{23}' \\ \varepsilon_{31}' & \varepsilon_{32}' & \varepsilon_{33}' \end{pmatrix} \\ &= \begin{pmatrix} a_{11} & a_{12} & a_{13} \\ a_{21} & a_{22} & a_{23} \\ a_{31} & a_{32} & a_{33} \end{pmatrix} \begin{pmatrix} \varepsilon_{11} & \varepsilon_{12} & \varepsilon_{13} \\ \varepsilon_{21} & \varepsilon_{22} & \varepsilon_{23} \\ \varepsilon_{31} & \varepsilon_{32} & \varepsilon_{33} \end{pmatrix} \begin{pmatrix} a_{11} & a_{12} & a_{13} \\ a_{21} & a_{22} & a_{23} \\ a_{31} & a_{32} & a_{33} \end{pmatrix}^{-1} \\ &= \begin{pmatrix} a_{11} & a_{12} & a_{13} \\ a_{21} & a_{22} & a_{23} \\ a_{31} & a_{32} & a_{33} \end{pmatrix} \begin{pmatrix} \varepsilon_{11} & \varepsilon_{12} & \varepsilon_{13} \\ \varepsilon_{21} & \varepsilon_{22} & \varepsilon_{23} \\ \varepsilon_{31} & \varepsilon_{32} & \varepsilon_{33} \end{pmatrix} \begin{pmatrix} a_{11} & a_{21} & a_{31} \\ a_{12} & a_{22} & a_{32} \\ a_{13} & a_{23} & a_{33} \end{pmatrix}, \end{aligned} \tag{3.11}$$

where we used $\begin{pmatrix} a_{11} & a_{12} & a_{13} \\ a_{21} & a_{22} & a_{23} \\ a_{31} & a_{32} & a_{33} \end{pmatrix}^{-1} \equiv \begin{pmatrix} a_{11} & a_{12} & a_{13} \\ a_{21} & a_{22} & a_{23} \\ a_{31} & a_{32} & a_{33} \end{pmatrix}^{t}$ (unitary matrix!). We can now understand that the transformation of the second-rank tensor can be calculated by

$$\varepsilon_{ij}' = \sum_{k,l} a_{ik} a_{jl} \varepsilon_{kl}. \tag{3.12}$$

Two-Fold Axisymmetry

When the crystal has a 2-fold axis along the z-axis, the dielectric permittivity should have the same tensor form in terms of this transformation, that is, the rotation matrix of Equation (3.5) for $\theta = 180°$:

$$\begin{pmatrix} -1 & 0 & 0 \\ 0 & -1 & 0 \\ 0 & 0 & 1 \end{pmatrix}.$$

From the condition in Equation (3.11):

$$\begin{pmatrix} \varepsilon_{11}' & \varepsilon_{12}' & \varepsilon_{13}' \\ \varepsilon_{21}' & \varepsilon_{22}' & \varepsilon_{23}' \\ \varepsilon_{31}' & \varepsilon_{32}' & \varepsilon_{33}' \end{pmatrix} = \begin{pmatrix} -1 & 0 & 0 \\ 0 & -1 & 0 \\ 0 & 0 & 1 \end{pmatrix} \begin{pmatrix} \varepsilon_{11} & \varepsilon_{12} & \varepsilon_{13} \\ \varepsilon_{21} & \varepsilon_{22} & \varepsilon_{23} \\ \varepsilon_{31} & \varepsilon_{32} & \varepsilon_{33} \end{pmatrix} \begin{pmatrix} -1 & 0 & 0 \\ 0 & -1 & 0 \\ 0 & 0 & 1 \end{pmatrix} = \begin{pmatrix} \varepsilon_{11} & \varepsilon_{12} & -\varepsilon_{13} \\ \varepsilon_{21} & \varepsilon_{22} & -\varepsilon_{23} \\ -\varepsilon_{31} & -\varepsilon_{32} & \varepsilon_{33} \end{pmatrix}. \quad (3.13)$$

Because this crystal has a 2-fold symmetry, $\varepsilon' \equiv \varepsilon$ or $\begin{pmatrix} \varepsilon_{11}' & \varepsilon_{12}' & \varepsilon_{13}' \\ \varepsilon_{21}' & \varepsilon_{22}' & \varepsilon_{23}' \\ \varepsilon_{31}' & \varepsilon_{32}' & \varepsilon_{33}' \end{pmatrix} = \begin{pmatrix} \varepsilon_{11} & \varepsilon_{12} & \varepsilon_{13} \\ \varepsilon_{21} & \varepsilon_{22} & \varepsilon_{23} \\ \varepsilon_{31} & \varepsilon_{32} & \varepsilon_{33} \end{pmatrix}$ must be held for this 180° rotation transformation. Thus, the following equivalency should be derived:

$$\begin{pmatrix} \varepsilon_{11} & \varepsilon_{12} & -\varepsilon_{13} \\ \varepsilon_{21} & \varepsilon_{22} & -\varepsilon_{23} \\ -\varepsilon_{31} & -\varepsilon_{32} & \varepsilon_{33} \end{pmatrix} = \begin{pmatrix} \varepsilon_{11} & \varepsilon_{12} & \varepsilon_{13} \\ \varepsilon_{21} & \varepsilon_{22} & \varepsilon_{23} \\ \varepsilon_{31} & \varepsilon_{32} & \varepsilon_{33} \end{pmatrix}. \quad (3.14)$$

Using the logic that $x = -x \rightarrow x = 0$, we can obtain

$$\begin{aligned} &\varepsilon_{31} = \varepsilon_{13} = \varepsilon_{32} = \varepsilon_{23} = 0 \\ &\varepsilon_{11}, \varepsilon_{22}, \varepsilon_{33} \neq 0, \\ &\varepsilon_{12} = \varepsilon_{21} \end{aligned}$$

The permittivity tensor form with four independent components is expressed by

$$\begin{pmatrix} \varepsilon_{11} & \varepsilon_{12} & 0 \\ \varepsilon_{12} & \varepsilon_{22} & 0 \\ 0 & 0 & \varepsilon_{33} \end{pmatrix}.$$

It is very important to note that most physical constants have a "symmetric tensor" form. The proof involves thermodynamical considerations. Refer to [1].

Four-Fold Axisymmetry

When the crystal has a 4-fold axis along the z-axis, the dielectric permittivity should have the same tensor form in terms of this transformation, that is, the rotation matrix of Equation (3.5) for $\theta = 90°$:

$$\begin{pmatrix} 0 & 1 & 0 \\ -1 & 0 & 0 \\ 0 & 0 & 1 \end{pmatrix}.$$

From the condition in Equation (3.11):

$$\begin{pmatrix} \varepsilon_{11}' & \varepsilon_{12}' & \varepsilon_{13}' \\ \varepsilon_{21}' & \varepsilon_{22}' & \varepsilon_{23}' \\ \varepsilon_{31}' & \varepsilon_{32}' & \varepsilon_{33}' \end{pmatrix} = \begin{pmatrix} 0 & 1 & 0 \\ -1 & 0 & 0 \\ 0 & 0 & 1 \end{pmatrix} \begin{pmatrix} \varepsilon_{11} & \varepsilon_{12} & \varepsilon_{13} \\ \varepsilon_{21} & \varepsilon_{22} & \varepsilon_{23} \\ \varepsilon_{31} & \varepsilon_{32} & \varepsilon_{33} \end{pmatrix} \begin{pmatrix} 0 & 1 & 0 \\ -1 & 0 & 0 \\ 0 & 0 & 1 \end{pmatrix}^{-1} = \begin{pmatrix} \varepsilon_{22} & -\varepsilon_{21} & \varepsilon_{23} \\ -\varepsilon_{12} & \varepsilon_{11} & -\varepsilon_{13} \\ \varepsilon_{32} & -\varepsilon_{31} & \varepsilon_{33} \end{pmatrix}. \tag{3.15}$$

Because this crystal has a 4-fold symmetry, $\varepsilon' \equiv \varepsilon$ or $\begin{pmatrix} \varepsilon_{11}' & \varepsilon_{12}' & \varepsilon_{13}' \\ \varepsilon_{21}' & \varepsilon_{22}' & \varepsilon_{23}' \\ \varepsilon_{31}' & \varepsilon_{32}' & \varepsilon_{33}' \end{pmatrix} = \begin{pmatrix} \varepsilon_{11} & \varepsilon_{12} & \varepsilon_{13} \\ \varepsilon_{21} & \varepsilon_{22} & \varepsilon_{23} \\ \varepsilon_{31} & \varepsilon_{32} & \varepsilon_{33} \end{pmatrix}$ must be held for this 90° rotation transformation. Thus, the following equivalency should be derived:

$$\begin{pmatrix} \varepsilon_{22} & -\varepsilon_{21} & \varepsilon_{23} \\ -\varepsilon_{12} & \varepsilon_{11} & -\varepsilon_{13} \\ \varepsilon_{32} & -\varepsilon_{31} & \varepsilon_{33} \end{pmatrix} = \begin{pmatrix} \varepsilon_{11} & \varepsilon_{12} & \varepsilon_{13} \\ \varepsilon_{21} & \varepsilon_{22} & \varepsilon_{23} \\ \varepsilon_{31} & \varepsilon_{32} & \varepsilon_{33} \end{pmatrix}. \tag{3.16}$$

Using the logic that $x = -x \rightarrow x = 0$, we can obtain

$\varepsilon_{12} = \varepsilon_{21} = \varepsilon_{32} = \varepsilon_{23} = \varepsilon_{13} = \varepsilon_{31} = 0,$
$\varepsilon_{11} = \varepsilon_{22},\ \varepsilon_{33} \neq 0.$

We again used the "symmetric property" of the permittivity tensor for this derivation. The permittivity tensor form with only two independent components is expressed by

$$\begin{pmatrix} \varepsilon_{11} & 0 & 0 \\ 0 & \varepsilon_{11} & 0 \\ 0 & 0 & \varepsilon_{33} \end{pmatrix}.$$

Example Problem 3.2

Tensile stress X and compressive stress $-X$ (with the same magnitude) are applied simultaneously along the (1 0 1) and ($\overline{1}$ 0 1) axes, respectively, to a cube specimen shown in Figure 3.3. When we take the prime coordinates (1′ and 3′), the stress tensor can be represented as

$$\begin{pmatrix} X & 0 & 0 \\ 0 & 0 & 0 \\ 0 & 0 & -X \end{pmatrix}. \tag{P3.2.1}$$

Using the transformation matrix A (i.e., $\theta = -45°$ rotation along the 2′-axis in Figure 3.3) $\begin{pmatrix} \cos\theta & 0 & \sin\theta \\ 0 & 1 & 0 \\ -\sin\theta & 0 & \cos\theta \end{pmatrix}$, calculate $A{\cdot}X{\cdot}A^{-1}$, and verify that the above stress is equivalent to a pure shear stress in the original (non-prime) coordinates.

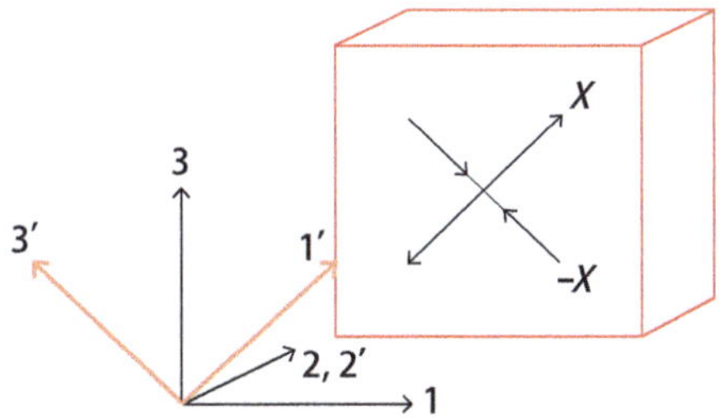

Figure 3.3. Application of a pair of stresses, X and $-X$, to a cube of material. Source: Figure by author.

<u>Solution</u>

Using $\theta = -45°$, we can obtain the transformed stress representation:

$$A{\cdot}X{\cdot}A^{-1} = \begin{pmatrix} 1/\sqrt{2} & 0 & -1/\sqrt{2} \\ 0 & 1 & 0 \\ 1/\sqrt{2} & 0 & 1/\sqrt{2} \end{pmatrix} \begin{pmatrix} X & 0 & 0 \\ 0 & 0 & 0 \\ 0 & 0 & -X \end{pmatrix} \begin{pmatrix} 1/\sqrt{2} & 0 & 1/\sqrt{2} \\ 0 & 1 & 0 \\ -1/\sqrt{2} & 0 & 1/\sqrt{2} \end{pmatrix} = \begin{pmatrix} 0 & 0 & X \\ 0 & 0 & 0 \\ X & 0 & 0 \end{pmatrix}. \tag{P3.2.2}$$

Note that the off-diagonal components X_{13} and X_{31} have the same magnitude X as the original tensile and compressive stresses, which represent a pure "shear stress" in the non-prime coordinate. A shear stress is equivalent to a combination of extension and contraction stresses. Though an extensional stress applied along a diagonal direction 1′ exhibits an apparently similar diagonal distortion of the crystal without contraction along the 3′ direction, a smaller contraction occurs only from the Poisson ratio of the extension. This is not exactly equivalent to the pure shear deformation, with a volume expansion.

Example Problem 3.3

Force is a vector, while stress (composed of a pair of forces) is a tensor. Suppose that a shear stress X_{13} is applied to a square crystal and the crystal is deformed by 1° angle as illustrated in Figure 3.4. Calculate the induced strain x_5 (=$2x_{31}$).

Solution

Since $x_5 = 2x_{31} = 2\tan, \varphi = 2\varphi = 1°$ and $1° = \pi/180$ radian, $x_5 = 0.017$. Typical strain in a piezoelectric ceramic is around 0.1% or 0.001, leading to the shear angle 0.1°. Thus, 1° is unrealistic in practice. Prior to reaching this deformation, crack/collapse will occur. Note that shear deformation is not accompanied by a volume change (the shadowed area is the same as that of the original square), different from the longitudinal deformation. Refer to Example Problem 3.2.

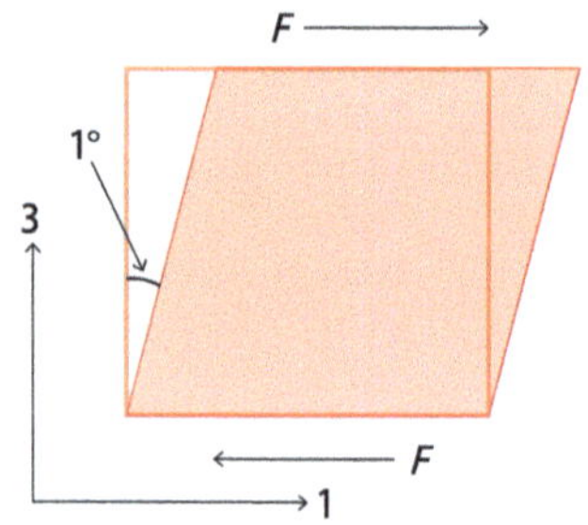

Figure 3.4. Shear stress and strain configuration. Source: Figure by author.

3.2.2. Piezoelectric Constant

Piezoelectric coefficients, providing there is a relation of the induced strain x (second-rank tensor) with the applied field $\mathbf{E}$ (vector), are represented by a third-rank tensor (i.e., 1 + 2 = 3):

$$x = d\mathbf{E}, \tag{3.17a}$$

or providing there is a relation of the induced polarization $\mathbf{P}$ with the applied stress X, as

$$\mathbf{P} = dX, \tag{3.17b}$$

or as

$$x_{jk} = \sum_i d_{ijk} E_i, \tag{3.18a}$$

$$P_i = \sum_{j,k} d_{ijk} X_{jk}. \tag{3.18b}$$

Note that the first suffix "i" in d_{ijk} corresponds to the electric component, while the second and third, "j,k", correspond to the stress and strain, which are "commutative" or "symmetric". The d tensor is composed of three layers of symmetrical matrices ("j,k" are commutative):

$$\text{First layer } (i=1) \begin{pmatrix} d_{111} & d_{112} & d_{113} \\ d_{121} & d_{122} & d_{123} \\ d_{131} & d_{132} & d_{133} \end{pmatrix},$$
$$\text{Second layer } (i=2) \begin{pmatrix} d_{211} & d_{212} & d_{213} \\ d_{221} & d_{222} & d_{223} \\ d_{231} & d_{232} & d_{233} \end{pmatrix}, \tag{3.19}$$
$$\text{Third layer } (i=3) \begin{pmatrix} d_{311} & d_{312} & d_{313} \\ d_{321} & d_{322} & d_{323} \\ d_{331} & d_{332} & d_{333} \end{pmatrix}.$$

Recall again that if two physical parameters are represented using tensors of the p-rank and q-rank, the property quantity which combines the two parameters in a linear relation is represented by a tensor of the $(p + q)$-rank.

For a third-rank tensor such as the piezoelectric tensor, a transformation due to a change in coordinate system is represented by

$$d_{ijk}' = \sum\nolimits_{l,m,n} a_{il} a_{jm} a_{kn} d_{lmn}. \tag{3.20}$$

Note that, though we can use a simple matrix product formula for the axis transformation of the vector and second-rank tensor, it is difficult to describe the transformation of the third- or higher-order tensors.

Four-Fold Axisymmetry

When the crystal has a 4-fold axis along the z-axis, the transformation matrix is given (Equation (3.5) for $\theta = 90°$) by

$$\begin{pmatrix} 0 & 1 & 0 \\ -1 & 0 & 0 \\ 0 & 0 & 1 \end{pmatrix}.$$

Taking into account the tensor symmetry in terms of the second and third suffixes such that $d_{123} = d_{132}$ and $d_{213} = d_{231}$ (each matrix of the i-th layer of the d tensor is symmetrical), we have "18 independent d_{ijk}'s" (i.e., each layer has 6 independent components). Notice initially that $a_{12} = 1$, $a_{21} = -1$, and $a_{33} = 1$, which means that the second suffix is automatically determined (2, 1 or 3) when the first suffix is given (1, 2, or 3) in the practical calculation.

- $d_{111}{}' = \sum_{l,m,n} a_{1l}a_{1m}a_{1n}d_{lmn} = a_{12}a_{12}a_{12}d_{222} = (+1)(+1)(+1)d_{222} = d_{222}$
  Since $d_{111}{}' \equiv d_{111}$, we obtain $d_{111} = d_{222}$. (3.21)
- $d_{122}{}' = \sum_{l,m,n} a_{1l}a_{2m}a_{2n}d_{lmn} = a_{12}a_{21}a_{21}d_{211} = (+1)(-1)(-1)d_{211} = d_{211}$
  Since $d_{122}{}' \equiv d_{122}$, we obtain $d_{122} = d_{211}$. (3.22)
- $d_{133}{}' = a_{12}a_{33}a_{33}d_{233} = (+1)(+1)(+1)d_{233} = d_{233}$
  Since $d_{133}{}' \equiv d_{133}$, we obtain $d_{133} = d_{233}$. (3.23)
- $d_{123}{}' = a_{12}a_{21}a_{33}d_{213} = (+1)(-1)(+1)d_{213} = -d_{213}$
  Since $d_{123}{}' \equiv d_{123}$, we obtain $d_{123} = -d_{213} = d_{132} = -d_{231}$. (3.24)
- $d_{131}{}' = a_{12}a_{33}a_{12}d_{232} = (+1)(+1)(+1)d_{232} = d_{232}$
  Since $d_{131}{}' \equiv d_{131}$, we obtain $d_{131} = d_{232} = d_{113} = d_{223}$. (3.25)
- $d_{112}{}' = a_{12}a_{12}a_{21}d_{221} = (+1)(+1)(-1)d_{221} = -d_{221}$
  Since $d_{112}{}' \equiv d_{112}$, we obtain $d_{112} = -d_{221} = d_{121} = -d_{212}$. (3.26)
- $d_{211}{}' = a_{21}a_{12}a_{12}d_{122} = (-1)(+1)(+1)d_{122} = -d_{122}$
  Since $d_{211}{}' \equiv d_{211}$, we obtain $d_{211} = -d_{122}$. (3.27)
- $d_{222}{}' = a_{21}a_{21}a_{21}d_{111} = (-1)(-1)(-1)d_{111} = -d_{111}$
  Since $d_{222}{}' \equiv d_{222}$, we obtain $d_{222} = -d_{111}$. (3.28)
- $d_{233}{}' = a_{21}a_{33}a_{33}d_{133} = (-1)(+1)(+1)d_{133} = -d_{133}$
  Since $d_{233}{}' \equiv d_{233}$, we obtain $d_{233} = -d_{133}$. (3.29)
- $d_{223}{}' = a_{21}a_{21}a_{33}d_{113} = (-1)(-1)(+1)d_{113} = d_{113}$
  Since $d_{223}{}' \equiv d_{223}$, we obtain $d_{223} = d_{113}$. (3.30)
- $d_{231}{}' = a_{21}a_{33}a_{12}d_{132} = (-1)(+1)(+1)d_{132} = -d_{132}$
  Since $d_{231}{}' \equiv d_{231}$, we obtain $d_{231} = -d_{132}$. (3.31)
- $d_{212}{}' = a_{21}a_{12}a_{21}d_{121} = (-1)(+1)(-1)d_{121} = d_{121}$
  Since $d_{212}{}' \equiv d_{212}$, we obtain $d_{212} = d_{121}$. (3.32)
- $d_{311}{}' = a_{33}a_{12}a_{12}d_{322} = (+1)(+1)(+1)d_{322} = d_{322}$
  Since $d_{311}{}' \equiv d_{311}$, we obtain $d_{311} = d_{322}$. (3.33)
- $d_{322}{}' = a_{33}a_{21}a_{21}d_{311} = (+1)(-1)(-1)d_{311} = d_{311}$
  Since $d_{322}{}' \equiv d_{322}$, we obtain $d_{322} = d_{311}$. (3.34)
- $d_{333}{}' = a_{33}a_{33}a_{33}d_{333} = (+1)(+1)(+1)d_{333} = d_{333}$
  Since $d_{333}{}' \equiv d_{333}$, we obtain the trivial $d_{333} = d_{333}$. (3.35)
- $d_{323}{}' = a_{33}a_{21}a_{33}d_{313} = (+1)(-1)(+1)d_{313} = -d_{313}$
  Since $d_{323}{}' \equiv d_{323}$, we obtain $d_{323} = -d_{313}$. (3.36)
- $d_{331}{}' = a_{33}a_{33}a_{12}d_{332} = (+1)(+1)(+1)d_{332} = d_{332}$
  Since $d_{331}{}' \equiv d_{331}$, we obtain $d_{331} = d_{332}$. (3.37)
- $d_{312}{}' = a_{33}a_{12}a_{21}d_{321} = (+1)(+1)(-1)d_{321} = -d_{321}$
  Since $d_{312}{}' \equiv d_{312}$, we obtain $d_{312} = -d_{321}$. (3.38)

From the above 18 total equations, we will obtain the necessary relations:

- From Equations (P2.1.2) and (P2.1.7), we obtain $d_{122} = d_{211} = -d_{122} = 0$.

- From Equations (P2.1.1) and (P2.1.8), we obtain $d_{111} = d_{222} = -d_{111} = 0$.
- From Equations (P2.1.6) and (P2.1.12), we obtain $d_{112} = -d_{221} = d_{121} = -d_{212} = d_{212} = 0$.
- From Equations (P2.1.3) and (P2.1.9), we obtain $d_{133} = d_{233} = -d_{133} = 0$.
- From Equations (P2.1.16) and (P2.1.17), we obtain $d_{323} = -d_{313} = -d_{331} = d_{331} = d_{332} = 0$.
- From Equation (P2.1.18), we obtain $d_{312} = d_{321} = -d_{321} = 0$.
- From Equation (P2.1.4), we obtain $d_{123} = -d_{213} = d_{132} = -d_{231}$.

Considering the tensor symmetry with m and n such that $d_{123} = d_{132}$ and $d_{213} = d_{231}$ (each matrix of the i-th layer of the d tensor is symmetrical), we can obtain:

$$\begin{aligned}
&d_{111} = d_{222} = d_{112} = d_{121} = d_{211} = d_{221} = d_{212} = d_{122} = d_{331} = d_{313} = d_{133} = d_{332} \\
&= d_{323} = d_{233} = d_{312} = d_{321} = 0, \\
&d_{333} \neq 0, \\
&d_{311} = d_{322}, \\
&d_{113} = d_{131} = d_{223} = d_{232}, \\
&d_{123} = d_{132} = -d_{213} = -d_{231}.
\end{aligned}$$

Then, we obtain the d tensor with four independent components (d_{333}, d_{311}, d_{123}, d_{131}) as follows:

$$\begin{aligned}
&\text{First layer } (i=1) \quad \begin{pmatrix} 0 & 0 & d_{131} \\ 0 & 0 & d_{123} \\ d_{131} & d_{123} & 0 \end{pmatrix}, \\
&\text{Second layer } (i=2) \quad \begin{pmatrix} 0 & 0 & -d_{123} \\ 0 & 0 & d_{131} \\ -d_{123} & d_{131} & 0 \end{pmatrix}, \\
&\text{Third layer } (i=3) \quad \begin{pmatrix} d_{311} & 0 & 0 \\ 0 & d_{311} & 0 \\ 0 & 0 & d_{333} \end{pmatrix}.
\end{aligned} \tag{3.39}$$

4mm Symmetry

Barium titanate introduced in Chapter 1 has a crystal symmetry of point group *4mm* at room temperature, which means that the crystal has additional mirror symmetry normal to the x-z plane and the y-z plane, in addition to the 4-fold axisymmetry around the z-axis. The additional mirror transformation matrix should be

$$\begin{pmatrix} -1 & 0 & 0 \\ 0 & 1 & 0 \\ 0 & 0 & 1 \end{pmatrix} \text{ and } \begin{pmatrix} 1 & 0 & 0 \\ 0 & -1 & 0 \\ 0 & 0 & 1 \end{pmatrix}.$$

We now consider the four previous independent components (d_{333}, d_{311}, d_{123}, d_{131}) for the transformation matrix; $a_{11} = -1, a_{22} = 1, a_{33} = 1$.

- $d_{333}' = a_{33}a_{33}a_{33}d_{333} = (+1)(+1)(+1)d_{333}$
  Since $d_{333}' \equiv d_{333}$, we obtain the trivial $d_{333} = d_{333}$. (3.40)
- $d_{311}' = a_{33}a_{11}a_{11}d_{311} = (+1)(-1)(-1)d_{311}$
  Since $d_{311}' \equiv d_{311}$, we obtain the trivial $d_{311} = d_{311}$. (3.41)
- $d_{113}' = a_{11}a_{11}a_{33}d_{113} = (-1)(-1)(+1)d_{113} = d_{113}$
  Since $d_{113}' \equiv d_{113}$, we obtain the trivial $d_{113} = d_{113}$. (3.42)
- $d_{123}' = a_{11}a_{22}a_{33}d_{123} = (-1)(+1)(+1)d_{123} = -d_{123}$
  Since $d_{123}' \equiv d_{123}$, we obtain $d_{123} = -d_{123} = 0$. (3.43)

In conclusion, the mirror symmetry further eliminates
$d_{123} = d_{132} = -d_{213} = -d_{231} = 0$.

3.2.3. Reduction in the Tensor (Matrix Notation)

A third-rank tensor has $3^3 = 27$ independent components in general. Since d_{ijk} is symmetrical in j and k (which correspond to stress and strain), some of the coefficients can be the same, leaving 18 independent d_{ijk} coefficients; this facilitates the use of the matrix notation.

Thus far, all the equations have been developed in the full tensor notation. However, when describing the tensor and/or calculating actual properties, it is advantageous to reduce the number of suffixes as much as possible. This is done by defining new symbols, for instance, $d_{21} = d_{211}$ and $d_{14} = 2d_{123}$: the second and third suffixes (stress/strain) in the full tensor notation are replaced by a single suffix, from 1 to 6, in the matrix notation, as follows:

Tensor Notation	11	22	33	23, 32	31, 13	12, 21
Matrix Notation	1	2	3	4	5	6

Note that only when the shear stress and strain (4, 5, 6) are included, the multiplication factor "1/2" is required in these new matrix array; Equation (3.19) is rewritten as:

$$\text{First layer } (i = 1) \quad \begin{pmatrix} d_{11} & \left(\frac{1}{2}\right)d_{16} & \left(\frac{1}{2}\right)d_{15} \\ \left(\frac{1}{2}\right)d_{16} & d_{12} & \left(\frac{1}{2}\right)d_{14} \\ \left(\frac{1}{2}\right)d_{15} & \left(\frac{1}{2}\right)d_{14} & d_{13} \end{pmatrix},$$

$$\text{Second layer } (i = 2) \quad \begin{pmatrix} d_{21} & \left(\frac{1}{2}\right)d_{26} & \left(\frac{1}{2}\right)d_{25} \\ \left(\frac{1}{2}\right)d_{26} & d_{22} & \left(\frac{1}{2}\right)d_{24} \\ \left(\frac{1}{2}\right)d_{25} & \left(\frac{1}{2}\right)d_{24} & d_{23} \end{pmatrix}, \qquad (3.44)$$

$$\text{Third layer } (i = 3) \quad \begin{pmatrix} d_{31} & \left(\frac{1}{2}\right)d_{36} & \left(\frac{1}{2}\right)d_{35} \\ \left(\frac{1}{2}\right)d_{36} & d_{32} & \left(\frac{1}{2}\right)d_{34} \\ \left(\frac{1}{2}\right)d_{35} & \left(\frac{1}{2}\right)d_{34} & d_{33} \end{pmatrix}.$$

The last two suffixes in the tensor notation correspond to those of the strain components; therefore, for consistency, we make the following change in the notation for the strain components:

$$\begin{pmatrix} x_{11} & x_{12} & x_{31} \\ x_{12} & x_{22} & x_{23} \\ x_{31} & x_{23} & x_{33} \end{pmatrix} = \begin{pmatrix} x_1 & \left(\frac{1}{2}\right)x_6 & \left(\frac{1}{2}\right)x_5 \\ \left(\frac{1}{2}\right)x_6 & x_2 & \left(\frac{1}{2}\right)x_4 \\ \left(\frac{1}{2}\right)x_5 & \left(\frac{1}{2}\right)x_4 & x_3 \end{pmatrix}. \tag{3.45}$$

The (1/2)s in Equations (3.44) and (3.45) originate from the shear strain definition, $x_6 = x_{12} + x_{21}$, etc. (i.e., strain is an extensive parameter). Then, we have

$$x_j = \sum_i d_{ij} E_i \quad (i = 1, 2, 3; j = 1, 2, \ldots, 6), \tag{3.46a}$$

or

$$\begin{pmatrix} x_1 \\ x_2 \\ x_3 \\ x_4 \\ x_5 \\ x_6 \end{pmatrix} = \begin{pmatrix} d_{11} & d_{21} & d_{31} \\ d_{12} & d_{22} & d_{32} \\ d_{13} & d_{23} & d_{33} \\ d_{14} & d_{24} & d_{34} \\ d_{15} & d_{25} & d_{35} \\ d_{16} & d_{26} & d_{36} \end{pmatrix} \begin{pmatrix} E_1 \\ E_2 \\ E_3 \end{pmatrix}. \tag{3.46b}$$

Concerning the stress components, the (1/2)s are unnecessary because the stress is an intensive parameter.

$$\begin{pmatrix} X_{11} & X_{12} & X_{31} \\ X_{12} & X_{22} & X_{23} \\ X_{31} & X_{23} & X_{33} \end{pmatrix} = \begin{pmatrix} X_1 & X_6 & X_5 \\ X_6 & X_2 & X_4 \\ X_5 & X_4 & X_3 \end{pmatrix}. \tag{3.47}$$

The matrix notation has the advantage of compactness over the tensor notation, and it makes it easy to display the coefficients on a plane diagram (the 3D d_{ijk} expression can be described by a 2D matrix expression). However, it must be remembered that in spite of their form, the d_{ij}'s do not transform like the components of a normal second-rank tensor. Piezoelectric matrices for the point groups *4* and *4mm* are written (from Equation (3.39)) as

$$\begin{pmatrix} 0 & 0 & 0 & d_{14} & d_{15} & 0 \\ 0 & 0 & 0 & d_{15} & -d_{14} & 0 \\ d_{31} & d_{31} & d_{33} & 0 & 0 & 0 \end{pmatrix}, \begin{pmatrix} 0 & 0 & 0 & 0 & d_{15} & 0 \\ 0 & 0 & 0 & d_{15} & 0 & 0 \\ d_{31} & d_{31} & d_{33} & 0 & 0 & 0 \end{pmatrix}. \tag{3.48}$$

Example Problem 3.4

The room temperature form of α-quartz belongs to class 32. Taking into account the crystal symmetry (refer to Figure 3.5), verify that the piezoelectric matrix (d_{ij}) is given by only two independent components, d_{11} and d_{14}:

$$\begin{pmatrix} d_{11} & -d_{11} & 0 & d_{14} & 0 & 0 \\ 0 & 0 & 0 & 0 & -d_{14} & -2d_{11} \\ 0 & 0 & 0 & 0 & 0 & 0 \end{pmatrix}. \quad \text{(P3.4.1)}$$

Notice that the piezoelectric tensor must be invariant for a 120° rotation around the 3-axis and for a 180° rotation around the 1-axis. The transformation matrices are respectively,

$$\begin{pmatrix} -1/2 & \sqrt{3}/2 & 0 \\ -\sqrt{3}/2 & -1/2 & 0 \\ 0 & 0 & 1 \end{pmatrix} \text{ and } \begin{pmatrix} 1 & 0 & 0 \\ 0 & -1 & 0 \\ 0 & 0 & -1 \end{pmatrix}.$$

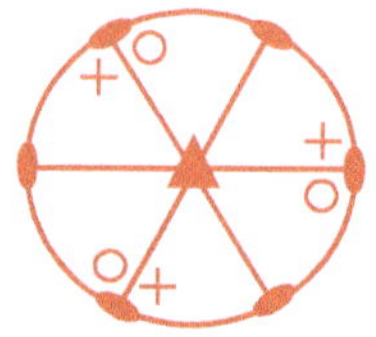

Figure 3.5. 32 symmetry. Source: Figure by author.

Solution

We start from the 2-fold symmetry analysis first, because the rotation matrix has a simple structure with only 3 components, 1 for each row and column, to eliminate as many components as possible from the initial 18 components (each layer matrix of the d_{ijk} tensor is symmetrical). The transformation change in the coordinate system can be expressed as

$$d'_{ijk} = \sum_{lmn} a_{il} a_{jm} a_{kn} d_{lmn}. \quad \text{(P3.4.2)}$$

In the 180° rotation matrix around the x-axis, all the elements equal zero except for $a_{11} = 1$, $a_{22} = -1$, and $a_{33} = -1$, which means in the original equation, $d'_{ijk} \neq 0$ only when $i = l,\ j = m,\ and\ k = n$. Thus, we can simplify the equation into:

$$d'_{ijk} = \sum_{ijk} a_{ii} a_{jj} a_{kk} d_{ijk}. \quad \text{(P3.4.3)}$$

Since each layer matrix ($i = 1, 2, 3$) is symmetric, there are 6 components in each layer, with 18 components in the whole tensor, thet are independent, which means $d'_{112} = d'_{121}, d'_{113} = d'_{131}, d'_{123} = d'_{132}, d'_{212} = d'_{221}, d'_{213} = d'_{231}, d'_{223} = d'_{232}, d'_{312} = d'_{321}$, $d'_{313} = d'_{331}$, and $d'_{323} = d'_{332}$. Then, we can use this equation to find all the elements in the new matrix:

- For the first layer,

  $d'_{111} = (1)(1)(1)d_{111} = d_{111}$
  $d'_{112} = a_{11}a_{11}a_{22}d_{112}$
  $d'_{112} = (1)(1)(-1)d_{112} = -d_{112}$
  $d'_{113} = a_{11}a_{11}a_{33}d_{113}$
  $d'_{113} = (1)(1)(-1)d_{113} = -d_{113}$
  $d'_{122} = a_{11}a_{22}a_{22}d_{122}$
  $d'_{122} = (1)(-1)(-1)d_{122} = d_{122}$
  $d'_{123} = a_{11}a_{22}a_{33}d_{123}$
  $d'_{123} = (1)(-1)(-1)d_{123} = d_{123}$
  $d'_{133} = a_{11}a_{33}a_{33}d_{133}$
  $d'_{133} = (1)(-1)(-1)d_{133} = d_{133}$

  we obtain:

$$\begin{pmatrix} d'_{111} = d_{111} & d'_{112} = -d_{112} & d'_{113} = -d_{113} \\ d'_{121} = -d_{112} & d'_{122} = d_{122} & d'_{123} = d_{123} \\ d'_{131} = -d_{113} & d'_{132} = d_{123} & d'_{133} = d_{133} \end{pmatrix} \rightarrow \begin{pmatrix} d_{111} & 0 & 0 \\ 0 & d_{122} & d_{123} \\ 0 & d_{132} & d_{133} \end{pmatrix}. \quad \text{(P3.4.4)}$$

- For the second layer,

  $d'_{211} = (-1)(1)(1)d_{211} = -d_{211}$
  $d'_{212} = a_{22}a_{11}a_{22}d_{212}$
  $d'_{212} = (-1)(1)(-1)d_{212} = d_{212}$
  $d'_{213} = a_{22}a_{11}a_{33}d_{213}$
  $d'_{213} = (-1)(1)(-1)d_{213} = d_{213}$
  $d'_{222} = a_{22}a_{22}a_{22}d_{222}$
  $d'_{222} = (-1)(-1)(-1)d_{222} = -d_{222}$
  $d'_{223} = a_{22}a_{22}a_{33}d_{223}$
  $d'_{223} = (-1)(-1)(-1)d_{223} = -d_{223}$
  $d'_{233} = a_{22}a_{33}a_{33}d_{233}$
  $d'_{233} = (-1)(-1)(-1)d_{233} = -d_{233}$

  we obtain

$$\begin{pmatrix} d'_{211} = -d_{211} & d'_{212} = d_{212} & d'_{213} = d_{213} \\ d'_{221} = d_{212} & d'_{222} = -d_{222} & d'_{223} = -d_{223} \\ d'_{231} = d_{213} & d'_{232} = -d_{223} & d'_{233} = -d_{233} \end{pmatrix} \rightarrow \begin{pmatrix} 0 & d_{212} & d_{213} \\ d_{221} & 0 & 0 \\ d_{231} & 0 & 0 \end{pmatrix}. \quad \text{(P3.4.5)}$$

- For the third layer,

  $d'_{311} = (-1)(1)(1)d_{311} = -d_{311}$
  $d'_{312} = a_{33}a_{11}a_{22}d_{312}$

$$d'_{312} = (-1)(1)(-1)d_{312} = d_{312}$$
$$d'_{313} = a_{33}a_{11}a_{33}d_{313}$$
$$d'_{313} = (-1)(1)(-1)d_{313} = d_{313}$$
$$d'_{322} = a_{33}a_{22}a_{22}d_{322}$$
$$d'_{322} = (-1)(-1)(-1)d_{322} = -d_{322}$$
$$d'_{323} = a_{33}a_{22}a_{33}d_{323}$$
$$d'_{323} = (-1)(-1)(-1)d_{323} = -d_{323}$$
$$d'_{233} = a_{22}a_{33}a_{33}d_{233}$$
$$d'_{333} = (-1)(-1)(-1)d_{333} = -d_{333}$$

we obtain

$$\begin{pmatrix} d'_{311} = -d_{311} & d'_{312} = d_{312} & d'_{313} = d_{313} \\ d'_{321} = d_{312} & d'_{322} = -d_{322} & d'_{323} = -d_{323} \\ d'_{331} = d_{313} & d'_{332} = -d_{323} & d'_{333} = -d_{333} \end{pmatrix} \to \begin{pmatrix} 0 & d_{312} & d_{313} \\ d_{321} & 0 & 0 \\ d_{331} & 0 & 0 \end{pmatrix}. \quad \text{(P3.4.6)}$$

In conclusion, knowing the tensor symmetry such as $d_{123} = d_{132}$ and $d_{312} = d_{321}$, the 2-fold symmetry reduces the independent components down to eight.

We will now work on the 3-fold symmetry. For a 120° rotation along the z-axis, we have the following rotation matrix:

$$\begin{pmatrix} -1/2 & \sqrt{3/2} & 0 \\ -\sqrt{3/2} & -1/2 & 0 \\ 0 & 0 & 1 \end{pmatrix}.$$

Therefore, $a_{11} = -1/2$, $a_{12} = -\sqrt{3/2}$, $a_{21} = \sqrt{3/2}$, $a_{22} = -1/2$, and $a_{33} = 1$. Note that from the previous solution, we obtained $d_{112} = d_{113} = d_{121} = d_{131} = d_{211} = d_{222} = d_{232} = d_{223} = d_{233} = d_{311} = d_{322} = d_{332} = d_{323} = d_{333} = 0$, $d'_{111} = d_{111}$, $d'_{122} = d_{122}$, $d'_{133} = d_{133}$, $d'_{123} = d_{123}$, $d'_{212} = d_{212}$, $d'_{213} = d_{213}$, $d'_{312} = d_{312}$, $d'_{313} = d_{313}$. We will calculate the eight non-zero components, d'_{111}, d'_{122}, d'_{133}, d'_{123}, d'_{212}, d'_{213}, d'_{312}, and d'_{313}, below.

- d'_{111}

$$\begin{aligned} d'_{111} &= \sum_{lmn} a_{1l}a_{1m}a_{1n}d_{lmn} = \sum_{mn} a_{11}a_{1m}a_{1n}d_{1mn} + \sum_{mn} a_{12}a_{1m}a_{1n}d_{2mn} \\ &= a_{11}a_{11}a_{11}d_{111} + a_{11}a_{12}a_{12}d_{122} + a_{11}a_{13}a_{13}d_{133} \\ &+2a_{11}a_{12}a_{13}d_{123} + 2a_{12}a_{11}a_{12}d_{212} + 2a_{12}a_{11}a_{13}d_{213}, \end{aligned} \quad \text{(P3.4.7)}$$

$$d'_{111} = \left(-\tfrac{1}{2}\right)\left(\tfrac{\sqrt{3}}{2}\right)\left(\tfrac{\sqrt{3}}{2}\right)d_{122} + \left(-\tfrac{1}{2}\right)\left(-\tfrac{1}{2}\right)\left(-\tfrac{1}{2}\right)d_{111} + 2\left(\tfrac{\sqrt{3}}{2}\right)\left(\tfrac{\sqrt{3}}{2}\right)\left(-\tfrac{1}{2}\right)d_{21},$$

$$d'_{111} = \left(-\tfrac{3}{8}\right)d_{122} + \left(-\tfrac{1}{8}\right)d_{111} + \left(-\tfrac{3}{4}\right)d_{212} \equiv d_{111}.$$

- d'_{122}

$$d'_{122} = \sum_{lmn} a_{1l}a_{2m}a_{2n}d_{lmn} = \sum_{mn} a_{11}a_{2m}a_{2n}d_{1mn} + \sum_{mn} a_{12}a_{2m}a_{2n}d_{2mn}$$

$$\begin{gathered} = a_{11}a_{21}a_{21}d_{111} + a_{11}a_{22}a_{22}d_{122} + a_{11}a_{23}a_{23}d_{133} + 2a_{11}a_{22}a_{23}d_{123} + \\ 2a_{12}a_{21}a_{22}d_{212} + 2a_{12}a_{21}a_{23}d_{213}, \\ d'_{122} = \left(-\tfrac{1}{2}\right)\left(-\tfrac{\sqrt{3}}{2}\right)\left(-\tfrac{\sqrt{3}}{2}\right)d_{111} + \left(-\tfrac{1}{2}\right)\left(-\tfrac{1}{2}\right)\left(-\tfrac{1}{2}\right)d_{122} + \\ 2\left(-\tfrac{\sqrt{3}}{2}\right)\left(\tfrac{\sqrt{3}}{2}\right)\left(-\tfrac{1}{2}\right)d_{212}, \\ d'_{122} = \left(-\tfrac{3}{8}\right)d_{111} + \left(-\tfrac{1}{8}\right)d_{122} + \left(\tfrac{3}{4}\right)d_{212} \equiv d_{122}. \end{gathered} \tag{P3.4.8}$$

- d'_{133}

$$d'_{133} = \sum_{lmn} a_{1l}a_{3m}a_{3n}d_{lmn} = \sum_{mn} a_{11}a_{3m}a_{3n}d_{1mn} + \sum_{mn} a_{12}a_{3m}a_{3n}d_{2mn}$$

$$\begin{gathered} = a_{11}a_{31}a_{31}d_{111} + a_{11}a_{32}a_{32}d_{122} + a_{11}a_{33}a_{33}d_{133} + 2a_{11}a_{32}a_{33}d_{123} + \\ 2a_{12}a_{31}a_{32}d_{212} + 2a_{12}a_{31}a_{33}d_{213}, \\ d'_{133} = \left(-\tfrac{1}{2}\right)(1)(1)d_{133} = \left(-\tfrac{1}{2}\right)d_{133} \equiv d_{133}. \end{gathered} \tag{P3.4.9}$$

- d'_{123}

$$d'_{123} = \sum_{lmn} a_{1l}a_{2m}a_{3n}d_{lmn} = \sum_{mn} a_{11}a_{2m}a_{3n}d_{1mn} + \sum_{mn} a_{12}a_{2m}a_{3n}d_{2mn}$$

$$\begin{gathered} = a_{11}a_{21}a_{31}d_{111} + a_{11}a_{22}a_{32}d_{122} + a_{11}a_{23}a_{33}d_{133} + a_{11}a_{22}a_{33}d_{123} + \\ a_{11}a_{23}a_{32}d_{132} + a_{12}a_{21}a_{32}d_{212} + a_{12}a_{22}a_{31}d_{221} + a_{12}a_{21}a_{33}d_{213} + \\ a_{12}a_{23}a_{31}d_{231}, \\ d'_{123} = \left(-\tfrac{1}{2}\right)\left(-\tfrac{1}{2}\right)(1)d_{123} + \left(-\tfrac{\sqrt{3}}{2}\right)\left(\tfrac{\sqrt{3}}{2}\right)(1)d_{213}, \\ d'_{123} = \tfrac{1}{4}d_{123} + \left(-\tfrac{3}{4}\right)d_{213} \equiv d_{123}. \end{gathered} \tag{P3.4.10}$$

- d'_{212}

$$d'_{212} = \sum_{lmn} a_{2l}a_{1m}a_{2n}d_{lmn} = \sum_{mn} a_{21}a_{1m}a_{2n}d_{1mn} + \sum_{mn} a_{22}a_{1m}a_{2n}d_{2mn}$$
$$= a_{21}a_{11}a_{21}d_{111} + a_{21}a_{12}a_{22}d_{122} + a_{21}a_{13}a_{23}d_{133} + a_{21}a_{12}a_{23}d_{123}$$
$$+a_{22}a_{11}a_{22}d_{212} + a_{22}a_{12}a_{21}d_{221} + a_{22}a_{11}a_{23}d_{213} + a_{22}a_{13}a_{21}d_{231},$$
$$d'_{212} = \left(-\tfrac{\sqrt{3}}{2}\right)\left(-\tfrac{\sqrt{3}}{2}\right)\left(-\tfrac{1}{2}\right)d_{111} + \left(-\tfrac{\sqrt{3}}{2}\right)\left(\tfrac{\sqrt{3}}{2}\right)\left(-\tfrac{1}{2}\right)d_{122}+$$
$$\left(-\tfrac{1}{2}\right)\left(-\tfrac{1}{2}\right)\left(-\tfrac{1}{2}\right)d_{212} + \left(-\tfrac{\sqrt{3}}{2}\right)\left(\tfrac{\sqrt{3}}{2}\right)\left(-\tfrac{1}{2}\right)d_{212},$$
$$d'_{212} = (-\tfrac{3}{8})d_{111} + (\tfrac{3}{8})d_{122} + \left(\tfrac{1}{4}\right)d_{212} \equiv d_{212}. \quad \text{(P3.4.11)}$$

- d'_{213}

$$d'_{213} = \sum_{lmn} a_{2l}a_{1m}a_{3n}d_{lmn} = \sum_{mn} a_{21}a_{1m}a_{3n}d_{1mn} + \sum_{mn} a_{22}a_{1m}a_{3n}d_{2mn}$$
$$= a_{21}a_{11}a_{31}d_{111} + a_{21}a_{12}a_{32}d_{122} + a_{21}a_{13}a_{33}d_{133} + a_{21}a_{12}a_{33}d_{123}$$
$$+a_{21}a_{13}a_{32}d_{132} + a_{22}a_{11}a_{32}d_{212} + a_{22}a_{12}a_{31}d_{221} + a_{22}a_{11}a_{33}d_{213}$$
$$+a_{22}a_{13}a_{31}d_{231},$$
$$d'_{213} = \left(-\tfrac{\sqrt{3}}{2}\right)\left(\tfrac{\sqrt{3}}{2}\right)(1)d_{123} + \left(-\tfrac{1}{2}\right)\left(-\tfrac{1}{2}\right)(1)d_{213},$$
$$d'_{213} = -\tfrac{3}{4}d_{123} + \tfrac{1}{4}d_{213} \equiv d_{213}. \quad \text{(P3.4.12)}$$

- d'_{312}

$$d'_{312} = \sum_{lmn} a_{3l}a_{1m}a_{2n}d_{lmn} = \sum_{mn} a_{33}a_{1m}a_{2n}d_{2mn}$$
$$= a_{33}a_{11}a_{22}d_{312} + a_{33}a_{12}a_{21}d_{321} + a_{33}a_{11}a_{23}d_{313} + a_{33}a_{13}a_{21}d_{331}, \quad \text{(P3.4.13)}$$
$$d'_{312} = (1)\left(-\tfrac{1}{2}\right)\left(-\tfrac{1}{2}\right)d_{312} + (1)\left(-\tfrac{\sqrt{3}}{2}\right)\left(\tfrac{\sqrt{3}}{2}\right)d_{321} = \tfrac{1}{4}d_{312} - \tfrac{3}{4}d_{321} \equiv d_{312}.$$

- d'_{313}

$$d'_{313} = \sum_{lmn} a_{3l}a_{1m}a_{3n}d_{lmn} = \sum_{mn} a_{33}a_{1m}a_{3n}d_{2mn}$$
$$= a_{33}a_{11}a_{32}d_{312} + a_{33}a_{12}a_{31}d_{321} + a_{33}a_{11}a_{33}d_{313} + a_{33}a_{13}a_{31}d_{331}, \quad \text{(P3.4.14)}$$
$$d'_{313} = (1)\left(-\tfrac{1}{2}\right)(1)d_{313} = -\tfrac{1}{2}d_{313} \equiv d_{313}.$$

We can summarize the eight obtained equations, Equations (P3.4.7)–(P3.4.14), as follows:

$$\begin{cases} 3d_{111} + d_{122} + 2d_{212} = 0 \\ d_{111} + 3d_{122} - 2d_{212} = 0 \\ d_{133} = 0 \\ d_{123} + d_{231} = 0 \\ d_{111} - d_{122} + 2d_{212} = 0 \\ d_{123} + d_{231} = 0 \\ d_{312} = 0 \\ d_{331} = 0 \end{cases} \rightarrow \begin{cases} d_{111} = -d_{122} \\ d_{212} = -d_{111} \\ d_{231} = -d_{123} \\ d_{133} = d_{312} = d_{331} = 0 \end{cases}. \tag{P3.4.15}$$

Using the matrix notation, $d_{111} = d_{11}$, $d_{122} = d_{12} = -d_{11}$, $d_{123} = \left(\frac{1}{2}\right)d_{14} = -d_{231} = -\left(\frac{1}{2}\right)d_{25}$, and $d_{212} = \left(\frac{1}{2}\right)d_{26} = -d_{111}$, we finally obtain the matrix form as follows:

$$\begin{pmatrix} d_{11} & -d_{11} & 0 & d_{14} & 0 & 0 \\ 0 & 0 & 0 & 0 & -d_{14} & -2d_{11} \\ 0 & 0 & 0 & 0 & 0 & 0 \end{pmatrix}. \tag{P3.4.16}$$

Note that α-quartz has only two independent tensor/matrix components, d_{11} and d_{14}.

3.3. Tensor Description of Constitutive Equations

Two piezoelectric constitutive equations are shown below:

$$x = s^E X + dE, \tag{3.49a}$$

$$D = dX + \varepsilon_0 \varepsilon^X E. \tag{3.49b}$$

By using the vector and tensor (reduced matrix) notation, we can obtain

$$\begin{pmatrix} x_1 \\ x_2 \\ x_3 \\ x_4 \\ x_5 \\ x_6 \end{pmatrix} = \begin{pmatrix} s_{11}^E & s_{12}^E & s_{13}^E & s_{14}^E & s_{15}^E & s_{16}^E \\ s_{21}^E & s_{22}^E & s_{23}^E & s_{24}^E & s_{25}^E & s_{26}^E \\ s_{31}^E & s_{32}^E & s_{33}^E & s_{34}^E & s_{35}^E & s_{36}^E \\ s_{41}^E & s_{42}^E & s_{43}^E & s_{44}^E & s_{45}^E & s_{46}^E \\ s_{51}^E & s_{52}^E & s_{53}^E & s_{54}^E & s_{55}^E & s_{56}^E \\ s_{61}^E & s_{62}^E & s_{63}^E & s_{64}^E & s_{65}^E & s_{66}^E \end{pmatrix} \begin{pmatrix} X_1 \\ X_2 \\ X_3 \\ X_4 \\ X_5 \\ X_6 \end{pmatrix} + \begin{pmatrix} d_{11} & d_{21} & d_{31} \\ d_{12} & d_{22} & d_{32} \\ d_{13} & d_{23} & d_{33} \\ d_{14} & d_{24} & d_{34} \\ d_{15} & d_{25} & d_{35} \\ d_{16} & d_{26} & d_{36} \end{pmatrix} \begin{pmatrix} E_1 \\ E_2 \\ E_3 \end{pmatrix} \tag{3.50a}$$

$$\begin{pmatrix} D_1 \\ D_2 \\ D_3 \end{pmatrix} = \begin{pmatrix} d_{11} & d_{12} & d_{13} & d_{14} & d_{15} & d_{16} \\ d_{21} & d_{22} & d_{23} & d_{24} & d_{25} & d_{26} \\ d_{31} & d_{32} & d_{33} & d_{34} & d_{35} & d_{36} \end{pmatrix} \begin{pmatrix} X_1 \\ X_2 \\ X_3 \\ X_4 \\ X_5 \\ X_6 \end{pmatrix} + \varepsilon_0 \begin{pmatrix} \varepsilon_{11}^X & \varepsilon_{12}^X & \varepsilon_{13}^X \\ \varepsilon_{21}^X & \varepsilon_{22}^X & \varepsilon_{23}^X \\ \varepsilon_{31}^X & \varepsilon_{32}^X & \varepsilon_{33}^X \end{pmatrix} \begin{pmatrix} E_1 \\ E_2 \\ E_3 \end{pmatrix} \tag{3.50b}$$

Remember that the elastic and permittivity tensors are symmetric, but the piezoelectric matrix is not symmetric, because "i" and "j" correspond to the electric field and strain, respectively, and not commutative. We can also describe these matrix expressions as

$$\begin{cases} x_i = s_{ij}^E X_j + d_{mi} E_m \\ D_m = d_{mi} X_i + \varepsilon_0 \varepsilon_{mk}^X E_k \end{cases}, \tag{3.51a}$$

$$(i, j = 1, 2, \cdots, 6; m, k = 1, 2, 3). \tag{3.51b}$$

Note also that for d_{mi}, $i = 4, 5, 6$ (i.e., shear mode), $d_{mi} = 2d_{mpq}$ (pq should be 23, 31, 12).

Example Problem 3.5

Measured piezoelectric constant d_{ij} values for right-handed quartz (crystal symmetry 32) are given by

$$\begin{pmatrix} -2.3 & 2.3 & 0 & -0.67 & 0 & 0 \\ 0 & 0 & 0 & 0 & 0.67 & 4.6 \\ 0 & 0 & 0 & 0 & 0 & 0 \end{pmatrix} \times 10^{-12}\ [\mathrm{C/N}].$$

(a) For the case where a compressive stress of 1 kg·f/cm^2 is applied along the 1-axis of a quartz crystal, find the polarization generated (kg·f = kilogram force = 9.8 N).

(b) For the case where an electric field of 100 V/cm is applied along the 1-axis, find the strains generated.

Solution

(a) Considering the "compressive stress" has a negative sign, the polarization can be expressed as

$$\begin{pmatrix} P_1 \\ P_2 \\ P_3 \end{pmatrix} = \begin{pmatrix} -2.3 & 2.3 & 0 & -0.67 & 0 & 0 \\ 0 & 0 & 0 & 0 & 0.67 & 4.6 \\ 0 & 0 & 0 & 0 & 0 & 0 \end{pmatrix} \times 10^{-12}[\mathrm{C/N}] \begin{pmatrix} -98{,}000 \\ 0 \\ 0 \\ 0 \\ 0 \\ 0 \end{pmatrix} \left[\mathrm{N/m^2}\right], \quad \text{(P3.5.1)}$$

$$\begin{pmatrix} P_1 \\ P_2 \\ P_3 \end{pmatrix} = \begin{pmatrix} 2.3 \\ 0 \\ 0 \end{pmatrix} \times 10^{-7} \left[\mathrm{C/m^2}\right]. \quad \text{(P3.5.2)}$$

(b) The strain can be calculated as:

$$\begin{pmatrix} x_1 \\ x_2 \\ x_3 \\ x_4 \\ x_5 \\ x_6 \end{pmatrix} = \begin{pmatrix} -2.3 & 0 & 0 \\ 2.3 & 0 & 0 \\ 0 & 0 & 0 \\ -0.67 & 0 & 0 \\ 0 & 0.67 & 0 \\ 0 & 4.6 & 0 \end{pmatrix} \times 10^{-12}[\mathrm{C/N}] \times \begin{pmatrix} 1 \\ 0 \\ 0 \end{pmatrix} \times 10^4\ [\mathrm{V/m}], \quad \text{(P3.5.3)}$$

$$\begin{pmatrix} x_1 \\ x_2 \\ x_3 \\ x_4 \\ x_5 \\ x_6 \end{pmatrix} = \begin{pmatrix} -2.3 \\ 2.3 \\ 0 \\ -0.67 \\ 0 \\ 0 \end{pmatrix} \times 10^{-8}. \quad \text{(P3.5.4)}$$

Example Problem 3.6

Barium titanate shows a tetragonal crystal symmetry (point group *4mm*) at room temperature. Therefore, its piezoelectric constant matrix is given by (Equation (3.48)):

$$\begin{pmatrix} 0 & 0 & 0 & 0 & d_{15} & 0 \\ 0 & 0 & 0 & d_{15} & 0 & 0 \\ d_{31} & d_{31} & d_{31} & 0 & 0 & 0 \end{pmatrix}$$

(a) Calculate the induced strain under an electric field applied along the crystal c-axis (E_3).

(b) Calculate the induced strain under an electric field applied along the crystal a-axis (E_1).

Solution

$$\begin{pmatrix} x_1 \\ x_2 \\ x_3 \\ x_4 \\ x_5 \\ x_6 \end{pmatrix} = \begin{pmatrix} 0 & 0 & d_{31} \\ 0 & 0 & d_{31} \\ 0 & 0 & d_{33} \\ 0 & d_{15} & 0 \\ d_{15} & 0 & 0 \\ 0 & 0 & 0 \end{pmatrix} \begin{pmatrix} E_1 \\ E_2 \\ E_3 \end{pmatrix} \quad \text{(P3.6.1)}$$

can be transformed into

$$\begin{aligned} x_1 = x_2 = d_{31}E_3,\ x_3 = d_{33}E_3, \\ x_4 = d_{15}E_2,\ x_5 = d_{15}E_1,\ x_6 = 0. \end{aligned} \quad \text{(P3.6.2)}$$

(a) When E_3 is applied, elongation in the c direction ($x_3 = d_{33}E_3$, $d_{33} > 0$) and contraction in the a and b directions ($x_1 = x_2 = d_{31}E_3$, $d_{31} < 0$) are induced. The ratio $|d_{31}/d_{33}|$ corresponds to "Poisson's ratio" σ.

(b) When E_1 is applied, shear strain x_5 ($=2x_{31}$) $= d_{15}E_1$ is induced. Figure 3.6a illustrates a case of $d_{15} > 0$ and $x_5 > 0$. The deformation can be intuitively understood by the polarization cant under the electric field.

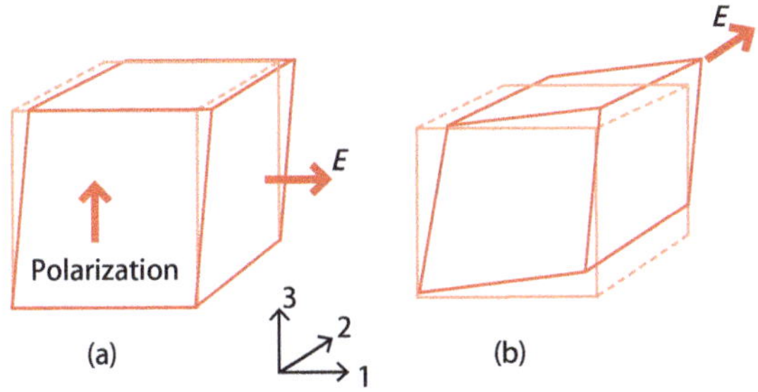

Figure 3.6. (**a**) Piezoelectric shear strain in the point group tetragonal *4mm*, and (**b**) [111] axis electrostrictive strain in the point group cubic *m3m*. Source: Figure by author.

3.4. Matrix Notation of Electrostrictive Coefficients

In the solid state theoretical treatment of the phenomenon of piezoelectricity (primary) or electrostriction (secondary electromechanical coupling), the strain x_{kl} is expressed in terms of the electric field $\boldsymbol{E}_i$ or electric polarization $\boldsymbol{P}_i$ as follows (refer to the previous Section 1.2.4):

$$x_{kl} = \sum_{i} d_{ikl}\boldsymbol{E}_i + \sum_{i,j} M_{ijkl}\boldsymbol{E}_i\boldsymbol{E}_j = \sum_{i} g_{ikl}\boldsymbol{P}_i + \sum_{i,j} Q_{ijkl}\boldsymbol{P}_i\boldsymbol{P}_j. \quad (3.52)$$

Here, d_{ikl} and g_{ikl} are called the "piezoelectric coefficients", and M_{ijkl} and Q_{ijkl} are the "electrostrictive coefficients". Since the $\boldsymbol{E}$ and x are first-rank and second-rank tensors, respectively, d should be a third-rank tensor. However, $\boldsymbol{E}_i\boldsymbol{E}_j$ and $\boldsymbol{P}_i\boldsymbol{P}_j$ are not tensors, precisely speaking, but we treat a combination of ($E_1{}^2$, $E_2{}^2$, $E_3{}^2$, E_2E_3, E_3E_1, E_1E_2) as if these are equivalent to a second-rank tensor. Note that these six components are not independent at all. This is a smart way to convert the non-linear behavior (electrostriction) to a linear algebra problem.

Using a similar reduction in the notation for the electrostrictive coefficients M_{ijkl}, we obtain the following equation corresponding to Equation (3.52):

$$\begin{pmatrix} x_1 \\ x_2 \\ x_3 \\ x_4 \\ x_5 \\ x_6 \end{pmatrix} = \begin{pmatrix} d_{11} & d_{21} & d_{31} \\ d_{12} & d_{22} & d_{32} \\ d_{13} & d_{23} & d_{33} \\ d_{14} & d_{24} & d_{34} \\ d_{15} & d_{25} & d_{35} \\ d_{16} & d_{26} & d_{36} \end{pmatrix} \begin{pmatrix} E_1 \\ E_2 \\ E_3 \end{pmatrix} + \begin{pmatrix} M_{11} & M_{21} & M_{31} & M_{41} & M_{51} & M_{61} \\ M_{12} & M_{22} & M_{32} & M_{42} & M_{52} & M_{62} \\ M_{13} & M_{23} & M_{33} & M_{43} & M_{53} & M_{63} \\ M_{14} & M_{24} & M_{34} & M_{44} & M_{54} & M_{64} \\ M_{15} & M_{25} & M_{35} & M_{45} & M_{55} & M_{65} \\ M_{16} & M_{26} & M_{36} & M_{46} & M_{56} & M_{66} \end{pmatrix} \begin{pmatrix} E_1{}^2 \\ E_2{}^2 \\ E_3{}^2 \\ E_2E_3 \\ E_3E_1 \\ E_1E_2 \end{pmatrix}. \quad (3.53)$$

Tables 3.1 and 3.2 summarize the matrix notations of d and M for all crystallographic point groups [1].

Table 3.1. Piezoelectric coefficient matrix. *

$$* \begin{cases} d_{mn} = d_{ijk} \ (n = 1, 2, 3) \\ d_{mn} = 2d_{ijk} \ (n = 4, 5, 6) \end{cases}$$

i — electric field / polarization
jk — strain / stress

Symbol meanings

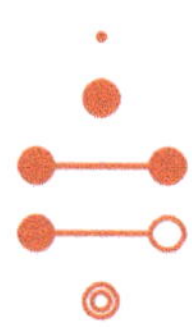

Zero component
Non-zero component
Equal components
Equal with opposite signs
−2 times of the ● connected point

I Centro symmetric point group

Point group $\bar{1}$, $2/m$, mmm, $4/m$, $4/mmm$, $m3$, $m3m$, $\bar{3}$, $\bar{3}m$, $6/m$, $6/mmm$. All components are zero.

II Non-centro symmetric point group

Triclinic

Point group *1*

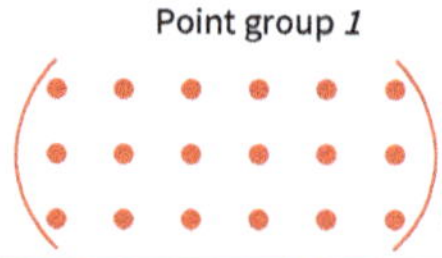
(18)

Monoclinic

Point group *2*

$2 \parallel x_2$ (Standard) orientation

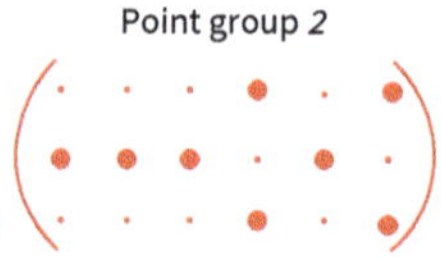
(8)

Point group *2*

$2 \parallel x_3$

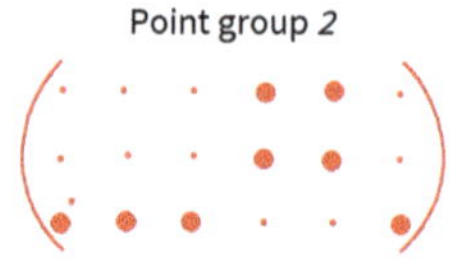
(8)

Point group m

$m \perp x_2$ (Standard) orientation

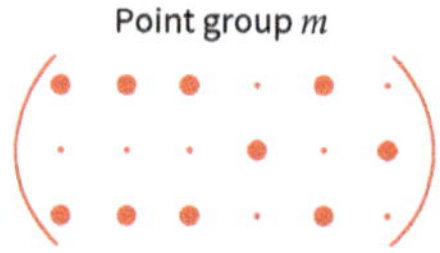
(10)

Point group m

$m \perp x_3$

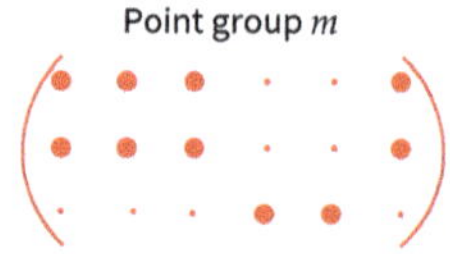
(10)

Orthorhombic

Point group *222*

(3)

Point group $mm2$

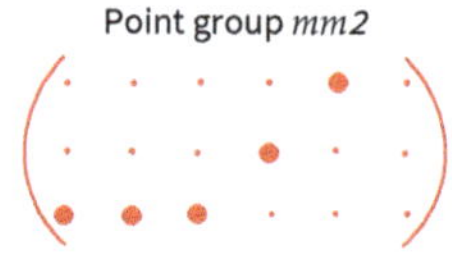
(5)

Tetragonal

Point group *4*

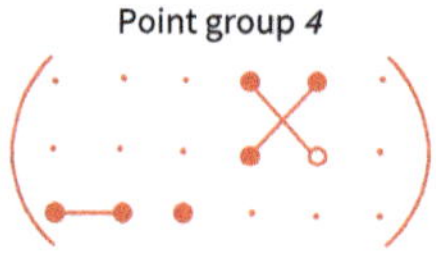
(4)

Point group $\bar{4}$

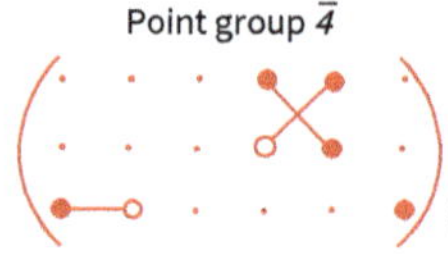
(4)

Table 3.1. *Cont.*

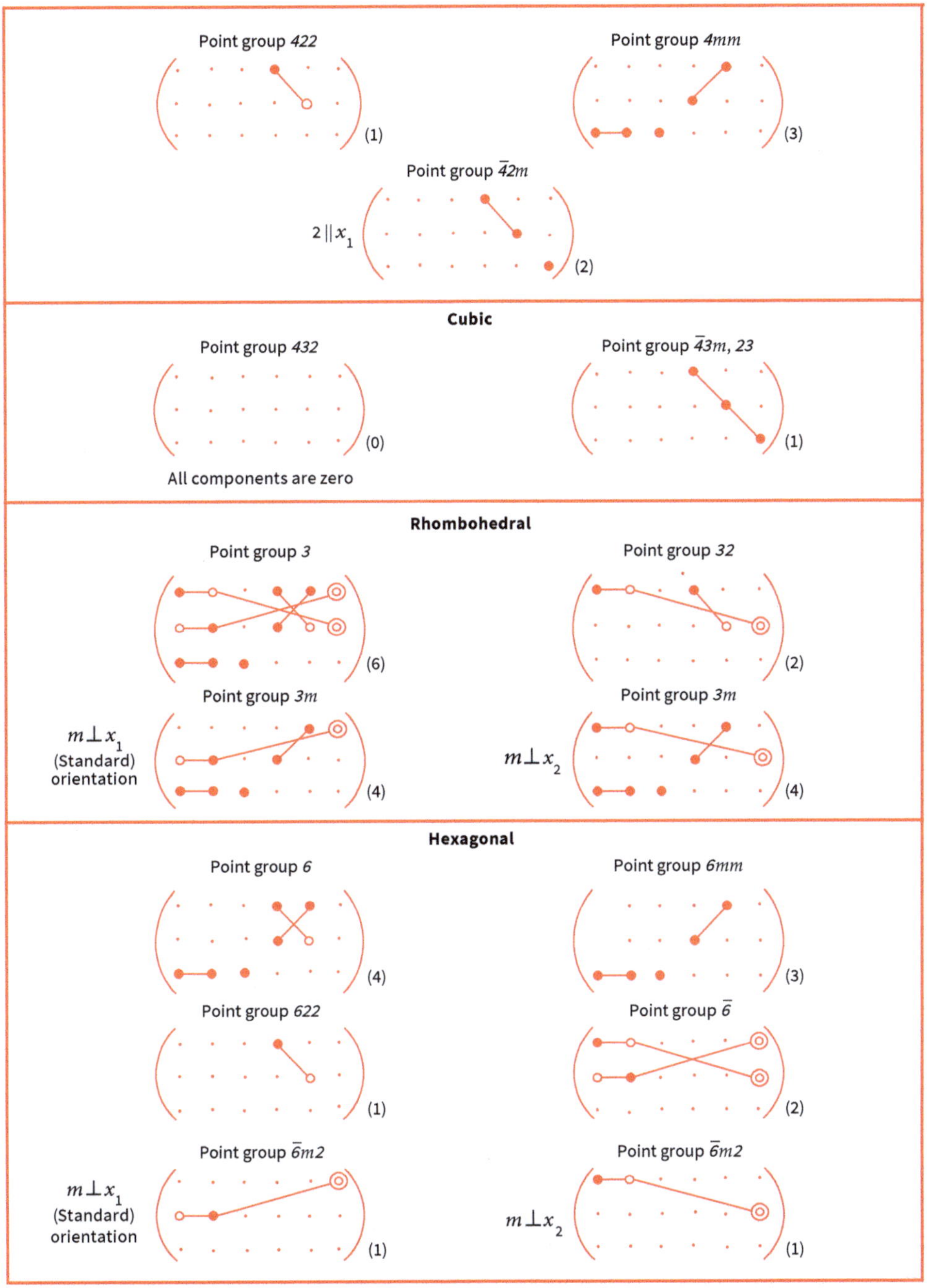

Source: [3] ©Uchino, K. *Micromechatronics*, 2nd ed. CRC Press, 2019; p. 50. Reproduced by permission of Taylor & Francis Group.

Table 3.2. Electrostrictive coefficient matrix. *

$$* \begin{cases} Q_{mn} = Q_{ijkl} & (m, n = 1, 2, 3) \\ Q_{mn} = 2Q_{ijkl} & (m \text{ or } n = 4, 5, 6) \\ Q_{mn} = 4Q_{ijkl} & (m, n = 4, 5, 6) \end{cases}$$

ij — strain
kl — electric field

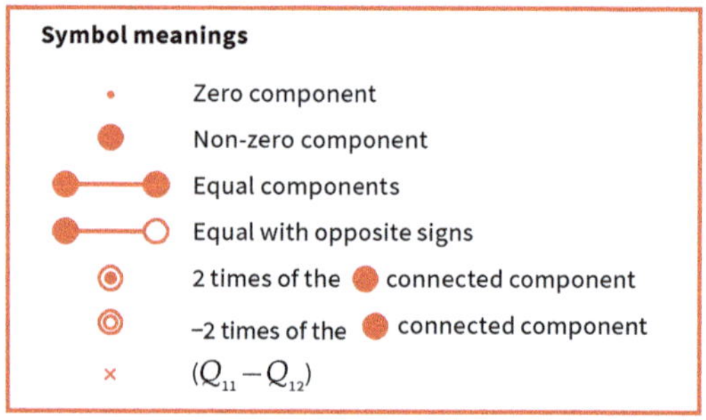

Trigonal
Point group *1*, *T*

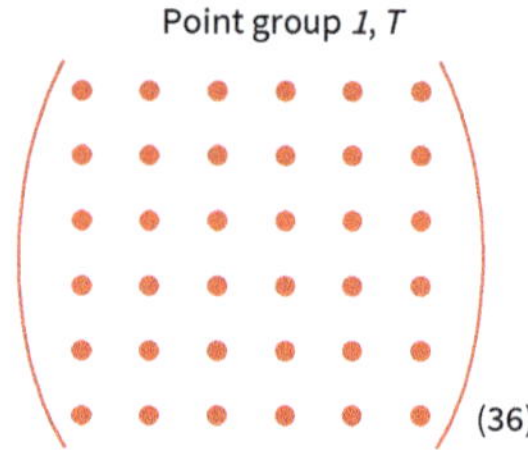

Monoclinic
Point group *2*, *m*, *2/m*

2 fold axis || x_2
Standard orientation

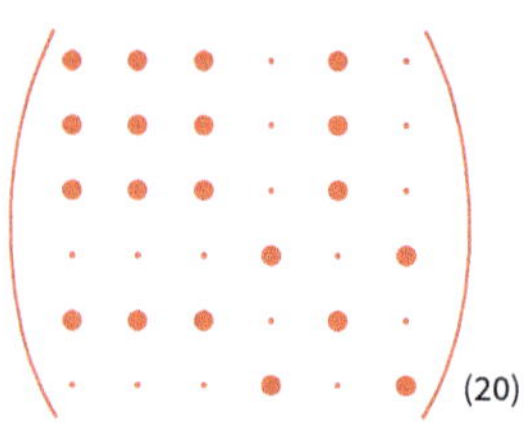

2 fold axis || x_3

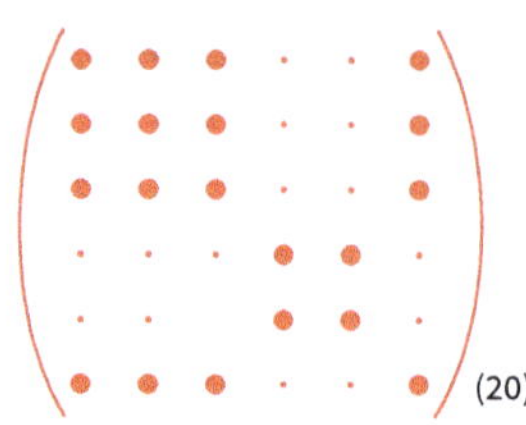

Trigonal
Point group *222*, *mm2*, *mmm*

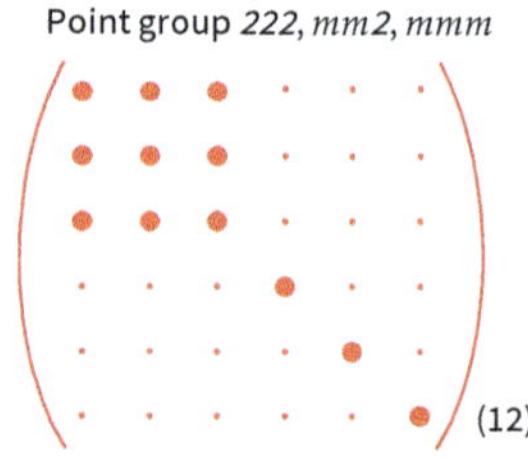

Table 3.2. *Cont.*

Teragonal	
Point group *4*, $\bar{4}$, *4/m*	Point group *4mm*, $\bar{4}2m$, *422*, *4/mmm*
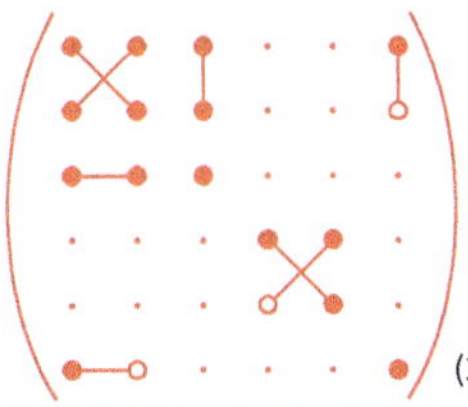 (10)	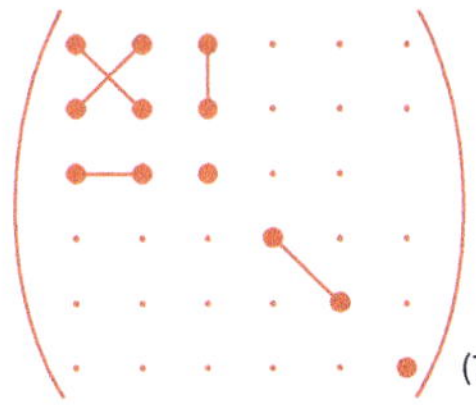 (7)
Rhombohedral	
Point group *3*, $\bar{3}$	Point group *3m*, *32*, $\bar{3}m$
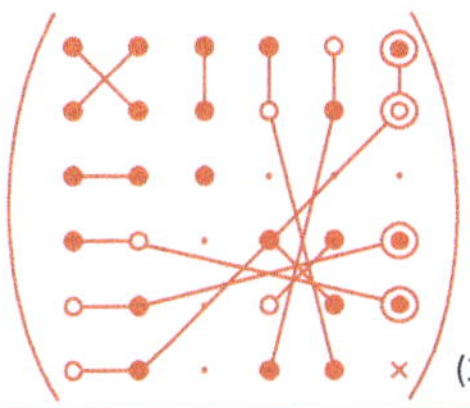 (12)	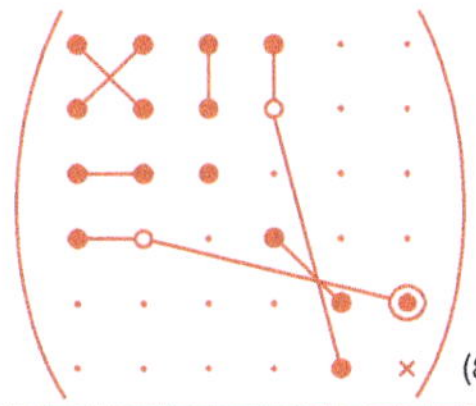 (8)
Hexagonal	
Point group *6*, $\bar{6}$, *6/m*	Point group $\bar{6}m2$, *6mm*, *622*, *6/mmm*
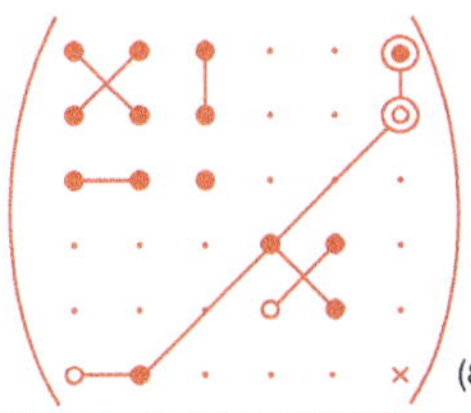 (8)	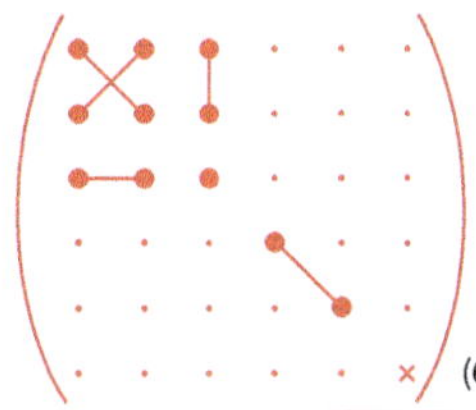 (6)
Cubic	
Point group *23*, *m3*	Point group $\bar{4}3m$, *432*, *m3m*
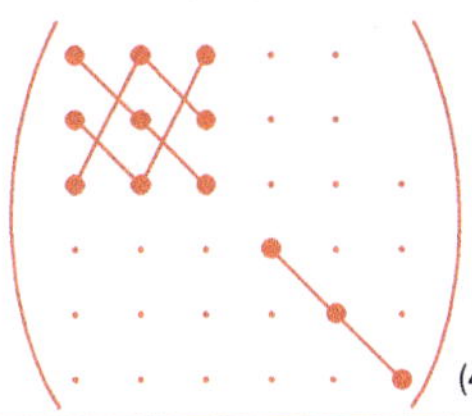 (4)	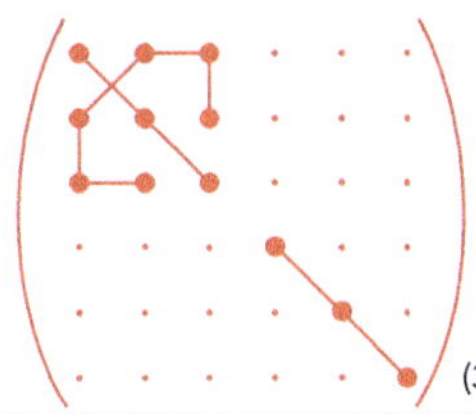 (3)
Isotropic	
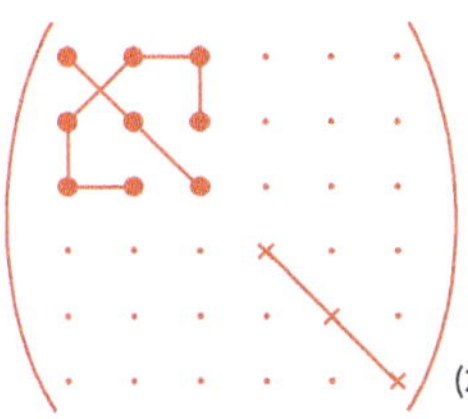 (2)	

Source: [3] ©Uchino, K. *Micromechatronics*, 2nd ed. CRC Press, 2019; p. 52. Reproduced by permission of Taylor & Francis Group.

Example Problem 3.7

Lead magnesium niobate ($Pb(Mg_{1/3}Nb_{2/3})O_3$) exhibits a cubic crystal symmetry (point group *m3m*) at room temperature and thus, does not show piezoelectricity. However, large electrostriction is induced under an applied electric field. The relation between the strain and the electric field is given by:

$$\begin{pmatrix} x_1 \\ x_2 \\ x_3 \\ x_4 \\ x_5 \\ x_6 \end{pmatrix} = \begin{pmatrix} M_{11} & M_{12} & M_{12} & 0 & 0 & 0) \\ M_{12} & M_{11} & M_{12} & 0 & 0 & 0 \\ M_{12} & M_{12} & M_{11} & 0 & 0 & 0 \\ 0 & 0 & 0 & M_{44} & 0 & 0 \\ 0 & 0 & 0 & 0 & M_{44} & 0 \\ 0 & 0 & 0 & 0 & 0 & M_{44} \end{pmatrix} \begin{pmatrix} E_1^2 \\ E_2^2 \\ E_3^2 \\ E_2E_3 \\ E_3E_1 \\ E_1E_2 \end{pmatrix}, \qquad \text{(P3.7.1)}$$

in a matrix representation (refer to Table 3.2, *m3m* symmetry). Calculate the induced strain under an electric field applied along the [111] direction (based on a cubic perovskite coordinate).

Solution

The electric field along the [111] direction, $\boldsymbol{E}_{[111]}$, is represented as ($E_{[111]}/\sqrt{3}$, $E_{[111]}/\sqrt{3}$, $E_{[111]}/\sqrt{3}$). Substituting $E_1 = E_2 = E_3 = E_{[111]}/\sqrt{3}$ into Equation (P3.7.1), we obtain

$$x_1 = x_2 = x_3 = (M_{11} + 2M_{12})\, E_{[111]}{}^2/3 \ (=x_{11} = x_{22} = x_{33}), \qquad \text{(P3.7.2)}$$

$$x_4 = x_5 = x_6 = M_{44}\, E_{[111]}{}^2/3 \ (=2x_{23} = 2x_{31} = 2x_{12}). \qquad \text{(P3.7.3)}$$

Extensional and shear strains occur in all perovskite primary axes. The distortion is illustrated in Figure 3.6b. The strain x induced along an arbitrary direction is given by

$$x = \sum_{i,j} x_{ij} l_i l_j, \qquad \text{(P3.7.4)}$$

where l_i is a *direction cosine* with respect to the i-axis. Therefore, the strain induced along the [111] direction, $x_{[111]//}$, is given by

$$\begin{aligned} x_{[111]//} &= \textstyle\sum_{i,j} x_{ij}\left(1/\sqrt{3}\right)\left(1/\sqrt{3}\right) \\ &= [x_1 + x_2 + x_3 + 2(x_4/2 + x_5/2 + x_6/2)]/3 \qquad \text{(P3.7.5)} \\ &= (M_{11} + 2M_{12} + M_{44})E_{[111]}{}^2/3. \end{aligned}$$

On the other hand, the strain induced perpendicular to the [111] direction, $x_{[111]\perp}$, is calculated in a similar fashion as

$$x_{[111]\perp} = (M_{11} + 2M_{12} - M_{44}/2)E_{[111]}^2/3. \tag{P3.7.6}$$

Figure 3.6b shows the distortion schematically. It is noteworthy that the volumetric strain ($\Delta V/V$) is given by

$$x_{[111]//} + 2x_{[111]\perp} = (M_{11} + 2M_{12})E_{[111]}^2. \tag{P3.7.7}$$

Note that this volumetric strain is the same for ($\Delta V/V$) under an electric field E_1:

$$x_1 + 2x_2 = (M_{11} + 2\,M_{12})E_1^2, \tag{P3.7.8}$$

leading to the following conclusion: volume expansion ($\Delta V/V$) is the same regardless of the applied field direction.

3.5. Alternative Elastic Property Representation

3.5.1. Elastic Compliance and Stiffness

The elastic compliance and stiffness tensors/reduced matrices can be described in general as

$$\begin{pmatrix} x_1 \\ x_2 \\ x_3 \\ x_4 \\ x_5 \\ x_6 \end{pmatrix} = \begin{pmatrix} s_{11} & s_{12} & s_{13} & s_{14} & s_{15} & s_{16} \\ s_{21} & s_{22} & s_{23} & s_{24} & s_{25} & s_{26} \\ s_{31} & s_{32} & s_{33} & s_{34} & s_{35} & s_{36} \\ s_{41} & s_{42} & s_{43} & s_{44} & s_{45} & s_{46} \\ s_{51} & s_{52} & s_{53} & s_{54} & s_{55} & s_{56} \\ s_{61} & s_{62} & s_{63} & s_{64} & s_{65} & s_{66} \end{pmatrix} \begin{pmatrix} X_1 \\ X_2 \\ X_3 \\ X_4 \\ X_5 \\ X_6 \end{pmatrix}, \tag{3.54}$$

$$\begin{pmatrix} X_1 \\ X_2 \\ X_3 \\ X_4 \\ X_5 \\ X_6 \end{pmatrix} = \begin{pmatrix} c_{11} & c_{12} & c_{13} & c_{14} & c_{15} & c_{16} \\ c_{21} & c_{22} & c_{23} & c_{24} & c_{25} & c_{26} \\ c_{31} & c_{32} & c_{33} & c_{34} & c_{35} & c_{36} \\ c_{41} & c_{42} & c_{43} & c_{44} & c_{45} & c_{46} \\ c_{51} & c_{52} & c_{53} & c_{54} & c_{55} & c_{56} \\ c_{61} & c_{62} & c_{63} & c_{64} & c_{65} & c_{66} \end{pmatrix} \begin{pmatrix} x_1 \\ x_2 \\ x_3 \\ x_4 \\ x_5 \\ x_6 \end{pmatrix}. \tag{3.55}$$

The compliance and stiffness are mutually related as inverse matrices:

$$\begin{pmatrix} c_{11} & c_{12} & c_{13} & c_{14} & c_{15} & c_{16} \\ c_{21} & c_{22} & c_{23} & c_{24} & c_{25} & c_{26} \\ c_{31} & c_{32} & c_{33} & c_{34} & c_{35} & c_{36} \\ c_{41} & c_{42} & c_{43} & c_{44} & c_{45} & c_{46} \\ c_{51} & c_{52} & c_{53} & c_{54} & c_{55} & c_{56} \\ c_{61} & c_{62} & c_{63} & c_{64} & c_{65} & c_{66} \end{pmatrix} = \begin{pmatrix} s_{11} & s_{12} & s_{13} & s_{14} & s_{15} & s_{16} \\ s_{21} & s_{22} & s_{23} & s_{24} & s_{25} & s_{26} \\ s_{31} & s_{32} & s_{33} & s_{34} & s_{35} & s_{36} \\ s_{41} & s_{42} & s_{43} & s_{44} & s_{45} & s_{46} \\ s_{51} & s_{52} & s_{53} & s_{54} & s_{55} & s_{56} \\ s_{61} & s_{62} & s_{63} & s_{64} & s_{65} & s_{66} \end{pmatrix}^{-1} . \tag{3.56}$$

Compared with the "electrostrictive coefficient matrix", which is not symmetric, the "elastic constant matrix" is symmetric. Thus, there are 21 independent components in the lowest symmetry crystals among 36 components.

A poled piezoelectric ceramic has a crystallographic (∞mm) symmetry (anisotropic) with the elastic constant matrix (five independent components, s_{11}, s_{33}, s_{12}, s_{13}, s_{44})

$$\begin{pmatrix} s_{11} & s_{12} & s_{13} & 0 & 0 & 0 \\ s_{12} & s_{11} & s_{13} & 0 & 0 & 0 \\ s_{13} & s_{13} & s_{33} & 0 & 0 & 0 \\ 0 & 0 & 0 & s_{44} & 0 & 0 \\ 0 & 0 & 0 & 0 & s_{44} & 0 \\ 0 & 0 & 0 & 0 & 0 & 2(s_{11}-s_{12}) \end{pmatrix} . \tag{3.57}$$

However, merely from the mathematical/analytical simplicity viewpoint, a treatment with "piezoelectrically anisotropic", but "elastically isotropic", assumption is often utilized in piezoelectric transducers. In an isotropic crystal, the elastic compliance matrix is simplified as follows, with only two independent components, s_{11} and s_{12}:

$$\begin{pmatrix} s_{11} & s_{12} & s_{12} & 0 & 0 & 0 \\ s_{12} & s_{11} & s_{12} & 0 & 0 & 0 \\ s_{12} & s_{12} & s_{11} & 0 & 0 & 0 \\ 0 & 0 & 0 & 2(s_{11}-s_{12}) & 0 & 0 \\ 0 & 0 & 0 & 0 & 2(s_{11}-s_{12}) & 0 \\ 0 & 0 & 0 & 0 & 0 & 2(s_{11}-s_{12}) \end{pmatrix} . \tag{3.58}$$

The reason why the shear component s_{66} is given by $2(s_{11}-s_{12})$ can be intuitively explained as follows (refer to Example Problem 3.2): the shear stresses X_{12}, X_{21} are equivalent to X_{11}' (tensile), $-X_{22}'$ (compressive) in a 45° rotated coordinate system. If the material is isotropic, since the 45° rotation will not change the elastic compliance, the strain x_6 should be the same for both stress conditions. We obtain

$$x_6 = x_{12} + x_{21} = s_{1212}(X_{12} + X_{21}) = s_{66}X_6 = x'_{11} + x'_{22} = (s_{1111}X'_{11} - s_{1122}X'_{22}) + (s_{1111}X'_{22} - s_{1122}X'_{11}) = 2(s_{11} - s_{12})X'_{11}.$$

Since $X_6 = X_{11}'$ (magnitude of the shear and longitudinal stresses should be equal for this 45° rotation), we can conclude that $s_{66} = 2(s_{11} - s_{12})$.

On the other hand, the elastic stiffness matrix (c_{11} and c_{12}) is expressed as

$$\begin{pmatrix} c_{11} & c_{12} & c_{12} & 0 & 0 & 0 \\ c_{12} & c_{11} & c_{12} & 0 & 0 & 0 \\ c_{12} & c_{12} & c_{11} & 0 & 0 & 0 \\ 0 & 0 & 0 & \frac{1}{2}(c_{11} - c_{12}) & 0 & 0 \\ 0 & 0 & 0 & 0 & \frac{1}{2}(c_{11} - c_{12}) & 0 \\ 0 & 0 & 0 & 0 & 0 & \frac{1}{2}(c_{11} - c_{12}) \end{pmatrix}. \tag{3.59}$$

From the condition $(s_{ij})\cdot(c_{ij}) = (I)$ (unity matrix), we obtain the following two equations:

$$\begin{cases} s_{11}c_{11} + 2s_{12}c_{12} = 1 \\ s_{12}c_{11} + s_{11}c_{12} + s_{12}c_{12} = 0 \end{cases}.$$

Accordingly, the relations between (s_{ij}) and (c_{ij}) are

$$\begin{cases} c_{11} = \frac{(s_{11}+s_{12})}{(s_{11}-s_{12})(s_{11}+2s_{12})} \\ c_{12} = -\frac{s_{12}}{(s_{11}-s_{12})(s_{11}+2s_{12})} \\ \frac{1}{2}(c_{11} - c_{12}) = \frac{1}{2(s_{11}-s_{12})} \end{cases} \quad \begin{cases} s_{11} = \frac{(c_{11}+c_{12})}{(c_{11}-c_{12})(c_{11}+2c_{12})} \\ s_{12} = -\frac{c_{12}}{(c_{11}-c_{12})(c_{11}+2c_{12})} \\ 2(s_{11} - s_{12}) = \frac{1}{\frac{1}{2}(c_{11}-c_{12})} \end{cases}. \tag{3.60}$$

3.5.2. *Young's Modulus and Poisson's Ratio*

"Young's modulus" (or the Young modulus) E is a mechanical property which measures the stiffness of a solid material. It is defined by the relationship between stress X and strain x in a material in the linear elasticity regime of a uniaxial deformation:

$$X = E\cdot x. \tag{3.61}$$

The reader is more familiar with the Young modulus in mechanical engineering from their high school age, rather than elastic compliance in the physics field. Because Young's modulus is defined by the free condition (no clamping) along the transversal direction, we had better consider that an inverse E corresponds to the elastic compliance (because it is a stress-free, rather than strain-free, condition) in practice. Taking into account the transversal shrinkage via Poisson's ratio

$$\sigma = -s_{12}/s_{11}, \tag{3.62}$$

the elastic compliance matrix is represented by two parameters, E and σ, in an isotropic material as

$$(s_{ij}) = \frac{1}{E}\begin{pmatrix} 1 & -\sigma & -\sigma & 0 & 0 & 0 \\ -\sigma & 1 & -\sigma & 0 & 0 & 0 \\ -\sigma & -\sigma & 1 & 0 & 0 & 0 \\ 0 & 0 & 0 & 2(1+\sigma) & 0 & 0 \\ 0 & 0 & 0 & 0 & 2(1+\sigma) & 0 \\ 0 & 0 & 0 & 0 & 0 & 2(1+\sigma) \end{pmatrix}. \tag{3.63}$$

On the contrary, the elastic stiffness matrix is slightly more complicated than the above, which can be derived from the relation $(s_{ij})\cdot(c_{ij}) = (I)$ (unity matrix):

$$(c_{ij}) = \begin{pmatrix} c_{11} & c_{12} & c_{12} & 0 & 0 & 0 \\ c_{12} & c_{11} & c_{12} & 0 & 0 & 0 \\ c_{12} & c_{12} & c_{11} & 0 & 0 & 0 \\ 0 & 0 & 0 & c_{44} & 0 & 0 \\ 0 & 0 & 0 & 0 & c_{44} & 0 \\ 0 & 0 & 0 & 0 & 0 & c_{44} \end{pmatrix}, \tag{3.64a}$$

where the matrix components are represented by Poisson's ratio with Young's moduli as

$$\begin{cases} c_{11} = \frac{1-\sigma}{(1+\sigma)(1-2\sigma)}E \\ c_{12} = \frac{\sigma}{(1+\sigma)(1-2\sigma)}E \\ c_{44} = \frac{1}{2(1+\sigma)}E \end{cases}. \tag{3.64b}$$

For the reader's reference, the following equations provide another important idea on c_{ij} and s_{ij}:

$$\begin{cases} c_{11} = \frac{1-\sigma}{(1+\sigma)(1-2\sigma)}\frac{1}{s_{11}} \\ c_{12} = \frac{\sigma^2}{(1+\sigma)(1-2\sigma)}\frac{1}{s_{12}} \end{cases}. \tag{3.65}$$

When we adopt $\sigma = 1/4 - 1/3$ (typical values for PZT's), $\frac{1-\sigma}{(1+\sigma)(1-2\sigma)} = 1.2 - 1.5$ and $\frac{\sigma^2}{(1+\sigma)(1-2\sigma)} = 0.1 - 0.25$. c_{11} is slightly larger than the inverse of s_{11}, while c_{12} may be neglected depending on Poisson's ratio σ.

3.5.3. *Lamé Parameters*

Another alternative representation often used is "Lamé parameters" (after Gabriel Lamé, a French mathematician) in an isotropic elastic material, which is analogous to the elastic stiffness from the viewpoint of the mechanical clamping (strain-free) condition [2]. The "first and second Lamé parameters", λ and μ, are defined by both shear parameters as

$$\lambda = c_{12}, \text{ and } \mu = c_{66} = \frac{1}{2}(c_{11} - c_{12}). \tag{3.66}$$

Though the physical meaning of μ is clear as the "shear modulus", $\lambda = c_{12}$ may not have a clear image. The elastic stiffness matrix is represented using the first and second Lamé parameters as follows in an isotropic symmetry:

$$(c_{ij}) = \begin{pmatrix} (\lambda+2\mu) & \lambda & \lambda & 0 & 0 & 0 \\ \lambda & (\lambda+2\mu) & \lambda & 0 & 0 & 0 \\ \lambda & \lambda & (\lambda+2\mu) & 0 & 0 & 0 \\ 0 & 0 & 0 & \mu & 0 & 0 \\ 0 & 0 & 0 & 0 & \mu & 0 \\ 0 & 0 & 0 & 0 & 0 & \mu \end{pmatrix}. \tag{3.67}$$

The diagonal c_{11} can be obtained from Equation (3.66) as

$$c_{11} = \lambda + 2\mu \tag{3.68}$$

The transformation relations between (E, σ) and (λ, μ) are summarized as:

$$\begin{cases} E = \frac{1}{s_{11}} = \frac{(c_{11}+c_{12})}{(c_{11}-c_{12})(c_{11}+2c_{12})} = \frac{\lambda+\mu}{\mu(\lambda+4\mu)} \\ \sigma = -\frac{s_{12}}{s_{11}} = \frac{c_{12}}{c_{11}+c_{12}} = \frac{\lambda}{2(\lambda+\mu)} \end{cases}. \tag{3.69}$$

Lamé parameters are preferably used in sound propagation in a material. Taking the material's mass density ρ, the sound velocity for the longitudinal and transverse waves is given by $c_l^2 = (\lambda + 2\mu)/\rho$ and $c_t^2 = \mu/\rho$.

3.6. The Magnitude Ellipsoid

We derived the permittivity tensor form for a crystal with a 4-fold symmetry with only two independent components in Subsection Four-Fold Axisymmetry (page 71):

$$\begin{pmatrix} D_1 \\ D_2 \\ D_3 \end{pmatrix} = \varepsilon_0 \begin{pmatrix} \varepsilon_{11} & 0 & 0 \\ 0 & \varepsilon_{11} & 0 \\ 0 & 0 & \varepsilon_{33} \end{pmatrix} \begin{pmatrix} E_1 \\ E_2 \\ E_3 \end{pmatrix}. \tag{3.70}$$

We know the principal permittivity along x-, y-, or z-axis from this representation. However, how can we obtain the permittivity along an arbitrary direction? The solution can be found by the elliptical surface, whose equation, when referring to the principal axes of $[\varepsilon_{ij}]$, is

$$\frac{x^2}{{\varepsilon_x}^2} + \frac{y^2}{{\varepsilon_y}^2} + \frac{z^2}{{\varepsilon_z}^2} = {\varepsilon_0}^2. \tag{3.71}$$

This is called the "magnitude ellipsoid", whose semi-axes are ε_x, ε_y, and ε_z, as illustrated in Figure 3.7.

The verification of this ellipsoid solution is conducted as follows. Let $\boldsymbol{E} = (E_x, E_y, E_z)$, and since a constant (unit) electric field is applied on this crystal in an arbitrary direction, ${E_x}^2 + {E_y}^2 + {E_z}^2 = 1$. From the relation $\boldsymbol{D} = (D_x, D_y, D_z) = (\varepsilon_0\varepsilon_{11}E_x, \varepsilon_0\varepsilon_{11}E_y, \varepsilon_0\varepsilon_{33}E_z)$, we obtain

$$\frac{{D_x}^2}{{\varepsilon_0}^2{\varepsilon_x}^2} + \frac{{D_y}^2}{{\varepsilon_0}^2{\varepsilon_y}^2} + \frac{{D_z}^2}{{\varepsilon_0}^2{\varepsilon_z}^2} = 1. \tag{3.72}$$

Hence, the extremity of the vector $\boldsymbol{D}$ lies on the ellipsoid of Equation (3.71) (see the details in Chapter 13).

In 4-fold tetragonal symmetry (4, $\bar{4}$, $4/m$, 422, $4mm$, $\bar{4}2m$, $4/mmm$), $\varepsilon_x = \varepsilon_y$, hence the permittivity ellipsoid is donut-shape (when $\varepsilon_x > \varepsilon_z$). On the contrary, in orthogonal symmetry (222, *mm2*, and *mmm*), all principal ε_x, ε_y, and ε_z are different. Thus, the three ellipsoid axes are all different.

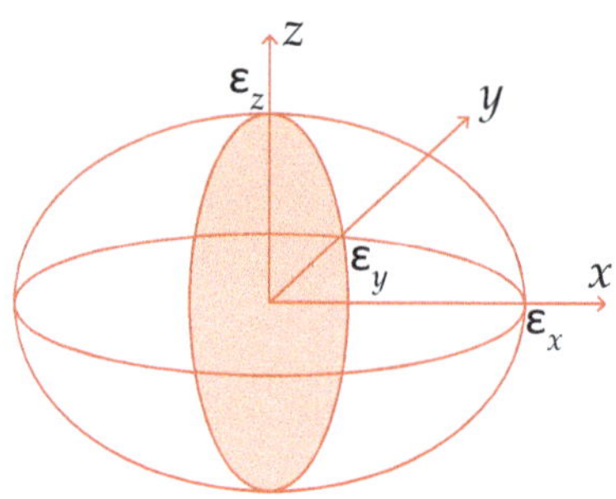

Figure 3.7. Permittivity ellipsoid for a crystal with a tetragonal 4-fold symmetry. Source: Figure by author.

Chapter Essentials

1. When we correlate one input physical parameter X with an output parameter Y, we introduce a proportional parameter A in a linear relation approximation:

   $Y = AX$.

   When X is a p-rank tensor, and Y is a q-rank tensor, A is supposed to be expressed by using a $(p + q)$-rank tensor:

   $Y_{ij...q} = \sum_{lm...p} A_{ij...qlm...p}\, X_{lm...p}$.

2. Transformation matrix: unitary

$$\begin{pmatrix} a_{11} & a_{12} & a_{13} \\ a_{21} & a_{22} & a_{23} \\ a_{31} & a_{32} & a_{33} \end{pmatrix}^{-1} = \begin{pmatrix} a_{11} & a_{12} & a_{13} \\ a_{21} & a_{22} & a_{23} \\ a_{31} & a_{32} & a_{33} \end{pmatrix}^{t},$$

centro-symmetry $\begin{pmatrix} -1 & 0 & 0 \\ 0 & -1 & 0 \\ 0 & 0 & -1 \end{pmatrix}$; mirror symmetry $\begin{pmatrix} -1 & 0 & 0 \\ 0 & 1 & 0 \\ 0 & 0 & 1 \end{pmatrix}$; rotation matrix $\begin{pmatrix} \cos\theta & \sin\theta & 0 \\ -\sin\theta & \cos\theta & 0 \\ 0 & 0 & 1 \end{pmatrix}$.

3. The shear stresses X_{12}, X_{21} are equivalent to X_{11}' (tensile), $-X_{22}'$ (compressive) in a 45° rotated coordinate system.
4. Reduction in the Tensor (Matrix Notation):

Tensor Notation	11	22	33	23, 32	31, 13	12, 21
Matrix Notation	1	2	3	4	5	6

Stress/strain, stress/strain reduced notation:

$$\begin{pmatrix} X_{11} & X_{12} & X_{31} \\ X_{12} & X_{22} & X_{23} \\ X_{31} & X_{23} & X_{33} \end{pmatrix} = \begin{pmatrix} X_1 & X_6 & X_5 \\ X_6 & X_2 & X_4 \\ X_5 & X_4 & X_3 \end{pmatrix},$$

$$\begin{pmatrix} x_{11} & x_{12} & x_{31} \\ x_{12} & x_{22} & x_{23} \\ x_{31} & x_{23} & x_{33} \end{pmatrix} = \begin{pmatrix} x_1 & \left(\frac{1}{2}\right)x_6 & \left(\frac{1}{2}\right)x_5 \\ \left(\frac{1}{2}\right)x_6 & x_2 & \left(\frac{1}{2}\right)x_4 \\ \left(\frac{1}{2}\right)x_5 & \left(\frac{1}{2}\right)x_4 & x_3 \end{pmatrix}$$

$(X_1, X_2, X_3, X_4, X_5, X_6)$, and $(x_1, x_2, x_3, x_4, x_5, x_6)$.

5. Tensor Description of Piezoelectric Constitutive Equations (*4mm* Symmetry Case)

$$\begin{pmatrix} x_1 \\ x_2 \\ x_3 \\ x_4 \\ x_5 \\ x_6 \end{pmatrix} = \begin{pmatrix} s_{11} & s_{12} & s_{13} & 0 & 0 & 0 \\ s_{12} & s_{11} & s_{13} & 0 & 0 & 0 \\ s_{13} & s_{13} & s_{33} & 0 & 0 & 0 \\ 0 & 0 & 0 & s_{44} & 0 & 0 \\ 0 & 0 & 0 & 0 & s_{44} & 0 \\ 0 & 0 & 0 & 0 & 0 & s_{66} \end{pmatrix} \begin{pmatrix} X_1 \\ X_2 \\ X_3 \\ X_4 \\ X_5 \\ X_6 \end{pmatrix} + \begin{pmatrix} 0 & 0 & d_{31} \\ 0 & 0 & d_{31} \\ 0 & 0 & d_{33} \\ 0 & d_{15} & 0 \\ d_{15} & 0 & 0 \\ 0 & 0 & 0 \end{pmatrix} \begin{pmatrix} E_1 \\ E_2 \\ E_3 \end{pmatrix},$$

$$\begin{pmatrix} D_1 \\ D_2 \\ D_3 \end{pmatrix} = \begin{pmatrix} 0 & 0 & 0 & 0 & d_{15} & 0 \\ 0 & 0 & 0 & d_{15} & 0 & 0 \\ d_{31} & d_{31} & d_{33} & 0 & 0 & 0 \end{pmatrix} \begin{pmatrix} X_1 \\ X_2 \\ X_3 \\ X_4 \\ X_5 \\ X_6 \end{pmatrix} + \varepsilon_0 \begin{pmatrix} \varepsilon_{11} & 0 & 0 \\ 0 & \varepsilon_{11} & 0 \\ 0 & 0 & \varepsilon_{33} \end{pmatrix} \begin{pmatrix} E_1 \\ E_2 \\ E_3 \end{pmatrix}.$$

6. Permittivity Ellipsoid:

$$\frac{x^2}{{\varepsilon_x}^2} + \frac{y^2}{{\varepsilon_y}^2} + \frac{z^2}{{\varepsilon_z}^2} = {\varepsilon_0}^2.$$

7. Alternative Elastic Property Representation in Isotropic Materials
   - Young's modulus and Poisson's ratio

$$(s_{ij}) = \frac{1}{E} \begin{pmatrix} 1 & -\sigma & -\sigma & 0 & 0 & 0 \\ -\sigma & 1 & -\sigma & 0 & 0 & 0 \\ -\sigma & -\sigma & 1 & 0 & 0 & 0 \\ 0 & 0 & 0 & 2(1+\sigma) & 0 & 0 \\ 0 & 0 & 0 & 0 & 2(1+\sigma) & 0 \\ 0 & 0 & 0 & 0 & 0 & 2(1+\sigma) \end{pmatrix} \left(E = \frac{1}{s_{11}},\ \sigma = -s_{12}/s_{11} \right)$$

   - Lamé Parameters

$$(c_{ij}) = \begin{pmatrix} (\lambda+2\mu) & \lambda & \lambda & 0 & 0 & 0 \\ \lambda & (\lambda+2\mu) & \lambda & 0 & 0 & 0 \\ \lambda & \lambda & (\lambda+2\mu) & 0 & 0 & 0 \\ 0 & 0 & 0 & \mu & 0 & 0 \\ 0 & 0 & 0 & 0 & \mu & 0 \\ 0 & 0 & 0 & 0 & 0 & \mu \end{pmatrix} \quad \left[\lambda = c_{12},\ \mu = c_{66} = \frac{1}{2}(c_{11} - c_{12})\right]$$

Check Point

1. (T/F) The following two force configurations are equivalent mathematically (Figure 3.8). True or false?

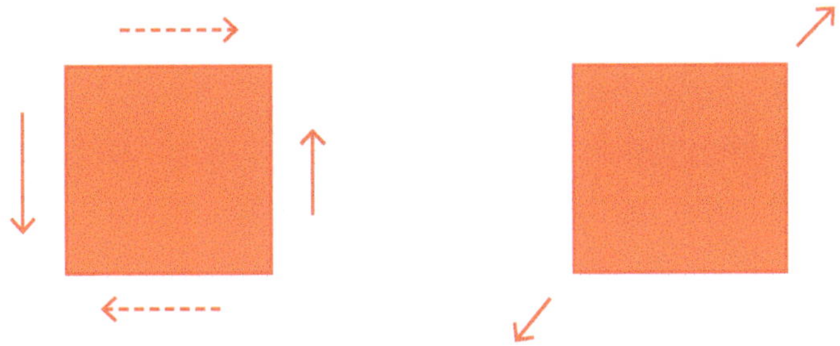

Figure 3.8. Shear stress (**left**) and uniaxial stress (**right**). Source: Figure by author.

2. The permittivity ε_{ij} tensor is a second-rank tensor. How many independent components are there in general (in the lowest symmetry)?
3. The piezoelectric d_{ijk} tensor is a third-rank tensor. How many independent components are there in general (in the lowest symmetry)?
4. The elastic compliance s_{ijkl} tensor is a fourth-rank tensor. How many independent components are there in general (in the lowest symmetry)?
5. Provide two independent permittivity tensor components for a *4mm* crystal symmetry using a tensor notation ε_{ij}.
6. Provide three independent piezoelectric tensor components for a *4mm* crystal symmetry using a reduced notation d_{ij}.
7. Provide two independent elastic compliance tensor components for an isotropic crystal symmetry using a reduced notation s_{ij}.
8. In an isotropic crystal symmetry, provide the Young modulus E and Poisson ratio in terms of the elastic compliance reduced notation s_{ij}.
9. In an isotropic crystal symmetry, provide the first and second Lamé parameters in terms of the elastic stiffness reduced notation c_{ij}.
10. (T/F) The rotation matrix (θ) around the x-axis is given by $\begin{pmatrix} \cos\theta & \sin\theta & 0 \\ -\sin\theta & \cos\theta & 0 \\ 0 & 0 & 1 \end{pmatrix}$.

    True or false?
11. Choose the correct answer. The transformation matrix $\begin{pmatrix} -1 & 0 & 0 \\ 0 & 1 & 0 \\ 0 & 0 & 1 \end{pmatrix}$ means:

    (a) centro symmetry with respect to the origin (0,0,0); (b) 180° rotation with respect to the x-axis; (c) mirror symmetry with respect to the y-z plane; (d) none of the above.

Chapter Problems

3.1 Derive the relations between the compliances and the stiffnesses for a cubic *m3m* symmetry.

Hint

The solution should be:

$$\begin{cases} c_{11} = \frac{(s_{11}+s_{12})}{(s_{11}-s_{12})(s_{11}+2s_{12})} \\ c_{12} = -\frac{s_{12}}{(s_{11}-s_{12})(s_{11}+2s_{12})} \\ c_{44} = \frac{1}{s_{44}} \end{cases}.$$

3.2 Knowing the permittivity tensor/matrix of a tetragonal (4-fold) symmetry:

$$\begin{pmatrix} \varepsilon_{11} & 0 & 0 \\ 0 & \varepsilon_{11} & 0 \\ 0 & 0 & \varepsilon_{33} \end{pmatrix},$$

calculate the permittivity of a crystal slab with the normal direction θ from the z-axis.

Hint

The permittivity ellipsoid for a tetragonal crystal is given by

$\frac{x^2}{\varepsilon_{11}{}^2} + \frac{y^2}{\varepsilon_{11}{}^2} + \frac{z^2}{\varepsilon_{33}{}^2} = \varepsilon_0{}^2.$

Since the direction θ condition is given by

$z^2 = (x^2 + y^2 + z^2)\cos^2\theta, (x^2 + y^2) = (x^2 + y^2 + z^2)\sin^2\theta,$

$(x^2 + y^2 + z^2)\left(\frac{\sin^2\theta}{\varepsilon_{11}{}^2} + \frac{\cos^2\theta}{\varepsilon_{33}{}^2}\right) = \varepsilon_0{}^2,$

$\varepsilon_{eff}{}^2 = 1/\left(\frac{\sin^2\theta}{\varepsilon_{11}{}^2} + \frac{\cos^2\theta}{\varepsilon_{33}{}^2}\right).$

3.3 Prove that the volume change of a cubic crystal under uniaxial tension X is independent of the direction of the tension and is given by $(s_{11} + 2s_{12})X$.

References

1. Nye, J. F. *Physical Properties of Crystals*; Oxford University Press: London, UK, 1972; pp. 123–140.
2. Jumonji, H.; Tomikawa, Y.; Mochizuki, Y. *Fundamentals of Solid Vibrations*; Morio, M., Ed.; Ohm Pub. Company: Tokyo, Japan, 1982.
3. Uchino, K. *Micromechatronics*, 2nd ed.; CRC Press: Boca Raton FL, USA, 2019.

4. Nonlinear Phenomenology—Taylor Expansion II

4.1. Fundamentals in Phenomenology

4.1.1. Introduction to Nonlinear Phenomenology

A thermodynamic phenomenological theory is discussed based on the free energy expressed in the form of an expansion series in terms of the intensive and extensive physical properties: one with electric field E (intensive) and polarization P (extensive), one with temperature T (intensive) and entropy S (extensive), one with stress X (intensive) and strain x (extensive), and, if applicable, one with magnetic field H (intensive) and magnetization M (extensive). In our ferroelectric discussion, the last parameters will be neglected.

In Chapter 2, we considered a practical formula of the Gibbs free energy $G(T, X, E)$ for the case of a small change in temperature $\theta = T - T_R$ (room temperature), external X, and E (1D case). If the change in parameters is small, we may adopt the three-parameter Taylor expansion approximation up to second derivatives in order to discuss just the linear relationships:

$$\begin{aligned} G(T,X,E) = G_0 &+ \left(\tfrac{\partial G}{\partial T}\right)\theta + \left(\tfrac{\partial G}{\partial X}\right)X + \left(\tfrac{\partial G}{\partial E}\right)E + \tfrac{1}{2}\left(\tfrac{\partial^2 G}{\partial T^2}\right)\theta^2 + \tfrac{1}{2}\left(\tfrac{\partial^2 G}{\partial X^2}\right)X^2 \\ &+ \tfrac{1}{2}\left(\tfrac{\partial^2 G}{\partial E^2}\right)E^2 + \left(\tfrac{\partial^2 G}{\partial T \partial X}\right)\theta X + \left(\tfrac{\partial^2 G}{\partial T \partial E}\right)\theta E + \left(\tfrac{\partial^2 G}{\partial X \partial E}\right)XE. \end{aligned} \tag{4.1}$$

Taking into account $dG = -SdT - xdX - DdE$, we first obtain the relations, $\left(\frac{\partial G}{\partial T}\right)_{\theta,X,E=0} = -S_0$, $\left(\frac{\partial G}{\partial X}\right)_{\theta,X,E=0} = -x_0$ and $\left(\frac{\partial G}{\partial E}\right)_{\theta,X,E=0} = -D_0$. Take these constants as the new "origins", and set them to "zero". Then, Equation (4.1) can be transformed as:

$$S = -\left(\frac{\partial G}{\partial T}\right) = -\left(\frac{\partial^2 G}{\partial T^2}\right)\theta - \left(\frac{\partial^2 G}{\partial T \partial X}\right)X - \left(\frac{\partial^2 G}{\partial T \partial E}\right)E, \tag{4.2a}$$

$$x = -\left(\frac{\partial G}{\partial X}\right) = -\left(\frac{\partial^2 G}{\partial T \partial X}\right)\theta - \left(\frac{\partial^2 G}{\partial X^2}\right)X - \left(\frac{\partial^2 G}{\partial X \partial E}\right)E, \tag{4.2b}$$

$$D = -\left(\frac{\partial G}{\partial E}\right) = -\left(\frac{\partial^2 G}{\partial T \partial E}\right)\theta - \left(\frac{\partial^2 G}{\partial X \partial E}\right)X - \left(\frac{\partial^2 G}{\partial E^2}\right)E. \tag{4.2c}$$

Based on the above linear relationships, we derived several types of "constitutive linear equations".

However, as the reader is familiar with so-called "hysteresis" in the polarization–electric-field and strain–electric-field relations, one of the characteristics in ferroelectrics is the nonlinear performances. For this purpose, we will take higher-order Taylor expansion terms in this chapter. Small hysteresis observed in small parameter modulation of the electric field or stress can be treated as the phase delay (e.g., viscoelastic damping) in the linear relationship in Equation (4.2) primarily by integrating complex parameters into the physical coefficients. This situation is discussed in Chapter 6 Loss in Piezoelectrics.

Let us start the fundamentals of Taylor expansion terms by taking Helmholtz free energy, $A = U - TS$ or $dA = -SdT + Xdx + EdD$ in derivative expression, which is useful for discussing the internal energy of material under an isothermal condition. Taylor expansion approximation up to higher-order terms is described as follows:

$$\begin{aligned} A(T,x,P) &= G_0 + \left(\tfrac{\partial A}{\partial T}\right)\theta + \left(\tfrac{\partial A}{\partial x}\right)x + \left(\tfrac{\partial A}{\partial P}\right)P + \tfrac{1}{2}\left(\tfrac{\partial^2 A}{\partial T^2}\right)\theta^2 \\ &+\tfrac{1}{2}\left(\tfrac{\partial^2 A}{\partial x^2}\right)x^2 + \tfrac{1}{2}\left(\tfrac{\partial^2 A}{\partial P^2}\right)P^2 + \left(\tfrac{\partial^2 A}{\partial T\partial x}\right)\theta x + \left(\tfrac{\partial^2 A}{\partial T\partial P}\right)\theta P + \left(\tfrac{\partial^2 A}{\partial x\partial P}\right)xP \\ &+\tfrac{1}{3!}\left(\tfrac{\partial^3 A}{\partial T^3}\right)\theta^3 + \tfrac{1}{3!}\left(\tfrac{\partial^3 A}{\partial x^3}\right)x^3 + \tfrac{1}{3!}\left(\tfrac{\partial^3 A}{\partial P^3}\right)P^3 + \tfrac{1}{2}\left(\tfrac{\partial^3 A}{\partial T^2\partial x}\right)\theta^2 x + \tfrac{1}{2}\left(\tfrac{\partial^3 A}{\partial T\partial x^2}\right)\theta x^2 \\ &+\tfrac{1}{2}\left(\tfrac{\partial^3 A}{\partial T^2\partial P}\right)\theta^2 P + \tfrac{1}{2}\left(\tfrac{\partial^3 A}{\partial T\partial P^2}\right)\theta P^2 + \tfrac{1}{2}\left(\tfrac{\partial^3 A}{\partial x^2\partial P}\right)x^2 P + \tfrac{1}{2}\left(\tfrac{\partial^3 A}{\partial x\partial P^2}\right)xP^2 + \cdots \end{aligned} \tag{4.2}$$

As you have learned, temperature is a scalar quantity (0th-rank tensor), polarization is a vector (1st-rank tensor), and strain is a tensor (2nd-rank tensor), and their product should have characteristics of a $(p+q)$-rank tensor. For example, when we take the transformation matrix on $P_iP_jP_k$ (equivalent to P^3 in 1D expression), we need to take the treatment similar to the 3rd-rank tensor, and the Taylor expansion coefficient $\left(\frac{\partial^3 A}{\partial P_i \partial P_j \partial P_k}\right)$ should be represented by three suffices as α_{ijk}, which are handled as the 3rd-rank tensor. When we discuss the crystal symmetry, the description of α_{ijk} on a new coordinate is expressed by the transformation matrix (a_{ij}) as $\alpha'_{ijk} = \sum\limits_{lmn} a_{il}a_{jm}a_{kn}\alpha_{lmn}$. As another example, when we take $x_iP_jP_k$ (i = 1, 2, $\cdots$, 6) or $x_{lm}P_jP_k$ (l,m = 1, 2, 3), the Taylor expansion coefficient $\left(\frac{\partial^3 A}{\partial x_i \partial P_j \partial P_k}\right)$ (or $\left(\frac{\partial^3 A}{\partial x_{lm} \partial P_j \partial P_k}\right)$) should be represented by four suffices as α_{lmjk}, which are handled as the 4th-rank tensor. When we discuss the crystal symmetry, the description of α_{lmjk} on a new coordinate system is expressed by the transformation matrix (a_{ij}) as $\alpha'_{lmjk} = \sum\limits_{opqr} a_{lo}a_{mp}a_{jq}a_{kr}\alpha_{opqr}$. In this sense, we categorize the higher-rank tensor terms under an isothermal condition ($\theta = 0$) as:

- $P_iP_jP_k$ (3); $x_iP_jP_k$ (4); $x_ix_jP_k$ (5); $x_ix_jx_k$ (6)
- $P_iP_jP_kP_l$ (4); $x_iP_jP_kP_l$ (5); $x_ix_jP_kP_l$ (6); $x_ix_jx_kP_l$ (7); $x_ix_jx_kx_l$ (8)
- $P_iP_jP_kP_lP_m$ (5); $x_iP_jP_kP_lP_m$ (6); $x_ix_jP_kP_lP_m$ (7); $\cdots$
- $P_iP_jP_kP_lP_mP_n$ (6); $x_iP_jP_kP_lP_mP_n$ (7); $x_ix_jP_kP_lP_mP_n$ (8); $\cdots$

4.1.2. Elimination Theorem of Taylor Expansion Terms

Theorem 1. *When the crystal possesses a "centrosymmetry", the odd power of the expansion tensor coefficient $\alpha_{ij\cdots l}$ becomes "zero".*

This theorem can be verified as follows: note the transformation matrix for centrosymmetry $\begin{pmatrix} -1 & 0 & 0 \\ 0 & -1 & 0 \\ 0 & 0 & -1 \end{pmatrix}$. As $\alpha'_{ij\cdots l} = \sum\limits_{lm\cdots p} a_{il}a_{jm}\cdots a_{lp}\alpha_{lm\cdots p}$, and $(ij\cdots l) \equiv$

$(lm \cdots p)$, the multiplication of $a_{il}a_{jm} \cdots a_{lp} = -1$ for the odd number of a_{il}'s. From $\alpha_{lm \cdots p} = -\alpha_{lm \cdots p}$, we can conclude that $\alpha_{lm \cdots p} = 0$. Another explanation is that the centrosymmetry transformation changes the polarization $\boldsymbol{P}$ polarity, that is, $P_iP_jP_k \rightarrow -P_iP_jP_k$. In order to keep the Helmholtz energy constant, we should eliminate the odd power of the polarization terms. Needless to say, the odd power of the strain terms remains, because x_i itself is the even-rank tensor.

4.1.3. Polarization Expansion Series

Let us start from the simplest model with only polarization as an "order parameter" in order to discuss the para- to ferroelectric phase transition. The order parameter is created and determined by the cooperation of microscopic quantities and yet governs the behavior of the whole system. Using the Taylor expansion series of the free energy in terms of the polarization P (a simple 1D model is initially adopted):

$$F(P) = F(0) + a_1P + a_2P^2 + a_3P^3 + a_4P^4 + a_5P^5 + a_6P^6 + \ldots \quad (4.3)$$

Theorem 2. *When we discuss the phase transition, we assume that energy description is common through the paraelectric and ferroelectric phases and that the reduction of the Taylor expansion terms follows the highest symmetry paraelectric phase. When the paraelectric phase is "centrosymmetric", the odd power of the expansion tensor coefficient $\alpha_{ij \ldots l}$ becomes "zero".*

We assume that the free energy of the crystal should not change with polarization reversal ($P \rightarrow -P$), because the charge or permittivity in the capacitance should not be changed according to the capacitor orientation/upside down. This is the key in practical electronic equipment. From the condition $F(\boldsymbol{P}) = F(-\boldsymbol{P})$, the expansion series should not contain the odd power of terms of P, only even powers of P:

$$F(P) = a_2P^2 + a_4P^4 + a_6P^6 + \ldots \quad (4.4)$$

4.1.4. Temperature Expansion Series

Next, we take into account the expansion series in terms of P and temperature θ ($\theta = T - T_0$):

$$F(P,\theta) = a_2P^2 + a_4P^4 + a_6P^6 + \ldots + b_1\theta + b_2\theta^2 + \ldots + c_1\theta P^2 + \ldots$$

From $S = -\left(\frac{\partial F}{\partial T}\right) = -b_1$, we set $b_1 = 0$, because a constant entropy is meaningless. The term $b_2\theta^2$ is a higher-order term of temperature to be neglected. Thus, we adopt only $c_1\theta P^2$. Note that a possible term θP is omitted from the reason $F(\boldsymbol{P}) = F(-\boldsymbol{P})$ again (as long as the higher temperature phase possesses centrosymmetry, such as a cubic perovskite). It is important to understand that the product θP^2 of the two parameters (P^2 and θ) explain the "coupling effect"; that is, T change causes P change to keep the same free energy (this effect is called the "pyroelectric" effect), or E application causes T change (this is called the "electrocaloric" effect). For simplicity's sake, we introduce a new notation α by combining a_2P^2 and $c_1\theta P^2$:

$$(1/2)\alpha P^2 = a_2P^2 + c_1TP^2 = (1/2)\left(\frac{T - T_0}{\varepsilon_0 C}\right)P^2.$$

The α is the only parameter with a temperature dependence. We also introduce the following notations:

$$(1/4)\beta P^4, (1/6)\gamma P^6.$$

4.1.5. Stress Expansion Series

Now, we construct the elastic Gibbs free energy form by adding the stress expansion series:

$$G_1(P,T,X) = (1/2)\alpha(T)P^2 + (1/4)\beta P^4 + (1/6)\gamma P^6 + \ldots + d_1 X + d_2 X^2 + \ldots + e_1 P^2 X + \ldots$$
$$[\alpha(T) = (T - T_0)/\varepsilon_0 C].$$

From $x = -(\frac{\partial F}{\partial X}) = -d_1$, and given that the constant strain is meaningless, we set $d_1 = 0$ (strain origin). P^2X is the fundamental electromechanical coupling (i.e., "electrostrictive coupling"), which explains the polarization generation under stress, or strain generation under an electric field. This argument is also valid when spontaneous polarization exists in the ferroelectric phase, in addition to the case that induced polarization exists in the paraelectric phase. Needless to say, it is not valid in quartz, which does not have the centrosymmetric paraelectric phase in the high temperature range (quartz is not even a ferroelectric). Quartz includes the PX coupling term in its discussion (i.e., the odd power of P can exist). Introducing new notations $d_2 = -(1/2)s$ (elastic compliance) and $e_1 = -Q$ (electrostrictive coefficient), we finally obtain popular "elastic Gibbs energy" G_1:

$$G_1(P,X,T) = (1/2)\alpha(T)P^2 + (1/4)\beta P^4 + (1/6)\gamma P^6 - (1/2)sX^2 - QP^2X \quad [\alpha(T) = (T - T_0)/\varepsilon_0 C]. \tag{4.5}$$

4.2. Landau Theory of the Phase Transition

We assume that the Landau free energy F in 1D is represented in terms of polarization P (excluding stress terms initially) as:

$$F(P,T) = (1/2)\alpha P^2 + (1/4)\beta P^4 + (1/6)\gamma P^6 \ [\alpha(T) = (T - T_0)/\varepsilon_0 C]. \tag{4.6}$$

The coefficients α, β, γ depend, in general, on the temperature; however, as discussed in the previous section, only α is assumed to be temperature dependent (linearly) in the following calculation. The phenomenological formulation should be applied for the whole temperature range over which the material is in the paraelectric and ferroelectric states (this is the fundamental assumption).

As the spontaneous polarization should be zero in the paraelectric state, the free energy should be zero in the paraelectric phase at any temperatures above its Curie temperature (or the phase transition temperature). To stabilize the ferroelectric state, the free energy for a certain polarization P should be lower than "zero". Otherwise, the paraelectric state should be realized without making the phase transition. Thus, at least, the coefficient α of the P^2 term must be negative for the polarized state to be stable, while in the paraelectric state, it must be positive, passing through zero at some temperature T_0 ("Curie–Weiss temperature"). In order to satisfy this argument, we introduce a linear relation in terms of temperature:

$$\alpha = (T - T_0)/\varepsilon_0 C, \tag{4.7}$$

where C is taken as a positive constant called the "Curie–Weiss constant" and T_0 is equal to or lower than the actual transition temperature T_C ("Curie temperature"). The temperature dependence of α is related on a microscopic level to the temperature dependence of the ionic polarizability coupled with thermal expansion and other effects of anharmonic lattice interactions. Refer to the discussion in Chapter 11 later.

The equilibrium polarization in an electric field E should satisfy the condition:

$$(\partial F/\partial P) = E = \alpha P + \beta P^3 + \gamma P^5. \tag{4.8}$$

With no electric field applied, Equation (4.8) provides two cases:

$$P(\alpha + \beta P^2 + \gamma P^4) = 0. \tag{4.9}$$

(i) $P = 0 \rightarrow$ This trivial solution corresponds to a paraelectric state.
(ii) $\alpha + \beta P^2 + \gamma P^4 = 0 \rightarrow$ This finite polarization solution corresponds to a ferroelectric state.

4.2.1. Second-Order Phase Transition (In the Case of $\beta > 0$)

When β is positive, γ is often neglected because nothing special is added by this term. There are not many material examples which show this "second-order" transition; however, triglycine sulphate (TGS) is an example of a ferroelectric exhibiting the second-order phase transition. We will discuss this in detail because this description provides intuitive ideas on the phase transition owing to its mathematical simplicity.

The second-order transition is based on the Landau expression:

$$F(P, T) = (1/2)\alpha P^2 + (1/4)\beta P^4 \quad [\alpha(T) = (T - T_0)/\varepsilon_0 C]. \tag{4.10}$$

Electric field is obtained by the first derivative of F in terms of P:

$$(\partial F/\partial P) = E = \alpha P + \beta P^3. \tag{4.11}$$

Taking another derivative of E with respect to P, inverse permittivity is obtained:

$$\frac{1}{\varepsilon_0 \varepsilon} = \frac{1}{\left(\frac{\partial P}{\partial E}\right)} = \left(\frac{\partial E}{\partial P}\right) = \alpha + 3\beta P^2. \tag{4.12}$$

Now, under zero applied field conditions, let us obtain the spontaneous polarization from Equation (4.11)

$$\alpha P_S + \beta P_S{}^3 = 0 \quad [\alpha = (T - T_0)/\varepsilon_0 C], \tag{4.13}$$

so that the following two states are possible:

$$\begin{cases} P_S = 0 \\ {P_S}^2 = -\frac{\alpha}{\beta} = \frac{T_0 - T}{\beta\varepsilon_0 C} \cdot \end{cases} \tag{4.14}$$

Landau Free Energy Change with Temperature

Figure 4.1 plots the Landau free energy $F(P, T) = (1/2)\alpha P^2 + (1/4)\beta P^4$ as a function of polarization P by changing the temperature T. Projected curves on the F vs. polarization P domain are shown in Figure 4.1a. When $T \gg T_0$, since the $(1/2)\alpha P^2$ positive term dominates over the $(1/4)\beta P^4$ term, the free energy curve is almost "convex" parabolic with single minimum at $P = 0$ (i.e., paraelectric phase). As the inverse permittivity is obtained from the second derivative of F (i.e., $\left(\frac{\partial^2 F}{\partial P^2}\right)$) and the curvature of F is given by $(\frac{\partial^2 F}{\partial P^2})/\left[1 + \left(\frac{\partial F}{\partial P}\right)^2\right]^{3/2}$, we can conclude that the inverse permittivity is visibly obtained from the "energy curvature" around the energy minimum point (that is, $\left(\frac{\partial F}{\partial P}\right) = 0$ point). With a decrease in temperature T, the parabolic curvature (inverse permittivity) decreases continuously, leading to the Curie–Weiss law. With a decrease in the temperature close to T_0 ($T \approx T_0$), the $(1/2)\alpha P^2$ positive term almost diminishes and the $(1/4)\beta P^4$ term exhibits a very flat potential minimum range, that is, the curvature becomes zero, or permittivity reaches infinite. With a decrease in temperature T below T_0, the situation is rather different: since the $(1/2)\alpha P^2$ term is now negative, the free energy curve becomes "concave" around $P = 0$, and the positive $(1/4)\beta P^4$ term competes and makes the curve "convex" in the large P range. Thus, the free energy curve should show double minima at $P_S = \pm\sqrt{-\frac{\alpha}{\beta}}$ in the ferroelectric phase. The minimum energy at these points is

$$F(P, T) = (1/2)\alpha P^2 + (1/4)\beta P^4 = -\left(\frac{1}{4}\right)\frac{\alpha^2}{\beta} = -\frac{(T_0 - T)^2}{4\beta{\varepsilon_0}^2 C^2}, \tag{4.15}$$

which indicates that the energy F is equal to "zero" (the F value in the paraelectric phase) at $T = T_0$ (phase transition temperature), and becomes lower in $T < T_0$ than that in the paraelectric phase. This is the reason why the phase transition from paraelectric to ferroelectric phase occurs.

Landau free energy change associated with the second-order phase transitions is shown in an extended form in terms of temperature in Figure 4.1b. The reader can notice the energy minimum point tracing line, which splits into two lines from a single line, resembling a Y-shape fork, at the phase transition temperature $T_C = T_0$, which is called "bifurcation". Mathematically, a bifurcation occurs when a small smooth change made to the parameter value ("bifurcation parameter", in this case "α") of a system causes a sudden topological change in its behavioral contour. The occurrence of the double minima generates P–E hysteresis, as discussed in Subsection Ferroelectric Phase (page 111).

The "order" of a phase transition was defined by Ehrenfest [1], who suggested that the "n-th" order transition exhibits "continuity" of the (n − 1)-th derivative of the Gibbs free energy G and "discontinuity" of the n-th derivative of G at the phase transition temperature. That is to say, the "first-order phase transition" will show the discontinuity of the first derivative of G (i.e., entropy), $\frac{\partial G}{\partial T} = -S$, while the second-order transition will show the discontinuity of the second derivative G (i.e., specific heat capacity), $c_p^E = -T\left(\frac{\partial^2 G}{\partial T^2}\right)_{X,E}$. We may translate this specific heat capacity into P (or D) constant specific heat capacity,

$$c_p^D = -T\left(\frac{\partial^2 G_1}{\partial T^2}\right)_{X,D}, \tag{4.16}$$

which is equivalent to Equation (4.15) without including the elastic energy term. From Equation (4.15), we can derive

- $F(P,T) = -\frac{(T_0-T)^2}{4\beta\varepsilon_0{}^2C^2} \to 0$ with $T \to T_0$: $F(P_S) \leq F(0) = 0$, continuous to the paraelectric phase.
- $\frac{\partial F(P,T)}{\partial T} = \frac{(T_0-T)}{2\beta\varepsilon_0{}^2C^2} \propto -S \to 0$ with $T \to T_0$, continuous to the paraelectric phase.
- $\frac{\partial^2 F(P,T)}{\partial T^2} = -\frac{1}{2\beta\varepsilon_0{}^2C^2} \propto -c_p^D$, discontinuous to the paraelectric phase (zero).

The above analysis can explain why the handling of Equation (4.15) is for the second-order transition.

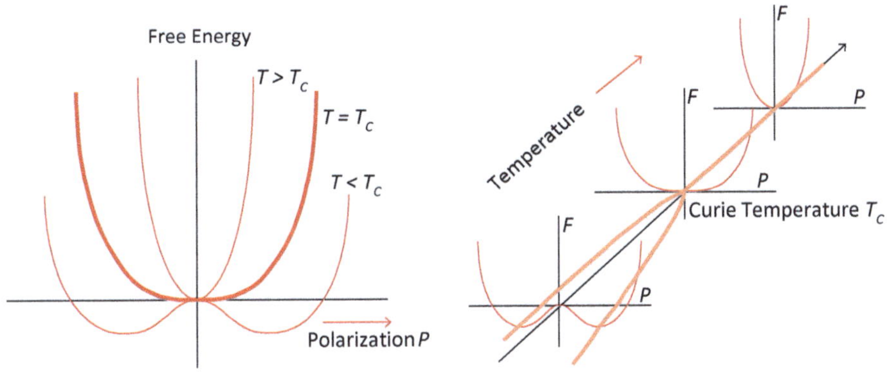

(a) (b)

Figure 4.1. Landau free energy change associated with the second-order phase transitions: (**a**) projected curves on F-P domain and (**b**) extended description with temperature axis. Source: Figure by author.

Paraelectric Phase

For $T > T_0$, the trivial solution $P_S = 0$ is obtained, because $P_S{}^2 = (T_0 - T)/\beta\varepsilon_0 C$ becomes negative (unrealistic in physics). Thus, from Equation (4.10), the reader can understand that the Landau free energy is zero in the whole range of the paraelectric phase. By putting $P_S = 0$ in Equation (4.12), the permittivity in this temperature range (i.e., paraelectric phase) is expressed by

$$\frac{1}{\varepsilon_0\varepsilon} = \alpha = (T - T_0)/\varepsilon_0 C, \text{ or } \varepsilon = \frac{C}{(T - T_0)}. \tag{4.17}$$

This permittivity relation in the paraelectric phase is popularly called the "Curie–Weiss law", where C is the "Curie–Weiss constant", and T_0 is the "Curie–Weiss temperature".

Ferroelectric Phase

For $T < T_0$, the solution

$$P_S{}^2 = -\frac{\alpha}{\beta} = (T_0 - T)/\beta\varepsilon_0 C \left[\text{or } P_S = \pm\sqrt{(T_0 - T)/(\beta\,\varepsilon_0\,C)}\right]. \quad (4.18)$$

provides the spontaneous polarization, which exhibits the minimum of the Landau free energy (Equation (4.15)):

$$F(P,\ T) = (1/2)\alpha P^2 + (1/4)\beta P^4 = \left(\tfrac{1}{2}\right)\alpha\left(-\tfrac{\alpha}{\beta}\right) + \left(\tfrac{1}{4}\right)\beta\left(-\tfrac{\alpha}{\beta}\right)^2 = -\frac{\left(\frac{1}{4}\right)\alpha^2}{\beta}$$
$$= -(1/4)(T - T_0)^2/\varepsilon_0{}^2 C^2 \beta.$$

The above energy is lower than "zero" in the paraelectric phase, which explains the phase transition from the paraelectric to ferroelectric phase.

The relative permittivity ε in the ferroelectric phase is calculated as:

$$\begin{gathered} 1/\varepsilon_0\varepsilon = 1/(\partial P/\partial E) = (\alpha + 3\beta P^2) = [\alpha + 3\beta(-\alpha/\beta)] = -2\alpha, \\ \frac{1}{\varepsilon_0\varepsilon} = -2\alpha = 2(T_0 - T)/\varepsilon_0 C, \text{ or } \varepsilon = \frac{C/2}{(T_0 - T)}. \end{gathered} \quad (4.19)$$

Figure 4.2 shows the variations of P_S and with temperature in the second-order phase transition. The spontaneous polarization P_S decreases with increasing temperature continuously (square root function) and becomes 0 at $T = T_0$. It is notable that the permittivity becomes infinite (i.e., inverse permittivity = 0) at the transition temperature ($T_C = T_0$) and that the slope of the inverse permittivity in the ferroelectric phase is twice that in the paraelectric phase.

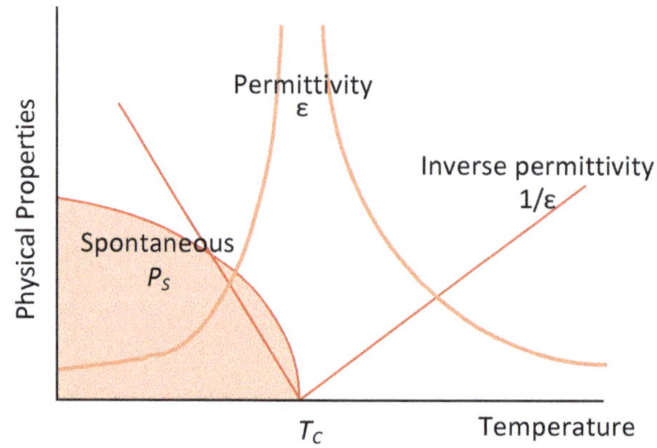

Figure 4.2. Spontaneous polarization and permittivity change associated with the second-order phase transitions in a ferroelectric. Source: Figure by author.

Let us now consider the polarization vs. electric field hysteresis curve at a temperature T. We start from the potential minima obtained from $(\partial F/\partial P) = E = \alpha P + \beta P^3$. By putting

$$y_1 = \alpha P + \beta P^3 \text{ and} \tag{4.20a}$$

$$y_2 = E, \tag{4.20b}$$

a visual geometrical solution technique can be used, as illustrated in Figure 4.3a; that is, the intersects of these two curves ($y_1 = y_2$) provide the solution points: only one intersect exists for $T > T_C$, while for $T < T_C$, there are three intersects. Under $E = 0$ at $T < T_C$, we obtain $P_S = \pm\sqrt{-\frac{\alpha}{\beta}}$, which correspond to the spontaneous polarization.

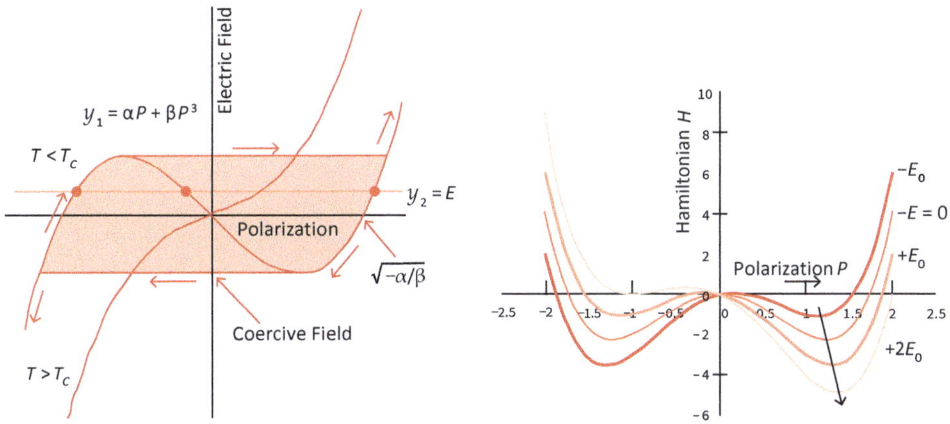

Figure 4.3. (**a**) Polarization vs. electric field hysteresis curve, obtained from a graphic technique. (**b**) Hamiltonian $F(P, E)$ under the external electric field E. Source: Figure by author.

Varying the electric field E up and down, we can understand that the shadowed area in Figure 4.3a shows the polarization vs. electric field hysteresis loop, when we assume the macroscopic all-polarization one-time reversal. The macroscopic coercive field is obtained from the maximum/minimum point of the y_1 curve:

$$\frac{\partial y_1}{\partial P} = 0 \rightarrow \alpha + 3\beta P^2 = 0 \rightarrow P = \sqrt{-\alpha/3\beta}. \tag{4.21}$$

Since the coercive field is obtained from the y_1 max point,

$$y_1 = \alpha P + \beta P^3 = \sqrt{-\alpha/3\beta}\,[\alpha + \beta(-\alpha/3\beta)] = \sqrt{-4\alpha^3/27\beta}. \tag{4.22}$$

The shadowed area in Figure 4.3a shows the polarization vs. electric field hysteresis loop, where arrows show the loop tracing way. The above coercive field is under the assumption that the macroscopic whole polarization reverses at one-time, which is 10 times higher than the experimentally obtained coercive field (1 kV/mm), where, by segmenting the domain into multidomain states, the required electric field is significantly reduced for the domain reversal in practice.

Figure 4.3b shows an alternative explanation for the domain reversal. Knowing the relation Equation (4.11)

$(\partial F/\partial P) = E = \alpha P + \beta P^3$,

we introduce the Gibbs free energy by integrating the potential energy $-E{\cdot}P$ under the external electric field E into Landau free energy:

$$G = \frac{1}{2}\alpha P^2 + \frac{1}{4}\beta P^4 - E{\cdot}P. \tag{4.23}$$

This Hamiltonian expression gives the negative slope line potential on the original Landau free energy curve under a positive electric field application, as illustrated in Figure 4.3b $E = +E_0$, which clearly indicates that the positive electric field decreases the Hamiltonian energy of the positive spontaneous polarization state. This is numerically obtained from the minimum energy point:

$$\frac{\partial G}{\partial P} = \alpha P + \beta P^3 - E = 0. \tag{4.24}$$

Since there are three roots a, b, and c ($a < b < c$) for Equation (4.24), we put

$$P^3 + (\alpha/\beta)P - E/\beta = (P-a)(P-b)(P-c) = 0. \tag{4.25}$$

Accordingly, we obtain the following three equations:

$$\begin{cases} a+b+c = 0 \\ ab+bc+ca = (\alpha/\beta). \\ abc = E/\beta \end{cases} \tag{4.26}$$

By solving the above, we obtain $a = -\sqrt{-\frac{\alpha}{\beta}} + \Delta_1(E^{\frac{1}{3}})$, $b = 0 + \Delta_2(E^{\frac{1}{3}})$, and $c = +\sqrt{-\frac{\alpha}{\beta}} + \Delta_3(E^{\frac{1}{3}})$. When $P = c$, we obtain the minimum energy. Note that with an increase in the electric field E, the polarization P (energy minimum point) is gradually increased. From the initial spontaneous polarization state at $P = a$, we will consider the coercive electric field E_C to change the spontaneous polarization state to $P = c$. This can be obtained when the energy curve at $P = a$ becomes "flat", that is, the minimum condition is resolved, and the $P = c$ point becomes a unique minimum energy state in the model. Figure 4.3b $E = 2E_0$ is rather close to this condition. The energy curve flatness is equivalent to "zero" curvature $\left[\left(\frac{\partial^2 F}{\partial P^2}\right) / \left[1 + \left(\frac{\partial F}{\partial P}\right)^2\right]^{3/2}\right]$ mathematically:

$$\frac{\partial^2 G}{\partial P^2} = \alpha + 3\beta P^2 = 0. \tag{4.27}$$

From the above, $P = -\sqrt{-\alpha/3\beta}$, leading to $E_C = \alpha P + \beta P^3 = \sqrt{-4\alpha^3/27\beta}$. This result is exactly the same as Equation (4.22).

4.2.2. First-Order Phase Transition (In the Case of $\beta < 0$)

We now consider the case of $\beta < 0$ in Equation (4.6)

$F(P, T) = (1/2)\alpha P^2 + (1/4)\beta P^4 + (1/6)\gamma P^6 \quad [\alpha(T) = (T - T_0)/\varepsilon_0 C]$.

In this case, γ should be taken as positive in order to keep the polarization P in a finite region around $P = 0$. As discussed later, this transition becomes "first order", because the first derivative of free energy, $\left(\frac{\partial F}{\partial P}\right)$, already exhibits discontinuity from the paraelectric to ferroelectric phase transition point (T_C). The equilibrium polarization in an electric field E should satisfy the condition Equation (4.8):

$(\partial F/\partial P) = E = \alpha P + \beta P^3 + \gamma P^5$.

With no electric field applied, Equation (4.8) provides the spontaneous polarization Equation (4.9):

$$P(\alpha + \beta P^2 + \gamma P^4) = 0. \tag{4.28}$$

We discuss two cases:

(i) $P = 0 \rightarrow$ This trivial solution corresponds to a paraelectric state.
(ii) $\alpha + \beta P^2 + \gamma P^4 = 0 \rightarrow$ This solution corresponds to a ferroelectric state.

The second case gives

$$P_{S^2} = \left[-\beta + \sqrt{\beta^2 - 4\gamma\alpha}\right]/2\gamma] = \left[-\beta + \sqrt{\beta^2 - 4\gamma(T - T_0)/\varepsilon_0 C}\right]/2\gamma]. \tag{4.29}$$

Example Problem 4.1

Is $P_S{}^2 = [-\beta - \sqrt{\beta^2 - 4\gamma\alpha}]/2\gamma$ not another root for solving Equation (4.28)?

Solution

Since low temperature range $(T - T_0) < 0$ and $\gamma > 0$, $\sqrt{\beta^2 - 4\gamma(T - T_0)/\varepsilon_0 C} > \sqrt{\beta^2} = -\beta$ (or $|\beta|$; note that $\beta < 0$). Thus, $[-\beta - \sqrt{\beta^2 - 4\gamma(T - T_0)/\varepsilon_0 C}\,]/2\gamma < 0$, which is contradictory with $P_S{}^2$ because the physical parameter P_S should be a real value. The spontaneous polarization should be positive or negative, but still a real number, never an imaginary number.

Landau Free Energy Curves and Critical Temperatures

Let us calculate the free energy curves for various temperatures:

$$F(P, T) = (1/2)\alpha P^2 + (1/4)\beta P^4 + (1/6)\gamma P^6 \quad [\alpha(T) = (T - T_0)/\varepsilon_0 C]. \tag{4.30}$$

As shown in Figure 4.4a, there are three critical temperatures, T_1, T_C, and T_0, in the first-order transition, in comparison with one unique temperature, $T_C = T_0$, in the second-order transition. As derived in Equation (4.9), there are three potential minima in general in Equation (4.30), $-P_s$, 0, and $+P_s$. T_1 is the temperature where the side minimum starts (though this minima energy is much higher than the energy at $P = 0$). T_C is the temperature where the side minimum minima energy becomes the same as the energy at $P = 0$ (paraelectric). We believe this is the phase transition condition, though some temperature hysteresis is observed between the rising and falling temperature process in practice. The lowest temperature T_0 is the point where the center ($P = 0$) minimum (convex) disappears or switches to the maximum (concave).

The following equation should be maintained for the energy minimum points:

$$(\partial F/\partial P) = E = \alpha P + \beta P^3 + \gamma P^5 = 0. \tag{4.31}$$

- T_1 Calculation

The T_1 can be calculated from the condition of "point of inflection" prior to making the minimum; that is, the second derivative of $F(P, T)$ is equal to 0:

$$\left(\frac{\partial^2 F}{\partial P^2}\right) = \alpha + 3\beta P^2 + 5\gamma P^4 = 0. \tag{4.32}$$

Note that this inflection point should correspond to the hypothetical inverse permittivity $\frac{1}{\varepsilon_0 \varepsilon} = 0$ point, as discussed later in Subsection Permittivity (page 118). Combining the above equation and

$$\alpha + \beta P^2 + \gamma P^4 = 0, \tag{4.33}$$

from Equation (4.31), we obtain $P^2 = -2\alpha/\beta$. Then, from $\alpha + \beta(-2\alpha/\beta)^2 + \gamma(-2\alpha/\beta)^4 = 0$, we obtain

$$\alpha = \beta^2/4\gamma, \text{ or } T_1 = T_0 + \beta^2 \varepsilon_0 C/4\gamma. \tag{4.34}$$

Note that the relation Equation (4.34) which can also be obtained from the condition of the inside term of the root $\sqrt{\ }$ in the spontaneous polarization solution $P_S{}^2 = \left[-\beta + \sqrt{\beta^2 - 4\gamma\alpha}\right]/2\gamma]$ should be ≥ 0.

- T_C Calculation

The transition temperature T_C is obtained from the condition that the Landau free energy of the paraelectric and ferroelectric phases are equal, i.e., $F = 0$:

$$(1/2)\alpha P_S{}^2 + (1/4)\beta P_S{}^4 + (1/6)\gamma P_S{}^6 = 0, \tag{4.35a}$$

which is valid only at $T = T_C$; the potential minima are obtained from

$$(\partial F/\partial P) = E = \alpha P + \beta P^3 + \gamma P^5 = 0. \tag{4.36a}$$

This equation is valid for any temperature below and above the Curie temperature.

Knowing $P_S \neq 0$, Equations (4.35) and (4.36) are reduced to

$$\alpha + (1/2)\beta P^2 + (1/3)\gamma P^4 = 0, \tag{4.35b}$$

$$\alpha + \beta P^2 + \gamma P^4 = 0. \tag{4.36b}$$

Note again that Equation (4.36b) is valid for all temperatures below T_C, but Equation (4.35b) is only valid at $T = T_C$. Eliminating the P^4 terms from these two equations [3 × (4.35b)–(4.36b)],

$$[(3/2) - 1]\beta P^2 + [3 - 1]\alpha = 0 \rightarrow P^2 = -4\alpha/\beta. \tag{4.37}$$

We then obtain the following equation from Equation (4.36b):

$$\alpha + \beta(-4\alpha/\beta) + \gamma(-4\alpha/\beta)^2 = 0 \rightarrow -3\alpha + \gamma \times 16\alpha^2/\beta^2 = 0 \rightarrow \alpha = \frac{3}{16}\frac{\beta^2}{\gamma}.$$

Taking into account our special case (valid only at $T = T_c$), $\alpha = (T - T_0)/\varepsilon_0 C = (T_C - T_0)/\varepsilon_0 C$, the Curie temperature T_C is calculated as

$$T_C = T_0 + (3/16)\left(\beta^2\varepsilon_0 C/\gamma\right). \tag{4.38}$$

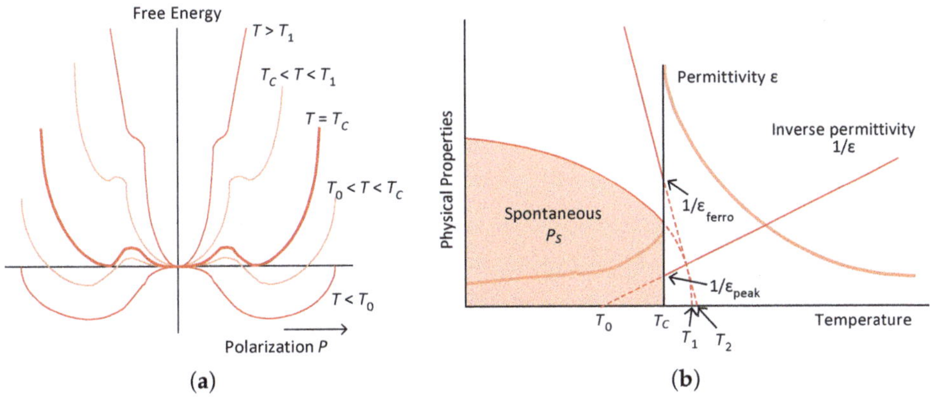

Figure 4.4. (**a**) Free energy as a function polarization P at various temperatures. (**b**) Spontaneous polarization and permittivity/inverse permittivity change associated with the first-order phase transitions in a ferroelectric. Source: [2] ©Uchino, K. *Ferroelectric Devices*, 2nd ed. CRC Press, 2010; p. 46. Reproduced by permission of Taylor & Francis Group.

Spontaneous Polarization

We discuss the spontaneous polarization and permittivity change associated with the first-order phase transitions in comparison with the second-order transition. The spontaneous polarization decreases in proportion to $\sqrt{T_0 - T}$ down to zero with an increase in temperature in the second-order transition, while in the first-order transition, as illustrated in Figure 4.4b, the lean parabolic-like (resembling to parabolic) curve is cut abruptly at the transition temperature $T = T_c$. From the spontaneous polarization expression in the first-order phase transition:

$$P_S = \sqrt{\left[-\beta + \sqrt{\beta^2 - 4\gamma\alpha}\right]/2\gamma]}. \tag{4.39}$$

By putting $\alpha = \frac{3}{16}\frac{\beta^2}{\gamma}$ at $T = T_c$ into Equation (4.39), we obtain the minimum realizable spontaneous polarization as

$$P_S = \sqrt{[-\beta + \sqrt{\beta^2 - 4\gamma(\frac{3}{16}\frac{\beta^2}{\gamma})}/2\gamma]} = \sqrt{-\frac{3}{4}\frac{\beta}{\gamma}}. \tag{4.40}$$

The Landau free energy minima start at $T = T_1$, and in the temperature range $T_c < T < T_1$, these minima are sustained, though these polarizations are not experimentally observed because the energy at $P = 0$ is lower, making the paraelectric phase more stable. It is also interesting that P_S minima start at $T = T_1$, where the condition $\beta^2 - 4\gamma\alpha = 0$ is sustained, leaving $P_S = \sqrt{(-\frac{\beta}{2\gamma})}$ as the minimum value. Note that the $P_S = 0$ state should not be realized in the ferroelectric phase in this first-order transition model.

Let us confirm the "order" of a phase transition: that is to say, will the above "first-order phase transition" treatment show the discontinuity of the first derivative of G (i.e., entropy), "$\frac{\partial G}{\partial T} = -S$"? We can derive:

- $F(P,T) = (1/2)\alpha {P_S}^2 + (1/4)\beta {P_S}^4 + (1/6)\gamma {P_S}^6 \to 0$ with $T \to T_C$: $F(P_S) = F(0) = 0$, continuous at $T = T_C$ to the paraelectric phase.
- $\frac{\partial F(P,T)}{\partial T} = \frac{1}{2\varepsilon_0 C}{P_S}^2 + (\alpha P_S + \beta {P_S}^3 + \gamma {P_S}^5)\frac{\partial P_S}{\partial T} \propto -S \to (-\frac{\beta}{4\gamma\varepsilon_0 C})$ with $T \to T_0$, because of the jump $P_S = \sqrt{(-\frac{\beta}{2\gamma})}$ and $\left(\alpha P_S + \beta {P_S}^3 + \gamma {P_S}^5\right) = 0$, discontinuous to the paraelectric phase.

The above analysis can explain why the handling of Equation (4.30) is for the first-order transition.

Permittivity

The permittivity is obtained as

$$\frac{1}{\varepsilon_0 \varepsilon} = \frac{1}{\left(\frac{\partial P}{\partial E}\right)} = \left(\frac{\partial E}{\partial P}\right) = \alpha + 3\beta P^2 + 5\gamma P^4. \tag{4.41}$$

In the paraelectric phase ($P_S = 0$)

$$\frac{1}{\varepsilon_0 \varepsilon} = \alpha = (T - T_0)/\varepsilon_0 C, \text{ or } \varepsilon = \frac{C}{(T - T_0)}. \tag{4.42}$$

This permittivity relation in the paraelectric phase is popularly called the "Curie–Weiss law", where C is the "Curie–Weiss constant" and T_0 is the "Curie–Weiss temperature". Different from the second-order transition, T will not reach T_0 but is stopped at T_C with decreasing temperature. Thus, there exists the minimum of $\frac{1}{\varepsilon_0 \varepsilon} = \frac{T_C - T_0}{\varepsilon_0 C} = \frac{3}{16}\frac{\beta^2}{\gamma}$, or the maximum of $\varepsilon_0 \varepsilon = \frac{16\gamma}{3\beta^2}$.

On the contrary, in the ferroelectric phase with

$${P_S}^2 = \left[-\beta + \sqrt{\beta^2 - 4\gamma\alpha}\right]/2\gamma] \text{ or } \alpha + \beta P^2 + \gamma P^4 = 0. \tag{4.43}$$

Using Equation (4.43), we can transform Equation (4.41) into

$$\frac{1}{\varepsilon_0\varepsilon} = \alpha + 3\beta P^2 + 5\left(-\alpha - \beta P^2\right) = -4\alpha - 2\beta P^2. \tag{4.44}$$

In order to calculate the $\frac{1}{\varepsilon_0\varepsilon}$ slope in the ferroelectric phase, we analyze the approximate formula around the phase transition temperature T_c (i.e., $T_0 < T < T_C$). Note here that $(T_C - T)$ is a small value, but $(T_0 - T)$ is not small, because of $T_C = T_0 + (3/16)(\beta^2\varepsilon_0 C/\gamma)$ (temperature difference is 30–40 °C). We transform α as

$$\alpha = \frac{T - T_0}{\varepsilon_0 C} = \frac{3\beta^2}{16\gamma} - \frac{T_C - T}{\varepsilon_0 C}, \tag{4.45}$$

to proceed with the small value approximation ($(T_C - \mathrm{T}) \ll 1$). Taking Equation (4.43) into Equation (4.44),

$$\frac{1}{\varepsilon_0\varepsilon} = -4\alpha - 2\beta {P_S}^2 = -4\left(\frac{3\beta^2}{16\gamma} - \frac{T_C - T}{\varepsilon_0 C}\right) + \frac{\beta^2}{\gamma} - \frac{\beta\sqrt{\beta^2 - 4\gamma\left(\frac{3\beta^2}{16\gamma} - \frac{T_C - T}{\varepsilon_0 C}\right)}}{\gamma}.$$

Considering (T_C − T) << 1, β < 0, i.e., $\sqrt{\beta^2} = -\beta$, and the approximation $\sqrt{1+x} = 1 + \frac{x}{2}$ (if x << 1):

$$\begin{aligned}
\frac{1}{\varepsilon_0\varepsilon} &= -4\left(\frac{3\beta^2}{16\gamma} - \frac{T_C - T}{\varepsilon_0 C}\right) + \frac{\beta^2}{\gamma} - \frac{\beta\sqrt{\beta^2\left(1 - \frac{4\gamma}{\beta^2}\left(\frac{3\beta^2}{16\gamma} - \frac{T_C - T}{\varepsilon_0 C}\right)\right)}}{\gamma} \\
&= -4\left(\frac{3\beta^2}{16\gamma} - \frac{T_C - T}{\varepsilon_0 C}\right) + \frac{\beta^2}{\gamma} - \frac{\beta\sqrt{\beta^2\left(1 - \frac{3}{4} + \frac{4\gamma(T_C - T)}{\beta^2\varepsilon_0 C}\right)}}{\gamma} \\
&= -4\left(\frac{3\beta^2}{16\gamma} - \frac{T_C - T}{\varepsilon_0 C}\right) + \frac{\beta^2}{\gamma} + \frac{\beta^2}{2\gamma}\sqrt{1 + \frac{16\gamma(T_C - T)}{\beta^2\varepsilon_0 C}} \\
&= -\frac{3\beta^2}{4\gamma} + \frac{4(T_C - T)}{\varepsilon_0 C} + \frac{\beta^2}{\gamma} + \frac{\beta^2}{2\gamma}\left(1 + \frac{16\gamma(T_C - T)}{2\beta^2\varepsilon_0 C}\right) \\
&= \frac{\beta^2}{4\gamma} + \frac{\beta^2}{2\gamma} + \frac{4(T_C - T)}{\varepsilon_0 C} + \frac{4(T_C - T)}{\varepsilon_0 C}.
\end{aligned}$$

Finally, we obtain

$$\frac{1}{\varepsilon_0\varepsilon} = \frac{3\beta^2}{4\gamma} + \frac{8(T_C - T)}{\varepsilon_0 C}. \tag{4.46}$$

Note first that the slope of the inverse permittivity vs. temperature in the ferroelectric phase is eight-times larger than that in the paraelectric phase (normal Curie–Weiss law with $1/C$ slope). The minimum inverse permittivity $\frac{1}{\varepsilon_0\varepsilon} = \frac{3\beta^2}{4\gamma}$ or the maximum permittivity $\varepsilon_0\varepsilon = \frac{4\gamma}{3\beta^2}$ (one-quarter of the paraelectric peak value) are obtained at $T = T_C$. The extrapolated inverse permittivity line intersect for the paraelectric phase is, of course, $T = T_0$, while that for the ferroelectric phase is

$T = T_2 = T_0 + \frac{9\varepsilon_0 C}{32\gamma}$, which is very close to $T_1 = T_0 + \frac{\varepsilon_0 C}{4\gamma}$ (with difference of only $\frac{\varepsilon_0 C}{32\gamma}$). This deviation may originate from the linear approximation used in the derivation process above, as discussed in Subsection Landau Free Energy Curves and Critical Temperatures.

In summary, in the "first-order phase transition", the Curie temperature T_C is slightly higher than the Curie–Weiss temperature T_0, and that a discrete jump of P_S appears at T_C. Additionally, the permittivity exhibits a finite maximum at T_C (Figure 4.4b). Barium titanate is an example of a ferroelectric that undergoes a first-order phase transition. Figure 4.4b also shows the variation in ε with temperature. The slope of the inverse permittivity $1/\varepsilon$ in the ferroelectric phase is eight times that in the paraelectric phase. The extrapolated temperature of the inverse permittivity in the paraelectric phase provides the normal Curie–Weiss temperature T_0, while the extrapolated temperature of the inverse permittivity in the ferroelectric phase gives the temperature T_2 (theoretically T_1), as discussed above.

The free energy curves are plotted for the second- and first-order phase transitions at various temperatures in Figures 4.1a and 4.4a, respectively. In the case of $\beta > 0$, the phase transition is not associated with a latent heat but with a jump in the specific heat; this is called a second-order transition. On the other hand, in the case of $\beta < 0$, the transition exhibits a latent heat (i.e., entropy S discontinuity), and is called a first-order transition, where the permittivity shows a maximum and a discontinuity of the spontaneous polarization appears at T_C. When $T > T_1$, there is only one free energy minimum; when $T_C < T < T_1$, there are three potential minima. $P = 0$ is the lowest energy solution for $T_C < T < T_1$, while $P = \pm P_S$ exhibits the lowest potential for $T_0 < T < T_C$; when $T < T_0$, there are double minima of the free energy (with the disappearance of the center minimum), which correspond to very stable spontaneous polarizations. Due to the potential gap between three potential minima, we observe significant temperature hysteresis of the phase transition between the cycles of rising and falling temperature.

$-E$ Hysteresis

Similar to Subsection Paraelectric Phase (page 111), we introduce electric Gibbs energy by adding $-EP$ to the Landau free energy, and we simulate the polarization P–electric field E hysteresis:

$$G_2 = \frac{1}{2}\alpha P^2 + \frac{1}{4}\beta P^4 + \frac{1}{6}\gamma P^6 - EP. \tag{4.47}$$

Figure 4.5 illustrates the polarization vs. electric field hysteresis curve in the "first-order" phase transition. Refer to the hysteresis curve of Figure 4.3a in the second-order transition. A significant difference in the $P-E$ hysteresis in the first-order transition can be found in a "double hysteresis" in the temperature range $T_C < T < T_1$, which cannot be observed in the second-order transition. The system with multiple potential minima in the Gibbs energy (Figure 4.4a) can exhibit discontinuous polarization induction (i.e., electric-field-induced ferroelectric phase) under a high electric field. As shown in Figure 4.5, the $P-E$ double hysteresis is observed in a narrow temperature range.

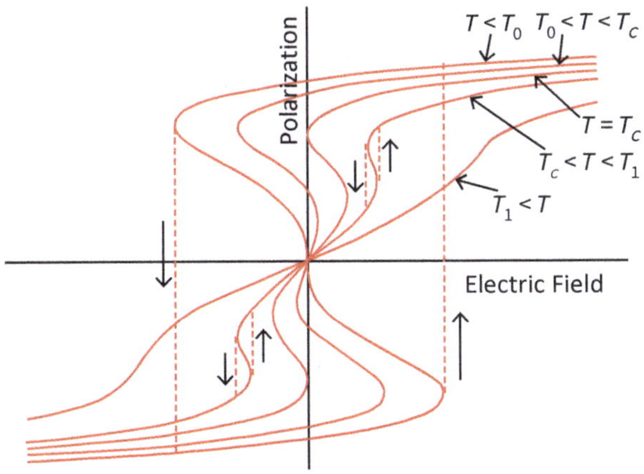

Figure 4.5. Polarization vs. electric field hysteresis curve in the first-order phase transition. Source: Figure by author.

4.3. Devonshire Theory of the Phase Transition

In a ferroelectric whose prototype phase (high-temperature paraelectric phase) is centrosymmetric and non-piezoelectric, the piezoelectric coupling term PX is omitted and only the electrostrictive coupling term P^2X is introduced. The theories for electrostriction in ferroelectrics were formulated in the 1950s by Devonshire [3] and Kay [4]. Let us assume that the elastic Gibbs energy (1D model) should be expanded in a one-dimensional form:

$$G_1(P,\ X,\ T) = \left(\tfrac{1}{2}\right)\alpha P^2 + \left(\tfrac{1}{4}\right)\beta P^4 + \left(\tfrac{1}{6}\right)\gamma P^6 - \left(\tfrac{1}{2}\right)sX^2 - QP^2X \quad [\alpha = (T - T_0)/\varepsilon_0 C], \tag{4.48}$$

where P, X, and T are the polarization, stress, and temperature, respectively, and s and Q are the elastic compliance and electrostrictive coefficient, respectively. This leads to the following three equations: Equations (4.49), (4.50), and (4.51):

$$E = \left(\frac{\partial G_1}{\partial P}\right) = \alpha P + \beta P^3 + \gamma P^5 - 2QPX, \tag{4.49}$$

$$x = -\left(\frac{\partial G_1}{\partial X}\right) = sX + QP^2, \tag{4.50}$$

$$\frac{1}{\varepsilon_0 \varepsilon} = \frac{1}{\left(\frac{\partial P}{\partial E}\right)} = \left(\frac{\partial E}{\partial P}\right) = \alpha + 3\beta P^2 + 5\gamma P^4 - 2QX. \tag{4.51}$$

4.3.1. *Case I: X = 0*

When the external stress X is zero, the following equations are derived:

$$E = \alpha P + \beta P^3 + \gamma P^5, \tag{4.52}$$

$$x = QP^2, \tag{4.53}$$

$$\frac{1}{\varepsilon_0\varepsilon} = \alpha + 3\beta P^2 + 5\gamma P^4. \tag{4.54}$$

Except for Equation (4.53), the analysis is exactly the same as that in the previous section. When the external electric field is equal to zero ($E = 0$), two different states are derived:

- $P = 0$
- $P^2 = (-\beta + \sqrt{\beta^2 - 4\alpha\gamma})/2\gamma$.

Paraelectric Phase

The paraelectric phase is analyzed under the condition:

$P_S = 0$ or $P = \varepsilon_0\varepsilon E$ (under small E modulation).

Equations (4.53) and (4.54) provide:

$$\text{Permittivity: } \varepsilon = C/(T - T_0) \quad \text{(normal Curie-Weiss law).} \tag{4.55}$$

$$\text{Electrostriction : } x = Q\varepsilon_0^2\varepsilon^2 E^2. \tag{4.56}$$

The "electrostrictive coefficient M" introduced in Equation (1.13) in Section 1.2.4 is related to this electrostrictive Q coefficient through

$$M = Q\varepsilon_0^2\varepsilon^2 E^2. \tag{4.57}$$

Ferroelectric Phase

Ferroelectric phase possesses:

$${P_S}^2 = \left(-\beta + \sqrt{\beta^2 - 4\alpha\gamma}\right)/2\gamma \text{ or } P = PS + \varepsilon_0\varepsilon E \text{ (under small } E \text{ modulation).}$$

Equations (4.52) and (4.53) provide:

$$x = Q(P_S + \varepsilon_0\varepsilon E)^2 = Q{P_S}^2 + 2\varepsilon_0\varepsilon Q P_S E + Q\varepsilon_0^2\varepsilon^2 E^2. \tag{4.58}$$

$$\frac{1}{\varepsilon_0\varepsilon} = \alpha + 3\beta P^2 + 5\gamma P^4 = -4\alpha - 2\beta {P_S}^2. \tag{4.59}$$

The total strain in Equation (4.58) is composed of three terms: the spontaneous strain x_S, the piezoelectric strain (proportional to E), and electrostriction (proportional to E^2; thus, we can define

$$\text{Spontaneous strain: } x_S = Q{P_S}^2, \tag{4.60}$$

$$\text{Piezoelectric constant: } d = 2\varepsilon_0\varepsilon Q P_S, \tag{4.61}$$

$$\text{Electrostrictive strain:} Q\varepsilon_0^2\varepsilon^2 E^2. \tag{4.62}$$

When the electric field E applied is much smaller than $P_S/\varepsilon_0\varepsilon$ (typically, 0.3 $(\mathrm{C/m^2})/2000\varepsilon_0$ $\sim$20 (kV/mm)), the third term in Equation (4.62) is neglected in comparison with the piezostriction dE. We understand from Equation (4.58) that "piezoelectricity" in a crystal with a centrosymmetric paraelectric phase is equivalent to the "electrostrictive phenomenon biased by the spontaneous polarization". Since the temperature dependence of spontaneous polarization and permittivity are already shown in Figure 4.4b, the temperature dependences of the mechanically related parameters, spontaneous strain, and the piezoelectric constant in the first-order phase transition are plotted in Figure 4.6b.

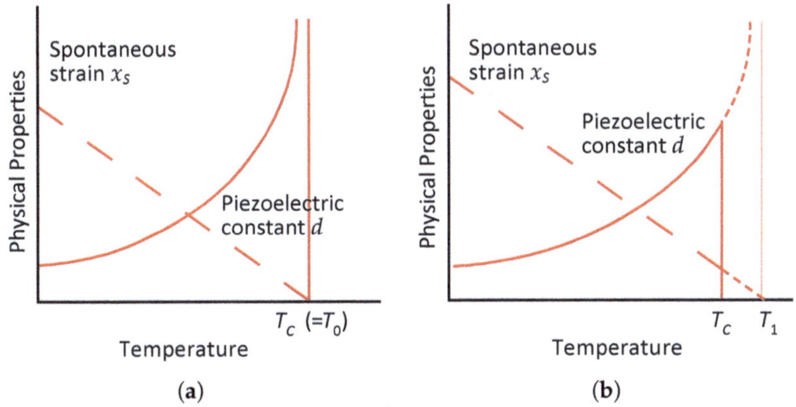

Figure 4.6. Temperature dependences of the spontaneous strain and the piezoelectric constant in the second- (**a**) and first-order phase transition (**b**). Source: [2] ©Uchino, K. *Ferroelectric Devices*, 2nd ed. CRC Press, 2010; p. 48. Reproduced by permission of Taylor & Francis Group.

Example Problem 4.2

In the case of a second-order phase transition, the elastic Gibbs energy is expanded in a 1D form as follows:

$$G_1(P, X, T) = (1/2)\alpha P^2 + (1/4)\beta P^4 - (1/2)sX^2 - QP^2X, \quad \text{(P4.2.1)}$$

where only the coefficient α is dependent on temperature, $\alpha = (T - T_0)/\varepsilon_0 C$, and $\beta > 0$. From this, obtain the temperature dependence of the dielectric constant, spontaneous polarization, spontaneous strain, and piezoelectric constant.

Solution

$$E = (\partial G_1/\partial P) = \alpha P + \beta P^3 - 2QPX, \quad \text{(P4.2.2)}$$

$$x = -(\partial G_1/\partial X) = sX + QP^2. \quad \text{(P4.2.3)}$$

When an external stress is zero, we can deduce the three characteristic equations:

$$E = \alpha P + \beta P^3, \quad \text{(P4.2.4)}$$

$$x = QP^2, \quad \text{(P4.2.5)}$$

$$1/\varepsilon_0\varepsilon = (\partial E/\partial P) = \alpha + 3\beta P^2. \quad \text{(P4.2.6)}$$

By initially setting $E = 0$, we obtain the following two stable states: $P_S{}^2 = 0$ and $-\alpha/\beta$

(i) Paraelectric phase ($T > T_0$): $P_S = 0$

$$1/\varepsilon_0\varepsilon = \alpha, \text{ then } \varepsilon = C/(T - T_0) \quad \text{(Curie-Weiss law)}. \quad \text{(P4.2.7)}$$

(ii) Ferroelectric phase ($T < T_0$):

$$P_S = \pm\sqrt{(T_0 - T)/\varepsilon_0 C\beta} \quad \text{(P4.2.8)}$$

$$1/\varepsilon_0\varepsilon = \alpha + 3\beta P^2 = -2\alpha, \text{ then } \varepsilon = C/2(T_0 - T), \quad \text{(P4.2.9)}$$

$$x_S = QP_S{}^2 = Q(T_0 - T)/\varepsilon_0 C\beta. \quad \text{(P4.2.10)}$$

From Equations (P4.2.8) and (P4.2.9), the piezoelectric constant is obtained as

$$d = 2\varepsilon_0\varepsilon QP_S = Q\sqrt{\varepsilon_0 C/\beta}(T_0 - T)^{-1/2}. \quad \text{(P4.2.11)}$$

The temperature dependence of the spontaneous strain x_S and the piezoelectric constant d in this second-order phase transition are plotted in Figure 4.6a. Refer to Figure 4.6b in the first-order transition.

4.3.2. Case II: $X \neq 0$

Here, we discuss the simplest case of hydrostatic pressure p in a 1D model. When a hydrostatic pressure p (usually by changing the sign, we define $X_1 = X_2 = X_3 = -p$) is applied, we obtain the following equations from Equations (4.49)–(4.51):

$$E = \alpha P + \beta P^3 + \gamma P^5 + 2QPp, \quad (4.63)$$

$$x = -\left(\frac{\partial G_1}{\partial X}\right) = -sp + QP^2, \quad (4.64)$$

$$\frac{1}{\varepsilon_0\varepsilon} = \alpha + 3\beta P^2 + 5\gamma P^4 + 2Qp. \quad (4.65)$$

Curie Temperature Shift

Equation (4.64) indicates the volumetric shrinkage under hydrostatic pressure p, which seems to be trivial. To the contrary, Equation (4.63) is very intriguing;

$(\alpha + 2Qp)P + \beta P^3 + \gamma P^5 = 0$ when the external electric field $E = 0$, which indicates that the Curie temperature decreases under hydrostatic pressure p, in the following:

$$(\alpha + 2Qp) = [T - (T_0 - 2Q\varepsilon_0 Cp)]/\varepsilon_0 C. \tag{4.66}$$

It is out of the scope of this book to go into, but the property issues of a few materials are described here for the reader's knowledge. We know an "empirical rule" on the hydrostatic pressure effect on ferroelectric perovskite materials, that is, a 50 °C Curie temperature decrease with 1 GPa hydrostric pressure application. This "50 °C/1 GPa rate" of the phase transition decrease can be derived as follows.

The author's group investigated electrostrictive coefficient Q and Curie–Weiss constant C on various perovskite-type oxides, the results of which are summarized in Table 4.1 [5,6]. It is important to note that the magnitude of the electrostrictive coefficient Q_h does not depend on whether the polar state is ferroelectric, antiferroelectric, or paraelectric, but strongly depends on the crystal structure, such as whether the two kinds of B and B′ ions are randomly distributed or ordered like B-B′-B-B′ (1:1 order) in the oxygen octahedra. The electrostrictive coefficient Q increases with the increasing degree of cation ordering and follows the sequence (1) disordered, (2) partially ordered, (3) simple, and (4) ordered-type perovskites. For the polar materials, their Curie–Weiss constants C are also listed in Table 4.1, showing a completely opposite trend to the Q_h values. Consequently, we found that the invariant for the complex perovskite-type oxide is the product of the electrostrictive coefficient and the Curie–Weiss constant:

$$Q_h C = 3.1(\pm 0.4) \times 10^3 \left[\mathrm{m^4C^{-2}K}\right]. \tag{4.67}$$

This "$Q_h C$ constant rule" can be understood intuitively if we accept the assumption that the material whose dielectric constant changes easily with pressure also exhibits a large change in the dielectric constant with the temperature, i.e., the proportionality between the following two equations (discussed in Subsection Direct Piezoelectric Effect):

$$\begin{cases} Q_h = \left[\frac{\partial(1/\varepsilon)}{\partial p}\right]/2\varepsilon_0 \\ 1/C = \left[\frac{\partial(1/\varepsilon)}{\partial T}\right] \end{cases}. \tag{4.68}$$

If we take $Q_h C = 3.1 \times 10^3 \left[\mathrm{m^4C^{-2}K}\right]$, and under $p = 1[\mathrm{GPa}]$, we calculate

$$2Q_h\varepsilon_0 Cp = 2 \times 3.1 \times 10^3 \left[\mathrm{m^4C^{-2}K}\right] \times 8.854 \times 10^{-12} \left[\mathrm{Fm^{-1}}\right] \times 1 \times 10^9\,[\mathrm{Pa}] = 55\,[\mathrm{K}]. \tag{4.69}$$

This explains a well-known "empirical rule" on the hydrostatic pressure effect on ferroelectric perovskite materials: that is, a 50 °C Curie temperature decrease with 1-GPa hydrostatic pressure application.

Table 4.1. Electrostrictive coefficient Q_h and Curie–Weiss constant C for various perovskite oxide crystals.

Polarity	Ordering	Material	Q_h [$\times 10^{-2}$ m^4C^{-2}]	C [$\times 10^5$ K]	Q_hC [$\times 10^3$ $m^4C^{-2}K$]	References
Ferroelectric	Order	$Pb(Mg_{1/3}Nb_{2/3})O_3$	0.60	4.7	2.8	[7,8]
		$Pb(Zn_{1/3}Nb_{2/3})O_3$	0.66	4.7	3.1	[9] [10]
	Partial Order	$Pb(Sc_{1/2}Ta_{1/2})O_3$	0.83	3.5	2.9	[11]
	Simple	$BaTiO_3$	2.0	1.5	3.0	[12] [13]
		$PbTiO_3$	2.2	1.7	3.7	[14,15]
		$SrTiO_3$	4.7	0.77	3.6	[16,17]
		$KTaO_3$	5.2	0.5	2.6	[18] [19]
Antiferroelectric	Partial Order	$Pb(Fe_{2/3}U_{1/3})O_3$	–	2.3	–	[20]
	Simple	$PbZrO_3$	2.0	1.6	3.2	[6,21]
	Order	$Pb(Co_{1/2}W_{1/2})O_3$	–	1.2	–	[22]
		$Pb(Mg_{1/2}W_{1/2})O_3$	6.2	0.42	2.6	[6] [8]
Non-Polar	Disorder	$(K_{3/4}Bi_{1/4})(Zn_{1/6}Nb_{5/6})O_3$	0.55–1.15	–	–	[23]
	Simple	$BaZrO_3$	2.3	–	–	[23]

Source: Table by author, based on data from [5,6].

Direct Piezoelectric Effect

A piezoelectric is occasionally used as a stress sensor, which is originated from Equation (4.63) in ferroelectric phase, $\alpha P_S + \beta {P_S}^3 + \gamma {P_S}^5 + 2QP_S p = E$. Under the external electric field zero condition, the hydrostatic pressure will shift the phase transition temperature in the form of $(T_0 - 2Q\varepsilon_0 Cp)$. Thus, a P_S decrease is expected under hydrostatic pressure. In a linear approximation, using $\left(\alpha P_S + \beta {P_S}^3 + \gamma {P_S}^5\right) \approx 0$, we can expect the "depolarization electric field" in the open-circuit crystal:

$$2QP_S p = -E \;\rightarrow\; \Delta P = \varepsilon_0 \varepsilon E = -2\varepsilon_0 \varepsilon Q P_S p. \tag{4.70}$$

The reader can now understand that the polarization change ΔP is generated in proportion to the pressure, and may also recall the relation of the piezoelectric constant d and electrostrictive coefficient Q as

$$d = 2\varepsilon_0 \varepsilon Q P_S. \tag{4.71}$$

Note here that above d and Q are $d_h = d_{33} + 2d_{31}$ and $Q_h = Q_{11} + 2Q_{12}$ under hydrostatic pressure. The piezoelectric stress sensor is to measure the charge or voltage generated on the crystal under the stress.

Permittivity Change with Pressure

Equation (4.65) indicates that the inverse permittivity changes linearly with hydrostatic pressure p:

$$1/\varepsilon_0\varepsilon = \alpha + 3\beta P_S{}^2 + 5\gamma P_S{}^4 + 2Qp \text{ (Ferroelectric state)}, \tag{4.72a}$$

$$\alpha + 2Qp = (T - T_0 + 2Q\varepsilon_0 Cp)/(\varepsilon_0 C) \text{ (Paraelectric state)}. \tag{4.72b}$$

Therefore, the pressure dependence of the Curie–Weiss temperature T_0 or the transition temperature T_C is derived as follows:

$$(\partial T_0/\partial p) = (\partial T_C/\partial p) = -2Q\varepsilon_0 C. \tag{4.73}$$

As already introduced, the ferroelectric Curie temperature is decreased with increasing hydrostatic pressure (when $Q_h > 0$).

Though we can measure the permittivity change with stress in the ferroelectric phase, since the piezoelectric effect can generate the charge or voltage (via a direct piezoelectric effect), we usually apply this effect to develop stress sensors. Let us consider here the converse effect of "electrostriction", that is, the paraelectric material's response to an external stress, which is also applicable to sensors. Since an electrostrictive material does not have a spontaneous polarization, it does not generate any charge under stress, but does exhibit a change in permittivity (see Equation (4.72b)):

$$\Delta(1/\varepsilon_0\varepsilon) = 2QX. \tag{4.74}$$

This is the "converse electrostrictive effect". A bimorph structure which can subtract the static capacitances of two dielectric ceramic plates can provide superior stress sensitivity and temperature stability [24]. The capacitance changes of the top and bottom plates in the bimorph have opposite signs for uniaxial stress (bending stress) and the same sign for temperature change. The response speed is limited by the capacitance measuring frequency to about 1 kHz. Unlike piezoelectric sensors, electrostrictive sensors are effective in the low frequency range (less than 1 kHz), especially pseudo-DC. On the contrary, the stress sensor made from a piezoelectric is suitable for higher frequency, above 10 Hz up to 10 kHz (i.e., the mechanical resonance frequency), because the piezo-generated charge leaks under very low frequency (e.g., less than 1 Hz) and loses accuracy.

Example Problem 4.3

Barium titanate has $d_{33} = 320 \times 10^{-12}$ C/N, ε_c (=ε) = 800 and $Q_{33} = 0.11$ m^{4}C^{-2} at room temperature. From this, estimate the spontaneous polarization P_S.

Solution

Let us use the relationship:

$$d_{33} = 2\varepsilon_0\varepsilon_3 Q_{33} P_S. \tag{P4.3.1}$$

P_S can be obtained as

$$P_S = d_{33}/2\varepsilon_0\varepsilon_3 Q_{33}$$
$$= 320 \times 10^{-12}\ [\mathrm{C/N}]/\{2 \times 8.854 \times 10^{-12}\ [\mathrm{F/m}] \times 800 \times 0.11\ [\mathrm{m^4C^{-2}}]\} = 0.21\ [\mathrm{C/m^2}]. \tag{P4.3.2}$$

4.3.3. Temperature Dependence of Electrostriction

We treat the "electrostrictive coefficient" Q as a temperature-independent constant in the Devonshire theory. How is the actual situation experimentally? Several expressions for the electrostrictive coefficient Q have been given so far, from the data obtained by independent experimental methods such as:

(1) electric-field-induced strain in the paraelectric phase;
(2) spontaneous polarization and spontaneous strain (X-ray diffraction) in the ferroelectric phase;
(3) d constants from the field-induced strain in the ferroelectric phase or from piezoelectric resonance;
(4) pressure dependence of permittivity in the paraelectric phase.

Nearly equal values of Q can be obtained by the above methods. Figure 4.7 shows the temperature dependence of the electrostrictive coefficients Q_{33} and Q_{31} observed for a complex perovskite $Pb(Mg_{1/3}Nb_{2/3})O_3$ single-crystal specimen whose Curie temperature is near 0 °C [25]. It is seen that there is no significant anomaly in the electrostrictive coefficient Q through the temperature range in which the paraelectric to ferroelectric phase transition occurs and piezoelectricity appears. Q is verified to be almost temperature-independent.

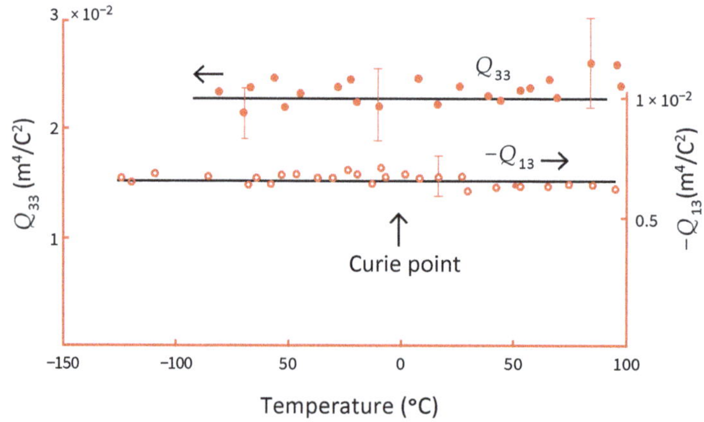

Figure 4.7. Temperature dependence of the electrostrictive constants Q_{33} and Q_{31} measured in a single crystal $Pb(Mg_{1/3}Nb_{2/3})O_3$. Source: [2] ©Uchino, K. *Ferroelectric Devices*, 2nd ed. CRC Press, 2010; p. 51. Reproduced by permission of Taylor & Francis Group.

4.4. Phenomenological Approach in Solid Solutions

One of the strategies for designing ferroelectric materials is to select a material with a suitable Curie temperature. As described in Chapter 1, for capacitor dielectrics, the peak dielectric constant around the transition (Curie) temperature is utilized, while for memory applications, the material must be ferroelectric at room temperature. A large temperature dependence of the spontaneous polarization below T_C is sought for pyroelectric sensors. On the other hand, piezoelectric materials are used as sensors and actuators, where the T_C should be much higher than room temperature. Electro-optic materials, which are key components in displays and optical communication systems, mostly use the Kerr effect, which requires a T_C lower than room temperature. Barium-titanate-based semiconductive ferroelectric ceramics are used for "thermistor" application by setting their T_C around the temperature at which a positive temperature coefficient (PTC) is desired. In this section, we consider how we can manipulate the Curie temperature by using the solid solution methodology.

Let us consider an example for piezoelectric application. In general, Pb(Zr,Ti)O_3 (*PZT*), PbTiO_3 (PT), (Pb,La)(Zr,Ti)O_3 (*PLZT*), and PZT-based ternary ceramics are utilized for piezoelectric applications. Their piezoelectric coefficients are summarized in the international data book:

K. H. Hellwege et al.: Landolt-Börnstein, Group III, Vol.11, Springer-Verlag, N.Y. (1979).

Figure 4.8 shows the composition dependence of the permittivity and the electromechanical coupling factor k_p for the PZT system [26].

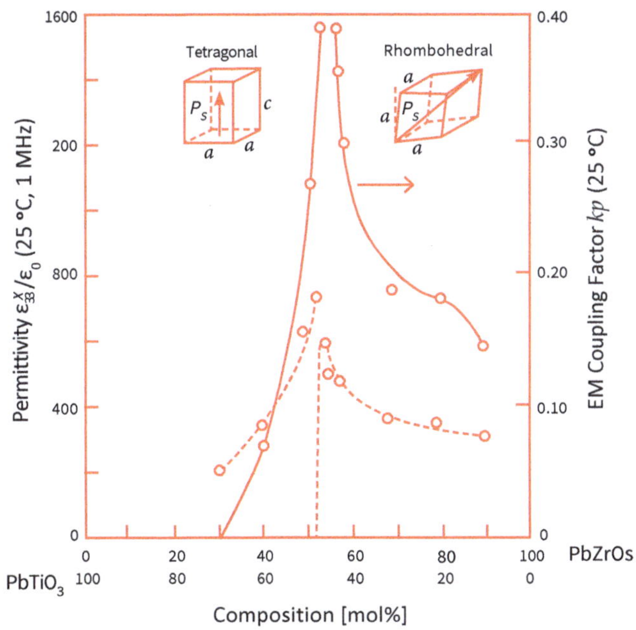

Figure 4.8. Composition dependence of the permittivity and the electromechanical coupling factor k_p in the PZT system. Source: [2] ©Uchino, K. *Ferroelectric Devices*, 2nd ed. CRC Press, 2010; p. 76. Reproduced by permission of Taylor & Francis Group.

If we do not have this sort of comprehensive experimental data, how can we estimate the values for the solid solutions between $PbTiO_3$ and $PbZrO_3$? In general, physical properties of a solid solution between A and B, $(1-x)A-xB$, can be estimated by a "phenomenological theory" [27,28]. Expanding the theories in Section 4.3, we assumed a linear combination of the elastic Gibbs energy of each component in terms of the molar fraction of two end-members. As described in the following Equation (4.75), the solid solution provides reasonable first-order estimates of the Curie temperature, spontaneous polarization and strain, permittivity, piezoelectric constant, and electromechanical coupling. Abe et al. reported a good example of theoretical fitting to experimental results for the solid solution $(1-x)Pb(Zn_{1/3}Nb_{2/3})O_3$-$xPbTiO_3$ [28], where the following linear summation of each energy term of both end-members, A and B, in terms of the molar ratio $(1-x){:}x$ is adopted:

$$G_1(P, X, T) = (1/2)[(1-x)\alpha_A + x\alpha_B]P^2 + (1/4)[(1-x)\beta_A + x\beta_B]P^4$$
$$+ (1/6)[(1-x)\gamma_A + x\gamma_B]P^6 - (1/2)[(1-x)s_A + xs_B]X^2 - [(1-x)Q_A + xQ_B]P^2X \quad (4.75)$$
$$(\alpha_A = (T - T_{0,A})/C_A, \alpha_B = (T - T_{0,B})/C_B).$$

This simplest assumption, that is, linear change of each parameter, α, β, γ, s, and Q, reduces the calculation process significantly, though this is not a precise energy combination procedure. By expanding Equation (4.75) into the 3D expression with P_1, P_2, P_3, X_{11}, X_{33}, X_{44}, etc. for realizing cubic, tetragonal, and rhombohedral symmetry phases, the elastic Gibbs energy is calculated for a certain composition x and temperature T. Then, the lower energy phase is taken as a stable phase at that particular point (x, T). Figures 4.9–4.12 show these fittings calculated on the basis of the end-member data listed in Table 4.2. The transition temperature from the tetragonal to cubic phase (Curie temperature) changes linearly with the composition x, as the reader can imagine, while the transition temperature from the rhombohedral to tetragonal phase is calculated by comparing the G_1 for both phases. We should point out some discrepancies in (1) the concave curvature of the MPB ("morphotropic phase boundary") with composition and (2) the maximum dielectric constant peak shape in the intermediate composition, which are different from the expectation deduced from the simplest linear summation of expansion coefficients.

Table 4.2. Coefficients for $Pb(Zn_{1/3}Nb_{2/3})O_3$ (PZN) and $PbTiO_3$ (PT) used in calculating the transition temperature and lattice parameters in $(1-x)$PZN-xPT.

Constants	PZN	PT
T_0 (°C)	130	478.8
C (10^5 °C)	4.7	1.5
ξ_{11} (10^7 $m^5C^{-2}F^{-1}$)	−13.7	−29.0
ξ_{12} (10^8 $m^5C^{-2}F^{-1}$)	−1.0	15.0
ζ_{111} (10^8 $m^9C^{-4}F^{-1}$)	10.3	15.6
ζ_{112} (10^8 $m^9C^{-4}F^{-1}$)	6.8	12.2
Q_{11} (10^{-2} m^4C^{-2})	2.4	8.9
Q_{12} (10^{-2} m^4C^{-2})	−0.86	−2.6
Q_{44} (10^{-2} m^4C^{-2})	1.6	6.75
a_c (Å)	4.058	3.957

Source: Table by author, based on data from [2].

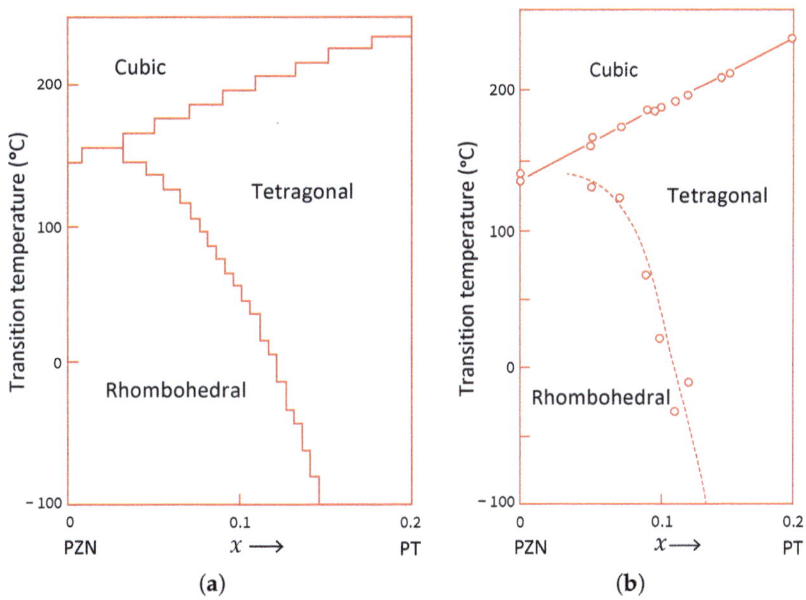

Figure 4.9. Phase diagram for $(1-x)Pb(Zn_{1/3}Nb_{2/3})O_{3-}xPbTiO_3$; (**a**) calculated and (**b**) experimental. Source: [2] ©Uchino, K. *Ferroelectric Devices*, 2nd ed. CRC Press, 2010; p. 77. Reproduced by permission of Taylor & Francis Group.

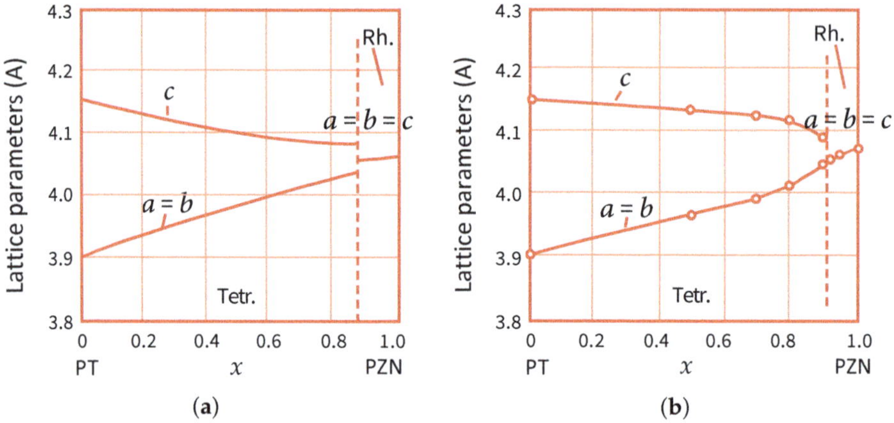

Figure 4.10. Lattice parameters for (1 − x)PZN-xPT; (**a**) calculated and (**b**) experimental. Source: Source: [2] ©Uchino, K. *Ferroelectric Devices*, 2nd ed. CRC Press, 2010; p. 78. Reproduced by permission of Taylor & Francis Group.

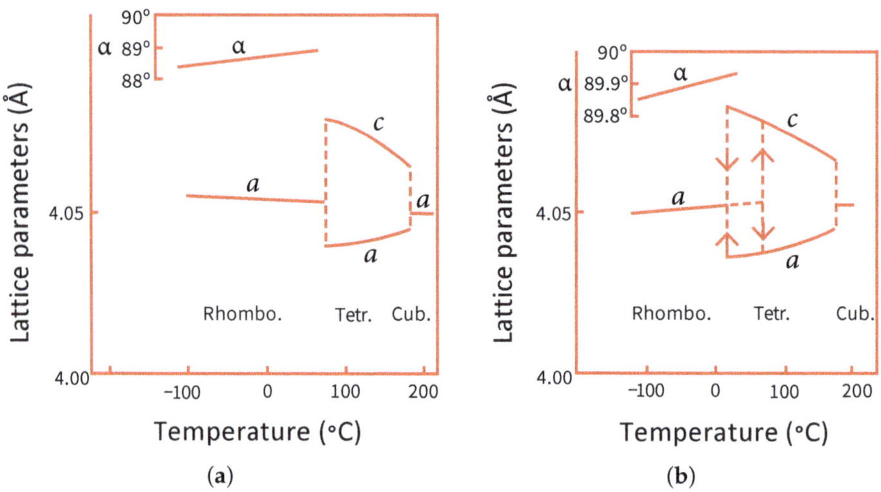

Figure 4.11. Temperature dependence of lattice parameters for 0.91PZN-0.09PT through two successive phase transitions; (**a**) theory and (**b**) measurement. Source: [2] ©Uchino, K. *Ferroelectric Devices*, 2nd ed. CRC Press, 2010; p. 78. Reproduced by permission of Taylor & Francis Group.

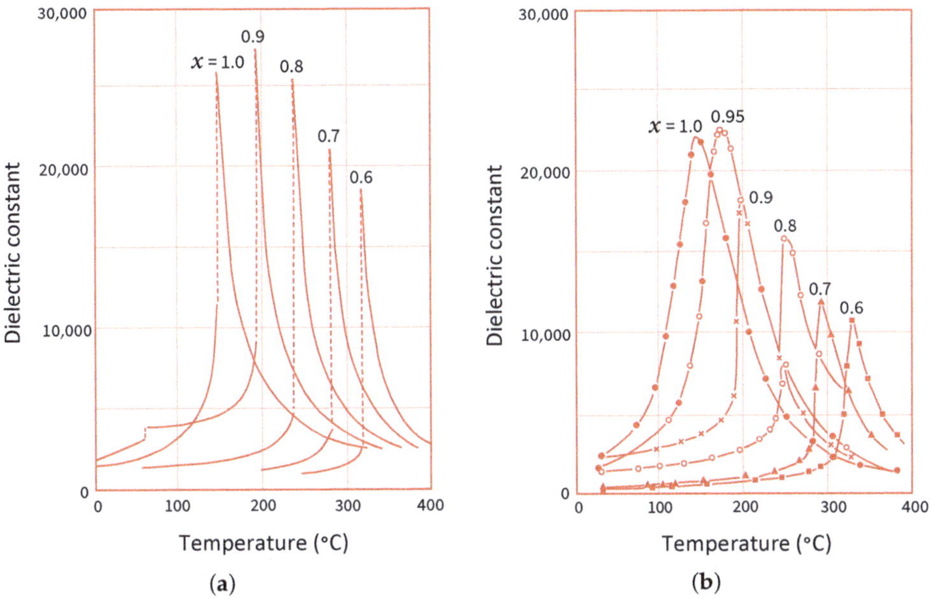

Figure 4.12. Temperature dependence of dielectric constant for xPZN − (1 − x)PT; (**a**) calculated and (**b**) experimental. Source: [2] ©Uchino, K. *Ferroelectric Devices*, 2nd ed. CRC Press, 2010; p. 79. Reproduced by permission of Taylor & Francis Group.

4.5. Phenomenology of Antiferroelectricity

4.5.1. Antiferroelectrics

The previous sections dealt with the case in which the directions of the spontaneous dipoles are parallel to each other in a crystal ("polar crystal"). In this section, we handle anti-parallel orientation, which lowers the "dipole–dipole interaction energy" ("antipolar" or "antiferroelectric" crystals). Figure 4.13 displays the orientation of the spontaneous electric dipoles in an antipolar state in comparison with a nonpolar and a polar state. In an antipolar crystal, where the free energy of an antipolar state does not differ appreciably from that of a polar state, the application of an external electric field or mechanical stress may cause a transition of the dipole orientation to a parallel state. Such crystals are called "antiferroelectrics".

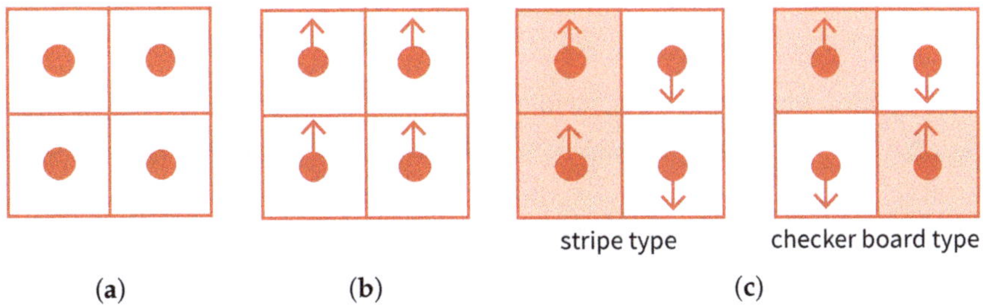

Figure 4.13. Schematic arrangement of the spontaneous dipoles in nonpolar (**a**), polar (**b**), and antipolar (**c**) materials. Source: Figure by author.

Figure 4.14 illustrates the relationship between E (applied electric field) and P (induced polarization) in paraelectric, ferroelectric, and antiferroelectric phases. In a paraelectric phase, the P–E relation is almost linear; in a ferroelectric phase, there appears to be a hysteresis caused by the transition of the spontaneous polarization between the positive and negative directions (see Figure 4.5); in an antiferroelectric phase, in a low electric field, the induced polarization is proportional to E (due to zero net spontaneous polarization), and when E exceeds a certain value E_{crit}, the crystal becomes ferroelectric (i.e., electric-field-induced phase transition), and the polarization shows hysteresis with respect to E. After removal of the electric field, the crystal returns to its antipolar state; hence, no spontaneous polarization can be observed as a whole. This is called a "double hysteresis curve".

We previously introduced the double-hysteresis in the first-order phase transition in Figure 4.5, where the paraelectric (zero spontaneous dipole) to ferroelectric phase transition is associated. Though the hysteresis curve is apparently similar, the double-hysteresis in this antiferroelectric is associated with the antipolar spontaneous dipole moment reoriented or realigned under a high electric field.

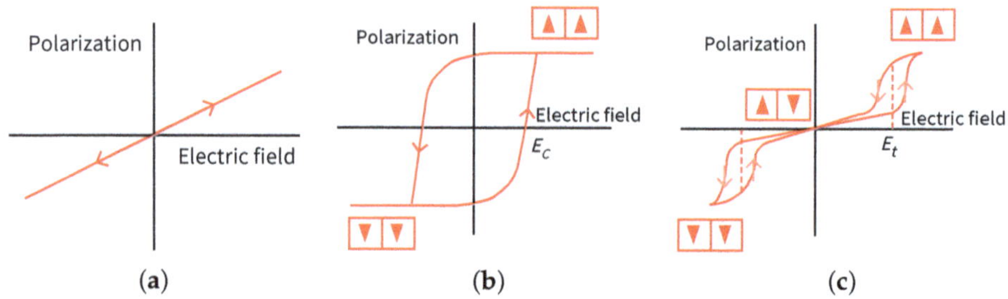

Figure 4.14. Polarization vs. electric field hysteresis curves in paraelectric (**a**), ferroelectric (**b**), and antiferroelectric (**c**) materials. Source: Figure by author.

4.5.2. Phenomenology of Antiferroelectrics

Here, we discuss the introduction of electrostrictive coupling to the Kittel's free energy expression for antiferroelectrics [29]. Though Suzuki and Okada discussed the antiferroelectric phenomenology, it was not sufficient because they did not include the sublattice coupling [30]. The simplest model for antiferroelectrics is the "one-dimensional two-sublattice model". It treats the coordinates as 1D, and a superlattice (twice the unit lattice) is formed from two neighboring sublattices, each having a sublattice polarization P_a and P_b. In comparison with the previous "intra-coupling" (or self-coupling) of single polarization P, the sublattice coupling handles the next-nearest-neighbor "inter-coupling". The state $P_a = P_b$ represents the ferroelectric phase, while $P_a = -P_b$, the antiferroelectric phase. For the electrostrictive effect, if we ignore the coupling between the two sublattices, the strains from the two sublattices are $QP_a{}^2$ and $QP_b{}^2$, respectively (assuming equal electrostrictive constants Q for both sublattices), leading to the total strain of the crystal, represented by

$$x = Q(P_a{}^2 + P_b{}^2)/2. \tag{4.76}$$

Uchino also modeled the sublattice coupling for the electrostrictive effect, since antiferroelectricity originates from the coupling between the sublattices [6]. The coupling term for the electrostriction Ω is introduced in the following form:

$$\begin{aligned} G_1 &= (1/4)\alpha(P_a^2 + P_b^2) + (1/8)\beta(P_a^4 + P_b^4) + (1/12)\gamma(P_a^6 + P_b^6) \\ &+(1/2)\eta P_a P_b - (1/2)\chi_T p^2 + (1/2)Q_h(P_a^2 + P_b^2 + 2\Omega P_a P_b)p, \end{aligned} \quad (4.77)$$

in which the hydrostatic pressure p is employed in this simple 1D model, χ_T is the isothermal compressibility, and Q_h ($=Q_{11} + 2Q_{12}$) and $Q_h \cdot \Omega$ are the intra- and inter-coupling electrostrictive constants. Introducing the transformations $P_F = (P_a + P_b)/2$ and $P_A = (P_a - P_b)/2$ leads to the following expression:

$$\begin{aligned} G_1 &= (1/2)\alpha(P_F^2 + P_A^2) + (1/4)\beta(P_F^4 + P_A^4 + 6\,P_F^2 P_A^2) \\ &+(1/6)\gamma(P_F^6 + P_A^6 + 15P_F^4 P_A^2 + 15P_F^2 P_A^4) + (1/2)\eta(P_F^2 - P_A^2) \\ &-(1/2)\chi_T p^2 + Q_h[P_F^2 + P_A^2 + \Omega(P_F^2 - P_A^2)]p. \end{aligned} \quad (4.78)$$

The dielectric and elastic relationships for the intensive parameters are as follows:

$$\begin{aligned} \partial G_1/\partial P_F = E = P_F[\alpha + \eta + 2Q_h(1+\Omega)p + \beta P_F^2 + 3\beta P_A^2 \\ + \gamma P_F^4 + 10\gamma P_F^2 P_A^2 + 5\gamma P_A^4], \end{aligned} \quad (4.79)$$

$$\partial G_1/\partial P_A = 0 = P_A[\alpha - \eta + 2Q_h(1-\Omega)p + \beta P_A^2 + 3\beta P_F^2 + \gamma P_A^4 + 10\gamma P_F^2 P_A^2 + 5\gamma P_F^4], \quad (4.80)$$

$$\partial G_1/\partial p = \Delta V/V = -\chi_T p + Q_h(1+\Omega)P_F^2 + Q_h(1-\Omega)P_A^2. \quad (4.81)$$

Hence, the induced volume change in the paraelectric phase can be related to the induced "ferroelectric" polarization by the following formula:

$$(\Delta V/V)_{ind} = Q_h(1+\Omega)P_{F,ind}^2. \quad (4.82)$$

On the contrary, below the phase transition temperature, which, for antiferroelectrics, is usually called the "Neel temperature", the spontaneous volume strain and the spontaneous antiferroelectric polarization are related as

$$(\Delta V/V)_S = Q_h(1-\Omega)P_{A,S}^2. \quad (4.83)$$

Even if the perovskite crystal shows $Q_h > 0$, in general, the spontaneous volume strain can be positive or negative, depending on the value of Ω ($\Omega < 1$ or $\Omega > 1$), that is, if the inter-sublattice coupling is stronger than the intra-sublattice coupling (i.e., $\Omega > 1$), a volume contraction is observed at the Neel point. This is quite different from ferroelectrics such as $BaTiO_3$ and $PbTiO_3$, which always show a volume expansion at the Curie temperature. Figure 4.15 schematically illustrates the spontaneous strains in 1D form in a crystal for $\Omega > 1$ (stronger inter-coupling). When P_a and P_b are in the parallel configuration (ferroelectric phase), the Ω-term acts to increase the spontaneous strain x_S, in comparison with $Q(P_a^2 + P_b^2)/2$; when they are in the anti-parallel configuration (antiferroelctric phase), the Ω-term acts to decrease the spontaneous strain, in comparison with $Q(P_a^2 + P_b^2)/2$.

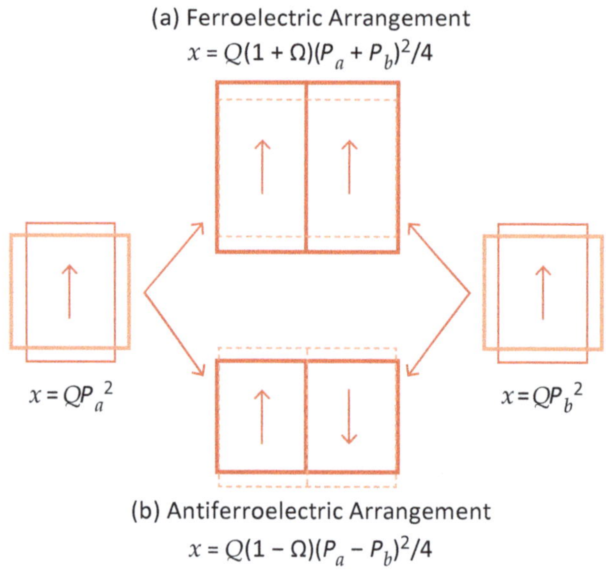

Figure 4.15. Intuitive explanation of the sublattice coupling with respect to electrostriction (for $\Omega > 0$). Source: Figure by author.

4.5.3. Electric Field-Induced Phase Transition: AFE—FE

Suggested from Equations (4.79) and (4.80), we can expect that the ferroelectric state (P_F) becomes more stable than the antiferroelectric state (P_A) under an electric field, because of the potential energy $-P_F E$ formula added onto the elastic Gibbs energy. Accordingly, we can induce the phase transition from antiferroelectric (AFE) to ferroelectric (FE) phase by increasing the applied electric field E, and the double-hysteresis in the P—E relation as shown in Figure 4.14. The isotropic volumetric change associated with the field-induced transition from the antiferro- to ferroelectric phase is estimated by the subtraction between Equations (4.82) and (4.83):

$$(\Delta V/V) = Q_h(1 + \Omega){P_{F,S}}^2 - Q_h(1 - \Omega){P_{A,S}}^2 = 2Q_h\Omega {P_{F,S}}^2. \tag{4.84}$$

Here, we assume that the magnitudes of P_a and P_b do not change drastically through the phase transition; that is, $P_{F,S} \approx P_{A,S}$.

Temperature Dependence of the Phase Transition

The phenomenological model in Section 4.5.2 effectively explains the experimental results for the $PbZrO_3$-based antiferroelectric perovskite crystal and other ceramics [6]. Introduced here are the results on the antiferroelectric ceramic $Pb_{0.99}Nb_{0.02}[(Zr_{0.6}Sn_{0.4})_{1-y}Ti_y]_{0.98}O_3$ [31,32]. Figure 4.16a shows the relation between the electric field and polarization in the AFE ceramic $y = 0.06$ (i.e., $Pb_{0.99}Nb_{0.02}[(Zr_{0.6}Sn_{0.4})_{0.94}$-$Ti_{0.06}]_{0.98}O_3$). The typical double and ferroelectric hysteresis loops are observed at room temperature and −76 °C, respectively, while a transitive shape with humps is observed at intermediate temperatures. The transitive process can be observed more clearly in the strain curve. Figure 4.16b shows the transversely induced strains. The forced transition from AFE to FE at room temperature is characterized by a huge discontinuous extension strain. On the other hand, a typical ferroelectric butterfly-type hysteresis is observed at −76 °C, corresponding to polarization reversal. It is important to note that the strain discontinuities associated with the phase transition have the same positive expansion in both longitudinal and transverse directions with respect to the electric field (i.e., the apparent Poisson's ratio is negative), while the piezostriction is negative and positive in the transverse (d_{31}) and longitudinal (d_{33}) directions, respectively, which will be further discussed in Section 4.5.4.

A sort of "shape memory effect" is observed on this loop at −4 °C. That is, when a large electric field is applied to an annealed AFE specimen, a massive strain $\Delta L/L$ of about 7×10^{-4} is produced and maintained metastably, even after the field is removed. After applying a small reverse field or thermal annealing, the original AFE shape is observed. In comparison with conventional "shape memory metal", the shape change is controlled by the electric field rather than the external stress or temperature.

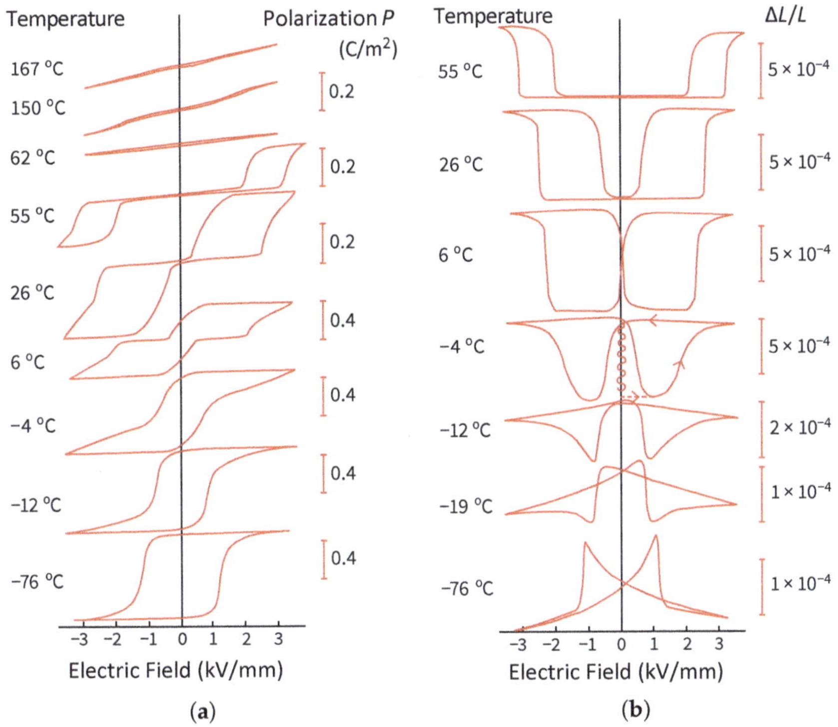

Figure 4.16. Polarization (**a**) and transverse elastic strain (**b**) induced by electric field for several temperatures in PNZST (y = 0.06). Source: Figure by author, adapted from [33].

Temperature Dependence of the Phase Transition

The reverse critical field related to the FE–AFE transition is plotted with solid lines in the phase diagram for the sample with y = 0.06 in Figure 4.17a, in which the temperature-field points are based on the measurements in permittivity, polarization and strain [32]. In the temperature range from −30 °C to 10 °C, a hump-type hysteresis in the field vs. polarization curve and an inverse hysteresis in the field-induced strain are observed: this has often previously been misinterpreted as another AFE phase, different from the phase above 10 °C. The annealed state below −30 °C down to −200 °C is AFE. However, once the FE state is induced, the AFE phase is never observed during a cycle of the rising and falling electric field. The critical field line for the FE-to-AFE transition (the solid line) in the temperature range −30 °C to 10 °C intersects the coercive field line for the + FE to − FE reversal (the dashed line) below −30 °C. Figure 4.17b visualizes a 3D phase diagram for understanding the bifurcation and the AFE–FE transformation hysteresis.

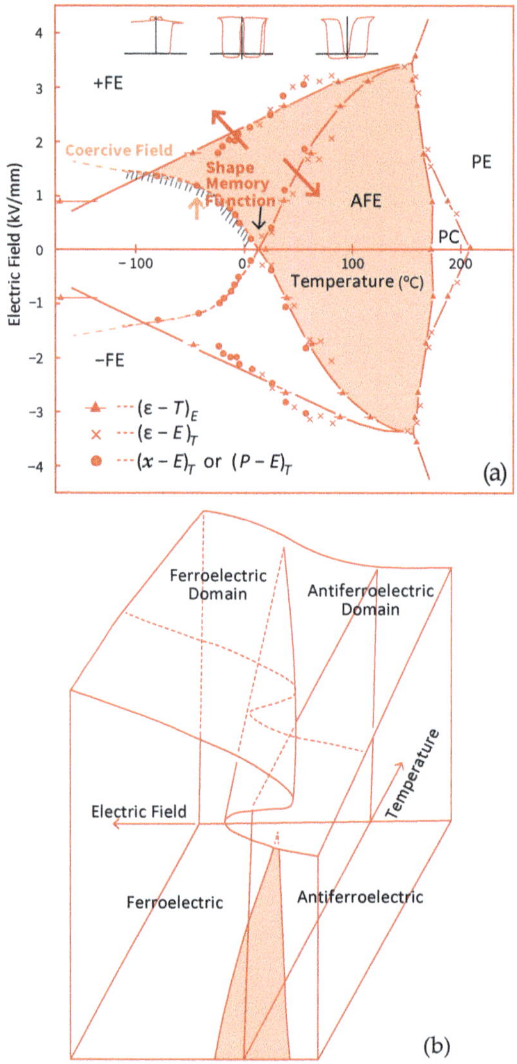

Figure 4.17. (**a**) Phase diagram with hysteresis on the temperature vs. bias electric field plane for the $Pb_{0.99}Nb_{0.02}[(Zr_{0.6}Sn_{0.4})_{0.94}Ti_{0.06}]_{0.98}O_3$ ceramic. (**b**) A schematic 3D view for understanding the bifurcation and the AFE–FE transformation hysteresis. Source: Figure by author, based on data from [32].

Composition Dependence of the Induced Strain

The strain curves induced transversely by the external field at room temperature for samples of several different compositions are shown in Figure 4.18 [32]. The molar fraction of Ti, y, is increased from 0.06 (Figure 4.18a) to 0.065 (Figure 4.18c). The initial state was obtained by annealing at 150 °C, which is above the Curie (or Neel) temperature for all the samples. A typical double hysteresis curve (Type I) is observed in the sample containing $y = 0.06$ (Figure 4.18a). Large jumps in the strain are observed at the forced phase transitions from the AFE to the FE phase ($\Delta L/L = 8 \times 10^{-4}$). In comparison, the strain change with electric field in either the AFE or FE state is rather small: this suggests a possible application for the material as a "digital displacement transducer", having OFF/ON displacement states. The difference in the strain between that occurring in the initial state and that appearing in a cyclic process at $E = 0$ kV/cm is also noteworthy, which is explained by the "antiferroelectric domain reorientation" via the field-induced phase transition from AFE to FE [31].

In the sample with $y = 0.063$, a Ti concentration slightly higher than that just described, the field-induced FE phase will not return to the AFE state, even after decreasing the field to zero (Type II, Figure 4.18b): this is called "memorizing" the FE strain state. In order to obtain the initial AFE state, a small reverse bias field is required. On the contrary, Figure 4.18c shows the strain curve for the sample with $y = 0.065$, which exhibits irreversible characteristics during an electric field cycle (Type III). The initial antiferroelectric strain state can only be recovered by thermal annealing up to 50 °C.

These strain curve data can construct a phase diagram of the system $Pb_{0.99}Nb_{0.02}[(Zr_{0.6}Sn_{0.4})_{1-y}Ti_y]_{0.98}O_3$ at room temperature with respect to the composition y and the applied electric field E (Figure 4.19). If the Ti concentration of the horizontal axis is redefined in terms of temperature and evaluated in the opposite direction, this phase diagram is topologically the same as the phase diagram of Figure 4.17 (if the horizontal axis is reversed). The key feature of this phase diagram is the existence of the three phases, namely the AFE, the positively poled FE (+FE), and the negatively poled FE (−FE) phases, the boundaries of which are characterized by the two transition lines corresponding to rising and falling electric fields; hysteresis originated from "bifurcation", similar to Figure 4.17b.

The composition regions I and IV exhibit the typical double hysteresis and ferroelectric "butterfly domain reversal", respectively. The shape memory effect is observed in regions II and III. It is important to consider the magnitude of the electric field associated with the +FE → AFE transition (notice the direction of the arrow). Let us consider the transition process under an inverse bias field after the +FE is induced by the positive electric field. If the magnitude of the field for the +FE → AFE transition is smaller than the coercive field for +FE → −FE (region II, $0.0625 < y < 0.065$), the AFE phase appears once under a small inverse field, then the −FE phase is induced at the AFE → −FE transition field. In this case, the shape memory is reversible to the initial state only with the application of a reverse electric field (Type II); this is very useful! On the other hand, if the +FE → −FE coercive field is smaller than the +FE → AFE field (region III, $0.0625 < y < 0.085$), the domain reversal to −FE appears without passing through the AFE phase. The initial state can be obtained by thermally annealing up to 50–70 °C (Type III).

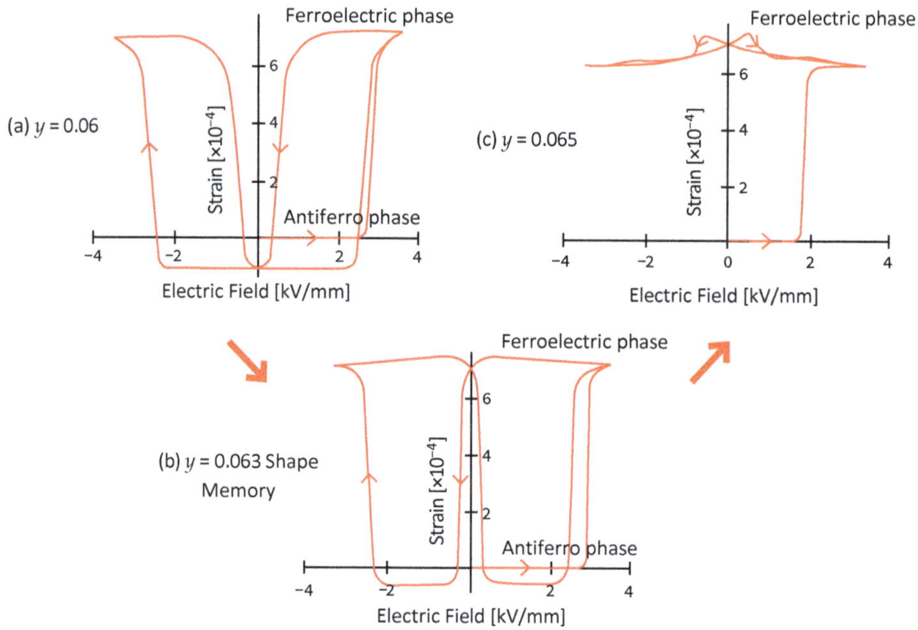

Figure 4.18. Electric-field-induced strain in $Pb_{0.99}Nb_{0.02}[(Zr_{0.6}Sn_{0.4})_{1\text{-}y}Ti_y]_{0.98}O_3$ antiferroelectric ceramics. Source: Figure by author, adapted from [33].

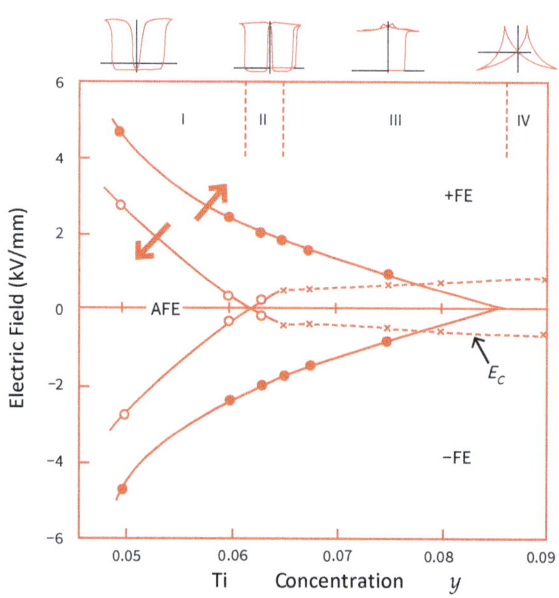

Figure 4.19. Phase diagram of $Pb_{0.99}Nb_{0.02}[(Zr_{0.6}Sn_{0.4})_{1-y}Ti_y]_{0.98}O_3$ at room temperature with respect to the composition y and the applied electric field E. Source: Figure by author, adapted from [33].

4.5.4. 3D Antiferroelectric Phenomenology

We expand the phenomenology to a three-dimensional formulation [34]. Considering the simplest case of a tetragonal spontaneous distortion of the primitive perovskite cell, let us start by reducing the 3D polarization (P_1 P_2 P_3) to a simple form (0 0 P_3). The elastic Gibbs free energy is represented by using two-sublattice polarization P_a and P_b, ad stress X under a cubical supposition that $s_{33}{}^E = s_{11}{}^E$, $s_{31}{}^E = s_{12}{}^E$, etc., for simplicity:

$$\begin{aligned} G_1 &= \tfrac{1}{4}\alpha(P_{a3}{}^2 + P_{b3}{}^2) + 1/8\beta(P_{a3}{}^4 + P_{b3}{}^4) + 1/12\gamma(P_{a3}{}^6 + P_{b3}{}^6) + \tfrac{1}{2}\eta P_{a3}P_{b3} \\ &- \tfrac{1}{2}s_{33}{}^E(X_1{}^2 + X_2{}^2 + X_3{}^2) - s_{31}{}^E(X_1X_2 + X_2X_3 + X_3X_1) - \tfrac{1}{2}s_{44}{}^E(X_4{}^2 + X_5{}^2 + X_6{}^2) \\ &- \tfrac{1}{2}Q_{33}(P_{a3}{}^2 + P_{b3}{}^2)X_3 - \tfrac{1}{2}Q_{31}(P_{a3}{}^2 + P_{b3}{}^2)(X_1 + X_2) - q_{33}P_{a3}P_{b3}X_3 - q_{31}P_{a3}P_{b3}(X_1 + X_2). \end{aligned} \quad (4.85)$$

Here, Q_{33} and Q_{31} denote the conventional longitudinal and transversal electrostrictive coefficients (intra-sublattice coupling), and q_{33} and q_{31} are the corresponding inter-sublattice coupling parameters (the ratio q/Q was denoted as Ω in the previous section). Introducing the transformations

$$P_{F3} = (P_{a3} + P_{b3})/2, P_{A3} = (P_{a3} - P_{b3})/2, \quad (4.86)$$

leads to four types of stable states under zero applied electric field: nonpolar ($P_{F3} = P_{A3} = 0$), polar ($P_{F3} \neq 0$, $P_{A3} = 0$), antipolar ($P_{F3} = 0$, $P_{A3} \neq 0$), and semipolar ($P_{F3} \neq 0$, $P_{A3} \neq 0$) states. The spontaneous polarization and strains derived from the free energy function are summarized as follows for the ferroelectric and antiferroelectric states:

- Ferroelectric:

$$\begin{aligned} P_{A3} &= 0 \\ P_{F3}{}^2 &= [-\beta + \{1/4\beta^2 - 4\gamma(T - T_C(X))/\varepsilon_0 C\}^{1/2}]/2\gamma, \end{aligned} \quad (4.87)$$

$$T_C(X) = T_C + 2\varepsilon_0 C\{(Q_{33} + q_{33})X_3 + (Q_{31} + q_{31})(X_1 + X_2)\}, \quad (4.88)$$

$$x_3 = s_{33}{}^E X_3 + s_{31}{}^E(X_1 + X_2) + (Q_{33} + q_{33})P_{F3}, \quad (4.89)$$

$$x_1 = s_{33}{}^E X_1 + s_{31}{}^E(X_2 + X_3) + (Q_{31} + q_{31})P_{F3}{}^2, \quad (4.90)$$

$$(\Delta V/V) = (s_{33}{}^E + 2s_{31}{}^E)(X_1 + X_2 + X_3) + (Q_{33} + 2Q_{31} + q_{33} + 2q_{31})P_{F3}{}^2. \quad (4.91)$$

- Antiferroelectric:

$$\begin{aligned} P_{F3} &= 0 \\ P_{A3}{}^2 &= [-\beta + \{1/4\beta^2 - 4\gamma(T - T_N(X))/\varepsilon_0 C\}^{1/2}]/2\gamma, \end{aligned} \quad (4.92)$$

$$T_N(X) = T_N + 2\varepsilon_0 C\{(Q_{33} - q_{33})X_3 + (Q_{31} - q_{31})(X_1 + X_2)\}, \quad (4.93)$$

$$x_3 = s_{33}{}^E X_3 + s_{31}{}^E(X_1 + X_2) + (Q_{33} - q_{33})P_{A3}{}^2, \quad (4.94)$$

$$x_1 = s_{33}{}^E X_1 + s_{31}{}^E (X_2 + X_3) + (Q_{31} - q_{31}) P_{A3}{}^2, \quad (4.95)$$

$$(\Delta V/V) = (s_{33}{}^E + 2s_{31}{}^E)(X_1 + X_2 + X_3) + (Q_{33} + 2Q_{31} - q_{33} - 2q_{31}) P_{A3}{}^2. \quad (4.96)$$

Here, T_C and T_N are the Curie and Neel temperatures, respectively, and C is the Curie–Weiss constant. Note again that we presume the cubical symmetry physical parameter components.

Estimation of q_{33} and q_{31}

The values of q_{33} and q_{31} can be obtained from the strain changes associated with the electric-field-induced and thermally induced phase transitions. The spontaneous strains generated at the phase transition from paraelectric to antiferroelectric are described as

$$x_3 = (Q_{33} - q_{33}) P_{A3}{}^2, \quad (4.97)$$

$$x_1 = (Q_{31} - q_{31}) P_{A3}{}^2. \quad (4.98)$$

On the contrary, the strain changes associated with the field-induced transition from antiferroelectric to ferroelectric are given by

$$\Delta x_3 = (Q_{33} + q_{33}) P_{F3}{}^2 - (Q_{33} - q_{33}) P_{A3}{}^2 = 2q_{33} P_{F3}{}^2, \quad (4.99)$$

$$\Delta x_1 = (Q_{31} + q_{31}) P_{F3}{}^2 - (Q_{31} - q_{31}) P_{A3}{}^2 = 2q_{31} P_{F3}{}^2. \quad (4.100)$$

Here, we have assumed that $P_{F3} \approx P_{A3}$ because only the flipping of polarizations P_a and P_b would occur at the transition. Let us estimate the q_{33} and q_{31} values using experimental strains and polarization data for $Pb_{0.99}Nb_{0.02}[(Zr_{0.6}Sn_{0.4})_{0.94}Ti_{0.06}]_{0.98}O_3$. The field-induced change in lattice parameters is plotted in Figure 4.20a [35]. The forced transition from the AFE to the FE phase gives rise to the simultaneous increase in a and c in the perovskite unit cell, thereby keeping the tetragonality, c/a, nearly constant. Since the angle γ makes only a negligible contribution to the volume change, the strain change at the phase transition is nearly isotropic with a magnitude of $\Delta L/L = 8.5 \times 10^{-4}$. It is noteworthy that this $\Delta L/L$ is the same observed in Figure 4.18a macroscopically. We observe minor changes in the parameters c, c/a, and γ between AFE–FE on-set and FE–AFE off-set electric fields. The intensity change in the X-ray reflections with the application of an electric field suggests that the spontaneous polarization in the FE state lies in the c-plane, parallel with the perovskite [110] axis, and that the sublattice polarization configuration in the AFE state is very similar to that of $PbZrO_3$ [36]. Figure 4.20b illustrates the simplest two-sublattice model.

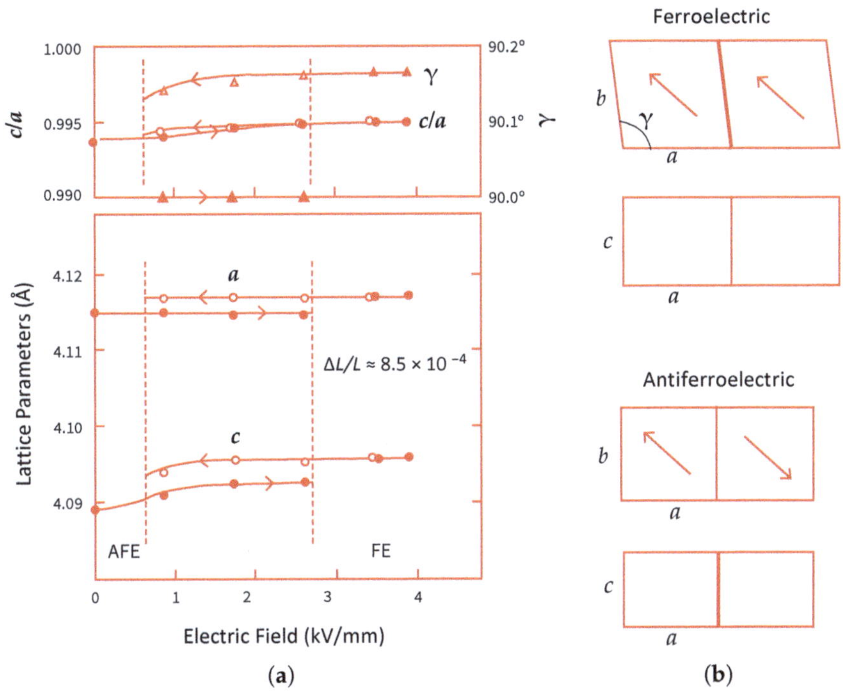

Figure 4.20. (**a**) Variation of lattice parameters with bias electric field at room temperature ($y = 0.06$). (**b**) Two-sublattice model of the polarization configuration for the AFE and FE states. Source: Figure by author, adapted from [33].

Using the above data and $(\delta T_N/\delta p)$ of the $PbZrO_3$-based sample [31], we derive:

$P_{F3} = P_{A3} = 0.4\ (\mathrm{C{\cdot}m^{-2}})$,

$\Delta x_3 = \Delta x_1 = 8 \times 10^{-4}$,

$Q_h = Q_{33} + 2Q_{31} = 0.5 \times 10^{-2}\ (\mathrm{m^4{\cdot}C^{-2}})$,

$q_h = q_{33} + 2q_{31} = 0.9 \times 10^{-2}\ (\mathrm{m^4{\cdot}C^{-2}})$.

We then derive the following parameter values:

$Q_{33} = 1.5 \times 10^{-2}\ (\mathrm{m^4{\cdot}C^{-2}})$, $Q_{31} = -0.5 \times 10^{-2}\ (\mathrm{m^4{\cdot}C^{-2}})$,

$q_{33} = 0.3 \times 10^{-2}\ (\mathrm{m^4{\cdot}C^{-2}})$, $q_{31} = 0.3 \times 10^{-2}\ (\mathrm{m^4{\cdot}C^{-2}})$.

It is noteworthy that q_{33} and q_{31} have the same positive sign (accidentally almost the same value), while Q_{33} and Q_{31} have the opposite sign with a "piezoelectric Poisson's" ratio of 1/3. Figure 4.21 illustrates the spontaneous strains in a crystal schematically for $\Omega > 0$ (you may interpret $\Omega = q_{33}/Q_{33}$ in the figure). When P_a and P_b are in the parallel configuration (ferroelectric phase), the Ω-term acts to increase the strain x_S; when they are in the anti-parallel configuration (antiferroelctric phase), the Ω-term acts to decrease the strain. The difference from Figure 4.15 (1D model) can be found in the isotropic volumetric expansion due the positive value of sublattice electrostrictive coupling coefficient q_{31}.

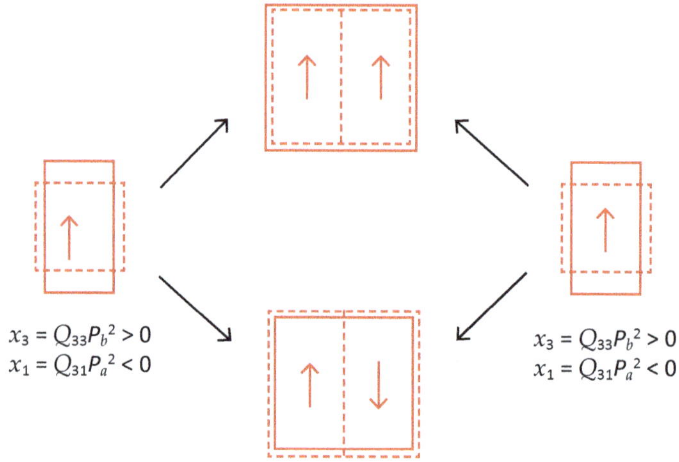

Figure 4.21. Spontaneous strain changes associated with sublattice interactions in the electrostrictive effect. Illustration is drawn in the case of q_{33} and $q_{31} > 0$. Source: Source: Figure by author, adapted from [34].

Piezoelectric Anisotropy Related to Sublattice Coupling

The PZT system possesses both ferroelectric and antiferroelectric phases depending on the composition. Thus, let us consider the piezoelectric coefficients in the "ferroelectric state" with the "sublattice polarization" coupling. Under a small external field E modulation, the polarization is given by

$$P_{F3} = P_{F3,S} + \varepsilon_0\varepsilon_3 E_3, \tag{4.101}$$

where ε_3 is the relative permittivity. Using Equations (4.89) and (4.90), longitudinal and transversal strains are represented as

$$x_3 = (Q_{33} + q_{33})P_{F3,S}^2 + 2(Q_{33} + q_{33})\varepsilon_0\varepsilon_3 P_{F3,S}E_3 + (Q_{33} + q_{33})\varepsilon_0^2\varepsilon_3^2 E_3^2, \tag{4.102}$$

$$x_1 = (Q_{31} + q_{31})P_{F3,S}^2 + 2(Q_{31} + q_{31})\varepsilon_0\varepsilon_3 P_{F3,S}E_3 + (Q_{31} + q_{31})\varepsilon_0^2\varepsilon_3^2 E_3^2. \tag{4.103}$$

The first term describes the spontaneous strains, and Figure 4.21 illustrates the spontaneous strain changes due to the sublattice interactions in the case of $q_{33}, q_{31} > 0$. When the spontaneous polarization $P_{F3,S}$ exists, the third term (pure electrostriction) may be negligibly small in comparison with the second term (piezostriction), and the piezoelectric d coefficients are denoted as

$$d_{33} = 2(Q_{33} + q_{33})\varepsilon_0\varepsilon_3 P_{F3,S}, \tag{4.104}$$

$$d_{31} = 2(Q_{31} + q_{31})\varepsilon_0\varepsilon_3 P_{F3,S}. \tag{4.105}$$

Different from the normal formula, $d_{3i} = 2Q_{3i}\varepsilon_0\varepsilon_3 P_{F3,S}$, the above equations include the sublattice coupling q_{3i} parameters. Using the above physical parameters in Subsection Estimation of q_{33} and q_{31} and $\varepsilon_3 = 600$, we can evaluate $d_{33} = 72 \times 10^{-12}$ m/V and $d_{31} = -8 \times 10^{-12}$ m/V.

This estimated value is close to the experimentally obtained $d_{31} = -7 \times 10^{-12}$ m/V, as shown in Figure 4.22, though we use a rough isotropic elastic approximation such as $s_{33}{}^E = s_{11}{}^E$, $s_{31}{}^E = s_{12}{}^E$, etc. The "piezoelectric Poisson's" ratio d_{31}/d_{33} is given by $(Q_{31} + q_{31})/(Q_{33} + q_{33})$, and it can differ from the usual value Q_{31}/Q_{33} ($\approx -1/3$) of the normal ferroelectrics, owing to the values of q_{33} and q_{31}. Using the above values again, we can estimate $d_{31}/d_{33} = -(1/9)$, that is, huge anisotropy.

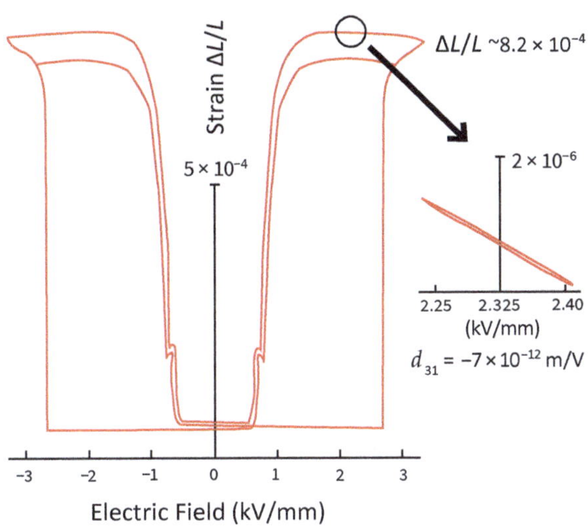

Figure 4.22. Piezoelectric d_{31} measurement in the induced ferroelectric phase in $Pb_{0.99}Nb_{0.02}[(Zr_{0.6}Sn_{0.4})_{0.94}Ti_{0.06}]_{0.98}O_3$. Source: Figure by author, adapted from [37].

Regarding the anisotropy of the electromechanical coupling factors k_t and k_p, which are represented as

$$k_t = \frac{d_{33}}{\sqrt{s_{33}^E \varepsilon_{33}^X}} \sqrt{\frac{\varepsilon_{33}^x}{c_{33}^D}}, \tag{4.106}$$

$$k_p = \frac{d_{31}}{\sqrt{s_{11}^E \varepsilon_{33}^X}} \sqrt{\frac{2}{1 - \sigma}}. \tag{4.107}$$

Then, supposing again that $s_{33}^E \approx s_{11}^E$, $\sqrt{\frac{\varepsilon_{33}^X}{c_{33}^D}} \approx 0.75$, and $\sigma \approx 1/3$, we obtain

$$k_t/k_p \approx 0.5 d_{33}/d_{31}. \tag{4.108}$$

For the antiferroelectric-based piezoelectrics, taking into account the above discussion $d_{31}/d_{33} = -(1/9)$, k_t/k_p will be equal to 4.5, much larger than the normal PZT value around 2.0.

Table 4.3 lists several anisotropic piezoelectric data for field-biased PNZSTs, $PbZrO_3$- and $PbTiO_3$-based ceramics [37,38]. The electromechanical coupling factors k_t (thickness mode) and k_p (planar mode) range from 0.5 to 0.6 and from 0.05 to 0.15, respectively, and the anisotropy (k_t/k_p) reaches more than 4.0. In contrast, the ratio (k_t/k_p) for the intermediate composition of the solid solution Pb(Zr,Ti)O_3 will not exceed 2.5, which is also listed in Table 4.3 [37].

Table 4.3. Anisotropic piezoelectric constants in field-biased PNZSTs, $PbZrO_3$- and $PbTiO_3$-based ceramics.

Composition	Electromechanical Coupling Factor		
	k_t	k_p	k_t/k_p
$Pb_{0.99}Nb_{0.02}[(Zr_{0.6}Sn_{0.4})_{0.937}Ti_{0.063}]_{0.98}O_3$ under 22.5 kV/cm	0.456	0.114	4.00
$Pb_{0.99}Nb_{0.02}[(Zr_{0.6}Sn_{0.4})_{0.936}Ti_{0.064}]_{0.98}O_3$ under 22.5 kV/cm	0.501	0.123	4.15
$Pb_{0.99}Nb_{0.02}[(Zr_{0.6}Sn_{0.4})_{0.934}Ti_{0.066}]_{0.98}O_3$ under 22.5 kV/cm	0.622	0.137	4.56
$Pb_{0.99}Nb_{0.02}[(Zr_{0.6}Sn_{0.4})_{0.920}Ti_{0.080}]_{0.98}O_3$ under 22.5 kV/cm	0.575	0.145	4.02
$Pb_{0.99}Nb_{0.02}[(Zr_{0.6}Sn_{0.4})_{0.910}Ti_{0.090}]_{0.98}O_3$ under 22.5 kV/cm	0.564	0.136	4.15
$Pb(Zr_{0.9}Ti_{0.1})O_3$ [38]	0.325	0.072	4.52
$(Pb_{0.8}Ca_{0.2})TiO_3$ [39]	0.530	0.050	10.60
$Pb(Zr_{0.5}Ti_{0.5})O_3$ [40]	0.752	0.388	1.938

Source: Table by author, based on data from [37].

It is interesting to note that most of the PZT-based compositions exhibiting "piezoelectric anisotropy" are closely related with "antiferroelectricity" or "sublattice" structure. Some of them based on $PbZrO_3$ are originally antiferroelectric at a low temperature or even at room temperature, and the ferroelectricity is induced under a high electric field applied (i.e., poling process). Ca-modified $PbTiO_3$ [$(Pb_{0.8}Ca_{0.2})TiO_3$] ceramics [39] possess huge anisotropy with a crystallographic superlattice structure observed in the annealed state, suggesting an antiferroelectric-like sublattice structure.

As a final remark, even if the sample is not originally antiferroelectric, the perovskite-type piezoelectric ceramics with large piezoelectric anisotropy ($k_t/k_p > 3$) may possess rather large "sublattice dipole coupling" as the microscopic origin.

4.6. Phenomenology of AFE–FE Solid Solution

A phenomenological theory for the solid solutions systems between the ferroelectric $Pb(Fe_{2/3}W_{1/3})O_3$ and antiferroelectric $Pb(M_{1/2}W_{1/2})O_3$ (M = Mn, Co, Ni) compositions is introduced in this section. These solid solution systems have been investigated to discover new multifunctional (ferromagnetic–ferroelectric) materials [22]. In this section, only ferroelectric properties are focused. The phase diagram of experimentally determined $Pb(Fe_{2/3}W_{1/3})O_3$- $Pb(M_{1/2}W_{1/2})O_3$ (M = Mn, Co, Ni) is shown in Figure 4.23a [27]. For mathematical simplicity, we introduce the second-order phase transition treatment [9].

We take Kittel's free energy expression in the 1D two-sublattice model for a ferro- or antiferroelectric crystal, analogous to Equation (4.85) with an $-EP$ potential energy term to discuss the electric field dependence of properties:

$$G_i = \alpha_i(T)(P_a{}^2 + P_b{}^2) + 1/2\beta_i(P_a{}^4 + P_b{}^4) + \eta_i P_a P_b + \zeta_i\,(P_a{}^2 + P_b{}^2)P_a P_b - E(P_a + P_b). \quad (4.109)$$

Here, $i = 1$ and 2 denote the suffixes for $Pb(Fe_{2/3}W_{1/3})O_3$ and $Pb(M_{1/2}W_{1/2})O_3$, respectively. P_a and P_b are the polarization of the two sublattices, and E is the externally applied electric field. The terms η and ζ are introduced to account for an antiferroelectric and a successive ferroelectric phase transition, respectively [27]. The $P_a{}^2P_b{}^2$ and $(P_a{}^6 + P_b{}^6)$ terms are omitted for simplicity. α is the only coefficient assumed to depend on temperature. Since the solid solution crystal (except the end member $Pb(Fe_{2/3}W_{1/3})O_3$) has the $2 \times 2 \times 2$ ordered structure, it is reasonable to adopt the two-sublattice mode for these systems.

4.6.1. Phenomenological Expression for the Solid Solution

We assume that the Gibbs free energy of the solid solution can be expressed as follows:

$$\begin{aligned} G &= (1 - x)G_1 + xG_2 \\ &= [\alpha_1 + x(\alpha_2 - \alpha_1)](P_a{}^2 + P_b{}^2) + 1/2[\beta_1 + x(\beta_2 - \beta_1)](P_a{}^4 + P_b{}^4) \\ &+ [\eta_1 + x(\eta_2 - \eta_1)]P_aP_b + [\zeta_1 + x(\zeta_2 - \zeta_1)](P_a{}^2 + P_b{}^2)P_aP_b - E(P_a + P_b), \end{aligned} \quad (4.110)$$

where x represents the mole faction of $Pb(M_{1/2}W_{1/2})O_3$. We also assume that the temperature-dependent coefficient α_i is

$$\alpha_i = \alpha_{0i}(T - T_i)[i = 1,2], \quad (4.111)$$

where T_i is the Curie–Weiss temperature, not equal to the actual transition temperature of crystal i, as shown later. Introducing new expressions for the coefficients:

$$\begin{aligned} \alpha(T,x) &= [\alpha_{01} + x(\alpha_{02} - \alpha_{01})](T - T_1) + (T_1 - T_2)\alpha_{02}x = a_0(1 + a_1x)(T - T_1) + a_2x, \\ \beta(x) &= \beta_1 + x(\beta_2 - \beta_1) = \beta_0(x - x_0), \\ \eta(x) &= \eta_1 + x(\eta_2 - \eta_1) = \eta_0(x - x_1), \\ \zeta(x) &= \zeta_1 + x(\zeta_2 - \zeta_1) = \zeta_0(x - x_2), \end{aligned} \quad (4.112)$$

we obtain a simple form of the free energy:

$$G = \alpha(T,x)(P_a{}^2 + P_b{}^2) + 1/2\beta(x)(P_a{}^4 + P_b{}^4) + \eta(x)P_aP_b + \zeta(x)(P_a{}^2 + P_b{}^2)P_aP_b - E(P_a + P_b). \quad (4.113)$$

It is essential to the expression that the physical properties of the solid solution are determined only for the linear combination of the expansion coefficients of the two end-members. Transformations $P = (P_a + P_b)/\sqrt{2}$, $p = (P_a - P_b)/\sqrt{2}$ lead to the following expression:

$$G(T, x, P, p) = (\alpha + \eta/2)P^2 + (\alpha - \eta/2)p^2 + (\beta/4 + \zeta/2)P^4 + (3/2)\beta P^2p^2 + (\beta/4 - \zeta/2)p^4 - EP. \quad (4.114)$$

4.6.2. Stable State under E = 0

The stable state conditions for $E = 0$ which give the minimum free energy in the P–p plane are as follows:

$$\left(\frac{\partial G}{\partial P}\right) = P\left[2\alpha + \eta + (\beta + 2\zeta)P^2 + 3\beta p^2\right] = 0, \quad (4.115)$$

$$\left(\frac{\partial G}{\partial p}\right) = p\left[2\alpha - \eta + (\beta - 2\zeta)P^2 + 3\beta P^2\right] = 0, \quad (4.116)$$

$$\left(\frac{\partial^2 G}{\partial P^2}\right) = (2\alpha + \eta) + 3(\beta + 2\zeta)P^2 + 3\beta p^2 > 0, \quad (4.117)$$

$$\left(\frac{\partial^2 G}{\partial p^2}\right) = (2\alpha - \eta) + 3(\beta - 2\zeta)p^2 + 3\beta P^2 > 0, \quad (4.118)$$

$$f = \left(\frac{\partial^2 G}{\partial P^2}\right)\left(\frac{\partial^2 G}{\partial p^2}\right) - \left(\frac{\partial^2 G}{\partial P \partial p}\right)^2 = \left(\frac{\partial^2 G}{\partial P^2}\right)\left(\frac{\partial^2 G}{\partial p^2}\right) - (6\beta Pp)^2 > 0. \quad (4.119)$$

Four types of polar state are possible from Equations (4.114)–(4.119):

I Nonpolar (Paraelectric)

$$P_S = 0, p_S = 0, \quad 2\alpha + \eta > 0, 2\alpha - \eta > 0, \quad \text{Minimum energy } G_n = 0. \quad (4.120)$$

II Polar (Ferroelectric)

$$P_S{}^2 = -(2\alpha+\eta)/(\beta+2\zeta),\ p_S = 0,$$
$$2\alpha+\eta<0, \left(\frac{\partial^2 G}{\partial p^2}\right) = (2\alpha-\eta) - 3\beta(2\alpha+\eta)/(\beta+2\zeta) > 0, \tag{4.121}$$
$$\text{Minimum energy } G_p = -\frac{1}{4}\frac{(2\alpha+\eta)^2}{(\beta+2\zeta)}.$$

III Antipolar (Antiferroelectric)

$$P_S = 0,\ p_S{}^2 = -(2\alpha-\eta)/(\beta-2\zeta),$$
$$2\alpha-\eta<0, \left(\frac{\partial^2 G}{\partial P^2}\right) = (2\alpha+\eta) - 3\beta(2\alpha-\eta)/(\beta-2\zeta) > 0, \tag{4.122}$$
$$\text{Minimum energy } G_a = -\frac{1}{4}\frac{(2\alpha-\eta)^2}{(\beta-2\zeta)}.$$

IV Semipolar (Ferrielectric)

$$P_S{}^2 = [(\beta-2\zeta)(2\alpha+\eta) - 3\beta(2\alpha-\eta)]/4(2\beta^2+\zeta^2)),$$
$$p_S{}^2 = [(\beta+2\zeta)(2\alpha-\eta) - 3\beta(2\alpha+\eta)]/4(2\beta^2+\zeta^2)), \tag{4.123}$$
$$(\beta+2\zeta)>0, (\beta-2\zeta)>0, f = -16(2\beta^2+\zeta^2\big)P_S{}^2 p_S{}^2.$$

Since $f < 0$ in Equation (4.123), the ferrielectric state is not realized as a stable state (i.e., metastable as the maximum point in these solid solutions.

4.6.3. Permittivity

Inverse permittivity $1/\varepsilon_0\varepsilon_n$ (nonpolar state), $1/\varepsilon_0\varepsilon_p$ (polar state), and $1/\varepsilon_0\varepsilon_a$ (antipolar state), defined as $\left(\frac{\partial E}{\partial P}\right)$, are calculated from Equation (4.114), and they prove to be expressed by the similar formula with Equation (4.117), i.e., for nonpolar, polar, and antipolar phases by

$$1/\varepsilon_0\varepsilon_n = (2\alpha+\eta),$$
$$1/\varepsilon_0\varepsilon_p = -2(2\alpha+\eta), \tag{4.124}$$
$$1/\varepsilon_0\varepsilon_a = (2\alpha+\eta) - 3\,\beta(2\alpha-\eta)/(\beta-2\zeta).$$

4.6.4. Phase Transition Temperature

Since the equations $(2\alpha+\eta)=0$ or $(2\alpha-\eta)=0$ are realized at the paraelectric–ferroelectric or antiferroelectric transition temperatures, respectively, we can derive the composition x dependence of the transition temperature:

(a) $x < x_1$: paraelectric – ferroelectric transition

$$T_C = T_1 - \left[a_2 x + \left(\frac{1}{2}\right)\eta_0(x-x_1)\right]/a_0(1+a_1 x), \tag{4.125}$$

(b) $x > x_1$: paraelectric – antiferroelectric transition

$$T_N = T_1 - \left[a_2 x - \left(\frac{1}{2}\right)\eta_0(x - x_1)\right] / a_0(1 + a_1 x). \quad (4.126)$$

It is noticeable that the prefixed signs of $\eta(x)$ are different in Equations (4.125) and (4.126), and $\eta(x)$ itself changes sign at $x = x_1$, which leads to a transition temperature curve anomaly (e.g., sometimes, the transition temperature is a minimum) at $x = x_1$. The relation $0 < x_1 (= -\eta_1/(\eta_2 - \eta_1)) < 1$ is always realized since $Pb(Fe_{2/3}W_{1/3})O_3$ and $Pb(M_{1/2}W_{1/2})O_3$ are ferro- and antiferroelectric, i.e., $\eta_1 < 0$ and $\eta_2 > 0$.

If $x > x_1$, another transition antiferroelectric–ferroelectric phase occurs at a temperature below T_N, owing to the existence of the ζ term. The temperature T_0 is calculated from the condition $G_a = G_p$ (see Equations (4.121) and (4.122)), as

$$T_0 = T_1 - \left[a_2 x + \left(\frac{\kappa}{2}\right)\eta_0(x - x_1)\right] / a_0(1 + a_1 x), \quad (4.127)$$

where

$$\kappa = \left(1 + \sqrt{\frac{\beta + 2\zeta}{\beta - 2\zeta}}\right) / \left(1 - \sqrt{\frac{\beta + 2\zeta}{\beta - 2\zeta}}\right), 0 < \frac{\beta + 2\zeta}{\beta - 2\zeta} < 1. \quad (4.128)$$

4.6.5. Comparison with Experimental Results

From the experimental data obtained from the phase diagrams listed in Table 4.4 and Equations (4.125)–(4.128), we obtain the significant coefficient ratios of the expansion coefficients of the free energy summarized in Table 4.5. The value of T_1 was assumed to be zero since T_1 was common to the three systems and was found to be nearly equal to zero from the average of the experimental data. The values of coefficients change systematically with the component M. The parameter η_2, considered to represent the degree of antiferroelectricity, shows an increase similar to η_0/a_0 in order of Mn, Co, and Ni.

Figure 4.23b shows the theoretical phase diagrams of the three systems calculated with the parameters listed in Table 4.5. Reasonable agreement is obtained between the calculated curves and the experimental ones (Figure 4.23a). Example calculations made for $0.15Pb(Fe_{2/3}W_{1/3})O_3$-$0.85Pb(Co_{1/2}W_{1/2})O_3$ are shown in Figure 4.24a–c. The free energies at three possible stable states are plotted as a function of temperature in Figure 4.24a, where the dashed (antiferroelectric) curve at $T = 87$ K, that is, successive phase transitions occur, such as para-(224 K)-antiferroelectric-(87 K)-ferroelectric. Figure 4.24b shows the ferroelectric spontaneous polarization P_S, and antiferroelectric p_S. Figure 4.24c shows the permittivity change, which peaks at both phase transition temperatures. The low-temperature peak is, however, too sharp and too large compared with the experimental curve shown in [27], probably due to neglecting the term $(P_a{}^6 + P_b{}^6)$.

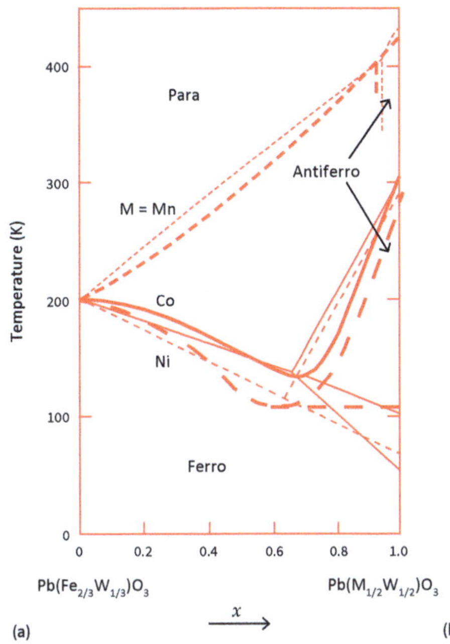

Figure 4.23. Phase diagrams of $Pb(Fe_{2/3}W_{1/3})O_3$- $Pb(M_{1/2}W_{1/2})O_3$ (M = Mn, Co, Ni): experimental results (thick curved lines), and calculated (fine linear lines) from the data in Table 4.5. Source: Figure by author, adapted from [27].

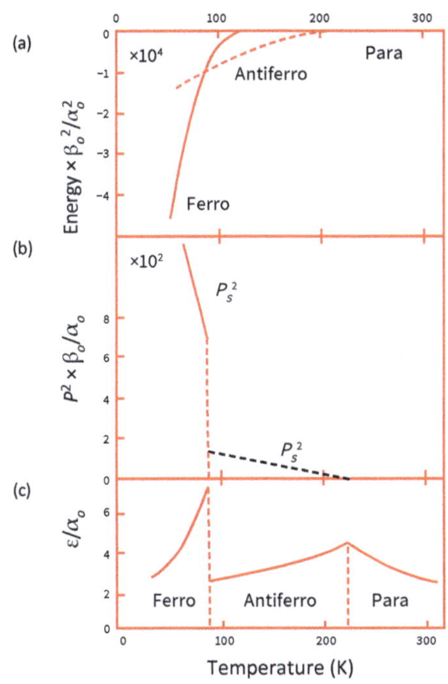

Figure 4.24. Calculations for $0.15Pb(Fe_{2/3}W_{1/3})O_3$-$0.85Pb(Co_{1/2}W_{1/2})O_3$: (**a**) free energy change, (**b**) spontaneous polarization, and (**c**) permittivity. Source: Figure by author, based on data from [27].

Table 4.4. Experimental data of phase diagrams for the systems $Pb(Fe_{2/3}W_{1/3})O_3$-$Pb(M_{1/2}W_{1/2})O_3$.

M	x_1	T_C ($x = 0$)	T_C ($x = x_1$)	T_N ($x = 0$)	T_0 ($x = 1$)
Mn	0.9–0.95	203 K	298–412 K	429 K	(<77 K)
Co	0.65–0.7	203	135	311	100
Ni	0.6–0.7	203	114	291	113

Source: Author's compilation based on data from [27].

Table 4.5. Theoretical data of phase diagrams used for the systems $Pb(Fe_{2/3}W_{1/3})O_3$-$Pb(M_{1/2}W_{1/2})O_3$.

M	x_1	T_1	a_1	a_2/a_0	η_0/a_0	κ ($x > x_1$)
Mn	0.95	0	0.06	−452	427	35.0
Co	0.67	0	0.02	−204	606	1.55
Ni	0.64	0	0.01	−179	634	1.01

Source: Author's compilation based on data from [27].

4.7. Advanced Phenomenology with Higher-Order Expansion

4.7.1. Bias Electric Field and Stress Dependence of Piezoelectric Properties

Taking into account the DC bias external electric field and stress dependence of the material property, an extended phenomenological formula should be required. Since most of the material properties show approximate linear changes under external biases, we can restrict the expansion functions of the material properties to merely the first order approximation. Therefore, the material properties can be expressed accordingly:

$$s_{ij}(E,X) = s_{ij}{}^{E} + s_{ijk}^{(E)} \cdot E_k + s_{ijk}^{(X)} \cdot X_k, \tag{4.129}$$

$$d_{ij}(E,X) = d_{ij} + d_{ijk}^{(E)} \cdot E_l + d_{ijk}^{(X)} \cdot X_l, \tag{4.130}$$

$$\varepsilon_i(E,X) = \varepsilon_i{}^{X} + \varepsilon_{ik}^{(E)} \cdot E_k + \varepsilon_{ik}^{(X)} \cdot X_k. \tag{4.131}$$

It should be noted that $s_{ijk}^{(E)}$ and $s_{ijk}^{(X)}$ are fifth rank and sixth rank tensors, respectively.

This section considers the higher-order material properties described in Equations (4.129)–(4.131), in addition to the primary $s_{ij}{}^{E}$, d_{ij}, and $\varepsilon_i{}^{X}$, based on the experimental data obtained for a soft PZT (PIC-255, PI Ceramics, Germany) [41]. Table 4.6 lists the DC electric field and compressive stress bias dependence of dielectric permittivity, elastic compliance, and piezoelectric constant. Note that the change in the parameters is only 2–3% of the original parameter values. We will discuss the higher-order expansion terms to explain these deviations under the DC bias conditions.

4.7.2. Phenomenological Higher-Order Integration

We adopt the Landau–Devonshire phenomenological theory to examine the first-order transition in the tetragonal–rhombohedral morphotropic phase boundary

(MPB) PZT composition behavior and material properties. Due to a lack of single crystal PZT data, the PZT Landau energy coefficients are mainly measured using indirect methods [42]. Haun et al. developed a comprehensive thermodynamic model for the entire solutions of PZT [43]. Though the current thermodynamic models are in good agreement with various experimental data, these models must be modified to explain the external bias dependency. Daneshpajooh et al. developed the phenomenological formula for the effect of nonlinearity observed by the application of DC stress and an electric field [41].

Table 4.6. Experimental and calculated higher-order thermodynamic terms.

Parameter	PIC-255 (Measured)	PIC-255 (Fitting)
$\partial\varepsilon_{33}/\partial E_3$ (10^{-4} m/V)	-2.02 ± 0.08	-0.8 ± 0.6
$\partial\lvert d_{31}\rvert/\partial E_3$ (10^{-17} C·m/N·V)	-3.3 ± 0.1	-7 ± 4.2
$\partial\varepsilon_{33}/\partial X_3$ (10^{-6} 1/Pa)	3.2 ± 0.2	2 ± 1.4
Q_{333} $\left(10^{-11}\ \mathrm{m^6/C^2N}\right)$	9 ± 7.1	
Q_{113} $\left(10^{-11}\ \mathrm{m^6/C^2N}\right)$	-6 ± 4.3	
s_{333} (10^{-20} 1/Pa^2)	-4 ± 3.0	
$(1/3\, s_{333}X_3^3)/(1/2\, s_{33}X_3^2)$	1.1–2.2%	
$(1/2\, Q_{333}X_3^2P_3^2)/(Q_{11}P_3^2X_3)$	1.9–3.8%	
$(1/2\, Q_{113}X_1^2P_3^2)/(1/2\, s_{11}^E X_1^2)$	0.6–1.2%	

Source: Table by author, based on data from [41].

Since we mainly focus on ferroelectricity phenomena, the thermodynamic model is described as a power series of polarization, stress, and electrostrictive coupling along the crystallographic axes. In order to explain the compliance change under external biases, higher-order piezoelectric coupling terms and higher-order elastic expansion terms should be introduced. Since our research focus is on k_{31} ($P_1 = P_2 = 0,\ X_3 = X_2 = 0$) and k_{33} ($P_1 = P_2 = 0,\ X_1 = X_2 = 0$) modes for the MPB composition PZT ceramic, taking into account PZT's crystallographic symmetry (∞mm or $6mm$ symmetry class) and the k_{31} and k_{33} mode geometric configurations, the thermodynamic elastic Gibbs free energy equation is modified with the following additional terms:

$$\begin{aligned}\Delta G_1(P,X) = {} & \tfrac{1}{2}\alpha_1 P_3^2 + \tfrac{1}{4}\beta_{11}P_3^4 + \tfrac{1}{6}\gamma_{111}P_3^6 - P_3\cdot\tfrac{1}{2}\left(s_{11}X_1^2 + s_{33}X_3^2\right) - \tfrac{1}{3}s_{333}X_3^3 \\ & - Q_{11}X_3P_3^2 - Q_{12}X_1P_3^2 - \tfrac{1}{2}\left(Q_{333}X_3^2P_3^2 + Q_{113}X_1^2P_3^2\right),\end{aligned} \tag{4.132}$$

where the "shaded" last terms on the first and second equation lines are newly introduced to the elastic Gibbs free energy description. It should be noted that only $\alpha_i = (T - T_0)/\varepsilon_0 C$ is considered to be temperature dependent, which represents the "Curie–Weiss" law in the paraelectric phase. The parameters T_0, s_{ij}, s_{ijk}, Q_{ij}, and Q_{ijk} are the Curie–Weiss temperature, fourth- and sixth-rank elastic compliance tensor components (reduced notation), and fourth- and sixth-rank electrostrictive coefficient tensor components (reduced notation), respectively ($i, j, k = 1, 2, \cdots, 6$). In materials which experience the first-order transition ($\beta < 0$), the elastic Gibbs function is expanded up to the sixth power of polarization. In the following sections, we discuss the phenomenology of ferroelectricity under external stress and an electric field, based on Equation (4.132).

4.7.3. Bias Electric Field and Stress Dependence of Physical Parameters

The external DC electric field and stress can considerably affect the piezoelectric material properties. The reader is first reminded of the following relations:

$$E_i = (\partial G_1 / \partial P_i), \quad (4.133)$$

$$x_i = -(\partial G_1 / \partial X_i), \quad (4.134)$$

$$1/\varepsilon_0 \varepsilon_i = \left(\partial^2 G_1 / \partial {P_i}^2\right). \quad (4.135)$$

From Equation (4.132), we obtain the following equations:

$$\begin{aligned} \mathrm{E}_3(P, X) &= \alpha_1 P_3 + \beta_{11} P_3^3 + \gamma_{111} P_3^5 - 2(Q_{11} X_3 P_3 + Q_{12} X_1 P_3) \\ &\quad - (Q_{333} X_3^2 P_3 + Q_{113} X_1^2 P_3) \\ &= \alpha^{eff} P_3 + \beta_{11} P_3^3 + \gamma_{111} P_3^5 \end{aligned} \quad (4.136a)$$

(applicable for both k_{31} and k_{33} modes),

$$x_1(X, P) = s_{11}^{eff} X_1 + Q_{12} P_3^2 \text{ (for } k_{31} \text{ mode)}, \quad (4.137a)$$

$$x_3(X, P) = s_{33}^{eff} X_3 + Q_{11} P_3^2 \text{ (for } k_{33} \text{ mode)}, \quad (4.138a)$$

where

$$\alpha_1^{eff} = \alpha_1 - 2Q_{11} X_3 - \left(Q_{333} X_3^2 + Q_{113} X_1^2\right) \text{ (for both } k_{31} \text{ and } k_{33} \text{ modes)}, \quad (4.136b)$$

$$s_{11}^{eff} = s_{11} + Q_{113} P_3^2 \text{ (for } k_{31} \text{ mode)}, \quad (4.137b)$$

$$s_{33}^{eff} = s_{33} + s_{333} X_3 + Q_{333} P_3^2 \text{ (for } k_{33} \text{ mode)}. \quad (4.138b)$$

The stress dependence of compliance is a combination of the primary and secondary elastic behavior and the higher-order electrostriction of the material. Since the spontaneous polarization changes under external electric field, the bias electric field dependence of material compliance is merely due to spontaneous polarization change. Therefore, the material properties including piezoelectric d constant ($d_{ij} = \varepsilon_0 \varepsilon_i \cdot g_{ij}$), g constant ($g_{ij} = -(\partial^2 G / \partial P_i \partial X_j)$), and inverse permittivity ($1/\varepsilon_0 \varepsilon_{ij} = \left(\partial^2 G / \partial P_i \partial P_j\right)$) can be calculated as follows:

$$1/\varepsilon_0 \varepsilon_3(X, E) = \alpha_1^{eff} + 3\beta_{11} P_3^3 + 5\gamma_{111} P_3^5, \quad (4.139)$$

$$g_{31} = 2Q_{12}P_3 + 2Q_{113}X_1P_3; d_{31} = 2\varepsilon_0\varepsilon_3(Q_{12} + Q_{113}X_1)P_3(k_{31}\text{ mode}), \tag{4.140}$$

$$g_{33} = 2Q_{11}P_3 + 2Q_{333}X_3P_3;\ d_{33} = 2\varepsilon_0\varepsilon_3(Q_{11} + Q_{333}X_3)P_3(k_{33}\text{ mode}). \tag{4.141}$$

In order to find the effect of the external electric field and stress effects on the polarization status inside material at room temperature, Equations (4.132)–(4.138) should be solved to find the equilibrium ferroelectric states under these biases. Accordingly, using the calculated spontaneous polarization at equilibrium states, the DC electric field and compressive stress dependence of material properties are calculated based on Equations (4.139)–(4.141).

External Electric Field Effect on k_{31} Mode PZT

The inverse permittivity should change under the presence of an external DC field. The electric field and dielectric stiffness in the presence of the external field (E_0) can be expressed in the k_{31} plate (from Equations (4.133)–(4.135)) as

$$E_0 = \alpha_1 P_3 + \beta_{11}P_3^3 + \gamma_{111}P_3^5, \tag{4.142}$$

$$x_1 = Q_{12}P_3^2, \tag{4.143}$$

$$1/\varepsilon_0\varepsilon_i = \alpha_1 + 3\beta_{11}P_3^2 + 5\gamma_{111}P_3^4. \tag{4.144}$$

Under a positive external electric field, the Curie temperature shifts to higher temperatures while showing a spontaneous polarization discontinuity at the Curie temperature. In order to calculate the material property behavior including inverse permittivity ($1/\varepsilon_0\varepsilon_i$), piezoelectric coefficients (d_{ij}), and elastic compliance (s_{ij}), it is necessary to find the free energy minima. Using numerical methods, the corresponding spontaneous polarization (P_S) under an external electric field can be calculated from Equation (4.142) and elastic Gibbs free energy minima. We conducted the first-order approximation of spontaneous polarization under an external field for a PZT 50/50 by referring to the paper by Amin et al. [44]. At room temperature, the first-order approximation of spontaneous polarization shows less than 0.2% deviation from numerical results. Accordingly, since the effect of the DC electric field on material properties is inherited by spontaneous polarization change, piezoelectric and permittivity also show little deviation (less than 1%). According to Equations (4.133)–(4.138), the inverse permittivity and piezoelectric coefficients under an external electric field at room temperature can be formulated as follows. The second-order material properties used in Equations (4.129)–(4.131) can be deduced as follows:

$$\varepsilon_{33}^{(E)} = \frac{\partial\varepsilon_3(E,X)}{\partial E_3} = -\left(\frac{\gamma_{111}}{A}\right)^3\sqrt{\frac{2(A-\beta_{11})}{\gamma_{111}}}\left(\frac{5A-2\beta_{11}}{(A-\beta_{11})^3}\right), \tag{4.145}$$

$$d_{333}^{(E)} = \frac{\partial d_{33}(E,X)}{\partial E_3} = -4Q_{11}\gamma_{111}^2\frac{3\beta_{11}^2 - 3\beta_{11}A - 8\alpha_1\gamma_{111}}{(A^2-\beta_{11}A)^3}, \tag{4.146a}$$

$$d_{313}^{(E)} = \frac{\partial d_{31}(E,X)}{\partial E_3} = -4Q_{12}\gamma_{111}^2\frac{3\beta_{11}^2 - 3\beta_{11}A - 8\alpha_1\gamma_{111}}{(A^2-\beta_{11}A)^3}, \tag{4.146b}$$

$$s_{113}^{(E)} = \frac{\partial s_{11}(E,X)}{\partial E_3} = \frac{Q_{113}}{A}\sqrt{\frac{2\gamma_{111}}{A-\beta_{11}}}, \tag{4.147}$$

where A is defined as

$$A = \sqrt{\beta_{11}^2 - 4\alpha_1\gamma_{111}}. \tag{4.148}$$

Based on Equation (4.147), in order to discuss the elastic compliance change under an electric field, the reader can now understand that a higher-order nonlinear electrostriction effect Q_{113} should be integrated.

External Stress Effect on the PZT Phenomenological Theory

The thermodynamic theory can also be applied for the explanation of stress effect on ferroelectric properties. The elastic Gibbs energy expressed in Equation (4.132) derives the electric field E_3 under external stress X_3,

$$\begin{aligned} E_3(P,X) &= \alpha_1 P_3 + \beta_{11}P_3^3 + \gamma_{111}P_3^5 - 2Q_{11}P_3X_3 - Q_{111}P_3X_3^2 \\ &= \alpha_1' P_3 + \beta_{11}P_3^3 + \gamma_{111}P_3^5, \end{aligned} \tag{4.149}$$

where $\alpha_1' = \alpha_1 - 2Q_{11}X_3 - Q_{111}P_3X_3^2$.

Similar to Equations (4.145)–(4.147), using the first-order approximation, the second-order material properties under a constant pre-stress condition at the ferroelectric phase can be derived as follows:

$$\varepsilon_{33}^{(X)} = \frac{\partial \varepsilon_3(E,X)}{\partial X_3} = -\frac{4Q_{11}\gamma_{111}^2}{A^3}\left(\frac{2A-\beta_{11}}{(A-\beta_{11})^2}\right), \tag{4.150}$$

$$d_{333}^{(X)} = \frac{\partial d_{33}(E,X)}{\partial X_3} \frac{-2\sqrt{2}Q_{11}^2(5\beta_{11}^2 - 5\beta_{11}A - 12\alpha_1\gamma_{111})}{A^3\gamma_{111}\left(\frac{A-\beta_{11}}{\gamma_{111}}\right)^{5/2}} + \frac{2\sqrt{2}Q_{111}(\beta_{11}^2 - \beta_{11}A - 2\alpha_1\gamma_{111})}{A\gamma_{111}^2\left(\frac{A-\beta_{11}}{\gamma_{111}}\right)^{5/2}}, \tag{4.151}$$

$$s_{333}^{(X)} = \frac{\partial s_{33}(E,X)}{\partial X_3} = s_{333} + 4\frac{Q_{111}\times Q_{11}}{A}, \tag{4.152}$$

where $A = \sqrt{\beta_{11}^2 - 4\alpha_1\gamma_{111}}$, as in the previous Subsection External Electric Field Effect on k_{31} Mode PZT. The permittivity change under external stress can be explained by the conventional thermodynamic models due to ready-integrated higher-order dielectric stiffness parameters. However, based on Equations (4.151) and (4.152), the piezoelectric constant d and elastic compliance s change under external stress can be obtained merely by integrating higher-order nonlinear elastic s_{333} and electrostriction Q_{111} coefficients.

Table 4.6 lists the above simulated permittivity, elastic compliance, and piezoelectric constant change with bias electric field and compressive stress in the measurements. Though the errors for these evaluations are not small, the general tendency can be explained. Note that the modulation by bias in the primary parameters is only 2–3% (not very large). Figure 4.25 shows the comparison of phenomenological model predictions vs. experimental data on ε_{33}^X, s_{33}^E, and d_{33} under DC electric field bias (Figure 4.25a–c) and under compressive stress bias (Figure 4.25d–f). Though the prediction bands are rather wide (due to the error propagation), the estimated trend lines are in relatively good agreement with the experimental data. The DC bias dependence of physical parameters will help with constructing the domain dynamic models, as discussed in Chapter 14.

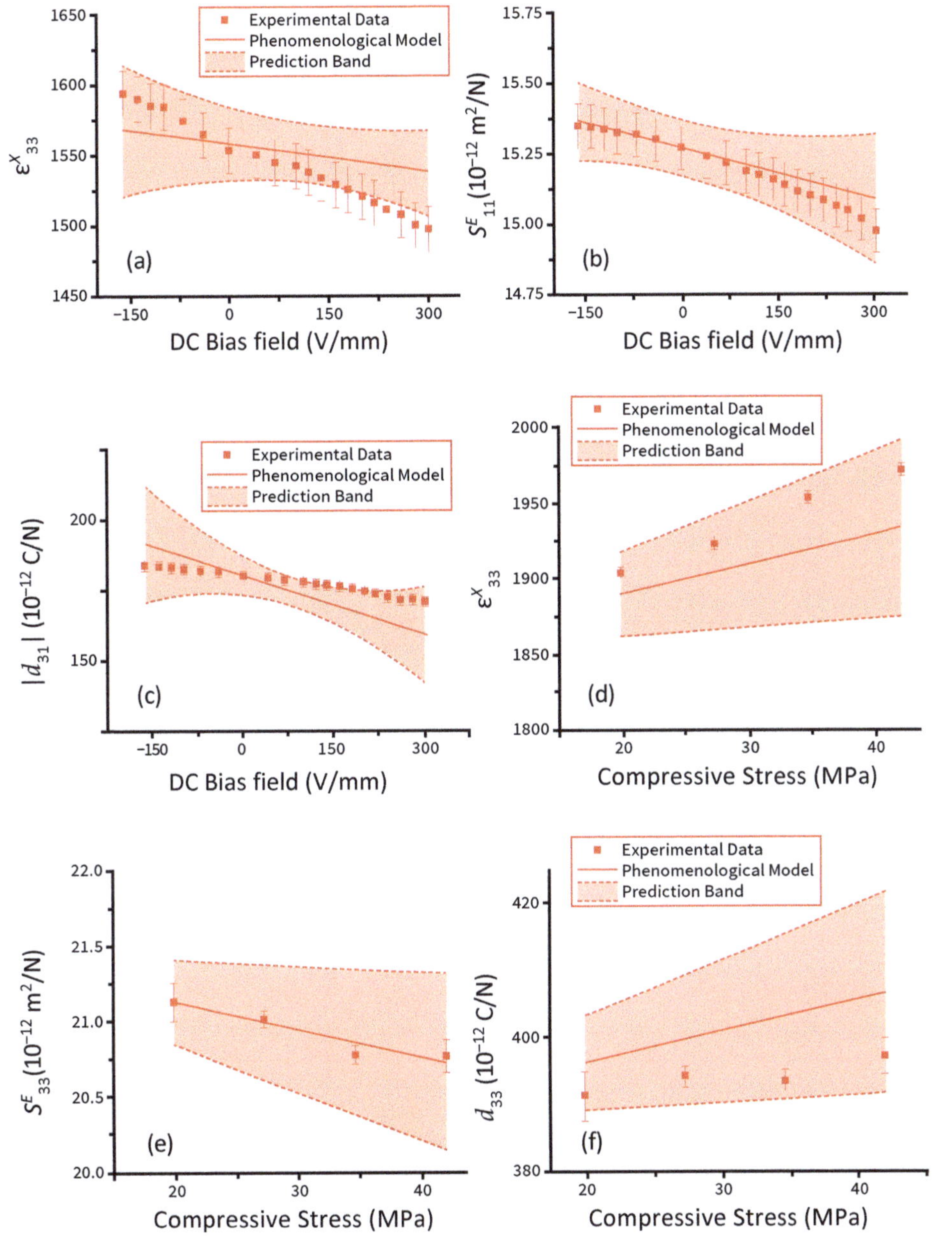

Figure 4.25. Comparison of phenomenological model predictions vs. experimental data on ε^X_{33}, s^E_{33}, and d_{33} under DC electric field bias (**a**–**c**); and under compressive stress bias (**d**–**f**). Source: Figure by author, adapted from [41].

Chapter Essentials

1. Elimination Theorem of Taylor Expansion Terms

Theorem 1. *When the crystal possesses a "centrosymmetry", the odd power of the expansion tensor coefficient $\alpha_{ij\cdots l}$ becomes "zero".*

Theorem 2. *When we discuss the phase transition, we assume that energy description is common through the paraelectric and ferroelectric phases and that the reduction in the Taylor expansion terms follows to the highest symmetry paraelectric phase. When the paraelectric phase is "centrosymmetric", the odd power of the expansion tensor coefficient $\alpha_{ij\cdots l}$ becomes "zero".*

2. Landau Phase Transition Theory

Second-Order Phase Transition (in the Case of $\beta > 0$) (Figure 4.2)

$F(P, T) = (1/2)\alpha P^2 + (1/4)\beta P^4$ $[\alpha(T) = (T - T_0)/\varepsilon_0 C]$

$(\partial F/\partial P) = E = \alpha P + \beta P^3$

$\frac{1}{\varepsilon_0 \varepsilon} = \left(\frac{\partial E}{\partial P}\right) = \alpha + 3\beta P^2$

- Paraelectric Phase ($T > T_0 = T_C$)

  $P_S = 0$

  $\frac{1}{\varepsilon_0 \varepsilon} = \alpha = (T - T_0)/\varepsilon_0 C$, or $\varepsilon = \frac{C}{(T - T_0)}$

- Ferroelectric Phase ($T < T_0 = T_C$)

  ${P_S}^2 = -\frac{\alpha}{\beta} = (T_0 - T)/\beta\varepsilon_0 C$, or $P_S = \pm\sqrt{(T_0 - T)/(\beta\, \varepsilon_0\, C)}$

  $\frac{1}{\varepsilon_0 \varepsilon} = -2\alpha = 2(T_0 - T)/\varepsilon_0 C$, or $\varepsilon = \frac{C/2}{(T - T_0)}$

  Coercive field: $E_C = \alpha P + \beta P^3 = \sqrt{-4\alpha^3/27\beta}$

First-Order Phase Transition (in the Case of $\beta < 0$) (Figure 4.4b)

$F(P, T) = (1/2)\alpha P^2 + (1/4)\beta P^4 + (1/6)\gamma P^6$ $[\alpha(T) = (T - T_0)/\varepsilon_0 C]$

$(\partial F/\partial P) = E = \alpha P + \beta P^3 + \gamma P^5 = 0$

$\frac{1}{\varepsilon_0 \varepsilon} = \left(\frac{\partial E}{\partial P}\right) = \alpha + 3\beta P^2 + 5\gamma P^4$

- Paraelectric Phase ($T > T_C$)

  $P_S = 0$

  $\frac{1}{\varepsilon_0 \varepsilon} = \alpha = (T - T_0)/\varepsilon_0 C$, or $\varepsilon = \frac{C}{(T - T_0)}$

  $T_1 = T_0 + \beta^2 \varepsilon_0 C/4\gamma$

  $T_C = T_0 + (3/16)(\beta\varepsilon_0 C/\gamma)$

- Ferroelectric Phase ($T < T_C$)

  $P_S{}^2 = [-\beta + \sqrt{\beta^2 - 4\gamma\alpha}]/2\gamma]$

  $\frac{1}{\varepsilon_0 \varepsilon} = -4\alpha - 2\beta P^2 \approx \frac{3\beta^2}{4\gamma} + \frac{8(T_C - T)}{\varepsilon_0 C}$

3. Devonshire Phase Transition Theory

$$G_1(P, X, T) = \left(\frac{1}{2}\right)\alpha P^2 + \left(\frac{1}{4}\right)\beta P^4 + \left(\frac{1}{6}\right)\gamma P^6 - \left(\frac{1}{2}\right)sX^2 - QP^2X$$

$[\alpha = (T - T_0)/\varepsilon_0 C]$

$$E = \left(\frac{\partial G_1}{\partial P}\right) = \alpha P + \beta P^3 + \gamma P^5 - 2QPX$$

$$x = -\left(\frac{\partial G_1}{\partial X}\right) = sX + QP^2$$

$$\frac{1}{\varepsilon_0 \varepsilon} = \left(\frac{\partial E}{\partial P}\right) = \alpha + 3\beta P^2 + 5\gamma P^4 - 2QX$$

- Paraelectric Phase ($T > T_C$)

  $P_S = 0$ or $P = \varepsilon_0 \varepsilon E$ (under small E modulation)

  Permittivity: $\varepsilon = C/(T - T_0)$ (normal Curie–Weiss law)

  Electrostriction: $x = Q\varepsilon_0^2 \varepsilon^2 E^2$

- Ferroelectric Phase ($T < T_C$)

  $P_S{}^2 = (-\beta + \sqrt{\beta^2 - 4\alpha\gamma})/2\gamma$ or $P = P_S + \varepsilon_0 \varepsilon E$ (under small E modulation)

  $x = Q(P_S + \varepsilon_0 \varepsilon E)^2 = QP_S{}^2 + 2\varepsilon_0 \varepsilon Q P_S E + Q\varepsilon_0^2 \varepsilon^2 E^2$

  $\frac{1}{\varepsilon_0 \varepsilon} = \alpha + 3\beta P^2 + 5\gamma P^4 = -4\alpha - 2\beta P_S{}^2$

  Spontaneous strain: $x_S = QP_S{}^2$

  Piezoelectric constant: $d = 2\, \varepsilon_0\, \varepsilon\, QP_S$

  Electrostrictive strain: $Q\varepsilon_0^2 \varepsilon^2 E^2$ (usually neglected)

4. Phenomenological Approach in Solid Solutions

$$G_1(P, X, T) = (1/2)[(1 - x)\alpha_A + x\alpha_B]P^2 + (1/4)[(1 - x)\beta_A + x\beta_B]P^4$$
$$+(1/6)[(1 - x)\gamma_A + x\gamma_B]P^6 - (1/2)[(1 - x)s_A + xs_B]X^2 - [(1 - x)Q_A + xQ_B]P^2X$$

$(\alpha_A = (T - T_{0,A})/\varepsilon_0 C_A, = (T - T_{0,B})/\varepsilon_0 C_B)$

5. Phenomenology of Antiferroelectrics

$$G_1 = (1/4)\alpha(P_a{}^2 + P_b{}^2) + (1/8)\beta(P_a{}^4 + P_b{}^4) + (1/12)\gamma(P_a{}^6 + P_b{}^6) + (1/2)\eta P_a P_b$$
$$- (1/2)\chi_T p^2 + (1/2)Q_h(P_a{}^2 + P_b{}^2 + 2\Omega P_a P_b)p$$

Introducing the transformations $P_F = (P_a + P_b)/2$ and $P_A = (P_a - P_b)/2$ leads to the following expression:

$$G_1 = (1/2)\alpha(P_F{}^2 + P_A{}^2) + (1/4)\beta(P_F{}^4 + P_A{}^4 + 6P_F{}^2P_A{}^2)$$
$$+ (1/6)\gamma(P_F{}^6 + P_A{}^6 + 15P_F{}^4P_A{}^2 + 15P_F{}^2P_A{}^4)$$
$$+ (1/2)\eta(P_F{}^2 - P_A{}^2) - (1/2)\chi_T p^2 + Q_h[P_F{}^2 + P_A{}^2 + \Omega(P_F{}^2 - P_A{}^2)]p.$$

The piezoelectric d coefficients in a sublattice material are denoted as $d_{33} = 2(Q_{33} + q_{33})\varepsilon_0\varepsilon_3 P_{F3,S}$, $d_{31} = 2(Q_{31} + q_{31})\varepsilon_0\varepsilon_3 P_{F3,S}$. Thus, when a large piezoelectric anisotropy ($|d_{33}/d_{31}| > 4$) is observed, we may anticipate positive inter-sublattice electrostrictive coupling q_{31} in the material with a sort of crystallographic superlattice structure.

Check Point

1. Elastic Gibbs energy is given by:

   $G_1 = (1/2)\alpha P^2 + (1/4)\beta P^4 + (1/6)\gamma P^6 - (1/2)sX^2 - QP^2X.$

   Why do we not include the "odd-number" power terms of P? Answer simply.
2. (T/F) The phenomenology suggests that the piezoelectric constant d of a ferroelectric material increases with a decrease in temperature below its Curie temperature. True or false?
3. (T/F) The phenomenology suggests that the Curie temperature of a ferroelectric material is always lower than (or equal to) the Curie–Weiss temperature. True or false?
4. How is the piezoelectric coefficient d related with the electrostrictive coefficient Q, spontaneous polarization P_S, and relative permittivity ε_r in a ferroelectric phase in the 1D phenomenology? Provide the simplest formula.
5. (T/F) The Landau phenomenology on the second-order phase transition derives the linear decrease in the spontaneous polarization with a temperature rise below T_C. True or false?
6. (T/F) The Landau phenomenology on the second-order phase transition derives the linear decrease in the spontaneous strain down to zero with a temperature rise below T_C. True or false?
7. (T/F) The Landau phenomenology on the second-order phase transition derives the linear decrease in the inverse permittivity down to zero with a temperature rise below T_C (ferroelectric phase). However, the slope is four-times steeper than the slope of that in the paraelectric phase. True or false?
8. (T/F) The MPB composition of the PZT system exhibits the maximum electromechanical coupling k, piezoelectric coefficient d, and the minimum permittivity ε. True or false?
9. (T/F) The electrostrictive coefficient M, defined by strain $x = ME^2$ (E: applied electric field), is rather insensitive to the temperature change, even through the phase transition temperature T_C. True or false?
10. (T/F) The phenomenology of antiferroelectrics with the sublattice coupling suggests a possibility of large piezoelectric anisotropy in the field-induced piezoelectric phase, in comparison with a normal ferroelectric material. True or false?

Chapter Problems

4.1 Referring to a paper by Amin et al. [44], consider the necessary expansion terms in 3D Devonshire phenomenological theory.

Hint

Consider which term stabilizes primarily, tetragonal ($P_1 = P_2 = 0,\ P_3 \neq 0$), orthorhombic ($P_2 = 0,\ P_3 = P_1 \neq 0$) or rhombohedral ($P_1 = P_2 = P_3 \neq 0$) symmetry structure?

$$\Delta G(P, X) = \tfrac{1}{2}(\alpha_1 P_1^2 + \alpha_2 P_2^2 + \alpha_3 P_3^2) + \tfrac{1}{4}(\beta_{11} P_1^4 + \beta_{22} P_2^4 + \beta_{33} P_3^4)$$
$$+\tfrac{1}{4}(\beta_{12} P_1^2 P_2^2 + \beta_{23} P_2^2 P_3^2 + \ldots) + \tfrac{1}{6}(\gamma_{111} P_1^6 + \gamma_{222} P_2^6 + \gamma_{333} P_3^6)$$
$$+\tfrac{1}{6}(\gamma_{121} P_1^2 P_2^2 P_2^2 + \gamma_{123} P_1^2 P_2^2 P_3^2 + \ldots) - \tfrac{1}{2}(s_{11} X_1^2 + s_{22} X_2^2 + s_{33} X_3^2)$$
$$-(s_{12} X_1 X_2 + s_{13} X_1 X_3 + s_{23} X_2 X_3) - \ldots - (Q_{11} P_1^2 X_1 + Q_{22} P_2^2 X_2 + Q_{33} P_3^2 X_3)$$
$$-(Q_{12} P_2^2 X_1 + Q_{13} X_1 P_3^2 + \ldots) - (Q_{44} X_4 P_2 P_3 + \ldots) + \ldots$$

4.2 Landau free energy for the first-order phase transition is given by

$F(P, T) = (1/2)\alpha P^2 + (1/4)\beta P^4 + (1/6)\gamma P^6 \quad [\alpha(T) = (T - T_0)/\varepsilon_0 C]$.

The temperature dependence of the spontaneous polarization is illustrated in the Figure 4.4b, the curve shape of which seems to be the lean parabola in the second-order phase transition shown in the Figure 4.2. If we approximate the spontaneous polarization in the first-order transition (Figure 4.4b) as the lean parabola of the second-order transition shifted along the positive temperature axis, what is the state of the numerical deviation from the real curve on the left? The temperature slope of the inverse permittivity in the $T_0 < T < T_C$ range gives 8 in the first-order transition theoretically. How about the lean-parabola approximation?

Hint

$$\text{First – order transition: } P_S = \sqrt{\left[-\beta + \sqrt{\beta^2 - 4\gamma\alpha}\right]/2\gamma]}, \qquad \text{(CP4.2.1)}$$

$$\text{Second – order transition: } P_S = \sqrt{-\alpha/\beta}. \qquad \text{(CP4.2.2)}$$

At $T = T_c$, we obtain $\alpha = \frac{T_c - T_0}{\varepsilon_0 C} = \frac{3}{16}\frac{\beta^2}{\gamma}$. The lean-parabola shifted curve is obtained from Equation (CP4.2.2) by this amount. Taking the Taylor expansion in terms of $(T_c - T)$ (a small value << 1) on this shifted curve and Equation (CP4.2.2), compare the deviation.

4.3 A significant difference in the P–E hysteresis in the first-order transition can be found in a "double hysteresis" in the temperature range $T_C < T < T_1$, which cannot be observed in the second-order transition. Gibbs energy by adding $-EP$ to the Landau free energy is given by

$$G = \frac{1}{2}\alpha P^2 + \frac{1}{4}\beta P^4 + \frac{1}{6}\gamma P^6 - EP.$$

The system with multiple potential minima in the Gibbs energy (Figure 4.4a) can exhibit discontinuous polarization induction (i.e., electric-field-induced ferroelectric phase) under a high electric field. As shown in Figure 4.5, the $P-E$ double hysteresis is observed in a narrow temperature range. Calculate the electric field for the double-hysteresis on-set and off-set at a temperature T, which is in the temperature range $T_C < T < T_1$.

References

1. Tisza, L. On the General Theory of Phase Transitions. In *Phase Transformations in Solids*; Smoluctowski, R., Mayer, J.E., Weyl, W.A., Eds.; Wiley: New York, NY, USA, 1951.
2. Uchino, K. *Ferroelectric Devices*, 2nd ed.; CRC Press: Boca Raton, FL, USA, 2010.
3. Devonshire, A.F. Theory of Ferroelectrics. *Adv. Phys.* **1954**, *3*, 85–130. [CrossRef]
4. Kay, H.F. Electrostriction. *Rep. Prog. Phys.* **1955**, *18*, 230–250. [CrossRef]
5. Uchino, K.; Nomura, S.; Cross, L.-E.; Newnham, R.-E.; Jang, S.-J. Electrostrictive Effect in Perovskites and Its Transducer Applications. *J. Mater. Sci.* **1981**, *16*, 569–578. [CrossRef]
6. Uchino, K.; Cross, L.E.; Newnham, R.E.; Nomura, S. Electrostrictive Effects in Antiferroelectric Perovskites. *J. Appl. Phys.* **1981**, *52*, 1455–1459. [CrossRef]
7. Uchino, K.; Nomura, S.; Cross, L.E.; Jang, S.J.; Newnham, R.E. Electrostrictive Effect in Lead Magnesium Niobate Single Crystals. *J. Appl. Phys.* **1980**, *52*, 1142–1145. [CrossRef]
8. Nomura, S.; Jang, S.J.; Cross, L.E.; Newnham, R.E. Structure and Dielectric Properties of Materials in the Solid Solution System $Pb(Mg_{1/3}Nb_{2/3})O_3$:$Pb(W_{1/2}Mg_{1/2})O_3$. *J. Am. Ceram. Soc.* **1979**, *62*, 485–488. [CrossRef]
9. Nomura, S.; Kuwata, J.; Jang, S.J.; Cross, L.E.; Newnham, R.E. Electrostriction in $Pb(Zn_{1/3}Nb_{2/3})O_3$. *Mater. Res. Bull.* **1979**, *14*, 769–774. [CrossRef]
10. Kuwata, J.; Uchino, K.; Nomura, S. Diffuse Transition in Lead Zinc Niobate. *Ferroelectrics* **1979**, *22*, 863–867. [CrossRef]
11. Setter, N.; Cross, L.E. Order-Disorder Perovskite Ferroelectrics. In Proceedings of the 82nd Annual Meeting of the American Ceramic Society, Chicago, IL, USA, 29 April 1980; p. 52-E-80.
12. Yamada, T. Electromechanical Properties of Oxygen-Octahedra Ferroelectric Crystals. *J. Appl. Phys.* **1972**, *43*, 328–338. [CrossRef]
13. Johnson, C.J. Some Dielectric and Electro-Optic Properties of $BaTiO_3$ Single Crystals. *Appl. Phys. Lett.* **1965**, *7*, 221–223. [CrossRef]
14. Gavrilyachenko, V.G.; Fesenko, E.G. Piezoelectric effect in lead titanate single crystals. *Sov. Phys. Chrystallogr.* **1971**, *16*, 549.
15. Fesenko, E.G.; Gavrilyachenko, V.G.; Zarochentsev, E.V. Ferroelectric Properties of Lead Titanate Single Crystals. *Bull. Acad. Sci. USSR, Phys. Ser.* **1970**, *34*, 2262–2549.
16. Samara, G.A. Pressure and Temperature Dependences of the Dielectric Properties of the Perovskites $BaTiO_3$ and $SrTiO_3$. *Phys. Rev.* **1966**, *151*, 378. [CrossRef]
17. Bell, R.O.; Rupprecht, G. Elastic Constants of Strontium Titanate. *Phys. Rev.* **1963**, *129*, 90. [CrossRef]
18. Uwe, H.; Sakudo, T. Electrostriction and Stress-Induced Ferroelectricity in $KTaO_3$. *J. Phys. Soc. Jpn.* **1975**, *38*, 183–189. [CrossRef]
19. Uwe, H.; Unoki, H.; Fujii, Y.; Sakudo, T. Stress induced ferroelectricity in $KTaO_3$. *Commun. Solid State Phys.* **1973**, *13*, 737–739. [CrossRef]
20. Uchino, K.; Kojima, F.; Nomura, S. Phase transition in the $Pb(Fe_{2/3}U_{1/3})O_3$-$PbZrO_3$ system. *Ferroelectrics*, **1977**, *15*, 69–71. [CrossRef]

21. Samara, G.A. Pressure and Temperature Dependence of the Dielectric Properties and Phase Transitions of the Antiferroelectric Perovskites: $PbZrO_3$ and $PbHfO_3$. *Phys. Rev.* **1970**, *B1*, 3777. [CrossRef]
22. Bokov, V.A.; Kizhaev, S.A.; Myl'nikova, I.E.; Totov, A.G. Magnetic and Electrical Properties of Antiferroelectric Lead Cobalt Tungstate. *Sov. Phys. Solid State* **1965**, *6*, 2419.
23. Uchino, K.; Cross, L.E.; Newnham, R.E.; Nomura, S. Electrostrictive Effects in Non-polar Perovskites. *Phase Transit.* **1980**, *1*, 333–341. [CrossRef]
24. Uchino, K. Force Sensor with Electrostrictive Bimorph Devices. In Proceedings of the Study Committee on Barium Titanate XXXI, Tokyo, Japan, 20 May 1983; pp. 171–1067.
25. Kuwata, J.; Uchino, K.; Nomura, S. Electrostrictive Coefficients of $Pb(Mb_{1/3}Nb_{2/3})O_3$ Ceramics. *Jpn. J. Appl. Phys.* **1980**, *19*, 2099. [CrossRef]
26. Jaffe, B.; Cook, W.R.; Jaffe, H. *Piezoelectric Ceramics*; Academic Press: New York, NY, USA, 1971; p. 142.
27. Uchino, K.; Nomura, S. Phenomenological Theory of Ferroelectricity in Solid Solution Systems $Pb(Fe_{2/3}W_{1/3})O_3$–$Pb(M_{1/2}W_{1/2})O_3$ (M = Mn, Co, Ni). *Jpn. J. Appl. Phys.* **1979**, *18*, 1493–1497. [CrossRef]
28. Abe, K.; Furukawa, O.; Inagawa, H. Calculations concerning the phase diagram, dielectric constant and lattice parameters for the $Pb(Zn_{1/3}Nb_{2/3})O_3$–$PbTiO_3$ solid solution. *Ferroelectrics* **1988**, *87*, 55–64. [CrossRef]
29. Kittel, C. Theory of Antiferroelectric Crystals. *Phys. Rev.* **1951**, *82*, 729. [CrossRef]
30. Suzuki, I.; Okada, K. Phenomenological Theory of Antiferroelectric Transition. IV. Ferrielectric. *J. Phys. Soc. Jpn.* **1978**, *45*, 1302–1308. [CrossRef]
31. Uchino, K. Electrostrictive Effect in Antiferroelectrics. *Solid State Phys.* **1982**, *17*, 371–380.
32. Uchino, K. Digital Displacement Transducer Using Antiferroelectrics. *Jpn. J. Appl. Phys.* **1985**, *24*, 460. [CrossRef]
33. Uchino, K. Shape Memory Ceramics. In *Shape Memory Materials*; Otsuka, K., Wayman, C.M., Eds.; Cambridge University Press: Cambridge, UK, 1998; pp. 184–202.
34. Uchino, K.; Oh, K.-Y. Piezoelectric Anisotrophy and Polarization Sublattice Coupling in Perovskite Crystals. *J. Am. Ceram. Soc.* **1991**, *74*, 1131–1134. [CrossRef]
35. Uchino, K.; Nomura, S. Electrostriction in PZT-Family Antiferroelectrics. *Ferroelectrics* **1983**, *50*, 191–196. [CrossRef]
36. Fujishita, H.; Hoshino, S. A Study of Structural Phase Transitions in Antiferroelectric $PbZrO_3$ by Neutron Diffraction. *J. Phys. Soc. Jpn.* **1984**, *53*, 226–234. [CrossRef]
37. Oh, K.-Y.; Saito, Y.; Furuta, A.; Uchino, K. Piezoelectricity in the Field-Induced Ferroelectric Phase of Lead Zirconate-Based Antiferroelectrics. *J. Am. Ceram. Soc.* **1992**, *75*, 795–799. [CrossRef]
38. Kobayashi, T.; Uchino, K. Piezoelectric Anisostropy with Sublattice Electrostrictive Coupling. In *Abstract of 48th Autumn Meeting of the Japan Society of Applied Physics, Nagoya, Japan, October 1987*; Japan Society of Applied Physics: Tokyo, Japan, 1987.
39. Yamamoto, T.; Saho, M.; Okazaki, K.; Goo, E. Electrical Properties and Microstructure of Ca Modified $PbTiO_3$ Ceramics. *Jpn. J. Appl. Phys.* **1987**, *26*, 57. [CrossRef]
40. Berlincourt, D.A.; Cmolik, C.; Jaffe, H. Piezoelectric Properties of Polycrystalline Lead Titanate Zirconate Compositions. *Proc. IRE* **1960**, *48*, 220. [CrossRef]
41. Daneshpajooh, H.; Park, Y.; Scholehwar, T.; Hennig, E.; Uchino, K. DC bias electric field and stress dependence of piezoelectric parameters in lead zirconate titanate ceramics–Phenomenological approach. *Ceram. Int.* **2020**, *46*, 15572–15580. [CrossRef]
42. Haun, M.J.; Furman, E.; Jang, S.J.; Cross, L.E. Thermodynamic theory of the lead zirconate-titanate solid solution system, part I: phenomenology. *Ferroelectrics* **1989**, *99*, 13–25. [CrossRef]

43. Haun, M.J.; Furman, E.; McKinstry, H.A.; Cross, L.E. Thermodynamic theory of the lead zirconate-titanate solid solution system, part II: tricritical behavior. *Ferroelectrics* **1989**, *99*, 27–44. [CrossRef]
44. Amin, A.; Haun, M.J.; Badger, B.; McKinstry, H.; Cross, L.E. A phenomenological Gibbs function for the single cell region of the $PbZrO_3$: $PbTiO_3$ solid solution system. *Ferroelectrics* **1985**, *65*, 107–130. [CrossRef]

5. Relaxation Phenomena—Time-Dependent Phenomenology

5.1. Introduction to Relaxation Phenomena

Phenomenology, as so far discussed, is used for an equilibrium status (no time dependence). However, if the deviation is small due to the equilibrium status, the material property may return to the stable point (due to the energy minimization condition). The "relaxation phenomenon" in physics and chemistry is an effect related to the delay between the application of an external controlable parameter to a material and its response. The easiest example is to consider what happens if the driving force such as the electrical field is suddenly switched off after it has been constant for a sufficiently long time so that an equilibrium distribution of dipoles has been realized. We handle the transident reponse of a physical parameter after slightly deviating from the equilibrium state in terms of the "relaxation" time in this chapter. In the latter part, we also discuss the relaxation phenomena from the viewpoint of the frequency dependence. This relaxation concept is essential to understand the domain wall dynamics (Chapter 14), loss mechanisms (Chapter 6), and heat conduction (Chapter 12).

5.2. Polarization Relaxation

5.2.1. Polarization Relaxation and Internal Energy

Landau and Khalatnikov developed a theory for the temperature dependence of the "ralaxation time" of the order parameter, P, based on the Ginzburg–Landau theory of phase transiditions [1,2]. This mean-field approach shows a divergence of $\tau \propto 1/(T_C - T)$ near a second-order phase transision point, T_C. The key assumption is that the change of polarization P with time (i.e., $\frac{\partial P}{\partial t}$) is proportional to the internal energy decrease rate with the unit order parameter change (i.e., $-\frac{\partial U}{\partial P}$). Around the equilibrium/stable-state $P = P_S$, $\frac{\partial U}{\partial P} = 0$, from which we obtain P_S. By shifting ΔP from this point, the internal energy should increase. By introducing the "relaxation time" τ, the inverse of which is taken as a proportional constant:

$$\frac{\partial P}{\partial t} = -\frac{1}{\tau}\left(\frac{\partial U}{\partial P}\right). \tag{5.1}$$

5.2.2. Analysis in the Second-Order Phase Transition

We use the simplest "second-order phase transition" model here for a practical calculation:

$$G(P, T) = (1/2)\alpha P^2 + (1/4)\beta P^4 - PE \quad [\alpha = (T - T_0)/\varepsilon_0 C]. \tag{5.2}$$

Recall the fact that in the ferroelectric phase ($T < T_0$), the spontaneous polarization is expressed as

$$P_S = \pm\sqrt{-\frac{\alpha}{\beta}} = \sqrt{(T_0 - T)/\varepsilon_0 C\beta}. \tag{5.3}$$

Equation (5.1) is expressed in practice by

$$\frac{\partial P}{\partial t} = -\frac{1}{\tau'}\frac{\partial G}{\partial P} = -\frac{1}{\tau'}(\alpha P + \beta P^3 - E). \tag{5.4}$$

We consider the initial polarization P_0 $(= P_S + \varepsilon_0\varepsilon^X E_0)$ by applying a small electric field E_0 on a ferroelectric specimen with $P_S = \sqrt{-\frac{\alpha}{\beta}}$. Then, we calculate the polarization change after a sudden reduction in E_0. The meaning of Equation (5.4) is to establish how quickly the P should return to the equilibrium state P_S after sudden termination of the field. Equation (5.4) can be solved by putting $E = 0$ as

$$\int_0^t \left(-\tfrac{1}{\tau'}\right)dt = \int_{P_0}^{P} \tfrac{dP}{(\alpha P+\beta P^3)} = \tfrac{1}{\beta {P_S}^2}\int_{P_0}^{P} [-\tfrac{1}{P} + \tfrac{1}{2}\tfrac{1}{(P-P_S)} + \tfrac{1}{2}\tfrac{1}{(P+P_S)}]dP - \tfrac{t}{\tau'}$$
$$= \tfrac{1}{-\alpha}\left[-\ln\left(\tfrac{P}{P_0}\right) + \tfrac{1}{2}\ln\left(\tfrac{P-P_S}{P_0-P_S}\right) + \tfrac{1}{2}\ln\left(\tfrac{P+P_S}{P_0+P_S}\right)\right].$$

Thus, we obtain

$$\sqrt{\left[1-\left(\frac{P_S}{P}\right)^2\right]/[1-(\frac{P_S}{P_0})^2]} = e^{-t/(\frac{\tau'}{-\alpha})}. \tag{5.5}$$

Thus, the actual "relaxation time" τ'' can be denoted by

$$\tau'' = \frac{\tau'}{-\alpha} = \frac{\tau'\varepsilon_0 C}{(T_0 - T)} \propto 1/(T_0 - T)\ [\alpha = (T - T_0)/\varepsilon_0 C] \tag{5.6}$$

From Equations (5.5) and (5.6), we can conclude the following items:

- The time constant is proportional to "permittivity" $\varepsilon_0\varepsilon^X$.
- $t \to \infty$ gives $P \to P_S$.
- With approaching $T \to T_0$, $\tau \to \infty$. The recovery time of P is very slow around $T_C = T_0$.

Note here that the relaxation time τ'' above is a measure of the time delay of $\sqrt{\left[1-\left(\frac{P_S}{P}\right)^2\right]}$. The relaxation time τ for $\Delta P = (P - P_S) = P_S[1 - \left(\frac{P_S}{P_0}\right)^2]e^{-t/(\frac{\tau'}{-2\alpha})}$ is half of the above τ''. The "relaxation time" corresponds to the "reaction resistance" or "dielectric loss". A similar concept is discussed in Chapter 6.

5.3. Temperature Relaxation

The time dependence of temperature (uniform temperature in a small volume) is considered in this section. For example, by the "electrocaloric effect", the ferroelectric material's temperature is changed with the electric field application under an adiabatic condition. We start from an equation similar to the one in the previous section.

$$\frac{\partial\theta}{\partial t} = -\frac{1}{\tau}(\frac{\partial U}{\partial\theta}). \tag{5.7}$$

The temperature change speed is proportional to the energy change per unit temperature increase (i.e., proportional to the specific heat capacity c_p). If we take the Gibbs energy transformed from Equation (2.11) in Chapter 2 under stress-free condition ($X = 0$),

$$\begin{aligned} G(T,X,E) &= \frac{1}{2}\left(\frac{\partial^2 G}{\partial T^2}\right)\theta^2 + \frac{1}{2}\left(\frac{\partial^2 G}{\partial E^2}\right)E^2 + \left(\frac{\partial^2 G}{\partial T\partial E}\right)\theta E \\ &= -\frac{1}{2}\left(\frac{c_p^E}{T}\right)\theta^2 - \frac{1}{2}\left(\varepsilon_0\varepsilon^X\right)E^2 + p\theta E, \end{aligned} \tag{5.8}$$

where p is pyroelectric coefficient.

Equation (5.7) is transformed into

$$\frac{\partial\theta}{\partial t} = \frac{1}{\tau'}[\left(\frac{c_p^E}{T}\right)\theta - pE]. \tag{5.9}$$

The meaning of Equation (5.9) is to provide how quickly the θ should approach the equilibrium status θ_s after sudden application of the field E. As you may realize, the electrocaloric effect under an adiabatic condition indicates the temperature change in the equilibrium status $((\frac{\partial\theta}{\partial t}) = 0$, in Equation (5.9)) as

$$\theta_s = \frac{pT}{c_p^E}E. \tag{5.10}$$

Equation (5.9) can be solved as

$$\begin{aligned} -\textstyle\int_0^t \frac{1}{\tau'}\left(\frac{c_p^E}{T}\right)dt &= \textstyle\int_0^\theta \frac{d\theta}{(\theta_s-\theta)}, \\ -\frac{1}{\tau'}\left(\frac{c_p^E}{T}\right)t &= ln(\theta_s-\theta) - ln(\theta_s), \\ (1-\theta/\theta_s) &= e^{-t/\tau'(\frac{T}{c_p^E})}. \end{aligned} \tag{5.11}$$

We denote the actual relaxation time constant τ expressed by

$$\tau = \tau'\left(\frac{T}{c_p^E}\right). \tag{5.12}$$

From Equations (5.11) and (5.12), we can conclude the following items:

- In a uniform (no space gradient) specimen, temperature change follows an exponential trend with time: $(1-\theta/\theta_s) = e^{-t/\tau}$.

- $t \to \infty$ gives $\theta \to \theta_S$. θ_s corresponds to the temperature change by the "electrocaloric effect".
- The time constant is proportional to the absolute temperature and inversely proportional to the specific heat capacity c_p^E. The larger the specific heat capacity c_p^E, and the lower the temperature, the lower the time constant τ. The recovery time of θ is quicker. This τ is a roughly suitable rise time period of applying a pseudo-step electric field.

5.4. From Time Dependence to Frequency Dependence

5.4.1. Time Dependence of Polarization Recovery

The "relaxation phenomenon" with a sudden switch-off of the electric field is taken into account again in a ferroelectric crystal, after it has been constant for a sufficiently long time. We expect that the electric-field-induced polarization ΔP will go to zero to approach the stable spontaneous polarization P_S. However, that cannot happen instantaneously; some time delay is included. See Figure 5.1. The polarization recovery, that is, relative ionic movement under the external field elimination, will take a characteristic time owing to the effective mass of ions in an atomic potential in a lattice, which we will call the "relaxation time τ" of the system. We expect a smooth recovery over the polarization with an electric field to zero within the relaxation time τ. As derived in Section 5.2, with this behavior, as shown in Figure 5.1, we expect that P decays starting at the time of the switch-off according to

$$\Delta P = \Delta P(t = 0)e^{-t/\tau}. \tag{5.13}$$

This simple equation describes the behavior of a system such as the polarization change. Nevertheless, we know that a relation such as this is found whenever we look at the decay of some ensemble of particles or objects from higher energy than the equilibrium condition, or the change from the excited state to the base state, i.e., that has to overcome some energy barrier.

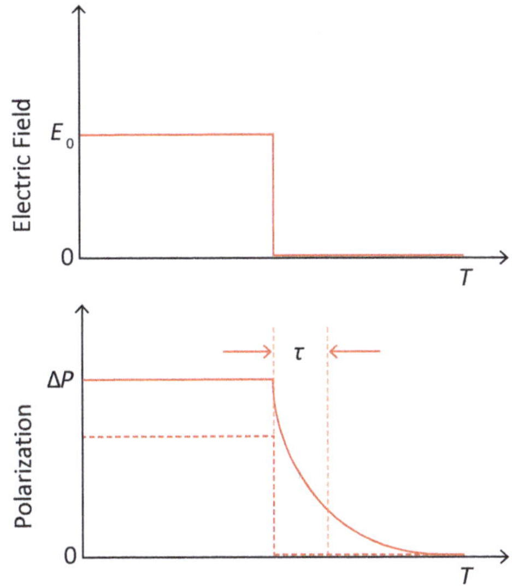

Figure 5.1. Polarization relaxation phenomenon for a sudden reduction of electric field. Source: Figure by author.

5.4.2. Frequency Dependence of Polarization

We described the "time dependent" $P(t)$ of the polarization when we applied some disturbance or E input to the material (switching the electrical field on–off). When we consider a cyclical application of electric field, this relaxation time will reflect the phase delay of the response. We now discuss the "frequency dependence" of $P(\omega)$ with angular frequency ω, i.e., the output to a periodic harmonic input, $E = E_0 \cdot \sin(\omega t)$. Fourier transform is suitable for analyzing a periodic steady phenomenon. By knowing $P(\omega)$, we can express the response to any signal just as well. In other words, we can "Fourier reverse-transform" $P(t)$ into $P(\omega)$.

Since we already know the time dependence $P(t)$ for a switch-off signal in the previous section, let us derive $P(\omega)$ from that. Knowing Equation (5.13) defined in the interval $0 < t < \infty$, we conduct Fourier transformation expressed by

$$P(\omega) = \int_{0}^{\infty} \Delta P_0 e^{-t/\tau} \cdot e^{-j\omega t} \cdot dt, \tag{5.14}$$

where ΔP_0 is the initial static polarization under a certain electric field E_0, i.e., the value of $P(\omega)$ for $\omega = 0$ Hz, and $j = \sqrt{-1}$. Thus, we obtain

$$P(\omega) = \frac{\Delta P_0}{\omega_0 + j\omega}, \tag{5.15a}$$

$$\omega_0 = 1/\tau. \tag{5.15b}$$

The reader can understand that $P(\omega)$ is the polarization response of the system when we jiggle it with an electrical field $E = E_0 \cdot \exp(j\omega t)$.

5.4.3. Complex Numbers and Debye Model

Complex Permittivity

Complex numbers are occasionally used in a "steady harmonic phenomenon" such as the voltage–current relation. In a complex impedance $Z^* = Z' + jZ''$, the real part Z' stands for the voltage/current magnitude ratio and the imaginary part Z''/Z' stands for the voltage vs. current phase lag.

Under the supposition $D \approx P$ in a high-permittivity ferroelectric, we have

$$P(\omega) = \varepsilon_0 \varepsilon(\omega) E(\omega). \tag{5.16}$$

The time dependence of $P(\omega)$ is assumed to be under the same ω as the electric field. It is either given by $e^{-j(\omega t - \varphi)}$, with φ accounting for a possible phase shift, or simply by $e^{-j\omega t}$, if we include the phase shift in $\varepsilon(\omega)$, which means it must be complex. The second possibility is more powerful and popular. By combining Equations (5.16) and (5.15a), we obtain

$$\varepsilon_0 \varepsilon(\omega) = \frac{\omega_0 P(\omega)}{E(\omega)} = \frac{\omega_0 P(\omega = 0)}{E_0} \frac{1}{\omega_0 + j\omega} = \varepsilon_0 \varepsilon_S \frac{1}{1 + j(\omega/\omega_0)}, \tag{5.17}$$

$\varepsilon_S = \Delta P_0 / \varepsilon_0 E_0$ ($P(\omega = 0) = \Delta P_0 / \omega_0$) is the "static permittivity", i.e., the value at zero frequency. Now, we can denote a complex permittivity as

$$\varepsilon(\omega) = \varepsilon_S \frac{1}{1 + j(\omega/\omega_0)}, \tag{5.18}$$

then decompose $\varepsilon(\omega)$ in a real and an imaginary part, i.e., write it as

$$\varepsilon(\omega)^* = \varepsilon(\omega)' - j\varepsilon(\omega)'', \tag{5.19}$$

we obtain

$$\varepsilon(\omega)^* = \varepsilon_S [\frac{1}{1 + \left(\frac{\omega}{\omega_0}\right)^2} - j \frac{\left(\frac{\omega}{\omega_0}\right)}{1 + \left(\frac{\omega}{\omega_0}\right)^2}] \tag{5.20}$$

or

$$\begin{cases} \varepsilon(\omega)' = \dfrac{\varepsilon_S}{1+\left(\frac{\omega}{\omega_0}\right)^2} \\ \varepsilon(\omega)'' = \dfrac{\varepsilon_S \left(\frac{\omega}{\omega_0}\right)}{1+\left(\frac{\omega}{\omega_0}\right)^2} \end{cases}. \tag{5.21}$$

Figure 5.2 plots the real and imaginary permittivity, $\varepsilon(\omega)'$ and $\varepsilon(\omega)''$, where a typical relaxation phenomenon can be found, i.e., permittivity change with frequency, around the characteristic frequency $\omega_0 = 1/\tau$, or $\omega\tau \approx 1$.

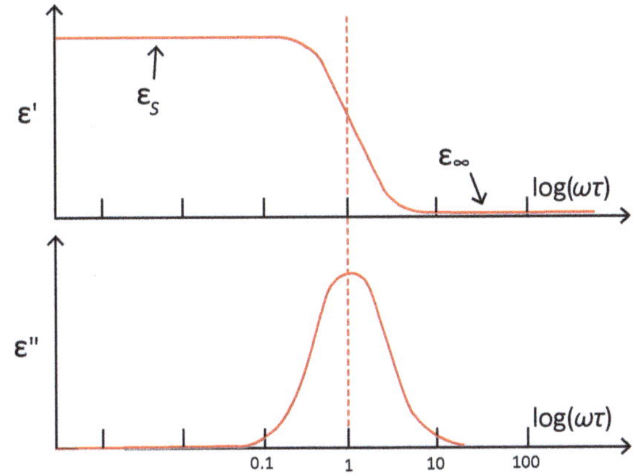

Figure 5.2. Frequency dependence of real and imaginary permittivity. Source: Figure by author.

Cole–Cole Circle

So far, we assumed that at high frequencies ($\omega_0 < \omega \to \infty$) the polarization is essentially zero (i.e., $\varepsilon(\omega)' \to 0$). That is not necessarily true in the most general case—when we primarily discuss "ionic polarization", "electronic polarization" still remains, even at a high frequencies such as THz. If we take this into account, we have to change our consideration of relaxation somewhat and introduce a new, simple parameter $\varepsilon'(\omega \gg \omega_0) = \varepsilon_\infty$. For the electronic polarization, we sometimes adopt $\varepsilon_\infty = n^2$, where n is the refractive index of this material. This reasoning follows the "Debye model", and the following equations are called "Debye equations":

$$\varepsilon(\omega)^* = [\frac{(\varepsilon_S - \varepsilon_\infty)}{1 + j\left(\frac{\omega}{\omega_0}\right)} + \varepsilon_\infty] \tag{5.22}$$

and

$$\begin{cases} \varepsilon(\omega)' = \varepsilon_\infty + \frac{(\varepsilon_S - \varepsilon_\infty)}{1+\left(\frac{\omega}{\omega_0}\right)^2} \\ \varepsilon(\omega)'' = \frac{(\varepsilon_S - \varepsilon_\infty)\left(\frac{\omega}{\omega_0}\right)}{1+\left(\frac{\omega}{\omega_0}\right)^2} \end{cases}. \tag{5.23}$$

Here, note that $\varepsilon'(\omega = 0) = \varepsilon_S$ and $\varepsilon'(\omega = \infty) = \varepsilon_\infty$. ε' is the real part of a complex amplitude, which gives the amplitude of the response that is in phase with the driving force, while ε'' is the imaginary part, which gives the amplitude of the response that is phase shifted by 90°. Finally, let us consider the graphical relationship between ε' and ε''. The reader can easily imagine the following relation:

$$\begin{aligned} &\left[\varepsilon(\omega)' - \frac{(\varepsilon_S + \varepsilon_\infty)}{2}\right]^2 + \left[\varepsilon(\omega)''\right]^2 \\ &= [-\frac{\varepsilon_S - \varepsilon_\infty}{2} + \frac{(\varepsilon_S - \varepsilon_\infty)}{1+\left(\frac{\omega}{\omega_0}\right)^2}]^2 + [\frac{(\varepsilon_S - \varepsilon_\infty)\left(\frac{\omega}{\omega_0}\right)}{1+\left(\frac{\omega}{\omega_0}\right)^2}]^2 = (\frac{\varepsilon_S - \varepsilon_\infty}{2})^2. \end{aligned} \tag{5.24}$$

The locus of $\varepsilon(\omega)^*$ is a simple half-circle, as illustrated in Figure 5.3. Note that the graph is characterized by the three numbers that define a particular material, ε_s, ε_∞, and $\omega_0 = 1/\tau$.

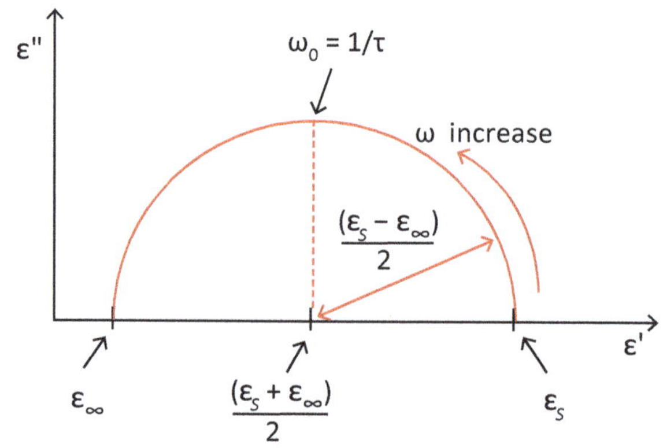

Figure 5.3. Cole-Cole plot based on the Debye model. Source: Figure by author.

So far, we have not discussed much on the microscopic origin of the "relaxation time". Through Example Problem 5.1, the reader is requested to learn how the macroscopic relaxation time is related with the microscopic potential minimum gap.

Example Problem 5.1

Consider an "order–disorder-type ferroelectric" with ions trapped in the same "double-minimum potential" with a relatively low barrier between the two minima (Figure 5.4). Thus, each unit lattice cell has a permanent dipole moment, and the dipole–dipole coupling is taken into account at a temperature lower than the Curie temperature. Under a quasi-DC field, the ion follows the electric field alternating between the positive and negative potentials. However, with increasing drive frequency, the ionic motion exhibits a delay with respect to the electric field due to the potential barrier ΔU. This is an intuitive explanation for the "dielectric relaxation" in a ferroelectric phase (refer to Mason's treatment [3]).

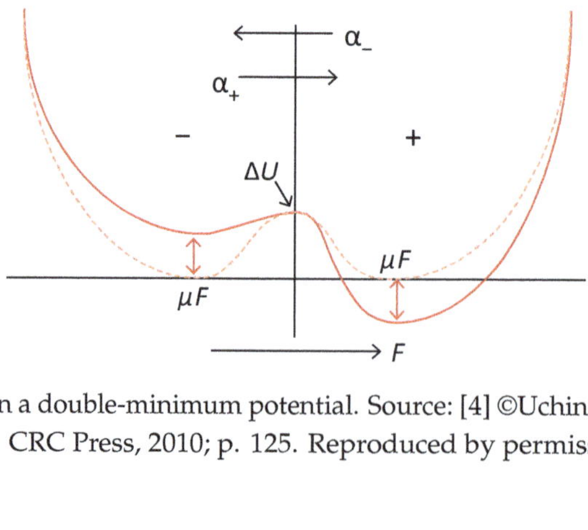

Figure 5.4. Ion in a double-minimum potential. Source: [4] ©Uchino, K. *Ferroelectric Devices*, 2nd ed. CRC Press, 2010; p. 125. Reproduced by permission of Taylor & Francis Group.

(1) Using a mathematical representation, derive the following "Debye dispersion relation" for a mono-dispersive case (equivalent to Equation (5.18)):

$$E(\omega) = \varepsilon_S/(1 + j\omega\tau). \tag{P5.1.1}$$

(2) Discuss how the above dispersion obeys the so-called "Cole–Cole relation" (i.e., the real and imaginary parts of permittivity trace a half circle on a complex permittivity plane).

Solution

When an external electric field E is applied, the local field F in the crystal is described by

$$F = E + \gamma P, \tag{P5.1.2}$$

where γ is the "Lorentz factor", a positive feedback amplifier for the local field. Refer to Section 1.2.3. The transition probability for an ion from the $-$ to the + in Figure 5.4, α_+, and the opposite transition probability, α_-, are expressed as

$$\alpha_+ = \Gamma\exp[-(\Delta U - \mu F)/kT], \text{ and} \tag{P5.1.3}$$

$$\alpha_- = \Gamma\exp[-(\Delta U + \mu F)/kT], \tag{P5.1.4}$$

respectively, based on the Boltzmann distribution. Here, ΔU is the barrier height between the two potential minima, μ is the dipole moment, and Γ is a constant for normalizing the probability. One example is the energy required to switch the leftward water molecule to the rightward water molecule in an ice crystal.

If we introduce the number of + (or $-$) direction dipoles per unit volume N_+ (or N_-), the total dipole number is given by $N = N_+ + N_-$, and the polarization (per unit volume) is represented as

$$P = (N_+ - N_-)\mu \tag{P5.1.5}$$

The time dependence will be expressed as

$$dN_+/dt = N_-\alpha_+ - N_+\alpha_-, \tag{P5.1.6}$$

$$dN_-/dt = N_+\alpha_- - N_-\alpha_+. \tag{P5.1.7}$$

Then,

$$dP/dt = \mu(dN_+/\mathrm{dt} - dN_-/\mathrm{dt}) = 2\mu(N_-\alpha_+ - N_+\alpha_-), \tag{P5.1.8}$$

where

$$N_+ = (1/2)(N + P/\mu), \tag{P5.1.9}$$

$$N_- = (1/2)(N - P/\mu). \tag{P5.1.10}$$

Suppose that the external electric field $E = E_0 e^{j\omega t}$ is small ($P_S \gg \varepsilon_0 \varepsilon E$) and that the polarization is given by

$$P = P_S + \varepsilon_0 \varepsilon E_0 e^{j\omega t}. \tag{P5.1.11}$$

From Equation (P5.1.8),

$$\begin{aligned}
&\text{Left side} = (j\omega)\varepsilon_0 Ee = \text{Right-side} \\
&= 2\mu(N_-\Gamma \exp[-(\Delta U - \mu F)/kT] - N_+\Gamma \exp[-(\Delta U + \mu F)/kT] \\
&= 2\mu(N_-\Gamma \exp[-(\Delta U - (E+\gamma P))/kT] - N_+\Gamma \exp[-(\Delta U + \mu(E+\gamma P))/kT] \\
&= 2\mu \exp(-\Delta U/kT)\{N_- \exp[\mu(E+\gamma(P_S+\varepsilon_0\varepsilon E))/kT] \\
&-N_+ \exp[-\mu(E+\gamma(P_S+\varepsilon_0\varepsilon E))/kT]\}
\end{aligned}$$

furthermore, using Equations (P5.1.9) and (P5.1.10),

$$\begin{aligned}
&= 2\mu\Gamma\exp(-\Delta U/kT)\{(1/2)(N - P/\mu)\exp(\mu\gamma P_S/kT)\exp[\mu(1+\gamma\varepsilon_0\varepsilon)E/kT] \\
&- (1/2)(N + P/\mu)\exp(-\mu\gamma P_S)/kT)\exp[-\mu(1+\gamma\varepsilon_0\varepsilon)E/kT].
\end{aligned}$$

Taking into account $P_S \gg \varepsilon_0\varepsilon E$ and $\exp(x) \approx 1 + x$ (for $x \ll 1$), the above calculation is transformed into:

$$\begin{aligned}
&(j\omega)\varepsilon_0\varepsilon E = 2\mu\Gamma\exp(-\Delta U/kT)\{(1/2)(N - P/\mu)\exp(\mu\gamma P_S/kT) \\
&[1 + \mu(1+\gamma\varepsilon_0\varepsilon)E/kT] - (1/2)(N + P/\mu)\exp(-\mu\gamma P_S)/kT)[1 - \mu(1+\gamma\varepsilon_0\varepsilon)E/kT] \\
&= 2\Gamma\exp(-\Delta U/kT)[\mu N\{\sinh(\mu\gamma P_S/kT) + \mu(1+\gamma\varepsilon_0\varepsilon)(E/kT)\cosh(\mu\gamma P_S/kT)\} \\
&- P\{\cosh(\mu\gamma P_S/kT) + \mu(1+\gamma\varepsilon_0\varepsilon)(E/kT)\sinh(\mu\gamma P_S/kT)\}].
\end{aligned} \tag{P5.1.12}$$

Using the relation $P = P_S + \varepsilon_0\varepsilon E$ on Equation (P5.1.12), we obtain

$$\begin{aligned}
&(j\omega)\varepsilon_0\varepsilon E = 2\Gamma\exp(-\Delta U/kT)[\mu N\{\sinh(\mu\gamma P_S/kT) \\
&+ \mu(1+\gamma\varepsilon_0\varepsilon)(E/kT)\cosh(\mu\gamma P_S/kT)\} - P_S\{\cosh(\mu\gamma P_S/kT) \\
&+ \mu(1+\gamma\varepsilon_0\varepsilon)(E/kT)\sinh(\mu\gamma P_S/kT)\} \\
&- \varepsilon_0\varepsilon E\{\cosh(\mu\gamma P_S/kT) + \mu(1+\gamma\varepsilon_0\varepsilon)(E/kT)\sinh(\mu\gamma P_S/kT)\}] \\
&= 2\Gamma\exp(-\Delta U/kT)[\mu N\mu(1+\gamma\varepsilon_0\varepsilon)(E/kT)\cosh(\mu\gamma P_S/kT) \\
&- P_S\mu(1+\gamma\varepsilon_0\varepsilon)(E/kT)\sinh(\mu\gamma P_S/kT)\} - \varepsilon_0\varepsilon E\cosh(\mu\gamma P_S/kT)].
\end{aligned} \tag{P5.1.13}$$

For the last transformation, we used the relationship of $\mu N\{\sinh(\mu\gamma P_S/kT) - P_S\{\cosh(\mu\gamma P_S/kT) = 0$ and the neglect of the higher order E^2. Introducing the static permittivity ε_S at $\omega = 0$, we obtain

$$\begin{aligned}
&\mu N\mu(1+\gamma\varepsilon_0\varepsilon_S)(E/kT)\cosh(\mu\gamma P_S/kT) \\
&- P_S\mu(1+\gamma\varepsilon_0\varepsilon_S)(E/kT)\sinh(\mu\gamma P_S/kT)\} - \varepsilon_0\varepsilon_S E\cosh(\mu\gamma P_S/kT) = 0.
\end{aligned} \tag{P5.1.14}$$

Now, for a high-frequency permittivity, from Equation (P5.1.13)

$$\varepsilon(\omega) = \varepsilon_S/(1 + j\omega\tau), \tag{P5.1.15}$$

where

$$\tau = (1 + \gamma\varepsilon_0\varepsilon_S)\tau_0/\cosh(\mu\gamma P_S/kT), \tag{P5.1.16a}$$

$$\tau_0 = 1/2\Gamma\exp(-\Delta U/kT). \tag{P5.1.16b}$$

The subscript "s" of ε_S stands for a static value ($\omega = 0$), and in the paraelectric phase, it should follow the Curie–Weiss law:

$$\varepsilon_0 \varepsilon_s = \varepsilon_0 C/(T - T_C). \tag{P5.1.17}$$

The relaxation time $\tau \propto 1/(T - T_C)$, which increases significantly when approaching $T \to T_C$. This means that the recovery to the equilibrium polarization is quite slow, which is called "critical slowing-down".

Equation (P5.1.15) can be rewritten as

$$\varepsilon(\omega) = \varepsilon'(\omega) - j\varepsilon''(\omega),$$

where

$$\varepsilon'(\omega) = \varepsilon_S/[1 + (\omega\tau)^2], \varepsilon''(\omega) = \omega\tau\varepsilon_S/[1 + (\omega\tau)^2]. \tag{P5.1.18}$$

The so-called "Cole–Cole relation" is obtained from Equation (P5.1.18), which is a half-circle with the following formula, and is illustrated in Figure 5.5.

$$(\varepsilon'(\omega) - \varepsilon_S/2)^2 + \varepsilon''(\omega)^2 = (\varepsilon_S/2)^2. \tag{P5.1.19}$$

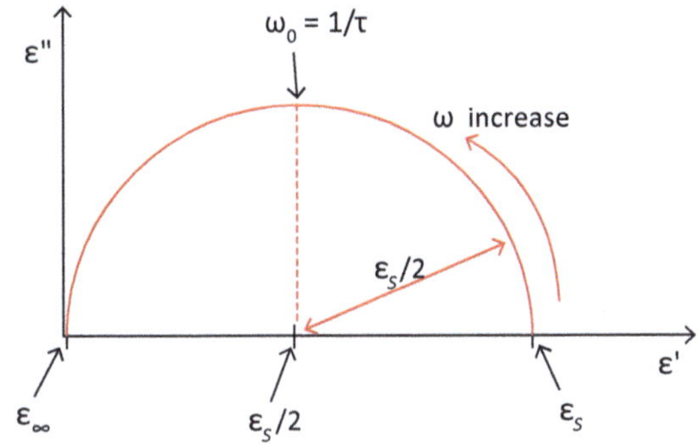

Figure 5.5. Cole–Cole plot for a double-minimum potential model. Source: Figure by author.

The permittivity for $\omega \to \infty$ is assumed to be $\varepsilon_\infty = 0$ in this case, and the maximum $\varepsilon'' = \varepsilon_S/2$ is obtained at $\omega = \omega_0 = 1/\tau$ or $\omega\tau = 1$. Equations (P5.1.16a) and (P5.1.16b) indicate that the relaxation time τ is proportional to (1) $\exp(\Delta/kT)$, in addition to (2) $1/(T_C - T)$. The larger the dipole moment barrier height ΔU, the longer the relaxation time τ.

Dipole Reorientation

Suffice it to say that typical relaxation times are around 10^{-11} s in dielectric materials, which corresponds to frequencies in the GHz range, i.e., "cm waves". We must, therefore, expect that typical materials exhibiting dipole reorientation such as "ice/water" will show some peculiar behavior in the "microwave range" of the electromagnetic spectrum. Water molecule flip-over, i.e., dipole reorientation, will not follow above this particular frequency $\omega_0 = 1/\tau$; thus, the imaginary permittivity, that is, loss, increases significantly. This is the meal heating mechanism of the "microwave oven". In mixtures of materials, or in complicated materials with several different dipoles and several different relaxation times, things become more complicated. The smooth curves shown above may no longer be smooth because they now result from a superposition of several smooth curves. Finally, it is also clear that τ may vary quite a bit, depending on the material and the temperature. As discussed in Section 5.2.2, the relaxation time is proportional to $1/\alpha$ in the second-order phase transition ferroelectrics:

$$\tau = \frac{\tau'}{-2\alpha} \propto \frac{1}{T_0 - T}. \tag{5.25}$$

When approaching the Curie temperature from low temperatures, the relaxation time increases significantly.

5.4.4. Distribution Function of Relaxation Time

We introduced the simplest Debye model with a single relaxation time τ, whose Cole–Cole plot of complex permittivity shows a perfect half-circle. However, when we plot $\varepsilon(\omega)'$ and $\varepsilon(\omega)''$ of the experimentally obtained data, the Cole–Cole plot is deviated from a half-circle, which requires consideration of the τ distribution. We can say that the permanent dipoles in a real dielectric material seem to have slightly deviated potential barriers ΔU, leading to the distribution of the relaxation time.

Figure 5.6 shows such an example, where the Cole–Cole plot of complex permittivity is observed by Hatta [5] in $NaNO_2$ above the Curie temperature (i.e., paraelectric phase). Sodium nitrite composed of NO_2 dipole moments is a water-soluble ferroelectric crystal with the Curie temperature at 163.4 °C [6]. The center of the complex permittivity circle seems to be located below the "real coordinate axis". Considering the line connecting the circle center and ε_∞ on the real axis, the angle of this line and the real coordinate axis is defined as α in "radian" (refer to Figure 5.6). We define a new parameter β as

$$\beta \equiv 1 - \frac{2}{\pi}\alpha. \tag{5.26}$$

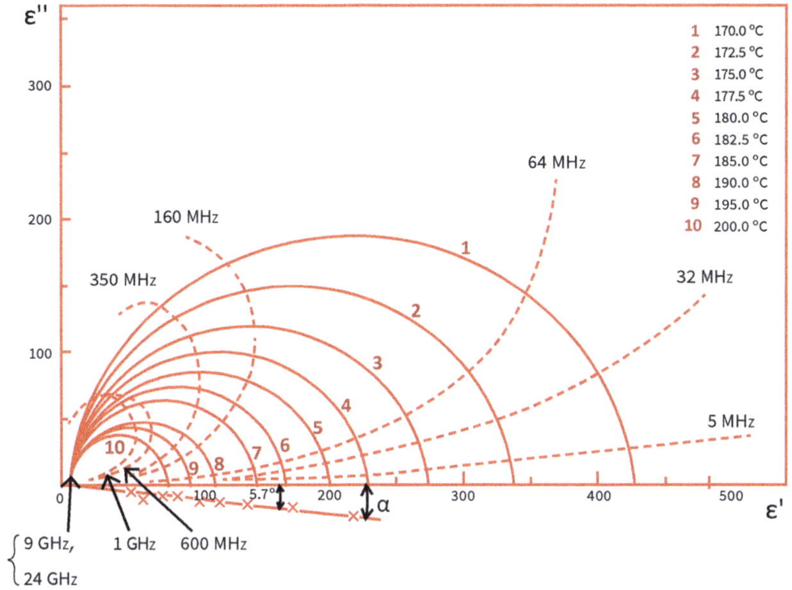

Figure 5.6. Cole–Cole plot of complex permittivity in $NaNO_2$. Source: Figure by author, adapted from [7].

This parameter β is a measure of distribution of the relaxation time; $\beta = 1$ corresponds to the single relaxation time, and with an increase in the distribution, the β value decreases. $\beta = 0.94$ in the case of $NaNO_2$, that is, the time distribution is rather small.

When the relaxation time has a distribution, Equation (5.23) is modified by introducing a distribution function $y(\tau)$ as the following equation:

$$\begin{cases} \frac{(\varepsilon(\omega)' - \varepsilon_\infty)}{(\varepsilon_S - \varepsilon_\infty)} = \int_0^\infty \frac{y(\tau)d\tau}{1+(\omega\tau)^2} \\ \frac{\varepsilon(\omega)''}{(\varepsilon_S - \varepsilon_\infty)} = \int_0^\infty \frac{\omega\tau y(\tau)d\tau}{1+(\omega\tau)^2} \end{cases}. \quad (5.27)$$

Hill and Ichiki adopted a Gaussian distribution to $y(\tau)$ [8]:

$$y(\tau) = Ae^{-(\tau/\tau_1)^2}, \quad (5.28)$$

where τ_1 is the standard deviation of the τ distribution and assumed to be temperature dependent as

$$\tau_1 = \frac{B}{T - T_C}, \quad (5.29)$$

where B is the constant.

The average relaxation time τ increases, as well as the standard deviation τ_1, when the temperature is reduced down to the Curie temperature.

Chapter Essentials

1. Basic Equations for Relaxation Phenomena:

The change of polarization P with time (i.e., $\frac{\partial P}{\partial t}$) is proportional to the internal energy decrease rate with the unit polarization change (i.e., $-\frac{\partial U}{\partial P}$).

$$\frac{\partial P}{\partial t} = -\frac{1}{\tau}\left(\frac{\partial U}{\partial P}\right),$$

$$\sqrt{\left[1-\left(\frac{P_S}{P}\right)^2\right]/[1-(\frac{P_S}{P_0})^2]} = e^{-t/(\frac{\tau'}{-\alpha})}.$$

The temperature change speed is proportional to the energy change per unit temperature increase (i.e., proportional to the specific heat capacity c_p).

$$\frac{\partial \theta}{\partial t} = -\frac{1}{\tau}\left(\frac{\partial U}{\partial \theta}\right),$$

$$(1-\theta/\theta_s) = e^{-t/\tau\prime(\frac{T}{c_p^E})}.$$

2. Time Dependence vs. Frequency Dependence:
   - Time dependence of polarization recovery:
     $\Delta P = \Delta P(t=0)e^{-t/\tau}$.
   - Frequency dependence of polarization:
     $P(\omega) = \int_0^\infty \Delta P_0 e^{-t/\tau} e^{-j\omega t} dt,$
     $$\left\{\begin{array}{c} P(\omega) = \frac{\Delta P_0}{\omega_0 + j\omega} \\ \omega_0 = \frac{1}{\tau} \end{array}\right.,$$
     $\omega_0 = 1/\tau$.

3. Complex Permittivity—Cole–Cole Plot (Refer to Figures 5.2 and 5.3)

$$\varepsilon(\omega)^* = \varepsilon(\omega)' - j\varepsilon(\omega)'',$$

$$\varepsilon(\omega)^* = [\frac{(\varepsilon_S - \varepsilon_\infty)}{1+j\left(\frac{\omega}{\omega_0}\right)} + \varepsilon_\infty]$$

$$\left\{\begin{array}{l} \varepsilon(\omega)' = \varepsilon_\infty + \frac{(\varepsilon_S - \varepsilon_\infty)}{1+\left(\frac{\omega}{\omega_0}\right)^2} \\ \varepsilon(\omega)'' = \frac{(\varepsilon_S - \varepsilon_\infty)\left(\frac{\omega}{\omega_0}\right)}{1+\left(\frac{\omega}{\omega_0}\right)^2} \end{array}\right..$$

4. Distribution Function of Relaxation Time

$$\left\{\begin{array}{l} \frac{(\varepsilon(\omega)' - \varepsilon_\infty)}{(\varepsilon_S - \varepsilon_\infty)} = \int\limits_0^\infty \frac{y(\tau)d\tau}{1+(\omega\tau)^2} \\ \frac{\varepsilon(\omega)''}{(\varepsilon_S - \varepsilon_\infty)} = \int\limits_0^\infty \frac{\omega\tau y(\tau)d\tau}{1+(\omega\tau)^2} \end{array}\right.,$$

Gaussian distribution to $y(\tau)$:

$$y(\tau) = Ae^{-(\tau/\tau_1)^2},$$

where τ_1 is the standard deviation of the τ distribution and is assumed to be temperature dependent as

$$tau_1 = \frac{B}{T-T_C},$$

where B is the constant.

Check Point

1. (T/F) The relaxation phenomenon is defined as a recovering phenomenon from a deviated status to an equilibrium status. True or false?
2. (T/F) When we consider the temperature recovery, the speed is proportional to free energy U change per temperature deviation θ, $\frac{\partial U}{\partial \theta}$. True or false?
3. (T/F) When we consider the polarization relaxation phenomenon in the ferroelectric phase after shutting off the external electric field, the relaxation time is directly proportional to $(T_C - T)$. True or false?
4. (T/F) When we consider the permittivity relaxation phenomenon in the paraelectric phase of an order–disorder-type phase transition material, the relaxation time is inversely proportional to $(T - T_C)$. That is, the recovery time is very slow when approaching the Curie temperature. True or false?
5. (T/F) The relaxor ferroelectric shows a decrease in permittivity with an increase in the measuring frequency. True or false?
6. (T/F) When we plot the real and imaginary parts of permittivity on a 2D map (Cole–Cole plot), the plots follow on an exact half-circle for all relaxor ferroelectrics. True or false?
7. (T/F) The inverse of the relaxation time τ provides the frequency wherein the maximum imaginary permittivity appears. True or false?
8. (T/F) Large imaginary permittivity stands for large dielectric loss, leading to the absorption of input electric energy at that frequency. This is the principle of "dielectric spectroscopy". True or false?
9. When we draw the Cole–Cole plot with
$$\begin{cases} \varepsilon(\omega)' = \frac{\varepsilon_S}{1+\left(\frac{\omega}{\omega_0}\right)^2} \\ \varepsilon(\omega)'' = \frac{\varepsilon_S\left(\frac{\omega}{\omega_0}\right)}{1+\left(\frac{\omega}{\omega_0}\right)^2} \end{cases}$$
we can obtain a half-circle. Provide the circle center position with a complex permittivity value.
10. When we draw the Cole–Cole plot with
$$\begin{cases} \varepsilon(\omega)' = \frac{\varepsilon_S}{1+\left(\frac{\omega}{\omega_0}\right)^2} \\ \varepsilon(\omega)'' = \frac{\varepsilon_S\left(\frac{\omega}{\omega_0}\right)}{1+\left(\frac{\omega}{\omega_0}\right)^2} \end{cases}$$
We can obtain a half-circle. Provide the angular frequency value that exhibits the maximum $\varepsilon(\omega)''$.

Chapter Problems

5.1 When the relaxation time is distributed, the permittivity dispersion can be approximated as

$\varepsilon(\omega) = \varepsilon_S/[1 + (j\omega\tau)^{\beta}]$,

where $0 < \beta < 1$. Discuss the Cole–Cole plot change in comparison with the case $\beta = 1$ in Figure 5.3 (mono-dispersion model). Does it resemble Figure 5.6 in shape with the relaxation time distribution? If so, what is the relationship with β and the angle α in the figure?

5.2 The "relaxor ferroelectrics" exhibit "dielectric relaxation" (frequency dependence of the permittivity) from which their name is derived. The temperature dependence of the permittivity for $Pb(Mg_{1/3}Nb_{2/3})O_3$ is plotted in Figure 5.7 at various measuring frequencies [9]. Thus, accordingly, the "Curie point" is not precisely defined, but the "Curie range" is sometimes adopted. The permittivity of relaxor ferroelectrics in the paraelectric region obeys the following quadratic or critical component relation [10,11]:

$1/\varepsilon = 1/\varepsilon_0 + (T - T_C)^2/C^*$,

$1/\varepsilon = 1/\varepsilon_0 + (T - T_C)^\beta/C^*$,

rather than the normal Curie–Weiss law

$1/\varepsilon = (T - T_C)/C$.

Based on the concept of the relaxation time distribution and the permittivity dispersion (modified Cole–Cole plot), discuss the phenomenological modified Curie–Weiss law.

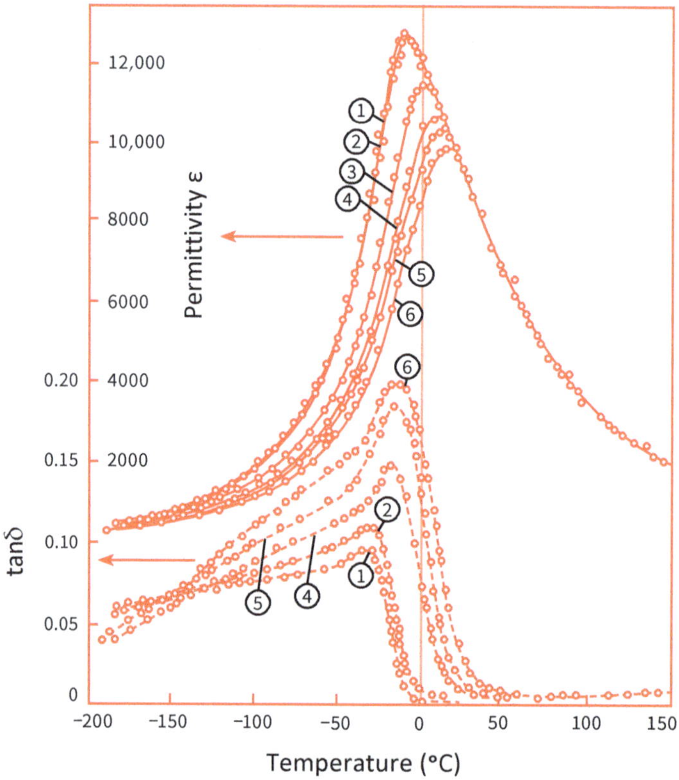

Figure 5.7. Temperature dependence of the permittivity and loss tanδ in $Pb(Mg_{1/3}Nb_{2/3})O_3$ for various measuring frequencies (kHz): (1) 0.4; (2) 1; (3) 45; (4) 450; (5) 1500; (6) 4500. Source: Source: [4] ©Uchino, K. *Ferroelectric Devices*, 2nd ed. CRC Press, 2010; p. 124. Reproduced by permission of Taylor & Francis Group.

Hint

We assumed the local composition distribution in complex perovskite crystals. By superimposing the "normal" Curie–Weiss law for each cluster with slightly different Curie temperatures, we obtain a rather broad permittivity peak as well as the quadratic relationship with temperature [10]. On the other hand, by using the "fractal analysis" of microdomains, we approached the critical exponent explanation [11,12].

References

1. Landau, L.D.; Khalatnikov, I.M. *Collected Papers of L. D. Landau*; ter Haar, D., Ed.; Gordon & Breach: New York, NY, UA, 1965.
2. Landau, L.D.; Khalatnikov, I.M. On the anomalous absorption of sound near a second order phase transition point. *Dokladii Academii Nauk CCCP* **1954**, *96*, 25.
3. Mason, W.P. Theory of the ferroelectric effect and clamped dielectric constant of Rochelle salt. *Phys. Rev.* **1947**, *72*, 854. [CrossRef]
4. Uchino, K. *Ferroelectric Devices*, 2nd ed.; CRC Press: Boca Raton, FL, USA, 2010.
5. Hatta, I.J. Experimental study on dielectric relaxation in $NaNO_2$. *Phys. Soc. Jpn.* **1968**, *24*, 1043. [CrossRef]
6. Sawada, S.; Nomura, S.; Asao, A. Dielectric Properties of Ferroelectric $NaNO_2$. *J. Phys. Soc. Jpn.* **1961**, *16*, 2207. [CrossRef]
7. Mitsui, T.; Tatsuzaki, T.; Nakamura, E. *Ferroelectrics*; Maki Publishing Co.: Tokyo, Japan, 1969.
8. Hill, R.M.; Ichiki, S.K. Paraelectric Response of KD_2PO_4. *Phys. Rev.* **1963**, *130*, 150. [CrossRef]
9. Smolensky, G.A.; Isupov, V.A.; Agranovskaya, A.I.; Popov, S.N. Ferroelectrics with diffuse phase transitions. *Sov. Phys.-Solid State* **1961**, *2*, 2584–2594. [CrossRef]
10. Uchino, K.; Cross, L.E.; Newnham, R.E.; Nomura, S. Electrostrictive effects in non-polar perovskites. *J. Phase Transit.* **1980**, *1*, 333. [CrossRef]
11. Uchino, K.; Nomura, S. Critical Exponents of the Dielectric Constants in Diffused-Phase-Transition Crystals. *Ferroelectr. Lett.* **1982**, *44*, 55–61. [CrossRef]
12. Uchino, K. Fractal Phenomena in Ferroelectrics. *J. Nanotechnol. Mater. Sci.* **2014**, *1*, 1–15.

6. Losses in Piezoelectrics—Complex Number Utilization

6.1. Dielectric Losses

6.1.1. Dielectric Materials

In highly resistive dielectric materials, the constituent atoms are considered to be ionized to a certain degree and are either positively or negatively charged (particularly ionic crystals). When an electric field is applied, cations are attracted to the cathode and anions to the anode due to electrostatic interaction. This phenomenon is known as "ionic polarization" of the dielectric, and the polarization is expressed quantitatively as the sum of the electric dipoles per unit volume (C/m^2). There are three types of polarization: electronic, ionic, and dipole reorientation. Electronic polarization is basically electron-cloud deformation under an electric field, which can follow alternating fields with frequencies up to THz–PHz (10^{12}–10^{15} cycle/sec, light wave range), while ionic polarization responds up to GHz–THz (10^9–10^{12} cycle/sec, microwave region). Permanent dipole reorientation can follow only up to MHz–GHz (10^6–10^9 cycle/sec). Refer to Figures 1.1 and 1.2. As is well known, a polar water molecule (H_2O) is excited in a microwave oven at around 2 GHz, which absorbs the electromagnetic energy to increase the water temperature. This is also the reason why ferroelectric materials with permanent dipoles cannot be used for microwave-frequency dielectric materials; though their permittivity is typically high at low frequencies (kHz), it decreases significantly when increasing the electric field frequency.

Compared with air-filled capacitors, dielectric capacitors can store more electric charge due to the dielectric polarization P induced by the external field, as schematically shown in Figure 6.1. The physical quantity corresponding to the total stored electric charge per unit area is called the "electric displacement", D, and is related to the externally applied electric field E by the following expression:

$$D = \varepsilon_0 E + P = \varepsilon_0 \varepsilon E. \tag{6.1}$$

Here, ε_0 is the vacuum permittivity (=8.854 × 10^{-12} F/m), ε is the material's "relative permittivity" (also simply called permittivity or "dielectric constant", and, in general, is a second-rank tensor property). In Figure 6.1, subscript "*b*" stands for "bound" charge originated from charge on the top of the induced dipole moment, and "*f*" is for "free" charge supplied from the coated electrode metal via the power supply, which usually screen/compensate the bound charge, leading to internal electric field $E = 0$. Without an electrode coat or environmental floating charge, there is no free charge, leading to electric displacement $D = 0$, or a so-called "depolarization field" in the crystal ($E_{dep} = -P/\varepsilon_0$).

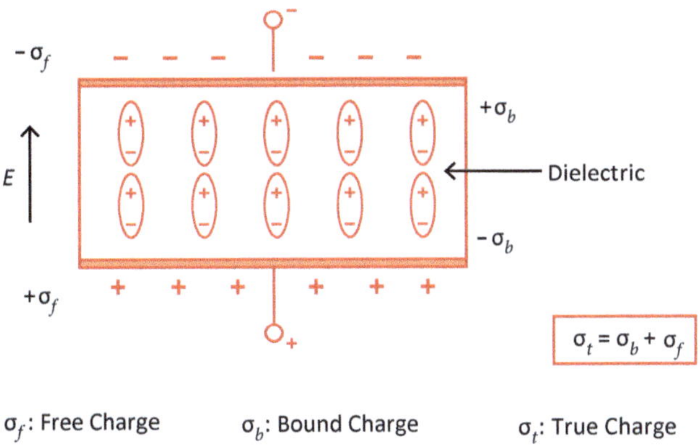

Figure 6.1. Charge accumulation in a dielectric capacitor. Source: [1] ©Uchino, K. *Ferroelectric Devices*, 2nd ed. CRC Press, 2010; p. 3. Reproduced by permission of Taylor & Francis Group.

6.1.2. Dielectric Loss

The magnitude of induced polarization P depends on the crystal structure. As discussed in Section 1.2.3, dielectric materials with high "Lorentz polarization factor" γ should induce high polarization, leading to high permittivity. As imagined from the response speed limitation of the ionic polarizability (GHz–THz) (Figure 1.2), polarization induction requires some delay time after the external electric field E application. In order to express the delay, we adopt the complex permittivity ε^* such that

$$D = \varepsilon^* \varepsilon_0 E = \varepsilon_0(\varepsilon' - j\varepsilon'')E = \varepsilon_0 \varepsilon'(1 - j\tan\delta)E. \quad (6.2)$$

Here, $j = \sqrt{-1}$, and $\tan\delta = \varepsilon''/\varepsilon'$ is called the "dielectric loss factor" or "dissipation factor". Note that until Section 6.4, we do not discuss the dissipation factor in terms of the intensive or extensive parameter's viewpoint.

Figure 6.2 illustrates the electric displacement D (almost the same as polarization P in ferroelectrics, because the permittivity is large ~1000) vs. the electric field E curve under stress-free conditions with some hysteresis. In a typical "delay" case of the D generation after the electric field E application, the hysteresis is the counterclockwise rotation (as indicated by arrows) on this narrow elliptic locus. Note also that the hysteresis shape should be an "ellipse" in this complex notation; that is, a rounded edge at the maximum field point, which suggests a discrepancy from the actual experimental result, and the limitation of this complex parameter approach. Typical ferroelectric P–E hysteresis curves usually exhibit a rather sharp edge shape in practice, as shown in Figure 6.2. Example Problem 6.1 further illustrates the numerical derivation of the loss factor from the observed D–E hysteresis curve.

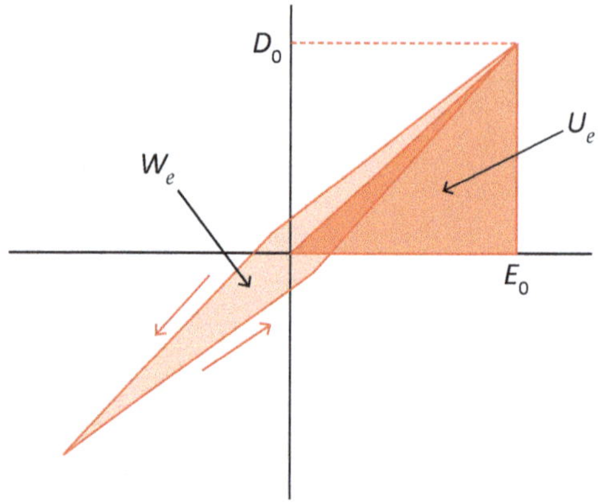

Figure 6.2. D vs. E (stress-free) curve with hysteresis. Source: Figure by author.

Example Problem 6.1

When the observed variation in electric displacement, D, can be represented as if it had a slight phase lag with respect to the applied electric field (i.e., harmonic approximation), we can describe the relation D vs. E as δ

$$E^* = E_0 e^{j\omega t}, \tag{P6.1.1}$$

$$D^* = D_0 e^{j(\omega t - \delta)}. \tag{P6.1.2}$$

We can rewrite the relationship between D and E by squeezing the phase lag into the "complex permittivity" ε:

$$D = \varepsilon^* \varepsilon_0 E, \tag{P6.1.3}$$

where the "complex dielectric constant", ε^*, is

$$\varepsilon^* = \varepsilon' - j\varepsilon'', \tag{P6.1.4}$$

$$\varepsilon''/\varepsilon' = \tan\delta. \tag{P6.1.5}$$

The integrated area inside the hysteresis loop, labeled w_e in Figure 6.2, is equivalent to the energy loss per cycle per unit volume of the dielectric. It is defined for an isotropic dielectric as:

$$w^e = -\int DdE = -\int_0^{\frac{2\pi}{\omega}} D\frac{dE}{dt}dt. \tag{P6.1.6}$$

(1) Substituting the electric field, E, and electric displacement, D, into Equation (P6.1.6), obtain the following equations:

$$w_e = \pi\varepsilon''\varepsilon_0 E_0^2 = \pi\varepsilon'\varepsilon_0 E_0^2 \tan\delta. \tag{P6.1.7}$$

(2) Verify an alternative expression (i.e., visual calculation from the hysteresis loop) for the dissipation factor:

$$\tan\delta = (1/2\pi)(w_e/U_e), \tag{P6.1.8}$$

where U_e, the integrated area so labeled in Figure 6.2, represents the energy stored during a quarter cycle.

<u>Solution</u>

The integrated area inside the hysteresis loop, labeled w_e in Figure 6.2, is equivalent to the energy loss per cycle per unit volume of the dielectric. It is defined as $w_e = -\int DdE = -\int_0^{\frac{2\pi}{\omega}} D\frac{dE}{dt}dt$. Substituting the real parts of the electric field, E^* (i.e., $E_0\cos(\omega t)$), and electric displacement, $D_0\cos(\omega t - \delta)$, into Equation (P6.1.6) yields:

$$\begin{aligned} w_e = \int_0^{\frac{2\pi}{\omega}} D_0\cos(\omega t - \delta)[E_0\omega\cdot\sin(\omega t)]dt\ E_0D_0\omega\sin(\delta)\cdot\int_0^{\frac{2\pi}{\omega}} \sin^2(\omega t)dt \\ = \pi E_0 D_0 \sin(\delta), \end{aligned} \tag{P6.1.9}$$

so that

$$w_e = \pi\varepsilon''\,\varepsilon_0 E_0{}^2 = \pi\varepsilon'\varepsilon_0 E_0{}^2\tan\delta. \tag{P6.1.10}$$

When there is a phase lag, an energy loss (or non-zero w_e) will occur for every cycle of the applied electric field, resulting in the heat generation in the dielectric material. The quantity $\tan\delta$ is referred to as the "dissipation factor". The electrostatic energy stored during a half cycle of the applied electric field is $2U_e$, where U_e, the integrated area so labeled in Figure 6.2, represents the energy stored during a quarter cycle.

$$2U_e = 2[(1/2)(E_0D_0\cos\delta)] = (E_0D_0)\cos\delta \tag{P6.1.11}$$

Knowing that $\varepsilon'\varepsilon_0 = (D_0/E_0)\cos\delta$, Equation (P6.1.11) may be rewritten in the form:

$$2U_e = \varepsilon'\varepsilon_0 E_0{}^2. \tag{P6.1.12}$$

Then, an alternative expression for the dissipation factor can be obtained:

$$\tan\delta = (1/2\pi)(w_e/U_e). \tag{P6.1.13}$$

Note that the factor 2π comes from the integration process for one cycle. In conclusion, the loss dissipation factor $\tan\delta$ is obtained by obtaining the area (equivalent to electric energy) ratio on the experimentally obtained $P-E$ hysteresis curve.

Ferroelectric materials are occasionally doped by donor or acceptor ions in order to enhance the piezoelectric performance, and polycrystalline (ceramic) specimens possess grain boundaries with various crystal dislocations/deficits. In these cases, the material's resistivity is occasionally degraded. Let us discuss the case of a slightly conductive (or semiconductive) dielectric material, where the hysteresis apparently becomes enhanced.

We start from Gauss law, $\nabla \cdot \boldsymbol{D} = \rho$, which is valid under the condition of equilibrium. Here, ρ is the true charge density. Taking a "continuity equation" of charge,

$$\frac{\partial \rho}{\partial t} + div(\boldsymbol{i}) = 0, \tag{6.3}$$

and the relations $\frac{\partial}{\partial t} \to j\omega$ (harmonic approximation) and $\boldsymbol{i} = \sigma \boldsymbol{E}$, we obtain

$$\nabla \cdot (\boldsymbol{D} - \left(\frac{j\sigma}{\omega}\right)\boldsymbol{E}) = 0 \text{ (Extended Gauss's law)}. \tag{6.4}$$

If we adopt $\boldsymbol{D} = \varepsilon^* \varepsilon_0 \boldsymbol{E}$, we rewrite the equation as

$$\varepsilon_0(\varepsilon' - j[\varepsilon'' + \left(\frac{\sigma}{\varepsilon_0 \omega}\right)])\nabla \cdot \boldsymbol{E} = 0. \tag{6.5}$$

Thus, conductance enhances the imaginary loss part ε'', leading to the phase lag increase and an apparently wider hysteresis curve. Note that the intrinsic dielectric loss tanδ is not directly related with the measuring frequency, but the conductivity-related "apparent dielectric loss" exhibits a significant frequency dependence (i.e., it diminishes with increasing the frequency ω). This is the experimental base to distinguish the conductance loss in a piezoelectric material.

6.1.3. LCR Circuit

Analysis with Differential Equations

Capacitors are made of dielectric materials. The reader is probably familiar with a resonance circuit composed of an inductor L and a capacitor C. Let us review the loss handling with a discreate electric component viewpoint. We discuss on a series LCR circuit (by adding a resistance R), as shown in Figure 6.3. Dielectric loss and resistive loss in the inductor are expressed by a discrete resistor in the "equivalent circuit" as introduced in Chapter 9. Under an applied voltage $V(t)$, denoting the common circuit current $I(t)$ and charge on a capacitor Q, we obtain the equation:

$$L\left(\frac{dI}{dt}\right) + \frac{Q}{C} + RI = V(t). \tag{6.6}$$

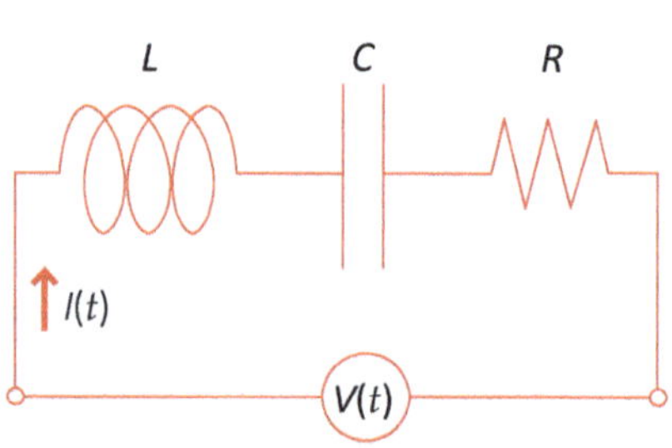

Figure 6.3. LCR circuit. Source: Figure by author.

Since $I = \frac{dQ}{dt}$, Equation (6.6) can be rewritten as

$$L\left(\frac{d^2Q}{dt^2}\right) + R(\frac{dQ}{dt}) + \frac{Q}{C} = V(t), \tag{6.7}$$

or

$$L\left(\frac{d^2I}{dt^2}\right) + R(\frac{dI}{dt}) + \frac{I}{C} = \frac{dV}{dt}. \tag{6.8}$$

When we apply a regular AC voltage $V(t) = V_0\sin\omega t$ and assume the steady current with the same frequency ω and the phase delay ϕ, $I(t) = I_0\sin(\omega t - \phi)$,

$-\omega^2 L I_0\sin(\omega t - \phi) + \omega R I_0\cos(\omega t - \phi) + I_0\sin(\omega t - \phi)/C = \omega V_0\sin\omega t.$

The solution is

$$I(t) = \frac{V_0}{Z}\sin(\omega t - \phi), \tag{6.9}$$

$$Z = \sqrt{R^2 + (L\omega - \frac{1}{C\omega})^2}, \tag{6.10}$$

$$\tan\phi = \frac{(L\omega - \frac{1}{C\omega})}{R}. \tag{6.11}$$

When $\left(L\omega - \frac{1}{C\omega}\right) = 0$, or $\omega = 1/\sqrt{LC}$, the impedance $Z = R$, which is the minimum in Z, and the current shows the maximum. This status is called "electric resonance". The frequency dependence of the impedance Z and phase $\tan\phi$ is discussed in Section 6.3.

Analysis with Complex Impedance

Equation (6.6) can be transformed as

$$L\left(\frac{dI}{dt}\right) + \frac{1}{C}\int Idt + RI = V(t). \tag{6.12}$$

Assuming a harmonic oscillation with ω, and taking $\frac{\partial}{\partial t} \rightarrow j\omega$ and $\int dt \rightarrow 1/j\omega$, we obtain

$$L(j\omega I) + \frac{1}{C}(\frac{I}{j\omega}) + RI = V(t). \tag{6.13}$$

Thus, we define the impedance of inductance L and capacitance C as

$$\begin{cases} j\omega L \\ 1/j\omega C \end{cases}. \tag{6.14}$$

Then, the total complex impedance is given under a harmonic operation by

$$Z^* = j\omega L + \frac{1}{j\omega C} + R, \tag{6.15}$$

which can also be expressed by

$$Z^* = Z(1 - j\tan\phi), \tag{6.16}$$

$$Z = \sqrt{R^2 + (L\omega - \frac{1}{C\omega})^2}, \tag{6.17}$$

$$\tan\phi = \frac{(L\omega - \frac{1}{C\omega})}{R}. \tag{6.18}$$

Note that Equations (6.17) and (6.18) are identical to Equations (6.10) and (6.11). The reader can now clearly understand the easier analytical process with the complex impedance usage.

6.2. Mechanical Loss/Damping Model

6.2.1. Mathematical Model of Mechanical Loss

The reader may remember the temple bell timbre. When hit suddenly, the sound pressure level decays gradually without changing its timbre, that is, all frequency components are damped in a similar fashion. On the contrary, in underwater acoustics, the acoustic absorption by water medium is accelerated when increasing the frequency. A lower-frequency sound navigation ranging (sonar) system is required for detecting an enemy submarine from as far as possible. We introduce three loss models in the following sections: solid damping, Coulomb damping, and viscous damping.

Figure 6.4 shows a simple mass–spring (m: mass, c: spring constant) harmonic vibration model (a) with a damper (ζ: damping factor) (b). Without a damper, using notations displacement u and force F, we can describe the Newton equation as:

$$m\frac{d^2u}{dt^2} + cu = F(t). \tag{6.19}$$

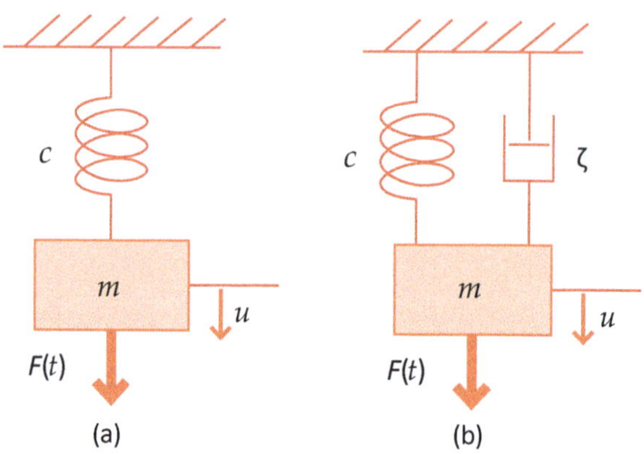

Figure 6.4. A simple mass–spring harmonic vibration model (**a**) and with a damper (**b**). Source: Figure by author.

When $F = 0$, assuming the harmonic solution $u(t) = u_0 e^{-i\omega t}$, Equation (6.19) can be solved as

$$\left(-m\omega^2 + c\right)u = 0 \rightarrow \omega = \sqrt{c/m}. \tag{6.20}$$

By keeping the initial displacement amplitude u_0, sinusoidal vibration with the above frequency ω will continue forever without damping. The above $\omega = \sqrt{c/m}$ is called the "resonance frequency" of this mechanical system.

Now, we consider a damper integration into Equation (6.19) as Figure 6.4b [2]. When the damping mechanism is associated directly with the displacement u, the damping factor is irrelevant to the frequency, which corresponds to the above temple bell case, and is called "solid damping". On the other hand, as you know, in the surface friction, the force direction changes sign (while keeping the force magnitude constant) according to the vibration direction. The vibration damping in this case does not behave in an exponential fashion with time, which is called "Coulomb damping". "Viscous damping" is observed occasionally for an object moving in liquid at a relatively low speed. The damping term is represented in proportion to the object velocity, ($\frac{du}{dt}$). Due to its mathematical simplicity (i.e., complex parameter integration), the viscous damping formula is most popularly used even for solid materials. These three models are further described in the following sections.

6.2.2. Solid Damping

Solid Damping/Structural Damping

The solid damping, sometimes called "structural damping", originates from the "internal friction" in the material, which is different from the "surface friction" introduced in Section 6.2.3. The solid damping does not change with the vibration frequency but is proportional to the "maximum stress" generated during the vibration cycle, which is also different from the "viscous damping" in Section 6.2.4. When we impact a solid suddenly, various vibration modes are excited, and their sound level decreases monotonously without changing the timbre. The temple bell does not change its "tone" during the sound level decay. That is, all frequency modes damp under a similar damping rate. Since the stress is almost proportional to the strain in the "elastic deformation" range, we can rephrase that the solid damping is proportional to the "maximum strain".

Here, we introduce the damping force in proportion to the strain, irrelevant to the operating frequency:

$$F = \zeta c x, \tag{6.21}$$

where ζ is the non-dimensional (i.e., normalized) damping factor and c is the spring constant. It is important to distinguish the situation from the modification of Equation (6.19) with an effective force constant $c(1 - \zeta)$. The vibration will diminish according to the damping force whilst keeping a similar resonance frequency of Equation (6.20). Since the sign of the damping force is not clear, different from the case in "Coulomb damping", it is better to use the energy consumption method because analyzing the damping procedure with normal kinetic equations is difficult.

Though the vibration is not perfectly harmonic, the damping vibration is supposed to be approximated by a harmonic model, if the damping factor ζ is reasonably small. The energy loss per cycle is approximated by

$$\Delta W = 2\pi \cdot (\frac{1}{2}) x_0 F_0 = \pi x_0 F_0 = \pi \zeta c x_0^2. \quad (6.22)$$

From the experiments, the solid damping energy loss is irrelevant to the operating frequency and proportional to the square of the maximum displacement x_0. The above harmonic assumption seems to be true in the case of small ζ of the system. The logarithmic damping rate δ ("logarithmic decrement" is defined as $ln\left(\frac{x_1}{x_2}\right)$, where x_1 and x_2 are the successive vibration amplitudes) of a free vibration via the solid damping mechanism can be estimated from the energy loss ΔW as

$$\delta = \frac{\Delta W}{2W} = \frac{\pi \zeta c x_0^2}{2 \times \frac{1}{2} c x_0^2} = \pi \zeta. \quad (6.23)$$

Equation (6.23) is occasionally utilized for determining the damping rate of structural components of an airplane, such as wing, tail wing, and body structure. The logarithmic damping factor δ is irrelevant to the frequency, similar to the case of viscous damping (refer to Section 6.2.4).

Piezoelectric Passive Damper

Though the mechanism is different from the solid damping, since the analytical process of energy loss per vibration cycle is analogous, the passive piezoelectric damper is introduced here [3,4]. The principle of the piezoelectric vibration damper is explained based on a piezoelectric ceramic single plate in Figure 6.5a. When an external pulse force is applied to the piezo-plate, an electric charge is produced by the direct piezoelectric effect (Figure 6.5b) [3]. Accordingly, the vibration remaining (i.e., ring-down vibration) after the removal of the external force induces an alternating voltage, which corresponds to the intensity of that vibration, across the terminals of the single plate. The electric charge produced is allowed to flow and is dissipated as Joule heat, when a resistor is placed between the terminals (see Figure 6.5c). When the external resistance is too large or small, the vibration intensity is not readily reduced, and we need to tune the resistance to match exactly to the piezo-plate impedance, that is, $|1/j\omega C|$, where ω is the cyclic frequency (i.e., the fundamental mechanical resonance of the piezo-plate in this case), and C is the piezo-plate capacitance. The reader might have learned that the electrical impedance matching indicates that the external impedance should be adjusted to the "conjugate" of the internal impedance "$1/j\omega C$", that is, the inductor with a value of "$j/\omega C$". However, in this case, the electric energy stored in the capacitor is not lost but flip-flops between the capacitor and inductor without losing total energy. The resistive impedance shunt is essential to dissipate the electrical energy via Joule heat.

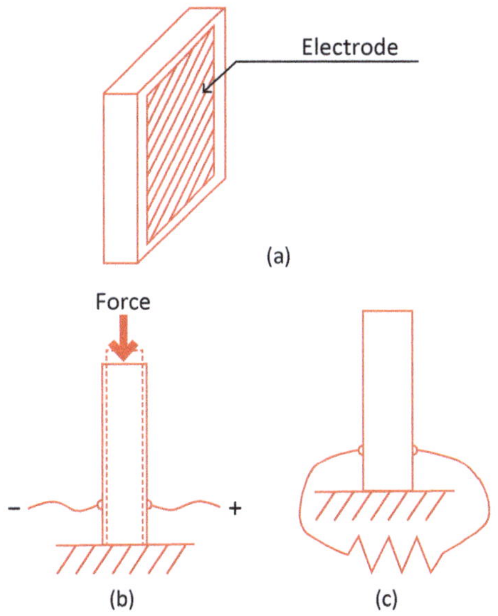

Figure 6.5. Mechanical damping concept with a piezoelectric. (**a**) A single plate piezoelectric sample; (**b**) direct piezoelectric effect; (**c**) electric energy dissipation through resistance. Source: [5] ©Uchino, K. *Micromechatronics*, 2nd ed. CRC Press, 2019; p. 399. Reproduced by permission of Taylor & Francis Group.

The bimorph piezoelectric component, which consists of an elastic beam sandwiched with two sheets of piezoelectric ceramic plates (Figure 6.6a), was utilized for the mechanical damping demonstraton. The bimorph edge was hit by an impulse force, and the transient vibration displacement decay was monitored by an eddy current-type non-contact displacement sensor. Figure 6.6b shows the measured displacement data which vibrates at the bimorph resonance frequency (295 Hz), and Figure 6.7 shows the relationship between the damping time constant and an external resistance. It can be seen that the damping time constant was minimized in the vicinity of 6.6 kΩ, which is close to the impedance $1/\omega C$. Try Example Problem 6.2 to better understand the resistive impedance matching.

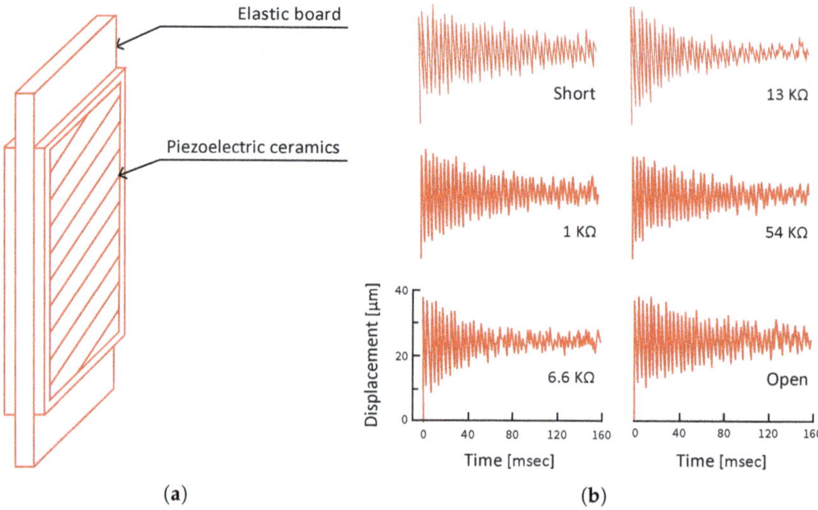

Figure 6.6. Vibration damping change associated with external resistance change. (**a**) Bimorph transducer for this measurement; (**b**) damped vibration with external resistor. Source: [5] ©Uchino, K. *Micromechatronics*, 2nd ed. CRC Press, 2019; p. 388. Reproduced by permission of Taylor & Francis Group.

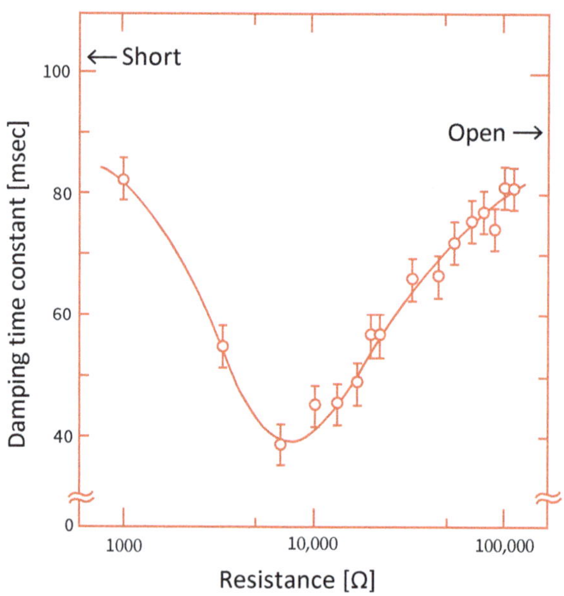

Figure 6.7. Relationship between the damping time constant and the external resistance. Source: [5] ©Uchino, K. *Micromechatronics*, 2nd ed. CRC Press, 2019; p. 399. Reproduced by permission of Taylor & Francis Group.

Let us evaluate the damping constant theoretically. The electric energy U_E generated can be expressed by using the electromechanical coupling factor k and the mechanical energy U_M:

$$U_E = U_M \times k^2. \tag{6.24}$$

The piezoelectric damper transforms electric energy into heat energy via Joule loss when the resistor R is connected, whilst the transforming rate of the damper can be raised to a level of up to 50% when the electrical impedance is exactly matched (refer to Example Problem 6.2). Accordingly, the vibration energy is transformed at a rate of $(1 - k^2/2)$ times with energy vibration repeated since $k^2/2$ multiplied by the amount of mechanical vibration energy is dissipated as heat energy. As the square of the amplitude is equivalent to the amount of energy, the amplitude decreases at a rate of $(1 - k^2/2)^{1/2}$ times with every vibration repeated. In comparison with Equation (6.21), the reader can understand that the damping factor, ζc in Equation (6.21), corresponds to $(k^2/4)$ when k is not large, and that the damping is proportional to the displacement x with no frequency dependence (merely electromechanical coupling factor k dependence). If the resonance period is taken to be T_0, the number of vibrations for t sec is $2t/T_0$, since one cycle includes twice (positive and negative) energy losing chance. Consequently, the amplitude in t sec is $(1 - k^2/2)^{t/T_0}$. If the residual vibration period is taken to be T_0, the damping in the amplitude of vibration is t sec can be expressed as follows:

$$(1 - k^2/2)^{t/T_0} = e^{-t/\tau}. \tag{6.25}$$

Thus, the following relationship for the time constant of the vibration damping is obtained:

$$\tau = -\frac{T_0}{\ln\left(1 - \frac{k^2}{2}\right)}. \tag{6.26}$$

Now, let us examine the time constant of the damping using the results for the bimorph. Substitution in Equation (6.26) of $k = 0.28$ and $T_0 = 3.4$ ms produces $\tau = 85$ ms, which seems to be considerably larger than the value of approximately 40 ms obtained experimentally for τ (Figure 6.7). This is because the theoretical derivation Equation (6.26) was conducted under the assumption of a loss-free (high Q_M) bimorph. In practice, however, it originally involved mechanical loss, the time constant of which can be obtained as the damping time constant under a short-circuited condition, i.e., $\tau_s = 102$ ms. The total vibration displacement can then be expressed as $e^{-t/\tau_{total}} = e^{-t/\tau_s} \times e^{-t/\tau}$. Accordingly,

$$\frac{1}{\tau_{total}} = \frac{1}{\tau_s} + \frac{1}{\tau}. \tag{6.27}$$

Substitution in Equation (6.27) of $\tau_s = 102$ ms and $\tau = 85$ ms produces $\tau_{total} = 46$ ms. This conforms to the experimental results shown in Figures 6.6b and 6.7.

Example Problem 6.2

We consider the piezoelectric mechanical damping from a k_{33}-type rod sample under a small cyclic stress $X = X_0 e^{j\omega t}$. See Figure 6.8. In order to obtain the maximum output electric power to consume as Joule heat, determine the external load impedance Z. Capacitance of the piezo-device is C. When we consider the output electric energy, we consider the electric displacement D vs. the electric field E domain as shown in Figure 6.9a. Answer the derivation process step-by-step as follows.

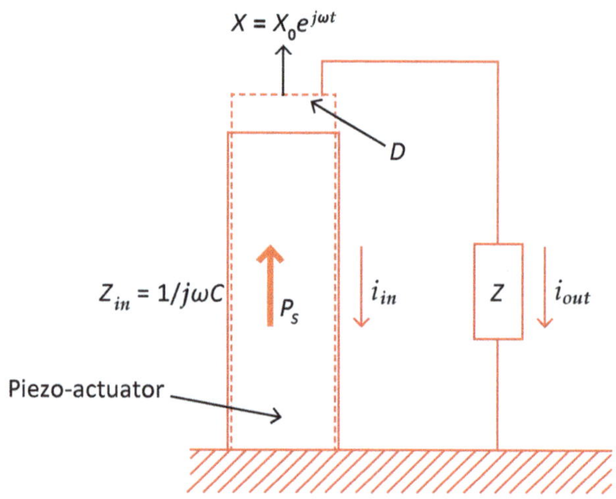

Figure 6.8. Piezoelectric energy harvesting model. Source: [5] ©Uchino, K. *Micromechatronics*, 2nd ed. CRC Press, 2019; p. 395. Reproduced by permission of Taylor & Francis Group.

(1) Calculate the "depolarization field" generated by the external stress for the open circuit ($Z = \infty$): $D = 0$.

(2) Calculate the electric displacement D for the short circuit ($Z = 0$): $E = 0$, using the piezoelectric constant d.

(3) Then, draw the D vs. E map under a certain load impedance Z.

(4) In order to maximize the consuming electric energy (i.e., hatched area in Figure 6.9a), we adopt: $X = X_0e^{j\omega t}$; $D = dX_0e^{j\omega t}$ (no phase lag, nor dielectric loss is considered). Since the total current generated by the piezoelectric transducer is given by $(\frac{\partial D}{\partial t})$

$$i = \frac{\partial D}{\partial t} = i_{in} + i_{out} = j\omega d X_0. \quad \text{(P6.2.1)}$$

Knowing the relationship, $Z_{in}i_{in} = Zi_{out}$, we obtain:

$$i_{out}(1 + j\omega CZ) = j\omega d X_0. \quad \text{(P6.2.2)}$$

Then, the power is calculated as

$$|P| = \frac{1}{2}Zi_{out}^2 = \frac{1}{2}Z\frac{(\omega d X_0)^2}{(1 + (\omega CZ)^2)}. \quad \text{(P6.2.3)}$$

After deriving the above equations by yourself, determine which Z value provides the maximum power and what the maximum power value is.

(5) Draw the output electric power vs. load Z curve.

Solution

(1) We start from the piezoelectric constitutive equations:

$$D_3 = \varepsilon_0\varepsilon_{33}^X E_3 + d_{33}X_3, \quad \text{(P6.2.4)}$$

$$x_3 = d_{33}E_3 + s_{33}^E X_3. \quad \text{(P6.2.5)}$$

The open-circuit condition satisfies $D_3 = 0$, leading to the depolarization field as

$$E_{3,dep} = -(d_{33}/\varepsilon_0\varepsilon_{33}^X)X_3. \quad \text{(P6.2.6)}$$

In this case, from Equation (P6.2.5),

$x_3 = -\frac{d_{33}{}^2}{\varepsilon_0\varepsilon_{33}^X}X_3 + s_{33}^E X_3 = (1-k_{33}{}^2)s_{33}^E X_3.$

Thus, we obtain the stiffened elastic compliance s_{33}^D of the piezo material:

$$s_{33}^D = (1-k_{33}{}^2)s_{33}^E. \quad \text{(P6.2.7)}$$

(2) Short-circuit condition satisfies $E_3 = 0$, leading to the charge generation $D_3 = d_{33}X_3$. In this case, the elastic compliance is s_{33}^E.

(3) Now, we draw the D vs. E map under a certain load impedance Z. Refer to Figure 6.9a. From (1), the intersect with the electric field axis is given by $E_{3,dep} = -\left(\frac{d_{33}}{\varepsilon_0\varepsilon_{33}^X}\right)X_3$; while from (2), the intersect with the electric displacement axis is given by $D_3 = d_{33}X_3$. The triangular area created by the origin and two intersects should be equal to the converted electrical energy per volume by the external stress:

$$U_{ME} = \left(\frac{1}{2}\right)E_{3,dep}D_3 = \left(\frac{1}{2}\right)(d_{33}{}^2/\varepsilon_0\varepsilon_{33}^X)X_3{}^2. \quad \text{(P6.2.8)}$$

Under a certain load impedance Z, the (D, E) point should be on the line passing through the above two intersect points, which is shown in Figure 6.9a.

(4) Figure 6.9a indicates that the maximum consumed energy (shadowed area) can be obtained at the (D, E) point, which is located at a half of both $E_{3,dep}$ and $D_{3,max}$, which is a half of U_{ME}. The maximum consumed electric energy should be a half of the input mechanical energy.

A detailed energy analysis is made below. When we assume the sinusoidal input stress $X = X_0e^{j\omega t}$ and output electric displacement $D = dX_0e^{j\omega t}$ via the direct piezoelectric effect (d constant), we can derive the following current and voltage relationships from Figure 6.8. We can understand that the piezo power-supply has the internal impedance $1/j\omega C$ under an off-resonance frequency (by neglecting the dielectric loss or effective conducting loss $\sigma = 0$), and this piezoelectric "current supply" generates the total current density per area:

$$i = \frac{\partial D}{\partial t} = j\omega dX_0. \quad \text{(P6.2.9)}$$

This current is split into internal "displacement current" i_{in} and external current i_{out},

$$i = i_{in} + i_{out}. \tag{P6.2.10}$$

Then, because the potential/voltage should be the same on the top electrode of the piezo component, we obtain:

$$Z_{in} i_{in} = Z i_{out}. \tag{P6.2.11}$$

Inserting the relation $i_{in} = \left(\frac{Z}{Z_{in}}\right) i_{out} = j\omega CZ \cdot i_{out}$ into Equation (P6.2.9),

$$i_{out}(1 + j\omega CZ) = j\omega d X_0. \tag{P6.2.12}$$

Thus, we can obtain the output electric energy as

$$|P| = \frac{1}{2}\left|Z \cdot i_{out}{}^2\right| = \frac{1}{2} Z \frac{(\omega d X_0)^2}{(1 + (\omega CZ)^2)}. \tag{P6.2.13}$$

(5) Figure 6.9b shows the electric load (resistive) dependence of the output electric energy, which concludes that the maximum electric energy $|P| = \frac{1}{4}\frac{\omega d^2 X_0^2}{C}$ can be obtained at $Z = 1/\omega C$, when we consider Z resistive, which is the situation for dissipating the electric energy via Joule heat. In other words, the generated electric energy in a piezo component can be spent maximum when the external load resistive impedance matches exactly to the internal capacitive impedance with a phase lag of $-j(-90°)$. The reader is reminded of the discussion in the beggining of (4), that is, the energy consumption is $\left(\frac{1}{4}\right)(d_{33}{}^2/\varepsilon_0\varepsilon_{33}^X)X_3{}^2$ from Equation (P6.2.8). This value is equivalent to $|P| = \frac{1}{4}\frac{\omega d^2 X_0^2}{C}$ by taking into account the piezoelectric rod size.

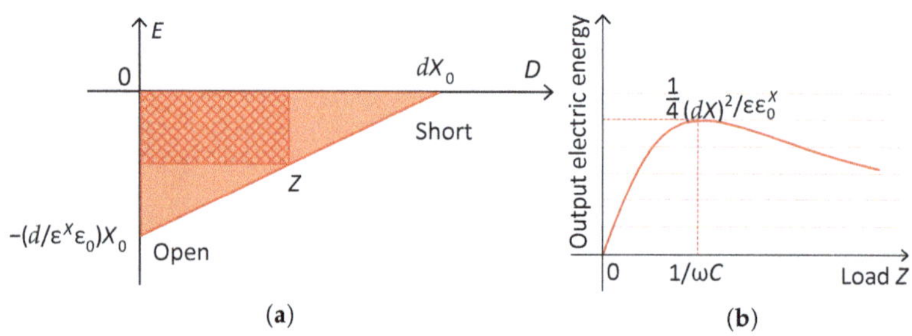

Figure 6.9. Output electric energy calculation process under different external impedances (**a**); output electric energy vs. external electrical load Z (**b**). Source: [5] ©Uchino, K. *Micromechatronics*, 2nd ed. CRC Press, 2019; p. 396. Reproduced by permission of Taylor & Francis Group.

In conclusion, a half of the converted electric energy ($k_{33}{}^2 U_M$), that is, $\left(\frac{1}{2}\right) U_{ME} = \left(\frac{1}{2}\right) k_{33}{}^2 U_M$, can be consumed in the external resistive impedance when the external impedance is adjusted to $Z = 1/\omega C$.

It is noteworthy that the input mechanical energy differs even if we keep the input stress constant according to the external electric impedance, because the elastic compliance is different depending on the electrical shunt condition; the elastic compliance under the short-circuit condition is given by s_{33}^E, and under the open-circuit condition by $s_{33}^D = (1 - k_{33}{}^2)s_{33}^E$. How about that under $Z = 1/\omega C$? We calculate the "input mechanical energy $\frac{1}{2}s_{33}^{eff}X_0^2$" under the Z-shunt condition from the second constitutive equation:

$$x = d_{33}E + s_{33}{}^E X = -d_{33}\left(\frac{V}{L}\right) + s_{33}{}^E X = -\left(\frac{d_{33}}{L}\right)\left[\frac{j\omega d_{33}X_0}{\frac{1}{Z} + j\omega C}\right] + s_{33}{}^E X. \quad \text{(P6.2.14)}$$

The last transformation used Equation (P6.2.11). We obtained the effective elastic compliance as

$$s_{eff}^E = \frac{x}{X} = s^E\left[1 - k_{33}{}^2\frac{j\omega CZ}{(1 + j\omega CZ)}\right]. \quad \text{(P6.2.15)}$$

You can verify the above "effective elastic compliance" is equal to s^E or $s^D = s^E(1 - k_{31}{}^2)$, when $Z = 0$ or ∞, respectively. Under $Z = 1/\omega C$.

$$s_{eff}^E = s^E\left(1 - \frac{1}{2}k_{33}{}^2 + \frac{j}{2}k_{33}{}^2\right) = s^E(1 - k_{33}{}^2 + \frac{1}{2}k_{33}{}^4)(1 - j\tan\varphi). \quad \text{(P6.2.16)}$$

Note that the stress–strain phase lag is zero for the short- or open-circuit condition, but it is not zero under $Z = 1/\omega C$. The softer the piezoelectric elasticity is, the higher the input mechanical energy is. Thus, from the "energy transmission coefficient" viewpoint, $Z = 1/\omega C$ is slightly off from the optimized electrical impedance condition.

6.2.3. Coulomb (Friction) Damping

Friction Damping Dynamic Equation

"Coulomb damping" occurs when the mechanical object is contacted on a "dry surface". As learned in high-school physics, the Coulomb friction force F is almost constant (irrelevant to the object speed) and is expressed by the product of the normal force N and the friction constant μ:

$$F = \mu N. \quad (6.28)$$

The friction constant changes from 0 to 1, but typical values are around 0.2–0.4. Most importantly, the force changes its sign according to the motion direction. We introduce the "Laplace transform" to solve this differential equation under this nonlinear force condition below, referring to Chapter 8 for the Laplace transform. You may skip this subsection tentatively because Chapter 14 gives the detailed solution process. Figure 6.10a,b show a commercial friction damper and a schematic model with mass m, spring constant c and friction contact, respectively. We can start from the differential equation by using mass displacement u:

$$m\ddot{u} + cu = \pm F. \quad (6.29)$$

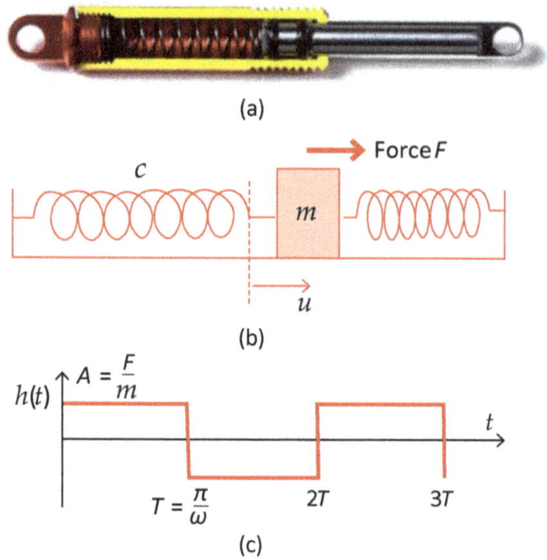

Figure 6.10. (**a**) Commercial friction damper; (**b**) schematic model with mass, spring, and friction contact; (**c**) rectangular wave function representing friction force. Source: [6] ©Uchino, K. *High-Power Piezoelectrics and Loss Mechanisms*. CRC Press, 2020; p. 92. Reproduced by permission of Taylor & Francis Group.

We can rewrite Equation (6.29) using $\omega = \sqrt{c/m}$ and a rectangular wave function $h(t)$ visualized in Figure 6.10c,

$$\ddot{u} + \omega^2 u = h(t). \tag{6.30}$$

Here, the amplitude A of $h(t)$ is set $F/m = \mu N/m$, and a cyclic period ($2T$) is taken as $2\pi/\omega$, corresponding to the resonance period of the original mass–spring system. We will adopt the initial conditions as:

$$u(t=0) = a,\ \dot{u}(t=0) = 0. \tag{6.31}$$

The initial mass position a (spring force $c \cdot a$) should be taken to be reasonably large so that the motion will start by competing with the frictional force μN:

$$a > A/\omega^2. \tag{6.32}$$

Transient Response Analysis with Laplace Transform

Let us solve the differential equation, Equation (6.30), using Laplace transform. Since a detailed solution is provided in Section 14.1.3, a brief introduction is given here. We denote the Laplace transforms of the displacement $u(t)$ and friction force $h(t)$ as $U(s)$ and $H(s)$: $U(s) = Lu(t)$, $H(s) = Lh(t)$. Equation (6.30) can be written as

$$L[\ddot{u}] + \omega^2 U(s) = H(s). \tag{6.33}$$

Taking into account the initial condition $u(t = 0) = a$ and $u'(t = 0) = 0$,

$$L[\ddot{u}] = s^2U - sa, \tag{6.34}$$

and the Laplace transform of a rectangular wave expressed by

$$H(s) = \frac{A}{s}\tanh(\frac{Ts}{2}) = \frac{A}{s}(1 - 2e^{-Ts}+2e^{-2Ts} - 2e^{-3Ts} + \cdots), \tag{6.35}$$

we obtain the following equation:

$$(s^2 + \omega^2)U - sa = \frac{A}{s}(1 - 2e^{-Ts}+2e^{-2Ts} - 2e^{-3Ts} + \cdots). \tag{6.36}$$

We can now solve Equation (6.36) in terms of $U(s)$

$$U = \frac{s \cdot a}{(s^2 + \omega^2)} + \frac{A}{s(s^2 + \omega^2)}(1 - 2e^{-Ts}+2e^{-2Ts} - 2e^{-3Ts} + \cdots). \tag{6.37}$$

Remember that $T = \pi/\omega$ (a half of the resonance period).

We can now obtain the displacement $u(t)$ solution for successive time intervals, $0 < t < T$, $T < t < 2T$, $2T < t < 3T$, $\cdots$, where T is a half of the resonance period (i.e., $\omega T = \pi$; refer to [5]):

$$\begin{array}{c} u = a\cos(\omega t) + \frac{A}{\omega^2}(1 - \cos(\omega t)) \\ \text{for } 0 < t < T;\ u(T) = -a + \frac{2A}{\omega^2}, \end{array} \tag{6.38}$$

$$\begin{array}{c} u = a\cos(\omega t) + \frac{A}{\omega^2}(1 - \cos(\omega t)) - \frac{2A}{\omega^2}(1 - \cos(\omega(t - T)) \\ \text{for } T < t < 2T;\ u(2T) = a - \frac{4A}{\omega^2} \end{array} \tag{6.39}$$

$$\begin{array}{c} u = a\cos(\omega t) + \frac{A}{\omega^2}(1 - \cos(\omega t)) - \frac{2A}{\omega^2}(1 - \cos(\omega(t - T)) \\ +\frac{2A}{\omega^2}(1 - \cos(\omega(t - 2T)) \\ \text{for } 2T < t < 3T;\ u(3T) = -a + \frac{6A}{\omega^2}. \end{array} \tag{6.40}$$

We find that

(1) The system exhibits sinusoidal vibration with the resonance frequency given by $\omega = \sqrt{c/m}$, determined by the original mass and spring.

(2) Each successive "sinusoidal" displacement swing is $(\frac{2A}{\omega^2})$ shorter than the preceding one, until inside the dead region, that is, linear decay with time, different from exponential decay in viscous damping in the next section. Figure 6.11 shows the linear vibration amplitude decay for the "Coulomb damping", in comparison with no damping-free vibration.

(3) There is the critical stop point of the vibration; that is, the minimum displacement $u(t) = A/\omega^2$, below which the spring force cannot compete with the friction force. This dead region is shown as a shadow band in Figure 6.11.

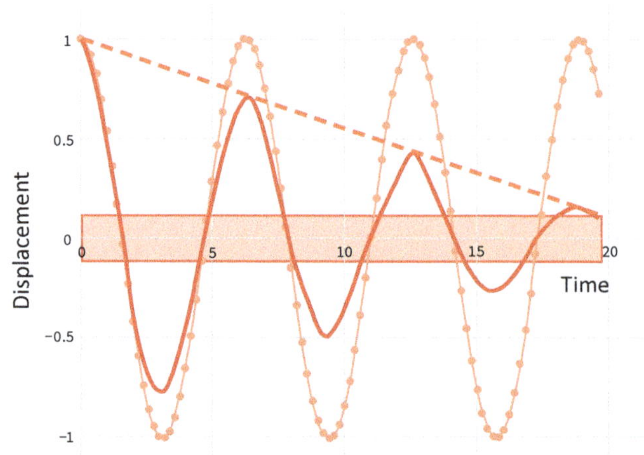

Figure 6.11. Linear vibration amplitude decay for Coulomb damping. Source: [6] ©Uchino, K. *High-Power Piezoelectrics and Loss Mechanisms*. CRC Press, 2020; p. 94. Reproduced by permission of Taylor & Francis Group.

6.2.4. Viscous Damping

Different from the Coulomb damping for a dry surface (i.e., constant force), "viscous damping" is applied for "lubricated surface" friction (i.e., time-dependent force); so-called "dashpots" (i.e., shock absorber, buffer), illustrated in Figure 6.4b, exhibit this behavior. It can also be applied for an object moving in viscous oil, or an electro-active object moving in a magnetic field with its damping force in proportion to the object speed. The damping force is introduced in proportion to the velocity v of the mass m as

$$F = -\xi v = -\xi \frac{du}{dt}, \tag{6.41}$$

where ξ is the viscous damping coefficient. Thus, the dynamic equation of the mass without external force in Figure 6.4b is described as

$$m\ddot{u} = -cu - \xi\dot{u}. \tag{6.42}$$

Taking the following notations,

$$\omega_0 = \sqrt{c/m} \text{ (base resonance frequency for zero damping)}, \tag{6.43}$$

$$\zeta = \xi/2m\omega_0 \text{ (normalized damping factor (no dimension))}, \tag{6.44}$$

we obtain the normalized equation as follows, which is a differential equation equivalent to the LCR circuit in Equation (6.7):

$$\ddot{u} + 2\zeta\omega_0\dot{u} + {\omega_0}^2 u = 0. \tag{6.45}$$

Due to the obedient characteristic of the damping formula, we can easily solve this differential equation using the Laplace transform, detailed in Section 8.2. Taking

$L[u(t)] = U(s)$, and Useful Theorem (b) in Section 8.2 with the initial conditions, $\dot{u}(t=0) = 0$, $u(t = 0) = u_0$,

$$\left[s^2U - su_0\right] + 2\zeta\omega_0[sU - u_0] + {\omega_0}^2 U = 0. \tag{6.46}$$

Then

$$\begin{aligned} &[s^2 + (2\zeta\omega_0)s + {\omega_0}^2]U(s) = (s + 2\zeta\omega_0)u_0, \text{ or} \\ &U(s) = \frac{(s+2\zeta\omega_0)u_0}{[s^2+(2\zeta\omega_0)s+{\omega_0}^2]}. \end{aligned} \tag{6.47}$$

Equation (6.47) is a general solution for $U(s)$. In order to apply the inverse Laplace transform, we need to consider three cases: $0 \le \zeta < 1$, $\zeta = 1$, and $1 < \zeta$.

Under Damping ($0 \le \zeta < 1$)

Rewriting Equation (6.47) as

$$U(s) = u_0\left[\frac{(s+\zeta\omega_0)}{(s+\zeta\omega_0)^2 + (1-\zeta^2){\omega_0}^2} + \frac{\zeta}{\sqrt{1-\zeta^2}}\frac{\sqrt{1-\zeta^2}\omega_0}{(s+\zeta\omega_0)^2 + (1-\zeta^2){\omega_0}^2}\right]. \tag{6.48}$$

then using the inverse Laplace transforms (numbers 9 and 10 in Table 8.1 in Chapter 8) for the first and second terms, we can obtain the solution:

$$\begin{aligned} u(t) = u_0[&\exp(-\zeta\omega_0 t)\cos\left(\sqrt{1-\zeta^2}\omega_0 t\right) + \\ &\tfrac{\zeta}{\sqrt{1-\zeta^2}}\exp(-\zeta\omega_0 t)\sin\left(\sqrt{1-\zeta^2}\omega_0 t\right)]. \end{aligned} \tag{6.49}$$

We can understand that only when $1-\zeta^2 > 0$, sinusoidal vibration can be observed, which is called "light damping" or "under damping". It is important to note that the resonance frequency of this system is not ω_0 but $\sqrt{1-\zeta^2}\omega_0$, as can been seen in Equation (6.49). Refer to Figure 6.12 for $u(0) = u_0\zeta = 0$ shows the calculated result for a simple cosine curve, $u(t) = \cos(\omega_0 t)$, and $\zeta = 0.1$ is for

$$u(t) = \exp(-0.1\omega_0 t)\cos\left(\sqrt{0.99}\omega_0 t\right) + \frac{0.1}{\sqrt{0.99}}\exp(-0.1\omega_0 t)\sin\left(\sqrt{0.99}\omega_0 t\right).$$

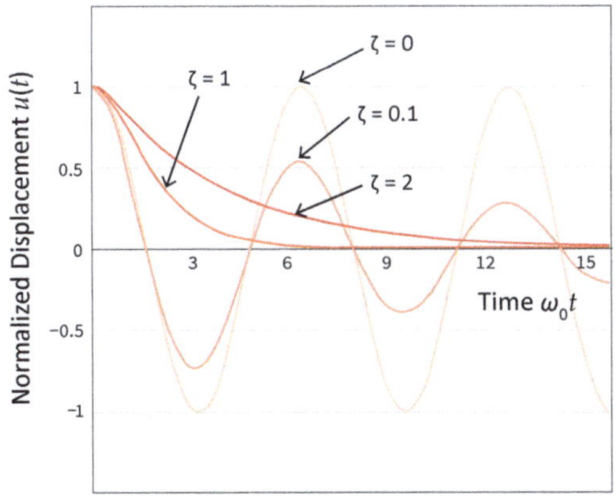

Figure 6.12. Free vibration amplitude decay for viscous damping. $\zeta = 1$ corresponds to the critical damping. Source: Figure by author.

Critical Damping ($\zeta = 1$)

Sinusoidal vibration can be observed only when $1 - \zeta^2 > 0$ is satisfied. When $\zeta = 1$, the vibration status is called "critical damping". The response speed is not as high as the "under damping" condition, but it is the quickest response without any ringing vibration associated (i.e., "aperiodic" motion). Equation (6.47) is transformed as

$$U(s) = \frac{(s + 2\omega_0)u_0}{[s^2 + (2\omega_0)s + \omega_0{}^2]} = u_0[\frac{1}{s + \omega_0} + \frac{\omega_0}{(s + \omega_0)^2}]. \tag{6.50}$$

Then, using the inverse Laplace transforms (numbers 3 and 4 in Table 8.1 in Chapter 8) for the first and second terms, we can obtain the solution:

$$u(t) = u_0[\exp(-\omega_0 t) + \omega_0 t \cdot \exp(-\omega_0 t)] = u_0(1 + \omega_0 t) \cdot \exp(-\omega_0 t) \tag{6.51}$$

The curve denoted $\zeta = 1$ in Figure 6.12 corresponds to the calculated result for $u(t) = (1 + \omega_0 t)\exp(\omega_0 t)$.

Note that the critical damping condition exhibits the quickest decay of the vibration without any ringing.

Over Damping ($\zeta > 1$)

When the damping factor $\zeta > 1$, "large damping" or "over damping" is observed. Rewriting Equation (6.57) as

$$U(s) = u_0\left[\frac{(s + \zeta\omega_0)}{(s + \zeta\omega_0)^2 - (\zeta^2 - 1)\omega_0{}^2} + \frac{\zeta\omega_0}{(s + \zeta\omega_0)^2 - (\zeta^2 - 1)\omega_0{}^2}\right]. \tag{6.52}$$

Then, using the inverse Laplace transforms (numbers **7** and **8** in Table 8.1 in Chapter 8) for the first and second terms, we can obtain the solution:

$$\begin{aligned} u(t) = u_0 \Big[&\exp(-\zeta\omega_0 t)\cosh(\sqrt{\zeta^2 - 1}\omega_0 t) + \\ &\tfrac{\zeta}{\sqrt{\zeta^2-1}}\exp(-\zeta\omega_0 t)\sinh(\sqrt{\zeta^2 - 1}\omega_0 t)\Big]. \end{aligned} \tag{6.53}$$

This motion is actually "aperiodic", without exhibiting any ringing. The curve denoted $\zeta = 2$ in Figure 6.12 corresponds to the calculated result for $u(t) = 1.08\exp\ (-0.27\omega_0 t) - 0.08\exp(-3.73\omega_0 t)$.

6.2.5. Logarithmic Decrement

Definition of Logarithmic Decrement

When the damping factor ζ is small, a sinusoidal vibration continues, as shown in Figure 6.13. Since Equation (6.49) can be rewritten as

$$u(t) = u_0\exp(-\zeta\omega_0 t)\cos\left(\sqrt{1 - \zeta^2}\omega_0 t - \phi\right),$$

the resonance angular frequency is given by $\sqrt{1-\zeta^2}\omega_0$, not by ω_0, and the vibration peak points which satisfy

$$\cos\left(\sqrt{1-\zeta^2}\omega_0 t - \phi\right) = 1,$$

are almost bounded by the envelope of $u(0)\exp(-\zeta\omega_0 t)$. Though the contact point on the envelope is slightly off from the amplitude maximum points, precisely speaking, the deviation is negligibly small. The "logarithmic decrement" δ is defined by the natural log of the ratio of two successive vibration amplitudes:

$$\delta = \ln\left(\frac{x_1}{x_2}\right) = \ln\frac{\exp(-\zeta\omega_0 t)}{\exp(-\zeta\omega_0(t+T_0))} = \ln[\exp(\zeta\omega_0 T_0)] = \zeta\omega_0 T_0. \tag{6.54}$$

Since the vibration resonance period T_0 is given by $T_0 = \frac{2\pi}{\sqrt{1-\zeta^2}\omega_0}$, the logarithmic decrement can be written as

$$\delta = \frac{2\pi\zeta}{\sqrt{1-\zeta^2}} \approx 2\pi\zeta. \tag{6.55}$$

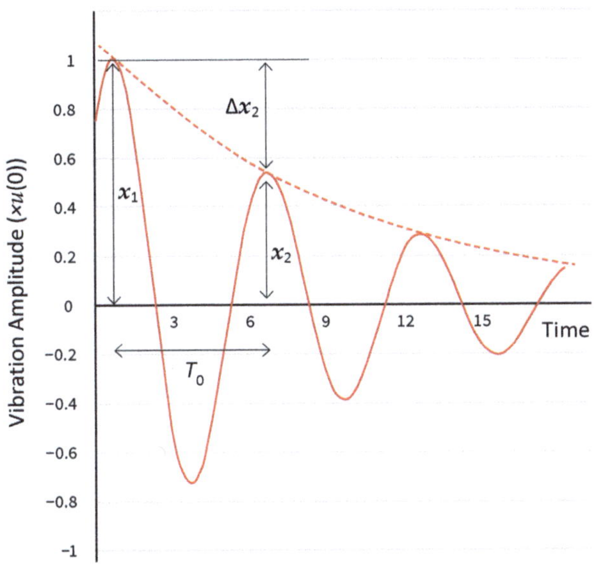

Figure 6.13. Damping factor determined by the logarithmic decrement. Source: Figure by author.

Experimental Determination

Refer to Figure 6.13 for the notations. When Δx_2 is small, δ can be experimentally obtained as follows:

$$\delta = \ln\left(\frac{x_1}{x_2}\right) = \ln\left(\frac{x_2+\Delta x_2}{x_2}\right) = \ln\left(1+\frac{\Delta x_2}{x_2}\right) \cong \frac{\Delta x_2}{x_2}. \tag{6.56}$$

The so-called time constant τ determined from the envelope curve, $\exp(-t/\tau)$, is experimentally related with the damping factor ζ as $\tau = 1/\zeta\omega_0$. The logarithmic decrement δ can also be determined from the energy loss. The total energy of this system is estimated as $\frac{1}{2}cx^2$. The energy loss per cycle ΔW can be estimated by

$$W - \Delta W = \frac{1}{2}c(x - \Delta x)^2. \tag{6.57}$$

Thus,

$$\delta \cong \frac{\Delta x_2}{x_2} \cong \frac{\Delta W}{2W}, \tag{6.58}$$

δ is obtained by a half of the ratio: lost energy/total energy.

6.3. Bode Plot—Frequency Response of a System

6.3.1. Steady-State Oscillation

In the previous Section 6.2, we considered "free" vibration of a mass–spring-damper system shown in Figure 6.14a (retaken from Figure 6.4b). Due to the damper, the system gradually loses energy and the vibration amplitude decreases. In this section, we consider steady-state forced oscillation under a harmonic force $f(t) = f_0\sin(\omega t)$.

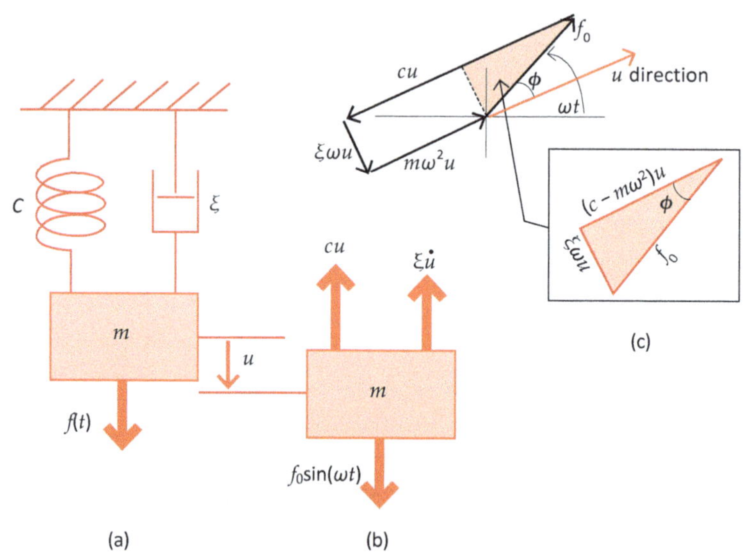

Figure 6.14. Mass–spring-damper model (**a**), and mass under forced oscillation (**b**). Force vector analysis under forced oscillation (**c**). Source: [6] ©Uchino, K. *High-Power Piezoelectrics and Loss Mechanisms*. CRC Press, 2020; p. 98. Reproduced by permission of Taylor & Francis Group.

Supposing the viscous damper, the sum of spring force, damping force, and external force will generate the mass acceleration (see Figure 6.14b for the force direction):

$$m\ddot{u} = -\xi\dot{u} - cu + f(t), \text{ or} \\ m\ddot{u} + \xi\dot{u} + cu = f(t). \tag{6.59}$$

In order to simplify the equation, we will adopt the following notations:

- Resonance angular frequency for zero damping:

$$\omega_0{}^2 = c/m \left[\omega_0 = \sqrt{c/m}\right]. \tag{6.60}$$

- Damping ratio ζ and damping factor ξ:

$$2\zeta\omega_0 = \xi/m \ [\zeta = \xi 2m\omega_0]. \tag{6.61}$$

Equation (6.59) is now transformed into

$$\ddot{u} + 2\zeta\omega_0\dot{u} + \omega_0{}^2 u = \frac{1}{m} f(t). \tag{6.62}$$

By taking $L[u(t)] = U(s)$, $L[f(t)] = F(s)$ with the initial conditions, $\dot{u}(t = 0) = 0$, $u(\mathrm{t} = 0) = u_0$, we obtain

$$\left[s^2 U - su_0\right] + 2\zeta\omega_0[sU - u_0] + \omega_0{}^2 U = (1/m)F(s), \text{ then} \\ \left[s^2 + (2\zeta\omega_0)s + \omega_0{}^2\right]U(s) = (s + 2\zeta\omega_0)u_0 + (1/m)F(s). \tag{6.63}$$

Thus, from the algebraic calculation, $U(s)$ is expressed by

$$U(s) = \frac{(s + 2\zeta\omega_0)u_0}{[s^2 + (2\zeta\omega_0)s + \omega_0{}^2]} + \frac{(1/m)F(s)}{[s^2 + (2\zeta\omega_0)s + \omega_0{}^2]}. \tag{6.64}$$

The first term on the right-hand side is called the "transient solution" (or "complementary function"), which is the solution when the external force $f(t) = 0$. As we have discussed in Section 6.2, all solutions for different damping factors ζ include the time dependence of $\exp(-\zeta\omega_0 t)$. Thus, the transient solution will disappear with a time lapse. On the contrary, the second term will remain even after a long time-lapse, called "steady-state oscillation".

We further consider only the second term (i.e., steady-state oscillation) below:

$$U(s) = G(s)F(s), \tag{6.65a}$$

$$G(s) = \frac{1}{m[s^2 + (2\zeta\omega_0)s + \omega_0{}^2]}. \tag{6.65b}$$

The Laplace function $G(s)$, relating the input function $F(s)$ to the output function $U(s)$, is called the "transfer function". As the denominator includes s^2, this function is called a "second-order system". Knowing that when $F(s) = 1$, that is, $f(t) = \delta(t)$ (impulse function), $U(s) = G(s)$, the $G(s)$ can be obtained experimentally by taking Laplace transform of the output $u(t)$ under the "impulse input" (hitting the system with a hammer!). When we consider only the "steady-state oscillation" under a harmonic input, $f(t) = f_0\sin(\omega t)$, since its Laplace transform is expressed by $\frac{\omega}{(s^2+\omega^2)}$ and its "pole" exists at "$s = \pm j\omega$", we can discuss the frequency dependence of the displacement $u(t)$ from the "transfer function" by replacing s by "$j\omega$", which corresponds to the "Fourier transform". By this replacement, Equation (6.65) can be transformed as

$$U(j\omega) = \frac{(f_0/\mathrm{m})}{[-\omega^2 + j2\zeta\omega_0\omega + \omega_0{}^2]}. \tag{6.66}$$

6.3.2. Steady State—Reconsideration

We considered the frequency dependency of the displacement in the previous section (Equation (6.66)). Direct displacement in the time domain is considered here. Supposing that the displacement $u(t)$ is excited with a slight delay after the force $f(t)$ $(= f_0\sin(\omega t))$, the steady-state vibration is described as

$$u(t) = u_0\sin(\omega t + \phi) \quad (\phi < 0, \text{delay}). \tag{6.67}$$

We consider four forces balance: inertial force, damping force, spring force, and external force; the total sum as vectors should be zero. Refer to Figure 6.14c. Knowing the phase change by the time derivative, we obtain

$\dot{u} = \omega u0\sin(\omega t + \phi + \frac{\pi}{2})$,
$\ddot{u} = \omega^2 u0\sin(\omega t + \phi + \pi) = -\omega^2 u0\sin(\omega t + \phi)$.

Now, the original equation, $m\ddot{u} + \xi\dot{u} + cu = f(t)$, is transformed to

$m\omega^2 u0\sin(\omega t + \phi) - 2\zeta m\omega_0\omega u0\sin(\omega t + \phi + \frac{\pi}{2}) - cu0\sin(\omega t + \phi) +$

$f_0\sin(\omega t) = 0$.

Figure 6.14c describes:

1. The output displacement $u(t)$ is delayed from the input force $f(t)$. The phase delay ϕ in the above equation is negative.
2. The spring force is opposite to the displacement.
3. The damping force is delayed 90° from the displacement and opposite to the velocity. This is the definition of the viscous damping.
4. The inertial force is in phase with the displacement and opposite to the acceleration.
5. Four force vectors rotate at the angular velocity ω by keeping the relative position fixed.

From the inserted triangle figure in Figure 6.14c, the following relations can be derived:

$$u_0 = \frac{f_0}{\sqrt{(c - m\omega^2)^2 + (2m\zeta\omega_0\omega)^2}}, \tag{6.68}$$

$$\tan\phi = -\frac{2m\zeta\omega_0\omega}{c - m\omega^2}, \tag{6.69}$$

$$u(t) = \frac{f_0\sin(\omega t + \phi)}{\sqrt{(c - m\omega^2)^2 + (2m\zeta\omega_0\omega)^2}}. \tag{6.70}$$

Introducing the non-dimensional normalized form, taking $u_0(\omega = 0)$, which is equal to f_0/c, and zero-damping resonance frequency $\omega_0 = \sqrt{c/m}$, the above equations are transformed as

$$\text{Magnification factor}: \frac{u_0}{u_0(\omega = 0)} = \frac{1}{\sqrt{[1 - (\frac{\omega}{\omega_0})^2]^2 + (2\zeta\frac{\omega}{\omega_0})^2}}, \tag{6.71}$$

$$\text{Phase}: \tan\phi = -\frac{2\zeta\frac{\omega}{\omega_0}}{1 - (\frac{\omega}{\omega_0})^2}. \tag{6.72}$$

Since we adopted $\sin(\omega t + \phi)$, negative ϕ is obtained for the phase delay.

Figure 6.15 illustrated the magnification factor ($\frac{u_0}{u_0(\omega=0)}$) and phase lag of the displacement as a function normalized frequency ($\frac{\omega}{\omega_0}$) for various damping ratios ζ (ζ = 0.1, 0.2, 0.5, 1 and 2). When $(\omega/\omega_0) << 1.0$, the inertial and damping force are small, leading to small phase deviation. The force vs. displacement relation is close to linear. When $(\omega/\omega_0) = 1.0$, the inertial force becomes large to balance with the spring force, and the external force compensates for the damping force, then the phase becomes $-90°$. The Lissajous curve between the force and displacement is a circle (or ellipse) with a significantly magnified displacement. When $(\omega/\omega_0) >> 1.0$, much higher than the mechanical resonance frequency, the magnification factor becomes small (displacement diminishing significantly, which approaches the mechanical clamping status), and the phase approaches $-180°$. The force–displacement curve slope is opposite in comparison with the case $(\omega/\omega_0) << 1.0$.

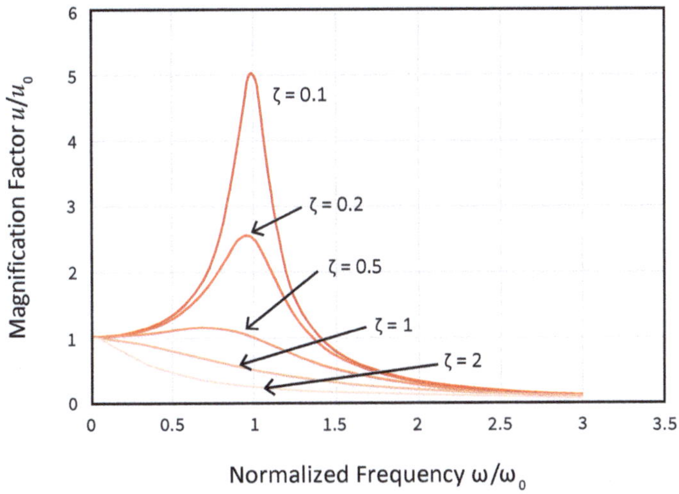

(a)

Figure 6.15. *Cont.*

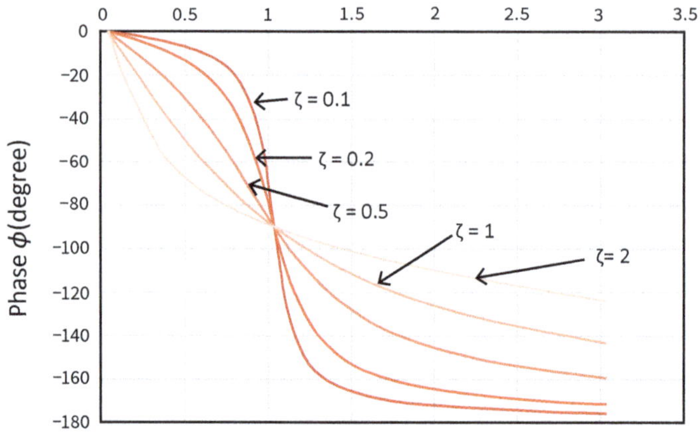

(b)

Figure 6.15. Magnification factor ($\frac{u_0}{u_0(\omega=0)}$) (**a**) and phase (**b**) as a function-normalized frequency ($\frac{\omega}{\omega_0}$) for various damping ratios ζ. Source: Figure by author.

6.3.3. Bode Plot

Equation (6.66) can also be written, using $T = 1/\omega_0$ (resonance period in radian scale):

$$G(j\omega) = \left(\frac{m}{f_0}\right)(m/f_0)U(j\omega) = \frac{1}{(-\omega^2T^2) + 2\zeta j\omega T + 1}. \quad (6.73)$$

The "Bode plot" is a representation of the transfer function (amplitude and phase) as a function of frequency on a logarithmic scale, as shown in Figure 6.16.

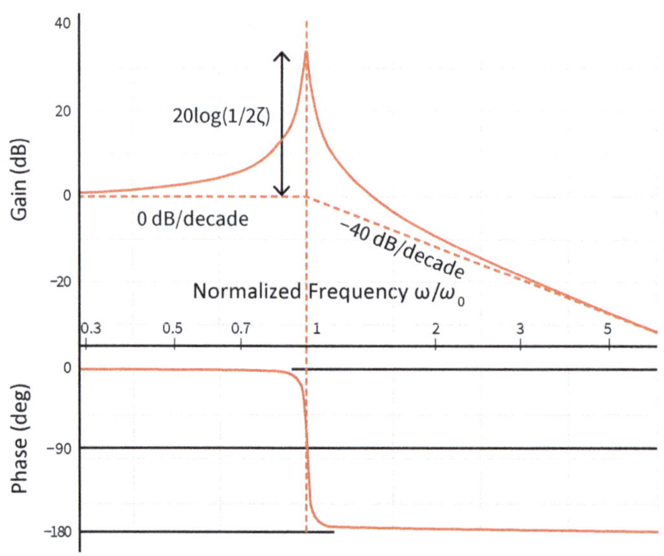

Figure 6.16. The Bode diagram for a standard second-order system. Source: Figure by author.

First, let us consider "asymptotic straight curves" of the "gain" for the "low" and "high" frequency regions.

- For $\omega \to 0$, $G(j\omega) \to 1$. Thus, gain $|G(j\omega)| = 1$, so that, in decibels:

$$\text{dB} = 20\log_{10}(1) = 0. \tag{6.74}$$

  "0 dB/decade", i.e., flat frequency dependence of the gain. Regarding the phase, the real number "1" corresponds to 0°. Gain and phase Bode plots are shown on the left-hand side in Figure 6.16.

- For $\omega \to \infty$, $G(j\omega) \to 1/(-\omega^2T^2)$ (N.B. do not immediately make $G(j\omega) \to 0$; otherwise, the frequency dependence of $G(j\omega)$ cannot be obtained).

$$\text{Gain}: \ |G(j\omega)| = \left|\frac{1}{(-\omega^2T^2)}\right|, \tag{6.75}$$

  so that in decibels:

$$\text{dB} = -20\log_{10}(\omega T)^2 = -40\log_{10}(\omega T). \tag{6.76}$$

  "−40 dB/decade" (or −12 dB/octave) with frequency. Regarding the phase, the negative real number corresponds to −180°, as indicated by the gain and phase curves appearing on the right-hand side in Figure 6.16.

  Second, we consider displacement for the resonance ω_0 frequency.

- Resonance range: we will now consider the deviation from these two asymptotic lines around the bend-point frequency, which is obtained from the relation $\omega T = 1$. Substituting the resonance condition $\omega T = 1$ in Equation (6.73) yields:

$$G(j\omega) = \frac{1}{(2\zeta j\omega T)} = \frac{1}{(2\zeta j)}, \tag{6.77a}$$

  so that the gain and phase become $[1/(2\zeta)]$ and −90°, respectively. The constant ζ is the damping ratio.

$$\text{dB} = 20\log_{10}(\frac{1}{(2\zeta)}). \tag{6.77b}$$

  If $\zeta = 0$ (loss-free), an infinite amplitude will occur at the bend-point frequency (i.e., resonance frequency); while ζ is large (>1), the resonance peak will disappear, and a monotonous decrease in amplitude is observed.

The "Lissajous curves" between the force and displacement are illustrated in Figure 6.17; when $(\omega/\omega_0) << 1.0$, there is a linear relation without a phase delay with a right-up positive slope, while for $(\omega/\omega_0) >> 1.0$, there is a linear relation with a right-down negative slope because of 180° phase delay (i.e., negative sign). At the resonance $(\omega/\omega_0) = 1.0$, there is an elliptical Lissajous relation with the magnification factor by $(1/2\zeta)$ along the displacement (under force f_0/c constant condition). The phase lag −90° indicates the locus in counterclockwise with timelapse. Since this Lissajous area on the force–displacement domain is related with the heat generation, the actual energy dissipation seems to be increased when approaching 90°. However, since the displacement is significantly amplified $(\times 1/2\zeta)$ under the constant force, the dissipation factor evaluated by (dissipation energy/input energy) is actually very similar.

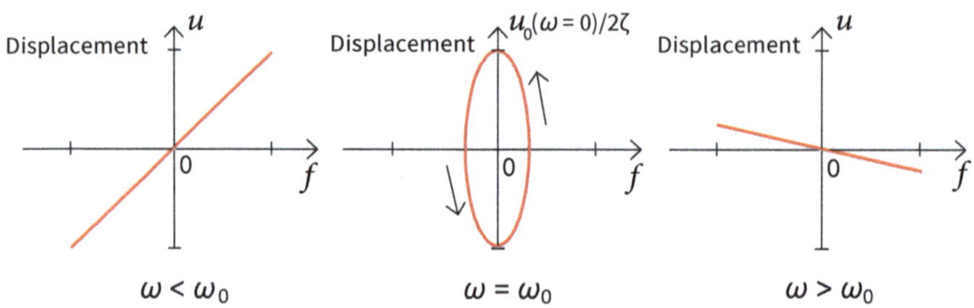

Figure 6.17. The Lissajous curves between force and displacement. Source: Figure by author.

6.3.4. Mechanical Quality Factor

There are multiple definitions for the "mechanical quality factor" Q, which are approximately but not exactly equivalent. One of these definitions is the frequency-to-bandwidth ratio of the mechanical resonator:

$$Q = \frac{f_r}{\Delta f} = \frac{\omega_r}{\Delta\omega}, \tag{6.78}$$

where f_r is the resonant frequency, Δf is the resonance width or "full width at half maximum" (FWHM), i.e., the bandwidth over which the power of vibration is greater than half the power at the resonant frequency, $\omega_r = 2\pi f_r$ is the angular resonant frequency, and $\Delta\omega$ is the angular half-power bandwidth. From the "Bode plot" of the displacement in Figure 6.16, $\Delta\omega$ should be obtained from $1/\sqrt{2}$ of the maximum displacement around the resonant frequency, which corresponds to 3 dB down level in a 20 dB type gain plot (recall the mechanical power ∝ (displacement)^2). Since $\frac{u_0(\omega_0)}{u_0(\omega=0)} = \frac{1}{2\zeta\frac{\omega}{\omega_0}}$, by putting $\frac{u_0}{u_0(\omega=0)} = \frac{1}{\sqrt{[1-(\frac{\omega}{\omega_0})^2]^2+(2\zeta\frac{\omega}{\omega_0})^2}} = \frac{1}{\sqrt{2}}\frac{1}{2\zeta\frac{\omega}{\omega_0}}$, we can obtain

$$1 - (\frac{\omega}{\omega_0})^2 = \pm 2\zeta\frac{\omega}{\omega_0}, \text{ depending on } \frac{\omega}{\omega_0} < 1 \text{ or } \frac{\omega}{\omega_0} > 1. \tag{6.79}$$

We obtain two roots, $\frac{\omega_1}{\omega_0} = \sqrt{1+\zeta^2} - \zeta$ or $\frac{\omega_2}{\omega_0} = \sqrt{1+\zeta^2} + \zeta$, for either $\frac{\omega}{\omega_0} < 1$ or $\frac{\omega}{\omega_0} > 1$, respectively. Thus, $\frac{\Delta\omega}{\omega_0} = \frac{\omega_2-\omega_1}{\omega_0} = 2\zeta$. The mechanical quality factor Q_m is expressed by

$$Q_m = \frac{\omega_0}{\Delta\omega} = 1/2\zeta. \tag{6.80}$$

The "mechanical quality factor" Q can also be obtained from the phase angle, that is, "quadrantal frequencies". Around the phase $-90°$ frequency, which corresponds to the resonance frequency, you can find the frequencies which provide the phases $-45°$ and $-135°$ (i.e., $\pm 45°$). These two frequencies correspond to the above

ω_1 and ω_2, respectively, which can be verified as follows. By inserting ω_1 and ω_2 into Equation (6.73),

$$G(j\omega_{1,2}) = \frac{1}{(-\omega_{1,2}{}^2T^2) + 2\zeta j\omega_{1,2}T + 1} = \frac{1}{2\zeta(\sqrt{1+\zeta^2} \pm \zeta)(\mp 1 + j)}. \tag{6.81}$$

Since the phases at ω_1 and ω_2 are determined by the denominator $(\mp 1 + j)$, we can obtain $-45°$ and $-135°$ immediately. The reader now understands the equivalency of the "quadrantal frequency method" to the above 3 dB down method. In experiments, the quadrantal frequency method provides more accurate results than the 3 dB up/down method.

6.3.5. Complex Algebra Method

Complex Displacement

The complex algebra method often facilitates solving differential equations, in the case of a forced oscillation under a harmonic external force, since the steady-state solution exhibits a "harmonic oscillation" with the same frequency as the input force. As explained in Figure 6.14c, the output displacement u is delayed from the input force f with phase lag ϕ, and keeping this phase lag, both vectors rotate at the angular frequency of ω. Supposing that these vectors are expressed by complex parameters such as

$$f(t) = f_0 e^{j\omega t}, \tag{6.82}$$

$$u(t) = u_0 e^{j(\omega t - \phi)} = u_0 e^{-j\phi} e^{j\omega t}. \tag{6.83}$$

f_0 and u_0 correspond to the absolute length of the force and displacement vectors, respectively. We write Equation (6.83) by using the complex vibration amplitude as

$$u(t) = u_0{}^* e^{j\omega t},\ u_0{}^* = u_0 e^{-j\phi}.$$

When we adopt Equations (6.82) and (6.83) into a mass–spring-damper model in Figure 6.14a,

$$m\ddot{u} + \xi\dot{u} + cu = f_0 e^{j\omega t}. \tag{6.84}$$

Using $u(t) = u_0{}^* e^{j\omega t}$, we obtain

$$\left(-m\omega^2 + j\xi\omega + c\right)u_0^* = f_0. \tag{6.85}$$

Accordingly,

$$u_0^* = \frac{f_0}{(-m\omega^2 + j\xi\omega + c)} = \frac{f_0 e^{-j\phi}}{\sqrt{(c - m\omega^2)^2 + (\xi\omega)^2}}. \tag{6.86}$$

The vibration amplitude and phase are obtained as:

$$u_0 = \frac{f_0}{\sqrt{(c - m\omega^2)^2 + (\xi\omega)^2}}, \tag{6.87a}$$

$$\phi = \tan^{-1} \frac{\xi\omega}{c - m\omega^2}. \tag{6.87b}$$

Complex Physical Parameter

From Equation (6.84), $m\ddot{u} + \xi\dot{u} + cu = f_0 e^{j\omega t}$, we assume harmonic vibration $u(t)$ with the same ω. Then,

$$\left(-m\omega^2 + j\xi\omega + c\right)u(t) = f_0 e^{j\omega t}. \tag{6.88}$$

We adopt a "complex spring constant" as

$$c^* = c(1 + j\frac{\xi\omega}{c}). \tag{6.89}$$

Note that the viscoelastic damping-related imaginary part is frequency dependent. Then, the dynamic equation is transformed as

$$\left(-m\omega^2 + c^*\right)u(t) = f_0 e^{j\omega t}. \tag{6.90}$$

We can understand that Equation (6.90) corresponds to a simple mass–spring oscillator with a complex spring constant. Under an assumption $u(t) = u_0 e^{j(\omega t - \phi)} = u_0 e^{-j\phi} e^{j\omega t}$, the remaining solution process is the same in the previous subsection, leading to the final results Equations (6.87a) and (6.87b).

Note that most of physical phenomena inevitably exhibit heat generation associated with losses or phase delay because a sort of delay in the output reaction occurs from the input electric or mechanical force.

6.4. Intensive and Extensive Losses in Piezoelectrics

6.4.1. *Energy Description of Intensive and Extensive Physical Parameters*

We will extend the loss formulation to "piezoelectric" materials, including "coupling phenomenon losses" in particular, by introducing complex numbers for physical parameters in this section. Complex parameter usage limits the applicability only for small damping situations, such as a damping ratio ζ less than 0.1 from a thermodynamic theory viewpoint. We need to obtain both "intensive" and "extensive" losses in the piezoelectric characterization to realize accurate analysis in piezo-device design by using computer simulation tools such as the "finite element method", because either loss will contribute in a different way depending on the realizing vibration mode in piezoelectrics. This loss distinction is also essential for creating a microscopic loss model in piezo materials; that is, in order to explain loss mechanisms theoretically, we usually utilize the "extensive" losses, which are calculated from "intensive" losses easily obtained experimentally.

According to IUPAC (The International Union of Pure, and Applied Chemistry), an "extensive parameter" depends on the volume of the material, while an "intensive parameter" is the ratio of two extensive ones and, therefore, is independent of the volume of the material [7]. If we cut an object in half, the mass, length, and displacement (extensive properties) would halve, while the temperature, force, and voltage (intensive properties) would not change. Consequently, the stress (X, first derivative of force) and electric field (E, first derivative of voltage) are intensive parameters, which are externally controllable, while the strain (x, first derivative of displacement) and dielectric displacement (D) (or polarization (P), as defined by the total dipole moments per volume) are extensive parameters, which are internally determined in the material.

We start with the Gibbs free energy, G, in terms of intensive parameters, in general differential form as:

$$dG = -xdX - DdE - SdT, \tag{6.91}$$

where x and X are the strain and stress, D and E are the electric displacement and electric field, and S and T are the entropy and temperature. Equation (6.91) is the energy expression in terms of the externally controllable (which is denoted as "intensive") physical parameters X, E, and T. If we assume the simplest linear phenomena for the elastic (Hooke's law), dielectric, and electromechanical coupling properties, we obtain the following Gibbs energy expression (refer to Chapter 2):

$$G = -(1/2)s^E X^2 - dXE - (1/2)\varepsilon_0 \varepsilon^X E^2. \tag{6.92}$$

The temperature dependence of the function is associated with the elastic compliance, s^E, the dielectric constant, ε^X, and the piezoelectric charge coefficient, d, and the direct entropy expression is omitted (refer to the Devonshire theory in Chapter 4). It is also noteworthy that the electromechanical coupling term XE (not XE^2) indicates the crystal symmetry (piezoelectrics belong to asymmetric class), which allows the sign change of X or x simultaneously for the E direction change. The following two piezoelectric equations (i.e., "piezoelectric constitutive equations") are derived from Equation (6.92):

$$x = -\frac{\partial G}{\partial X} = s^E X + dE, \tag{6.93}$$

$$D = -\frac{\partial G}{\partial E} = dX + \varepsilon_0 \varepsilon^X E. \tag{6.94}$$

Note that the Gibbs energy function provides intensive physical parameters: E—constant elastic compliance s^E, and X—constant permittivity ε^X.

On the other hand, when we consider the free energy in terms of the "extensive" (that is, material-related) parameters of the strain, x, and electric displacement, D, we start from the differential form of the Helmholtz free energy designated by A (refer to Chapter 2), such that:

$$dA = Xdx + EdD - SdT. \tag{6.95}$$

We now assume

$$A = (1/2)c^D x^2 - hxD + (1/2)\kappa_0 \kappa^x D^2 \ \ [\kappa_0 = (\frac{1}{\varepsilon_0})]. \tag{6.96}$$

From this energy function, we obtain another pair of piezoelectric constitutive equations:

$$X = \frac{\partial A}{\partial x} = c^D x - hD, \tag{6.97}$$

$$E = \frac{\partial A}{\partial D} = -hx + \kappa_0 \kappa^x D. \tag{6.98}$$

where c^D is the elastic stiffness at constant electric displacement (open-circuit conditions), h is the inverse piezoelectric charge coefficient, and κ^x is the inverse dielectric constant at a constant strain (mechanically clamped conditions).

Equations (6.93), (6.94), (6.97), and (6.98) should be written in tensor or matrix notations in 3D description, precisely speaking, and the reader can imagine that these pairs are mutually inverse tensor matrix relations. However, we initially obtain the interrelations between the intensive and extensive physical parameters in the one-dimensional form, simply for mathematical simplicity.

6.4.2. Piezoelectric Constitutive Equations with Losses

Intensive Losses

Since the detailed mathematical treatment has been described in a previous paper [8], we summarize the essential results in this subsection. We start from the "piezoelectric constitutive equation":

$$\begin{pmatrix} x \\ D \end{pmatrix} = \begin{pmatrix} s^E & d \\ d & \varepsilon_0 \varepsilon^X \end{pmatrix} \begin{pmatrix} X \\ E \end{pmatrix}, \tag{6.99}$$

where x is the strain, X is the stress, D is the electric displacement, and E is the electric field. Note that the original piezoelectric constitutive equations cannot yield a delay–time-related loss, in general, without taking into account irreversible thermodynamic equations or dissipation functions. However, the "dissipation functions" are mathematically equivalent to the introduction of "complex physical constants" into the phenomenological equations, if the loss is small and can be treated as a perturbation ("dissipation factor tangent" << 0.1).

Therefore, we will introduce complex parameters ε^{X*}, s^{E*}, and d^*, using *, in order to consider the small hysteresis losses in dielectric, elastic, and piezoelectric constants:

$$\varepsilon^{X*} = \varepsilon^X (1 - j\tan\delta'), \tag{6.100}$$

$$s^{E*} = s\,(1 - j\tan\phi'), \tag{6.101}$$

$$d^* = d(1 - j\tan\theta'). \tag{6.102}$$

θ' is the phase delay of the strain under an applied electric field, or the phase delay of the electric displacement under an applied stress. Both delay phases should be exactly the same if we introduce the same complex piezoelectric constant d^* into two constitutive equations of Equation (6.99). δ' is the phase delay of the electric displacement to an applied electric field under a constant stress (e.g., zero stress) condition, and ϕ' is the phase delay of the strain to an applied stress under a constant electric field (e.g., short-circuit) condition. We will consider these phase delays as "intensive losses" because these losses are related with the intensive physical parameters, ε^X, s^E, and d. Note here that though the "loss factor" is not a volume-dependent parameter, we will denote "intensive (or extensive) parameter-related loss" as "intensive (or extensive) loss" for short. We take a negative sign in front of the loss tangent, supposing that the extensive parameters are induced after the intensive parameters are applied. So far, no negative "intensive loss factor" has been reported experimentally.

Figure 6.18a–d correspond to the hysteresis model curves for practical experiments: D vs. E curve under a stress-free condition, x vs. X under a short-circuit condition, x vs. E under a stress-free condition, and D vs. X under a short-circuit condition (D is calculated from measured current integration), respectively. Note that these measurements are easily conducted in practice by changing the externally controllable intensive parameters (E, X). The average slope of the D–E hysteresis curve in Figure 6.18a corresponds to the permittivity $\varepsilon^X \varepsilon_0$ where the superscript stands for X = constant (occasionally zero). Thus, $\tan\delta'$ is called the "intensive dielectric loss tangent", or "dissipation factor". The situation of s^E is similar; the slope of the x–X relation is the elastic compliance under the E = constant condition. Though Figure 6.18a illustrates a sharp hysteresis edge around the maximum (and minimum) electric field, similar to the actually observed hysteresis curve, the complex parameter representation in Equation (6.100) indicates an elliptic shape (counterclockwise rotation) with rounded edges. Though this discrepancy implies a modeling inaccuracy (i.e., "viscoelastic damping" may not be a real phenomenon in piezoelectrics), we will adopt the complex parameter method for the loss analysis for mathematical simplicity.

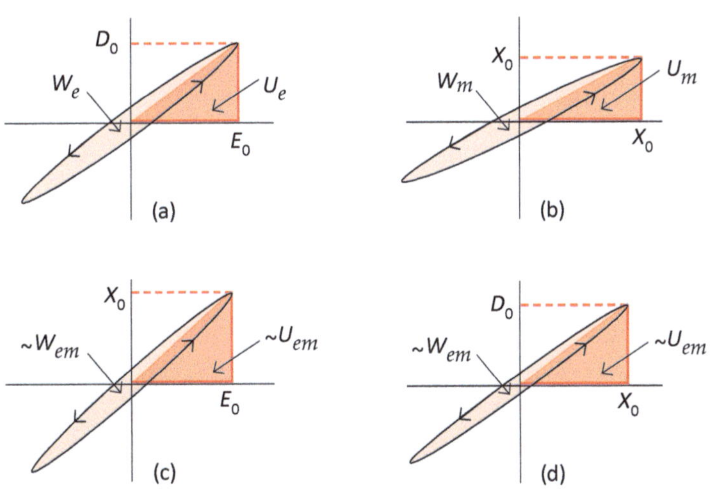

Figure 6.18. (**a**) D vs. E (stress free), (**b**) x vs. X (short circuit), (**c**) x vs. E (stress free), and (**d**) D vs. X (short circuit) curves with a slight hysteresis in each relation. Source: Figure by author, adapted from [5].

Since the areas on the D–E and x–X domains directly exhibit the electrical and mechanical energies, respectively (see Figure 6.18a,b), the stored energies (during a quarter cycle) and hysteresis losses (during a full electric or stress cycle) for pure dielectric and elastic energies can be calculated as (refer to Example Problem 6.1 for the detailed calculation process):

$$U_e = (1/2)\varepsilon^X \varepsilon_0 E_0{}^2, \quad (6.103)$$

$$w_e = \pi\varepsilon^X \varepsilon_0 E_0{}^2 \tan\delta', \quad (6.104)$$

$$U_m = (1/2)s^E X_0{}^2, \quad (6.105)$$

$$w_m = \pi s^E X_0{}^2 \tan\phi'. \quad (6.106)$$

Here, U_e and U_m stand for electrical and mechanical energy stored during a quarter cycle, and w_e and w_m are the electrical and mechanical hysteresis losses, respectively. The dissipation factors, $\tan\delta'$ and $\tan\phi'$, can be experimentally obtained by measuring the dotted hysteresis area and the stored energy area, that is, $(1/2\pi)(w_e/U_e)$ and $(1/2\pi)(w_m/U_m)$, respectively. Note that the factor (2π) comes from the integral per cycle.

The electromechanical hysteresis loss calculations, however, are more complicated, because the areas on the x–E and P–X domains do not directly provide energy. The areas on these domains can be calculated as follows, depending on the measuring methods: when measuring the induced strain under an electric field, the electromechanical conversion energy can be calculated as follows, by converting E to stress X:

$$U_{em} = \int x dX = \left(\frac{1}{s^E}\right) \int x dx = (d^2/s^E) \int_0^{E_0} E dE = (1/2)(d^2/s^E) E_0{}^2, \quad (6.107)$$

where $x = dE$. Then, using Equations (6.101) and (6.102), and from the imaginary part, we obtain the loss during a full cycle as

$$w_{em} = \pi(d^2/s^E) E_0{}^2 (2\tan\theta' - \tan\phi'). \quad (6.108)$$

Note that the area ratio in the strain vs. electric field measurement should provide the combination of piezoelectric loss $\tan\theta'$ and elastic loss $\tan\phi'$ (not $\tan\theta'$ directly!). When we measure the induced charge under stress, the stored energy U_{me} and the hysteresis loss w_{me} during a quarter and a full stress cycle, respectively, obtained similar results:

$$U_{me} = \int P dE = (1/2)(d^2/\varepsilon_0 \varepsilon^X) X_0{}^2, \quad (6.109)$$

$$w_{me} = \pi(d^2/\varepsilon_0 \varepsilon^X) X_0{}^2 (2\tan\theta' - \tan\delta'). \quad (6.110)$$

Now, the area ratio in the charge vs. stress measurement provides the combination of piezoelectric loss $\tan\theta'$ and dielectric loss $\tan\delta'$. Hence, from the measurements of D vs. E and x vs. X, we obtain $\tan\delta'$ and $\tan\phi'$, respectively, and either the piezoelectric (D vs. X) or converse piezoelectric measurement (x vs. E) provides $\tan\phi'$ through a numerical subtraction. The above equations provide a traditional loss-measuring technique on piezoelectric actuators, that is, measurement of polarization and strain induced by an electric field under the mechanical-free condition, and measurement of polarization and strain induced by the external stress under the short-circuit condition. You may recognize that the "piezoelectric" loss is a sort of "hidden" parameter, which cannot be directly measured but is obtained from the measurable combination loss. Another intriguing point is the loss subtraction: the piezoelectric coupling loss contributes oppositely to the elastic or electric loss, which means that normal electric and mechanical losses (these are merely added together) can be cancelled somewhat by the piezoelectric loss.

Extensive Losses

In the previous subsection, we discussed the "intensive" dielectric, mechanical, and piezoelectric losses (with prime notation) in terms of "intensive parameters" X and E. In order to consider "physical meanings" of the losses (microscopic or semi-macroscopic model) in the material (e.g., domain dynamics), we will introduce the "extensive losses" [4] in terms of "extensive parameters" x and D. In practice, intensive losses are easily measurable; extensive losses are not in the pseudo-DC measurement but are obtainable from the intensive losses by using the so-called "K-matrix" introduced later. When we start from the 1D piezoelectric equations in terms of extensive physical parameters x and D,

$$\begin{pmatrix} X \\ E \end{pmatrix} = \begin{pmatrix} c^D & -h \\ -h & \kappa_0\kappa^x \end{pmatrix} \begin{pmatrix} x \\ D \end{pmatrix}, \tag{6.111}$$

where c^D is the elastic stiffness under D = constant condition (i.e., electrically open circuit), κ^x is the inverse dielectric constant under x = constant condition (i.e., mechanically clamped), and h is the inverse piezoelectric constant d. We introduce the "extensive" dielectric, elastic, and piezoelectric losses as

$$\kappa^{x*} = \kappa^x(1 + j\tan\delta), \tag{6.112}$$

$$c^{D*} = c^D(1 + j\tan\phi), \tag{6.113}$$

$$h^* = h(1 + j\tan\theta). \tag{6.114}$$

The sign "+" in front of the imaginary "j" is taken by a general induction principle: "polarization induced after electric field application" and "strain induced after stress application". However, in terms of the "extensive piezoelectric loss" $\tan\theta$, in the relation among electric displacement D (or polarization P) and strain x, we have no idea which comes earlier, either D or x. In other words, is it polarization-originated ferroelasticity or ferroelasticity-originated ferroelectricity?

It is notable that the permittivity under a constant strain (e.g., zero strain or completely clamped) condition, ε^{x*}, and the elastic compliance under a constant electric displacement (e.g., open-circuit) condition, s^{D*}, can be provided as an inverse value of κ^{x*} and c^{D*}, respectively, in this simplest one-dimensional expression. Thus, using exactly the same losses in Equations (6.112) and (6.113),

$$\varepsilon^{x*} = \varepsilon^x(1 - j\tan\phi), \tag{6.115}$$

$$s^{D*} = s^D(1 - \tan\phi), \tag{6.116}$$

we will consider these phase delays again as "extensive losses". Care should be taken in the case of a general 3D expression, where this part must be translated as "inverse matrix components" of κ^{x*} and c^{D*} tensors. In order to realize an x-constant status, we need to clamp 3D precisely, not just 1D, as introduced in the longitudinally clamped capacitance in the k_{31} mode plate specimen in Chapter 7.

In order to obtain the interrelationship between the intensive and extensive losses, we remind the reader of the physical property difference according to the boundary conditions: E constant and D constant, or X constant and x constant in the simplest 1D model. When an electric field is applied on a piezoelectric sample as illustrated in the top part of Figure 6.19, this state will be equivalent to the superposition of the following two steps: first, the sample is completely clamped and the field E_0 is applied (pure electrical energy $(1/2)\varepsilon^x\varepsilon_0 E_0{}^2$ is stored); second, keeping the field at E_0, the mechanical constraint is released (additional mechanical energy $(1/2)(d^2/s^E)E_0{}^2$ is necessary). The total energy should correspond to the total input electrical energy $(1/2)\varepsilon^X\varepsilon_0 E_0{}^2$ under stress-free conditions (left figure). That is, $(1/2)\varepsilon^X\varepsilon_0 E_0{}^2 = (1/2)\varepsilon^x\varepsilon_0 E_0{}^2 + (1/2)(d^2/s^E)E_0{}^2$. A similar energy calculation can be obtained from the bottom part of Figure 6.19, leading to the following equations:

$$\varepsilon^x/\varepsilon^X = (1-k^2), \quad (6.117)$$

$$s^D/s^E = (1-k^2), \quad (6.118)$$

$$\kappa^X/\kappa^x = (1-k^2), \quad (6.119)$$

$$c^E/c^D = (1-k^2), \quad (6.120)$$

where

$$k^2 = d^2/(s^E\varepsilon_0\varepsilon^X) = h^2/(c^D\kappa_0\kappa^x)\ [\kappa_0 = (\frac{1}{\varepsilon_0})]. \quad (6.121)$$

This k is called the "electromechanical coupling factor", which is handled as a real number in most of the cases in this book.

It is noteworthy that losses are not actual "intensive" or "extensive" parameters at all, but define the "losses associated with the intensive or extensive parameters" as "intensive or extensive losses" in simple expressions.

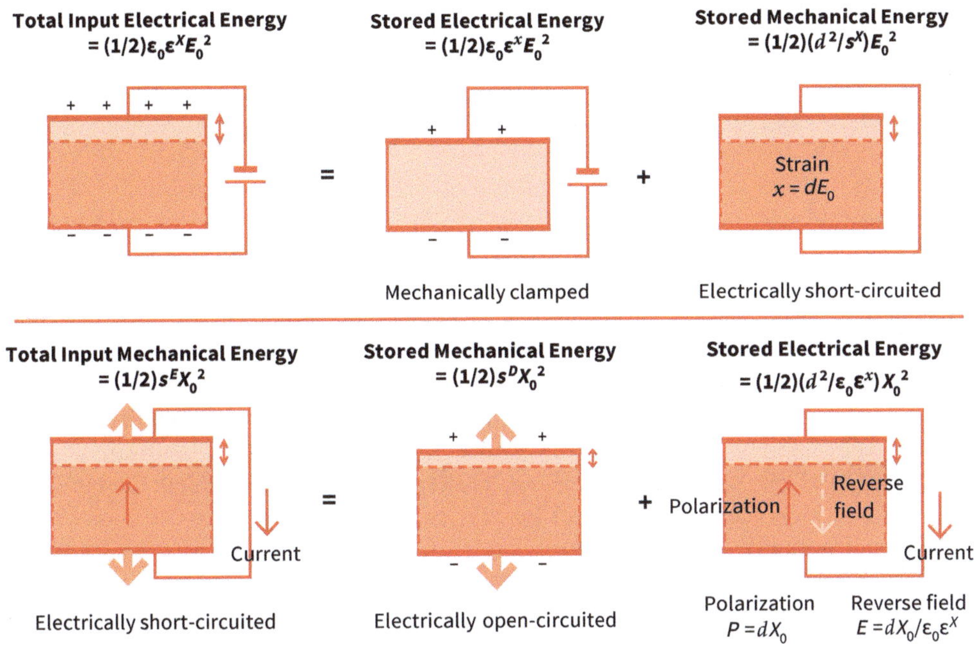

Figure 6.19. Conceptual figure for explaining the relation between ε^X and ε^x, s^E, and s^D. Source: [5] ©Uchino, K. Micromechatronics, 2nd ed. CRC Press, 2019; p. 76. Reproduced by permission of Taylor & Francis Group.

K-Matrix in the Intensive and Extensive Losses

In order to obtain the relationships between the intensive and extensive losses, the following three equations derived from Equations (6.99) and (6.111) are essential (derivation process in Example Problem 6.3):

$$s^E = \frac{1}{c^D}\frac{1}{\left(1 - \frac{h^2}{(c^D\kappa_0\kappa^x)}\right)}, \tag{6.122}$$

$$\varepsilon_0\varepsilon^X = \frac{1}{\kappa_0\kappa^x}\frac{1}{\left(1 - \frac{h^2}{(c^D\kappa_0\kappa^x)}\right)}, \tag{6.123}$$

$$d = \frac{1}{d}\frac{\frac{h^2}{(c^D\kappa_0\kappa^x)}}{\left(1 - \frac{h^2}{(c^D\kappa_0\kappa^x)}\right)}. \tag{6.124}$$

Replacing the parameters in Equations (6.122)–(6.124) by the complex parameters in Equations (6.100)–(6.102), (6.112)–(6.114), we obtain the relationships between the intensive and extensive losses:

$$\tan\delta' = (1/(1-k^2))\left[\tan\delta + k^2(\tan\phi - 2\tan\theta)\right], \tag{6.125}$$

$$\tan\phi' = (1/(1-k^2))\left[\tan\phi + k^2(\tan\delta - 2\tan\theta)\right], \quad (6.126)$$

$$\tan\theta' = (1/(1-k^2))\left[\tan\delta + \tan\phi - (1+k^2)\tan\theta\right], \quad (6.127)$$

where k is the "electromechanical coupling factor" defined by Equation (6.121), and here as a real number. It is important that the "intensive dielectric, elastic, and piezoelectric losses" (with prime) are mutually correlated with the "extensive dielectric, elastic, and piezoelectric losses" (non-prime) through the electromechanical coupling k^2, and that the denominator $(1 - k^2)$ basically comes from the ratios, $\varepsilon^x/\varepsilon^X = (1-k^2)$ and $s^D/s^E = (1-k^2)$, and this real part reflects the dissipation factor when the imaginary part is divided by the real part.

Knowing the relationships between the intensive and extensive physical parameters (Equations (6.99) and (6.111)), and the electromechanical coupling factor k (Equation (6.121)), we introduce the so-called "[K]-matrix" to interrelate the intensive (prime) and extensive (non-prime) loss factors (attempt Example Problem 6.3 to further understand the derivation process):

$$\begin{bmatrix} \tan\delta' \\ \tan\phi' \\ \tan\theta' \end{bmatrix} = [K] \begin{bmatrix} \tan\delta \\ \tan\phi \\ \tan\theta \end{bmatrix}, \quad (6.128)$$

$$[K] = \frac{1}{1-k^2}\begin{bmatrix} 1 & k^2 & -2k^2 \\ k^2 & 1 & -2k^2 \\ 1 & 1 & -1-k^2 \end{bmatrix}, \quad k^2 = \frac{d^2}{s^E(\varepsilon^X\varepsilon_0)} = \frac{h^2}{c^D(\kappa^x\kappa_0)}. \quad (6.129)$$

The matrix [K] is proven to be "invertible", i.e., $K^2 = I$, or $K = K^{-1}$, where I is the identity matrix. Hence, the conversion relationship between the intensive (prime) and extensive (non-prime) exhibits full symmetry:

$$\begin{bmatrix} \tan\delta \\ \tan\phi \\ \tan\theta \end{bmatrix} = [K] \begin{bmatrix} \tan\delta' \\ \tan\phi' \\ \tan\theta' \end{bmatrix}, \text{ and } \begin{bmatrix} \tan\delta' \\ \tan\phi' \\ \tan\theta' \end{bmatrix} = [K] \begin{bmatrix} \tan\delta \\ \tan\phi \\ \tan\theta \end{bmatrix} \quad (6.130)$$

The author again emphasizes that the extensive losses are more important for considering the physical micro/macroscopic models and can be obtained mathematically from a set of intensive losses, which are obtained directly from the experiments (in particular, pseudo-DC measurement).

Though we handle the electromechanical coupling factor k as a real parameter in the above, if we introduce a sort of "electromechanical coupling loss", it will be derived as follows from Equation (6.121):

$$\left(\frac{k^{2\prime\prime}}{k^{2\prime}}\right) = \tan\chi = (2\tan\theta' - \tan\delta' - \tan\phi') = -(2\tan\theta - \tan\delta - \tan\phi). \quad (6.131)$$

Note that the electromechanical coupling loss is an eigen function of Equation (6.129) with the [K] matrix, that is, the unique constant, irrelevant of the intensive or extensive description. The loss $\tan\chi$ can be either positive or negative, depending on the piezoelectric loss magnitute tan θ', which contributes to the mechanical quality factor spectrum around the resonance and antiresonance frequencies, as discussed in Chapter 7.

Example Problem 6.3

---

(1) Derive the [K]-matrix to interrelate the intensive and extensive losses:

$$[K] = \frac{1}{1-k^2}\begin{bmatrix} 1 & k^2 & -2k^2 \\ k^2 & 1 & -2k^2 \\ 1 & 1 & -1-k^2 \end{bmatrix}. \tag{P6.3.1}$$

(2) Verify the following relationship first:

$$k^2 = \frac{d^2}{(s^E \varepsilon_0 \varepsilon^X)} = \frac{h^2}{(c^D \kappa_0 \kappa^x)}, \tag{P6.3.2}$$

then, verify the "electromechanical coupling loss" relation:

$$(2\tan\theta' - \tan\delta' - \tan\phi') = -(2\tan\theta - \tan\delta - \tan\phi). \tag{P6.3.3}$$

Hint

From the following pairs of equations, eliminate the parameters, X, E, x, and D.

$$x = s^E X + dE, \tag{P6.3.4}$$

$$D = dX + \varepsilon_0 \varepsilon^X E, \tag{P6.3.5}$$

$$X = c^D x - hD, \tag{P6.3.6}$$

$$E = -hx + \kappa_0 \kappa^x D. \tag{P6.3.7}$$

Solution

(1) From Equations (6.99) and (6.111)

$$\begin{pmatrix} x \\ D \end{pmatrix} = \begin{pmatrix} s^E & d \\ d & \varepsilon_0 \varepsilon^X \end{pmatrix}\begin{pmatrix} X \\ E \end{pmatrix} = \begin{pmatrix} s^E & d \\ d & \varepsilon_0 \varepsilon^X \end{pmatrix}\begin{pmatrix} c^D & -h \\ -h & \kappa_0 \kappa^x \end{pmatrix}\begin{pmatrix} x \\ D \end{pmatrix}. \tag{P6.3.8}$$

Thus, the product of the matrix should be the identity matrix:

$$\begin{pmatrix} s^E c^D - dh & -s^E h + d\kappa_0 \kappa^x \\ dc^D - \varepsilon_0 \varepsilon^X h & -dh + \varepsilon_0 \varepsilon^X \kappa_0 \kappa^x \end{pmatrix} = \begin{pmatrix} 1 & 0 \\ 0 & 1 \end{pmatrix}. \tag{P6.3.9}$$

From these four component equations, we can derive the following equations easily:

$$\varepsilon^X \varepsilon_0 = \frac{1}{\kappa_0 \kappa^x \left[1 - \frac{h^2}{c^D \kappa_0 \kappa^x}\right]} = \frac{1}{\kappa_0 \kappa^x (1-k^2)}, \tag{P6.3.10}$$

$$s^E = \frac{1}{c^D\left[1 - \frac{h^2}{c^D \kappa_0 \kappa^x}\right]} = \frac{1}{c^D(1-k^2)}, \quad \text{(P6.3.11)}$$

$$d = \frac{\frac{h^2}{c^D \kappa_0 \kappa^x}}{h\left[1 - \frac{h^2}{c^D \kappa_0 \kappa^x}\right]} = \frac{k^2}{h(1-k^2)}. \quad \text{(P6.3.12)}$$

Introducing the complex parameters, with prime losses on the left-hand side, and non-prime losses on the right-hand side (the middle terms) of the above three equations, we can obtain the following:

$$\tan\delta' = (1/(1-k^2))\left[\tan\delta + k^2(\tan\phi - 2\tan\theta)\right], \quad \text{(P6.3.13)}$$

$$\tan\phi' = (1/(1-k^2))\left[\tan\phi + k^2(\tan\delta - 2\tan\theta)\right], \quad \text{(P6.3.14)}$$

$$\tan\theta' = (1/(1-k^2))\left[\tan\delta + \tan\phi - (1+k^2)\tan\theta\right]. \quad \text{(P6.3.15)}$$

The $[K]$-matrix (Equation (P6.3.1)) is automatically obtained from Equations (P6.3.13)–(P6.3.15):

$$[K] = \frac{1}{1-k^2}\begin{bmatrix} 1 & k^2 & -2k^2 \\ k^2 & 1 & -2k^2 \\ 1 & 1 & -1-k^2 \end{bmatrix} \quad \text{(P6.3.1)}$$

(2) Substituting X, E in Equations (P6.3.4) and (P6.3.5) by Equations (P6.3.6) and (P4.3.7), we obtain

$x = s^E(c^D x - hD) + d(-hx + \kappa_0\kappa^x D)$,
$D = d(c^D x - hD) + \varepsilon_0\varepsilon^X(-hx + \kappa_0\kappa^x D)$.

Upon rearranging,

$(1 + dh - s^E c^D)x = \left[d\kappa_0\kappa^x - hs^E\right]D$,
$(dc^D - h\varepsilon_0\varepsilon^X)x = \left[1 + dh - \kappa_0\kappa^x\varepsilon_0\varepsilon^X\right]D$.

Thus, from $(1 + dh - s^E c^D)\left[1 + dh - \kappa_0\kappa^x\varepsilon_0\varepsilon^X\right] = (dc^D - h\varepsilon_0\varepsilon^X)\left[d\kappa_0\kappa^x - hs^E\right]$; finally,

$$\frac{d^2}{(s^E\varepsilon_0\varepsilon^X)} = \frac{h^2}{(c^D\kappa_0\kappa^x)}. \quad \text{(P6.3.16)}$$

Let us verify that Equation (P6.3.16) corresponds to the electromechanical coupling factor, which is defined by k^2 = (stored electrical energy/input mechanical energy) or (stored mechanical energy/input electrical energy). We demonstrate the electric energy input case (try for the mechanical energy input case by yourself). See Figure 6.20a first, when we apply an electric field on the top and bottom electrodes under a stress-free condition ($X = 0$). The input electric energy must be equal to $(1/2)\varepsilon_0\varepsilon^X E^2$ from Equation (6.92), and the strain generated by E should be dE from

Equation (P6.3.4). Since the converted/stored mechanical energy is obtained as $(1/2s^E)x^2$ (E-constant or short-circuit condition), we obtain:

$$k^2 = \left[(1/2)(dE)^2/s^E\right]/\left[(1/2)\varepsilon_0\varepsilon^X E^2\right] = d^2/\varepsilon_0\varepsilon^X s^E \tag{P6.3.17}$$

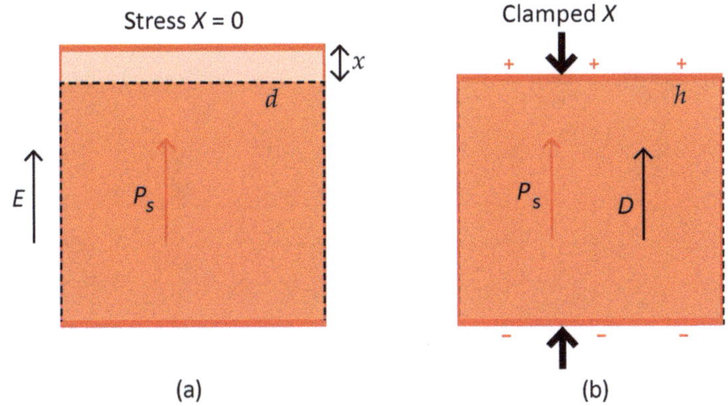

Figure 6.20. Calculation models of electromechanical coupling factor k for (**a**) electric field input and (**b**) electric displacement input. Source: Figure by author.

On the contrary, we now consider the extensive parameter description. See Figure 6.20b. The specimen generates delectric displacement D (under the open-circuit condition) first along the spontanous polarization direction under the completely clamped condition (x = 0). The input electric energy must be equal to $(1/2)\kappa_0\kappa^x D^2$ from Equation (6.96). Since the blocking force (for clamping) is given by $X = -hD$ and the converted/stored mechanical energy is obtained as $\frac{1}{2}\left(\frac{1}{c^D}\right)X^2 = \frac{1}{2}\left(\frac{1}{c^D}\right)(hD)^2$, we obtain:

$$k^2 = \left[\frac{1}{2}\left(\frac{1}{c^D}\right)X^2\right]/\left[(1/2)\kappa_0\kappa^x D^2\right] = \frac{h^2}{(c^D\kappa_0\kappa^x)}. \tag{P6.3.18}$$

We can now understand that both $\frac{d^2}{(s^E\varepsilon_0\varepsilon^X)}$ and $\frac{h^2}{(c^D\kappa_0\kappa^x)}$ mean the electromechanical coupling factor, and the values are exactly the same.

Introducing the complex parameters, on both sides of Equation (P6.3.16), it is obvious to derive the electromechanical coupling loss equation:

$$(2\tan\theta' - \tan\delta' - \tan\phi') = -(2\tan\theta - \tan\delta - \tan\phi). \tag{P6.3.19}$$

Example Problem 6.4

Verify that the following $[K]$ matrix is "invertible", i.e., $K = K^{-1}$.

$$[K] = \frac{1}{1-k^2}\begin{bmatrix} 1 & k^2 & -2k^2 \\ k^2 & 1 & -2k^2 \\ 1 & 1 & -1-k^2 \end{bmatrix}. \tag{P6.4.1}$$

Then, obtain the eigen function in terms of the vector component $(\tan\delta', \tan\phi', \tan\theta')$.

<u>Solution</u>

We calculate K^2.

$$[K]\times[K] = \frac{1}{1-k^2}\begin{bmatrix} 1 & k^2 & -2k^2 \\ k^2 & 1 & -2k^2 \\ 1 & 1 & -1-k^2 \end{bmatrix} \times \frac{1}{1-k^2}\begin{bmatrix} 1 & k^2 & -2k^2 \\ k^2 & 1 & -2k^2 \\ 1 & 1 & -1-k^2 \end{bmatrix}$$

$$= \frac{1}{(1-k^2)^2}\begin{bmatrix} 1+k^4-2k^2 & 0 & 0 \\ k^2+k^2-2k^2 & k^4+1-2k^2 & 0 \\ 0 & 0 & -2k^2-2k^2+(-1-k^2)^2 \end{bmatrix}$$

$$= \begin{bmatrix} 1 & 0 & 0 \\ 0 & 1 & 0 \\ 0 & 0 & 1 \end{bmatrix} = I.$$

It is also interesting to obtain the eigen value and eigen vector of Equation (P6.4.1). Taking the determinant

$$\begin{vmatrix} \frac{1}{1-k^2}-\lambda & \frac{k^2}{1-k^2} & \frac{-2k^2}{1-k^2} \\ \frac{k^2}{1-k^2} & \frac{1}{1-k^2}-\lambda & \frac{-2k^2}{1-k^2} \\ \frac{1}{1-k^2} & \frac{1}{1-k^2} & \frac{-1-k^2}{1-k^2}-\lambda \end{vmatrix} = 0, \tag{P6.4.2}$$

we obtain the three eigen values of $\lambda_1 = \lambda_2 = 1$, $\lambda_3 = -1$, and the eigen vector for $\lambda_1 = \lambda_2 = 1$ as

$$x_1 = -x_2 + 2x_3,\ x_2 = x_2, \text{ and } x_3 = x_3. \tag{P6.4.3}$$

This results in the value $(2\tan\theta' - \tan\delta' - \tan\phi') = -(2\tan\theta - \tan\delta - \tan\phi)$ being invariant, which corresponds to the loss for the electromechanical coupling factor $d^2/(s^E\varepsilon_0\varepsilon^X) = h^2/(c^D\kappa^x\kappa^0)$. Note that the negative sign in this loss equation comes from the definition difference of intensive and extensive losses in Equations (6.100)–(6.102) and (6.112)–(6.114).

Example Problem 6.5

In this chapter, the piezoelectric coupling loss $\tan\theta'$ was introduced, in addition to the well-known elastic loss $\tan\phi'$ and dielectric loss $\tan\delta'$. Describe why the inclusion of $\tan\theta'$ is essential. The motivation is to explain the difference of Q_m at the resonance and at the antiresonance experimentally observed in most of the PZT-based ceramics.

Hint

The major problem is found in the present IEEE Standard on Piezoelectricity, ANSI/IEEE Std. 176-1987, which many engineers are still using as the standard. Figure 6.21 shows an equivalent circuit for a k_{31}-type piezoelectric resonator, for example, proposed by the IEEE Standard on Piezoelectricity. Only one loss parameter R_1 results in the same mechanical quality factor Q_m for both resonance and antiresonance peaks in its admittance/impedance spectrum, as suggested in the following forms for the k_{31} mode:

$$s_{11}^E = 1/\left(4\rho f_r^2 l^2\right), \tag{P6.5.1}$$

$$K_{31}^2 = \frac{\pi}{2}\frac{f_{ar}}{f_r}\tan\left(\frac{\pi}{2}\frac{\Delta f}{f_r}\right) \text{ where, } K_{31}^2 = \frac{k_{31}^2}{1-k_{31}^2}, \tag{P6.5.2}$$

$$Q_m = \frac{Y_m^{max^2}}{8\cdot\omega_0\cdot C\cdot K_{31}^2}. \tag{P6.5.3}$$

This "Standard" does not include the terminology "piezoelectric loss", nor does it discuss the difference of mechanical quality factors Q_A (at resonance) and Q_B (at antiresonance); that is, both are exactly the same, against many of the practical experimental results and reports. Chapter 7 is devoted to solving this IEEE Standard dilemma.

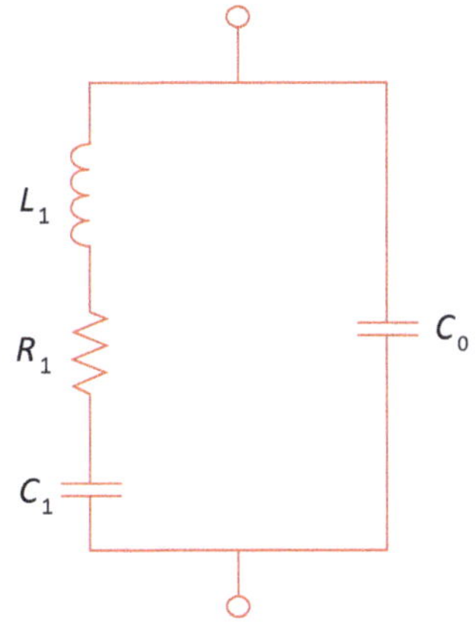

Figure 6.21. An equivalent circuit for a k_{31}-type piezo-resonator by the IEEE Standard on Piezoelectricity. Source: Figure by author, adapted from [1].

Solution

The mechanical quality factors Q_A at the resonance and at the antiresonance Q_B are expressed by using the three losses (piezoelectric tan θ', elastic tan ϕ', and dielectric tan δ') as follows (see Section 7.3.1 for the details):

$$Q_{A,31} = \frac{1}{\tan\phi_{11}'}, \ \Omega_{A,31} = \frac{\omega_a l}{2v_{11}^E} = \frac{\pi}{2}, \ \left[v_{11}^E = 1/\sqrt{\rho s_{11}^E}\right], \tag{P6.5.4}$$

$$\frac{1}{Q_{B,31}} = \frac{1}{Q_{A,31}} - \frac{2}{1+(\frac{1}{k_{31}} - k_{31})^2 \Omega_{B,31}{}^2} (2\tan\, \theta_{31}{}' - \tan\, \delta_{33}{}' - \tan\, \phi_{11}{}'), \quad \text{(P6.5.5)}$$

$$\Omega_{B,31} = \frac{\omega_b l}{2v_{11}^E}, \quad 1 - k_{31}{}^2 + k_{31}{}^2 \frac{\tan\, \Omega_B}{\Omega_B} = 0. \quad \text{(P6.5.6)}$$

The mechanical quality factor $Q_{A,31}$ is given only by the elastic loss $\tan\, \phi_{11}{}'$, while $Q_{B,31}$ at the antiresonance is given by the coupling of three losses (i.e., "electromechanical coupling loss" $[2\tan\theta' - (\tan\phi' + \tan\delta')]$). It is essential to mention that the coupling loss $\tan\theta'$ is subtracted from the average of the normal elastic and dielectric $\frac{1}{2}(\tan\phi' + \tan\delta')$ so that the electromechanical coupling loss $[\tan\theta' - \frac{1}{2}(\tan\phi' + \tan\delta')]$ can be either positive or negative, which induces $Q_{A,31} < Q_{B,31}$ or $Q_{A,31} > Q_{B,31}$, respectively, as demonstrated in Figure 6.22. Note again that regardless of each loss value (even rather large), as long as the subtracted result is small, the mechanical quality factor $Q_{B,31}$ at the antiresonance can be significantly large (i.e., the heat generation is very small). All three losses are not always added, but the coupling loss behaves for deducing the total loss.

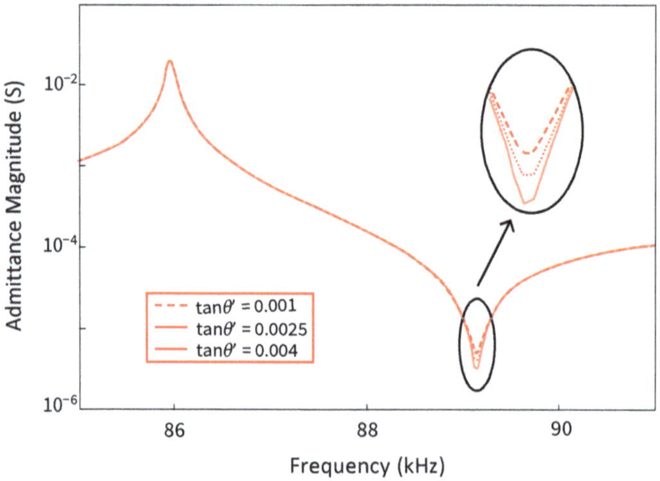

Figure 6.22. Admittance simulation of a k_{31}-type PZT plate by changing only the piezoelectric loss $\tan\, \theta'$. Source: Figure by author, adapted from [1].

Chapter Essentials

1. Dielectric loss: though electronic polarization responds up to Peta Hertz, ionic and dipolar polarization do have response limits, which provide the intrinsic dielectric loss. Small conductance in the material contributes additional effective dielectric loss.
2. LCR circuit: $L\left(\frac{d^2Q}{dt^2}\right) + R(\frac{dQ}{dt}) + \frac{Q}{C} = V(t)$ or $L\left(\frac{d^2I}{dt^2}\right) + R(\frac{dI}{dt}) + \frac{I}{C} = \frac{dV}{dt}$

   $I(t) = \frac{V_0}{Z}\sin(\omega t - \phi)$; $Z = \sqrt{R^2 + (L\omega - \frac{1}{C\omega})^2}$, $\tan\phi = \frac{(L\omega - \frac{1}{C\omega})}{R}$.
3. Three mechanical loss models:
   a. Solid damping – damping force $F = \zeta c u_{max}$,

b. Coulomb damping – damping force constant $\pm F$ – linear decay of the displacement amplitude,

c. Viscous damping – damping force proportional to velocity $F = \xi \dot{u}$ – exponential decay of the displacement amplitude.

4. Steady-state oscillation for a mass–spring–dashpot model: $m\ddot{u} + \xi\dot{u} + cu = f(t)$.
$\omega_0 = \sqrt{c/m}$ (ω_0: resonance angular frequency for zero damping)
$\zeta = \xi/2m\omega_0$ (ξ, ζ: damping factor, ratio) (refer to Figure 6.16)

$$u(t) = \frac{f_0 \sin\,(\omega t+\phi)}{\sqrt{(c-m\omega^2)^2+(2m\zeta\omega_0\omega)^2}},$$

$$u_0 = \frac{f_0}{\sqrt{(c-m\omega^2)^2+(2m\zeta\omega_0\omega)^2}},$$

$$\tan\phi = -\frac{2m\zeta\omega_0\omega}{c-m\omega^2}.$$

5. Bode plot: asymptotic curves – 0 dB/decade, −40 dB/decade.
Resonance peak height = $20\log_{10}(\frac{1}{2\zeta})$.

6. Mechanical quality factor:
$$Q_m = \frac{\omega_0}{\Delta\omega} = 1/2\zeta.$$

7. Complex algebra method, including a complex physical parameter such as a complex elastic stiffness, is a useful tool for harmonic steady-state oscillation to calculate the vibration amplitude and phase lag as a function of frequency.
→ the Bode diagram is a logarithmic plot of these parameters.

8. Piezoelectric constitutive equations:
Intensive parameter description $x = -\frac{\partial G}{\partial X} = s^E X + dE$,
$D = -\frac{\partial G}{\partial E} = dX + \varepsilon_0\varepsilon^X E$,
s^E—elastic compliance under constant field, ε^X—dielectric constant under constant stress, d—piezoelectric charge coefficient.

9. Interrelationship between intensive and extensive parameters:

$$c^D = \frac{1}{s^E}\frac{1}{(1-\frac{d^2}{(s^E\varepsilon_0\varepsilon^X)})},\ \kappa_0\kappa^x = \frac{1}{\varepsilon_0\varepsilon^X}\frac{1}{(1-\frac{d^2}{(s^E\varepsilon_0\varepsilon^X)})},\ h = \frac{1}{d}\frac{\frac{d^2}{(s^E\varepsilon_0\varepsilon^X)}}{(1-\frac{d^2}{(s^E\varepsilon_0\varepsilon^X)})}.$$

10. Electromechanical coupling factor:

$$k^2 = \frac{d^2}{(s^E\varepsilon_0\varepsilon^X)} = \frac{h^2}{(c^D\kappa_0\kappa^x)}.$$

11. Constraint dependence of permittivity and elastic compliance:

$$\varepsilon^x/\varepsilon^X = (1-k^2),\ s^D/s^E = (1-k^2),\ \kappa^X/\kappa^x = (1-k^2),\ c^E/c^D = (1-k^2).$$

12. Intensive and extensive loss definitions:

$$\varepsilon^{X*} = \varepsilon^X(1 - j\tan\delta') \quad \kappa^{x*}\kappa^x(1 + j\tan\delta),$$
$$s^{E*} = s^E(1 - j\tan\phi') \quad c^{D*} = c^D(1 + j\tan\phi),$$
$$d^* = d(1 - j\tan\theta') \quad h^* = h(1 + j\tan\theta).$$

13. Intensive and extensive loss interrelation:

$$\begin{bmatrix} \tan \delta' \\ \tan \phi' \\ \tan \theta' \end{bmatrix} = [K] \begin{bmatrix} \tan \delta \\ \tan \phi \\ \tan \theta \end{bmatrix} \text{ or } \begin{bmatrix} \tan \delta \\ \tan \phi \\ \tan \theta \end{bmatrix} = [K] \begin{bmatrix} \tan \delta' \\ \tan \phi' \\ \tan \theta' \end{bmatrix},$$

$$\text{where } [K] = \frac{1}{1-k^2} \begin{bmatrix} 1 & k^2 & -2k^2 \\ k^2 & 1 & -2k^2 \\ 1 & 1 & -1-k^2 \end{bmatrix}.$$

14. The loss of the electromechanical coupling factor k is represented by $(2\tan \theta' - \tan \delta' - \tan \phi') = -(2\tan \theta - \tan \delta - \tan \phi)$, which is an eigen function of the $[K]$ matrix and invariant.

Check Point

1. (T/F) When we add a Coulomb damper to a mass–spring system under free vibration (no external force), the vibration amplitude decreases exponentially. True or false?
2. (Fill in the blank) There are three mechanical damping mechanisms: solid damping, Coulomb (friction) damping, and [ ].
3. What is the Laplace transform for the Impulse $\delta(t)$ function?
4. What is the Laplace transform for the Heaviside Step function?
5. (T/F) The Laplace transform for $\sin(at)$ is $1/(s^2 + a^2)$. True or false?
6. (T/F) When $L[u(t)] = U(s)$, its first differentiation with respect to t is given by $L\left[\frac{du(t)}{dt}\right] = sU(s) - u(0)$. True or false?
7. (T/F) The mechanical quality factor and the damping ratio ζ are related as $Q_m = \frac{\omega_0}{\Delta\omega} = 1/\zeta$. True or false?
8. (T/F) The complex spring constant is equivalent to the viscoelastic damping model. True or false?
9. (T/F) The high-frequency portion of the Bode plot for the second-order system is approximated with an asymptotic straight line having a negative slope of 20 dB/decade. True or false?
10. (T/F) As the polarization is induced after the electric field is applied (time delay), the P vs. E hysteresis loop should show the clockwise rotation. True or false?
11. We observed electric displacement D and applied an electric field E relation as shown in Figure 6.2. Using the area of U_e and w_e, describe the dielectric loss $\tan\delta'$.
12. (T/F) The hysteresis area of the strain x vs. electric field E corresponds directly to the piezoelectric loss factor $\tan\theta'$. True or false?
13. (T/F) The permittivity of a piezoelectric under the mechanically clamped condition is smaller than that under the mechanically free condition. True or false?
14. (T/F) The elastic compliance of a piezoelectric under the open-circuit condition is larger than that under the short-circuit condition. True or false?
15. Provide the inverse matrix of the following $[K]$ matrix:

$$[K] = \frac{1}{1-k^2} \begin{bmatrix} 1 & k^2 & -2k^2 \\ k^2 & 1 & -2k^2 \\ 1 & 1 & -1-k^2 \end{bmatrix}.$$

Chapter Problems

6.1 (a) In a mass–spring-damper model in the free vibration condition, starting from the initial displacement u_0, verify that the logarithmic decrement δ given by the following equation, where u_n is the vibration amplitude after the n cycles:

$$\delta = \frac{1}{n}\ln\left(\frac{u_0}{u_n}\right).$$

(b) The above δ is related with the damping ratio ζ as $\delta = 2\pi\zeta$. In the free vibration condition, starting from the initial u_0, calculate the required cycle number for reducing the displacement by half (50%) as a function of the damping ratio ζ.

6.2 Let us consider a damper, the force of which is proportional to the displacement with a phase in the same as velocity. This damper is modeled as a complex spring constant $c(1 + j\gamma)$. Solve the dynamic equation in a mass–spring-damper system given as follows:

$$m\ddot{u} + c(1 + j\gamma)u = 0.$$

Hint

Suppose that $u(t) = u_0 e^{(\alpha + j\beta)t}$, then determine α and β.

$$\alpha = \sqrt{\frac{c}{2m}}\sqrt{-1 + \sqrt{1+\gamma^2}} \cong \frac{\gamma}{2}\sqrt{\frac{c}{m}},\ \beta = \pm\sqrt{\frac{c}{2m}}\sqrt{1 + \sqrt{1+\gamma^2}} \cong \pm\sqrt{\frac{c}{m}};$$

$$\delta = \ln\left(\frac{u_1}{u_2}\right) \cong \pi\gamma.$$

6.3 Let us consider a mass–spring–dashpot system (Figure 6.14a). We apply a sinusoidal force $f_0\sin(\omega t)$ from the initial position $u(t = 0) = u_0$. Verify the following arguments:

(a) Transient response (vibration amplitude and phase) strongly depends on the initial condition.

(b) Steady-state oscillation (vibration amplitude and phase) is irrelevant to the initial condition.

6.4 The electrical LCR circuit and mechanical mass–spring–dashpot model are shown in Figures 6.3 and 6.4b. Provide the dynamic equations (under the input sinusoidal voltage or harmonic force) for both electric and mechanical systems. Then, discuss the equivalency for obtaining the steady-state solutions for both systems. This approach is the key to understanding the "equivalent circuit" concept introduced in Chapter 9.

6.5 Consider an "order–disorder-type ferroelectric" with ions trapped in the same "double-minimum potential" with a relatively low barrier between the two minima (Figure 6.23). Thus, each unit lattice cell has a permanent dipole moment, and the dipole–dipole coupling is taken into account at a temperature lower than the Curie temperature. Under a quasi-DC field, the ion follows the electric field alternating between the positive and negative potentials. However, increasing drive frequency the ionic motion exhibits a delay with respect to the electric field due to the potential barrier ΔU. This is an intuitive explanation for the "dielectric relaxation" in a ferroelectric phase.

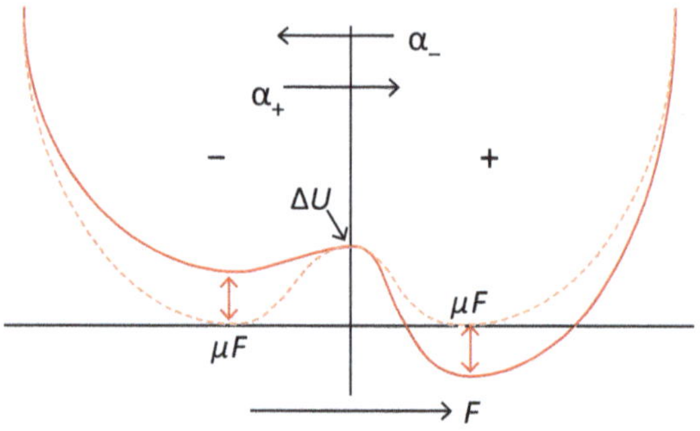

Figure 6.23. Ion in a double-minimum potential. Source: Figure by author.

In Example Problem 5.1, we derived the following "Debye dispersion relation" for a mono-dispersive case:

$$\varepsilon(\omega) = \varepsilon_S/(1 + j\omega\tau). \tag{P6.5.1}$$

where

$$\tau = (1 + \gamma\varepsilon_0\varepsilon_S)\tau_0/\cosh(\mu\gamma P_S/kT), \tag{P6.5.2a}$$

$$\tau_0 = 1/2\Gamma\exp(-\ \Delta U/kT). \tag{P6.5.2b}$$

The subscript "s" of ε_S stands for a static value ($\omega = 0$), and in the paraelectric phase, it should follow the Curie–Weiss law:

$$\varepsilon_0\varepsilon_S = \varepsilon_0 C/(T - T_C). \tag{P6.5.3}$$

The relaxation time $\tau \propto 1/(T - T_C)$, which increases significantly when approaching $T \to T_C$. This means that the recovery to the equilibrium polarization is quite slow.

When we transform the permittivity $\varepsilon(\omega)$ as

$$\varepsilon(\omega) = \varepsilon'(\omega) - j\varepsilon''(\omega), \tag{P6.5.4}$$

where

$$\varepsilon'(\omega) = \varepsilon_S/[1 + (\omega\tau)^2], \tag{P6.5.5}$$

$$\varepsilon''(\omega) = \omega\tau\varepsilon_S/[1 + (\omega\tau)^2]. \tag{P6.5.6}$$

The so-called "Cole–Cole relation" is obtained from Equations (P6.5.5) and (P6.5.6), which is a half-circle with the following formula, and illustrated in Figure 6.24.

(1) Draw the D vs. E hysteresis curve. (2) Derive the dielectric loss tan δ' formula. Do you think this loss generated the heat in the sample? (3) Obtain $\omega_0 = 1/\tau$, then calculate a practical number using a particular material.

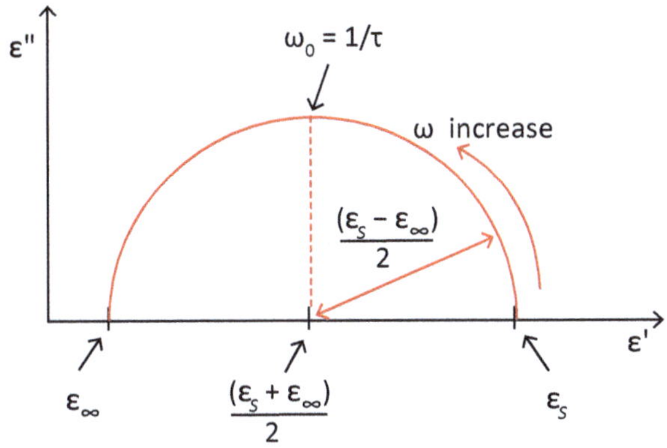

Figure 6.24. Cole–Cole plot for the Debye model. Source: Figure by author.

References

1. Uchino, K. *Ferroelectric Devices*, 2nd ed.; CRC Press: Boca Raton, FL, USA, 2010.
2. Thomson, W.T. *Mechanical Vibrations*; Prentice-Hall Inc.: Englewood Cliffs, NJ, USA, 1953.
3. Uchino, K.; Ishii, T. Mechanical Damper Using Piezoelectric Ceramics. *J. Ceram. Soc. Jpn.* **1988**, *96*, 863. [CrossRef]
4. Uchino, K. Piezoelectric Energy Harvesting Systems–Essentials to Successful Developments. *J. Energy Technol.* **2018**, *6*, 829–848. [CrossRef]
5. Uchino, K. *Micromechatronics*, 2nd ed.; CRC Press: Boca Raton, FL, USA, 2019.
6. Uchino, K. *High-Power Piezoelectrics and Loss Mechanisms*; CRC Press: Boca Raton, FL, USA, 2020; ISBN 978-0-367-54069-2.
7. Tobergte, D.R.; Curtis, S. *IUPAC Compendium of Chemical Terminology—The "Gold Book"*; International Union of Pure and Applied Chemistry: Zurich, Switzerland, 2013; p. 53.
8. Uchino, K.; Hirose, S. Loss Mechanisms in Piezoelectrics: How to Measure Different Losses Separately. *IEEE Trans. Ultrason. Ferroelectr. Freq. Control* **2001**, *48*, 307–321. [CrossRef] [PubMed]

7. AC Drive on Piezoelectrics—Fourier Transform

We discuss the AC drive, in particular around the resonance frequency, on piezoelectric devices by using Fourier transform analysis from both electrical and mechanical excitation viewpoints. The reader will learn the difference between the resonance and antiresonance operations.

7.1. Driving Methods of Piezoelectric Devices

7.1.1. Classification of Piezoelectric Actuators

Piezoelectric and electrostrictive actuators are classified into two major categories based on the type of drive voltage applied to the device and the nature of the strain induced by the voltage, as depicted in Figure 7.1. They are: (1) "rigid displacement devices", for which the strain is induced unidirectionally, aligned with the applied DC field, and (2) "resonant displacement devices", for which an alternating strain is excited by an AC field, in particular at the mechanical resonance frequency ("ultrasonic motors"). The first category can be further divided into two general types: "servo displacement transducers" (positioners), which are controlled by a feedback system through a position detection signal, and "pulse drive motors", which are operated in a simple on/off switching mode. Since recent energy harvesting devices require the AC stress drive of the piezoelectric components, we also discuss this drive in this chapter in parallel to the electric field drive.

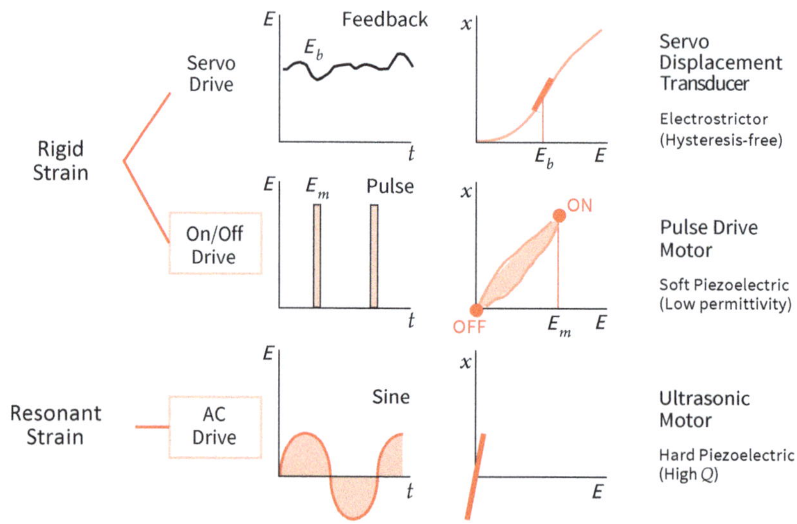

Figure 7.1. Classification of piezoelectric/electrostrictive actuators according to the type of drive voltage and the nature of the induced strain. Source: [1] ©Uchino, K. *Micromechatronics*, 2nd ed.; CRC Press, 2019; p. 268. Reproduced by permission of Taylor & Francis Group.

The response of the resonant displacement device is not directly proportional to the applied voltage, but is strongly dependent on the drive frequency. Although the positioning accuracy of this class of devices is not as high as that of the rigid displacement devices, ultrasonic motors are able to produce very rapid motion due to their high-frequency operation. Servo displacement transducers, which are controlled by a feedback voltage superimposed on a DC bias, are used as positioners for optical and precision machinery systems. In contrast, a pulse drive motor generates only on/off strains, suitable for the impact elements of inkjet printers or injection valves. The inertial motors used in camera zoom/focus mechanisms belong to this pulse drive category, as discussed in Chapter 8.

The material requirements for each class of devices are different, and certain compositions will be better suited for particular applications [1]. Because the servo displacement transducer suffers from "strain hysteresis" the most, a $Pb(Mg_{1/3}Nb_{2/3})O_3$-$PbTiO_3$ [PMN] "electrostrictive material" is preferred for this application. It should be noted that even when a feedback system is employed, the presence of pronounced strain hysteresis generally results in a much slower response speed. The pulse drive motor, for which a quick response rather than a small hysteresis is desired, requires a low-permittivity material under a current limitation of a power supply. "Soft piezoelectrics" $Pb(Zr,Ti)O_3$ (PZT) are preferred over the high-permittivity PMN for this application. The ultrasonic motor, on the other hand, requires a very "hard piezoelectric" with a high mechanical quality factor, Q_m, in order to maximize the AC strain and to minimize heat generation (from low elastic loss). Note that the figure of merit for the resonant strain (i.e., displacement amplification factor) is characterized by $(\frac{8}{\pi^2})Q_m dEL$ (d: piezoelectric strain coefficient, E: applied electric field, L: sample length, Q_m: mechanical quality factor). Although hard PZT materials have smaller d coefficients in comparison with soft PZT, they also have significantly larger Q_m values, thus providing the high resonant strains needed for the motor devices.

7.1.2. Piezoelectric Driving Methods

There are three methods for actuator drive/control that are most commonly employed: (1) pseudo-DC drive, (2) pulse drive, and (3) AC drive, which are typically used for displacement transducers, pulse drive motors, and ultrasonic motors, respectively. Displacement transducers are usually controlled in a closed-loop mode. Open-loop control can also be employed, but only when strain hysteresis is negligible and temperature fluctuation during operation is very small. Closed-loop control is a feedback method whereby the electric field-induced displacement of a ceramic actuator is monitored, deviation from the desired displacement is detected, and an electric signal proportional to this deviation is fed back to the ceramic actuator through an amplifier to effectively correct the deviation. Since the "feedback control" systems of piezoelectric devices have been described in detail in [1], we will skip this category. The pulse drive motor is typically operated in an open-loop mode, but special care must be taken to suppress displacement overshoot and/or vibration ringing that can occur after the pulse voltage is applied, which is discussed in Chapter 8. The AC electric voltage around the resonance frequency range applied to ultrasonic motors is not very large, but significantly amplified displacement can be excited due to an amplified current under constant voltage drive, where the drive frequency must be precisely matched with the resonance frequency of the device for the optimum performance. Heat generation, which is a potentially significant problem with this design, can be effectively minimized with the proper selection of operating parameters in the range around the resonance and antiresonance. In this chapter, we will discuss the AC drive around the resonance and antiresonance frequency range.

7.1.3. Mechanical Resonance

Let us recall the elementary physics on the mechanical resonance of a length L rod with sound velocity v. The reader still remembers that the fundamental resonance frequency is expressed by

$$f = v/2L. \quad (7.1)$$

Knowing $v = f\lambda$, we obtain $\lambda = 2L$. Thus, the fundamental resonance mode means that a standing wave with a half of the wavelength λ on the length L of the specimen, as illustrated in Figure 7.2a $m = 1$. Figure 7.2a shows the strain distribution of harmonic mechanical resonance modes from the fundamental $m = 1$ to second, third, and fourth ($m = 4$) modes. Figure 7.2b illustrates the fundamental resonance frequency ($v/2L$) derivation intuitively. Let us assume to apply a sudden tensile stress (X) on the rod specimen, by applying a pair of step-function pulling forces F, $-F$ on both sides of the rod (top figure). This sudden stress application generates a sort of shockwave-like wall between the extended portion (initiated at the rod end) and the original zero strain portion close to both rod ends, as shown in the second top figure (Chapter 8 provides the detailed analysis on the pulse drive). These strain (x)-gap walls move inwards with the sound velocity v in the specimen, crossing over at the rod center at a quarter of a cycle period. Further extension of the rod is followed (which corresponds to the "overshoot") until the maximum length (100% overshoot of the expected length by the stress, i.e., sX) at half of the cycle period. Then, the strain-gap walls are reflected at the rod ends and change the translation direction to start the rod shrinkage. At the time of three-quarters of the cycle period, the rod length returns to the expected length by the stress (i.e., $x = sX$, s: elastic compliance). In order to return to the original status, the strain-gap wall needs to travel the distance $2L$ with the sound velocity v, leading to the necessary cyclic time period of $2L/v$. In other words, the cyclic frequency should be $v/2L$, which is called the "fundamental resonance frequency".

As the reader remembers, the child swing does not need a large force, but a large swing amplitude is obtained as long as you choose a suitable pushing frequency. When the sinusoidal stress X is applied along the rod length, the same phenomenon happens. With sweeping the drive frequency ω from low to the fundamental resonance frequency ω_r, the strain and displacement is significantly enhanced under the constant cyclical stress X. The strain enhancement is owing to the "synchronous" (i.e., the same frequency and phase) mechanical energy input to the specimen, leading to infinite displacement if no loss is included. In practice, the amplification factor is proportional to the mechanical quality factor Q_m, inverse of the elastic loss. When $Q_m = 1000$, roughly 1000 small stress cycles are required to reach 1000-times amplification. We can say "the displacement amplification in terms of "time". When the drive frequency is increased beyond ω_r, the strain/displacement decreases quickly with the rate of −40 dB/decade approaching the clamped condition. This phenomenon was discussed with the "Bode plot" in Section 6.3.3.

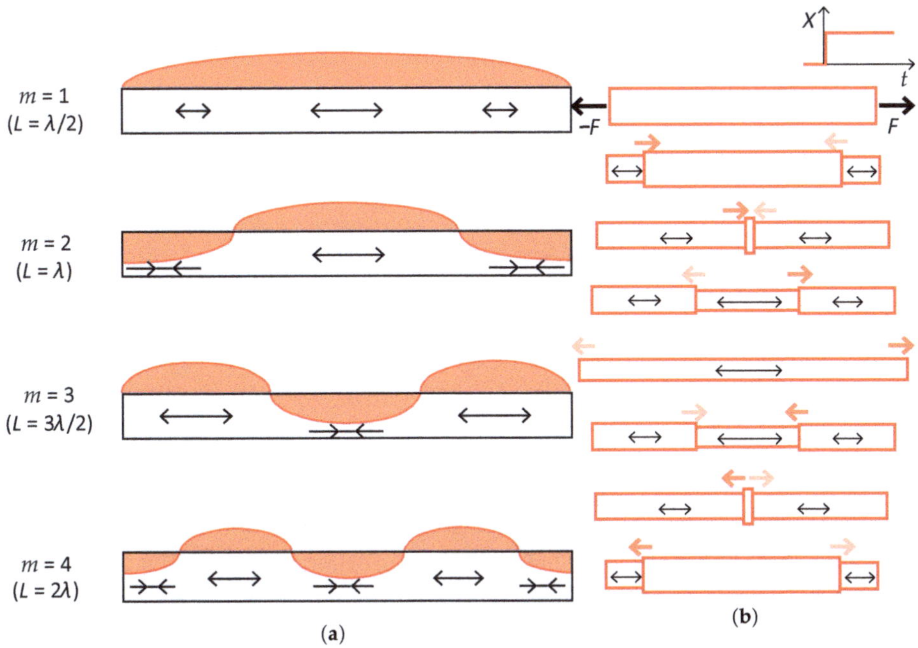

Figure 7.2. Mechanical resonance in a rod specimen: (**a**) harmonic resonance modes; (**b**) strain response to the step strain. Source: Figure by author.

When we increase the drive frequency further, up to $2\omega_r$, the second harmonic resonance appears and the strain/displacement is enhanced again. The vibration mode includes a full wavelength λ on a length L specimen. Note, however, from the second top figure of Figure 7.2a that the total rod length does not change because both the rod ends become nodal lines, because the strain generated inside the rod cancels out completely even though the local strain inside the rod is significant. As you can imagine from this argument, $m = 3$ and $m = 4$ modes in Figure 7.2a exhibit similar behavior to the cases of $m = 1$ and $m = 2$, respectively; The odd-number harmonic resonance modes generate the total rod length enhancement, while the even-number resonance modes keep the rod length constant (i.e., both rod ends are the nodal lines) even though the inside local strain/displacement is largely excited. The number of nodal lines N for the m-th mode is presented by

$$N = 2 \cdot \left[\frac{m}{2}\right] + 1. \quad (7.2)$$

Here $[\frac{m}{2}]$ is the "Gauss symbol", which means the maximum integer number $\leq m/2$, which is popularly used when the odd and even number states are differentiated.

We define the mechanical impedance as follows near the resonant frequency of the rod: $F(\omega) = Z_m(\omega)v(\omega)$, where $F(\omega)$ and $v(\omega)$ are the force and velocity on the rod edges. $Z_m(\omega)$ is the impedance as a function of ω. When $Z_m(\omega)$ is minimum or maximum, these frequencies are called "resonance" and "antiresonance" in the mechanical vibration.

7.1.4. Piezoelectric Resonance and Antiresonance

There are various methods for characterizing piezoelectric performances in piezoelectric materials: (1) pseudo-static, (2) admittance/impedance spectrum, and (3) transient/ burst mode methods [2]. The admittance/ impedance spectrum method is further classified into (1) constant voltage, (2) constant current, and (3) constant vibration velocity methods. Piezoelectric resonance can be excited by either electrical or mechanical driving, as shown in Figure 7.3. In a k_{31} mode piezoelectric plate, for example, as long as the surface is electroded, the sound velocity along the length direction is v^E originated from ${s_{11}}^E$, while in the no-electrode specimen, they are v^D and ${s_{11}}^D$. In the normal IEEE Standard measuring technique [3], the specimen should have electrodes and be excited by an electrical AC signal, while the resonance on a no-electrode specimen can be excited only by the mechanical excitation. A short-circuit condition realizes the resonance and an open-circuit condition provides the antiresonance mode under the mechanical excitation method. In order to measure the D-constant parameters (${s_{11}}^D$ and its extensive elastic loss tanϕ) directly, we need to use a non-electrode sample under the mechanical driving method.

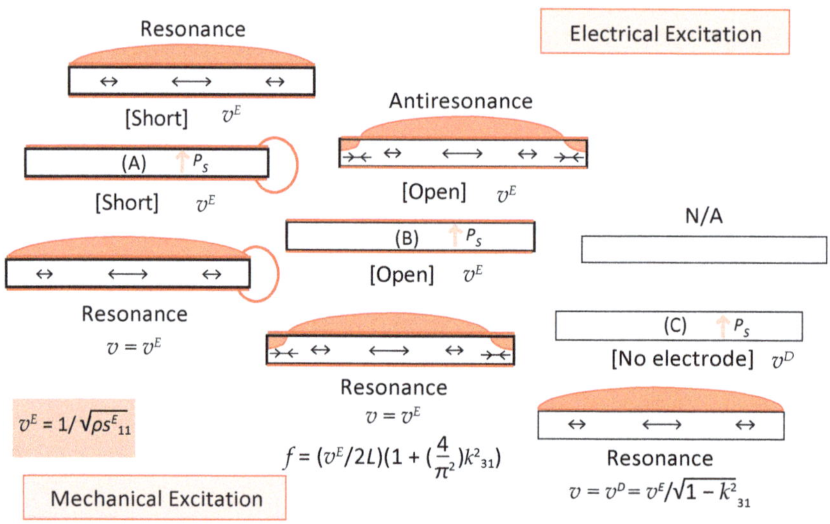

Figure 7.3. Resonance and antiresonance mode excitation under electrical or mechanical driving methods (visualization for k_{31} mode). Source: [1] ©Uchino, K. *Micromechatronics*, 2nd ed.; CRC Press, 2019; p. 269. Reproduced by permission of Taylor & Francis Group.

Figure 7.4 shows an example admittance spectrum of a 20 mm long k_{31} type piezoelectric (PZT) plate specimen with the resonance frequency around 86 kHz.

Measurement was performed under the vibration velocity/amplitude constant condition (i.e., output mechanical energy constant). When the operating frequency is lower than 10 kHz, this is considered an "off-resonance" drive, and its characteristic is purely "capacitive" with the admittance phase lag of 90° [4]. When the operating frequency is 86 or 89 kHz, the characteristic becomes "resistive" with a phase lag of 0°, which corresponds to the resonance or antiresonance frequency, respectively. In order to induce the same level of vibration velocity, low voltage and high current or high voltage and low current are required in the resonance or antiresonance drive (i.e., both are the mechanical resonance modes), respectively. We also introduced an operating frequency at 88 kHz in the "inductive" region to minimize the required input drive power in order to obtain the same vibration level. To the contrary, the pulse drive of electric field includes a wide range of frequencies (pseudo-DC to multiple higher-order resonance frequencies), which exhibit linear or parabolic total displacement (not sinusoidal), in addition to the overshoot and/or vibration ringing (discussed in Chapter 8).

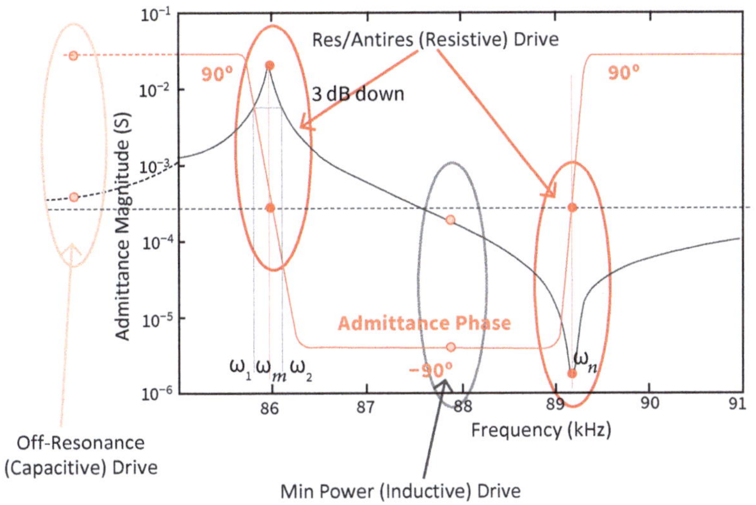

Figure 7.4. Application frequency ranges for displacement transducers, pulse drive motors and ultrasonic motors. Source: [1] ©Uchino, K. *Micromechatronics*, 2nd ed.; CRC Press, 2019; p. 268. Reproduced by permission of Taylor & Francis Group.

7.2. Piezoelectric Equations and Vibration Modes—Loss Free

7.2.1. Piezoelectric Constitutive Equations

When the applied electric field, E, and the stress, X, are small, the strain, x, and the electric displacement, D, induced in a piezoelectric can be represented by the following linear equations:

$$x_i = s_{ij}{}^E X_j + d_{mi} E_m, \tag{7.3}$$

$$D_m = d_{mi} X_i + \varepsilon_0 \varepsilon_{mk}{}^X E_k, \tag{7.4}$$

where ($i, j = 1, 2, \ldots, 6$; $m, k = 1, 2, 3$). These are the "piezoelectric constitutive equations". There are 21 independent $s_{ij}{}^{E}$ coefficients, 18 d_{mi} coefficients, and 6 $\varepsilon_{mk}{}^{X}$ coefficients for the lowest symmetry "trigonal" crystal. When considering polycrystalline ceramic specimens such as PZT ($Pb(Zr,Ti)O_3$, lead zirconate titanate), the poling direction is typically designated as the z-axis. Poled ceramic is isotropic with respect to this z-axis and has a Curie group designation $C_{\infty v}$ (∞m). There are 10 non-zero matrix elements ($s_{11}{}^{E}$, $s_{12}{}^{E}$, $s_{13}{}^{E}$, $s_{33}{}^{E}$, $s_{44}{}^{E}$, d_{31}, d_{33}, d_{15}, $\varepsilon_{11}{}^{X}$, and $\varepsilon_{33}{}^{X}$) that apply in the following discussion.

7.2.2. Longitudinal Vibration Mode via Transverse Piezoelectric Effect (k_{31} Mode)—Loss Free

This section and the next, Section 7.2.3, discuss the key difference between the wave propagation direction "perpendicular (k_{31})" and "parallel (k_{33})" to the spontaneous direction.

Vibration Modes

Let us consider a longitudinal mechanical vibration in a simple piezoelectric ceramic plate via the transverse piezoelectric effect d_{31} with thickness b, width w, and length L ($b << w << L$), pictured in Figure 7.5. When the polarization is in the z direction and the x–y planes are the planes of the electrodes, the extensional vibration along the x direction (1D model) is represented by the following dynamic equation:

$$\rho \frac{\partial^2 u}{\partial t^2} = F = \frac{\partial X_{11}}{\partial x} + \frac{\partial X_{12}}{\partial y} + \frac{\partial X_{13}}{\partial z}, \tag{7.5}$$

where u is the displacement in the x direction of a small-volume element in the ceramic plate, ρ is density of the piezoelectric material, and X_{ij}'s are stresses (only the force along the x direction is our target). The relations between the stress, electric field (only E_z exists, because $E_x = E_y = 0$ due to the electrodes on the top and bottom), and the induced strains are described by the following set of equations:

$$\begin{bmatrix} x_1 \\ x_2 \\ x_3 \\ x_4 \\ x_5 \\ x_6 \end{bmatrix} = \begin{bmatrix} s_{11}{}^{E} & s_{12}{}^{E} & s_{13}{}^{E} & 0 & 0 & 0 \\ s_{12}{}^{E} & s_{11}{}^{E} & s_{13}{}^{E} & 0 & 0 & 0 \\ s_{13}{}^{E} & s_{13}{}^{E} & s_{33}{}^{E} & 0 & 0 & 0 \\ 0 & 0 & 0 & s_{44}{}^{E} & 0 & 0 \\ 0 & 0 & 0 & 0 & s_{44}{}^{E} & 0 \\ 0 & 0 & 0 & 0 & 0 & 2(s_{11}{}^{E} - s_{12}{}^{E}) \end{bmatrix} \begin{pmatrix} X_1 \\ X_2 \\ X_3 \\ X_4 \\ X_5 \\ X_6 \end{pmatrix} + \begin{pmatrix} 0 & 0 & d_{31} \\ 0 & 0 & d_{31} \\ 0 & 0 & d_{33} \\ 0 & d_{15} & 0 \\ d_{15} & 0 & 0 \\ 0 & 0 & 0 \end{pmatrix} \begin{bmatrix} E_1 \\ 0 \\ 0 \end{bmatrix}. \tag{7.6}$$

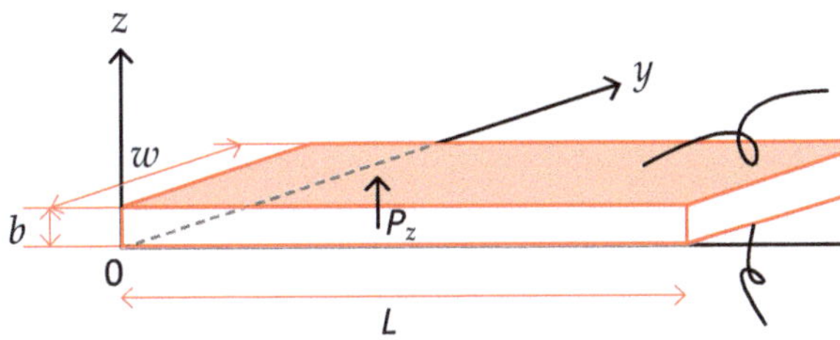

Figure 7.5. Longitudinal vibration k_{31} mode of a rectangular piezoelectric plate. Source: [1] ©Uchino, K. *Micromechatronics*, 2nd ed.; CRC Press, 2019; p. 111. Reproduced by permission of Taylor & Francis Group.

Let us review the resonance of a piezoelectric plate when an AC electric field of increasing frequency is applied. The length, width, and thickness extensional resonance vibrations are excited successively. Consider a PZT plate with dimensions 100 mm × 10 mm × 1 mm; these resonance frequencies correspond roughly to 10 kHz, 100 kHz, and 1 MHz for the fundamental length extensional mode. When the frequency of the applied field is well below 10 kHz, the induced displacement follows the AC field cycle, and the displacement magnitude is given by $d_{31}E_3L$. As we approach the fundamental resonance frequency, a delay in the length displacement with respect to the applied field begins to develop, and the amplitude of the displacement becomes enhanced, showing the peak value of $(\frac{8}{\pi^2})Q_m dEL$. At frequencies above 10 kHz, the length displacement no longer follows the applied field and the amplitude of the displacement is significantly reduced. With a further increase in the frequency up to 100 kHz, now the width vibration is amplified (by neglecting the higher-order harmonics of the length modes). Finally, around 1 MHz, the thickness mode is excited by clamping the displacement both length- and widthwise.

When a very long, thin thickness and width plate (Figure 7.5) is driven in the vicinity of this length fundamental resonance, X_2 and X_3 may be considered zero (a free condition) throughout the plate. Since shear stress will not be generated by the applied electric field E_z, only the following single equation applies:

$$X_1 = x_1/s_{11}{}^E - (d_{31}/s_{11}{}^E)E_z. \tag{7.7}$$

Substituting Equation (7.7) into Equation (7.5), and assuming that strain $x_1 = \partial u/\partial x$ and $\partial E_z/\partial x = 0$ (since each electrode is at the same potential), we obtain the following dynamic equation:

$$\rho \frac{\partial^2 u}{\partial t^2} = \frac{1}{s_{11}^E} \cdot \frac{\partial^2 u}{\partial x^2}. \tag{7.8}$$

Remember that the "E-constant" condition "s_{11}^E" is the key characteristic in the k_{31} mode. Assuming a harmonic vibration equation of $u(x,t)$ (i.e., sinusoidal vibration in terms of both space x and time t) under an electric field E, Equation (7.8) is transformed to:

$$-\omega^2 \rho s_{11}{}^E u = \partial^2 u/\partial x^2. \tag{7.9}$$

Here, ω is the angular frequency of the sinusoidal drive field E_z and the displacement u. Supposing the displacement u also vibrates with the frequency of ω, a general solution $u = u_1(x)e^{j\omega t} + u_2(x)e^{-j\omega t}$ is substituted into Equation (7.9), and with the boundary condition $X_1 = 0$ at $x = 0$ and L (sample length) (due to the mechanically free condition at the plate end), the following solution can be obtained (refer to Example Problem 7.1):

$$\text{(Strain)} \quad \partial u/\partial x = x_1 = d_{31}E_z\,(\frac{\cos[\frac{\omega(2x-L)}{2v}]}{\cos(\frac{\omega L}{2v})}), \tag{7.10}$$

$$\text{(Displacement)} \quad u(x) = d_{31}E_z(\frac{v}{\omega})\frac{\sin[\frac{\omega(2x-L)}{2v}]}{\cos(\frac{\omega L}{2v})}, \tag{7.11}$$

$$\text{(Total Displacement)} \quad \Delta L = \int_0^L x_1 dx = d_{31}E_z L(2v/\omega L)\tan(\omega L/2v). \tag{7.12}$$

Here, v is the "sound velocity" (or "group velocity") in the piezo-ceramic given by

$$v = 1/\sqrt{\rho s_{11}{}^E}. \tag{7.13}$$

The strain distribution in Equation (7.10) is symmetrically sinusoidal in respect of $x = L/2$ position, and the maximum strain (i.e., the "nodal line") exists at least on this line. Note that $\omega \to 0$ (i.e., pseudo-DC) makes Equation (7.10) equal to $x_1 = d_{31}E_z$; that is, uniform strain distribution on the piezo-plate. It is also obvious that $\Delta L \to d_{31}EzL$ under $\omega \to 0$.

Example Problem 7.1

Let us consider a piezo-ceramic plate which vibrates via the transverse piezoelectric effect (d_{31}). Substituting a general solution $u = u_1(x)e^{j\omega t} + u_2(x)e^{-j\omega t}$ into

$$-\omega^2 \rho s_{11}{}^E u = \partial^2 u/\partial x^2, \tag{P7.1.1}$$

then with the boundary condition $X_1 = 0$ at $x = 0$ and L, derive the strain

$$x_1 = d_{31}E_z\,(\frac{\cos[\frac{\omega(L-2x)}{2v}]}{\cos(\frac{\omega L}{2v})}); \quad (v = 1/\sqrt{\rho s_{11}{}^E}). \tag{P7.1.2}$$

Solution

Substituting a general solution $u = u_1(x)e^{j\omega t} + u_2(x)e^{-j\omega t}$ into $-\omega^2\rho s_{11}{}^E u = \partial^2 u/\partial x^2$, we obtain

$$-(\frac{\omega^2}{v^2})(u_1(x)e^{j\omega t} + u_2(x)e^{-j\omega t}) = (\frac{\partial^2 u_1}{\partial x^2})e^{j\omega t} + (\frac{\partial^2 u_2}{\partial x^2})e^{-j\omega t}. \tag{P7.1.3}$$

Since this equation should be satisfied for any time, u_1 and u_2 should satisfy $(\frac{\partial^2 u_1}{\partial x^2}) = -(\frac{\omega^2}{v^2})u_1$ and $(\frac{\partial^2 u_2}{\partial x^2}) = -(\frac{\omega^2}{v^2})u_2$, respectively. If we consider only the standing wave as a solution, $u(x)$ should be a "real" parameter, leading to the relation $u_1(x) = u_2(x)$ and $u(x,t) = 2u_1(x)\cos(\omega t)$. We will neglect $\cos(\omega t)$ hereafter because this is included in the $\cos(\omega t)$ of the electric field. Thus, we suppose a general solution:

$$u_1 = u_2 = A_1\cos(\frac{\omega}{v}x) + A_2\sin(\frac{\omega}{v}x). \quad \text{(P7.1.4)}$$

Now, the strain distribution on the plate can be calculated as

$$x_1 = \partial u/\partial x = 2(\frac{\partial u_1}{\partial x}) = 2\left(\frac{\omega}{v}\right)[-A_1\sin(\frac{\omega}{v}x) + A_2\cos(\frac{\omega}{v}x)]. \quad \text{(P7.1.5)}$$

Let us consider the boundary condition. From $X_1 = 0 = x_1/s_{11}{}^E - (d_{31}/s_{11}{}^E)E_z$ at $x = 0$ and L, $x_1 = d_{31}E_z$ (i.e., $E_z = E_{max}\cos(\omega t)$) is obtained at both plate edges (without considering the time lag or loss, the strain response should be simultaneous with the electric field):

$2(\frac{\omega}{v})[-A_1\sin(\frac{\omega}{v}0) + A_2\cos(\frac{\omega}{v}0)] = 2(\frac{\omega}{v})A_2 = d_{31}E_z$,

$2(\frac{\omega}{v})[-A_1\sin(\frac{\omega}{v}L) + A_2\cos(\frac{\omega}{v}L)] = d_{31}E_z$.

Thus, we obtain $A_1 = (\frac{1}{2})(\frac{v}{\omega})d_{31}E_z\frac{[\cos(\frac{\omega L}{v})-1]}{\sin(\frac{\omega L}{v})}$, and $A_2 = (\frac{1}{2})(\frac{v}{\omega})d_{31}E_z$. Finally, inserting A_1 and A_2 into Equation (P7.1.5), we derive

$$\text{(Strain)}\ x_1 = d_{31}E_z\ [\sin\omega(L-x)/v + \sin(\omega x/v)]/\sin(\omega L/v) = d_{31}E_z\ (\frac{\cos[\frac{\omega(L-2x)}{2v}]}{\cos(\frac{\omega L}{2v})}), \quad \text{(P7.1.6)}$$

$$\text{(Displacement)}\ u(x) = d_{31}E_z(\frac{v}{\omega})\frac{\sin[\frac{\omega(2x-L)}{2v}]}{\cos(\frac{\omega L}{2v})}. \quad \text{(P7.1.7)}$$

Remember that E_z is an AC field with the frequency ω. With increasing ω, the stress concentration at the nodal line ($x = L/2$) will be enhanced. The strain distribution on a rectangular plate is illustrated in Figure 7.6 for the resonance and antiresonance frequencies; cosine shape with respect to the plate center ($x = L/2$) and the amplitude depends on the drive frequency around the resonance frequency (∞ amplitude at the resonance, $cos\left(\frac{\omega L}{2v}\right) = 0$).

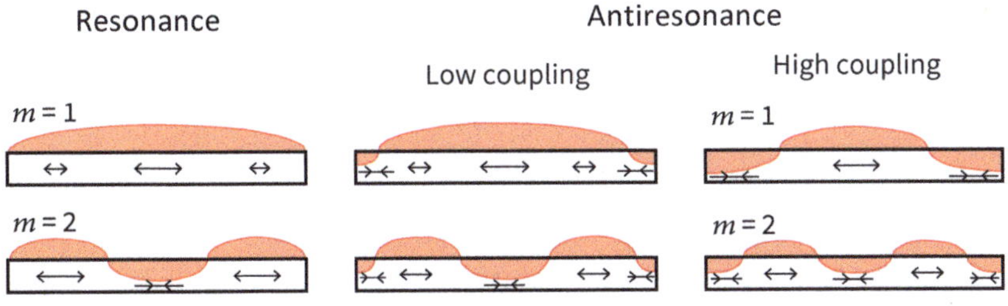

Figure 7.6. Strain distribution in the resonant and antiresonant states for a k_{31} type piezoelectric plate. Source: [1] ©Uchino, K. *Micromechatronics*, 2nd ed.; CRC Press, 2019; p. 113. Reproduced by permission of Taylor & Francis Group.

When the specimen is utilized as an electrical component such as a filter or a vibrator, the electrical admittance ((induced current/applied voltage) ratio) plays an important role. We will establish the formula for characterizing the admittance spectrum obtained from the k_{31} type piezo-plate specimen. Now, the electric displacement constitutive equation (Equation (7.4)) is essential. Since the electrodes are on the top and bottom of the piezo-plate, as shown in Figure 7.5, the required equation is only D_3:

$$D_3 = d_{31}X_1 + \varepsilon_{33}{}^X \varepsilon_0 E_3. \tag{7.14}$$

Only E_3 and X_1 are active ($X_2 = X_3 = 0$) in this case. The current flow into the specimen is described by the surface charge increment, $\partial D_3/\partial t$. Note that D_3 is position dependent, though $\partial E_3/\partial x = 0$, since the stress is sinusoidally distributed in the specimen, which generates polarization via a direct piezoelectric effect. Thus, the total current is given by:

$$\begin{aligned} i &= j\omega w \int_0^L D_3 dx = j\omega w \int_0^L (d_{31}X_1 + \varepsilon_{33}{}^X\varepsilon_0 E_z)dx \\ &= j\omega w \int_0^L [d_{31}\{x_1/s_{11}{}^E - (d_{31}/s_{11}{}^E)E_z\} + \varepsilon_{33}{}^X\varepsilon_0 E_z]dx. \end{aligned} \tag{7.15}$$

Using Equation (7.10), the admittance Y for the mechanically free sample is calculated to be:

$$\begin{aligned} Y &= (-i/V) = (i/Ezb) \\ &= (j\omega wL/Ezb)\int_0^L [(d_{31}{}^2/s_{11}{}^E)(\frac{\cos\left[\frac{\omega(2x-L)}{2v_{11}^E}\right]}{\cos\left(\frac{\omega L}{2v_{11}^E}\right)})E_z + [\varepsilon_{33}{}^X\varepsilon_0 - (d_{31}{}^2/s_{11}{}^E)]E_z]dx \\ &= (j\omega wL/b)\varepsilon_0\varepsilon_{33}{}^{LC}[1 + (d_{31}{}^2/\varepsilon_0\varepsilon_{33}{}^{LC}s_{11}{}^E)(\tan(\omega L/2v_{11}{}^E)/(\omega L/2v_{11}{}^E)] \\ &= j\omega C_d[1 + \frac{k_{31}^2}{1-k_{31}^2}\frac{\tan(\Omega_{11})}{\Omega_{11}}] \qquad [\Omega_{11} = (\omega L/2v_{11}^E)] \\ &= j\omega C_0[(1 - k_{31}^2) + k_{31}^2\frac{\tan(\Omega_{11})}{\Omega_{11}}] \qquad [k_{31}{}^2 = d_{31}{}^2/\varepsilon_0\varepsilon_{33}^X s_{11}^E], \end{aligned} \tag{7.16}$$

where w is the width, L the length, b the thickness of the rectangular piezo sample, and V is the applied voltage. Note that $E_z = -grad(V)$ (i.e., $V = -E_z b$), and the current direction measured externally should be taken in opposition to the internal flow. $\varepsilon_{33}{}^{LC}$ is the permittivity in a "longitudinally clamped" sample, which is given by

$$\varepsilon_{33}{}^{LC} = \varepsilon_{33}{}^X - \left(\frac{d_{31}{}^2}{\varepsilon_0 s_{11}{}^E}\right) = \varepsilon_0\varepsilon_{33}{}^X(1 - k_{31}{}^2); [k_{31}{}^2 = d_{31}{}^2/\varepsilon_0\varepsilon_{33}^X s_{11}^E]. \tag{7.17}$$

Note, however, that this is not three-dimensionally clamped permittivity ε_{33}^x, precisely speaking, which also reflects the later dielectric loss. Accordingly, Equation (7.16) can be understood as follows, under a constant input voltage/electric field: the first term $(j\omega wL/b)\varepsilon_0\varepsilon_{33}{}^{LC} = j\omega C_d$ is called "damped (or longitudinally clamped) capacitance", which is directly proportional to ω, while the second term $j\omega C_0 k_{31}^2 \frac{\tan(\Omega_{11})}{\Omega_{11}}$ is called "motional capacitance", which originates from the resonator's size (length) change via the mechanical vibration and is strongly dependent on ω like $\tan(\omega L/2v_{11}{}^E)$. When ω is small, $\frac{\tan(\Omega_{11})}{\Omega_{11}} \to 1$, then the motional admittance becomes $j\omega C_0 k_{31}^2$. The total input energy will split into the motional (mechanical) and damped (electric) energy with the ratio $k_{31}{}^2$ vs. $(1 - k_{31}{}^2)$, respectively. However, as ω approaches the resonance frequency, motional admittance (or capacitance) increases dramatically like $\tan(\omega L/2v_{11}{}^E)$, for which we can understand the accumulation/amplification of energy with respect to "time". Figure 7.4 shows an example admittance magnitude and phase spectra for a rectangular piezo-ceramic plate (L = 20) for a fundamental longitudinal mode (k_{31}) through the transverse piezoelectric effect (d_{31}), on the basis is Equation (7.16). Note that the shown data include losses, and the 3 dB down method to obtain mechanical quality factor Q_m is also inserted in advance (Discussion is in Section 7.3).

The piezoelectric resonance is achieved when the admittance becomes infinite or the impedance is zero (when the loss is negligible). The resonance frequency f_A is calculated from Equation (7.16) ($\tan(\omega L/2v_{11}{}^E) = \infty$ by putting $\omega L/2v_{11}{}^E = \pi/2$), and the fundamental frequency is given by

$$f_A = \omega_A/2\pi = v_{11}{}^E/2L = 1/(2L\sqrt{\rho s_{11}{}^E}). \tag{7.18}$$

This resonance mode corresponds to the fundamental standing wave ($\lambda/2$ on L) with the velocity $v_{11}{}^E$ on a rod with length L (i.e., $f_A = v_{11}{}^E/2L$). On the other hand, the antiresonance state is generated for zero admittance or infinite impedance:

$$(\omega_B L/2v_{11}{}^E)\cot(\omega_B L/2v_{11}{}^E) = -d_{31}{}^2/\varepsilon_0\varepsilon_{33}{}^{LC}s_{11}{}^E = -k_{31}{}^2/(1 - k_{31}{}^2). \tag{7.19}$$

The final transformation is provided by the definition,

$$k_{31} = d_{31}/\sqrt{s_{11}{}^E \cdot \varepsilon_{33}{}^X \varepsilon_0}. \tag{7.20}$$

Resonance and Antiresonance Vibration Modes

The resonance and antiresonance states are both mechanical resonance states with amplified strain/displacement states, but they are very different from the driving viewpoints. The mode difference is described by the following intuitive model. In a high electromechanical coupling material with k almost equal to one, the resonance or antiresonance states appear for $\tan(\omega L/2v) = \infty$ or 0 (i.e., $\omega L/2v = (m - 1/2)\pi$ or $m\pi$ (m: integer)), respectively. The strain amplitude x_1 distribution for each state (calculated using Equation (7.10)) is illustrated in Figure 7.6. In the resonance state, the strain distribution is basically sinusoidal with the maximum at the center of the plate ($x = L/2$) (see the numerator). When ω is close to ω_A, $(\omega_A L/2v) = \pi/2$, leading to the denominator $\cos(\omega_A L/2v) \to 0$. Significant strain magnification is obtained. It is worth noting that the stress X_1 is zero at the plate ends (x = 0 and L), but the strain x_1 is not zero, but is equal to $d_{31}E_Z$. According to these large strain amplitudes, large capacitance changes (called "motional capacitance") are induced, and under a constant applied voltage the current can easily flow into the device (i.e., admittance Y is infinite). To the contrary, at the antiresonance, the strain induced in the device compensates completely in the plate (because extension and compression are compensated. Recall Figure 7.2, even the harmonic modes), resulting in no motional capacitance change in the total plate, and the current cannot flow easily into the sample (i.e., admittance Y zero). Thus, for a high k material the first antiresonance frequency f_B should be twice as large as the first resonance frequency f_A.

It is notable that both resonance and antiresonance states are in the mechanical resonance, which can create large strain inside the sample under the minimum input of electrical energy. When we use a constant voltage supply, the specimen vibration is excited only at the resonance mode, because the electrical power is very small at the antiresonance mode (due to high impedance). This provides a common misconception to junior engineers that "the antiresonance is not a mechanical resonance". In contrast, when we use a constant current supply, the vibration is excited only at the antiresonance, instead, because of the large input voltage. The stress X_1 at the plate ends ($x = 0$ and L) is supposed to be zero in both cases. However, though the strain x_1 at the plate ends is zero/very small (precisely, $d_{31}E_z$, because of low voltage and high current drive) for the resonance, the strain x_1 at the plate ends is not zero (actually the maximum, or the nodal lines) for the antiresonance (because of high voltage and low current drive). This means that there is only one vibration node at the plate center for the fundamental resonance (top left in Figure 7.6), and there are additional two nodes at both plate ends for the first antiresonance (top right in Figure 7.6). The reason is from the antiresonance drive, i.e., high voltage/low current (minimum power) drive due to the high impedance. The converse piezo effect strain under E directly via d_{31} (uniform strain in the sample) superposes on the mechanical resonance strain distribution (distributed strain with nodes in the sample), two strains of which have exactly the same level theoretically at the antiresonance for $k_{31} \approx 1$.

In a typical case, where $k_{31} = 0.3$, the antiresonance state varies from the previously mentioned (high k_{31}) mode and becomes closer to the resonance mode (top center in Figure 7.6). The low-coupling material exhibits an antiresonance mode where the capacitance change due to the size change ("motional capacitance") is compensated completely by the current required to charge up the static capacitance (called "damped capacitance"). Thus, the antiresonance frequency f_B will approach the resonance frequency f_A. The vibration mode of the antiresonance resembles that of the resonance with slight shift of the anti-nodal lines into the plate.

7.2.3. Longitudinal Vibration Mode via Longitudinal Piezoelectric Effect (k_{33} Mode)—Loss Free

Piezoelectric Dynamic Equation

Let us now consider the longitudinal vibration k_{33} mode in comparison with the k_{31} mode. When the resonator is long in the z direction and the electrodes are deposited on each end of the rod, as shown in Figure 7.7, the following stress conditions are satisfied:

$$X_1 = X_2 = X_4 = X_5 = X_6 = 0 \text{ and } X_3 \neq 0.$$

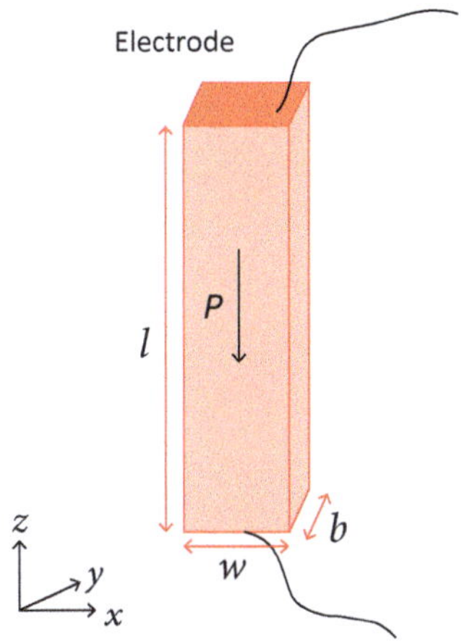

Figure 7.7. Longitudinal vibration through the piezoelectric effect (d_{33}) in a rod ($L \gg w \approx b$). Source: [1] ©Uchino, K. *Micromechatronics*, 2nd ed.; CRC Press, 2019; p. 116. Reproduced by permission of Taylor & Francis Group.

Thus, the constitutive equations are

$$X_3 = (x_3 - d_{33}E_z)/s_{33}{}^E, \tag{7.21}$$

$$D_3 = \varepsilon_0\varepsilon_{33}{}^X E_z + d_{33}X_3, \tag{7.22}$$

for this configuration. Assuming a local displacement u in the z direction, from Equation (7.21) ($E_z \neq 0$ in this no-electrode along the wave propagation direction Z) the dynamic equation is expressed by:

$$\rho\frac{\partial^2 u}{\partial t^2} = \frac{1}{s_{33}^E}\left[\frac{\partial^2 u}{\partial z^2} - d_{33}\frac{\partial E_z}{\partial z}\right]. \tag{7.23}$$

The electrical condition for the longitudinal vibration is not $(\partial E_z/\partial z) = 0$, but rather $(\partial D_z/\partial z) = 0$. Inserting Equation (7.21) into Equation (7.22):

$$\begin{gathered}\varepsilon_0\varepsilon_{33}^X\tfrac{\partial E_Z}{\partial z} + \tfrac{d_{33}}{s_{33}^E}[(\tfrac{\partial^2 u}{\partial z^2}) - d_{33}(\tfrac{\partial E_Z}{\partial z})] = 0, \text{ or}\\ \varepsilon_0\varepsilon_{33}^X(1-k_{33}^2)(\tfrac{\partial E_Z}{\partial z}) = -\tfrac{d_{33}}{s_{33}^E}(\tfrac{\partial^2 u}{\partial z^2}).\end{gathered} \tag{7.24}$$

Thus, Equation (7.23) becomes:

$$\rho\frac{\partial^2 u}{\partial t^2} = \frac{1}{s_{33}^D}\frac{\partial^2 u}{\partial z^2} \quad (s_{33}^D = (1-k_{33}^3)s_{33}^E). \tag{7.25}$$

Compared with Equation (7.13) ($v = 1/\sqrt{\rho s_{11}{}^E}$) in the surface electroded (E-constant) sample along the vibration direction, the non-electrode (D-constant) k_{33}

sample exhibits $v_{33}{}^D = 1/\sqrt{\rho s_{33}{}^D}$, which is faster (elastically stiffened) than in the E-constant condition. Taking a similar calculation process to the k_{31} mode, we obtain

$$(\text{Strain})\ x_3 = \frac{d_{33}}{\varepsilon_0\varepsilon_{33}^X} D_3[\cos\left(\frac{\omega}{2v_{33}^D}(2z-L)\right)/\cos\left(\frac{\omega L}{2v_{33}^D}\right)], \quad (7.26)$$

$$(\text{Displacement})\ u_3 = \frac{d_{33}}{\varepsilon_0\varepsilon_{33}^X}\frac{v_{33}^D}{\omega} D_3[\sin\left(\frac{\omega}{2v_{33}^D}(2z-L)\right)/\cos\left(\frac{\omega L}{2v_{33}^D}\right)]. \quad (7.27)$$

In comparison with the resonance/antiresonance strain distribution status in the k_{31} mode in Figure 7.6, Figure 7.8 illustrates the strain distribution status in the k_{33} mode. Because k_{31} and k_{33} modes possess E-constant and D-constant constraints, respectively, in k_{31}, the resonance frequency is directly related to $v_{11}{}^E$ or $s_{11}{}^E$, while in k_{33}, the antiresonance frequency is directly related to $v_{33}{}^D$ or $s_{33}{}^D$, $c_{33}{}^D$. The antiresonance in k_{31} and the resonance in k_{33} are subsidiary, originating from the electromechanical coupling factors. It is also worth noting that with increasing the k value toward 1, the ratio f_B/f_A approaches two in k_{31}, while it can reach ∞ in k_{33}, and that the strain distribution at the resonance becomes almost flat or uniform in k_{33}, though the stress distributes sinusoidally with zero at the plate ends. The "extensive parameters" $s_{33}{}^D$, $c_{33}{}^D$ can be determined experimentally using the high-frequency measurement, when the "depolarization field" cannot be compensated by the free charge (no side electrode in the k_{33} specimen).

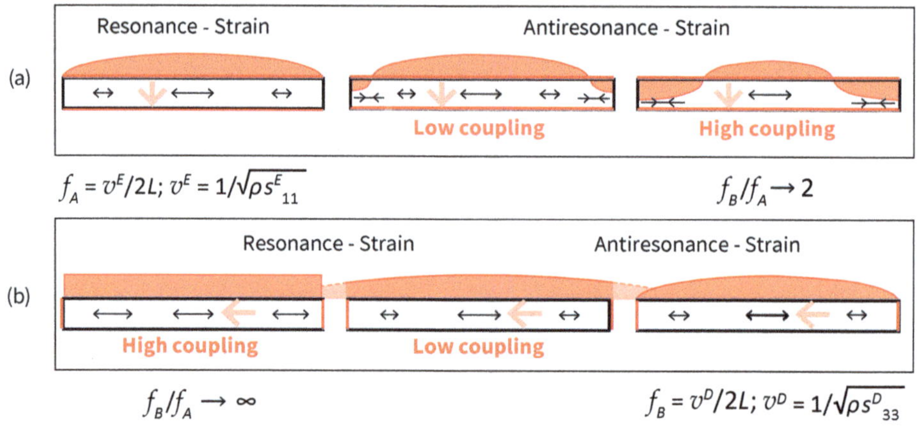

Figure 7.8. Strain distribution in the resonance and antiresonance states. Longitudinal vibration through the transverse d_{31} (**a**) and longitudinal d_{33} (**b**) piezo effect in a rectangular plate. Source: [1] ©Uchino, K. *Micromechatronics*, 2nd ed.; CRC Press, 2019; p. 117. Reproduced by permission of Taylor & Francis Group.

Electrical Admittance around Resonance and Antiresonance

Admittance can also be calculated from $(\partial D_3/\partial t)$ with $D_3 = \varepsilon_0\varepsilon_{33}{}^X E_z + d_{33}X_3$ as follows:

$$Y = \frac{i}{-V} = \frac{j\omega\varepsilon_0\varepsilon_{33}^{LC}\left(\frac{wb}{L}\right)}{\left[1-k_{33}^2\left\{\frac{\tan\left(\frac{\omega L}{2v_{33}^D}\right)}{\left(\frac{\omega L}{2v_{33}^D}\right)}\right\}\right]} = j\omega C_d + \frac{j\omega C_d}{[-1+1/k_{33}^2\{\frac{\tan(\Omega_{33})}{(\Omega_{33})}\}]}$$
$$= j\omega C_d + \frac{1}{[-\frac{1}{j\omega C_d}+1/j\omega C_d k_{33}^2\{\frac{\tan(\Omega_{33})}{(\Omega_{33})}\}]}. \tag{7.28}$$

Here we used $\Omega_{33} = \left(\frac{\omega L}{2v_{33}^D}\right)$, $\varepsilon_{33}^{LC} = \varepsilon_{33}^X(1-k_{33}^2)$, $s_{33}^D = s_{33}^E(1-k_{33}^2)$, $k_{33}^2 = \frac{d_{33}^2}{\varepsilon_0\varepsilon_{33}^X s_{33}^E}$, $v_{33}^D = 1/\sqrt{\rho s_{33}^D}$, and $C_d = \varepsilon_0\varepsilon_{33}^{LC}\left(\frac{wb}{L}\right)$. The first expression is to obtain the resonance and antiresonance frequencies from $Y = \infty$ and 0 conditions. The second expression is to show the "damped admittance" and the "motional admittance", separately, and the final expression is for an equivalent circuit construction, explicitly revealing that the motional admittance branch should include the "negative capacitance" (with exactly the same damped capacitance value) in series with the pure vibration related contribution proportional to $\tan(\Omega_{33})/(\Omega_{33})$.

The resonance frequency is obtained from $Y = \infty$, that is, from Equation (7.28)

$$\left(\frac{\omega L}{2v_{33}^D}\right) = k_{33}^2\tan\left(\frac{\omega L}{2v_{33}^D}\right). \tag{7.29}$$

To the contrary, the antiresonance frquency is obtained from $Y = 0$; that is,

$$\tan\left(\frac{\omega L}{2v_{33}^D}\right) = \infty,\ \text{or}\ \frac{\omega L}{2v_{33}^D} = \frac{\pi}{2},\ \text{leading to}\ f_B = \frac{v_{33}^D}{2L}. \tag{7.30}$$

Unlike the k_{31} case, the k_{33} mode exhibits the antiresonance as a primary mechanical resonance frequency with a half-wavelength exactly on the rod length under the sound velocity of v_{33}^D (i.e., stiffened vibration), and the resonance is a subsidiary vibration mode associated with the electromechanical coupling.

Boundary Condition: *E*-Constant vs. *D*-Constant

Both dielectric permittivity ε and elastic compliance s exhibit significant difference in terms of electromechanical coupling factor k under different boundary conditions: mechanically stress-free or clamped; electrical short circuit or open circuit, as described in Subsection Extensive Losses in Chapter 6. The reader is reminded of the relations:

$\varepsilon^x/\varepsilon^X = (1-k^2)$, $s^D/s^E = (1-k^2)$, where $k^2 = d^2/(s^E\varepsilon_0\varepsilon^X)$.

We discussed the k_{31} mode vibrator with *E*-constant $s_{11}{}^E$ and k_{33} mode with *D*-constant $s_{33}{}^D$ for analyzing the dynamic equations in sections 7.2.2 and 7.2.3. Here, we reconsider the relation between these status differences from the "depolarization field" viewpoint.

Let us consider boundary conditions in a piezoelectric plate with or without a surface electrode, in which a mechanical longitudinal vibration wave is propagating along the plate, as shown in Figure 7.9, where the spontaneous polarization P_S axis is perpendicular to the plate in (a) and (b), while in parallel to the plate in (c). Figures merely illustrate the induced polarization ΔP and field E visually, with the arrows. The "Gauss law", static electromagnetic Maxwell relation, $div\mathbf{D} = \rho$; or $div\mathbf{E} = \frac{1}{\varepsilon_0}(\rho - div\mathbf{P})$ indicates the depolarization field $E_{dep} = -(\frac{\Delta P}{\varepsilon_0})$ originated from the induce polarization by the piezoelectricity $\Delta P = d\Delta X$, for instance, in a resistive ferroelectric single crystal without surface electrodes (i.e., $\rho = 0$). Because this stationary E_{dep} is compensated by the migrating charge in a short period (~minutes), we consider only AC ΔP associated with the mechanical vibration (i.e., D-constant).

If there are free charges ρ in the specimen plate, $div\mathbf{E}$ can be equal to zero by compensating induced ΔP (induced by the stress as $\Delta P = d\Delta X$) with ρ, leading to an E-constant with respect to space/coordinate. In contrast, if there are no charges, $div\mathbf{D} = 0$ (D-constant), by generating a so-called "depolarization electric field". With piezoelectric coupling, $D = \varepsilon_0\varepsilon^X E + dX$ should be integrated into above $div\mathbf{D} = 0$, leading to

$$E_{dep} = -(\frac{\Delta P}{\varepsilon_0\varepsilon^X}), \text{where } \Delta P = d\Delta X. \tag{7.31}$$

When the surface is electroded in k_{31} mode (Figure 7.9a), charges ρ can easily be supplied through the electrodes, as illustrated. Thus, $(\frac{\partial E_Z}{\partial x}) = 0$, or E-constant is derived when the electrodes are connected to a voltage supply (small constant E_Z shown in the figure is from the power supply for exciting the mechanical wave), or E_Z = zero in the short circuit between the top and bottom electrodes. When the surface does not have an electrode, no charge is supplied (Figure 7.9b). Thus, the depolarization/reverse field is induced to maintain $(\frac{\partial D_Z}{\partial x}) = 0$, leading to D-constant condition. That is, as shown in Figure 7.9b, both the induced polarization ΔP and depolarization field E are positively and negatively proportional to the stress distribution, and cancel each other out. In the case of k_{33} mode (Figure 7.9c), though the plate edges are electroded, there is no electrode along the wave propagation z axis (parallel to the plate). Thus, no charge is available to compensate the polarization modulation along the z direction, and the sound velocity along the polarization direction should be a D-constant sound velocity based on ${s_{33}}^D$. Needless to say, when we made electrodes on the side of this k_{33} rod, free charge compensated the depolarization field, leading to the E-constant ${v_{33}}^E$ and ${s_{33}}^E$.

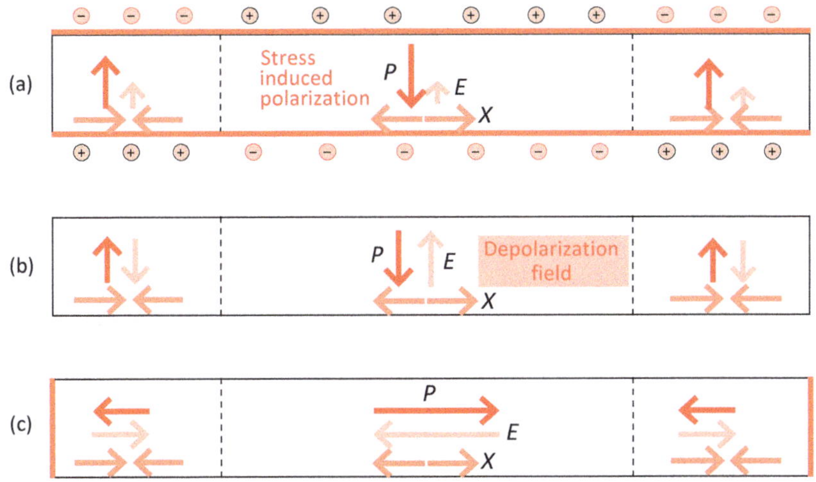

Figure 7.9. Boundary conditions: *E*-constant vs. *D*-constant under dynamic waves. (**a**) *E*-constant (≈0): k_{31} mode (Electrode); (**b**) *D*-constant (=0): k_{31} mode (No Electrode); (**c**) *D*-constant (=0): k_{33} mode (No Side Electrode; Edge Electrode). Source: [1] ©Uchino, K. *Micromechatronics*, 2nd ed.; CRC Press, 2019; p. 118. Reproduced by permission of Taylor & Francis Group.

However, it is noteworthy that the situation is different when the driving frequency is pseudo-DC. Even in a k_{33} rod specimen, when the operating frequency is low, the depolarization field attracts "stray" charges in the specimen or on the specimen surface from the surrounding atmosphere, and it is canceled out (i.e., so-called "screening"); that is, approaching to the *E*-constant condition, rather than *D*-constant status. The elasticity seems to change from the original ${s_{33}}^D$ to ${s_{33}}^E$ when the operating frequency decreases from >1 kHz down to 0.001 Hz, in practice. In this sense, remember that the electromechanical coupling factors k_{31} and k_{33} are defined at pseudo-static (pseudo-DC) operation, described with the *E*-constant elastic compliances:

$$\begin{cases} k_{31} = \dfrac{d_{31}}{\sqrt{s_{11}^E \varepsilon_0 \varepsilon_{33}^X}} \\ k_{33} = \dfrac{d_{33}}{\sqrt{s_{33}^E \varepsilon_0 \varepsilon_{33}^X}} \end{cases}. \tag{7.32}$$

7.2.4. Other Vibration Modes—Loss Free

In addition to the k_{31} and k_{33} modes, there are several piezoelectric ceramic resonators with different shapes and sizes. In order to determine both dielectric permittivities (ε_{33}^X, ε_{11}^X), five elastic compliances (s_{33}^E, s_{11}^E, s_{13}^E, s_{12}^E, and s_{44}^E), and three piezoelectric constants (d_{33}, d_{31} and d_{15}) in piezo-ceramic materials with ∞mm symmetry, the measurements on "five" vibration modes are required, the specimen configurations of which are illustrated in Figure 7.10, which correspond to (a), (b), (c), (d), and (j) in Table 7.1. Table 7.1 summarizes the electromechanical coupling factor definitions of various piezoelectric resonators with different shapes and electrode configurations.

Table 7.1. The electromechanical coupling factor definitions of various piezoelectric resonators with different shapes and sizes.

	Factor	Boundary Conditions	Resonator Shape	Definition
(a)	k_{31}	$X_1 \neq 0, X_2 = X_3 = 0$ $x_1 \neq 0, x_2 \neq 0, x_3 \neq 0$	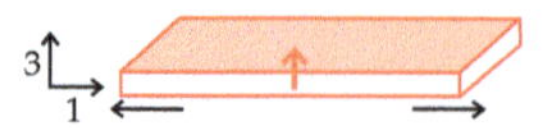	$\frac{d_{31}}{\sqrt{S^E{}_{11}\varepsilon_0\varepsilon^X{}_{33}}}$
(b)	k_{33}	$X_1 = X_2 = 0, X_3 \neq 0$ $x_1 = x_2 \neq 0, x_3 \neq 0$		$\frac{d_{33}}{\sqrt{S^E{}_{33}\varepsilon_0\varepsilon^X{}_{33}}}$
(c)	k_p	$X_1 = X_2 \neq 0, X_3 = 0$ $x_1 = x_2 \neq 0, x_3 \neq 0$	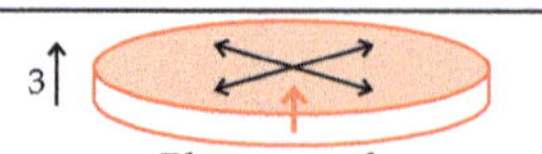 Planar mode	$k_{31}\sqrt{\frac{2}{1-\sigma}}$
(d)	k_t	$X_1 = X_2 \neq 0, X_3 \neq 0$ $x_1 = x_2 = 0, x_3 \neq 0$	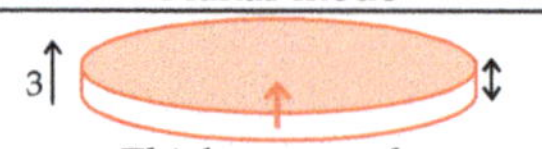 Thickness mode	$k_{33}\sqrt{\frac{\varepsilon_0\varepsilon^X{}_{33}}{C^D{}_{33}}}$
(e)	k_p'	$X_1 = X_2 \neq 0, X_3 \neq 0$ $x_1 = x_2 \neq 0, x_3 = 0$	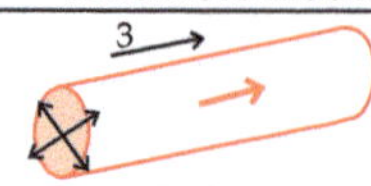 Radial mode	$\frac{k_p - Ak_{33}}{\sqrt{1-A^2}\sqrt{1-k^2{}_{33}}}$
(f)	k_{31}'	$X_1 \neq 0, X_2 \neq 0, X_3 = 0$ $x_1 \neq 0, x_2 = 0, x_3 \neq 0$	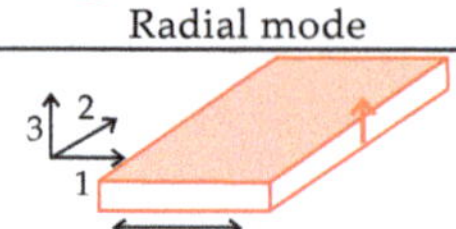 Width mode	$\frac{k_{31}}{\sqrt{1-k^2{}_{31}}}\sqrt{\frac{1+\sigma}{1-\sigma}}$
(g)	k_{31}''	$X_1 \neq 0, X_2 = 0, X_3 \neq 0$ $x_1 \neq 0, x_2 \neq 0, x_3 = 0$	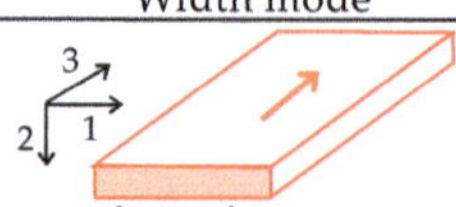 Width mode	$\frac{k_{31} \quad Bk_{33}}{\sqrt{1-k^2{}_{33}}}$
(h)	k_{31}'''	$X_1 \neq 0, X_2 \neq 0, X_3 \neq 0$ $x_1 \neq 0, x_2 = 0, x_3 = 0$	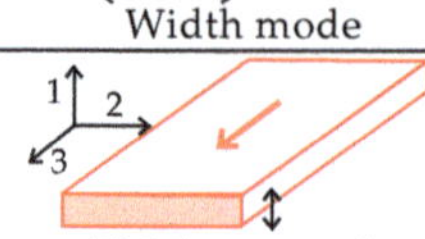 Thickness mode	$\frac{\sqrt{\frac{(k_p - Ak_{33})^2}{1-A^2} - (k_{31} - Bk_{33})^2}}{1 - k^2{}_{33} - (k_{31} - Bk_{33})^2}$
(i)	k_{33}'	$X_1 \neq 0, X_2 = 0, X_3 \neq 0$ $X_1 = 0, X_2 \neq 0, X_3 \neq 0$	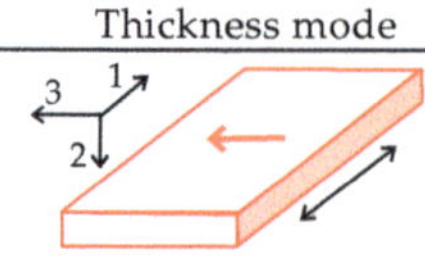 Width mode	$\frac{k_{33} - \mathrm{B}k_{31}}{\sqrt{1-B^2}\sqrt{1-k^2{}_{31}}}$
(j)	$k_{24} = k_{15}$	$X_1 = X_2 = X_3 = 0, X_4 \neq 0$ $X_1 = X_2 = X_3 = 0, X_5 \neq 0$	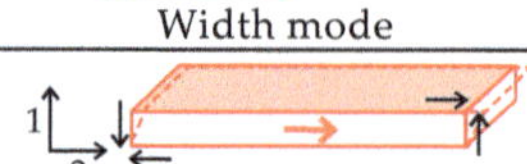 Shear mode	$\frac{d_{15}}{\sqrt{S^E{}_{55}\varepsilon_0\varepsilon^X{}_{11}}}$

Note: Above $A = \frac{\sqrt{2}S^E_{13}}{\sqrt{S^E_{33}(S^E_{11}+S^E_{12})}}$, $B = \frac{S^E_{13}}{S^E_{11}S^E_{33}}$. Source: Table by author.

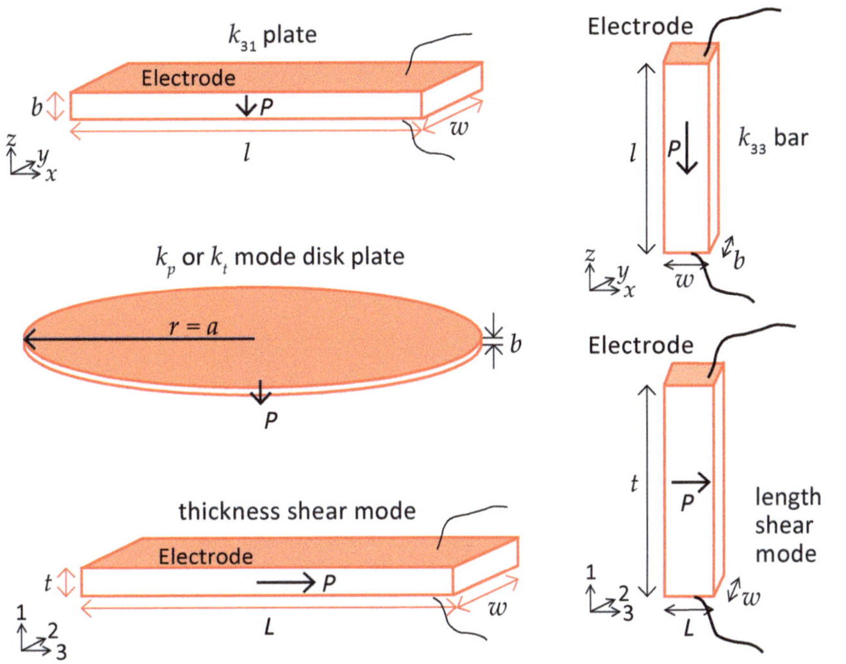

Figure 7.10. Sketches of the sample geometries for five required vibration modes. Source: [1] ©Uchino, K. *Micromechatronics*, 2nd ed.; CRC Press, 2019; p. 179. Reproduced by permission of Taylor & Francis Group.

7.3. Piezo Equations and Vibration Modes—With Losses

7.3.1. Longitudinal Vibration Mode via Transverse Piezoelectric Effect (k_{31} Mode)—With Losses

Resonance Mode—Q_A

Now, we introduce the complex parameters into the admittance formula Equation (7.16) around the resonance frequency [5,6]: $\varepsilon_3{}^{X*} = \varepsilon_3{}^X(1 - j\tan\delta_{33}')$, $s_{11}{}^{E*} = s_{11}{}^E(1 - j\tan\phi_{11}')$, and $d_{31}{}^* = d_{31}(1 - j\tan\theta_{31}')$.

$$Y = Y_d + Y_m = j\omega C_d(1 - j\tan\delta_{33}''') + j\omega C_d K_{31}{}^2[(1 - j(2\tan\theta_{31}' - \tan\phi_{11}')][(\tan(\omega L/2v_{11}{}^{E*})/(\omega L/2v_{11}{}^{E*})], \tag{7.33}$$

where

$$C_0 = (wL/t)\varepsilon_0\varepsilon_{33}{}^X \text{ (free electrostatic capacitance, real number)}, \tag{7.34}$$

$$C_d = (1 - k_{31}{}^2)C_0 \text{ (damped/clamped capacitance, real number)}, \tag{7.35}$$

$$k_{31}{}^2 = \frac{k_{31}^2}{1 - k_{31}^2}. \tag{7.36}$$

Note that the loss for the first term ("damped/clamped admittance") is represented by the dielectric loss $\tan\delta'''$:

$$\tan\delta_{33}''' = [1/(1 - k_{31}^2)][\tan\delta_{33}' + k_{31}^2(\tan\phi_{11}' - 2\tan\theta_{31}')]. \quad (7.37)$$

Though the formula is identical to Equation (6.135) in 1D expression through the $[K]$ matrix, $\tan\delta_{33}'''$ is not exactly to the "extensive" non-prime loss $\tan\delta$, because the extensive loss should be under a three-dimensionally clamped condition, not just 1D longitudinally clamped (Recall we used ε_{33}^{LC}).

Regarding the motional admittance term, taking into account

$$v_{11}^{E*} = \frac{1}{\sqrt{\rho s_{11}^E(1 - j\tan\phi_{11}')}} = v_{11}^E\left(1 + j\frac{\tan\phi_{11}'}{2}\right), \quad (7.38)$$

we further calculate $1/[\tan(\omega L/2v^*)]$ with an expansion-series approximation around the A-type resonance frequency $(\omega_A L/2v) = \pi/2$. Using new frequency parameters,

$$\Omega_A = \omega_A L/2v_{11}{}^E = \pi/2,\ \Delta\Omega = \Omega - \pi/2\ (<<1), \quad (7.39)$$

we obtain

$$\frac{1}{\tan\Omega^*} = \cot\left(\frac{\pi}{2} + \Delta\Omega_A - j\frac{\pi}{4}\tan\phi_{11}'\right) = \Delta\Omega_A - j\frac{\pi}{4}\tan\phi_{11}'. \quad (7.40)$$

Thus, the "motional admittance" Y_m is approximated around the first resonance frequency ω_A by

$$Y_m = j(8/\pi^2)\omega_A C_d K_{31}^2[(1 - j(2\tan\theta_{31}' - \tan\phi_{11}')]/[(4/\pi)\Delta\Omega_A - j\tan\phi_{11}']. \quad (7.41)$$

The maximum Y_m is obtained at $\Delta\Omega_A = 0$:

$$Y_m{}^{max} = (8/\pi^2)\omega_A C_d K_{31}^2(\tan\phi_{11}')^{-1} = (8/\pi^2)\omega_A C_d K_{31}^2 Q_A. \quad (7.42)$$

The mechanical quality factor for A-type resonance $Q_A = (\tan\phi_{11}')^{-1}$ can be proved as follows: Q_A is defined by $Q_A = \omega_A/2\Delta\omega$, where $2\Delta\omega$ is a full width of the 3 dB down (i.e., $1/\sqrt{2}$, because $20\log_{10}(1/\sqrt{2}) = -3.01$) of the maximum value $Y_m{}^{max}$ at $\omega = \omega_A$. Since $|Y| = |Y|^{max}/\sqrt{2}$ can be obtained when the "conductance = susceptance"; $\Delta\Omega_A = \pi/4)\tan\phi_{11}'$ (see the denominator of Equation (7.41)),

$$Q_A = \Omega_A/2\Delta\Omega_A = (\pi/2)/2(\pi/4)\tan\phi_{11}' = (\tan\phi_{11}')^{-1}. \quad (7.43)$$

Similarly, the maximum displacement u^{max} is obtained at $\Delta\Omega = 0$:

$$u^{max} = (8/\pi^2)d_{31}E_Z L Q_A. \quad (7.44)$$

The maximum displacement at the resonance frequency is $(8/\pi^2)Q_A$ times larger than that at a non-resonance frequency, $d_{31}E_Z L$. Under the constant voltage/field drive, the displacement is amplified at the resonance frequency, while under the constant current drive, the displacement u and the impedance Z are amplified at the antiresonance frequency by the factor of $(8/\pi^2)Q_B$. Example Problem 7.2 provides the origin of the calibration factor $(8/\pi^2)$ for both maximum values of $Y_m{}^{max}$ and u^{max} at the fundamental resonance mode.

Example Problem 7.2

Under pseudo-DC operation, the input electric energy is split into the converted mechanical energy by k^2 and the stored electric energy by $(1 - k^2)$, leading to the damped and motional capacitance ratio $(1 - k^2)$ vs. k^2. However, under the resonance drive, though the damped admittance is provided by $\omega_A C_0(1 - k_{31}{}^2)$, the maximum of the motional admittance for the fundamental resonance frequency is described by

$$Y_m{}^{max} = (8/\pi^2)\omega_A C_0 k_{31}{}^2 Q_A. \tag{P7.2.1}$$

The calibration factor $(8/\pi^2)$ ($\approx$0.81) is required for the fundamental resonance frequency, rather than just one. Explain why this calibration factor is required for the fundamental resonance condition.

Hint

Calculate the motional admittance for higher-order resonance harmonics. The fundamental resonance mode does not spend all mechanically converted energy, but it is also shared by harmonics. Use the relation:

$$\Sigma[\frac{1}{(2m-1)^2}] = (\frac{\pi^2}{8}). \tag{P7.2.2}$$

Solution

We start from Equation (7.33):

$$Y_m = j\omega C_d K_{31}{}^2[(1 - j(2\tan\theta_{31}{}' - \tan\phi_{11}{}'))][(\tan(\omega L/2v_{11}{}^{E*})/(\omega L/2v_{11}{}^{E*})]. \tag{P7.2.3}$$

Note that the A-type resonance is obtained at $\left(\frac{\omega_{A,n}L}{2v_{11}^E}\right) = n(\frac{\pi}{2})$, where $n = 1, 3, 5, \ldots$ (the n-th higher-order harmonics) and $v_{11}^E{}^2 = 1/\rho s_{11}^E$. Then, taking into account the complex elastic compliance

$$v_{11}^{E*} = \frac{1}{\sqrt{\rho s_{11}^E(1 - j\tan\phi_{11}{}')}} = v_{11}^E\left(1 + j\frac{\tan\phi_{11}{}'}{2}\right), \tag{P7.2.4}$$

we further calculate $1/[\tan(\omega L/2v^*)]$ with an expansion-series approximation around the A-type resonance frequency $(\omega_A L/2v_{11}^E) = n(\pi/2)$, taking into account that the resonance state is defined in this case for the minimum impedance (maximum admittance) point. Using new frequency parameters, $\Omega_A = \omega_A L/2v_{11}{}^E = n(\pi/2)$, $\Delta\Omega_A = \Omega - n(\pi/2)$ (<<1), we obtain the approximation

$$\frac{1}{\tan\Omega^*} = \cot\left(n\frac{\pi}{2} + \Delta\Omega_A - j\frac{1}{2}(n\frac{\pi}{2})\tan\phi_{11}{}'\right) = \Delta\Omega_A - j\frac{n\pi}{4}\tan\phi_{11}{}' \quad \text{(P7.2.5)}$$

the "motional admittance" Y_m is approximated around the n-th resonance frequency $\omega_{A,n}$ by

$$Y_{m,n} = j(8/\pi^2 n^2 \omega_A C_0 k_{31}{}^2/[(4/n\pi)\Delta\Omega_A - j\tan\phi_{11}{}']. \quad \text{(P7.2.6)}$$

The maximum Y_m is obtained at $\Delta\Omega_A = 0$:

$$Y_{m,n}^{max} = (8/\pi^2 n^2)\omega_A C_0 k_{31}{}^2(\tan\phi 11')^{-1} = (8/\pi^2 n^2)\omega_A C_0 k_{31}{}^2 Q_m. \quad \text{(P7.2.7)}$$

Supposing that the intensive elastic loss tan $\phi_{11}{}'$ or the mechanical quality factor Q_m is insensitive to the frequency difference among the higher-order harmonic resonance frequencies, we can understand that each harmonic mode is originated from the effective motional capacitance equal to $(8/\pi^2 n^2)C_0 k_{31}{}^2$, and the admittance is enhanced by the factor of Q_m. Under the resonance, the input cyclic electric energy will excite the mechanical vibration and motional capacitance synchronously by a factor of Q_m by spending the cyclic excitation number proportional to Q_m. The motional capacitance is proportional to $(1/n^2)$ for the n-th order harmonic resonance mode. Knowing a general relationship $\Sigma[\frac{1}{(2m-1)^2}] = (\frac{\pi^2}{8})$ (m—positive integer), when we add motional capacitances for all harmonic resonance modes:

$$(8/\pi^2)C_0 k_{31}{}^2 \sum_{n=1,\,3,5,\ldots} (\frac{1}{n^2}) = C_0 k_{31}{}^2. \quad \text{(P7.2.8)}$$

Since the total motional capacitance for all harmonic resonance modes corresponds exactly to the free capacitance minus damped capacitance, the calibration factor $(8/\pi^2 n^2)$ can be understood as the distribution ratio of the mechanical energy to all n-th harmonic modes. The above concept on the higher order harmonic modes will be used in the Equivalent Circuit Model explained in Chapter 9.

Antiresonance Mode—Q_B

On the other hand, in PZT ceramics a higher quality factor at the antiresonance is usually observed in comparison with that at the resonance point [7,8], the reason for which was interpreted by Mezheritsky from the combination of three loss factors [8]. In this subsection, we provide an alternative and, more importantly, a user-friendly formula to determine piezoelectric losses by analyzing the admittance/impedance spectra at resonance and antiresonance [9]. The antiresonance corresponds to the minimum admittance of Equation (7.33):

$$Y = (j\omega w L/b)\varepsilon_0\varepsilon_{33}{}^X[(1-k^2) + k^2\tan(\omega L/2v_{11}{}^E)/(\omega L/2v_{11}{}^E)],$$
$$(v_{11}{}^E = 1/\sqrt{\rho s_{11}^E}) = j\omega C_0[(1-k_{31}^2) + k_{31}^2\frac{\tan(\Omega_{11})}{\Omega_{11}}].$$

Here, $v_{11}{}^{E} = 1/\sqrt{\rho s_{11}^{E}}$, $\Omega_{11} = (\omega L/2v_{11}^{E})$, and $k_{31}{}^{2} = d_{31}{}^{2}/\varepsilon_0\varepsilon_{33}^{X}s_{11}^{E}$.

In the resonance discussion, we neglected the damped admittance, because the motional admittance is significantly large due to $\tan(\omega L/2v_{11}{}^{E*}) \nearrow \infty$. On the contrary, in the antiresonance discussion, we basically consider the subtraction between the damped and motional admittances; that is, the admittance should be exactly zero when the loss is not included, or is only the minimum when we consider the losses (that is, complex parameters) in Equation (7.33).

We introduce the normalized admittance Y' for further calculation:

$$Y' = 1 - k_{31}{}^{2} + k_{31}{}^{2}\frac{\tan(\omega l/2v_{11}^{E})}{\omega l/2v_{11}^{E}} = 1 - k_{31}{}^{2} + k_{31}{}^{2}\frac{\tan(\Omega)}{\Omega}. \tag{7.45}$$

Since the expansion series of $\tan\Omega$ is convergent in this case, taking into account

$$1/v_{11}^{E*} = \sqrt{\rho s_{11}^{E}(1 - j\tan\phi_{11}{}')} = (1/v_{11}^{E})\left(1 - j\tfrac{\tan\phi_{11}{}'}{2}\right),$$

we can apply the following expansion approximation in terms of $\tan\phi_{11}{}'$:

$$\tan(\Omega^*) = \tan\left(\Omega - j\tfrac{\Omega\tan\phi_{11}{}'}{2}\right) = \tan\Omega - j\tfrac{\Omega\tan\phi_{11}{}'}{2\cos^2\Omega}.$$

Introducing losses for the parameters in Equation (7.45) leads to

$$\begin{aligned} Y' &= 1 - k_{31}{}^{2}\left[1 - j(2\tan\theta_{31}' - \tan\delta_{33}' - \tan\phi_{11}{}')\right] \\ &+ k_{31}{}^{2}\left[1 - j(2\tan\theta_{31}{}' - \tan\delta_{33}{}' - \tan\phi_{11}{}')\right]\tfrac{\tan\Omega^*}{\Omega^*}. \end{aligned} \tag{7.46}$$

Note that the "electromechanical coupling loss" $(2\tan\theta_{31}{}' - \tan\delta_{33}{}' - \tan\phi_{11}{}')$ contributes significantly in this antiresonance discussion. We separate Y' into conductance G (real part) and susceptance B (imaginary part) as $Y' = G + jB$:

$$G = 1 - k_{31}{}^{2} + k_{31}{}^{2}\frac{\tan\Omega}{\Omega}. \tag{7.47}$$

$$B = \left(k_{31}{}^{2} - k_{31}{}^{2}\frac{\tan\Omega}{\Omega}\right)(2\tan\theta_{31}{}' - \tan\delta_{33}' - \tan\phi_{11}{}') - \frac{k_{31}{}^{2}}{2}\left(\frac{1}{\cos^2\Omega} - \frac{\tan\Omega}{\Omega}\right)\tan\phi_{11}{}'. \tag{7.48}$$

The antiresonance frequency Ω_b is initially determined from $G = 0$ (refer to Subsection Resonance/Antiresonance Frequency Definitions), and

$$1 - k_{31}{}^{2} + k_{31}{}^{2}\frac{\tan\Omega_B}{\Omega_B} = 0. \tag{7.49}$$

Using new parameters,

$$\Omega = \Omega_B + \Delta\Omega_B, \tag{7.50}$$

similar to $\Delta\Omega_A$ for the resonance, $\Delta\Omega_B$ is also a small number, and the first-order approximation of $(\frac{\tan\Omega}{\Omega})$ in Equation (7.45) can be utilized.

$$\frac{\tan\Omega}{\Omega} = \frac{\tan\Omega_B}{\Omega_B} + \frac{1}{\Omega_B}\left(\frac{1}{\cos^2\Omega_B} - \frac{\tan\Omega_B}{\Omega_B}\right)\Delta\Omega_B.$$

Neglecting the high order term, which has two or more small factors (loss factor or $\Delta\Omega_B$),

$$G = \frac{k_{31}{}^2}{\Omega_B}\left(\frac{1}{\cos^2\Omega_B} - \frac{\tan\Omega_B}{\Omega_B}\right)\Delta\Omega_B. \tag{7.51}$$

$$B = (2\tan\theta_{31}{}' - \tan\delta_{33}{}' - \tan\phi_{11}{}') - \frac{k_{31}{}^2}{2}\left(\frac{1}{\cos^2\Omega_B} - \frac{\tan\Omega_B}{\Omega_B}\right)\tan\phi_{11}{}'. \tag{7.52}$$

Consequently, the minimum absolute value of admittance can be achieved when $\Delta\Omega_B$ is zero. The antiresonance frequency Ω_B is determined by Equation (7.49). In order to find the 3 dB-up point, let $G = B$, where $\sqrt{G^2 + B^2} = \sqrt{2}B$ is satisfied:

$$\begin{aligned}\tfrac{k_{31}{}^2}{\Omega_B}\left(\tfrac{1}{\cos^2\Omega_B} - \tfrac{\tan\Omega_B}{\Omega_B}\right)\Delta\Omega_B = (2\tan\theta_{31}{}' - \tan\delta_{33}{}' - \tan\phi_{11}{}') - \\ \tfrac{k_{31}{}^2}{2}\left(\tfrac{1}{\cos^2\Omega_B} - \tfrac{\tan\Omega_B}{\Omega_B}\right)\tan\phi_{11}{}'.\end{aligned} \tag{7.53}$$

Further, since the antiresonance quality factor is given by

$$Q_{B,31} = \frac{\Omega_B}{2|\Delta\Omega_B|}. \tag{7.54}$$

Equation (7.53) can be represented as

$$\begin{aligned}&\tfrac{k_{31}{}^2}{2Q_{B,31}}\left(\tfrac{1}{\cos^2\Omega_B} - \tfrac{\tan\Omega_B}{\Omega_B}\right) \\ &= -(2\tan\theta_{31}{}' - \tan\delta_{33}{}' - \tan\phi_{11}{}') + \tfrac{k_{31}{}^2}{2}\left(\tfrac{1}{\cos^2\Omega_B} - \tfrac{\tan\Omega_B}{\Omega_B}\right)\tan\phi_{11}{}'.\end{aligned}$$

We can now obtain the result as

$$\frac{1}{Q_{B,31}} = \tan\phi_{11}{}' - \frac{2}{k_{31}{}^2}(2\tan\theta_{31}{}' - \tan\delta_{33}{}' - \tan\phi_{11}{}')/\left(\frac{1}{\cos^2\Omega_B} - \frac{\tan\Omega_B}{\Omega_B}\right).$$

Or, as a final formula:

$$\frac{1}{Q_{B,31}} = \frac{1}{Q_{A,31}} - \frac{2}{1 + \left(\frac{1}{k_{31}} - k_{31}\right)^2 \Omega_B{}^2}(2\tan\theta_{31}{}' - \tan\delta_{33}{}' - \tan\phi_{11}{}'). \tag{7.55}$$

Note the following relation used in the formula transformation:

$$\frac{1}{\cos^2\Omega_B} - \frac{\tan\Omega_B}{\Omega_B} = \frac{(1 - k_{31}{}^2)^2\Omega_B{}^2 + k_{31}{}^2}{k_{31}{}^4}. \tag{7.56}$$

You may understand that in k_{31} mode, where the wave propagation direction with the electrode is perpendicular to the spontaneous polarization direction, the primary mechanical resonance (a half-wavelength vibration of the plate length) corresponds to the "resonance" mode with the sound velocity $v_{11}{}^E$, and the "antiresonance" mode corresponds to the subsidiary mode via the electromechanical coupling. Additionally, from Equation (7.55), we can understand that when $(2\tan\theta'_{31} - \tan\delta'_{33} - \tan\phi'_{11}) > 0$, $Q_{B,31} > Q_{A,31}$; while $(2\tan\theta'_{31} - \tan\delta'_{33} - \tan\phi'_{11}) < 0$, $Q_{B,31} < Q_{A,31}$. From Figure 7.4, it is experimentally obvious that $Q_{B,31} > Q_{A,31}$ in PZT piezo-ceramics, leading to a conclusion that the piezoelectric loss is larger than the average of the dielectric and elastic losses: $(2\tan\theta'_{31} - \tan\delta'_{33} - \phi'_{11}) > 0$.

7.3.2. Vibration Mode via Longitudinal Piezoelectric Effect (k_{33} Mode)—With Losses

The length extensional mode is shown in Figure 7.7, where $L >> w, b$. Recall that the vibration velocity along the spontaneous polarization is given by $v^D = 1/\sqrt{\rho s_{33}^D}$. Taking into account the admittance formula given by Equation (7.28), we can derive the impedance expression of the k_{33} mode bar in a similar fashion to k_{31} mode [10].

$$Z(\omega) = \frac{1}{j\omega C_d}\left(1 - {k_{33}}^2 \frac{\tan\Omega}{\Omega}\right), \tag{7.57}$$

where

$$C_d = \frac{wb}{L}\varepsilon_0 {\varepsilon_{33}}^X\left(1 - k_{33}^2\right), \tag{7.58}$$

$$\Omega = \frac{\omega L}{2}\sqrt{\rho s_{33}^D} = \frac{\omega L}{2}\sqrt{\rho s_{33}^E (1 - k_{33}^2)}, \tag{7.59}$$

$${k_{33}}^2 = \frac{{d_{33}}^2}{\varepsilon_0 \varepsilon_{33}^X s_{33}^E}. \tag{7.60}$$

By introducing the complex parameters,

$$\left({k_{33}}^2\right)^* = {k_{33}}^2(1 - j\chi_{33}), \tag{7.61}$$

$$\chi_{33} = 2\tan\theta_{33}' - \tan\delta_{33}' - \tan\phi_{33}' \text{ (“electromechanicalcouplingloss”)}, \tag{7.62}$$

$$C_d^* = C_d(1 - j\tan\delta_{33}''') \text{ (dampedcapacitanceloss)}, \tag{7.63}$$

$$\tan\delta_{33}''' = \frac{1}{1 - {k_{33}}^2}\left[\tan\delta_{33}' - {k_{33}}^2(2\tan\theta_{33}' - \tan\phi_{33}')\right], \tag{7.64}$$

$$\Omega^* = \Omega\sqrt{1 - j\tan\phi_{33}'''}, \tag{7.65}$$

$$\tan\phi_{33}''' = \frac{1}{1 - {k_{33}}^2}\left[\tan\phi_{33}' - {k_{33}}^2(2\tan\theta_{33}' - \tan\delta_{33}')\right]. \tag{7.66}$$

Note again that the parameters in k_{33} mode have similar forms to k_{31} mode, and the difference is that the loss factors by $-\chi_{33}$, $\tan\delta_{33}'''$, $\tan\phi_{33}'''$, which show identical forms to the “extensive loss” parameters in terms of “intensive losses”, but are not the same, strictly speaking. The difference between the extensive (non-prime) losses and these triple-prime losses comes from the 3D or 1D mechanically clamped conditions. Refer to the k_t mode in the next subsection, where the loss factors are purely "extensive losses" since the elastic stiffness $c_{33}{}^D$ is the primary parameter, and the mechanical 3D clamp is practically satisfied. Compare the formula (b) and (d) in Table 7.1. The thickness resonance frequency is high enough to suppress the length/width vibration excitation. Therefore, a similar derivation process to the k_{31} mode can be applied, and the results for the k_{33} are given by

$$Q_{B,33} = \frac{1}{\tan\phi_{33}'''} = \frac{1-k_{33}{}^2}{\tan\phi_{33}' - k_{33}{}^2(2\tan\theta_{33}' - \tan\delta_{33}')}, \tag{7.67}$$

$$\frac{1}{Q_{A,33}} = \frac{1}{Q_{B,33}} + \frac{2}{k_{33}{}^2 - 1 + \Omega_A{}^2/k_{33}{}^2}(2\tan\theta_{33}' - \tan\delta_{33}' - \tan\phi_{33}'). \tag{7.68}$$

Unlike in the k_{31} mode, you may approximately understand that in k_{33} and k_t modes, where the wave propagation direction is parallel to the spontaneous polarization direction, the primary mechanical resonance (a half-wavelength vibration of the length or thickness) corresponds to the "antiresonance" mode with the sound velocity $v_{33}{}^D$, and the "resonance" state is the subsidiary mode via the piezoelectric coupling. Additionally, from Equation (7.68) we can understand that when $(2\tan\theta_{33}' - \tan\delta_{33}' - \tan\phi_{33}') > 0$, $Q_{B,33} > Q_{A,33}$; while $(2\tan\theta_{33}' - \tan\delta_{33}' - \tan\phi_{33}') < 0$, $Q_{B,31} < Q_{A,31}$. From Equation (7.57) and setting $Z = 0$, the resonance frequency is provided simply by

$$\Omega_A = k_{33}{}^2 \tan\Omega_A \quad [k_{33}{}^2 = \frac{d_{33}{}^2}{\varepsilon_0 \varepsilon_{33}^X s_{33}^E}]. \tag{7.69}$$

Note again that a half-wavelength of the vibration is longer than the rod length at the resonance frequency (more uniform strain distribution than the sinusoid); a half-wavelength is realized at the antiresonance frequency.

7.3.3. Loss and Mechanical Quality Factor in Other Modes

To obtain the loss factor matrix, "five vibration modes" need to be characterized in PZT ceramics with ∞mm crystallographic symmetry (independently, two dielectric, five elastic, and three piezoelectric loss components for either intensive and extensive parameters), as summarized in Figure 7.10 and Table 7.1. The methodology is based on the equations of quality factors Q_A (resonance) and Q_B (antiresonance) in various modes with regard to loss factors and other properties [10]. We can measure Q_A and Q_B for each mode by using the "3 dB-up/down method" (or "quadrantal frequency method") in the impedance/admittance spectra (see an example in Figure 7.4). The experimental techniques to determine the mechanical quality factors are described in Section 7.4. In addition to some derivations based on fundamental relations of the material properties, all 20 loss factors (prime and non-prime $\tan\delta_{33}$, $\tan\delta_{11}$; $\tan\phi_{33}$, $\tan\phi_{11}$, $\tan\phi_{12}$, $\tan\phi_{13}$, $\tan\phi_{55}$; $\tan\theta_{33}$, $\tan\theta_{31}$, $\tan\theta_{15}$) can be obtained for piezoelectric ceramics. We derived the relationships between mechanical quality factors Q_A (resonance) and Q_B (antiresonance) in all five required modes shown in Table 7.1. The results for Q_A (resonance) and Q_B (antiresonance) formulae are summarized below [10]:

(a) k_{31} mode: (intensive elastic loss)

$$Q_{A,31} = \frac{1}{\tan\phi_{11}'}$$
$$\frac{1}{Q_{B,31}} = \frac{1}{Q_{A,31}} - \frac{2}{1+(\frac{1}{k_{31}}-k_{31})^2\Omega_{B,31}{}^2}(2\tan\theta_{31}' - \tan\delta_{33}' - \tan\phi_{11}')$$
$$\Omega_{A,31} = \frac{\omega_a l}{2v_{11}^E} = \frac{\pi}{2}, \left[v_{11}^E = 1/\sqrt{\rho s_{11}^E}\right]$$
$$\Omega_{B,31} = \frac{\omega_b l}{2v_{11}^E}, 1 - k_{31}{}^2 + k_{31}{}^2\frac{\tan\Omega_B}{\Omega_B} = 0$$

(b) k_t mode: (extensive elastic loss)

$$Q_{B,t} = \frac{1}{\tan\phi_{33}}$$
$$\frac{1}{Q_{A,t}} = \frac{1}{Q_{B,t}} - \frac{2}{k_t{}^2-1+\Omega_{A,t}{}^2/k_t{}^2}(2\tan\theta_{33} - \tan\delta_{33} - \tan\phi_{33})$$
$$\Omega_{B,t} = \frac{\omega_b l}{2v_{33}^D} = \frac{\pi}{2}, \left[v_{33}^D = 1/\sqrt{\rho/c_{33}^D}\right]$$
$$\Omega_{A,t} = \frac{\omega_a l}{2v_{33}^D}, \Omega_{A,t} = k_t{}^2\tan\Omega_{A,t}$$

(c) k_{33} mode:

$$Q_{B,33} = \frac{1}{\tan\phi'''_{33}} = \frac{1-k_{33}{}^2}{\tan\phi_{33}'-k_{33}{}^2(2\tan\theta_{33}'-\tan\delta_{33}')}$$
$$\frac{1}{Q_{A,33}} = \frac{1}{Q_{B,33}} + \frac{2}{k_{33}{}^2-1+\Omega_A{}^2/k_{33}{}^2}(2\tan\theta_{33}' - \tan\delta_{33}' - \tan\phi_{33}')$$
$$\Omega_{B,33} = \frac{\omega_b l}{2v_{33}^D} = \frac{\pi}{2}, \left[v_{33}^D = 1/\sqrt{\rho s_{33}^D}\right],$$
$$\Omega_{A,33} = \frac{\omega_a l}{2v_{33}^D}\Omega_{A,33}, \Omega_{A,33} = k_{33}{}^2\tan\Omega_{A,33}$$

(d) k_{15} mode (constant E—length shear mode): (intensive elastic loss)

$$Q_{A,15}^E = \frac{1}{\tan\phi_{55}'}$$
$$\frac{1}{Q_{B,15}^E} = \frac{1}{Q_{A,15}^E} - \frac{2}{1+(\frac{1}{k_{15}}-k_{15})^2\Omega_B{}^2}(2\tan\theta_{15}' - \tan\delta_{11}' - \tan\phi_{55}')$$
$$\Omega_B = \frac{\omega_b L}{2v_{55}^E} = \frac{\omega_b L}{2}\sqrt{\rho s_{55}^E}, 1 - k_{15}{}^2 + k_{15}{}^2\frac{\tan\Omega_B}{\Omega_B} = 0$$

(e) k_{15} mode (constant D—thickness shear mode): (extensive elastic loss)

$$Q_{B,15}^D = \frac{1}{\tan\phi_{55}}$$
$$\frac{1}{Q_{A,15}^D} = \frac{1}{Q_{B,15}^D} - \frac{2}{k_{15}{}^2-1+\Omega_A{}^2/k_{15}{}^2}(2\tan\theta_{15} - \tan\delta_{11} - \tan\phi_{55})$$
$$\Omega_A = \frac{\omega_a t}{2v_{55}^D} = \frac{\omega_a t}{2}\sqrt{\frac{\rho}{c_{55}^D}}, \Omega_A = k_{15}{}^2\tan\Omega_A$$

Note again that because k_{31} and k_{33}/k_t modes possess E-constant and D-constant constraints, respectively, in k_{31}, the resonance frequency is directly related to $v_{11}{}^E$ or $s_{11}{}^E$ as $f_A = \frac{v_{11}^E}{2L} = 1/2L\sqrt{\rho s_{11}^E}$, while in k_{33}/k_t, the antiresonance frequency is directly related to $v_{33}{}^D$ or $s_{33}{}^D$, $c_{33}{}^D$ as $f_B = \frac{v_{33}^D}{2L} = 1/2L\sqrt{\rho s_{33}^D}$ or $1/2b\sqrt{\rho/c_{33}^D}$. It is important to distinguish k_{33} ($X_1 = X_2 = 0$, $x_1 = x_2 \neq 0$) from k_t ($X_1 = X_2 \neq 0$, $x_1 = x_2 = 0$) from the boundary conditions. Note the relations: $s_{33}^D = s_{33}^E(1 - k_{33}^2)$ and $c_{33}^E = c_{33}^D(1 - k_t^2)$, and $k_{33} > k_t$ in general. The pure "extensive loss" $\tan\phi_{33}$ is obtained from the loss relating to c_{33}^D from the definition, that is, in the k_t mode. When the length of a rod k_{33} is not very long, the mode approaches the k_t, and $c_{33}{}^D \approx 1/s_{33}{}^D$. The antiresonance in k_{31} and the resonance in k_{33}/k_t are subsidiary, originating from the electromechanical coupling factors. We also remind the reader the relation for the "electromechanical coupling factor losses" from Equation (6.131):

$$\left(2\tan\theta' - \tan\delta' - \tan\phi'\right) = -(2\tan\theta - \tan\delta - \tan\phi). \quad (7.70)$$

Since the side is not clamped ($x_1 = x_2 \neq 0$) in the k_{33} mode (different from the k_t mode), the triple-prime losses in the previous section are not exactly equal to non-prime extensive losses. The 3D-clamped k_t mode exhibits the purely "extensive" non-prime losses, though the Q_m formulae for the k_{33} mode seems to be rather similar to the extensive losses transformed from the intensive losses.

7.3.4. Q_A and Q_B in the IEEE Standard

It is also important to discuss the assumption in the IEEE Standard [3], where the difference in the mechanical quality factors among the resonance and antiresonance modes is neglected: that is, $Q_A = Q_B$. This historically originates from the neglection of the coupling loss (i.e., "piezoelectric loss") and the assumption of $\tan\phi' \gg \tan\delta'$ around the resonance region, leading to only one loss factor; that is, the intensive elastic loss. However, if we adopt our three-loss model, this situation ($Q_A = Q_B$) occurs only when $\left(2\tan\theta' - \tan\delta' - \tan\phi'\right) = 0$, or $\tan\theta' = (\tan\delta' + \tan\phi')/2$. The IEEE Standard corresponds only when the piezoelectric loss is equal to the average value of the dielectric and elastic losses, which exhibits a serious contradiction to the well-known PZT experimental results; that is, $Q_A < Q_B$. As we can realize in Figure 7.4 from the peak sharpness, the PZTs exhibit Q_A (resonance) < Q_B (antiresonance), irrelevant to the vibration mode (Figure 7.4 is an example of the k_{31} mode). This concludes that ($\tan\delta_{33}' + \tan\phi_{11}' - 2\tan\theta_{31}'$) < 0, or ($\tan\delta_{33}' + \tan\phi_{11}')/2 < \tan\theta_{31}'$ for k_{31}, and ($\tan\delta_{33} + \tan\phi_{33} - 2\tan\theta_{33}$) > 0, or ($\tan\delta_{33} + \tan\phi_{33})/2 > \tan\theta_{33}$ for k_t. It is worth noting that the intensive piezoelectric loss is larger than the average of the dielectric and elastic intensive losses in Pb-contained piezo-ceramics.

7.4. Admittance Spectrum Characterization Method

7.4.1. Real Parameter Determination Method

Firstly, we introduce piezoelectric characterization methods of the real parameters, and we describe how to calculate the electromechanical parameters in the k_{31} mode specimen (k_{31}, d_{31}, s_{11}^E, *and* ε_{33}^X) from the admittance/impedance spectrum measurement for the reader's convenience in getting acquainted. When we measure the admittance/impedance of a piezoelectric specimen by changing the frequency, a frequency spectrum similar to Figure 7.4 is observed, where the first and second max/min peaks correspond to the resonance and antiresonance, respectively. The parameters used in the following procedure are shown in the Figure 7.5 k_{31} mode.

(1) The sound velocity v in the specimen is obtained from the resonance frequency f_A (admittance peak frequency): $f_A = v/2L$.
(2) Knowing the density ρ, the elastic compliance s_{11}^E can be calculated from the sound velocity v: $v = 1/\sqrt{\rho s_{11}^E}$.
(3) The electromechanical coupling factor k_{31} is calculated from the v value and the antiresonance frequency f_A through Equation (7.19): $(\omega_B L/2v_{11}^E)\cot(\omega_B L/2v_{11}^E)$

$= -k_{31}{}^2/(1-k_{31}{}^2)$; or $k_{31}{}^2/(1-k_{31}{}^2) = (\pi^2/4)(\Delta f/f_R)$, $(\Delta f = f_B - f_A)$ (Approximation when k_{31} is not large.)

(4) Knowing the permittivity $\varepsilon_{33}{}^X$ from the independent measurement such as an LCR meter or the admittance value $j\omega C = j\omega\varepsilon_0\varepsilon(\frac{Lw}{b})$ under an off-resonance condition, the d_{31} is calculated from k_{31}: $k_{31} = d_{31}/\sqrt{s_{11}{}^E \cdot \varepsilon_{33}{}^X}$.

7.4.2. Resonance/Antiresonance under Constant Vibration Velocity

The admittance/impedance frequency spectrum is obtained conventionally by measuring current under a constant voltage, sweeping the drive frequency around the resonance/antiresonance frequency range. The admittance can also be determined by measuring the voltage under a constant current. However, with an increase in the input power energy and vibration velocity of the piezoelectric specimen, significant spectrum distortion emerges around the resonance peak under constant voltage, while significant distortion is exhibited around the antiresonance peak under constant current [1,2]. Therefore, in order to identify both mechanical quality factors Q_A and Q_B precisely, Uchino's group developed the High-Power Piezoelectric Characterization System (HiPoCS), shown in Figure 7.11. One of the key pieces of equipment includes NF Corporation's power supply, which satisfies: maximum voltage: 200 (V), maximum current: 10 (A), frequency range: 0–500 (kHz), and output impedance: <1 (Ω). In addition, the system is equipped with an infrared image sensor to monitor the heat generation distributed in the test specimen. The impedance/admittance curves by keeping the following various conditions: (1) constant voltage, (2) constant current, (3) constant vibration velocity of a piezoelectric sample, and (4) constant input power [11]. The key is that the values Q_A and Q_B can be different, and if we precisely measure both values, the information on the piezoelectric loss $\tan\theta'$ can be obtained. Thus, we proposed a simple, easy and user-friendly method to determine the piezoelectric loss factor $\tan\theta'$ in k_{31} mode through admittance/impedance spectrum analysis. Adopting the useful formulae proposed by Zhuang and Uchino [6,7], the intensive losses are obtained from the mechanical quality factor Q_A and Q_B for the rectangular k_{31} mode:

$$Q_{A,31} = \frac{1}{\tan\phi_{11}{}'} \tag{7.71}$$

$$\frac{1}{Q_{B,31}} = \frac{1}{Q_{A,31}} - \frac{2}{1+(\frac{1}{k_{31}} - k_{31})^2 \Omega_{B,31}{}^2}(2\tan\theta_{31}{}' - \tan\delta_{33}{}' - \tan\phi_{11}{}'), \tag{7.72}$$

where $\tan\delta_{33}{}'$, $\tan\phi_{11}{}'$, $\tan\theta_{31}{}'$ are intensive loss factors for $\varepsilon_{33}{}^T$, $s_{11}{}^E$, d_{31}, and $\Omega_{B,31}$ is the normalized antiresonance frequency given by

$$\Omega_{B,31} = \frac{\omega_b l}{2v_{11}^E}\ [v_{11}{}^E = 1/\sqrt{\rho\, s_{11}{}^E}], \tag{7.73a}$$

which should satisfy

$$1 - k_{31}{}^2 + k_{31}{}^2 \frac{\tan\Omega_B}{\Omega_B} = 0, \tag{7.73b}$$

while the normalized resonance frequency is given by

$$\Omega_{A,31} = \frac{\omega_a l}{2v_{11}^E} = \frac{\pi}{2}[v_{11}{}^E = 1/\sqrt{\rho\, s_{11}{}^E}]. \tag{7.74}$$

Figure 7.12 shows an interface display of HiPoCS, demonstrating a rectangular k_{31} plate measurement under a "constant vibration velocity" condition (i.e., output mechanical displacement or converted mechanical energy is maintained and remains almost constant). In order to keep the vibration velocity constant (i.e., stored/converted mechanical energy is constant), the current is almost constant, and the voltage is minimized around the resonance, while the voltage is almost constant and the current is minimized around the antiresonance frequency (bottom of Figure 7.12). The apparent power is shown in the top of Figure 7.12 (for a specimen of 80 mm L), which clearly indicates that the antiresonance operation requires less power than the resonance mode to generate the same vibration velocity or stored mechanical energy. We can conclude that the PZT transducer should be operated at the antiresonance frequency, rather than the resonance mode, from the energy efficiency viewpoint [12].

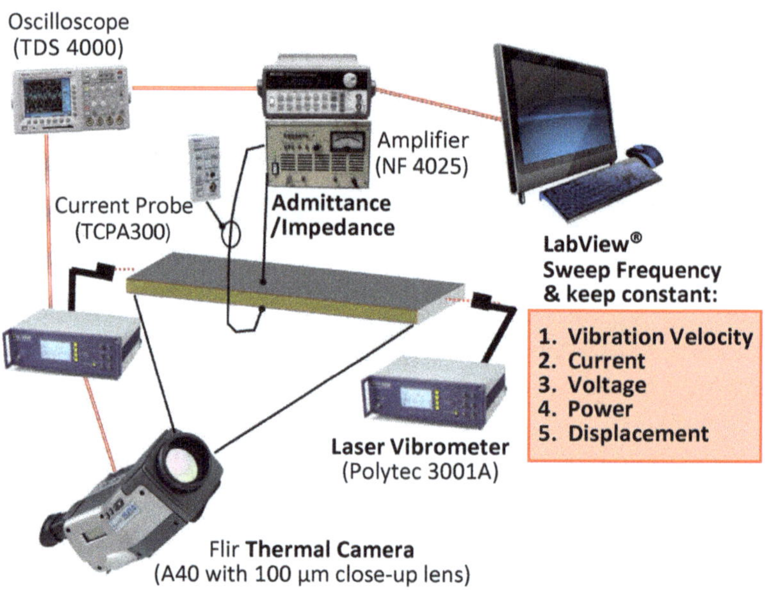

Figure 7.11. Setup of the High-Power Piezoelectric Characterization System (HiPoCS). Source: Figure by author, based on data from [11].

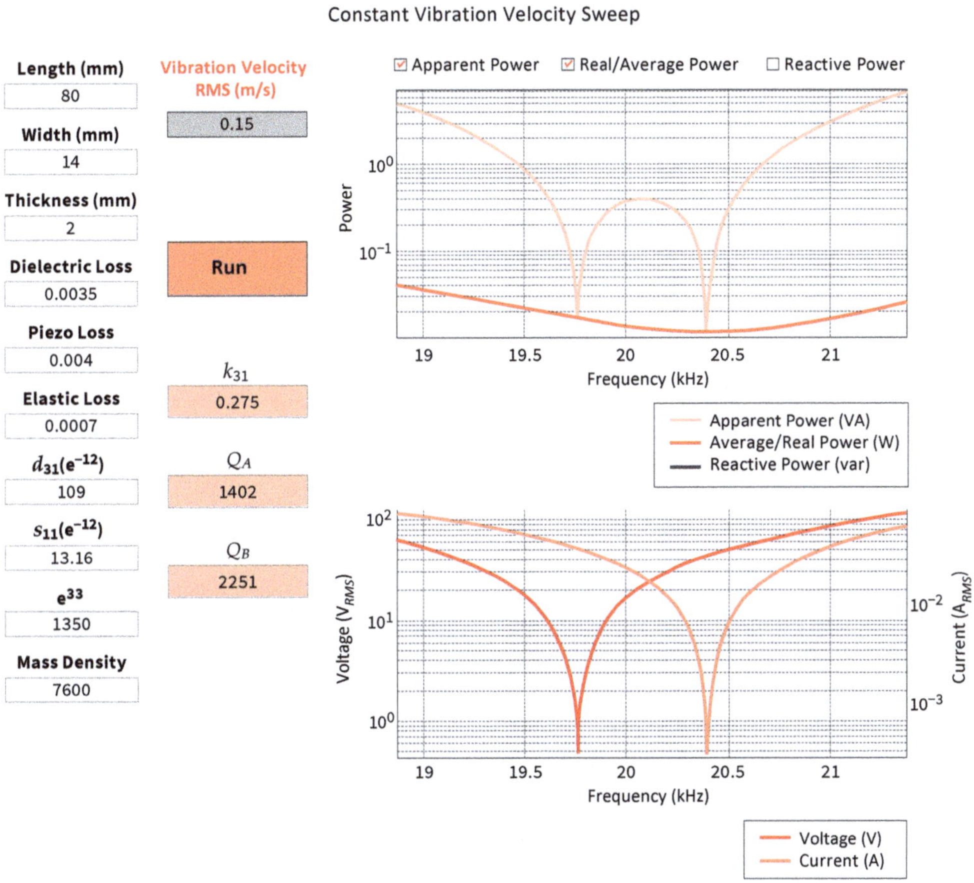

Figure 7.12. Voltage and current change with frequency under the constant vibration velocity condition. Source: [2] ©Uchino, K. *High-Power Piezoelectrics and Loss Mechanisms*; CRC Press, 2020; p. 196. Reproduced by permission of Taylor & Francis Group.

The admittance can be calculated from the voltage and current data at each frequency from the bottom of Figure 7.12, which is plotted in Figure 7.13 (data are for a specimen of 20 mm L). Note that this admittance curve is obtained by keeping the same vibration velocity in all the frequency ranges below the resonance to above the antiresonance frequencies, so that no significant spectrum distortion is recognized. In order to obtain the Q_A and Q_B, 3 dB-down and -up methods are used for the resonance and antiresonance frequencies, as indicated in Figure 7.13.

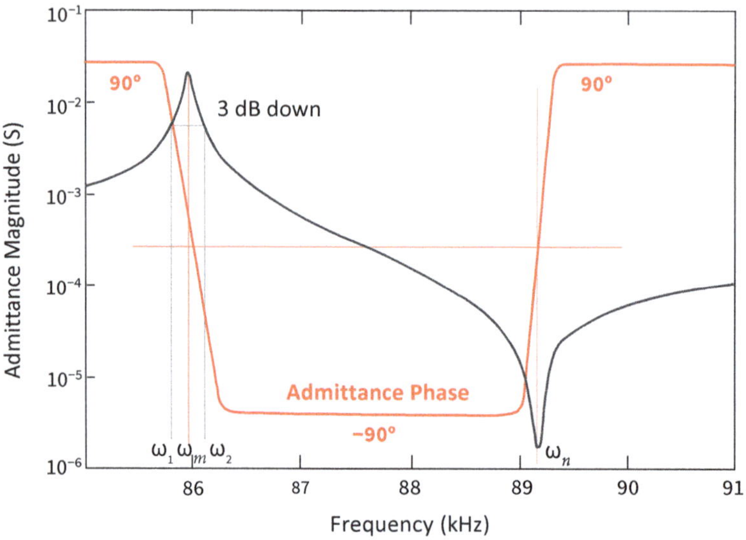

Figure 7.13. Admittance magnitude and admittance phase spectra for a rectangular piezo-ceramic plate for a fundamental longitudinal mode (k_{31}) through the transverse piezoelectric effect (d_{31}). Source: [1] ©Uchino, K. *Micromechatronics*, 2nd ed.; CRC Press, 2019; p. 181. Reproduced by permission of Taylor & Francis Group.

7.4.3. Real Electric Power Method

Because the conventional admittance spectrum method can provide the mechanical quality factors only at two frequency points; that is, resonance Q_A and antiresonance Q_B, knowing the Q_m at any frequency was frustrating. A unique methodology for characterizing the quality factor in piezoelectric materials was developed in the ICAT by utilizing "real electrical power" measurements (including the phase lag), e.g., $P = V{\cdot}I\cos\varphi$, rather than the "apparent power" $V{\cdot}I$, as shown in the top of Figure 7.12 [13].

The mechanical quality factor, Q_m, can be defined in general as

$$Q_m = 2\pi \frac{Energy\ Stored/Cycle}{Energy\ Lost/Cycle}. \tag{7.75a}$$

The ratio of elastic stored energy of an oscillator to the power being dissipated electrically provides the mechanical quality factor:

$$Q_m = 2\pi f_r \frac{U_e}{P_d}, \tag{7.75b}$$

where U_e is the maximum stored mechanical energy and P_d is the dissipated power, measured in this experiment by P_d = electrically spent energy [13]. Because the compliance of a piezoelectric material exhibits nonlinearity, the maximum kinetic energy is used to define the stored energy term. For a longitudinally vibrating k_{31}

plate (see Figure 7.5 or the inserted figure in Figure 7.6 with the plate center $x = 0$), the kinetic energy as a function of displacement, u_x, is

$$U_e = \frac{1}{2}A\int_{-\frac{L}{2}}^{\frac{L}{2}} \rho\left(\frac{\partial u_x}{\partial t}\right)^2 dx. \tag{7.76}$$

Using the geometry of the rectangular plate with length L, width w, thickness b, and assuming sinusoidal forcing at a frequency near the fundamental resonance (or even near the antiresonance mode as shown in the center of Figure 7.6, as long as k_{31} is not large <40%), the spatial vibration is approximated as

$$u_x(x,t) = V_{RMS}\sqrt{2}\sin\left(\frac{\pi x}{L}\right)\sin(2\pi f t). \tag{7.77}$$

The maximum kinetic energy can be calculated as

$$U_e = \frac{1}{2}A\int_{-\frac{L}{2}}^{\frac{L}{2}} \rho\left(V_{RMS}\sqrt{2}\sin\left(\frac{\pi x}{L}\right)\right)^2 dx = V_{RMS}^2\rho A\frac{L}{2}, \tag{7.78}$$

where V_{RMS} is the vibration velocity at the edge of the plate (RMS value of m/s), and ρ, A, L are the mass density, cross-section area (=wb), and length of the specimen. The relation between mechanical quality factor and real electrical power and mechanical vibration is based on two concepts: (1) at equilibrium, the power input is the power lost, and (2) the stored mechanical energy can be predicted using the known vibration mode shape, as we did in Equation (7.78), which is almost valid even around the antiresonance frequency in less than 1% accuracy. We can derive the following equation from these concepts, which allows the calculation of the mechanical quality factor at any frequency from the real electrical power (P_d) and tip RMS vibration velocity (V_{RMS}) measurements for a longitudinally vibrating piezoelectric resonator (k_t, k_{33}, k_{31}):

$$Q_{m,l} = 2\pi f\frac{\frac{1}{2}\rho V_{RMS}^2}{P_d/Lwb}. \tag{7.79}$$

The change in mechanical quality factor was measured for an 80 mm long Hard PZT (APC 851) ceramic plate (k_{31}) under constant vibration condition of 100 mm/s RMS tip vibration velocity (i.e., stored mechanical energy constant). The experimental key in the HiPoCS usage is to determine the phase difference φ precisely to obtain the $\cos(\varphi)$ value. The required power and mechanical quality factor Q_m are shown in Figure 7.14. The quality factor obtained at the resonance is within 2% agreement with results from the impedance spectrum method (3 dB-down bandwidth). This technique reveals the behavior of the mechanical quality factor at any frequency from "below the resonance" to "above the antiresonance" frequencies. Moreover, very interestingly, the mechanical quality factor reaches a maximum value between the resonance and the antiresonance frequency, the point of which may suggest the optimum condition for the transducer operation merely from an efficiency viewpoint, also for understanding the behavior of piezoelectric material properties under high-power excitation.

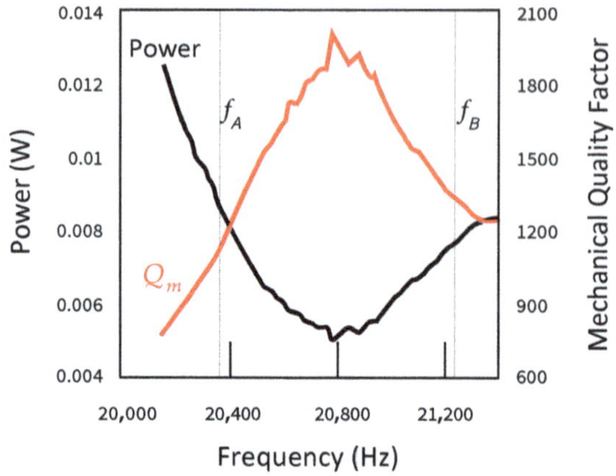

Figure 7.14. Mechanical quality factor measured using real electrical power (including the phase lag) for a hard PZT APC 851 k_{31} plate. Source: [2] ©Uchino, K. *High-Power Piezoelectrics and Loss Mechanisms*; CRC Press, 2020; p. 198. Reproduced by permission of Taylor & Francis Group.

7.4.4. Determination Methods of the Mechanical Quality Factor

Let us review the precise determination method of the mechanical quality factor from the admittance or impedance spectrum around the resonance and antiresonance frequencies. The admittance spectrum on the k_{31} mode is shown in Figure 7.13. Figure 7.15a,b show the admittance circle and its magnified vision around the antiresonance frequency. The admittance circle acts as a plot of "conductance" G in the horizontal axis and "susceptance" jB in the vertical axis by sweeping the frequency. Though the "admittance circle" is useful for the Q_A around the resonance peak, the "impedance circle" ("impedance" R vs. "reactance" X) is better for the Q_B around the antiresonance peak, as illustrated in Figure 7.15c.

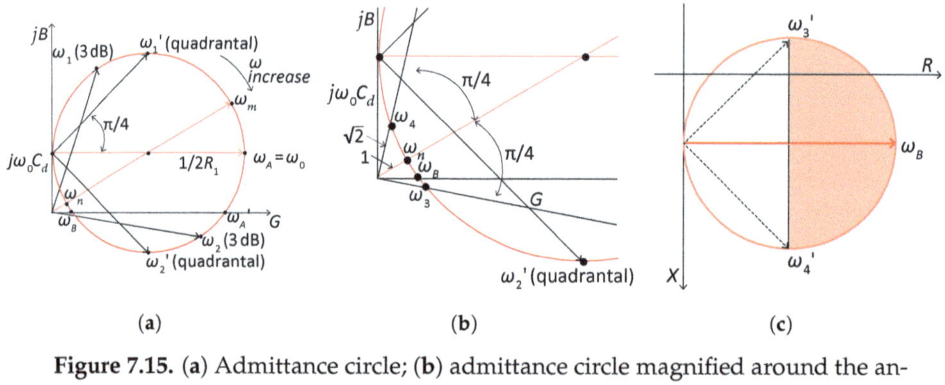

Figure 7.15. (**a**) Admittance circle; (**b**) admittance circle magnified around the antiresonance; (**c**) impedance circle for the antiresonance peak. Source: [2] ©Uchino, K. *High-Power Piezoelectrics and Loss Mechanisms*; CRC Press, 2020; p. 198. Reproduced by permission of Taylor & Francis Group.

Resonance/Antiresonance Frequency Definitions

The resonance angular frequency is defined by ω_A, the most right on the motional admittance circle (the intersect (higher G) between the admittance circle and the susceptance $B = 0$, ω_A', is another definition as the resonance), while the antiresonance frequency is defined by ω_B, the intersect (lower G) between the admittance circle and the susceptance $B = 0$. Popularly used maximum and minimum frequencies of the admittance magnitude (i.e., absolute value in the admittance spectrum), ω_m and ω_n, are not exactly the resonance and antiresonance frequencies, precisely speaking. Note the relationship: $\omega_m < \omega_A = \omega_0 < \omega_B < \omega_n$.

Mechanical Quality Factor Determination

(a) Q_A Determination (see Figure 7.15a)

- 3 dB down method around ω_m

$$(Q_A{}^{-1}) = (\omega_2 - \omega_1)/\omega_m. \quad (7.80)$$

- Quadrantal frequency method around ω_A ($\pm 45°$ phase difference on the admittance circle)

$$(Q_A{}^{-1})' = (\omega_2' - \omega_1')/\omega_A. \quad (7.81)$$

Note ω_1 (3 dB) < ω_1' (quadrantal) < ω_2 (3 dB) < ω_2' (quadrantal). The difference between $(Q_A{}^{-1})$ and $(Q_A{}^{-1})'$ can be estimated as

$$(Q_A{}^{-1})/(Q_A{}^{-1})' = 1 + 1/2M^2, \quad (7.82)$$

where $M = |Y_m|/|Y_d| = 1/R_1\omega_R C_d = Q_A K$ and $K = C_1/C_d$ ($1/K$: capacitance ratio). When we consider $Q_A \approx 1000$, the deviation of Q_A values among these two ways is less than 1 ppm (negligibly small).

(b) Q_B Determination (see Figure 7.15b,c):

- 3 dB up method around ω_n

$$(Q_B{}^{-1}) = (\omega_4 - \omega_3)/\omega_n. \quad (7.83)$$

- Quadrantal frequency method around ω_A ($\pm 45°$ phase difference on the impedance circle)

$$(Q_B{}^{-1})' = (\omega_4' - \omega_3')/\omega_B. \quad (7.84)$$

In summary, in Figure 7.15 the admittance circle is useful for the Q_A around the resonance peak, while the impedance circle is better for the Q_B around the antiresonance peak.

7.4.5. Determination of the Three Losses from the Mechanical Quality Factors

A method for determining the piezoelectric loss is summarized for a piezoelectric k_{31} mode plate sample here (refer to [14] for other modes):

(1) Obtain $\tan\delta'$ from an impedance analyzer or a capacitance meter at a frequency away (lower range) from the resonance/antiresonance range;
(2) Obtain the following parameters experimentally from an admittance/impedance spectrum around the resonance (A-type) and antiresonance (B-type) range (3 dB bandwidth method): ω_a, ω_b, Q_A, Q_B, and the normalized frequency $\Omega_b = \omega_b l/2v$;
(3) Obtain $\tan\phi'$ from the inverse value of Q_A (quality factor at the resonance) in the k_{31} mode;
(4) Calculate electromechanical coupling factor k_{31} from the ω_a and ω_b with the IEEE Standard equation in the k_{31} mode:

$$\frac{{k_{31}}^2}{1-{k_{31}}^2} = \frac{\pi}{2}\frac{\omega_b}{\omega_a}\tan[\frac{\pi(\omega_b-\omega_b)}{2\omega_a}]. \quad (7.85)$$

(5) Finally obtain $\tan\theta'$ by the following equation in the k_{31} mode:

$$\tan\theta' = \frac{\tan\delta' + \tan\phi'}{2} + \frac{1}{4}\left(\frac{1}{Q_A} - \frac{1}{Q_B}\right)[1 + (\frac{1}{k_{31}} - k_{31})^2 {\Omega_b}^2]. \quad (7.86)$$

As long as we have accurate ω_a, ω_b, Q_A, and Q_B, the above procedure can be used. A general problem in determining accurate piezoelectric and loss parameters is found in the k_{33} rod specimen, in which a relatively large electric field leak is anticipated according to the aspect ratio (rod length/width).

Example Problem 7.3

The electromechanical coupling factor k can basically be obtained from the resonance and antiresonance frequencies. However, there are several formulae for this calculation, depending on the approximation level, which directly reflects the accuracy of the piezoelectric loss $\tan\theta$, as indicated in the above section. Knowing the experimental result on the impedance spectrum for a PZT-5 k_{33} rod specimen shown in Figure 7.16: $f_A = 1.3 f_R$ (Antiresonance, Resonance frequencies), calculate the k_{33} value of this PZT-5H by using the following three different formulae:

$${k_{33}}^2/(1-{k_{33}}^2) = (\pi^2/4)(\Delta f/f_R), \quad (P7.3.1)$$

$${k_{33}}^2/(1-{k_{33}}^2) = (\pi^2/8)({f_A}^2 - {f_R}^2)/{f_R}^2, \quad (P7.3.2)$$

$${k_{33}}^2 = (\pi/2)(f_R/f_A)\tan[(\pi/2)(\Delta f/f_A)], \quad (P7.3.3)$$

where $\Delta f = f_A - f_R$.

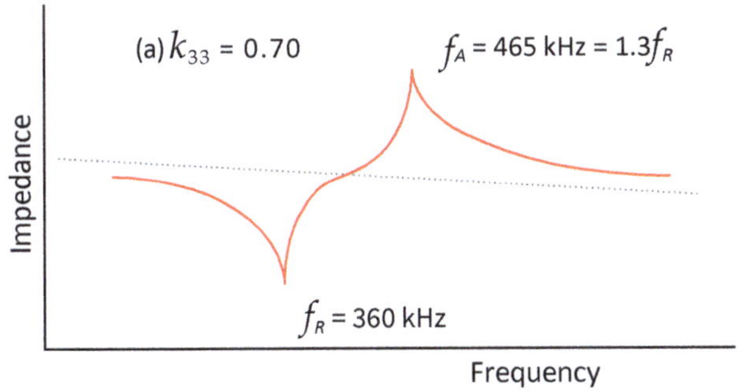

Figure 7.16. Impedance spectrum for (a) k_{33} PZT-5 rod specimen. Source: [1] ©Uchino, K. *Micromechatronics*, 2nd ed.; CRC Press, 2019; p. 119. Reproduced by permission of Taylor & Francis Group.

Solution

(1) Similar to the most rough approximation for small k_{31}, $k_{31}^2/(1 - k_{31}^2) = (\pi^2/4)(\Delta f/f_R)$, we use the following approximation for k_{33} mode:
$k_{33}^2/(1 - k_{33}^2) = (\pi^2/4)(\Delta f/f_R) = (\pi^2/4) \times 0.3 = 0.749$.
Thus, $k_{33} = 0.654$ (underestimation).

(2) When we use a better approximation (IRE Standard, "Marutake Approximation"):
$k_{33}^2/(1 - k_{33}^2) = (\pi^2/8)(f_A^2 - f_R^2)/f_R^2 = 0.851$,
we obtain $k_{33} = 0.678$, higher value than the above (1) and close to the accurate (3) (slightly over).

(3) When we use the accurate formula:
$k_{33}^2 = (\pi/2)(f_R/f_A)\tan[(\pi/2)(\Delta f/f_A)] = 0.458$,
we can obtain $k_{33} = 0.677$. Note that $k_{33}^2/(1 - k_{33}^2) = -(2\pi f_A L/2v)\cot(2\pi f_A L/2v)$ is another accurate formula for the k_{33} mode. Different from the k_{31} mode formula ($k_{31}^2/(1 - k_{31}^2) = (\pi/2)(f_A/f_R)\tan[(\pi/2)(\Delta f/f_R)]$), in the k_{33} mode formula, the denominator is f_A (not f_R) because the antiresonance is the primary vibration mode (the resonance is the primary vibration mode in the k_{31} case).

The reader should understand that the k value deviates from the accurate one (the larger k, larger error) according to the approximation formula.

7.5. Vibration Characterization under Cyclic Stress

Let us start again from the piezoelectric constitutive equations for the k_{31} type plate sample, shown in Figure 7.5:

$$x_1 = s_{11}^E X_1 + d_{31} E_z, \tag{7.87a}$$

$$D_3 = d_{31} X_1 + \varepsilon_0 \varepsilon_{33}^X E_z. \tag{7.87b}$$

In Section 7.4, with the change in the operating frequency of the external electric field E, exciting the mechanical resonance, we measure the electrical admittance/impedance. Then, we analyze the vibration modes under resonance and antiresonance frequencies. We distinguish $\varepsilon_0\varepsilon_{33}{}^X$ and $\varepsilon_0\varepsilon_{33}{}^x$ under elastic compliance $s_{11}{}^E$ constant condition. In the k_{33} type rod sample, the elastic compliance $s_{33}{}^D$ is constant.

This section concerns the external mechanical operation, practically found in piezoelectric energy harvesting systems. With the change in the drive frequency of the external stress X, exciting the mechanical resonance, we measure the strain/displacement or electrically generated power depending on the external impedance, generated strain, and stored/output electric energy changes. Analogous to the case, the piezoelectric specimen changes its elastic compliance significantly from $s_{11}{}^E$ to $s_{11}{}^D$ with or without surface electrodes; the strain frequency spectrum in the k_{31} specimen shows one enhancement peak at the resonance under the short condition, while at the antiresonance it is shown under the open condition due to the effective elastic compliance difference. Needless to say, neither case generates the output electric energy, but merely stored electric energy in the piezo-device. In order to maximize the output electric energy in the energy harvesting system, we need to choose an electric impedance (resistive, in particular) that is matched to the internal electric impedance of the piezoelectric specimen. This section describes the mechanical resonance frequency and the corresponding effective elastic compliance under a matched electrical impedance shunted on the piezoelectric device.

7.5.1. Piezoelectric Dynamic Equation for the k_{31} Mode Plate

Let us consider the same piezo-ceramic k_{31} plate, as shown in Figure 7.5. Sinusoidal force/pressure F and $-F$ (angular frequency ω) are applied on the plate ends at $x = 0$ and L along the length direction x. Thus,

$$F(t) = -bwX_1(t), \tag{7.88}$$

where the negative sign above is adopted merely due to the opposite direction definition between pressure and stress. If the polarization is in the z direction and x–y planes are the planes of the electrodes, the extensional vibration in the x (length) direction is represented by the following dynamic equations (when the length L is more than 4–6 times of the width w or the thickness b, we can neglect the coupling modes with width or thickness vibrations):

$$\rho(\partial^2 u/\partial t^2) = (\partial X_{11}/\partial x), \tag{7.89}$$

where ρ is the density of the piezo-ceramic, and u is the displacement of a small-volume element in the ceramic plate in the x direction. Since Equation (7.87a) is transformed into $X_1 = x_1/s_{11}{}^E - (d_{31}/s_{11}{}^E)E_z$, we obtain

$$\frac{\partial X_1}{\partial x} = \frac{1}{s_{11}^E}\frac{\partial x_1}{\partial x} - \frac{d_{31}}{s_{11}^E}\frac{\partial E_z}{\partial x}. \tag{7.90}$$

Because of the equal potential on each electrode, $\partial E_z/\partial x = 0$, and knowing the strain definition $x_1 = \partial u/\partial x$ along the 1 (x) direction (non-suffix x corresponds to the Cartesian coordinate), Equation (7.89) is transformed into

$$\rho\frac{\partial^2 u}{\partial t^2} = \frac{1}{s_{11}^E}\frac{\partial^2 u}{\partial x^2}. \tag{7.91}$$

The following derivation is close to that which was performed in Subsection Vibration Modes. If we assume a "harmonic vibration" equation at the angular frequency ω, displacement u under a sinusoidal force application, we can simplify Equation (7.91):

$$-\omega^2 \rho s_{11}{}^E u = \partial^2 u/\partial x^2 \text{ or } -\left(\frac{\omega}{v_{11}^E}\right)^2 u(x) = \frac{\partial^2 u(x)}{\partial x^2}. \tag{7.92}$$

Here, v_{11}^E is the "sound velocity" along the length x direction in the piezo-ceramic plate, expressed by

$$v_{11}^E = 1/\sqrt{\rho s_{11}{}^E}. \tag{7.93}$$

The reader can easily understand that the above process corresponds to the Fourier transform; that is, the time domain to frequency domain. Supposing the displacement u also vibrates with the frequency of ω, a general solution of Equation (7.92) is expressed by

$$u(x) = A\sin\left(\frac{\omega}{v_{11}^E}x\right) + B\cos\left(\frac{\omega}{v_{11}^E}x\right). \tag{7.94}$$

The strain $x_1(x)$ is given by taking the first derivative of $u(x)$ of Equation (7.94) as

$$x_1(x) = \frac{\partial u}{\partial x} = A\frac{\omega}{v_{11}^E}\cos\left(\frac{\omega}{v_{11}^E}x\right) - B\frac{\omega}{v_{11}^E}\sin\left(\frac{\omega}{v_{11}^E}x\right). \tag{7.95}$$

In order to determine the above two parameters, A and B, the boundary condition under harmonic stress is imposed: $X_1 = X_0 e^{j\omega t}$ at $x = 0$ and L (both plate ends). Here, we will consider three cases: (1) short-circuit condition of the piezo-plate, where $E_z = 0$, (2) open-circuit condition of the piezo-plate, where the current $I = \frac{\partial Q}{\partial t} = 0$ (or D_z = constant), and (3) matching impedance shunt condition.

Solution under Short-Circuit Condition

Since $E_z = 0$, $x_1 = s_{11}{}^E X_1$ and $D_3 = d_{31} X_1$ are the necessary equations. From the first strain Equation (7.78a) at $x = 0$ and L, we obtain the following two equations:

$$\begin{cases} A\frac{\omega}{v_{11}^E} = s_{11}^E X_0 \\ A\frac{\omega}{v_{11}^E}cos\left(\frac{\omega}{v_{11}^E}L\right) - B\frac{\omega}{v_{11}^E}sin\left(\frac{\omega}{v_{11}^E}L\right) = s_{11}^E X_0 \end{cases}. \tag{7.96}$$

Thus,

$$\begin{cases} A = (\frac{v_{11}^E}{\omega}) s_{11}^E X_0 \\ B = -(\frac{v_{11}^E}{\omega}) s_{11}^E X_0 \frac{\sin\left(\frac{\omega}{2v_{11}^E} L\right)}{\cos\left(\frac{\omega}{2v_{11}^E} L\right)} \end{cases}, \tag{7.97}$$

$$\text{(Displacement) } u(x) = (\frac{v_{11}^E}{\omega}) s_{11}^E X_0 \frac{\sin[\frac{\omega(2x-L)}{2v_{11}^E}]}{\cos(\frac{\omega L}{2v_{11}^E})}, \tag{7.98}$$

$$\text{(Strain) } x_1 = \partial u / \partial x = s_{11}^E X_0 \, (\frac{\cos[\frac{\omega(2x-L)}{2v_{11}^E}]}{\cos(\frac{\omega L}{2v_{11}^E})}). \tag{7.99}$$

First, the displacement and strain are proportional to the external stress X_0. Second, their distributions in terms of x in Equations (7.98) and (7.99) are antisymmetrically and symmetrically sinusoidal in respect of $x = L/2$ position (the numerator becomes maximum, cos(0) = 1), and the maximum strain (i.e., "nodal line") exists on this line. Note that $\omega \to 0$ (i.e., pseudo-DC) makes Equation (7.99) $x_1 = s_{11}^E X_0$; that is, uniform strain distribution on the whole piezo-plate. For $\omega \to \left(\frac{\omega L}{2v_{11}^E}\right) = n\frac{\pi}{2}$ [n: 1, 3, 5, ...], the denominator of both Equations (7.98) and (7.99) approaches zero and the strain becomes infinite, which is called the "resonance" frequency. The resonance frequency under a closed circuit is given by

$$f_A = \frac{v_{11}^E}{2L}. \tag{7.100}$$

Now we use another set of constitutive equations with respect to electric displacement $D_3 = d_{31}X_1$. Taking into account $E_z = 0$, we calculate the total electric current under AC stress $X_1 = X_0 e^{j\omega t}$:

$$I = \frac{\partial Q}{\partial t} = j\omega w \int_0^L D_3 dx = j\omega w d_{31} \int_0^L X_1 dx = j\omega w \frac{d_{31}}{s_{11}^E} \int_0^L x_1 dx. \tag{7.101}$$

From Equation (7.99), we obtain $\int_0^L x_1 dx = \Delta L = s_{11}^E X_0 \frac{2v_{11}^E}{\omega} \tan(\frac{\omega L}{2v_{11}^E})$.
Thus, the total current is represented by

$$I = j\omega w \frac{d_{31}}{s_{11}^E} s_{11}^E X_0 \frac{2v_{11}^E}{\omega} \tan(\frac{\omega L}{2v_{11}^E}) = j(\frac{2wd_{31}}{s_{11}^E}) s_{11}^E X_0 v_{11}^E \tan(\frac{\omega L}{2v_{11}^E}). \tag{7.102}$$

Here, $(\frac{2wd_{31}}{s_{11}^E})$ is called the "force factor" to convert the mechanical input to the electrical output, and "j" stands for 90° phase ahead to the total displacement change. When ω is small the current increases in proportion to the frequency ω,

$$I = j\omega (\frac{wd_{31}}{s_{11}^E}) s_{11}^E X_0 L, \tag{7.103}$$

and for $\omega \rightarrow \left(\frac{\omega L}{2v_{11}^{E}}\right) = n\frac{\pi}{2}$ [n: 1, 3, 5, ...]; that is, approaching the resonance, I becomes infinite, similar to the total displacement behavior. Note that the short-circuit condition merely exhibits the current output, and no electrical output due to zero voltage.

Solution under Open-Circuit Condition

Since $E_z \neq 0$, we should use the original $x_1 = s_{11}{}^{E}X_1 + d_{31}E_z$, and $D_3 = d_{31}X_1 + \varepsilon_0\varepsilon_{33}{}^{X}E_z$, and calculate the voltage generated on the electrode under AC stress on both ends of the piezo-plate. An open-circuit condition means $I = \frac{\partial Q}{\partial t} = 0$ (Q: total charge collected from the surface electrodes). Integrating the constitutive equation of the electric displacement, $D_3 = d_{31}X_1 + \varepsilon_0\varepsilon_{33}{}^{X}E_z$, with respect to the electrode area

$$Q = w\int_0^L D_3 dx = w\int_0^L [d_{31}X_1 + \varepsilon_0\varepsilon_{33}^{X}E_z]dx. \quad (7.104)$$

Meanwhile, from $X_1 = x_1/s_{11}{}^{E} - (d_{31}/s_{11}{}^{E})E_z$, we obtain

$$\int_0^L X_1 dx = \frac{1}{s_{11}^{E}}\int_0^L (x_1 - d_{31}E_z)dx. \quad (7.105)$$

Knowing that $\int_0^L x_1 dx = \Delta L = 2u(t,L)$ and $E_z(t)$ = constant in terms of the coordinate x (electrode on the surface along x), inserting Equation (7.105) into Equation (7.104), we obtain

$$Q = w\left\{\left(\frac{d_{31}}{s_{11}^{E}}\right)[2u(t,L) - d_{31}E_zL] + \varepsilon_0\varepsilon_{33}^{X}E_zL\right\} = w\left\{\left(\frac{d_{31}}{s_{11}^{E}}\right)2u(t,L) + \varepsilon_0\varepsilon_{33}^{X}(1-k_{31}^2)E_z(t)L\right\} \quad (7.106)$$
$$[k_{31} = d_{31}/\sqrt{s_{11}{}^{E}\cdot\varepsilon_{33}{}^{X}}].$$

Equation (7.106) indicates that the total Q consists of the charge accumulated in the "damped (clamped) capacitance" (the second term of the right-hand formula) and the additional charge induced by the mechanical vibration (the first term, which is called "motional capacitance"). Note the "force factor" $\left(2w\frac{d_{31}}{s_{11}^{E}}\right)$ which converts the mechanical input u to electrical output Q (or equivalently, vibration velocity $\dot{u}$ to current I in Equation (7.102)). The open-circuit condition, $I = \frac{\partial Q}{\partial t} = j\omega Q = 0$, results in the relation between the output electric field E_z and the total displacement $2u(t,L)$ as

$$E_z = -\frac{k_{31}^2}{(1-k_{31}^2)}\frac{1}{Ld_{31}}2u(t,L). \quad (7.107)$$

It should also be noted that $u(t,L) = -u(t,0)$, symmetric for the displacement profile.

Taking into account the electric field generated on the piezo-plate, we derive a mechanical resonance frequency (which corresponds to the piezoelectric "antiresonance frequency"). The displacement u and strain $x_1(x)$ are assumed to be expressed by

$$u(x) = A\sin\left(\frac{\omega}{v_{11}^E}x\right) + B\cos\left(\frac{\omega}{v_{11}^E}x\right)$$
$$x_1(x) = \frac{\partial u}{\partial x} = A\frac{\omega}{v_{11}^E}\cos\left(\frac{\omega}{v_{11}^E}x\right) - B\frac{\omega}{v_{11}^E}\sin\left(\frac{\omega}{v_{11}^E}x\right)$$

We start from $x_1 = s_{11}{}^E X_1 + d_{31}E_z$, or $X_1 = x_1/s_{11}{}^E - (d_{31}/s_{11}{}^E)E_z$. This equation should be satisfied under $X_0(t)$ at $x = 0$ and L, and we obtain the following two equations:

$$\begin{cases} s_{11}^E X_0 = A\frac{\omega}{v_{11}^E} - \frac{k_{31}^2}{(1-k_{31}^2)}\frac{1}{L}2u(t,0) = A\frac{\omega}{v_{11}^E} - B\frac{k_{31}^2}{(1-k_{31}^2)}\frac{2}{L} \\ s_{11}^E X_0 = A\frac{\omega}{v_{11}^E}cos\left(\frac{\omega}{v_{11}^E}L\right) - B\frac{\omega}{v_{11}^E}sin\left(\frac{\omega}{v_{11}^E}x\right) + \frac{k_{31}^2}{(1-k_{31}^2)}\frac{2}{L}[Asin\left(\frac{\omega}{v_{11}^E}L\right) + Bcos\left(\frac{\omega}{v_{11}^E}L\right)] \end{cases}.$$

Thus,

$$\begin{cases} A = s_{11}^E X_0/[\frac{\omega}{v_{11}^E} + \frac{k_{31}^2}{(1-k_{31}^2)}\frac{2}{L}tan\left(\frac{\omega L}{2v_{11}^E}\right)] \\ B = -s_{11}^E X_0 tan\left(\frac{\omega L}{2v_{11}^E}\right)/[\frac{\omega}{v_{11}^E} + \frac{k_{31}^2}{(1-k_{31}^2)}\frac{2}{L}tan\left(\frac{\omega L}{2v_{11}^E}\right)] \end{cases}, \quad (7.108)$$

$$(\text{Displacement})\ u(x) = s_{11}^E X_0 \frac{\sin[\frac{\omega(2x-L)}{2v_{11}^E}]}{[\frac{\omega}{v_{11}^E}\cos\left(\frac{\omega L}{2v_{11}^E}\right) + \frac{k_{31}^2}{(1-k_{31}^2)}\frac{2}{L}\sin\left(\frac{\omega L}{2v_{11}^E}\right)]}, \quad (7.109)$$

$$(\text{Strain})\ x_1 = \frac{\partial u}{\partial x} = s_{11}^E X_0 \frac{(\frac{\omega}{v_{11}^E})\cos[\frac{\omega(2x-L)}{2v_{11}^E}]}{[\frac{\omega}{v_{11}^E}\cos\left(\frac{\omega L}{2v_{11}^E}\right) + \frac{k_{31}^2}{(1-k_{31}^2)}\frac{2}{L}\sin\left(\frac{\omega L}{2v_{11}^E}\right)]}. \quad (7.110)$$

The mechanical resonance—that is, the displacement or strain maximum (∞)—can be obtained when the denominator of Equations (7.109) and (7.110) $[\frac{\omega}{v_{11}^E}\cos\left(\frac{\omega L}{2v_{11}^E}\right) + \frac{k_{31}^2}{(1-k_{31}^2)}\frac{2}{L}\sin\left(\frac{\omega L}{2v_{11}^E}\right)]$ is equal to zero, which is obtained by the following equation:

$$(\omega_B L/2v_{11}^E)\cot(\omega_B L/2v_{11}^E) = -k_{31}{}^2/(1-k_{31}{}^2) = -d_{31}{}^2/\varepsilon_{33}{}^{LC}s_{11}{}^E, \quad (7.111)$$

where ω_B is the "antiresonance frequency". You are reminded that under the short-circuit condition the denominator of the displacement formula is $\cos\left(\frac{\omega L}{2v_{11}^E}\right)$, then the resonance condition $\left(\frac{\omega L}{2v_{11}^E}\right) = \frac{\pi}{2}$. Taking the first approximation on Equation (7.111) for a small k_{31}, we obtain

$$\begin{cases} f_A = v_{11}^E/2L \\ f_B = (v_{11}^E/2L)(1 + \frac{4}{\pi^2}k_{31}^2) \quad (\text{for small } k_{31}) \end{cases}. \quad (7.112)$$

Example Problem 7.4

In a piezo-ceramic k_{31} plate, as shown in Figure 7.5, the fundamental resonance frequency is given by $f_A = v_{11}^E/2L$, while the fundamental antiresonance frequency is approximated as $f_B = f_A(1 + \frac{4}{\pi^2}k_{31}^2)$. Derive this formula from the exact solution equation: $(\omega_B L/2v_{11}^E)\cot(\omega_B L/2v_{11}^E) = -k_{31}{}^2/(1 - k_{31}{}^2)$.

Solution

Introducing $\Delta\omega = (\omega_B - \omega_A)$, and knowing $\omega_A = \pi v_{11}^E/L$, the equation $(\omega_B L/2v_{11}^E)\cot(\omega_B L/2v_{11}^E) = -k_{31}{}^2/(1 - k_{31}{}^2)$ is transformed into

$$-\frac{k_{31}^2}{(1-k_{31}^2)} = \left(\frac{\pi}{2} + \frac{\Delta\omega L}{2v_{11}^E}\right)\frac{\cos\left(\frac{\pi}{2} + \frac{\Delta\omega L}{2v_{11}^E}\right)}{\sin\left(\frac{\pi}{2} + \frac{\Delta\omega L}{2v_{11}^E}\right)} = -\left(\frac{\pi}{2} + \frac{\Delta\omega L}{2v_{11}^E}\right)\tan\left(\frac{\Delta\omega L}{2v_{11}^E}\right). \quad \text{(P7.4.1)}$$

Supposing that $\left(\frac{\Delta\omega L}{2v_{11}^E}\right) = \Delta\omega/4f_A << 1$, we use the Taylor expansion to $\tan(x) = x + \frac{x^3}{3} + \frac{2x^5}{15} + \cdots$ into Equation (P7.4.1):

$$\left(\frac{\pi}{2} + \frac{\Delta\omega L}{2v_{11}^E}\right)\tan\left(\frac{\Delta\omega L}{2v_{11}^E}\right) = \left(\frac{\pi}{2} + \Delta\omega/4f_A\right)\left[(\Delta\omega/4f_A) + \frac{1}{3}\left(\frac{\Delta\omega}{4f_A}\right)^3 + \cdots\right] = \frac{k_{31}^2}{(1-k_{31}^2)}. \quad \text{(P7.4.2)}$$

Then,

$$\frac{\pi}{2}\left(\frac{\Delta\omega}{4f_A}\right) = \frac{k_{31}^2}{(1-k_{31}^2)}. \quad \text{(P7.4.3)}$$

Finally, we obtain the following relation for the case $k_{31}^2 << 1$:

$$f_B = f_A + \Delta\omega/2\pi = f_A(1 + \frac{4}{\pi^2}k_{31}^2). \quad \text{(P7.4.4)}$$

Solution under Z-Shunt Condition

An external electrical impedance Z is connected to a piezoelectric k_{31} plate (Figure 7.5). We start from the constitutive equations: $x_1 = s_{11}{}^E X_1 + d_{31}E_z$, and $D_3 = d_{31}X_1 + \varepsilon_0\varepsilon_{33}{}^X E_z$. When we assume sinusoidal input force $F(t) = -bwX_1(t)$, and stress $X_1(t) = X_0 e^{j\omega t}$ at both ends of the piezo-plate symmetrically, we can also assume the displacement $u(x)e^{j\omega t}$ and strain $x_1(x)e^{j\omega t}$ as:

$$u(x) = A\sin\left(\frac{\omega}{v_{11}^E}x\right) + B\cos\left(\frac{\omega}{v_{11}^E}x\right), \quad \text{(7.113)}$$

$$x_1(x) = \frac{\partial u}{\partial x} = A\frac{\omega}{v_{11}^E}\cos\left(\frac{\omega}{v_{11}^E}x\right) - B\frac{\omega}{v_{11}^E}\sin\left(\frac{\omega}{v_{11}^E}x\right). \quad \text{(7.114)}$$

Knowing $E_z(t)$ = constant in terms of the coordinate x, owing to the surface electrode, at $x = 0$ and L, $X_1 = x_1/s_{11}{}^E - (d_{31}/s_{11}{}^E)E_z = X_0$:

$$\begin{cases} s_{11}^E X_0 = A\frac{\omega}{v_{11}^E} - d_{31}E_z \\ s_{11}^E X_0 = A\frac{\omega}{v_{11}^E}cos\left(\frac{\omega}{v_{11}^E}L\right) - B\frac{\omega}{v_{11}^E}sin\left(\frac{\omega}{v_{11}^E}L\right) - d_{31}E_z \end{cases}. \tag{7.115}$$

The output electric charge Q (i.e., no loss, no time lag) can be described as:

$$Q = w\int_0^L D_3 dx = w\int_0^L [d_{31}X_1 + \varepsilon_0\varepsilon_{33}^X E_z]dx. \tag{7.116}$$

While, from $X_1 = x_1/s_{11}{}^E - (d_{31}/s_{11}{}^E)E_z$, we obtain

$$\int_0^L X_1 dx = \frac{1}{s_{11}^E}\int_0^L (x_1 - d_{31}E_z)dx. \tag{7.117}$$

Knowing that $\int_0^L x_1 dx = 2u(L)$ and E_z = constant, we obtain

$$\begin{aligned} I = \dot{Q} &= \left\{\left(\frac{2wd_{31}}{s_{11}^E}\right)\dot{u}(L) + \varepsilon_0\varepsilon_{33}^X(1-k_{31}^2)\dot{E}_z wL\right\} \\ &= j\omega\left(\frac{2wd_{31}}{s_{11}^E}\right)u(L) + j\omega\varepsilon_0\varepsilon_{33}^X(1-k_{31}^2)E_z wL. \end{aligned} \tag{7.118}$$

Using $V = bE_z = Z{\cdot}I$ and $C_d = \varepsilon_0\varepsilon_{33}^X(1-k_{31}^2)wL/b$, Equation (7.118) leads to the following relations:

$$j\omega\left(\frac{2wd_{31}}{s_{11}^E}\right)\left[A\sin\left(\frac{\omega}{v_{11}^E}L\right) + B\cos\left(\frac{\omega}{v_{11}^E}L\right)\right] + j\omega C_d E_z b - \frac{b}{Z}E_z = 0. \tag{7.119}$$

From Equations (7.115) and (7.119) we can derive A, B and E_z as follows:

$$\begin{pmatrix} \frac{\omega}{v_{11}^E} & 0 & -d_{31} \\ \frac{\omega}{v_{11}^E}cs & -\frac{\omega}{v_{11}^E}sn & -d_{31} \\ j\omega\left(\frac{2wd_{31}}{s_{11}^E}\right)sn & j\omega\left(\frac{2wd_{31}}{s_{11}^E}\right)cs & b\left(j\omega C_d - \frac{1}{Z}\right) \end{pmatrix}\begin{pmatrix} A \\ B \\ E_z \end{pmatrix} = \begin{pmatrix} s_{11}^E X_0 \\ s_{11}^E X_0 \\ 0 \end{pmatrix}, \tag{7.120}$$

where the symbols $sn = \sin\left(\frac{\omega}{v_{11}^E}L\right)$ and $cs = \cos\left(\frac{\omega}{v_{11}^E}L\right)$. Thus

$$\begin{cases} A = \dfrac{s_{11}^E X_0 b(j\omega C_d - \frac{1}{Z})\cos\left(\frac{\omega L}{2v_{11}^E}\right)}{\triangle} \\ B = -\dfrac{s_{11}^E X_0 b(j\omega C_d - \frac{1}{Z})\sin\left(\frac{\omega L}{2v_{11}^E}\right)}{\triangle} \\ E_z = -\dfrac{s_{11}^E X_0 (j\omega\frac{2wd_{31}}{s_{11}^E})\sin\left(\frac{\omega L}{2v_{11}^E}\right)}{\triangle} \\ \triangle = \left(\frac{\omega}{v_{11}^E}\right)b\left(j\omega C_d - \frac{1}{Z}\right)cos\left(\frac{\omega L}{2v_{11}^E}\right) + d_{31}j\omega\left(\frac{2wd_{31}}{s_{11}^E}\right)sin\left(\frac{\omega L}{2v_{11}^E}\right) \end{cases}. \tag{7.121}$$

The denominator $\triangle = 0$ gives the resonance condition for the stress operation. When $Z \approx 0$, a major contribution comes from the first term. Thus, $\cos\left(\frac{\omega L}{2v_{11}^E}\right) = 0$ corresponds to the piezo resonance condition. While $Z \to \infty$, the last equation is transformed to

$$\left(1-k_{31}^2\right)\left(\frac{\omega L}{2v_{11}^E}\right)\cos\left(\frac{\omega L}{2v_{11}^E}\right) + k_{31}^2 \sin\left(\frac{\omega L}{2v_{11}^E}\right) = 0, \text{ or } \left(\frac{\omega L}{2v_{11}^E}\right)\cot\left(\frac{\omega L}{2v_{11}^E}\right) = -\frac{k_{31}^2}{\left(1-k_{31}^2\right)}, \quad (7.122)$$

which is a familiar formula for calculating the antiresonance frequency.

Now, by connecting $Z = 1/\omega C_d$ (the supposed electrical matching resistive impedance), we consider the minimization of the magnitude of $\triangle$ for obtaining the resonance condition.

$$\begin{aligned}\triangle = j\omega 2w\varepsilon_0\varepsilon_{33}^X[(1-k_{31}^2)\left(\frac{\omega L}{2v_{11}^E}\right)\cos\left(\frac{\omega L}{2v_{11}^E}\right) + k_{31}^2\sin\left(\frac{\omega L}{2v_{11}^E}\right) \\ +j(1-k_{31}^2)\left(\frac{\omega L}{2v_{11}^E}\right)\cos\left(\frac{\omega L}{2v_{11}^E}\right)].\end{aligned} \quad (7.123)$$

- For a small ω (much lower than the resonance frequency),

$$\begin{aligned}\triangle = j\omega 2w\varepsilon_0\varepsilon_{33}^X[(1-k_{31}^2)\left(\frac{\omega L}{2v_{11}^E}\right) + k_{31}^2\left(\frac{\omega L}{2v_{11}^E}\right) + j(1-k_{31}^2)\left(\frac{\omega L}{2v_{11}^E}\right)] \\ = j\omega 2w\varepsilon_0\varepsilon_{33}^X\left(\frac{\omega L}{2v_{11}^E}\right)[1+j(1-k_{31}^2)].\end{aligned} \quad (7.124)$$

  The apparent dissipation factor $\tan\varphi = (1-k_{31}^2)$ is quite high under $Z = 1/\ \omega C_d$ resistive shunt case.

- For a frequency around the resonance frequency ($\frac{\omega_R L}{2v_{11}^E} = \frac{\pi}{2}, \Delta\omega = \omega - \omega_R$), taking $\frac{\omega L}{2v_{11}^E} = \left(\frac{\pi}{2} + \frac{\Delta\omega L}{2v_{11}^E}\right)$, $\cos\left(\frac{\omega L}{2v_{11}^E}\right) = -\sin\left(\frac{\Delta\omega L}{2v_{11}^E}\right)$, and $\sin\left(\frac{\omega L}{2v_{11}^E}\right) = \cos\left(\frac{\Delta\omega L}{2v_{11}^E}\right)$ into account

$$\begin{aligned}\triangle = j(\omega_R + \Delta\omega)2w\varepsilon_0\varepsilon_{33}^X[-(1-k_{31}^2)\left(\frac{\pi}{2} + \frac{\Delta\omega L}{2v_{11}^E}\right)\sin\left(\frac{\Delta\omega L}{2v_{11}^E}\right) \\ +k_{31}^2\cos\left(\frac{\Delta\omega L}{2v_{11}^E}\right) - j(1-k_{31}^2)\left(\frac{\pi}{2} + \frac{\Delta\omega L}{2v_{11}^E}\right)\sin\left(\frac{\Delta\omega L}{2v_{11}^E}\right)] \\ \approx j\omega_R 2w\varepsilon_0\varepsilon_{33}^X[-(1-k_{31}^2)\left(\frac{\pi}{2}\right)\left(\frac{\Delta\omega L}{2v_{11}^E}\right) + k_{31}^2 - j(1-k_{31}^2)\left(\frac{\pi}{2}\right)\left(\frac{\Delta\omega L}{2v_{11}^E}\right)].\end{aligned} \quad (7.125)$$

The external impedance Z connection is equivalent to the loss tangent increase, and

$$\begin{aligned}\tan\varphi = (1-k_{31}^2)\left(\frac{\omega L}{2v_{11}^E}\right)\cos\left(\frac{\omega L}{2v_{11}^E}\right)/[(1-k_{31}^2)\left(\frac{\omega L}{2v_{11}^E}\right)\cos\left(\frac{\omega L}{2v_{11}^E}\right) + k_{31}^2\sin\left(\frac{\omega L}{2v_{11}^E}\right)] \\ \approx -(1-k_{31}^2)\left(\frac{\pi}{2}\right)\left(\frac{\Delta\omega L}{2v_{11}^E}\right)/[-(1-k_{31}^2)\left(\frac{\pi}{2}\right)\left(\frac{\Delta\omega L}{2v_{11}^E}\right) + k_{31}^2] \\ \approx -\frac{(1-k_{31}^2)}{k_{31}^2}\left(\frac{\pi}{2}\right)\left(\frac{\Delta\omega L}{2v_{11}^E}\right).\end{aligned} \quad (7.126)$$

It is very interesting that the resistive shunt contributes largely to the dissipation, but its contribution is small around the mechanical resonance frequency range, mainly due to significant enhancement of the real elastic compliance s_{11}^E at the resonance by a factor of Q_m.

The displacement $u(x)$ and strain $x_1(x)$ are summarized here:

$$\begin{cases} u(x) = \dfrac{s_{11}^E X_0 b\omega C_d (j-1)\cos\left(\frac{\omega L}{2v_{11}^E}\right)}{\Delta} sin\left(\frac{\omega}{v_{11}^E}x\right) + \dfrac{s_{11}^E X_0 b\omega C_d (j-1)\sin\left(\frac{\omega L}{2v_{11}^E}\right)}{\Delta} cos\left(\frac{\omega}{v_{11}^E}x\right) \\ x_1(x) = \dfrac{s_{11}^E X_0 b\omega C_d (j-1)\cos\left(\frac{\omega L}{2v_{11}^E}\right)}{\Delta} \frac{\omega}{v_{11}^E} cos\left(\frac{\omega}{v_{11}^E}x\right) - \dfrac{s_{11}^E X_0 b\omega C_d (j-1)\sin\left(\frac{\omega L}{2v_{11}^E}\right)}{\Delta} \frac{\omega}{v_{11}^E} sin\left(\frac{\omega}{v_{11}^E}x\right) \end{cases}. \quad (7.127)$$

The energy spent in the resistive shunt $Z = 1/\ \omega C_d$ can be calculated from Equation (7.121) as

$$P_{out}| = Re\left[\frac{1}{2}\frac{VV^*}{Z}\right] = Re\left[\frac{b^2}{2Z}\left[\frac{s_{11}^E X_0\left(j\omega\frac{2wd_{31}}{s_{11}^E}\right)\sin\left(\frac{\omega L}{2v_{11}^E}\right)}{\left(\frac{\omega}{v_{11}^E}\right)b\left(j\omega C_d - \frac{1}{Z}\right)\cos\left(\frac{\omega L}{2v_{11}^E}\right) + d_{31}j\omega\left(\frac{2wd_{31}}{s_{11}^E}\right)\sin\left(\frac{\omega L}{2v_{11}^E}\right)}\right]^2\right]. \quad (7.128)$$

If we consider a small ω (much lower than the resonance frequency),

$$\begin{aligned} |P_{out}| &= \tfrac{b^2}{2}\omega\tfrac{Lw}{b}\varepsilon_0\varepsilon_{33}^X(1-k_{31}^2)Re\left[\frac{s_{11}^E X_0(j\omega\frac{2wd_{31}}{s_{11}^E})}{(\frac{2}{L})b\omega\frac{Lw}{b}\varepsilon_0\varepsilon_{33}^X(1-k_{31}^2)(j-1)+d_{31}j\omega\left(\frac{2wd_{31}}{s_{11}^E}\right)}\right]^2 \\ &= \tfrac{1}{2}\omega(Lwb)\varepsilon_0\varepsilon_{33}^X(1-k_{31}^2)Re\left[\frac{d_{31}X_0(j\omega 2w)}{\omega 2w\varepsilon_0\varepsilon_{33}^X(1-k_{31}^2)(j-1)+j\omega 2w\varepsilon_0\varepsilon_{33}^X\left(\frac{d_{31}{}^2}{\varepsilon_0\varepsilon_{33}^X s_{11}^E}\right)}\right]^2 \\ &= \tfrac{1}{2}\omega(Lwb)Re\left[\frac{(d_{31}X_0)^2(1-k_{31}^2)}{\varepsilon_0\varepsilon_{33}^X[-(1-k_{31}^2)+j]}\right] = \tfrac{1}{2}\omega(Lwb)\frac{(d_{31}X_0)^2}{\varepsilon_0\varepsilon_{33}^X}\frac{1}{(1-k_{31}^2)+\frac{1}{(1-k_{31}^2)}}. \end{aligned} \quad (7.129)$$

Equation (7.129) can be understood as follows: because $d_{31}X_0 = P_3$, and $\frac{1}{2}\frac{(d_{31}X_0)^2}{\varepsilon_0\varepsilon_{33}^X}$ corresponds to the electric energy per cycle per unit volume converted via the piezoelectric effect, the total power $|P_{out}|$ can be obtained by multiplying the volume (Lwb) and frequency ω. The last additional calibration factor by the electromechanical coupling factor, $\frac{1}{(1-k_{31}^2)+\frac{1}{(1-k_{31}^2)}} = \frac{1}{2+\frac{k_{31}^4}{(1-k_{31}^2)}}$, is intriguing. When k_{31}^2 is not large ($k_{31} < 30\%$), $|P_{out}|$ becomes roughly 1/2 of the converted energy via the "resistive Z" which matches the piezoelectric damped capacitance.

Example Problem 7.5

We consider the piezoelectric energy harvesting from a k_{33} type rod (unit area) sample under a small cyclic stress $X = X_0 e^{j\omega t}$. See Figure 7.17. In order to obtain the maximum output electric power, determine the external load impedance Z. Answer the derivation process step by step as follows. First "Constitutive Equations" are provided as:

$$x_s = s_{33}{}^E X_3 + d_{33}E_z, \quad (P7.5.1)$$

$$D_3 = d_{33}X_3 + \varepsilon_0\varepsilon_{33}{}^X E_z. \quad \text{(P7.5.2)}$$

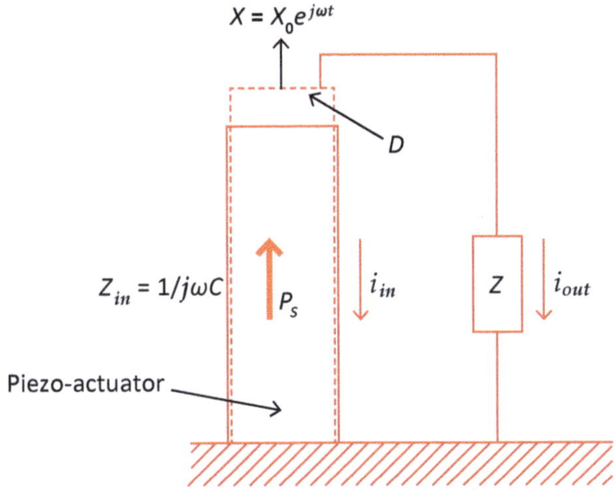

Figure 7.17. Piezoelectric energy harvesting model. Source: [1] ©Uchino, K. *Micromechatronics*, 2nd ed.; CRC Press, 2019; p. 395. Reproduced by permission of Taylor & Francis Group.

(1) When we consider the output electric energy, we consider the electric displacement D vs. electric field E domain as shown in the bottom figure. Calculate the depolarization field for the open circuit ($Z = \infty$): $D = 0$. In this condition, provide the elastic compliance s_{33}^D.
(2) Calculate the electric displacement D for the short circuit ($Z = 0$): $E = 0$, using the piezoelectric constant d_{33}. In this condition, provide the elastic compliance s_{33}^E.
(3) Draw the D vs. E map under a certain load impedance Z. Then calculate the output power under the external load Z, and obtain the maximum power condition; that is, the matching impedance Z.
(4) Calculate the input mechanical power under the load of the matching impedance Z, then calculate the energy transmission coefficient λ defined by

$$\lambda_{max} = \left(\frac{\text{Output electrical energy}}{\text{Input mechanical energy}}\right)_{max}. \quad \text{(P7.5.3)}$$

Solution

(1) Under the open-circuit condition, $D = 0$, leading to

$$E = -\frac{d}{\varepsilon_0\varepsilon^X}X, \quad \text{(P7.5.4)}$$

as depolarization field from Equation (P7.5.2). Inserting this depolarization field to Equation (7.5.1), we obtain $x = s^E X + d\left(-\frac{d}{\varepsilon_0 \varepsilon^X} X\right) = s^E(1 - \frac{d^2}{s^E \varepsilon_0 \varepsilon^X})X$ Thus, we obtain

$$s^D = (1 - \frac{d^2}{s^E \varepsilon_0 \varepsilon^X}) = s^E(1 - k^2). \tag{P7.5.5}$$

(2) Under short-circuit condition, $E = 0$ (this is true for k_{31} mode, but partially true for k_{33} mode only for low-frequency operation). From Equation (P7.5.2) we obtain

$$D = dX. \tag{P7.5.6}$$

Under this condition, it is obvious that the elastic compliance is s^E from Equation (P7.5.1).

(3) Figure 7.18c shows the $D-E$ map to calculate the output electrical energy. The intersect with the vertical line (E) should be $(-\frac{d}{\varepsilon_0 \varepsilon^X} X)$ and the intersect with the horizontal line (D) should be (dX). Under the shunt condition with Z, the tracing line with changing Z should be on the straight line connecting these intersects. At which point can we obtain the maximum output energy; that is, the maximum rectangular area hatched on the figure? From simple mathematical intuition, obviously this point should be a half of the vertical and horizontal intersects, which leads to the area

$$U = \frac{1}{2} \frac{d}{\varepsilon_0 \varepsilon^X} X \cdot \frac{1}{2} dX = \frac{1}{4} \frac{d^2}{\varepsilon_0 \varepsilon^X} X^2. \tag{P7.5.7}$$

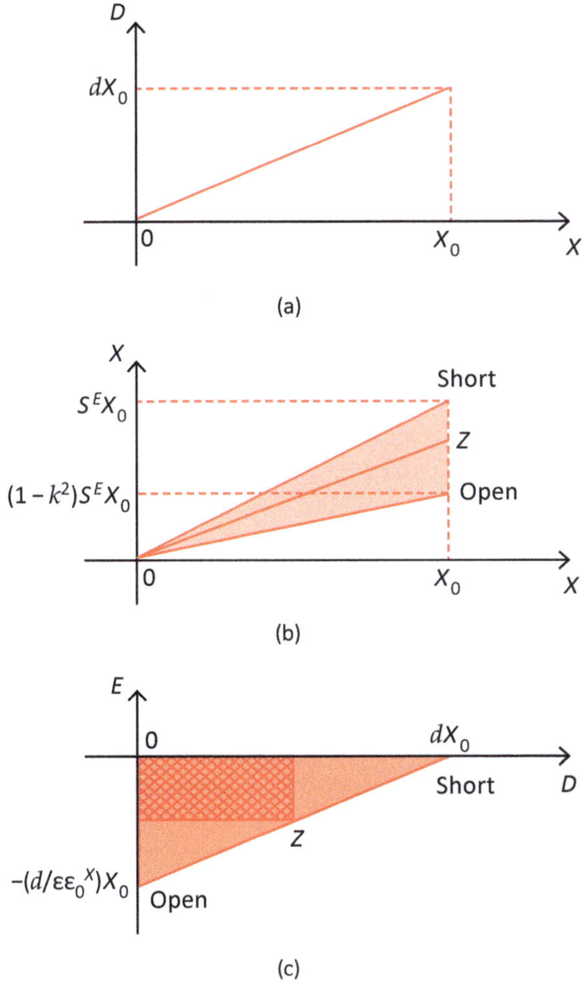

Figure 7.18. Calculation models of the input mechanical and output electric energy. (**a**) Stress vs. electric displacement; (**b**) stress vs. strain; (**c**) electric displacement vs. field. Source: [1] ©Uchino, K. *Micromechatronics*, 2nd ed.; CRC Press, 2019; p. 396. Reproduced by permission of Taylor & Francis Group.

More precisely, under an impedance Z shunt condition, we can expect a point (E, D) on the line between the intersects of the above $D_0 = dX_0$ and $E_0 = -\frac{d}{\varepsilon_0\varepsilon^X}X_0$:

$$E = \frac{1}{\varepsilon_0\varepsilon}(D - dX_0). \qquad \text{(P7.5.8)}$$

The output electrical energy can be calculated as

$$U = -DE = -\frac{D}{\varepsilon_0\varepsilon}(D - dX_0) = -\frac{1}{\varepsilon_0\varepsilon}\left(D - \frac{1}{2}dX_0\right)^2 + \frac{1}{4}\frac{(dX_0)^2}{\varepsilon_0\varepsilon}. \qquad \text{(P7.5.9)}$$

which is exactly the same result as Equation (P7.5.7). When the "ambient vibration energy is unlimited", the above maximum output energy condition is the final targeted status. Using Figure 7.17, let us calculate the output electric energy. Sinusoidal input stress $X = X_0 e^{j\omega t}$ generates output electric displacement $D = dX_0 e^{j\omega t}$ via direct piezoelectric effect (d constant). We can understand that the piezo power supply has the internal impedance $1/j\omega C$ under an off-resonance frequency (by neglecting the dielectric loss or effective conducting loss $\sigma = 0$), and this piezoelectric "current supply" generates the total current

$$i = \frac{\partial D}{\partial t} = j\omega d X_0. \quad \text{(P7.5.10)}$$

This current is split into internal "displacement current" i_{in} and external current i_{out},

$$i = i_{in} + i_{out}. \quad \text{(P7.5.11)}$$

Then, because of the potential/voltage should be the same on the top electrode of the piezo component, we get

$$Z_{in} i_{in} = Z i_{out}. \quad \text{(P7.5.12)}$$

Inserting the relation $i_{in} = \left(\frac{Z}{Z_{in}}\right) i_{out} = j\omega CZ \cdot i_{out}$ into Equation (P7.5.11),

$$i_{out}(1 + j\omega CZ) = j\omega d X_0. \quad \text{(P7.5.13)}$$

Thus, we can obtain the output electric energy as

$$|P| = Re[\frac{1}{2}|Z i_{out} \cdot i_{out}{}^*|] = \frac{1}{2} Z \frac{(\omega d X_0)^2}{(1 + (\omega CZ)^2)}. \quad \text{(P7.5.14)}$$

Figure 7.19 shows the electric load (resistive) dependence of the output electric energy, which concludes that the maximum electric energy

$$|P| = \frac{1}{4} \frac{\omega d^2 X_0^2}{C}, \quad \text{(P7.5.15)}$$

can be obtained at $Z = 1/\omega C$, when we consider Z resistive, which is the situation for charging a rechargeable battery. In other words, the generated electric energy in a piezo component can be spent maximally when the external load resistive impedance exactly matches the internal impedance (absolute value). Note the internal impedance is capacitive with phase lag of $-j$ $(-90°)$. Note that Equation (P7.5.15) is equivalent to Equation (P7.5.7), taking into account the difference in the specimen size/volume and one cycle and per unit time (second).

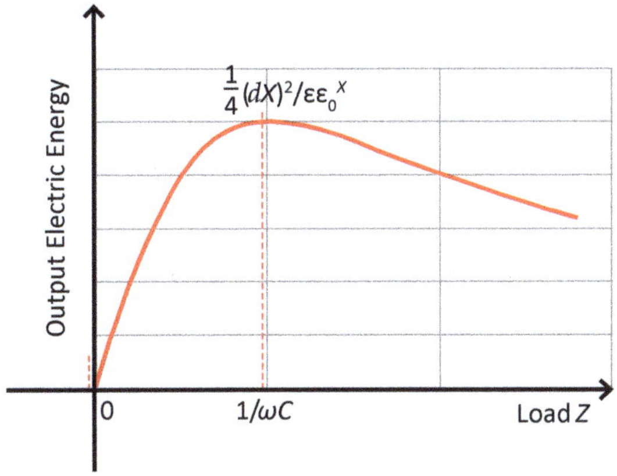

Figure 7.19. Output electric energy vs. external electrical load Z. Source: [1] ©Uchino, K. *Micromechatronics*, 2nd ed.; CRC Press, 2019; p. 396. Reproduced by permission of Taylor & Francis Group.

The reader is also reminded of the discussion in Subsection Solution under Z-Shunt Condition, calculated from the piezoelectric constitutive equations for the k_{31} mode. The difference in the above Equation (P7.5.15) from Equation (7.129) can be found in the following calibration factor $\frac{1}{(1-k_{31}^2)+\frac{1}{(1-k_{31}^2)}}$, originating from the difference between "constant capacitance" here and "stress dependent mechanical constraint" (such as ε_{33}^X or $\varepsilon_{33}^{x_1}$). Thus, precisely speaking, the above conclusion should be modified as follows:

(a) Matching impedance is to be replaced by the "damped capancitance" C_d from just capacitance C,

(b) The calibration factor $\frac{1}{(1-k_{31}^2)+\frac{1}{(1-k_{31}^2)}}$ is more precise, rather than $1/2$ in $|P| = \frac{1}{2}\frac{\omega d^2 X_0^2}{C}\frac{1}{(1-k_{31}^2)+\frac{1}{(1-k_{31}^2)}}$.

We consider further two additional impedances matching: $Z = \left(\frac{1}{j\omega C}\right)^*$ and $Z = \left(\frac{1}{j\omega C}\right)$. When we consider Z "complex", $Z = Z_{in}{}^* = \left(\frac{1}{j\omega C}\right)^* = j\omega\left(\frac{1}{\omega^2 C}\right)$ provides the original electrical impedance matching. This condition corresponds to LC series connection (i.e., $(\frac{1}{j\omega C})$ and $j\omega L$), where $L = 1/\omega^2 C$ is satisfied, leading to the LC resonance frequency exactly equal to the stress application frequency ω. The energy generated by a piezo component will be exchanged between the internal capacitance and external inductance, like a "catch-ball", without losing energy nor providing work externally. The effective elastic compliance s_{eff}^E approaches infinity. To the contrary, when we consider $Z = \left(\frac{1}{j\omega C}\right)$, the same capacitance as the internal one is connected to the external load, since converted energy is split to two equal capacitances, $s_{eff}^E = s^E(1 - \frac{1}{2}k^2)$, in between the short- and open-circuit conditions. In order to take the energy out into a rechargeable battery, it is essential to connect the resistive load.

(4) Energy Transmission Coefficient (Section 10.5.2 describes a more detailed derivation process). Since we need to use or accummulate energy externally, we consider "resistive shunt". Let us reconsider the power expendable on the external electrical load Z from the "energy transmission coefficient" viewpoint. Figure 7.18 summarizes the calculation processes of the input mechanical and output electric energy under various impedance Zs: (a) the stress vs. electric displacement relation; the area on this domain does not mean the energy, thus, we need to translate this plot into (b) stress vs. strain relation to calculate the input mechanical energy, and (c) electric displacement vs. electric field to calculate the output electric energy. No electrically converted energy can actually be spent under the short-circuit (zero impedance) or open-circuit (infinite impedance) condition in the energy harvesting case. The "energy transmission coefficient" is defined by

$$\lambda_{max} = (\text{Output electrical energy}/\text{Input mechanical energy})_{max}. \quad \text{(P7.5.16)}$$

The output electric energy has been calculated above as $|P| = \frac{1}{2}Z\frac{(\omega d X_0)^2}{(1+(\omega CZ)^2)}$. Now, we will calculate the input mechanical energy. You should notice that the input mechanical energy also differs significantly depending on the external electrical load Z. If you recall that the tunable elasticity according to the electric constraint is s^E (short circuit) or s^D(open circuit), and further $s^D = s^E(1-k^2)$ in particular, you can understand that the input mechanical energy (e.g., triangular area made by OX_0x_0 for a short-circuit condition) differs largely depending on the electrical load Z, as illustrated in Figure 7.18b (the slope; elastic compliance changes according to Z). Now, second, let us calculate the load-Z dependence of the input mechanical energy. We now calculate the "input mechanical energy" from the second constitutive equation in Equation (P7.5.1):

$$x = dE + s^E X = -d\left(\frac{V}{t}\right) + s^E X = -\left(\frac{d}{t}\right)\left[\frac{j\omega d X_0}{\frac{1}{Z} + j\omega C}\right] + s^E X. \quad \text{(P7.5.17)}$$

The last transformation used Equation (P7.5.13). We obtained effective elastic compliance as

$$s^E_{eff} = \frac{x}{X} = s^E\left[1 - \left(\frac{S}{t}\right)\frac{j\omega Z d^2}{s^E(1+j\omega CZ)}\right]. \quad \text{(P7.5.18)}$$

You can verify the above "effective elastic compliance" is equal to ${s_{11}}^E$ or $s^D = s^E(1-k^2)$ (no electrode on the surface ideally), when Z = 0 or ∞, respectively. Meanwhile, under $Z = 1/\omega C$,

$$s^E_{eff} = s^E\left(1 - \frac{1}{2}k^2 + \frac{j}{2}k^2\right). \quad \text{(P7.5.19)}$$

The resonance frequency f under the Z-shunt condition may be estimated as

$$f = \frac{1}{2L\sqrt{\rho s_{eff}^{E}}} = f_R\left(1 + \frac{1}{4}k^2\right), \quad \text{(P7.5.20)}$$

which is higher than the short-circuit f_A, but lower than the open-circuit condition $f_A(1 + \frac{4}{\pi^2}k_{31}^2)$. The input mechanical power under the Z-shunt condition is derived as

$$|P|_{in} = \frac{\omega}{2}s_{eff}^{E}X_0{}^2 = \frac{\omega}{2}\left|s^E[1 - \left(\frac{S}{t}\right)\frac{j\omega Zd^2}{s^E(1 + j\omega CZ)}]X_0{}^2\right|. \quad \text{(P7.5.21)}$$

The "energy transmission coefficient" λ_{max} can be calculated from

$$\lambda = \frac{|P|_{out}}{|P|_{in}} = \frac{1}{2}Z\frac{(\omega dX_0)^2}{(1 + (\omega CZ)^2)} / \frac{\omega}{2}\left|s^E[1 - \left(\frac{S}{t}\right)\frac{j\omega Zd^2}{s^E(1 + j\omega CZ)}]X_0{}^2\right|. \quad \text{(P7.5.22)}$$

Taking the maximization process in terms of Z, we can obtain the energy transmission coefficient as

$$\lambda_{max} = [(1/k) - \sqrt{(1/k^2) - 1}]^2 = [(1/k) + \sqrt{(1/k^2) - 1}]^{-2}. \quad \text{(P7.5.23)}$$

We need to be aware that since the input mechanical energy is changed (even if we keep the stress/force constant) due to the elastic compliance change with the external electrical impedance, the condition for realizing the "maximum transmission coefficient" is slightly off from the electrical impedance matching point for the output energy maximum. When we take the matched electrical impedance $Z = 1/\omega C$, we obtain

$$\lambda = \frac{k^2}{2}\frac{1}{(2 - k^2)}, \quad \text{(P7.5.24)}$$

which is slightly amaller than λ_{max} of Equation (P7.5.23). We can also notice that

$$k^2/4 < \lambda_{max} < k^2/2,$$

depending on the k value ($k < 0.95$).

Chapter Essentials

1. Mechanical fundamental resonance frequency of a length L rod with sound velocity v: $f = v/2L$. Knowing $v = f\cdot\lambda$, we obtain $\lambda = 2L$, or the mode is exact a half-wavelength standing wave on the rod.
2. Steady AC Drive methods of a piezoelectric component:
   - Mechanical Drive
     - Short-circuit condition with surface electrodes (E-constant) $\rightarrow$ Resonance mode

- Open-circuit condition with surface electrodes (partially (1D) D-constant) $\rightarrow$ Antiresonance mode
- No surface electrodes (D-constant)

- Electrical Drive
  - Admittance peak $\rightarrow$ Resonance mode (Resistive characteristic)
  - Impedance peak $\rightarrow$ Antiresonance mode (Resistive characteristic)
  - Intermediate frequency between Res and AntiRes $\rightarrow$ Max efficiency (Inductive)
  - Off-resonance (low frequency) $\rightarrow$ (Capacitive characteristic)

3. Electric Excitation k_{31} Mode: Vibration direction perpendicular to P_S

(a) Strain $x_1 = d_{31}E_z\,(\frac{\cos[\frac{\omega(2x-L)}{2v}]}{\cos(\frac{\omega L}{2v})})$,

Displacement $u(x) = d_{31}E_z(\frac{v}{\omega})\frac{\sin[\frac{\omega(2x-L)}{2v}]}{\cos(\frac{\omega L}{2v})}$,

(b) Admittance $Y = j\omega C_d[1+\frac{k_{31}^2}{1-k_{31}^2}\frac{\tan(\Omega_{11})}{\Omega_{11}}]$ $[\Omega_{11} = (\omega L/2v_{11}^E)]$,

(c) Resonance/Antiresonance Frequencies

Resonance: $\omega_A = \pi v_{11}{}^E/L = \pi/(L\sqrt{\rho s_{11}{}^E})$,

Antiresonance: $(\omega_B L/2v_{11}{}^E)\cot(\omega_B L/2v_{11}{}^E) = -k_{31}{}^2/(1-k_{31}{}^2)$,

$k_{31} = d_{31}/\sqrt{s_{11}{}^E\cdot\varepsilon_{33}{}^X\varepsilon_0}$.

(d) Loss Factors

$$Q_{A,31} = \frac{1}{\tan\phi_{11}{}'}$$

$$\frac{1}{Q_{B,31}} = \frac{1}{Q_{A,31}} - \frac{2}{1+(\frac{1}{k_{31}}-k_{31})^2\Omega_{B,31}{}^2}\left(2\tan'\theta_{31} - \tan'\delta_{33} - \tan'\phi_{11}\right),$$

$$\Omega_{A,31} = \frac{\omega_a l}{2v_{11}^E} = \frac{\pi}{2}\quad\left[v_{11}^E = 1/\sqrt{\rho s_{11}^E}\right],$$

$$\Omega_{B,31} = \frac{\omega_b l}{2v_{11}^E},\quad 1-k_{31}{}^2+k_{31}{}^2\frac{\tan\Omega_B}{\Omega_B} = 0.$$

4. Electric Excitation k_{33} Mode: Vibration direction parallel to P_S

(a) Strain $x_3 = \frac{d_{33}}{\varepsilon_0\varepsilon_{33}^X}D_3[\cos\left(\frac{\omega}{2v_{33}^D}(2z-L)\right)/\cos\left(\frac{\omega L}{2v_{33}^D}\right)]$,

Displacement $u_3 = \frac{d_{33}}{\varepsilon_0\varepsilon_{33}^X}\frac{v_{33}^D}{\omega}D_3[\sin\left(\frac{\omega}{2v_{33}^D}(2z-L)\right)/\cos\left(\frac{\omega L}{2v_{33}^D}\right)]$,

(b) Admittance $Y = \frac{i}{-V} = \frac{j\omega\varepsilon_0\varepsilon_{33}^{LC}(\frac{wb}{L})}{\left[1-k_{33}^2\left\{\frac{\tan\left(\frac{\omega L}{2v_{33}^D}\right)}{\left(\frac{\omega L}{2v_{33}^D}\right)}\right\}\right]} = j\omega C_d + \frac{j\omega C_d}{[-1+1/k_{33}^2\{\frac{\tan(\Omega_{33})}{(\Omega_{33})}\}]}$

$[\Omega_{33} = (\omega L/2v_{33}^D)]$,

(c) Resonance/Antiresonance Frequencies

Resonance: $\left(\frac{\omega_A L}{2v_{33}^D}\right) = k_{33}^2\tan(\frac{\omega_A L}{2v_{33}^D})$

Antiresonance: $\frac{\omega_B L}{2v_{33}^D} = \frac{\pi}{2}$

$k_{33} = d_{33}/\sqrt{s_{33}{}^E\cdot\varepsilon_{33}{}^X\varepsilon_0}$

(d) Loss Factors

$$Q_{B,33} = \frac{1}{\tan\phi'''_{33}} = \frac{1-k_{33}{}^2}{\tan'\phi_{33}-k_{33}{}^2(2\tan\theta_{33}'-\tan\delta_{33}')},$$
$$\frac{1}{Q_{A,33}} = \frac{1}{Q_{B,33}} + \frac{2}{k_{33}{}^2-1+\Omega_A{}^2/k_{33}{}^2}(2\tan\theta_{33}' - \tan\delta_{33}' - \tan\phi_{33}'),$$
$$\Omega_{B,33} = \frac{\omega_b l}{2v_{33}^D} = \frac{\pi}{2} \quad \left[v_{33}^D = 1/\sqrt{\rho s_{33}^D}\right],$$
$$\Omega_{A,33} = \frac{\omega_a l}{2v_{33}^D}, \quad \Omega_{A,33} = k_{33}{}^2\tan\Omega_{A,33}.$$

5. Admittance/Impedance Spectrum Measurement:
   - Constant voltage method—suitable for antiresonance range
   - Constant current method—suitable for resonance range
   - Constant vibration velocity method—suitable for all resonance and antiresonance ranges.
6. Mechanical Quality Factor Determination:
   - "3 dB down/up method" on the admittance/impedance spectrum
   - "Quadrantal frequency method" on the admittance (resonance) and impedance circles (antiresonance)
7. Loss Determination Process from the Admittance Spectrum – k_{31} Case
   (1) Obtain tanδ' from an impedance analyzer or a capacitance meter at a frequency away (lower range) from the resonance/antiresonance range;
   (2) Obtain the following parameters experimentally from an admittance/impedance spectrum around the resonance (A-type) and antiresonance (B-type) range (3 dB bandwidth method): ω_a, ω_b, Q_A, Q_B, and the normalized frequency $\Omega_b = \omega_b l/2v$;
   (3) Obtain tanϕ' from the inverse value of Q_A (quality factor at the resonance) in the k_{31} mode;
   (4) Calculate the electromechanical coupling factor k_{31} from the ω_a and ω_b with the IEEE Standard equation in the k_{31} mode: $\frac{k_{31}{}^2}{1-k_{31}{}^2} = \frac{\pi}{2}\frac{\omega_b}{\omega_a}\tan[\frac{\pi(\omega_b-\omega_b)}{2\omega_a}]$;
   (5) Finally, obtain tanθ' using the following equation in the k_{31} mode: $\tan\theta' = \frac{\tan\delta'+\tan\phi'}{2} + \frac{1}{4}\left(\frac{1}{Q_A} - \frac{1}{Q_B}\right)[1 + (\frac{1}{k_{31}} - k_{31})^2\Omega_b{}^2]$.
8. Mechanical Excitation k_{31} Mode: Vibration direction perpendicular to P_S
   (a) Short Circuit—Resonance

$$\text{Strain } x_1 = s_{11}^E X_0 \left(\frac{\cos[\frac{\omega(2x-L)}{2v_{11}^E}]}{\cos(\frac{\omega L}{2v_{11}^E})}\right),$$

$$\text{Displacement } u(x) = \left(\frac{v_{11}^E}{\omega}\right)s_{11}^E X_0 \frac{\sin[\frac{\omega(2x-L)}{2v_{11}^E}]}{\cos(\frac{\omega L}{2v_{11}^E})},$$

$$\text{Resonance Frequency } \left(\frac{\omega_A L}{2v_{11}^E}\right) = \frac{\pi}{2}.$$

   (b) Open Circuit—Antiresonance

$$\text{Strain } x_1 = s_{11}^E X_0 \frac{(\frac{\omega}{v_{11}^E})\cos[\frac{\omega(2x-L)}{2v_{11}^E}]}{[\frac{\omega}{v_{11}^E}\cos\left(\frac{\omega L}{2v_{11}^E}\right) + \frac{k_{31}^2}{(1-k_{31}^2)}\frac{2}{L}\sin\left(\frac{\omega L}{2v_{11}^E}\right)]},$$

$$\text{Displacement } u(x) = s_{11}^E X_0 \frac{\sin[\frac{\omega(2x-L)}{2v_{11}^E}]}{[\frac{\omega}{v_{11}^E}\cos\left(\frac{\omega L}{2v_{11}^E}\right) + \frac{k_{31}^2}{(1-k_{31}^2)}\frac{2}{L}\sin\left(\frac{\omega L}{2v_{11}^E}\right)]},$$

Antiresonance Frequency $(\omega_B L/2v_{11}^E)\cot(\omega_B L/2v_{11}^E) = -k_{31}{}^2/(1-k_{31}{}^2)$,

Approximate: $f_B = f_A(1 + \frac{4}{\pi^2}k_{31}^2)$.

(c) $$\text{Z-shunt Strain } x_1(x) = \frac{s_{11}^E X_0 b\omega C_d (j-1)\cos\left(\frac{\omega L}{2v_{11}^E}\right)}{\triangle}\frac{\omega}{v_{11}^E}\cos\left(\frac{\omega}{v_{11}^E}x\right) - \frac{s_{11}^E X_0 b\omega C_d (j-1)\sin\left(\frac{\omega L}{2v_{11}^E}\right)}{\triangle}\frac{\omega}{v_{11}^E}\sin\left(\frac{\omega}{v_{11}^E}x\right),$$

$$\text{Displacement } u(x) = \frac{s_{11}^E X_0 b\omega C_d (j-1)\cos\left(\frac{\omega L}{2v_{11}^E}\right)}{\triangle}\sin\left(\frac{\omega}{v_{11}^E}x\right) + \frac{s_{11}^E X_0 b\omega C_d (j-1)\sin\left(\frac{\omega L}{2v_{11}^E}\right)}{\triangle}\cos\left(\frac{\omega}{v_{11}^E}x\right)$$

$$\triangle = \left(\frac{\omega}{v_{11}^E}\right)b\left(j\omega C_d - \frac{1}{Z}\right)\cos\left(\frac{\omega L}{2v_{11}^E}\right) + d_{31}j\omega\left(\frac{2wd_{31}}{s_{11}^E}\right)\sin\left(\frac{\omega L}{2v_{11}^E}\right),$$

Matching Impedance $Z = 1/\omega C_d$,

Resonance Frequency $f = f_A(1 + \frac{1}{4}k^2)$,

Elastic Compliance $s_{eff}^E = s^E(1 - \frac{1}{2}k^2 + \frac{j}{2}k^2)$,

Maximum Output Power $|P| = \frac{1}{2}\frac{\omega d^2 X_0^2}{C}\frac{1}{(1-k_{31}^2)+\frac{1}{(1-k_{31}^2)}} \approx \frac{1}{4}\frac{\omega d^2 X_0^2}{C}$.

Check Point

1. (T/F) Piezoelectric "resonance" is a mechanical resonance mode, but the "antiresonance" is not a mechanical resonance, at which the vibration amplitude is not enhanced. True or false?
2. In a k_{31} piezo-ceramic plate, the first antiresonance frequency f_A is observed higher than the resonance frequency f_R. What value does the ratio f_A/f_R approach with an increase in the electromechanical coupling factor k_{31}?
3. (T/F) When we measure the admittance spectrum on a k_{31} type piezoelectric plate specimen, the admittance minimum point corresponds to the resonance point. True or false?
4. When we measure the admittance spectrum on a k_{31} type piezoelectric plate, the phase changes from +90 to $-90°$ around the resonance point with an increase in drive frequency. What is the phase lag at the resonance point?
5. When we measure the admittance spectrum on a k_{31} type piezoelectric plate, the phase changes from +90 to $-90°$ around the resonance point with an increase in drive frequency. What do you call the frequencies that provide the phase $\pm 45°$?
6. (T/F) The fundamental resonance mode of the k_{33} mode has an exact half-wavelength vibration on the rod specimen. True or false?
7. (T/F) The fundamental resonance mode of the k_{31} mode has an exact half-wavelength vibration on the plate specimen. True or false?
8. Provide the relationship between the mechanical quality factor Q_M at the resonance frequency and the intensive elastic loss in the k_{31} type specimen.
9. Provide the relationship between the mechanical quality factor Q_M at the antiresonance frequency and the extensive elastic loss in the k_t type specimen.
10. (T/F) The strain distribution in a high k_{33} rod specimen is more uniform at the antiresonance mode than that at the resonance mode. True or false?
11. When $(\tan\delta_{33}' + \tan\phi_{11}')/2 < \tan\theta_{31}'$ is satisfied, which is larger for the k_{31} type specimen—Q_A or Q_B?

12. (T/F) When we drive the piezoelectric k_{31} plate mechanically under a sinusoidal force, the resonance frequency should be the same for both the short-circuit and open-circuit condition. True or false?
13. (T/F) When we drive the piezoelectric k_{31} plate electrically under constant voltage condition, the admittance spectrum shows significant skew distortion at the antiresonance frequency. True or false?
14. (T/F) The mechanical quality factors Q_A (at resonance) and Q_B (at antiresonance) should be the same in a piezoelectric k_{33} rod specimen. True or false?
15. (T/F) The mechanical quality factor Q_A at resonance is larger than Q_B at antiresonance in a PZT piezoelectric k_{31} plate specimen. True or false?
16. (T/F) To generate the same vibration velocity of a piezoelectric transducer, the resonance drive is the most efficient, rather than the antiresonance drive in PZT based materials. True or false?
17. Can you find a more energy-efficient frequency for driving a PZT piezoelectric k_{31} plate specimen than its resonance or antiresonance frequencies? If so, where do you find this most efficient frequency?
18. (T/F) There is a highly resistive (no electric carrier/impurity in a crystal) piezoelectric single crystal (spontaneous polarization P_S) with a mono-domain state without a surface electrode. The "depolarization electric field" in the crystal is given by $E = -(\frac{P_S}{\varepsilon_r \varepsilon_0})$. True or false?
19. (T/F) In a k_{31} piezo-ceramic plate, the first antiresonance frequency f_B and the resonance frequency f_A are related as $f_B = f_A(1 + \frac{4}{\pi^2}k_{31}^2)$ when the electromechanical coupling factor k_{31} is not large. True or false?
20. (T/F) In a k_{31} piezo-ceramic plate shunted by the external impedance Z, the mechanical resonance exhibits between the piezoelectric resonance and antiresonance frequencies. True or false?

Chapter Problems

7.1 When we neglect the piezoelectric loss $\tan\theta'$ (i.e., $\tan\theta' = 0$) among three losses, $\tan\delta'$, $\tan\phi'$, and $\tan\theta'$, discuss the relation of the mechanical quality factors at the resonance Q_A and antiresonance frequencies Q_B. In the case of $\tan\delta' > 0$, $\tan\phi' > 0$, which is larger—Q_A or Q_B?

7.2 The piezoelectric component with the capacitance C is driven by the external stress $X_0 e^{j\omega t}$. The input mechanical power $|P|_{in}$ and the output electric power $|P|_{out}$ through the external impedance Z are calculated as

$|P|_{in} = \frac{\omega}{2} s_{eff}^E X_0{}^2 = \frac{\omega}{2}\left| s^E[1 - \left(\frac{S}{t}\right)\frac{j\omega Z d^2}{s^E(1+j\omega CZ)}]X_0{}^2\right|,$

$|P|_{out} = \frac{1}{2}Z\frac{(\omega d X_0)^2}{(1+(\omega CZ)^2)}.$

The "energy transmission coefficient" λ_{max} can be calculated from

$\lambda = \frac{|P|_{out}}{|P|_{in}} = \frac{1}{2}Z\frac{(\omega d X_0)^2}{(1+(\omega CZ)^2)} / \frac{\omega}{2}\left| s^E[1 - \left(\frac{S}{t}\right)\frac{j\omega Z d^2}{s^E(1+j\omega CZ)}]X_0{}^2\right|.$

Taking the maximization process in terms of Z, verify the energy transmission coefficient as

$\lambda_{max} = [(1/k) - \sqrt{(1/k^2) - 1}]^2 = [(1/k) + \sqrt{(1/k^2) - 1}]^{-2}.$

References

1. Uchino, K. *Micromechatronics*, 2nd ed.; CRC Press: Boca Raton, FL, USA, 2019.
2. Uchino, K. *High-Power Piezoelectrics and Loss Mechanisms*; CRC Press: Boca Raton, FL, USA, 2020.
3. *ANSI/IEEE Standards 176-1987*; IEEE Standard on Piezoelectricity. The Institute of Electrical and Electronics Engineers: New York, NY, USA, 1988.
4. Zheng, J.; Takahashi, S.; Yoshikawa, S.; Uchino, K.; de Vries, J.W.C. Heat Generation in Multilayer Piezoelectric Actuators. *J. Am. Ceram. Soc.* **1996**, *79*, 3193–3198. [CrossRef]
5. Uchino, K.; Zheng, J.; Joshi, A.; Chen, Y.H.; Yoshikawa, S.; Hirose, S.; Takahashi, S.; de Vries, J.W.C. High Power Characterization of Piezoelectric Materials. *J. Electroceram.* **1998**, *2*, 33–40. [CrossRef]
6. Uchino, K. *Ferroelectric Devices*, 2nd ed.; CRC: Boca Raton, FL, USA, 2010.
7. Hirose, S.; Aoyagi, M.; Tomikawa, Y.; Takahashi, S.; Uchino, K. High Power Characteristics at Antiresonance of Piezoelectric Transducers. *Ultrasonics* **1996**, *34*, 213. [CrossRef]
8. Mezheritsky, A.V. Efficiency of excitation of piezoceramic transducers at antiresonance frequency. *IEEE Trans. Ultrason. Ferroelectr. Freq. Control* **2002**, *49*, 484. [CrossRef] [PubMed]
9. Zhuang, Y.; Ural, S.O.; Rajapurkar, A.; Tuncdemir, S.; Amin, A.; Uchino, K. Derivation of Piezoelectric Losses from Admittance Spectra. *Jpn. J. Appl. Phys.* **2009**, *48*, 041401. [CrossRef]
10. Zhuang, Y.; Ural, S.O.; Tuncdemir, S.; Amin, A.; Uchino, K. Analysis on Loss Anisotropy of Piezoelectrics with ∞mm Crystal Symmetry. *Jpn. J. Appl. Phys.* **2010**, *49*, 021503. [CrossRef]
11. Ural, S.O.; Tuncdemir, S.; Zhuang, Y.; Uchino, K. Development of a High Power Piezoelectric Characterization System and Its Application for Resonance/Antiresonance Mode Characterization. *Jpn. J. Appl. Phys.* **2009**, *48*, 056509. [CrossRef]
12. Hirose, S.; Aoyagi, M.; Tomikawa, Y.; Takahashi, S.; Uchino, K. High Power Characteristics at Antiresonance Frequency of Piezoelectric Transducers. In Proceedings of the Ultrasonics International 1995, Edinburgh, UK, 5–7 July 1995; Elsevier: Amsterdam, The Netherlands, 1996; pp. 213–217.
13. Shekhani, H.N.; Uchino, K. Evaluation of the mechanical quality factor under high power conditions in piezoelectric ceramics from electrical power. *J. Eur. Ceram. Soc.* **2014**, *35*, 541–544. [CrossRef]
14. Uchino, K.; Zhuang, Y.; Ural, S.O. Loss Determination Methodology for a Piezoelectric Ceramic: New Phenomenological Theory and Experimental Proposals. *J. Adv. Dielectr.* **2011**, *1*, 17–31. [CrossRef]

8. Pulse Drive on Piezoelectrics—Laplace Transform

8.1. Impulse Applications of Piezoelectric Actuators

Many of the million-selling piezoelectric actuators are driven by "pulse drive". Electric field-controlled actuators include inkjet printers and diesel injection valves. Diesel engines are recommended rather than regular gasoline cars from an energy conservation and global warming viewpoint. When we consider the total energy of gasoline production, both well-to-tank and tank-to-wheel, the energy efficiency, measured by the total energy required to realize unit drive distance for a vehicle (MJ/km), is of course better for high-octane gasoline than diesel oil. However, since the electric energy required for purification is significant, the gasoline is inferior to diesel fuel. As is well known, the conventional diesel engine, however, generates toxic exhaust gases such as SO_X and NO_X due to insufficient burning of the fuel. In order to solve this problem, new diesel injection valves with piezoelectric multilayered actuators were developed by Siemens, Bosch, and Toyota [1,2]. Figure 8.1 shows such a common rail-type diesel injection valve with a multilayer (ML) piezo-actuator which produces high-pressure fuel and quick injection control. The piezoelectric actuator is namely the key to increasing burning efficiency and minimizing the toxic exhaust gases. The author's contribution to this project was the "pulse drive technique" of the ML actuator without generating troublesome vibration ringing after the quick actuation. On the other hand, a stress-controlled impulse drive is utilized in PABM (programmable air-burst munition for 25 mm ϕ caliber) and a lightning switch (remote control relay switch) [3,4].

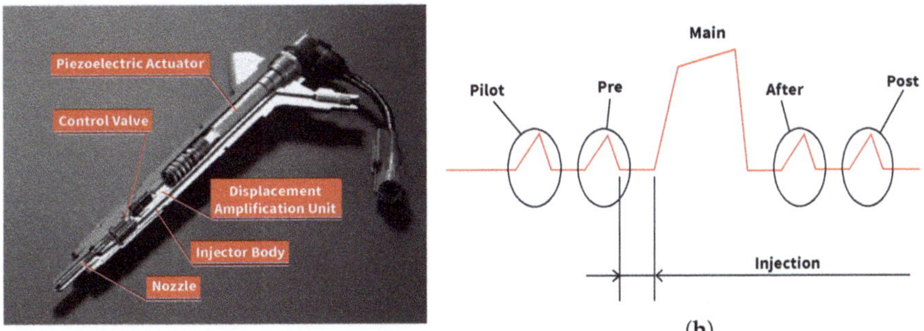

(a) (b)

Figure 8.1. (**a**) Common rail-type diesel injection valve with a piezoelectric multilayer actuator (courtesy of Denso Corporation); (**b**) diesel injection timing chart. Source: [2] ©Uchino, K. *Micromechatronics*, 2nd ed. CRC Press, 2019; pp. 460-461. Reproduced by permission of Taylor & Francis Group.

In this chapter, after the review of the "Laplace transform", we consider the pulse electric field control of a piezo component in Section 8.3, then the stress-controlled energy harvesting process on a piezoelectric specimen under an impulse stress application is considered theoretically in Section 8.4.

8.2. The Laplace Transform

Let us first review an important mathematical tool, the "Laplace transform". The Laplace transform is generally employed to treat the "transient response" to a pulse input. The "Fourier transform" is preferred for cases where a continuous sinusoidal input is applied, such as for resonance-type actuators, which was discussed in Chapter 7.

We consider a function $u(t)$ which is defined for $t \geq 0$ ($u(t) = 0$ for $t < 0$), and satisfies $|u(t)| \leq ke^{\delta t}$ for all δ no less than a certain positive real number δ_0. When these conditions are satisfied, $e^{-st}u(t)$ is absolutely integrable for $Re(s) \geq \delta_0$. We define the Laplace transform:

$$U(s) = L[u(t)] = \int_0^\infty e^{-st}u(t)dt. \tag{8.1}$$

It is noteworthy that the input function $u(t)$ should satisfy $u(t) = 0$ for $t < 0$. The inverse Laplace transform is represented as $L^{-1}[U(s)]$. Application of the useful theorems for the Laplace transform that are listed below reduces the work of solving certain differential equations by reducing them to simpler algebraic forms. The procedure is applied as follows:

1. Transform the differential equation to the "s"-domain by means of the appropriate Laplace transform.
2. Manipulate the transformed "algebraic equation" using the useful "Theorems".
3. The boundary conditions at $t = 0$, $u(0)$ and $\dot{u}(0)$, are integrated in the above.
4. Then, obtain $L^{-1}[U(s)]$ as an algebraic form of "s".
5. Obtain the inverse Laplace transform from Table 8.1.

Useful Theorems for the Laplace Transform:

(a) Linearity:

$L[au_1(t) + bu_2(t)] = aU_1(s) + bU_2(s)$

$L^{-1}[aU_1(s) + bU_2(s)] = au_1(t) + bu_2(t)$

(b) Differentiation with respect to t:

$$L\left[\frac{du(t)}{dt}\right] = sU(s) - u(0)$$

$$L\left[\frac{d^n u(t)}{dt^n}\right] = s^n U(s) - \sum s^{n-k} u^{k-1}(0)$$

(c) Integration:

$$L\left[\int u(t)dt\right] = U(s)/s + (1/s)\left[\int u(t)dt\right]_{t=0}$$

(d) Scaling formula:

$L[u(t/a)] = aU(sa)$ $(a > 0)$

(e) Shift formula with respect to t:

$u(t-k) = 0$ *for* $t < k$ [k: positive real number]. The $u(t)$ curve shifts by k along the positive t axis.

$L[u(t-k)] = e^{-ks}U(s)$

(f) Differentiation with respect to an independent parameter:

$$L\left[\frac{\partial u(t,x)}{\partial x}\right] = \frac{\partial U(s,x)}{\partial x}$$

(g) Initial and final values:

$$\lim_{t\to 0}[u(t)] = \lim_{|s|\to\infty}[sU(s)]$$

$$\lim_{t\to\infty}[u(t)] = \lim_{|s|\to 0}[sU(s)]$$

Table 8.1. Some common forms of the Laplace transform.

	$H(t)$	$G(s)$
1	$1(t)$: *Heaviside Step function* $1(t) = 1, t > 0; 1(t) = 0, t < 0$	$1/s$
2	$\delta(t)$: Dirac *Impulse function* $\delta(t) = \infty, \ t = 0; \ \delta(t) = 0, \ t \neq 0$	1
3	$t^n/n!$ (n: positive integer)	$1/s^{n+1}$
4	e^{-at} (a: complex)	$1/(s + a)$
5	$\cos(at)$	$s/(s^2 + a^2)$
6	$\sin(at)$	$a/(s^2 + a^2)$
7	$\cosh(at)$	$s/(s^2 - a^2)$
8	$\sinh(at)$	$a/(s^2 - a^2)$
9	$e^{-bt}\cos(at) \ a^2 > 0$	$\frac{s+b}{(s+b)^2+a^2}$
10	$e^{-bt}\sin(at) \ a^2 > 0$	$\frac{a}{(s+b)^2+a^2}$
11		$\frac{1}{s}(e^{-as} - e^{-bs})$
12	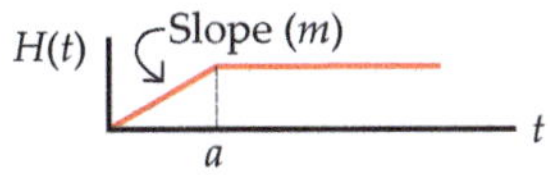	$\frac{m}{s^2}(1 - e^{-as})$
13	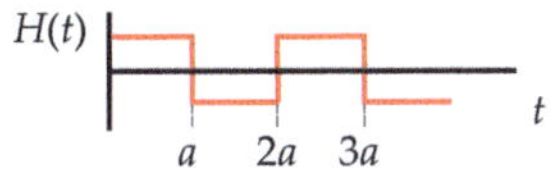	$\frac{1}{s}\tanh(\frac{as}{2})$
14	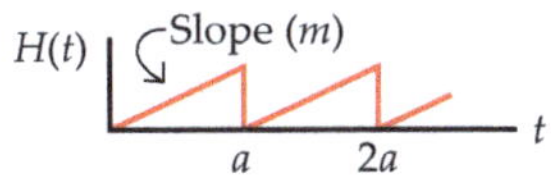	$\frac{m}{s^2} - \frac{ma}{2s}[\coth(\frac{as}{2}) - 1]$

Source: Table by author.

Example Problem 8.1

Compute the Laplace transform of the Heaviside function ("step function"): $1(t) = 0$ when $t < 0$ and $1(t) = 1$ when $t \geq 0$.

<u>Solution</u>

$$L[1(t)] = \int_0^\infty e^{-st}1(t)dt = \int_0^\infty e^{-st}dt = (\frac{1}{s})e^{-st}|_0^\infty = 1/s. \quad \text{(P8.1.1)}$$

Example Problem 8.2

Using the result from the previous problem, $L[1(t)] = 1/s$, obtain the Laplace transform for a pulse function defined by the following:
$P(t) = 0$ when $t < a$ and $t > b$ (here, $0 < a < b$),
$P(t) = 1$ when $a < t < b$.

Solution

$P(t)$ is obtained by superimposing the two step functions, $1(t - a)$ and $-1(t - b)$. Using the shift formula (Theorem (e)), we obtain the Laplace transform of $P(t)$:

$$L[P(t)] = e^{-as}(1/s) - e^{-bs}(1/s) = (1/s)(e^{-as} - e^{-bs}). \quad \text{(P8.2.1)}$$

8.3. Electric Pulse Drive on Piezoelectrics

8.3.1. General Solution for Longitudinal Vibration k_{31} Mode

Vibration Equation of the k_{31} Mode

Let us consider a longitudinal mechanical vibration in a simple piezoelectric ceramic plate via the transverse piezoelectric effect d_{31} with thickness b, width w, and length L ($b << w << L$), pictured in Figure 8.2. This specimen configuration is the same as the one in Chapter 7. When the polarization is in the z direction and the x–y planes are the planes of the electrodes, the extensional vibration along the x direction (1D model) is represented by the following dynamic equation:

$$\rho\frac{\partial^2 u}{\partial t^2} = F = \frac{\partial X_{11}}{\partial x} + \frac{\partial X_{12}}{\partial y} + \frac{\partial X_{13}}{\partial z}, \quad (8.2)$$

where u is the displacement in the x direction of a small-volume element in the ceramic plate, ρ is the density of the piezoelectric material, and Xij's are stresses (only the force along the x direction is our target). The relations between the stress, electric field (only E_z exists, because $E_x = E_y = 0$ due to the electrodes on the top and bottom), and the induced strains are described by the following set of equations:

$$\begin{bmatrix} x_1 \\ x_2 \\ x_3 \\ x_4 \\ x_5 \\ x_6 \end{bmatrix} = \begin{bmatrix} s_{11}{}^E & s_{12}{}^E & s_{13}{}^E & 0 & 0 & 0 \\ s_{12}{}^E & s_{11}{}^E & s_{13}{}^E & 0 & 0 & 0 \\ s_{13}{}^E & s_{13}{}^E & s_{33}{}^E & 0 & 0 & 0 \\ 0 & 0 & 0 & s_{44}{}^E & 0 & 0 \\ 0 & 0 & 0 & 0 & s_{44}{}^E & 0 \\ 0 & 0 & 0 & 0 & 0 & 2(s_{11}{}^E - s_{12}{}^E) \end{bmatrix} \begin{pmatrix} X_1 \\ X_2 \\ X_3 \\ X_4 \\ X_5 \\ X_6 \end{pmatrix} + \begin{pmatrix} 0 & 0 & d_{31} \\ 0 & 0 & d_{31} \\ 0 & 0 & d_{33} \\ 0 & d_{15} & 0 \\ d_{15} & 0 & 0 \\ 0 & 0 & 0 \end{pmatrix} \begin{bmatrix} E_1 \\ 0 \\ 0 \end{bmatrix}. \quad (8.3)$$

When a very long, thin thickness and width plate is driven in the vicinity of this fundamental resonance, X_2 and X_3 may be considered zero throughout the plate. Since shear stress will not be generated by the applied electric field E_z, only the following single equation applies:

$$X_1 = x_1/s_{11}{}^E - (d_{31}/s_{11}{}^E)E_z. \quad (8.4)$$

Substituting Equation (8.4) into Equation (8.3), and assuming that strain $x_1 = \partial u/\partial x$ and $\partial E_z/\partial x = 0$ (since each electrode is at the same potential), we obtain the following dynamic equation:

$$\rho \frac{\partial^2 u}{\partial t^2} = \frac{1}{s_{11}^E} \frac{\partial^2 u}{\partial x^2}. \tag{8.5}$$

Remember that the "E-constant" condition "s_{11}^E" is the key characteristic in the k_{31} mode.

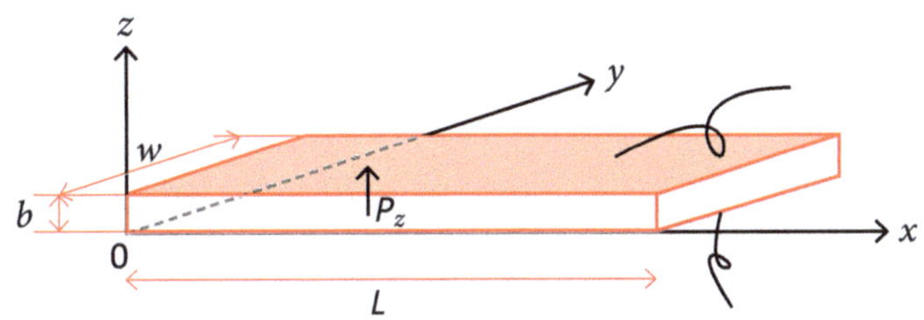

Figure 8.2. Longitudinal vibration k_{31} mode of a rectangular piezoelectric plate. Source: [2] ©Uchino, K. *Micromechatronics*, 2nd ed. CRC Press, 2019; p. 111. Reproduced by permission of Taylor & Francis Group.

Laplace Transform of the k_{31} Mode Vibration Equation

Let us solve Equation (8.5) of Figure 8.2 using the Laplace transform. Denoting the Laplace transforms of $u(t,x)$ and $E_z(t)$ as $U(s,x)$ and $\widetilde{E}(s)$, respectively (x: coordinate along plate length), Equation (8.5) is transformed by Theorem (f) to:

$$\rho s_{11}^E s^2 U(s,x) = \frac{\partial^2 U(s,x)}{\partial x^2}. \tag{8.6}$$

We assume the following "initial conditions":

$$\text{Displacement}: \ u(0,x) = 0 \text{ and velocity}: \ \frac{\partial[u(0,x)]}{\partial t} = 0. \tag{8.7}$$

We may also make use of the fact that:

$$\rho s_{11}{}^E = 1/v^2, \tag{8.8}$$

where v is the speed of sound in the piezoelectric ceramic under the E-constant condition. To obtain a general "algebraic" solution of Equation (8.6) in terms of space coordinate x, we assume:

$$U(s,x) = Ae^{(sx/v)} + Be^{-(sx/v)}. \tag{8.9}$$

The constants A and B can be determined by applying the "boundary conditions" $X_1 = 0$ at $x = 0$ and L:

$$X_1 = \frac{(x_1 - d_{31}E_z)}{s_{11}^E} = 0. \tag{8.10}$$

We also utilize the fact on the strain (Theorem (f)) that:

$$L[x_1] = (\partial U/\partial x) = A(s/v)e^{(sx/v)} - B(s/v)e^{-(sx/v)}. \tag{8.11}$$

In conjunction with the boundary conditions at $x = 0$ and L of Equation (5.91) to yield:

$$A(s/v) - B(s/v) = d_{31}\widetilde{E}, \tag{8.12a}$$

$$A(s/v)e^{(sl/v)} - B(s/v)e^{-(sl/v)} = d_{31}\widetilde{E}. \tag{8.12b}$$

Thus, we obtain

$$A = \frac{d_{31}\widetilde{E}(1 - e^{-sL/v})}{(s/v)(e^{sL/v} - e^{-sL/v})}, \tag{8.13a}$$

$$B = \frac{d_{31}\widetilde{E}(1 - e^{sL/v})}{(s/v)(e^{sL/v} - e^{-sL/v})}, \tag{8.13b}$$

and, consequently, Equations (8.9) and (8.11) become:

$$U(s,x) = \frac{d_{31}\widetilde{E}(v/s)[e^{-s(L-x)/v} + e^{-s(L+x)/v} - e^{-sx/v} - e^{-s(2L-x)/v}]}{(1 - e^{-2sL/v})}, \tag{8.14}$$

$$L[x_1] = \frac{d_{31}\widetilde{E}[e^{-s(L-x)/v} + e^{-s(L+x)/v} - e^{-sx/v} - e^{-s(2L-x)/v}]}{(1 - e^{-2sL/v})}. \tag{8.15}$$

The inverse Laplace transforms of Equations (8.14) and (8.15) now provide the displacement $u(t,x)$ and strain $x_1(t,x)$. Making use of the Taylor expansion series

$$1/(1 - e^{-2sl/v}) = 1 + e^{-2sl/v} + e^{-4sl/v} + e^{-6sl/v}\ldots, \tag{8.16}$$

the strain, $x_1(t,x)$, can now be obtained by shifting the $d_{31}E_z(t)$ curves with respect to t according to Theorem (e). We may also consider that since $u(t,L/2) = 0$ (from $U(s,L/2) = 0$) and $u(t,0) = -u(t,L)$ (from $U(s,0) = -U(s,L)$), the total displacement of the plate device ΔL becomes equal to $2u(t,L)$. We finally arrive at the following:

$$U(s,L) = \frac{d_{31}\widetilde{E}(v/s)(1 - e^{-sL/v})}{(1 + e^{-sL/v})} = d_{31}\widetilde{E}(v/s)[\tanh(sL/2v)]. \tag{8.17}$$

8.3.2. Displacement Response to a Step Voltage in the k_{31} Mode

We consider first a particular input of a "Heaviside step" electric field $E(t) = E_0 H(t)$. Since the Laplace transform of the step function is given by $(1/s)$, Equation (8.17) can be expressed by

$$\begin{aligned} U(s,x = L) &= d_{31}E_0(v/s^2)(1 - e^{-(sL/v)})/(1 + e^{-(sL/v)}) \\ &= d_{31}E_0(v/s^2)(1 - 2e^{-(sL/v)} + 2e^{-(2sL/v)} - 2e^{-3sL/v} + 2e^{-4sL/v}\ldots). \end{aligned} \tag{8.18}$$

Note that the base function of $U(s,L)$, $1/s^2$, gives the base function of $u(t,L)$ in terms of t (i.e., $\propto t$). It should also be noted that the final expansion terms will provide the time shift of the base function; for example, "$-2e^{-(sL/v)}$" means the time shift by (L/v) of the base function multiplied by the factor of "-2". The inverse Laplace transform of Equation (8.18) yields by segmenting the time interval of (L/v) (by superposing the e^{-sk} terms):

$$
\begin{aligned}
&u(t,L) = d_{31}E_0vt && 0 < t < L/v,\\
&u(t,L) = d_{31}E_0v[t - 2(t - L/v)] && L/v < t < 2L/v,\\
&u(t,L) = d_{31}E_0v[t - 2(t - L/v) + 2(t - 2L/v)] && 2L/v < t < 3L/v,\\
&u(t,L) = d_{31}E_0v[t - 2(t - L/v) + 2(t - 2L/v) - 2(t - 3L/v)] && 3L/v < t < 4L/v,\\
&\qquad\cdots\cdots\cdots\cdots
\end{aligned}
\tag{8.19}
$$

The transient displacement, ΔL ($= 2\cdot u(t,L)$), produced by the step voltage, is pictured in Figure 8.3 (since d_{31} is usually negative, Figure 8.3 is for $E_0 < 0$). The resonance period T of this piezoelectric plate corresponds to $(2L/v)$, and the time interval in Equation (8.19) is every $(T/2)$. It is worth noting that the displacement changes linearly, not sinusoidally. On the contrary, the displacement of a discrete-component system changes sinusoidally, as demonstrated in Example Problem 8.3. This transient response difference comes from the vibration medium difference: continuum or discrete mechanical medium. In either case, continuous ringing occurs under a step input when the loss is neglected.

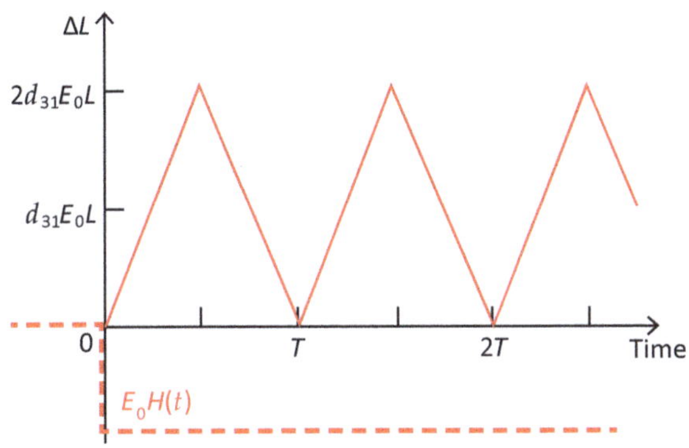

Figure 8.3. Triangular displacement response to a Heaviside step function voltage in a k_{31} piezoelectric plate. Source: [2] ©Uchino, K. *Micromechatronics*, 2nd ed. CRC Press, 2019; p. 312. Reproduced by permission of Taylor & Francis Group.

The strain distribution on a piezoelectric plate is also intriguing for this step excitation case. From Equation (8.15), $L(x_1)$ is directly proportional to $\tilde{E}$; that is, the strain distribution $x_1(x)$ follows exactly to $E(t)$, the Heaviside step function. The strain x_1 at a certain point x suddenly becomes "$d_{31}E_0$" from "zero" with a certain time lag depending on its coordinate x. Thus, as illustrated in Figure 8.4a, the strained portion starts from both ends ($x = 0$ and L) of the piezo-plates at the time of step voltage applied. These two symmetrical boundaries/walls between the strained and strain-free portion (analogous to a shockwave) propagate with a piezo material's sound velocity, v, in opposition to each other, crossing over at the plate center, then generating the doubly strained part in the center area (i.e., $2d_{31}E_0$). Thus, when the walls reach the plate ends, the plate length becomes the maximum ($\Delta L = 2d_{31}E_0L$), and we can understand the reason why 100% overshoot occurs under the step voltage applied. After that, the walls bounce back in the opposite directions, and the plate starts to shrink linearly according to the shrinkage of the strained portion. The linear displacement change originates from the constant wall velocity (which is equal to the piezo material's sound velocity under the E-constant condition in this case). This triangular vibration ringing will continue to be long when the loss is small. Figure 8.4b,c show the strain distribution on a piezo-plate under a pseudo-DC triangular voltage, and under a sinusoidal voltage at its resonance frequency, respectively, as references. The strain is uniformly generated in the plate ($x_1 = d_{31}E_3$) under a pseudo-CD condition (no stress appears in the plate), while the strain and stress distribute sinusoidally with the maximum at the center part (i.e., nodal line) under the resonance drive. The resonance mode can be understood as a standing wave generated by the superposition of right-ward and left-ward traveling waves with a half-wavelength exactly match to the rod length, so that the center node strain is amplified significantly by the factor of $(8/\pi^2)Q_m$.

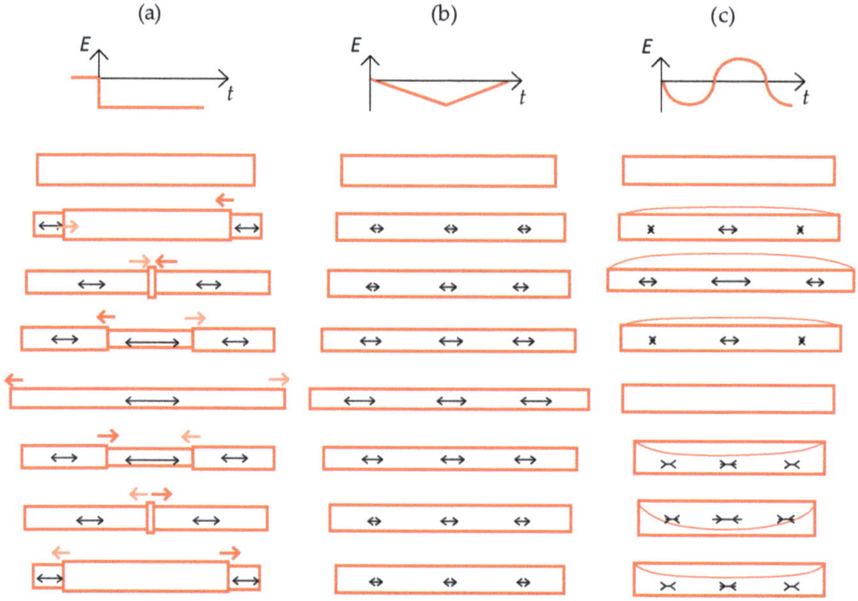

Figure 8.4. Strain distribution on a piezo-plate during the deformation process under voltage: (**a**) step; (**b**) pseudo DC triangle; (**c**) resonance sine. Source: [2] ©Uchino, K. *Micromechatronics*, 2nd ed. CRC Press, 2019; p. 113. Reproduced by permission of Taylor & Francis Group.

Example Problem 8.3

The dynamic equation for a mechanical or an electrical system, composed of discrete components; mass and spring (damper is neglected for simplicity); or inductor, capacitor and resistor, shown in Figure 8.5a,b, are expressed by

$$M(d^2u/dt^2) + cu = F(t), \quad \text{(P8.3.1)}$$

where u: mass displacement, M: mass, c: spring constant, F: external force,

$$L(d^2Q/dt^2) + R(dQ/dt) + (1/C)Q = V(t), \quad \text{(P8.3.2)}$$

where Q: charge, L: inductance, C: capacitance, R: resistance, V: voltage.

Consider the transient response $u(t)$ and $Q(t)$ in the case of Heaviside step function of the force and voltage.

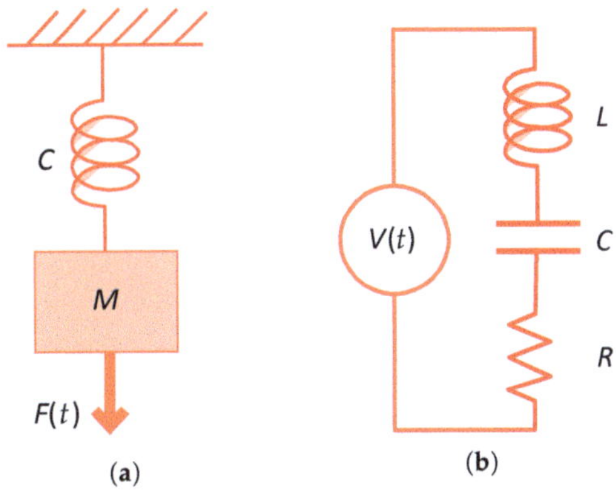

Figure 8.5. Discrete mechanical (**a**) and electrical (**b**) component systems. Source: Source: [2] ©Uchino, K. *Micromechatronics*, 2nd ed. CRC Press, 2019; p. 314. Reproduced by permission of Taylor & Francis Group.

Solution

Because these two second differential equations are basically the same, we will consider them only for the mechanical system. Since the force is a Heaviside step function $F(t) = F_0H(t)$, the Laplace transform of the force is given by F_0/s. Equation (P8.3.1) can be expressed by taking the Laplace transformation as:

$$M[s^2 + (c/M)]\,U = F_0/s, \quad \text{(P8.3.3)}$$

where U is the Laplace transform of the displacement u. U can be calculated by

$$U = F_0/Ms(s^2 + \omega_0{}^2) = (F_0/M\omega_0{}^2)\{1/s - (1/2)[1/(s + j\omega_0) + 1/(s - j\omega_0)]\}, \quad [\omega_0{}^2 = c/M]. \quad \text{(P8.3.4)}$$

Accordingly, using the inverse Laplace transforms (Item (1) and (5) of Table 6.1), we can obtain:

$$u(t) = (F_0/c)[H(t) - \cos\omega_0 t]. \quad \text{(P8.3.5)}$$

As illustrated in Figure 8.6, the step force excites a sinusoidal displacement vibration of a discrete component of mass M, superposed on a step bias position. Here, the time scale T is equal to the resonance period, $2\pi/\omega_0$ $(=2\pi\sqrt{M/c})$. When we neglect the damping factor, the vibration ringing will continue forever. Note 100% overshoot for every vibration. When we consider the damping factor ζ, as in the LCR circuit in Figure 8.5b, the ringing will diminish gradually with the exponential envelope curve of the time constant τ inversely proportional to the damping factor. Unlike the "continuum media" in Section 8.3.2, the "discrete component" system (such as "equivalent circuits") does not generate linear displacement, but a sinusoidal response.

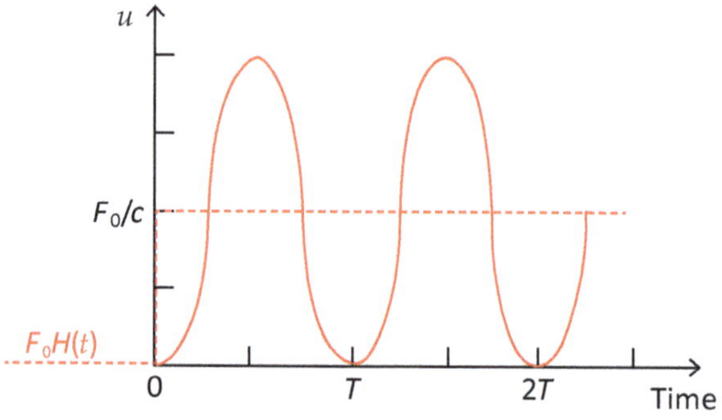

Figure 8.6. Sinusoidal displacement response to Heaviside step function force in a discrete component system. Source: [2] ©Uchino, K. *Micromechatronics*, 2nd ed. CRC Press, 2019; p. 314. Reproduced by permission of Taylor & Francis Group.

8.3.3. Displacement Response to a Pulse Drive in the k_{31} Mode

Next, let us consider the response to a rectangular pulse voltage such as the one pictured in the top left-hand corner of Figure 8.7a [5]. From (11) of Table 6.1, we begin by substituting

$$\widetilde{E} = (E_0/s)(1 - e^{-(nsL)/v}), \tag{8.20}$$

into Equation (8.17), which allows us to obtain the displacement ΔL for $n = 1$, 2, and 3. The quantity n is a time scale based on a half of the resonance period ($=T/2$) of the piezoelectric plate.

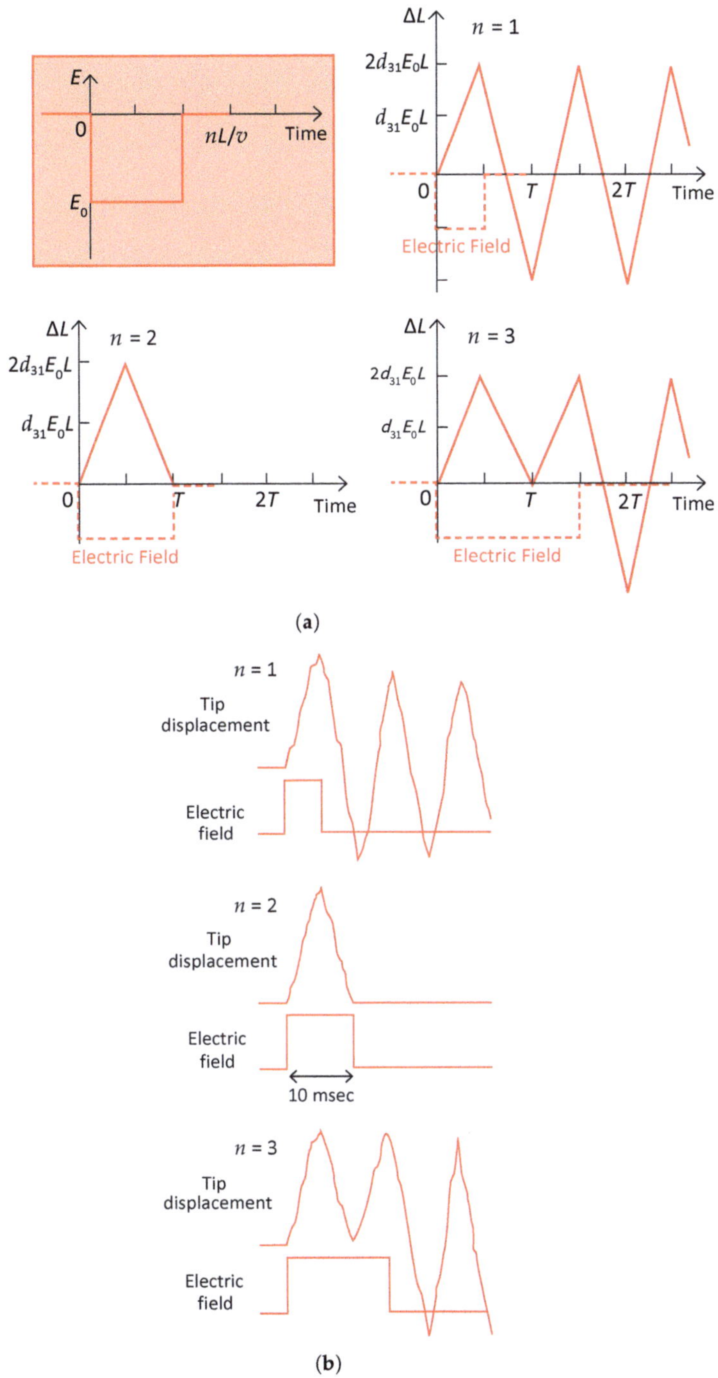

Figure 8.7. (**a**) Transient displacement ΔL produced by a rectangular pulse voltage. (Note that the time interval, $T = (2L/v)$, corresponds to the resonance period of the piezoelectric plate.) (**b**) Measurement on a bimorph tip displacement produced by a pulse voltage. Source: [2] ©Uchino, K. *Micromechatronics*, 2nd ed. CRC Press, 2019; p. 316. Reproduced by permission of Taylor & Francis Group.

For $n = 1$,

$$U(s,x = L) = d_{31}E_0(v/s^2)(1 - e^{-(sL/v)})^2/(1 + e^{-(sL/v)})$$
$$= d_{31}E_0(v/s^2)(1 - 3e^{-sL/v} + 4e^{-2sL/v} - 4e^{-3sL/v} + \cdots). \quad (8.21)$$

Similar to the "Heaviside Step" case, the base function of $U(s,L)$, $1/s^2$, gives the base function of $u(t,L)$ in terms of t. The inverse Laplace transform of Equation (8.21) yields:

$$u(t,L) = d_{31}E_0vt \qquad 0 < t < L/v,$$
$$u(t,L) = d_{31}E_0v[t - 3(t - L/v)] \qquad L/v < t < 2L/v,$$
$$u(t,L) = d_{31}E_0v[t - 3(t - L/v) + 4(t - 2L/v)] \qquad 2L/v < t < 3L/v. \quad (8.22)$$
$$\cdots\cdots\cdots\cdots$$

The transient displacement, ΔL, produced by the rectangular pulse voltage is pictured in Figure 8.7a (top-right) for $n = 1$. Only during the first $(T/2)$ period (i.e., the field pulse applied period) the edge vibration velocity $(\partial u/\partial t)$ is one half of the following continuous ringings with the resonance period of $T = (2L/v)$.

For $n = 2$, since $\widetilde{E} = (E_0/s)(1 - e^{-(2Ls)/v})$ includes the denominator of Equation (8.17),

$$U(s,L) = d_{31}E_0(v/s^2)\,(1 - 2e^{-sL/v} + e^{-2sL/v}). \quad (8.23)$$

Thus,

$$u(t,L) = d_{31}E_0vt \qquad 0 < t < L/v,$$
$$u(t,L) = d_{31}E_0v[t - 2(t - L/v)] \qquad L/v < t < 2L/v, \quad (8.24)$$
$$u(t,L) = d_{31}E_0v[t - 2(t - L/v) + (t - 2L/v)] = 0 \qquad 2L/v < t < 3L/v.$$

In this case, the displacement, ΔL, occurs in a single pulse and does not exhibit ringing as depicted in Figure 8.7a (bottom left). Remember that the applied field $\widetilde{E}$ should include the denominator term $(1 + e^{-sL/v})$ to realize finite expansion terms, leading to a complete suppression of vibrational ringing.

For $n = 3$, $U(s,L)$ is again expanded as an infinite series:

$$U(s,x = L) = d_{31}E_0\,(v/s^2)(1 - e^{-(3sL/v)})(1 - e^{-(sL/v)})/(1 + e^{-(sL/v)})$$
$$= d_{31}E_0(v/s^2)(1 - 2e^{-sL/v} + 2e^{-2sL/v} - 3e^{-3sL/v} + 4e^{-4sL/v} - 4e^{-5sL/v}\ldots). \quad (8.25)$$

The displacement response for this case is pictured in Figure 8.7a (bottom right). Note the displacement slope (plate edge vibration velocity) has twice the difference among the field applied period and zero field.

Figure 8.7b shows the measurement data collected on a PZT bimorph tip displacement produced by a pulse voltage; 10 ms corresponds to the resonance period of this bimorph. Notice that the ringing is completely eliminated for $n = 2$; the pulse width is adjusted exactly to the resonance period, and that the displacement curve is linear or a triangular sequence. Though the bimorph configuration is different from the k_{31} plate, the transient response mechanism seems to be similar to handle.

How precisely does the pulse width need to be adjusted? The calculated transient vibration for $n = 1.9$ appears in Figure 8.8. Notice the small amount of ringing that occurs after the main pulse. The actual choice of n, then, will depend on the amount of ringing that can be tolerated for a given application.

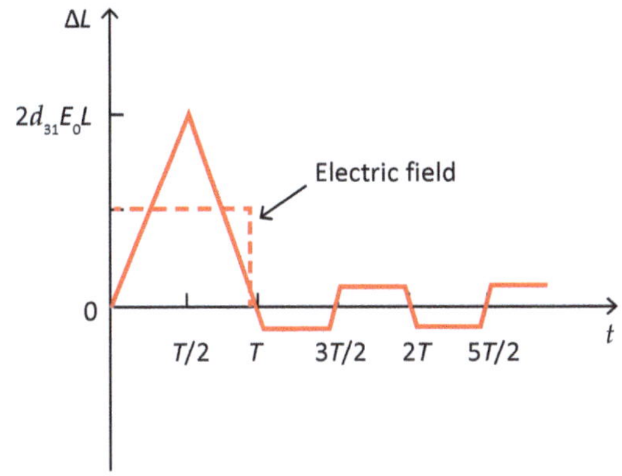

Figure 8.8. Transient displacement, ΔL, produced by a rectangular pulse voltage (n = 1.9). Source: [2] ©Uchino, K. *Micromechatronics*, 2nd ed. CRC Press, 2019; p. 317. Reproduced by permission of Taylor & Francis Group.

8.3.4. Displacement Response to a Pseudo-Step Drive in the k_{31} Mode

Next, we consider the displacement response of a rectangular plate to "pseudo-step voltage" as illustrated in the top left of Figure 8.9a. The Laplace transform is provided by the subtraction of a straight line $1/s^2$ with the time difference of (nL/v) ((12) of Table 6.1):

$$\widetilde{E} = (E_0 v/nLs^2)(1 - e^{-nsL/v}). \tag{8.26}$$

Substituting Equation (8.26) into Equation (8.17), we will repeat similar calculations to the above to obtain the displacement ΔL for the time scale n = 1, 2, and 3 (the time unit is one half of the resonance period (L/v). The difference from Section 8.3.2 is in the base function of $U(s,L)$, $1/s^3$, which gives the base function of $u(t,L)$ as $t^2/2$ (parabolic curve).

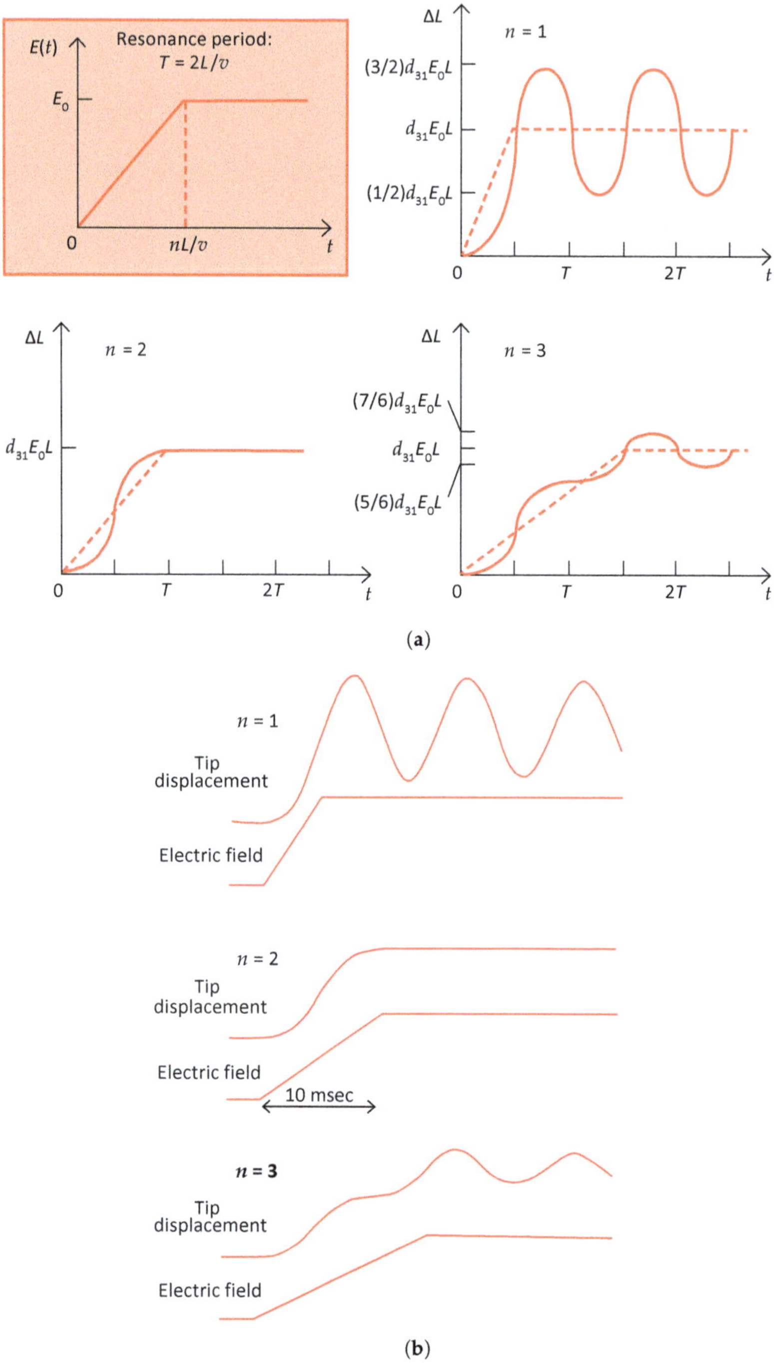

Figure 8.9. (**a**) Transient displacement ΔL induced in a rectangular plate for a pseudo-step voltage. The time scale n is based on $1/2$ of the resonance period T. (**b**) Measurement on a bimorph tip displacement produced by a pseudo step voltage. Source: Source: [2] ©Uchino, K. *Micromechatronics*, 2nd ed. CRC Press, 2019; p. 318. Reproduced by permission of Taylor & Francis Group.

For $n = 1$,

$$U(s,L) = \frac{(d_{31}E_o/L)(v^2/s^3)(1-e^{-sL/v})^2}{(1+e^{-sL/v})}$$
$$= (d_{31}E_o/L)(v^2/s^3)[1 - 3e^{-sL/v} + 4e^{-2sL/v} - 4e^{-3sL/v} + \cdots]. \quad (8.27)$$

Notice that the base function of $U(s,L)$, $1/s^3$, will lead to a base function of $u(t,L)$ in the form $t^2/2$ (parabolic curve), such that:

$$\begin{aligned}
&u(t,L) = (d_{31}E_0v^2/2L)t^2 && 0 < t < L/v,\\
&u(t,L) = (d_{31}E_0v^2/2L)[t^2 - 3(t - L/v)^2] && L/v < t < 2L/v,\\
&u(t,L) = (d_{31}E_0v^2/2L)[t^2 - 3(t - L/v)^2 + 4(t - 2L/v)^2] && 2L/v < t < 3L/v.\\
&\cdots\cdots\cdots\cdots
\end{aligned} \quad (8.28)$$

The transient displacement for an actuator driven by the pseudo-step voltage pictured in the top right of Figure 8.9a is seen to exhibit continuous ringing. Notice that this curve is actually a sequence of parabolic curves. It is "not"sinusoidal!

For $n = 2$,

$$U(s,L) = (d_{31}E_0/2L)(v^2/s^3)[1 - 2e^{-sL/v} + e^{-2sL/v}]. \quad (8.29)$$

Thus,

$$\begin{aligned}
&u(t,L) = (d_{31}E_0v^2/4L)t^2 && 0 < t < L/v,\\
&u(t,L) = (d_{31}E_0v^2/4L)[t^2 - 2(t - L/v)^2] && L/v < t < 2L/v,\\
&u(t,L) = (d_{31}E_0v^2/4L)[t^2 - 2(t - L/v)^2 + (t - 2L/v)^2] = (d_{31}E_0L/2) && 2L/v < t.\\
&\cdots\cdots\cdots\cdots
\end{aligned} \quad (8.30)$$

Neither overshoot nor ringing is apparent in the response for this case (i.e., the rise time is set exactly to the resonance period) represented in Figure 8.9a (bottom left). "When the Laplace transform of applied field $\widetilde{E}$ includes the term $(1 + e^{-sL/v})$, the expansion series terminates in finite terms, leading to a complete suppression of mechanical ringing".

For $n = 3$, $U(s,L)$ is again expanded as an infinite series:

$$U(s,L) = (d_{31}E_0/3L)(v^2/s^3)[1 - 2e^{-sL/v} + 2e^{-2sL/v} - 3e^{-3sL/v} + 4e^{-4sL/v} - 4e^{-5sL/v} \ldots]. \quad (8.31)$$

The displacement response for this condition is represented by the curve appearing in Figure 8.9a (bottom right).

As shown in Figure 8.9a, ΔL does not exhibit overshoot nor ringing for $n = 2$. However, for $n = 1$ and 3, the overshoot and ringing follow continuously. Note again that all the curves are composed of parabolic curves ("not" sinusoidal!) and that the heights of the overshoot are 1/2 (50%) and 1/6 (17%) of $d_{31}E_0L$, respectively, for $n = 1$ and 3.

You can also understand that the strain in the specimen is generated linearly (not suddenly) with time, since the electric field changes such. Figure 8.9b shows the measurement data collected on a PZT bimorph tip displacement produced by a pseudo-step voltage; 10 ms corresponds to the resonance period of this bimorph.

This derivation process suggests an empirical process on how to suppress the overshoot and/or ringing in a piezoelectric actuator system:

(1) By applying a relatively steep rising voltage to the actuator, we can obtain the resonance period first from the time period between the overshoot peak and the successive peak point.
(2) Next, by adjusting the voltage rise time exactly to the resonance period, we can eliminate the overshoot and/or ringing of the system vibration.

In other words, without using a mechanical damper (which loses energy), we can diminish vibration overshoot or ringing just by adjusting the pulse width or rise time of the applied voltage, which does not in fact lose energy. This procedure is the key to the system development, having already been adopted to the diesel injection valve control, inkjet printer, and cutting edge/tool position change with a piezoelectric actuator in lathes, or other cutting machines.

8.3.5. Consideration of the Loss in Transient Response

In order to integrate elastic loss into Equation (8.5), $\rho\frac{\partial^2 u}{\partial t^2} = \frac{1}{s_{11}^E}\frac{\partial^2 u}{\partial x^2}$, we add a viscous damping force term in proportion to the time derivative as

$$\rho\frac{\partial^2 u}{\partial t^2} = \frac{1}{s_{11}^E}\frac{\partial^2 u}{\partial x^2} + \eta\frac{\partial^3 u}{\partial x^2 \partial t}. \tag{8.32}$$

Taking the Laplace transformation, we obtain

$Us^2 = v^2\frac{\partial^2 U}{\partial x^2} + \left(\frac{\eta}{\rho}\right)s\frac{\partial^2 U}{\partial x^2} = v^2\frac{\partial^2 U}{\partial x^2}[1 + \left(\frac{\eta}{\rho v^2}\right)s]$.

Then,

$$U\frac{s^2}{(1 + \varsigma s)} = v^2\frac{\partial^2 U}{\partial x^2}. \tag{8.33}$$

The displacement $U(s,L)$ can then be obtained by making the following substitution in Equation (8.17):

$$s \quad \rightarrow \quad \frac{s}{\sqrt{1 + \zeta s}}. \tag{8.34}$$

Since this solution includes a complicated "error function", an approximate solution for the piezoelectric resonance state was determined by Ogawa [6]. Recall the "discrete component" system introduced in Chapter 6, with which we could properly account for loss effects. With the damping factor ζ, the following equation has been solved rather easily:

$\ddot{u} + 2\zeta\omega_0\dot{u} + {\omega_0}^2 u = f(x)$ or $Us^2 + 2\zeta\omega_0 Us + {\omega_0}^2 U = F(s)$.

This indicates the application limitation of the "equivalent circuit" to a continuum media specimen.

Experimental results appear in Figure 8.10 [7]. The displacement ΔL produced by a rectangular pulse voltage observed in this investigation is similar to the results shown in Figure 8.9, except for the vibrational damping. With the loss inclusion, the triangular shape is rounded and the amplitude is significantly damped. However, we still see that when the pulse width of this rectangular voltage is adjusted to the piezoelectric resonance period, T, or integral multiples of it, the vibrational ringing is eliminated.

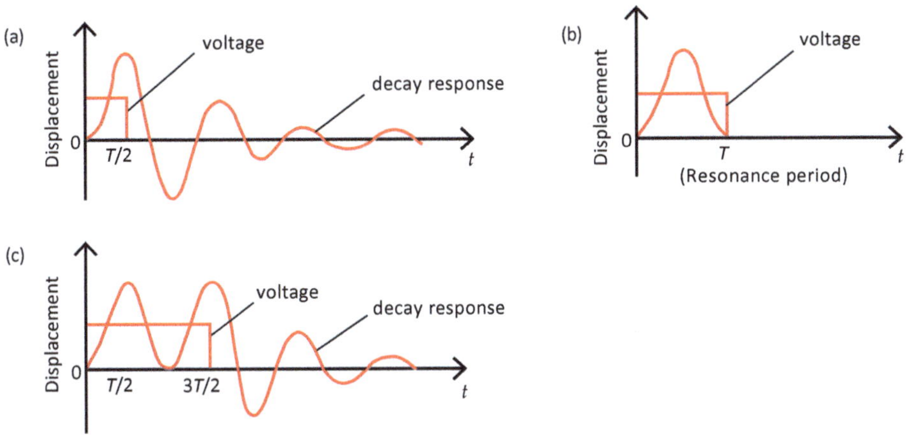

Figure 8.10. Displacement response of a lossy piezoelectric actuator under a rectangular pulse voltage. (**a**) Pulsewidth = $T/2$; (**b**) pulsewidth = T; (**c**) pulsewidth = $3T/2$. Source: [2] ©Uchino, K. *Micromechatronics*, 2nd ed. CRC Press, 2019; p. 320. Reproduced by permission of Taylor & Francis Group.

8.4. Mechanical Pulse Drive on Piezoelectrics

In this section, we consider "impulse stress" applications, such as in a PABM (programmable air-burst munition for 25 mm ϕ caliber) and a lightning switch (remote control relay switch) [8]. This analysis is the basic theoretical approach of the electric energy process on a piezoelectric specimen under an impulse stress application.

When an impulse force is applied to a piezoelectric actuator, an electric voltage/current vibration is excited via a mechanical vibration, the characteristics of which depend on the pulse profile. Voltage overshoot and ringing are frequently observed in piezoelectric "igniters", even if we start from a compressive stress input. Because the pulse drive may lead to the destruction of the piezo-actuator due to the large tensile stress and high voltage associated with the vibration overshoot, we need to more precisely examine the transient response of a piezoelectric device driven by pulse stress. The reader is reminded that an "equivalent circuit" with a discrete component cannot be adopted in the transient response analysis (including the stress wave propagation) under the impulse drive.

8.4.1. Vibration Mode in the k_{31}-Type Plate

Once again, we consider a longitudinal mechanical vibration in a simple piezoelectric ceramic plate via the transverse piezoelectric effect d_{31} with thickness b, width w, and length L ($b << w << L$), pictured in Figure 8.2. If we summarize the assumptions again:

(1) Only E_z exists, because $E_x = E_y = 0$ due to the electrodes on the top and bottom, and;

(2) Only X_1 exists, because X_2 and X_3 may be set equal to zero through the plate because the plate is very long with thin thickness and width. Under a low to fundamental resonance frequency range, only the following two equations are

essential to solve the dynamic equation around the resonance/antiresonance frequencies:

$$x_1 = s_{11}{}^E X_1 + d_{31} E_z, \tag{8.35}$$

$$D_3 = d_{31} X_1 + \varepsilon_0 \varepsilon_{33}{}^X E_z. \tag{8.36}$$

We start from the following dynamic equation for the stress operation:

$$\rho \frac{\partial^2 u}{\partial t^2} = \frac{1}{s_{11}^E} \frac{\partial^2 u}{\partial x^2}. \tag{8.37}$$

General Solution for Longitudinal Vibration k_{31} Mode

We solve Equation (8.35) for a piezo-plate, using the "Laplace transform". Equation (8.35) can be transformed by Laplace Theorem (b), by denoting the Laplace transforms of $u(t,x)$ and $E_z(t)$ as $U(s,x)$ and $\widetilde{E}(s)$, respectively (x: coordinate along plate length):

$$\rho s_{11}^E s^2 U(s,x) = \frac{\partial^2 U(s,x)}{\partial x^2}. \tag{8.38}$$

We assume the following initial ($t = 0$) conditions:

Displacement: $u(0,x) = 0$ and velocity: $\frac{\partial[u(0,x)]}{\partial t} = 0$.

We also make use of the sound velocity v along the x direction that:

$$\rho s_{11}{}^E = 1/v^2. \tag{8.39}$$

To obtain a general solution of Equation (8.36) in terms of space coordinate x, we assume:

$$U(s,x) = Ae^{(sx/v)} + Be^{-(sx/v)}. \tag{8.40}$$

Now we consider the input force (pressure) $F(t)$ on the both ends of the piezo-plate. Since the stress is defined as positive for the tensile, we obtain

$$F(t) = -bwX_1(t), \tag{8.41}$$

and Equation (8.33) is transformed with the geometrical boundary condition $X_1 = X(t)$ at $x = 0$ and L:

$$X(t) = \frac{(x_1 - d_{31}E_z)}{s_{11}^E}. \tag{8.42}$$

We denote the Laplace transform of external stress $X(t)$ as $\widetilde{X}(s)$. We also utilize the fact on the strain that:

$$L[x_1] = (\partial U/\partial x) = A(s/v)e^{(sx/v)} - B(s/v)e^{-(sx/v)}. \tag{8.43}$$

Short-Circuit Condition

Equation (8.42) is reduced to $x_1 = s_{11}{}^E X(t)$ at $x = 0$ and L, because of $E_z = 0$. Thus, using Equation (8.43) yields the following two equations to solve the parameters A and B at $x = 0$ and L:

$A(s/v) - B(s/v) = s_{11}{}^{E}\widetilde{X},$
$A(s/v)e^{(sL/v)} - B(s/v)e^{-(sL/v)} = s_{11}{}^{E}\widetilde{X}.$

Thus, we obtain

$$A = \frac{s_{11}^{E}\widetilde{X}(1 - e^{-sL/v})}{(s/v)(e^{sL/v} - e^{-sL/v})}, \tag{8.44a}$$

$$B = \frac{s_{11}^{E}\widetilde{X}(1 - e^{sL/v})}{(s/v)(e^{sL/v} - e^{-sL/v})}, \tag{8.44b}$$

and, consequently, Equations (8.40) and (8.43) become:

$$U(s,x) = s_{11}^{E}\widetilde{X}\left(\frac{v}{s}\right)\frac{\cosh\left[\frac{s(2x-L)}{2v}\right]}{\cosh\left(\frac{sL}{2v}\right)}, \tag{8.45a}$$

$$L[x_1(s,x)] = s_{11}^{E}\widetilde{X}\frac{\sinh\left[\frac{s(2x-L)}{2v}\right]}{\cosh\left(\frac{sL}{2v}\right)}. \tag{8.45b}$$

By transforming the above equations into

$$U(s,x) = \frac{s_{11}^{E}\widetilde{X}(v/s)[e^{-\frac{s(L-x)}{v}} + e^{-\frac{s(L+x)}{v}} - e^{-\frac{sx}{v}} - e^{-\frac{s(2L-x)}{v}}]}{(1 - e^{-\frac{2sL}{v}})}, \tag{8.46a}$$

$$L[x_1] = \frac{s_{11}^{E}\widetilde{X}[e^{-\frac{s(L-x)}{v}} - e^{-\frac{s(L+x)}{v}} + e^{-\frac{sx}{v}} - e^{-\frac{s(2L-x)}{v}}]}{(1 - e^{-\frac{2sL}{v}})}, \tag{8.46b}$$

and making use of the expansion series
$1/(1 - e^{-2sl/v}) = 1 + e^{-2sl/v} + e^{-4sl/v} + e^{-6sl/v} \ldots,$

the strain, $x_1(t,x)$, can now be obtained by shifting the $s_{11}^{E}X(t)$ curve with respect to t according to Laplace Theorem (e). That is to say, the strain profile $x_1(t,x)$ should be exactly the same as the stress profile $X(t)$, and the displacement profile is the inverse Laplace of $s_{11}^{E}\widetilde{X}(\frac{v}{s})$. We may also consider that since $u(t,L/2) = 0$ (from $U(s,L/2) = 0$) and $u(t,0) = -u(t,L)$ (from $U(s,0) = -U(s,L)$) (i.e., symmetrical vibration), the total displacement of the plate device ΔL becomes equal to $2u(t,L)$. We finally arrive at the following relation:

$$\Delta L = 2U(s,L) = \frac{2s_{11}^{E}\widetilde{X}(\frac{v}{s})\left(1 - e^{-\frac{sL}{v}}\right)}{\left(1 + e^{-\frac{sL}{v}}\right)} = 2s_{11}^{E}\widetilde{X}(v/s)[\tanh(sL/2v)]. \tag{8.47}$$

(a) First, we consider a particular input of "Heaviside step stress" $X(t) = X_0H(t)$. Since the Laplace transform of the step function is given by $(1/s)$ (Item 1 of Table 8.1), the total displacement Equation (8.47) can be expressed by

$$\begin{aligned} 2U(s,x=L) &= 2s_{11}{}^{E}X_0(v/s^2)(1 - e^{-(sL/v)})/(1 + e^{-(sL/v)}) \\ &= 2s_{11}{}^{E}X_0(v/s^2)(1 - 2e^{-(sL/v)} + 2e^{-(2sL/v)} - 2e^{-3sL/v} + 2e^{-4sL/v} \ldots). \end{aligned} \tag{8.48}$$

Note that the base function of $U(s,L)$, $1/s^2$, gives the base function of $u(t,L)$ in terms of t (i.e., $\propto t$, Item 3 in Table 8.1). The inverse Laplace transform of Equation (8.48) yields (by superposing the e^{-sk} terms via the Laplace transformation Theorem (e)):

$$\begin{aligned}
2u(t,L) &= 2s_{11}{}^{E}X_0vt && 0 < t < L/v,\\
2u(t,L) &= 2s_{11}{}^{E}X_0v[t - 2(t - L/v)] && L/v < t < 2L/v,\\
2u(t,L) &= 2s_{11}{}^{E}X_0v[t - 2(t - L/v) + 2(t - 2L/v)] && 2L/v < t < 3L/v,\\
2u(t,L) &= 2s_{11}{}^{E}X_0v[t - 2(t - L/v) + 2(t - 2L/v) - 2(t - 3L/v)] && 3L/v < t < 4L/v.\\
&\cdots\cdots\cdots\cdots
\end{aligned} \quad (8.49)$$

The transient displacement, ΔL (=$2u(t,L)$), produced by the step stress is pictured in Figure 8.11a (here X_0 is positive for the tensile). The fundamental resonance period of this piezoelectric plate corresponds to ($2L/v$), and the time interval in Equation (8.49) is every ($T/2$). It is worth noting that the displacement changes "linearly", not sinusoidally. Note that the vibration "ringing" will continue permanently when we neglect the loss.

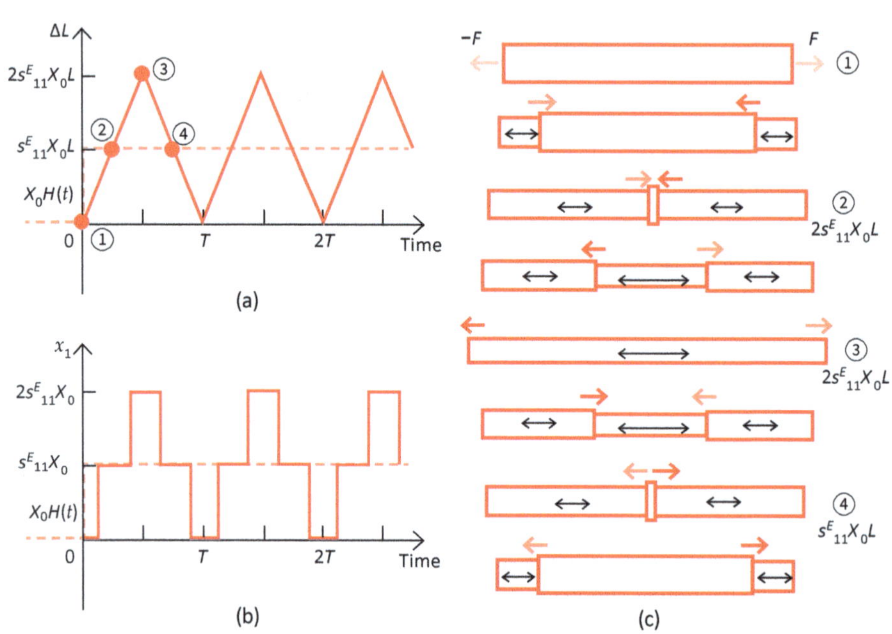

Figure 8.11. (**a**) Total displacement ΔL; (**b**) strain x_1 at the point $x = L/4$; (**c**) strain wave dynamic profile, responding to a Heaviside step input stress in a continuum piezoelectric plate (the k_{31} mode). Source: Figure by author.

The strain distribution on a piezoelectric plate is also intriguing for this step excitation case. From Equation (8.45b), $L(x_1)$ is directly proportional to $\widetilde{X}$; that is the strain distribution $x_1(x)$ exactly follows $X(t)$, the Heaviside step function. The strain x_1 at a certain point x becomes "$s_{11}{}^{E}X_0$" suddenly from "zero" with a certain time lag depending on its coordinate x. Figure 8.11b shows the strain change with time at the point $x = L/4$, which indicates two discrete strain levels $s_{11}{}^{E}X_0$, and $2s_{11}{}^{E}X_0$ for different time intervals. Strain wave dynamic modes are illustrated in Figure 8.11c.

The strained portion starts from both ends ($x = 0$ and L) of the piezo-plates at the time of step force applied at these ends. These two symmetrical boundaries/walls between the strained and strain-free portion (analogous to a shockwave) propagate with a piezo material's sound velocity, v_{11}^E, in opposition to each other, crossing over at the plate center, then generating the doubly strained part in the center area (i.e., $2s_{11}{}^E X_0$). Thus, when the wall reaches the plate end, the plate length becomes the maximum ($\Delta L = 2s_{11}{}^E X_0 L$), and we can understand the reason why 100% overshoot occurs under the step force applied. Note also that a minimum of one half of the resonance period $T/2$ is required to reach to the maximum total displacement.

Because the ceramic is weaker for the tensile stress than for the compressive stress, the ceramic plate may collapse $T/4$ later after the initial pressure applied (i.e., when the doubly strained part is initiated). After $T/2$, the wall bounces back in the opposite direction, and the plate starts to shrink linearly according to the shrinkage of the strained portion. The linear displacement change is originated from the constant wall velocity (which is equal to the piezo material's sound velocity). This triangular vibration ringing will remain long if the loss is small. The reader is reminded that the step-like force/stress application generates a distinct step-like strain discontinuity in the specimen, and this wave front propagates in the specimen with a sound velocity. The vibration ringing will continue for a long period with the average bias displacement at $\Delta L = s_{11}{}^E X_0 L$, as seen in Figure 8.11a. When you use an Equivalent Circuit (EC) analysis, you will only obtain the sinusoidal vibration ringing even under a step stress, because it cannot handle the step-like strain discontinuity inside the ceramic specimen (the EC will handle a specimen just as a discrete spring without the spring size and position).

(b) Next, let us consider the response to a "rectangular pulse stress" such as that pictured in the top left-hand corner of Figure 8.12. This model corresponds to practical clicking, kicking the piezo-plate. We begin by substituting

$$\widetilde{X} = (X_0/s)(1 - e^{-(nsL)/v}), \tag{8.50}$$

into Equation (8.47), which allows us to obtain the displacement ΔL for $n = 1$, 2 and 3. The quantity n is a time scale based on a half of the resonance period ($=T/2$) of the piezoelectric plate.

For $n = 1$,

$$\begin{aligned} U(s,x = L) &= s_{11}{}^E X_0(v/s^2)(1 - e^{-(sL/v)})^2/(1 + e^{-(sL/v)}) \\ &= s_{11}{}^E X_0(v/s^2)(1 - 3e^{-sL/v} + 4e^{-2sL/v} - 4e^{-3sL/v} + \ldots). \end{aligned} \tag{8.51}$$

Similar to the step case, the base function of $U(s,L)$, $1/s^2$, gives the base function of $u(t,L)$ in terms of t. The inverse Laplace transform of Equation (8.51) yields:

$$\begin{aligned} 2u(t,L) &= 2s_{11}{}^E X_0 vt && 0 < t < L/v, \\ 2u(t,L) &= 2s_{11}{}^E X_0 v[t - 3(t - L/v)] && L/v < t < 2L/v, \\ 2u(t,L) &= 2s_{11}{}^E X_0 v[t - 3(t - L/v) + 4(t - 2L/v)] && 2L/v < t < 3L/v. \\ &\cdots\cdots\cdots\cdots \end{aligned} \tag{8.52}$$

The transient displacement, ΔL, produced by the rectangular pulse stress, is pictured in Figure 8.12 (top right) for $n = 1$. The resonance period of this piezoelectric plate corresponds to $(2L/v)$. Notice how continuous ringing occurs under this condition.

For $n = 2$, since $\widetilde{X} = (X_0/s)(1 - e^{-(2Ls)/v})$ includes the denominator of Equation (8.47),

$$U(s,L) = s_{11}{}^{E}X_0(v/s^2)(1 - 2e^{-sL/v} + e^{-2sL/v}). \tag{8.53}$$

Thus,

$$\begin{aligned} 2u(t,L) &= 2s_{11}{}^{E}X_0vt & 0 < t < L/v,\\ 2u(t,L) &= 2s_{11}{}^{E}X_0v[t - 2(t - L/v)] & L/v < t < 2L/v,\\ 2u(t,L) &= 2s_{11}{}^{E}X_0v[t - 2(t - L/v) + (t - 2L/v)] = 0 & 2L/v < t < 3L/v.\\ &\cdots\cdots\cdots\cdots \end{aligned} \tag{8.54}$$

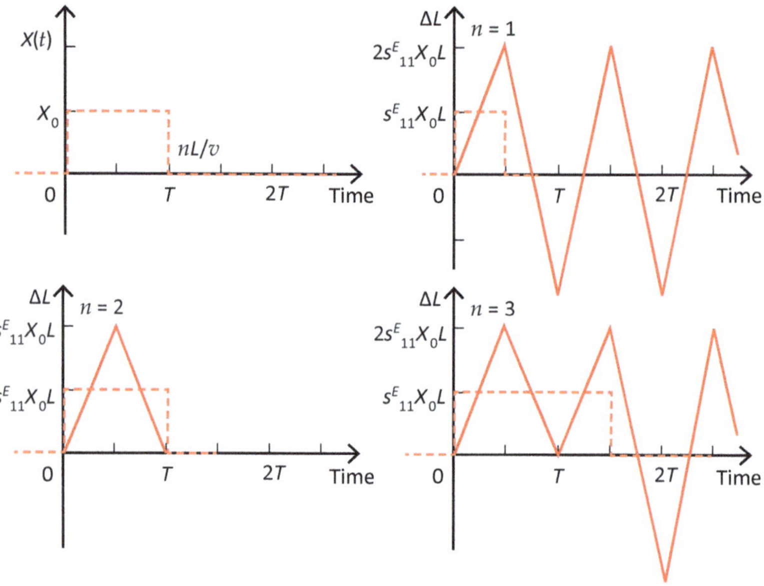

Figure 8.12. Transient displacement ΔL produced by a rectangular pulse stress with the pulse width of 1, 2, 3 of $n(T/2)$. Note that the time interval, $T = (2L/v)$, corresponds to the fundamental resonance period of the piezoelectric plate. Source: Figure by author.

In this case, the displacement, ΔL, occurs in a single pulse and does not exhibit ringing as depicted in Figure 8.12 (bottom left). Remember again that the applied field $\widetilde{X}$ should include the denominator term $(1 + e^{-sL/v})$ to realize finite expansion terms, leading to a complete suppression of vibrational ringing.

For $n = 3$, $U(s,L)$ is again expanded as an infinite series:

$$\begin{aligned} 2U(s,x = L) &= 2s_{11}{}^{E}X_0(v/s^2)(1 - e^{-(3sL/v)})(1 - e^{-(sL/v)})/(1 + e^{-(sL/v)})\\ &= 2s_{11}{}^{E}X_0(v/s^2)(1 - 2e^{-sL/v} + 2e^{-2sL/v} - 3e^{-3sL/v} + 4e^{-4sL/v} - 4e^{-5sL/v} \ldots). \end{aligned} \tag{8.55}$$

The displacement response for this case is pictured in Figure 8.12 (bottom right). Note the displacement slope (plate edge vibration velocity) has twice difference among the stress applied period and zero stress.

The short-circuit condition, $E_z = 0$, yields the current response. The constitutive equation of the electric displacement, $D_3 = d_{31}X_1 + \varepsilon_0\varepsilon_{33}{}^X E_z$, becomes simply $D_3 = d_{31}X_1$. Integrating this equation with respect to the electrode area

$Q = w\int_0^L D_3 dx$,

and from $x_1 = s_{11}{}^E X_1$, we obtain

$$Q = wd_{31}\int_0^L X_1 dx = w\frac{d_{31}}{s_{11}^E}\int_0^L x_1 dx = w\frac{d_{31}}{s_{11}^E}\Delta L. \tag{8.56}$$

Since the total current is provided by $I = \frac{\partial Q}{\partial t}$, and $\Delta L = 2u(t, L)$,

$$I = \frac{\partial Q}{\partial t} = w\frac{d_{31}}{s_{11}^E}\frac{\partial}{\partial t}(2u(t,\ L)). \tag{8.57}$$

The total current response profile with time is given by the slope of the total displacement ΔL. The proportionality constant $(\frac{2wd_{31}}{s_{11}^E})$ against the vibration velocity $\dot{u}(t, L)$ at the plate edge is called the "force factor". Or, since the Laplace transform of the total displacement is expressed by

$$2U(s, L) = \frac{2s_{11}^E\widetilde{X}(v/s)(1-e^{-sL/v})}{(1+e^{-sL/v})} = 2s_{11}^E\widetilde{X}(v/s)[\tanh(sL/2v)],$$

we may express the Laplace transform of the total current $\widetilde{I}$ as

$$\widetilde{I} = 2wd_{31}\widetilde{X}v\tanh(\frac{sL}{2v}). \tag{8.58}$$

Here $L[\frac{\partial}{\partial t}(u(t,\ L))] = sU(s, L)$ was used. Figure 8.13 illustrates the transient displacement ΔL (top) and current I (bottom) produced by rectangular pulse stress with a pulse width of 1, 2 of $n(T/2)$. Note that the time interval, $T = (2L/v)$, corresponds to the resonance period of the piezoelectric plate.

In conclusion, when we use the impulse stress input, the pulse width is important: when the pulse width is exactly equal to the resonance period of the device, no vibration ringing is followed, which is helpful to stop the temple bell timbre echo completely. On the contrary, in order to generate "large displacement continuous vibration ringing" for purpose of energy harvesting (Subsection Impedance Matching Load Condition), the pulse width should be adjusted to:

(1) Exactly $T/2$ to obtain 100% overshoot (never take exactly to the resonance period T);
(2) Longer than $100T$ (with high Q_m) to practically realize the "negative Step-force" ($T \approx 0.01$ ms).

When we account for loss effects, the Laplace transform of the displacement $U(s,L)$ can be obtained by making the following substitution in Equation (8.38):

$$s \rightarrow \frac{s}{\sqrt{1 + \varsigma s}}. \tag{8.59}$$

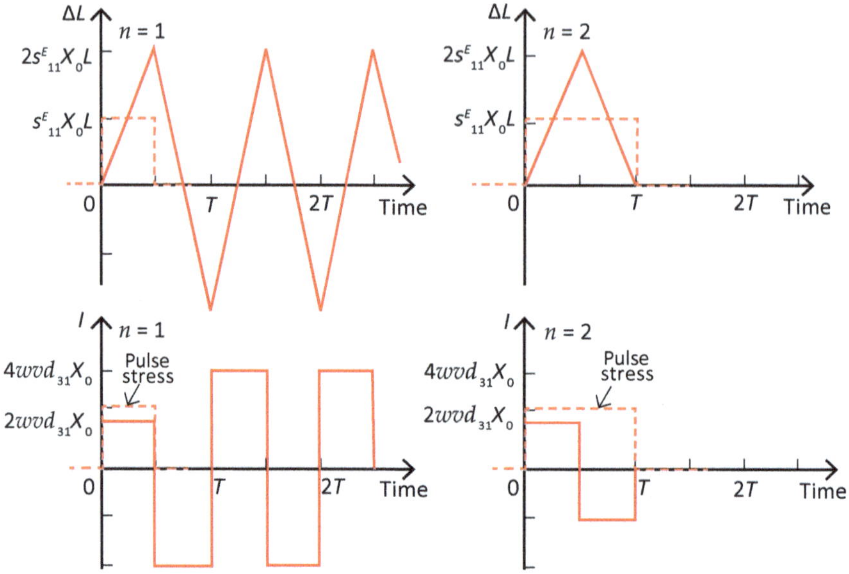

Figure 8.13. Transient displacement ΔL (top) and current I (bottom) produced by a rectangular pulse stress with the pulse width of 1, 2 of $n(T/2)$. Note that the time interval, $T = (2L/v)$, corresponds to the resonance period of the piezoelectric plate. Source: Figure by author.

Open-Circuit Condition

The open-circuit condition means the total current $I = 0$, which yields the voltage response generated on the electrode. Remember that the mechanical resonance under the short or open circuit corresponds to the piezoelectric "resonance" or "antiresonance" frequency, respectively, which indicates that the vibration ringing time period under the open-circuit condition should be "shorter" (i.e., elastically stiffer!) than that under the short-circuit condition. When the electromechanical coupling factor is not large, the antiresonance frequency is given by $f_B \approx \ (v^E/2L)(1+(\frac{4}{\pi^2})k_{31}^2)$, higher than the resonance frequency $f_A = (v^E/2L)$. Integrating the constitutive equation of the electric displacement, $D_3 = d_{31}X_1 + \varepsilon_0\varepsilon_{33}{}^X E_z$, with respect to the electrode area

$$Q = w\int_0^L D_3 dx = w\int_0^L [d_{31}X_1 + \varepsilon_0\varepsilon_{33}^X E_z]dx. \tag{8.60}$$

While, from $X_1 = x_1/s_{11}{}^E - (d_{31}/s_{11}{}^E)E_z$, we obtain

$$\int_0^L X_1 dx = \frac{1}{s_{11}^E}\int_0^L (x_1 - d_{31}E_z)dx. \tag{8.61}$$

Knowing that $\int_0^L x_1 dx = 2u(t, L)$ and $E_z(t)$ = constant in terms of the coordinate x, inserting Equation (8.61) into Equation (8.60), we obtain

$$Q = w\left\{\left(\frac{d_{31}}{s_{11}^E}\right)[2u(t,L) - d_{31}E_zL] + \varepsilon_0\varepsilon_{33}^X E_z L\right\} = w\left\{\left(\frac{d_{31}}{s_{11}^E}\right)2u(t,L) + \varepsilon_0\varepsilon_{33}^X(1-k_{31}^2)E_z(t)L\right\}. \quad (8.62)$$

The open-circuit condition, $I = \frac{\partial Q}{\partial t} = 0$, results in the relation between the electric field E_z and the total displacement $2u(t,L)$ as

$$\frac{\partial E_z}{\partial t} = -\frac{k_{31}^2}{(1-k_{31}^2)}\frac{1}{Ld_{31}}\frac{\partial}{\partial t}2u(t,L). \quad (8.63)$$

Thus, the open-circuit boundary condition indicates that time dependence of E_z is negatively proportional to the time dependence of average strain $\Delta L/L$. It should also be noted that $u(t,L) = -u(t,0)$, symmetric for the displacement profile. In other words, the Laplace transform describes

$$\widetilde{E} = -\frac{k_{31}^2}{(1-k_{31}^2)}\frac{2}{Ld_{31}}U(s,L). \quad (8.64)$$

This electric field is a sort of "depolarization field" along the thickness direction, originating from the D-constant condition merely along the z direction. If the D-constant condition is held for all x, y, and z directions, the sound velocity will be v^D. However, in this k_{31} case, the sound velocity along the x direction is still v^E, because of the top electrode covering all length directions.

Thus, we solve the same dynamic equation as that under the short-circuit condition,

$$\rho\frac{\partial^2 u}{\partial t^2} = \frac{\partial X_1}{\partial x}. \quad (8.65)$$

Since $\frac{\partial X_1}{\partial x} = \frac{1}{s_{11}^E}\frac{\partial x_1}{\partial x} - \frac{d_{31}}{s_{11}^E}\frac{\partial E_z}{\partial x}$, and the top and bottom electrodes keep the potential/voltage constant along the x direction, $\frac{\partial E_z}{\partial x} = 0$, the dynamic equation (Equation 8.65) is reduced to:

$$\rho\frac{\partial^2 u}{\partial t^2} = \frac{1}{s_{11}^E}\frac{\partial^2 u}{\partial x^2}. \quad (8.66)$$

Note here again that $x_1 = \frac{\partial u}{\partial x}$. To obtain a general solution of Equation (8.66) in terms of space coordinate x, we assume:

$$U(s,x) = Ae^{(sx/v)} + Be^{-(sx/v)}. \quad (8.67)$$

Here, we denote the sound velocity $v = 1/\sqrt{\rho s_{11}^E}$ along x axis. Since the plate surface is electroded, the sound velocity along the length direction is the same for both short- and open-circuit conditions. Now we consider the input force (pressure) $F(t)$ on both ends of the piezo-plate. Since the stress is defined as positive for the tensile, we obtain

$$F(t) = -bwX_1(t), \quad (8.68)$$

and the "geometrical boundary condition" $X_1 = X(t)$ at $x = 0$ and L:

$$X(t) = \frac{(x_1 - d_{31}E_z)}{s_{11}^E}. \tag{8.69}$$

We denote the Laplace transform of external stress $X(t)$ as $\widetilde{X}(s)$. We also utilize the fact on the strain that:

$$L[x_1] = (\partial U/\partial x) = A(s/v)e^{(sx/v)} - B(s/v)e^{-(sx/v)}. \tag{8.70}$$

If we rewrite Equation (8.69) as $s_{11}^E\widetilde{X}(s) = L[x_1] - d_{31}\widetilde{E}$, and using Equation (8.64), we obtain

$$s_{11}^E\widetilde{X}(s) = L[x_1] + \frac{k_{31}^2}{(1-k_{31}^2)}\frac{2}{L}U(s,L). \tag{8.71}$$

Different from the short-circuit condition, the external stress under the open-circuit condition generates the total displacement term (second term of Equation (8.71)) originating from the induced electric field E_z (depolarization field). Using Equations (8.67) and (8.70), and $U(s,L) = -U(s,0)$ yields the following two equations for the condition at $x = 0$ and L to solve the parameters A and B:

$$A(s/v) - B(s/v) - \frac{k_{31}^2}{(1-k_{31}^2)}\frac{2}{L}[A+B] = s_{11}{}^E\widetilde{X},$$

$$A(s/v)e^{(sL/v)} - B(s/v)e^{-(sL/v)} + \frac{k_{31}^2}{(1-k_{31}^2)}\frac{2}{L}[Ae^{(sL/v)} + Be^{-(sL/v)}] = s_{11}{}^E\widetilde{X}.$$

Thus, we obtain

$$A = \frac{s_{11}^E\widetilde{X}[\left(\frac{s}{v}\right)\left(1 - e^{-\frac{sL}{v}}\right) + \left(\frac{2K_{31}^2}{L}\right)\left(1 + e^{-\frac{sL}{v}}\right)]}{e^{sL/v}[\left(\frac{s}{v}\right) + (2K_{31}^2/L)]^2 - e^{-sL/v}[\left(\frac{s}{v}\right) - (2K_{31}^2/L)]^2}, \tag{8.72a}$$

$$B = \frac{s_{11}^E\widetilde{X}[\left(\frac{s}{v}\right)\left(1 - e^{\frac{sL}{v}}\right) - \left(\frac{2K_{31}^2}{L}\right)\left(1 + e^{\frac{sL}{v}}\right)]}{e^{sL/v}[\left(\frac{s}{v}\right) + (2K_{31}^2/L)]^2 - e^{-sL/v}[\left(\frac{s}{v}\right) - (2K_{31}^2/L)]^2}, \tag{8.72b}$$

where we use a new notation

$$K_{31}^2 = \frac{k_{31}^2}{(1-k_{31}^2)}, \tag{8.73}$$

and, consequently, $U(s, \mathrm{L})$ is expressed as:

$$U(s,\ x) = Ae^{\frac{sL}{v}} + Be^{-\left(\frac{sL}{v}\right)} = \frac{s_{11}^E\widetilde{X}\{-2\left(\frac{s}{v}\right) + e^{\frac{sL}{v}}\left[\left(\frac{s}{v}\right) + \left(\frac{2K_{31}^2}{L}\right)\right] + e^{-\frac{sL}{v}}\left[\left(\frac{s}{v}\right) - \left(\frac{2K_{31}^2}{L}\right)\right]\}}{e^{sL/v}[\left(\frac{s}{v}\right) + (2K_{31}^2/L)]^2 - e^{-sL/v}[\left(\frac{s}{v}\right) - (2K_{31}^2/L)]^2}. \tag{8.74}$$

It is important to note that when we consider the $e^{-\frac{sL}{v}}$ term, which is essential to sum up the time shift functions for future intervals with the unit of $T/2 = L/v$, the term is composed of $[s - (2K_{31}^2 v/L)]$, not merely of s. When we take into account s on the (angular) frequency domain replaced by ω, the new ω at the antiresonance condition $[\omega_A - (2K_{31}^2 v/L)]$ seems to be equal to the resonance frequency ω_R, which was discussed in the previous section; that is, the antiresonance frequency is higher than the resonance frequency, and the difference is proportional to K_{31}^2 (modified electromechanical coupling factor). Since further calculations are complicated, only the expected results are described here. Figure 8.14 illustrates the transient displacement ΔL produced by a rectangular pulse stress under open-circuit conditions excited by the pulse width slightly shorter than $(T/2) = L/v^E$, that is, half of the fundamental antiresonance time period $T_A/2 = \frac{L}{v^E}/(1 + \frac{4}{\pi^2}k_{31}^2)$. We expect similar triangular (linear) displacement change to the case in the short-circuit condition. The voltage/electric field change with time should be a similar triangular shape expected from Equation (8.64).

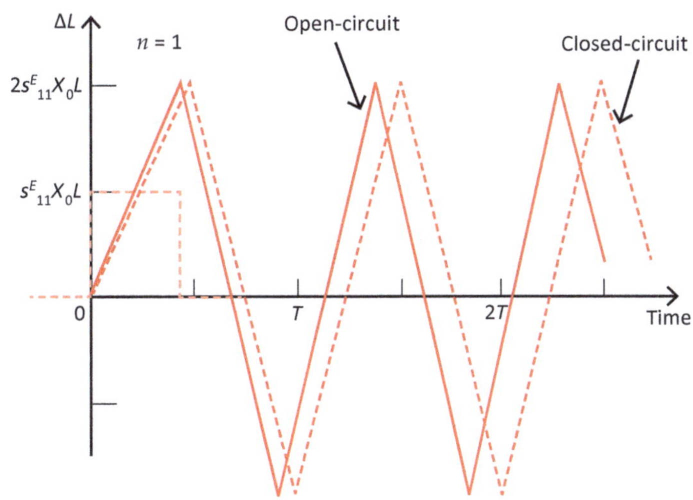

Figure 8.14. Transient displacement ΔL produced by a rectangular pulse stress under open- and short-circuit conditions with the pulse width close to $(T/2)$. Source: Figure by author.

We discussed Subsections Short-Circuit Condition and Open-Circuit Condition under short-circuit and open-circuit conditions, in both of which we cannot expect any electric energy harvesting in practice. In order to cultivate the energy, a suitable electrical resistive impedance should be connected in the external circuit.

Impedance Matching Load Condition

An external electrical impedance Z is connected to a piezoelectric k_{31} plate (Figure 8.15). When we assume impulse input stress $X = X_0(t)$, the output electric charge Q (i.e., no loss, no time lag) under the vibration ringing-down process at almost the fundamental resonance frequency can be described as:

$$Q = w\int_0^L D_3 dx = w\int_0^L [d_{31}X_1 + \varepsilon_0\varepsilon_{33}^X E_z]dx. \tag{8.75}$$

While, from $X_1 = x_1/s_{11}{}^E - (d_{31}/s_{11}{}^E)\,E_z$, we obtain

$$\int_0^L X_1 dx = \frac{1}{s_{11}^E}\int_0^L (x_1 - d_{31}E_z)dx. \tag{8.76}$$

Knowing that $\int_0^L x_1 dx = 2u(t,L)$ and $E_z(t)$ = constant in terms of the coordinate x, and inserting Equation (8.76) into Equation (8.75), we obtain

$$Q = w\left\{\left(\frac{d_{31}}{s_{11}^E}\right)2u(t,L) + \varepsilon_0\varepsilon_{33}^X(1-k_{31}^2)E_z(t)L\right\}. \tag{8.77}$$

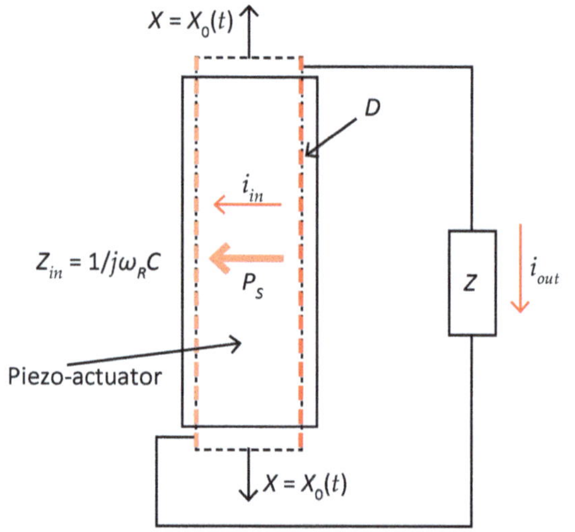

Figure 8.15. Electric energy harvesting model under the external electrical impedance Z on a piezoelectric actuator. Source: Figure by author.

Note here that the motional capacitance enhancement can be neglected in this off-resonance scenario due to no vibration enhancement via the mechanical quality factor Q_m during the ringing-down process after impulse stress. Taking Laplace transform formulation for the force $\widetilde{X_0}$ and total polarization $\widetilde{Q}$, $\widetilde{Q} = d_{31}\widetilde{X_0}$,

$I = \frac{\partial Q}{\partial t} = i_{in} + i_{out}$,

$Z_{in}i_{in} = Zi_{out}$,

$\widetilde{I} = s\widetilde{Q} = Cs\widetilde{V} + \frac{\widetilde{V}}{Z} = sd_{31}\widetilde{X_0}$.

Thus, the effective impedance and the voltage/force relation is obtained as

$$\frac{\widetilde{V}}{\widetilde{I}} = \frac{1}{sC + \frac{1}{Z}}, \tag{8.78}$$

$$\frac{\widetilde{V}}{\widetilde{X_0}} = \frac{sd_{31}}{sC + \frac{1}{Z}}. \tag{8.79}$$

- When we adopt the step force, that is $\widetilde{X_0} = X_0/s$, we can obtain the voltage

$\widetilde{V} = \frac{d_{31}X_0}{(sC+\frac{1}{Z})} = \frac{d_{31}X_0}{C}\frac{1}{s+\frac{1}{ZC}}$.

Taking an inverse Laplace transform, we obtain the voltage change with time for the first impact as

$$V = (d_{31}X_0/C)e^{-t/ZC}. \tag{8.80}$$

However, this analysis leads the reader in the wrong direction: we do not consider the vibration and voltage ringing with the resonance frequency, but consider just one-time polarization generation.

- When we approximate the vibration ringing after the impulse force as cyclic (sinusoidal) natural (resonance) vibration (though the actual displacement behavior is linear, not sinusoidal), we may adopt Fourier transform by replacing the above Laplace form with $s = j\omega$ for relatively long time-period. Here, ω is considered to be the natural resonance frequency under the Z-shunt condition. The dynamic impedance of the piezo component (off-resonance) becomes $1/j\omega C$. From $V = \frac{I}{j\omega C+\frac{1}{Z}} = \frac{j\omega d_{31}X_0}{j\omega C+\frac{1}{Z}}$ and $I = i_{out}(1 + j\omega CZ)$, the output electric energy is described as

$$|P|_{out} = \frac{1}{2}\,Re[\frac{1}{2}Vi_{out}{}^*] = \frac{1}{2}\,Z\,\frac{(\omega dX_0)^2}{(1+(\omega CZ)^2)}. \tag{8.81}$$

The maximum power energy $|P| = \frac{1}{4}\frac{\omega d^2X_0^2}{C}$ can be obtained when the external impedance is adjusted to

$$Z = 1/\omega C. \tag{8.82}$$

In other words, the maximum "stored" electric energy can be spent by half when the external resistive load impedance matches exactly to the internal impedance. This is called resistive "electrical impedance matching".

We now calculate the "input mechanical energy" under Z-shunt condition from the second constitutive equation:

$$x = d_{31}E + s_{11}{}^EX = -d_{31}\left(\frac{V}{b}\right) + s_{11}{}^EX = -\left(\frac{d_{31}}{b}\right)\left[\frac{j\omega d_{31}X_0}{\frac{1}{Z} + j\omega C}\right] + s_{11}{}^EX. \tag{8.83}$$

The last transformation used Equation (8.79). We obtained effective elastic compliance as

$$s_{eff}^{E} = \frac{x}{X} = s^{E}[1 - k_{31}{}^{2}\frac{j\omega CZ}{(1 + j\omega CZ)}]. \tag{8.84}$$

Under $Z = 1/\omega C$, Equation (8.84) becomes

$$s_{eff}^{E} = s^{E}(1 - \frac{1}{2}k_{31}{}^{2} + \frac{j}{2}k_{31}{}^{2}). \tag{8.85}$$

The resonance period T may be estimated as

$$T = 2L\sqrt{\rho s_{eff}^{E}} = T_{0}(1 - \frac{1}{4}k_{31}{}^{2}), \tag{8.86}$$

which is shorter than the short-circuit condition T_0, but longer than the open-circuit condition $T_0(1 - \frac{4}{\pi^2}k_{31}^2)$.

Let us calculate the energy spent in the external impedance Z, which should be the matched external impedance of the piezoelectric energy harvesting system. The "impulse" vibration energy U_M (time averaged by $\int_{half\ cycle}\frac{1}{2}\frac{x_0^2}{s^E}dt$) is transformed into electric energy U_E by the factor of k^2 ($U_E = U_M \times k^2$), then a half of this energy can be spent accumulating into a rechargeable battery ($(1/2)k^2 \times U_M$) when we take the exact matching impedance condition for the piezo component. For the next half cycle (i.e., opposite voltage and current during shrinkage), we start from the mechanical energy $(1 - k^2/2)U_M$, without taking into account the elastic loss ($\tan\phi' \ll 1$) in the system. As the square of the amplitude is equivalent to the amount of energy, the amplitude decreases at a rate of $(1 - k^2/2)^{1/2}$ times with every vibration repeated. If the resonance period is taken to be T_0, the number of vibrations for t sec is $2t/T_0$. Consequently, the amplitude in t sec is $(1 - k^2/2)^{t/T_0}$. If the residual vibration period is taken to be T_0, the damping in the amplitude of vibration is t sec and can be expressed as follows:

$$(1 - k^2/2)^{t/T_0} = e^{-t/\tau}. \tag{8.87}$$

Thus, the following relationship for the time constant of the vibration damping is obtained.

$$\tau = -\frac{T_0}{\ln(1 - k^2/2)}. \tag{8.88}$$

If we consider the elastic loss ($\tan\phi'$ which corresponds to the damping constant τ_S), the energy decay will be $(1 - k^2/2)e^{-T_0/2\tau_S}U_M$ every half cycle. Note that elastic loss or its inverse "mechanical quality factor" Q_M are related with τ_S as

$$\frac{T_0}{\tau_S} = \frac{\pi}{Q_M}. \tag{8.89}$$

A similar process will be repeated every half cycle during the ringing-down process after the step force is applied. The sequential energy ring-down process can be summarized in Table 8.2. The total loss energy (after n time sequences) can be calculated as

$$\frac{1}{2}k^2U_M\sum_{n=0}^{n}\left[\left(1-\frac{1}{2}k^2\right)e^{-\frac{\pi}{2Q_M}}\right]^n=\frac{1}{2}k^2U_M\frac{1-\left[\left(1-\frac{1}{2}k^2\right)e^{-\frac{\pi}{2Q_M}}\right]^n}{1-\left(1-\frac{1}{2}k^2\right)e^{-\frac{\pi}{2Q_M}}}. \quad (8.90)$$

Table 8.2. Electromechanical properties of the commercial PZT ceramics.

Sequence n	Mechanical Energy	Electrical Energy	Spent/Accumulated Energy
0	U_M	k^2U_M	$\frac{1}{2}k^2U_M$
1	$(1-\frac{1}{2}k^2)e^{-\pi/2Q_M}U_M$	$k^2(1-\frac{1}{2}k^2)e^{-\pi/2Q_M}U_M$	$\frac{1}{2}k^2(1-\frac{1}{2}k^2)e^{-\pi/2Q_M}U_M$
2	$[(1-\frac{1}{2}k^2)e^{-\frac{\pi}{2Q_M}}]^2U_M$	$k^2[(1-\frac{1}{2}k^2)e^{-\frac{\pi}{2Q_M}}]^2U_M$	$\frac{1}{2}k^2[(1-\frac{1}{2}k^2)e^{-\frac{\pi}{2Q_M}}]^2U_M$
3	$[(1-\frac{1}{2}k^2)e^{-\frac{\pi}{2Q_M}}]^3U_M$	$k^2[(1-\frac{1}{2}k^2)e^{-\frac{\pi}{2Q_M}}]^3U_M$	$\frac{1}{2}k^2[(1-\frac{1}{2}k^2)e^{-\frac{\pi}{2Q_M}}]^3U_M$
⋮	⋮	⋮	⋮
n	$[(1-\frac{1}{2}k^2)e^{-\frac{\pi}{2Q_M}}]^nU_M$	$k^2[(1-\frac{1}{2}k^2)e^{-\frac{\pi}{2Q_M}}]^nU_M$	$\frac{1}{2}k^2[(1-\frac{1}{2}k^2)e^{-\frac{\pi}{2Q_M}}]^nU_M$

Source: Table by author.

This indicates the following results according to the mechanical quality factor:

- High Q_M (~10,000) → Since the energy loss is small, the total energy accumulated will reach almost the input mechanical energy U_M after more than 10,000 ring-down processes.
- Low Q_M (~0.5) → Since the original damping is large, the total energy loss will be $\frac{1}{2}k^2\frac{1}{0.96+0.02k^2}$, just slightly larger than $\frac{1}{2}k^2$. This situation corresponds to only one-time pulse displacement, discussed in Equation (8.80).

Figure 8.16 compares the transient displacement ΔL produced by rectangular pulse stress under Z-shunt and short-circuit conditions with a pulse width close to $(T/2)$. When we use a matching impedance, the vibration amplitude decay rate is determined by $k^2/2$. Note the resonance period is shorter for the Z-shunt than for the short-circuit condition, while it is longer than that of the open-circuit condition. The total energy accumulation reaches almost the input mechanical energy U_M after multiple (~100 cycles) ring-down processes.

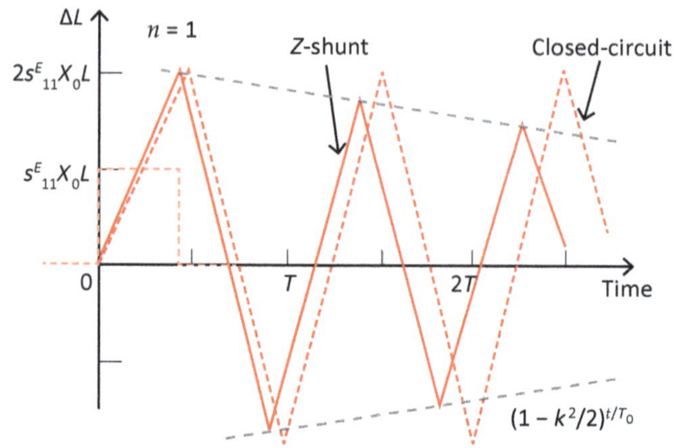

Figure 8.16. Transient displacement ΔL produced by rectangular pulse stress under Z-shunt and short-circuit conditions with the pulse width close to $(T/2)$. Source: Figure by author.

Example Problem 8.4

In order to develop a piezoelectric energy harvesting device, a bimorph piezoelectric element was prepared as shown in Figure 8.17a. An elastic beam was sandwiched with two sheets of piezoelectric ceramic plates, the characteristics of which are summarized as:

Length (mm)	Width (mm)	Thickness (mm)	Resonance	k_{eff}	Mechanical Q_m
25	16	0.5	294 Hz	0.28	30

Now, the bimorph edge was hit by an impulse force, and the transient vibration displacement decay (i.e., damping performance) was monitored under several connected external resistances, including short- and open-circuit conditions. Figure 8.17b shows the measured displacement data, which vibrate at almost the bimorph fundamental resonance frequency (295 Hz). The damping time constant was minimized in the vicinity of 7 kΩ, which is close to the resistive impedance $1/\omega C$ (C: bimorph capacitance). From the data under short-circuit conditions, we obtain the damping time constant $\tau_s = 102$ ms, while under a matching impedance 6.6 kΩ, the damping time constant is $\tau = 40$ ms. Calculate the possible electric energy harvested during the vibration ring-down process under the matching impedance condition.

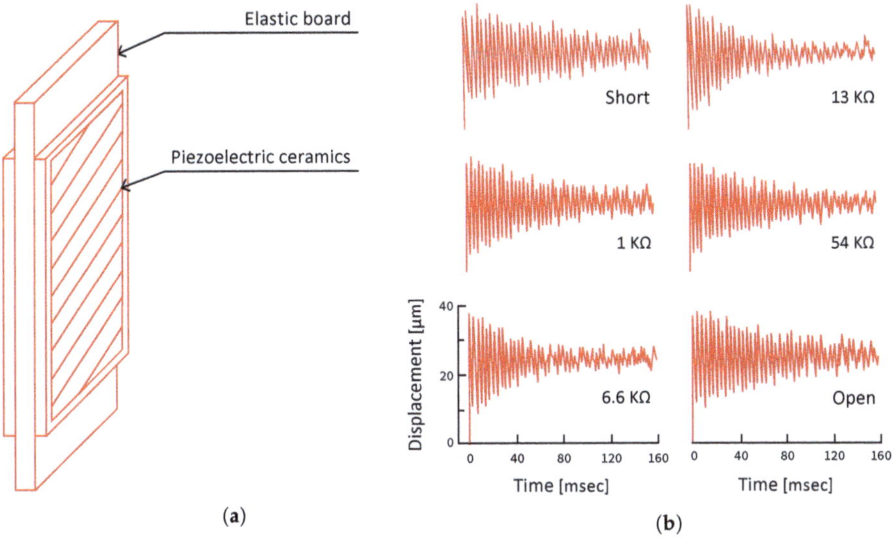

Figure 8.17. Vibration damping change associated with external resistance change. (**a**) Bimorph transducer for this measurement; (**b**) damped vibration with external resistor. Source: [2] ©Uchino, K. *Micromechatronics*, 2nd ed. CRC Press, 2019; p. 388. Reproduced by permission of Taylor & Francis Group.

Solution

Since the bimorph exhibits the intrinsic damping time constant $\tau_s = 102$ ms, the observed damping time constant $\tau = 40$ ms includes the intrinsic one. From the relation

$$\frac{1}{\tau_{total}} = \frac{1}{\tau_s} + \frac{1}{\tau_k}. \tag{P8.4.1}$$

The electromechanical coupling-factor-related damping time constant is obtained as $\tau_k = 85$ ms, which actually corresponds to the electric energy harvesting contribution.

Taking into account the resonance period $T_0 = 3.4$ ms, from the equation for the damping related with the electromechanical coupling factor,

$$\tau = -\frac{T_0}{\ln\left(1 - \frac{k^2}{2}\right)}, \tag{P8.4.2}$$

we obtain $k = 0.28$, exactly the same as this bimorph k_{eff} obtained from the impedance spectrum analysis.

Therefore, the total loss energy (after n time sequences) is given in Equation (8.90):

$$\frac{1}{2}k^2 U_M \frac{1 - \left[\left(1 - \frac{1}{2}k^2\right)e^{-\frac{\pi}{2Q_M}}\right]^n}{1 - \left(1 - \frac{1}{2}k^2\right)e^{-\frac{\pi}{2Q_M}}}. \tag{P8.4.3}$$

After the impulse mechanical energy U_M on this bimorph with $Q_M \sim 30$ and $k = 0.28$, Equation (P8.4.3) becomes $0.22U_M$ (summation from the first 30 pulses), which is between $\frac{1}{2}k^2 U_M$ ($\frac{1}{2}k^2 = 0.039$) and U_M. Because of low Q_M, the loss seems to be significant in comparison with loss-free (high Q_M) piezoelectric element.

Example Problem 8.5

We have a rectangular k_{31} piezo-ceramic plate (Figure 8.5). Using a Heaviside voltage drive technique, the transient length displacement change is measured as a function of time, and the displacement curve pictured in Figure 8.18 is obtained. Explain how to determine the k_{31}, d_{31} and Q_m values from these data. The density ρ, and dielectric constant $\varepsilon_{33}{}^X$, of the ceramic must be known prior to the experiments. You may also use the relationship: $Q_m = (1/2)\omega_0\tau$, where ω_0 is the resonance angular frequency (i.e., $2\pi/\omega_0$ is the resonance period) and τ is the damping time constant.

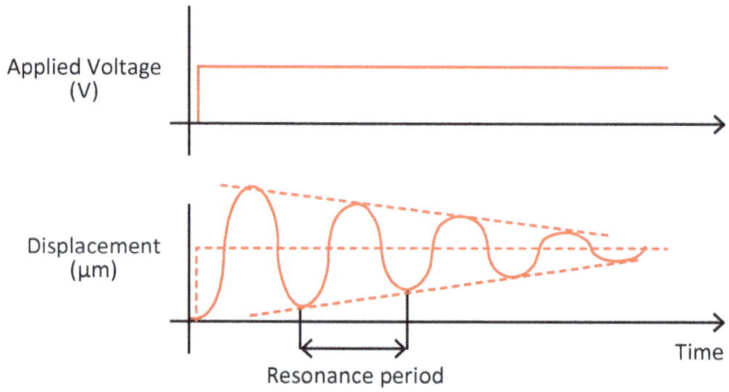

Figure 8.18. Pulse drive technique for measuring the electromechanical parameters. Source: [2] ©Uchino, K. *Micromechatronics*, 2nd ed. CRC Press, 2019; p. 279. Reproduced by permission of Taylor & Francis Group.

Solution

The pulse drive method is a simple method for measuring high voltage piezoelectric characteristics, developed in the ICAT/Penn State in the early 1990s. By applying a step electric field to a piezoelectric sample, the transient vibration displacement (i.e., "ringing-down") corresponding to the desired mode (extensional, bending, etc.) is measured under a short-circuit condition (see Figure 8.18). Because the equipment cost could be minimized (in comparison with a commercialized expensive "impedance analyzer"), this method was used previously. Notice that one-time high-voltage application (though multiple time measurements are technically accumulated with a certain interval) and the following short period (~ms) ringing vibration do not generate a measurable temperature rise experimentally (<0.2 °C). The resonance period, stabilized displacement, and damping time constant are obtained experimentally, from which the elastic compliance s^E, piezoelectric constant d, mechanical quality factor Q_m and electromechanical coupling factor k can be calculated. Using a rectangular k_{31} piezoelectric ceramic plate (length: L; width: w; and thickness: b; poled along the thickness, as in the inserted figure in Figure 8.2), we explain how to determine the electromechanical coupling parameters k_{31}, d_{31}, and Q_m step by step below. The density ρ, permittivity $\varepsilon_{33}{}^X$, and size (L, w, b) of the ceramic plate must be known prior to the experiments.

1. From the stabilized displacement D_s, we obtain the piezoelectric coefficient d_{31}:

$$D_s = d_{31}EL. \quad \text{(P8.5.1)}$$

2. From the ringing period, we obtain the elastic compliance $s_{11}{}^E$:

$$T_0 = 2L/v_{11}{}^E = 2L(\rho s_{11}{}^E)^{1/2}. \quad \text{(P8.5.2)}$$

3. From the damping time constant, which is determined by the time interval to decrease the displacement amplitude by $1/e$, we obtain the mechanical quality factor Q_m:

$$Q_m = (1/2)\omega_0\tau, \quad \text{(P8.5.3)}$$

where the resonance angular frequency $\omega_0 = 2\pi/T_0$.

4. From the piezoelectric coefficient d_{31}, elastic compliance $s_{11}{}^E$, and permittivity $\varepsilon_3{}^X$, we obtain the electromechanical coupling factor k_{31}:

$$k_{31} = d_{31}/(\varepsilon_0\varepsilon_3{}^X s_{11}{}^E)^{1/2}. \quad \text{(P8.5.4)}$$

On the other hand, the antiresonance Q_m can be obtained as follows: by suddenly removing a large electric field from a piezoelectric sample, and keeping the open circuit, the transient vibration displacement corresponds to the antiresonance mode. The bias electric field (and the vibration velocity) dependence of piezoelectricity can be measured. One drawback is the vibration velocity level: due to just one-time high-voltage application, the induced displacement or strain level is limited.

Chapter Essentials

1. The Laplace transform—Beneficial to impulse transient analysis
$U(s) = L[u(t)] = \int_0^\infty e^{-st}u(t)dt.$
   - Differentiation with respect to t:
   $L\left[\frac{du(t)}{dt}\right] = sU(s) - u(0),$
   $L\left[\frac{d^n u(t)}{dt^n}\right] = s^n U(s) - \sum s^{n-k}u^{k-1}(0);$
   - Integration:
   $L[\int u(t)dt] = U(s)/s + (1/s)[\int u(t)dt]_{t=0};$
   - Shift formula with respect to t:
   $L[u(t-k)] = e^{-ks}U(s).$
2. Laplace Transform of the k_{31} Mode Vibration Equation—Electric Field Drive:
$\rho s_{11}^E s^2 U(s,x) = \frac{\partial^2 U(s,x)}{\partial x^2},$
$U(s,L) = \frac{d_{31}\tilde{E}(v/s)(1-e^{-sL/v})}{(1+e^{-sL/v})} = d_{31}\tilde{E}(v/s)[\tanh(sL/2v)].$
3. Pulse and Pseudo-Step Response of the k_{31} Mode—Electrical Drive (summarized in Figures 8.7a and 8.9a).

4. Laplace Transform of the k_{31} Mode Vibration Equation—Mechanical Stress Drive (Summarized in Figure 8.13).
$U(s,x) = s_{11}^E \widetilde{X}(\frac{v}{s}) \frac{\cosh[\frac{s(2x-L)}{2v}]}{\cosh(\frac{sL}{2v})}$,
$L[x_1(s,x)] = s_{11}^E \widetilde{X} \frac{\sinh[\frac{s(2x-L)}{2v}]}{\cosh(\frac{sL}{2v})}$.
5. Stress Pulse Response of the k_{31} Mode: Under matching impedance Z conditions:
$s_{eff}^E = s^E[1 - k_{31}{}^2 \frac{j\omega CZ}{(1+j\omega CZ)}]$,
when $Z = 1/\omega C$, $s_{eff}^E = s^E(1 - \frac{1}{2}k_{31}{}^2 + \frac{j}{2}k_{31}{}^2)$, and $T = 2L\sqrt{\rho s_{eff}^E} = T_0(1 - \frac{1}{4}k_{31}{}^2)$.
6. Total electric energy (after n time sequences) harvested in the matched impedance $Z = 1/\omega C$:
$\frac{1}{2}k^2 U_M \frac{1-[(1-\frac{1}{2}k^2)e^{-\frac{\pi}{2Q_M}}]^n}{1-(1-\frac{1}{2}k^2)e^{-\frac{\pi}{2Q_M}}}$,
which ranges between $\frac{1}{2}k^2 U_M$ (low Q_M) and U_M (high Q_M).

Check Point

1. Using the Laplace transformation definition: $U(s) = L[u(t)] = \int_0^\infty e^{-st}u(t)dt$, calculate $U(s)$ for the Heaviside step function $u(t) = 1(t)$ [$u(t) = 0$ ($t < 0$); $u(t) = 1$ ($t > 0$)].
2. Derive the function $u(t)$ for the Laplace Transform: $U(s) = (m/s^2)e^{-as}$. Note a kink on the curve.
3. (T/F) When a piezoelectric actuator is driven by a rectangular pulse voltage, the mechanical ringing is completely suppressed when the pulse width is adjusted to exactly half of the resonance period of the sample. True or false?
4. When a piezoelectric actuator is driven by a Heaviside step voltage, the vibration displacement overshoot is excited (by neglecting mechanical loss). What is the maximum overshoot range (percentage), in comparison with the normal (pseudo-static) operation? Is it 10, 16.7, 33, 50, 100, or 200% larger than the normal displacement?
5. (T/F) When a piezoelectric k_{31} plate is driven by Heaviside step mechanical stress on the plate edges, the vibration displacement is exhibited linearly with time. True or false?
6. (T/F) When a piezoelectric k_{31} plate is driven by a Heaviside step mechanical stress on the plate edges, the resonance period under the short condition is shorter than that under the open-circuit condition. True or false?
7. (T/F) Total electric energy (after n time sequences) harvested in a high Q_m piezo component under the pulse stress drive in the matched impedance $Z = 1/\omega C$ reaches almost total input mechanical energy, irrelevant to the electromechanical coupling factor k. True or false?
8. (T/F) When a piezoelectric k_{31} plate is driven by a "pulse" mechanical stress with the pulse width exactly matching the resonance period, the electric energy

harvested in the matched impedance $Z = 1/\omega C$ connected reaches $\frac{1}{2}k_{31}^2 U_M$. U_M: input mechanical energy. True or false?

9. A piezoelectric plate was excited by a Heaviside step mechanical stress. We observed the resonance period ω_0 and the damping time constant τ of the total displacement, which is determined by the time interval to decrease the displacement amplitude by $1/e$. Obtain the mechanical quality factor Q_m from these data.
10. (T/F) The resonance frequency of the k_{31} type piezo-plate excited by the stress pulse drive under the matching impedance Z (=$1/\omega C$) condition ranges between the piezoelectric resonance and antiresonance frequencies. True or false?

Chapter Problems

8.1 Using the k_{31} type piezo-plate (Figure 8.5), we consider the Heaviside step stress application on the length edges. Calculate the total displacement ring-down behavior under the open-circuit condition in comparison with the short-circuit condition, the result of which is illustrated in Figure 8.14. Using a notation, $K_{31}^2 = \frac{k_{31}^2}{(1-k_{31}^2)}$, the Laplace form of displacement U(s,L) (=(1/2)ΔL) is expressed as: $U(s,L) = \frac{s_{11}^E \widetilde{X}\left\{-2\left(\frac{s}{v}\right)+e^{\frac{sL}{v}}\left[\left(\frac{s}{v}\right)+\left(\frac{2K_{31}^2}{L}\right)\right]+e^{-\frac{sL}{v}}\left[\left(\frac{s}{v}\right)-\left(\frac{2K_{31}^2}{L}\right)\right]\right\}}{e^{\frac{sL}{v}}\left[\left(\frac{s}{v}\right)+\left(\frac{2K_{31}^2}{L}\right)\right]^2 - e^{-\frac{sL}{v}}\left[\left(\frac{s}{v}\right)-\left(\frac{2K_{31}^2}{L}\right)\right]^2}$.

<u>Hint</u>

Use $f(s-a) \to e^{at}F(t)$ for the $[\left(\frac{s}{v}\right) \pm \left(\frac{2K_{31}^2}{L}\right)]$ terms to convert the resonance frequency $\omega_A = v/2L$ to the antiresonance frequency ω_B, which satisfies the relation: $(\omega_B L/2v_{11}{}^E)\cot(\omega_B L/2v_{11}{}^E) = -k_{31}{}^2/(1 - k_{31}{}^2)$. Since $\widetilde{X} \propto 1/s$ and $U(s,L) \propto s_{11}^E \widetilde{X}(1/s) \propto 1/s^2$, we can get the basic function $\propto t$; linear relation with time lapse.

References

1. Uchino, K. *Ferroelectric Devices*, 2nd ed.; CRC Press: Boca Raton, FL, USA, 2010.
2. Uchino, K. *Micromechatronics*, 2nd ed.; CRC Press: Boca Raton, FL, USA, 2020.
3. Uchino, K. Piezoelectric Actuator Renaissance. *J. Energy Harvest. Syst.* **2014**, *1*, 45–56. [CrossRef]
4. Uchino, K. *High-Power Piezoelectrics and Loss Mechanisms*; CRC Press: Boca Raton, FL, USA, 2020.
5. Sugiyama, S.; Uchino, K. Pulse Driving Method of Piezoelectric Actuators. In Proceedings of the Sixth IEEE International Symposium on Applications of Ferroelectrics, Bethlehem, PA, USA, 8–11 June 1986; p. 637. [CrossRef]
6. Ogawa, T. *Crystal Physical Engineering*; Shokabo Pub.: Tokyo, Japan, 1976.
7. Smiley, S. Lever Motion Multiplier Driven by Electroexpansive Material. US Patent No. 3614486, 19 October 1971.
8. Uchino, K. Piezoelectric Energy Harvesting Systems—Essentials to Successful Developments. *J. Energy Technol.* **2018**, *6*, 829–848. [CrossRef]

9. Uchino, K.; Ishii, T. Mechanical Damper Using Piezoelectric Ceramics. *J. Ceram. Soc. Japan* **1988**, *96*, 863. [CrossRef]

9. Equivalent Circuit

Mechanical and electrical systems are occasionally equivalent from the viewpoint of a mathematical formula. Therefore, an electrician tries to understand mechanical system behavior from a more familiar LCR electrical circuit analysis, or vice versa: a mechanic uses a mass-spring-damper model to understand an electric circuit. However, because discrete components are used in the analysis, the "equivalent circuit" analysis cannot provide the spatial analysis of the strain/displacement or current/voltage in the specimen, as demonstrated in Chapter 8. Two important notes must be taken into account: (1) mechanical loss is handled as "viscous damping", though the losses in piezoelectric ceramics may be "solid damping" in reality; (2) an equivalent circuit approach is almost successful, as long as we consider a steady sinusoidal (harmonic) vibration. Because the "equivalent circuit" approach is the handling simplification from the "continuum media" to "discrete component", some discrepancies arise. For example, when we consider a transient response, such as a pulse drive of a mechanical system with a finite specimen size, the equivalent circuit analysis cannot generate a time-linear response of the specimen's displacement.

The equivalent (electric) circuit (EC) is a commonly used tool which can greatly simplify the process of design and analysis of the piezoelectric devices, in which the circuit, in a standard form, reference [1] can only graphically characterize the mechanical loss by applying a resistor (and sometimes dielectric loss). Different from a pure mechanical system, a piezoelectric vibration exhibits an "antiresonance mode" in addition to a "resonance mode", due to the existence of the damped capacitance (i.e., only part of the input electric energy is transduced into the mechanical energy). As discussed in Chapter 6, without introducing the "piezoelectric loss" it is difficult to explain the difference of the mechanical quality factors at the resonance and antiresonance modes. Damjanovic therefore introduced an additional branch into the standard circuit, which is used to present the influence of the piezoelectric loss [2]. However, concise and decoupled formulae of three (dielectric, elastic, and piezoelectric) losses have not been derived, which can be used for the measurement of losses in piezoelectric material as a user-friendly method. We consider new equivalent circuits of piezoelectric devices with these three losses in this chapter.

9.1. Equivalency between Mechanical and Electrical Systems

There are two classifications of LCR electrical circuits: series connection and parallel connection for the equivalent circuit analysis. Though both circuits are equivalent, in general, focused usage is different.

9.1.1. LCR Series Connection Equivalent Circuit

The dynamic equation for a pure mechanical system composed of a mass, a spring, and a damper, illustrated in Table 9.1a, is expressed by

$$M(d^2u/dt^2) + \zeta(du/dt) + c \cdot u = F(t), \text{ or} \quad (9.1a)$$

$$M(dv/dt) + \zeta v + c\int_0^t v\,dt = F(t), \tag{9.1b}$$

where u is the displacement of a mass M, v is the velocity (= du/dt), c spring constant, ζ damping constant of the dashpot, and F is the external force. Note that when a continuum elastic material is considered, the actual damping may be "solid damping" (as we discussed in the previous Section 6.2.2), but here we consider or approximate the "viscous damping", where the damping force is described in proportion to the velocity, from a mathematical simplicity viewpoint.

On the other hand, the dynamic equation for an electrical circuit composed of a "series connection" of an inductance L, a capacitance C, and a resistance R, illustrated in Table 9.1b, is expressed by

$$L(d^2q/dt^2) + R(dq/dt) + (1/C)q = V(t), \text{ or} \tag{9.2a}$$

$$L(dI/dt) + RI + (1/C)\int_0^t I\,dt = V(t), \tag{9.2b}$$

where q is charge, I is the current (= dq/dt), and V is the external voltage. Taking into account the equation similarity (in this case, force vs. voltage and vibration velocity vs. current), the engineer introduces an equivalent circuit; consider a mechanical system using an equivalent electrical circuit, which is intuitively simpler for an electrical engineer. In contrast, consider an electrical circuit using an equivalent mechanical system, which is intuitively simpler for a mechanical engineer. Equivalency between these two systems is summarized in the center column in Table 9.1. We consider the "parallel connection" model in the next section, where force vs. current and vibration velocity vs. voltage correlations are treated.

Table 9.1. Equivalency between mechanical and electrical systems, composed of M (mass); c (spring constant); ζ (viscous damper); L (inductance); C (capacitance); R (resistance). (**a**) Mechanical system; (**b**) LCR series connection; (**c**) LCR parallel connection.

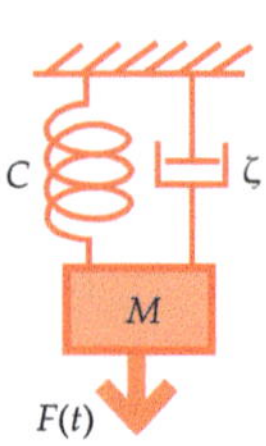

(a)

Mechanical	Electrical ($F - V$)	Electrical ($F - I$)
Force $F(t)$	Voltage $V(t)$	Current $I(t)$
Velocity $v/\dot{u}$	Current I	Voltage V
Displacement u	Charque q	--
Mass M	Inductance L	Capacitance C
Spring Compliance $1/c$	Capacitance C	Inductance L
Damping ζ	Resisance R	Conductance G

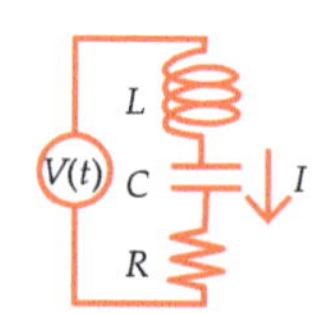

(b)

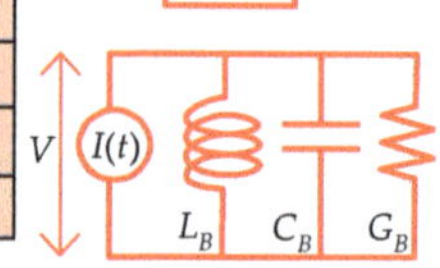

(c)

Source: [3] ©Uchino, K. *Micromechatronics*, 2nd ed. CRC Press, 2019; p. 325. Reproduced by permission of Taylor & Francis Group.

When we consider "steady sinusoidal vibrations" of the system at the frequency ω ($V(t) = V_0 e^{j\omega t}$, $I(t) = I_0 e^{i\omega t - \delta}$), Equation (9.2) can be transformed into

$$[j\omega L + R + (1/j\omega C)]I = V, \text{ or} \tag{9.3a}$$

$$Y = I/V = [j\omega L + R + (1/j\omega C)]^{-1}. \tag{9.3b}$$

Under a constant unit voltage (such as 1 V), the current (A) behavior provides the frequency dependence of the "circuit admittance". Thus, this series connection equivalent circuit (EC) is useful to discuss the piezoelectric resonance mode with the admittance maximum peak.

We consider the "Bode plot" of Equation (9.3b). A "Bode plot" is a graph of the frequency response of a system, usually a combination of a magnitude and phase angle, as introduced in Section 6.3. The admittance $|Y|$ gain (i.e., $20 \log_{10}|Y|$) is plotted in Figure 9.1a as a function of frequency ω in a logarithmic scale. The steady-state oscillation plot exhibits:

(1) A 20 dB/decade ($\propto \omega C$) asymptotic curve with 90° phase in the low-frequency region.

(2) The peak at ω_0, resonance angular frequency for zero damping, given by $\omega_0 = 1/\sqrt{LC}$, with the peak height $|Y|_{max} = (1/R)$, and $Q = \sqrt{L/C}/R$, which corresponds to the quality factor.

(3) A -20 dB/decade ($\propto 1/\omega L$) asymptotic curve with $-90°$ phase in the high frequency region.

Let us calculate the quality factor Q in the LCR circuit defined by $\omega_R/2\Delta\omega_R$, where $\Delta\omega_R$ is the half width of the admittance frequency spectrum to provide the $1/\sqrt{2}$ (3 dB down) of the maximum admittance $(1/R)$ at the resonance frequency ω_R. Since these cut-off frequencies are provided by

$$\frac{1}{\sqrt{2}} = \frac{1}{\sqrt{\left[\left(\frac{\omega_C L}{R}\right)-\left(\frac{1}{\omega_C RC}\right)\right]^2+1}}.$$

Then, two roots for the cut-off frequency ω_C are given by

$$\omega_{c1,c2} = \mp\frac{R}{2L} + \sqrt{\left(\frac{R}{2L}\right)^2 + \left(\frac{1}{LC}\right)}.$$

Since $2\Delta\omega_R = \omega_{c2} - \omega_{c1}$ and $\omega_R = 1/\sqrt{LC}$, the quality factor is expressed by

$$Q = \omega R/2\Delta\omega R = \left(1/\sqrt{LC}\right)/(R/L) = \sqrt{L/C}/R. \quad (9.4)$$

When we consider the charge q (which corresponds to u), rather than current I under the voltage (Equation (9.2a)):

$$L(d^2q/dt^2) + R(dq/dt) + (1/C)q = V(t).$$

Taking the harmonic oscillation, the above equation is transformed to

$$[-\omega^2 L + j\omega R + (1/C)]q = V, \text{ or} \quad (9.5a)$$

$$q/V == [-\omega^2 L + j\omega R + (1/C)]^{-1}. \quad (9.5b)$$

The Bode plot of Equation (9.5b), known as a "standard second-order system" (because of ω^2 in the denominator), is shown in Figure 9.1b, where the gain of charge q is plotted in a logarithmic scale and phase in a linear scale as a function of frequency ω. The steady state oscillation plot exhibits:

(1) A 0 dB/decade asymptotic curve in the low frequency region.

(2) A peak at ω_0, resonance angular frequency for zero damping, given by $\omega_0 = 1/\sqrt{LC}$, with the peak height $(1/2\zeta) = \sqrt{L/C}/R = Q$, which corresponds to the quality factor.
(3) A -40 dB/decade asymptotic curve in the high-frequency region.

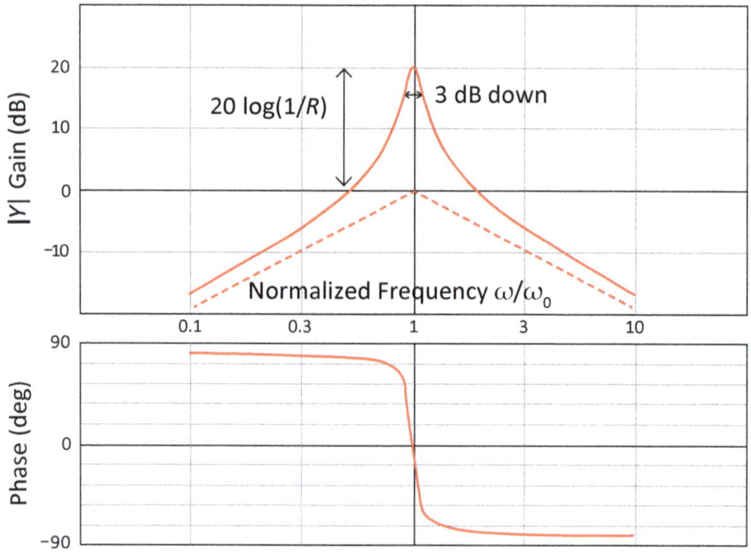

(**a**)

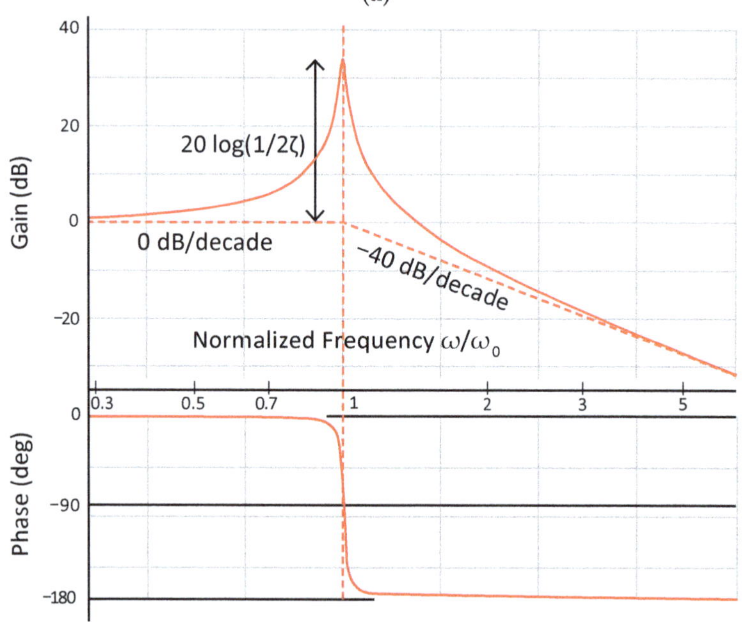

(**b**)

Figure 9.1. Bode diagram for a series LCR circuit: (**a**) admittance; (**b**) charge (second-order system). Source: Figure by author, adapted from [4].

9.1.2. LCR Parallel Connection Equivalent Circuit

Let us now consider the dynamic equation for an electrical circuit composed of a "parallel connection" of an inductance L_B, a capacitance C_B, and a conductance G_B illustrated in Table 9.1c:

$$C_B(dV/dt) + G_B\, V + (1/L_B)\int_0^t V dt = I(t), \quad (9.6)$$

where I is the current from the current supply, and V is the same voltage applied on three components. In comparison with Equation (9.1b), equivalency between the two mechanical and electrical systems is summarized in the last column in Table 9.1. When we consider steady sinusoidal vibrations of the system at the frequency ω ($I(t) = I_0 e^{j\omega t}$, $V(t) = V_0 e^{i\omega t - \delta}$), Equation (9.6) can now be transformed into

$$[j\omega C_B + G_B + (1/j\omega L_B)]V = I, \text{ or} \quad (9.7a)$$

$$Z = V/I = [j\omega C_B + G_B + (1/j\omega L_B)]^{-1}. \quad (9.7b)$$

Under a unit constant current (such as 1 A), the voltage (V) behavior provides the frequency dependence of the "circuit impedance". Thus, this parallel connection EC is preferred to discuss the piezoelectric "antiresonance mode" (i.e., *B*-type resonance) with the impedance maximum peak.

Example Problem 9.1.

Two equivalent circuits in Table 9.1b,c are modeled for the same mechanical system in Table 9.1a. Therefore, we can expect mutual relationships between these inductance, capacitance, and resistance/conductance values. Obtain the mutual relationships.

Hint

Since the voltage–current behavior should be equivalent in these series and parallel connection circuits, the admittance in Equation (9.3b) should be an inverse of the impedance in Equation (9.7b).

Solution

Equating Z with $1/Y$:

$$Z = [j\omega C_B + G_B + (1/j\omega L_B)]^{-1} = 1/Y = [j\omega L + R + (1/j\omega C)], \quad (P9.1.1)$$

we obtain the following equation:

$$C_B\left(\frac{1}{C} - \omega^2 L\right) + \frac{1}{L_B}\left(L - \frac{1}{\omega^2 C}\right) + RG_B + j\left[G_B\left(\omega L - \frac{1}{\omega C}\right) + R\left(\omega C_B - \frac{1}{\omega L_B}\right)\right] = 1. \quad (P9.1.2)$$

In order to keep the same resonance frequency in both circuits,

$$\omega^2 = \frac{1}{LC} = \frac{1}{L_B C_B}, \tag{P9.1.3}$$

should be maintained. Thus, Equation (P9.1.2) indicates another equation,

$$RG_B = 1. \tag{P9.1.4}$$

Though we have the circuit component flexibility, as long as $LC = L_B C_B$, the simplest solution is the utilization of the same L, C, and R for L_B, C_B, and $1/G_B$.

Example Problem 9.2.

Knowing the mechanical system (mass M, spring c, and damper ζ) and the electric circuit (inductance L, capacitance C, and resistance R) equivalency, as shown in Figure 9.2a, generate the electrical equivalent circuit corresponding to the mechanical system described in Figure 9.2b.

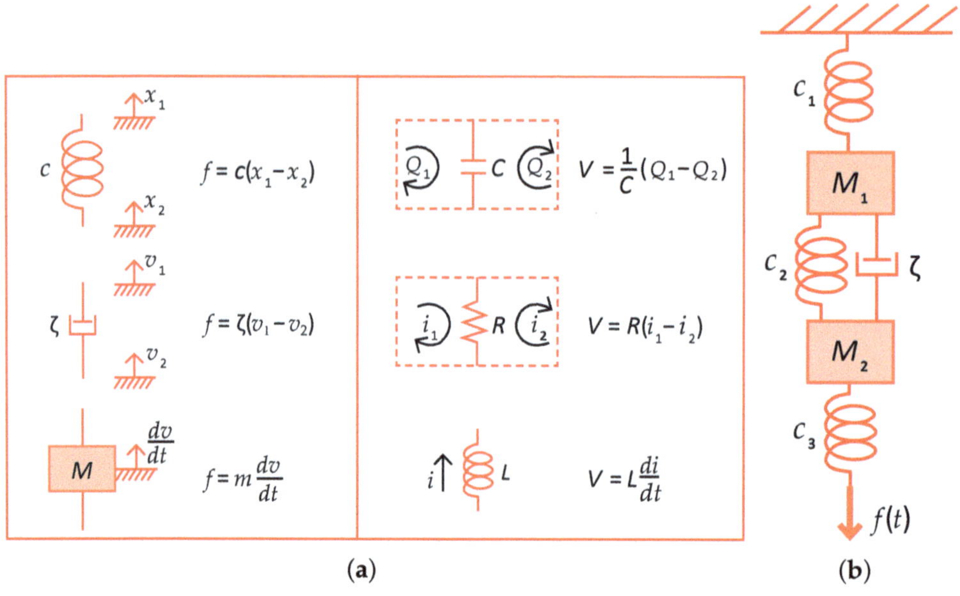

Figure 9.2. (**a**) Equivalency between mechanical components (mass M, spring c, and damper ζ) and electric components (inductance L, capacitance C, and resistance R). (**b**) Example problem. Source: Figure by author, adapted from [4].

<u>Solution</u>

Mass M, spring c, and damper ζ in a mechanical system are converted to inductance L, inverse capacitance $1/C$, and resistance R, respectively, as shown in Figure 9.2a. Note here that only the mass is dependent on one displacement parameter, while the spring and damper are expressed by the subtractions among two displacement parameters, which also reflect on the LCR components. Basically, the force should be the same in the series connection of the mechanical components, while the voltage should be the same in the electrical component circuit. Figure 9.3a shows the mechanical system of the problem under the same force condition, then Figure 9.3b shows transformation process into the electric components. Note that the spring-damper parallel connection is transformed into a capacitor–resistor series connection parallelly inserted to cover "two" closed circuit loops, while the mass (i.e., L) should be inserted independently in one circuit loop. The final equivalent circuit is shown in Figure 9.3c.

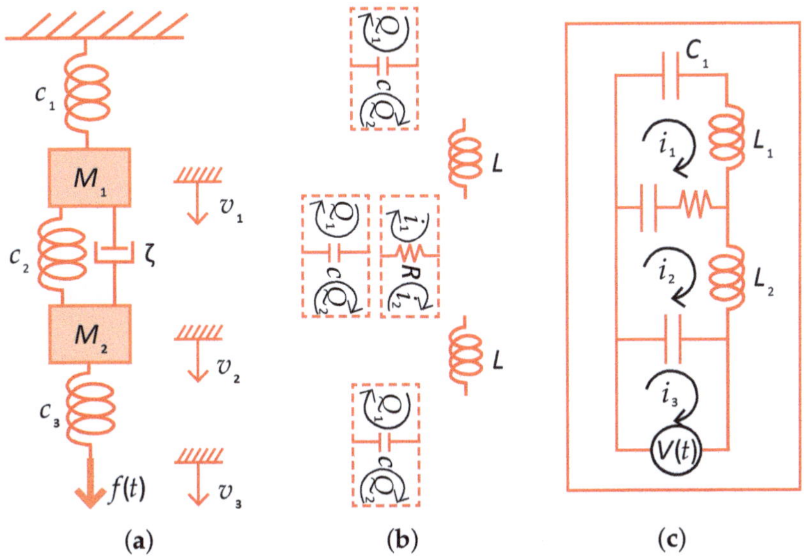

Figure 9.3. (**a**) Mechanical system of the problem; (**b**) transformation process into the electric components; (**c**) the final electrical equivalent circuit. Source: Figure by author.

9.2. Equivalent Circuit (Loss Free) of the k_{31} mode

In Section 9.1, we handled purely mechanical and electrical systems separately, where the principle equations are:

- Mechanical System:
  $\rho \frac{\partial^2 u_i}{\partial t^2} = F_i = \frac{\partial X_{i1}}{\partial x} + \frac{\partial X_{i2}}{\partial y} + \frac{\partial X_{i3}}{\partial z}$: Dynamic equation
  $\boldsymbol{x} = grad(\boldsymbol{u})$ $[x_1 = \frac{\partial u}{\partial x}, x_2 = \frac{\partial v}{\partial y}, x_3 = \frac{\partial w}{\partial z}]$: Strain and displacement
- Electrical System:
  $div(\boldsymbol{D}) = \sigma$: Gauss Law
  $\boldsymbol{E} = -grad(V)$: Electric field and potential/voltage
- Piezoelectric System:
  In addition to the above condition requirements, the following "piezoelectric constitutive equations" must be satisfied in a piezoelectric system (polycrystalline ceramic case):

$$\begin{bmatrix} x_1 \\ x_2 \\ x_3 \\ x_4 \\ x_5 \\ x_6 \end{bmatrix} = \begin{bmatrix} s_{11}{}^E & s_{12}{}^E & s_{13}{}^E & 0 & 0 & 0 \\ s_{12}{}^E & s_{11}{}^E & s_{13}{}^E & 0 & 0 & 0 \\ s_{13}{}^E & s_{13}{}^E & s_{33}{}^E & 0 & 0 & 0 \\ 0 & 0 & 0 & s_{44}{}^E & 0 & 0 \\ 0 & 0 & 0 & 0 & s_{44}{}^E & 0 \\ 0 & 0 & 0 & 0 & 0 & 2\left(s_{11}{}^E - s_{12}{}^E\right) \end{bmatrix} \begin{pmatrix} X_1 \\ X_2 \\ X_3 \\ X_4 \\ X_5 \\ X_6 \end{pmatrix} + \begin{pmatrix} 0 & 0 & d_{31} \\ 0 & 0 & d_{31} \\ 0 & 0 & d_{33} \\ 0 & d_{15} & 0 \\ d_{15} & 0 & 0 \\ 0 & 0 & 0 \end{pmatrix} \begin{bmatrix} E_1 \\ E_2 \\ E_3 \end{bmatrix},$$

$$\begin{bmatrix} D_1 \\ D_2 \\ D_3 \end{bmatrix} = \begin{pmatrix} 0 & 0 & 0 & 0 & d_{15} & 0 \\ 0 & 0 & 0 & d_{15} & 0 & 0 \\ d_{31} & d_{31} & d_{33} & 0 & 0 & 0 \end{pmatrix} \begin{pmatrix} X_1 \\ X_2 \\ X_3 \\ X_4 \\ X_5 \\ X_6 \end{pmatrix} + \varepsilon_0 \begin{bmatrix} \varepsilon_{11} & 0 & 0 \\ 0 & \varepsilon_{11} & 0 \\ 0 & 0 & \varepsilon_{33} \end{bmatrix} \begin{bmatrix} E_1 \\ E_2 \\ E_3 \end{bmatrix}.$$

Now, we introduce the equivalent circuit (EC) of piezoelectric devices, a widely used tool which can greatly simplify the process of designing the devices. The key in a piezoelectric device is illustrated schematically in Figure 9.4, where the input electric energy is partially converted to the output mechanical energy by the factor or k^2, while the remaining energy $(1 - k^2)$ is stored in a capacitor (so-called damped capacitance). Taking the above energy distribution condition into account, the converted mechanical energy part is represented by the above-introduced LCR EC, while the remaining electrical energy part is represented merely by an additional capacitor (i.e., damped capacitance), then these two branches are connected in parallel to keep the applied voltage constant for constructing the total system EC. The loss observed as heat generation is usually small (around a couple of %), which is proportional to the loss tangent/dissipation factor. Different from the previous section of a simple LCR series connection, where only the resonance mode appears, when we include the damped capacitance, the antiresonance mode appears, where the damped (pure electrical component) and motional (originated from mechanical vibration) capacitances are basically canceled out. In other words, the existence of the damped capacitance is essential to generate the antiresonance mode.

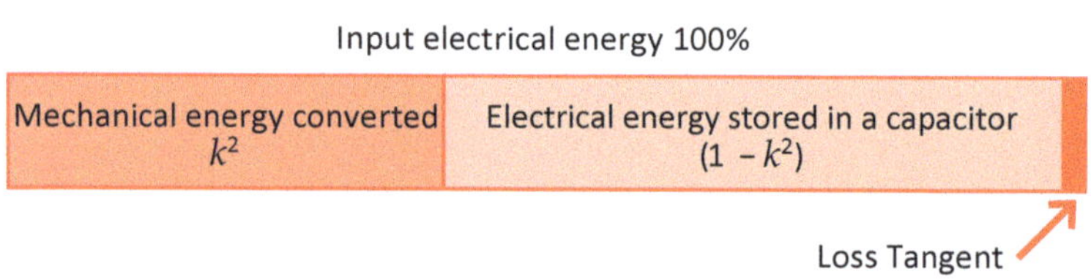

Figure 9.4. Energy conversion in a piezoelectric. Source: Figure by author, adapted from [4].

Next, we consider how to translate the physical parameters in a continuum medium into discrete component parameters, L, C, and R. First, we take the simplest equivalent circuit (loss-free) for the k_{31} mode piezo-plate, as shown in Figure 9.5, on which we already analyzed the resonance/antiresonance modes in detail in Section 7.2.2. Because of the surface electrode, the elastic compliance and sound velocity along the wave propagation direction are E-constant; that is, s_{11}^E and v_{11}^E. You are reminded of the admittance equation:

$$\begin{aligned} Y &= (j\omega wL/b)\varepsilon_0\varepsilon_{33}{}^{LC}\left[1 + \left(d_{31}{}^2/\varepsilon_0\varepsilon_{33}{}^{LC}s_{11}{}^E\right)\left(\tan\left(\omega L/2v_{11}^E\right)/\left(\omega L/2v_{11}^E\right)\right)\right] \\ &= (j\omega wL/b)\varepsilon_0\varepsilon_{33}{}^X\left[(1-k_{31}) + k_{31}{}^2\left(\tan\left(\omega L/2v_{11}^E\right)/\left(\omega L/2v_{11}^E\right)\right)\right] \\ &= j\omega C_d\left[1 + \frac{k_{31}^2}{1-k_{31}^2}\frac{\tan(\Omega_{11})}{\Omega_{11}}\right] = j\omega C_0\left[(1-k_{31}^2) + k_{31}^2\frac{\tan(\Omega_{11})}{\Omega_{11}}\right], \end{aligned} \tag{9.8}$$

where w is the width, L the length, and b the thickness of the rectangular piezo sample. We adopt the following notations to make the formulae simpler:

$k_{31}{}^2 = d_{31}{}^2/\varepsilon_0\varepsilon_{33}^X s_{11}^E$,
$\varepsilon_0\varepsilon_{33}{}^{LC} = \varepsilon_0\varepsilon_{33}{}^X\left(1 - k_{31}{}^2\right)$,
$C_0 = \varepsilon_0\varepsilon_{33}^X\frac{Lw}{b}$ (Free capacitance),
$C_d = \varepsilon_0\varepsilon_{33}^{LC}\frac{Lw}{b}$ (Damped capacitance),
$\Omega_{11} = \left(\omega L/2v_{11}^E\right)$.

Equation (9.8) indicates that the first term originates from the "clamped capacitance" (proportional to $(1 - k^2)$), and the second term is the "motional capacitance" associated with the mechanical vibration (proportional to k^2). By splitting Y into the damped admittance Y_d and the motional part Y_m,

$$Y_d = j\omega C_d = j\omega C_0\left(1 - k_{31}^2\right), \tag{9.9}$$

$$Y_m = j\omega C_d\left[\frac{k_{31}^2}{1-k_{31}^2}\frac{\tan(\Omega_{11})}{\Omega_{11}}\right] = j\omega C_0\left[\frac{\tan(\Omega_{11})}{\Omega_{11}}\right]k_{31}^2. \tag{9.10}$$

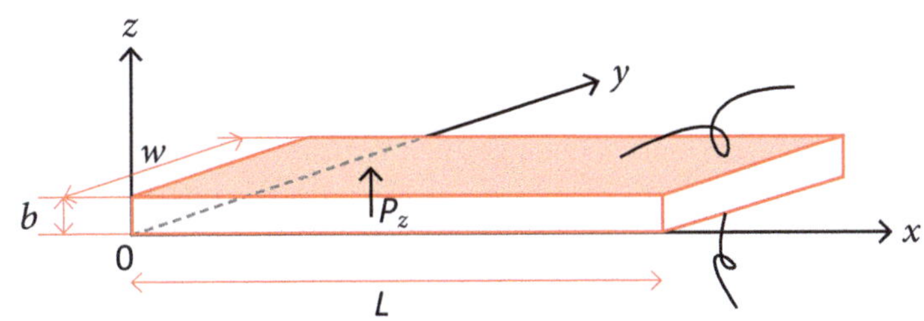

Figure 9.5. A rectangular piezo-ceramic plate ($L \gg w \gg b$) for a longitudinal mode through the transverse piezoelectric effect (d_{31}). Source: [3] ©Uchino, K. *Micromechatronics*, 2nd ed. CRC Press, 2019; p. 111. Reproduced by permission of Taylor & Francis Group.

The damped branch can be represented by a capacitor with "damped capacitance" C_d in Figure 9.6a. We connect the motional branch (mechanical vibration) in "parallel" to this damped capacitance, because Equation (9.8) indicates the summation of these two admittances originated from two current flows under a constant externally applied voltage. The formula of Y_m is derived in the next section.

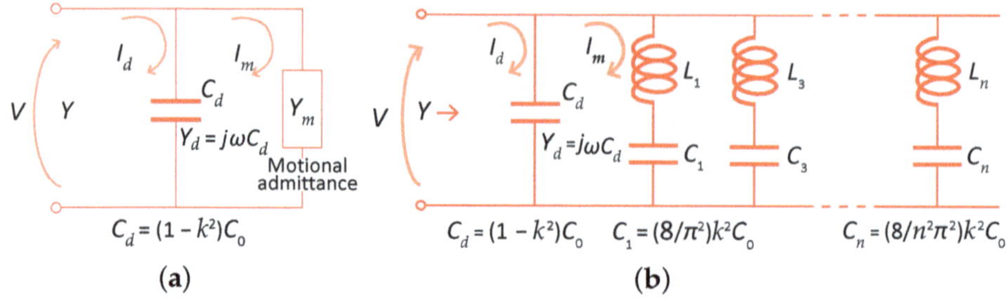

Figure 9.6. Equivalent circuit for the k_{31} mode (loss-free): (**a**) conceptual EC; (**b**) LC series EC. Source: Figure by author, adapted from [4].

9.2.1. *Resonance Mode*

Because the maximum Y corresponds to the resonance mode, we can analyze merely the motional Y_m, which is much larger than Y_d. $Y_m = j\omega C_d \left[\frac{k_{31}^2}{1-k_{31}^2}\frac{\tan(\Omega_{11})}{\Omega_{11}}\right]$ is infinite (∞) around the "A-type resonance" frequency, that is, $\omega_A L/2{v_{11}}^E = \Omega_{11,A,n} = n\pi/2$ ($n = 1, 3, 5, \ldots$). Taking "Mittag-Leffler's theorem" of $\frac{\tan(\Omega_{11})}{\Omega_{11}}$ around $\omega_{A,n}$,

$$\frac{\tan(\Omega_{11})}{\Omega_{11}} = \sum_{n:odd}^{\infty}\left(\frac{8}{n^2\pi^2}\right)/\left\{1-\left(\frac{\Omega_{11}}{\Omega_{11,A,n}}\right)^2\right\}. \quad (9.11)$$

When we use a LC series connection equivalent circuit (EC) model in Table 9.1b on the motional (mechanical vibration) branch, we convert the mass contribution to L and elastic compliance to C, then construct L_n and C_n series connections as shown in Figure 9.6b. Note here that a similar approach can be made for the parallel connection EC, because of the equivalency among the series and parallel ECs (refer to Example Problem 9.1). Each pair of (L_1,C_1), (L_3,C_3), ... (L_n,C_n) contributes to the fundamental, the second, and the n-th resonance vibration mode, respectively. Remember that n is only for the odd number, or even number n does not show up in the piezoelectric resonance, which corresponds basically to the antiresonance mode. Though each branch is activated only at its own n-th resonance frequency, the capacitance's contribution remains even at an inactive frequency range, and in particular at a low-frequency range (note the impedance of capacitance, $1/j\omega C$, and inductance, $j\omega L$. Under a low-frequency region, the inductance contribution will disappear). Neglecting the damped admittance, the motional impedance of this LC circuit around the A-type resonance $\omega_{A,n}$ is approximated by

$$1/Y_{m,n} = j\omega L_n + 1/j\omega C_n \approx j(L_n + 1/{\omega_{A,n}}^2 C_n)(\omega - \omega_{A,n}), \quad (9.12)$$

where ${\omega_{A,n}}^2 = 1/L_n C_n$. Using Equations (9.11) and (9.12), we can obtain the following equation:

$$Y_m = j\omega C_d\left[\frac{k_{31}^2}{1-k_{31}^2}\sum_{n:odd}^{\infty}\frac{\frac{8}{n^2\pi^2}}{\left\{1-\left(\frac{\Omega_{11}}{\Omega_{11,A,n}}\right)^2\right\}}\right] = \sum_{n:odd}^{\infty}\frac{j}{\left(L_n+\frac{1}{{\omega_{A,n}}^2 C_n}\right)(\omega_{A,n}-\omega)}. \quad (9.13)$$

Taking into account further approximation, $\frac{1}{\left\{1-\left(\frac{\Omega_{11}}{\Omega_{11,A,n}}\right)^2\right\}} \approx \frac{\omega_{11,A,n}}{2(\omega_{11,A,n}-\omega_{11})}$ for each n-th branch, we can obtain the following two equations which express the L_n, C_n in terms of the transducer's physical parameters:

$$L_n = \left(bLs_{11}^E/4v_{11}^{E\,2}wd_{31}^2\right)/2 = (\rho/8)(Lb/w)\left(s_{11}^{E2}/d_{31}^2\right), \quad (9.14)$$

$$\begin{aligned} C_n = 1/\omega_{A,n}^2 L_n &= \left(L/n\pi v_{11}^E\right)^2(8/\rho)(w/Lb)\left(d_{31}^2/s_{11}^{E2}\right) \\ &= (8/n^2\pi^2)(Lw/b)\left(d_{31}^2/s_{11}^{E2}\right)s_{11}^E, \end{aligned} \quad (9.15)$$

$$\omega_{A,n} = 1/\sqrt{L_n C_n} = n\pi/L\sqrt{\rho s_{11}^E}. \quad (9.16)$$

Note initially that L_n is a constant, irrelevant to n. All harmonics have the same L, which is originated from the ceramic density ρ or the specimen mass M. C_n is proportional to $1/n^2$ and the elastic compliance $s_{11}{}^E$. Note that the parameter $(d_{31}/s_{11}{}^E)$ is distinguished in both Equations (9.14) and (9.15), which will be explained in the next Section 9.3 as a "force factor" $\Phi = 2wd_{31}/s_{11}{}^E$. The total motional capacitance $\sum_n C_n$ is calculated as follows, using an important relation $\Sigma\left[\frac{1}{(2m-1)^2}\right] = \left(\frac{\pi^2}{8}\right)$:

$$\sum_n C_n = \sum_n \frac{1}{n^2}\left(\frac{8}{\pi^2}\right)\left(\frac{Lw}{b}\right)\left(\frac{d_{31}^2}{s_{11}^E}\right) = \left(\frac{Lw}{b}\right)\left(\frac{d_{31}^2}{s_{11}^E}\right) = k_{31}{}^2 C_0 \quad \left[k_{31}^2 = d_{31}^2/s_{11}^E\varepsilon_0\varepsilon_{33}{}^X\right]. \quad (9.17)$$

Therefore, we can understand that the total capacitance $C_0 = (wL/b)\,\varepsilon_0\varepsilon_{33}{}^X$ is split into the damped capacitance $C_d = (1 - k_{31}{}^2)C_0$ and the total motional capacitance $k_{31}{}^2C_0$, which is reasonable from the energy conservation viewpoint. You have now learned how the continuum medium parameters are converted to discrete components.

9.2.2. Antiresonance Mode

Next, we consider the antiresonance n-th mode, where the total admittance $Y = 0$ in Equations (9.8) and (9.12):

$$Y = j\omega C_d\left[1 + \frac{k_{31}^2}{1-k_{31}^2}\frac{\tan(\Omega_{11})}{\Omega_{11}}\right] = j\omega C_d + \frac{1}{\frac{1}{j\omega C_n} + j\omega L_n} = 0. \quad (9.18)$$

This admittance corresponds to the closed-circuit admittance under an externally open-circuit condition (i.e., the smallest admittance condition). Accordingly, we obtain the antiresonance (B-type) frequency ω_B in terms of the EC circuit parameters:

$$\omega_B = \sqrt{\left(1+\frac{C_n}{C_d}\right)/L_nC_n} = \sqrt{\left(\frac{1}{C_n}+\frac{1}{C_d}\right)/L}. \quad (9.19)$$

9.3. Equivalent Circuit of the k_{31} Mode with Losses

9.3.1. IEEE Standard Equivalent Circuit

Figure 9.7 shows the IEEE Standard equivalent circuit (EC) for the k_{31} mode with only one elastic loss ($\tan\phi'$) [5]. This elastic loss introduction in the mechanical branch is based on the assumption that the elastic loss in a piezoelectric material follows a "viscous damping" model, merely from the viewpoint of mathematical simplicity. The dielectric or piezoelectric losses are neglected. In this EC model, merely for the fundamental resonance mode, in addition to Equations (9.9), (9.14) and (9.15) in the loss-free EC, the circuit analysis provides the following R and Q (electrical quality factor, which corresponds to the mechanical quality factor in the piezo-plate) relation:

$$Q = \sqrt{L_A/C_A}/R_A. \quad (9.20)$$

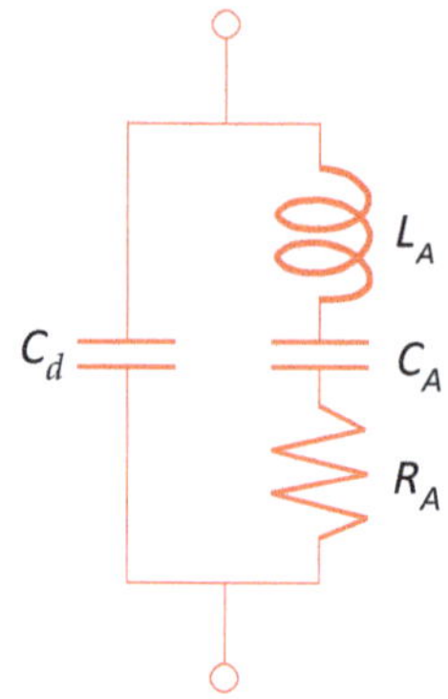

Figure 9.7. Equivalent circuit for the k_{31} mode (IEEE). Source: [3] ©Uchino, K. *Micromechatronics*, 2nd ed. CRC Press, 2019; p. 328. Reproduced by permission of Taylor & Francis Group.

This R introduction means the inclusion of merely the elastic loss (i.e., $\tan\phi_{11}'$ in the k_{31} mode), leading automatically to the relation Q_A (resonance) = Q_A (antiresonance). In order to demonstrate the usefulness of the equivalent circuit model for the piezoelectric device analysis, a simulation tool is introduced. The PSpice is a popular circuit analysis software code for simulating the performance of electrical circuits, which is widely distributed to students in the university Electrical Engineering department. EMA Design Automation, Inc. in the United State (http://www.ema-eda.com, accessed on 4 October 2022) is distributing a free download "OrCAD Capture", for this circuit-design solution software. The reader can access to the download site, if you wish: http://www.orcad.com/products/orcad-lite-overview?gclid=COaXitWJp9ECFcxKDQodCGMB0w (accessed on 4 October 2022).

Figure 9.8 shows the PSpice simulation process of the IEEE Standard k_{31} type. Figure 9.8a shows an equivalent circuit for the k_{31} mode. L, C and R values were calculated for PZT4 with 40 × 6 × 1 mm^3 (Equations (9.14), (9.15), and (9.20)), where the following data are used: Density—7500 kg/m^3, s_{11}^E—1.23 $\times 10^{-11}$ (m^2/N), d_{31}—1.23 $\times 10^{-10}$ (m/V), ε_{33}^X—1300, $\tan\phi_{11}'$—0.002, Q_m—500.

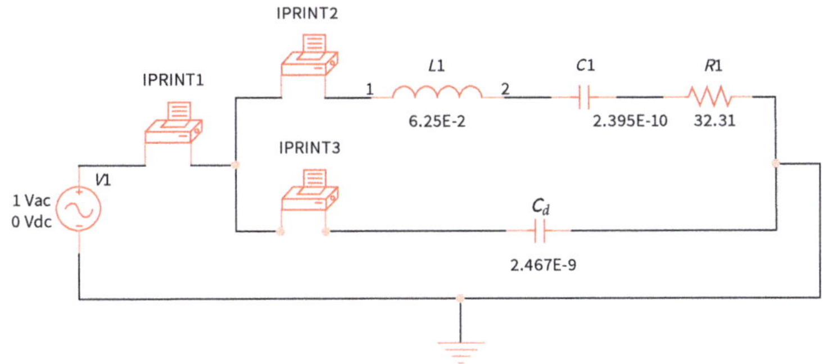

(a)

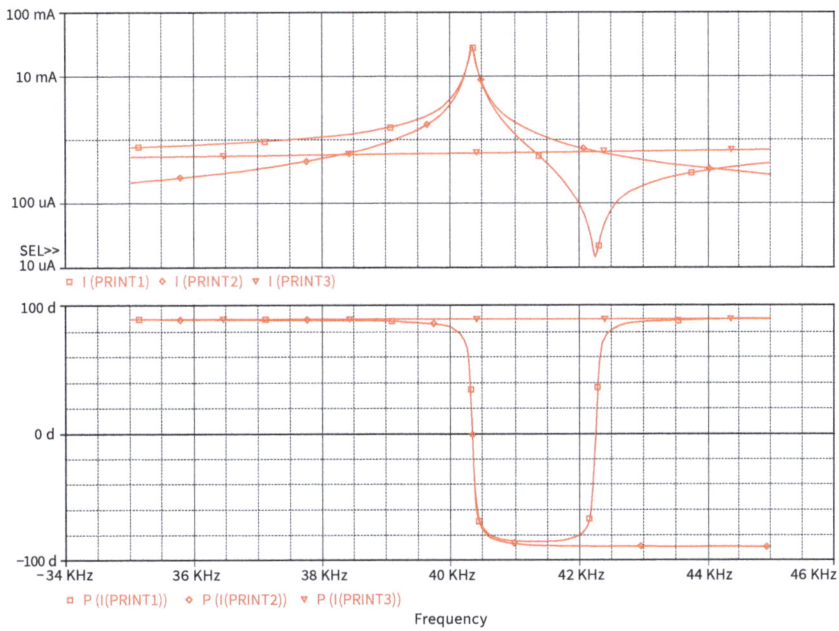

(b)

Figure 9.8. PSpice simulation of the IEEE type k_{31} mode. (**a**) Equivalent circuit for the k_{31} mode. *L*, *C* and *R* values were calculated for PZT4 with $40 \times 6 \times 1$ mm^3. (**b**) Simulation results on admittance magnitude and phase spectra. Source: [3] ©Uchino, K. *Micromechatronics*, 2nd ed. CRC Press, 2019; p. 329. Reproduced by permission of Taylor & Francis Group.

Figure 9.8b plots the simulation results of the current under 1V; that is, admittance magnitude and phase spectra. IPRINT1 (current measurement), IPRINT2, and IPRINT3 are the current meters of the total admittance (□ line), motional admittance (○ line), and damped admittance (∇ line), respectively. First, the damped admittance shows a slight linear increase with the frequency ($j\omega C_d$) with +90° phase in a full frequency range. Second, the motional admittance shows a peak at the resonance frequency, where the phase changes from +90° (i.e., capacitive) to –90° (i.e., inductive). In other words, the phase is exactly zero at the resonance frequency. The admittance magnitude decreases above the resonance frequency with a rate of

−20 dB down in a "Bode plot". Third, by adding the above two, the total admittance is obtained. The admittance magnitude shows two peaks, maximum and minimum, which correspond to the resonance and antiresonance points, respectively. You can find that the peak sharpness (i.e., the mechanical quality factor) is the same for both peaks, because only one loss is included in the equivalent circuit. The antiresonance frequency is obtained at the intersect of the damped and motional admittance curves. Because of the phase difference between the damped (+90°) and motional (–90°) admittance, the phase is exactly zero at the antiresonance, and changes to +90° above the antiresonance frequency. Remember that the phase is –90° (i.e., inductive) at a frequency between the resonance and antiresonance frequencies.

9.3.2. Equivalent Circuit (EC) with Three Losses

Hamilton's Principle

In Section 7.3.1, we derived the difference between the mechanical quality factor Q_A at the resonance and Q_B at the antiresonance in the k_{31} specimen, based on the three dielectric, elastic, and piezoelectric loss factors, $\tan\delta'$, $\tan\phi'$ and $\tan\theta'$. Recall the following formulae Equations (7.43) and (7.55) for the k_{31} type specimen:

$$Q_{A,31} = \frac{1}{\tan\phi_{11}{}'},$$

$$\frac{1}{Q_{B,31}} = \frac{1}{Q_{A,31}} - \frac{2}{1+\left(\frac{1}{k_{31}}-k_{31}\right)^2 \Omega_{B,31}{}^2}\left(2\tan\theta_{31}{}' - \tan\delta_{33}{}' - \tan\phi_{11}{}'\right),$$

$$\begin{cases} \Omega_{A,31} = \frac{\omega_a l}{2v_{11}^E} = \frac{\pi}{2}, & \left[v_{11}^E = 1/\sqrt{\rho s_{11}^E}\right] \\ \Omega_{B,31} = \frac{\omega_b l}{2v_{11}^E}, & 1-k_{31}{}^2 + k_{31}{}^2\frac{\tan\Omega_B}{\Omega_B} = 0 \end{cases}.$$

We now consider how to generate an EC with these three losses in order to realize the difference between Q_A and Q_B even in the EC. We start from the "Hamilton's Principle", a powerful tool for "mechanics" problem solving, which can transform a physical system model to "variational problem" solving. We integrate loss factors directly into the Hamilton's Principle for a piezoelectric k_{31} plate (Figure 9.5) [6]. Referring to reference [6], the following admittance expression can be derived, which is equivalent to Equation (7.33) in Section 7.3:

$$\begin{aligned} Y^* = {} & j\omega\cdot\frac{lw}{b}\cdot\left(\varepsilon_0\varepsilon_{33}^{X}{}' - Re\left[\frac{\left(d_{31}^*\right)^2}{s_{11}^{E}{}^*}\right]\right) + \omega\cdot\frac{lw}{b}\cdot\left(\varepsilon_0\varepsilon_{33}^{X}{}'' + Im\left[\frac{\left(d_{31}^*\right)^2}{s_{11}^{E}{}^*}\right]\right) \\ & + j\omega\cdot\frac{8lw}{b\pi^2}\cdot Re\left[\frac{\left(d_{31}^*\right)^2}{s_{11}^{E}{}^*}\right]\cdot\frac{\frac{\pi^2}{l^2\rho s_{11}^{E}{}^*}}{\frac{\pi^2}{l^2\rho s_{11}^{E}{}^*}-\omega^2} + j\omega\cdot\frac{8lw}{b\pi^2}\cdot\left(jIm\left[\frac{\left(d_{31}^*\right)^2}{s_{11}^{E}{}^*}\right]\right)\cdot\frac{\frac{\pi^2}{l^2\rho s_{11}^{E}{}^*}}{\frac{\pi^2}{l^2\rho s_{11}^{E}{}^*}-\omega^2}. \end{aligned} \quad (9.21)$$

Among the above 4 terms in Equation (9.21), the first and second terms correspond to the damped capacitance and its dielectric loss (i.e., the "extensive"—like dielectric loss ($\tan\delta'''$) in Equation (7.33) in Section 7.3), respectively, while the third and fourth terms correspond to the motional capacitance and the losses combining with "intensive" elastic and piezoelectric losses.

k_{31} Equivalent Circuit with Three Losses

Damjanovic [2] introduced a motional branch to describe the third term in Equation (9.21), which contains a motional resistor, a motional capacitor, and a motional inductor. Meanwhile, an additional branch is also injected into the classical circuit [1] to pictorially express the last term in Equation (9.21) to present the influence of the piezoelectric loss, where the new resistance, capacitance, and inductance are all proportional to corresponding motional elements, with the proportionality constant being $jIm\left[\frac{(d_{31}^{*})^2}{s_{11}^{E}{}^{*}}\right] / Re\left[\frac{(d_{31}^{*})^2}{s_{11}^{E}{}^{*}}\right]$.

Shi et al. proposed a concise equivalent circuit (EC) shown in Figure 9.9a with three losses [6]. Compared with the IEEE Standard EC with only one elastic loss or the Damjanovic's EC with a full set of L, C, R, only one additional electrical element G'_m is introduced into the classical circuit [6]. The new coupling conductance can reflect the coupling effect between the elastic and the piezoelectric losses. The admittance of this new EC can be mathematically expressed as:

$$Y^* = G_d + j\omega C_d + \frac{G'_m + j\omega C_m}{(1 + G'_m/G_m - \omega^2 L_m C_m) + j(\omega C_m/G_m + \omega L_m G'_m)}. \quad (9.22)$$

The parameters of the new EC can therefore be obtained by comparing Equation (9.21) with Equation (9.22) as new expressions of three "intensive" loss factors:

$$\tan\phi' = \omega C_m/G_m \quad [Gm = 1/Rm], \quad (9.23a)$$

$$\tan\theta' = \tan(\phi' - \beta'), \quad (9.23b)$$

$$\tan\delta' = k_{31}^2 \tan(2\theta' - \phi') + \frac{G_d}{\omega C_d}, \quad (9.23c)$$

where the phase delay $\tan\beta' = \frac{\omega C_m}{G'_m} - \sqrt{\left(\frac{\omega C_m}{G'_m}\right)^2 + 1}$ denotes the disparity between the piezoelectric and elastic components. From Equation (9.18), we learned that the piezoelectric loss and elastic loss are always coupled in the E excitation measurement. The value of β' generally holds negative or approaches zero (when $G'_m \to 0$) in PZT based piezo-ceramics, which implies that the piezoelectric loss is persistently larger than or equal to the elastic component. The significance of the piezoelectric loss has been therefore verified in theory from the equivalent circuit viewpoint.

Using the experimental data in Figure 9.9b, almost frequency-independent circuit parameters as $C_d = 3.2$ nF, $C_m = 0.29$ nF, $L_m = 210$ mH, and $G_d = 0$ (extensive dielectric loss $\tan\delta'''$ is small) can be obtained, and the frequency dependent parameters (G_m and G'_m) [6]. By manipulating Equations (9.23a)–(9.23c), we determined intensive dielectric, elastic, and piezoelectric losses as a function of frequency, as shown in Figure 9.9c.

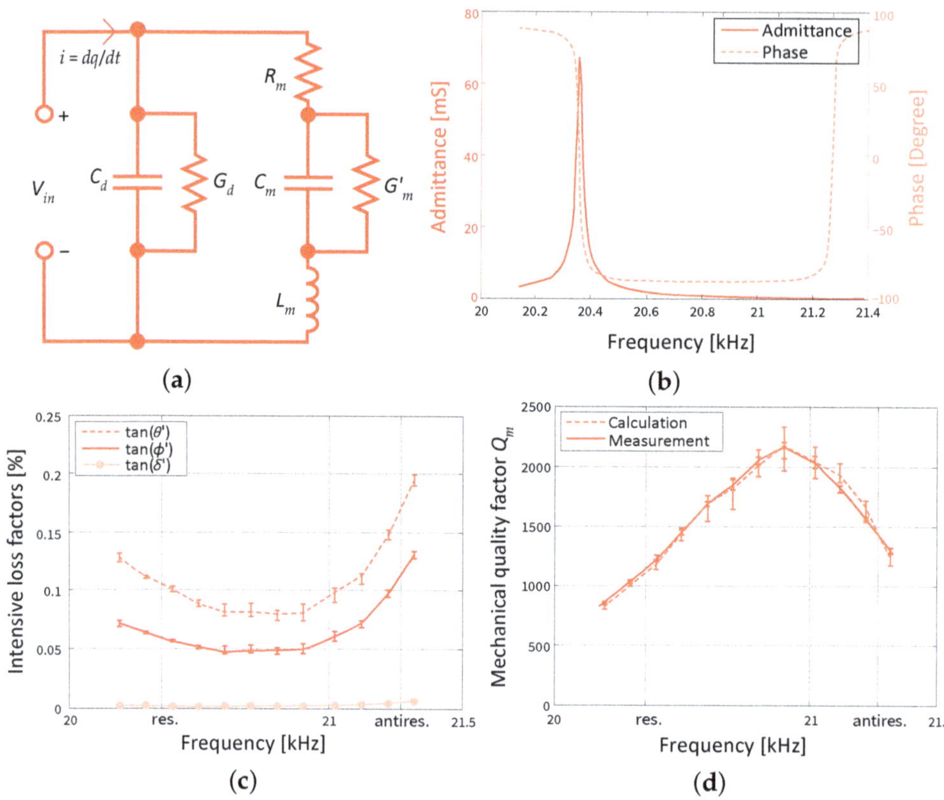

Figure 9.9. (**a**) Equivalent circuit proposed with three intensive loss factors; (**b**) admittance spectrum to be used in the simulation; (**c**) frequency spectra of intensive loss dielectric, elastic and piezoelectric loss factors obtained from the admittance spectrum (**b**) fitting, and (**d**) calculated mechanical quality factor Q_m as a function frequency around the resonance and antiresonance frequencies. Source: [3] ©Uchino, K. *Micromechatronics*, 2nd ed. CRC Press, 2019; p. 330. Reproduced by permission of Taylor & Francis Group.

Quality Factor in the Equivalent Circuit

The mechanical quality factor, Q_m, is always applied to evaluate the effect of losses. When arriving at steady state, it can be expressed by:

$$Q_m = 2\pi \cdot \frac{\text{energy stored/cycle}}{\text{energy lost/cycle}}. \tag{9.24a}$$

The denominator is supposed to compensate for the dissipation, w_{loss}; that is, $\int_V w_{loss} dV = \frac{\pi}{2}\left|v_3^*\right|\left|q_3^*\right| \cos\varphi$, where the phase difference between current and input voltage, φ, ranges within $\left[-\frac{\pi}{2}, \frac{\pi}{2}\right]$. Meanwhile, the reactive portion of the input energy returns to the amplifier and is neither used nor dissipated. Furthermore, the maximum stored and kinetic energies also reach equilibrium in an electrical cycle. With definitions of energy items and appropriate substitutions, Q_m can be calculated as [7]:

$$Q_m = \frac{\omega_a^2 - \omega_r^2}{\cos\varphi} \cdot \frac{\omega^2}{\left|\omega^2 - (\omega_r^*)^2\right|\left|\omega^2 - (\omega_a^*)^2\right|}. \quad (9.25)$$

As ω^2 approaches ω_r^2 or ω_a^2, the phase difference will approach zero. $(\omega_r^*)^2$ and $(\omega_a^*)^2$ are a sort of imaginary frequency including the loss factors, as described in [7]. Therefore, for low k_{31}^2 materials, substituting Equation (9.25), mechanical quality factors at the resonance and antiresonance frequencies can be calculated as:

$$Q_A = \frac{1}{\tan\phi'} = \frac{1}{R_m}\sqrt{\frac{L_m}{C_m}}, \quad (9.26)$$

$$Q_B = \frac{1}{\tan\phi' + \frac{8K_{31}^2}{\pi^2}\left[\tan\phi' + \tan\delta' - 2\tan\theta'\right]} \quad \left[{K_{31}}^2 = {K_{31}}^2/\left(1 - {K_{31}}^2\right)\right]. \quad (9.27)$$

Equations (9.26) and (9.27) obtained from a new equivalent circuit are basically the same as we derived analytically in Section 7.3.1, Equations (7.43) and (7.55). Hence, the calculation of Q_m at these special frequencies has been verified by the well-accepted conclusion. Not only at these frequencies, Equation (9.25) also infers an advanced calculation method of Q_m for a wide bandwidth. Figure 9.9d shows the frequency spectrum of the mechanical quality factor Q_m calculated from Equation (9.25). You can clearly find that (1) the Q_B at antiresonance is larger than Q_A at resonance, and (2) the maximum Q_m (i.e., the highest efficiency) can be obtained at a frequency between the resonance and antiresonance frequencies. This frequency can theoretically be obtained by taking the first derivative of Equation (9.25) in terms of ω as equal to zero, which suggests the best operating frequency of the transducer to realize the maximum efficiency.

We derived the following equation from Equation (9.24a) as shown in Section 7.4.3, which allows the calculation of the mechanical quality factor at any frequency from the real electrical power (P_d) and tip RMS vibration velocity (V_{RMS}) measurements for a longitudinally vibrating piezoelectric resonator (k_t, k_{33}, k_{31}):

$$Q_{m,l} = 2\pi f \frac{\frac{1}{2}\rho V_{RMS}^2}{P_d/Lwb}. \quad (9.24b)$$

The change in mechanical quality factor was measured for an 80 mm long hard PZT (APC 851) ceramic plate (k_{31}) under constant vibration condition of 100 mm/s RMS tip vibration velocity (i.e., stored mechanical energy constant). The required power and mechanical quality factor Q_m are shown in Figure 9.10. Notice the curve resemblance between Figures 9.9d and 9.10. The quality factor obtained at the resonance is within 2% agreement with results from the impedance spectrum method (3 dB down bandwidth). This technique reveals the behavior of the mechanical quality factor at any frequency from "below the resonance" to "above the antiresonance" frequencies. Moreover, very interestingly, the mechanical quality factor reaches a maximum value between the resonance and the antiresonance frequency, the point of which may suggest the optimum condition for the transducer operation from an efficiency viewpoint.

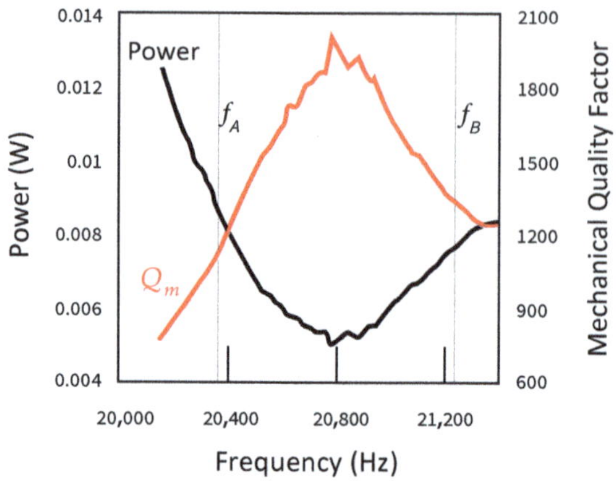

Figure 9.10. Mechanical quality factor measured using real electrical power (including the phase lag) for a Hard PZT APC 851 k_{31} plate. Source: [4] ©Uchino, K. *High-Power Piezoelectrics and Loss Mechanisms*. CRC Press, 2020; p. 198. Reproduced by permission of Taylor & Francis Group.

9.4. Equivalent Circuit of the k_{33} Mode with Losses

Remember that the k_{33} mode is governed by the sound velocity v^D, not by v^E, and that the antiresonance is the primary mechanical resonance given by $f = v^D/2L$, and the resonance is the subsidiary mode originated from the electromechanical coupling factor k_{33}. The difference from the k_{31} type oscillator with the "transversal" piezoelectric effect is that the k_{33} type is primarily associated with the "depolarization field" (that is, $E_{dep} = -\Delta P_3/\varepsilon_0\varepsilon_{33}^E$, where ΔP_3 is excited by the AC stress) created in the "longitudinal" piezoelectric effect (k_{33}, k_t) oscillator, so that the sound velocity is a D-constant, not an E-constant parameter. Let us consider the formulation of the equivalent circuit (EC) for the k_{33} mode, in particular how to integrate the "depolarization field effect", using specimen geometry shown in Figure 9.11a.

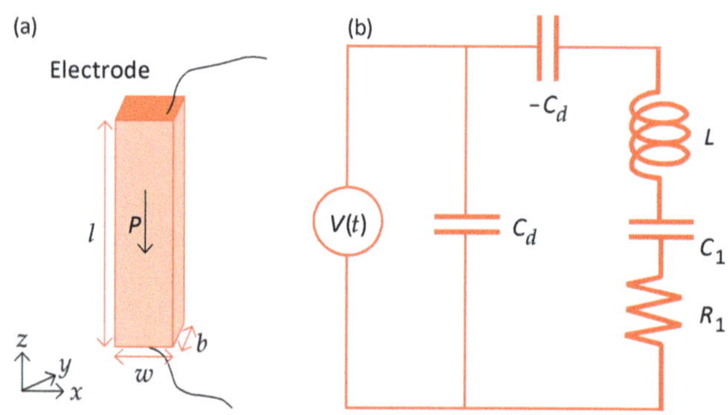

Figure 9.11. (**a**) k_{33} mode piezo-ceramic rod; (**b**) equivalent circuit for the k_{33} mode. Source: [3] ©Uchino, K. *Micromechatronics*, 2nd ed. CRC Press, 2019; p. 333. Reproduced by permission of Taylor & Francis Group.

9.4.1. Resonance/Antiresonance of the k_{33} Mode

Referring to the derivation process introduced in Section 7.2.3, we first summarize the key formulae.

- The constitutive equations

$$X_3 = (x_3 - d_{33}E_z)/s_{33}{}^E, \tag{9.28}$$

$$D_3 = \varepsilon_0 \varepsilon_{33}{}^X E_z + d_{33}X_3. \tag{9.29}$$

- Dynamic equation

$$\rho \frac{\partial^2 u}{\partial t^2} = \frac{1}{s_{33}^D} \frac{\partial^2 u}{\partial z^2} \quad \left(s_{33}^D = \left(1 - k_{33}^3\right) s_{33}^E\right). \tag{9.30}$$

- Admittance is expressed as

$$Y = \frac{j\omega\varepsilon_0\varepsilon_{33}^{LC}\left(\frac{wb}{L}\right)}{\left[1 - k_{33}^2\left\{\frac{\tan\left(\frac{\omega L}{2v_{33}^D}\right)}{\left(\frac{\omega L}{2v_{33}^D}\right)}\right\}\right]} = j\omega C_d + \frac{j\omega C_d}{\left[-1 + 1/k_{33}^2\left\{\frac{\tan(\Omega_{33})}{(\Omega_{33})}\right\}\right]}. \tag{9.31}$$

Here, we used $\Omega_{33} = \left(\frac{\omega L}{2v_{33}^D}\right)$, $\varepsilon_{33}^{LC} = \varepsilon_{33}^X(1 - k_{33}^2)$, $s_{33}^D = s_{33}^E(1 - k_{33}^2)$, $k_{33}^2 = \frac{d_{33}^2}{\varepsilon_0\varepsilon_{33}^X s_{33}^E}$, $v_{33}^D = 1/\sqrt{\rho s_{33}^D}$, and $C_d = \varepsilon_0\varepsilon_{33}^{LC}\left(\frac{wb}{L}\right)$. The second expression is to show the "damped admittance" and the "motional admittance" separately.

9.4.2. Resonance/Antiresonance of the k_{33} Mode

When we consider the resonance condition, $Y = \infty$, the resonance frequency is obtained from Equation (9.31) as

$$\left(\frac{\omega L}{2v_{33}^D}\right)\cot\left(\frac{\omega L}{2v_{33}^D}\right) = k_{33}{}^2 \quad \left(v_{33}^D = 1/\sqrt{\rho s_{33}^D}\right). \tag{9.32}$$

Since the resonance is the subsidiary mode, the resonance frequency of the k_{33} mode depends strongly on the electromechanical coupling factor k_{33} value.

To the contrary, the antiresonance mode is obtained by putting $Y = 0$, which provides the condition, $\tan\left(\frac{\omega L}{2v_{33}^D}\right) = \infty$. Thus, the antiresonance frequency is determined by $n(v_{33}^D/2L)$ (n = 1, 3, 5, ...), and the vibration mode shows an exact half-wavelength on the specimen with length L under sound velocity v_{33}^D, while the resonance is the subsidiary vibration mode as discussed above. This provides an intriguing contrast to the k_{31} mode, where the resonance mode is the primary vibration with a half-wavelength of the specimen of L, and the antiresonance is the subsidiary vibration mode.

9.4.3. Equivalent Circuit of the k_{33} Mode

We can rewrite Equation (9.31) further, as follows:

$$Y = j\omega C_d + \frac{1}{-\frac{1}{j\omega C_d} + \frac{1}{j\tan\left(\frac{\omega L}{2v_{33}^D}\right)\frac{2bwd_{33}{}^2}{\rho v_{33}^D L^2 s_{33}^E{}^2}}}, \quad (9.33)$$

where $C_d = \left(\frac{\varepsilon_0 \varepsilon_{33}^{x3} bw}{L}\right)$. The parameter ε_{33}^{x3} is the same as the longitudinally clamped permittivity, $\varepsilon_{33}^{LC} = \varepsilon_{33}^{X}(1 - k_{33}^2)$. From Equation (9.33), we can understand that the equivalent circuit of the k_{33} mode is composed of the first-term damped admittance with a "damped capacitance" and the second term "motional admittance". Additionally, the motional branch is obtained by a series connection of so-called "negative capacitance $-C_d$" (exactly the same absolute value of the damped capacitance in the electric branch) and the pure motional admittance, $j\tan\left(\frac{\omega L}{2v_{33}^D}\right)\frac{2bwd_{33}{}^2}{\rho v_{33}^D L^2 s_{33}^E{}^2}$. Figure 9.11b illustrates the fundamental mode equivalent circuit (EC) by translating the motional admittance with only a pair of L and C. The IEEE Standard model includes only one resistance R_1, which corresponds to the elastic loss $\tan\phi'''$ in the material's parameter. The admittance should be the minimum at the antiresonance frequency, where the pure mechanical resonance status is realized, because the damped capacitance should be compensated by the negative capacitance $-C_d$ in the closed loop circuit. On the contrary, the admittance should be the maximum at the resonance, and the effective motional capacitance in the motional branch is provided by $1/\left(\frac{1}{C_1} + \frac{1}{-C_d}\right)$, which provides $s_{33}{}^D$ ($=s_{33}{}^E(1 - k_{33}{}^2)$), rather than $s_{33}{}^E$ (i.e., origin of C_1). The reader can understand intuitively that the negative capacitance comes from the "depolarization field", or the D-constant status of the k_{33} vibration mode, different from the k_{31} E-constant mode. Figure 9.11b integrated a resistance R_1 in series with L_1 and C_1 in the pure mechanical branch. In comparison with Equations (9.14), (9.15), and (9.20) in the k_{31} mode, the EC components, L, C, and R of the k_{33} mode can be denoted as:

$$L_n = \left(bLs_{33}^D / 4v_{33}^D{}^2 wd_{33}^2\right)/2 = (\rho/8)(Lb/w)\left(s_{33}^{D2}/d_{33}^2\right), \quad (9.34)$$

$$\begin{aligned} C_n = 1/\omega_{A,n}^2 L_n &= \left(L/n\pi v_{33}^D\right)^2 (8/\rho)(w/Lb)\left(d_{33}^2/s_{33}^{D2}\right) \\ &= \left(8/n^2\pi^2\right)(Lw/b)\left(d_{33}^2/s_{33}^{D2}\right)s_{33}^D, \end{aligned} \quad (9.35)$$

$$Rn = \sqrt{L_n/C_n}/Q. \quad (9.36)$$

Here, $s_{33}^D = s_{33}^E(1 - k_{33}^2)$, $k_{33}^2 = \frac{d_{33}^2}{\varepsilon_0 \varepsilon_{33}^X s_{33}^E}$ and $Q = \tan\phi'''$ as the material's constants.

9.5. Four- and Six-Terminal Equivalent Circuits (ECs)—k_{31} Case

Though the new two-terminal EC with three dielectric, elastic, and piezoelectric losses is useful for basic no-load piezoelectric samples or the specimen characterization process, we need to extend it to four- and six-terminal EC models in order to consider the load effect for practical transducer/actuator applications with composite structures such as Langevin transducers.

9.5.1. *Four-Terminal Equivalent Circuit*

Four-Terminal Equivalent Circuit (Zero Loss)

We again consider the k_{31} type piezoelectric plate, whose admittance is described by Equation (9.8). When we consider the damped electric branch and the motional mechanical branch together, we can generate a two-terminal equivalent circuit (EC) as shown in Figure 9.12a. However, since the electric and mechanical branches are physically different, it is more reasonable to discuss these branches separately, which intuitively creates a four-terminal (or two-port) equivalent circuit, as exemplified in Figure 9.12b. The electric branch (left-hand side) is separated from the mechanical branch (right-hand side) by a transformer, which transforms voltage and current (electrical energy) to force and vibration velocity (mechanical energy), respectively, with the transformer ratio of Φ and $1/\Phi$, in order to change the unit from the electric to mechanical parameters (i.e., converse piezoelectric effect). This Φ is called the "force factor". In this case, the port on the mechanical branch can be mechanically loaded (symmetrically in the four-terminal model), depending on the piezoelectric composite structure. Vice versa, when the mechanical branch (right-hand-side) is excited initially, the same transformer converts the input force and vibration velocity to the output voltage and current by the same transformer ratios $1/\Phi$ and Φ, respectively. In this case, the port on the electrical branch can be loaded by a combination of L, C, and R.

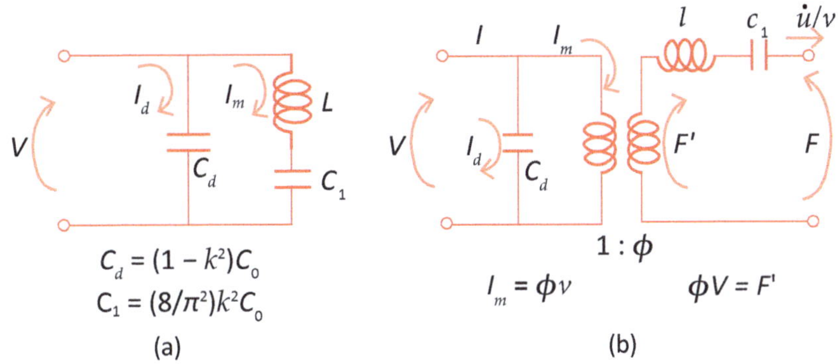

Figure 9.12. (**a**) 2- and (**b**) 4-terminal ECs for k_{31} mode (zero loss). Source: [4] ©Uchino, K. *High-Power Piezoelectrics and Loss Mechanisms*. CRC Press, 2020; p. 158. Reproduced by permission of Taylor & Francis Group.

Let us formulate electric component parameters of the four-terminal EC of the k_{31} plate in Figure 9.5. The motional current I_m is given by

$$I_m = E_z b Y_m = E_z b j\omega C_d \left(\frac{k_{31}^2}{1 - k_{31}^2} \right) \frac{\tan(\omega L/2v_{11})}{(\omega L/2v_{11})}, \tag{9.37}$$

while the vibration velocity $\dot{u}$ at the "plate edge" is described from Equation (7.11) in Chapter 7 as

$$(\partial u/\partial t)_{x=L} = j d_{31} E_z v_{11} \tan(\omega L/2v_{11}). \tag{9.38}$$

Taking into account the definition of the transformer ratio Φ in terms of current and vibration velocity by

$$I_m = \Phi \dot{u} = \Phi(\partial u/\partial t)_{x=L}, \tag{9.39}$$

Φ can be obtained as

$$\Phi = \frac{2wd_{31}}{s_{11}^E}. \tag{9.40}$$

Note the general relations: $F' = \Phi V$ and $I_m = \dot{u}/\Phi$. Using the former in terms of voltage V and force F' by

$$\Phi V = F', \tag{9.41a}$$

$$\Phi E_z b = \left(j\omega l + \frac{1}{j\omega c_1}\right)(\partial u/\partial t)_{x=L}. \tag{9.41b}$$

Note here that mechanical force F' at the plate edge is obtained by the product of vibration velocity $(\partial u/\partial t)_{x=L}$ and the "mechanical impedance" $\left(j\omega l + \frac{1}{j\omega c_1}\right)$. The mechanical impedance is defined by

$$F' = Z_m \dot{u} \text{ (on the plate edge plane)}. \tag{9.42}$$

In a popular mass-spring model, since the loss-free dynamic equation is given by $m\frac{\partial \dot{u}}{\partial t} + c\int \dot{u}dt = F'$, we obtain $F' = \left(j\omega m + \frac{c}{j\omega}\right)\dot{u}$. By converting m and c to l and $1/c_1$ in the EC, we obtain the mechanical impedance notation. Since the voltage is given by the product of motional current I_m and the impedance in the two-terminal model,

$$V = E_z b = \left(j\omega L + \frac{1}{j\omega C_1}\right) I_m, \tag{9.43}$$

we obtain the relationship between the L, C_1 in the two-terminal model and l, c_1 in the four-terminal model:

$$\left(j\omega l + \frac{1}{j\omega c_1}\right) = \left(j\omega L + \frac{1}{j\omega C_1}\right)\Phi^2. \tag{9.44}$$

We finally obtain the following relations in terms of the "force factor" Φ:

$$\Phi^2 L = l,\ C_1\ /\Phi^2 = c_1. \tag{9.45}$$

The force factor $= 2wd_{31}/s_{11}^E$ has a practical value around 0.1 in the MKS unit for PZTs.

Example Problem 9.3.

Figure 9.13 shows a composite piezoelectric oscillator, which is composed of the k_{31} type piezoelectric plate and two metal plates bonded on both ends of the piezo-plate. Supposing the piezo-plate length L and the metal length is $L/2$ symmetrically on both ends, consider the equivalent circuit of this composite oscillator with a metal load to analyze the vibration mode.

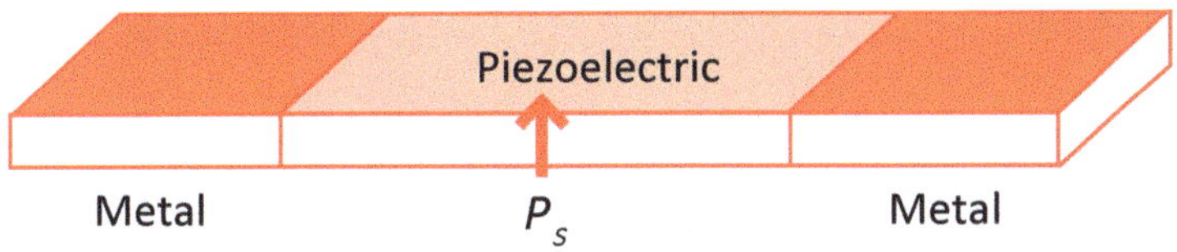

Figure 9.13. Composite piezoelectric oscillator. Source: [4] ©Uchino, K. *High-Power Piezoelectrics and Loss Mechanisms*. CRC Press, 2020; p. 160. Reproduced by permission of Taylor & Francis Group.

Hint

A four-terminal (two-port) equivalent circuit (EC) for the k_{31} mode is given by Figure 9.14a. Consider the elastic material's equivalent circuit.

Solution

Figure 9.14a shows a four-terminal (two-port) EC for the k_{31} mode, on which mechanical load can be applied. The resistance connected in series corresponds to the mechanical loss. We consider load application cases. Based on the LCR parameters in the two-terminal model:

$L_n = (\rho/8)(Lb/w)(s_{11}^{E2}/d_{31}^2)$,
$C_n = (8/n^2\pi^2)(Lw/b)(d_{31}^2/s_{11}^{E2})s_{11}^E$,
$R_n = \sqrt{l_n/c_n}/Q$,

we obtain the force factor, inductance, capacitance, and resistance on the mechanical branch:

$$\Phi = \frac{2wd_{31}}{s_{11}^E} \quad \text{(P9.3.1)}$$

$$l_n = \Phi^2 L_n = (\rho/2)(Lbw), \quad \text{(P9.3.2)}$$

$$c_n = C_n/\Phi^2 = \left(2/n^2\pi^2\right)(L/wb)s_{11}^E, \quad \text{(P9.3.3)}$$

$$r_n = \Phi^2 R_n = \sqrt{l_n/c_n}/Q. \quad \text{(P9.3.4)}$$

Note the difference from the two-terminal model: the L, C components in Figure 9.12a include the piezoelectric d constant explicitly, but the l, c components above do not, because the electromechanical coupling is defined in the "force factor" of the transformer. The mechanical branch parameters should be only pure elastic parameters. l_n is given by (1/2) of the piezo-plate total mass, while c_n corresponds to the inverse of the spring constant ($2/\pi^2$ is the calibration factor in addition to the normalization in terms of cross-section area wb and length L).

When the mechanical branch of the four-terminal EC is short circuited (Figure 9.14b), i.e., reaches a mechanically free condition (the force F on the piezo-plate ends is zero), this will be transformed to the two-terminal EC. On the contrary, when the mechanical branch is open circuited, this condition corresponds to completely clamped (strain-free) on both plate ends.

Figure 9.14c shows the model where the metal plate with the same width, thickness, and length $L/2$ is bonded symmetrically on both ends of the piezoelectric plate (total metal length L). The load is modeled by the LC "parallel" connection in this case with the parameters l_{elast}, c_{elast}, and r_{elast}, where ρ, s_{metal} and Q are the metal's density, elastic compliance, and the inverse elastic loss, respectively:

$$l_{elast} = \rho(Lbw), \tag{P9.3.5}$$

$$c_{elast} = \left(1/n^2\pi^2\right)(L/wb)s_{metal}, \tag{P9.3.6}$$

$$r_{elast} = \sqrt{l_{elast}/c_{elast}}/Q. \tag{P9.3.7}$$

For the reader's reference, if the metal plate is bonded symmetrically by cutting half of the thickness on both the top and bottom surfaces of the piezo-plate, the load is modeled by the above LC components in the "series" connection. You may understand this situation by taking into account the mechanical impedance series or parallel connection.

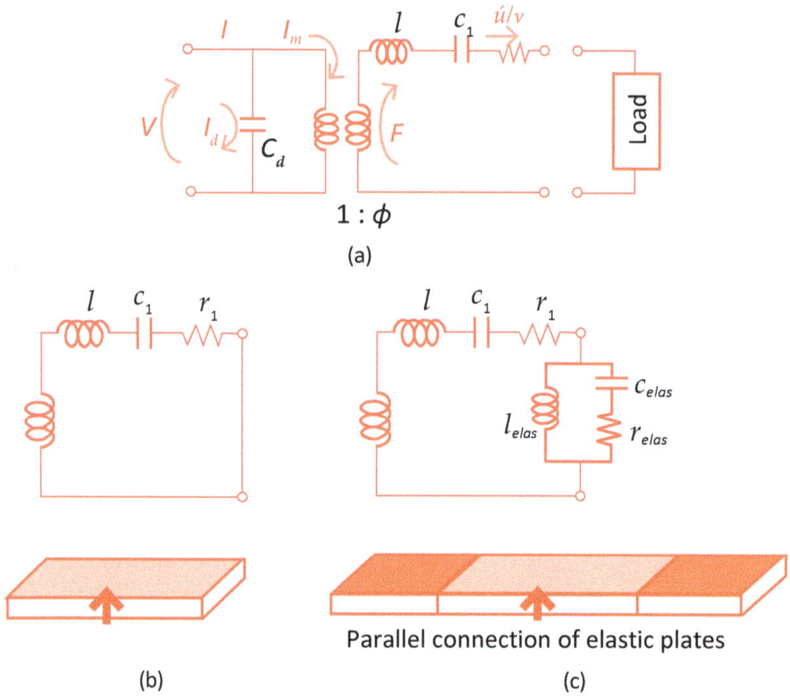

Figure 9.14. (**a**) 4-terminal equivalent circuit for the k_{31} mode; (**b**) a no load (short-circuit) condition; (**c**) elastic plates attached in parallel. Source: [4] ©Uchino, K. *High-Power Piezoelectrics and Loss Mechanisms*. CRC Press, 2020; p. 160. Reproduced by permission of Taylor & Francis Group.

Four-Terminal Equivalent Circuit with Three Losses

Uchino proposed a *four-terminal equivalent circuit* for a k_{31} mode plate, including elastic, dielectric, and piezoelectric losses (Figure 9.15a), which can handle symmetrical external mechanical losses [3]. The four-terminal EC includes an ideal transformer with a voltage step-up ratio Φ to connect the electric (damped capacitance) and the mechanical (motional capacitance) branches, where $\Phi = 2wd_{31}/s_{11}{}^{E}$, called "force factor" in this "electromechanical transformer". New capacitances l, c_1, and r_1 are related to L, C_1 and R_1 in the two-terminal EC given in Equations (9.14), (9.15), and (9.20). Here, r_1 and R_1 correspond to the intensive elastic loss $\tan\phi_{11}'$, which is introduced in IEEE Standard mode:

$$l = \Phi^2 L;\ c_1 = C_1/\Phi^2;\ r_1 = \Phi^2 R_1, \tag{9.46}$$

where Φ is the so-called "force factor". Regarding the three losses, as shown in Figure 9.15a in a k_{31} piezo-plate, in addition to the IEEE standard "elastic" loss r_1 and "dielectric" loss R_d, we introduce the "coupling loss" r_{cpl} in the force factor ($\Phi = 2wd_{31}/s_{11}{}^{E}$) as inversely proportional to ($\tan\phi_{11}' - \tan\theta_{31}'$), which can be either positive or negative, depending on the $\tan\theta_{31}'$ magnitude. Figure 9.15b shows the PSpice software simulation results for three values of r_{cpl}. We can find that (1) the resonance Q_A does not change with changing r_{cpl}, (2) when r_{cpl} = 100 kΩ (i.e., $\tan\theta_{31}' \approx 0$), $Q_A > Q_B$, (3) when r_{cpl} = 1 GΩ (i.e., $\tan\phi_{11}' - \tan\theta_{31}' \approx 0$), $Q_A = Q_B$, and (4) when r_{cpl} = −100 kΩ (i.e., $\tan\phi_{11}' - \tan\theta_{31}' < 0$), $Q_A < Q_B$. Taking into account a typical PZT case, where $\tan\theta' > (1/2)(\tan\delta' + \tan\phi')$, the well-known experimental result $Q_A < Q_B$ can be expected from the negative r_{cpl}. Thus, the large piezoelectric loss $\tan\theta_{31}'$ in PZTs is the key to exhibiting the negative force factor loss, which leads to the mechanical quality factor relation $Q_A < Q_B$.

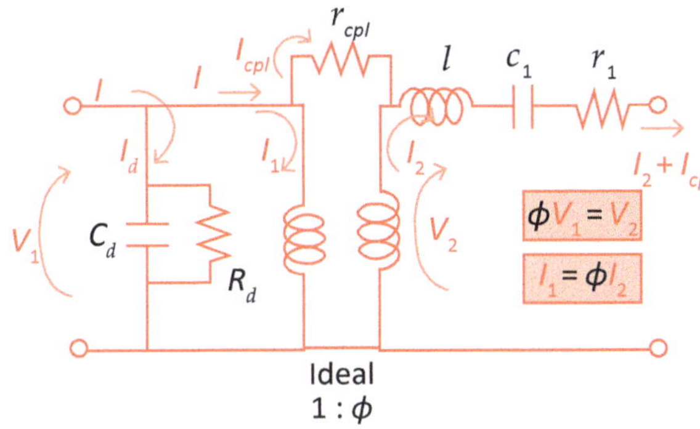

(a)

Figure 9.15. *Cont.*

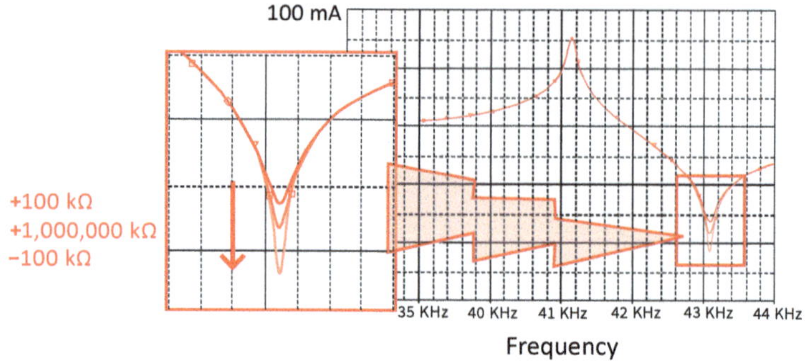

(b)

Figure 9.15. (**a**) 4-terminal (2-port) EC for a k_{31} plate, including three losses (r_1, R_d, and r_{cpl}); (**b**) PSpice simulation results on admittance for a k_{31} type PZT4 $40 \times 6 \times 1$ mm^3 plate. Source: [2] ©Uchino, K. *Micromechatronics*, 2nd ed. CRC Press, 2019; p. 332. Reproduced by permission of Taylor & Francis Group.

9.5.2. Six-Terminal Equivalent Circuit

Mason's Equivalent Circuit

Mason introduced a famous six-terminal (3-port) equivalent circuit (EC) model, relating to a "distributed element model" [8]. As illustrated in Figure 9.16, two ports in the mechanical branch of the six-terminal (three-port) EC for the k_{31} piezoelectric plate correspond to the two edges of the plate, on which different mechanical loads can individually be applied, exemplified by a "Langevin transducer" with different head and tail masses (i.e., "Tonpilz transducer"). Additionally, Mason's EC does not include any approximation, such as L and C component combination, which limits the usage only for a particular resonance mode, and can be applied to any frequency.

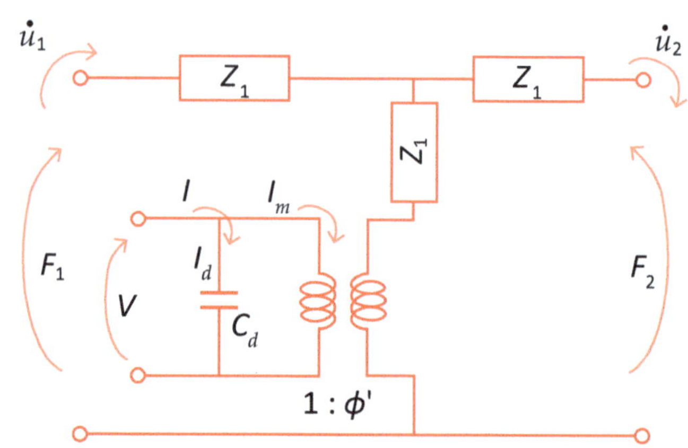

Figure 9.16. 6-terminal equivalent circuit for a k_{31} mode. Source: Figure by author, adapted from [3].

Let us determine the electronic components, Z_1, Z_2, and the force factor Φ' in the six-terminal EC model. We denote the displacement along the length of a plate specimen (Figure 9.5), u, force, and vibration velocity on the edge, F_1 and $\dot{u}_1$ at $x = 0$,

F_2 and $\dot{u}_2$ at $x = L$, in addition to the input voltage V and motional current I_m, damped current I_d. Supposing a general solution of the displacement as

$$u = A\cos(\omega x/v) + B\sin(\omega x/v), \tag{9.47}$$

and the boundary condition at $x = 0$,

$$A = u_1,\ B = (\partial u/\partial x)_1(v/\omega)$$

we obtain

$$\partial u/\partial x = -(\omega/v)u_1\sin(\omega x/v) + (\partial u/\partial x)_1\cos(\omega x/v), \tag{9.48}$$

$$\partial u/\partial t = \dot{u} = j\omega[u_1\cos(\omega x/v) + (\partial u/\partial x)_1(v/\omega)\sin(\omega x/v)]. \tag{9.49}$$

Now, we consider the force on the cross-section (wb) F is given by the stress (tensile is positive)

$$F = -wbX_1. \tag{9.50}$$

Since strain is given as $\partial u/\partial x = d_{31}E_z + s_{11}^E X_1$,

$$F = -\frac{wb}{s_{11}^E}\left[\left(\frac{\partial u}{\partial x}\right) - d_{31}E_z\right], \tag{9.51}$$

or

$$F - \Phi' V = -\frac{wb}{s_{11}^E}(\partial u/\partial x), \tag{9.52}$$

where the force constant Φ' is given by a half of Φ on the four-terminal EC, because the mechanical branch in the four-terminal model is the combination of Φ' of the two ports in the six-terminal model.

$$\Phi' = \Phi/2 = \frac{wd_{31}}{s_{11}^E}. \tag{9.53}$$

When we adopt the boundary conditions at $x = 0$:

$$\frac{\partial u}{(\partial x)_1} = -\frac{s_{11}^E}{wb}(F_1 - \Phi' V), \tag{9.54}$$

$$\dot{u}_1 = j\omega u_1. \tag{9.55}$$

Now Equation (9.49) becomes

$$\frac{\partial u}{\partial t} = \dot{u}_1\cos\left(\frac{\omega x}{v}\right) - j\frac{vs_{11}^E}{wb}(F_1 - \Phi' V)\sin\left(\frac{\omega x}{v}\right). \tag{9.56}$$

At x = L,

$$\dot{u}_2 = \dot{u}_1\cos(\omega L/v) - j\frac{vs_{11}^E}{wb}(F_1 - \Phi' V)\sin\left(\frac{\omega L}{v}\right). \tag{9.57}$$

Additionally, at $x = L$, using Equation (9.48):

$$F_2 - \Phi' V = -\frac{wb}{s_{11}^E}(\partial u/\partial x)_2 = \left(-\frac{wb}{s_{11}^E}\right)\left[-\left(\frac{\omega}{v}\right)u_1 \sin\left(\frac{\omega L}{v}\right) + \dot{u}_1 \cos\left(\frac{\omega L}{v}\right)\right]. \quad (9.58)$$

Now we can rewrite the relationship among F_1, F_2, $\dot{u}_1$, $\dot{u}_2$:

$$\dot{u}_2 = \dot{u}_1 \cos(\omega L/v) - j\frac{1}{Z_0}(F_1 - \Phi' V)\sin\left(\frac{\omega L}{v}\right), \quad (9.59)$$

$$F_2 - \Phi' V = (F_1 - \Phi' V)\cos(\omega L/v) - j\dot{u}_1 Z_0 \sin(\omega L/v), \quad (9.60)$$

$$I = j\omega C_d V + \Phi'(\dot{u}_2 - \dot{u}_1). \quad (9.61)$$

Note that the motional current is given by $\Phi'(u_2 - u_1)$. Now we can construct the six-terminal EC as shown in Figure 9.16. In order to satisfy Equations (9.59)– (9.61), we obtain all the components including Z_1, Z_2:

$$C_d = \frac{Lw\varepsilon_0\varepsilon_{33}^X(1 - k_{31}^2)}{b}, \quad (9.62)$$

$$Z_0 = wb\rho v = wb\left(\frac{\rho}{s_{11}^E}\right)^{1/2} = \frac{wb}{v_{11}^E s_{11}^E}, \quad (9.63)$$

$$Z_1 = jZ_0 \tan\left(\frac{\omega L}{2v_{11}^E}\right), \quad (9.64)$$

$$Z_2 = \frac{Z_0}{j\sin\left(\frac{\omega L}{v_{11}^E}\right)}, \quad (9.65)$$

$$\Phi' = \frac{wd_{31}}{s_{11}^E}. \quad (9.66)$$

Though the Mason's equivalent circuit includes the frequency dependent Z_1 and Z_2, these impedances can be translated into a pair of L and C for each individual fundamental or higher order harmonic mode, if required.

Application of Six-Terminal EC

Dong et al. constructed a six-terminal equivalent circuit with three (dielectric, elastic and piezoelectric) losses, which can handle symmetric external loads for a k_{31} mode plate [9] and Langevin transducer by integrating the head and tail mass loads [10], then estimate the optimum (i.e., minimum required input electrical energy) driving frequency at which we can drive the transducer, as demonstrated with the highest efficiency. In order to verify the feasibility of the EC circuit, a partial electrode configuration was designed (Figure 9.17a), which reflects intensive and extensive loss behavior on the electrode (center) and non-electrode (side) parts, respectively. The center part was electrically excited, which actuates the side non-electrode elastic load, then the vibration status was monitored from the admittance from this center portion. The non-electrode side portions were merely the mechanical load. Figure 9.17b shows a combination of six-terminal ECs which model the center constant E element (i.e., intensive losses, $\tan\phi_{11}'$, $\tan\delta_{33}'$, $\tan\theta_{31}'$) and the side constant D elements (i.e., extensive losses, $\tan\phi_{11}$, $\tan\delta_{33}$, $\tan\theta_{31}$) by integrating loss factors into Equations (9.62)–(9.66). Note that the non-electrode part was segmented into 20 parts on each side to calculate the voltage distribution generated on the surface during the center actuation. The resonance and antiresonance frequencies and their corresponding mechanical quality factors derived from the circuits are compared with the actual sample with the load and boundary conditions [9]. The voltage distribution of the non-electrode sample is simulated with the proposed equivalent circuit (Figure 9.18) under the supposition that 20 segmented parts are covered by narrow separated electrodes, which generates a discrete staircase curve. The voltage simulation results have the same sinusoidal distribution trend (neglecting small stepwise modulation) as the experiments, and the admittance curves show a good agreement between the simulation and the measurements.

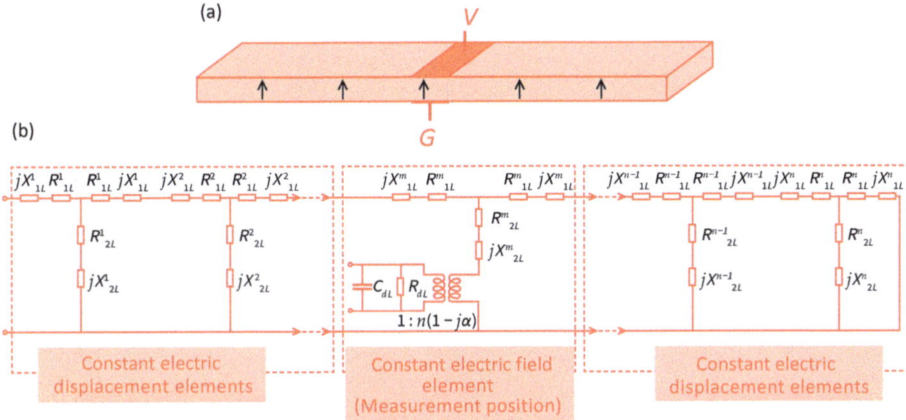

Figure 9.17. A partial electrode configuration (**a**) and its EC (**b**) of a combination of 6-terminal ECs which models the center constant E element (i.e., intensive losses) and the side constant D elements (i.e., extensive losses) by integrating loss factors. Source: [4] ©Uchino, K. *High-Power Piezoelectrics and Loss Mechanisms*. CRC Press, 2020; p. 164. Reproduced by permission of Taylor & Francis Group.

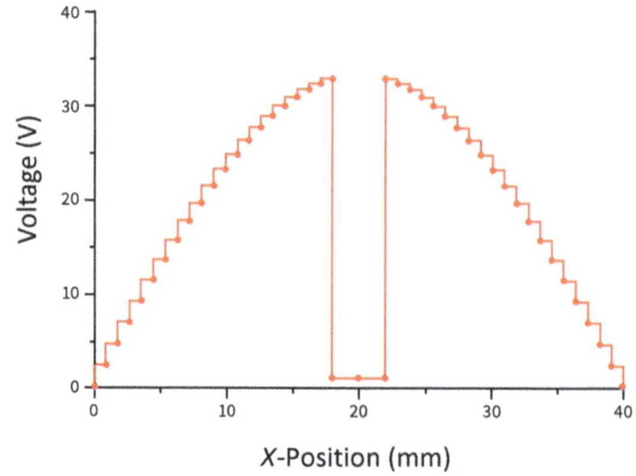

Figure 9.18. Voltage distribution of non-electrode sample simulated with the new 6-terminal equivalent circuit. Source: [4] ©Uchino, K. *High-Power Piezoelectrics and Loss Mechanisms*. CRC Press, 2020; p. 165. Reproduced by permission of Taylor & Francis Group.

9.6. Four- and Six-Terminal Equivalent Circuits (ECs)—k_{33} Case

The k_{33} mode requires a "negative capacitance" inclusion in the equivalent circuit (EC) in order to reflect a *D*-constant condition, or a "depolarization field". Since the sound velocity of the k_{33} mode is given by $1/\sqrt{\rho s_{33}^{D}}$, which is larger than $1/\sqrt{\rho s_{11}^{E}}$ of the k_{31} mode, the k_{33} mode is occasionally called a "stiffened mode". Equivalent circuits for the k_{33} mode are summarized for (a) a two-terminal model, (b) a four-terminal model, and (c) a six-terminal model in Figure 9.19. There are two possibilities to install the negative capacitor; the top and bottom show these differences with the negative capacitor in the electric branch and in the mechanical branch, respectively.

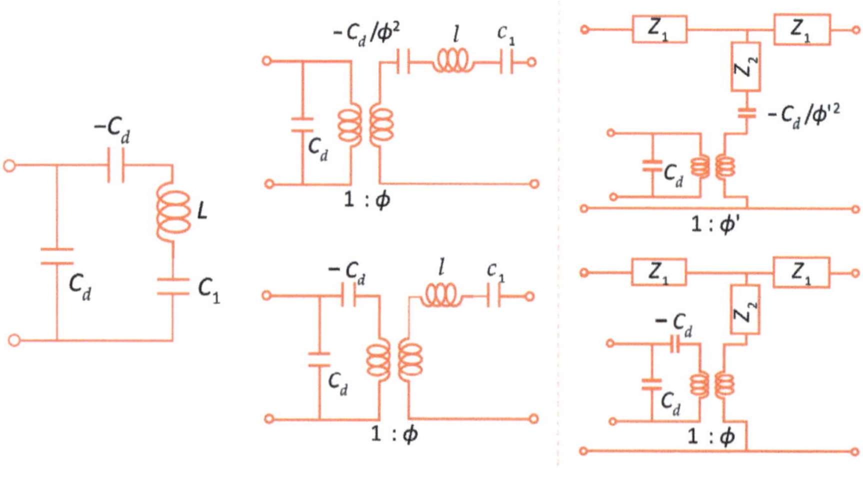

Figure 9.19. Equivalent circuits for the k_{33} mode: Top and bottom show the difference with the negative capacitor installation. Source: Figure by author, adapted from [4].

When the negative capacitance is installed in the electrical branch, $-C_d$ is directly inserted, while when it is installed in the mechanical branch, $-C_d/\Phi^{2}$ or $-C_d/\Phi'^{2}$ are inserted in series with other electrical components.

Note the difference between Φ and Φ' in the four- and six-terminal models:

$$\Phi' = \frac{\Phi}{2} = \frac{wbd_{33}}{Ls_{33}^{D}}. \quad (9.67)$$

Z_1 and Z_2 in the six-terminal model are described as follows:

$$C_d = \frac{wb\varepsilon_0\varepsilon_{33}^{X}\left(1-k_{33}^{2}\right)}{L}, \quad (9.68)$$

$$Z_0 = wb\rho v = wb\left(\frac{\rho}{s_{33}^{D}}\right)^{1/2} = \frac{wb}{v_{33}^{D}s_{33}^{D}}, \quad (9.69)$$

$$Z_1 = jZ_0\tan\left(\frac{\omega L}{2v_{33}^{D}}\right), \quad (9.70)$$

$$Z_2 = \frac{Z_0}{j\sin\left(\frac{\omega L}{v_{33}^{D}}\right)}. \quad (9.71)$$

We can integrate three losses, $\varepsilon_{33}^{X*} = \varepsilon_{33}^{X}(1 - j\tan\delta_{33}')$, $s_{33}^{E*} = s_{33}^{E}(1 - j\tan\phi_{33}')$, $d_{33}^{*} = d_{33}(1 - j\tan\theta_{33}')$, since the k_{33} mode does not strictly have the "extensive" non-prime losses, and the electromechanical coupling factor k_{33} loss in the above six-terminal circuit components, then simulate admittance/impedance response from the circuit. Alternatively, we may integrate three losses as R_{1L}, R_{2L} separately from X_{1L}, X_{2L}, as shown in Figure 9.17.

Chapter Essentials

1. Equivalency between mechanical and electrical systems (Refer to Table 9.1):
   $M(d^2u/dt^2) + \zeta(du/dt) + cu = F(t)$, or $M(dv/dt) + \zeta v + c\int_0^t v dt = F(t)$
   $L(d^2q/dt^2) + R(dq/dt) + (1/C)\, q = V(t)$, or $L(dI/dt) + RI + (1/C)\int_0^t I\, dt = V(t)$
2. Equivalent circuits of a piezoelectric k_{31} plate (Figure 9.5):

   $$Y = j\omega C_d\left[1 + \frac{k_{31}^{2}}{1-k_{31}^{2}}\frac{\tan\left(\frac{\omega L}{2v_{11}^{E}}\right)}{\left(\frac{\omega L}{2v_{11}^{E}}\right)}\right].$$

   Refer to Figures 9.12a, 9.7 and 9.12b, Figure 9.14a, respectively, for 2- and 4-terminal models below.

- Two-Terminal
- Four-Terminal

$$C_d = (wL/b)\varepsilon_0\varepsilon_{33}{}^{LC} = (wL/b)\varepsilon_0\varepsilon_{33}{}^{X}(1-k_{31}{}^2)$$

$$\Phi = \frac{2wd_{31}}{s_{11}^E}$$

$$L_n = (\rho/8)(Lb/w)(s_{11}^{E2}/d_{31}^2) \qquad l_n = \Phi^2 L_n = (\rho/2)(Lbw)$$

$$C_n = \frac{1}{\omega_{A,n}^2 L_n} = \left(\frac{8}{n^2\pi^2}\right)\left(\frac{Lw}{b}\right)(d_{31}^2/s_{11}^{E2})s_{11}^E \qquad c_n = C_n/\Phi^2 = (2/n^2\pi^2)(Lw/b)s_{11}^E$$

$$R_n = \sqrt{L_n/C_n}/Q \qquad r_n = \Phi^2 R_n = \sqrt{l_n/c_n}/Q$$

$$\omega_{A,n} = 1/\sqrt{L_n C_n} = 1/\sqrt{l_n/c_n} = n\pi/L\sqrt{\rho s_{11}^E}$$

3. Equivalent circuits of a piezoelectric k_{33} rod (Figure 9.11a):
$$Y = j\omega C_d + \frac{1}{-\frac{1}{j\omega C_d} + \frac{1}{j\tan\left(\frac{\omega L}{2v_{33}^D}\right)\frac{2bwd_{33}{}^2}{\rho v_{33}^D L^2 s_{33}^E{}^2}}}.$$

The negative capacitance $-C_d$ is inserted into the electrical branch in the two-, four- or six-terminal circuit, or $-C_d/\Phi^2$ or $-C_d/\Phi'^2$ into the mechanical branch in the four- or six-terminal circuit, respectively. Refer to Figure 9.19a, Figure 9.11b, Figure 9.19b, and Figure 9.19c, respectively, for 2-, 4- and 6-terminal models below.

- Two-Terminal
- Four-Terminal

$$C_d = (wb/L)\varepsilon_0\varepsilon_{33}^X(1-k_{33}^2)$$

$$\Phi = \frac{2wd_{33}}{s_{33}^D}$$

$$L_n = (\rho/8)(L^3/wb)(s_{33}^{E2}/d_{33}^2) \qquad l_n = \Phi^2 L_n = (\rho/2)(Lbw)$$

$$C_n = (8/n^2\pi^2)(wb/L)\left(\frac{d_{33}^2}{s_{33}^{E2}}\right)s_{33}^E(1-k_{33}^2) \qquad c_n = C_n/\Phi^2 = (2/n^2\pi^2)(L/wb)s_{33}^D$$

$$R_n = \sqrt{L_n/C_n}/Q \qquad r_n = \Phi^2 R_n = \sqrt{l_n/c_n}/Q$$

$$\omega_{A,n} = 1/\sqrt{L_n C_n} = 1/\sqrt{l_n/c_n} = n\pi/L\sqrt{\rho s_{33}^D}$$

- Six-Terminal

$$\Phi' = \Phi/2 = \frac{wd_{33}}{s_{33}^D}$$

$$Z_0 = wb\rho v = wb\sqrt{\frac{\rho}{s_{33}^D}} = \frac{wb}{v_{33}^D s_{33}^D}, \quad Z_1 = jZ_0\tan\left(\frac{\omega L}{2v_{33}^D}\right), \quad Z_2 = \frac{Z_0}{j\sin\left(\frac{\omega L}{v_{33}^D}\right)}$$

Check Point

1. (T/F) When we consider an equivalent electric circuit of a mechanical system in terms of LCR series connection, the inverse of the spring constant c corresponds to capacitance C. True or false?
2. (T/F) Because of the damped capacitance in the equivalent circuit of a piezoelectric oscillator, the antiresonance mode emerges in addition to the resonance mode. True or false?
3. (T/F) The permittivity under a mechanically clamped condition is larger than that under a mechanically free condition. True or false?

4. (T/F) The elastic compliance under an open-circuit condition is larger than that that under a short-circuit condition. True or false?
5. How can you describe the quality factor Q in a series connected LCR circuit?
6. In the k_{33} type two-terminal equivalent circuit, in addition to the damped capacitance C_d and motional capacitance C_m, we need to insert a negative capacitance. What should be the value of this negative capacitance?
7. Provide the force factor formula in the k_{31} type four-terminal equivalent circuit, in terms of d_{31}, ε_{33}^X, s_{11}^E and the specimen size, w, b, and L.
8. (T/F) The fundamental resonance mode of the k_{31} mode has an exact half-wavelength vibration on the plate specimen. True or false?
9. Provide the relationship between the mechanical quality factor Q_M at the resonance frequency with the intensive elastic loss in the k_{31} type specimen.
10. When $(\tan\delta_{33}' + \tan\phi_{11}')/2 < \tan\theta_{31}'$ is satisfied, which is larger for the k_{31} type specimen—Q_A or Q_B?

Chapter Problems

9.1 When a piezoelectric actuator is driven by a step pulse voltage with the pulse width exactly adjusted to the resonance period, the vibration displacement ΔL is generated linearly with time, and only one triangular shape displacement is realized without any vibration ringing (refer to Chapter 8). However, when a step pulse voltage with the pulse width exactly adjusted to the resonance period is applied on an equivalent circuit (L, C, R, and C_d) of this piezo-actuator, the resulting displacement is a sinusoidal pulse (not a triangular shape), as shown in Figure 9.20. Derive the time dependence of these displacements, then understand the limitation of the EC model for the transient vibration analysis.

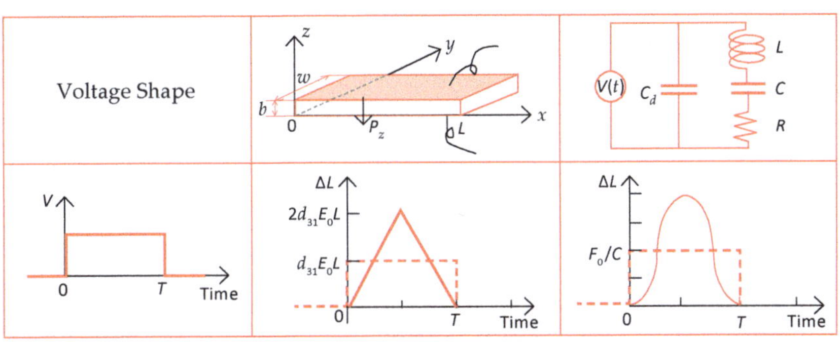

Figure 9.20. Comparison among continuous solid state model and equivalent circuit model. Source: Figure by author, adapted from [4].

9.2 The Rosen type transformer is a combination of the k_{31} (thin electrode gap) and k_{33} (large electrode gap) transducers boded at one end of each other, as illustrated in Figure 9.21a. In the EC of the transformer in Figure 9.21b, impedance parameters in Table 9.2 below can be applied. When k_{31} side (thin electrode gap) is used for the input, and k_{33} side (large electrode gap) for the output, large voltage step-up is expected. Using Mason's equivalent circuits for these two length expander bars, calculate the maximum step-up voltage ratio for this Rosen-type transformer under an open-circuit condition.

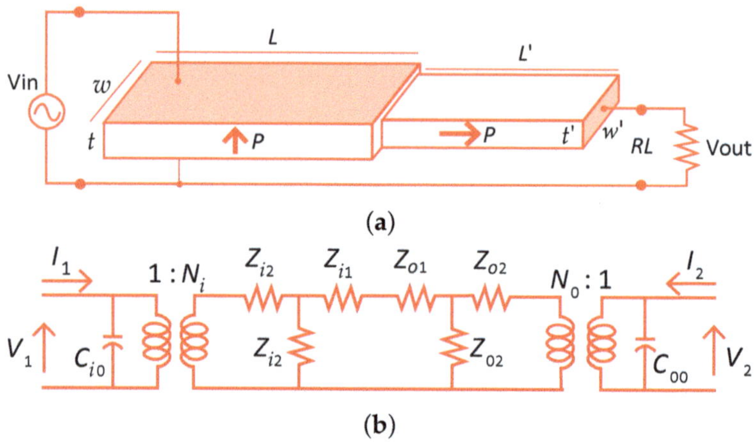

Figure 9.21. (**a**) Structure of the Rosen-type piezoelectric transformer; (**b**) Equivalent circuit of the piezo-transformer. Source: [4] ©Uchino, K. *High-Power Piezoelectrics and Loss Mechanisms*. CRC Press, 2020; p. 170. Reproduced by permission of Taylor & Francis Group.

Table 9.2. Parameters in the equivalent circuit of Rosen-type piezo-transformer.

	k_{31} Part	**k_{33} Part**
Clamped capacitance	$C_{io} = \frac{Lw\varepsilon_0\varepsilon_{33}^X(1-k_{31}^2)}{2t}$	$C_{oo} = \frac{2w't'\varepsilon_0\varepsilon_{33}^X(1-k_{33}^2)}{L'}$
Characteristic mechanical impedance	$Z_0 = wt\left(\frac{\rho}{s_{11}^E}\right)^{1/2}$	$Z_0^! = w't'\rho v_b^D = w't'\left(\frac{\rho}{s_{33}^D}\right)^{1/2}$
Other mechanical equivalent impedances	$Z_{i2} = \frac{jZ_0}{j\sin\left(\frac{\omega L}{4v_b^E}\right)}$	$Z_{02} = \frac{jZ_0^!}{j\sin\left(\frac{\omega L'}{4v_b^D}\right)}$
	$Z_{i1} = jZ_0\tan\left(\frac{\omega L}{4v_b^E}\right)$	$Z_{01} = jZ_0^!\tan\left(\frac{\omega L'}{4v_b^D}\right)$
Force factor	$N_i = \frac{wd_{31}}{s_{11}^E} = \frac{wd_{31}}{s_{11}^E}\sqrt{\frac{\varepsilon_0\varepsilon_{33}^X}{s_{11}^E}}k_{31}$	$N_0 = \frac{2w't'd_{33}}{L's_{33}^D} = \frac{w't'}{L'}\left(\frac{\varepsilon_0\varepsilon_{33}^X}{s_{33}^D}\right)^{1/2}k_{33}$
Wave velocity	$v_b^E = \left(\frac{1}{\rho s_{11}^E}\right)^{1/2}$	$v_b^D = \left(\frac{1}{\rho s_{33}^D}\right)^{1/2}$

Source: Table by author, adapted from [11].

References

1. Mason, W.P. An Electromechanical Representation of a Piezoelectric Crystal Used as a Transducer. *Proc. Inst. Radio Eng.* **1935**, *23*, 1252–1263. [CrossRef]
2. Damjanovic, D. An Equivalent Electric-Circuit of a Piezoelectric Bar Resonator with a Large Piezoelectric Phase-Angle. *Ferroelectrics* **1990**, *110*, 129–135. [CrossRef]
3. Uchino, K. *Micromechatronics*, 2nd ed.; CRC Press: Boca Raton, FL, USA, 2019.
4. Uchino, K. *High-Power Piezoelectrics and Loss Mechanisms*; CRC Press: Boca Raton, FL, USA, 2020.
5. *ANSI/IEEE Std 176-1987*; IEEE Standard on Piezoelectricity. The Institute of Electrical and Electronics Engineers: New York, NY, USA, 1987; p. 56.
6. Shi, W.; Shekhani, H.N.; Zhao, H.; Ma, J.; Yao, Y.; Uchino, K. Losses in piezoelectrics derived from a new equivalent circuit. *J. Electroceram.* **2015**, *35*, 1–10. [CrossRef]
7. Shi, W.; Zhao, H.; Ma, J.; Yao, Y.; Uchino, K. Investigating the Frequency Spectrum of Mechanical Quality Factor for Piezoelectric Materials Based on Phenomenological Model. *Jpn. J. Appl. Phys.* **2015**, *54*, 101501. [CrossRef]
8. Mason, W.P. *Electromechanical Transducers and Wave Filters*; D. Van Norstrand Company Inc.: New York, NY, USA, 1948.
9. Dong, X.; Majzoubi, M.; Choi, M.; Ma, Y.; Hu, M.; Jin, L.; Xu, Z.; Uchino, K. A new equivalent circuit for piezoelectrics with three losses and external loads. *Sens. Actuators A Phys.* **2017**, *256*, 77–83. [CrossRef]
10. Dong, X.; Yuan, T.; Hu, M.; Shekhani, H.; Maida, Y.; Tou, T.; Uchino, K. Driving frequency optimization of a piezoelectric transducer and the power supply development. *Rev. Sci. Instrum.* **2016**, *87*, 105003. [CrossRef] [PubMed]
11. Koc, B. Miniature Piezoelectric Ultrasonic Rotary Motors. Ph.D. Thesis, The Pennsylvania State University, State College, PA, USA, August 1999.

10. Impedance Matching—Transmittance and Reflectance

Consider the stored electric energy in a battery or the stored mechanical energy in a spring. Can we spend 100% of the stored energy as the output work? The simplest answer is NO! Then, how much potential energy can we use as output work? 70, 50, 30%, or less? This chapter will find the answer to this question.

10.1. Principles of Electric Impedance Matching

10.1.1. Electric Impedance Matching with a Battery

Let us start from a fundamental knowledge check on this issue with a battery in Example Problem 10.1 [1,2].

Example Problem 10.1.

Given a power supply (such as a DC battery) with an internal impedance, Z_0, what is the optimum circuit impedance, Z_1, required for maximum power transfer?

Refer to Figure 10.1.

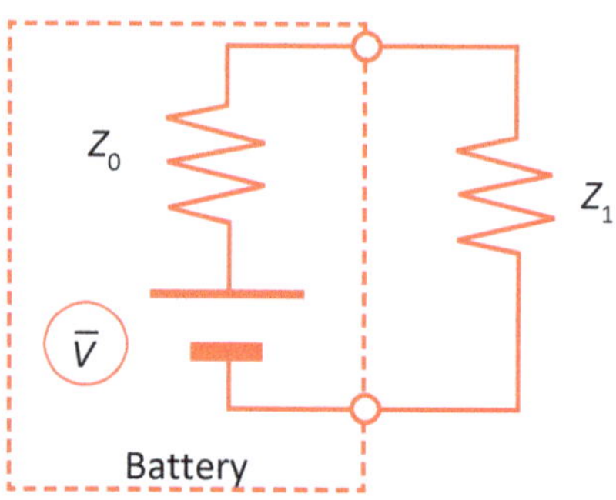

Figure 10.1. Impedance matching with a power supply. Source: Figure by author.

Solution

A battery is a constant voltage (V) supply with an internal impedance Z_0 during a suitable time period. Referring to Figure 10.1, the current and voltage associated with an external impedance Z_1 are expressed by $V/(Z_0 + Z_1)$ and $[Z_1/(Z_0 + Z_1)]V$, respectively. The product of these yields the power spent in this external load Z_1:

$$P = \left[\frac{V}{Z_0 + Z_1}\right] \cdot \frac{Z_1 V}{Z_0 + Z_1} = \frac{Z_1}{(Z_0 + Z_1)^2} V^2. \quad \text{(P10.1.1)}$$

To maximize the power (or most effectively spend the battery energy), the following maximization relation should be satisfied:

$$\frac{\partial P}{\partial Z_1} = \frac{Z_0 - Z_1}{(Z_0 + Z_1)^3} V^2 = 0. \tag{P10.1.2}$$

When impedance is resistive, the power will be maximum at $Z_1 = Z_0$, with $P_{max} = \left(\frac{1}{4}\right)\frac{V^2}{Z_0}$. To adjust the external impedance exactly to the internal impedance, $(Z_1 = Z_0)$ is called "impedance matching". Note that the same amount of power $P = \left(\frac{1}{4}\right)\frac{V^2}{Z_0}$ is spent inside the battery (usually this is converted to the heat generation), leading to the total power $P = \left(\frac{1}{2}\right)\frac{V2}{Z_0}$. With an open-circuit condition, the battery has the total power capability of $\left(\frac{1}{2}\right)\frac{V^2}{Z_0}$, while with a short-circuit condition, this power is consumed completely as joule heat in the battery. This is the primary reason for the battery fire of smartphones or laptops.

10.1.2. Electric Impedance Matching in AC Circuits

Impedance is the disturbance rate of electric energy or current from a voltage source. For AC signals, it usually changes with frequency ω. The impedances of three basic components—inductor, capacitor, and resistor—are represented by $j\omega L$, $1/j\omega C$, and R. The unit of electrical impedance is (ohm), similar to resistance. Thus, in general, impedance has a complex value.

$$Z^* = R + jX, \tag{10.1}$$

where real part R is "resistance", and imaginary part X is called "reactance". In a simple case under low-frequency ω (i.e., direct-current (DC)-like) drive, the reactance of the inductor ($j\omega L$) may be negligible or zero, leading to the pure resistive scenario, as demonstrated in Example Problem 10.1, while the reactance of the capacitor ($1/j\omega C$) approaches very large or infinite, leading to zero current or an open-circuit condition.

Let us now calculate the maximum power transfer in the case of a complex source and load impedance Z_S and Z_L, as illustrated in Figure 10.2. Similar to Example Problem 10.1, the complex AC current I^* and complex AC voltage V^* associated with an external impedance Z_L are expressed by $V^*/(Z_S + Z_L)$ and $[Z_L/(Z_S + Z_L)]V^*$, respectively. Referring to Example Problem 10.2, the "active power" spent in this external load Z_L can be provided by the real part of $\left(\frac{1}{2}\right)\left(V^*\overline{I}^*\right)$, where the "top bar" $\overline{I}^*$ is the "conjugate" of I^* as follows:

$$P = Re\left\{\left(\frac{1}{2}\right)\left(V^*\overline{I}^*\right)\right\} = Re\left\{\left(\frac{1}{2}\right)\frac{Z_L V}{Z_S+Z_L}\cdot\left[\frac{\overline{V}}{\overline{Z_S+Z_L}}\right]\right\} = Re\left\{\left(\frac{1}{2}\right)\frac{R_L+jX_L}{\left[(R_S+R_L)^2+(X_S+X_L)^2\right]}V^2\right\} = \left(\frac{1}{2}\right)\frac{R_L}{\left[(R_S+R_L)^2+(X_S+X_L)^2\right]}V^2. \tag{10.2}$$

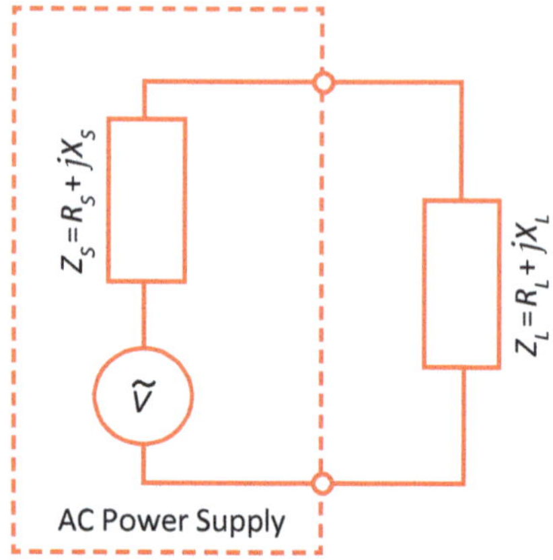

Figure 10.2. Impedance matching with an AC power supply. Source: Figure by author.

The imaginary part of Equation (10.2) is identified as "reactive power". To maximize the power transfer, the following maximization relations should be satisfied:

$$\text{Imaginary parameter} \quad (X_S + X_L)^2 = 0 \rightarrow X_L = -X_S, \tag{10.3}$$

$$\text{Real parameter} \quad \frac{\partial P}{\partial R_L} = \left(\frac{1}{2}\right) \frac{R_S - R_L}{(R_S + R_L)^3} V^2 = 0 \rightarrow R_L = R_S. \tag{10.4}$$

In the impedance matching case, the external and internal power rates are the same, $(1/8)V^2/R_S$, leading to the total power of $(1/4)V^2/R_S$ or $(1/2){V_{rms}}^2/R_S$ using the effective voltage V_{rms} $\left(= V/\sqrt{2}\right)$, equivalent description to the pure resistive DC circuit in Example Problem 10.1. Factor $(1/2)$ comes from the integral operation $\int IdV$ for obtaining the power. In conclusion, in order to maximize power transfer (i.e., "impedance matching"), the external impedance should be adjusted to the "conjugate of the internal impedance", that is,

$$Z_L = \overline{Z_S} \text{ or } R_L + jX_L = R_S - jX_S, \tag{10.5}$$

when the output power in the load shares half of the total power while keeping the same amount of power in the source circuit.

Example Problem 10.2.

When we apply complex AC voltage $V^* = Ve^{j\omega t}$ between two terminals, we obtain the complex current I^*. Verify that the expended electric power between these two terminals can be expressed by the real part of the product $\left(\frac{1}{2}\right)\left(V^* {\cdot} \overline{I}^*\right)$, where the "top bar" $\overline{I}^*$ is the conjugate of I^*.

Solution

Denoting φ for the delay phase angle of the current against the voltage, we can describe

$$V^* = Ve^{j\omega t},\ I^* = Ie^{j(\omega t-\varphi)}. \quad \text{(P10.2.1)}$$

Now, the real part of the product $\left(\frac{1}{2}\right)\left(V^*\cdot\overline{I}^*\right)$ is calculated as

$$\begin{gathered}
\mathrm{Re}\left[\left(\tfrac{1}{2}\right)\left(V^*\cdot\overline{I}^*\right)\right] = \left(\tfrac{1}{2}\right)\tfrac{V^*\cdot\overline{I}^*+\overline{V}^*\cdot I^*}{2} = \left(\tfrac{1}{2}\right)\left(\tfrac{1}{2}\right) \\
\left[Ve^{j\omega t}Ie^{-j(\omega t-\varphi)} + Ve^{-j\omega t}Ie^{j(\omega t-\varphi)}\right] = \left(\tfrac{1}{2}\right)\left(\tfrac{1}{2}\right) \\
\left[VIe^{j(\varphi)} + VIe^{-j(\varphi)}\right] = \left(\tfrac{1}{2}\right)V\cdot I\cdot\cos(\varphi).
\end{gathered} \quad \text{(P10.2.2)}$$

As the final formula of Equation (P10.2.2) is the "average electric power" of the voltage–current relation, we can conclude that Re$\left[\left(\frac{1}{2}\right)\left(V^*\cdot\overline{I}^*\right)\right]$ should be the average electric power. Here, (1/2) is the origin of the "effective RMS voltage", and the current is $1/\sqrt{2}$.

In an alternating current (AC) circuit, the reactance depends on frequency, so circuits that are impedance matched at one frequency may not be impedance matched if the frequency is changed. Impedance matching over a wide band will generally require complex, filter-like structures with many components, except in the trivial case of constant source and load resistances, when a transformer can be used.

The concept of impedance matching found its first applications in electrical engineering but is also relevant in other applications in which a form of energy, not necessarily electrical, is transferred between a source and a load.

10.2. Transmission/Reflection of Elastic Waves

10.2.1. Mechanical Wave Equations in an Isotropic Material

We discussed the equivalency among the electric circuit and mechanical system in Chapter 9: Equivalent Circuit. Ohm's law between the voltage and current ($V = RI$) corresponds to the relationship between force and vibration velocity ($F = Z_m v$, Z_m: "mechanical impedance") originated from Hooke's law between force and displacement ($F = c\Delta L$). Knowing the vibration velocity given by $v = \frac{\partial \Delta L}{\partial t} = j\omega\Delta L$ in alternating displacement, we may introduce mechanical impedance as $Z_m = c/j\omega$, which is consistent to $Z = 1/j\omega C$ of an electric capacitor. When the source mechanical system has the internal mechanical impedance, we need to consider the external mechanical impedance for optimizing the mechanical energy transfer.

We consider the "elastically isotropic" assumption in this chapter because of its simplicity. Then, we can adopt the simple Hooke's law using only two "elastic stiffnesses", c_{11} and c_{12} as follows:

$$\begin{bmatrix} X_1 \\ X_2 \\ X_3 \\ X_4 \\ X_5 \\ X_6 \end{bmatrix} = \begin{bmatrix} c_{11} & c_{12} & c_{12} & 0 & 0 & 0 \\ c_{12} & c_{11} & c_{12} & 0 & 0 & 0 \\ c_{12} & c_{12} & c_{11} & 0 & 0 & 0 \\ 0 & 0 & 0 & \frac{1}{2}(c_{11}-c_{12}) & 0 & 0 \\ 0 & 0 & 0 & 0 & \frac{1}{2}(c_{11}-c_{12}) & 0 \\ 0 & 0 & 0 & 0 & 0 & \frac{1}{2}(c_{11}-c_{12}) \end{bmatrix} \begin{pmatrix} x_1 \\ x_2 \\ x_3 \\ x_4 \\ x_5 \\ x_6 \end{pmatrix}. \quad (10.6)$$

In isotropic elastic materials, "Lamé parameters" (first parameter λ and shear modulus μ) are often utilized conventionally. The first and second parameters, λ and μ, are defined by both shear parameters as

$$\lambda = c_{12}, \text{ and } \mu = c_{66} = \frac{1}{2}(c_{11} - c_{12}). \quad (10.7)$$

The elastic stiffness matrix can also be represented as follows in the isotropic symmetry:

$$(c_{ij}) = \begin{pmatrix} (\lambda+2\mu) & \lambda & \lambda & 0 & 0 & 0 \\ \lambda & (\lambda+2\mu) & \lambda & 0 & 0 & 0 \\ \lambda & \lambda & (\lambda+2\mu) & 0 & 0 & 0 \\ 0 & 0 & 0 & \mu & 0 & 0 \\ 0 & 0 & 0 & 0 & \mu & 0 \\ 0 & 0 & 0 & 0 & 0 & \mu \end{pmatrix}. \quad (10.8)$$

The above Lamé parameters definitions derive Poisson's ratio:

$$\sigma = \frac{c_{12}}{c_{11} + c_{12}} = \frac{\lambda}{2(\lambda + \mu)}. \quad (10.9)$$

The sound velocity for the longitudinal and transverse waves in isotropic materials is $c_l^2 = (\lambda + 2\mu)/\rho$ and $c_t^2 = \mu/\rho$, taking the material's mass density ρ, as we derive them in the next section.

On the contrary, when we use the inverse notations with elastic compliances, we denote

$$\begin{bmatrix} x_1 \\ x_2 \\ x_3 \\ x_4 \\ x_5 \\ x_6 \end{bmatrix} = \begin{bmatrix} s_{11} & s_{12} & s_{12} & 0 & 0 & 0 \\ s_{12} & s_{11} & s_{12} & 0 & 0 & 0 \\ s_{12} & s_{12} & s_{11} & 0 & 0 & 0 \\ 0 & 0 & 0 & 2(s_{11}-s_{12}) & 0 & 0 \\ 0 & 0 & 0 & 0 & 2(s_{11}-s_{12}) & 0 \\ 0 & 0 & 0 & 0 & 0 & 2(s_{11}-s_{12}) \end{bmatrix} \begin{pmatrix} X_1 \\ X_2 \\ X_3 \\ X_4 \\ X_5 \\ X_6 \end{pmatrix}. \quad (10.10)$$

An alternative set of elastic parameters in isotropic materials is composed of "Young's modulus" E and "Poisson's ratio" σ, where $E = 1/s_{11}$ and $\sigma = -s_{12}/s_{11}$.

$$(s_{ij}) = \frac{1}{E}\begin{pmatrix} 1 & -\sigma & -\sigma & 0 & 0 & 0 \\ -\sigma & 1 & -\sigma & 0 & 0 & 0 \\ -\sigma & -\sigma & 1 & 0 & 0 & 0 \\ 0 & 0 & 0 & 2(1+\sigma) & 0 & 0 \\ 0 & 0 & 0 & 0 & 2(1+\sigma) & 0 \\ 0 & 0 & 0 & 0 & 0 & 2(1+\sigma) \end{pmatrix}. \tag{10.11}$$

We have also the following relations: $c_{11} = \frac{1-\sigma}{(1+\sigma)(1-2\sigma)}E$, $c_{12} = \frac{\sigma}{(1+\sigma)(1-2\sigma)}E$.

Knowing the strain and displacement relations as $x_1 = \frac{\partial u}{\partial x}$, $x_2 = \frac{\partial v}{\partial y}$, and $x_3 = \frac{\partial w}{\partial z}$, the following stress vs. displacement relations are obtained using the Lamé parameters:

$$\begin{cases} X_1 = \lambda\Delta + 2\mu\frac{\partial u}{\partial x} \\ X_2 = \lambda\Delta + 2\mu\frac{\partial v}{\partial y} \\ X_3 = \lambda\Delta + 2\mu\frac{\partial w}{\partial z} \end{cases}, \quad \begin{cases} X_4 = \mu\left(\frac{\partial v}{\partial z} + \frac{\partial w}{\partial y}\right) \\ X_5 = \mu\left(\frac{\partial w}{\partial x} + \frac{\partial u}{\partial z}\right) \\ X_6 = \mu\left(\frac{\partial u}{\partial y} + \frac{\partial v}{\partial x}\right) \end{cases}, \tag{10.12}$$

where $\Delta = \frac{\partial u}{\partial x} + \frac{\partial v}{\partial y} + \frac{\partial w}{\partial z}$.

In order to discuss the mechanical/sound energy transfer, we now introduce the dynamic equation in a continuum elastic media with isotropic elastic properties. Newton equation is adopted to a small volume element at the position (x, y, z), taking into account the force that is provided by the stress gradient in terms of the coordinate as follows:

$$\begin{cases} \rho\left(\frac{\partial^2 u}{\partial t^2}\right) = \left(\frac{\partial X_{11}}{\partial x}\right) + \left(\frac{\partial X_{12}}{\partial y}\right) + \left(\frac{\partial X_{13}}{\partial z}\right) \\ \rho\left(\frac{\partial^2 v}{\partial t^2}\right) = \left(\frac{\partial X_{21}}{\partial x}\right) + \left(\frac{\partial X_{22}}{\partial y}\right) + \left(\frac{\partial X_{23}}{\partial z}\right) \\ \rho\left(\frac{\partial^2 w}{\partial t^2}\right) = \left(\frac{\partial X_{31}}{\partial x}\right) + \left(\frac{\partial X_{32}}{\partial y}\right) + \left(\frac{\partial X_{33}}{\partial z}\right) \end{cases}, \tag{10.13}$$

where ρ is the density of the elastic material; u, v, and w are the displacements of a small volume element in the material in the x-, y- and z-directions, respectively. In the pure mechanical wave discussion, we tentatively neglect the electromechanical coupling (i.e., piezoelectric effect) in order to simplify the analysis. Using the Lamé parameters, Equation (10.13) can be rewritten as

$$\rho\frac{\partial^2}{\partial t^2}\begin{pmatrix} u \\ v \\ w \end{pmatrix} = (\lambda+\mu)\begin{pmatrix} \frac{\partial}{\partial x} \\ \frac{\partial}{\partial y} \\ \frac{\partial}{\partial z} \end{pmatrix}\Delta + \mu\nabla^2\begin{pmatrix} u \\ v \\ w \end{pmatrix}, \tag{10.14}$$

where $\nabla^2 = \frac{\partial^2}{\partial x^2} + \frac{\partial^2}{\partial y^2} + \frac{\partial^2}{\partial z^2}$.

10.2.2. Plane Wave Propagation

The propagating plane wave in an isotropic elastic material keeps the "equi-phase plane" always in a parallel plane. Thus, if we assume a sinusoidal harmonic wave with time dependence of $e^{-j\omega t}$, and denote the "direction cosine" of the normal axis to the equi-phase plane as (l, m, n), this equi-phase plane can be described as

$$lx + my + nz = p, \tag{10.15}$$

where $l^2 + m^2 + n^2 = 1$. The displacement (u, v, w) can be described as

$$\begin{pmatrix} u \\ v \\ w \end{pmatrix} = \begin{pmatrix} u_0 \\ v_0 \\ w_0 \end{pmatrix} e^{-j\{\omega t - k(lx+my+nz)\}}. \tag{10.16}$$

Here, ω is the angular frequency, and k is the wave vector with the following relations:

$$k_1^2 + k_2^2 + k_3^2 = k^2\left(l^2 + m^2 + n^2\right) = k^2. \tag{10.17}$$

Since the dynamic Equation (10.13) can be rewritten as

$$\begin{gathered} \text{Left-side} : \rho\left(\frac{\partial^2 u_i}{\partial t^2}\right) = -\rho\omega^2 u_i, \\ \text{Right-side} : \frac{\partial X_{ij}}{\partial x_j} = \frac{\partial\left(c_{ijmn} x_{mn}\right)}{\partial x_j} = c_{ijmn}\frac{\partial^2 u_m}{\partial x_j \partial x_n} = -\frac{1}{2}k^2 c_{ijmn}\left(l_m l_j u_n + l_n l_j u_m\right). \end{gathered} \tag{10.18}$$

By putting the above equation as

$$k^2\begin{pmatrix} A_{11} & A_{12} & A_{13} \\ A_{21} & A_{22} & A_{23} \\ A_{31} & A_{32} & A_{33} \end{pmatrix}\begin{pmatrix} u \\ v \\ w \end{pmatrix} = \rho\omega^2\begin{pmatrix} u \\ v \\ w \end{pmatrix}, \tag{10.19}$$

let us solve this eigenvalue problem. In the isotropic material expressed in Equation (10.6), the A_{ij} can be given by

$$\left\{\begin{array}{l} A_{11} = c_{11}l^2 + c_{66}m^2 + c_{66}n^2 \\ A_{22} = c_{66}l^2 + c_{11}m^2 + c_{66}n^2 \\ A_{33} = c_{66}l^2 + c_{66}m^2 + c_{11}n^2 \end{array}\right., \quad \left\{\begin{array}{l} A_{12} = A_{21} = (c_{12} + c_{66})lm \\ A_{23} = A_{32} = (c_{12} + c_{66})mn \\ A_{31} = A_{13} = (c_{12} + c_{66})nl \end{array}\right.. \tag{10.20}$$

Note $c_{66} = \frac{1}{2}\left(c_{11} - c_{12}\right)$. Thus, denoting the eigenvalue as C, we solve the following equation:

$$\begin{vmatrix} c_{11}l^2 + c_{66}m^2 + c_{66}n^2 - C & (c_{12} + c_{66})lm & (c_{12} + c_{66})nl \\ (c_{12} + c_{66})lm & c_{66}l^2 + c_{11}m^2 + c_{66}n^2 - C & (c_{12} + c_{66})mn \\ (c_{12} + c_{66})nl & (c_{12} + c_{66})mn & c_{66}l^2 + c_{66}m^2 + c_{11}n^2 - C \end{vmatrix} = 0.$$

Three eigenvalues of the above equation, C_1, C_2, and C_3, can be obtained irrelevant to (l, m, n) as

$$C_1 = c_{11}, \text{ and } C_2 = C_3 = c_{66}. \tag{10.21}$$

From $C = \frac{\rho\omega^2}{k^2}$ and the phase velocity $v_p = \frac{\omega}{k} = \sqrt{\frac{C}{\rho}}$, we obtain two characteristic sound (phase) velocities, that is, longitudinal (primary (P) wave) and transversal (two secondary (S) waves, orthogonal each other) types:

$$v_{p1} = \sqrt{\frac{c_{11}}{\rho}} = \sqrt{\frac{\lambda + 2\mu}{\rho}}, \text{ and } v_{p2} = v_{p3} = \sqrt{\frac{c_{66}}{\rho}} = \sqrt{\frac{\mu}{\rho}}. \quad (10.22)$$

You recognize that $v_{p1} > v_{p2} = v_{p3}$; the P wave propagates faster than the S wave. As the longitudinal P wave reaches the target point first in the "earthquake", this wave was, in fact, named "primary" historically.

10.2.3. Elastic Wave Transmission/Reflection at the Interface

There exists only the transverse electromagnetic wave in an isotropic material, while both longitudinal and transverse elastic waves exist in an elastic material, which makes the situation more complicated in the analysis. We consider here the transmission/reflection of three different waves: (1) secondary-horizontal (SH), (2) primary (P), and (3) secondary-vertical (SV) waves between two phases [3]. In an infinite elastic medium, these three waves exist independently, but in a finite size medium, P and SV waves are usually coupled at the medium interface, depending on the beam angle.

SH Waves

We consider first the SH wave because of the simplicity. SH has the displacement direction perpendicular to the wave propagation direction and in parallel to the interface plane (sound velocity $\sqrt{\frac{c_{66}}{\rho}}$), which exhibits an equivalent "Snell's law" in optics. The model of this analysis is illustrated in Figure 10.3, where two material phases 1 and 2 (with density, elastic shear stiffness μ ("Lamé shear modulus"), and wavenumbers k, $\rho_1, \mu_1, k_1, \rho_2, \mu_2, k_2$) create an interface on the x-y plane, and incident, reflection, and transmission waves are illustrated with cant angles θ θ_i, ${\theta_t}^1$, and ${\theta_t}^2$, respectively. Since the SH wave is the transverse type, only the shear elastic stiffness is sufficient for the analysis. We neglect the wave absorption during the propagation tentatively in the following analysis. We may assume the displacements v (only along the y-direction, normal to Figure 10.3 plane; $u = w = 0$) of the incident, reflection (phase 1), and transmission (phase 2) waves as

$$v_i = v_{i0} e^{-i\{\omega t - k_1(\sin\theta_i \cdot x + \cos\theta_i \cdot z)\}}, \quad (10.23)$$

$$v_r = v_{r0} e^{-i\{\omega t - k_1(\sin\theta_t^1 \cdot x - \cos\theta_t^1 \cdot z)\}}, \quad (10.24)$$

$$v_t = v_{t0} e^{-i\{\omega t - k_2(\sin\theta_t^2 \cdot x + \cos\theta_t^2 \cdot z)\}}. \quad (10.25)$$

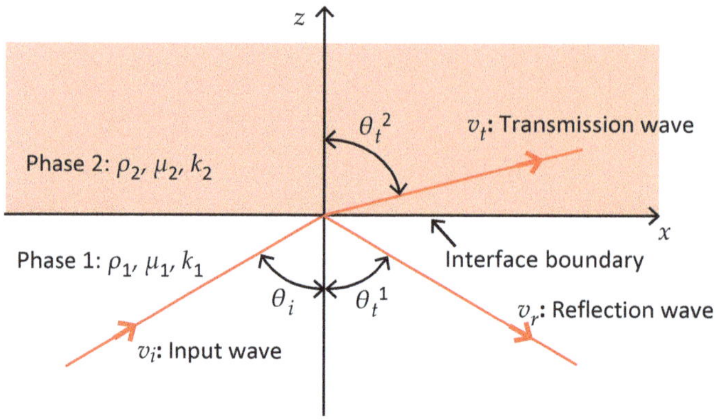

Figure 10.3. Transmission/reflection of SH acoustic wave. Source: Figure by author.

The stress boundary conditions at $z = 0$ (interface between phases 1 and 2) should satisfy

$$\begin{cases} X_3^{(i)} + X_3^{(r)} = X_3^{(t)} \\ X_4^{(i)} + X_4^{(r)} = X_4^{(t)} \\ X_5^{(i)} + X_5^{(r)} = X_5^{(t)} \end{cases}, \quad v_i + v_r = v_t. \tag{10.26}$$

Here, the boundary conditions for X_3 and X_5 are automatically satisfied because all stress components are zero. Regarding the X_4 (shear stress on the $z - x$ plane) boundary condition, the displacement continuity should be maintained at $z = 0$ (on the interface plane), so that displacement v should satisfy the above condition on a plane $z = 0$; that is, the relation

$$v_{i0}e^{-i\{\omega t - k_1(\sin\theta_i \cdot x)\}} + v_{r0}e^{-i\{\omega t - k_1(\sin\theta_t^1 \cdot x)\}} = v_{t0}e^{-i\{\omega t - k_2(\sin\theta_t^2 \cdot x)\}}, \tag{10.27}$$

should be satisfied for any time t and position x, leading to the following relations:

$$\theta_i = \theta_t^1, \tag{10.28}$$

$$v_{i0} + v_{r0} = v_{t0}, \tag{10.29}$$

$$k_1\left(\sin\theta_t^1\right) = k_2\left(\sin\theta_t^2\right). \tag{10.30}$$

Here, the wavenumber k_1 and k_2 are given by

$$k_1 = \frac{\omega}{c_{t1}} = \omega\sqrt{\frac{\rho_1}{\mu_1}}, \quad k_2 = \frac{\omega}{c_{t2}} = \omega\sqrt{\frac{\rho_2}{\mu_2}}. \tag{10.31}$$

In order for stress X_4 to satisfy the continuity condition on a plane $z = 0$

$$\mu_1 v_{i0} k_1 \cos\theta_t^1 - \mu_1 v_{r0} k_1 \cos\theta_t^1 = \mu_2 v_{t0} k_2 \cos\theta_t^2. \tag{10.32}$$

Then, we can obtain the following reflectance and transmittance relations:

$$\frac{v_{r0}}{v_{i0}} = \frac{\left(1 - \sqrt{\frac{\rho_2\mu_2}{\rho_1\mu_1}} \cdot \frac{\cos\theta_t^2}{\cos\theta_t^1}\right)}{\left(1 + \sqrt{\frac{\rho_2\mu_2}{\rho_1\mu_1}} \cdot \frac{\cos\theta_t^2}{\cos\theta_t^1}\right)}, \quad \frac{v_{t0}}{v_{i0}} = \frac{2}{\left(1 + \sqrt{\frac{\rho_2\mu_2}{\rho_1\mu_1}} \cdot \frac{\cos\theta_t^2}{\cos\theta_t^1}\right)}. \tag{10.33}$$

Note that Equation (10.33) indicates the energy conservation; that is, the incident wave energy is equal to the sum of the reflected and transmitted wave energy $[\frac{v_{t0} - v_{r0}}{v_{i0}} = 1]$. In order to minimize the reflectance (or 100% transmittance), the following relation must be maintained:

$$\sqrt{\frac{\rho_2\mu_2}{\rho_1\mu_1}} \cdot \frac{\cos\theta_t^2}{\cos\theta_t^1} = 1. \tag{10.34}$$

When the incident wave is normal to the phase boundary plane ($\theta_t^1 = 0$), in particular, knowing $\mu = c_{66}$,

$$\sqrt{\rho_1\mu_1} = \sqrt{\rho_2\mu_2} \text{ or } \sqrt{\rho_1 c_{66,1}} = \sqrt{\rho_2 c_{66,2}}. \tag{10.35}$$

Since we define the "mechanical/acoustic impedance" by the form of $\sqrt{\rho c}$, the reader can understand that the mechanical energy (SH wave) efficient transfer requires the "mechanical impedance matching" between the adjacent two phases.

P and SV Waves

Next, we consider the P wave with the displacement in parallel to the wave propagation direction (sound velocity $\sqrt{c_{11}/\rho}$), and the SV wave with a displacement direction perpendicular to the wave propagation direction and perpendicular to the interface plane (the same sound velocity $\sqrt{c_{66}/\rho}$ as the SH wave). Both the displacements u and w of the incident, as well as reflection and transmission waves, should be taken into account, with full descriptions as follows [3]:

- Incident

$$\text{P Wave}: \begin{cases} u_i^{(P)} = A_i^{(P)} \sin\theta_p^1 e^{-i\{\omega t - k_p^1(\sin\theta_p^1 \cdot x + \cos\theta_p^1 \cdot z)\}} \\ w_i^{(P)} = A_i^{(P)} \cos\theta_p^1 e^{-i\{\omega t - k_p^1(\sin\theta_p^1 \cdot x + \cos\theta_p^1 \cdot z)\}} \end{cases}, \tag{10.36}$$

$$\text{SV Wave}: \begin{cases} u_i^{(S)} = A_i^{(S)} \cos\theta_t^1 e^{-i\{\omega t - k_t^1(\sin\theta_t^1 \cdot x + \cos\theta_t^1 \cdot z)\}} \\ w_i^{(S)} = -A_i^{(S)} \sin\theta_t^1 e^{-i\{\omega t - k_t^1(\sin\theta_t^1 \cdot x + \cos\theta_t^1 \cdot z)\}} \end{cases}. \tag{10.37}$$

- Reflection

$$\text{P Wave}: \begin{cases} u_r^{(P)} = A_r^{(P)} \sin\theta_p^1 e^{-i\{\omega t - k_p^1(\sin\theta_p^1 \cdot x - \cos\theta_p^1 \cdot z)\}} \\ w_r^{(P)} = -A_r^{(P)} \cos\theta_p^1 e^{-i\{\omega t - k_p^1(\sin\theta_p^1 \cdot x - \cos\theta_p^1 \cdot z)\}} \end{cases}, \tag{10.38}$$

$$\text{SV Wave}: \begin{cases} u_r^{(S)} = A_r^{(S)} \cos\theta_t^1 e^{-i\{\omega t - k_t^1(\sin\theta_t^1 \cdot x - \cos\theta_t^1 \cdot z)\}} \\ w_r^{(S)} = A_r^{(S)} \sin\theta_t^1 e^{-i\{\omega t - k_t^1(\sin\theta_t^1 \cdot x - \cos\theta_t^1 \cdot z)\}} \end{cases}. \tag{10.39}$$

- Transmission

$$\text{P Wave}: \begin{cases} u_t^{(P)} = A_t^{(P)} \sin\theta_p^2 e^{-i\{\omega t - k_p^2(\sin\theta_p^2\cdot x + \cos\theta_p^2\cdot z)\}} \\ w_t^{(P)} = A_t^{(P)} \cos\theta_p^2 e^{-i\{\omega t - k_p^2(\sin\theta_p^2\cdot x + \cos\theta_p^2\cdot z)\}} \end{cases}, \tag{10.40}$$

$$\text{SV Wave}: \begin{cases} u_t^{(S)} = A_t^{(S)} \cos\theta_t^2 e^{-i\{\omega t - k_t^2(\sin\theta_t^2\cdot x + \cos\theta_t^2\cdot z)\}} \\ w_t^{(S)} = -A_t^{(S)} \sin\theta_t^2 e^{-i\{\omega t - k_t^2(\sin\theta_t^2\cdot x + \cos\theta_t^2\cdot z)\}} \end{cases}. \tag{10.41}$$

We can solve the waveforms based on the boundary conditions at $z = 0$.

$$\begin{cases} u_i^{(P)} + u_i^{(S)} + u_r^{(P)} + u_r^{(S)} = u_t^{(P)} + u_t^{(S)} \\ w_i^{(P)} + w_i^{(S)} + w_r^{(P)} + w_r^{(S)} = w_t^{(P)} + w_t^{(S)} \end{cases}, \tag{10.42}$$

$$X_3^{(i)} + X_3^{(r)} = X_3^{(t)},\ X_5^{(i)} + X_5^{(r)} = X_5^{(t)}. \tag{10.43}$$

As further analyses are lengthy, we skip the derivation step and leave it for the reader to carry out by referring to [3]. Instead, we introduce the simplest transmission/reflection model of the P acoustic wave under the normal incident wave situation illustrated in Figure 10.4. We describe the incident, reflected, and transmitted stress waves with normalized w displacement notations (which are proportional to the stress) as

$$\begin{cases} w_i = e^{ik_p^1\cdot z} \\ w_r = Re^{-ik_p^1\cdot z} \\ w_t = Te^{ik_p^2\cdot z} \end{cases}, \tag{10.44}$$

where R and T denote the reflectance and transmittance coefficients, respectively. The total normalized stress values in Phase 1 and Phase 2 (the equi-stress wave plane is parallel to the phase boundary) are expressed as

$$\begin{cases} X^1(z) = e^{ik_p^1\cdot z} + Re^{-ik_p^1\cdot z} \\ X^2(z) = Te^{ik_p^1\cdot z} \end{cases}. \tag{10.45}$$

From the stress continuation boundary condition at $z = 0$, we first obtain the relation

$$1 + R = T. \tag{10.46}$$

Second, taking into account $\rho\left(\frac{\partial^2 w}{\partial t^2}\right) = \left(\frac{\partial X_3}{\partial z}\right)$, and imposing continuity of particle velocity (along the z direction), we need also the following relation:

$$\left(k_p^1/\rho_1\right)(1 - R) = \left(k_p^2/\rho_2\right)T. \tag{10.47}$$

Knowing the "phase velocity" (i.e., "sound velocity") $v_p = \frac{\omega}{k}$, Equations (10.46) and (10.47) result in

$$\begin{cases} R = \frac{\rho_2 v_{p2} - \rho_1 v_{p1}}{\rho_2 v_{p2} + \rho_1 v_{p1}} \\ T = \frac{2\rho_2 v_{p2}}{\rho_2 v_{p2} + \rho_1 v_{p1}} \end{cases}. \tag{10.48}$$

Thus, minimizing the reflectance (or 100% transmittance), the following relation must be maintained:

$$\rho_1 v_{p1} = \rho_2 v_{p2}. \tag{10.49}$$

We may define the mechanical impedance by the product of density and phase sound velocity $\rho \cdot v_p$. As $v_{p1} = \sqrt{\frac{c_{11}{}^1}{\rho_1}}$ and $v_{p2} = \sqrt{\frac{c_{11}{}^2}{\rho_2}}$, the above condition is equivalent to

$$\sqrt{\rho_1 c_{11}{}^1} = \sqrt{\rho_2 c_{11}{}^2}. \tag{10.50}$$

We can also define the mechanical/acoustic impedance by the form of $\sqrt{\rho c}$ (c: elastic stiffness). The reader can again understand that the efficient transfer of mechanical energy requires the mechanical impedance matching between two phases, irrelevant to the longitudinal (P wave) or transverse (SH, SV) waves.

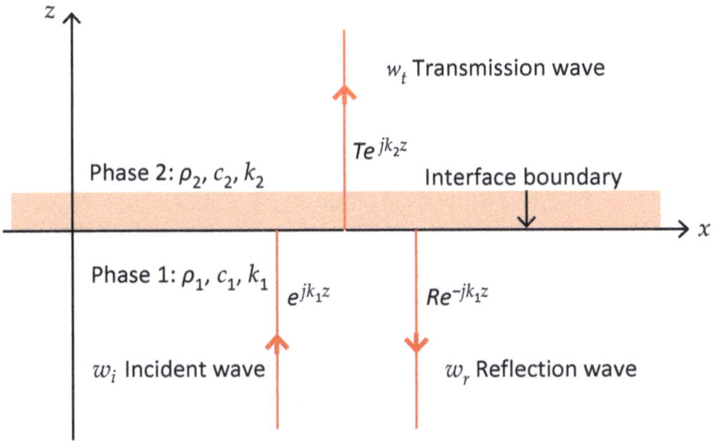

Figure 10.4. Transmission/reflection of P acoustic wave. Source: Figure by author.

10.3. Acoustic Impedance Matching

The "acoustic impedance" parameter is a measure of the impedance that a system presents to the acoustic flow against an acoustic pressure applied to the system. This concept is important, for example, in designing the piezoelectric energy harvesting systems, where the environmental mechanical energy is converted into electrical energy. The acoustic impedance Z_m is used for evaluating the acoustic energy transfer between two "continuum materials", which is defined, in general, by

$$Z_m = \text{(pressure/volume velocity)}. \tag{10.51a}$$

Recall the mechanical impedance in a "discrete component" system is defined by

$$Z_m = \text{(force/vibration velocity) or } F = Z_m v. \tag{10.51b}$$

In a simple mass–spring model, the mechanical impedance is given by the spring constant c as $Z_m = c/j\omega$.

10.3.1. Acoustic/Mechanical Impedance Derivation

In an isotropic, solid material, the dynamic equation is expressed by

$$\rho\left(\frac{\partial^2 u}{\partial t^2}\right) = \left(\frac{\partial X_{11}}{\partial x}\right) + \left(\frac{\partial X_{12}}{\partial y}\right) + \left(\frac{\partial X_{13}}{\partial z}\right) = -\left(\frac{\partial p}{\partial x}\right), \tag{10.52}$$

in a 1D form. From $p = X_{11}$, $X_{11} = c_{11}x_{11}$, we obtain

$$\rho\left(\frac{\partial^2 u}{\partial t^2}\right) = c_{11}\left(\frac{\partial^2 u}{\partial x^2}\right) \text{ or } \left(\frac{\partial^2 u}{\partial t^2}\right) = {v_{11}}^2\left(\frac{\partial^2 u}{\partial x^2}\right) \left[\text{sound velocity} v_{11} = \sqrt{\frac{c_{11}}{\rho}}\right]. \tag{10.53}$$

The constitutive law of non-dispersive linear acoustics in 1D gives a relation between stress (pressure) and strain from Equations (10.52) and (10.53) as follows:

$$p = -\rho v^2\left(\frac{\partial u}{\partial x}\right), \tag{10.54}$$

where p is the acoustic pressure, ρ mass density, and v is the sound wave speed in the medium. This equation is valid both for fluids and solids.

- Fluids – $\rho v^2 = K$ (K: bulk modulus);
- Solids – $\rho v^2 = K + 4/3G$ (G: shear modulus) for longitudinal waves and $\rho v^2 = G$ for transverse waves.

From Equation (10.53), we assume a general displacement solution $u(x,t)$ for a traveling plane wave as

$$u(x,t) = f(x - vt). \tag{10.55}$$

Then, we obtain pressure $p(x,t)$ and each "volume/particle velocity" $v(x,t) = \frac{\partial u}{\partial t}$ are represented by

$$\begin{cases} p(x,t) = -\rho v^2 f'(x - vt) \\ v(x,t) = -vf'(x - vt) \end{cases}. \tag{10.56}$$

From the definition in Equations (10.51) and (10.56), the acoustic/mechanical impedance defined by pressure/volume velocity is obtained as follows:

$$Z = \frac{p(x,t)}{v(x,t)} = \rho v. \tag{10.57}$$

Since $v = \sqrt{c/\rho}$ in a solid material, Z can be translated to

$$Z = \sqrt{\rho c}, \tag{10.58}$$

where ρ is the density, and c is the elastic stiffness of the material.

10.3.2. Designing Acoustic Impedance Matching

Concept of Acoustic Impedance Matching

Acoustic (or mechanical) impedance matching is necessary for transferring mechanical energy from one material to the other efficiently. Figure 10.5 illustrates a conceptual cartoon for two extreme cases. The mechanical work performed by one material on the other is evaluated by the product of the applied force F and the displacement ΔL: $W = F \times \Delta L$. If the material is very soft, the force F can be very small, leading to a very small W (practically, no work!). This corresponds to "pushing a curtain", exemplified by the case in which the acoustic wave is generated in water directly by an elastically hard PZT transducer. Most of the acoustic energy generated in the PZT (large force and small displacement) is reflected at the interface, and only a small portion of acoustic energy transfers into water (large displacement is required). On the other hand, if the material is very hard, the displacement ΔL will be very small, again leading to a very small W. This corresponds to "pushing a wall". Polymer piezoelectric polyvinylidene di-fluoride (PVDF) (large displacement and small force) cannot drive a hard steel part effectively (large force is required). Therefore, the "acoustic impedance" must be adjusted between the transducer and acoustic energy transferring medium to maximize the output mechanical power.

$$\sqrt{\rho_1 c_1} = \sqrt{\rho_2 c_2}, \tag{10.59}$$

where ρ and c are the density and elastic stiffness, and subscripts 1 and 2 denote the two materials. In practice, an acoustic impedance matching layer (elastically intermediate material between PZT and water, such as a polymer) is inserted between two phases (1 and 2). More precisely, the acoustic impedance Z should be chosen the geometrical average $\sqrt{Z_1 Z_2}$ of Z_1 in phase 1 and Z_2 in phase 2 so that the transfer of mechanical energy in the PZT to water will be optimized.

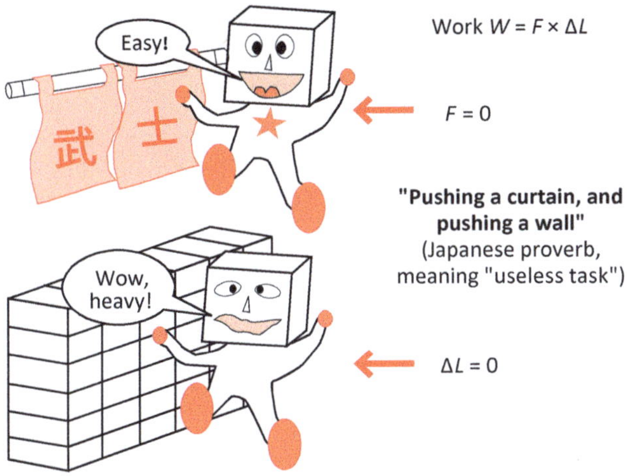

Figure 10.5. Mechanical impedance matching. Source: Figure by author.

In more advanced discussions, there are three kinds of impedances; specific acoustic impedance (pressure/particle speed), acoustic impedance (pressure/volume speed), and radiation impedance (force/speed). See reference [4] for the details.

Acoustic Impedance of Piezoelectric Materials

(a) PZT Ceramics

The acoustic-wave-transmitting object in medical diagnostic and underwater sonar applications is basically water. First, let us calculate the acoustic impedance of water. Taking into account ρ = 1000 kg/m^3 and the sound velocity v = 1.5 km/s, we obtain Z = ρv = 1.5 × 10^6 kg/m^2·s = 1.5 MRayls. The unit (Rayl) = (kg/m^2·s) is used for the acoustic impedance, named after John William Strutt, third Baron Rayleigh. On the other hand, the acoustic impedance of the PZT's is calculated from ρ = 7750 kg/m^3, $s_{33}{}^E$ = 18.8 × 10^{-12} m^2/N for "soft" PZT 5A, and ρ = 7600 kg/m^3, $s_{33}{}^E$ = 13.9 × 10^{-12} m^2/N for "hard" PZT 8, for example; $Z = \sqrt{\rho c} \approx \sqrt{\rho / s_{33}^E} =$ 20 MRayls and 24 MRayls, respectively. Due to this large difference in the acoustic impedance in the PZT ceramics and water, the energy transmission problem occurs if we set the PZT transducer directly on the water medium.

(b) Piezoelectric Polymers

Polymer piezoelectric transducer materials such as polyvinylidene difluoride (PVDF) are more suitable from the acoustic impedance matching viewpoint, because of ρ = 1780 kg/m^3, Young's modulus Y = 8.3 × 10^9 N/m^2, and $Z = \sqrt{\rho Y}$ = 3.8 MRayls, much closer to water. However, due to small piezoelectric actuator figures of merit, that is, piezoelectric d constants, their application is limited to sensors such as heart-rate/pulse measurements or hydrophones.

(c) PZT: Polymer Composites

Piezocomposites comprising a piezoelectric ceramic and a polymer phase are promising materials because of their excellent and readily tailored properties. The geometry for two-phase composites can be classified according to the dimensional connectivity of each phase into 10 structures: 0-0, 0-1, 0-2, 0-3, 1-1, 1-2, 1-3, 2-2, 2-3 and 3-3 [5]. A 1-3 piezocomposite such as the PZT-rod/polymer composite is the most promising candidate, which is composed of PZT fibers embedded in a polymer matrix, as shown in Figure 10.6a. The original fabrication process involves the injection of epoxy resin into an array of PZT fibers assembled with a special rack [6]. After the epoxy is cured, the sample is cut, polished, electroded on the top and bottom, and finally, electrically poled. The die-casting technique has also been employed to make rod arrays from a PZT slurry [7].

The effective piezoelectric coefficients d^* and g^* of the composite can be interpreted as follows: When an electric field E_3 is applied to this composite, the piezo-ceramic rods extend easily because the polymer is elastically very soft (assuming the electrode plates that are bonded to its top and bottom are rigid enough). Thus, $d_{33}{}^*$ is almost the same as ${}^1d_{33}$ of the PZT itself.

$$d_{33}{}^* = {}^1d_{33}. \tag{10.60}$$

Similarly,

$$d_{33}{}^* = {}^1V\,{}^1d_{33}, \tag{10.61}$$

where ${}^1V$ is the volume fraction of phase 1 (piezoelectric). On the other hand, when an external stress load is applied to the composite, the elastically stiff piezo-ceramic rods will support most of the load, and the effective stress is drastically enhanced and inversely proportional to the volume fraction. Thus, larger induced electric fields and larger g^* constants are expected, defined as follows:

$$g_{33}{}^* = d_{33}{}^* / \varepsilon_0 \varepsilon^* = {}^1d_{33} / {}^1V \varepsilon_0^1 \varepsilon_3 = {}^1g_{33} / {}^1V. \quad (10.62)$$

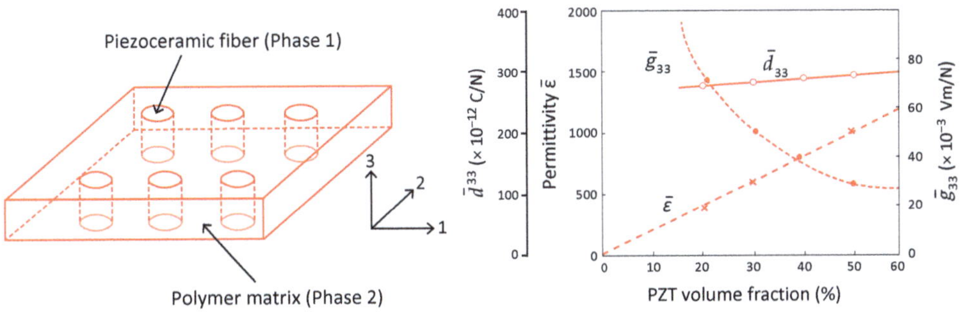

(a) (b)

Figure 10.6. (**a**) A 1-3 composite of PZT rods and polymer. The top and bottom planes are rigid electrodes; (**b**) volume fraction dependence of the permittivity ε and the piezoelectric constants d_{33} and g_{33} in the 1-3 PZT: polymer composite. Source: [8] ©Uchino, K. *Piezoelectric Composite Materials*. Woodhead Publishing, 2010; p. 318. Reproduced by permission of Elsevier B.V.

Figure 10.6b shows the piezoelectric coefficients for a PZT–Spurr epoxy composite with 1-3 connectivity, measured with a Berlincourt d_{33} meter [6]. As predicted by the model for this composite, the measured $d_{33}{}^*$ values are almost independent of volume fraction but are only about 75% of the d_{33} value of the PZT 501A ceramic. This discrepancy may be due to incomplete poling of the rods. A linear relation between the permittivity and the volume fraction ${}^1V$ is satisfied, resulting in a significant increase in $g_{33}{}^*$ with decreasing fraction of PZT. Therefore, 1-3 composites can enhance the piezoelectric g coefficient by an order of magnitude with decreasing volume fraction of PZT, while the d coefficient remains constant.

The advantages of this composite are high coupling factors, low acoustic impedance, good matching to water or human tissue (more than 70% of a human body is water!), mechanical flexibility, broad bandwidth in combination with a low mechanical quality factor, and the possibility of making un-diced arrays by simply patterning the electrodes. The thickness-mode electromechanical coupling of the composite can exceed the k_t (0.40~0.50) of the constituent ceramic, approaching almost the value of the rod-mode electromechanical coupling, k_{33} (0.70~0.80) of that ceramic [9]. The acoustic impedance matching to tissue or water (1.5 MRayls) of the typical piezo-ceramics (20~30 MRayls) is significantly improved when they are incorporated in forming a composite structure, that is, by replacing the dense, stiff ceramic with a low density, soft polymer. Piezoelectric composite materials are especially useful for underwater sonar and medical diagnostic ultrasonic transducer applications. This composite design is suitable for energy harvesting under plate-perpendicular force (cyclic or impact) because of the very high effective thickness electromechanical coupling factor, close to k_{33} value of the PZT ceramic with much lower effective acoustic impedance.

Although the PZT composites are very useful for acoustic transducer applications, care must be taken when using them in continuously operating transducer applications. Under an applied DC field, the field-induced strain exhibits large hysteresis and creep due to the "viscoelastic property" of the polymer matrix. More serious problems are found when they are driven under a high AC field, related to the generation of heat. The heat generated by ferroelectric hysteresis in piezo-ceramics cannot be dissipated easily due to the very low thermal conductivity of the polymer matrix, which results in rapid degradation of piezoelectricity.

Several flexible PZT composites such as "Active Fiber Composite" (AFC) and "Macro Fiber Composite" (MFC) (Figure 10.7) are commercially available and used for high-bending displacement actuators and transducers even for energy harvesting systems. Major advantages of those fiber composites over conventional piezoelectric elements are their flexibility and toughness, both far superior, compared with monolithic PZT bulk ceramics, although fiber composites fail to drive elastically hard metal or ceramic structures. Furthermore, due to their thin, planar geometry, fiber composites can easily be integrated into composite laminates [10]. Previously, a PVDF film was used for implantable physiological power supply [11] and inserted for recovering some of the mechanical power in the process of human walking [12]. For the alternative, the advanced piezo fiber composite (MFC) commercialized from Smart Material Corporation (Sarasota, FL) was experimentally demonstrated and confirmed for the energy conversion component by the Penn State group [13].

The MFC is an actuator design that was developed at the NASA Langley Research Center. The piezoelectric fibers, manufactured by a computer-controlled dicing saw (rectangular cross-section) and embedded in the epoxy matrix, were sandwiched between two layers of polyimide film that had a conductive interdigitated electrode pattern printed on the inner surface. There are two types of MFC, depending on the polling direction. The poling direction of the d_{33} type is parallel along the fiber length, and each segment has an opposite polling direction by interdigitated electrodes, as shown in Figure 10.7a. For the d_{31} type, the poling direction is from the top to the bottom along the fiber thickness. The MFC is extremely flexible, durable, and has the advantage of higher electromechanical coupling coefficients granted through the interdigitated electrodes (Figure 10.7b).

Previously, the d_{33} mode type of the MFC was tested to charge batteries, but Sodano et al. [14] claimed that the MFC did not produce a high current because of the construction of the MFC. As the interdigitated electrodes of the original d_{33} type made the small segments connect in series, high voltage but a low current is obtained, owing to small capacitance in the d_{33} type. By contrast, the d_{31} mode type of MFC (M8528 P2), fabricated by Smart Material Corp., is composed of the piezo-ceramic fibers in the MFC cut by 350 μm width and 170 μm thickness from the piezoelectric wafer by a computer-controlled dicing saw. The total dimensions of MFC are 85 mm in length, 28 mm in width, and 0.3 mm in thickness. Uchino et al. tested the d_{31} mode type of MFC under a small mechanical vibration source to generate enough current for mobile phone battery charging owing to its reasonably large capacitance [13].

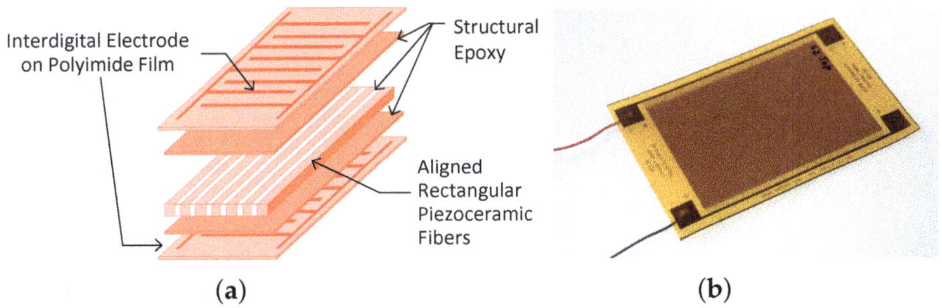

Figure 10.7. Macro Fiver Composite (MFC) by Smart Material Corporation: (**a**) composite structure; (**b**) photo of MFC (Courtesy by Smart Material Corp.). Source: [2] ©Uchino, K. *Micromechatronics*, 2nd ed. CRC Press, 2019; p. 403. Reproduced by permission of Taylor & Francis Group.

10.3.3. Acoustic Impedance Matching Layer in Ultrasonic Transducers

Ultrasonic waves are now used in various fields. The sound source is made from piezoelectric ceramics with high acoustic impedance. In particular, hard piezoelectric materials with a high Q_M are preferable because of high-power generation without heat generation. A liquid medium (water) is usually used for sound energy transfer. Ultrasonic washers/cleaners, ultrasonic hydrophones/microphones, sonars for short-distance remote control, underwater detection, fish finding, and non-destructive testers are typical applications. The applicationtion of Piezoelectric materials as ultrasonic scanning detectors is useful in medical electronics for clinical purposes ranging from diagnosis to therapy and surgery.

Medical Ultrasonic Probe

One of the most important applications is based on the ultrasonic echo field [15,16]. Ultrasonic transducers convert electrical energy into mechanical form when generating an acoustic pulse and convert mechanical energy into an electrical signal when detecting its echo. The transmitted waves propagate into a body, and echoes are generated, which travel back to be received by the same transducer. These echoes vary in intensity according to the type of tissue or body structure based on the acoustic impedance mismatch between two tissue phases, thereby creating images. An ultrasonic image represents the mechanical properties of the tissue, such as density and elasticity (i.e., "acoustic impedance"). For example, the cancer tissue is stiffer than the normal tissue. We can recognize anatomical structures in an ultrasonic image since the organ boundaries and fluid-to-tissue interfaces are easily discerned. The ultrasonic imaging process can also be carried out in real time. This means we can follow rapidly moving structures such as the heart valve without motion distortion. In addition, ultrasound is one of the safest diagnostic imaging techniques. It does not use ionizing radiation, in contrast to X-rays; thus, it is routinely used for fetal and obstetrical imaging. Useful areas for ultrasonic imaging include cardiac structures, the vascular systems, the fetus, and abdominal organs such as the liver and kidney.

Figure 10.8 shows the basic ultrasonic transducer geometry. The transducer is mainly composed of (1) "matching", (2) "piezoelectric material", and (3) "backing layers" [17]. One or more matching layers are used to increase sound transmissions into tissues. The backing is added to the rear of the transducer in order to dampen the acoustic back wave and to reduce the pulse duration (i.e., quick decay of the ring-down vibration). Piezoelectric materials are used to generate and detect ultrasound (f = 2~4 MHz, λ = 0.4~0.7 mm). In general, broadband transducers should be used for medical ultrasonic imaging. The broad bandwidth response corresponds to a short pulse length (due to low Q_m or large elastic loss), resulting in better axial resolution. Three factors are important in designing broad bandwidth transducers; "acoustic impedance matching", a "high electromechanical coupling coefficient" of the transducer, and "electrical impedance matching". These "pulse-echo transducers" operate based on thickness k_t mode resonance of the piezoelectric thin plate. Further, a low planar mode coupling coefficient k_p (or k_{31}) is beneficial for limiting energies being expended in non-productive lateral mode, which generates a so-called "ghost image" [18]. A large dielectric constant is necessary to enable a good electrical impedance match to the system, especially with tiny piezoelectric sizes.

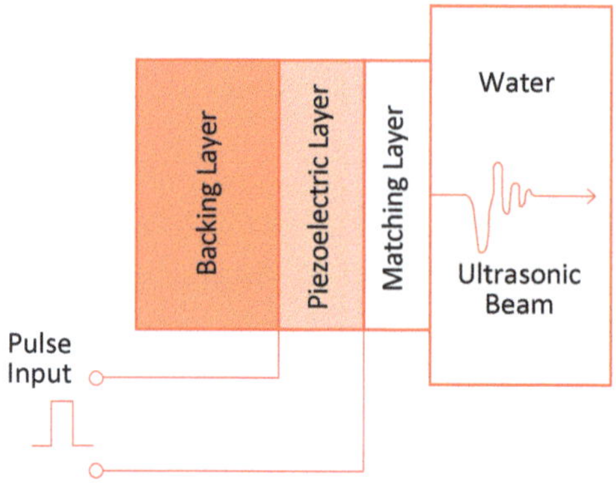

Figure 10.8. Basic transducer geometry for acoustic imaging applications. Source: Figure by author, based on data from [1].

There are various types of transducers used in ultrasonic imaging. Multiple element array transducers permit discrete elements to be individually accessed by the imaging system and enable electronic focusing in the scanning plane to various adjustable penetration depths through the use of phase delays. A linear array is a collection of elements (Figure 10.9a) arranged in one direction, producing a rectangular display. As illustrated in Figure 10.9b, a thin PZT (thickness 0.3 mm for 2~4 MHz ultrasonic wave) wafer is segmented into 128 elements with the separation pitch of 0.3~0.5 mm. In a phased array transducer, the acoustic beam is steered by signals that are applied to the elements with delays, creating a sector display. This segmentation also enhances the electromechanical coupling much higher from k_t, approaching k_{33} mode. The acoustic impedance of the "matching layer" is to be chosen as a "geometric average" value of the piezoelectric element impedance Z_1 (~20 MRayls) and the water impedance Z_2 (~1.5 MRayls), that is, $\sqrt{Z_1 Z_2}$ (~5.5 MRayls). In practice, the PZT thin wafer is initially coated by epoxy-based polymer (glass-filled type to tune Young's modulus) with the acoustic impedance 3–7 MRayls. Then, the rubber covers as the second impedance matching layer (see the center photo of Figure 10.9c). A curved linear (or convex) array is a modified linear array whose elements are arranged along an arc to permit an enlarged trapezoidal field of view (Figure 10.9c).

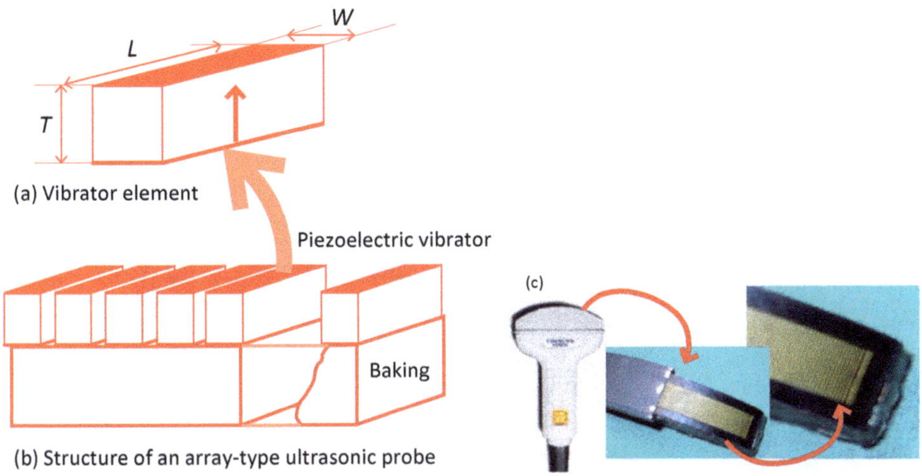

Figure 10.9. (**a**) Basic transducer geometry for acoustic imaging applications; (**b**) linear array type ultrasonic probe; (**c**) photos of convex linear array ultrasonic probes. Source: Figure by author, based on data from [1].

Cymbal Underwater Sonar

In contrast to the flexural bimorph designs, flextensional "cymbal" transducers use the flexural motion of only the metal shells by keeping the PZT disk with longitudinal vibration mode (much higher electromechanical coupling factor k_{eff}). The use of metal endcap motion offers one great advantage over the flexural disks, that is, no bending deformation on the ceramic material. Cymbal transducers consist of a piezoelectric disk (poled in the thickness direction) sandwiched between two metal endcaps (Figure 10.10a). The caps contain a shallow cavity on their inner surface. When acting as a sensor or energy harvesting device, the cavities allow the incident axial stress to be converted into large radial and tangential stresses of opposite signs, causing d_{31} and d_{33} contributions of the piezoelectric to add in the effective sensitivity of the device (i.e., force amplification mechanism). Conversely, the presence of the cavities allows the caps to convert and amplify the small radial displacement of the disk into a much larger axial displacement normal to the surface of the caps when used as an actuator (i.e., displacement amplifier) [19].

For underwater sonar applications, in the low-frequency range, the flextensional transducer is one of the competing technologies with 1-3 composites or Langevin/Tonpilz transducers. The cymbal, which is a miniaturized class V flextensional transducer, has received attention because of its small size, low cost and weight, and thin profile. There are no other technologies that can match these characteristics, which are key to some applications in the Navy, including underwater automated vehicles (UAVs). However, single cymbal transducers are not well suited for most underwater applications because of their high Q_m and low bandwidth. Thus, cymbal transducer elements were built into 3 × 3 arrays to enhance their underwater characteristics in terms of the power level and acoustic beam directivity. Figure 10.10b shows a photo of the 3 × 3 arrays. We used "polyurethane" for potting material of the cymbal transducers for the following three reasons: (1) fixing structure of the 3 × 3 arrays, (2) electric insulation, and (3) acoustic impedance matching to water [20]. The acoustic impedance of polyurethane is rather tunable from 1.6 to 6.9 MRayls depending on the foam rate prepared in the polymeric material.

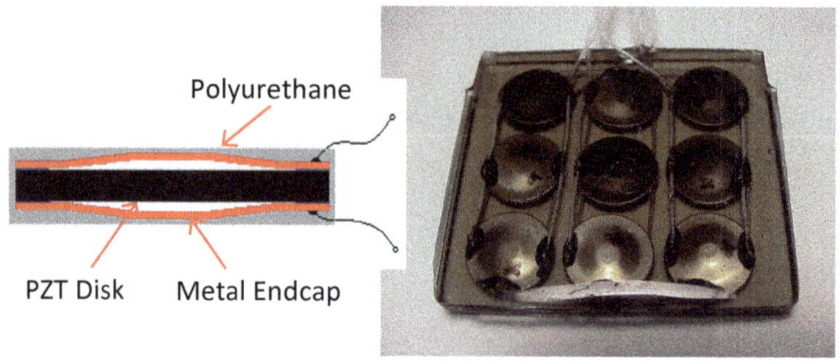

(a) (b)

Figure 10.10. (**a**) Single cymbal potted in polyurethane; (**b**) 3 × 3 arrays, potted in polyurethane. Source: Figure by author.

10.4. Impedance Matching in Piezoelectric Energy Harvesting

10.4.1. Impedance Matching in Piezoelectric Devices

Piezoelectric devices convert the input electric energy to the output mechanical energy or vice versa. The complex matter exists in the situation that the elastic compliance depends on the electric external load and the permittivity depends on the mechanical external load, owing to the electromechanical coupling (piezoelectric) effect. This section will discuss both the electrical and mechanical impedance matching in the piezoelectric devices, in particular in the case of piezoelectric energy harvesting.

Energy harvesting from unused mechanical power has been a recently developed topic in industrial and academic research units, in particular by using piezoelectric transducers, aiming at elimination of "environmentally hazardous" small batteries. There are three major phases/steps associated with piezoelectric energy harvesting: (1) mechanical–mechanical energy transfer, including mechanical stability of the piezoelectric transducer under large stresses, and mechanical impedance matching; (2) mechanical–electrical energy transduction, relating with the electromechanical coupling factor in the composite transducer structure; (3) electrical–electrical energy transfer, including electrical impedance matching, such as a DC–DC converter to accumulate the energy into a rechargeable battery. The reader needs to first understand the concept of "mechanical transformer" and "electrical transformer" to tune the mechanical and electrical impedance for obtaining the maximum energy transfer rate.

10.4.2. "Pushing a Curtain and Pushing a Wall"

Wasted or unused mechanical energy (vibration source) should be transferred properly to the energy converter such as piezoelectric devices. Mechanical impedance matching is one of the important factors we have to take into account. The mechanical impedance of the material is defined by $Z = (\rho c)^{1/2}$, where ρ and c are the density and elastic stiffness, respectively, or "effective parameter" values in a composite structure. The receiving part of the mechanical energy in a piezoelectric device should be designed to match the mechanical/acoustic impedance with the vibration source. Otherwise, most of the vibration energy will be reflected at the interface between the vibration source and the harvesting piezoelectric device. Remember a Japanese proverb, "pushing a curtain and pushing a wall [useless task!]", both cases of which will not transfer mechanical energy efficiently (Figure 10.5). Figure 10.11a,b exhibit these two extreme examples we consider in this section: (a) high energy harvesting from a "hard machine", such as an engine, and (b) low energy harvesting from a "soft machine", such as human motion. In addition to mechanical impedance matching, mechanical strength and damping factor (i.e., loss) of the device are also important.

The "cymbal transducer" is a preferred device for high-power purposes [21,22]. A cymbal transducer consists of a piezoelectric ceramic disk and a pair of metal end-caps. The metal endcaps play important roles as displacement-direction convertors and displacement amplifiers under electric field operation (Figure 10.11c). For the energy harvesting application, the cymbal structure behaves as a force amplifier and an effective "mechanical impedance transformer/tuner", as well as protecting the PZT ceramic from the impact force. The cymbal transducer has a relatively high coupling factor (k_{eff}) and high effective stiffness (but tunable!), in comparison with unimorphs/ bimorphs, which makes it suitable for a high force mechanical source. On the contrary, the flexible transducer is a preferred device for elastically soft applications [23]. The Macro Fiber Composite (MFC) is an actuator that offers reasonably high performance and flexibility in a cost-competitive manner (Smart Material Corp.) (Figure 10.11d). The MFC consists of rectangular piezo-ceramic rods sandwiched between layers of adhesive and electroded polyimide film. This film contains interdigitated electrodes that transfer the applied voltage directly to and from the ribbon-shaped rods. This assembly enables in-plane poling, actuation, and sensing in a sealed, durable, ready-to-use package. The MFC composites are useful for harvesting energy in flexible, large bending structures, though the effective electromechanical coupling factor k_{eff} is not large. However, usage with metal or ceramic elastically stiff structures is not recommended due to the mechanical impedance mismatch. Uchino et al. developed intelligent clothing ("IC", i.e., "wearable energy harvesting system") with piezoelectric energy harvesting system of flexible piezoelectric textiles [24], aiming at a power source for charging up portable equipment such as cellular phones, health monitoring units, or medical drug delivery devices.

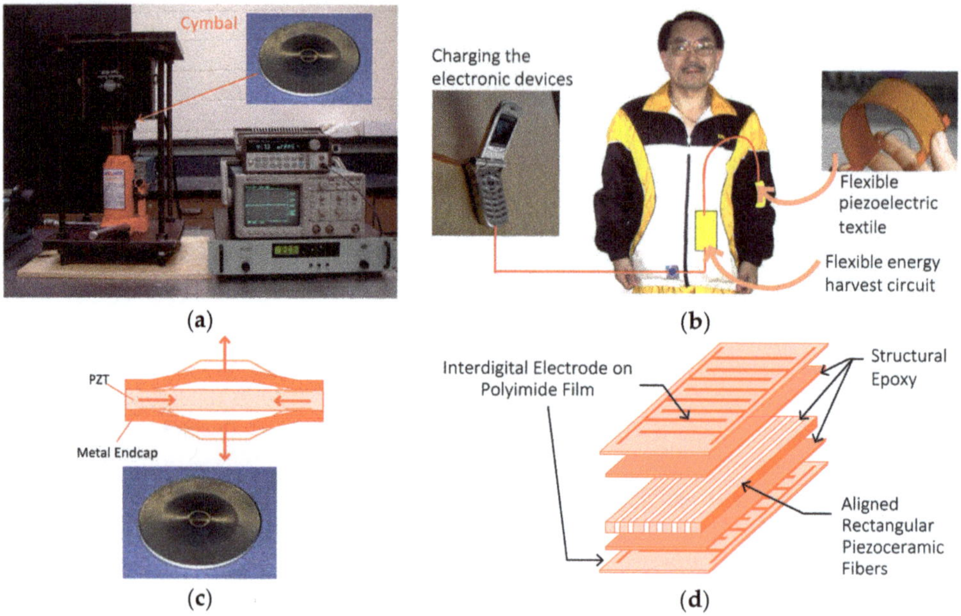

Figure 10.11. Two extreme vibration source examples: (**a**) high energy harvesting from a "hard" machine, such as an engine, and (**b**) low energy harvesting from a "soft" machine, such as human motion; (**c**) operating principle of the cymbal and its photo; (**d**) Macro Fiber Composite (MFC) (Courtesy by Smart Materials Corp.). Source: Figure by author.

10.4.3. Energy Transfer Measurement for the Case of Cymbal

Energy transfer or reflection rate from the "stiff" electromagnetic shaker to a cymbal was analyzed by changing the rigidity of the cymbal endcap (i.e., by changing the endcap thickness, 0.3, 0.4, and 0.5 mm). The characterization system used for measuring the response of the cymbal under a controlled stress environment is shown in Figure 10.11a. The mounting assembly was designed to transfer the maximum mechanical energy onto the piezoelectric transducer. The vibration generated using the mechanical shaker resembles that of a car engine and was applied to the cymbal without any damping material. A large, amplitude shaker (model type 4808, Bruel and Kjaer Instruments Inc., Norcross, GA) has the capability of applying a high force level up to 112 N in a frequency range of 5 Hz to 10 kHz. The shaker was driven at various voltages and frequencies using a function generator (HP 33120A, Agilent Technologies, Santa Clara, CA) and a high-power current amplifier (type 2719, Bruel and Kjaer Instruments Inc.) to produce a cyclic force of the required magnitude and frequency. The output signal from the cymbal was monitored using a digital oscilloscope (TDS 420A, Tektronix, Richardson, TX). The output voltage generated from the cymbal was passed through the rectifier and charged to a capacitor and successively discharged through a resistive load. The cymbal transducers were tested under a high vibration source with prestressed conditions applied using a hydraulic press (Fred S. Carver Inc.). All experiments were performed on an isolated bench to avoid mechanical interference from the surrounding environment.

Figure 10.12 shows the example output voltage waveforms from the cymbal transducer under a cyclic force depending on prestress condition at 100 Hz frequency. Prestress is the pressure applied by the mass of the vibration source to the cymbal transducer. AC forces of 7.8 N and 40 N at 100 Hz were applied for zero-prestress and prestressed (67 N) conditions, respectively. Under the zero-prestress condition, intermittent, spiky, high voltage was observed because the vibration source bottom block hit the cymbal similar to a bang-bang mode, while under prestress (larger than the AC amplitude), steady ± sinusoidal voltage was observed, which seems to be much stable as the energy harvesting system.

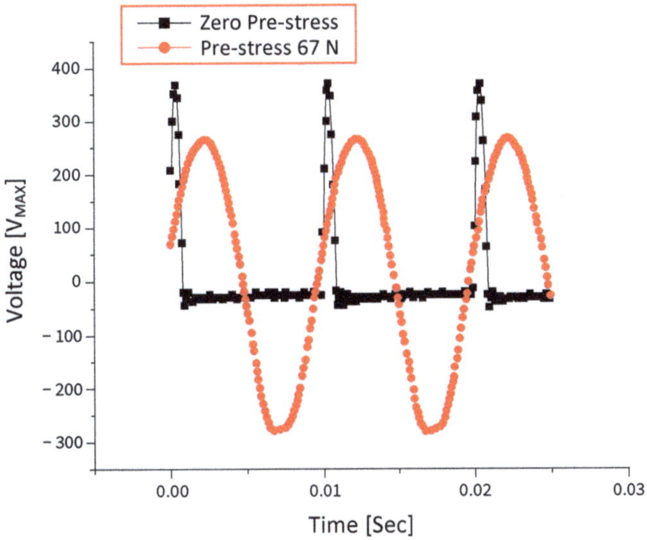

Figure 10.12. Output voltage of the cymbal transducer under two prestressed conditions. A force of 7.8 N and 40 N at 100 Hz was applied for zero-prestress and prestressed conditions, respectively. Source: [25] ©Uchino, K. *Essentials of Piezoelectric Energy Harvesting*. World Scientific, 2021; p. 133. Reproduced by permission of World Scientific Publishing.

Once we obtain the sinusoidal vibration on the cymbal device, we can evaluate the transferred mechanical energy into the cymbal transducer as follows: Refer to Figure 10.13. In order to obtain the source energy, we measure initially the free vibration amplitude u of the load mass M at the angular frequency ω (here at 100 Hz). Then, the average kinetic energy (per second, i.e., "power") can be evaluated as

$$\int_0^1 \frac{1}{2}M\left(\frac{du}{dt}\right)^2 dt = \frac{1}{4}M\omega^2{u_0}^2. \tag{10.63}$$

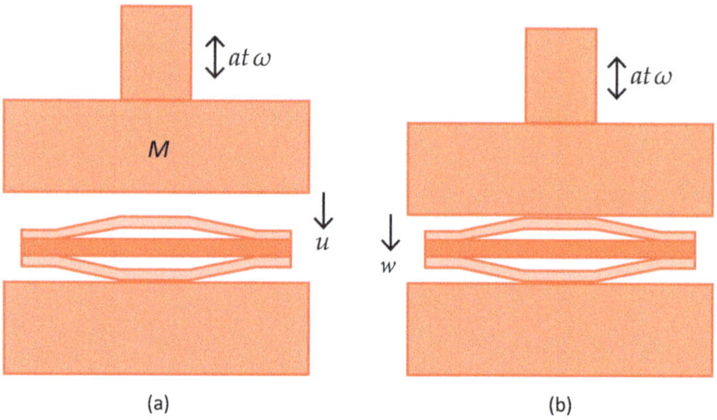

Figure 10.13. Energy evaluation methods for the vibration source (**a**) and for the transferred energy to the cymbal (**b**). Source: [25] ©Uchino, K. *Essentials of Piezoelectric Energy Harvesting*. World Scientific, 2021; p. 133. Reproduced by permission of World Scientific Publishing.

To obtain the transferred mechanical energy to the cymbal, we now measure the cymbal AC displacement w change under prestressed condition at the angular frequency ω. Knowing the effective spring constant c^{eff} (i.e., effective elastic stiffness) of the cymbal transducer by measuring the displacement w and force F beforehand, $F = c^{eff} \cdot w$, we can evaluate the mechanical energy in the cymbal (per second) from

$$\int_0^1 \frac{1}{2} c^{eff} (w)^2 dt = \frac{\omega}{8\pi} c^{eff} (w_0)^2. \tag{10.64}$$

10.4.4. Endcap Thickness Dependence of Mechanical Energy Transmission

The force generated by the electromagnetic shaker is proportional to the payload mass M and the generated acceleration, which is controlled by the applied voltage. The acceleration of the payload was computed by performing the real-time differentiation of measured vibration velocity. The vibration velocity was measured by using Polytec Vibrometer (Tustin, CA). Several payload masses (100–1000 g) were used in the experiment. The cymbal transducer was bonded on the payload by using a silicone rubber sealer. A bias DC force was applied on the transducer using a hydraulic system (Fred S. Carver INC.) to avoid the separation problem, i.e., bang-bang shock (demonstrated in Figure 10.12). The mechanical energy transferred to the cymbal was evaluated from the cymbal deformation and its effective stiffness.

Figure 10.14 shows mechanical energy flow analysis from the vibration source to the cymbal transducer, measured on three types of cymbal transducers: endcap thickness of 0.3 mm and 0.4 mm with and without bias force under various cyclic vibration levels and drive durations. We used a "burst" drive from 1 to 20 second time period for accumulating the mechanical energy by using payload masses of 120 g (for low stress) or 820 g (for high stress). This limited-time measurement originated from the used capacitor's specification; the rectified voltage was used for charging the capacitor C_{rec} of 10 μF in open condition during the charging time (t), for which the capacitor was charged up to 200 V. Note that the measurement results in Figure 10.14 include the energy joule (not the power W, joule per second) during a certain charging period.

(1) The energy transmission rate depends significantly on the endcap thickness (for 0.3 mm, 83–87%, while for 0.4 mm, 46%), because of the "effective elastic stiffness" difference, that is, 0.4 mm may be too thick/rigid from the optimized "mechanical impedance matching" to the shaker's effective elasticity.
(2) With increasing the bias stress level, the handling mechanical energy level by changing the payload mass increases significantly by suppressing the bang-bang shock.
(3) However, when we increased the AC force level up to 70 N by using a payload mass of 820 g, the sample with 0.3 mm thick endcaps was damaged, because it is too fragile for this high stress.

Therefore, we need to take a compromised strategy between the two strategies, that is, (1) keeping the "mechanical impedance matching" by reducing the applying stress level for thinner endcaps, or (2) increasing the applying stress level for thicker endcaps by sacrificing the impedance matching.

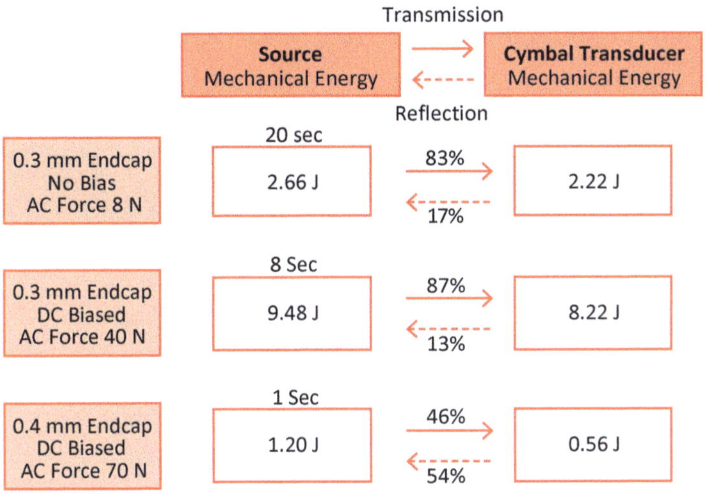

Figure 10.14. Energy flow on three types of cymbal transducers: endcap thickness of 0.3 mm and 0.4 mm with and without bias force under various vibration levels and drive durations. Source: [25] ©Uchino, K. *Essentials of Piezoelectric Energy Harvesting*. World Scientific, 2021; p. 134. Reproduced by permission of World Scientific Publishing.

The above discussion is supported by the generated electrical energy level in the cymbal transducers, as shown in Figure 10.15 [22]. A rectification circuit is composed of a full-wave rectifier and a capacitor for storing generated electrical energy of the cymbal transducer in the case of off-resonance (Details are described in Section 10.5). Using this circuit, the output power was measured across the resistive load directly without any amplification circuit to characterize the performance of different cymbal transducers. The maximum rectified voltage V_{rec} of a capacitor C_{rec} (10 μF) was charged up to 248 V after saturation. Figure 10.15 shows the output electrical power from various cymbal transducers under AC and DC mechanical loads as a function of external load resistance. Endcap thickness made of steel was changed from 0.3 mm to 0.5 mm. Prestress (DC bias load) to the cymbal was set constant at 66 N, and applied AC (100 Hz) force was varied experimentally from 40 N to 70 N by changing the load mass. For a small force drive (40 and 55 N), the power level increased with decreasing the endcap thickness (from 0.5, then 0.4, and finally 0.3 mm), which is due to the energy transmission rate from the vibration source via the mechanical impedance matching. With increasing the force level up to 70 N, the maximum power of 53 mW was obtained at an electric load of 400 kΩ with a 0.4 mm steel endcap, because the cymbal sample with a 0.3 mm thick endcap could not endure under this high force drive (i.e., the cavity depth is collapsed). The electric impedance matching is described in the next section. Note that the maximum power was obtained due to the large input mechanical vibration level (via mechanical impedance matching) and also due to the effective electromechanical coupling factor k_{eff} of the cymbal design with different endcap thickness. From only the energy efficiency viewpoint, the 0.3 mm thick sample is the best because of the best electromechanical coupling factor k_{eff} and mechanical impedance matching, though it is too fragile for practical high-power-level applications.

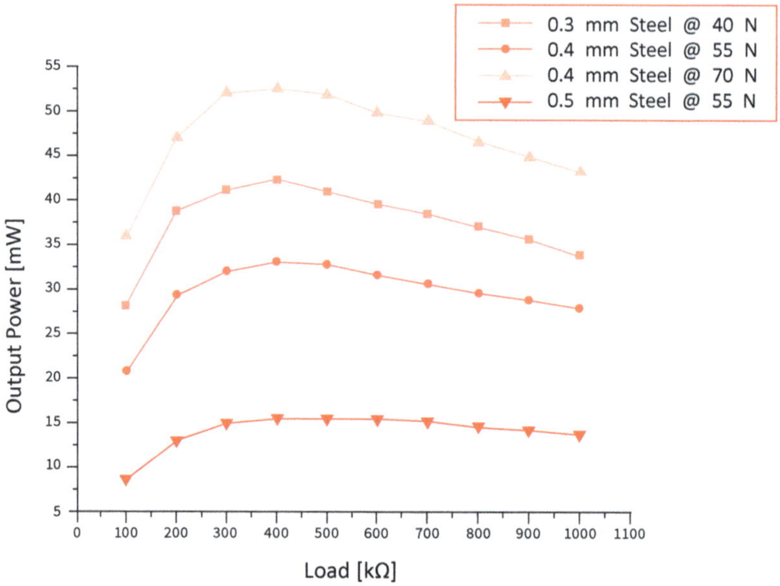

Figure 10.15. Change in output electrical power from the various cymbal transducers under different 100 Hz AC mechanical load (shown as @ xx N under 66 N constant DC bias) with external electrical load resistance. Source: [25] ©Uchino, K. *Essentials of Piezoelectric Energy Harvesting*. World Scientific, 2021; p. 134. Reproduced by permission of World Scientific Publishing.

10.4.5. Electrical Impedance Matching in Piezoelectric Energy Harvesting

A piezoelectric energy harvesting system under sinusoidal stress application on a piezoelectric component connected with the external electrical impedance Z is shown in Figure 10.16. When we assume sinusoidal input stress $X = X_0 e^{j\omega t}$ and output electric displacement $D = dX_0 e^{j\omega t}$ via direct piezoelectric effect (d constant), we can derive current and voltage relationships from Figure 10.16 (supposing that ω is low enough not to cause the resonance). We can understand that the piezoelectric power supply has the internal impedance $1/j\omega C$ under an off-resonance frequency (by neglecting the dielectric loss or effective conducting loss $\sigma = 0$), and this piezoelectric "current supply" generates the total current

$$i = \frac{\partial D}{\partial t} = j\omega d X_0. \quad (10.65)$$

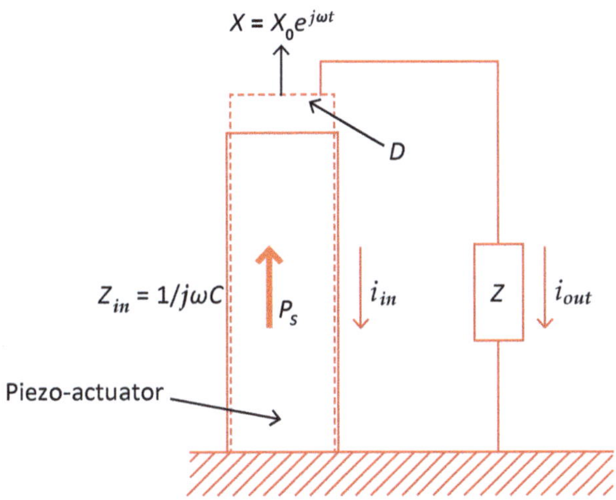

Figure 10.16. Piezoelectric energy harvesting model. Source: [2] ©Uchino, K. *Micromechatronics*, 2nd ed. CRC Press, 2019; p. 395. Reproduced by permission of Taylor & Francis Group.

This current is split into internal "displacement current" i_{in} and external current i_{out},

$$i = i_{in} + i_{out}. \quad (10.66)$$

Then, because the potential/voltage should be the same on the top electrode of the piezoelectric component, we obtain

$$Z_{in} i_{in} = Z i_{out}\,. \quad (10.67)$$

Inserting the relation $i_{in} = \left(\frac{Z}{Z_{in}}\right) i_{out} = j\omega CZ \cdot i_{out}$ into Equation (10.66),

$$i_{out}(1 + j\omega CZ) = j\omega d X_0. \quad (10.68)$$

Thus, we can obtain the output electric energy as

$$|P| = \frac{1}{2}\left|Z \cdot i_{out}{}^{2}\right| = \frac{1}{2} Z \frac{(\omega d X_0)^2}{\left(1 + (\omega C Z)^2\right)}. \tag{10.69}$$

Figure 10.17 shows the electric load (resistive) dependence of the output electric energy, which concludes that the maximum electric energy $|P| = \frac{1}{4}\frac{\omega d^2 X_0^2}{C}$ can be obtained at $Z = 1/\omega C$, when we consider Z resistive, which is the situation for charging up a rechargeable battery. In other words, the "generated" electric energy in a piezo component can be spent maximum when the external load impedance matches exactly to the internal impedance absolute value. Note the internal impedance is capacitive with a phase lag of $-j$ (i.e., $-90°$).

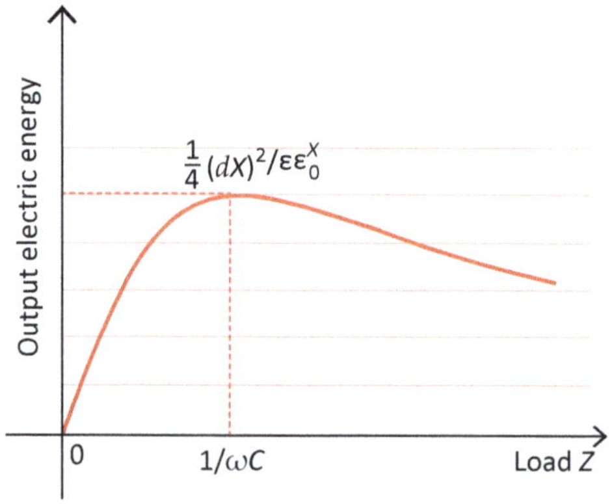

Figure 10.17. Output electric energy vs. external electrical load Z. Source: [2] ©Uchino, K. *Micromechatronics*, 2nd ed. CRC Press, 2019; p. 396. Reproduced by permission of Taylor & Francis Group.

We further consider two additional impedance matching: $Z = \left(\frac{1}{j\omega C}\right)^*$ (i.e., conjugate) and $Z = \left(\frac{1}{j\omega C}\right)$. When we consider the Z "complex", $Z = Z_{in}{}^* = \left(\frac{1}{j\omega C}\right)^* = j\omega\left(\frac{1}{\omega^2 C}\right)$ provides the traditional electrical impedance matching. This condition corresponds to LC series connection (i.e., $\left(\frac{1}{j\omega C}\right)$ and $j\omega L$), where $L = 1/\omega^2 C$ is satisfied, leading to the LC resonance frequency exactly equal to the stress application frequency ω. The energy generated by a piezo component will be exchanged between the internal capacitance and external inductance, similar to a "catch ball", while neither losing energy nor providing work externally. On the contrary, when we consider $Z = \left(\frac{1}{j\omega C}\right)$, the same capacitance as internal is connected to the external load. The converted energy is just split into two equal capacitances. In order to take the energy out into a rechargeable battery, a resistive load is essential to connect.

10.4.6. DC–DC Converters

The reader has learned that the "acoustic impedance matching" layer (such as silicon rubber) should be inserted between a high acoustic impedance PZT and a low impedance water medium in order to maximize the mechanical energy transfer. In a similar sense, you can imagine that we need an "electrical impedance converter" between a high electrical impedance piezoelectric transducer (~300 kΩ) and a low impedance rechargeable battery (~50 Ω). This component may be called a digital "electric transformer". However, different from the conventional analog double-coil transformer, this "converter" can be applied for DC voltage.

High-frequency "switching converters" are power conditioning circuits whose semiconductor devices operate at a frequency that is "fast compared to the variation of input and output waveforms" [26]. They are used most often over linear regulators as a more efficient interface between DC systems operating at disparate voltage levels and are the workhorse of computer and consumer electronic power supply circuitry today. Switching power supplies offer the following two distinct advantages over linear voltage regulators:

(1) As they are truly power converters and not simply voltage regulators, switching converters are quite efficient even when the difference between input and output voltages is large. On the other hand, the average values of the input and output currents in a linear regulator must be the same. Therefore, the power lost through a linear regulator is the product of the input current with the difference between the input and regulated output voltages. As piezoelectric voltage signals typically have a relatively large domain, and it is disadvantageous to clamp this signal, linear regulators encounter some obvious drawbacks that switching converters are well suited to meet.

(2) Switching converters conserve input-to-output power, regulating either voltage or current at the output stage. In contrast, a linear regulator is an active resistive divider in series with the load. They regulate the output voltage by dissipating excess power for a given input current. The switching converter can be thought of as "impedance converters" because the average DC output current can be smaller or larger (step-up or step-down converter, respectively) than the average DC input current [27]. This impedance conversion property is the second notable advantage to using a switching converter over a linear regulator with direct discharge because of the large impedance mismatch inherent in this design.

Analysis of DC–DC Converters

Three kinds of DC–DC converters were analyzed by the author's group for the piezoelectric energy harvesting circuit application [28].

- Buck PWM DC–DC converter;
- Buck–boost PWM DC–DC converter;
- Transformer-isolated buck–boost PWM converter or a flyback converter.

Their circuit designs are shown in Figure 10.18. A "buck converter" (a) is identical to the switching regulator. Try Example Problem 10.1 for refreshing your knowledge on switching regulator. A "buck–boost converter" (b) is a type of DC–DC converter that has an output voltage magnitude that is either greater than or less than the input voltage magnitude. Note the position exchange between the diode and inductance from the buck converter. A "flyback converter" (c) is a kind of buck–boost converter with a slight difference in the usage of a transformer, instead of a single inductor.

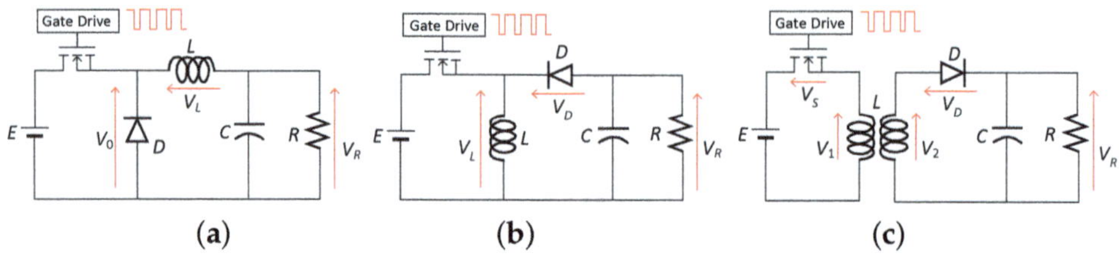

Figure 10.18. DC–DC converters: (**a**) buck converter, (**b**) buck–boost converter, and (**c**) flyback converter. Source: [25] ©Uchino, K. *Essentials of Piezoelectric Energy Harvesting*. World Scientific, 2021; p. 234. Reproduced by permission of World Scientific Publishing.

Example Problem 10.3.

On the basis of the current switching function of the MOSFET, explain the function of the "switching regulators" (also called "step-down buck choppers") shown in Figure 10.18a.

Hint

Let us review a "power MOSFET", which is popularly used in the piezoelectric actuator drive [2]. The symbol of the MOSFET is shown in Figure 10.19a, and its drain current vs. drain-source voltage characteristics are plotted in (b), which corresponds to 500 V, 50 A class power MOSFET. By keeping the drain-source voltage (V_{DS}) at 5 V, the drain current can be significantly changed from 0 to 60 A by changing the gate-source voltage (V_{GS}) from 0 to 5.5 V, which creates the current ON–OFF switch by controlling the gate-source voltage.

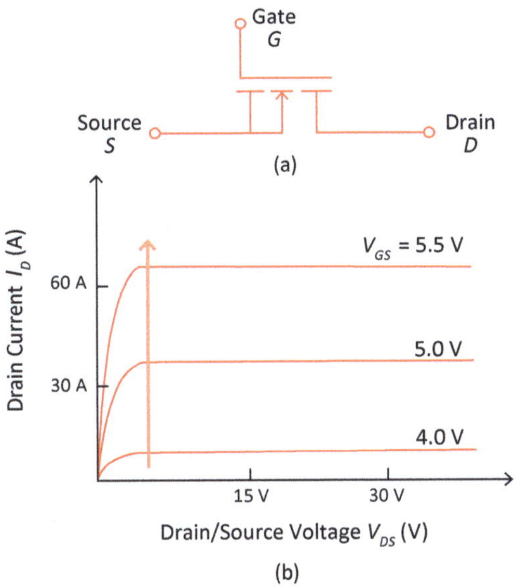

Figure 10.19. (**a**) MOSFET and (**b**) its output characteristics. Source: [2] ©Uchino, K. *Micromechatronics*, 2nd ed. CRC Press, 2019; p. 344. Reproduced by permission of Taylor & Francis Group.

Solution

The switching regulator is occasionally used as a step-down voltage/step-up current converter (popular DC–DC converter), significant output impedance modulation, without using an electromagnetic transformer, which kills the size and weight in a power system. Figure 10.20 shows the simplest switching regulator composed of only a single MOSFET, inductor L, diode, and the resistive load R (capacitor C is occasionally added to stabilize the ripple waveform) under a DC constant voltage (battery). (a) and (b) illustrate the operations for the MOSFET on and off stages, respectively. When the gate-source voltage with a rectangular waveform (reasonably high carrier frequency with the "duty ratio" $d = (\frac{T_{on}}{T_{on}+T_{off}})$) is applied, the MOSFET behaves as an ON-and-OFF switch. During the ON stage (Figure 10.20a), *E–FET–L–R* is the current flow route, so that $v_0 = E$, but v_R does not reach E so quickly because of the inductor (which needs to accumulate the electrical energy first), while during OFF state (Figure 10.20b), $v_0 = 0$, but v_R does not reach to 0 so quickly; moreover, because the inductor will release the electrical energy, or generate the "reverse electromotive force", the current still continues to flow in the route *L–R–D* now. Note first that the average voltage of a rectangular waveform (0–E) with the duty ratio (d) is estimated as $d{\cdot}E$. Voltage waveforms of v_0, v_L, and v_R of the step-down buck chopper are illustrated as a function of time in Figure 10.20c, where you can find first v_0 as exactly the "similar" rectangular waveform to the MOSFET gate voltage with 0 to E voltage height (unipolar). On the contrary, v_L shows the same waveform but a negative bias voltage equal to v_R. Since v_R is obtained as the subtraction v_0–v_L, we can conclude that the v_R is almost constant around the average voltage $d{\cdot}E$. More detailed information on the v_R behavior is described using Figure 10.20c. Without using a capacitance, the v_R exhibits a ripple mode of an exponential curve with a time constant $\tau = (L/R)$ in an L–R circuit. In order to minimize the ripple level, the carrier time period (inverse of the carrier frequency) should be chosen much less than the circuit time constant (L/R) first. An additional smoothing capacitance C helps more with realizing almost constant output voltage $d{\cdot}E$. Carrier frequency is set at 1 kHz in our cymbal energy harvesting system, which is high enough, compared with the operating frequency 100 Hz, but should be as low as possible not to increase the switching losses.

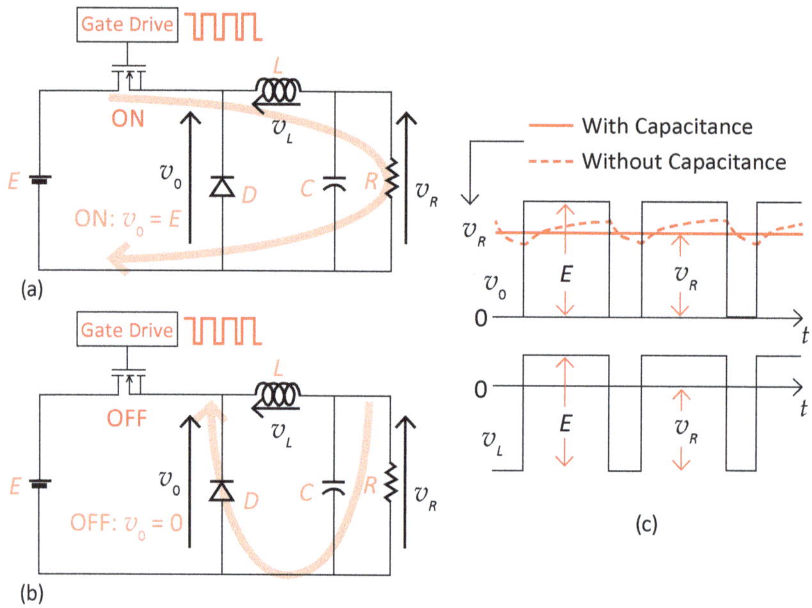

Figure 10.20. Switching regulator: (**a**) ON and (**b**) OFF operation; (**c**) voltage waveforms of v_0, v_L, and v_R of the step-down buck chopper. Source: [25] ©Uchino, K. *Essentials of Piezoelectric Energy Harvesting*. World Scientific, 2021; p. 232. Reproduced by permission of World Scientific Publishing.

Each converter's analysis is divided into the following four main categories:

(a) Converter description (see Figure 10.18);
(b) Analysis of ideal converter in discontinuous conduction mode;
(c) Determination of optimal duty cycle of the converter for energy harvesting;
(d) Loss analysis of a non-ideal converter in discontinuous conduction mode.

For the sake of simplicity, all the converters considered here are fixed frequency. Given below is the origin of losses in a conventional fixed-frequency DC–DC converter:

- Load-Dependent (Conduction) Losses
  - MOSFET "ON" resistance;
  - Diode forward drop;
  - Inductor/transformer winding resistance;

- Capacitor ESR.

- Frequency-Dependent (Switching) Losses
  - MOSFET output capacitance;
  - MOSFET gate capacitance;
  - Diode capacitance;
  - Diode stored minority charge;
  - Inductor and transformer core loss;
  - Snubber loss;
  - Gate driver loss.
- Other Fixed Losses
  - Controller circuitry losses;
  - MOSFET, diode, and capacitor leakage currents.

Reference [28] contains the detailed derivation of the optimal duty cycle, operation, and estimated power loss of the converters in the "Discontinuous Conduction" chapter for the buck–boost and flyback converter topologies. Table 10.1 summarizes the conduction losses in buck, buck–boost, and flyback converters operating in discontinuous conduction mode.

Losses in almost all the cases have the following correlations:

- Proportional to the cube of input voltage: Losses increase with high-voltage-generating devices;
- Inversely proportional to the square root of the inductance value and switching frequency;
- Inversely proportional to the output voltage.

Assuming input voltage ~150 V (~310/2) and output voltage ~12 V, the losses in a buck converter are 10% less than buck–boost converter under optimal operating conditions. More precisely, we obtained the following results, where the loss is compared with the rate (buck converter/buck–boost converter):

Conduction Loss		Switching Loss
Inductor Loss	0.83	0.83
MOSFET Loss	0.91	Assuming same t_{off} and L
Diode Loss	0.90	

Based on the loss analysis for the DC–DC converters above the following results can be drawn:

- Strong arguments can be made to show "buck converter" is better than "buck–boost" in terms of conduction and switching losses;
- Buck converter is even a better choice for devices that do not generate high voltages;
- For "flyback converters", however, the design is not optimized, so a direct comparison is not possible. However, strong intuitive arguments can be made to show higher losses associated with this converter.

Table 10.1. Conduction losses in the three converters operating in discontinuous conduction mode.

Converter	Diode Loss	Inductor Loss	MOSFET Loss
Buck	$\frac{8R_F\left(\frac{\omega C_{cymbal}}{\pi}\right)^{\frac{3}{2}}(V_g-V_o)^{\frac{3}{2}}V_g^{\frac{3}{2}}}{3\sqrt{Lf_s}\cdot V_o}+\frac{\left(\frac{2\omega C_{cymbal}}{\pi}\right)V_g(V_g-V_o)V_f}{V_o}$	$\frac{8R_L\left(\frac{\omega C_{cymbal_s}}{\pi}\right)^{\frac{3}{2}}(V_g-V_o)^{\frac{1}{2}}V_g^{\frac{5}{2}}}{3\sqrt{Lf_s}\cdot V_o}$	$\frac{8R_{DS}(\omega C_{cymbal_s})^{\frac{3}{2}}(V_g-V_o)^{\frac{1}{2}}V_g^{\frac{3}{2}}}{3\sqrt{Lf_s}}$
Buck–Boost	$\frac{8R_F\left(\frac{\omega C_{cymbal}}{\pi}\right)^{\frac{3}{2}}V_g^3}{3\sqrt{Lf_s}\cdot V_o}+\frac{V_g^2\left(\frac{2\omega C_{cymbal}}{\pi}\right)}{V_o}\cdot V_f$	$\frac{8R_L\left(\frac{\omega C_{cymbal}}{\pi}\right)^{\frac{3}{2}}V_g^2(V_g-V_o)}{3\sqrt{Lf_s}\cdot V_o}$	$\frac{8R_{DS}\left(\frac{\omega C_{cymbal}}{\pi}\right)^{\frac{3}{2}}V_g^2}{3\sqrt{Lf_s}}$
Flyback	$\frac{8R_F V_g^3\left(\frac{N_p}{N_s}\right)\left(\frac{\omega C_{cymbal}}{\pi}\right)^{\frac{3}{2}}}{3\sqrt{Mf_s}\cdot V_o}+\frac{V_g^2\left(\frac{2\omega C_{cymbal}}{\pi}\right)}{V_o}\cdot V_f$	$\frac{8R_p\left(V_g+\left(\frac{N_p}{N_s}\right)V_o\right)^2\left(\frac{\omega C_{cymbal}}{\pi}\right)^{\frac{3}{2}}}{3\sqrt{Mf_s}}+\frac{8V_g^3R_s\left(\frac{\omega C_{cymbal}}{\pi}\right)^{\frac{3}{2}}}{3\sqrt{Mf_s}\cdot V_o}\left(\frac{N_p}{N_s}\right)$	$\frac{8R_{DS}V_g^2\left(\frac{\omega C_{cymbal}}{\pi}\right)^{\frac{3}{2}}}{3\sqrt{Mf_s}}$

Source: Table by author, based on data from [28].

Cymbal Energy Harvesting into Rechargeable Battery

A buck DC–DC converter was chosen for the cymbal energy harvesting systems in order to store the energy into a rechargeable battery [21]. The beneficial reasons include the following advantages:

- Low power loss: ~3 mW for the gate drive circuitry;
- Inexpensive and small: component count for the entire circuit = 8;
- Operates at a fixed "optimal duty cycle" of 2% for high excitation: no complicated control of frequency generation is required;
- Very reliable and durable: the circuit had been tested for several hours, and it works without any performance degradation;
- Low stress on the MOSFET switch and other components: better efficiency and cheap components.

The basic theory for the converter is summarized as follows: (1) The purpose of the external circuit is to maximize the "average power" transferred to the electrical load. (2) The condition for maximum average power transfer requires that the load impedance must be equal to the complex conjugate of the "Thevenin impedance". (3) The optimal duty cycle of the converter is calculated to be as the following equation, using the mechanical excitation frequency ω, inductance value of Buck filter L, and the switching frequency of the converter f_S:

$$D_{optimal}=\sqrt{\frac{4\omega LV_gC_{cymbal}\,f_s}{\pi(V_g-V_o)}}. \tag{10.70}$$

Figure 10.21 shows an electrical energy harvesting circuit composed of a full-wave rectifier, a rechargeable battery, and a DC–DC buck converter designed on the basis of the "maximum power transfer theorem" at an "optimal duty cycle". We chose the switching frequency ~1 kHz, high enough in comparison with the operating frequency of the piezoelectric component (~100 Hz) but low enough to reduce the switching losses. The "duty cycle" ~2% can be calculated by substituting the values in $D_{optimal}$ in Equation (10.70). We may expect a 50-time voltage step-down and 50-time current step-up, leading to the 2500-time impedance reduction ideally, if we neglect any losses in the circuit. Since the matching impedance to the cymbal component is 400 kΩ, we may expect the matching impedance down to 200 Ω. Figure 10.22 plots the duty cycle (1–5%) dependence of the obtained power through the buck converter. Irrelevant to the electrical load, 2% provides the maximum, as Equation (10.70) indicates. However, from Figure 10.22, the maximum output power can be obtained at 5 kΩ (i.e., matching impedance), which is an order of magnitude higher than ideally expected above. The sizes of the inductor and filter capacitor were set to 33 mH and 100 μF, which are high enough inductance to reduce the output current ripple and high enough capacitance to keep the output voltage ripple-free. Low power consumption PWM ("pulse width modulation") generator "LM555" was used then for the "duty cycle" generation. Amplified output current was applied for charging the battery, with the power increase by approximately 10 times, compared with direct charging. Power supply continued to the load irrespective of the mechanical input fluctuations. A DC–DC buck converter designed to allow transfer of 43 mW power out of 53 mW from the cymbal (81% efficiency) by converting the original impedance 300 kΩ down to 5 kΩ, with a 2% duty cycle and at a switching frequency of 1 kHz. The power loss in the gate drive circuit of the buck converter was estimated at ~3 mW, which is much smaller than the cultivated energy of 43 mW into a rechargeable battery.

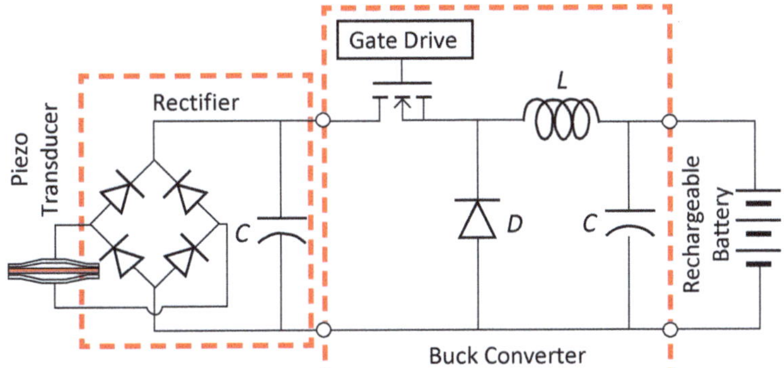

Figure 10.21. DC–DC buck converter designed for converting the original impedance 300 kΩ down to 5 kΩ with a 2% duty cycle. Source: [25] ©Uchino, K. *Essentials of Piezoelectric Energy Harvesting*. World Scientific, 2021; p. 236. Reproduced by permission of World Scientific Publishing.

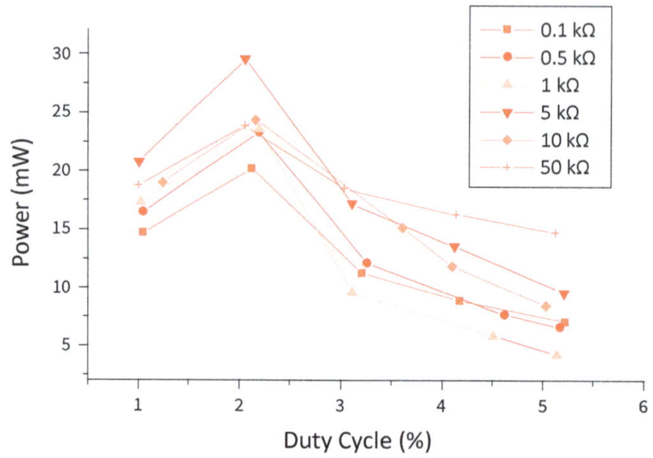

Figure 10.22. Duty cycle dependence of the obtained power through the buck converter. Source: [25] ©Uchino, K. *Essentials of Piezoelectric Energy Harvesting*. World Scientific, 2021; p. 237. Reproduced by permission of World Scientific Publishing.

Multilayered Cymbal

Since the "buck converter" introduced in the previous subsection cannot reduce the output impedance sufficiently to match with the rechargeable battery (~50 Ω), we should further reduce the output impedance. However, reducing the duty ratio to much less than 2% is not practically feasible. Thus, an alternative strategy is to reduce the output impedance of the piezoelectric transducer by changing the piezoelectric transducer structure. Multilayered (ML) cymbal structures have lower impedance [29], different from a popular reason for the ML usage to reduce the driving voltage for actuator applications. Figure 10.23a,b show cross-sectional views of single- and multilayered (ML) cymbal transducers. With increasing the number n of the layers by keeping the total thickness constant, output impedance decreases by the factor of $(1/n^2)$, owing to their capacitance increase in an opposite way, as you are familiar with. As shown in Figure 10.23c, the maximum output power shifts to the lower resistance direction with an increase in the layer number, which means output impedance can be controlled by the number of layers in the piezoelectric transducer structure. You can find that the matching impedance 300 kΩ in the single-layer cymbal is reduced down to 3 kΩ by using a 10-layer cymbal. Note that the total power is the same for all ML piezoelectric components, as long as we keep the same total PZT volume.

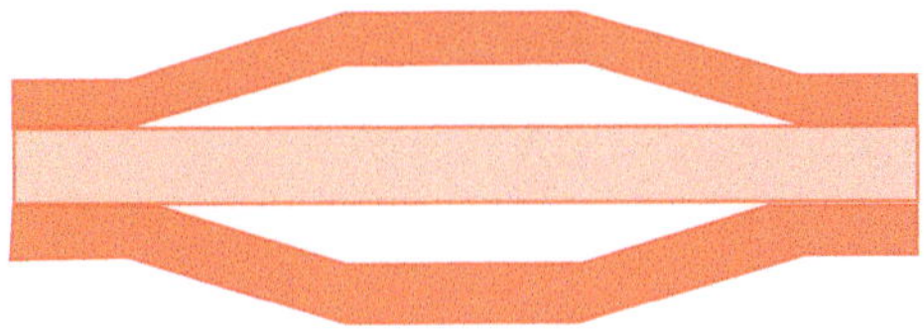

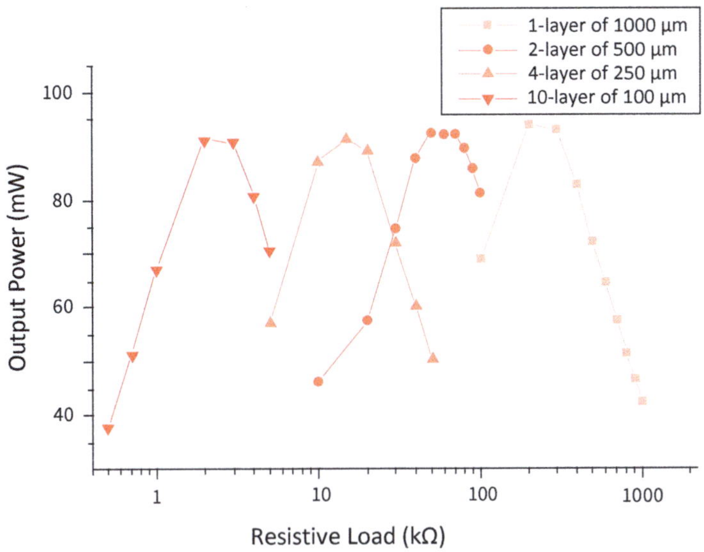

Figure 10.23. (**a**) Single-layer cymbal and (**b**) multilayered (ML) cymbal transducer; (**c**) output power characteristics of the ML cymbal transducers. Source: [25] ©Uchino, K. *Essentials of Piezoelectric Energy Harvesting*. World Scientific, 2021; p. 237. Reproduced by permission of World Scientific Publishing.

It is worth noting that the performance becomes much superior by combining the ML cymbal structure and the DC–DC buck converter, as shown in Figure 10.24. When we compare first the output voltage from the 10-layer cymbal with or without the DC–DC converter, no significant difference can be found, only a continuous increase in the output voltage for both cases with increasing the resistive load. On the contrary, the output power of the 10-layer cymbal with or without the DC–DC converter presents significant differences—using the buck converter reduces the maximum power level from 100 mW to 80 mW, with the matching load shift from 5 kΩ to 2 kΩ. However, the output power around 50 Ω ("matching impedance" to the rechargeable battery) differs significantly—50 mW with the converter and less than 10 mW without the converter. This load-insensitive broadening effect is essential to the usage of the DC–DC buck converter, but the reason needs to be clarified in the future.

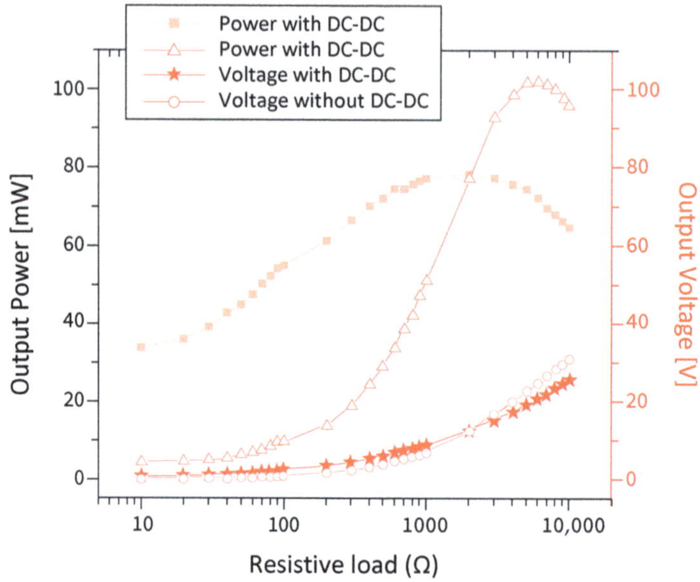

Figure 10.24. Load resistance dependence of the harvesting energy from the ML piezoelectric component. Source: [25] ©Uchino, K. *Essentials of Piezoelectric Energy Harvesting*. World Scientific, 2021; p. 238. Reproduced by permission of World Scientific Publishing.

10.5. Energy Transmission Coefficient

10.5.1. Modification of the Piezoelectric Dynamic Analysis

In the previous section, we modeled the piezoelectric energy harvesting system on an external electrical load Z, where a piezoelectric device with piezoelectric constant d and capacitance C is excited by a constant cyclic stress X at a frequency of ω. we can obtain the output electric energy as

$$|P| = \frac{1}{2}\left|Z{\cdot}{i_{out}}^2\right| = \frac{1}{2}Z\frac{(\omega d X_0)^2}{\left(1+(\omega C Z)^2\right)}. \tag{10.71}$$

Equation (10.71) concludes that the maximum electric energy $|P| = \frac{1}{4}\frac{\omega d^2 X_0^2}{C}$ can be obtained at $Z = 1/\omega C$, which corresponds to the "electrical impedance matching".

However, the above derivation was made from a rough approximation on the basis of two assumptions or simplifications: (1) The elasticity of the piezoelectric does not change with the external load Z and (2) the capacitance (or permittivity) of the piezoelectric does not change under alternating stress application. If the reader recalls the following relations with the "electromechanical coupling factor" k:

$$\varepsilon^x/\varepsilon^X = \left(1-k^2\right), \tag{10.72a}$$

$$s^D/s^E = \left(1-k^2\right), \tag{10.72b}$$

where k is given by

$$k^2 = \frac{d^2}{s^E \varepsilon^X \varepsilon_0}, \tag{10.73}$$

it is obvious that the above assumption is only valid for a small coupling factor k. When the external load Z is large ($Z = \infty$), the elasticity becomes "stiff" (i.e., s^D), while when $Z = 0$ (short circuited), the elasticity becomes "soft" (i.e., s^E). The reader can speculate that when the load Z is intermediate, the elasticity will be also in the middle of s^D and s^E. Therefore, even though the stress is maintained constant X_0, the transferred mechanical energy from the vibration source to the piezoelectric differs, largely depending on the external impedance. We may need to normalize the input mechanical energy constant for maximizing the output harvesting electric energy. On the other hand, when the stress is zero, the permittivity should be large (i.e., ε^X), while when large "blocking stress" (which clamps the strain completely, $x = 0$) is applied, the permittivity becomes stiff or as small as ε^x. Thus, under AC stress application, since the permittivity depends on the stress modulation, the reader can easily understand that we cannot use constant free permittivity ε^X or capacitance C in order to obtain the power maximization external impedance.

Since we need to use or accumulate energy externally, we consider "resistive shunt" for further discussions. When the vibration source generates sinusoidal continuous force, not all the electrically stored energy (in this case, "power") in the piezoelectric can be actually taken out under the mechanical drive, and the actual work performed by the piezoelectric component depends on the external electrical load, as we roughly derive the electrical impedance matching above. Let us reconsider the power expendable on the external electrical load Z from the "energy transmission coefficient" viewpoint in this section. Figure 10.25 summarizes the calculation processes of the input mechanical and output electric energy under various impedance Zs—namely, (a) in the stress X vs. electric displacement D relation, the area on this domain does not mean the energy; thus, we need to translate this plot into (b) stress X vs. strain x relation, to calculate the input mechanical energy. Note that the input mechanical energy differs depending on the external load Z (the triangle area made of $0X_0Z$); (c) electric displacement D vs. electric field E to calculate the output electric energy. Similar to the situation in an electrically driven piezo-actuator, in which with a zero mechanical load or a complete clamp (no strain), no output work ("pushing a curtain and pushing a wall") is performed, no electrically converted energy can be actually spent under the short-circuit (zero impedance) or open-circuit (infinite impedance) condition in the energy harvesting case. Let us consider the formula derivation for Figure 10.18c. First, the electrical energy output can be calculated from the constitutive equations.

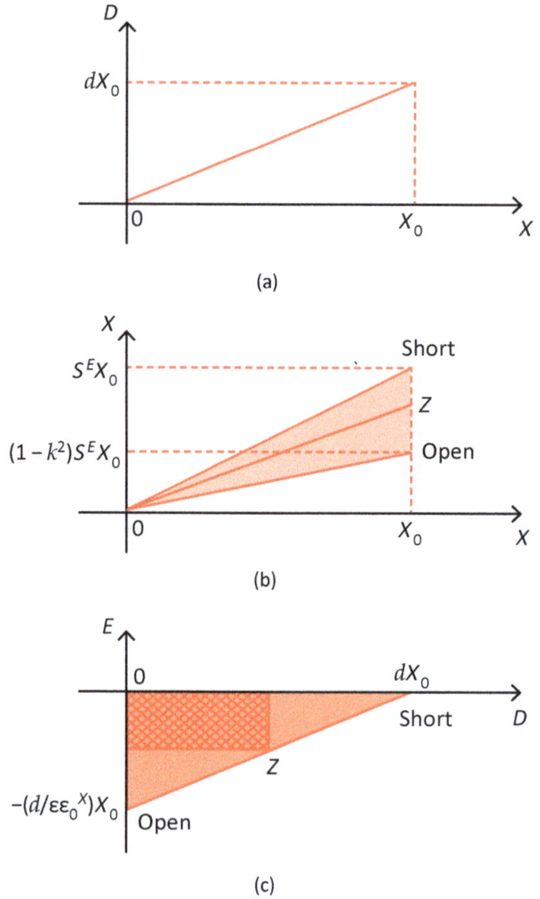

Figure 10.25. Calculation models of the input mechanical and output electric energy. (**a**) Stress vs. electric displacement; (**b**) stress vs. strain; (**c**) electric displacement vs. field. Source: [2] ©Uchino, K. *Micromechatronics*, 2nd ed. CRC Press, 2019; p. 396. Reproduced by permission of Taylor & Francis Group.

$$\begin{pmatrix} D \\ x \end{pmatrix} = \begin{pmatrix} \varepsilon_0\varepsilon & d \\ d & s^E \end{pmatrix} \begin{pmatrix} E \\ X \end{pmatrix}. \tag{10.74}$$

The short-circuit condition ($E = 0$) gives $D_0 = dX_0$, while the open-circuit condition ($D = 0$) gives $E_0 = -dX_0/\varepsilon_0\varepsilon$. The triangular area of OD_0E_0 ($\frac{1}{2}dX_0 \cdot \left(\frac{dX_0}{\varepsilon_0\varepsilon}\right) = \frac{1}{2}\frac{(dX_0)^2}{\varepsilon_0\varepsilon}$) means the total electric energy converted from the mechanical vibration. Thus, under an impedance Z shunt condition, we can expect a point (E, D) on the straight line [$E = \left(\frac{1}{\varepsilon_0\varepsilon}\right)D - \left(\frac{d}{\varepsilon_0\varepsilon}\right)X$)] between the terminals of the above D_0 and E_0, with the slope $\left(\frac{1}{\varepsilon_0\varepsilon}\right)$ (i.e., inverse permittivity) of the line D_0E_0 under the supposition of constant permittivity of ε^X, irrelevant to the stress modulation.

The "energy transmission coefficient" λ is related to the electromechanical coupling factor k but defined differentially by

$$\lambda_{max} = \text{(Output mechanical energy/Input electrical energy)}_{max}, \tag{10.75a}$$

in the actuator application or alternatively by

$$\lambda_{max} = \text{(Output electrical energy/Input mechanical energy)}_{max}, \tag{10.75b}$$

in the energy harvest application. The difference of the above from the definition of electromechanical coupling factor k^2 is "stored/converted energy" in the numerator in k^2 or "output/spent energy" in λ.

10.5.2. Piezoelectric Dynamic Equation under Resistive Shunt Condition

Though Subsection Solution under Z-Shunt Condition in Chapter 7 handles the electrical energy analysis under the AC stress conditions, we analyze it in this section again in detail from the electric impedance matching viewpoint. We now analyze the piezoelectric vibration mode under AC stress application with the external electrical load Z. Let us consider a piezo-ceramic k_{31} plate, as shown in Figure 10.26. Sinusoidal force/pressure F and $-F$ (angular frequency ω) are applied on the plate ends at $x = 0$ and L along the length direction x.

$$F(t) = -bwX_1(t). \tag{10.76}$$

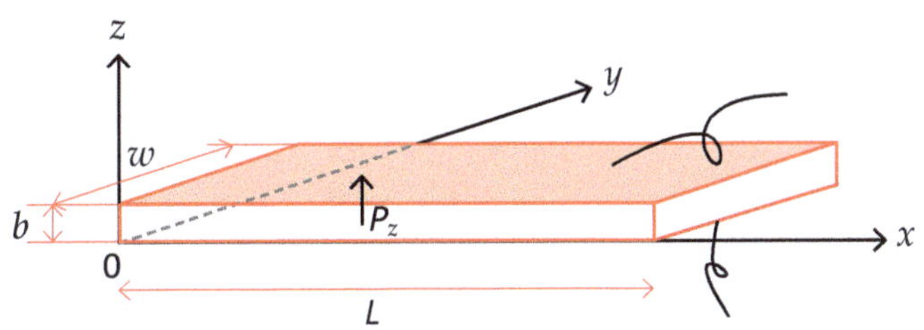

Figure 10.26. Longitudinal vibration k_{31} mode of a rectangular piezoelectric plate. Source: [2] ©Uchino, K. *Micromechatronics*, 2nd ed.; CRC Press, 2019; p. 111. Reproduced by permission of Taylor & Francis Group.

If the polarization is in the z-direction and x-y planes are the planes of the electrodes, the extensional vibration in the x (length) direction is represented by the following dynamic equations (when the length L is more than 4~6 times of the width w or the thickness b, we can neglect the coupling modes with width or thickness vibrations):

$$\rho\left(\partial^2 u/\partial t^2\right) = (\partial X_{11}/\partial X), \tag{10.77}$$

where ρ is the density of the piezo-ceramic, and u is the displacement of a small volume element in the ceramic plate in the x-direction. Only the following two equations are essential to solve the dynamic equation around the resonance/antiresonance frequencies:

$$x_1 = s_{11}{}^E X_1 + d_{31} E_z, \tag{10.78a}$$

$$D_3 = d_{31}\, X_1 + \varepsilon_0 \varepsilon_{33}{}^X E_z. \tag{10.78b}$$

Since Equation (10.78a) is transformed into $X_1 = x_1/s_{11}{}^E - (d_{31}/s_{11}{}^E)E_z$, we obtain

$$\frac{\partial X_1}{\partial x} = \frac{1}{s_{11}^E}\frac{\partial x_1}{\partial x} - \frac{d_{31}}{s_{11}^E}\frac{\partial E_z}{\partial x}. \tag{10.79}$$

Due to the equal potential on each electrode, $\partial E_z/\partial x = 0$, and knowing the strain definition $x_1 = \partial u/\partial x$ along the 1 (x) direction (non-suffix x corresponds to the Cartesian coordinate), Equation (10.77) is transformed into

$$\rho \frac{\partial^2 u}{\partial t^2} = \frac{1}{s_{11}^E}\frac{\partial^2 u}{\partial x^2}. \tag{10.80}$$

If we assume a "harmonic vibration" equation of u under a sinusoidal force application, we can simplify Equation (10.80) as

$$-\omega^2 \rho s_{11}{}^E u = \partial^2 \mathrm{u}/\partial \mathrm{x}^2 \text{ or } -\left(\frac{\omega}{v_{11}^E}\right)^2 u(x) = \frac{\partial^2 u(x)}{\partial x^2}, \tag{10.81}$$

where ω is the angular frequency of the sinusoidal force, u displacement, and v_{11}^E is the "sound velocity" along the length x-direction in the piezo-ceramic plate, expressed by

$$v_{11}^E = 1/\sqrt{\rho s_{11}{}^E}. \tag{10.82}$$

Supposing the displacement u also vibrates with the frequency of ω, a general solution of Equation (10.81) is expressed by

$$u(x) = \mathrm{A}\sin\left(\frac{\omega}{v_{11}^E}x\right) + \mathrm{B}\cos\left(\frac{\omega}{v_{11}^E}x\right). \tag{10.83}$$

From Equation (10.83), the strain $x_1(x)$ is given by

$$x_1(x) = \frac{\partial u}{\partial x} = A\frac{\omega}{v_{11}^E}\cos\left(\frac{\omega}{v_{11}^E}x\right) - B\frac{\omega}{v_{11}^E}\sin\left(\frac{\omega}{v_{11}^E}x\right). \tag{10.84}$$

In order to determine the above two parameters, A and B, the boundary condition is imposed: $X_1 = X_0 e^{j\omega t}$ at $x = 0$ and L (both plates' ends). We consider here the impedance (Z) shunt condition. Knowing the piezoelectric constitutive equation

$s_{11}{}^{E}X_1 = x_1 - d_{31}E_z$, where $E_z(t)$ = constant in terms of the coordinate x, owing to the surface electrode,

$$\begin{cases} s_{11}^{E}X_0 = A\frac{\omega}{v_{11}^{E}} - d_{31}E_z \\ s_{11}^{E}X_0 = A\frac{\omega}{v_{11}^{E}}\cos\left(\frac{\omega}{v_{11}^{E}}L\right) - B\frac{\omega}{v_{11}^{E}}\sin\left(\frac{\omega}{v_{11}^{E}}L\right) - d_{31}E_z \end{cases}. \quad (10.85)$$

The output electric charge Q (i.e., no loss, no time lag) can be described from the piezoelectric constitutive equation (Equation (10.78b)) $D_3 = d_{31}X_1 + \varepsilon_0\varepsilon_{33}{}^{X}E_z$ as

$$Q = w\int_0^L D_3dx = w\int_0^L \left[d_{31}X_1 + \varepsilon_0\varepsilon_{33}^{X}E_z\right]dx. \quad (10.86)$$

While, from $X_1 = x_1/s_{11}{}^{E} - (d_{31}/s_{11}{}^{E})E_z$, we obtain

$\int_0^L X_1dx = \frac{1}{s_{11}^{E}}\int_0^L (x_1 - d_{31}E_z)dx.$

Knowing that $\int_0^L x_1dx = 2u(L)$ and E_z = constant, we obtain

$I = \dot{Q} = \left\{\left(\frac{2wd_{31}}{s_{11}^{E}}\right)\dot{u}(L) + \varepsilon_0\varepsilon_{33}^{X}\left(1-k_{31}^2\right)\dot{E}_zwL\right\}$

$= j\omega\left(\frac{2wd_{31}}{s_{11}^{E}}\right)u(L) + j\omega\varepsilon_0\varepsilon_{33}^{X}\left(1-k_{31}^2\right)E_zwL.$

Using $V = bE_z = Z{\cdot}I$ and $C_d = \varepsilon_0\varepsilon_{33}^{X}\left(1-k_{31}^2\right)wL/b$, Equation (10.86) leads to the following relations:

$$j\omega\left(\frac{2wd_{31}}{s_{11}^{E}}\right)\left[A\sin\left(\frac{\omega}{v_{11}^{E}}L\right) + B\cos\left(\frac{\omega}{v_{11}^{E}}L\right)\right] + j\omega C_dE_zb - \frac{b}{Z}E_z = 0. \quad (10.87)$$

From Equations (10.85) and (10.87), we can derive A, B, and E_z as follows:

$$\begin{pmatrix} \frac{\omega}{v_{11}^{E}} & 0 & -d_{31} \\ \frac{\omega}{v_{11}^{E}}cs & -\frac{\omega}{v_{11}^{E}}sn & -d_{31} \\ j\omega\left(\frac{2wd_{31}}{s_{11}^{E}}\right)sn & j\omega\left(\frac{2wd_{31}}{s_{11}^{E}}\right)cs & b\left(j\omega C_d - \frac{1}{Z}\right) \end{pmatrix}\begin{pmatrix} A \\ B \\ E_z \end{pmatrix} = \begin{pmatrix} s_{11}^{E}X_0 \\ s_{11}^{E}X_0 \\ 0 \end{pmatrix}, \quad (10.88)$$

where $sn = \sin\left(\frac{\omega}{v_{11}^{E}}L\right)$ and $cn = \cos\left(\frac{\omega}{v_{11}^{E}}L\right)$. Thus, we can obtain

$$\begin{cases} A = \frac{s_{11}^{E}X_0b\left(j\omega C_d - \frac{1}{Z}\right)\cos\left(\frac{\omega L}{2v_{11}^{E}}\right)}{\Delta} \\ B = -\frac{s_{11}^{E}X_0b\left(j\omega C_d - \frac{1}{Z}\right)\sin\left(\frac{\omega L}{2v_{11}^{E}}\right)}{\Delta} \\ E_z = -\frac{s_{11}^{E}X_0\left(j\omega\frac{2wd_{31}}{s_{11}^{E}}\right)\sin\left(\frac{\omega L}{2v_{11}^{E}}\right)}{\Delta} \end{cases}, \quad (10.89)$$

where the denominator Δ is the determinant of the matrix of Equation (10.88) calculated as

$$\begin{aligned}\Delta &= \left(\frac{\omega}{v_{11}^E}\right)b\left(j\omega C_d - \frac{1}{Z}\right)\cos\left(\frac{\omega L}{2v_{11}^E}\right) + d_{31}j\omega\left(\frac{2wd_{31}}{s_{11}^E}\right)\sin\left(\frac{\omega L}{2v_{11}^E}\right) \\ &= j\omega 2w\varepsilon_0\varepsilon_{33}^X\left[\left(1-k_{31}^2\right)\left(\frac{\omega L}{2v_{11}^E}\right)\cos\left(\frac{\omega L}{2v_{11}^E}\right) + k_{31}^2\sin\left(\frac{\omega L}{2v_{11}^E}\right)\right] + \left(\frac{\omega}{v_{11}^E}\right)\frac{b}{Z}\cos\left(\frac{\omega L}{2v_{11}^E}\right).\end{aligned} \tag{10.90}$$

When $\Delta \to 0$, the displacement amplitudes A, B, and the generated electric field E_z will approach infinite if we neglect the loss. This condition is considered to be mechanical resonance.

(a) When $Z \to 0$ (i.e., short circuited), the last term $\left(\frac{\omega}{v_{11}^E}\right)\frac{b}{Z}\cos\left(\frac{\omega L}{2v_{11}^E}\right)$ is the major contribution, which leads to the resonance condition of $\cos\left(\frac{\omega L}{2v_{11}^E}\right) = 0$, or $\frac{\omega L}{2v_{11}^E} = \frac{\pi}{2}$. This is the piezoelectric resonance mode condition in the k_{31} plate.

(b) When $Z \to \infty$ (i.e., open circuited), since the last term is neglected, the resonance condition should be:

$$\begin{aligned}\left(1-k_{31}^2\right)\left(\frac{\omega L}{2v_{11}^E}\right)\cos\left(\frac{\omega L}{2v_{11}^E}\right) + k_{31}^2\sin\left(\frac{\omega L}{2v_{11}^E}\right) &= 0, \text{ or} \\ \left(\frac{\omega L}{2v_{11}^E}\right)\cot\left(\frac{\omega L}{2v_{11}^E}\right) &= -\frac{k_{31}^2}{\left(1-k_{31}^2\right)},\end{aligned} \tag{10.91}$$

which is the familiar formula for calculating the piezoelectric antiresonance frequency.

(c) Now, by connecting $Z = 1/\omega C_d$ to combine the $\cos\left(\frac{\omega L}{2v_{11}^E}\right)$ terms together, we consider the minimization of the magnitude of Δ for obtaining the mechanical resonance condition as follows:

$$\begin{aligned}\Delta = j\omega 2w\varepsilon_0\varepsilon_{33}^X\Big[&\left(1-k_{31}^2\right)\left(\frac{\omega L}{2v_{11}^E}\right)\cos\left(\frac{\omega L}{2v_{11}^E}\right) + k_{31}^2\sin\left(\frac{\omega L}{2v_{11}^E}\right) + \\ &j\left(1-k_{31}^2\right)\left(\frac{\omega L}{2v_{11}^E}\right)\cos\left(\frac{\omega L}{2v_{11}^E}\right)\Big].\end{aligned} \tag{10.92a}$$

- For a small ω (much lower than the resonance frequency),

$$\begin{aligned}\Delta &= j\omega 2w\varepsilon_0\varepsilon_{33}^X\left[\left(1-k_{31}^2\right)\left(\frac{\omega L}{2v_{11}^E}\right) + k_{31}^2\left(\frac{\omega L}{2v_{11}^E}\right) + j\left(1-k_{31}^2\right)\left(\frac{\omega L}{2v_{11}^E}\right)\right] \\ &= j\omega 2w\varepsilon_0\varepsilon_{33}^X\left(\frac{\omega L}{2v_{11}^E}\right)\left[1 + j\left(1-k_{31}^2\right)\right].\end{aligned} \tag{10.92b}$$

The apparent dissipation factor $\tan\varphi = \left(1-k_{31}^2\right)$ is quite high under $Z = 1/\omega C_d$ resistive shunt case.

- For a frequency around the resonance frequency $\left(\frac{\omega_R L}{2v_{11}^E} = \frac{\pi}{2}, \Delta\omega = \omega - \omega_R \right)$, taking $\frac{\omega L}{2v_{11}^E} = \left(\frac{\pi}{2} + \frac{\Delta\omega L}{2v_{11}^E} \right)$, $\cos\left(\frac{\omega L}{2v_{11}^E} \right) = -\sin\left(\frac{\Delta\omega L}{2v_{11}^E} \right)$, and $\sin\left(\frac{\omega L}{2v_{11}^E} \right) = \cos\left(\frac{\Delta\omega L}{2v_{11}^E} \right)$ into account

$$\begin{aligned} \Delta &= j(\omega_R + \Delta\omega)2w\varepsilon_0\varepsilon_{33}^X \left[-(1-k_{31}^2)\left(\frac{\pi}{2} + \frac{\Delta\omega L}{2v_{11}^E} \right) \sin\left(\frac{\Delta\omega L}{2v_{11}^E} \right) + \right. \\ &\left. k_{31}^2 \cos\left(\frac{\Delta\omega L}{2v_{11}^E} \right) - j(1-k_{31}^2)\left(\frac{\pi}{2} + \frac{\Delta\omega L}{2v_{11}^E} \right) \sin\left(\frac{\Delta\omega L}{2v_{11}^E} \right) \right] \\ &\approx j\omega_R 2w\varepsilon_0\varepsilon_{33}^X \left[-(1-k_{31}^2)\left(\frac{\pi}{2}\right)\left(\frac{\Delta\omega L}{2v_{11}^E} \right) + k_{31}^2 - j(1-k_{31}^2)\left(\frac{\pi}{2}\right)\left(\frac{\Delta\omega L}{2v_{11}^E} \right) \right]. \end{aligned} \quad (10.93)$$

The external impedance Z connection is equivalent to the loss tangent increase, and

$$\begin{aligned} \tan\varphi &= (1-k_{31}^2)\left(\frac{\omega L}{2v_{11}^E} \right) \cos\left(\frac{\omega L}{2v_{11}^E} \right) / \left[(1-k_{31}^2)\left(\frac{\omega L}{2v_{11}^E} \right) \cos\left(\frac{\omega L}{2v_{11}^E} \right) + k_{31}^2 \sin\left(\frac{\omega L}{2v_{11}^E} \right) \right] \\ &\approx -(1-k_{31}^2)\left(\frac{\pi}{2}\right)\left(\frac{\Delta\omega L}{2v_{11}^E} \right) / \left[-(1-k_{31}^2)\left(\frac{\pi}{2}\right)\left(\frac{\Delta\omega L}{2v_{11}^E} \right) + k_{31}^2 \right] \\ &\approx -\frac{(1-k_{31}^2)}{k_{31}^2}\left(\frac{\pi}{2}\right)\left(\frac{\Delta\omega L}{2v_{11}^E} \right). \end{aligned} \quad (10.94)$$

It is important to note that the resistive shunt contributes largely to the apparent dissipation. In other words, this large dissipation in the piezoelectric component stands for efficient piezoelectric energy harvesting in the external load. However, the apparent dissipation becomes small around the mechanical resonance frequency range, compared with the amplified motional current (note that we neglected the piezo material-originated losses).

The displacement $u(x)$ and strain $x_1(x)$ under the external impedance Z are summarized as follows:

$$\begin{cases} u(x) = \dfrac{s_{11}^E X_0 b\omega C_d (j-1)\cos\left(\frac{\omega L}{2v_{11}^E} \right)}{\Delta} \sin\left(\frac{\omega}{v_{11}^E} x \right) + \dfrac{s_{11}^E X_0 b\omega C_d (j-1)\sin\left(\frac{\omega L}{2v_{11}^E} \right)}{\Delta} \cos\left(\frac{\omega}{v_{11}^E} x \right) \\ x_1(x) = \dfrac{s_{11}^E X_0 b\omega C_d (j-1)\cos\left(\frac{\omega L}{2v_{11}^E} \right)}{\Delta} \frac{\omega}{v_{11}^E} \cos\left(\frac{\omega}{v_{11}^E} x \right) - \dfrac{s_{11}^E X_0 b\omega C_d (j-1)\sin\left(\frac{\omega L}{2v_{11}^E} \right)}{\Delta} \frac{\omega}{v_{11}^E} \sin\left(\frac{\omega}{v_{11}^E} x \right) \end{cases} . \quad (10.95)$$

The electric power spent in the resistive shunt $Z = 1/\omega C_d$ can be calculated by

$$|P_{out}| = Re\left[\left(\frac{1}{2} \right) \left(V^* \cdot \overline{I}^* \right) \right], \quad (10.96)$$

from Example Problem 10.2., initially, we obtain the following from Equation (10.89):

$$\frac{1}{2}\frac{V^2}{Z} = \frac{1}{2}\frac{(bE_z)^2}{Z} = \frac{b^2}{2Z} \left[\frac{s_{11}^E X_0 \left(j\omega \frac{2wd_{31}}{s_{11}^E} \right) \sin\left(\frac{\omega L}{2v_{11}^E} \right)}{\left(\frac{\omega}{v_{11}^E} \right) b \left(j\omega C_d - \frac{1}{Z} \right) \cos\left(\frac{\omega L}{2v_{11}^E} \right) + d_{31} j\omega \left(\frac{2wd_{31}}{s_{11}^E} \right) \sin\left(\frac{\omega L}{2v_{11}^E} \right)} \right]^2 . \quad (10.97)$$

If we consider a small ω (much lower than the resonance frequency),

$$\begin{aligned}\frac{1}{2}\frac{V^2}{Z} &= \frac{b^2}{2}\omega\frac{Lw}{b}\varepsilon_0\varepsilon_{33}^X(1-k_{31}^2)\left[\frac{s_{11}^E X_0\left(j\omega\frac{2wd_{31}}{s_{11}^E}\right)}{\left(\frac{2}{L}\right)b\omega\frac{Lw}{b}\varepsilon_0\varepsilon_{33}^X(1-k_{31}^2)(j-1)+d_{31}j\omega\left(\frac{2wd_{31}}{s_{11}^E}\right)}\right]^2 \\ &= \frac{1}{2}\omega(Lwb)\varepsilon_0\varepsilon_{33}^X(1-k_{31}^2)\left[\frac{d_{31}X_0(j\omega 2w)}{\omega 2w\varepsilon_0\varepsilon_{33}^X(1-k_{31}^2)(j-1)+j\omega 2w\varepsilon_0\varepsilon_{33}^X\left(\frac{d_{31}{}^2}{\varepsilon_0\varepsilon_{33}^X s_{11}^E}\right)}\right]^2 \\ &= \frac{1}{2}\omega(Lwb)\frac{(d_{31}X_0)^2(1-k_{31}^2)}{\varepsilon_0\varepsilon_{33}^X\left[-(1-k_{31}^2)+j\right]}.\end{aligned} \quad (10.98)$$

Thus, the output electrical power is given by

$$|P_{out}| = Re\left[\left(\frac{1}{2}\right)\left(V^*\cdot I^*\right)\right] = \frac{1}{2}\omega(Lwb)\frac{(d_{31}X_0)^2}{\varepsilon_0\varepsilon_{33}^X}\frac{1}{(1-k_{31}^2)+\frac{1}{(1-k_{31}^2)}}. \quad (10.99)$$

In Equation (10.99), because $d_{31}X_0 = P_3$, and $\frac{1}{2}\frac{(d_{31}X_0)^2}{\varepsilon_0\varepsilon_{33}^X}$ corresponds to the electric energy per unit volume converted via the piezoelectric effect with some calibration factor by the electromechanical coupling factor, $\frac{1}{(1-k_{31}^2)+\frac{1}{(1-k_{31}^2)}} = \frac{1}{2+\frac{k_{31}^4}{(1-k_{31}^2)}}$. The power obtained from this piezoelectric k_{31} specimen is expressed by the product of frequency ω and volume (Lwb). When k_{31}^2 is not large (k_{31} < 30%), $|P_{out}|$ becomes roughly 1/2 of the converted energy via the resistance Z, which matches the piezoelectric damped capacitance.

Differently from Equations (10.69) and (10.71), in which we did not consider the difference depending on the mechanical constraint (i.e., ε_{33}^X or $\varepsilon_{33}^{x_1}$) from the exact solution, in Equation (10.99), the following factors are considered:

(1) Matching impedance should be replaced by the "damped" capacitance C_d rather than only a capacitance C;

(2) The calibration factor $\frac{1}{(1-k_{31}^2)+\frac{1}{(1-k_{31}^2)}}$ is more precise, rather than 1/2 in $|P| = \frac{1}{2}\frac{\omega d^2 X_0^2}{C}\frac{1}{(1-k_{31}^2)+\frac{1}{(1-k_{31}^2)}}$.

Recall that the mechanical excitation of a piezoelectric plate under a short-circuit condition exhibits a so-called "piezoelectric resonance mode" with the elastic compliance $s_{11}{}^E$, while the mechanical excitation of a piezoelectric plate under an open-circuit condition exhibits a so-called "piezoelectric antiresonance mode" with lower "effective elastic compliance" $s_{11,\,eff}{}^E$ (i.e., higher peak frequency, though the device elastic compliance should be $s_{11}{}^E$ theoretically). We now calculate the "input mechanical energy" under a Z-shunt condition from the second constitutive equation (Equation (10.78b) and Equation (10.92)) under the low frequency ω:

$$\begin{aligned} x &= d_{31}E_z + s_{11}{}^E X = d_{31}\left[-\frac{s_{11}^E X_0\left(j\omega\frac{2wd_{31}}{s_{11}^E}\right)\sin\left(\frac{\omega L}{2v_{11}^E}\right)}{\Delta}\right] + s_{11}{}^E X \\ &= d_{31}\left[-\frac{s_{11}^E X_0\left(j\omega\frac{2wd_{31}}{s_{11}^E}\right)\sin\left(\frac{\omega L}{2v_{11}^E}\right)}{j\omega 2w\varepsilon_0\varepsilon_{33}^X\left(\frac{\omega L}{2v_{11}^E}\right)\left[1+j\left(1-k_{31}^2\right)\right]}\right] + s_{11}{}^E X = s_{11}{}^E X_0\left[1-\frac{k_{31}{}^2}{1+j\left(1-k_{31}{}^2\right)}\right]. \end{aligned} \quad (10.100)$$

We can obtain effective elastic compliance as

$$s_{eff}^E = \frac{x}{X} = s^E\left[1-\frac{k_{31}{}^2}{1+j\left(1-k_{31}{}^2\right)}\right] = s^E\left[1-\frac{k_{31}{}^2}{1+\left(1-k_{31}{}^2\right)^2} + j\frac{\left(1-k_{31}{}^2\right)}{1+\left(1-k_{31}{}^2\right)^2}\right]. \quad (10.101)$$

Thus, under $Z = 1/\omega C$, we can conclude that the real part of the effective elastic compliance is given by

$$Re\left[s_{eff}^E\right] = s^E\left[1-\frac{k_{31}{}^2}{1+\left(1-k_{31}{}^2\right)^2}\right] \approx s^E\left(1-\frac{1}{2}k_{31}{}^2\right) \quad [\text{for small } k_{31}]. \quad (10.102)$$

Though the above derivation was made under a low-frequency region, if we extrapolate the idea to high frequency, the mechanical resonance frequency f may be estimated as

$$f = 1/2L\sqrt{\rho s_{eff}^E} = f_R\left(1+\frac{1}{4}k_{31}{}^2\right) \quad [\text{for small } k_{31}], \quad (10.103)$$

which is higher than the short-circuit condition f_R (i.e., piezoelectric resonance frequency) but lower than the open-circuit condition f_A (i.e., piezoelectric antiresonance frequency), approximated as $f_A = f_R\left(1+\frac{4}{\pi^2}k_{31}^2\right)$. Under the resistive shunt condition, the elastic compliance exhibits intermediate between s^E and s^D, then the mechanical resonance frequency seems to exist also in between the resonance and antiresonance frequencies.

Thus far, in the above, we concentrated only on the maximization of the output electrical energy. Now, we will consider the maximization of the "energy transmission coefficient", taking into account the input mechanical energy. Though we already handled this concept in Example Problem 7.5, we describe here a more detailed derivation. The "energy transmission coefficient" in the piezoelectric energy harvesting system is defined by Equation (10.75b) as follows:

λ_{max} = (Output electrical energy/Input mechanical energy)$_{max}$.

As you have learned above, the input mechanical energy differs significantly depending on the external electrical load Z, even under the constant AC stress condition, because the elastic compliance changes with Z. If you recall that the tunable elasticity according to the electric constraint is s^E (short circuit) or s^D (open circuit), and further $s^D = s^E(1-k^2)$ in particular, in the transverse effect k_{31} case, you can understand that the input mechanical energy (e.g., the triangular area made by OX_0x_0) differs largely depending on the electrical load Z, as illustrated in Figure 10.18b (the slope, elastic compliance changes according to Z). Let us calculate the load Z dependence of the input mechanical energy. Instead of Equation (10.89) in the precise analysis, we will use the simplified electric field for the simple analysis. From Equations (10.67) and (10.68) for the low k condition,

$$V_z = SZi_{out} = S\frac{j\omega dX_0 Z}{(1 + j\omega CZ)}. \tag{10.104}$$

Note that since i_{out} is originally derived from $\frac{\partial D}{\partial t}$, the total current requires to be multiplied by the area S. Thus, we can obtain the output electric energy as

$$|P|_{out} = Re\left[\frac{S^2}{2}\left(\overline{Z\cdot i_{out}}\right)\cdot i_{out}\right] = \frac{S^2}{2}Z\frac{(\omega dX_0)^2}{\left(1+(\omega CZ)^2\right)}, \tag{10.105}$$

where $\overline{i_{out}}$ stands for the conjugate of i_{out}. Then, the second constitutive equation in Equation (10.78b) leads to the following equation:

$$x = dE + s^E X = -d\left(\frac{V}{t}\right) + s^E X = -\left(\frac{d}{t}\right)\left[\frac{j\omega dX_0}{\frac{1}{Z} + j\omega C}\right] + s^E X. \tag{10.106}$$

We obtain effective elastic compliance as

$$s^E_{eff} = \frac{x}{X} = s^E\left[1 - \left(\frac{S}{t}\right)\frac{j\omega Zd^2}{s^E(1 + j\omega CZ)}\right]. \tag{10.107}$$

You can verify that the above "effective elastic compliance" is equal to s^E or $s^D = s^E\left(1 - k_{31}{}^2\right)$, when $Z = 0$ or ∞, respectively, using $C = \varepsilon_0\varepsilon^X_{33}\left(\frac{S}{t}\right)$ and $k_{31}{}^2 = d_{31}{}^2/s^E\varepsilon_0\varepsilon^X_{33}$. The total input mechanical power under the Z-shunt condition can be derived as

$$|P|_{in} = Re\left[(St)\frac{\omega}{2}\left(\overline{X_0 s^E_{eff}}\right)X_0\right] = (St)\frac{\omega}{2}s^E\left[1 - \left(\frac{S}{t}\right)\frac{C\left(\omega Zd\right)^2}{s^E\left[1 + (\omega CZ)^2\right]}\right]X_0{}^2. \tag{10.108}$$

The volume $(S\cdot t)$ was multiplied by the unit volume elastic energy. The "energy transmission coefficient", defined by

λ_{max} = (Output electrical energy/Input mechanical energy)$_{max}$.

in the energy harvesting application, can now be calculated from

$$\begin{aligned}\lambda = \frac{|P|_{out}}{|P|_{in}} &= S^2\frac{1}{2}\,Z\frac{(\omega dX_0)^2}{\left[1+(\omega CZ)^2\right]}/(St)\frac{\omega}{2}s^E\left[1 - \left(\frac{S}{t}\right)\frac{C(\omega Zd)^2}{s^E\left[1+(\omega CZ)^2\right]}\right]X_0{}^2 \\ &= \omega CZk^2/\left[1 + (\omega CZ)^2(1 - k^2)\right].\end{aligned} \tag{10.109}$$

Taking the maximization process in terms of Z, we can obtain the optimized impedance Z as follows:

$$\frac{\partial \lambda}{\partial Z} = 0 \rightarrow Z = \frac{1}{\sqrt{1-k^2}}\frac{1}{\omega C}. \quad (10.110)$$

This impedance value is in between the free capacitance C and the damped capacitance $(1-k^2)C$. Then, the energy transmission coefficient is expressed as

$$\lambda_{max} = \left[(1/k) - \sqrt{(1/k^2) - 1}\right]^2 = \left[(1/k) + \sqrt{(1/k^2) - 1}\right]^{-2}. \quad (10.111)$$

However, we need to be aware that since the input mechanical energy is changed (even if we keep the stress/force constant), due to the elastic compliance change with the external electrical impedance (see Equation (6.16)), the condition for realizing the "maximum transmission coefficient" is slightly off from the electrical impedance matching point. When we take the matched electrical impedance $Z = 1/\omega C$, we obtain

$$\lambda = \frac{k^2}{2}\frac{1}{(2-k^2)}, \quad (10.112)$$

which is slightly smaller than λ_{max} of Equation (10.111). We can also notice that from Equation (10.111) (monotonous increase with respect to k increase),

$$k^2/4 < \lambda_{max} < k^2/2,$$

depending on the k value. For a small k (< 0.3), $\lambda_{max} \approx k^2/4$, and for a large k (up to 0.9), $\lambda_{max} \approx k^2/3 \sim k^2/2$. When k is unrealistically high (~0.98), λ_{max} approaches 1.

Example Problem 10.4.

Not all converted/stored energy can be actually used, and the actual work performed depends on the mechanical load under an electric field application. With a zero mechanical load or a complete clamp (no strain) condition, no output mechanical work is performed, and even a strain is generated under an electric field. Remember that the work is given by (Force) × (Displacement). The energy transmission coefficient for the actuator is defined by

$$\lambda_{max} = (\text{Output mechanical energy/Input electrical energy})_{max}. \quad (P10.4.1)$$

Based on Figure 10.27, which illustrates the calculation process of the input electrical and output mechanical energy in a piezoelectric actuator, derive the energy transmission coefficient expressed as

$$\lambda_{max} = \left[(1/k) - \sqrt{(1/k^2) - 1}\right]^2 = \left[(1/k) + \sqrt{(1/k^2) - 1}\right]^{-2}. \quad (P10.4.2)$$

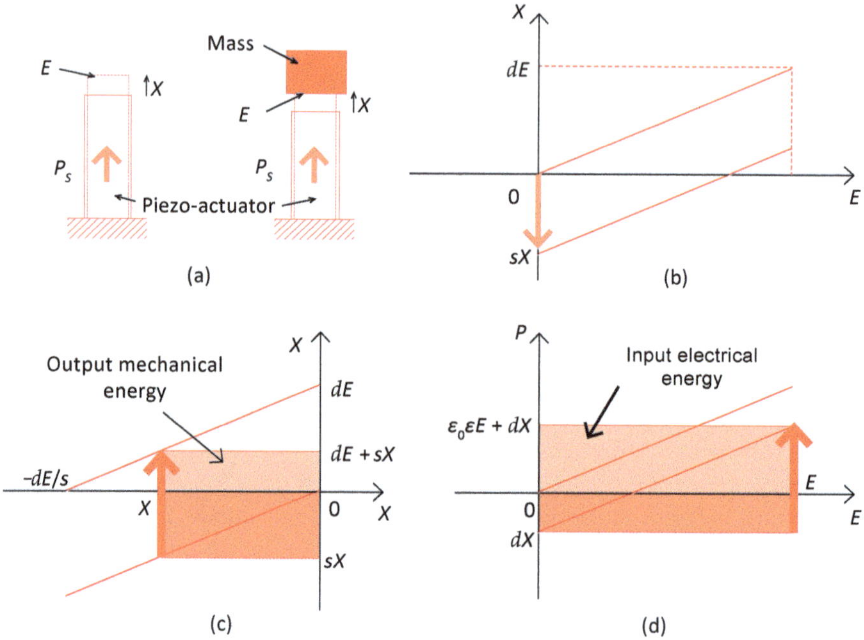

Figure 10.27. Calculation of the input electrical and output mechanical energy: (**a**) load mass model for the calculation, (**b**) electric field vs. induced strain curve, (**c**) stress vs. strain curve, and (**d**) electric field vs. polarization curve. Source: [2] ©Uchino, K. *Micromechatronics*, 2nd ed.; CRC Press, 2019; p. 131. Reproduced by permission of Taylor & Francis Group.

Hint

Let us consider the case where an electric field E is applied to a piezoelectric under constant external stress X (< 0, because compressive stress is necessary to output work). This corresponds to the situation that a mass is put suddenly on the actuator, as shown in Figure 10.27a. Figure 10.27b shows two electric-field vs. induced-strain curves, corresponding to two conditions—under a mass load and no load. As the area on the "field-strain" domain does not mean the energy, we should use the "stress–strain" and "field-polarization" domains in order to discuss the mechanical and electrical energy, respectively. Figure 10.27c illustrates how to calculate mechanical energy. Note that the mass shrinks the actuator first by sX (s: piezo material's compliance, and $X < 0$). This mechanical energy sX^2 is a sort of "loan" of the actuator credited from the mass, which should be subtracted later (i.e., "paying back"). This energy corresponds to the bottom hatched area in Figure 10.27c. By applying the step electric field, the actuator expands by the strain level dE under a constant stress condition. This is the mechanical energy provided from the actuator to the mass, which corresponds to $|dEX|$. Similar to paying back the initial "loan", the output work (from the actuator to the mass) can be calculated as the area subtraction (shown by the top dotted area in Figure 10.27c).

$$\int (-X)\,dx = -(dE + sX)X. \quad \text{(P10.4.3)}$$

We can now initially consider this equation merely to maximize the output mechanical energy. The maximum output energy can be obtained when the top dotted area in Figure 10.27c becomes maximum under the constraint of the rectangular corner point tracing on the line (from dE on the vertical axis to $-dE/s$ on the horizontal axis). Since the work–energy Equation (P10.4.3) can be transformed as $-s(X + \frac{dE}{2s})^2 + \frac{(dE)^2}{4s}$, $X = -\frac{dE}{2s}$ provides the maximum mechanical energy of $\frac{(dE)^2}{4s}$. Therefore, the load should be half of the maximum generative stress when we apply the maximum electric field E.

The above mechanical energy maximization condition is not the best condition from the "energy transmission coefficient" viewpoint; that is, input electric energy is overspent. Figure 10.27d illustrates how to calculate the electrical energy spent. The mass load X generates the "loaned" electrical energy by inducing $P = dX$ (see the bottom hatched area in Figure 10.27d). By applying a sudden electric field E, the actuator (such as a capacitor) receives the electrical energy of $\varepsilon_0\varepsilon E^2$. Thus, the total energy is given by the area subtraction (shown by the top dotted area in Figure 10.27d)

$$\int (E)dP = (\varepsilon_0\varepsilon E + dX)E. \quad \text{(P10.4.4)}$$

Now, from the maximization condition of (Output mechanical energy/Input electrical energy),

$$\lambda = -(dE + sX)X/(\varepsilon_0\varepsilon E + dX)E, \quad \text{(P10.4.5)}$$

choose a proper load X, which corresponds to a sort of matching mechanical impedance.

Solution

The energy transmission coefficient is defined by

λ = (Output mechanical energy/Input electrical energy).

Considering the case where an electric field E is applied to a piezoelectric under a constant external stress X, λ can be calculated as

$$\begin{aligned}\lambda &= -x\cdot X/P\cdot E = -(dE + sX)X/(\varepsilon_0\varepsilon E + dX)E \\ &= -[d(X/E) + s(X/E)^2]/[\varepsilon_0\varepsilon + d(X/E)].\end{aligned} \quad \text{(P10.4.6)}$$

We need to determine an appropriate stress X under a certain applied field E so as to maximize the λ value. Letting $y = X/E$, then

$$\lambda = -(sy^2 + dy)/(dy + \varepsilon_0\varepsilon). \quad \text{(P10.4.7)}$$

The maximum λ can be obtained when y satisfies

$$(d\lambda/dy) = [-(2sy + d)\cdot(dy + \varepsilon_0\varepsilon) + (sy^2 + dy)d]/(dy + \varepsilon_0\varepsilon)^2 = 0. \quad \text{(P10.4.8)}$$

Then, from $y_0{}^2 + 2(\varepsilon_0\varepsilon/d)y_0 + (\varepsilon_0\varepsilon/s) = 0$,

$$y_0 = (\varepsilon_0\varepsilon/d)\left[-1 + \sqrt{(1-k^2)}\right], \quad \text{(P10.4.9)}$$

where $k^2 = d^2/(s\cdot\varepsilon_0\varepsilon)$ [electromechanical coupling factor]. Note that among the two roots $y_0 = (\varepsilon_0\varepsilon/d)[-1 \pm \sqrt{(1-k^2)}]$, only $y_0 = (\varepsilon_0\varepsilon/d)[-1 + \sqrt{(1-k^2)}]$ is valid for realizing the meaningful maximum point, since the "$-$" root provides $(d^2\lambda/dy^2) > 0$, that is, λ minimum position.

By inserting $y = y_0$ into $\lambda(y)$, we can obtain the maximum value of λ as follows:

$$\begin{aligned}\lambda_{max} &= -\{s[-2(\varepsilon_0\varepsilon/d)y_0 - (\varepsilon_0\varepsilon/s)] + dy_0\}/(dy_0 + \varepsilon_0\varepsilon)\\ &= \left[dy_0(2/k^2 - 1) + \varepsilon_0\varepsilon\right]/(y_0 + \varepsilon_0\varepsilon)\\ &= \left\{\left[-1 + \sqrt{(1-k^2)}\right](2/k^2 - 1) + 1\right\}/\left\{\left[-1 + \sqrt{(1-k^2)}\right] + 1\right\}\\ &= \left[(1/k) - \sqrt{(1/k^2) - 1}\right]^2.\end{aligned} \quad \text{(P10.4.10)}$$

The relation between energy transmission coefficient λ_{max} and electromechanical coupling factor k is plotted in Figure 10.28, where you can also find the ratio λ_{max}/k^2, which changes from 1/4 for small k to 1/2 for large k (<0.9). Though the λ_{max}/k^2 approaches 1, when k is very close to 1, this is very unrealistic in most piezoelectric applications. It is also worth noting that the maximum condition stated above does not agree precisely with the condition that provides the "maximum output mechanical energy". The maximum output energy can be obtained when the dotted area in Figure 10.27c becomes maximum under the constraint of the rectangular corner point tracing on the strain line, which corresponds to $(1/2)k^2$. Therefore, the load should be half of the maximum generative stress (i.e., "blocking stress"), and the mechanical energy at that point: $-[dE - s(dE/2s)](-dE/2s) = (dE)^2/4s$. In this case, since the input electrical energy is given by $[\varepsilon_0\varepsilon E + d(-dE/2s)]E$, the energy transmission coefficient λ is calculated as

$$\lambda = 1/2[(2/k^2) - 1] = (1/4)k^2 + (1/8)k^4 + (4/64)k^6 + \ldots \quad \text{(P10.4.11)}$$

The above λ is close to the value λ_{max} when k is small but has a slightly different value when k is large, as predicted theoretically.

$$\lambda_{max} = \left[(1/k) - \sqrt{(1/k^2) - 1}\right]^2 = (1/4)k^2 + (1/8)k^4 + (5/64)k^6 + \ldots \quad \text{(P10.4.12)}$$

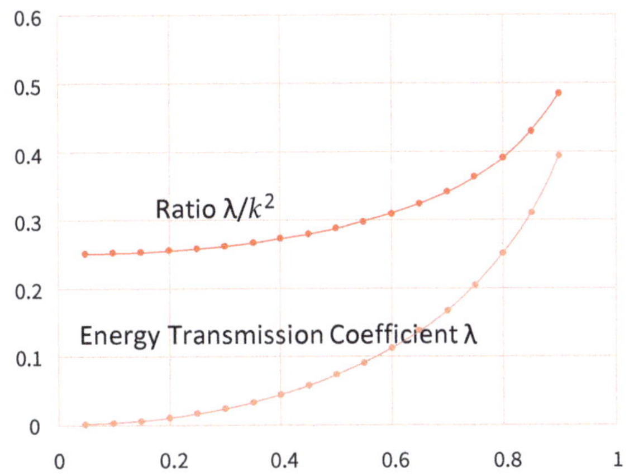

Figure 10.28. Energy transmission coefficient λ_{max} vs. electromechanical coupling factor k. Source: [2] ©Uchino, K. *Micromechatronics*, 2nd ed.; CRC Press, 2019; p. 134. Reproduced by permission of Taylor & Francis Group.

Chapter Essentials

Mechanical Impedance Matching

1. Improvement of mechanical-to-mechanical energy transfer between two phases requires the concept of "mechanical impedance matching".
2. The mechanical/acoustic impedance is expressed by
   $Z = \rho v_p$ (including liquid, ρ: mass density, v_p: sound phase velocity) or
   $Z = \sqrt{\rho c}$ (solid material, c: elastic stiffness).
3. Example of acoustic impedance:
   Water: $Z = 1.5 \times 10^6$ kg/m^2·s = 1.5 MRayls;
   Polymer: 3.8 MRayls;
   PZT: 20–24 MRayls;
   Steel: 45 MRayls.
4. Acoustic piezoelectric medical and underwater transducer is mainly composed of three layers: (1) impedance matching, (2) piezoelectric material, and (3) backing layers. One or more matching layers are used to increase sound transmissions from the piezoelectric material to the medium, or vice versa. The backing is added to the rear of the transducer in order to dampen the acoustic back wave and to reduce the pulse duration. Piezoelectric materials are used to generate and detect ultrasound (20~40 kHz for SONAR, 2~4 MHz for medical diagnosis).

Electrical Impedance Matching

5. The internal impedance of a piezoelectric component is "capacitive" under an off-resonance operation, $1/j\omega C$, with an absolute value of 100s kΩ at 100 Hz (in piezoelectric energy harvesting).

6. Electric Impedance Matching: External impedance Z_1 is adjusted to "conjugate" of the internal impedance Z_0^*, in general. However, in this impedance matching, energy will make a catch-ball between the internal capacitance and external inductance. A resistive load is essential to harvest the energy and adjusted to the "absolute internal impedance" of the piezoelectric component ($1/\omega C$) for obtaining the maximum output power.
7. When the input mechanical energy is unlimited (such as environmental water or wind flow), the impedance matching for obtaining the maximum output power is the primary target.
8. MOSFET is popularly used for an ON–OFF switching regulator.
9. As the output impedance from the piezoelectric energy harvesting device is too high to accumulate the energy directly into a rechargeable battery, we should adopt a DC–DC converter for the impedance matching purpose.
10. DC–DC converters: Among forward converter, buck converter, buck–boost converter, flyback converter, the buck converter is the best suited for piezoelectric energy harvesting, from the simplest design and high-efficiency viewpoints.

Impedance Matching in Piezoelectrics

11. Under a constant force X_0, the input mechanical energy into a piezoelectric transducer changes with the shunted external impedance Z as follows:

$$|P|_{in} = Re\left[(St)\frac{\omega}{2}\left(X_0 s_{eff}^E\right)X_0\right] = (St)\frac{\omega}{2}s^E\left[1-\left(\frac{S}{t}\right)\frac{C(\omega Z d)^2}{s^E\left[1+(\omega CZ)^2\right]}\right]X_0{}^2,$$

where S: area, t: electrode gap of piezoelectric component, and the volume ($S{\cdot}t$) is multiplied on the unit volume elastic energy. This is originated from the effective complex elastic compliance s_{eff}^E under Z shunt expressed as

$$s_{eff}^E = \frac{x}{X} = s^E\left[1-\left(\frac{S}{t}\right)\frac{j\omega Zd^2}{s^E(1+j\omega CZ)}\right].$$

Recall that s_{eff}^E approaches s^E or $s^D = s^E(1-k^2)$, when $Z = 0$ or ∞, respectively.

12. When the input mechanical/electrical energy is limited, the "energy transmission coefficient" is the FOM:

- λ_{max} = (Output electrical energy/Input mechanical energy)$_{max}$ (piezoelectric energy harvesting);
- λ_{max} = (Output mechanical energy/Input electrical energy)$_{max}$ (actuator/transducer application).

Both are expressed with the electromechanical coupling factor k as

$$\lambda_{max} = \left[(1/k)-\sqrt{(1/k^2)-1}\right]^2 = \left[(1/k)+\sqrt{(1/k^2)-1}\right]^{-2}.$$

When the input energy is unlimited, $|P|_{out} = \left(\frac{1}{2}\right)k^2|P|_{in}$ (under the impedance matching condition).

Check Point

1. (T/F) Mechanical impedance in a solid material is given by $Z = \sqrt{\rho s}$ (solid material, s: elastic compliance). True or false?

2. Knowing $\rho = 7750\ kg/m^3$, $s_{33}{}^E = 18.8 \times 10^{-12}\ m^2/N$ for "soft" PZT 5A, calculate its acoustic impedance.
3. (T/F) When we consider a mechanical wave transmission from one phase to another, as long as the incident wave is normal to the boundary interface, 100% energy transmittance is expected. True or false?
4. What is the unit of mechanical impedance Z, which is equivalent to the MKS unit of ($kg/m^2 \cdot s$)?
5. Acoustic impedance definition has two ways in solid materials, $Z = \rho v_p$ and $Z = \sqrt{\rho c}$. Derive the sound velocity formula v_p in terms of density ρ and elastic stiffness c.
6. Fill in the blank: An acoustic piezoelectric medical and underwater transducer is mainly composed of three layers: (1) ( ), (2) piezoelectric material, and (3) backing layers.
7. (T/F) External load resistance should be adjusted to the internal impedance of the piezo-energy harvesting component for obtaining the maximum output power. True or false?
8. There is a battery (total energy = 1 kJ) with an internal impedance of 75 Ω. How much energy can be spent for the external work roughly by matching the external load impedance?
9. Calculate the electrical impedance $1/j\omega C$ of a piezoelectric component with capacitance 1 nF at the off-resonance frequency of 100 Hz.
10. The above impedance is significantly larger than the internal impedance of rechargeable batteries (~50 Ω). What kind of circuit is required to match the impedance between the piezoelectric component and the battery?
11. Among three DC–DC converters—buck, buck–boost, and Flyback—which is the best suitable converter for the piezoelectric energy harvesting system?
12. Fill in the blank: A DC–DC converter is composed of (a) MOSFET switching device, (b) inductor, (c) capacitor, and (d) ( ).
13. (T/F) A full-wave rectifier is represented by the following circuit (Figure **??**). True or false?
14. (T/F) When the losses of the electronic components are neglected, input power = output power is ideally expected in a Buck converter. When we take the duty ratio (on/off time period ratio) as 2%, the impedance can be reduced by 50 theoretically. True or false?
15. The effective elastic compliance under Z shunt is expressed as
$s_{eff}^E = \frac{x}{X} = s^E\left[1 - \left(\frac{s}{t}\right)\frac{j\omega Z d^2}{s^E(1+j\omega CZ)}\right]$.
Calculate s_{eff}^E for $Z = \infty$.
16. In the above effective complex elastic compliance, when we choose $Z = 1/j\omega C$ (capacitive load), calculate s_{eff}^E, which should be between s^E and $s^D = s^E(1 - k^2)$.

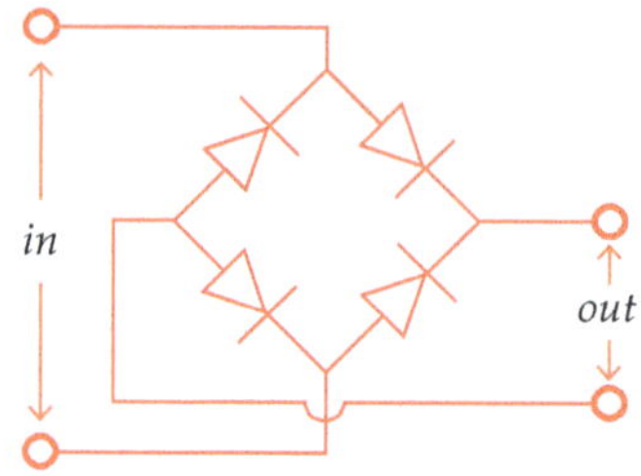

Figure 10.29. A full-wave rectifier. Source: Figure by author.

Chapter Problems

10.1 Figure 10.30 shows a piezoelectric energy harvesting system with an elastically soft (polyimide-base) piezoelectric composites (MFCs) bonded on the steel beam structure, a part of machinery vibrating at 50 Hz. Discuss why this system is NOT recommended in terms of the "mechanical impedance matching" step by step.

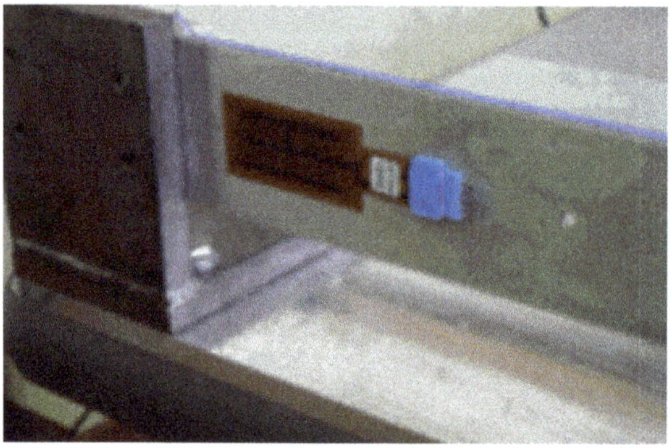

Figure 10.30. Piezoelectric energy harvesting system. Source: Image by author.

(1) Calculate the acoustic impedance of steel from the following data: $\rho = 8000\ \mathrm{kg/m^3}$, $Y\ (\sim c_{11}) = 200$ GPa.

(2) Calculate the acoustic impedance of polyimide from the following data: $\rho = 1450\ \mathrm{kg/m^3}$, $Y\ (\sim c_{11}) = 2.5$ GPa.

(3) Supposing the SH wave (transversal wave) from the steel and using the transmittance ratio equation for the normal elastic wave, $\frac{v_{t0}}{v_{i0}} = \frac{2}{\left(1+\sqrt{\frac{\rho_2 c_{66.2}}{\rho_1 c_{66.1}}}\right)}$, calculate the transmittance ratio, taking into account the acoustic impedances in (1) and (2). You can find very small mechanical energy is transmitted into the piezoelectric component due to the large acoustic impedance mismatch.

10.2 A "monolithic hinge lever mechanism" is applied to amplify a small displacement generated in a piezoelectric multilayer (ML) actuator. Figure 10.31 illustrates a structure of the hinge lever used in a dot-matrix printer in the 1980s.

Discuss the design principle of the mechanism in terms of the concept of "mechanical impedance matching".

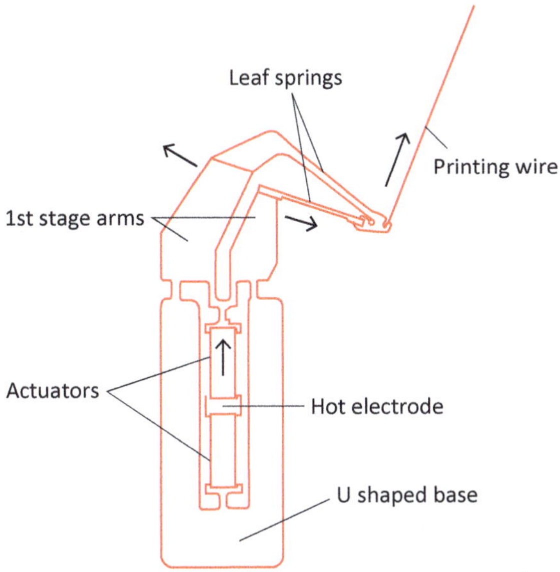

Figure 10.31. Hinge lever mechanism with multilayer actuators. Source: [25] ©Uchino, K. *Essentials of Piezoelectric Energy Harvesting*. World Scientific, 2021; p. 136. Reproduced by permission of World Scientific Publishing.

Hint

The displacement 20 μm generated in an ML with the blocking force of 200 N (with the elastic stiffness constant $200/20 \times 10^{-6}$ (N/m)) is amplified to 500 μm (amplification × 25) at the tip of the printing wire, by sacrificing the force level a little less than 8 N. The first-stage arms generate × 5 displacement via the geometric distance ratio, and the push–pull leaf springs provide additional × 5 amplification. Thus, the effective elastic stiffness constant can be estimated by $8/500 \times 10^{-6}$ (N/m). Using this mechanical amplifier (sometimes called "mechanical transformer") with a total displacement amplification ratio of 25, we can generate effective elastic compliance by a factor of $(25)^2$. Supposing that the mass density of the materials is the same order, we can expect the effective mechanical impedance ($F/\dot{u}$) reduction by a factor of $1/(25)^2$ in order to transfer mechanical energy of the printing wire onto the soft paper. The "mechanical transformer" can be recognized as a "mechanical impedance converter", analogous to the relation of an "electromagnetic transformer" with an "impedance/admittance converter". Similar to the electromagnetic transformer, which exhibits $V_{in}I_{in} \approx V_{out}I_{out}$ when the loss is neglected, the mechanical transformer exhibits $F_{in}\Delta L_{in} \approx F_{out}\Delta L_{out}$ when the energy transfer loss (from the actuator to the tip of the printing wire) is neglected. Note that the effective elastic stiffness is equivalent to $F/\Delta L$.

References

1. Uchino, K. *Ferroelectric Devices*, 2nd ed.; CRC Press: Boca Raton, FL, USA, 2010.
2. Uchino, K. *Micromechatronics*, 2nd ed.; CRC Press: Boca Raton, FL, USA, 2020.
3. Onoe, M. *Fundamentals of Solid State Vibrators for Electric & Electronic Engineers*; Ohm Publ. Company: Tokyo, Japan, 1982.
4. Kinsler, L.E.; Frey, A.R.; Coppens, A.B.; Sanders, J.V. *Fundamentals of Acoustics*; John Wiley & Sons: New York, NY, USA, 1982.
5. Newnham, R.E.; Skinner, D.P.; Cross, L.E. Connectivity and piezoelectric-pyroelectric composites. *Mater. Res. Bull.* **1978**, *13*, 525. [CrossRef]
6. Klicker, K.A.; Biggers, J.V.; Newnham, R.E. Composites of PZT and Epoxy for Hydrostatic Transducer Applications. *J. Am. Ceram. Soc.* **1981**, *64*, 5. [CrossRef]
7. Bowen, L.J. Method for Making Piezoelectric Ceramic/Polymer Composite Transducers. U.S. Patent 5,340,510, 23 August 1994. Available online: https://patents.google.com/patent/US5340510A/en (accessed on 25 January 2015).
8. Uchino, K. Chapter 9 of Advanced Piezoelectric Materials. In *Piezoelectric Composite Materials*; Uchino, K., Ed.; Woodhead Publishing: Cambridge, UK, 2010; p. 318.
9. Smith, W.A. The role of piezocomposites in ultrasonic transducers. In Proceedings of the IEEE Ultrasonics Symposium, Montreal, QC, Canada, 3–6 October 1989; pp. 755–766.
10. Nelson, L.J. Smart piezoelectric Fibre composites. *Mater. Sci. Technol.* **2002**, *18*, 1245. [CrossRef]
11. Hausler, E.; Stein, L.; Harbauer, G. Implantable physiological power supply with PVDF film. *Ferroelectrics* **1984**, *60*, 277. [CrossRef]
12. Kymissis, J.; Kendall, C.; Paradiso, J.; Gershenfield, N. Digest of Papers. In Proceedings of the Second IEEE International Symposium on Wearable Computers, Pittsburgh, PA, USA, 19–20 October 1998; p. 132.
13. Uchino, K. Piezoelectric Composite Materials. In Proceedings of the 9th Japan International SAMPE Symposium, Tokyo, Japan, 18–21 November 2005; pp. 11–14.
14. Sodano, H.A.; Park, G.; Leo, D.J.; Inman, D.J. Smart Structure and Materials: Smart Sensor Technology and Measurement Systems. *Proc. SPIE* **2003**, *5050*, 101.
15. Auld, B.A. *Acoustic Fields and Waves in Solids*, 2nd ed.; Robert E. Krieger: Melbourne, Australia, 1990.
16. Kino, G.S. *Acoustic Waves: Device Imaging and Analog Signal Processing*; Prentice-Hall: Englewood Cliffs, NJ, USA, 1987.
17. Desilets, C.S.; Fraser, J.D.; Kino, G.S. The Design of Efficient Broad-Band Piezoelectric Transducers. *IEEE Trans. Sonics Ultrason.* **1978**, *SU-25*, 115. [CrossRef]
18. Saitoh, S.; Takeuchi, T.; Kobayashi, T.; Harada, K.; Shimanuki, S.; Yamashita, Y. An improved phased array ultrasonic probe using $0.91Pb(Zn_{1/3}Nb_{2/3})O_3$–$0.09PbTiO_3$ single crystal. *Jpn. J. Appl. Phys.* **1999**, *38*, 3380–3384. [CrossRef]
19. Sugawara, Y.; Onitsuka, K.; Yoshikawa, S.; Xu, Q.C.; Newnham, R.E.; Uchino, K. Metal-Ceramic Composite Actuators. *J. Am. Ceram. Soc.* **1992**, *75*, 996–998. [CrossRef]
20. Zhang, J. Cymbal Transducers and Arrays. Ph.D. Thesis, The Pennsylvania State University, State College, PA, USA, 2000.
21. Kim, H.-W.; Batra, A.; Priya, S.; Uchino, K.; Markley, D.; Newnham, R.E.; Hofmann, H.F. Energy Harvesting Using a Piezoelectric "Cymbal" Transducer in Dynamic Environment. *Jpn. J. Appl. Phys.* **2004**, *43*, 6178–6183. [CrossRef]
22. Kim, H.W.; Priya, S.; Uchino, K.; Newnham, R.E. Piezoelectric Energy Harvesting under High Pre-stressed Cyclic Vibrations. *J. Electroceram.* **2005**, *15*, 27–34. [CrossRef]
23. Available online: http://www.smart-material.com/Smart-choice.php?from=MFC (accessed on 20 February 2015).

24. Uchino, K. Piezoelectric Actuators 2004—Materials, Design, Drive/Control, Modeling and Applications. In Proceedings of the 9th International Conference New Actuators, A1.0, Bremen, Germany, 14–16 June 2004; pp. 38–48.
25. Uchino, K. *Essentials of Piezoelectric Energy Harvesting*; World Scientific: Singapore, Singapore, 2021.
26. Kassakian, J.; Schlecht, M.; Verghese, G. *Principles of Power Electronics*; Addison-Wesley Publishing Company, Inc.: Reading, MA, USA, 1991; p. 103.
27. Horowitz, P.; Hill, W. *The Art of Electronics*; Cambridge University Press: Cambridge, UK, 1980; p. 360.
28. Batra, A. Energy Harvesting Using a Piezoelectric "Cymbal" Transducer in a Dynamic Environment. Master's Thesis, The Pennsylvania State University, State College, PA, USA, August 2004.
29. Kim, H.-W.; Priya, S.; Stephanau, H.; Uchino, K. Consideration of Impedance Matching Techniques for Efficient Piezoelectric Energy Harvesting. *IEEE Trans. UFFC* **2007**, *54*, 1851–1859. [CrossRef] [PubMed]

11. Lattice Vibration—Linear Differential Equation in Periodic Phenomena

Based on the linear differential equation under harmonic spring in periodic phenomena, we describe the lattice vibration and the concept of "phonon" in this chapter, which is interrelated with the ferroelectric transition. Specific heat can be derived from the harmonic oscillation. We describe briefly the nonlinear atomic spring in the periodic lattice (i.e., anharmonic phonon), which is essential to explain "thermal conductivity", to connect with the detailed description in Chapter 14 "Nonlinear Oscillatory Systems".

Remember the fact that ferroelectric-originated piezoelectric materials exhibit the phase transition associated with phonon mode "softening" (in particular, transversal optical phonon mode), as introduced in Section 1.2.3. Using the "first-principle" calculations, Zhang et al. obtained elastic compliances, heat capacity, and thermal expansion coefficient, based on phonon dispersion curves [1]. Though the detailed discussion is beyond our target in this chapter, we introduce here briefly basic concepts on the lattice vibration and "phonon", based on books by Ashcroft and Mermin [2], Ishii [3], and Kittel [4]. This chapter treats mainly "harmonic" (i.e., linear spring constant) oscillations with a brief description of the anharmonic oscillations in the last part.

11.1. Lattice Vibration—Monatomic Chain Model

A simple mass M—spring K model was discussed in Chapter 9, which gives the resonance angular frequency of $\omega_0 = \sqrt{K/M}$. The lattice vibration in a crystal is modeled by cascading a large number of these mass–spring units. Since 3D modeling is beyond the level of this textbook, we discuss the 1D chain model in this chapter. As an infinite size of crystals is difficult to be modeled, we introduce a particular boundary condition in a finite-sized crystal.

11.1.1. Solution under Free-End Boundary Condition

With increasing the component atom number in a crystal, a relatively cooperative phenomenon occurs as a whole system. We consider first the simplest one-atom (mass M) 1D chain (number of atoms N) connected by a harmonic spring (spring constant K), as shown in Figure 11.1a (first, note two end atoms in a free condition). We consider free lattice vibration with no external force, such as stress or electric field. When we denote the displacement of the n-th atom from the equilibrium position as u_n, we can obtain the following set of Newton equations:

$$\begin{gathered} M\ddot{u}_1 = -K(u_1 - u_2), \\ M\ddot{u}_n = -K(u_n - u_{n-1}) - K(u_n - u_{n+1})(n = 2, 3, \cdots, N-1), \\ M\ddot{u}_N = -K(u_N - u_{N-1}). \end{gathered} \tag{11.1a}$$

Note that the force is always created by the subtraction of the adjacent atom's displacement. Assuming a harmonic vibration, $u_n \propto e^{j\omega t}$, where ω is the frequency,

$$\begin{aligned} -M\omega^2 u_1 &= -K(u_1 - u_2), \\ -M\omega^2 u_n &= -K(u_n - u_{n-1}) - K(u_n - u_{n+1}) \ (n = 2, 3, \cdots, N-1), \\ -M\omega^2 u_N &= -K(u_N - u_{N-1}). \end{aligned} \tag{11.1b}$$

Thus, we can write the following matrix formula:

$$\omega^2 \boldsymbol{u} = [F]\boldsymbol{u}, \tag{11.2}$$

where $\boldsymbol{u}$ is an N-dimensional vector with the components of u_n, and $[F]$ is a symmetric matrix with the components.

$$F_{nm} = \left(\frac{K}{M}\right)\{(2 - \delta_{n1} - \delta_{nN})\delta_{nm} - \delta_{n,m-1} - \delta_{n,m+1}\}. \tag{11.3}$$

Here, we used "Kronecker δ_{nm}", which means that $\delta_{nm} = 1$ for $n = m$; $\delta_{nm} = 0$ for $n \neq m$. If we explicitly write Equation (11.2) in the matrix notation,

$$\omega^2 \begin{pmatrix} u_1 \\ u_2 \\ \vdots \\ u_N \end{pmatrix} = \left(\frac{K}{M}\right) \begin{pmatrix} 1 & -1 & 0 & \cdots \\ -1 & 2 & -1 & \cdots \\ \vdots & \vdots & \vdots & \vdots \\ \cdots & 0 & -1 & 1 \end{pmatrix} \begin{pmatrix} u_1 \\ u_2 \\ \vdots \\ u_N \end{pmatrix}. \tag{11.4}$$

We will now solve the "eigenvalue equation" of Equation (11.2). Knowing the matrix component relation

$$\left(\frac{K}{M}\right)\left[\left(\frac{M\omega^2}{K} - 2\right)u_n + u_{n-1} + u_{n+1}\right] = 0, \tag{11.5}$$

and the boundary condition for the "free end" ($u_0 - u_1 = u_N - u_{N+1} = 0$), assuming a general solution of "difference equation" as Equation (11.5) in the form of $u_n \propto P^n$, we obtain the following characteristic equation:

$$P^2 + \left(\frac{M\omega^2}{K} - 2\right)P + 1 = 0. \tag{11.6}$$

When $\left|\frac{M\omega^2}{K} - 2\right| < 2$, we can put

$$\left(\frac{M\omega^2}{K} - 2\right) \equiv -2\cos ka \equiv -\left(e^{jka} + e^{-jka}\right) \ (0 < ka < \pi) \tag{11.7}$$

where k and a are the "wavenumber" and the "lattice unit size". The solution of Equation (11.6) is expressed as

$$P = \exp(\pm jka). \tag{11.8}$$

Then, we can express a general solution of Equation (11.2) as

$$u_n = A\exp(jkan) + B\exp(-jkan). \tag{11.9}$$

The "free-end" boundary condition ($u_0 - u_1 = u_N - u_{N+1} = 0$) gives the following relations:

$$\begin{cases} u_0 = A + B = u_1 = A\exp(jka) + B\exp(-jka) \\ u_{N+1} = A\exp(jka(N+1)) + B\exp(-jka(N+1)) \\ \quad = u_N = A\exp(jkaN) + B\exp(-jkaN). \end{cases}$$

To realize the meaningful solution (or A and B values), at least the following "determinant = 0" should be satisfied:

$$\begin{vmatrix} 1-\exp(jka) & 1-\exp(-jka) \\ \exp(jkaN)[1-\exp(jka)] & \exp(-jkaN)[1-\exp(-jka)] \end{vmatrix} = 0. \tag{11.10}$$

This requirement determines the solutions regarding the k value

$$ka = \left(\frac{\alpha}{N}\right)\pi \ (\alpha = 1, 2, \cdots, N-1), \tag{11.11}$$

and for u_n,

$$u_n \propto [1-\exp(-jka)]\exp(jkan) - [1-\exp(jka)]\exp(-jkan) = 4j\sin\left(\tfrac{ka}{2}\right)\cos ka\left(n - \tfrac{1}{2}\right). \tag{11.12}$$

Notice that Equation (11.12) means a "standing wave". Taking the normalizing factor determined by $\sum_{n=1}^{N} {u_n}^2 = 1$, we obtain the eigenvectors and eigenfrequencies as follows:

$$u_n(\alpha) = \sqrt{\frac{2}{N}}\cos\frac{\alpha\pi}{N}\left(n - \frac{1}{2}\right) \ (\alpha = 1,\ 2,\ \cdots,\ N-1), \tag{11.13}$$

$$\omega_\alpha = 2\sqrt{\frac{K}{M}}\sin\frac{\alpha\pi}{2N} = 2\sqrt{\frac{K}{M}}\sin\frac{k_\alpha a}{2}. \tag{11.14}$$

Note here that when we adopt the "free-end" boundary condition, N atoms create $(N-1)$ freedom ($\alpha = 1, 2, \cdots, N-1$) for $\left|\frac{M\omega^2}{K} - 2\right| < 2$. When $\left|\frac{M\omega^2}{K} - 2\right| = 2$, unique solution $\omega_0 = 0$, $u_n(0) = \sqrt{\frac{1}{N}}$ exists. However, when $\left|\frac{M\omega^2}{K} - 2\right| > 2$, no solution exists to satisfy the "free-end" boundary condition.

$k_\alpha a \equiv \left(\frac{\alpha}{N}\right)\pi$ is called "wavenumber", and the relationship between the frequency and wavenumber (Equation (11.4)) is called the "dispersion relation". As shown in Figure 11.2a, $\omega \propto k$ is valid only for a low k range (long wavelength λ); that is, a "wave packet" (a mixture of low- and high-frequency waves) shape distorts significantly via frequency dispersion. This is the reason why "$\omega(k)$ vs. k" curve is called the "dispersion relation". Since a crystal has a large N, ω_α exists densely ((N − 1) modes) just $0 \le \omega_\alpha \le \omega_L = 2\sqrt{K/M}$, in particular, close to the maximum ω_L. The density of modes is discussed in Section 11.1.3.

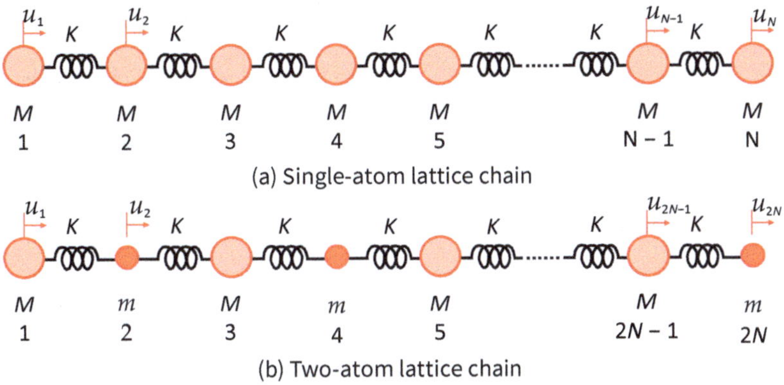

Figure 11.1. Monatomic (**a**) and diatomic (**b**) linear chain lattice models connected by the same springs. Source: Figure by author.

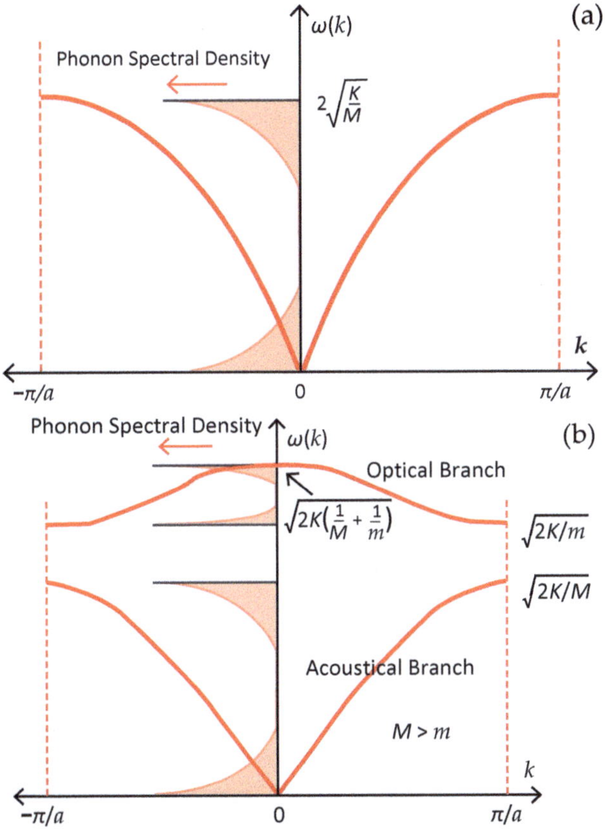

Figure 11.2. ω–k dispersion curve and photon spectral density for (**a**) monatomic 1D lattice chain model and (**b**) diatomic 1D lattice change model. Notice the ω gap between the acoustical and optical branches in the diatomic chain model. Source: Figure by author.

11.1.2. Solution under Periodic Boundary Condition

In the case of large crystal ($N \rightarrow \infty$), we occasionally use the so-called "periodic boundary condition", instead of the "end-free" condition; that is, the end atom (N-th) is connected with the first atom with a spring K to the lattice chain as a "ring". Refer to Figure 14.29 in Chapter 14. In this case, Equation (11.3) is modified as

$$F_{nm} = \left(\frac{K}{M}\right)(2\delta_{nm} - \delta_{n,m-1} - \delta_{n,m+1} - \delta_{n1}\delta_{mN} - \delta_{nN}\delta_{m1}), \tag{11.16}$$

and Equation (11.4) is modified as

$$\omega^2 \begin{pmatrix} u_1 \\ u_2 \\ \vdots \\ u_N \end{pmatrix} = \left(\frac{K}{M}\right) \begin{pmatrix} 2 & -1 & 0 & \cdots \\ -1 & 2 & -1 & \cdots \\ \vdots & \vdots & \vdots & \vdots \\ \cdots & 0 & -1 & 2 \end{pmatrix} \begin{pmatrix} u_1 \\ u_2 \\ \vdots \\ u_N \end{pmatrix}. \tag{11.17}$$

Different from Equation (11.4), the [F] matrix now keeps the $[\cdots -1\, 2 -1\, \cdots]$ sequence for all—no stop end of the crystal lattice. We now solve the above "difference equation" under the "periodic boundary condition", $u_0 - u_N = u_{N+1} - u_1 = 0$.

The results are slightly different from Equations (11.13) and (11.14).

$$u_n(\alpha) = \begin{cases} \sqrt{\frac{2-\delta_{\alpha,0}-\delta_{2[\frac{\alpha}{2}],N}}{N}} \cos \frac{2\pi n}{N}\left[\frac{\alpha}{2}\right] \ (\alpha = \text{even number}) \\ \sqrt{\frac{2}{N}} \sin \frac{2\pi n}{N}\left[\frac{\alpha}{2}\right] \ (\alpha = \text{odd number}) \end{cases}, \tag{11.18}$$

$$\omega_\alpha = 2\sqrt{\frac{K}{M}} \sin \frac{\pi}{N}\left[\frac{\alpha}{2}\right] (\alpha = 1,\ 2,\ 3,\ \cdots,\ N), \tag{11.19}$$

where $\left[\frac{\alpha}{2}\right]$ is the "Gauss symbol", which means the maximum integer number $\leq \alpha/2$. The key difference due to the boundary condition change is the "doubled unit cell"; that is, even and odd number position atoms are not identical (Equation (11.18)). The wavenumber $k_\alpha a \equiv \left(\frac{2\pi}{N}\right)\left[\frac{\alpha}{2}\right]$ exhibits "double-degenerated" eigenvalues, which correspond to the following two eigenfunctions:

$$u_n(t) = A\cos(k_\alpha a n \pm \omega_\alpha t). \tag{11.20}$$

These waves correspond to left-ward and right-ward propagating waves. Since the "periodic boundary" condition has a somewhat ring shape, clockwise and counterclockwise waves can exist, which provide the "degeneration" of the two modes. In contrast, the "free end" or "fixed end" condition results in "standing waves". Taking an atomic distance "a", the wavelength Λ and wave "group velocity" v are expressed by

$$\Lambda = 2\pi a / k_\alpha, \tag{11.21a}$$

$$v = \Lambda\left(\frac{\omega_\alpha}{2\pi}\right) = 2\sqrt{\frac{K}{M}} \frac{\sin(k_\alpha/2)}{k_\alpha} a. \tag{11.21b}$$

Equation (11.21b) means that the wave velocity depends on the wavenumber; thus, a wave packet with a different frequency mixture distorts with time lapse. When considering only a long-wavelength range ($k_\alpha a \ll 1$), the wave velocity approaches $v_0 = 2\sqrt{K/M}a$, and $\omega \propto k$ is valid (no dispersion), which provides the Debye approximation for heat capacitance calculation in Section 11.1.4.

11.1.3. Phonon Spectral Density

1D Lattice Chain Model—Boundary Condition Difference

The density of modes in the 1D monatomic chain is considered. In this case, 1D chain with length L (Figure 11.1a) carries $(N - 1)$ modes under the "free end" condition. Each normal mode is a "standing wave" as follows:

$$u_n(\alpha) = \sqrt{\tfrac{2}{N}}\cos\tfrac{\alpha\pi}{N}\left(n-\tfrac{1}{2}\right) = \sqrt{\tfrac{2}{N}}\cos k_\alpha a\left(n-\tfrac{1}{2}\right)e^{-j\omega_a t} \quad (\alpha = 1,\ 2,\ \cdots,\ N-1), \tag{11.22}$$

$$\omega_\alpha = 2\sqrt{\frac{K}{M}}\sin\frac{k_\alpha a}{2}, \tag{11.23}$$

$$ka = \left(\frac{\alpha}{N}\right)\pi \text{ or} k_\alpha = \alpha\left(\frac{\pi}{L}\right)\ [L = Na]. \tag{11.24}$$

From Equation (11.24), eigenvalues (α = 1, 2, $\cdots$, $N - 1$) of a 1D lattice chain on the wave vector k distribute uniformly, as illustrated in Figure 11.3a(1). One eigenmode exists per every $\left(\frac{\pi}{L}\right)$ interval of wave vector k.

On the contrary, the results under "periodic" condition are slightly different, shown as follows:

$$u_n(\alpha) = \begin{cases} \sqrt{\frac{2-\delta_{\alpha,0}-\delta_{2[\frac{\alpha}{2}],N}}{N}}\cos\frac{2\pi n}{N}\left[\frac{\alpha}{2}\right] & (\alpha = \text{even number}) \\ \sqrt{\frac{2}{N}}\sin\frac{2\pi n}{N}\left[\frac{\alpha}{2}\right] & (\alpha = \text{odd number}) \end{cases}, \tag{11.25}$$

$$\omega_\alpha = 2\sqrt{\frac{K}{M}}\sin\frac{\pi}{N}\left[\frac{\alpha}{2}\right]\ (\alpha = 1,\ 2,\ 3,\ \cdots,\ N), \tag{11.26}$$

$$k_\alpha = \alpha'\left(\frac{2\pi}{L}\right)\alpha' = 0,\ \pm 1,\ \pm 2,\ \pm 3,\ \cdots,\ \pm N. \tag{11.27}$$

The Gauss symbol $\left[\frac{\alpha}{2}\right]$ usage in Equation (11.26) means two modes (even number n mode and smaller odd number $(n - 1)$ mode) give the same ω_α, that is, "double-degenerated" eigenvalues. Due to a "ring" connection of atom 1 and atom N, the clockwise and counterclockwise rotating waves generate the same energy (or frequency) wave on the ring (i.e., "degeneration"). The situation is visualized in Figure 11.3a(2). Refer also to Figure 14.29 in Chapter 14. From Equation (11.27), eigenvalues (α' = 1, 2, $\cdots$, $N - 1$, N) of a 1D lattice chain on the wave vector k distribute uniformly, but in this case, two eigenmodes exist per every $\left(\frac{2\pi}{L}\right)$ interval of wave vector k. Note again here that because "odd" and "even" number atoms are not identical in Equation (11.25), the unit cell size "a" seems to behave "$2a$", which provides the doubled interval ($2\pi/L$) in the k space.

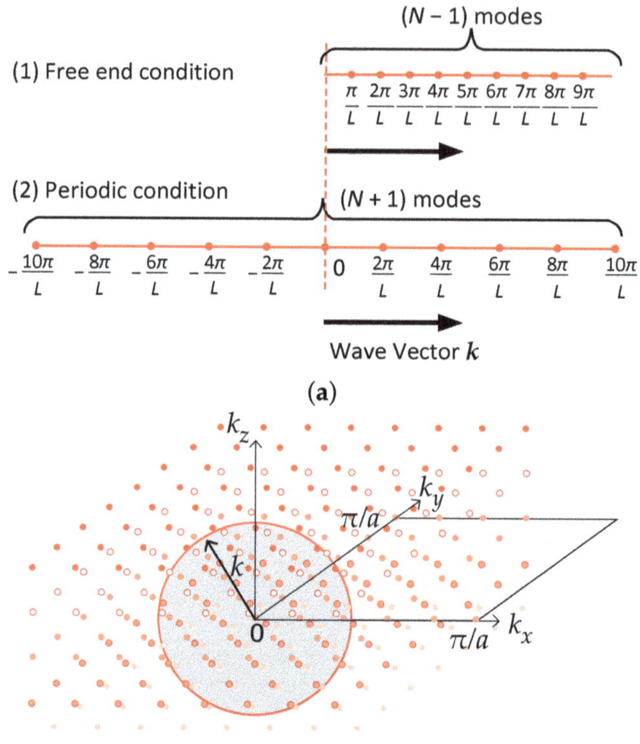

Figure 11.3. (**a**) Eigenvalue distribution difference of a 1D lattice chain on the wave vector k, depending on the boundary conditions: (1) free end and (2) periodic condition; (**b**) eigenvalue distribution of a 3D lattice on the wave vector $\boldsymbol{k}$. Source: Figure by author.

1D Lattice Chain Model—Density of Modes

Both "free-end" and "periodic" boundary conditions give basically similar mode density on the wave vector domain: one eigenmode per every $\left(\frac{\pi}{L}\right)$ interval of wave vector k $(0 < k < \pi/a)$ in the free end, and one eigenmodes per $\left(\frac{2\pi}{L}\right)$ interval of wave vector k $(-\pi/a < k < \pi/a)$ in the periodic (in other words, the same frequency has double-generated modes). As expressed in Equations (11.11) and (11.27), the phonon modes are uniformly distributed in terms of wavenumber k. However, in terms of frequency ω, the distribution is not uniform. Due to the sinusoidal relationship, $\omega \propto \sin\frac{ka}{2}$, the flat part of the dispersion curve in Figure 11.2a condenses phonon modes significantly.

Since the accumulated mode number N is expressed as $= N(k_\alpha) = \sum_0^{k_\alpha}(1) = \left(\frac{L}{\pi}\right)k_\alpha$, the mode density $D(k)$ in the integral form is uniform, given by $D(k)dk = \frac{\partial N}{\partial k}dk = \left(\frac{L}{\pi}\right)dk$. We are interested in the density of modes $D(\omega)$, which is defined as the number of modes per unit frequency range. From $D(k)dk = \left(\frac{L}{\pi}\right)dk$, the number of modes $D(\omega)d\omega$ in the interval ω to $\omega + d\omega$ is calculated in 1D lattice model by

$$D(\omega)d\omega = \left(\frac{L}{\pi}\right)\frac{dk}{d\omega}d\omega = \left(\frac{L}{\pi}\right)\frac{d\omega}{(d\omega/dk)}. \tag{11.28}$$

From Equation (11.23), $\omega_\alpha = 2\sqrt{\frac{K}{M}}\sin\frac{k_\alpha a}{2}$,

$$\left(\frac{d\omega}{dk}\right) = 2\sqrt{\frac{K}{M}}\frac{a}{2}\cos\frac{ka}{2} = \sqrt{\frac{K}{M}}a\sqrt{1-\left(\frac{M}{4K}\right)\omega^2}. \tag{11.29}$$

Accordingly,

$$D(\omega) = 2\left(\frac{N}{\pi}\right)/\sqrt{\left(\frac{4K}{M}\right)-\omega^2}. \tag{11.30}$$

The number of phonon eigenvalues that exist between the frequency ω and $(\omega + d\omega)$ is denoted as $Ng(\omega)d\omega$, where N is the total number of atoms and $g(\omega)$ is called "spectral density".

$$g(\omega) = \frac{D(\omega)}{N} = \left(\frac{2}{\pi}\right)/\sqrt{\omega_L{}^2-\omega^2}\left[\omega_L = 2\sqrt{K/M}\right] \tag{11.31}$$

Figure 11.2a inserted a "modified phonon spectral density" (i.e., "frequency square spectral density"), $G(\omega^2)$, which is defined as

$$\begin{aligned} G(\omega^2)d(\omega^2) &= 2\omega G(\omega^2)d\omega = g(\omega), \\ G(\omega^2) &= \tfrac{g(\omega)}{2\omega} = \tfrac{1}{\pi\omega\sqrt{\omega_L{}^2-\omega^2}}. \end{aligned} \tag{11.32}$$

As the reader can notice, there are two singularities in Equation (11.32); $\omega = 0$ and $\omega = \omega_L = 2\sqrt{K/M}]$ (ω_L is the maximum frequency of all eigenmodes). The modified phonon spectral density in Figure 11.2a exhibits two peaks around $\omega = 0$ and $\omega = \omega_L$, and symmetrical with respect to $\omega = \omega_L/2 = \sqrt{K/M}$, as anticipated.

3D Lattice Model—Density of Modes

We apply periodic boundary conditions on N^3 monatomic cells within a cube of side length L, so that $\mathbf{k}$ can be determined by the condition (similar to Equation (11.10)) as follows:

$$\exp\left[j(k_x x + k_y y + k_z z)\right] = \exp\left[j(k_x(x+L) + k_y(y+L) + k_z(z+L))\right]. \tag{11.33}$$

Thus,

$$k_x,\ k_y,\ k_z = 0,\ \pm\frac{2\pi}{L},\ \pm\frac{4\pi}{L},\ \pm\frac{6\pi}{L},\ \cdots,\ \pm\frac{N\pi}{L}. \tag{11.34}$$

We can state that there is one allowed mode per volume $\left(\frac{2\pi}{L}\right)^3$ in the $\boldsymbol{k}$ space of $-\frac{\pi}{a} < k_x, k_y, k_z < \frac{\pi}{a}$. Refer to Figure 11.3b. In other words, the mode density per unit volume of $\boldsymbol{k}$ can be described as

$$\left(\frac{L}{2\pi}\right)^3 = \frac{V}{8\pi^3}. \tag{11.35}$$

11.1.4. Lattice Heat Capacitance

Phonon Introduction

The reader now understands that there are N lattice vibration eigenmodes for N eigenvalues in the N-chain crystal lattice. As the actual crystal size includes the Avogadro number (10^{23} per mol) of atoms of N, the energy gap among eigenvalues is very small. It is worth noting that the vibration mode/energy discretization does not need to deduce the quantization. However, merely due to the analogy to the "photon" introduction by A. Einstein, who introduced the famous energy description with lightwave frequency as

$$E = \hbar\omega \left[\hbar = h/2\pi\,,\ \text{and } h = 6.626 \times 10^{-34}\text{J·s}\right], \tag{11.36}$$

the energy of a lattice vibration can be quantized. The quantum of energy is called a "phonon". Thermal vibrations in crystals can be explained by thermally excited phonons, such as the thermally excited photons of black-body electromagnetic radiation in a cavity. The reader may recall the "particle and wave duality" concept. The energy of an elastic model of angular frequency ω is expressed with using Planck's constant again,

$$E = \left(n + \frac{1}{2}\right)\hbar\omega \left[\hbar = h/2\pi\,,\ \text{and } h = 6.626 \times 10^{-34}\text{J·s}\right], \tag{11.37}$$

when the mode is excited to quantum number n, that is, when the mode is occupied by n phonons. The term $\left(\frac{1}{2}\right)\hbar\omega$ is the "zero-point energy" of the mode.

Planck Distribution

Let us consider a set of identical harmonic oscillators in thermal equilibrium. The ratio of the phonons (vibration modes) in their $(n+1)$th quantum state of excitation to the number of the n-th state is assumed to follow the Boltzmann (or Gibbs) distribution (the probability of a state is proportional to the Boltzmann factor related with its state energy), as shown below:

$$\frac{N_{n+1}}{N_n} = e^{-\frac{\hbar\omega}{k_B T}}, \tag{11.38}$$

where k_B is the Boltzmann constant, 1.381×10^{-23} (J/K). Thus, the fraction of the total number of phonons in the n-th quantum state is given by

$$\frac{N_n}{\sum_{\alpha=0}^{\infty} N_\alpha} = \frac{e^{-n\frac{\hbar\omega}{k_BT}}}{\sum_{\alpha=0}^{\infty} e^{-\alpha\frac{\hbar\omega}{k_BT}}} = \left(1 - e^{-\frac{\hbar\omega}{k_BT}}\right)e^{-n\frac{\hbar\omega}{k_BT}}. \quad (11.39)$$

Here, we used a formula $\sum_{\alpha=0}^{\infty} x^\alpha = \frac{1}{1-x}$ (assuming $x < 1$). The average excitation quantum number of a phonon can now be calculated as

$$\langle n \rangle = \frac{\sum_{n=0}^{\infty} ne^{-n\frac{\hbar\omega}{k_BT}}}{\sum_{\alpha=0}^{\infty} e^{-\alpha\frac{\hbar\omega}{k_BT}}} = \frac{\left[\frac{x}{(1-x)^2}\right]}{\left[\frac{1}{1-x}\right]} = \frac{e^{-\frac{\hbar\omega}{k_BT}}}{1 - e^{-\frac{\hbar\omega}{k_BT}}} = \frac{1}{e^{\frac{\hbar\omega}{k_BT}} - 1}. \quad (11.40)$$

Here, we used the first derivative of the above formula in terms of x, then multiplied by x: $\sum_{\alpha=0}^{\infty} \alpha x^\alpha = \frac{x}{(1-x)^2}$.

Lattice Heat Capacitance—Einstein Model

"Heat capacitance" of a material C_p is defined per unit volume (J/Km^3), while the "specific heat capacity" c_p is defined per unit mass (J/K·kg) so that $C_p = c_p \times \rho$, where ρ is mass density (kg/m^3). C_p is defined as the number of heat units to raise block of unit area and unit length (i.e., per unit volume) 1 °C in temperature (refer to next Chapter 12 for the details), formulated as

$$C_p = \frac{\partial Q}{\partial T} = T\frac{\partial S}{\partial T}, \quad (11.41)$$

where Q, S, and T are the heat quantity, entropy per volume (J/K·m^3), and absolute temperature (K).

According to the Gibbs (or Boltzmann) statistical dynamics for the equilibrium status, thermodynamical properties in a crystal lattice vibration are determined by the eigenvalues of the phonons. If we adopt the Planck distribution formula Equation (11.40),

$$\langle n \rangle = \frac{\sum_{n=0}^{\infty} ne^{-n\frac{\hbar\omega}{k_BT}}}{\sum_{\alpha=0}^{\infty} e^{-\alpha\frac{\hbar\omega}{k_BT}}} = \frac{1}{e^{\frac{\hbar\omega}{k_BT}} - 1} = \frac{1}{2}\left[\coth\left(\frac{\hbar\omega}{2k_BT}\right) - 1\right]. \quad (11.42)$$

Here, the final transformation used is

$$\frac{1}{e^{\frac{\hbar\omega}{k_BT}}-1} = \frac{1}{2}\frac{\left(1+e^{\frac{\hbar\omega}{k_BT}}\right)+\left(1-e^{\frac{\hbar\omega}{k_BT}}\right)}{e^{\frac{\hbar\omega}{k_BT}}-1} = \frac{1}{2}\left[\frac{\left(1+e^{\frac{\hbar\omega}{k_BT}}\right)}{e^{\frac{\hbar\omega}{k_BT}}-1} - 1\right] = \frac{1}{2}\left[\frac{\left(e^{\frac{\hbar\omega}{2k_BT}}+e^{-\frac{\hbar\omega}{2k_BT}}\right)}{\left(e^{\frac{\hbar\omega}{2k_BT}}-e^{-\frac{\hbar\omega}{2k_BT}}\right)} - 1\right].$$

As the average internal energy (i.e., thermal energy) of a phonon at frequency ω is expressed by $\langle n \rangle \hbar\omega$, for total N phonons, we may assume (under the supposition that phonons occupy all eigenmodes)

$$U = N\langle n \rangle \hbar\omega = \frac{N\hbar\omega}{e^{\frac{\hbar\omega}{k_B T}} - 1}. \tag{11.43}$$

The heat capacitance of the phonons is obtained as

$$C_p = \frac{\partial U}{\partial T} = Nk_B \left(\frac{\hbar\omega}{k_B T} \right)^2 \frac{e^{\frac{\hbar\omega}{k_B T}}}{\left[e^{\frac{\hbar\omega}{k_B T}} - 1 \right]^2}. \tag{11.44}$$

This simplest model is called the "Einstein model". In 3D and $3N$ degree of freedom's case, the above Nk_B should be replaced by $3Nk_B$. Figure 11.4 shows the temperature dependence of the heat capacitance calculated by the Einstein model in an insulating solid material, in comparison with that by the Debye approximation introduced in the next section. Temperature is normalized by $\theta_E = \hbar\omega / k_B$. At high temperature, both models approach $C_p = 3Nk_B$. Though it is not the real heat capacitance "per volume" when we use the Avogadro number N_A =6.022 × 10^{23} (Mole^{-1}), $3Nk_B$ is equal to 24.94 (J/K/mol) for any materials theoretically. This heat capacitance per mole is called the "Dulong–Petit value". At low temperature, Equation (11.44) decreases exponentially, as

$$C_p \propto e^{-\frac{\hbar\omega}{k_B T}}, \tag{11.45}$$

which is actually contradictory to the experimentally obtained results, that is, the empirical rule of $C_p \propto T^3$. Thus, the Debye model is proposed in the next subsection.

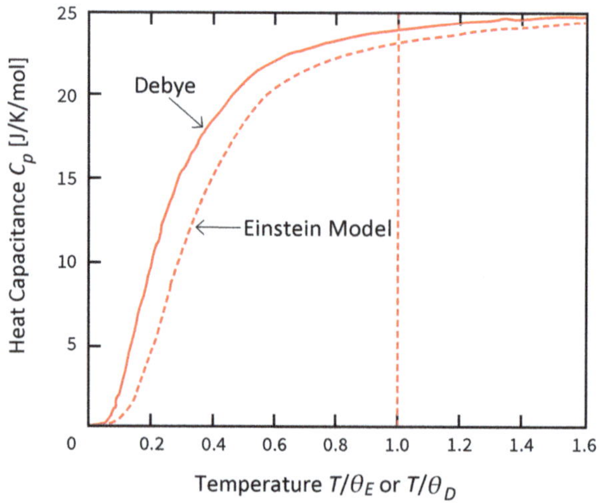

Figure 11.4. Comparison of the Einstein and Debye models' approximation to the heat capacitance. Source: Figure by author.

Lattice Heat Capacitance—Debye Model

Introduction to the Debye Model

Let us recall the semiconductor physics you have learned. Refer to Figure 11.5a, where the density of orbitals of the electron is plotted as a function of energy. The "Fermi level" is defined as almost the top electron energy level occupied by actual electrons in the bandgap structure (possible eigenmode alignment on the energy scale). As one eigenenergy level can be occupied by two electrons (up and down spin), in general (i.e., "degeneration"), about a half lower energy levels are occupied by the electrons, and the higher band part will be empty at low temperature. However, with increasing the temperature, owing to the thermal energy $k_B T$, trapped electrons (area 1) are excited to a higher level (area 2) according to Boltzmann distribution. The Debye model of phonon mode is analogous to this electron band occupancy model.

We have discussed monatomic lattice vibration discrete eigenmodes so far. The Einstein model calculated the average number $\langle n \rangle$ for all energy levels. Supposing that if the actual phonons occupy only lower energy levels (considering the degeneration), higher energy levels will be empty. The Debye model introduces this type of top frequency, which modifies the lattice heat capacitance formula from the Einstein model.

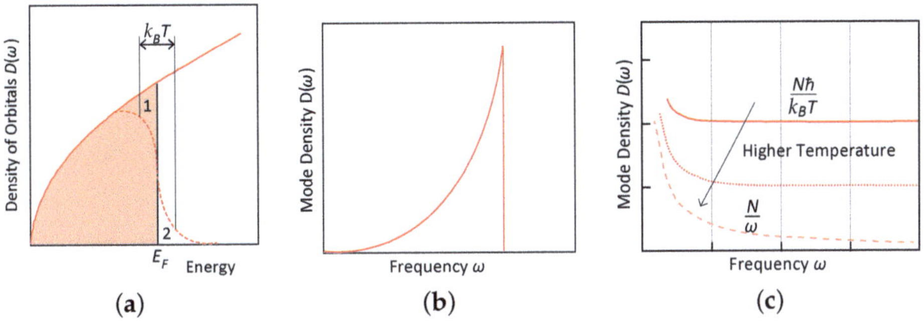

Figure 11.5. (**a**) Density of orbitals of electron as a function of energy; (**b**) phonon mode density as a function of frequency (Debye model); (**c**) phonon mode density vs. frequency (Einstein model). Source: Figure by author.

Mode Density Inclusion

The energy in thermal equilibrium of a collection of phones with various frequencies ω_k is given by

$$U = \sum_k n_k \hbar \omega_k. \tag{11.46}$$

It is mathematically convenient to replace the summation with an integral when the frequency discretion $\Delta\omega$ is sufficiently narrow in comparison with the frequency value ω, which is

$$\begin{aligned} U = \int dk[n(k)\hbar\omega(k)] = \int d\omega \left(\frac{\partial k}{\partial \omega}\right)[n(\omega,T)\hbar\omega] \\ = \int d\omega D(\omega)[n(\omega,T)\hbar\omega], \end{aligned} \tag{11.47}$$

where we defined

$$D(\omega) = \left(\frac{\partial k}{\partial \omega}\right). \tag{11.48}$$

The "mode density" $D(\omega)$ means that the crystal has $D(\omega)d\omega$ modes of vibration in the frequency range $(\omega,\ \omega + d\omega)$. This definition is equivalent to Equation (11.30) already discussed in the previous section.

Though we have not considered $D(\omega)$ explicitly in the Einstein's model calculation, we can obtain the mode density under the following assumption:

$$U = \int d\omega \frac{1}{\langle n \rangle}\left(\frac{\partial \langle n \rangle}{\partial \omega}\right)[N\langle n \rangle \hbar\omega] = \int d\omega D(\omega)[n(\omega, T)\hbar\omega]. \tag{11.49}$$

Recall that $\langle n \rangle$ is the average excitation quantum number of a phonon. Therefore,

$$D(\omega) = \frac{N}{\langle n \rangle}\left(\frac{\partial \langle n \rangle}{\partial \omega}\right) = N\left(\frac{\partial \ln \langle n \rangle}{\partial \omega}\right). \tag{11.50}$$

Knowing $\langle n \rangle = \frac{1}{e^{\frac{\hbar\omega}{k_B T}} - 1}$ (from Equation (11.42)), we obtain

$$D(\omega) = \frac{\hbar}{k_B T}\frac{N}{1 - e^{-\frac{\hbar\omega}{k_B T}}}. \tag{11.51}$$

Equation (11.51) is plotted for different temperatures in Figure 11.5c. For a low temperature

$$D(\omega) \rightarrow \frac{N\hbar}{k_B T}, \tag{11.52}$$

(the mode density is almost constant), while for a high temperature,

$$D(\omega) \rightarrow \frac{N}{\omega}. \tag{11.53}$$

The mode density decreases rapidly with frequency; the higher frequency modes will not contribute much.

Debye Approximation

In the Debye approximation, the "group velocity" of sound is constant: $\omega = v{\cdot}k$. This sound velocity (non-dispersive) formula can be derived from a general displacement description $u(x,t) \propto e^{j(kx-\omega t)}$ and $v = \frac{\partial x}{\partial t}$; that is, we consider only lower frequency range in Figure 11.2a, where we can keep $\sin x \approx x$,

$$\omega = 2\sqrt{\frac{K}{M}}\sin\frac{ka}{2} \approx \sqrt{\frac{K}{M}}ka. \tag{11.54}$$

In other words, the highest frequency ω_D mode occupied is lower than the sinusoidally saturating range. The total number of modes with wave vector less than k is given by the product of mode density Equation (11.35)

$\left(\frac{L}{2\pi}\right)^3 = \frac{V}{8\pi^3}$,

and the sphere volume of radius k_D in Figure 11.3b.

$$N = \frac{V}{8\pi^3}\left(\frac{4\pi}{3}k^3\right) = \frac{V}{6\pi^2 v^3}\omega^3. \quad (11.55)$$

The phonon mode density can be calculated as

$$D(\omega) = \frac{dN}{d\omega} = \frac{V}{2\pi^2 v^3}\omega^2, \quad (11.56)$$

which is illustrated in Figure 11.5b.

Using $\langle n \rangle$ in Equation (11.40), the thermal energy for 1D linear chain is given by

$$U = \int d\omega D(\omega)[n(\omega, T)\hbar\omega] = \int_0^{\omega_D} d\omega \left(\frac{V}{2\pi^2 v^3}\omega^2\right)\left(\frac{\hbar\omega}{e^{\frac{\hbar\omega}{k_B T}} - 1}\right). \quad (11.57)$$

The major difference from the "Einstein model" in Equation (11.43) can be found in (1) the limited integration range (up to ω_D) and (2) the mode density $D(\omega)$ introduction. Assuming again the sound velocity v is isotropic for 3D, the energy for 3D may be obtained just by multiplying factor three (each phonon has three degrees of freedom) on Equation (11.57) as follows:

$$U = \left(\frac{3V\hbar}{2\pi^2 v^3}\right)\int_0^{\omega_D} d\omega \left(\frac{\omega^3}{e^{\frac{\hbar\omega}{k_B T}} - 1}\right) = \left(\frac{3V(k_B T)^4}{2\pi^2 v^3 \hbar^3}\right)\int_0^{x_D} dx \left(\frac{x^3}{e^x - 1}\right), \quad (11.58)$$

where $x = \frac{\hbar\omega}{k_B T}$ and

$$x_D = \frac{\hbar\omega_D}{k_B T} = \theta_D / T. \quad (11.59)$$

Since the Debye temperature θ_D can be expressed as

$$\theta_D = \frac{\hbar v}{k_B} \cdot \left(\frac{6\pi^2 N}{V}\right)^{1/3}, \quad (11.60)$$

so that

$$U = 9Nk_B T (T/\theta_D)^3 \int_0^{x_D} dx \left(\frac{x^3}{e^x - 1}\right), \quad (11.61)$$

where N is the number of atoms in the specimen and $x_D = \theta_D / T$. The heat capacitance can be calculated by taking the first derivative of U in terms of T. As Equation (11.61) includes the integral, which is also dependent on T, we had better use the first equation in Equation (11.58) for further calculation.

$$C_p = \frac{\partial U}{\partial T} = \left(\frac{3V\hbar^2}{2\pi^2 v^3 k_B T^2}\right)\int_0^{\omega_D} d\omega \left(\frac{\omega^4 e^{\frac{\hbar\omega}{k_B T}}}{\left(e^{\frac{\hbar\omega}{k_B T}} - 1\right)^2}\right) = 9Nk_B (T/\theta_D)^3 \int_0^{x_D} dx \frac{x^4 e^x}{(e^x - 1)^2}. \quad (11.62)$$

The calculated result of C_p is shown in Figure 11.4. At high temperature $T \gg \theta_D$ the heat capacitance approaches the classical value $3Nk_B$, which is equal to 24.94 J/mole/K. At very low temperature, since x_D is large, the integral region can be approximated $x_D \to \infty$. Knowing a general relation $\int_0^\infty dx\left(\frac{x^3}{e^x-1}\right) = 6\sum_1^\infty \alpha^{-4} = \pi^4/15$, we obtain $U = 3\pi^4 Nk_B T^4/5\theta_D{}^3$, leading to

$$C_p = \frac{\partial U}{\partial T} = \frac{12\pi^4}{5} Nk_B (T/\theta_D)^3. \tag{11.63}$$

This is a famous "Debye T^3 Law".

11.2. Lattice Vibration—Diatomic Chain Model

11.2.1. 1D Lattice Diatomic Chain Model

We now consider the two-atom (mass M and m, rock-salt-like) 1D chain (total number of atoms $2N$) connected by a harmonic spring (spring constant K), as shown in Figure 11.1b [2,3]. The two-species atom, a closer model to actual "ionic" crystals, introduces a new concept on two categories, "acoustic" and "optical" branches, into the lattice vibration, which suggests a better idea on the spontaneous polarization induction. When we denote the displacement of the n-th atom from the equilibrium position as u_n in two species aligned alternately, the dynamic equations are expressed as

$$\begin{cases} -m\omega^2 u_{2n} = -K(u_{2n} - u_{2n+1}) - K(u_{2n} - u_{2n-1}) \\ -M\omega^2 u_{2n+1} = -K(u_{2n+1} - u_{2n}) - K(u_{2n+1} - u_{2n+2}) \end{cases}. \tag{11.64}$$

Mass m (or M) is located at an even (or odd) number lattice position and assuming the solutions

$$\begin{cases} \sqrt{m}u_{2n} = Qe_1 \exp(jkan) \\ \sqrt{M}u_{2n+1} = Qe_2 \exp(jkan) \end{cases}. \tag{11.65}$$

Note here that the unit cell length "a" above is doubled length in comparison with the monatomic chain model. Equation (11.64) can be calculated as

$$\begin{cases} \omega^2 e_1 = \frac{2K}{m} e_1 - \frac{K}{\sqrt{Mm}}[1 + exp(-jka)]e_2 \\ \omega^2 e_2 = -\frac{K}{\sqrt{Mm}}[1 + \exp(jka)]e_1 + \frac{2K}{M} e_2 \end{cases}. \tag{11.66}$$

In the matrix notation,

$$\omega^2 \boldsymbol{e} = D(k)\boldsymbol{e}, \tag{11.67}$$

$$\boldsymbol{e} \equiv \begin{pmatrix} e_1 \\ e_2 \end{pmatrix} \left(e_1{}^2 + e_2{}^2 = 1\right), \tag{11.68}$$

$$D(k) = \begin{pmatrix} \frac{2K}{m} & -\frac{K}{\sqrt{Mm}}[1 + \exp(-jka)] \\ -\frac{K}{\sqrt{Mm}}[1 + \exp(jka)] & \frac{2K}{M} \end{pmatrix}. \tag{11.69}$$

The lattice chain has a unit cell of size a with M and m atoms, which is double in comparison with the monatomic model, and e_1 and e_2 are the "polarization (displacement) vectors" of m (even number position) and M (odd number position), respectively. From Equation (11.67), the eigenvalue ω should satisfy

$$\omega^4 - 2K\left(\frac{1}{M} + \frac{1}{m}\right)\omega^2 + \frac{4K^2}{Mm}\sin^2\left(\frac{ka}{2}\right) = 0. \tag{11.70a}$$

The solution of the above equation is given by

$$\omega_{\pm}{}^2(k) = K\left\{\frac{1}{m} + \frac{1}{M} \pm \sqrt{\left(\frac{1}{m} + \frac{1}{M}\right)^2 - \frac{4}{Mm}\sin^2\left(\frac{ka}{2}\right)}\right\}. \tag{11.70b}$$

We assume there are N unit cells with two M and m atoms in the unit cell ($2N$ atoms in total), with a unit cell size of a, and the "period boundary condition" is adopted in this model. For $N \to \infty$, the summation equation is converted to an integral equation, and ka will vary from $-\pi$ to π. At $k = 0$,

$$\omega_{\pm}{}^2(0) = \begin{cases} 0 \\ 2K\left(\frac{1}{m} + \frac{1}{M}\right) \end{cases}, \tag{11.71a}$$

while, at $k = \pi/a$, from $\omega_{\pm}{}^2(\pi/a) = K\left[\left(\frac{1}{m} + \frac{1}{M}\right) \pm \left(\frac{1}{m} - \frac{1}{M}\right)\right]$ [supposing $M > m$]

$$\omega_{\pm}{}^2(\pi/a) = \begin{cases} 2K/M \\ 2K/m \end{cases}. \tag{11.71b}$$

11.2.2. Dispersion Curve of Diatomic Chain Model

Comparison of the Dispersion Curves among Diatomic and Nonatomic Models

Figure 11.2b illustrates the dispersion curves, plotted in the ka range of $-\pi \sim \pi$ (because of the period symmetry). There are two branches in the vibration modes with a frequency gap between $\sqrt{2K/M}$ and $\sqrt{2K/m}$ at the "Brillouin zone" ends $k = -\pi/a$ and π/a, where no solution (i.e., phonon mode) exists.

If we take the case of $M = m$, this gap should disappear and the dispersion curve should also be equivalent to that of the one-atom model in Figure 11.2a. How should we translate the still-remaining two branches in the diatomic model into one branch in the monatomic model? The reader can imagine the twofold sine curve in Figure 11.2a at $k = -\pi/2a$ or$\pi/2a$, so that we can generate basically two branches. Since the unit cell of the diatomic chain "a" is actually "$2a$" in the monatomic model, the unit cell in the k space should correspond to "$\pi/2a$" in the monatomic model.

Origin of Frequency Gap

Basically, there are two different resonance frequency oscillators—one is mass M connected with two springs $2K$ ($\omega = \sqrt{2K/M}$), and the other is mass m connected with two springs $2K$ ($\omega = \sqrt{2K/m}$). Depending on the mode (optical or acoustic), these resonance frequencies reflect directly without allowing the vibration frequencies in between. The frequency in between these two frequencies becomes "imaginary" from Equation (11.70b).

Flatness of the Dispersion Curves at the Brillouin Zone

In addition to the frequency gap at the Brillouin zone, the reader can notice the flatness of the dispersion curves, which indicates a somewhat "singularity" of the mode density such as

$$D(\omega) = \left(\frac{2N}{\pi}\right) / \sqrt{\omega_m{}^2 - \omega^2}, \tag{11.72}$$

similar to Equation (11.31). This can be verified from Equation (11.70b): by taking the first derivative of Equation (11.70b), then putting $k = -\pi/a$ or π/a, we can obtain "zero" as follows:

$$\begin{aligned} \frac{d}{dk}\omega_\pm{}^2(k) &= \frac{d}{dk}\left[K\left(\frac{1}{m}+\frac{1}{M}\right)^2 \pm \sqrt{\left(\frac{1}{m}+\frac{1}{M}\right)^2 - \frac{4}{Mm}\sin^2\left(\frac{ka}{2}\right)}\right] \\ &= \mp\frac{\frac{4a}{Mm}\sin\left(\frac{ka}{2}\right)\cos\left(\frac{ka}{2}\right)}{\sqrt{\left(\frac{1}{m}+\frac{1}{M}\right)^2 - \frac{4}{Mm}\sin^2\left(\frac{ka}{2}\right)}} \\ &= 0 \leftarrow \left[\cos\left(\frac{\pi}{2}\right) = 0\right]. \end{aligned} \tag{11.73}$$

11.2.3. Optical and Acoustic Modes

Difference among Optical and Acoustic Modes

$\omega_+{}^2(k)$ corresponds to the upper curve, which is called the "optical branch". This branch approaches to ω_L with $k \to 0$

$$\omega_L = \sqrt{2K\left(\frac{1}{m}+\frac{1}{M}\right)}. \tag{11.74}$$

Around $k = 0$, the "polarization vector" e satisfies

$$\sqrt{m}e_1 + \sqrt{M}e_2 = 0, \tag{11.75}$$

which indicates that the two species of atoms move in opposite directions by keeping the center of gravity position. When we consider ionic crystals such as rock salt (or PZT), Na^+ and Cl^- ions move in opposite directions, leading to the electric polarization deviation. This phonon mode can easily couple with the external electric field such as "optical light" electric wave, in particular, "infrared" light; thus, it is called the "optical branch".

On the contrary, the lower branch $\omega_-{}^2(k)$ in Figure 11.2b is called the "acoustic branch". This branch approaches $\omega \propto k$ with $k \to 0$, which is a long-wavelength vibration transfer with a constant wave speed. The polarization vector $\boldsymbol{e}$ satisfies the following condition at $k = 0$:

$$\sqrt{m}e_1 = \sqrt{M}e_2. \tag{11.76}$$

Two species of atoms displace in the same direction with the same amplitude. Thus, no electric polarization is induced.

Visualization of Optical and Acoustical Modes

The above argument is visualized in Figure 11.6, which shows acoustical and optical waves in a 1D diatomic lattice chain, illustrated by the mass (shown as + and − ions) displacements (longitudinal displacements are illustrated vertically for the visual simplicity) for the modes for different wavelengths near zero to the "Brillouin zone edge" ($k = \pi/a$). The optical mode at $k \approx 0$ (Figure 11.6, top-right image) seems to be a ferroelectric phase with spontaneous polarization if this mode is "softening", while the acoustic modes do not generate the electric dipole moments (Figure 11.6, top-left image). In this simple illustration, the acoustical and optical modes at $k = \pi/a$ are apparently indistinguishable (Figure 11.6, bottom).

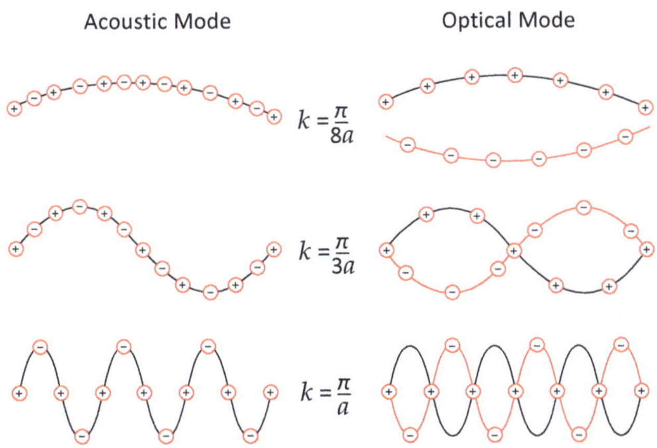

Figure 11.6. Optical and acoustical waves in a 1D diatomic lattice chain, illustrated by the mass displacements for the modes for different wavelengths near zero to the Brillouin zone ($k = \pi/a$). Source: Figure by author.

11.2.4. Phonon Spectral Density

As you may recognize, the phonon modes are uniformly distributed in terms of "wave number" k. However, in terms of frequency ω, the distribution is not uniform but clustered. Due to the sinusoidal relationship, $\omega \propto \sin\frac{ka}{2}$ (Equation (11.28b)), the flat parts of the dispersion curve in Figure 11.2b condense phonon modes significantly. The number of phonon eigenvalues that exist between the frequency ω and $(\omega + d\omega)$ is denoted as $D(\omega)d\omega = Ng(\omega)d\omega$, where N is the total number of atoms and $g(\omega)$ is called "spectral density". Figure 11.2b inserted a "frequency square spectral density", $G(\omega^2) = \frac{g(\omega)}{2\omega} = \frac{1}{\pi\omega\sqrt{\omega_L{}^2-\omega^2}}$. Notice the difference from Figure 11.2a, that is, the peak of $D(\omega)$ can be found in both acoustical and optical branches.

11.3. Ferroelectric Phase Transition

11.3.1. "Soft Phonon" Mode

Recall the discussion on the origin of spontaneous polarization in Section 1.2.3. Why does a particular crystal experience the shifting of cations and anions and become spontaneously polarized? The reason is briefly explained below. For simplicity, we assume that dipole moments result from the displacement of one type of ion relative to the crystal lattice. This kind of ionic displacement can be expected through lattice vibrations at a finite temperature. Figure 11.7 shows some of the possible "eigen-lattice vibrations" in a perovskite-like crystal: (a) shows an initial cubic (symmetrical) structure; (b) is a symmetrically elongated one (i.e., no polarization is generated), which corresponds to an "acoustic mode"; (c) has coherently shifted center cations (i.e., the right-ward polarization), which corresponds to an "optical mode"; (d) exhibits an antipolarized shift of the center cations (i.e., no net polarization). You can imagine easily the similarity of Figure 11.7 to the discussions conducted on the "two-atom chain mode" above. If one particular lattice vibration lowers the crystal energy, the ions will shift and stabilize the crystal structure so as to minimize the energy. Starting from the original cubic structure (a), if (b) is stabilized (acoustical mode at $k \approx 0$), only a phase with oxygen octahedra distorted with no dipole moment (acoustic mode) is induced, that is, "structural phase transition". On the other hand, when (c) (optical mode at $k \approx 0$) or (d) (optical mode at $k = \pi/a$) is stabilized, dipole moments are generated, leading to "polar/ferroelectric" and "antipolar/antiferroelectric" states, respectively. If a particular mode becomes stabilized, the vibration mode frequency decreases (i.e., "soft phonon mode"), and finally at a certain phase transition temperature, this frequency approaches zero. The phonon softening is originated from the phonon–phonon coupling under a nonlinear spring model, as we will discuss in Chapter 14.

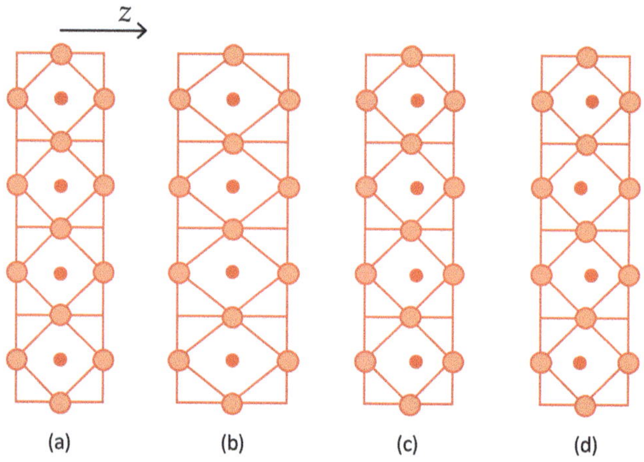

Figure 11.7. Some possible eigen-lattice vibration modes in a perovskite crystal. Source: [5] ©Uchino, K. *Ferroelectric Devices*, 2nd ed. CRC Press, 2010; p. 4. Reproduced by permission of Taylor & Francis Group.

11.3.2. Local Field Lorentz Factor

What kind of energy motivates the dipole generation in a crystal? In a simple word, it is the "Lorentz factor". At any individual ion site, there exists a local field from the surrounding polarization $\boldsymbol{P}$, even if there is no external field. The "local field" can be described as

$$\boldsymbol{E}^{loc} = \boldsymbol{E_0} + \sum\nolimits_{i}[3(\boldsymbol{p_i}\cdot\boldsymbol{r_i})\boldsymbol{r_i} - \boldsymbol{r_i}^2\boldsymbol{p_i}]/4\pi\varepsilon_0\boldsymbol{r_i}^5 = (\gamma/3\varepsilon_0)\boldsymbol{P}. \tag{11.77}$$

Here, γ is called the "Lorentz factor" (tensor parameter in general). Though the electric field from the dipole moment diminishes rather quickly with increasing the distance r ($\propto 1/r^3$), since there are so many dipoles in a condensed material as the Avogadro number (6.022×10^{23} mol^{-}1), the local field E^{loc} is sometimes much larger than the externally applied field E_0. For an ideally isotropic cubic system, it is known that $\gamma = 1$, but in some crystals, $\gamma = 10$ (significantly large) [6]. ε_0 is the permittivity of vacuum and is equal to 8.854×10^{-12} F/m. If the "ionic polarizability" of our focusing ion is α, then the dipole moment of the unit cell of this crystal is given by

$$\mu = (\alpha\gamma/3\varepsilon_0)\boldsymbol{P}. \quad (11.78)$$

Thus, the energy of this dipole moment ("dipole–dipole coupling") is given by

$$w_{dip} = -\boldsymbol{\mu}\boldsymbol{E}^{loc} = -(\alpha\gamma^2/9\varepsilon_0{}^2)\boldsymbol{P}^2. \quad (11.79)$$

We can understand that the mechanism seems to be a "positive feedback"; that is, once a small fluctuation of P occurs in a crystal, which enhances the local field E^{loc} by a factor of γ, then the dipole–dipole coupling energy w_{dip} decreases by a factor of "γ squared". In other words, the polarized state becomes stabilized with an increase in P. Defining N to be the number of atoms per unit volume, the dipole–dipole coupling energy per unit volume is expressed as

$$W_{dip} = Nw_{dip} = -(N\alpha\gamma^2/9\varepsilon_0{}^2)\boldsymbol{P}^2. \quad (11.80)$$

This is the spontaneous polarization motivation principle. However, the ionic separation does not continue but stops because of the suppression force from the atomic spring property. When the ions are displaced from their nonpolar equilibrium positions, the elastic energy also increases, which stops the cation–anion ionic separation (see Figure 11.1b). Different from the pure harmonic spring model in Section 11.1.2, we introduce higher-order anharmonicity, force constants k and k', for the ionic displacement u. Then, the increase in the elastic energy per unit volume can be expressed as

$$W_{elas} = N[(k/2)\boldsymbol{u}^2 + (k'/4)\boldsymbol{u}^4], \quad (11.81)$$

where k' (>0) is the higher-order force constant. It should be noted that in pyroelectrics (i.e., polar status), k' plays an important role in determining the magnitude of the dipole moment (i.e., "electrothermal coupling"). Rewriting Equation (11.81) with polarization, we obtain

$$\boldsymbol{P} = Nq\boldsymbol{u}, \quad (11.82)$$

where q and N are the electric charges and the number of dipoles per unit volume, and combining with Equation (11.80), the total energy can be expressed as follows (see Figure 11.8):

$$W_{tot} = W_{dip} + W_{elas} = [(k/2Nq^2) - (N\alpha\gamma^2/9\varepsilon_0{}^2)]\boldsymbol{P}^2 + [k'/4N^3q^4]\boldsymbol{P}^4. \quad (11.83)$$

From this, one can see that if the coefficient of the harmonic term ($k/2Nq^2$) of the elastic energy is equal to or greater than the coefficient of the dipole–dipole coupling ($N\alpha\gamma^2/9\varepsilon_0{}^2$), then $P = 0$; the ions are stable and remain at the nonpolar equilibrium positions. However, if $[(k/2Nq^2) - (N\alpha\gamma^2/9\varepsilon_0{}^2)] < 0$, because W_{tot} exhibits negative parabolic around the region $P \approx 0$, more stable state can be found with a shift from the equilibrium position (from $\frac{\partial W_{tot}}{\partial P} = 0$) as

$$\boldsymbol{P_S}^2 = [(2N\alpha\gamma^2/9\varepsilon_0{}^2) - (k/Nq^2)]/[k'/N^3q^4]. \tag{11.84}$$

Therefore, in order to realize the above spontaneous polarization stabilization, the following conditions should be satisfied:

(1) The Lorentz factor γ should be sufficiently large (crystal structure dependent);
(2) The ionic polarizability α of the focusing ion should be sufficiently large (ionic species dependent);
(3) If the polarizability α decreases with an increase in temperature, "double-minima" to "single-minimum" phase transition is expected at a certain temperature, which satisfies Equation (11.84) = 0.

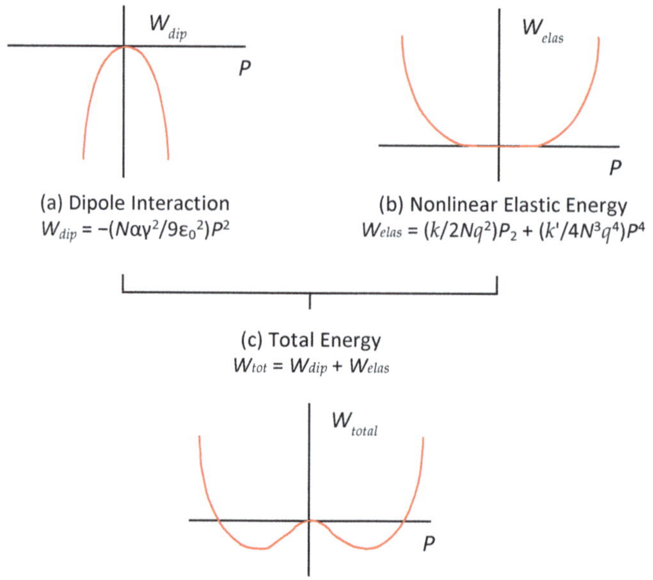

Figure 11.8. Energy explanation of the origin of spontaneous polarization: (**a**) dipole interaction—motivation to promote the dipole moment; (**b**) elastic energy—deceleration not to increase the dipole; (**c**) total energy—double minima to realize the spontaneous polarization. Source: Figure by author, adapted from [5].

Example Problem 11.1.

Knowing that the electric field at a distance $\boldsymbol{r}$ from a dipole moment $\boldsymbol{p}$ is given by $[3(\boldsymbol{p}\cdot\boldsymbol{r})\boldsymbol{r} - r^2\boldsymbol{p}]/4\pi\varepsilon_0 r^5$ (see Example Problem 1.1), the Lorentz local field in a crystal is described as

$$\boldsymbol{E}^{loc} = \boldsymbol{E}_0 + \sum_i \left[3(\mathbf{p_i}\cdot\mathbf{r}_i)\boldsymbol{r}_i - \mathbf{r}_i^2\mathbf{p}_i\right]/4\pi\varepsilon_0 \boldsymbol{r}^5. \tag{P11.1.1}$$

Calculate the Lorentz field along the z-axis E_z^{loc} for a uniform (simple cubic) crystal with all $\boldsymbol{p}_z$ parameters aligned.

Solution

Under an external electric field $\boldsymbol{E}_0$, dipole moment $\boldsymbol{p}$ is induced along the z-axis in a uniform crystal. We consider a small hypothetical sphere cavity in the crystal. Since the dipole charges are compensated in a uniform crystal, the bound charges existing on the cavity surface, as illustrated in Figure 11.9, will be the origin of the local field. We consider the charge distribution on a narrow ring band because of the z-axis crystal symmetry. The surface charge density (per unit area) of the cavity should be effectively "$-P\cos\theta$" (think + and − charge distribution), resulting in charge on the ring ($2\pi a\sin\theta \cdot ad\theta \cdot P\cos\theta$). Considering Coulomb's law from a charge, $E_r = q/4\pi\varepsilon_0 r^2$, the z-component is given by the direction cosine component, $E_z = E_r\cos\theta$.

Now, the local field E_z^{loc} can be calculated as

$$\begin{aligned} E_z^{loc} &= E_0 + \left(\frac{1}{4\pi\varepsilon_0}\right)\int_0^\pi [2\pi a\sin\theta \cdot ad\theta \cdot P\cos\theta]\cdot(\cos\theta)/a^2 \\ &= E_0 + \left(\frac{P}{2\varepsilon_0}\right)\int_0^\pi (\sin\theta\cdot\cos\theta\cdot\cos\theta)d\theta = E_0 + \left(\frac{P}{2\varepsilon_0}\right)\left(\frac{1}{4}\right)\int_0^\pi (\sin\theta + \sin 3\theta)d\theta \\ &= E_0 + \left(\frac{1}{3\varepsilon_0}\right)P. \end{aligned} \quad \text{(P11.1.2)}$$

In consideration of the Lorentz factor definition Equation (11.77), the $\gamma = 1$ is a uniform cubic symmetry dielectric.

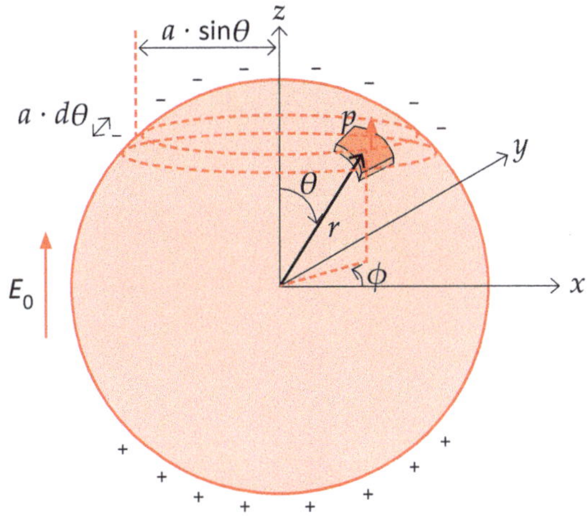

Figure 11.9. Spherical coordinate for the Lorentz field calculation. Source: Figure by author.

11.3.3. Modified Lorentz Factor in Barium Titanate

We consider now why $BaTiO_3$ (BT) exhibits extraordinarily large Lorentz factor γ, in comparison with NaCl, where $\gamma = 1$. This is the key to slowing down the phonon frequency and stabilizing the ferroelectric phase. We introduce here the Devonshire–Slater theory [7,8], in which it is assumed that the BT crystal is electrically poled along the z-axis; thus, all the ions are polarized also along the z-axis. All equivalent ions are assigned from 1 to 5 (Ba = 1, Ti = 2, O = 3, 4, and 5) in the mother phase cubic BT crystal, as shown in Figure 11.10. Knowing each ionic sublattice in a "simple cubic structure", which results in $\gamma = 1$ at each lattice point, the founders of the theory assumed the local electric field at an off-lattice point (u, v, w) to be different from $\left(\frac{P}{3\varepsilon_0}\right)$, expressed as

$$E^{loc} = E_0 + \left(\frac{1}{\varepsilon_0}\right)\left[\frac{1}{3} + S(u, v, w)\right]P, \tag{11.85}$$

where $S(u, v, w)$ is the crystal-structure-dependent modulation of the γ factor from (1/3). The normalized coordinates, (u, v, w), are based on the unit lattice parameter. McKeehan [9,10] and Luttinger–Tisza [11] calculated $S(u, v, w)$ when the dipoles are aligned also along the z-axis and obtained the following results:

$$\begin{cases} S(0, 0, 0) = S\left(\frac{1}{2}, \frac{1}{2}, \frac{1}{2}\right) = 0 \\ S\left(0, \frac{1}{2}, \frac{1}{2}\right) = 0.3448 \\ S\left(\frac{1}{2}, \frac{1}{2}, 0\right) = -0.6896 \\ S\left(\frac{1}{2}, 0, 0\right) = -1.196 \\ S\left(0, 0, \frac{1}{2}\right) = 2.392 \end{cases}. \tag{11.86}$$

Note that the structural relations $S\left(\frac{1}{2}, \frac{1}{2}, 0\right) = -2 \cdot S\left(0, \frac{1}{2}, \frac{1}{2}\right)$ and $S\left(0, 0, \frac{1}{2}\right) = -2 \cdot S\left(\frac{1}{2}, 0, 0\right)$. It is important to understand that the detailed crystal structure (here, perovskite) exhibits the enhancement of the local field, different from the situation in a simple cubic NaCl type (i.e., $\gamma = 1$).

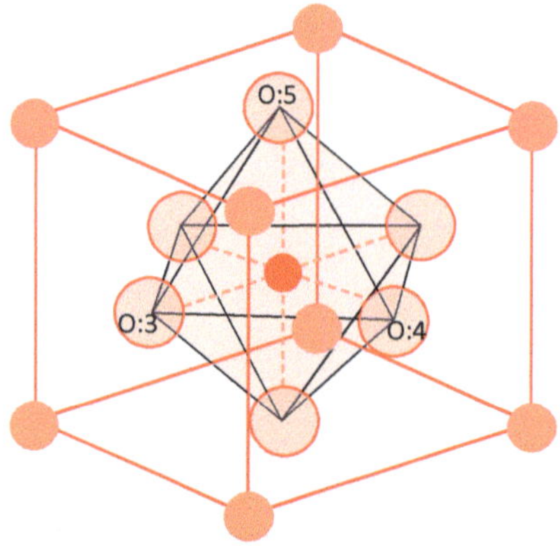

Figure 11.10. Unit cell of $BaTiO_3$ with numbers on the ions: Ba: 1, Ti: 2, and O: 3, 4, 5. Source: Figure by author.

Let us calculate the local field explicitly for each ion position. For example, E_1^{loc} at the Ba ion position can be calculated from self P_1, Ti ion P_2, and three O ion P_3, P_4 and P_5. Since $S(0, 0, 0) = S\left(\frac{1}{2}, \frac{1}{2}, \frac{1}{2}\right) = 0$, the first two contributions are purely 1/3 (simple cubic structure). While the contributions from equivalent P_3 and P_4 are $S\left(\frac{1}{2}, 0, \frac{1}{2}\right)$ and $S\left(0, \frac{1}{2}, \frac{1}{2}\right)$, respectively, and that from P_5 is $S\left(\frac{1}{2}, \frac{1}{2}, 0\right)$. It is important to take into account the number of ions and their unit lattice contribution; that is, O is aligned in two symmetric positions and the oxygen ion is situated on the face center (i.e., a half contribution), leading to "one" contribution to a unit cell. For another example, E_2^{loc} at the Ti ion position can be calculated from self P_2, Ba ion P_1, and three O ion P_3, P_4 and P_5. Since $S(0,\ 0,\ 0) = S\left(\frac{1}{2},\ \frac{1}{2},\ \frac{1}{2}\right) = 0$, the first two contributions are again purely 1/3 (simple cubic structure), while the contributions from equivalent P_3 and P_4 are $S\left(0,\ \frac{1}{2},\ 0\right)$ and $S\left(\frac{1}{2},\ 0,\ 0\right)$, respectively, and that from P_5 is $S\left(0,\ 0,\ \frac{1}{2}\right)$. All results including other local fields at oxygen positions are summarized as follows:

$$\begin{pmatrix} E_1^{loc} \\ E_2^{loc} \\ E_3^{loc} \\ E_4^{loc} \\ E_5^{loc} \end{pmatrix} = E_0 + \left(\frac{1}{\varepsilon_0}\right) \begin{pmatrix} \frac{1}{3} & \frac{1}{3} & \frac{1}{3}+\frac{1}{2}p & \frac{1}{3}+\frac{1}{2}p & \frac{1}{3}-p \\ \frac{1}{3} & \frac{1}{3} & \frac{1}{3}-\frac{1}{2}q & \frac{1}{3}-\frac{1}{2}q & \frac{1}{3}+q \\ \frac{1}{3}+\frac{1}{2}p & \frac{1}{3}-\frac{1}{2}q & \frac{1}{3} & \frac{1}{3}-p & \frac{1}{3}+\frac{1}{2}p \\ \frac{1}{3}+\frac{1}{2}p & \frac{1}{3}-\frac{1}{2}q & \frac{1}{3}-p & \frac{1}{3} & \frac{1}{3}+\frac{1}{2}p \\ \frac{1}{3}-p & \frac{1}{3}+q & \frac{1}{3}+\frac{1}{2}p & \frac{1}{3}+\frac{1}{2}p & \frac{1}{3} \end{pmatrix} \begin{pmatrix} P_1 \\ P_2 \\ P_3 \\ P_4 \\ P_5 \end{pmatrix}. \tag{11.87}$$

Here, we used the notations, $p = -S\left(\frac{1}{2},\ \frac{1}{2},\ 0\right) = 0.6896$ and $q = S\left(0,\ 0,\ \frac{1}{2}\right) = 2.392$ for simplicity. The reader can notice that the contribution of q is significant and that the most amplified Lorentz factor $\left(\frac{1}{3}+q\right)$ is found in two terms, $E_2^{loc} = \cdots\cdots + \left(\frac{1}{3}+q\right)P_5$ and $E_5^{loc} = \cdots + \left(\frac{1}{3}+q\right)P_2 + \cdots$. We may conclude that the Lorentz field enhancement is primarily originated from Ti: 2 and O: 5 (aligned along the z-axis) interaction, which may be originated from the hybridization among the dumbbell shape d_z orbital of the Ti^{4+} and the dumbbell shape p_z orbital of the O^{2-}.

Both large γ and large polarizability are essential to amplify the dipole coupling energy to promote the ionic separation to initiate the spontaneous polarization in a crystal. Taking into account the polarizability α_k of the ion k, we can denote the polarization as

$$P_k = \alpha_k E_k^{loc}/v \quad (v : \text{unit cell volume}). \tag{11.88}$$

Inserting Equation (11.88) into Equation (11.87), we can obtain the simultaneous equations of P_k in terms of E_0 and α_k. Then, we obtain the total polarization $P = \sum_k P_k$ as a function of the external field E_0 and obtain the permittivity equation. As the Lorentz field enhancement is primarily originated from Ti: 2 and O: 5 (aligned along the z-axis) interaction, Slater assumed that the polarizabilities of Ba and O are merely from electronic polarization, but only the Ti polarizability is composed of both ionic and electronic polarizations, which is

$$\alpha_2 = \alpha_2^{ion} + \alpha_2^{el}. \tag{11.89}$$

By using the electronic polarizabilities of all ions obtained from optical measurement, he obtained the permittivity expression as a function of α_2^{ion}

$$\varepsilon = 3.84 + \frac{1.93}{1 - 5.39\left(\frac{4\pi\alpha_2^{ion}}{v}\right)}. \tag{11.90}$$

His conclusion is summarized as follows:

(1) Overall, 37% of the spontaneous polarization comes from Ti ion (31% from α_2^{ion} and 6% from α_2^{el});

(2) A total of 59% of P_S comes from α_5^{el} of O: 5, and 6% from other oxygens α_3^{el} and α_4^{el};

(3) Only 2% is from α_1^{el} of Ba: 1.

The origin of the spontaneous polarization in $BaTiO_3$ comes primarily from (1) enhanced Lorentz factor γ at the Ti position and (2) enhanced ionic polarizability of the Ti ion (i.e., Ti ion shift is easiest among all ions) in the z-direction chain Ti-O-Ti-O of a $BaTiO_3$ crystal.

In order to simulate the spontaneous polarization magnitude, we also need to find out the origin of nonlinear elastic constant k' (i.e., anharmonicity) in Equation (11.81), which is considered in Chapter 14.

11.4. Nonlinear Elastic Performances in the Crystal Lattice

Important nonlinear equilibrium effects include the "thermal expansion" and "electrostriction" originated from the lattice spring nonlinearity and nonequilibrium effect, whereas the "thermal conductivity" originated from the anharmonic dynamic lattice vibration. Heat transport in dielectric solids is by way of elastic dynamic vibrations of the lattice (i.e., phonons) [2], which is discussed in Chapter 12. Since Chapter 14 describes the details of "nonlinear oscillatory systems", this section provides a simple introduction to them.

11.4.1. Nonlinearity in Crystal Potential

When we use the theory of cohesive forces in ionic crystals, proposed by Born [12], we can set the potential function involving an inverse power type of repulsive energy of the form in a simple crystal-like NaCl as

$$U = -\frac{Mq^2}{r} + \frac{Nb}{r^n}, \tag{11.91}$$

where M is the Madelung constant for Coulombic energy, N is the coordination number, and b is the potential constant for the quantum mechanical energy [13]. We assume a relatively large number, 9–11, for quantum mechanical repulsive potential $1/r^n$. Expanding the potential function around the equilibrium position ($r_0^{n-1} = nNb/Mq^2$), we obtain the following form as a function of Δr (= $r - r_0$):

$$\Delta U = U(r) - U(r_0) = f(\Delta r)^2 - g(\Delta r)^3, \tag{11.92}$$

where $f = (n-1)Mq^2/2r_0^3$ and $g = (n+4)(n-1)Mq^2/6r_0^4$. It is essential to realize the curvature difference in the positive and negative region; that is, the lattice spring is softer for extension than for contraction.

11.4.2. Thermal Expansion and Electrostriction

The ionic displacement Δr is supposed to be generated under small electric field (E) applied and under finite temperature T. Using the Boltzmann distribution for

Gibbs energy $\Delta V_{\pm} = \Delta U \pm qE\Delta r$, the average equilibrium separation at an elevated temperature under an applied electric field E is approximated as follows:

$$\begin{aligned} < \Delta r_{\pm} > &\sim \int_{-\infty}^{\infty} \Delta r \exp\left(-\frac{\Delta V_{\pm}}{kT}\right) d\Delta r / \int_{-\infty}^{\infty} \exp\left(-\frac{\Delta V_{\pm}}{kT}\right) d\Delta r \\ &\sim \frac{3gk}{4f^2} T \pm \frac{q}{2f} E + \frac{3gq^2}{4f^3} E^2, \end{aligned} \tag{11.93}$$

where subscripts $\pm$ denote the ion pairs in the positive and negative directions of the electric field, respectively. The strain is therefore given by

$$\frac{< \Delta r_{+} > + < \Delta r_{-} >}{2r_0} = \frac{3gk}{4f^2 r_0} T + \frac{3gq^2}{4f^3 r_0} E^2, \tag{11.94}$$

where the first term represents thermal expansion and the second term, electrostriction (no piezoelectricity is expected in this cubic symmetry). Due to the softer lattice spring performance for extension, thermal expansion (i.e., positive strain) is observed. The reader can understand that both coefficients are originated from "g", which is an anharmonic term $g(\Delta r)^3$ in Equation (11.92), and that neither thermal expansion nor electrostriction occurs when the crystal is rigorously harmonic (that is, only $f(\Delta r)^2$ term in Equation (11.92)).

11.4.3. Anharmonic Phonon Modes and Thermal Conductivity

Thermal energy can be stored in the lattice vibration normal phonon modes (i.e., harmonic) as a vibration amplitude. We obtained heat capacitance for harmonic lattice vibration models in this chapter. However, in a rigorously harmonic crystal, the phonon states are stationary (i.e., "standing wave"), widespread in the crystal uniformly with a monotone frequency as a wave (not an isolated wave packet or particle-like phonon). Since phonon vibration is not disturbed by dopants, for example, we can state that the thermal resistance is zero, or thermal conductivity is infinite, leading to a completely uniform temperature distribution in a crystal [2]. However, when the atomic energy potential includes nonlinear term, "cubic" anharmonic term just introduced in Equation (11.92) or "quartic" term in Equation (11.81), the resonance frequency should include at least $2\omega_0$ or $3\omega_0$, and higher-order harmonic modes. According to the uncertainty of the resonance frequency from the definite $\omega = \omega_0$ to $\Delta\omega = |\omega - \omega_0|$, the phonon distribution changes from an infinitely widespread state in a crystal to a relatively packet status (i.e., localized existence). From Equation (11.13), we assume the normal phonon eigenfunctions as

$$u_\alpha(t) \propto \sin k_\alpha a \cdot \cos \omega_\alpha t. \tag{11.95}$$

Taking into account a modified "phonon spectral density" (i.e., frequency square spectral density), $\frac{g(\omega)}{2\omega}$ as the summation weight, and the low-frequency acoustic mode dispersion relation $k_\alpha \propto \omega_\alpha$, we calculate the sum of $u_n(t)$'s, which exist in $\Delta\omega$

$$\sum_{\alpha=1}^{n} u_\alpha(t) \propto \sum_{\alpha=1}^{n} \frac{\sin \omega_\alpha a \cos \omega_\alpha t}{\omega_\alpha}. \tag{11.96}$$

Once multiple phonons are generated synchronously via the anharmonic potential interactions, the phonon energy localization is expected (not uniformly distributed as a separated harmonic vibration), leading to the concept of wave-to-particle transition (i.e., the reason for the terminology introduction of "phonon" from the elastic lattice vibration wave). If we rephrase the above argument in a reverse way, by having an excess of phonons with similarly directed group velocities (i.e., by touching a heat source on the solid crystal), the anharmonic part of the ionic interaction plays the wave packet into creation, destruction, or scattering of various frequency phonons, which corresponds to "thermal resistivity" (i.e., the inverse of thermal conductivity).

Chapter Essentials

1. One-atom (a) and two-atom (b) linear chain lattice models connected by the same springs provide the dispersion curves, plotted in the ka range of $-\pi \sim \pi$ (see figure below). Frequency gap between $\sqrt{2K/M}$ and $\sqrt{2K/m}$, where no solution (i.e., phonon mode) exists, can be found in the two-atom model (Figures 11.1 and 11.2).
2. Heat capacitance: Both models reach $C_p \to 3Nk_B$ at high temperature.

   (a) Einstein model—$C_p = \frac{\partial U}{\partial T} = Nk_B\left(\frac{\hbar\omega}{k_B T}\right)^2 \frac{e^{\frac{\hbar\omega}{k_B T}}}{\left[e^{\frac{\hbar\omega}{k_B T}}-1\right]^2}$

   (b) Debye model—$C_p = 9Nk_B(T/\theta_D)^3 \int_0^{x_D} dx \frac{x^4 e^x}{(e^x-1)^2}$ Debye's "T^3 law" is applied at low temperatures.
3. The Lorentz factor γ (local field amplification factor) in a simple cubic crystal is 1, leading to the local field given by $E_0 + \left(\frac{1}{3\varepsilon_0}\right)P$. The Lorentz factor is enhanced depending on the crystal structure. The perovskite $BaTiO_3$ exhibits $\gamma \approx 10$.
4. The origin of the spontaneous polarization in $BaTiO_3$ comes primarily from (1) enhanced Lorentz factor γ at the Ti position and (2) enhanced ionic polarizability of the Ti ion (i.e., Ti ion shift is easiest among all ions) in the z-direction chain Ti-O-Ti-O of a $BaTiO_3$ crystal.
5. Nonlinearity in crystal lattice: Born's model is

   $$U = -\frac{Mq^2}{r} + \frac{Nb}{r^n},$$

   where M is the Madelung constant for Coulombic energy, N is the coordination number, and b is the potential constant for the quantum mechanical energy.
6. Taking the Taylor expansion of the Born's model around $r = r_0$ (potential minimum point), we obtain

   $$\Delta U = U(r) - U(r_0) = f(\Delta r)^2 - g(\Delta r)^3,$$

where $f = (n-1)Mq^2/2r_0^3$ and $g = (n+4)(n-1)Mq^2/6r_0^4$. Based on Boltzmann distribution, we can derive the lattice parameter change with temperature T (i.e., thermal expansion) and external field E (i.e., electrostriction) as follows:

$$\frac{<\Delta r_+> + <\Delta r_->}{2r_0} = \frac{3gk}{4f^2 r_0}T + \frac{3gq^2}{4f^3 r_0}E^2.$$

7. (a) An ideal crystal with rigorously harmonic atomic potential should exhibit zero thermal resistance, or infinite thermal conductivity, leading to completely uniform temperature distribution in a crystal.
(b) An actual crystal with an anharmonic atomic potential exhibits a localized phonon packet, leading to the thermal distribution in a crystal and the finite thermal conductivity.

Check Point

1. (T/F) One-atom 1D lattice chain model with N atoms connected by the same lattice spring results in N eigenfrequencies and vibration eigenmode in general. True or false?
2. (T/F) The boundary condition difference, "free-end atoms" or "periodic (ring-connected) atoms", in the one-atom 1D lattice chain model connected by the same lattice spring is found in double-degenerated eigenvalues in the former boundary condition. True or false?
3. (T/F) Two-atom 1D lattice chain model connected by the same lattice spring results in the frequency gap between $\sqrt{2K/M}$ and $\sqrt{2K/m}$, where no solution (i.e., phonon mode) exists. True or false?
4. There exist two categories of the lattice vibration modes around the low k region in a two-atom 1D lattice chain model connected by the same lattice spring: (1) two species of atoms displace in the same direction and (2) two species of atoms displace in the opposite directions each other. Which is called the "optical" branch?
5. The Lorentz factor γ is defined in the relationship between the local field and polarization as $E^{loc} = (\gamma/3\varepsilon_0)P$. Provide the value of γ in a simple cubic crystal.
6. (T/F) A large Lorentz factor γ in $BaTiO_3$ is one of the reasons why it transforms into a ferroelectric phase from a cubic phase with reducing the temperature. True or false?
7. (T/F) The equivalent lattice spring in a crystal seems to have a tendency to be "softer" for extension than for contraction. True or false?
8. The strain in a crystal under electric field E and finite temperature T is expressed by

$$\frac{<\Delta r_+> + <\Delta r_->}{2r_0} = \frac{3gk}{4f^2 r_0}T + \frac{3gq^2}{4f^3 r_0}E^2,$$

in the Born atomic model, where f and g are the harmonic and cubic anharmonic terms of the lattice springs. How do you call the first and second terms with phenomenological terminologies (such as "piezoelectric strain")?

9. (T/F) An ideal crystal with rigorously harmonic atomic potential should exhibit zero thermal conductivity or infinite thermal resistivity. True or false?
10. (T/F) The finite thermal conductivity introduces the temperature distribution in a crystal, which is originated from a phonon phenomenon in an anharmonic lattice potential. True or false?

Chapter Problems

11.1 Consider a diatomic linear chain of identical atoms (mass M) connected by two types of springs of alternating strengths (K and G), as shown in the Figure 11.11. Calculate the dispersion curve (i.e., ω vs. k relation) for this 1D lattice model.

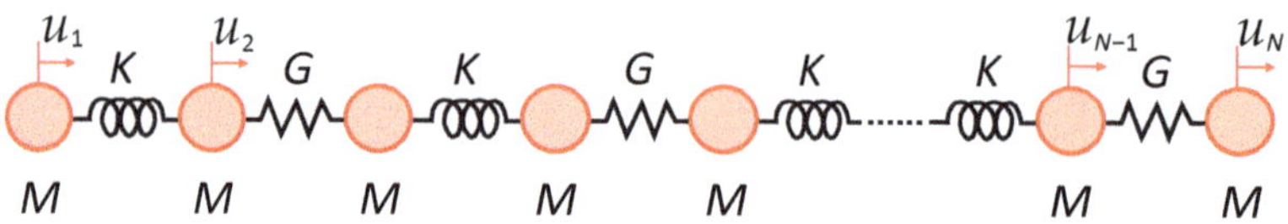

Figure 11.11. A diatomic linear chain of identical atoms (mass M) connected by springs of alternating strengths. Source: Figure by author.

Hint

We take a unit cell length "a" for the diatomic cell with two springs, K and G. The harmonic potential energy can be written as

$$U^{harm} = \left(\frac{K}{2}\right)\sum_n [u_1(na) - u_2(na)]^2 + \left(\frac{G}{2}\right)\sum_n [u_2(na) - u_1((n+1)a)]^2,$$

where we write $u_1(na)$ for the displacement of the atom that oscillates about the site na (n-th lattice cell site) and $u_2(na)$ for the displacement of the atom that locates in the center of the lattice cell. We assume $K \geq G$ without losing generality. The equations of atomic motion are now expressed as

$$M\ddot{u}_1(na) = -\frac{\partial U^{harm}}{\partial u_1(na)} = -K[u_1(na) - u_2(na)] - G[u_1(na) - u_2((n-1)a)],$$
$$M\ddot{u}_2(na) = -\frac{\partial U^{harm}}{\partial u_2(na)} = -K[u_2(na) - u_1(na)] - G[u_2(na) - u_1((n+1)a)].$$

Assuming wave solutions with frequency ω and wave vector k,

$$u_1(na) = u_1 e^{j(kna-\omega t)},$$

$$u_2(na) = u_2 e^{j(kna-\omega t)},$$

we need to determine u_1 and u_2 on the basis of the Born–von Karman periodic boundary condition. By substituting above $u_1(na)$ and $u_2(na)$ expression into the dynamic equations, we can obtain the following two coupled equations:

$$\left[M\omega^2 - (K+G)\right]u_1 + \left(K + Ge^{-jka}\right)u_2 = 0,$$

$$\left(K + Ge^{jka}\right)u_1 + \left[M\omega^2 - (K+G)\right]u_2 = 0.$$

Similar to the discussion in Section 11.1.1, To realize the meaningful solution (or u_1 and u_2 values), at least the following "determinant = 0" should be satisfied:

$$\begin{vmatrix} [M\omega^2 - (K+G)] & \left(K + Ge^{-jka}\right) \\ \left(K + Ge^{jka}\right) & [M\omega^2 - (K+G)] \end{vmatrix} = 0.$$

The above leads to the following relation:

$$\left[M\omega^2 - (K+G)\right]^2 = \left|K + Ge^{-jka}\right|^2 = K^2 + G^2 + 2KG{\cdot}\cos(ka).$$

We can obtain two positive solutions for ω^2,

$$\omega_{\pm}{}^2(k) = \frac{K+G}{M} \pm \left(\frac{1}{M}\right)\sqrt{K^2 + G^2 + 2KG{\cdot}\cos(ka)}\Big\},$$

with the following relation according to the above solutions:

$$\frac{u_2}{u_1} = \mp\left(K + Ge^{jka}\right)/\left|K + Ge^{-jka}\right|.$$

The negative – sign means the vibration mode with the adjacent atoms displacing in opposite direction each other (i.e., "optical branch"), while + corresponds to the mode with the adjacent atoms displacing in the same direction (i.e., "acoustic branch"). We assume there are N unit cells with two springs (K and G) in the unit cell with a unit cell size of a, and the "period boundary condition" is adopted in this model. For $N \to \infty$; ka will vary from 0 to π. At $k = 0$,

$$\omega_{\pm}{}^2(0) = \begin{cases} \frac{2(K+G)}{M} \\ 0 \end{cases},$$

while at $k = \pi/a$, from $\omega_{\pm}{}^2(\pi/a) = \frac{K+G}{M} \pm \frac{K-G}{M}\Big]$ (supposing $K > G$),

$$\omega_{\pm}{}^2(\pi/a) = \begin{cases} 2K/M \\ 2G/M \end{cases}.$$

The frequency gap exists between $\sqrt{2K/M}$ and $\sqrt{2G/M}$, where no solution (i.e., phonon mode) exists.

References

1. Zhang, H.; Shang, S.L.; Wang, Y.; Saengdeejing, A.; Chen, L.Q.; Liu, Z.K. First-principles calculations of the elastic, phonon and thermodynamic properties of $Al_{12}Mg_{17}$. *Acta Mater.* **2010**, *58*, 4012–4018. [CrossRef]
2. Ashcroft, N.W.; Mermin, N.D. *Solid State Physics*; W. B. Saunders Co.: Orlando, FL, USA, 2022.
3. Ishii, K. Vibration and Eigenvalue Problem. *Mod. Math.* **1972**, *5*, 24–32.
4. Kittel, C. *Solid State Physics*, 5th ed.; John Wiley & Sons, Inc.: New York, NY, USA, 1976.
5. Uchino, K. *Ferroelectric Devices*, 2nd ed.; CRC Press: Boca Raton, FL, USA, 2010.
6. Kinase, W.; Uemura, Y.; Kikuchi, M. Correction of dipole field due to lattice deformation of a perovskite-type crystal. *J. Phys. Chem. Solids* **1969**, *30*, 441–447. [CrossRef]
7. Devonshire, A.F. XCVI. Theory of barium titanate: Part I. *Philos. Mag.* **1949**, *40*, 1040–1063. [CrossRef]
8. Slater, J.C. The Lorentz correction in barium titanate. *Phys. Rev.* **1950**, *78*, 748. [CrossRef]
9. McKeehan, L.W. Magnetic dipole fields in unstrained cubic crystals. *Phys. Rev.* **1933**, *43*, 913. [CrossRef]
10. McKeehan, L.W. Magnetic dipole fields in unstrained cubic crystals. *Phys. Rev.* **1947**, *72*, 78. [CrossRef]
11. Littinger, J.M.; Tisza, L. Theory of dipole interaction in crystals. *Phys. Rev.* **1946**, *70*, 954, Erratum in *Phys. Rev.* **1947**, *72*, 257. [CrossRef]
12. Born, M.; Göppert-Mayer, M. *Handbuch der Physik*; Springer: Berlin/Heidelberg, Germany, 1933; Volume 24, p. 623.
13. Uchino, K.; Cross, L.E. Electrostriction and its Interrelation with Other Anharmonic Properties of Materials. *Jpn. J. Appl. Phys.* **1980**, *19*, L171–L173. [CrossRef]

12. Heat Conduction—Linear Differential Equation II

We discussed so far the equilibrium and time-dependent (dynamic) phenomenology in the uniform ferroelectric specimen (that is, the uniform temperature distribution in a specimen). We will discuss spatially nonuniform (i.e., "space-gradient") phenomenology in this chapter. The concept of "heat flow" is introduced, where the exponential trend with time such as $(1 - \theta/\theta_s) = e^{-t/\tau}$ is not sustained correctly. The secondary electrothermal coupling factor k^{λ} is also discussed in this chapter, the PZT value of which seems to be much larger than the primary electrothermal coupling factor $k^{ET^2} = \frac{p^2}{(C_p^E/T)\varepsilon_0\varepsilon^X}$ introduced in Chapter 2. It is noted that thermal conductivity varies significantly with the electric boundary condition (i.e., short or open circuit), as well as with the ferroelectric compositions. Heat generation analyses in practical piezoelectric devices are also introduced in the last part of this chapter.

12.1. Heat Conduction Model

12.1.1. 1D Heat Transfer Model

We develop a simple 1D heat transfer model, as shown in Figure 12.1a, where a uniform disk or rod is thermally isolated so that no heat escapes (i.e., impervious) from its sides hypothetically [1]. The temperature gradient is introduced, and we define the temperature function $\theta(x,t)$ ($= (T - T_R)$ difference from the T_R) at a point a distance x from one end of a rod, assuming isotropic thermal conductivity. We introduce the following three parameters:

- Q—"Heat quantity". Scalar quantity. The unit of heat quantity is usually calorie (cal), and 1 cal corresponds to 4.186 J in energy; q—"Heat flow" (or "flux"). Vector quantity $= -grad(Q)$. Quantity of heat passing through the cross-section of rod per unit area per unit time; that is, q is the thermal energy flow from Q (J), the unit should be (J/m^2/s) = (W/m^2);
- λ—"Thermal conductivity". Second rank tensor quantity. Thermal or heat conductance per unit length of material. The unit is (W/m·K). The inverse $1/\lambda$ (inverse tensor, in general) is the "thermal resistance", which measures the temperature drop per unit length when heat flux is unity;
- C_p—"Heat capacitance" of material per unit volume. Scalar quantity = specific heat capacity c_p (c_p^E, c_p^D) × density ρ, number of heat units to raise block of unit area and unit length (i.e., per unit volume) 1 °C in temperature, formulated as $C_p = \frac{\partial q}{\partial T}$;
- c_p—"Specific heat capacity" per unit mass. Scalar quantity. The specific heat capacity (J/(kg·K)) is determined per unit mass (kg), which must be multiplied by density (kg/m^3) to obtain the heat capacitance per unit volume (J/(m^3·K)).

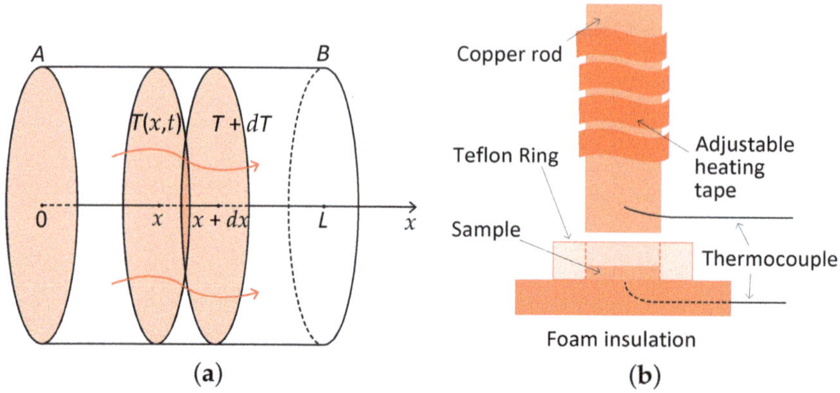

Figure 12.1. (**a**) The 1D thermal diffusion model; (**b**) experimental setup for determining directional thermal diffusivity. Source: [2] ©Uchino, K. *High-Power Piezoelectrics and Loss Mechanisms*; CRC Press, 2020; pp. 183, 184. Reproduced by permission of Taylor & Francis Group.

The total heat quantity Q is transferred from T_1 on A to T_0 on B through the area S along the length L during the time t; the "thermal conductivity" λ is defined as a proportional constant in the following equation:

$$Q = \lambda S \frac{T_1 - T_0}{L} t. \tag{12.1}$$

If we convert this macroscopic formula into derivative form, taking heat quantity Q along a short distance interval x and $x + dx$ in the time duration dt, then the temperature difference $\theta(x,t)$ and $\theta(x+dx,t)$, or $\theta(x,t) - \theta(x+dx,t) = \theta(x,t) - \left[\theta(x,t) + \left(\frac{\partial\theta}{\partial x}\right)dx\right] = -\left(\frac{\partial\theta}{\partial x}\right)dx$. Equation (12.1) is converted as

$$q = \lambda \frac{\theta(x,t) - \theta(x+dx,t)}{dx} dt = -\lambda\left(\frac{\partial\theta}{\partial x}\right)dt. \tag{12.2}$$

The above equation is considered as input heat quantity at x, $q(x,t)$. As the same formula may be valid at $(x+dx)$ as output from this narrow slab, total heat quantity increase dq can be evaluated as the following subtraction:

$$dq = q(x,t) - q(x+dx,t) = -\lambda\left[\left(\frac{\partial\theta}{\partial x}\right) - \left\{\left(\frac{\partial\theta}{\partial x}\right) + \left(\frac{\partial^2\theta}{\partial x^2}\right)dx\right\}\right]dt = \lambda\left(\frac{\partial^2\theta}{\partial x^2}\right)dxdt, \tag{12.3}$$

where dq is the thermal energy flow per unit "volume", given by the total energy flow $dQ = vdq$ (v: volume). Heat capacitance C_p is defined by

$$C_p = \frac{\partial q}{\partial T} = T(\frac{\partial S}{\partial T})_{X,E}. \tag{12.4}$$

Here, we used the thermodynamic relation $dq = TdS$. When we introduce heat capacitance (required heat quantity for increasing 1 °C) per unit volume C_p,

$$dq = C_p d\theta dv = C_p d\theta dx. \tag{12.5}$$

Note here that $dv = Sdx$, and $S = 1$ in our model. Equation (12.3) can be transformed as

$C_p d\theta dx = \lambda\left(\frac{\partial^2\theta}{\partial x^2}\right)dxdt.$

We finally obtain a 1D heat transfer equation as

$$\left(\frac{\partial\theta}{\partial t}\right) = \frac{\lambda}{C_p}\left(\frac{\partial^2\theta}{\partial x^2}\right) = \frac{\lambda}{c_p\rho}\left(\frac{\partial^2\theta}{\partial x^2}\right) = \alpha_T\left(\frac{\partial^2\theta}{\partial x^2}\right). \quad (12.6)$$

The proportional constant $\frac{\lambda}{c_p\rho}$ is called "thermal diffusivity" α_T, which is practically measured by temperature monitoring by the setup shown in Figure 12.1b. The Teflon ring suppresses the side thermal dissipation. Specific heat capacity c_p is defined per unit mass, related with heat capacitance C_p as C_p/ρ. Units and typical numbers of the necessary parameters in PZT's are summarized as follows:

- Thermal conductivity λ—0.6~1.3 (W/(m·K));
- Specific heat capacity c_p—340~420 (J/(kg·K));
- Mass density ρ—7600 (kg/m^3);
- Thermal diffusivity α_T—2.7~5.1 × 10^{-7} (m^2/s).

12.1.2. Solution of 1D Heat Transfer Equation

Let us now solve the heat Equation (12.6) in this section.

$\left(\frac{\partial\theta}{\partial t}\right) = \alpha_T\left(\frac{\partial^2\theta}{\partial x^2}\right).$

We adopt the initial and boundary conditions as follows:

- At $x = 0$: $\theta(x = 0, t) = \theta_0$, and $\frac{\partial\theta(x,t)}{\partial t} = 0$ ("isothermal condition": by attaching a large heat reservoir on $x = 0$ at $t = 0$, high temperature θ_0 is maintained continuously);
- At $x = L$: $\frac{\partial\theta(x,t)}{\partial x} = -\left(\frac{1}{\lambda}\right)q = 0$ ("isolated condition": impervious (i.e., no heat transfer) at $x = L$, thus, θ is time dependent, started from room temperature T_R (i.e., $\theta(L, t = 0) = 0$));
- At $t = 0$: $\theta(x > 0, t = 0) = 0$ (initial temperature of the whole part starts from room temperature).

Fourier Expansion Series Approach

Since the solution $\theta(x,t)$ of Equation (12.6) should be less than the maximum temperature θ_0 at surface A, and with $t \to \infty$, it should approach θ_0, we assume the following form:

$$\theta(x,t) = \theta_0 - e^{-mt}u(x), \quad (12.7)$$

where m is a constant and $u(x)$ is the function of x to be determined. On substituting Equation (12.7) in Equation (12.6), we obtain the following equation of the time-independent function:

$$\left(\frac{\partial^2 u}{\partial x^2}\right) = -\left(\frac{m}{\alpha_T}\right)u. \quad (12.8)$$

Using a new parameter p,

$$p^2 = (\frac{m}{\alpha_T}). \tag{12.9}$$

The above equation becomes

$$\left(\frac{\partial^2 u}{\partial x^2}\right) + p^2 u = 0. \tag{12.10}$$

Then, the general solution can be assumed in the Fourier series as

$$u(x) = A\sin(px) + B\cos(px), \tag{12.11a}$$

$$\frac{\partial u(x)}{\partial x} = p[A\cos(px) - B\sin(px)]. \tag{12.11b}$$

Taking into account the boundary conditions: (a) $\theta(x = 0, t) = \theta_0$ requires $\frac{\partial \theta(x,t)}{\partial t} = me^{mt} u(x) = 0$, we can obtain $u(x = 0) = 0$, (b) $\frac{\partial \theta(x,t)}{\partial x} = 0$ at $x = L$ requires $\frac{\partial u(x)}{\partial x} = 0$,

$$\begin{cases} A\sin(0) + B\cos(0) = 0 \\ A\cos(pL) - B\sin(pL) = 0 \end{cases}. \tag{12.12}$$

Thus, the following condition should be satisfied, in addition to $B = 0$:

$$A\cos(pL) = 0. \tag{12.13}$$

Nontrivial solutions for p are

$$pL = (n + \frac{1}{2})\pi, \text{ or } p = (n + \frac{1}{2})\pi/L \ (n = 0,\ 1,\ 2,\ 3,\ \cdots). \tag{12.14}$$

For each value of n, the n-th solution can be identified as

$$u_n(x) = A_n\sin((n + \frac{1}{2})\pi/L)x. \tag{12.15}$$

Then,

$$m_r = \alpha_T p^2 = \alpha_T((n + \frac{1}{2})\pi/L)^2. \tag{12.16}$$

Now, the solution of $\theta(x, t)$ is expressed by the summation of all $u_n(x)$ weighted by $e^{-m_r t}$ as

$$\theta(x, t) = \theta_0 - \sum_{n=1}^{\infty} A_n e^{-\alpha_T((n+\frac{1}{2})\pi/L)^2 t}\sin((n + \frac{1}{2})\pi/L)x, \tag{12.17}$$

where A_n parameters are determined from the initial condition, $\theta(x, t = 0) = 0$; that is $\sum_{n=1}^{\infty} A_n\sin((n + \frac{1}{2})\pi/L)x = \theta_0$.

Merely for the simplicity, taking only the first term in the series ($n = 0$) as an approximation [3], we derive the temperature profile at $x = L$ (isolated end) as follows:

$$\theta(L,t) = \theta_0 - A_0 e^{-\alpha_T(\pi/2L)^2 t}\sin(\pi/2L)L = \theta_0[1 - e^{-\alpha_T(\frac{\pi}{2L})^2 t}]. \quad (12.18)$$

By examining the transient temperature profile at the "insulated side" of the sample (see Figure 12.1b), the thermal diffusivity α_T can directly be calculated by finding the time constant τ experimentally. By fitting the temperature profile at $x = L$ with $\theta_0[1 - e^{-t/\tau}]$, we can obtain τ, leading to α_T from

$$\alpha_T = \frac{L^2}{(\frac{\pi}{2})^2 \tau}. \quad (12.19)$$

Laplace Transform Approach

Let us now solve the heat Equation (12.6) using the Laplace operator.

$\left(\frac{\partial \theta}{\partial t}\right) = \alpha_T \left(\frac{\partial^2 \theta}{\partial x^2}\right)$.

Taking Θ as the Laplace transform of $\theta(x,t)$ (i.e., $\Theta = L[\theta(x,t)]$) [1], we have

$$\left(\frac{\partial^2 \Theta}{\partial x^2}\right) = \frac{s}{\alpha_T}\Theta. \quad (12.20)$$

We may assume the solution form as

$$\Theta = Ae^{\sqrt{\frac{s}{\alpha_T}}x} + Be^{-\sqrt{\frac{s}{\alpha_T}}x}. \quad (12.21)$$

Knowing the inverse Laplace transform found in Laplace transform Table in Reference [1],

$$L^{-1}\left[e^{-a\sqrt{s}}\right] = \frac{a}{2\sqrt{\pi t^3}}e^{-a^2/4t}, \quad (12.22)$$

and $a = \mp\frac{x}{\sqrt{\alpha_T}}$, Equation (12.18) can be transformed into

$$\theta(x,t) = -A\frac{\frac{x}{\sqrt{\alpha_T}}}{2\sqrt{\pi t^3}}e^{-x^2/4t\alpha_T} + B\frac{\frac{x}{\sqrt{\alpha_T}}}{2\sqrt{\pi t^3}}e^{-x^2/4t\alpha_T}. \quad (12.23a)$$

We consider the following boundary condition: A large heat source ($\theta = \theta_0$) is attached suddenly ($t = 0$) on surface A ($x = 0$) in Figure 12.1a; that is, heat flux is given as a step function with respect to time (i.e., "isothermal condition" at $x = 0$). Excluding immediately after $t = 0$ and adjacent to $x = 0$ point, we consider the region $t > \delta, x > \delta'$ and assume the following equation in most of the rod material's length:

$$\theta(x,t) = \theta_0 e^{-x^2/4t\alpha_T}. \quad (12.23b)$$

Equation (12.23b) is rather an "error function" in terms of coordinate x, and indicates that

- At $x = 0$, $\theta(x = 0, t) = \theta_0$—the temperature is constant at θ_0 (i.e., "isothermal"), irrelevant to time after attaching to a large heat source;
- At $x = L$, $\theta(L, t) = \theta_0 e^{-L^2/4t\alpha_T}$—isolated or "impervious condition" (i.e., no heat transfer) at $x = L$, started from room temperature T_R (i.e., $\theta(L, t = 0) = 0$). By measuring temperature change with t at $x = L$, we can obtain the thermal diffusivity α_T.

Figure 12.2a shows temperature distribution profiles as functions of position x for various time lapses, and Figure 12.2b shows the temperature change with time at the position $x = L$. This simulation used the following values: $\theta_0 = 15$ °C, $L = 2 \times 10^{-3}$ (m), $\alpha_T = 8 \times 10^{-7}$ (m^2/s). As can be seen, heat flux penetration speed for a 2 mm thick sample does not take longer than 0.5 s, and the temperature monitoring finishes in less than 3 s. Even in a thicker specimen with 10 mm, the measuring time is still shorter than 30~40 s. It is noteworthy that the temperature distribution profile as a function of position x is not a simple exponential curve but resembles a half positive part of the so-called "error function" when the abrupt step-function heat flux is inserted from the position $x = 0$ at $t = 0$. As the curve profile of Figure 12.2b resembles a simple exponential curve, we used the approximate formula Equation (12.18) in Subsection Fourier Expansion Series Approach, which is

$$\theta(L, t) = \theta_0[1 - e^{-t/(\frac{L^2}{\alpha_T(\pi/2)^2})}]. \tag{12.24a}$$

We can verify this handling equivalency with the exact formula,

$$\theta(L, t) = \theta_0 e^{-L^2/4t\alpha_T}. \tag{12.24b}$$

By putting $A = e^{-(\frac{L^2}{4\alpha_T})/t}$, we obtain $\frac{1}{\ln A} = -\frac{t}{(\frac{L^2}{4\alpha_T})}$, then $e^{-t/(\frac{L^2}{4\alpha_T})} = e^{\frac{1}{\ln A}}$. Taking Taylor expansion,

$$e^{\frac{1}{\ln A}} \approx 1 - A + \cdots$$

we verify the relation

$$e^{-L^2/4t\alpha_T} \approx [1 - e^{-t/(\frac{L^2}{4\alpha_T})}]. \tag{12.25}$$

Thus, the thermal diffusivity α_T is obtained from the experimentally obtained time constant τ as

$$\alpha_T = \frac{L^2}{4\tau}. \tag{12.26}$$

However, note the numerical factor difference; that is, $(\pi/2)^2$ in Equation (12.24a), and 4 in Equation (12.25). This means that the α_T determined with Equation (12.19) from the experimental time constant τ is overestimated in comparison with the α_T value with Equations (12.26) by the factor of $4/(\pi/2)^2$. This difference is originated from the neglection of the higher-order harmonic terms ($n = 1, 2, \cdots$) in Equation (12.17). The absolute α_T values may need to be modified by this factor from the previously reported values in Reference [3] if required.

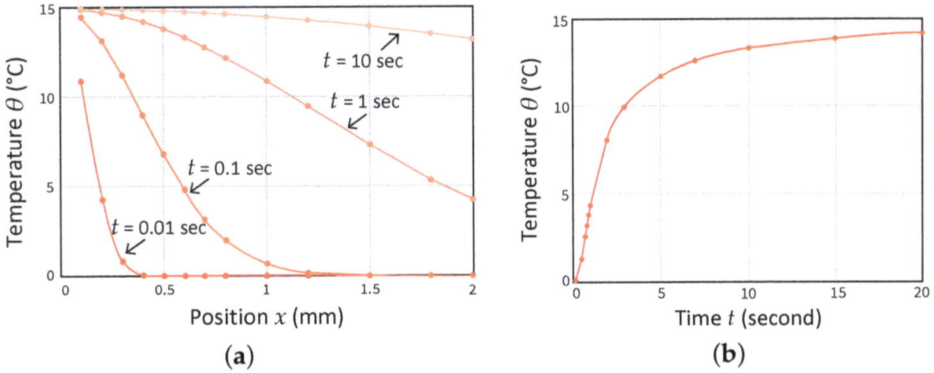

Figure 12.2. (**a**) Temperature distribution profiles as a function of position x for various time lapses and (**b**) temperature change with time at the position $x = L$. Source: Figure by author.

Example Problem 12.1.

Two material disks with different thermal conductivities, λ_1 and λ_2, are laminated with thicknesses L_1 and L_2, as shown in Figure 12.3; then, outer surfaces A and C (area S is common) are maintained at T_1 and T_2 ($T_1 > T_2$), respectively. Calculate temperature T and thermal energy flow Q on contact surface B.

Hint

When the two-surface temperature of a disk specimen (thickness L) is maintained at T_1 and T_2 ($T_1 > T_2$), the thermal conductivity λ is defined as

$$Q = \lambda\, t\, S \frac{T_1 - T_2}{L}, \tag{P12.1.1}$$

where Q is the quantity of heat transferred from high-temperature surface to low-temperature surface via surface S in time duration t.

Solution

Supposing that $T_1 > T_2$, and the temperature on contact surface B is T, the thermal energy flow Q via the surface area S in time duration t should be expressed by the following equations under a steady state:

$$Q = \lambda_1 t S \frac{T_1 - T}{L_1} = \lambda_2 t S \frac{T - T_2}{L_2}. \tag{P12.1.2}$$

Thus, temperature T is obtained from $\lambda_1 \frac{T_1 - T}{L_1} = \lambda_2 \frac{T - T_2}{L_2}$; then,

$$T = \frac{\frac{\lambda_1}{L_1} T_1 + \frac{\lambda_2}{L_2} T_2}{\frac{\lambda_1}{L_1} + \frac{\lambda_2}{L_2}}. \tag{P12.1.3}$$

Accordingly, the normalized energy flow q per unit area and unit time defined by Q/St is calculated as

$$q = \frac{\lambda_1 \lambda_2}{L_1 \lambda_2 + L_2 \lambda_1}(T_1 - T_2). \quad \text{(P12.1.4)}$$

The effective thermal conductivity of the series connection composite material is expressed by

$$\kappa_{eff} = \frac{1}{\frac{L_1}{\lambda_1} + \frac{L_2}{\lambda_2}}. \quad \text{(P12.1.5)}$$

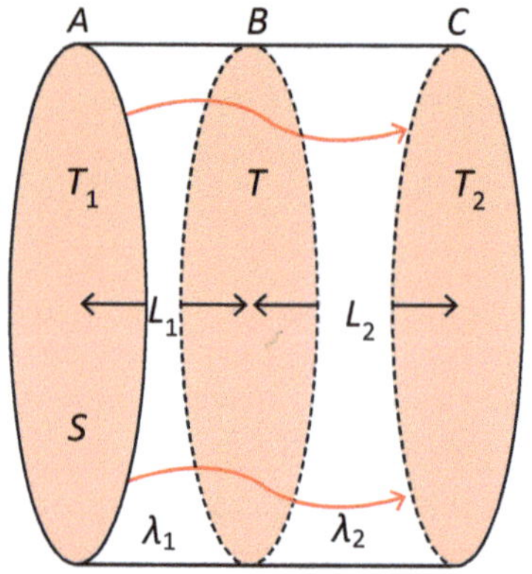

Figure 12.3. Thermal conductivity model. Source: Figure by author.

Example Problem 12.2.

Referring to Figure 12.1a, we consider a particular case that the length L is long enough in comparison with the radius r. The end surface A is maintained at θ_0 (high temperature) from the heat source, and another end surface B is kept at $\theta = 0$ (room temperature) after obtaining the steady temperature profile on this sample rod. Use the bulk thermal conductivity λ, surface thermal conductivity α_S, and mass density ρ in the calculation.

Hint

The rate at which heat is lost from a rod as a consequence of surface radiation into the surrounding air at a constant temperature T_R is proportional to the difference in temperature $(T - T_R) = \theta$ and to the surface area of the element. Therefore, the 1D heat transfer equation may be modified as

$$\left(\frac{\partial \theta}{\partial t}\right) = \alpha_T \left(\frac{\partial^2 \theta}{\partial x^2}\right) - \alpha_S \theta. \quad \text{(P12.2.1)}$$

Solution

Taking the x-axis along the rod length, we consider the quantity of heat passing through a cross-section of rod per unit time on the x to $x + dx$ narrow slab. First, the heat transfer quantity rate is calculated as

$$\frac{dQ}{dt} = \lambda S\left(\frac{\partial^2\theta}{\partial x^2}\right)dx \text{ (Here, } S = \pi r^2\text{)}. \tag{P12.2.2}$$

Second, heat dissipation from the side surface is expressed as

$$\alpha_S S'\theta dt(\text{here, } S' = 2\pi r dx). \tag{P12.2.3}$$

Thus, the change rate of the quantity of heat per unit area ($S = \pi r^2 = 1$) in this slab is expressed as

$$\frac{dq}{dt} = \lambda\left(\frac{\partial^2\theta}{\partial x^2}\right) - \frac{2\alpha_S}{r}\theta. \tag{P12.2.4}$$

Under a steady state,

$$\left(\frac{\partial^2\theta}{\partial x^2}\right) = \frac{2\alpha_S}{\lambda r}\theta. \tag{P12.2.5}$$

Equation (P12.2.5) is solved under the boundary conditions $\theta = \theta_0$ at $x = 0$, and $\theta = 0$ at $x = \infty$. Since a general solution is expressed by

$$\theta = A\cdot exp\left(\sqrt{\frac{2\alpha_S}{\lambda r}}x\right) + B\cdot exp\left(-\sqrt{\frac{2\alpha_S}{\lambda r}}x\right). \tag{P12.2.6}$$

$A = 0$, $B = \theta_0$ are derived. The temperature profile under the steady state is provided as

$$\theta(x) = \theta_0\cdot exp\left(-\sqrt{\frac{2\alpha_S}{\lambda r}}x\right). \tag{P12.2.7}$$

12.1.3. Thermal Diffusivity Measurements

We can find previous papers [4,5], which report on the thermal properties of PZT ceramics at low temperature (20–300 K), indicating a transition temperature between 50 K and 80 K, and at high temperature (300–800 K), characterizing the effect of phase transition on the thermal properties. Uchino's group investigated the relationship of thermal properties with electrical boundary conditions (a short- or open-circuit condition) and poling status in the PZTs and other ferroelectric piezoelectric ceramics, which are described in this chapter. A significantly large "secondary electrothermal coupling factor" ${k_{33}^{\lambda}}^2$ is introduced, much larger than the primary electrothermal coupling factor ${k^{ET}}^2$ introduced in Chapter 2.

A user-friendly new experimental setup for measuring the thermal diffusivity of PZTs is introduced. Though Reference [3] reported the details of the experimental setup, we summarize it briefly for the reader's sake (see Figure 12.1b). The hot isothermal condition was imposed on a flat disk sample in our experiments by suddenly being applied on the top surface ($x = 0$) at $t = 0$. The increase in transient temperature of the bottom side of the disk specimen is analytically similar to an exponential formulation with a classic time constant, as described in the previous section in Equations (12.18) and (12.19), which provides the time constant τ, then $\alpha_T = \frac{L^2}{(\frac{\pi}{2})^2\tau}$ (this value may need to be calibrated with Equation (12.26) for the absolute value analysis). The thermal diffusivity is given proportionally to the "inverse time constant $1/\tau$". This method hosts a variety of advantages over other methods such as (1) high accuracy, (2) low cost, (3) elimination of interface effects, and (4) small specimen size. Best of all, (5) the measuring time period is short (10~20 s) enough for measuring the difference between the short- and open-circuit conditions. The accuracy of this setup has already been demonstrated in several materials with low-to-medium thermal diffusivity ($0.1 \sim 3 \times 10^{-6}$ m^2/s). The thermal diffusivity measurements in this experiment have an accuracy of 5% or better for some standard materials such as Fused Quartz and Pyrex 7740, in comparison with the literature values [3].

Using this method, the thermal diffusivity α_T was measured on "poled" and "unpoled" commercially available hard PZT ceramic disks, APC 841 (APC Int'l., Mackeyville, PA USA), of a diameter of 51 mm with thickness 2–5 mm [6]. The "unpoled" sample was "depoled" by heating the specimen, annealing, and then checking their no piezoelectric response on a conventional d_{33} meter. The thermal diffusivity was measured in the direction of polarization for the poled samples. In parallel, the absolute value of heat capacity of a small specimen was measured using the DSC Q2000 (TA Instruments, New Castle, DE, USA) by comparing it to a sapphire reference sample. The "specific heat capacity (per mass)" and density are, respectively, c_p = 340 J/kg·K and ρ = 7600 kg/m^3. The specific heat capacity difference between c_p^E and c_p^D could not be detected under electrical boundary condition difference (short and open circuit) because the differential scanning calorimetry (DSC) took too long (5 min) to keep the "depolarization field", as well as unmeasurably small difference theoretically, as shown below. Table 12.1 summarizes thermal diffusivity, specific heat capacity, and thermal conductivity of a hard PZT (APC 841), for unpoled and poled under different electrical boundary conditions (open and short circuit) [6]. Note the significant difference in "thermal diffusivity" obtained experimentally in these three electrical constraint conditions. The origin of this difference is discussed in the following section.

Table 12.1. Thermal diffusivity, specific heat capacity, and thermal conductivity of a Hard PZT, for unpoled and poled under different electrical boundary conditions.

Hard PZT	Thermal Diffusivity α_T (10^7 m^2/s)	+/−	Specific Heat Capacity c_p (J/kg K)	Thermal Conductivity λ (W/m K)	+/−
Unpoled	4.32	0.34	c_p^{UP} = 340	1.12	0.10
Open Circuit	5.02	0.23	c_p^D = 340	1.30	0.06
Short Circuit	8.25	0.78	c_p^E = 340	2.13	0.23

Source: Table by author.

12.1.4. Thermal Diffusivity under Different Electrical Constraints

It is an intriguing fact that experimentally obtained "thermal diffusivity" exhibits the largest in a poled specimen under short-circuit condition, followed by a poled specimen under open-circuit condition, and the smallest in an unpoled specimen; all disk samples have electrodes on both the top and bottom surfaces. As the thermal diffusivity is expressed by (repeated from Equation (12.6))

$$\alpha_T = \frac{\lambda}{c_p \rho}, \tag{12.27}$$

where λ, c_p, and ρ are thermal conductivity, specific heat capacity, and mass density, respectively. The difference in α_T must be the combined effect of λ and c_p differences (the density ρ may not be changed by the electric constraint condition).

Specific Heat Capacity—Scalar Parameter

Recall the two types of "specific heat capacity" in Section 2.4.2, c_p^E and c_p^D. We introduced c_p^E for specific heat capacity (per unit mass) under $X = 0$ and $E = 0$, that is, under a short-circuit condition of a ferroelectric specimen's surface electrodes. We consider a different specific heat capacity under an open-circuit condition (i.e., D = constant or zero). If we denote $C_p^D = \rho c_p^D = T(\frac{\partial S}{\partial T})_{X,D}$, we can obtain

$$\rho c_p^D = \rho c_p^E - \frac{T p^2}{\varepsilon_0 \varepsilon^X} = \rho c_p^E (1 - k^{ET^2}) \alpha_T = \frac{\lambda}{c_p \rho}. \tag{12.28}$$

Here, the primary "electrothermal coupling factor" k^{ET} is given by

$$k^{ET^2} = \frac{p^2}{\left(\frac{\rho c_p^E}{T}\right) \varepsilon_0 \varepsilon^X}. \tag{12.29}$$

We decided first $c_p^E = 340$ J/kg·K from the DSC equipment on the short-circuit specimen. Then, let us calculate c_p^D for the open-circuit specimen, using the following PZT-APC841 specimen values:

Pyroelectric coefficient $p = 0.5 \times 10^{-4}$ (C/m^2·K);
Specific heat capacity $c_p^E = 340$ (J/kg·K);
Mass density $\rho = 7600$ (kg/m^3);
Permittivity $\varepsilon^X = 1375$.

Thus, the primary electrothermal coupling factor is calculated as

$$k^{ET^2} = \frac{\left(0.5 \times 10^{-4} \mathrm{C/m^2 \cdot K}\right)^2}{\left(\frac{7600 \frac{\mathrm{kg}}{\mathrm{m}^3} \cdot 340 \frac{\mathrm{J}}{\mathrm{kg}} \cdot \mathrm{K}}{300\ K}\right) (8.854 \times 10^{-12} \frac{F}{m}) \times 1375} = 0.11 \times 10^{-6},$$

then, $c_p^D = c_p^E \left(1 - k^{ET^2}\right) = 340$ J/kg·K. We can conclude that c_p^D and c_p^E show no measurable difference in this PZT. Finally, an unpoled specimen is supposed to be composed of a mixture of c_p^D and c_p^E, such as $\frac{1}{3}\left(c_p^D + 2c_p^E\right)$, which is also the same value as above. See the center column data of Table 12.1.

Thermal Conductivity—Tensor Parameter

Using $\alpha_T = \frac{\lambda}{c_p \rho}$ with $\rho = 7600$ kg/m^3, we calculated thermal conductivity λ, as listed in the last column of Table 12.1. First, note that the thermal conductivity λ_{ij} is a second-rank tensor, different from the scalar "specific heat capacity". Second, notice that the thermal diffusivity difference is mainly attributed to the thermal conductivity λ difference, depending on the electrical constraint conditions, even after reasonable calibration with c_p^E and c_p^D (no distinguishable difference).

Let us discuss the difference among the measured thermal conductivity λ values for poled short-circuit, poled open-circuit, and unpoled specimens. Note that once poled, the piezo-ceramic crystallographic symmetry becomes ∞mm (equivalent symmetry to 6 mm in terms of tensor notations). First, the open-circuit thermal conductivity $\lambda_{33}^D = 1.30$ is 0.61 times of the short-circuit conductivity $\lambda_{33}^E = 2.13$. We denote the superscripts E and D of the conductivity λ, supposing that the sample is roughly maintained "electric field E constant" and "electric displacement D (or P) constant" during a rather short experimental time period less than 10 s. Subscript "33" stands for the tensor component relating to heat flux vector q_3 and x-component of the temperature gradient $-grad(\theta)$ (i.e., vector) along the spontaneous polarization P_S direction. Second, the unpoled specimen exhibits a crystallographic symmetry of isotropic cubic $m3m$ (different from the poled specimens), and the thermal conductivity $\lambda_{11}^u = 1.12$ shows the smallest value, 14% less than that of the poled open-circuit case (See the last column of Table 12.1). Different from the scalar analysis, the tensor analysis is directly coupled with the material's crystallographic symmetry. The unpoled specimen cannot be discussed in parallel with the poled specimens because of the crystallographic symmetry difference. Shekhani et al. proposed a new dynamic "secondary electrothermal coupling factor" k_{33}^λ [6], in the relationship between the open-circuit $\lambda^D{}_{33}$ and short-circuit thermal conductivity $\lambda^E{}_{33}$ such as

$$\lambda_{33}^D = \lambda_{33}^E (1 - k_{33}^{\lambda\,2}). \tag{12.30}$$

This secondary electrothermal coupling factor $k_{33}^\lambda = 62\%$ calculated for the above PZT-APC841 is remarkably higher than the primary electrothermal coupling factor $k^{ET} = 0.105$ % of the same PZT specimen. The background theoretical approach is discussed in Section 12.2.

Thermal Conductivity in Pb-Free Piezoelectrics

In 2006, European Union started Restrictions on the use of certain Hazardous Substances (RoHS), which explicitly limits the usage of lead (Pb) in electronic equipment. Basically, we may need to regulate the usage of lead zirconate titanate (PZT), currently, the most widely used piezoelectric ceramics, in the future. Due to this background, research on Pb-free piezoelectrics is now accelerated, including their high-power performance. A comparison between the maximum vibration velocity in Pb-free piezoelectric and PZTs indicates 1 m/s (rms) vs. 0.6 m/s in k_{31}-type plate specimens. Table 12.2 summarizes the preliminary data on thermal conductivity in NKN-based materials with the PZT value (both unpoled samples). Pb-free piezoceramics such as (Na,K)NbO_3- and (Bi,Na)TiO_3-based materials show much higher maximum vibration velocity than the PZTs [7,8]. The much larger thermal conductivity found in NKN-based materials, compared with PZTs, may also contribute to this good high-power performance in NKN-based ceramics, because of the definition of the maximum vibration velocity, which is defined under the maximum temperature rise 20 °C from room temperature. The heat generated at the nodal point diffuses quickly due to large thermal conductivity. Try Chapter Problem 12.1 to learn how the conductivity decreased the maximum temperature at the nodal point.

Table 12.2. Thermal properties of NKN-Cu in comparison with Hard PZT.

Thermal Properties	c_p (J/kg·K)	λ (W/m/K)
Hard PZT	420	1.25
NKN-Cu	580	3.10

Source: Table by author.

12.2. Dynamic Electrothermal Coupling Factor

This section handles the "steady state" of the heat conduction process in order to establish the steady-state comprehensive equations; that is, in the heat transfer equation, $\left(\frac{\partial\theta}{\partial t}\right) = \frac{\lambda}{c_p\rho}\left(\frac{\partial^2\theta}{\partial x^2}\right) = \alpha_T\left(\frac{\partial^2\theta}{\partial x^2}\right)$, the case of $\left(\frac{\partial\theta}{\partial t}\right) = 0$ is in consideration. The time dependence $\left(\frac{\partial}{\partial t}\right)$ will not show up. Try Example Problem 12.3, where the thermal conductivity can be obtained from the temperature profile θ as a function of coordinate x, without time dependence monitoring of temperature.

Example Problem 12.3.

Referring to Figure 12.1a, we consider a particular disk specimen case with the length L area S. The end surface A is maintained at θ_0 (high temperature) with a heat source, and another end surface B is kept at $\theta = 0$ (room temperature) with a heat sink. After obtaining the steady temperature profile, calculate the temperature distribution as a function of coordinate x in this disk specimen by using the thermal conductivity λ, specific heat capacity c_p, and mass density ρ.

Solution

We will start from a general thermal conduction equation, taking an x-axis along the rod length

$$\left(\frac{\partial\theta}{\partial t}\right) = \alpha_T\left(\frac{\partial^2\theta}{\partial x^2}\right), \quad \text{(P12.3.1)}$$

under the steady-state condition and $\alpha_T = \frac{\lambda}{c_p\rho}$:

$$\frac{\lambda}{c_p\rho}\left(\frac{\partial^2\theta}{\partial x^2}\right) = 0. \tag{P12.3.2}$$

It is important to remember that the time dependency is not exactly an exponential function but an "error function" and that the "steady-state" space dependency is expressed correctly by an exponential function. Equation (P12.3.2) is solved under the boundary conditions $\theta = \theta_0$ at $x = 0$ and $\theta = 0$ at $x = L$. Since a general solution is expressed by

$$\theta = A\cdot exp\left(\sqrt{\frac{\lambda}{c_p\rho}}x\right) + B\cdot exp\left(-\sqrt{\frac{\lambda}{c_p\rho}}x\right), \tag{P12.3.3}$$

we obtain the following requirements:

$$\begin{cases} A + B = \theta_0 \\ A\cdot exp\left(\sqrt{\frac{\lambda}{c_p\rho}}L\right) + B\cdot exp\left(-\sqrt{\frac{\lambda}{c_p\rho}}L\right) = 0 \end{cases}. \tag{P12.3.4}$$

Taking into account the determinant $\begin{vmatrix} 1 & 1 \\ exp\left(\sqrt{\frac{\lambda}{c_p\rho}}L\right) & exp\left(-\sqrt{\frac{\lambda}{c_p\rho}}L\right) \end{vmatrix} = exp\left(-\sqrt{\frac{\lambda}{c_p\rho}}L\right) - exp\left(\sqrt{\frac{\lambda}{c_p\rho}}L\right)$,

$$\begin{cases} A = -\theta_0 exp\left(-\sqrt{\frac{\lambda}{c_p\rho}}L\right) / \left[exp\left(\sqrt{\frac{\lambda}{c_p\rho}}L\right) - exp\left(-\sqrt{\frac{\lambda}{c_p\rho}}L\right)\right] \\ B = \theta_0 exp\left(\sqrt{\frac{\lambda}{c_p\rho}}L\right) / \left[exp\left(\sqrt{\frac{\lambda}{c_p\rho}}L\right) - exp\left(-\sqrt{\frac{\lambda}{c_p\rho}}L\right)\right] \end{cases}. \tag{P12.3.5}$$

Thus, the temperature profile under the steady state is provided as

$$\begin{aligned} \theta(x) &= [-\theta_0 exp\left(-\sqrt{\tfrac{\lambda}{c_p\rho}}L\right)\cdot exp\left(\sqrt{\tfrac{\lambda}{c_p\rho}}x\right) + \theta_0 exp\left(\sqrt{\tfrac{\lambda}{c_p\rho}}L\right)\cdot exp\left(-\sqrt{\tfrac{\lambda}{c_p\rho}}x\right)] \\ &\quad /[exp\left(\sqrt{\tfrac{\lambda}{c_p\rho}}L\right) - exp\left(-\sqrt{\tfrac{\lambda}{c_p\rho}}L\right)] \\ &= \theta_0[exp\left(-\sqrt{\tfrac{\lambda}{c_p\rho}}(x-L)\right) - exp\left(\sqrt{\tfrac{\lambda}{c_p\rho}}(x-L)\right)]/[exp\left(\sqrt{\tfrac{\lambda}{c_p\rho}}L\right) - exp\left(-\sqrt{\tfrac{\lambda}{c_p\rho}}L\right)]. \end{aligned} \tag{P12.3.6}$$

Since the solution formula is $\sinh\left(\sqrt{\frac{\lambda}{c_p\rho}}(x-L)\right)$, as long as we measure temperature $\theta(x_0)$ at one point $x = x_0$, we can determine α_T and then λ value.

12.2.1. Thermal Conductivity Tensor

When a difference of temperature θ is maintained between different parts of a material, there is a flow of heat q per unit surface area per unit time period, in general [9]. The heat flow (i.e., heat flux) (unit: W/m^2) is defined by $-grad(Q)/S$

(Q: heat quantity per unit time, S: cross-sectional area) and also expressed in terms of temperature gradient in Equation (12.2)

$$q = -\lambda\left(\frac{\partial\theta}{\partial x}\right), \tag{12.31a}$$

where the proportional constant λ is called "thermal conductivity" (unit: W/K·m). If we extend this formula into 3D form, a thermal conductivity tensor can be obtained. If q_1, q_2, and q_3 are the quantities of heat traversing, unit time, and unit areas (called "heat flux") perpendicular to Ox_1, Ox_2, Ox_3, respectively, we can define the heat flux vector $\boldsymbol{q}$ described by (q_1, q_2, q_3). In a thermally isotropic material, the heat conduction obeys the following law:

$$\boldsymbol{q} = -\lambda\, grad(T). \tag{12.31b}$$

On the other hand, in an anisotropic material in general, the heat conduction law is modified as

$$\boldsymbol{q} = -[\boldsymbol{\lambda}]\, grad(T), \text{ or } \begin{pmatrix} q_1 \\ q_2 \\ q_3 \end{pmatrix} = -\begin{pmatrix} \lambda_{11} & \lambda_{12} & \lambda_{13} \\ \lambda_{21} & \lambda_{22} & \lambda_{23} \\ \lambda_{31} & \lambda_{32} & \lambda_{33} \end{pmatrix} \begin{pmatrix} \frac{\partial T}{\partial x_1} \\ \frac{\partial T}{\partial x_2} \\ \frac{\partial T}{\partial x_3} \end{pmatrix}, \tag{12.31c}$$

where the vector $\boldsymbol{q}$ is not parallel to $grad(T)$, in general. $[\boldsymbol{\lambda}]$ is the "thermal conductivity tensor". We adopt the so-called "Onsager's principle", that is, the symmetry of the thermal conductivity tensor (see Section 12.2.3).

$$\lambda_{ij} = \lambda_{ji}. \tag{12.32}$$

It is important to note here that when the off-diagonal components exist in the $[\boldsymbol{\lambda}]$ matrix, the two vectors, $\boldsymbol{q}$ and $grad(T)$, are not in parallel but keep a cant angle, in general. Remember that a symmetric tensor can be transformed into a "diagonal tensor" by referring to its "principal axes" as follows:

$$\begin{pmatrix} \lambda_{11} & \lambda_{12} & \lambda_{31} \\ \lambda_{12} & \lambda_{22} & \lambda_{23} \\ \lambda_{31} & \lambda_{23} & \lambda_{33} \end{pmatrix} \to \begin{pmatrix} \lambda_1 & 0 & 0 \\ 0 & \lambda_2 & 0 \\ 0 & 0 & \lambda_3 \end{pmatrix},$$

which helps us handle the analysis in a much simpler way. Try Example Problem 12.4 for this diagonalization.

Example Problem 12.4.

Verify that a symmetric matrix can be "diagonalized" using a "unitary matrix"; thus, if $\boldsymbol{A}$ is a symmetric matrix, there is a unitary matrix $\boldsymbol{U}$ such that $\boldsymbol{UAU}^t$ is a diagonal matrix with non-negative entries.

Solution

Symmetric matrix: $A = A^t$; unitary matrix: $U^* = U^{-1}$ (for real matrix, $U = U^{-1}$), where the superscripts, t, *, and -1 stand for "transposed", "conjugate", and "inverse" matrix, respectively.

We consider here so-called "transformation matrices" with real components (see Section 3.1 in Chapter 3), in particular, such as point symmetric, mirror-symmetric, and rotation matrices.

$$\begin{pmatrix} -1 & 0 & 0 \\ 0 & -1 & 0 \\ 0 & 0 & -1 \end{pmatrix}, \begin{pmatrix} 1 & 0 & 0 \\ 0 & 1 & 0 \\ 0 & 0 & -1 \end{pmatrix}, \text{ and } \begin{pmatrix} \cos\theta & \sin\theta & 0 \\ -\sin\theta & \cos\theta & 0 \\ 0 & 0 & 1 \end{pmatrix}$$

The transformation matrices are all "unitary" (not "symmetric"!). Let us demonstrate the rotation matrix U on the thermal conductivity matrix (under the symmetric assumption) in a simple 2D model. Taking the operation $U[\lambda]U^{-t}$, the original coordinate axes are rotated by angle θ, leading to

$$\begin{pmatrix} \cos\theta & \sin\theta \\ -\sin\theta & \cos\theta \end{pmatrix} \begin{pmatrix} \lambda_{11} & \lambda_{12} \\ \lambda_{12} & \lambda_{22} \end{pmatrix} \begin{pmatrix} \cos\theta & -\sin\theta \\ \sin\theta & \cos\theta \end{pmatrix} =$$
$$\begin{pmatrix} [\lambda_{11}\cos^2\theta + 2\lambda_{12}\sin\theta\cos\theta + \lambda_{22}\sin^2\theta] & [-\lambda_{11}\sin\theta\cos\theta + \lambda_{12}(\cos^2\theta - \sin^2\theta) + \lambda_{22}\sin\theta\cos\theta] \\ [-\lambda_{11}\sin\theta\cos\theta + \lambda_{12}(\cos^2\theta - \sin^2\theta) + \lambda_{22}\sin\theta\cos\theta] & [\lambda_{11}\sin^2\theta - 2\lambda_{12}\sin\theta\cos\theta + \lambda_{22}\cos^2\theta] \end{pmatrix}. \quad \text{(P12.4.1)}$$

In order to obtain the diagonal matrix, the off-diagonal component should be zero, that is,

$$-\lambda_{11}\sin\theta\cos\theta + \lambda_{12}(\cos^2\theta - \sin^2\theta) + \lambda_{22}\sin\theta\cos\theta = 0.$$

Note that because of $\lambda_{12} = \lambda_{21}$ (symmetry), $U[\lambda]U^t$ becomes also symmetric. Then, the off-diagonal components of $U[\lambda]U^t$ can be "zero" simultaneously. Thus, we obtain the rotation angle θ, which satisfies

$$\tan 2\theta = -2\lambda_{12}/(\lambda_{11} + \lambda_{22}). \quad \text{(P12.4.2)}$$

A similar process can be expanded for obtaining the principal axes in the 3D tensor.

12.2.2. Two Special Cases of Steady Heat Flow

Since the two vectors q and $grad(T)$ are not in parallel, in general, to simplify the analysis, we usually consider two special sample geometries: (a) flat plate and (b) long rod.

Heat Flow across a Flat Plate

The first geometry is illustrated in Figure 12.4a. As two surfaces of a large flat plate of crystal are in contact with two good conductors that maintain the surfaces at different temperatures, the isothermal contour must run parallel to the surfaces of the crystal (except for the edge parts). Thus, the temperature gradient is assumed to be perpendicular to the plate, and the heat flow vector lies in some other direction. In the analysis, our focus is merely $-(\frac{\partial T}{\partial x_1})$, and the following three equations stand:

$$q_1 = -\lambda_{11}(\frac{\partial T}{\partial x_1}),\ q_2 = -\lambda_{12}(\frac{\partial T}{\partial x_1}),\ q_3 = -\lambda_{31}(\frac{\partial T}{\partial x_1}). \tag{12.33}$$

Since the transverse heat flow is measured, λ_{11} is the quantity most readily measured in the experiment. Refer to Figure 12.1b.

Heat Flow Down a Long Rod

Figure 12.4b illustrates a crystal in a long-rod form with the same crystal orientation as in Figure 12.4a. If a temperature difference is maintained between the two ends of the rod, the conductivity of the crystal is supposed to be much larger than that of its surroundings. Thus, the direction of heat flow must be parallel to the rod axis. In this case, our focus is merely q_1, and the following equation is obtained:

$$q_1 = -\left[\lambda_{11}\left(\frac{\partial T}{\partial x_1}\right) + \lambda_{12}\left(\frac{\partial T}{\partial x_2}\right) + \lambda_{31}\left(\frac{\partial T}{\partial x_3}\right)\right]. \tag{12.34}$$

Or, using the "thermal resistivity" defined by the inverse conductivity matrix as

$$\begin{pmatrix} \lambda_{11} & \lambda_{12} & \lambda_{31} \\ \lambda_{12} & \lambda_{22} & \lambda_{23} \\ \lambda_{31} & \lambda_{23} & \lambda_{33} \end{pmatrix}^{-1} = \begin{pmatrix} r_{11} & r_{12} & r_{31} \\ r_{12} & r_{22} & r_{23} \\ r_{31} & r_{23} & r_{33} \end{pmatrix}, \tag{12.35}$$

the following three equations are obtained:

$$\left(\frac{\partial T}{\partial x_1}\right) = -r_{11}q_1,\ \left(\frac{\partial T}{\partial x_2}\right) = -r_{21}q_1,\ \left(\frac{\partial T}{\partial x_3}\right) = -r_{31}q_1. \tag{12.36}$$

Since the temperature gradient along the length of the rod $\left(\frac{\partial T}{\partial x_1}\right)$ is most easily measured in the experiment, the thermal resistivity component r_{11} is immediately obtained from this rod measurement. Though the isothermal contour is not precisely perpendicular to the rod axis x_1, because the rod diameter is not large in comparison with the length, the temperature deviation in the cross-section is not measurably large.

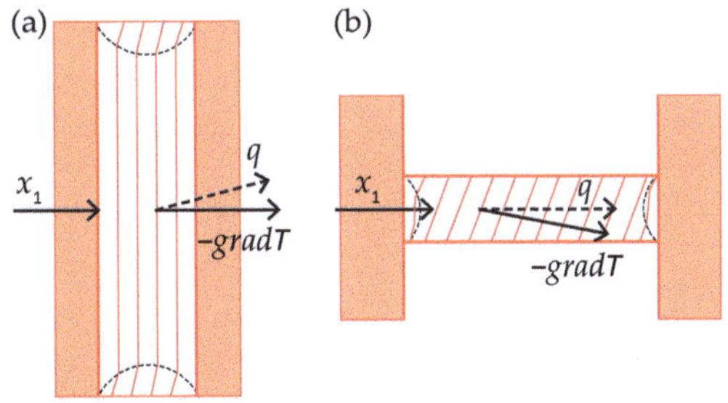

Figure 12.4. Heat flow models: (**a**) across a flat plate and (**b**) down a long rod. Source: Figure by author.

12.2.3. Thermodynamical Arguments—Onsager's Principle

We have discussed the symmetry of tensors such as permittivity, elastic compliance, and piezoelectric constant in Chapter 3. The symmetry of these tensors follows because we are able to write the expression for the energy of a crystal as a function of the electric field and stresses. We need to emphasize the fact that energy is a function only of these variables (provided they are not too large to keep the linear relationship).

For instance (refer to Chapter 2), the Gibbs free energy ($dG = -SdT - xdX - DdE$) can be represented in the Taylor expansion series in terms of only electric field (E_1, E_2, E_3) as

$$G(E_1, E_2, E_3) = \sum_{i,j} \frac{1}{2} \left(\frac{\partial^2 G}{\partial E_i \partial E_j} \right) E_i E_j. \tag{12.37}$$

Taking the first derivative in terms of E_i, we obtain

$$D_i = -\left(\frac{\partial G}{\partial E_i} \right) = -\sum_j \left(\frac{\partial^2 G}{\partial E_i \partial E_j} \right) E_j. \tag{12.38}$$

From the definition of the linear permittivity,

$$\begin{pmatrix} D_1 \\ D_2 \\ D_3 \end{pmatrix} = \varepsilon_0 \begin{pmatrix} \varepsilon_{11} & \varepsilon_{12} & \varepsilon_{13} \\ \varepsilon_{21} & \varepsilon_{22} & \varepsilon_{23} \\ \varepsilon_{31} & \varepsilon_{32} & \varepsilon_{33} \end{pmatrix} \begin{pmatrix} E_1 \\ E_2 \\ E_3 \end{pmatrix}, \tag{12.39}$$

we can understand the interrelation of the permittivity with the Gibbs energy as

$$\varepsilon_{ij} = -\left(\frac{\partial^2 G}{\partial E_i \partial E_j} \right). \tag{12.40}$$

As we believe the exchangeable relation in the energy derivative equations, $\left(\frac{\partial^2 G}{\partial E_i \partial E_j} \right) = \left(\frac{\partial^2 G}{\partial E_j \partial E_i} \right)$,

we can derive the symmetric property of the permittivity matrix, which is

$$\varepsilon_{ij} = \varepsilon_{ji}. \tag{12.41}$$

Such a procedure used above cannot be used in a dynamic transfer phenomenon such as thermal conduction, because no such energy expression exists, though we introduced the symmetry of the thermal conductivity matrix in advance, in Example Problem 12.4.

Another important issue of the aforementioned tensors is related to the "equilibrium state"; for example, when we describe "elasticity", we strain the crystal, and we can work as slowly as we want from one equilibrium state to another. Conventional "thermodynamics" is almost equivalent to a "reversible phenomenon". We may call it, in fact, a "thermostatic" theory. On the other hand, thermal conduction cannot be described as an equilibrium state. In the 1930s, Onsager formulated advanced thermodynamics of "irreversible processes", which is expanded further for the purpose of our thermal conduction in the next section.

12.2.4. Thermodynamical Treatment of Thermal Conductivity

Based on the discussion conducted by Nye [9], we consider here the thermodynamical treatment of thermal conductivity in piezo-ceramic PZTs.

Review of Electrothermal Effect

First, we review the content of the primary electrothermal effect discussed in Chapter 2, that is, a "reversible phenomenon". Under the stress-free condition (neglecting piezoelectric effect), we can obtain the following constitutive equations in pyroelectric materials, in terms of temperature $\theta = (T - T_R)$, electric field E, entropy S per unit volume (J/K/m^3), and electric displacement D per unit area (C/m^2):

$$S = -\left(\frac{\partial^2 G}{\partial T^2}\right)\theta - \left(\frac{\partial^2 G}{\partial T \partial E}\right)E, \tag{12.42a}$$

$$D = -\left(\frac{\partial^2 G}{\partial T \partial E}\right)\theta - \left(\frac{\partial^2 G}{\partial E^2}\right)E, \tag{12.42b}$$

or

$$S = (C_p^E/T)\theta - pE, \tag{12.43a}$$

$$D = -p\theta + \varepsilon_0 \varepsilon^X E, \tag{12.43b}$$

where the following notations are used and denoted as C_p^E: "heat capacitance" (per unit volume) under $X = 0$ and $E = 0$ ($C_p^E = \rho c_p^E$, c_p^E : "specific heat capacity"), $\varepsilon_0\varepsilon^X$: permittivity under constant stress X, p: pyroelectric coefficient. Though all C_p, ε^X and p are temperature and the electric field dependent in general on large modulation of θ and E, we adopt the followings as a matter of fact,

$$\begin{cases} \rho c_p^E = -T\left(\frac{\partial^2 G}{\partial T^2}\right)_{X,E} \\ \varepsilon_0 \varepsilon^X = -\left(\frac{\partial^2 G}{\partial E^2}\right)_{T,X} \\ p = \left(\frac{\partial^2 G}{\partial T \partial E}\right)_X \end{cases}. \tag{12.44}$$

The primary "electrothermal coefficient" p is usually called "pyroelectric coefficient", defined by

$$p = \left(\frac{\partial^2 G}{\partial T \partial E}\right)_X = -\left(\frac{\partial P}{\partial T}\right)_X, \tag{12.45}$$

where we used the relation $\left(\frac{\partial G}{\partial E}\right)_X = D\ (\approx P)$.

We can denote the primary "electrothermal coupling factor" k^{ET} from Equations (12.43a) and (12.43b) as

$$k^{ET2} = \frac{(\text{Couplingfactor})^2}{(\text{Productofthediagonalparameters})} = \frac{p^2}{\left(\rho c_p^E/T\right)\varepsilon_0\varepsilon^X}. \quad (12.46)$$

Utilizing typical values of coefficients in a PZT (APC 841), we obtain $p = 0.5 \times 10^{-4}$ [C/m^2·K], $c_p^E = 340$ (J/kg·K), $\rho = 7600$ (kg/m^3), $\varepsilon^X = 1375$, and the primary electrothermal coupling factor is calculated as $k^{ET2} = 0.11 \times 10^{-6}$—a very small energy transduction rate!

Constraint Heat Capacitance and Permittivity

In Equation (12.44), we introduced C_p^E heat capacitance (per unit volume) under $X = 0$ and $E = 0$, that is, under a short-circuit condition of a ferroelectric specimen's surface electrodes. We may consider a different specific heat capacity under an open-circuit condition or no surface electrode, ideally (i.e., D = constant or zero). Taking the first derivative of Equation (12.43a) with respect to T by keeping $X = D = 0$,

$$\left(\frac{\partial S}{\partial T}\right)_{X,D} = \left(\frac{C_p^E}{T}\right)\left(\frac{\partial \theta}{\partial T}\right)_{X,D} - p\left(\frac{\partial E}{\partial T}\right)_{X,D}. \quad (12.47)$$

From Equation (12.43b) at $D = 0$, we obtain

$$E = \frac{p}{\varepsilon_0\varepsilon^X}\theta, \quad (12.48)$$

$$\left(\frac{\partial E}{\partial T}\right)_{X,D} = \frac{p}{\varepsilon_0\varepsilon^X}. \quad (12.49)$$

If we denote $C_p^D = T\left(\frac{\partial S}{\partial T}\right)_{X,D}$ and $\left(\frac{\partial \theta}{\partial T}\right)_{X,D} = 1$, we can obtain

$$C_p^D = C_p^E - \frac{Tp^2}{\varepsilon_0\varepsilon^X} = C_p^E\left[1 - \frac{p^2}{\left(C_p^E/T\right)\varepsilon_0\varepsilon^X}\right] = C_p^E\left(1 - k^{ET2}\right). \quad (12.50)$$

Though heat capacitance C_p changes theoretically depending on the E-constant or D-constant condition, a distinguishable difference cannot be anticipated because of the small value of the "primary electrothermal coupling factor", $k^{ET2} = 0.11 \times 10^{-6}$.

On the other hand, permittivity defined isothermally may change in an adiabatic condition theoretically when no heat flow is hypothesized, such as the case where a ferroelectric specimen is suspended in a vacuum chamber [10]. From Equation (12.43b), isothermal permittivity ($\theta = 0$) is given by

$$\varepsilon_0\varepsilon^{X,T} = \left(\frac{\partial D}{\partial E}\right)_{X,T}. \quad (12.51)$$

Under "adiabatic condition", by putting $S = 0$ in Equation (12.43a), we obtain the temperature θ change under electric field E applied as

$$\theta = \frac{pT}{C_p^E} E. \tag{12.52}$$

Inserting Equation (12.52) into Equation (12.43b),

$$D = -p\frac{pT}{C_p^E}E + \varepsilon_0 \varepsilon^{X,T} E = \varepsilon_0 \varepsilon^{X,T}\left[1 - \frac{Tp^2}{C_p^E \varepsilon_0 \varepsilon^X}\right] E. \tag{12.53}$$

Thus, "adiabatic (S = constant) permittivity" is related to "isothermal (T = constant) permittivity" again by using the primary electrothermal coupling factor k^{ET} as

$$\varepsilon_0 \varepsilon^{X,S} = \varepsilon_0 \varepsilon^{X,T}(1 - k^{ET^2}). \tag{12.54}$$

We have learned above that if the electrothermal effect exists in a crystal, its heat capacitance C_p and permittivity ε^X are changed theoretically by the external electric constraint (E- or D-constant condition), though the difference is not distinguishably large due to the small value of k^{ET^2}.

Modified Onsager's Principle

Let us now consider the "irreversible thermodynamics" of thermal conductivity and derivation of the "secondary coupling factor $k^{\lambda}{}_{33}$" by using a "space-gradient model" in Figure 12.5. Note again that the time dependence is not considered in the steady-state analysis, but the energy flow per second is considered (unit: W = J/s).

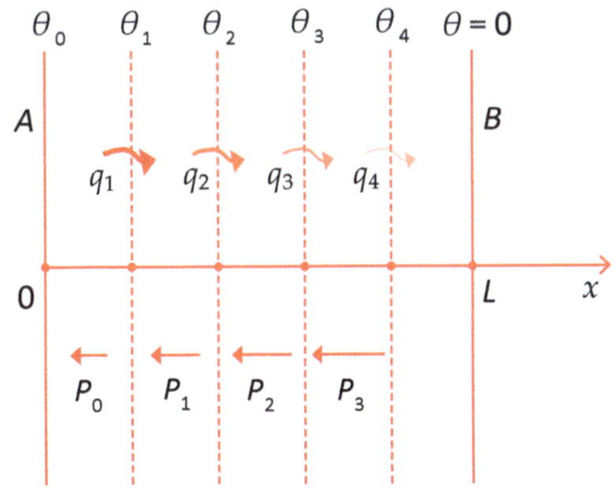

Figure 12.5. A 1D thermal conduction model of an electrothermal material under open-circuit condition. Source: Figure by author.

Electrothermal Equations

To refresh the reader's mind, the reversible phenomenon (no heat flow), i.e., Equations (12.43a) and (12.43b), are repeated below ($\theta = (T - T_R)$):

$$\begin{cases} S = (C_p^E/T)\theta - pE \\ D = -p\theta + \varepsilon_0\varepsilon^X E \end{cases}.$$

Note here that we consider basically unit volume values such as $S = (\mathrm{J/Km^3})$.

The 1D Thermal Conduction Model

We will now consider thermal conduction equation derivation under a "steady-state" condition, by converting the thermal parameters into "space-gradient" components. As shown in Figure 12.5, when the end surfaces A and B of a flat-plate crystal are maintained isothermally at $\theta = \theta_0$ (high temperature) and at $\theta = 0$ (room temperature), with heat source and sink (i.e., "heat reservoir") contacted, the temperature distribution in space (recall Example Problem 12.3) generates also the spatial distribution of heat flux, polarization, and electric field, as illustrated in Figure 12.5.

Thermal Conductivity Equations

Initially, entropy $dS = dQ/T$ is considered in a unit volume. Then, heat flux, defined by $\boldsymbol{q} = -grad(Q)$, is the quantity of heat passing through the cross-section of rod per unit area per unit time (unit: $\mathrm{W/m^4}$); that is, dq is the thermal energy flow from unit "volume" Q, given by the total energy flow $dQ = Sdqdx$ (S: surface).

$$\begin{pmatrix} q_1 \\ q_2 \\ q_3 \end{pmatrix} = -T\nabla(S) = -T\begin{pmatrix} \frac{\partial S}{\partial x_1} \\ \frac{\partial S}{\partial x_2} \\ \frac{\partial S}{\partial x_3} \end{pmatrix} [q : \mathrm{W/m^4}, \mathrm{S} : \mathrm{W/K/m^3}]. \tag{12.55}$$

On the other hand, thermal conductivity is defined in the following equation:

$$\boldsymbol{q} = -[\boldsymbol{\lambda}]\nabla(T), \text{or}$$
$$\begin{pmatrix} q_1 \\ q_2 \\ q_3 \end{pmatrix} = -\begin{pmatrix} \lambda_{11} & 0 & 0 \\ 0 & \lambda_{22} & 0 \\ 0 & 0 & \lambda_{33} \end{pmatrix}\begin{pmatrix} \frac{\partial T}{\partial x_1} \\ \frac{\partial T}{\partial x_2} \\ \frac{\partial T}{\partial x_3} \end{pmatrix} [\mathrm{W/m^4}] \tag{12.56}$$

In parallel, the temperature gradient is introduced as

$$\nabla(\theta) = \begin{pmatrix} \frac{\partial \theta}{\partial x_1} \\ \frac{\partial \theta}{\partial x_2} \\ \frac{\partial \theta}{\partial x_3} \end{pmatrix} [\mathrm{K/m}] \tag{12.57}$$

The operator "Del" or "Nabra" ∇ is the "space gradient", $\nabla = \boldsymbol{i}\frac{d}{dx} + \boldsymbol{j}\frac{d}{dy} + \boldsymbol{k}\frac{d}{dz}$, which is also expressed by $grad(scalar)$. Next, we introduce the "space-gradient" parameters into the vector, and electric parameters, $\boldsymbol{D}$ (or $\boldsymbol{P}$), and $\boldsymbol{E}$, with "$div\boldsymbol{P}$" and $div\boldsymbol{E}$ for the conversion. Referring to Table 12.3, the conversion principle is summarized as follows:

$S \to -\nabla(S)$, $\theta \to -\nabla(\theta)$; $\boldsymbol{P} \to \nabla\cdot\boldsymbol{P}$, $\boldsymbol{E} \to \nabla\cdot\boldsymbol{E}$.

Let us now consider the parameter exchanges from Equations (12.43a) and (12.43b):

$$-\nabla(S) = \frac{q}{T} = (\lambda'/T)(-\nabla(T)) + p'(div\boldsymbol{E}), \quad (12.58a)$$

with unit of [WK^{-1}m^{-3}/m] = [Wm^{-4}/K] = [λ'/K]·[K/m] + [p'·Vm^{-1}/m] = total unit [W/Km^4],

$$div\boldsymbol{P} = p'(-\nabla(T)) + \varepsilon_0\varepsilon'(div\boldsymbol{E}), \quad (12.58b)$$

With unit of [Cm^{-2}/m] = [p'·K/m] + [CV^{-1}m^{-1}·Vm^{-1}/m] = total unit [C/m^3].

Table 12.3. Space-gradient-related equations of physical parameters.

		Integral Form	Derivative Form
Thermal Properties	Entropy	$S = \iiint (Q_{th}/T)dV$ (unit: J/K)	(unit volume) $grad(s) = \boldsymbol{q}/T$ (unit: J/K·m^4)
Electric Properties	Potential	$V = -\int \boldsymbol{E}\cdot dx$ (unit: V)	$\boldsymbol{E} = -grad(V)$ (unit: V/m)
	Charge	$Q_e = \iint \boldsymbol{P}dS$ (unit: C)	(unit volume) $\boldsymbol{P} = grad'(Q_e)$ (unit: C/m^2)
	Polarization		(unit volume) $div\ \boldsymbol{P} = \sigma$ (unit: C/m^3)

Source: Table by author.

New parameters, λ', $\varepsilon_0\varepsilon'$, and p' are introduced above, relating to the non-prime parameters, but due to the difference in driving force parameters ($(-\nabla(T))$ and $(div\boldsymbol{E})$) and in base units (volume and time), modification from the original parameters may be required. If we confirm the (unit) of all parameters, by referring to the following lines of Equations (12.58a) and (12.58b), we can derive the unit of λ' = (W/K·m^3), $\varepsilon_0\varepsilon = $ (C/Vm) without particular discrepancy. However, regarding the coupling parameter p', Equation (12.58a) gives (C/m^{2}K·s), while Equation (12.58b) gives (C/m^2·K), having discrepancy with (1/s) because the heat energy is defined per second. If we admit this discrepancy due to the steady state, taking the permission (W) equivalent to (J), p' has the same unit of the pyroelectric coefficient. Note also that because the polarization equation is based on unit volume, the thermal energy equation is also normalized as the unit volume energy density (J/m^3) intentionally.

In our simple model, we focus only on the x-direction component, which we assume in the spontaneous polarization direction P_S. Temperature gradient provides the polarization modulation $\Delta\boldsymbol{P}$ locally and equivalent charge $\sigma = div(\boldsymbol{P})$, which may also generate depolarization field $\boldsymbol{E}$ in the specimen, depending on the open- or short-circuit condition. By keeping the temperature distribution, we consider the driving parameters (such as intensive parameters) as $(-\nabla(T))$ (vector parameter) and $(div\boldsymbol{E})$ (scalar parameter) for determining the extensive-like parameters $-\nabla(S) = (\frac{q_3}{T})$ and $(div\boldsymbol{P})$. Knowing the facts in the 1D model—namely, that (1) $q_x = -\lambda\ \nabla(\theta)$, and

(2) heat flux seems to be controlled by the electric field E (or $(div\mathbf{E})$), the difference between λ_{33}^{D} and λ_{33}^{E} may be derived. Note that the above equations are valid merely when the room temperature is reasonably low from the Curie temperature, enough to satisfy $\nabla\left(p'\right), \nabla(\varepsilon_0\varepsilon) \ll p', \varepsilon_0\varepsilon$; that is, the change in pyroelectric-like coefficient and permittivity with temperature (or space coordinate x) is reasonably small.

Secondary Electrothermal Coupling Coefficient k_{33}^{λ}

From Equations (12.58a) and (12.58b), we define a new "secondary electrothermal coupling coefficient" $k^{\lambda}{}_{33}$ as

$$k_{33}^{\lambda\ 2} = \frac{(\text{Coupling factor})^2}{(\text{Product of the diagonal parameters})} = \frac{Tp'^2}{\lambda\varepsilon_0\varepsilon^X}. \tag{12.59}$$

This is a significant assumption in order to explain the difference experimentally observed between λ_{33}^{E} under a short-circuit condition and λ_{33}^{D} under an open-circuit condition, though Equations (12.58a) and (12.58b) are not in an equilibrium state but in an irreversible state. If we assume $div\mathbf{P} = 0$ under an open-circuit condition, we obtain

$$(div\mathbf{E}) = \frac{p'}{\varepsilon_0\varepsilon^X}(\nabla(\theta)), \tag{12.60}$$

from Equation (12.58b); then, Equation (12.58a) is transformed into

$$q = \lambda(-\nabla(T)) + Tp'(div\mathbf{E}) = \lambda(1 - \frac{Tp'^2}{\lambda\varepsilon_0\varepsilon^X})(-\nabla(T)). \tag{12.61}$$

Thus, we can derive the following equation:

$$\lambda_{33}^{D} = \lambda_{33}^{E}\,(1 - k_{33}^{\lambda\ 2}). \tag{12.62}$$

The reader can understand that Equation (12.59) provides the support for Equation (12.62) formula. The experimental result $\lambda^{D}{}_{33} = 0.61\ \lambda^{E}{}_{33}$ gives $k_{33}^{\lambda\ 2} = \frac{Tp'^2}{\lambda_{33}^{E}\varepsilon_0\varepsilon^X} = 0.39$. Knowing $\lambda_{33}^{E} = 2.13$ W/K·m/m^2 and $\varepsilon^X = 1375$, $T = 300$K, we can obtain $p' = 0.58 \times 10^{-5}$ (C/m^{2}K·s), which is 1/10 smaller than the "reversible" pyroelectric coefficient $p = 0.5 \times 10^{-4}$ (C/m^2·K). Significant enhancement of the "secondary electrothermal coupling" comes from the very small thermal conductivity λ in comparison with heat capacitance C_p.

12.2.5. Thermal Conductivity Dependence on Electric Constraint Condition

Thermal Conductivity Review

Thus far, we have introduced reversible electrothermal phenomenon equations, Equations (12.43a) and (12.43b),

$$\begin{cases} S = (C_p^E/T)\theta - pE \\ D = -p\theta + \varepsilon_0\varepsilon^X E\ ' \end{cases}$$

followed by the irreversible electrothermal phenomenon equations, Equations (12.58a) and (12.58b),

$$\begin{cases} -\nabla(S) = (\lambda/T)(-\nabla(T)) + p'(div\mathbf{E}) \\ divP = p'(-\nabla(T)) + \varepsilon_0\varepsilon_0\varepsilon^X(div\mathbf{E}) \end{cases}.$$

Then, we introduced the primary and secondary electrothermal coupling factors as follows:

$$k^{ET^2} = \frac{p^2}{\left(\rho c_p^E/T\right)\varepsilon_0\varepsilon^X},$$

$$k_{33}^{\lambda\ 2} = \frac{Tp'^2}{\lambda\varepsilon_0\varepsilon^X},$$

which show practical values of $k^{ET^2} = 0.11 \times 10^{-6}$ and $k_{33}^{\lambda\ 2} = 0.39$, originated from very small thermal conductivity λ in comparison with the heat capacitance C_p, as well as the difference among the pyroelectric coefficient p and p' in the irreversible phenomenon. Though theoretical and experimental background has not been clarified yet, we will discuss below a possible model of why this amplified coupling parameter $k_{33}^{\lambda\ 2}$ is derived, which leads to the thermal conductivity changes depending on the electrical boundary condition on the specimen from the microscopic viewpoint.

Grain/Domain Model

We propose an assumption on the "depolarization field" generation during sudden temperature rise by pyroelectric effect, as shown in Figure 12.6: (a) a poled specimen under the short-circuit condition, (b) a poled specimen under the open-circuit condition, and (c) unpoled specimen. As a polycrystalline PZT specimen is composed of multiple microcrystals, the situation is not actually so simple as described here. However, we assume that poled specimens are handled as a completely aligned single-crystal-like with monodomain, while the unpoled specimens have no net polarization, but each grain (i.e., microcrystal) generates the polarization change with temperature, which generates the so-called "depolarization field", described as $E_{dep} = -(\frac{\Delta P}{\varepsilon_0\varepsilon^X})$ in each domain and grain if no free charge is migrating in the crystal.

Note first that the "heat capacity" is a "scalar" parameter, the value of which is not affected by the specimen orientation. When a specimen is poled and short circuited with electrodes on the whole specimen (except for the narrow specimen sides) in Figure 12.6a, the depolarization field inside the material should be zero because the free charge in the electrode covers the bound charge on the surface and compensate the internal field; thus, c_p^E is expected to be observed. On the contrary, under the open-circuit condition, despite the surface electrode, which provides E-constant two-dimensionally on the disk surface, along the heat flow direction, D-constant seems to be maintained (at least a short time period) by the depolarization field generation, as illustrated in Figure 12.6b. We can expect to observe c_p^D in the short experimental period (such as 10 seconds). Remember that with or without the internal electric field depending on the open- or short-circuit conditions, $c_p^E \approx c_p^D$ in practice. A complex situation is expected in an unpoled specimen: Though the polarization directions are randomly aligned in the specimen, since each grain experiences the polarization reduction ΔP with temperature, the internal depolarization field may be generated in each grain. We assume no free charge on the grain boundary region inside the specimen to compensate for the depolarization field, though the total macroscopic field may be zero. However, because the adjacent grain exhibits the random direction of local polarization, the bound charge on a single grain edge may partially be concealed by the adjacent grain/domain bound charges (Figure 12.6c). Thus, the specific heat capacity c_p^D is expected to be observed as the value in between c_p^D and c_p^E. Note, however, that the short measuring time is essential to find the c_p^D value.

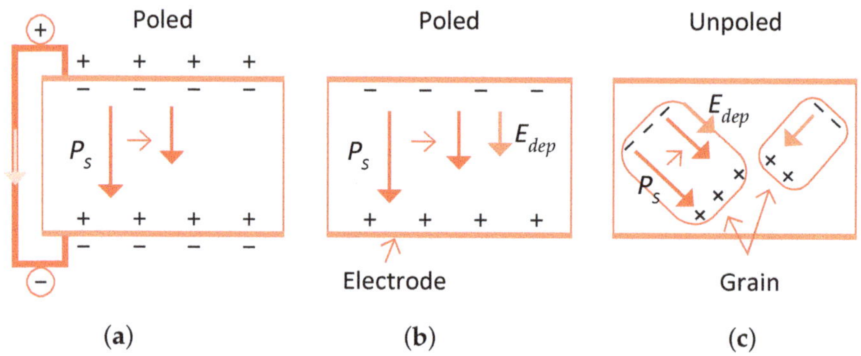

Figure 12.6. Depolarization field generation during temperature rise by pyroelectric effect: (**a**) poled specimen under short-circuit condition, (**b**) poled specimen under open-circuit condition, and (**c**) unpoled specimen. Source: Figure by author.

Though the practical values of c_p^D and c_p^E in PZTs are not measurably different because of a small primary electrothermal coupling factor k_{33}^{ET}, the above grain/domain configuration model on the *E*-constant or *D*-constant situation has been supported by Park's recent report on the elastic performances [11]. The study reported the elastic compliances and elastic losses on various PZT piezo-ceramic specimens: (1) poled/short-circuited, (2) poled/open-circuited, and (3) unpoled k_{31} and k_{33} specimens. Due to the large electromechanical coupling factor k_{33} and k_{31} in PZTs, the difference among s_{33}^D and s_{33}^E can easily be distinguished. The following inequality relationship holds, regardless of hard and soft type PZT:

1. $s_{33}^D < s_{11}^D < s_{eff} < s_{11}^E < s_{33}^E$,
2. $\tan\phi_{33}''' < \tan\phi_{11} < \tan\phi_{eff} < \tan\phi_{11}' \approx \tan\phi_{33}'$.

Here, the subscript "*eff*" means the values on unpoled specimens. From the inequality relationship above, we can conclude that elastic compliance and elastic loss of unpoled piezoelectric ceramics are not simply derived from a statistical average of s_{33}^D and s_{11}^D or corresponding elastic losses but "intermediate" between intensiveness and extensiveness; the electrical constraint condition of unpoled piezo-ceramics is not purely the *D*-constant condition. Relationship 1 was proposed by Fett et al. [12], and relationship 2 was demonstrated by Xie [13] in the measurement of elastic loss of unpoled piezoelectric ceramic. The intermediate elastic property of unpoled piezoelectric ceramic can be explained with a simplified assumption—i.e., each grain is treated as being a microscale single crystal with a multidomain state that has no net polarization (Figure 12.6c). For unpoled cases, even though the polarization is randomly assigned, each domain in a grain possesses spontaneous polarization and generates a "depolarization field" for a short period, in general, if the grain boundary is highly insulative with no migrating charge. However, there are two possibilities—namely, that the surface-bound charges between the adjacent grains have either the same polarity (++ or − −) or opposite polarity (+ and −). The grain boundary with the same polarity area may exhibit a D-constant condition, while the boundary with the opposite polarity will screen the depolarization field effectivity (similar to the surface electrode), leading to the E-constant condition. Therefore, unpoled piezoelectric ceramic shows a mix of D- and E-constant behaviors in terms of elasticity (elastic compliance and elastic loss).

Heat Flux in Grain/Domain Model

Now, we will touch upon large differences between λ_{33}^D and λ_{33}^E with large "secondary electrothermal coupling factor" k_{33}^{λ}= 0.62, comparable to the electromechanical coupling factor k_{33}. Why does this significant enhancement come in the "irreversible" process, in comparison with the "reversible" phenomenon with "primary electrothermal coupling factor" $k^{ET} = 0.105$ %? We discuss a microscopic "phonon model" on the heat flow in conjunction with the above phenomenological explanation. Refer to Chapter 14 on the phonon interaction with anharmonic lattice springs.

A significant difference in magnitude between "specific heat capacity" and "thermal conductivity" exists in a flow of heat energy; that is, "phonon" is always propagating in a crystal from high temperatures to low temperatures in the heat flow process (i.e., heat flux q), even though the "steady-state" condition is realized. In "unpoled" specimens, owing to the random alignment of grain/domain orientations, the propagating phonon is reflected and/or scattered at the grain/domain boundaries in a bulk specimen because of the acoustic impedance ($\sqrt{\rho c}$, c: elastic stiffness) mismatch between the adjacent grains and domains (recall $s_{33}^D < s_{11}^D$). Thus, thermal resistivity increase (or conductivity decrease) is anticipated, compared with poled specimens. Refer to the thermal conductivity data of unpoled specimens in Table 12.1.

Once poled, due to the better crystallographic alignment, thermal conductivity should increase significantly, though the grain boundary reflections still remain. The difference between λ_{33}^D and λ_{33}^E may be attributed to the "depolarization field" generated by temperature gradient via the primary pyroelectric effect. Temperature gradient generates the polarization deviation ΔP, which generates the depolarization field $E_{dep} = -(\frac{\Delta P}{\varepsilon_0 \varepsilon^X})$ in parallel to the spontaneous polarization, in order to satisfy the D-constant condition, when the top and bottom electrodes are open circuited. On the other hand, when the electrodes are short circuited, the depolarization field is canceled, leading to the E-constant condition. Compared with a normal (E = 0) phonon propagation speed, the local electric field (constraint condition) in a crystal may impede the lattice vibration or phonon propagation suppression. This may explain the difference between λ_{33}^D and λ_{33}^E and large "secondary electrothermal coupling factor" k_{33}^{λ}, though this is just one of the explanation possibilities.

12.3. Thermal Analysis on Piezoelectric Transducers

Based on the aforementioned knowledge, we introduce two practical thermal analysis case studies in piezoelectric transducers in this section. Heat generation in piezoelectric materials originates from three losses—dielectric, elastic, and piezoelectric losses. The hysteresis curves—dielectric displacement D vs. electric field E, elastic strain x vs. stress X, and piezoelectric x vs. E under a stress-free condition, and D vs. X under a short-circuit condition—correspond to the dielectric, elastic, and piezoelectric coupling losses, respectively.

We discuss the heat generation mechanisms of piezoelectric actuators under (1) off-resonance operation for actuator applications (under a large electric field, 1 kV/mm or higher), where the dielectric loss is the primary origin, and (2) resonance (or antiresonance) operation for ultrasonic transducer applications (under a high vibration condition at a low electric field, 100 V/mm or lower), where the elastic loss is the primary heat generation factor. The temperature distribution profile on the piezoelectric specimen was simulated with three terms: (1) heat generation from the material's losses, (2) thermal diffusion/conduction in a specimen, and (3) thermal radiation into the environment. As the thermal diffusion/conduction coefficients significantly affect the temperature profile analysis, the contents discussed in the previous sections are very essential.

12.3.1. Pseudo-DC Piezoelectric Actuators

Heat Generation from Multilayer Actuators

Zheng et al. reported the heat generation at an off-resonance frequency from various configurations of multilayer (ML)-type piezoelectric ceramic (soft PZT) actuators [14]. Figure 12.7 shows the structure of the multilayer piezoelectric actuators. The temperature change with time in the actuators was monitored when driven at 3 kV/mm (high electric field) and 300 Hz (much lower frequency than the resonance frequency) (Figure 12.8a). The specimen temperature reached 140 °C, depending on the size, showing an exponential increase with the operation time lapse. Figure 12.8b plots the saturated temperature as a function of V_e/A, where V_e is the effective volume (electrode overlapped part, abL in the figure), and A is the all-surface area. As the temperature was uniformly generated in a bulk sample (no significant stress distribution, except for the small inactive portion of the external electrode sides), this linear relation is reasonable because the volume V_e generates the heat, which is dissipated through area A. Thus, if we need to suppress the temperature rise, a small V_e/A design is preferred. Instead of a single ML, four (1/4) small MLs connected in parallel are preferred.

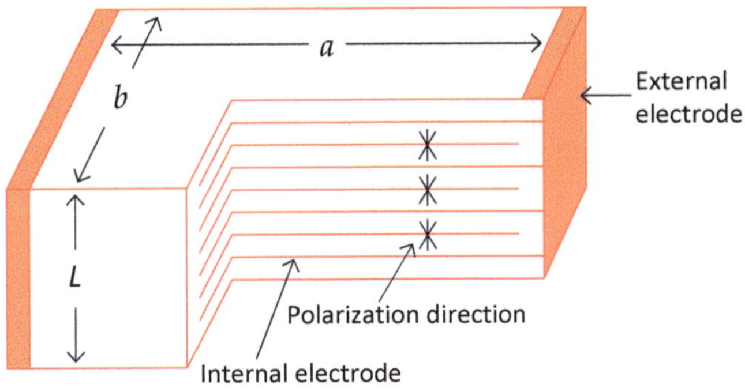

Figure 12.7. Multilayer piezoelectric actuator structure. Source: [2] ©Uchino, K. *High-Power Piezoelectrics and Loss Mechanisms*; CRC Press, 2020; p. 174. Reproduced by permission of Taylor & Francis Group.

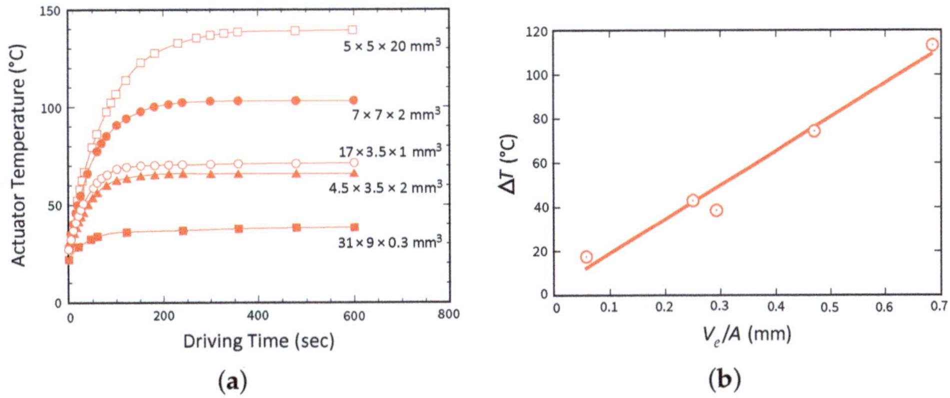

Figure 12.8. (**a**) Temperature change with driving time for ML actuators; (**b**) temperature rise at off-resonance vs. V_e/A in various size soft PZT ML actuators (V_e: volume, A: surface area). Source: [2] ©Uchino, K. *High-Power Piezoelectrics and Loss Mechanisms*; CRC Press, 2020; p. 174. Reproduced by permission of Taylor & Francis Group.

Thermal Analysis on ML Actuators

According to the law of energy conservation, the amount of heat stored in the piezoelectric, which is just the difference between the rate at which heat is generated, Q_g, and that at which the heat is dissipated, Q_d, can be expressed as

$$Q_g - Q_d = V\rho c_p(dT/dt), \tag{12.63}$$

where it is assumed that a "uniform temperature distribution" exists throughout the sample, and V is the total volume, ρ is the mass density, and c_p is the specific heat capacity (per mass) of the specimen. The heat generation in the piezoelectric is attributed to losses. Thus, the rate of heat generation, Q_g, is expressed as

$$Q_g = wfV_e, \tag{12.64}$$

where w is the loss per driving cycle per unit volume, f is the driving frequency, and V_e is the effective volume of active ceramic (no-electrode parts are omitted). According to the measurement conditions (no significant stress in the sample at off-resonance), w may correspond primarily to the dielectric hysteresis loss (i.e., P-E hysteresis), w_e, which is expressed in terms of the intensive dielectric loss $\tan\delta'$ as

$$w = w_e = \pi\varepsilon^X\varepsilon_0 E_0{}^2\tan\delta'. \quad (12.65)$$

If we neglect the transfer of heat through conduction, the rate of heat dissipation (Q_d) from the sample is the sum of the rates of heat flow by radiation (Q_r) and by convection (Q_c), that is,

$$Q_d = Q_r + Q_c = eA\sigma(T^4 - T_o{}^4) + h_c A(T - T_o), \quad (12.66)$$

where e is the emissivity of the sample, A is the sample surface area, σ is the Stefan–Boltzmann constant, T_o is the initial sample temperature, and h_c is the average "convective heat transfer coefficient". Thus, Equation (12.63) can be written in the following form:

$$wfV_e - Ak(T)(T - T_o) = V\rho c_p(dT/dt), \quad (12.67)$$

where the quantity

$$k(T) = \sigma e(T^2 + T_o{}^2)(T + T_o) + h_c, \quad (12.68)$$

is the overall "heat transfer coefficient". If we assume that $k(T)$ is relatively insensitive to temperature change (if the temperature rise is not large), solving Equation (12.67) for the rise in temperature of the piezoelectric sample yields

$$T - T_o = [wfV_e/k(T)A](1 - e^{-t/\tau}), \quad (12.69)$$

where the time constant τ is expressed as

$$\tau = \rho c_p V/k(T)A. \quad (12.70)$$

We can understand that the specimen temperature rise follows only when the heat transfer coefficient $k(T)$ is nearly constant.

As $t \rightarrow \infty$ the maximum temperature rise in the sample becomes

$$\Delta T = wfV_e k(T)A, \quad (12.71a)$$

while, as $t \rightarrow 0$, the initial rate of temperature rise is given by

$$dT/dt = (w_T fV_e/\rho c_p V) = \Delta T/\tau, \quad (12.71b)$$

where w_T can be regarded under these conditions as a measure of the total loss of the piezoelectric. The dependence of $k(T)$ on applied electric field and frequency is shown in Figure 12.9a,b, respectively. Note that $k(T)$ is almost constant, as long as the driving voltage or frequency is not very high ($E < 1$ kV/mm, $f < 2$ kHz). The total loss, w_T, as calculated from Equation (12.71b), is given for three multilayer specimens in Table 12.4, three values of which are almost the same in less than 2% deviation. In parallel, we measured the P-E hysteresis losses under stress-free conditions. The w_e

values obtained using Equation (12.65) are also listed in Table 12.4 for comparison. It is intriguing that the extrinsic *P-E* hysteresis loss contributes more than 90% of the calculated total loss associated with the heat generated in the operating piezoelectric specimen [14,15]. We can conclude that the heat generation of the piezoelectric specimen under high-electric field off-resonance operation is primarily originated from the intensive dielectric loss factor, $\tan\delta'$.

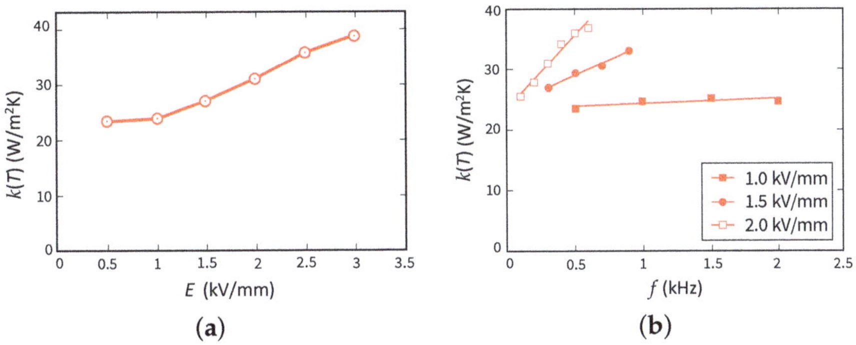

Figure 12.9. Overall heat transfer coefficient, $k(T)$, plotted as a function of applied electric field (**a**), and of frequency (**b**) for a PZT ML actuator with $7 \times 7 \times 2$ mm^3 driven at 400 Hz. Source: [2] ©Uchino, K. *High-Power Piezoelectrics and Loss Mechanisms*; CRC Press, 2020; p. 176. Reproduced by permission of Taylor & Francis Group.

Table 12.4. Loss and overall heat transfer coefficient for PZT multilayer samples (under $E = 3$ kV/mm, $f = 300$ Hz) [14].

Actuator	4.5 × 3.5 × 2.0 mm³	7.0 × 7.0 × 2.0 mm³	17 × 3.5 × 1.0 mm³
w_T (kJ/m^3) $[= \frac{\rho c_p V}{f V_e}(\frac{dT}{dt})_{t\to 0}]$	19.2	19.9	19.7
P-E hysteresis loss (kJ/m^3)	18.5	17.8	17.4
$k(T)$ (W/m^2 K)	38.4	39.2	34.1

Source: [2] ©Uchino, K. High-Power Piezoelectrics and Loss Mechanisms; CRC Press, 2020; p. 176. Reproduced by permission of Taylor & Francis Group.

12.3.2. Resonance Drive Piezoelectric Transducers

Heat Generation from a Resonating Piezoelectric Specimen

Tashiro et al. observed the heat generation in a rectangular piezoelectric plate during a resonating drive [16]. Even though the electric field is not large, considerable heat is generated due to the large induced strain/stress at the resonance. The maximum heat generation was observed at the nodal regions for the resonance vibration, which correspond to the locations where the maximum strains/stresses are generated.

The ICAT at Penn State University also worked on the heat generation comprehensively in rectangular piezoelectric k_{31} plates (Figure 12.10) when driven at the resonance [17]. The temperature distribution profile in a PZT-based plate sample was observed with a pyroelectric infrared camera (FLIR Systems ThermaCAM S40 outfitted with a 200 mm lens), as shown in Figure 12.11, where the temperature variations are shown in a sample driven at (a) the first (28.9 kHz) and (b) second resonance (89.7 kHz) modes, respectively. The highest temperature (bright spot) is evident at the nodal line areas of the length resonance for the specimen in Figure 12.11a,b. This observation supports that the heat generated in a resonating sample is primarily originated from the intensive elastic loss, $\tan\phi'$. Remember that the "maximum vibration velocity" is defined as the velocity under which 20 °C temperature rise occurs at the maximum temperature point (i.e., nodal line!) in the sample.

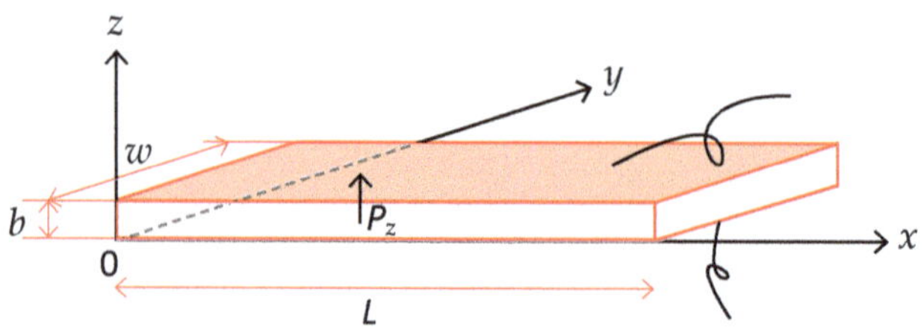

Figure 12.10. A rectangular piezo-ceramic plate ($L \gg w \gg b$) for a longitudinal mode through the transverse piezoelectric effect (d_{31}). Source: [18] ©Uchino, K. *Micromechatronics*, 2nd ed.; CRC Press, 2019; p. 111. Reproduced by permission of Taylor & Francis Group.

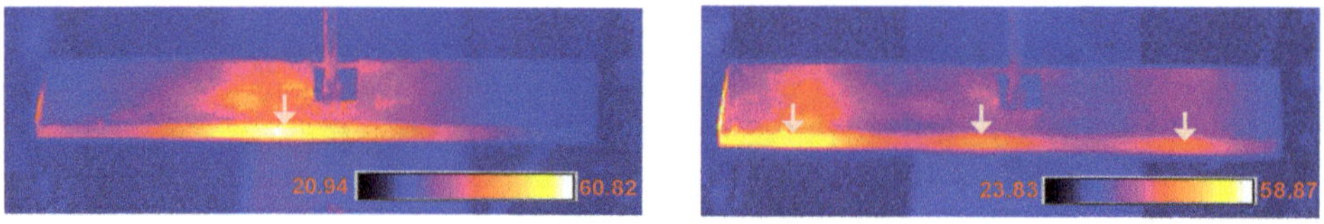

(**a**) (**b**)

Figure 12.11. Temperature variations in a PZT-based plate sample observed with an infrared camera, driven at (**a**) first resonance and (**b**) second resonance mode. Source: [2] ©Uchino, K. *High-Power Piezoelectrics and Loss Mechanisms*; CRC Press, 2020; p. 177. Reproduced by permission of Taylor & Francis Group.

Heat Generation at the Antiresonance Mode

The resonance and antiresonance are both mechanical resonances with the electrical admittance maximum and almost zero (or maximum), respectively, when electrically excited. We can amplify the generating displacement (or vibration velocity) significantly by the factor of mechanical quality factor Q_A at the resonance under constant voltage drive, while by Q_B at the antiresonance under constant current drive. In the k_{31} mode, we derived the mechanical quality factors Q_A and Q_B as follows [19]:

$$Q_{A,31} = \frac{1}{\tan\phi_{11}'}, \tag{12.72a}$$

$$\frac{1}{Q_{B,31}} = \frac{1}{Q_{A,31}} - \frac{2}{1+(\frac{1}{k_{31}} - k_{31})^2 \Omega_{B,31}{}^2}\left(2\tan'\theta_{31} - \tan'\delta_{33} - \tan'\phi_{11}\right), \tag{12.72b}$$

where $\tan\delta_{33}'$, $\tan\phi_{11}'$, $\tan\theta_{31}'$ are intensive loss factors for $\varepsilon_{33}{}^X$, $s_{11}{}^E$, d_{31}, respectively, and $\Omega_{B,31}$ is the normalized antiresonance frequency as follows:

$$\Omega_{A,31} = \frac{\omega_a l}{2v_{11}^E} = \frac{\pi}{2}, \; [v_{11}{}^E = 1/\sqrt{\rho s_{11}{}^E}] \tag{12.73a}$$

$$\Omega_{B,31} = \frac{\omega_b l}{2v_{11}^E}, \; [1 - k_{31}{}^2 + k_{31}{}^2 \frac{\tan\Omega_B}{\Omega_B} = 0] \tag{12.73b}$$

where the antiresonance (normalized) frequency $\Omega_{B,31}$ is k_{31} dependent and can be obtained from the equation, $1 - k_{31}{}^2 + k_{31}{}^2 \frac{\tan\Omega_B}{\Omega_B} = 0$. As the intensive dielectric loss $\tan\theta_{31}'$ is larger than $(\tan\delta_{33}' + \tan\phi_{11}')/2$ in PZT piezo-ceramics, Q_B at antiresonance is higher than Q_A at resonance; that is, the antiresonance operation seems to be more efficient than the resonance drive.

Figure 12.12a,b show temperature variations in a PZT-based plate specimen driven at the (a) antiresonance and (b) resonance frequency under the same vibration velocity (i.e., almost the same output mechanical energy), which clearly exhibit lower temperature rise in the antiresonance, than that in the resonance drive. Remember the similar resonance and antiresonance vibration modes for a reasonable electromechanical coupling factor k_{31} = 30% [17]. In comparison with the fundamental resonance mode, though the antiresonance mode exhibits the strain-zero lines (i.e., anti-node lines) slightly inside from the plate edges for this small k_{31} case, the overall vibration configurations for resonance and antiresonance modes are rather close to each other—more specifically, as long as the vibration velocity at the plate edge is the same, the total mechanical energy is assumed to be the same for both resonance and antiresonance operations. Numerical profiles of the temperature distribution for the A- and B-type resonance modes are shown in Figure 12.12c for various vibration velocity, which seems to be pseudo-sinusoidal curves in terms of the length position coordinate. Under the same vibration velocity, 550 mm/s RMS, the resonance nodal line area shows the temperature up to 100 °C, while the antiresonance mode shows the maximum around 60 °C, indicating a dramatic reduction in heat generation under the antiresonance drive.

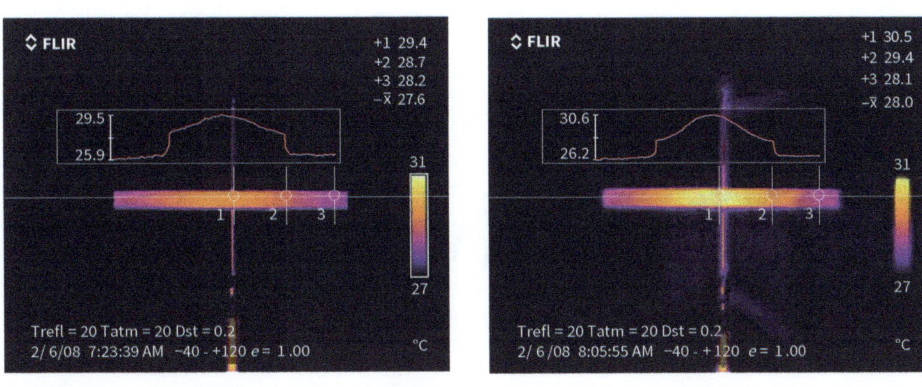

(a) (b)

Figure 12.12. *Cont.*

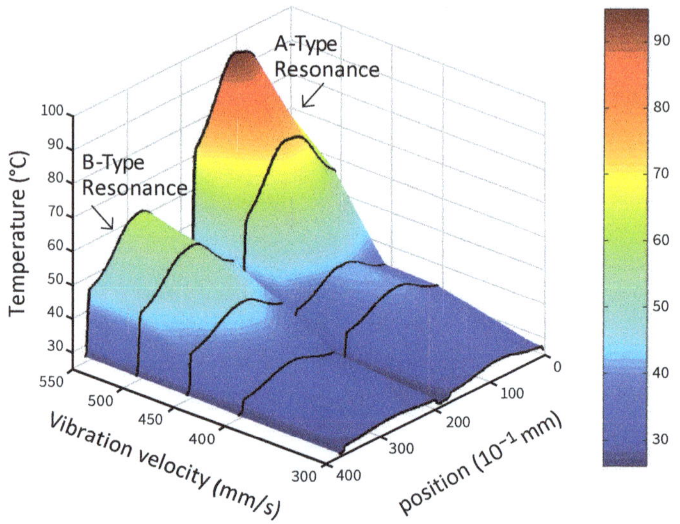

(c)

Figure 12.12. Temperature variations in a PZT-based plate specimen observed with a pyroelectric infrared camera when driven at the (**a**) antiresonance and (**b**) resonance frequency; (**c**) numerical temperature profile for the A- and B-type resonance modes. Source: [2] ©Uchino, K. *High-Power Piezoelectrics and Loss Mechanisms;* CRC Press, 2020; p. 178. Reproduced by permission of Taylor & Francis Group.

Thermal Analysis on the Resonance Mode

Heat Transfer Modeling

We developed a 1D heat transfer model for the k_{31} mode piezoelectric rectangular plate around the resonance/antiresonance frequency range [20]. In comparison with the off-resonance model, where the heat is generated primarily from the dielectric loss and the uniform temperature distribution profile due to no particular stress in the specimen, the resonance case generates the heat originated from the intensive elastic loss on sinusoidal stress distribution of a specimen. Since the initial heat source is sinusoidally distributed in the specimen, we need to integrate the thermal diffusivity of the piezo-ceramic in order to analyze the temperature distribution of the sample. We set the following assumptions for developing the heat diffusion equation:

(1) The 1D heat conduction of the specimen takes the coordinate x-axis along the length of the k_{31} specimen;
(2) Heat generation is proportional to strain squared (i.e., elastic energy), distributed on the specimen;
(3) Heat dissipation occurs via convection (to air) and radiation. Conduction is neglected.

Using a temperature parameter $T(x,t)$, which is defined as the temperature of a sliced volume Δx from the position coordinate x to $(x + \Delta x)$ at time t, the following equation is assumed:

$$\frac{\partial T(x,t)}{\partial t} = \frac{\lambda}{c_p\rho}\frac{\partial^2 T(x,t)}{\partial x^2} + \frac{q_g(x)}{c_p\rho} - \frac{h_d}{c_p\rho}[T(x,t) - T_{air}], \tag{12.74}$$

where λ is thermal conductivity (unit: W/m·K); c_p (c^E in the k_{31} case) is specific heat capacity (unit: J/kg·K; ρ is the density; $(\lambda/c_p\rho) = \alpha_T$ is called thermal diffusivity (unit: m^2/s). The first term of the right-hand side of Equation (12.74) describes the temperature distribution in respect of position x, which changes the shape with time. The second term corresponds to the temperature increment caused by heat generation per unit volume (divided by $c_p\rho$), which may exhibit a sinusoidal distribution. The third term indicates the heat dissipation proportional to the temperature difference ΔT from the ambient temperature T_{air}. The main difference from the heat generation model of ML actuators under off-resonance is the integration of the thermal conductivity due to the temperature distribution in a specimen. Recall Example Problem 12.2 for the dissipation treatment.

Regarding heat generation, we further assume that $q_g(x)$ is expressed in proportion to the square of the sinusoidally distributing strain, as visualized in Figure 12.13, because the applied electric field is small

$$q_g(x) = g_h \cos^2\left(\frac{\pi x}{L}\right). \tag{12.75}$$

Heat dissipation h_d is a proportional constant to $(T - T_{air})$, similar to "surface thermal conductivity" introduced in Example Problem 12.2.

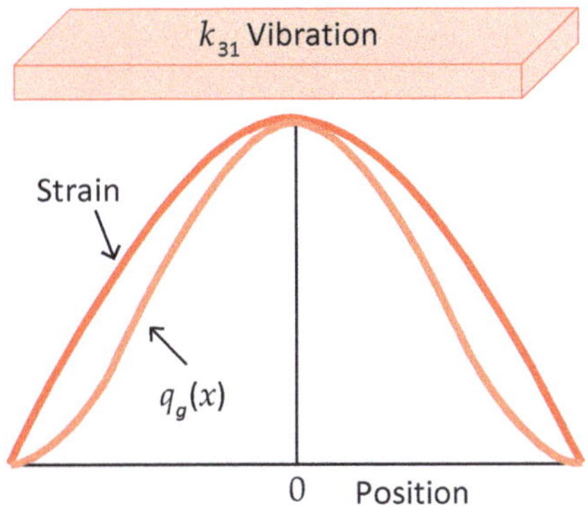

Figure 12.13. Heat generation modeling in proportion to strain square. Source: Figure by author.

Temperature Distribution Profile Change with Time

We prepared a piezoelectric k_{31} rectangular plate specimen with $80 \times 14 \times 2$ mm^3 in size with a hard PZT composition (APC 841, American Piezo Company, USA) for both admittance and thermal imaging observation purposes. We used a constant vibration velocity method for the measurements under 300 mm/s RMS, which stands for keeping the mechanical vibration energy constant. Figure 12.14a shows the temperature distribution profile change with time after driving. You can notice that the plate edge temperature increases significantly with time lapse, primarily due to the thermal diffusion in the PZT from the nodal highest point to the edge lowest temperature point. The saturated temperature distribution profile for the k_{31} specimen is shown in Figure 12.14b, which can be used for calculating the total thermal dissipation energy g_h. A small temperature dent at $x = 0$ originated from the heat dissipation by the center sample-holding rod conduction, which is neglected in the simulation [18].

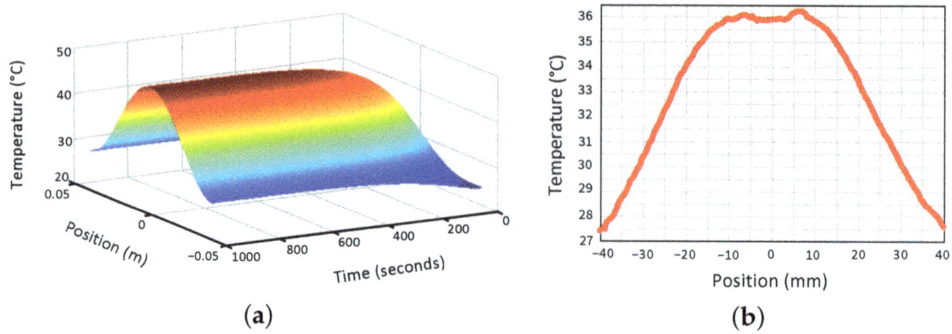

Figure 12.14. (**a**) Temperature distribution profile change with time after driving; (**b**) the saturated temperature distribution profile for k_{31} specimen with $80 \times 14 \times 2 mm^3$. Source: [2] ©Uchino, K. *High-Power Piezoelectrics and Loss Mechanisms*; CRC Press, 2020; p. 180. Reproduced by permission of Taylor & Francis Group.

If we adopt the most general definition of the mechanical quality factor as

$$Q_m = 2\pi \frac{Energy\ Stored/Cycle}{Energy\ Lost/Cycle}, \tag{12.76}$$

we can obtain Q_m from

$$Q_m = 2\pi f(\frac{\rho V_{rms}^2}{h_g}). \tag{12.77}$$

Note that this is the unique approach to determine the mechanical quality factor by using merely the thermal data, without using any electrical energy information.

Shekhani et al. measured the admittance spectrum on the above PZT sample ($80 \times 14 \times 2\ mm^3$) with the resonance frequency at 20.04 kHz at room temperature and obtained Q_m = 507 by a 3 dB down method on an admittance spectrum. Then, the sample was excited under the vibration velocity of 400 mm/s for 30 s, which corresponds to the heat dissipation of 11.6 W/m^2. Figure 12.15 shows the Q_m obtained at three frequencies slightly above the resonance frequency (20.04 kHz). The Q_m values around 550 agree with the extrapolated values from the above 507. Thus, we can conclude that this thermal method can determine Q_m reasonably at any frequency around the resonance and antiresonance region. An increase in Q_m with increasing the frequency suggests that the maximum Q_m frequency (i.e., the highest efficiency) exists between the resonance and antiresonance frequencies [20]. Figure 12.15 suggests that the maximum mechanical quality factor should be obtained in between the resonance and antiresonance frequencies, as Yuan et al. demonstrated in Langevin transducers [21].

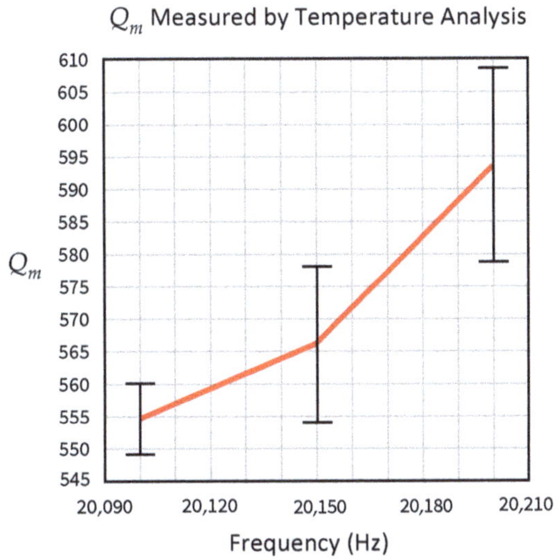

Figure 12.15. Change in Q_m with frequency ($f_r \approx 20.006$ kHz). Source: [2] ©Uchino, K. *High-Power Piezoelectrics and Loss Mechanisms*; CRC Press, 2020; p. 181. Reproduced by permission of Taylor & Francis Group.

12.4. Electrothermal Conductivity—Future Research

The primary and secondary electrothermal coupling phenomena in ferroelectrics were introduced in this chapter from the viewpoint of thermodynamics, in particular, thermal property differences among unpoled and poled PZTs in the poling direction for open-circuit and short-circuit conditions. The derivation processes for the primary electrothermal "coupling factor" k^{ET} was discussed comprehensively, the rather small values of which concluded that the specific heat capacity under both E-constant c_p^E and D-constant c_p^D condition are not distinguishably different in PZTs. On the contrary, the secondary electrothermal effect (i.e., thermal conductivity) exhibits a significant difference between λ_{33}^E and λ_{33}^D ($\lambda^D{}_{33} = 0.61\ \lambda^E{}_{33}$) depending on the short- or open-circuit conditions. We proposed a new secondary "electrothermal coupling factor" k^λ for thermal conductivity analysis so that the relationship $\lambda_{33}^D = \lambda_{33}^E\ (1 - {k_{33}^\lambda}^2)$ is sustained. The significant difference between the primary and secondary electrothermal coupling factors may be related to the microscopic phonon transfer mechanisms, the details of which should be explored in future research. The primary effect includes "pyroelectric" and "electrocaloric" phenomena, and the secondary effect includes the space-gradient (i.e., first-derivative) phenomena, such as "thermal conductivity" and local "electric displacement" gradient. The reader learned also how to simulate the temperature distribution profile on a piezoelectric specimen driven under off-resonance and resonance frequency conditions. The author expects to investigate further theoretical expansion in the application areas of electrothermal coupling and industrial products.

Chapter Essentials

1. Heat transfer equation:

$$\left(\frac{\partial\theta}{\partial t}\right) = \frac{\lambda}{C_p}\left(\frac{\partial^2\theta}{\partial x^2}\right) = \frac{\lambda}{c_p\rho}\left(\frac{\partial^2\theta}{\partial x^2}\right) = \alpha_T\left(\frac{\partial^2\theta}{\partial x^2}\right),$$

α_T: thermal diffusivity (m^2/s); λ: thermal conductivity (W/K/m); C_p: heat capacitance ($J/K/m^3$); c_p: specific heat capacity (J/K/kg); $c_p = C_p/\rho$, ρ: density (kg/m^3).

2. (a) Solution $\theta(x,t)$ at $x = L$ for high temperature θ_0 isothermal, low temperature $\theta = 0$ isolated:

Solution 1: $\theta(L,t) = \theta_0[1 - e^{-\alpha_T(\frac{\pi}{2L})^2 t}]$,
Solution 2: $\theta(x,t) = \theta_0 e^{-x^2/4t\alpha_T}$.

(b) Solution $\theta(x, t = \infty)$ for high temperature θ_0 isothermal, low temperature $\theta = 0$ isothermal:

$$\theta(x) = \theta_0[exp(-\sqrt{\alpha_T}(x-L)) - exp(\sqrt{\alpha_T}(x-L))]/[exp(\sqrt{\alpha_T}L) - exp(-\sqrt{\alpha_T}L)].$$

3. Thermal conductivity λ (W/m K) change with electric constraint in PZT:

Unpoled	Open Circuit	Short Circuit
1.12	1.30	2.13

4. Primary electrothermal effect:

$$\begin{cases} S = (C_p^E/T)\theta - pE \\ D = -p\theta + \varepsilon_0\varepsilon^X E \end{cases},$$

Pyroelectric coefficient $p = -(\frac{\partial P}{\partial T})_X$;
Primary electrothermal coupling factor: $k^{ET^2} = \frac{p^2}{(C_p^E/T)\varepsilon_0\varepsilon^X} = 0.11 \times 10^{-6}$;

Heat capacitance: $C_p^D = C_p^E(1 - k^{ET^2})$;
Permittivity: $\varepsilon_0\varepsilon^{X,S} = \varepsilon_0\varepsilon^{X,T}(1 - k^{ET^2})$.

5. Secondary electrothermal effect:

$$\begin{cases} -\nabla(S) = \frac{q}{T} = (\lambda'/T)(-\nabla(T)) + p'(divE) \\ divP = p'(-\nabla(T)) + \varepsilon_0\varepsilon'(divE) \end{cases},$$

Secondary electrothermal coupling factor: $k_{33}^{\lambda\,2} = \frac{Tp'^2}{\lambda\varepsilon_0\varepsilon^X} = 0.39$;
Thermal conductivity: $\lambda_{33}^D = \lambda_{33}^E\,(1 - k_{33}^{\lambda\,2})$;
Isothermal, adiabatic permittivity may be different, reflecting k_{33}^{λ}.

6. Origins of piezo-ceramic heat generation:
(a) Off-resonance: intensive dielectric loss tanδ';
(b) Resonance/antiresonance: intensive elastic loss tanϕ';

7. Heat flow equation $u(x,t)$ in a k_{31} type rectangular piezoelectric plate:

$$\frac{\partial u(x,t)}{\partial t} = \frac{\kappa}{c_p\rho}\frac{\partial^2 u(x,t)}{\partial x^2} + \frac{q_g(x)}{c_p\rho} - \frac{h_d P}{c_p\rho A}[u(x,t) - T_{air}],$$

where λ: thermal conductivity (unit: W/m K); c_p: specific heat capacity (J/kg·K); ρ: mass density (kg/m^3). At the resonance (due to the temperature distribution in a specimen) thermal conductivity/diffusivity is essential to discuss the "maximum vibration velocity".

Check Point

1. (T/F) Thermal energy drifts merely from high-temperature to low-temperature region. True or false?
2. (T/F) One-dimensional heat transfer equation is expressed as $\left(\frac{\partial^2\theta}{\partial t^2}\right) = \alpha_T\left(\frac{\partial^2\theta}{\partial x^2}\right)$, where $\theta = T - T_R$, t and x are time and 1D coordinate, and α_T is the thermal diffusivity. True or false?
3. (T/F) We consider a particular disk specimen case with the length L area S. The end surface A is maintained at θ_0 (high temperature) with a heat source, and another end surface B is kept at $\theta = 0$ (room temperature) with a heat sink. After obtaining the steady temperature profile, the temperature distribution as a function of coordinate x in this disk specimen is given by the exponential function of x. True or false?
4. (T/F) Heat capacitance C_p of material is defined per unit volume as $C_p = \frac{\partial Q}{\partial T}$, where Q is the heat quantity per volume. True or false?
5. What is the difference between specific heat capacity c_p and heat capacitance C_p? Provide the relationship equation using the material's mass density ρ.
6. (T/F) Thermal conductivity λ is defined as a proportional constant between the heat flux (heat flow) and the temperature gradient; $q = -\lambda\left(\frac{\partial\theta}{\partial x}\right)$. The λ has a "scalar" property. True or false?
7. (T/F) When we describe the thermal conductivity λ in a matrix form, the thermal conductivity matrix becomes symmetric, because we are able to write the expression for the heat energy of a crystal as potential energy. True or false?
8. Whose name is crowned on the principle that provides the symmetric property of the thermal conductivity λ matrix? Provide the scientist's name.
9. In a pyroelectric crystal, provide the relationship equation between the specific heat capacity under E-constant c_p^E and D-constant c_p^D conditions in terms of the primary electrothermal coupling factor k^{ET}, which is given by $k^{ET^2} = \frac{p^2}{\left(\rho c_p^E/T\right)\varepsilon_0\varepsilon^X}$ (p: pyroelectric coefficient; c_p^E: specific heat capaticy).
10. Which loss factor among dielectric tanδ', elastic tanϕ', and piezoelectric tanθ' contributes primarily to the piezoelectric k_{31} specimen driven under off-resonance (100 Hz) and high electric field (1 kV/mm)?
11. Which loss factor among dielectric tanδ', elastic tanϕ', and piezoelectric tanθ' contributes primarily to the piezoelectric k_{31} specimen driven under its mechanical resonance and low electric field (30 V/mm)?
12. (T/F) When a piezoelectric plate specimen is driven under its mechanical resonance, the maximum temperature rise is observed at its anti-node lines because of the largest vibration amplitude. True or false?

Chapter Problems

12.1 Heat flow equation ($T(x,t)$ is the temperature parameter) is given by

$$\frac{\partial T(x,t)}{\partial t} = \frac{\lambda}{c_p\rho}\frac{\partial^2 T(x,t)}{\partial x^2} + \frac{q_g(x)}{c_p\rho} - \frac{h_d P}{c_p\rho A}[T(x,t) - T_{air}],$$

where λ is thermal conductivity (unit: W/m·K), c_p is specific heat (unit: J/kg·K), and a coupled parameter $\frac{\lambda}{c_p\rho} = \alpha_T$ is called thermal diffusivity (unit: m^2/s). Based on the data in Table 12.2, for the thermal conductivity of NKN-Cu and Hard PZT, simulate the saturated temperature distribution profile difference between NKN-Cu and Hard PZT specimens, similar to Figure 12.16.

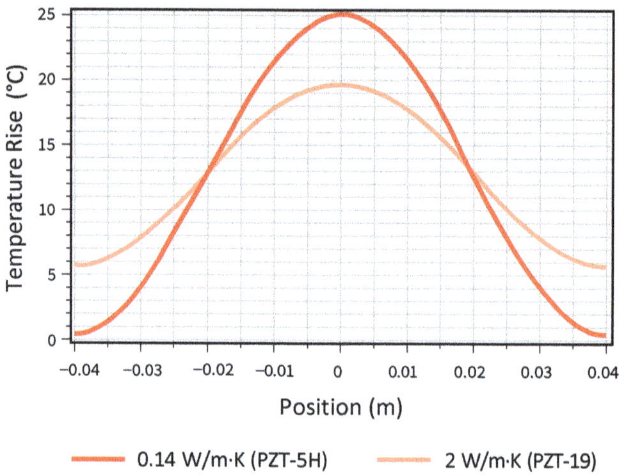

Figure 12.16. Saturated temperature distribution profile difference between PZT-5H and PZT-19. Source: [2] ©Uchino, K. *High-Power Piezoelectrics and Loss Mechanisms;* CRC Press, 2020; p. 182. Reproduced by permission of Taylor & Francis Group.

Hint

In addition to a large difference in thermal conductivity λ, a large difference even in the mass density ρ (check the mass density of NKN and PZT by yourself) provides a significant difference in the thermal diffusivity α_T. You should obtain a much larger difference in the temperature profile than Figure 12.16, where merely the difference in thermal conductivity (with almost the same density of PZT's) was demonstrated.

12.2 A thin bar of the uniform section is bent into the form of a circular ring of large radius r. At one point, P, in the ring, steady temperature θ_0 is maintained. Heat is assumed to radiate from the ring surface to the air. Assuming that the air is at zero θ temperature (i.e., room temperature), show that when a steady state is established, the temperature of the ring is given by

$$\theta = \theta_0 \frac{\cosh\sqrt{\alpha_S}(x-\pi r)}{\cosh\sqrt{\alpha_S}\pi r},$$

where α_S is the radiation coefficient (or surface conductivity), defined by the following equation (refer to Example Problem 12.2):

$$\left(\frac{\partial\theta}{\partial t}\right) = \alpha_T\left(\frac{\partial^2\theta}{\partial x^2}\right) - \alpha_S\theta$$

The coordinate x is measured around the ring so that $x = 0$ at P.

References

1. Pipes, L.A. *Applied Mathematics for Engineers and Physicists*, 2nd ed.; McGraw-Hill Book Company: New York, NY, USA, 1958.
2. Uchino, K. *High-Power Piezoelectrics and Loss Mechanisms*; CRC Press: Boca Raton, FL, USA, 2020.
3. Shekhani, H.N.; Uchino, K. Thermal diffusivity measurements using insulating and isothermal boundary conditions. *Rev. Sci. Instrum.* **2014**, *85*, 015117. [CrossRef] [PubMed]
4. Yarlagadda, S.; Chan, M.; Lee, H.; Lesieutre, G.A.; Jensen, D.W.; Messer, R.S. Low temperature thermal conductivity, heat capacity, and heat generation of PZT. *J. Intell. Mater. Syst. Struct.* **1995**, *6*, 757–764. [CrossRef]
5. Kallaev, S.N.; Gadzhiev, G.G.; Kamilov, I.K.; Omarov, Z.M.; Sadykov, S.A.; Reznichenko, L.A. Thermal properties of PZT-based ferroelectric ceramics. *Phys. Solid State* **2006**, *48*, 1169–1170. [CrossRef]
6. Shekhani, H.N.; Gurdal, E.A.; Ganapatibhotla, L.; Maranas, J.K.; Staut, R.; Uchino, K. Thermal conductivities of PZT piezoelectric ceramics under different electrical boundary conditions. *Insight-Mater. Sci.* **2020**, *3*, 10–14. [CrossRef]
7. Gurdal, E.A.; Ural, S.O.; Park, H.Y.; Nahm, S.; Uchino, K. High power characterization of $(Na_{0.5}K_{0.5})NbO_3$ based lead-free piezoelectric ceramics. *Sens. Actuators A Phys.* **2013**, *200*, 44–46. [CrossRef]
8. Hejazi, M.; Taghaddos, E.; Gurdal, E.; Uchino, K.; Safari, A. High power performance of manganese-doped BNT-Based Pb-free piezoelectric ceramics. *J. Am. Ceram. Soc.* **2014**, *97*, 3192–3196. [CrossRef]
9. Nye, J.F. *Physical Properties of Crystals*; Oxford University Press: London, UK, 1957.
10. Mitsui, T.; Tatsuzaki, T.; Nakamura, E. *Ferroelectrics*; Maki Pub. Co.: Tokyo, Japan, 1969.
11. Park, Y.; Daneshpajooh, H.; Scholehwar, T.; Hennig, E.; Uchino, K. Depolarization Field Effect on Elasticity of Unpoled Piezoelectric Ceramics. *Appl. Mater. Today* **2021**, *23*, 101020. [CrossRef]
12. Fett, T.; Munz, D. Measurement of Young's moduli for lead zirconate titanate (PZT) ceramics. *J. Test. Eval.* **2000**, *28*, 27–35.
13. Xie, M.; Li, F. Anomalous elastic moduli and internal frictions in unpoled and poled lead titanate zirconate ceramics near the Curie temperature. *AIP Adv.* **2020**, *10*, 045007. [CrossRef]
14. Zheng, J.; Takahashi, S.; Yoshikawa, S.; Uchino, K.; de Vries, J.W.C. Heat generation in multilayer piezoelectric actuators. *J. Am. Ceram. Soc.* **1996**, *79*, 3193–3198. [CrossRef]
15. Uchino, K.; Zheng, J.; Joshi, A.; Chen, Y.H.; Yoshikawa, S.; Hirose, S.; Takahashi, S.; de Vries, J.W.C. High power characterization of piezoelectric materials. *J. Electroceramics* **1998**, *2*, 33–40. [CrossRef]
16. Tashiro, S.; Ikehiro, M.; Igarashi, H. Influence of temperature rise and vibration level on electromechanical properties of high-power piezoelectric ceramics. *Jpn. J. Appl. Phys.* **1997**, *36*, 3004–3009. [CrossRef]
17. Ural, S.O.; Tuncdemir, S.; Zhuang, Y.; Uchino, K. Development of a high power piezoelectric characterization system and its application for resonance/antiresonance mode characterization. *Jpn. J. Appl. Phys.* **2009**, *48*, 056509. [CrossRef]
18. Uchino, K. *Micromechatronics*, 2nd ed.; CRC Press: Boca Raton, FL, USA, 2019; ISBN-13: 978-0-367-20231-6.

19. Zhuang, Y.; Ural, S.O.; Tuncdemir, S.; Amin, A.; Uchino, K. Analysis on loss anisotropy of piezoelectrics with ∞mm crystal symmetry. *Jpn. J. Appl. Phys.* **2010**, *49*, 021503. [CrossRef]
20. Shekhani, H.N.; Uchino, K. Characterization of mechanical loss in piezoelectric materials using temperature and vibration measurements. *J. Am. Ceram. Soc.* **2014**, *97*, 2810–2814. [CrossRef]
21. Yuan, T.; Dong, X.; Shekhani, H.; Li, C.; Maida, Y.; Tou, T.; Uchino, K. Driving an inductive piezoelectric transducer with class E inverter. *Sens. Actuators A Phys.* **2017**, *261*, 219–227. [CrossRef]

13. Electro-Optic Effect—The Indicatrix

Among various application fields of ferroelectric materials, electro-optic devices have been focused recently from the optical information technology boom. Since the newcomers are occasionally embarrassed by various math equations, as the author felt 50 years ago, this chapter is for the sake of these readers.

13.1. Optical Birefringence

Let me remind you of some physical phenomena, which you already experienced at your middle/high school age.

13.1.1. Double Refraction

Figure 13.1 shows the "double refraction" demonstration observed in calcite ($CaCO_3$). The characters are seen doubly through this crystal, which is known as "double refraction". Double refraction originates from "birefringence", which means the anisotropic refractive indices in the crystal. When a light ray incidents upon a birefringent material, the ray is split by polarization into two rays taking slightly different paths. This effect was first described by the Danish scientist Rasmus Bartholin in 1669, who observed it in calcite. This phenomenon indicates that the light beam can be modified by the refractive index change.

Figure 13.1. Double refraction demonstration in calcite. Source: Photo by author.

13.1.2. Optical Polarizer

In order to assemble an electro-optic device/system, a pair of so-called polarizers (which are usually denoted "polarizer and analyzer") are mandatory components. An optical polarizer is an optical filter that lets light waves (i.e., electromagnetic waves) of a specific polarization with such electric field orientation pass through while blocking light waves of other polarizations, which is visually shown in Figure 13.2. It can filter a beam of light of undefined or mixed polarization into a beam of well-defined polarization, which is "polarized light". In Figure 13.2, the original unpolarized light includes the rays with randomly oriented electric field (E) directions, only the horizontally aligned E component of which (i.e., optical polarization direction) can pass this polarizer. Due to this E field alignment, the incident optical beam intensity reduced by 1/2 (i.e., the average of direction cosine square, $\cos^2\theta$) after passing this filter theoretically. The magnetic field (H) keeps close to orthogonal to the E field direction.

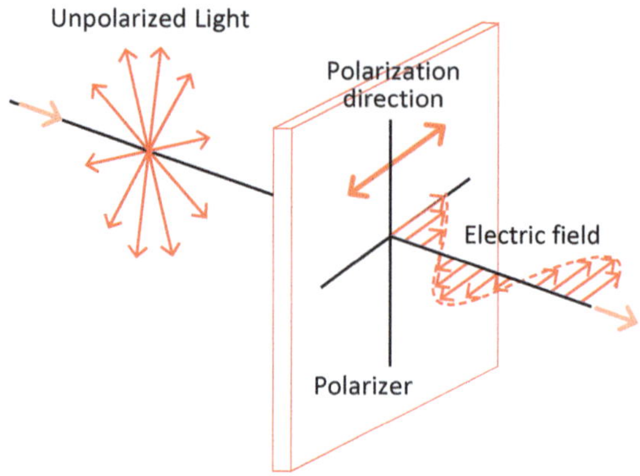

Figure 13.2. Function of an optical polarizer. Source: Figure by author.

The common types of polarizers are linear polarizers and circular polarizers. Certain crystals, due to the effects described by crystal optics, show "dichroism", preferential absorption of light, which is polarized in particular directions. They can therefore be used as linear polarizers. The well-known crystal of this type is tourmaline. A Polaroid polarizing filter functions similarly on an atomic scale to the wire-grid polarizer. It was originally made of microscopic herapathite crystals. Its current H-sheet form is made from polyvinyl alcohol (PVA) plastic with iodine doping. Stretching of the sheet during manufacture causes the PVA chains to align in one particular direction. Valence electrons from the iodine dopant are able to move linearly along the polymer chains, but not transverse to them. Therefore, incident light polarized parallel to the chains is absorbed by the sheet; while light polarized perpendicularly to the chains is transmitted. The durability and practicality of Polaroid makes it the most common type of polarizer in use, for example for sunglasses, liquid crystal displays, and the electro-optic devices. It is also much cheaper than other types of polarizers.

Example Problem 13.1

Transmitting light intensity change of a pair of optical polarizers is monitored with changing of the angle of the two polarization directions, demonstrated in Figure 13.3. Neglecting uniform light absorption by the polarizer sheet, the transmittance changes from 100% to 0% with changing the cant angle from 0° to 90°. Provide the intensity formula as a function of the cant angle.

Solution

Through one polarizer, only the electromagnetic wave with the electric field E direction along page top-down direction can pass, so that the light intensity I_{out}^1 will be a half in comparison with the incident beam:

$$I_{out}^1 = I_{in}\left(\frac{1}{2\pi}\right)\int_0^{2\pi}\cos^2\theta d\theta = I_{in}\left(\frac{1}{2\pi}\right)\int_0^{2\pi}\frac{1+\cos 2\theta}{2}d\theta = I_{in}/2. \quad \text{(P13.1.1)}$$

The light ray already aligned along page top-down direction will pass through the second polarizer with a cant angle θ. Since the electric field along the polarization direction of the second polarizer is given by $E{\cdot}\cos\theta$, the output ray intensity I_{out}^2 should be provided by

$$I_{out}^2 = I_{out}^1{\cdot}\cos^2\theta = I_{out}^1\frac{1+\cos 2\theta}{2}. \quad \text{(P13.1.2)}$$

With changing the cant angle θ from 0°, 45°, 90°, I_{out}^2 changes sinusoidally from 1, 0.5, and down to 0.

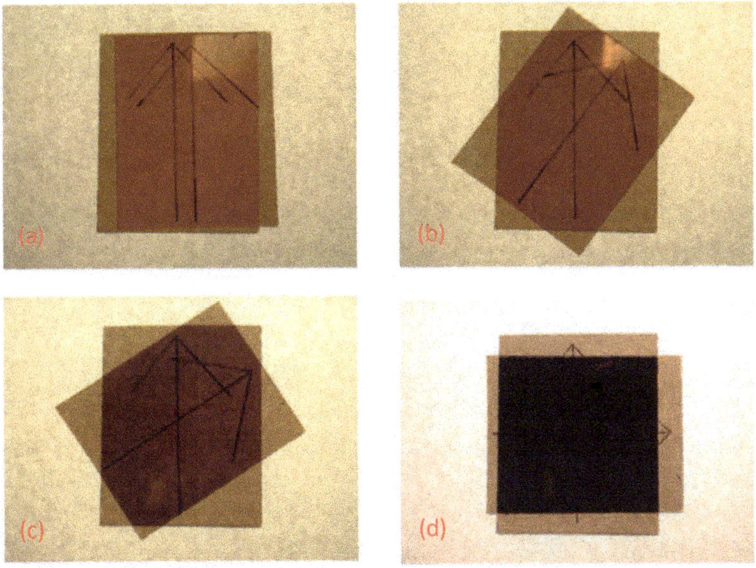

Figure 13.3. Transmitting light intensity change of a pair of optical polarizers with changing the angle. (**a**) $\theta = 0^\circ$; (**b**) $\theta = 30^\circ$; (**c**) $\theta = 60^\circ$; (**d**) $\theta = 90^\circ$. Source: [1] ©Uchino, K. *Ferroelectric Devices*, 2nd ed. CRC Press, 2010; p. 16. Reproduced by permission of Taylor & Francis Group.

13.1.3. Magic with "Scotch Tape"

The author demonstrates "Scotch Tape magic" in the class, which other manufacturers' products have not succeeded with so far. A Scotch Tape (put on an isotropic thin glass plate) is sandwiched by a pair of polarizers. Dark and bright conditions are reversed in comparison with Example Problem 13.1, as demonstrated in Figure 13.4a,b. When the analyzer (second polarizer) is arranged along the tape's extended direction (i.e., 45° cant), no Scotch Tape shadow is observed, but the intensity is reduced by half (Figure 13.4c). This is the base for understanding the "birefringence" and "retardation" of the inserted optical material between a pair of polarizers.

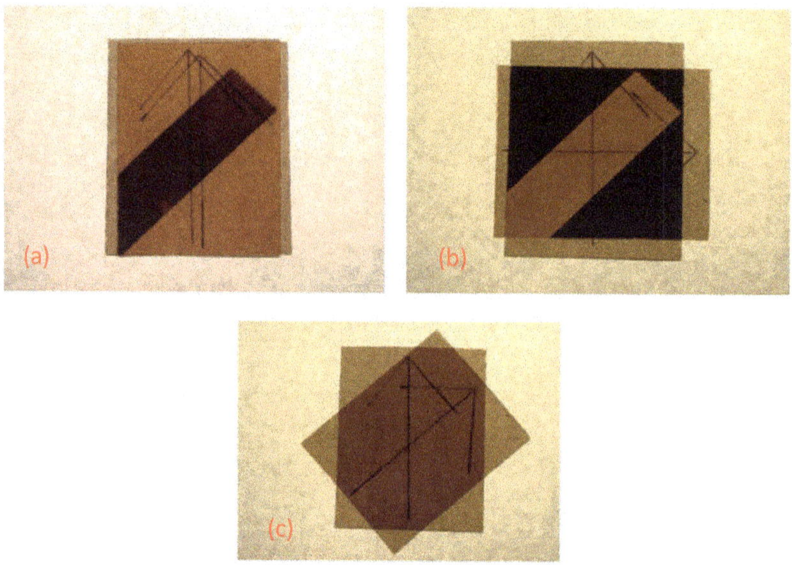

Figure 13.4. Demo with a pair of optical polarizers by changing the angle, with sandwiching of a Scotch Tape. (**a**) $\theta = 0^{\circ}$; (**b**) $\theta = 90^{\circ}$; (**c**) $\theta = 45^{\circ}$. Source: [1] ©Uchino, K. *Ferroelectric Devices*, 2nd ed. CRC Press, 2010; p. 16. Reproduced by permission of Taylor & Francis Group.

What is the reason for this effect? Scotch Tape is manufactured by stretching the tape, so that the refractive index along the tape is different from that of the width direction. This refractive index difference between different crystallographic axes (i.e., birefringence) and the optical path length (i.e., tape thickness) "accidentally" generates the phase "retardation" in Scotch Tape (not in other manufacturers' products); in other words, the polarization direction (E component plane of the electromagnetic wave) is rotated (or retarded) by $\pi/2$, 90°. That is why the "crossed-nicols" (90° cant) polarizer/analyzer arrangement provides the light transmission (Figure 13.4b); or why the parallel polarizer/analyzer arrangement provides the light shutting (Figure 13.4a). This type of optical component is called a "quarter-wave plate" (that causes $\pi/2$ phase retardation). This situation exhibits the above-mentioned "Scotch Tape magic". It is essential to note that the refractive index principal axis (extension direction) of the Scotch tape should be arranged with 45° with respect to the polarizer directions. By inserting an electro-optic PLZT (replacing Scotch Tape) and inducing the birefringence under an electric field, a similar dark and bright conversion can be introduced continuously by changing the applied electric field in a PLZT light valve.

13.2. Refractive Indicatrix

13.2.1. Refractive Index Definition

Since light is an alternating electromagnetic wave with electric and magnetic field vibration directions mutually perpendicular to one another, the electric field induces an electric polarization in a dielectric crystal, and the light itself is influenced by the crystal. Let us start from "Maxwell's electromagnetic wave equations" in vacuum:

$$\frac{\partial^2 E}{\partial x^2} = (\frac{1}{c^2})\frac{\partial^2 E}{\partial t^2}, \text{ and } \frac{\partial^2 B}{\partial x^2} = (\frac{1}{c^2})\frac{\partial^2 B}{\partial t^2}. \tag{13.1}$$

Note here that c is the light velocity [3×10^8 m/s], which is provided in vacuum by $1/\sqrt{\varepsilon_0 \mu_0}$ (ε_0: vacuum permittivity, 8.854×10^{-12} F/m; μ_0: vacuum permeability, $4\pi \times 10^{-7}$ H/m). When we consider a dielectric crystal, the permittivity is defined as a proportional constant in the electric displacement D and electric field E with the unit of ε_0:

$$D = \varepsilon_0 \varepsilon E. \tag{13.2}$$

The Maxwell's equation for E in Equation (13.1) can be rewritten in a dielectric crystal as

$$\frac{\partial^2 E}{\partial x^2} = \varepsilon_0 \varepsilon \mu_0 \mu \frac{\partial^2 E}{\partial t^2} = (\frac{n}{c})^2 \frac{\partial^2 E}{\partial t^2}. \tag{13.3}$$

Thus, the light velocity in a dielectric crystal (under the assumption of magnetic inactivity $\mu \cong 1$) is expressed by

$$v = c/\sqrt{\varepsilon}. \tag{13.4}$$

As the refractive index n is defined by (c/v), we obtain the relation between the permittivity and refractive index:

$$n = \sqrt{\varepsilon}. \tag{13.5}$$

The alternating frequency of the light is so high (PHz = 10^{15} Hz) that only the "electronic polarization" can follow the electric field change (refer to Figure 1.2), and the relative permittivity of an optically transparent crystal is small, not exceeding 10. The well-known electro-optic material, PLZT's (Pb-doped PZT), have $n = 2.4 \sim 2.5$, which are in the highest group in dielectric crystals, though semiconductor crystals exhibit higher values such as 3.42–3.48 in silicon, and 4.05–4.01 in germanium. Note that the relative permittivity value of 1000 in ferroelectrics such as barium titanate and

PZT's are originated from "ionic polarization", as we detailed in Subsection Lattice Heat Capacitance—Einstein Model in Chapter 11 Equation (13.5) is equivalent to:

$$\varepsilon = n^2. \tag{13.6}$$

Since we can understand that the refractive index comes from a coupling phenomenon between the electromagnetic wave and crystal electrons, the higher electron density should exhibit the higher refractive index, in general. As the reader has learned in your school age, silica glass has only $n \approx 1.5$, which has much smaller mass density and electron density than PLZT.

13.2.2. Refractive Indicatrix Construction

Refractive Indicatrix Definition

Remember that the permittivity tensor is a symmetric matrix, which can be converted to a "diagonal matrix". Thus, n^2 should also have a symmetry property, and through the crystal axis rotation, we should obtain only the three diagonal components (n_1, n_2, n_3) along the principal axes.

If x, y, z are the principal exes of the dielectric permittivity (or the refractive index) tensor, the "indicatrix" is defined by the equation:

$$\frac{x^2}{{n_1}^2} + \frac{y^2}{{n_2}^2} + \frac{z^2}{{n_3}^2} = 1. \tag{13.7}$$

Equation (13.7) shows a "Biaxial ellipsoid", the most general case.

Inverse Permittivity Ellipsoid

The representation of Equation (13.7) is equivalent to the following expression: [2]

$$B_1 x^2 + B_2 y^2 + B_3 z^2 = 1, \tag{13.8}$$

where $B_1 = \frac{1}{{n_1}^2} = \frac{1}{\varepsilon_1}$, $B_2 = \frac{1}{{n_2}^2} = \frac{1}{\varepsilon_2}$ and $B_3 = \frac{1}{{n_3}^2} = \frac{1}{\varepsilon_3}$. This expression is called an "inverse permittivity ellipsoid", which covers a wider concept of "quadrics (or conicoids)" introduced by Eisenhart in the 1930s [3].

A general quadric formula

$$B_{11}x^2 + B_{12}xy + B_{13}xz + B_{21}yx + B_{22}y^2 + B_{23}yz + B_{31}zx + B_{32}zy + B_{33}z^2 = 1. \tag{13.9}$$

Reminds the reader the symmetric matrix of B_{ij}, because of the permittivity matrix symmetry and obvious relations $xy = yx$, etc.

$$\begin{pmatrix} B_{11} & B_{12} & B_{31} \\ B_{12} & B_{22} & B_{23} \\ B_{31} & B_{23} & B_{33} \end{pmatrix}. \tag{13.10}$$

A symmetric matrix can be transformed into a diagonal matrix (refer to Example Problem 12.4):

$$\begin{pmatrix} B_1 & 0 & 0 \\ 0 & B_2 & 0 \\ 0 & 0 & B_3 \end{pmatrix}. \tag{13.11}$$

The final diagonal matrix corresponds to the "representation quadric" of the "inverse permittivity ellipsoid".

13.2.3. *Effect of Crystal Symmetry*

Thus far, we have handled the general case where the optical properties of the crystal are not restricted by crystal symmetry. In this section, we will consider the crystal symmetry on the refractive indexes.

Cubic Crystals

The refractive indicatrix for a cubic symmetry crystal is a "sphere" and, since all directions show a uniform refractive index, there is no "double refraction" or "birefringence".

Hexagonal, Tetragonal, Trigonal Crystals

For hexagonal, tetragonal and trigonal crystals, the indicatrix is the indicatrix that becomes a symmetric ellipsoid of revolution about the principal symmetry axis. With z as this rotation axis, the Equation (13.7) is rewritten:

$$\frac{x^2+y^2}{{n_o}^2} + \frac{z^2}{{n_e}^2} = 1. \tag{13.12}$$

Figure 13.5 illustrates refractive indicatrix configurations for a uniaxial crystal: (a) negative indicatrix, and (b) positive indicatrix. "Negative" or "positive" are defined by the difference between two refractive indexes; when $(n_e - n_o)$ is negative or positive, "negative" or "positive", respectively. The indicatrix is an ellipsoid of revolution, and the radius of the central circular section is n_o (suffix "o" stands for "ordinary" ray). The two rays polarized along x and y directions will transmit the crystal with the velocity of c/n_o (slower speed in Figure 13.5a), while one ray polarized along the z direction will transmit the crystal with the velocity of c/n_e (faster speed in Figure 13.5a), where the suffix "e" stands for an "extraordinary" ray; that is, only a unique polarized light ray with faster light velocity. Suppose a point light source is situated in the center of the crystal, the wave front surface should form a "positive ellipse" in the case of Figure 13.5a, the opposite shape of the refractive indicatrix. A similar discussion is sustained in a "positive" crystal in Figure 13.5b.

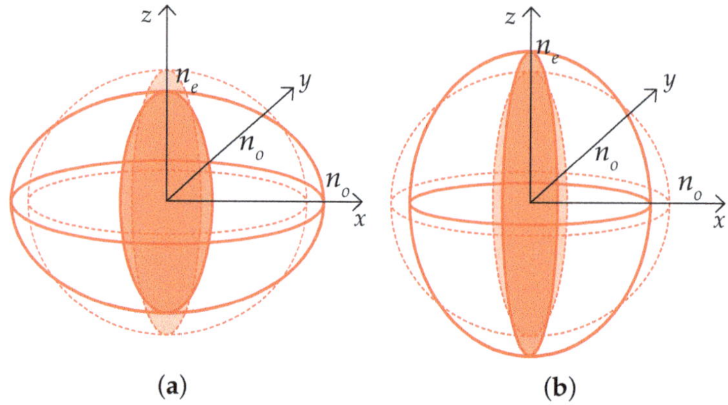

Figure 13.5. Indicatrix configurations for a uniaxial crystal: (**a**) negative crystal and (**b**) positive crystal. Source: Figure by author.

Biaxial Crystals

The refractive indicatrix shape and wave surface for a biaxial crystal is not as simple as that for a uniaxial crystal. The reader is requested to show from the indicatrix construction that the wave surface consists of two sheets, and that each principal plane cuts the sheets in a circle and an ellipse.

Example Problem 13.2

Ordinary and extraordinary rays are incident on a $BaTiO_3$ single crystal, as shown in Figure 13.6.

(1) Which ray, horizontally polarized or vertically polarized ray, is the extraordinary ray? Explain the physical reason for this decision.
(2) Which ray, horizontally polarized or vertically polarized ray, transmits faster? Explain the physical reason for this decision.
(3) Explain why "birefringence" $(n_e - n_o)$ causes "phase retardation" intuitively.

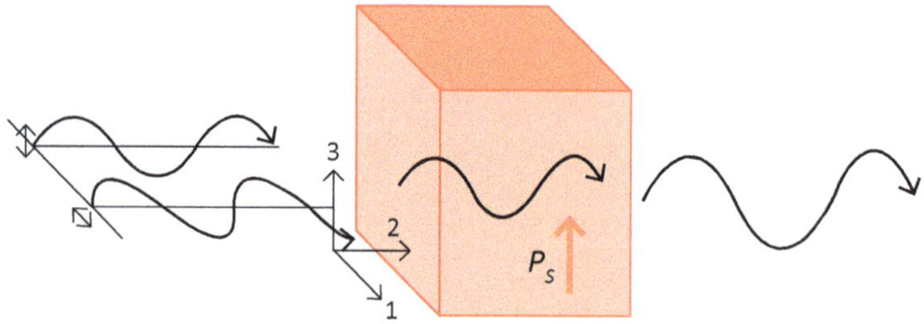

Figure 13.6. Ordinary and extraordinary incident rays into a $BaTiO_3$ single crystal. Source: Figure by author.

Solution

(1) $BaTiO_3$ has tetragonal *4mm* symmetry at room temperature with the spontaneous polarization direction along the 3 axis. As the revolution axis is the 3 axis, the extraordinary ray should be the vertically (3 axis) polarized ray, and the remaining two horizontally polarized rays, one with E direction in the 1 axis (on Figure 13.6) and the other with E polarized in the 2 axis, which is the ray propagating from the page-normal direction (not on this figure).

(2) The tetragonality in BT occurs at the phase transition (Curie) temperature with spontaneous strain, extension along the 3 axis, in parallel shrinkage along the 1 and 2 axes, as schematically illustrated in Figure 13.7a. The electron density dilution along the 3 axis and concentration along the 1 and 2 axes may exhibit the decrease and increase in the refractive index, as shown in Figure 13.7b. The horizontally polarized extraordinary ray experiences the lower n_e, leading to the faster transmitting speed in the BT crystal. On the contrary, the vertically polarized (with E in 1 direction) ordinary ray experiences the higher n_o, leading to the slower transmitting speed in the BT crystal.

(3) Refer to Figure 13.7c [1]. As the light velocity of the extraordinary and ordinary rays is given by c/n_e (faster) and c/n_o (slower), considering the same frequency ($v = f\lambda$), the wavelengths of the extraordinary (polarized along z-direction) and the ordinary (polarized along x) waves are described as

$$\lambda_z = \lambda_0/n_e, \tag{P13.2.1}$$

$$\lambda_x = \lambda_0/n_o, \tag{P13.2.2}$$

where λ_0 is the wavelength of the incident light, and the numbers of waves existing in the crystal with an optical path length of L are L/λ_z and L/λ_x, respectively, the phase difference between these waves ("retardation" Γ_y) is given by

$$\Gamma_y = 2\pi(L/\lambda_z - L/\lambda_x) = (2\pi/\lambda_0)L(n_e - n_o). \tag{P13.2.3}$$

The retardation Γ_y is proportional to the "birefringence" $\Delta n = (n_e - n_o)$.

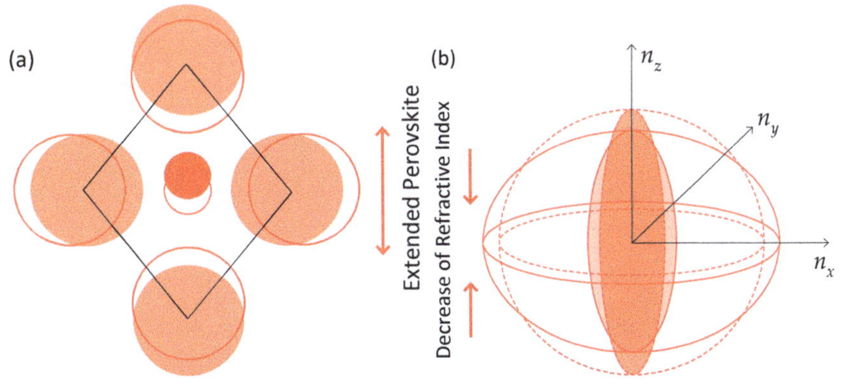

Figure 13.7. *Cont.*

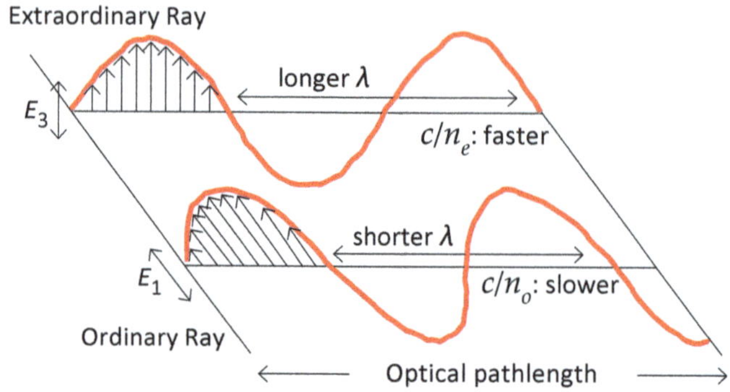

(c)

Figure 13.7. (**a**) Barium titanate (BT) elongated tetragonal symmetry. (**b**) Refractive indicatrix configuration of BT. (**c**) Ordinary and extraordinary incident ray transmission in BT single crystal. Source: Figure by author, adapted from [1].

13.3. Electro-Optic Effect

13.3.1. Introduction to the Electro- and Elasto-Optic Effects

Electro- and Elasto-Optic Effects

When an external electric field is applied to a crystal, ionic displacement is induced, deforming the shape of the electron cloud, and consequently the "refractive index" is changed. This phenomenon is called the "electro-optic effect". Similarly, when an external stress is applied to a crystal elastic deformation, it also generates the electron cloud and electron density modulation in a crystal, leading to the "elasto-optic effect".

Assuming small modulation under the electric field E and strain x, we consider the "inverse permittivity ellipsoid" deformation under Taylor expansion series. Let us start from the general quadric representation:

$$B_{ij}x_ix_j \ (= \sum_{i,j} B_{ij}x_ix_j) = 1, \tag{13.13}$$

where $B_{ij} = \varepsilon_0(\frac{\partial E_i}{\partial D_j})$ is the inverse permittivity symmetric matrix. Recall that in a uniaxial crystal such as ∞mm (piezo-ceramics), $4mm$ ($BaTiO_3$, $PbTiO_3$), the refractive indicatrix has a simple form with the principal axes, which will be utilized in practical electro-optic devices:

$$\frac{x^2+y^2}{{n_1}^2} + \frac{z^2}{{n_3}^2} = 1. \tag{13.14a}$$

In general, the change of refractive index produced by electric field and stress is small (i.e., a small change in the shape, size and orientation of the indicatrix), and we can introduce this change in the coefficients B_{ij}. If we take just lower-order terms of the electric field E and strain x, the change in B_{ij} may be represented by

$$\Delta B_{ij} = r'_{ijk}E_k + R'_{ijkl}E_kE_l + \cdots + p_{ijkl}x_{kl} + \cdots \tag{13.14b}$$

It is noteworthy that the electro-optic materials we consider here are "piezoelectric or ferroelectric" in many cases, which possess the following constitutive equation:

$$x_{ij} = s_{ijkl}X_{kl} + d_{kij}E_k + M_{klij}E_kE_l. \tag{13.15}$$

Even if we consider that the external stress X_{kl} is zero, the crystal under electric field E applied exhibits the induced strain, which reflects to ΔB_{ij} via elasto-optic effect as:

$$\Delta B_{ij} = (r'_{ijk} + p_{ijmn}d_{kmn})E_k + (R'_{ijkl} + p_{ijmn}M_{klmn})E_kE_l. \tag{13.16}$$

Thus, we will define new electro-optic coefficients r_{ijk} and R_{ijkl} by combining primary (pure, intrinsic) electro-optic coefficient and secondary (via elasto-optic effect through crystal deformation) effect:

$$\Delta B_{ij} = \Delta(1/n_{ij}^2) = \sum_k r_{ijk}E_k + \sum_{k,l} R_{ijkl}E_kE_l. \tag{13.17}$$

The linear electro-optic effect (first term) is observed in asymmetric crystals (such as in a ferroelectric phase), and called "Pockels effect", while the quadratic electro-optic effect (second term) is observed in symmetric crystals (such as in a paraelectric cubic phase), and called "Kerr effect", according to the discoverers.

Primary and Secondary Electro-Optic Effects

Though the author mentions r'_{ijk} and R'_{ijkl} as "primary", and $p_{ijmn}d_{kmn}$ and $p_{ijmn}M_{klmn}$ as "secondary" electro-optic effect, the secondary effect is not much smaller than the primary effect.

Let us evaluate the primary and secondary effect contributions. Refer to Table 13.1, which lists Pockels (1st) and Kerr (2nd) electro-optic coefficients for various materials. In typical PLZT specimens, $r = 5 \times 10^{-10}$ m/V, when we apply $E = 10^6$ V/m, we expect $\Delta B = \Delta\left(\frac{1}{n^2}\right) = 5 \times 10^{-4}$. Since PLZT has the piezoelectric strain level $x = 0.1\%$ under $E = 10^6\ V/m$, and elasto-optic coefficient $p \approx 10^{-1}$, we expect $\Delta B = \Delta\left(\frac{1}{n^2}\right) = 10^{-4}$. Among $\Delta B = 5 \times 10^{-4}$, 20% are from the secondary electro-optic effect. In the PLZT "Kerr" optical shutter explained in the next section, when we measure the electro-optic Kerr coefficient R_{ijkl}, roughly a half reduction is observed typically for the completely clamped (no strain induction) specimen. Care must be taken for holding the electro-optic specimen in the device holder so as not to generate stress by the holding jig.

Table 13.1. Pockels (1st) and Kerr (2nd) electro-optic coefficients for various materials.

	Materials	r ($\times 10^{-10}$ m/V)
Pockels Electro-optic Coefficient	$LiNbO_3$	0.17
	PLZT 8/65/35 (GS = 10 μm)	5.23
	PLZT 8/65/35 (GS = 3 μm)	6.12
	Materials	R ($\times 10^{-16}$ m^2/V^2)
Kerr Electro-optic Coefficient	$KTa_{065}Nb_{0.35}O_3$	5.30
	PLZT 9/65/35 (GS = 2 μm)	9.12
	PLZT 10/65/35 (GS = 2 μm)	1.07

Source: Table by author.

Example Problem 13.3

In a cubic crystal, the refractive index change for the z-polarized wave (i.e., extraordinary ray) under an external electric field along z-axis is expressed by the following equation:

$$1/n_z^2(E_z) - 1/n_0^2 = R_{11}E_z^2, \tag{P13.3.1}$$

where n_0 stands for the refractive index at $E_z = 0$. Derive the direct formula of $n_z(E_z)$.

Solution

Taking into account the derivative relation, $\Delta\left(\frac{1}{n^2}\right) = -(2/n^3)\Delta n$, we obtain

$$\Delta(1/n^2) = R_{11}E_z^2 = -\left(\frac{2}{n^3}\right)\Delta n. \tag{P13.3.2}$$

Thus,

$$\begin{aligned} \Delta n = n_z(E_z) - n_0 = -(n^3/2)R_{11}E_z^2, \text{ or} \\ n_z(E_z) = n_0 - (n^3/2)R_{11}E_z^2. \end{aligned} \tag{P13.3.3}$$

Do not forget the factor of $[-(2/n^3)]$, when Δn is discussed.

13.3.2. Electro-Optic Device—Light Intensity Modulator

Electro-Optic Device—Overview

With the application of an electric field E, the change in refractive index is given by a Taylor expansion expression in terms of E [1]:

$$1/n_{ij}^2(E) - 1/n_{ij}^2(0) = \Sigma r_{ijk}Ek + \Sigma R_{ijkl}E_kE_l. \tag{13.18}$$

Here, $n(E)$ and $n(0)$ (n_0) are the refractive indices at E and zero field, respectively, r_{ijk} is the linear "electro-optic coefficient" ("Pockels effect"), and R_{ijkl} is the quadratic coefficient (Kerr effect). Remember that the expansion is not based on n_{ij}, but on $1/n_{ij}{}^2$.

Using the controllable refractive index, we can develop two categories of electro-optic devices: (1) light intensity modulator, and (2) light beam deflector. The first devices utilize the phase retardation of ordinary and extraordinary rays coupled with crossed-nicols polarizer/analyzer in order to modulate the light beam intensity, occasionally called "light valves" or "light shutter". Giant Kerr effects in PLZT ceramics or in $KTa_{065}Nb_{0.35}O_3$ single crystals are popularly utilized.

On the contrary, the beam deflector is used to change the light propagation direction (i.e., the light bends toward higher refractive index side). Waveguides prepared on a single crystal $LiNbO_3$ are rather popular, which is discussed in Section 13.3.3.

Electro-Optic Coefficient Tensor

Let us consider the symmetry of the electro-optic coefficient tensors. Equation (13.17) is reminded

$$\Delta B_{ij} = \Delta\left(\frac{1}{n_{ij}^2}\right) = \sum_k r_{ijk} E_k + \sum_{k,l} R_{ijkl} E_k E_l.$$

First, n_{ij} and B_{ij} are a symmetric matrix, we can denote them as n_i and B_i with $i = 1, 2, \cdots, 5, 6$. Then, since $E_k E_l = E_l E_k$, we may also adopt E_m^2 with $m = 1, 2, \cdots, 6$ for convenience's sake. Finally, we obtain

$$\Delta B_i = \Delta(1/n_i^2) = \sum_k r_{ik} E_k + \sum_{k,l} R_{im} E_m^2 \; [i, m = 1, 2, \cdots, 5, 6; k = 1, 2, 3]. \quad (13.19)$$

We can describe r_{ik} with (6 × 3) matrix, and R_{im} with (6 × 6) matrix.

(a) Linear electro-optic coefficient

The refractive indicatrix under an electric field applied is expressed as:

$$\begin{pmatrix} \Delta(1/n_1^2) \\ \Delta(1/n_2^2) \\ \Delta(1/n_3^2) \\ \Delta(1/n_4^2) \\ \Delta(1/n_5^2) \\ \Delta(1/n_6^2) \end{pmatrix} = \begin{pmatrix} r_{11} & r_{12} & r_{13} \\ r_{21} & r_{22} & r_{23} \\ r_{31} & r_{32} & r_{33} \\ r_{41} & r_{42} & r_{43} \\ r_{51} & r_{52} & r_{53} \\ r_{61} & r_{62} & r_{63} \end{pmatrix} \begin{pmatrix} E_1 \\ E_2 \\ E_3 \end{pmatrix}. \quad (13.20)$$

Single crystal $LiNbO_3$ belongs to the crystal symmetry $3m$ and is optically uniaxial, with ordinary refractive indexes $n_{11} = n_{22} = n_o$, and extraordinary index $n_{33} = n_e$. In this case, the electro-optic coefficient matrix is

$$\begin{pmatrix} 0 & -r_{22} & r_{13} \\ 0 & r_{22} & r_{13} \\ 0 & 0 & r_{33} \\ 0 & r_{51} & 0 \\ r_{51} & 0 & 0 \\ -r_{22} & 0 & 0 \end{pmatrix}.$$

When we consider only E_3 as a non-zero field with keeping $E_1 = E_2 = 0$, we obtain only two applicable equations:

$$\begin{cases} \Delta\left(\frac{1}{n_3^2}\right) = r_{33}E_3 \\ \Delta\left(\frac{1}{n_1^2}\right) = \Delta\left(\frac{1}{n_2^2}\right) = r_{13}E_3 \end{cases}. \quad (13.21)$$

Thus,

$$\begin{cases} n_e(E_z) = n_e - ({n_e}^3/2)r_{33}E_3 \\ n_o(E_z) = n_o - ({n_o}^3/2)r_{13}E_3 \end{cases}. \quad (13.22)$$

Taking into account the electro-optic data for $LiNbO_3$ at room temperature, $\lambda = 632.8$ nm:

- $n_e = 2.200$, $n_o = 2.286$
- $r_c^X = r_{33} - (n_o/n_e)^3 r_{13} = 0.19 \times 10^{-10}$m/V

under the electric field $E_z = 10^5$ V/m applied, the refractive index changes for extraordinary and ordinary rays are roughly $\Delta n_e = 20 \times 10^{-6}$ and $\Delta n_o = 5 \times 10^{-6}$.

(b) Quadratic electro-optic coefficient

Considering the paraelectric phase of a perovskite crystal ($m3m$) as an example, the Kerr coefficients are represented in the following matrix with only three independent components:

$$\begin{pmatrix} R_{11} & R_{12} & R_{12} & 0 & 0 & 0 \\ R_{12} & R_{11} & R_{12} & 0 & 0 & 0 \\ R_{12} & R_{12} & R_{11} & 0 & 0 & 0 \\ 0 & 0 & 0 & R_{44} & 0 & 0 \\ 0 & 0 & 0 & 0 & R_{44} & 0 \\ 0 & 0 & 0 & 0 & 0 & R_{44} \end{pmatrix},$$

so that the refractive indicatrix under an electric field applied is expressed as:

$$\begin{pmatrix} \Delta(1/n_1^2) \\ \Delta(1/n_2^2) \\ \Delta(1/n_3^2) \\ \Delta(1/n_4^2) \\ \Delta(1/n_5^2) \\ \Delta(1/n_6^2) \end{pmatrix} = \begin{pmatrix} R_{11} & R_{12} & R_{12} & 0 & 0 & 0 \\ R_{12} & R_{11} & R_{12} & 0 & 0 & 0 \\ R_{12} & R_{12} & R_{11} & 0 & 0 & 0 \\ 0 & 0 & 0 & R_{44} & 0 & 0 \\ 0 & 0 & 0 & 0 & R_{44} & 0 \\ 0 & 0 & 0 & 0 & 0 & R_{44} \end{pmatrix} \begin{pmatrix} E_1^2 \\ E_2^2 \\ E_3^2 \\ E_4^2 \\ E_5^2 \\ E_6^2 \end{pmatrix}. \quad (13.23)$$

If we consider only E_3^2 as a non-zero field with keeping $E_1^2 = E_2^2 = 0$, we obtain only two applicable equations:

$$\begin{cases} \Delta\left(\frac{1}{n_3^2}\right) = R_{11}E_3^2 \\ \Delta\left(\frac{1}{n_1^2}\right) = \Delta\left(\frac{1}{n_2^2}\right) = R_{12}E_3^2 \end{cases}. \tag{13.24}$$

Thus,

$$\begin{cases} n_z(E_z) = n_0 - (n^3/2)R_{11}E_z^2 \\ n_x(E_z) = n_0 - (n^3/2)R_{12}E_z^2 \end{cases}. \tag{13.25}$$

Or in an indicatrix formula,

$$\frac{x^2 + y^2}{n_0{}^2\left[1 - \left(\frac{n_0{}^2}{2}\right)R_{12}E_z{}^2\right]^2} + \frac{z^2}{n_0{}^2\left[1 - \left(\frac{n_0{}^2}{2}\right)R_{11}E_z{}^2\right]^2} = 1. \tag{13.26}$$

Light Shutter Construction

The refractive index change under an external electric field is explained intuitively as follows. When an electric field E_z is applied to a cubic perovskite crystal, the crystal is elongated along the z-axis and contracted along both the x and y axes. Consequently, the material's density or compactness will be decreased along the z axis and densified along the x and y axes, leading to a decrease in the refractive index nz and an increase of the indices n_x and n_y, as shown in Figure 13.7b (Sphere becomes a doughnut-shape), and expressed in Equation (13.23). Note that the refractive index is proportional to the electron density or ion compactness along the polarized light electric field direction, which is perpendicular to the light propagation direction. Taking into account the above description, R_{11} and R_{12} in Equation (13.22) should be positive and negative, respectively.

(a) EO device setup

Refer to Figure 13.8. When light is transmitted along the y direction, a cubic electro-optic (EO) specimen (such as PLZT) with a rectangular shape (optical path length: L) is put between two crossed-nicols polarizer/analyzer arranged at $\pm 45°$ with respect to the z-axis. Assuming voltage V_z applied to the specimen with an electrode gap d, and light with a wavelength of λ (incident intensity: I_0) is transmitted through it, we will derive the output light intensity $I(V_z)$ by neglecting light absorption in the EO specimen. We denote the necessary parameters as listed below:

- Refractive index at $E = 0 : n_0$,
- Electro-optic Kerr coefficients : R_{11}, R_{12},
- Phase retardation: Γ_y,
- Reflectance at the crystal surface (normal incidence): $Re = [(n - 1)/(n + 1)]^2$.

The output light intensity is reduced twice, once at the inlet, and once again at the outlet crystal surfaces by a factor of $(1 - Re)^2$. The reader should also notice that the incident light (after passing through the first polarizer) has ordinary and extraordinary light components of equal magnitudes, because of the 45° cant angle of the polarizer.

(b) Retardation calculation

In a cubic structure, the refractive index change under an external electric field along the z-axis is expressed by the following two equations:

$$1/n_z^2(E_z) - 1/n_0^2 = R_{11}E_z^2, \tag{13.27}$$

$$1/n_x^2(E_z) - 1/n_0^2 = R_{12}E_z^2. \tag{13.28}$$

Taking into account the relation, $d(1/n^2) = -(2/n^3)dn$,

$$n_z(E_z) = n_0 - (1/2)\, n_0^3 R_{11} E_z^2, \tag{13.29}$$

$$n_x(E_z) = n_0 - (1/2)\, n_0^3 R_{12} E_z^2, \tag{13.30}$$

where $R_{11} > 0$ and $R_{12} < 0$ in most cases. Since the wavelengths of the extraordinary (polarized along z-direction) and the ordinary (polarized along x) waves are described as

$$\lambda_z = \lambda_0/n_z, \tag{13.31}$$

$$\lambda_x = \lambda_0/n_x, \tag{13.32}$$

where λ_0 is the vacuum wavelength of the incident light, and the numbers of waves existing in the crystal with an optical path length of L are L/λ_z and L/λ_x, respectively, the phase difference between these waves ("retardation" Γ_y) is described by

$$\Gamma_y = 2\pi(L/\lambda_x - L/\lambda_z) = (2\pi/\lambda_0)L\Delta n = (2\pi/\lambda_0)L(1/2)n_0^3(R_{11} - R_{12})(V_z/d)^2. \tag{13.33}$$

The retardation is proportional to the birefringence Δn ($=n_x - n_z$).

(c) Polarizer/analyzer arrangement

First, in comparison with the unpolarized light intensity, the intensity after one polarizer is just a half (by neglecting the light absorption by the polarizer). We will take this intensity after one polarizer as the incident light intensity I_0. Second, we describe the linearly polarized light incident on the PLZT in terms of its electric field vector as

$$\begin{pmatrix} e_x \\ e_z \end{pmatrix} \sqrt{I_0} \begin{pmatrix} \sin[(\frac{2\pi}{\lambda_0})y - \omega t] \\ \sin[(\frac{2\pi}{\lambda_0})y - \omega t] \end{pmatrix}. \tag{13.34}$$

Note here that 45° arrangement generates the same electric field amplitude along x and z directions, and that the relationship $I = e^2/2$, i.e., the intensity is an average of e^2 in terms of time. Third, the output light from the PLZT can be described as

$$\begin{pmatrix} e_x \\ e_z \end{pmatrix} \sqrt{(1 - Re)^2\, I_0} \begin{pmatrix} \sin[(\frac{2\pi}{\lambda_0})y - \omega t + \phi] \\ \sin[(\frac{2\pi}{\lambda_0})y - \omega t + \phi - \Gamma_y] \end{pmatrix}. \tag{13.35}$$

Remember to consider twice reflections on the front and backside of the PLZT sample, which reduces the light intensity by $(1 - Re)^2$. Additionally, basically the extraordinary ray speed corresponding to output e_z is faster than the ordinary ray speed (e_x), leading to the phase delay of Γ_y in e_z when we consider the optical path length L, which reflects in the term $\sin[\left(\frac{2\pi}{\lambda_0}\right)y - \omega t + \phi - \Gamma_y]$. Fourth, through the second polarizer (i.e., analyzer) arranged now at the $-45°$ orientation, the electric field component in this direction $e_{-45cant}$ is represented (taking into account the electric field vector projection on this $-45°$ orientation) by:

$$\begin{aligned} e_x/\sqrt{2} - e_z/\sqrt{2} &= (1-Re)\sqrt{I_0/2}\{\sin[(2\pi/\lambda_0)y - \omega t + \phi] - \sin[(2\pi/\lambda_0)y - \omega t + \phi - \Gamma]\} \\ &= (1-Re)\sqrt{I_0/2}[(1-\cos\Gamma_y)\sin[(2\pi/\lambda_0)y - \omega t + \phi] + \sin\Gamma_y \cos[(2\pi/\lambda_0)y - \omega t + \phi]. \end{aligned} \quad (13.36)$$

Finally, the output intensity through the 2nd polarizer ($-45°$ cant) is obtained from the relation $I = {e_{-45\text{cant}}}^2/2$:

$$I = (1/2)(1-Re)^2(I_0/2)[(1-\cos\Gamma_y)^2 + (\sin\Gamma_y)^2] = (1-Re)^2 I_0\left(\frac{1-\cos\Gamma_y}{2}\right) \quad (13.37)$$

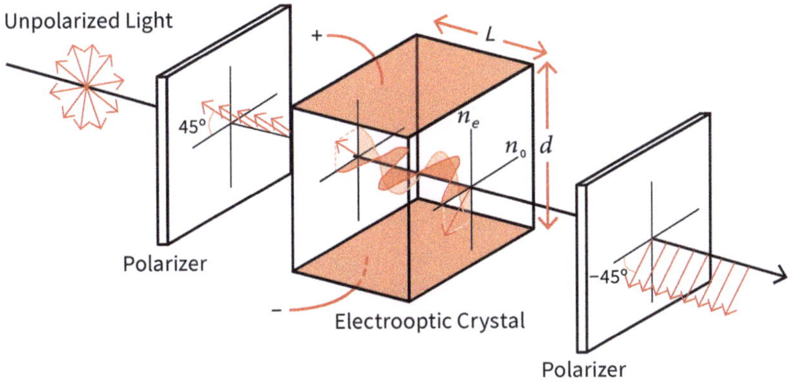

Figure 13.8. Optical phase retardation through an electro-optic crystal. Notice the crossed-nicols polarizer/analyzer configuration with the principal optical axis ±45° cant. Source: [1] ©Uchino, K. *Ferroelectric Devices*, 2nd ed. CRC Press, 2010; p. 13. Reproduced by permission of Taylor & Francis Group.

(d) Half-wave voltage

Remember that the retardation Γ_y is given by Equation (13.30), $\Gamma_y = (2\pi/\lambda_0)L(1/2)$ ${n_0}^3(R_{11} - R_{12})(V_z/d)^2$. Note that by increasing Γ_y from 0, $\pi/2$ and π, $(\frac{1-\cos\Gamma_y}{2})$ value increases from 0, 1/2, then 1. Figure 13.9 shows the output intensity I (actually $(1 - Re)^2 I_0$) as a function of applied voltage V_z, which exhibits maximum and minimum successively. The "half-wave voltage", which is defined as the voltage required to exhibit the first maximum in the transmitted light intensity, is given from the condition, $\cos\Gamma_y = -1$ or $\Gamma_y = \pi$. When we use a sample with Keer (secondary) electro-optic effect, Γ_y is expressed by Equation (13.30), and the half-wave voltage can be obtained as

$$V_{z,\lambda/2} = d\sqrt{\frac{\lambda_0}{L{n_0}^3(R_{11} - R_{12})}}. \quad (13.38)$$

The intensity maxima can be sequentially obtained with increasing the applied voltage. Notice that these half-wave, one-and-a-half-wave, and two-and-a-half-wave voltages are not arranged linearly, due to the nonlinear (quadratic) Kerr electro-optic effect.

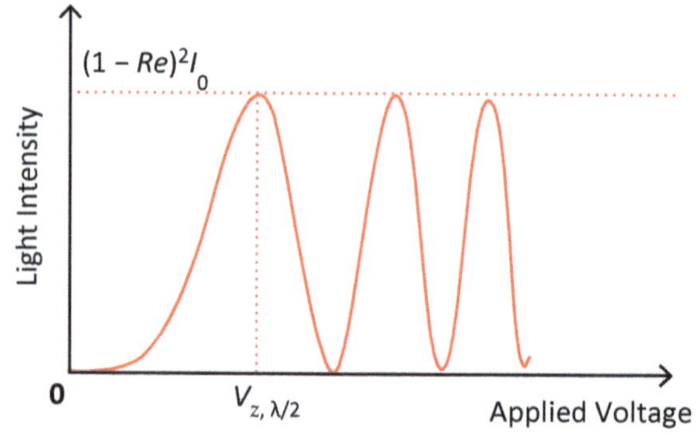

Figure 13.9. Variation in the light intensity of a Kerr-effect electro-optic shutter with applied voltage. Source: Figure by author, adapted from [1].

Example Problem 13.4

A PLZT specimen with a cubic symmetry has the refractive index $n_0 = 2.49$. A specimen with light pass-length $L = 5$ mm and electrode gap $d = 1$ mm was set in Figure 13.10a system. When $\lambda = 633$ nm laser light was transmitted perpendicular to the electric field, we obtained the light intensity change with applied voltage as shown in Figure 13.10b. Note that the maximum intensity voltage (i.e., half-wave voltage) was 150 V. Calculate the electro-optic coefficient $(R_{11} - R_{12})$ for this PLZT specimen.

Solution

The half-wave voltage is determined from the following condition on the retardation Γ_y:

$$\Gamma_y = (\pi/\lambda){n_0}^3{E_3}^2(R_{11} - R_{12})L = \pi. \tag{P13.4.1}$$

The electro-optic coefficient $(R_{11} - R_{12})$ is calculated from

$$(R_{11} - R_{12}) = \lambda/n_0^3E_3^2L. \tag{P13.4.2}$$

Putting $E_3 = \frac{150\text{ V}}{1\text{ mm}} = 1.5 \times 10^5\frac{\text{V}}{\text{m}}$, $\lambda = 633 \times 10^{-9}$ m, $n_0 = 2.49$ and $L = 5 \times 10^{-3}$ m into Equation (P13.4.2), the electro-optic coefficient can be calculated as

$$(R_{11} - R_{12}) = 633 \times 10^{-9}/2.49^3 \cdot (1.5 \times 10^5)^2 \cdot 5 \times 10^{-3} = 3.6 \times 10^{-16}\ [\text{m}^2/\text{V}^2]$$

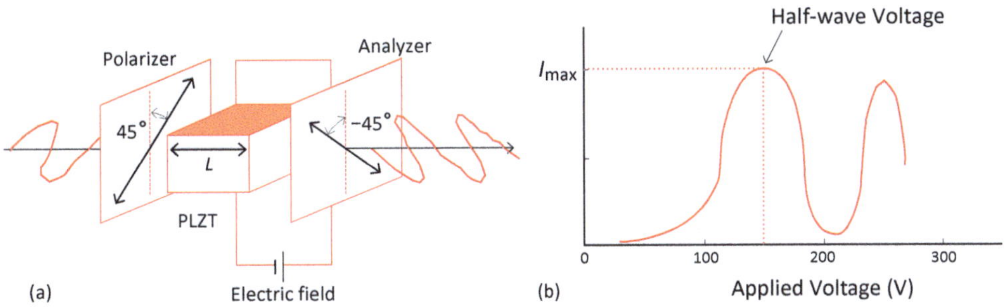

Figure 13.10. (**a**) Construction of an electro-optic light shutter. (**b**) Light intensity change with applied voltage. Source: Figure by author.

Example Problem 13.5

PLZT light valve 2D array with a multilayer pixel structure was developed for a projection-type color display, as shown in Figure 13.11a. Under the luminous flux of light source 10^4 lm, and distance from the projector 1.5 m, the brightness on a screen vs. applied voltage for red, green and blue lights was measured as in Figure 13.11b. The half-wave voltages among three lights were different. The first maximum in the light intensity was obtained at 160 V for red, 150 V for green and 130 V for blue light.

(1) Explain the reason physically why the half-wave voltage differs according to red, green and blue lights.

(2) Supposing that the refractive index n (=2.49), and that the electro-optic coefficient $(R_{11} - R_{12})$ [$= 3.6 \times 10^{-16}$ (m^2/V^2)] does not change significantly around the wavelength range of these three lights, calculate the wavelength of these three lights from the half-wave voltage observed.

Solution

The half-wave voltage is obtained from
$\Gamma_y = (\pi/\lambda) n_0{}^3 E_3{}^2 (R_{11} - R_{12}) L = \pi$.

(1) Since the half-wave voltage is provided by the above equation, according to the illumination light wavelength, the required voltage differs, as formulated in Equation (P13.5.1):

$$\lambda = n_0{}^3 E_3{}^2 (R_{11} - R_{12}) L. \quad \text{(P13.5.1)}$$

Thus, for a shorter wavelength, a smaller electric field is required.

(2) Taking into account the electrode gap of 0.45 mm, $E_3 = 3.55$, 3.33 and 2.89×10^5 [V/m] for R, G and B, respectively, and a path length L given by (1.0 − 0.1) mm (note that the surface depth 0.1 mm is an inactive layer):

$$\begin{gathered} \lambda = 2.49^3 \times (3.55 \times 10^5)^2 (3.6 \times 10^{-16})(0.9 \times 10^{-3}), \\ \lambda = 630 \text{ [nm] (for red)}, \\ \lambda = 555 \text{ [nm] (for green)}, \\ \lambda = 418 \text{ [nm] (for blue)}. \end{gathered} \quad \text{(P13.5.2)}$$

13.3.3. Electro-Optic Device—Light Deflector

There are three categories for deflecting optical beam direction [4]: (1) electro-optic crystal prism usage, (2) space gradient of refractive index, and (3) digital light deflection with birefringent crystal prisms.

Electro-Optic Crystal Prism

We fabricate an isosceles triangular prism from an electro-optic crystal such as KTN [$K(Ta,Nb)O_3$], as shown in Figure 13.12. Then, putting electrodes on the top and bottom of the triangular surface, we apply the electric field along the normal direction of the triangle. If the strain is positive, the refractive index n_e for the extraordinary ray should be reduced. The light beam polarized along the page-normal direction should deflect from the dashed line (high n) to the sold line (low n). If we denote the beam size ω, light wavelength λ, and the refractive index change under electric field Δn, resolution point number N can be evaluated by

$$N = (\Delta n / n^2 \lambda)(\frac{L}{W})\omega. \tag{13.39}$$

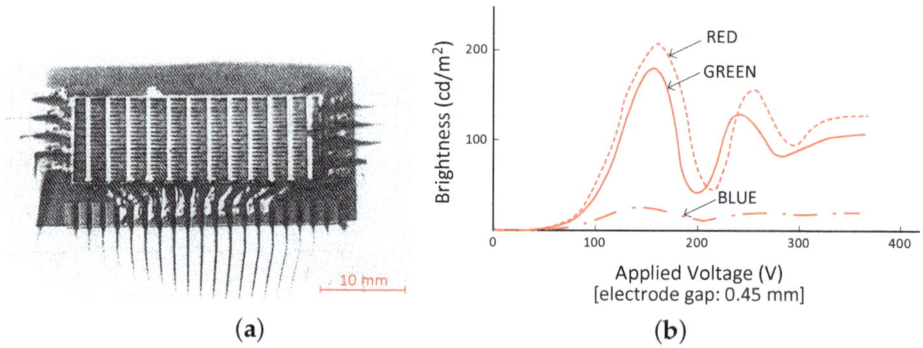

Figure 13.11. (**a**) PLZT light valve array with a multilayer pixel structure. (**b**) Brightness on a screen vs. applied voltage for red, green, and blue lights. The half-wave voltages among three lights are different. [Luminous flux of light source: 10^4 lm, distance from the projector: 1.5 m]. Source: ©Uchino, K. *Ferroelectric Devices*, 2nd ed. CRC Press, 2010; pp. 246–247. Reproduced by permission of Taylor & Francis Group.

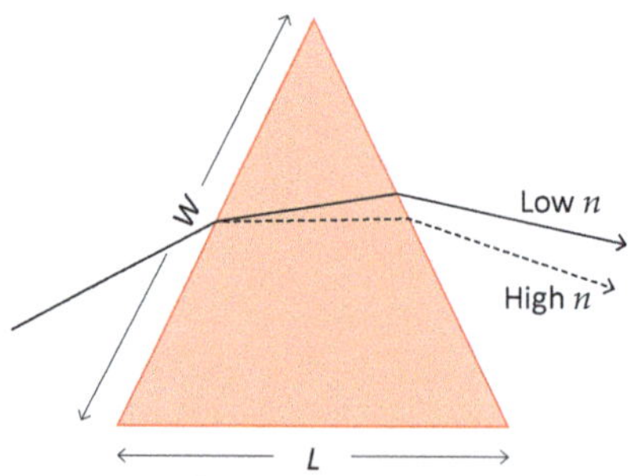

Figure 13.12. Light beam deflection with an electro-optic crystal prism. Source: Figure by author.

LiNbO$_3$ Waveguide

Light waveguides can be fabricated by depositing a high-refractive index layer on a substrate. The principle of the waveguide is shown schematically in Figure 13.13 [5]. Like an optical fiber, the light tends to bend toward high refractive-index side, so that the light should be confined in the narrow high refractive-index layer fabricated on the crystal. Two diagrams of (a) slab and (b) graded-index waveguide are shown in this figure. Nb-diffused LiNbO$_3$ single crystals are commonly used, in which high density Nb-concentrating in LN layer exponentially decreased from the top to bottom layer. Note that the higher atomic number ion should have the higher electron density and refractive index. Wave-functions for the TE$_0$ and TE$_1$ mode are also shown in the refractive-index profiles [5]. Note that the graded refractive index exhibits the continuous light beam deflection toward the high refractive index layer. This is the principle of how to trap the light beam in thin surface layer, and the waveguide principle.

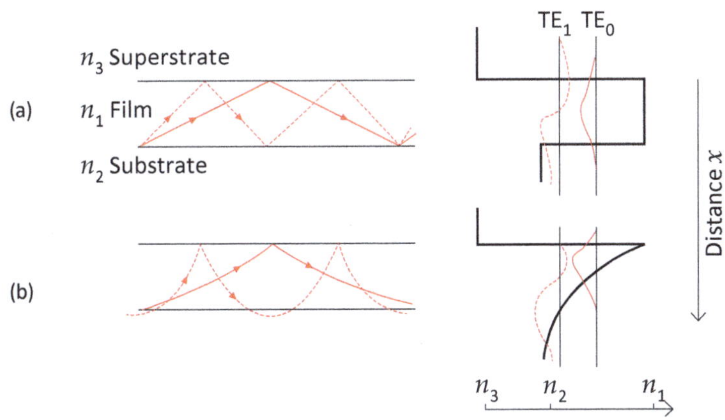

Figure 13.13. Diagrams of (**a**) slab and (**b**) graded-index waveguides. The wave-functions for the TE$_0$ and TE$_1$ modes are shown in the refractive-index profiles. Source: ©Uchino, K. *Ferroelectric Devices*, 2nd ed. CRC Press, 2010; p. 253. Reproduced by permission of Taylor & Francis Group.

Figure 13.14a,b are typical "planar" and "ridge type electro-optic waveguides", which are the way to apply electric field on the electro-optic crystal [6]. Though fabrication of a planar type is easy, the non-uniform distribution of the applied electric field is a problem. On the other hand, as you can imagine, the ridge type requires a sophisticated manufacturing technology, but the device function is close to the ideal. The c-axis is the extraordinary ray direction in LiNbO$_3$. The transmitted light intensity is 45° cant from the *c*-axis so that the retardation is easily modulated by applying a relatively low voltage via the change in the extra- and ordinary refractive indexes (Equation (13.22)).

$$\begin{cases} n_e(E_z) = n_e - ({n_e}^3/2)r_{33}E_3 \\ n_o(E_z) = n_o - ({n_o}^3/2)r_{13}E_3 \end{cases}.$$

Using the $-45°$ cant analyzer, the output light intensity is monitored. Phase modulation by 1 radian can be achieved by applying a voltage of 0.3 V with power consumption of several μW/MHz.

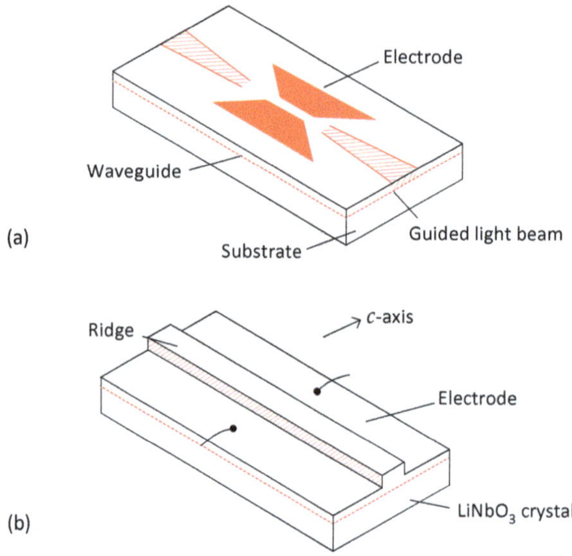

Figure 13.14. Electro-optic waveguides: (**a**) planar-type and (**b**) ridge-type. Source: ©Uchino, K. *Ferroelectric Devices*, 2nd ed. CRC Press, 2010; p. 254. Reproduced by permission of Taylor & Francis Group.

PZT Thin-Film Waveguide

With improving the film quality of PZT/PLZT, electro-optic applications have been investigated. Figure 13.15a illustrates a fundamental structure of an optical waveguide fabricated on a semiconductor substrate, and Figure 13.15b shows the SEM picture of the ridge-type PLZT thin-film optical waveguide [7]. Note that no columnar-like microstructure can be observed, which, once it exists, increases light scattering. A Y-type 1×2 optical switch using a PLZT thin-film waveguide was developed by Nashimoto et al. [7], as shown in Figure 13.16a. By applying electric voltage, the refractive index below is decreased, leading to the laser beam channel selection to a higher refractive index channel. Y separation length is a half of the digital switch using $LiNbO_3$ (LN), because the electro-optic coefficient is larger in PLZT. Figure 13.16b shows its optical transmission loss of a slab-type PLZT thin-film optical waveguide, demonstrating its optical high quality. Figure 13.17a demonstrates voltage response of the optical switch. Under 10 V applied, -22 dB cross talk (contrast ratio) can be obtained, which is compared with several tens volts in the conventional LN switch. The response speed 20 ns shown in Figure 13.17b corresponds to the RC time constant.

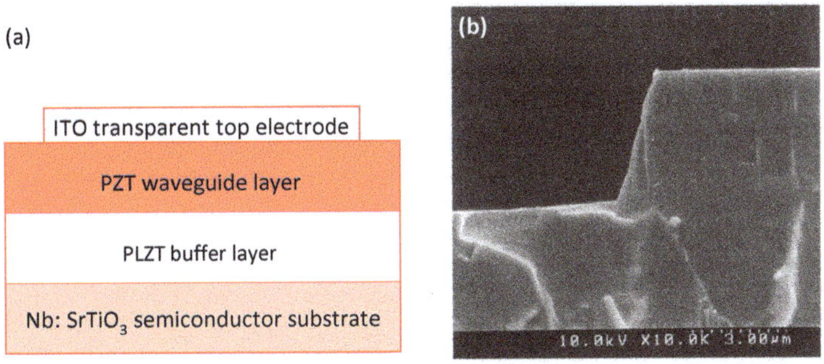

Figure 13.15. (**a**) Fundamental structure of an optical waveguide fabricated on a semiconductor substrate. (**b**) SEM picture of the ridge-type PLZT thin-film optical waveguide. Source: ©Uchino, K. *Ferroelectric Devices*, 2nd ed. CRC Press, 2010; p. 254. Reproduced by permission of Taylor & Francis Group.

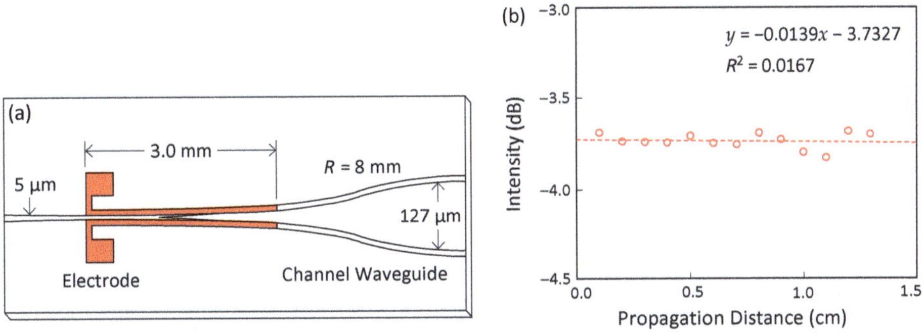

Figure 13.16. (**a**) Y-type 1 × 2 optical switch using a PLZT thin-film waveguide. (**b**) Optical transmission loss characteristics of a slab-type PLZT thin-film optical waveguide. Source: ©Uchino, K. *Ferroelectric Devices*, 2nd ed. CRC Press, 2010; p. 255. Reproduced by permission of Taylor & Francis Group.

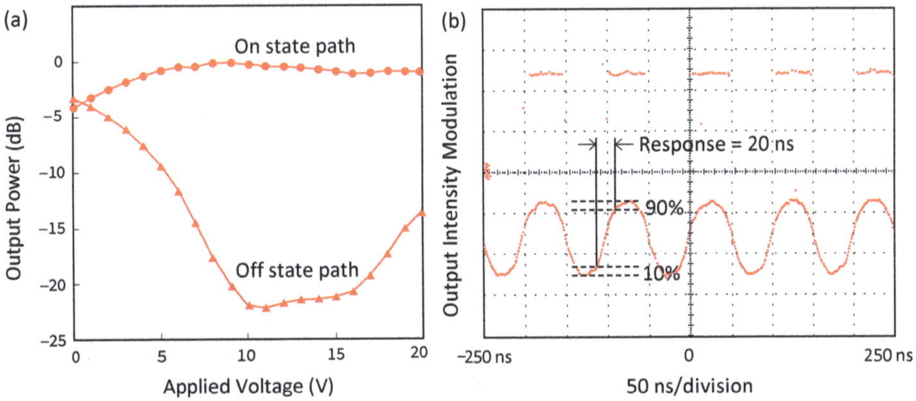

Figure 13.17. (**a**) Voltage response of the Y-type 1 × 2 optical switch. Under 10 V applied, −22 dB cross talk (contrast ratio) can be obtained. (**b**) Response speed demonstration. Source: ©Uchino, K. *Ferroelectric Devices*, 2nd ed. CRC Press, 2010; p. 256. Reproduced by permission of Taylor & Francis Group.

Chapter Essentials

1. The refractive index n of a material is a reflection of the dielectric constant (i.e., relative permittivity) ε, which exhibits interaction with the electromagnetic wave (~PHz). The formula: $\varepsilon = n^2$.
2. Quadric formula of "inverse permittivity ellipsoid":

$$B_{11}x^2 + B_{12}xy + B_{13}xz + B_{21}yx + B_{22}y^2 + B_{23}yz + B_{31}zx + B_{32}zy + B_{33}z^2 = 1,$$

or

$$\begin{pmatrix} B_{11} & B_{12} & B_{31} \\ B_{12} & B_{22} & B_{23} \\ B_{31} & B_{23} & B_{33} \end{pmatrix} \rightarrow \begin{pmatrix} B_1 & 0 & 0 \\ 0 & B_2 & 0 \\ 0 & 0 & B_3 \end{pmatrix}$$ [Symmetric matrix is transformed into a diagonal matrix].

Refer to Figure 13.5.

3. Refractive indicatrix:

$\frac{x^2}{n_1{}^2} + \frac{y^2}{n_2{}^2} + \frac{z^2}{n_3{}^2} = 1$ [Biaxial],

$\frac{x^2+y^2}{n_1{}^2} + \frac{z^2}{n_3{}^2} = 1$ [Uniaxial],

$\frac{x^2+y^2+z^2}{n_0{}^2} = 1$ [Isotropic].

4. Electro-optic Effect: Combination of primary electro-optic and secondary effect via elasto-optic effect:

$\Delta B_{ij} = r'_{ijk}E_k + R'_{ijkl}E_kE_l + p_{ijkl}x_{kl}$.

Strain follows "piezoelectric/electrostrictive" constitutive equation:

$x_{ij} = d_{kij}E_k + M_{klij}E_kE_l$.

Thus,

$\Delta B_{ij} = (r'_{ijk} + p_{ijmn}d_{kmn})E_k + (R'_{ijkl} + p_{ijmn}M_{klmn})E_kE_l = r_{ijk}E_k + R_{ijkl}E_kE_l$.

The secondary effect is comparable with the primary electro-optic effect.

5. Kerr effect formula in a cubic crystal:

$$\begin{pmatrix} \Delta(1/n_1^2) \\ \Delta(1/n_2^2) \\ \Delta(1/n_3^2) \\ \Delta(1/n_4^2) \\ \Delta(1/n_5^2) \\ \Delta(1/n_6^2) \end{pmatrix} = \begin{pmatrix} R_{11} & R_{12} & R_{12} & 0 & 0 & 0 \\ R_{12} & R_{11} & R_{12} & 0 & 0 & 0 \\ R_{12} & R_{12} & R_{11} & 0 & 0 & 0 \\ 0 & 0 & 0 & R_{44} & 0 & 0 \\ 0 & 0 & 0 & 0 & R_{44} & 0 \\ 0 & 0 & 0 & 0 & 0 & R_{44} \end{pmatrix} \begin{pmatrix} E_1^2 \\ E_2^2 \\ E_3^2 \\ E_4^2 \\ E_5^2 \\ E_6^2 \end{pmatrix}.$$

Under E_3^2 as non-zero field ($E_1^2 = E_2^2 = 0$):

$$\begin{cases} \Delta\left(\frac{1}{n_3^2}\right) = R_{11}E_3^2 \\ \Delta\left(\frac{1}{n_1^2}\right) = \Delta\left(\frac{1}{n_2^2}\right) = R_{12}E_3^2 \end{cases} \rightarrow \begin{cases} n_z(E_z) = n_0 - (n^3/2)R_{11}E_z^2 \\ n_x(E_z) = n_0 - (n^3/2)R_{12}E_z^2 \end{cases}'$$

$$\frac{x^2+y^2}{n_0{}^2[1-\left(\frac{n_0{}^2}{2}\right)R_{12}E_z{}^2]^2} + \frac{z^2}{n_0{}^2[1-\left(\frac{n_0{}^2}{2}\right)R_{11}E_z{}^2]^2} = 1 \quad \text{[Indicatrix form]}.$$

6. Light Shutter/Valve: Crossed-nicols polarizer/analyzer setup (Refer to Figures 13.8 and 13.9).
   $I = (1 - Re)^2\ I_0\ (\frac{1-\cos\Gamma_y}{2})^2$,
   where the phase retardation Γ_y is given by
   $\Gamma_y = (2\pi/\lambda_0)L(1/2)n_0{}^3(R_{11} - R_{12})(V_z/d)^2$.
7. Half-wave voltage: from $\Gamma_y = \pi$ condition $V_{z,\lambda/2} = d\sqrt{\frac{\lambda_0}{L\ n_0{}^3\ (R_{11}-R_{12})}}$
8. Electro-optic Devices:
   (a) Light intensity modulation.
   (b) Light beam deflection.

Check Point

1. (T/F) The refractive index is roughly determined by the electron density (per volume) of the material. True or false?
2. We apply the electric field on cubic PLZT 9/65/35 along the 3 axis direction. Does the refractive index for the polarized light along the 3 axis (i.e., extraordinary light) increase or decrease with the electric field?
3. The randomly oriented light passed through a polarizer. When we neglect the light absorption by the polarizer, what % of the light intensity can we obtain theoretically after one polarizer, in comparison with the input intensity.
4. (T/F) The definition of Pockels electro-optic coefficient r_{1jk} is given by an expansion expression: $1/n_{ij}(E) - 1/n_{ij}(0) = \Sigma r_{ijk}E_k$. True or false?
5. (T/F) Suppose a point light source is situated in the center of a uniaxial crystal with a "negative" refractive indicatrix, the light wave front should form a "negative ellipse". True or false?
6. In a uniaxial crystal with "negative" refractive indicatrix, which light wave travels faster, the extraordinary or ordinary ray?
7. Which PLZT composition is most popularly used for making a Kerr electro-optic device, 7/62/38, 7/65/35, 8/65/35, 9/65/35, or none of them?
8. Which color light has the lowest half-wave voltage, red, green, or blue, supposing that the electro-optic coefficient is almost the same for all three colors?
9. (T/F) A lower refractive index layer is fabricated on the top surface layer of $LiNbO_3$ single crystal substrate in order to trap the light in this low index thin layer. True or false?

10. We fabricate two optical switches by using KTN 65/35 and PLZT 9/65/35, respectively. The Kerr electro-optic coefficients ($R_{11} - R_{12}$) for KTN and PLZT are 5.3×10^{-16} m^2/V^2 and 9.1×10^{-16} m^2/V^2. Suppose that the same electric field is applied for both optical switches, which device can reduce the optical path length (i.e., device thickness), KTN or PLZT?

Chapter Problems

13.1 Let us consider a cubic PLZT thin film (1 μm in thickness) deposited on a semiconductive $SrTiO_3$ substrate with the following two electrode configurations: (a) surface electrode for lateral electric field and (b) surface electrode for normal electric field (Refer to Figure 13.18a,b).

(1) Discuss the merits and demerits of the above two electrode configurations.

(2) Suppose that the substrate is made of transparent single crystal and the electrode in Figure 13.18b is made of a transparent material such as SnO_2. Do you think the device will work as a light intensity modulator for light transmitted normally to the PLZT film?

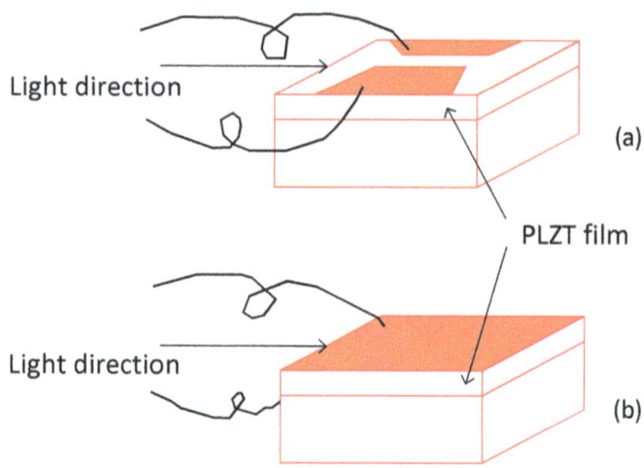

Figure 13.18. Two electrode configurations for PLZT thin-film optical waveguides: (**a**) surface electrode and (**b**) surface electrode. Source: Figures by author.

Hint

(1) Consider the birefringence and the shape of the refractive indicatrix induced by the electric field. Uniform electric field distribution is better for precise control of the light beam.

(2) Consider the phase retardation equation: $\Gamma_y = (\pi/\lambda)n_0{}^3E_3{}^2(R_{11} - R_{12})L$. The retardation comes from the existence of both extraordinary and ordinary rays in the light beam. When the incident beam from the normal to the electrode, that is, in parallel to the electric field, the light beam faces to both ordinary refractive indexes in cross direction. No Kerr effect will work in this situation.

Even if the PLZT with uniaxial composition (8/65/35) exhibits a Pockels effect with the optical principal axis on the film, is the path length L = 1 μm sufficient for obtaining $\Gamma_y = \pi$? How high of an electric field is required in this case? Is this field a realistic number achievable on the PLZT film specimen?

References

1. Uchino, K. *Ferroelectric Devices*, 2nd ed.; CRC Press: Boca Raton, FL, USA, 2010.
2. Nye, J.F. *Physical Properties of Crystals*; Oxford University Press: London, UK, 1957.
3. Eisenhart, L.P. *Coordinate Geometry*; Ginn: Boston, MA, USA, 1939.
4. Applied Physics Optical Study Committee. *Crystal Optics*; Morikita Pub. Co.: Tokyo, Japan, 1975.
5. Lines, M.E.; Glass, A.M. *Principles and Applications of Ferroelectrics and Related Materials*; Clarendon Press: Oxford, UK, 1977; p. 604.
6. Kaminow, I.P. Optical Waveguide Modulators. *IEEE Trans. Microw. Theory Tech.* **1975**, *23*, 57. [CrossRef]
7. Nashimoto, K. Optical Wave Guide Devices with PLZT Thin Films, *J. Ceram. Soc. Jpn.* **2002**, *37*, 538.

14. Nonlinear Oscillatory Systems—Nonlinear Differential Equation

Ferroelectricity originates from nonlinear self-coupling of the polarizations, while the electric-field-induced strain is a coupled phenomenon of linear piezoelectric and nonlinear electrostriction with the mechanical parameter. In this chapter, we handle nonlinear oscillatory phenomena related to ferroelectrics and piezoelectrics. We cover (1) mechanical nonlinear vibration systems in piezoelectric devices with friction damping, frequency spectrum skew/hysteresis phenomena in impedance/admittance at the piezoelectric resonance, (2) domain wall structure and dynamics, (3) nonlinear lattice spring effect, thermal expansion and electrostriction, and (4) lattice vibration with phonon localization in crystal imperfections, and phonon transfer in nonlinear potential to explain the thermal conductivity.

14.1. Mechanical Nonlinear Oscillatory Systems

Piezoelectric devices are often coupled with mechanical structures that include various nonlinear phenomena, such as snap-switch function and surface friction. We start to handle the mechanical nonlinear systems to be acquainted with mathematical procedures on nonlinear differential equations.

14.1.1. Elementary Oscillations

One of the oldest oscillating systems the reader learned in middle to high school is the so-called "simple pendulum", as illustrated in Figure 14.1. This consists of a "light-weight" rigid rod of length L (no length change) with a point mass m at one end, the other end being hinged at a fixed-point O, so that the pendulum can axially swing freely in on particular vertical planes under gravity conditions. Most of you still remember the famous "Foucault pendulum" in the museum.

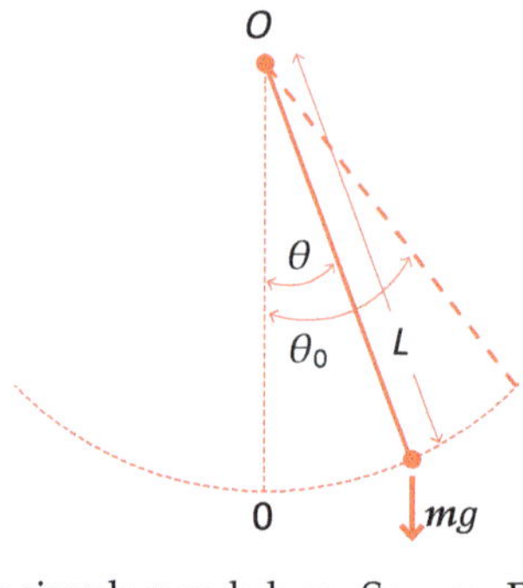

Figure 14.1. The simple pendulum. Source: Figure by author.

Using Newton dynamic equation, we can describe this simple pendulum as:

$$m\frac{\partial^2 L\theta}{\partial t^2} = -mg\cdot\sin\theta. \tag{14.1}$$

Or

$$\frac{\partial^2\theta}{\partial t^2} + \left(\frac{g}{L}\right)\cdot\sin\theta = 0. \quad (14.2)$$

You have learned the solution when $\theta \ll 1$, and $\sin\theta \approx \theta$ even in high school physics:

$$\frac{\partial^2\theta}{\partial t^2} + \left(\frac{g}{L}\right)\theta = 0. \quad (14.3)$$

This is a simple harmonic oscillation, and the general solution can be represented by a sinusoidal equation:

$$\theta(t) = A\sin(\omega t) + B\cos(\omega t). \quad (14.4)$$

Here, the angular frequency ω, which corresponds to the natural resonance frequency, should satisfy

$$\omega = \sqrt{g/L}. \quad (14.5)$$

If we take the initial condition, $\theta = \theta_0$ and $\frac{\partial\theta}{\partial t} = \dot{\theta} = 0$ (start from the rest) at $t = 0$,

$\theta(0) = A\sin(0) + B\cos(0) = \theta_0 \rightarrow B = \theta_0$
$\dot{\theta}(0) = A\cos(0) - B\sin(0) = 0 \rightarrow A = 0$

we finally obtain

$$\theta(t) = \theta_0\cos(\sqrt{g/L}\cdot t). \quad (14.6)$$

so that the pendulum resonance period becomes

$$T_{period} = 2\pi\sqrt{L/g}. \quad (14.7)$$

Note that T_{period} is proportional to $\sqrt{L}$, independent of the amplitude θ_0, in the simplest pendulum (harmonic) oscillation case.

14.1.2. Large Swings of the Pendulum—Nonlinear Dynamic Equation

Resonance Frequency Modification—Complete Elliptic Integral

Let us now consider the large swinging situation of Equation (14.2) to consider the nonlinear oscillation behavior:

$$\frac{\partial^2\theta}{\partial t^2} = -\left(\frac{g}{L}\right)\cdot\sin\theta = -\omega^2\sin\theta. \quad (14.8)$$

Multiplying $2(\frac{\partial\theta}{\partial t})$ on both sides of Equation (14.8), we integrate both sides, taking into account the boundary conditions: $\theta = \theta_0$ and $\frac{\partial\theta}{\partial t} = 0$ at $t = 0$:

$$\left(\frac{\partial\theta}{\partial t}\right)^2 = -2\omega^2\int_0^t \sin\theta\left(\frac{\partial\theta}{\partial t}\right)dt = 2\omega^2[\cos\theta]_{\theta_0}^{\theta} = (\omega^2/2)[\cos\theta - \cos\theta_0].$$

As a consequence,

$$\left(\frac{\partial\theta}{\partial t}\right) = \sqrt{2}\omega\sqrt{\cos\theta - \cos\theta_0},$$

or (14.9)

$$dt = \sqrt{\frac{L}{2g}}\frac{d\theta}{\sqrt{(\cos\theta - \cos\theta_0)}}.$$

Anticipating the amplitude dependence of the resonance period, the period T_{θ_0} is calculated as "twice the time taken by the pendulum to swing from $\theta = -\theta_0$ to $\theta = +\theta_0$":

$$T_{\theta_0} = 2\sqrt{\frac{L}{2g}}\int_{-\theta_0}^{\theta_0}\frac{d\theta}{\sqrt{(\cos\theta - \cos\theta_0)}}. \quad (14.10)$$

Using the trigonometric relations: $\cos\theta = 1 - 2\sin^2(\frac{\theta}{2})$ and $\cos\theta_0 = 1 - 2\sin^2(\frac{\theta_0}{2})$, Equation (14.10) is transformed into

$$T_{\theta_0} = \sqrt{\frac{L}{g}}\int_{-\theta_0}^{\theta_0}\frac{d\theta}{\sqrt{\sin^2\left(\frac{\theta_0}{2}\right) - \sin^2(\frac{\theta}{2})}}. \quad (14.11)$$

In order to utilize so-called "complete elliptic integral of the first kind", $K(k)$, defined by

$$K(k) = \int_0^{\pi/2}\frac{d\phi}{\sqrt{1 - k^2\sin^2\phi}}, \quad (14.12)$$

we further transform Equation (14.11). First, the initial condition reflects to k as

$$k = \sin\left(\frac{\theta_0}{2}\right). \quad (14.13)$$

Then, we introduce new angle parameter ϕ as

$$\sin\left(\frac{\theta}{2}\right) = k\cdot\sin\phi. \quad (14.14)$$

Hence,

$$d\theta = \frac{2k\cos\phi d\phi}{\cos\left(\frac{\theta}{2}\right)} = \frac{2k\cos\phi d\phi}{\sqrt{1 - k^2\sin^2\phi}}.$$

we can finally obtain with "complete elliptic integral of the first kind", $K(k)$,

$$T_{\theta_0} = 4\sqrt{\frac{L}{g}}\int_0^{\pi/2}\frac{d\phi}{\sqrt{1 - k^2\sin^2\phi}} = 4\sqrt{\frac{L}{g}}\cdot K(k). \quad (14.15)$$

$K(k = \sin(\theta_0/2))$ is tabulated as a function θ_0 in Table 14.1 [1].

- For $\theta_0 = 0$: The value of $K(k = 0) = \pi/2$, so that $T_{\theta_0 = 0} = 2\pi\sqrt{L/g}$, exactly the same as Equation (14.7).

- For $\theta_0 = 2°$: we have $T_{\theta_0=2°} = 1.000076 \cdot T_{\theta_0=0}$.
- For $\theta_0 = 60°$: we have $T_{\theta_0=60°} = 1.073 \cdot T_{\theta_0=0}$. Up to 60°, we may handle the linear dynamic equation.
- For $\theta_0 = 90°$: we have $T_{\theta_0=90°} = 1.18 \cdot T_{\theta_0=0}$. Note that even for $\theta_0 = \pi/2$ (large amplitude), the resonance frequency modification is only 18%.
- For $\theta_0 = 178°$: we have $T_{\theta_0=178°} = 3.46 \cdot T_{\theta_0=0}$. Now the resonance frequency is significantly decreased, when the initial position approaches an upside-down point (180°), because the staying time around the upside-down position is elongated significantly.

Vibration Mode Change

Complete elliptic integral of First kind $K(k)$ merely provides the resonance period change. Now we introduce so-called "phase plane" concept to obtain the phase paths and vibration modes [2].

Table 14.1. Complete elliptic integrals of First kind: $K(k) = \int_0^{\pi/2} \frac{d\phi}{\sqrt{1-k^2\sin^2\phi}}$ and $k = \sin\left(\frac{\theta_0}{2}\right)$.

θ_0	0°	2°	4°	6°	8°	10°	12°	14°	16°	18°
K	1.5708	1.5709	1.5713	1.5719	1.5727	1.5738	1.5751	1.5767	1.5785	1.5805
θ_0	20°	30°	40°	50°	60°	70°	75°	80°	85°	90°
K	1.5828	1.5981	1.6200	1.6490	1.6858	1.7312	1.7578	1.7868	1.8189	1.8541
θ_0	100°	110°	120°	130°	140°	150°	160°	170°	178°	180°
K	1.9356	2.0347	2.1565	2.3088	2.5046	2.7681	3.1534	3.8317	5.4349	∞

Source: Table by author.

First, Equation (14.8) $\frac{\partial^2\theta}{\partial t^2} = -\left(\frac{g}{L}\right) \cdot \sin\theta$ can be transformed into

$$\ddot{\theta} + \sin\theta = 0, \tag{14.16}$$

by introducing a reduced notation of time $\tilde{t}$:

$$\tilde{t} = t/\sqrt{L/g}. \tag{14.17}$$

Next, Equation (14.16) is recast as a first-order system [2]:

$$\begin{cases} y = \dot{\theta} \\ \dot{y} = -\sin\theta \end{cases}. \tag{14.18}$$

A "phase plane" is a graphical display of a differential equation, typically of a nonlinear type. Using the improved "Euler method" (see Subsection Euler's Method), Acheson integrated under the boundary conditions: $\theta = \theta_0$, and $\dot{\theta} = 0$ at $\tilde{t} = 0$; that is, the pendulum is released from rest [2], which is introduced below. Euler method is a first-order numerical procedure to solve "ordinary differential equations" under an initial condition (such as angle $\theta(0)$ and $\dot{\theta}(0)$). Since the error per step is proportional to the square of the step size, the accumulated error at a given time is also proportional to the step size, as introduced in the next section.

When θ_0 is small, the result is an oscillation that is nearly simple harmonic (i.e., linear!), as shown in Figure 14.2a for $\theta_0 = -\frac{\pi}{4}$. Even when θ_0 is $\frac{\pi}{2}$, we see from Figure 14.2b that the form of the oscillation is not much changed, with an almost circular path in the phase plane (θ vs.$\dot{\theta}$), and a resonance period only 18% larger than the small amplitude value $T_{\theta_0=0}$. However, when the pendulum is released very close to its "upside-down" position ($\theta_0 = 179°$), Figure 14.2c exhibits a significantly different oscillation mode: (1) the resonance period is much longer, and (2) the vibration amplitude change with time is not sinusoidal anymore, but approaches a rectangular pulse-like mode. We can understand that around $\theta_0 = \pm 179°$ (i.e., almost upside-down position), the pendulum motion is very slow, which appears as sharp bends at $\theta \approx \pm\pi$ (or $\pm 179°$) and $\dot{\theta} = 0$ position in Figure 14.2c.

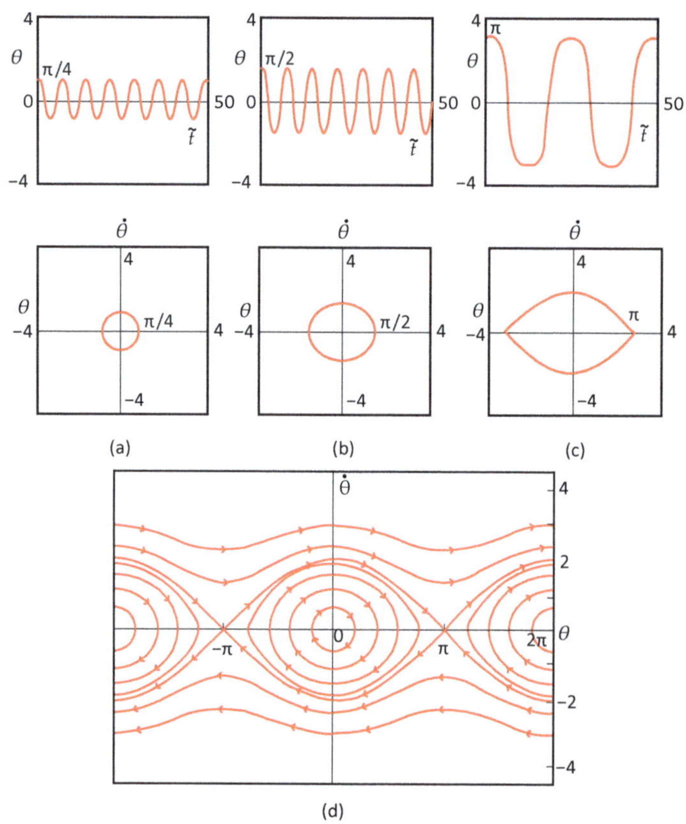

Figure 14.2. θ vs.$\tilde{t}$ and phase plane (θ vs.$\dot{\theta}$) plots for the pendulum equation: (**a**) $\theta_0 = \pi/4$ or 45°; (**b**) $\theta_0 = \pi/2$ or 90°, and (**c**) $\theta_0 = 3.124139$ or 179°. (**d**) Direction field in the phase plane and traces out various phase paths starting from different initial conditions. Source: Figure by author, adapted from [2].

If we simulate this problem under the boundary conditions: $\theta = \theta_0$, and $\dot{\theta} \neq 0$ at $\tilde{t} = 0$, this initial angular velocity creates different results. Figure 14.2d shows a direction field in the phase plane and traces out various phase paths starting from different initial conditions. For example, let us consider the initial position $\theta = 0$ at $\tilde{t} = 0$. When the initial angular velocity $\dot{\theta} < 2$, closed curves around the origin can be traced in the phase plane, denoting to-and-fro pendulum swing. Note the orthogonal crossing at two positions, $\dot{\theta} = 0$ and $\theta = \pm\pi$, which we have discussed above in Figure 14.2d. However, when the initial velocity $\dot{\theta} > 2$, the phase paths show periodical increase and decrease in $\dot{\theta}$, but never change the sign; that is, persistent whirling motions of the pendulum around the hinge. As $\theta = \pm\pi$ represent the identical position of the pendulum in space (exactly the upside-down position), it is in fact good to roll the portion of the phase plane $-\pi < \theta < \pi$ around a cylinder, and view the phase space as the surface of a cylinder. All periodic motions are then represented by topologically closed curves, the ones encircling the cylinder being "whirling" ones, the others corresponding to motions in which the pendulum swings to-and-fro.

Euler's Method

Though introduction to the computer simulation software is not the objective of this textbook, we briefly introduce an approximation technique here for the reader's reference. If the reader is not interested in obtaining the actual calculation technique, you may skip this subsection. "Euler's method" is one of the most famous calculation techniques to be utilized for solving the nonlinear differential equations. Figure 14.3 illustrates this process visually.

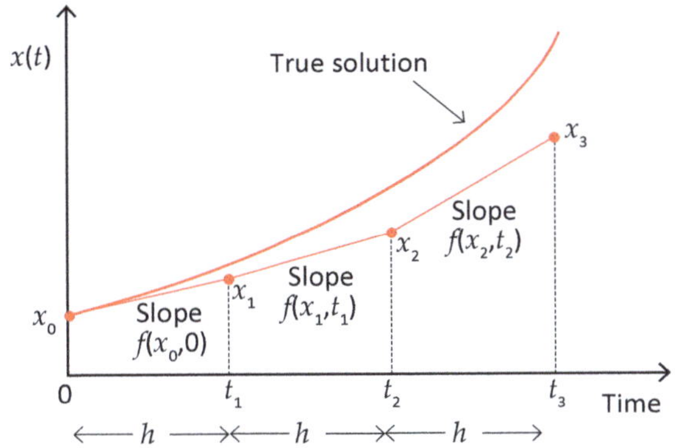

Figure 14.3. Euler's method. Source: Figure by author, adapted from [2].

Merely for the simplicity, we consider the first-order derivative equation:

$$\frac{dx}{dt} = f(x,t), \text{ with } x = x_0 \text{ at } t = 0. \tag{14.19}$$

In order to obtain the time dependence of $x(t)$, it may not be difficult for the reader to approach the following "broken sequential line" method, by referring to Figure 14.3. From the initial condition: $x = x_0$ at $t = 0$, we may approximate $x = x_1$

at $t = t_1$ (just small time interval h after the origin) by using the slope $\left(\frac{dx}{dt}\right)_{t=0}$. Since $\left(\frac{dx}{dt}\right)_{t=0} = f(x_0, 0)$, the following equation seems to be the first approximation:

$$x_1 = x_0 + h \cdot f(x_0, 0). \tag{14.20}$$

We take another step forward in the same way: from x_1 at t_1 to t_2 at the same interval h after. Using a new slope at the point (x_1, t_1), that is $\left(\frac{dx}{dt}\right)_{t=t_1} = f(x_1, t_1)$, we can obtain

$$x_2 = x_1 + h \cdot f(x_1, t_1). \tag{14.21}$$

Now the reader can understand how we can estimate the next point value with the time interval h,

$$x_{new} = x_{old} + h \cdot f(x_{old}, t_{old}). \tag{14.22}$$

Knowing the old values (x_{old}, t_{old}), we can estimate the future values successively. Two points to be mentioned for this approximation method:

(1) The deviation from the true function $x(t)$ becomes larger when the time interval h is not sufficiently small. The smaller the increment step is, the better accuracy. However, because of the increase of the calculation point number, the calculation time becomes long.

(2) When the function $x(t)$ is monotonous as changing time, the accuracy becomes high. In order to improve the calculation accuracy, instead of $h \cdot f(x_{old}, t_{old})$ in Equation (14.22), $\frac{1}{2} h \cdot [f(x_{old}, t_{old}) + f(x_{new}, t_{new})]$ is suggested. Refer to Reference [2] for further learning. If the reader uses "MatLab" software (MathWorks Inc., Natick, MA, USA) for solving nonlinear differential equations, this advanced Euler's method is adopted in it.

14.1.3. Oscillatory System with Friction

Different from a "simple pendulum" that handles "nonlinear force $\sin\theta$" in the previous section, the "mass–spring" model in this section treats a "linear spring" coupled with a sort of damper, which includes linear (viscous damping) or nonlinear friction (Coulomb damping) in this section. Though we described the damping mechanisms in Chapter 6, the reader is reminded of this topic here again from a different angle.

Viscous Damping—Conventional Approach

Figure 14.4a shows the simplest "mass–spring" model, which the reader is very familiar with. Denoting the mass displacement as u, the Newton dynamic equation of this system is expressed by neglecting losses:

$$m\ddot{u} = -cu. \tag{14.23}$$

Thus, by using

$$\omega_0 = \sqrt{c/m}, \tag{14.24}$$

we obtain the equation

$$\ddot{u} + {\omega_0}^2 u = 0. \tag{14.25}$$

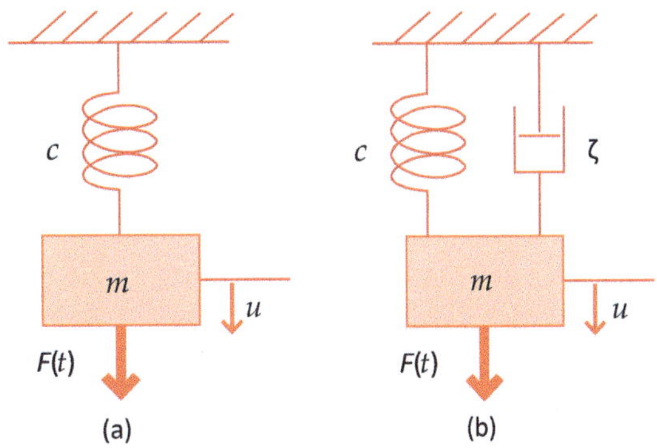

Figure 14.4. A simple mass–spring harmonic vibration model (**a**) and with a damper (**b**). Source: Figure by author.

We now understand that the solution $u(t)$ as

$$u(t) = u_0 \cos(\omega_0 t), \tag{14.26}$$

if we take the initial condition at $t = 0$: $u(0) = u_0$, $\dot{u}(0) = 0$. Additionally, ω_0 means the natural mechanical resonance angular frequency.

The "viscous damping" is applied for "lubricated surface" friction (i.e., time-dependent force); so-called "dash pot" (i.e., shock absorber, buffer), illustrated in Figure 14.4b, exhibits this behavior. It can also be applied for an object moving in viscous oil, or an electro-active object moving in a magnetic field with its damping force in proportion to the object speed. Though the loss mechanisms observed in piezoelectric materials are not actually "viscous", we occasionally adopt this model often just from a mathematical simplicity viewpoint, as introduced in Chapter 6. The damping force is introduced in proportion to the velocity v of the mass m as

$$F = -\xi v = -\xi \frac{du}{dt}, \tag{14.27}$$

where ξ is called viscous damping coefficient. Thus, the dynamic equation of the mass without external force in Figure 14.4b is described as

$$m\ddot{u} = -cu - \xi \dot{u}. \tag{14.28}$$

Taking the following normalized notations,

$$\omega_0 = \sqrt{c/m} \text{ (base resonance frequency for zero damping)}, \tag{14.29}$$

$$\zeta = \xi / 2m\omega_0 \text{ (normalized damping factor (no dimension))}, \tag{14.30}$$

we obtain the normalized equation,

$$\ddot{u} + 2\zeta\omega_0\dot{u} + {\omega_0}^2 u = 0. \tag{14.31}$$

Due to the obedient characteristic of the damping formula, we can easily solve this differential equation using the Laplace transform (refer to Section 8.2). Taking $L[u(t)] = U(s)$, and Theorem "differentiation with respect to t": $L\left[\frac{d^n u(t)}{dt^n}\right] = s^n U(s) - \sum s^{n-k} u^{k-1}(0)$ with the initial conditions, $\dot{u}(t = 0) = 0$, $u(t = 0) = u_0$,

$$[s^2U - su_0] + 2\zeta\omega_0[sU - u_0] + {\omega_0}^2U = 0. \tag{14.32}$$

Then,

$$U(s) = \frac{(s + 2\zeta\omega_0)u_0}{[s^2 + (2\zeta\omega_0)s + {\omega_0}^2]}. \tag{14.33}$$

- *Under Damping* $(0 \leq \zeta < 1)$

  Rewriting Equation (14.33) as

$$U(s) = u_0\left[\frac{(s + \zeta\omega_0)}{(s + \zeta\omega_0)^2 + (1 - \zeta^2){\omega_0}^2} + \frac{\zeta}{\sqrt{1 - \zeta^2}}\frac{\sqrt{1 - \zeta^2}\omega_0}{(s + \zeta\omega_0)^2 + (1 - \zeta^2){\omega_0}^2}\right], \tag{14.34}$$

then using the inverse Laplace transforms (#9 in Table 8.1), we can obtain the solution:

$$\begin{aligned} u(t) = u_0[&exp(-\zeta\omega_0 t)\cos\left(\sqrt{1 - \zeta^2}\omega_0 t\right) + \\ &\tfrac{\zeta}{\sqrt{1-\zeta^2}}exp(-\zeta\omega_0 t)\sin\left(\sqrt{1 - \zeta^2}\omega_0 t\right)]. \end{aligned} \tag{14.35}$$

- *Critical Damping* $(\zeta = 1)$

  Equation (14.33) is transformed as

$$U(s) = \frac{(s + 2\omega_0)u_0}{[s^2 + (2\omega_0)s + {\omega_0}^2]} = u_0[\frac{1}{s + \omega_0} + \frac{\omega_0}{(s + \omega_0)^2}], \tag{14.36}$$

then, using the inverse Laplace transforms (#3 and 4 in Table 8.1), we can obtain the solution:

$$u(t) = u_0[exp(-\omega_0 t) + \omega_0 t \cdot exp(-\omega_0 t)] = u_0(1 + \omega_0 t) \cdot exp(-\omega_0 t). \tag{14.37}$$

- *Over Damping* $(\zeta > 1)$

$$U(s) = u_0\left[\frac{(s + \zeta\omega_0)}{(s + \zeta\omega_0)^2 - (\zeta^2 - 1){\omega_0}^2} + \zeta\omega_0\frac{1}{(s + \zeta\omega_0)^2 - (\zeta^2 - 1){\omega_0}^2}\right]. \tag{14.38}$$

From the inverse Laplace transforms (#7 and 8 in Table 8.1), we can obtain the solution:

$$\begin{aligned} u(t) = u_0\Big[&exp(-\zeta\omega_0 t)\cosh\left(\sqrt{\zeta^2 - 1}\omega_0 t\right) + \\ &\tfrac{\zeta}{\sqrt{\zeta^2-1}}exp(-\zeta\omega_0 t)\sinh(\sqrt{^2 - 1}\omega_0 t)\Big]. \end{aligned} \tag{14.39}$$

Figure 14.5 shows free vibration amplitude decay in viscous damping models for the above three cases: $0 \leq \zeta < 1$, $\zeta = 1$, and $1 < \zeta$. The key in the viscous damping is an "exponential decay" of vibration like $exp(-\zeta\omega_0 t)$. Three important issues to note here:

(1) The case $\zeta = 1$ corresponds to the critical damping, at which the oscillation becomes actually "aperiodic", without exhibiting any ringing.
(2) In the cases $0 \leq \zeta < 1$, the oscillation is periodic. However, the resonance frequency is not the base $\omega_0 = \sqrt{c/m}$, but $\sqrt{1-\zeta^2}\omega_0$. The damping factor actually modulates the resonance frequency.
(3) The "logarithmic decrement" δ is defined by the natural log of the ratio of two successive vibration amplitudes (useful in experimental data analysis):

$$\delta = ln\left(\frac{x_1}{x_2}\right) = ln\frac{exp(-\zeta\omega_0 t)}{exp(-\zeta\omega_0(t+T_0))} = ln[exp(\zeta\omega_0 T_0)] = \zeta\omega_0 T_0. \quad (14.40)$$

Since the vibration resonance period T_0 is given by $T_0 = 2\pi/\sqrt{1-\zeta^2}\omega_0$, the logarithmic decrement can be written with the damping factor ζ as

$$\delta = \frac{2\pi\zeta}{\sqrt{1-\zeta^2}} \approx 2\pi\zeta. \quad (14.41)$$

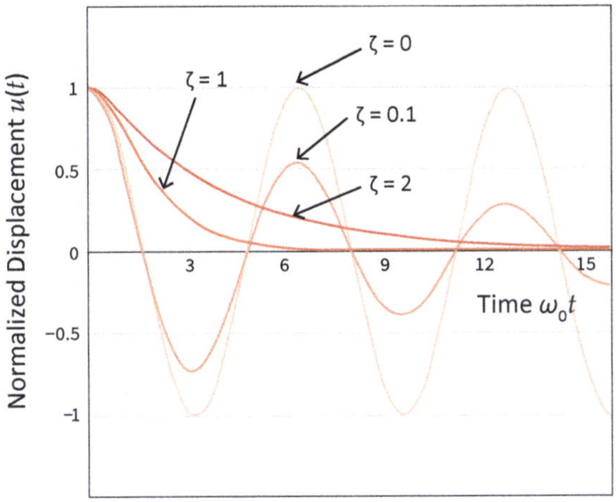

Figure 14.5. Free vibration amplitude decay for viscous damping. Source: Figure by author.

Coulomb (Friction) Damping

Now, we consider a nonlinear friction model, different from the "viscous" damping. Coulomb damping occurs when the mechanical object is contacted on a "dry surface". As learned in high school physics, the Coulomb friction force F is almost constant (irrelevant to the object speed), and expressed by the product of the normal force N and the friction constant μ:

$$F = \mu N.$$

The friction constant changes from 0 to 1, but typical values are around 0.2–0.4. Instead of the dashpot in Figure 14.3b, new illustrations are given in Figure 14.6 for your easy recognition. Figure 14.6a,b show a commercial friction damper and a schematic model with mass m, spring constant c and friction contact, respectively. We can start from the differential equation by using mass displacement u:

$$m\ddot{u} + cu = \pm F. \tag{14.43}$$

We can rewrite Equation (14.43) using $\omega = \sqrt{c/m}$ and a rectangular wave function $h(t)$ visualized in Figure 14.6c,

$$\ddot{u} + \omega^2 u = h(t). \tag{14.44}$$

Here, the amplitude A of $h(t)$ is set $F/m = \mu N/m$ (constant force with sign change with the moving direction), and a cyclic period ($2T$) is taken as $2\pi/\omega$, corresponding to the resonance period of the original mass–spring system. We will adopt the initial conditions as:

$$u(t = 0) = a, \dot{u}(t = 0) = 0. \tag{14.45}$$

The initial mass position a (spring force $c \cdot a$) should be taken as reasonably large, so that the motion will start by competing the frictional force μN:

$$a > A/\omega^2. \tag{14.46}$$

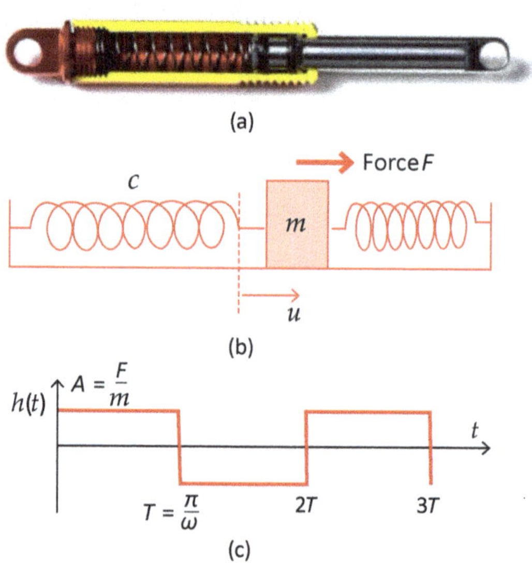

Figure 14.6. (**a**) Commercial friction damper, (**b**) schematic model with mass, spring, and friction contact, and (**c**) rectangular wave function representing friction force. Source: [3] ©Uchino, K. *High-Power Piezoelectrics and Loss Mechanisms*. CRC Press, 2020; p. 92. Reproduced by permission of Taylor & Francis Group.

Let us solve the differential equation, Equation (14.44), using "Laplace transform", which is a useful mathematical tool for this sort of non-sinusoidal, anharmonic input force. We denote the Laplace transforms of the displacement $u(t)$ and friction force $h(t)$ as $U(s)$ and $H(s)$: $U(s) = Lu(t)$, $G(s) = Lh(t)$. Equation (14.46) can be written as [4]

$$L\ddot{u} + \omega^2 U(s) = H(s). \tag{14.47}$$

Taking into account the initial condition $u(t=0) = a$ and $\dot{u}(t=0) = 0$ ([from Theorem: $L\left[\frac{d^n u(t)}{dt^n}\right] = s^n U(s) - \sum s^{n-k} u^{k-1}(0)$),

$$L\ddot{u} = s^2 U - sa, \tag{14.48}$$

and the Laplace transform of a rectangular wave expressed by (from #13 in Table 8.1)

$$H(s) = \frac{A}{s}\tanh\left(\frac{Ts}{2}\right) = \frac{A}{s}\left(1 - 2e^{-Ts} + 2e^{-2Ts} - 2e^{-3Ts} + \cdots\right), \tag{14.49}$$

we obtain the following equation:

$$(s^2 + \omega^2)U - sa = \frac{A}{s}\left(1 - 2e^{-Ts} + 2e^{-2Ts} - 2e^{-3Ts} + \cdots\right). \tag{14.50}$$

We can now solve it in terms of $U(s)$

$$U = \frac{s \cdot a}{(s^2 + \omega^2)} + \frac{A}{s(s^2 + \omega^2)}\left(1 - 2e^{-Ts} + 2e^{-2Ts} - 2e^{-3Ts} + \cdots\right). \tag{14.51}$$

Remember $T = \pi/\omega$ ("a half of the resonance period").

Knowing $\frac{1}{s(s^2+\omega^2)} = \frac{1}{\omega^2}\left[\frac{1}{s} - \frac{s}{(s^2+\omega^2)}\right]$, and the famous inverse Laplace transforms as follows (Table 8.1):

$$L^{-1}\frac{1}{s} = 1 \text{ (step function, } t > 0\text{)}; L^{-1}\frac{s}{(s^2 + \omega^2)} = \cos(\omega t);$$

and the "time-shift theorem" $L[u(t-a)] = e^{-as}U(s)$, we can obtain the displacement $u(t)$ solution for successive time intervals, $0 < t < T$, $T < t < 2T$, $2T < t < 3T$, $\cdots$, where T is a half of the resonance period (i.e., $\omega T = \pi$, $\cos \omega T = -1$) (refer to Reference [4]):

$$u = a\cos(\omega t) + \frac{A}{\omega^2}(1 - \cos(\omega t)) \text{ for } 0 < t < T; \; u(T) = -a + \frac{2A}{\omega^2} \tag{14.52}$$

$$u = a\cos(\omega t) + \frac{A}{\omega^2}(1 - \cos(\omega t)) - \frac{2A}{\omega^2}(1 - \cos(\omega(t - T)) \text{ for } T < t < 2T; \quad u(2T) = a - \frac{4A}{\omega^2} \tag{14.53}$$

$$\cdots\cdots\cdots\cdots\cdots$$

We find that

(1) The system has the resonance frequency provided by $\omega = \sqrt{c/m}$, determined by the original mass and spring.

(2) Each successive sinusoidal swing is $\left(\frac{2A}{\omega^2}\right)$ shorter than the preceding one, until inside the dead region, that is, "linearly decay" with time, different from popular "exponential decay" in the viscous damping in the previous section.

Figure 14.7 shows the linear vibration amplitude decay for the Coulomb damping, in comparison with no damping free vibration.

(3) There is the critical stop point of the vibration; that is, the minimum displacement $u(t) = A/\omega^2$, below which the spring force cannot compete with the friction force.

We can derive the displacement amplitude decay by $2(\frac{2A}{\omega^2})$ per cycle from the energy consumption analysis. We consider here the vibration amplitude decrease from the work by the friction force. When we consider a half cycle from the mass velocity zero to the next zero state (from $t = 0$ to $t = T$), the kinetic energy change should be zero. Supposing that the vibration amplitude is reduced by Δu from the initial $u_0 = a$ to $-u_0$ (but not reaching to $-a$), the spring potential energy change should equate to the work by the friction force F times moving distance $(2u_0 - \Delta u)$:

$$\frac{1}{2}c\left[u_0^2 - (u_0 - \Delta u)^2\right] = F(2u_0 - \Delta u). \tag{14.54}$$

Thus, neglecting $(\Delta u)^2$, Equation (14.54) gives

$$\Delta u = 2F/c. \tag{14.55}$$

This implies that the vibration amplitude is reduced by $2F/c$ per a half cycle, which is exactly the same conclusion from the above summary item (2), taking into account $2F/c = (\frac{2A}{\omega^2})$. The last relation can be derived from the definitions: $A = F/m$ and $\omega^2 = c/m$. The Coulomb damping exhibits linear vibration amplitude decay of the sinusoidal oscillation (Figure 14.7), rather than exponential amplitude decay (Figure 14.5)!

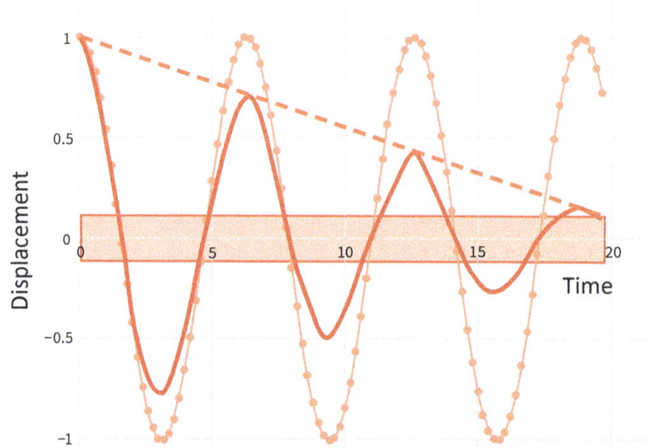

Figure 14.7. Linear vibration amplitude decay for Coulomb damping. Source: [3] ©Uchino, K. *High-Power Piezoelectrics and Loss Mechanisms*. CRC Press, 2020; p. 94. Reproduced by permission of Taylor & Francis Group.

Example Problem 14.1

We proposed a simple "stick–slick motion" analysis model. Figure 14.8a shows a model via friction model, where M is the slider mass, N, normal force, and $D(t)$ and $V(t)$ are the displacement and velocity of the moving base. Friction constant μ can be different for static and dynamic conditions, but we handle them as the same and constant regardless of velocity (Figure 14.8b). When we drive the moving base (displacement and velocity) with an ideal sawtooth shape as a function of time, as shown in Figure 14.8c, impact force can be estimated as a function of time (Figure 14.8d). Under the above assumption, derive the slider position $x(t)$ as a function time [5,6].

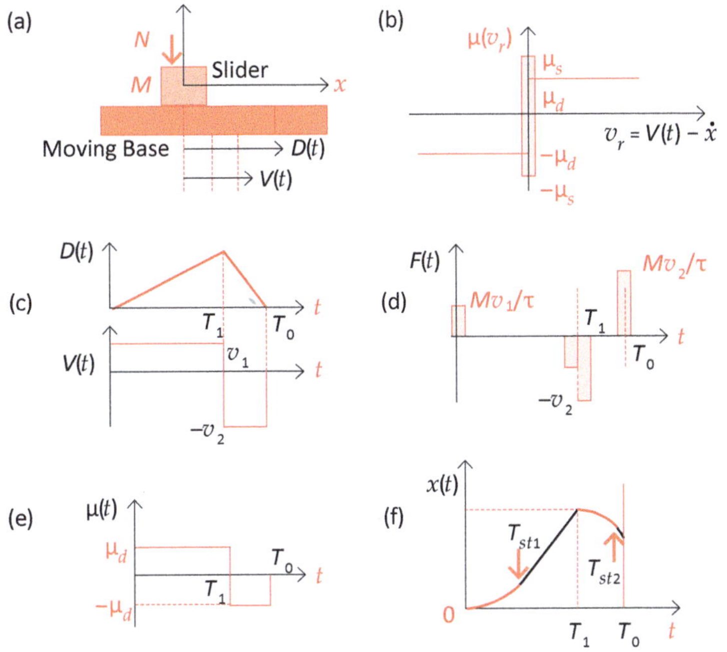

Figure 14.8. Stick–slick motion analysis via friction model (**a**): friction constant as a function of velocity (**b**), sawtooth displacement and velocity—as a function of time (**c**), impact force as a function of time (**d**), friction constant vs. time (**e**), and slider position change as a function of time. Source: [4] ©Uchino, K. *Micromechatronics*, 2nd ed. CRC Press, 2019; p. 512. Reproduced by permission of Taylor & Francis Group.

Solution

First, the moving base (stator) is assumed to be operated like a saw-tooth displacement motion (slow $0 < t < T_1$ and quick $T_1 < t < T_0$) shown in Figure 14.8c, so that the constant velocity rightward v_1 and leftward $-v_2$. Note $v_1 < v_2$ for the "slow and quick" sequence.

Second, we assume the two mass motion equations for the "slick" and "stick" conditions. We define the velocity v_r of the mass relative to the base velocity:

$$v_r = V(t) - \dot{x}. \tag{P14.1.1}$$

When $v_r \neq 0$, that is, under "slick/slip" condition, we adopt

$$M\ddot{x} = N\mu(v_r) = \text{sgn}(v_r)N\mu_d. \tag{P14.1.2}$$

We use the same dynamic friction constant μ_d to the static friction constant μ_d from the formula simplicity, while when $v_r = 0$, that is, under "stick" condition:

$$x = D(t) \text{ and } \dot{x} = V(t). \tag{P14.1.3}$$

Third, we consider abrupt force at the time when the base velocity suddenly changes. Recall the fundamental relation between the impact force and momentum change:

$$F{\cdot}\Delta t = \Delta(Mv). \tag{P14.1.4}$$

- At $t = 0$: Velocity sudden change (step function) from 0 to v_1 is assumed to be made during a short time period τ. The impulse force is estimated as Mv_1/τ.
- At $t = T_1$: Velocity change from v_1 to 0 provides the impulse force of $-Mv_1/\tau$, supposing the time duration τ. Immediately after $-v_2$ is applied, which generates the impulse force of $-Mv_2/\tau$.
- At $t = T_2$: Velocity change from $-v_2$ to 0 provides the impulse force of Mv_2/τ.

The above impulse forces are illustrated in Figure 14.8d. According to the friction force vs. momentum, we categorize the situation into three:

(1)	Stick and stick (no slip)	$N\mu_s(> N\mu_d) > \frac{Mv_2}{\tau}\left(> \frac{Mv_1}{\tau}\right)$
(2)	Stick and slick	$\frac{Mv_2}{\tau} > N\mu_s(> N\mu_d) > \frac{Mv_1}{\tau}$
(3)	Slick and slick	$\frac{Mv_2}{\tau} > \frac{Mv_1}{\tau} > N\mu_s(> N\mu_d)$

Case (1) does not provide the slider motion relative to the moving base (no interest!), while case (3) can provide the slider motion, but no large thrust of the slider is expected in practice because of the slick condition (useless from the application viewpoint!). Thus, we consider the case (2) stick and slick combination in more details.

The initial impact force (Mv_1/τ) generates a constant acceleration slipping motion of the slider (thus, parabolic increase in displacement) until T_{st1}, where $\dot{x} = V(t)$ (catching the speed of the base), then the slider is sticked on the moving base with almost constant velocity. We formulate the above address mathematically. Let the dynamic equation

$$M\ddot{x} = N\mu(v_r) = N\mu(t), \tag{P14.1.5}$$

be converted into the Laplace transform formula, knowing $\mu(t)$ as a rectangular wave shape illustrated in Figure 14.8e, which is expressed by $\left(\frac{1}{s}\right)\left[\left(1 - e^{-T_1 s}\right) - \left(e^{-T_1 s} - e^{-T_0 s}\right)\right]$ in the Laplace transform:

$$Ms^2\tilde{x} = N\mu_d\left(\frac{1}{s}\right)\left[\left(1 - e^{-T_1 s}\right) - \left(e^{-T_1 s} - e^{-T_0 s}\right)\right], \tag{P14.1.6}$$

where $\tilde{x}(s)$ is the Laplace transform of mass position $x(t)$. Thus, the solution of the position under a one-time pulse drive is expressed by

$$\tilde{x} = \frac{N\mu_d}{M}\left(\frac{1}{s^3}\right)\left(1 - 2e^{-T_1 s}\right) + e^{-T_0 s}. \quad \text{(P14.1.7a)}$$

Or under a period/cyclic pulse drive with the periodicity T_0:

$$\tilde{x} = \frac{N\mu_d}{M}\left(\frac{1}{s^3}\right)\left(1 - 2e^{-T_1 s} + e^{-T_0 s}\right)\left(1 + e^{-T_0 s}\right), \quad \text{(P14.1.7b)}$$

Knowing the inverse Laplace transform $\left(\frac{1}{s^3}\right) \to (\frac{1}{2})t^2$, in the initial interval (i.e., slipping) $0 < t < T_{st1}$, the position change will follow:

$$x(t) = (\frac{1}{2})\frac{N\mu_d}{M}t^2,\ \dot{x}(t) = \frac{N\mu_d}{M}t. \quad \text{(P14.1.8)}$$

Once the time reaches T_{st1}, since the mass velocity catches up to the base speed, the stick mode arrives, then the constant velocity $\dot{x}(t) = v_1$ is continued during $T_{st1} < t < T_1$. T_{st1} is obtained from

$$\dot{x}(T_{st1}) = \frac{N\mu_d}{M}T_{st1} = v_1 \to T_{st1} = \frac{M}{N\mu_d}v_1. \quad \text{(P14.1.9)}$$

The initial part $0 < t < T_1$ of $x(t)$ is drawn in Figure 14.8f, which consists of a parabolic (slick) and a linear curve (stick) connection. The position $x(t)$ and acceleration $\dot{x}(t)$ at $t = T_1$ are given by the following equations, which are the initial condition of the following interval $T_1 < t < T_0$:

$$\begin{cases} x(T_1) = \left(\frac{1}{2}\right)\frac{N\mu_d}{M}{T_1}^2 + v_1(T_1 - T_{st1}) = \left(\frac{1}{2}\right)\frac{N\mu_d}{M}{T_1}^2 + v_1 T_1 - \frac{M}{N\mu_d}v_1^2. \\ \dot{x}(T_1) = v_1 \end{cases} \quad \text{(P14.1.10)}$$

Let us now elaborate similarly on the time period $T_1 < t < T_0$. After T_1, the base moves backward very quickly with the velocity v_2 (in addition to the reduction of v_1), which should induce at least slicking condition on the slider mass until T_{st2} (rather close to T_0, since the base motion speed is very quick). The dragging friction is shown in Figure 14.8e with using the same friction constant μ_d:

$$\tilde{x} = \frac{N\mu_d}{M}\left(\frac{1}{s^3}\right)\left(1 - 2e^{-T_1 s} + e^{-T_0 s}\right). \quad \text{(P14.1.11)}$$

We solve Equation (P14.1.11) under the initial conditions in Equation (P14.1.10). Thus, $T_1 < t < T_{st2}$, and we may obtain

$$\begin{cases} x(t) = \left[\left(\frac{1}{2}\right)\frac{N\mu_d}{M}{T_1}^2 + v_1 T_1 - \frac{M}{N\mu_d}v_1^2\right] - \left(\frac{1}{2}\right)\frac{N\mu_d}{M}\left[2(t - T_1)^2\right] \\ \dot{x}(t) = v_1 + \frac{N\mu_d}{M}(-t + T_1) \end{cases}. \quad \text{(P14.1.12)}$$

T_{st2} can be determined by

$$\dot{x}(t_{st2}) = v_1 + \frac{N\mu_d}{M}(-t_{st2} + T_1) = -v_2.$$

Thus,

$$T_{st2} = T_1 + \frac{M}{N\mu_d}(v_1 + v_2). \quad \text{(P14.1.13)}$$

The slider is again sticked from T_{st2} to T_0, but this period may be short because of $v_2 > v_1$. Or, if v_2 is too large, $T_{st2} > T_0$ may happen; that is, no stick may be realized. The slider motion for this latter time period is schematically shown in Figure 14.8f again by a combination of quadratic and linear lines [5,6].

Practical slider translational motion was tested on a rod-type stator piezo-impact motor [5]. Figure 14.9 demonstrates the tip displacement of the base rod by supporting the slider ring. In the test setup, from the experimental simplicity, the motor is held from the mobile ring (slider) element and the stator rod movement was monitored by a laser vibrometer under a drive condition of 59 kHz. The linear average speed of the mobile element, superposed with zig-zag vibrational displacement, can be calculated as 5 mm/s under a condition of 4 mN thrust or blocking force, which basically comes from the friction force $N\mu_d$. Since the moving base displacement (sawtooth shape) does not have a sufficient "fall" slope, T_{st2} comes early, then the slider seems to be stuck, which reflects linear decrease after a small hump.

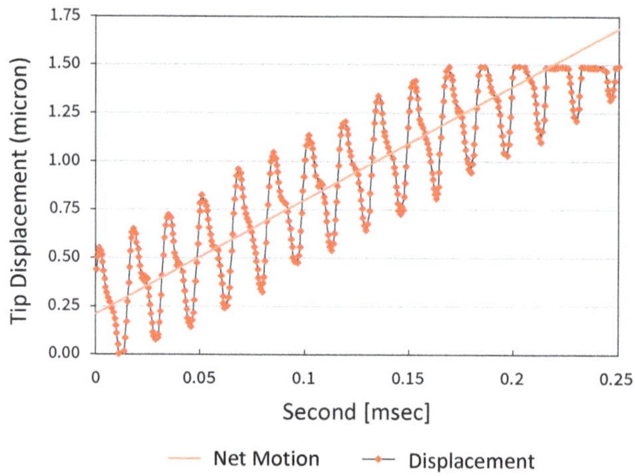

Figure 14.9. Practical slider motion of the "translational-rotary" inertial motor. Source: [4] ©Uchino, K. *Micromechatronics*, 2nd ed. CRC Press, 2019; p. 513. Reproduced by permission of Taylor & Francis Group.

14.1.4. Oscillatory System with Elastic Nonlinearity

Admittance Frequency Spectrum Distortion Phenomena

When we measure the admittance (i.e., current/voltage) frequency spectrum for a piezoelectric device, we observe a peak around its resonance frequency. However, with increasing the drive voltage (leading to the vibration amplitude increase), (1) the peak frequency shifts to a lower frequency and (2) the peak admittance decreases significantly, as demonstrated in Figure 14.10. The PZT specimen used here is a k_{31} type rectangular plate with 80 $mm{\cdot}L \times 10\ mm{\cdot}w \times 1\ mm{\cdot}t$ in size. In order to explain these behaviors, we provided an equivalent electric circuit model with variable parameters with applied voltage/current (see Figure 14.11) [7]. Recall that C_d is the damped capacitance (real electric capacitance of the piezo-ceramic), and C_A, L_A, and R_A are the motional components, corresponding to elastic compliance, mass, and elastic loss, respectively. The fundamental equations for the current (which corresponds to the admittance under a constant voltage condition) for both motional and electrical branches in the equivalent circuit are given by

$$\begin{cases} L_A \frac{d^2 I_1}{dt^2} + R_A \frac{dI_1}{dt} + \frac{I_1}{C_1} = \omega V \\ \frac{I_2}{C_d} = \omega V \\ I = I_1 + I_2 \end{cases} . \quad (14.56)$$

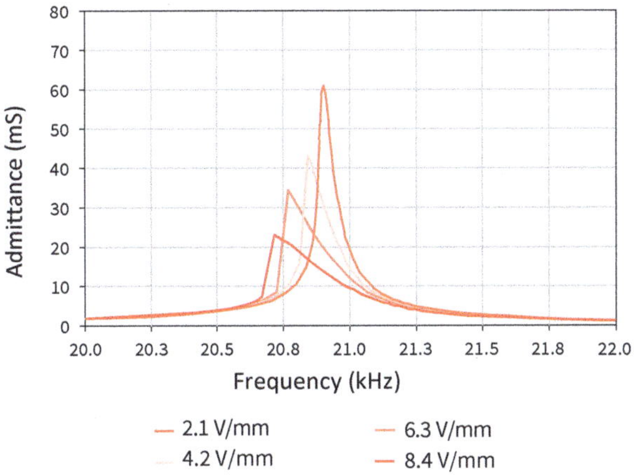

Figure 14.10. Experimental admittance frequency spectra under constant voltage condition in a piezoelectric ceramic PZT. Source: [3] ©Uchino, K. *High-Power Piezoelectrics and Loss Mechanisms*. CRC Press, 2020; p. 192. Reproduced by permission of Taylor & Francis Group.

Since the motional branch contributes primarily to the resonance mode, we focus on the top equation of Equation (14.56). Introducing the nonlinear characteristics to the capacitor and resistor elements (no change on inductor, because of mass) [7],

$$L_A \frac{d^2 I_1}{dt^2} + (R_{A1} + R_{A2} {I_1}^2) \frac{dI_1}{dt} + \frac{I_1}{C_1} + \frac{{I_1}^3}{C_2} = \omega V, \quad (14.57)$$

where both values of R_{A2} and C_2 are positive in most of the cases. The nonlinearity of the resistance, which corresponds to the increase in elastic loss factor of the PZT by increasing the vibration level, decreases the mechanical quality factor Q_m, and the admittance peak value, as well as broadening the spectrum peak significantly. To the contrary, the nonlinearity of the capacitance, which corresponds to the increase in the elastic compliance, provides significant skewness of the spectrum, also admittance jump and spectrum hysteresis under high vibration level with respect to frequency sweep.

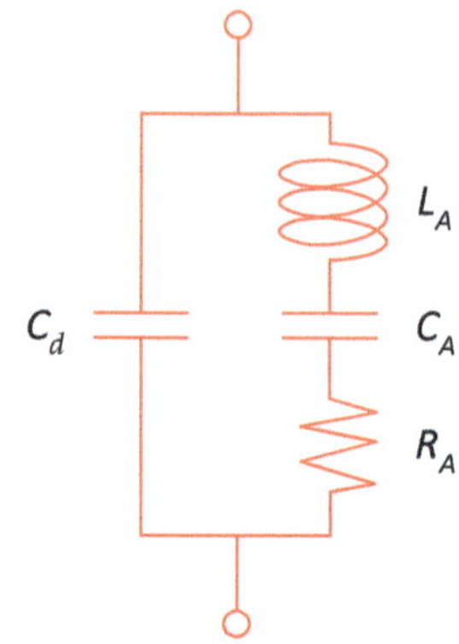

Figure 14.11. Equivalent circuit for the k_{31} mode (IEEE). Source: Figure by author.

Forced Duffing Equation

As we focus on the resonance peak frequency shift and the admittance spectrum skew primarily, we focus merely on the motional branch, and neglect the resistance nonlinearity (i.e., the admittance peak value does not decrease) and normalize with respect to L_A (such as $r = (R_{A1}/L_A)$ and $c_1 = (1/C_1 L_A)$). Equation (14.57) is transformed into the following simpler equation merely with the capacitance nonlinearity ("Forced Duffing Equation") [2]:

$$\ddot{I} + r\dot{I} + c_1 I + c_2 I^3 = \omega V, \tag{14.58}$$

where c_1 and c_2 are elastic stiffness parameters, and c_2 may be negative, so that the elastic softening (leading to the resonance frequency decrease) is induced with the current I (i.e., corresponding to vibration velocity) increase. When the external voltage V is provided by $V\cos(\omega t - \phi)$, we assume that the final steady state of current is expressed as:

$I = I\cos\omega t,$

as the first approximation. Taking into account the trigonometric relation:

$\cos^3\omega t = \left(\frac{1}{4}\right)\cos(3\omega t) + \left(\frac{3}{4}\right)\cos(\omega t).$

Equation (14.58) can be transformed into

$$\left(-\omega^2 + j\omega r + c_1\right)I + \left(\frac{3}{4}\right)c_2 I^3 + \left(\frac{1}{4}\right)c_2 I^3\cos(3\omega t) = \omega V. \tag{14.59a}$$

Supposing that an impedance analyzer only selectively monitors the fundamental frequency ω, we must have

$$-\left(\frac{3}{4}\right)c_2 I^3 + \left(\omega^2 - j\omega r - {\omega_0}^2\right)I + \omega V = 0 \tag{14.59b}$$

Here, ${\omega_0}^2 = c_1$ is the natural angular frequency of the system without the nonlinear term. Equation (14.60) provides the amplitude of the current I with the frequency of the external voltage V. The solutions of the above cubical equation can be obtained by a visual analysis illustrated in Figure 14.12a, which shows two curves:

Cubic curve: $y = -\left(\frac{3}{4}\right)(c_2/c_1)\cdot I^3$, and

Straight line: $y = \left(1 - \frac{\omega^2}{\omega_0^2} - \frac{j\omega r}{c_1}\right)\cdot I - \frac{\omega V}{c_1}$

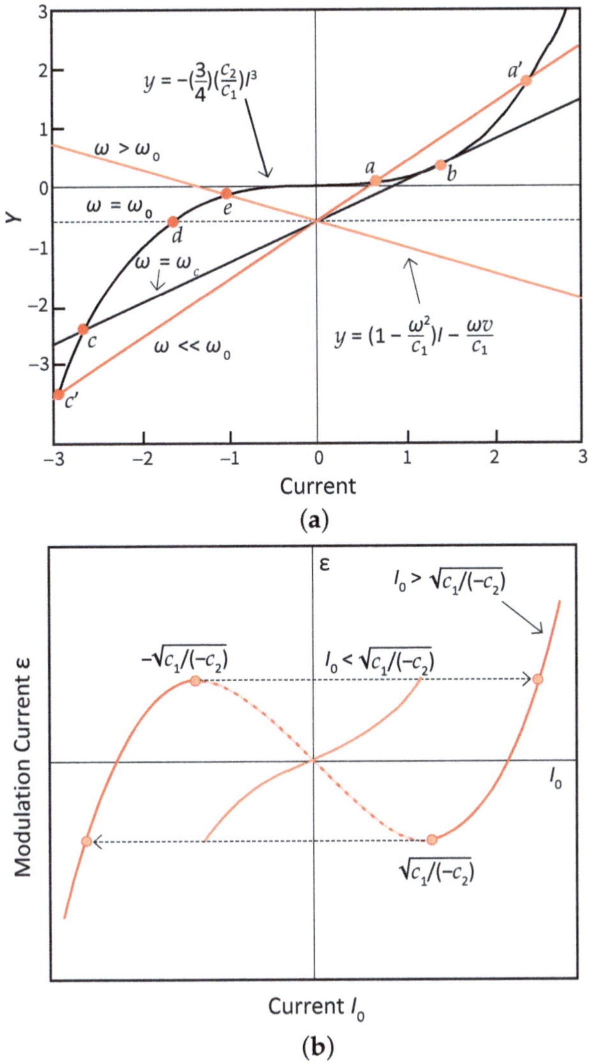

Figure 14.12. (**a**) Visual solution technique of the cubical equation. (**b**) The relation between the equilibrium current I_0 and the modulation current ε. Source: Figure by author.

The figure is drawn by neglecting the loss term r and keeping $-\frac{\omega V}{c_1}$ almost constant around $\omega = \omega_0$ just from the simplicity. The roots of the current I are obtained from the abscissa of the intersecting points of these two curves. When the frequency is small ($\omega \ll \omega_0$), under the straight-line slope slightly lower than "1", there are three roots (a, a' and c'). In practice, we may start from the point "a" (low current). With increasing the frequency, that is, with reducing the straight-line slope, two points "a" and "a'" start to merge into "b", the specific frequency at which is ω_c, slightly lower than ω_0. Above ω_c, there exists only one solution at the point "c", which causes a sudden current jump with a 180° phase change. We may call this transition as "positive to negative current branch transition". A further frequency increase to ω_0 gives the slope "0", leading to the current decrease from "c" to "d". When the frequency is larger ($\omega > \omega_0$), the straight-line slope becomes negative, and the current magnitude becomes monotonously decreased to zero. Now, we consider the frequency decreasing process. At a high frequency ($\omega > \omega_0$) there is only one solution. By reducing the frequency, the current will be gradually increased from the point "e", "d" to "c". Although at this point the straight-line touches on the cubic curve, the current position may go up to "c'". However, since another solution at the point "a" seems to be more stable (i.e., lower energy), the status will be transitioned from the negative current branch to the positive current branch with some frequency lag (that is, "hysteresis"), which shows the admittance spectrum simulation as a function of drive frequency ω using MatLab (an abbreviation of "matrix laboratory", developed by MathWorks, MA, USA) R2020a version. MatLab software integrates the advanced "Euler" approximation method, which can help with solving the normal differential equations and algebraic equations numerically, and plotting on the figure. The figure is made under a constant damping factor r = 0.01 (i.e., Q_m = 100) and $c_1 = 1$ (i.e., normalized). We change the nonlinear elasticity $c_2 = 0, -0.01$, and $-$ 0.05, and voltage = 0.1 and 0.5, the results of which are superposed on one figure. First, comparing three graphs of $c_2 = 0, -0.01$, and -0.05, the reader can recognize that the skewness and hysteresis of the admittance frequency spectrum are enhanced significantly with an increase of the nonlinear elasticity ($-c_2$); in addition, the peak admittance value decreases. Notice also that the transition temperature ω_c from the positive current branch to the negative branch (i.e., 180° phase change) is decreased with ($-c_2$), which is expected from the effective elastic stiffness decrease with nonlinearity. Second, the increase of applied voltage increases overall admittance value, also exhibits the ω_c decrease and hysteresis increase. These simulations explain the experimental results shown in Figure 14.10, where the admittance peak shift and skewness increase was obtained with an increase of the vibration velocity (i.e., applied voltage). The peak value decrease cannot be explained by the elastic nonlinearity, but by the loss parameter r increase (equivalent to the increase in the elastic loss factor $\tan\phi'$ physically).

Concept of the "Bifurcation"

Let us consider the admittance spectrum hysteresis from the concept of "bifurcation" theory. Starting from the linear resonance relation, $I = V/\sqrt{r^2 + (\omega - \frac{c_1}{\omega})^2}$, Equation (14.58) may be modified with the addition of the nonlinear elastic contribution c_2 as

$$I_0 + (\frac{c_2}{c_1})I_0{}^3 = \varepsilon \equiv \omega V_0/\sqrt{r^2 + (\omega - \frac{c_1}{\omega})^2}, \tag{14.60}$$

where subscript "0" stands for the peak values of sinusoidal voltage/current, and the right-hand-side term ε is the external modulation of current induced by the applied voltage via impedance. Note that ε is varied with the voltage proportionally, and with frequency ω significantly around the resonance frequency $\omega_0 = \sqrt{c_1}$.

To obtain the equilibrium current I_0, if it exists because of the nonlinear coupling term, let us modulate the current by ε with the external voltage/current. To see how I_0 depends on ε, let us consider reversely from the mathematical simplicity (see Figure 14.12b); that is, ε as a function of I_0,

$$\frac{d\varepsilon}{dI_0} = 1 + (c_2/c_1){I_0}^2. \tag{14.61}$$

Since the primary elastic stiffness is always positive, we set $c_1 > 0$. If $c_2 > 0$, $\frac{d\varepsilon}{dI_0} > 0$ is sustained for any I_0; that is, the value of ε increases steadily with I_0 (see Figure 14.12b, monotonous curve), while if $c_2 < 0$,

(1) $I_0 < \sqrt{-c_1/c_2}$: The value of ε increases steadily with I_0 (see Figure 14.12b).

(2) $I_0 > \sqrt{-c_1/c_2}$: There are two stationary solutions from $\frac{d\varepsilon}{dI_0} = 0$:

$$I_0 = \pm\sqrt{-c_1/c_2}. \tag{14.62}$$

Refer to Figure 14.12b (wider scale curve). The value of ε hypothetically decreases (dashed line) with an increase in I_0 for small I_0 (dashed line), which changes the sign at $I_0 = \pm\sqrt{-c_1/c_2}$. Once this condition occurs, I_0 value between $-\sqrt{-c_1/c_2}$ and $+\sqrt{-c_1/c_2}$ does not show up, but a current jump (which corresponds to the admittance jump under constant voltage operation).

If we turn the graphs of Figure 14.12b through 90° and plot them together in a 3D way, so that the equilibrium current I_0 states can be seen as a function of both modulation current ε and higher-order elastic parameter $(-c_2/c_1){I_0}^2$ (Figure 14.13b). The key feature is the fold in the surface (i.e., so-called "bifurcation"), and if we project this part down onto the ε vs. $(-c_2/c_1){I_0}^2$ plane, we obtain the cusped region shown in the figure. For any pair of values , $(-c_2/c_1){I_0}^2$ outside this region, there is just one equilibrium solution I_0, but for any $(\varepsilon,(-c_2/c_1){I_0}^2)$ within the cusped region, there are three equilibrium I_0 solutions. The "intermediate" one of these, corresponding to some point on the "middle" (shaded) section of the fold in Figure 14.13b, can be shown to be unstable (unrealizable in practice), while the other two are stable.

Bearing the previous analysis in mind, we can then consider the admittance spectrum skew and hysteresis with sweeping the drive frequency around the resonance frequency. According to the simulation in Figure 14.13b shown for the normalized parameters, the original resonance frequency under low oscillation level [i.e., $\omega_r = \sqrt{c_1}$] is "1", and admittance is in an arbitrary unit. First, regarding the admittance peak shift, if we assume $\omega_r = \sqrt{c_1 + c_2{I_0}^2}$, the elastic softening ($c_2 < 0$) with the current level increase leads to the shift to the lower frequency. Under a very low voltage and vibration level (that is, $I_0 < \sqrt{-c_1/c_2}$ even around the resonance frequency when r is reasonably large), we observe an almost symmetrical admittance frequency spectrum at the resonance frequency $\omega_0 = \sqrt{c_1}$ for the linear equation (i.e., nonlinearity is negligible). With increasing the voltage, because the current is significantly amplified by a factor of the mechanical quality factor (Q_m) around the resonance region (with the drive frequency sweep), $(1 + (c_2/c_1)I_0{}^2)$ will approach "zero", leading to the bifurcation critical point 1 $(= -(c_2/c_1)I_0{}^2)$ on Figure 14.13a. Considering the horizontal axis, we move from the left-corner to the "1" point, where the route bifurcates. Once the voltage and corresponding $(-c_2/c_1)I_0{}^2$ exceeds 1, there are two stable solutions, which generates a current jump and frequency spectrum hysteresis of the current (which is equivalent to "admittance" under constant voltage drive condition) between $-\sqrt{-c_1/c_2}$ and $+\sqrt{-c_1/c_2}$ theoretically, depending on the frequency sweep direction, increasing or decreasing. In practice, the hysteresis also depends on the frequency sweep speed, and on the environmental temperature (higher temperature, lower hysteresis due to the thermal fluctuation k_BT).

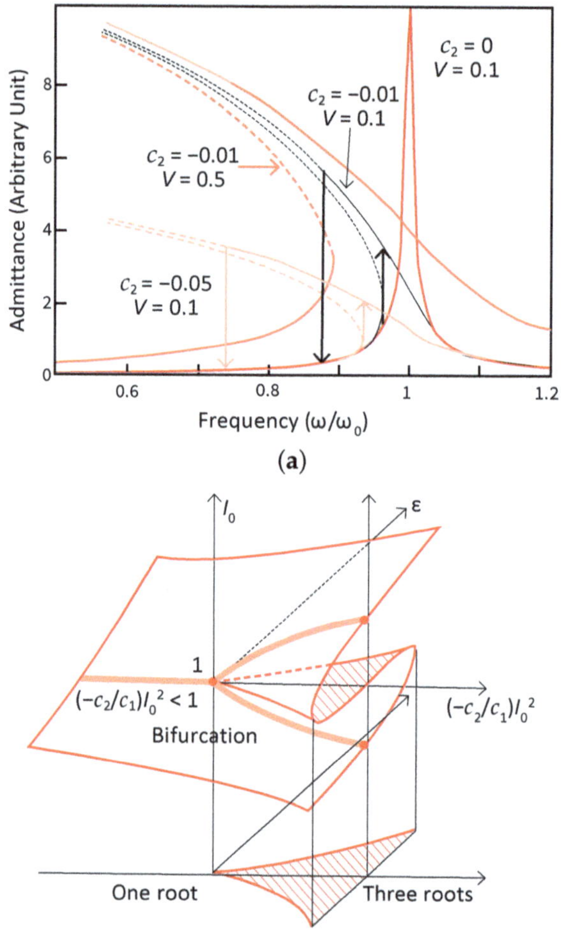

Figure 14.13. (**a**) Admittance spectrum simulation as a function of drive frequency. (**b**) Illustration of the equilibrium I_0 states as a function of both modulation current ε and higher-order elastic parameter $(-c_2/c_1)I_0{}^2$. Source: Figure by author.

Example Problem 14.2

In order to solve the "Forced Duffing Equation"

$$\ddot{I} + r\dot{I} + c_1 I + c_2 I^3 = \omega V, \tag{P14.2.1}$$

where c_1 and c_2 are elastic stiffness parameters, and c_2 may be negative, we assumed that the final steady state of the current is expressed as:

$$I = I_0 \cos\omega t, \tag{P14.2.2}$$

as the first approximation, under the external voltage V expressed as $V\cos(\omega t - \varphi)$. However, we neglected the higher order frequency contribution $\left(\frac{1}{4}\right) c_2 {I_0}^3 \cos(3\omega t)$ and obtained the following equation:

$$\left(-\omega^2 + j\omega r + c_1\right) I_0 = \left(\frac{3}{4}\right) c_2 {I_0}^3 = \omega V_0, \tag{P14.2.3}$$

Obtain the higher approximation by taking into account the higher order harmonic contribution.

Solution

The forced Duffing equation in Equation (14.58) can be transformed as

$$\frac{d^2 I}{dt^2} = \omega V_0 \cos\omega t - (j\omega r + c_1) I_0 \cos\omega t - \left(\frac{3}{4}\right) c_2 {I_0}^3 \cos\omega t - \left(\frac{1}{4}\right) c_2 {I_0}^3 \cos(3\omega t). \tag{P14.2.4a}$$

Knowing the relation in Equation (P14.2.3) in the first approximation, we obtain

$$\frac{d^2 I}{dt^2} = -\omega^2 I_0 \cos\omega t - \left(\frac{1}{4}\right) c_2 {I_0}^3 \cos(3\omega t). \tag{P14.2.4b}$$

Integrating Equation (P14.2.4a,b) in terms of t, we obtain a higher approximation:

$$I = I_0 \cos\omega t + \left(\frac{1}{36}\right) (c_2/\omega^2)\, {I_0}^3 \cos(3\omega t) \tag{P14.2.5}$$

This second approximation can be substituted into the original Equation (14.58) for obtaining the third approximation.

14.1.5. Mechanical Bistability

Mechanical Bistability Function

Mechanical bistability, such as a snap-action switch, has been used in many places, including a historical toy music instrument known as "Pop-Pen", even from the 18th century in Japan. Figure 14.14a shows an Utamaro Kitagawa's "Ukiyoe" picture drawing a lady playing "Pop-Pen". A slightly dented thin glass bottom plate of a flask (so-called "Biedro") has bistable positions. Light exhale and inhale air pressure can easily exchange the dent position up-or-down, during which action, a rather loud audible sound like "Pop" and "Pen" comes out. Piezoelectric actuator devices occasionally utilize mechanical bistability to save the operating energy. Figure 14.14b illustrates a mechanical latching relay developed by Omron Corporation, Japan, in the 1980s [8]. The latch mechanism possesses two mechanically stable positions, one ON-position and the other OFF-position on the "Movable Piece", so that no continuous electric voltage is required on the "piezoelectric unimorph", except for only switching the contact condition between ON and OFF. We discuss the analysis of the "mechanical bistability" in this section. Chapter Problem 14.1 shows an advanced model in practical designs; a stressed beam with slight bent.

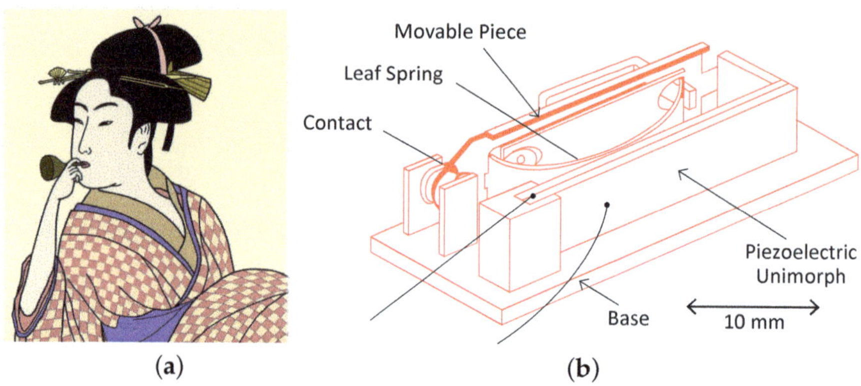

Figure 14.14. (**a**) "Pop-Pen", a mechanical bistability toy music instrument in the 18th century in Japan. (**b**) Piezoelectric mechanical relay (snap-action) developed by Omron Corporation, Japan. Source: [4] ©Uchino, K. *Micromechatronics*, 2nd ed. CRC Press, 2019; p. 452. Reproduced by permission of Taylor & Francis Group.

Two-Spring–Mass Model

A two-spring–mass model can be considered for the mechanical latching relay, as illustrated in Figure 14.15. Two springs with lengths a little longer than R are connected with the distance $2R$. The original angle set is denoted as α. When we push down the center light mass (mass is supposed to be neglected in the analysis), we denote the angle θ. Since the spring shrinkage is estimated by

$$\Delta L = \frac{R}{\cos\alpha} - \frac{R}{\cos\theta}. \tag{14.63}$$

Spring elastic energy in the two springs will be calculated as

$$U(\theta) = 2\cdot\frac{1}{2}k\left(\frac{R}{\cos\alpha} - \frac{R}{\cos\theta}\right)^2, \tag{14.64a}$$

where k is the spring constant. Using $\cos\theta = 1 - \frac{1}{2}\theta^2$ for a small angle, Equation (14.64a) is transformed into

$$U(\theta) = kR^2\left(1 + \frac{1}{2}\alpha^2 - 1 - \frac{1}{2}\theta^2\right)^2 = \frac{1}{4}kR^2\left(\alpha^4 - 2\alpha^2\theta^2 + \theta^4\right). \tag{14.64b}$$

On the other hand, the work on the mass from the force is evaluated by the product of force and displacement. Since the displacement is given by

$$\text{Displacement} = R(\tan\alpha - \tan\theta) = R(\alpha - \theta). \tag{14.65}$$

Now, the total energy of the springs and mass is represented by

$$V(\theta) = U(\theta) - FR(\alpha - \theta) \ = \frac{1}{4}kR^2(\alpha^4 - 2\alpha^2\theta^2 + \theta^4) - FR(\alpha - \theta). \tag{14.66}$$

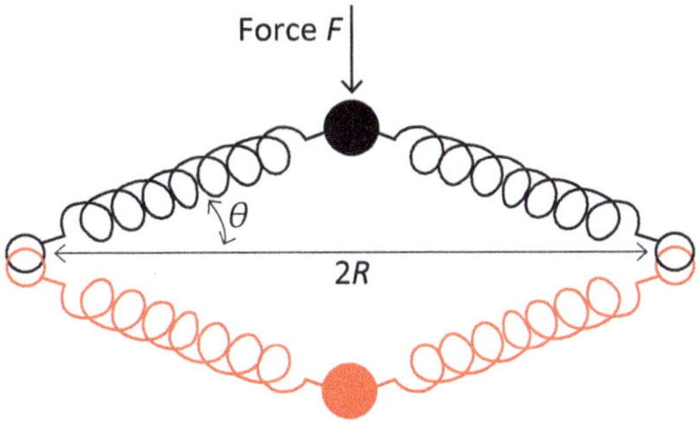

Figure 14.15. Two springs and mass model for the mechanical bistability. Source: Figure by author.

Total energy of the springs and mass as a function of $(\alpha - \theta)$ for changing F is shown in Figure 14.16a. The initial single minimum at $\theta = \alpha$ (case (1)) starts to generate another minimum around $\theta = -\alpha$ with the application of F (case (2)). Then, case (3) shows that the minimum at $\theta = -\alpha$ is deeper than that at $\theta = \alpha$, but due to the small potential barrier, the status is still maintained at $\theta = \alpha$. By increasing F further, and diminishing the potential barrier, the status changes suddenly from α to $-\alpha$ (case (4)).

Taking the first derivative of Equation (14.66) to find the potential minimum points:

$$\frac{\partial}{\partial x}V(\theta) = kR^2\left(-\alpha^2\theta + \theta^3\right) + FR = 0. \tag{14.67}$$

We obtain the

$$F = kR\left(\alpha^2\theta - \theta^3\right). \tag{14.68}$$

Finally, using Figure 14.16b, let us understand the mechanical bistability. First, load force F vs. angle θ dependence follows a "symmetric cubic equation", Equation (14.68). Second, when the load $F = 0$, there are three solution statuses: $\theta = \alpha$, 0, and $-\alpha$, among which $\theta = 0$ is a hypothetical solution, or cannot be observed in practice. Third, the snapping action process with increasing the load force F is shown by arrows in Figure 14.16b. With increasing the load force F, angle θ gradually decreases from the initial α. When the load F reaches the local maximum, Position 1, angle θ suddenly jumps to less than $-\alpha$. Once this jump occurs, even the load F is decreased to zero, $\theta = -\alpha$ (another stable position) is realized. Since the curve is point symmetry, it is easy to understand the opposite snap-action from $\theta = -\alpha$ to α.

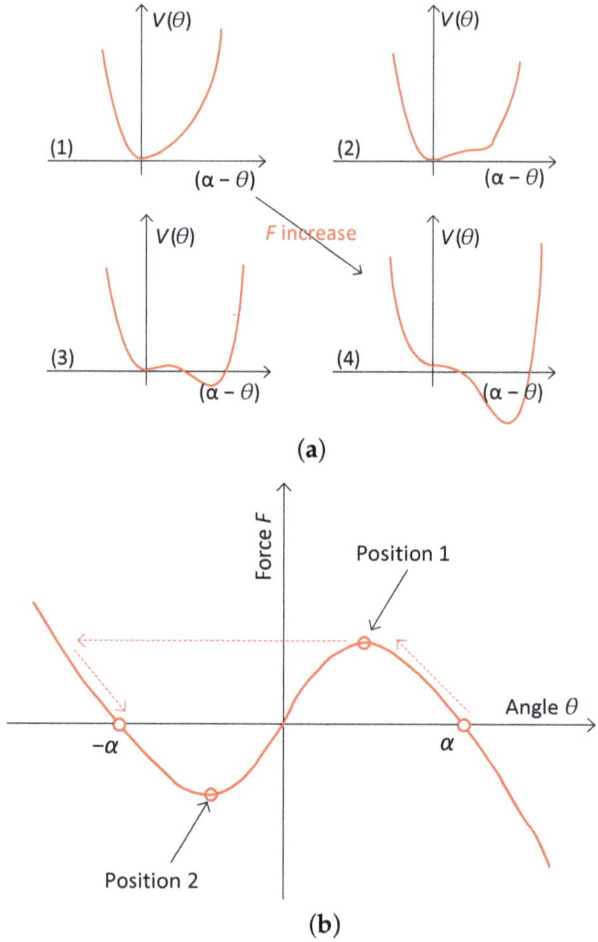

Figure 14.16. (**a**) Total energy of the springs and mass as a function of $(\alpha - \theta)$ for changing F. (**b**) Force vs. angle dependence of the mechanical bistability model. Source: Figure by author.

14.2. Domain Wall Structures and Dynamics

Chapter 4 described how nonlinear phenomenology induces the paraelectric-to-ferroelectric transition. However, that phenomenology assumed a mono-domain state in a single crystal, where the coercive field derived is 10 times higher than practically observed in a single crystal. The key reason comes from the domain segmentation due to the total crystal energy minimization. This section treats the dynamic phenomenology with domain walls. We describe first on the static domain formation, and the domain wall models, then discuss the domain wall dynamics. This section is largely devoted to a comprehensive domain structure textbook, "Domain Structure in Ferroelectrics and Related Materials" by Sidorkin [9].

14.2.1. Ginzburg–Landau Functional—Domain Wall Structure Phenomenology

Formulation of Ginzburg–Landau Functional

Landau phenomenological theory was introduced in Chapter 4, where we assume that the Landau free energy F in 1-D is represented in terms of polarization P as:

$$F(P,T) = (1/2)\alpha P^2 + (1/4)\beta P^4, \tag{14.69}$$

in the simplest second-order phase transition's case. That is, only the intra-coupling in the uniform polar cluster distribution (i.e., mono-domain state) is taken into account. Only the coefficient α is temperature dependent,

$$\alpha = (T - T_0)/\varepsilon_0 C \tag{14.70}$$

where C is taken as a positive constant called the "Curie–Weiss constant" and T_0 is equal to or lower than the actual transition temperature T_C ("Curie temperature"), in general (the first-order transition). β is supposed to be constant, and positive in this second-order transition case. The phenomenological formulation should be applied for the entire temperature range over which the infinitely large crystal is uniformly in its paraelectric and ferroelectric states. We discuss the form of this expansion in the case of multidomain status in a finite-size specimen shown in Figure 14.17a, without taking into account the depolarization energy initially (that is, a rather thick single crystal specimen). Taking the Cartesian coordinate, z: polarization direction, and x: perpendicular to the 180° domain wall planes, we consider the $P(x)$ distribution function in a narrow slab x to $x + \Delta x$ (Figure 14.17b). If, as the first approximation, we assume that the cells (or slabs), x, do not influence each other, the free energy can be decomposed into a sum (or an integral in a continuum approximation) of contributions of each cell. Since $+P_S$ and $-P_S$ do not change the energy in Equation (14.69) at all, the energy form is exactly the same. In the second step, we take the inter-coupling between neighboring cells into account by a term describing an increase of free energy if the polarization $P(x)$ in neighboring cells differ from each other. $x = 0$ is taken at the domain boundary center point, and $P(x) = +P_S$ at $x = \infty$, and $P(x) = -P_S$ at $x = -\infty$, without losing generality. This is achieved by a term $\kappa(\nabla P(x))^2$; that is, "second power" (symmetry with respect to the crystal up-side-down) of grad $(P(x))$. Thus, we represent F in the form of the famous "Ginzburg–Landau functional":

$$F(P(x),T) = \int dx[\frac{\alpha}{2}P(x)^2 + \frac{\beta}{4}P(x)^4 + \frac{\kappa}{2}(\nabla P(x))^2]. \tag{14.71}$$

We consider the minimization of the Ginzburg–Landau functional $F(P(x),T)$ with respect of P. If the existence of the κ term reduces the free energy, these guarantees "multidomain status" stability in practical single crystals. The minimization condition, $(\partial F/\partial P) = 0$, provide the following relation (Derivation process is in Example Problem 14.2):

$$\kappa\left(\frac{d^2P}{dx^2}\right) = \alpha P + \beta P^3. \tag{14.72}$$

If we adopt the equation for the relaxation of $P(x)$, that is, if we assume that the polarization change ΔP with time Δt is proportional to the free energy decrease with respect to the polarization change ΔP, we obtain the "time-dependent Ginzburg–Landau equation":

$$\frac{dP}{dt} = -\frac{\partial F}{\partial P} = -\alpha P - \beta P^3 + \kappa \Delta P, \tag{14.73}$$

where the proportional constant is taken as (− 1) from the simplicity viewpoint, and P is now treated as a function of space, x, and time, t. The time dependent equations are handled in Section 14.2.3. The typical features of Equation (14.73) in the static condition are:

- A linear term, $-\alpha P$, where the coefficient α changes its sign at the Curie–Weiss temperature $T = T_0$,
- A nonlinear term, $-\beta P^3$, which serves for a stabilization of the system,
- A "diffusion" term, $\kappa \Delta P$, where Δ is the Laplacian operator.

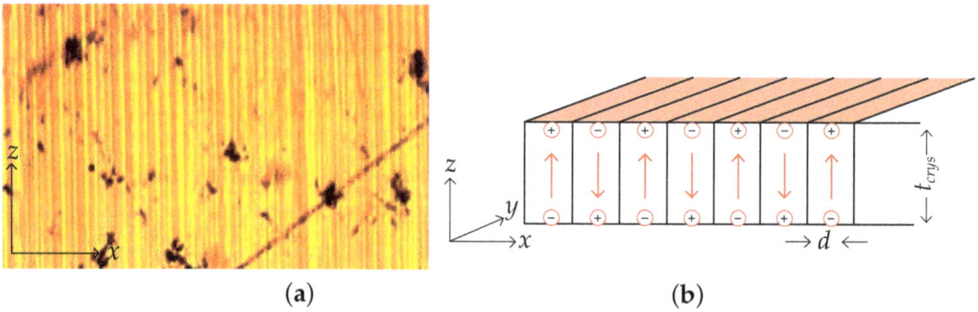

Figure 14.17. (**a**) The 180° domain walls in $BaTiO_3$ (001) plate (top view, no electrode). (**b**) Multidomain model of 180° domain walls on a ferroelectric plate (no electrode). Source: Figure by author.

Example Problem 14.3

In order to derive the following second-derivative equation (Equation (14.72)), which is equivalent to Equation (14.73) under steady state condition (i.e., $\frac{dP}{dt} = 0$):

$$\kappa\left(\frac{d^2P}{dx^2}\right) = \alpha P + \beta P^3, \tag{P14.3.1}$$

we consider the minimization of the time-independent Ginzburg–Landau functional with respect of P,

$$F(P(x), T) = \int_{-\infty}^{\infty} \left[\frac{\alpha}{2}P(x)^2 + \frac{\beta}{4}P(x)^4 + \frac{\kappa}{2}\left(\frac{dP}{dx}\right)^2\right]dx. \tag{P14.3.2}$$

Using the minimization condition, $(\partial F/\partial P) = 0$, derive Equation (P14.3.1) [8].

Solution

We denote $f(P) = \frac{\alpha}{2}P(x)^2 + \frac{\beta}{4}P(x)^4$. Then, we consider a slight change of polarization δP around the energy minimum point P. Let us take the expansion series:

$$f(P+\delta P) = f(P) + \frac{f'(P)}{1!}\delta P + \frac{f''(P)}{2!}(\delta P)^2, \tag{P14.3.3}$$

$$\frac{\kappa}{2}[\frac{d(P+\delta P)}{dx}]^2 = \frac{\kappa}{2}[\frac{dP}{dx} + \frac{d(\delta P)}{dx}]^2 = \frac{\kappa}{2}(\frac{dP}{dx})^2 + \kappa\left(\frac{dP}{dx}\right)\frac{d(\delta P)}{dx} + \frac{\kappa}{2}[\frac{d(\delta P)}{dx}]^2. \tag{P14.3.4}$$

Then, we obtain

$$\begin{aligned} F(P+\delta P) &= \textstyle\int_{-\infty}^{\infty} [f(P+\delta P) + \frac{\kappa}{2}(\frac{d(P+\delta P)}{dx})^2] \\ dx = \textstyle\int [f(P) + \frac{\kappa}{2}(\frac{dP}{dx})^2]dx &+ \textstyle\int [f'(P)\delta P + \kappa(\frac{dP}{dx})\frac{d(\delta P)}{dx}]dx + \cdots \\ &= F(P) + \delta F + \delta^2 F + \cdots \end{aligned} \tag{P14.3.5}$$

The first term in the right-hand-side of Equation (P14.3.5) describes the thermodynamic potential of the optimum distribution $P(x)$, with respect to which the variation is performed. It coincides with the original Equation (P14.3.2). The following terms represent, respectively, the first and second variations of the free energy.

The equality to zero of the first variation $\delta F = 0$ enables us to find the distribution $P(x)$, corresponding to the minimum F. Taking into account integration by parts

$$\int [f'(P)\delta P + \kappa(\frac{dP}{dx})\frac{d(\delta P)}{dx}]dx = \int [f'(P) - \kappa(d^2P/dx^2)](\delta P)dx. \tag{P14.3.6}$$

The derivation of the above Equation (P14.3.6) is from the two facts that $\frac{d}{dx}\left(\frac{dP}{dx}\delta P\right) = \frac{d^2P}{dx^2}\delta P + \frac{dP}{dx}\frac{d(\delta P)}{dx}$, and that $\int_{-\infty}^{\infty} \frac{d}{dx}\left(\frac{dP}{dx}\delta P\right)dx = \frac{dP}{dx}\delta P|_{-\infty}^{\infty} = 0$ (note that the slope $\frac{dP}{dx}$ should be zero at a point far from $x = 0$). Since Equation (P14.3.6) should be zero for any δP, the expression in the braces is equal to zero:

$$\kappa\left(\frac{d^2P}{dx^2}\right) = \frac{df}{dx} = \alpha P + \beta P^3. \tag{P14.3.7}$$

The sign of the second variation $\delta^2 F$ makes it possible to evaluate the stability (maximum or minimum) of the corresponding solution. We will skip this process here and remain for Chapter Problem 14.2.

Domain Wall Formula

We now solve the static domain wall structure equation from Equation (14.72):

$$\kappa(\frac{d^2P}{dx^2}) = \alpha P + \beta P^3. \tag{14.74}$$

The domain wall exists at $x = 0$, and away from the boundary where the homogeneous state is implemented, that is, the second derivative $(\frac{d^2P}{dx^2}) = 0$. The value of P at a point far from the wall can be determined from the conventional equation:

$$\alpha P_0 + \beta {P_0}^3 = 0, \tag{14.75}$$

which in the case of ferro-phase with the spontaneous polarization P_0 gives

$${P_0}^3 = -\alpha/\beta(\alpha < 0). \tag{14.76}$$

To determine the structure of the 180° domain wall in the vicinity of $x = 0$, we use the following boundary conditions:

$$\begin{cases} P(+\infty) = P_0 \\ P(-\infty) = -P_0 \end{cases}. \tag{14.77}$$

First, both parts of Equation (14.74) are multiplied by (dP/dx) and integrated with respect to dx, taking into account the conditions Equation (14.77). Consequently, we obtain

$$\frac{\kappa}{2}\left(\frac{dP}{dx}\right)^2 = f[P(x)] - f[P_0] \tag{14.78}$$

where $f(P) = \frac{\alpha}{2}P(x)^2 + \frac{\beta}{4}P(x)^4$. Separating the variables in Equation (14.78) gives

$$\int \frac{dP}{\sqrt{f[P(x)] - f[P_0]}} = \int \frac{dx}{\sqrt{\kappa/2}}. \tag{14.79}$$

Taking into account the specific value ${P_0}^2$, the difference $f[P(x)] - f[P_0]$ is transformed to the form

$$f[P(x)] - f[P_0] = \frac{\beta}{4}[P_0^2 - P^2]^2 \tag{14.80}$$

Expanding the resultant difference of the squares into multipliers

$$\frac{1}{P_0^2 - P^2} = \frac{1}{2P_0(P_0 + P)} + \frac{1}{2P_0(P_0 - P)}, \tag{14.81}$$

and integrating Equation (14.79), taking Equations (14.80) and (14.81) into account, we obtain

$$\frac{1}{\sqrt{\beta}P_0}\int\left[\frac{dP}{(P_0 + P)} + \frac{dP}{(P_0 - P)}\right] = \frac{1}{\sqrt{\beta}P_0} ln\frac{(P_0 + P)}{(P_0 - P)} = \sqrt{\frac{2}{\kappa}}x. \tag{14.82}$$

Assuming that the center of the domain boundary is situated at $x = 0$, where $P = 0$, we obtain the following distribution of polarization around the boundary.

$$P(x) = P_0 \tanh\left(\frac{x}{\delta}\right) \quad \left[\text{Note that } \tanh x = \frac{e^x - e^{-x}}{e^x + e^{-x}}\right], \tag{14.83}$$

$$\delta = \frac{1}{P_0}\sqrt{\frac{2\kappa}{\beta}} = \sqrt{\frac{2\kappa}{-\alpha}}. \tag{14.84}$$

It is important to note that the polarization distribution around the domain wall follows a hyperbolic tangent function in this simple "Ginzburg–Landau Functional" case. In accordance with Equation (14.83) and Figure 14.18, quantity δ is naturally referred to as the half of the domain boundary thickness. As indicated by Equation (14.84), this thickness depends greatly on temperature and increases significantly when approaching the Curie point T_C (= T_0 in our simplest second-order transition) due to $\alpha \to 0$. Figure 14.19 illustrates expected polarization distribution configurations in a multiple domain structure with the width d, and domain wall thickness δ at a low temperature (a), at an intermediate temperature (b), and a temperature close to the Curie temperature (c). A step function-like thin domain wall at a low temperature becomes diffused with increasing the temperature, exhibiting the polarization $P(x)$ distribution in a hyperbolic tangent in terms of position coordinate x. When approaching the Curie temperature, the domain wall becomes very vague, as though the polarization distribution is sinusoidal with the periodicity of $2d$ (Figure 14.19c). This model suggests the optical lattice vibration mode (i.e., optical phonon) "softening", that is, vibration frequency "slowing down" (at small wave vector $k = 2\pi/\lambda = \pi/d$) of a ferroelectric during cooling process from the paraelectric to the ferroelectric phase.

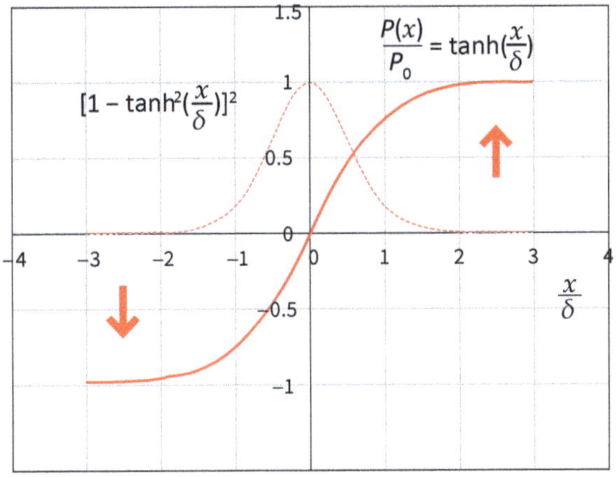

Figure 14.18. Domain wall models: polarization distribution (solid line) and domain wall energy distribution (dashed line). Source: [3] ©Uchino, K. *High-Power Piezoelectrics and Loss Mechanisms*. CRC Press, 2020; p. 294. Reproduced by permission of Taylor & Francis Group.

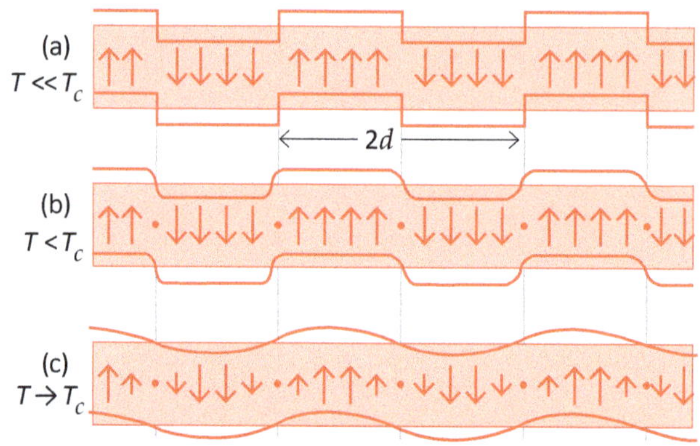

Figure 14.19. Polarization distribution configurations in a multidomain structure with the width d at various temperatures. Source: [3] ©Uchino, K. *High-Power Piezoelectrics and Loss Mechanisms*. CRC Press, 2020; p. 294. Reproduced by permission of Taylor & Francis Group.

Domain Wall Energy

The surface density of the energy of the stationary wall γ_0 is obtained as a result of substituting the distribution Equation (14.83) into Equation (14.71), and is less than the energy of the homogeneous state. Consequently, taking into account that $dP_0/dx = 0$, the first integral Equation (14.78) and the ratio Equation (14.80), we find

$$\begin{aligned}
\gamma_0 = \textstyle\int_{-\infty}^{\infty}\left[f[P(x)] - f[P_0] + \frac{\kappa}{2}\left(\frac{dP}{dx}\right)^2\right]dx \qquad & [\text{from Equation (14.78)}] \\
2\textstyle\int_{-\infty}^{\infty}[f[P(x)] - f[P_0]]dx \quad [\text{using Equation (14.80)} & f[P(x)] - f[P_0] = \tfrac{\beta}{4}\left[P_0^2 - P^2\right]^2] \\
= \tfrac{\beta}{2}P_0^4\textstyle\int_{-\infty}^{\infty}\left[1 - \tanh^2\left(\frac{x}{\delta}\right)\right]^2 dx = -\frac{\alpha P_0^2\delta}{2}\int_{-\infty}^{\infty}\frac{\frac{dx}{\delta}}{\cosh^4\left(\frac{x}{\delta}\right)} \quad & [\text{using Equation (14.76) } P_0^2 = -\alpha/\beta] \\
= -\tfrac{2}{3}\alpha P_0^2\delta = \tfrac{4}{3}P_0^2\left(\tfrac{\kappa}{\delta}\right) \qquad & [\text{from Equation (14.84)}].
\end{aligned} \tag{14.85}$$

Note here that a general integral relation, $\int_{-\infty}^{\infty}\frac{dx}{\cosh^4(x)} = \frac{\sinh x}{3\cosh^3 x}\Big|_{-\infty}^{\infty} + \frac{2}{3}\int_{-\infty}^{\infty}\frac{dx}{\cosh^2(x)} = \frac{2}{3}\tanh x\Big|_{-\infty}^{\infty} = \frac{4}{3}$.

14.2.2. Static Domain Structures

Since we obtain the domain wall energy from the phenomenology in Equation (14.85), we consider the static domain structures of a finite size single crystal by integrating all energy terms. We will work again on a simple 180° domain arrangement shown in Figure 14.17b with domain width d and domain crystal thickness t_{crys}. Following the Chenskii's approach [10], we describe the

$$G_1 - G_1^0 = \int \left(\frac{\alpha}{2}P^2 + \frac{\beta}{4}P^4\right)dV + W_e + W_{dip} + W_x. \tag{14.86}$$

Here, W_e, W_{dip}, and W_x are "depolarization energy", "dipole interaction energy" (that is, the "domain wall energy", given in Equation (14.85), excluding the polarization energy $[\frac{\alpha}{2}P_0^2 + \frac{\beta}{2}P_0^4]$ term), and "elastic energy" (via piezoelectric effect, $x_i = g_{ij}P_j$), which are provided, respectively, by

$$W_e = \varepsilon^* P_0^2 V(\frac{d}{t_{crys}}), \tag{14.87}$$

$$W_{dip} = -K\alpha P_0^2 \delta\left(\frac{V}{d}\right) \tag{14.88}$$

$[K = \frac{2}{3}$ in Equation (14.85), but different for the first-order transition.],

$$W_x = \frac{1}{2}\int_V X \cdot x dV = \frac{1}{2}\int_V c_{ij} x_i x_j dV = \frac{1}{2} c_{ij} g_{ij} P_{j} g_{jk} P_k. \tag{14.89}$$

Now, Equation (14.86) can be rewritten as

$$G_1 - G_1^0 = \frac{\alpha}{2} P_0^2 + \frac{\beta}{4} P_0^4 + \varepsilon^* P_0^2 V\left(\frac{d}{t_{crys}}\right) - K\alpha P_0^2 \delta\left(\frac{V}{d}\right) + \frac{1}{2} c g^2 P_0^2. \tag{14.90}$$

From the static condition, $\frac{dP}{dt} = -\frac{\partial G_1}{\partial P} = 0$, we obtain

$\frac{\partial G_1}{\partial P} = 0 = (2\frac{\varepsilon^* d}{t_{crys}} - 2K\delta\alpha/\mathrm{d} + \alpha + cg^2)P_0 + \beta P_0^3$,

$P_0^2 = -\frac{1}{\beta}\left(\alpha + cg^2 + 2\frac{\varepsilon^* d}{t_{crys}} - 2K\delta\alpha/\mathrm{d}\right)$.

Then, the equilibrium domain width d and the polarization P_0 can be obtained from the minimization condition $\frac{\partial G_1}{\partial d} = 0$;

$$d = \sqrt{\frac{-K\delta\alpha t_{crys}}{\varepsilon^*}}, \tag{14.91}$$

$$P_0^2 = -\frac{\alpha + cg^2}{\beta}. \tag{14.92}$$

Note that the spontaneous polarization is slightly modified by the existence of the piezoelectricity under the multidomain configuration, and the elastic energy term cg^2 should be replaced, depending on the crystal symmetry, by $(c_{33}{g_{33}}^2 + 2c_{11}{g_{31}}^2)$ in the *4 mm* case, for example.

14.2.3. Domain Wall Dynamics in Phenomenology

We now aim to determine the parameters of the moving domain wall. We will assume the effective mass of the domain wall, m^*, and its displacement u, with effective kinetic energy like $(\frac{1}{2})m^*(\frac{du}{dt})^2$ in a periodic potential modulated by the distance a (maybe the crystal unit cell). We further assume the effective charge, e^*, which links u with polarization P and a.

Domain Wall Dynamic Equation

In order to discuss the dynamic response, we introduce the kinetic energy T into the potential energy expressed in Equation (14.71). A general expression of the kinetic energy $T = \frac{1}{2}\rho(\frac{\partial u}{\partial t})^2$ (ρ: density of the crystal) can be rewritten as

$$T = \frac{1}{2}\mu(\frac{\partial P}{\partial t})^2, \tag{14.93}$$

taking into account $P = e^*u/a^3$ (proportional to the displacement), and a new parameter μ is a sort of mass proportional to the material's density normalized by the effective charge, which is verified as the "mobility" later, and is provided by

$$\mu = \rho a^6/e^{*2}. \tag{14.94}$$

The full energy expression (kinetic and potential energy) can be provided by

$$\Phi = \int dx[F+T] = \int dx[\frac{1}{2}\mu\left(\frac{\partial P}{\partial t}\right)^2 + \frac{1}{2}\kappa\left(\frac{\partial P}{\partial x}\right)^2 + \frac{\alpha}{2}P^2 + \frac{\beta}{4}P^4]. \tag{14.95}$$

Note that we neglect the depolarization energy and elastic energy in the present discussion. Under the energy minimum condition, $\frac{\partial \Phi}{\partial P} = 0$, we derive

$$\mu\frac{\partial^2 P}{\partial t^2} - \kappa\frac{\partial^2 P}{\partial x^2} + \alpha P + \beta P^3 = 0 \ \ [\text{refer to Example Problem 14.3}]. \tag{14.96}$$

When we consider the dissipation Γ and the presence of the external electric field E, which is actually essential to discuss the dielectric loss, we can expand the formula as follows:

$$\mu\frac{\partial^2 P}{\partial t^2} + \Gamma\frac{\partial P}{\partial t} - \kappa\frac{\partial^2 P}{\partial x^2} + \alpha P + \beta P^3 = E. \tag{14.97}$$

Domain Wall Motion under Zero Field

In order to understand the domain wall configuration change with the motion, we initially consider the simpler Equation (14.96) (i.e., no loss), where no external electric field is applied. That is, free domain wall vibration, after the initial sudden strain release. We will adopt an assumption that the distribution profile of polarization in the moving wall maintains $P(x,v) = P(x - vt)$, where v is the velocity of the domain wall motion; that is, the domain wall behaves as a "travelling wave" by keeping the wall structure. This leads to a general relation,

$$\frac{\partial P}{\partial t} = -v\frac{\partial P}{\partial x}. \tag{14.98}$$

Then, taking new parameters

$$x' = x - vt, \tag{14.99}$$

$$\kappa' = \kappa - \mu v^2 = \kappa(1 - v^2/{c_0}^2) \ \ [{c_0}^2 = \kappa/\mu], \tag{14.100}$$

we can rewrite Equation (14.96) in the following equation:

$$\kappa'\frac{\partial^2 P}{\partial x'^2} = \alpha P + \beta P^3. \tag{14.101}$$

The solution is obvious from Equation (14.83), and expressed as

$$P(x,v) = P_0\tanh(\frac{x - vt}{\delta'}), \tag{14.102}$$

$$\delta' = \sqrt{\frac{2\kappa'}{-\alpha}} = \sqrt{\frac{2\kappa(1 - v^2/c_0^2)}{-\alpha}} = \delta\sqrt{(1 - v^2/c_0^2)} \ [\alpha < 0]. \tag{14.103}$$

The limiting velocity of the domain wall motion is $c_0 = \sqrt{\kappa/\mu}$, and the domain wall width seems to be reduced by the factor of $\sqrt{(1 - v^2/c_0^2)}$, a similar formula to the relativistic "Lorentz factor". Let us determine the domain wall energy under the velocity v: from $\Phi - \Phi(P_0)$, obtain as

$$\gamma(v) = -\frac{2}{3}\alpha P_0^2 \delta \cdot \frac{1}{\sqrt{(1 - v^2/c_0^2)}} = \frac{\gamma_0}{\sqrt{(1 - v^2/c_0^2)}}. \tag{14.104}$$

where $\gamma_0 = -\frac{2}{3}\alpha P_0^2 \delta$ as given in Equation (14.85). If we adopt a similar relationship among "energy and the mass" to the relativity theory (i.e., energy = mc^2), we may introduce the effective mass m^* as follows:

$$\gamma(v) = \frac{\gamma_0}{\sqrt{(1 - v^2/c_0^2)}} = m^*(v)c_0^2. \tag{14.105}$$

The effective mass is expressed as

$$m^*(v) = \frac{\gamma_0/c_0^2}{\sqrt{(1 - v^2/c_0^2)}} = \frac{m_0^*}{\sqrt{(1 - v^2/c_0^2)}} \ [m_0^* = \gamma_0/c_0^2], \tag{14.106}$$

which increases with increasing the velocity. When the velocity is small, the kinetic energy is estimated by

$$T = (m^*(v) - m_0^*)\, c_0^2 \approx \frac{1}{2} m_0^* v^2, \tag{14.107}$$

which re-proves the validity of the effective mass description, taking into account the initial introduction of the kinetic energy $T = \frac{1}{2}\rho\left(\frac{\partial u}{\partial t}\right)^2$.

Domain Wall Motion with Dissipation under an Electric Field

Taking into account the dissipation and the electric field application, let us derive the dielectric loss from the formula expressed in Equation (14.97):

$\mu\frac{\partial^2 P}{\partial t^2} + \Gamma\frac{\partial P}{\partial t} - \kappa\frac{\partial^2 P}{\partial x^2} + \alpha P + \beta P^3 = E.$

We first examine its asymptotic solution. Away from the boundary, where all the derivatives are equal to zero, the asymptotic values of the polarization are the roots of the equation:

$$\alpha P + \beta P^3 = E. \tag{14.108}$$

As the derivation process is schematically illustrated in Figure 14.20a, under $E \neq 0$, the three roots, P_1, P_2, and P_3, have no longer the symmetry: "$P_0 = P_1 = -P_2 = \sqrt{-\frac{\alpha}{\beta}}$ and $P_3 = 0$ under $E = 0$" changes to "$P_1 > P_0$, $|P_2| < P_0$ and $P_3 \neq 0$".

Figure 14.20b shows the expected distribution of polarization in a domain wall under the external electric field E (solid line), in comparison with the stationary profile under $E = 0$ (dashed line).

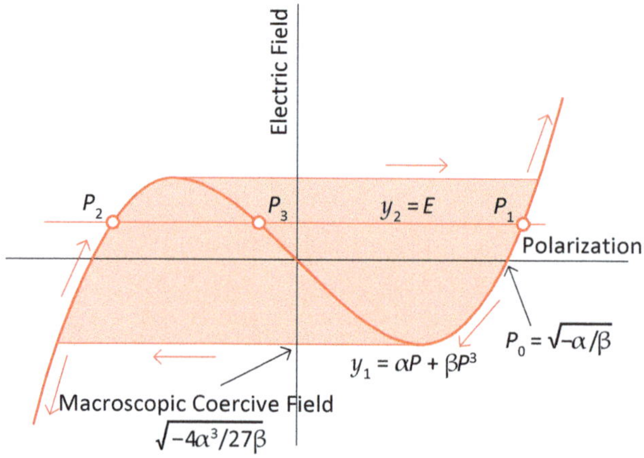

(**a**)

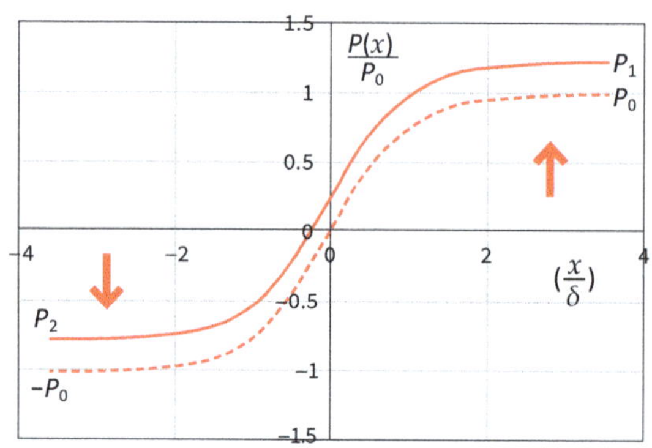

(**b**)

Figure 14.20. (**a**) Roots of the polynomial $\alpha P + \beta P^3 = E$ under various external field E. (**b**) Distribution of polarization in a stationary domain wall and in a domain wall under the external electric field. Source: Figure by author.

Absolute permittivity $\varepsilon \cdot \varepsilon_0$ is obtained from $(\frac{\partial P}{\partial E})$, and from Equation (14.108),

$$\varepsilon\varepsilon_0 = (\frac{\partial E}{\partial P} = 1/(\alpha + 3\beta P^2) \qquad (14.109)$$

Thus, the relative permittivity under very small electric field E at P_1, P_2, and P_3 is given, respectively, by taking into account $P_1 = -P_2 = \sqrt{-\alpha/\beta}$ and $P_3 = 0$, as follows:

$$P_1, P_2\text{: } \varepsilon\varepsilon_0 = 1/(-2\alpha) = C/2(T_0 - T). \qquad (14.110)$$

$$P_3\text{: } \varepsilon \cdot \varepsilon_0 = 1/(\alpha) = -C/(T_0 - T) \text{ [hypothetical negative capacitance at } T < T_0]. \qquad (14.111)$$

On the other hand, the macroscopic coercive field is obtained from the maximum/minimum point of $y_1 = \alpha P + \beta P^3$ curve: that is, from $\frac{\partial y_1}{\partial P} = 0$, $\alpha + 3\beta P^2 = 0$. Then, $P = \sqrt{-\alpha/3\beta}$. Since the coercive field is obtained from the maximum y_1 point,

$$y1 = \alpha P + \beta P3 = \sqrt{-\alpha/3\beta}\ [+(-\alpha/3\beta)] = \sqrt{-4\alpha^3/27\beta}. \tag{14.112}$$

We may not need to consider the AC electric field amplitude higher than this macroscopic coercive field (usually >10 kV/mm).

As the second step, we rewrite Equation (14.97) by using the normalized parameters, $p = P/P_0$, $E' = E/(-\alpha)P_0$:

$$\frac{1}{2}\frac{\delta^2}{c_0^2}\frac{\partial^2 p}{\partial t^2} + \frac{\Gamma}{\alpha}\frac{\partial p}{\partial t} - \frac{1}{2}\delta^2\frac{\partial^2 p}{\partial x^2} + p + p^3 = E'. \tag{14.113}$$

Further taking a new position/time parameter ξ for the moving domain wall with the velocity v,

$$\xi = \sqrt{2}(x - vt)/\delta\sqrt{(1 - v^2/c_0^2)}, \tag{14.114}$$

and the relationships,

$$\frac{\partial^2 p}{\partial t^2} = \frac{\partial^2 p}{\partial \xi^2}\frac{2v^2}{\delta^2(1 - v^2/c_0^2)}, \tag{14.115}$$

$$\frac{\partial^2 p}{\partial x^2} = \frac{\partial^2 p}{\partial \xi^2}\frac{2}{\delta^2(1 - v^2/c_0^2)}. \tag{14.116}$$

Equation (14.113) can be transformed into

$$\frac{\partial^2 p}{\partial \xi^2} + \overline{v}\frac{\partial p}{\partial \xi} - p - p^3 + E' = 0, \tag{14.117}$$

where

$$\overline{v} = \frac{\sqrt{2}\Gamma}{\alpha\delta\sqrt{(1 - v^2/c_0^2)}}v \quad [\text{Since } \alpha < 0, \overline{v} < 0]. \tag{14.118}$$

Due to the damping factor Γ, the domain wall experiences a sort of dragging force proportional to $\overline{v}$, which is also proportional to the wall velocity v with an opposite direction (i.e., viscous damping).

When the electric field E is not large, the solution of Equation (14.117) may be modified from the asymptotic solution for $\overline{v} = 0$ (no dissipation), and $E' = 0$: that is,

$$\frac{p}{p_0} = \tanh\left(\frac{x}{\delta}\right) = \frac{\exp\left(\frac{x}{\delta}\right) - \exp\left(-\frac{x}{\delta}\right)}{\exp\left(\frac{x}{\delta}\right) + \exp\left(-\frac{x}{\delta}\right)} = 1 - \frac{2}{\exp\left(\frac{2x}{\delta}\right) + 1}. \tag{14.119}$$

Denoting the three roots under E by

$$P_1/P_0 = a,\ P_2/P_0 = b,\ P_3/P_0 = c, \tag{14.120}$$

let us find the solution of Equation (14.117) in the following form, according to Reference [11]:

$$p(\xi) = a + \frac{\mathrm{b} - \mathrm{a}}{\exp\left(\frac{(b-a)\xi}{\sqrt{2}}\right) + 1}. \tag{14.121}$$

Then, the dimensionless roots of the polynomial should satisfy the following relation:

$$p^3 + p - E' = (p-a)(p-b)(p-c). \tag{14.122}$$

We can initially obtain the following general relationship among a, b, and c:

$$a + b + c = 0, ab + bc + ca = 1, \text{ and } abc = \mathrm{E}'. \tag{14.123}$$

Substitution of Equation (14.121) into Equation (14.117) verifies that the function of Equation (14.121) is the solution of Equation (14.117) only when

$$\overline{v} = -\frac{(a+b-2c)}{\sqrt{2}} = \frac{3c}{\sqrt{2}}. \tag{14.124}$$

By equating Equation (14.118) and Equation (14.124), and $c = P_3/P_0 \approx \varepsilon_0 \varepsilon E/P_0 = (1/\alpha)E/P_0$, we obtain.

Thus, when $v << c_0$, we can write the velocity in proportion to the applied electric field E:

$$v = \frac{3}{2}\frac{E}{P_0}\frac{\delta}{\Gamma} = \mu E, \tag{14.125}$$

where the proportional constant—mobility—can be expressed by

$$\mu = \frac{3}{2}\frac{\delta}{P_0}\frac{1}{\Gamma}. \tag{14.126}$$

It is interesting to note that the mobility expression, Equation (14.126), can be directly derived from the original equation, Equation (14.97), by assuming the following items:

(1) The external field and the dissipation factor have little influence on the moving domain wall profile,
(2) The domain wall profile is determined by Equation (14.96) without field nor dissipation,
(3) The dissipation term and electric field may be equivalent; $\Gamma\frac{\partial P}{\partial t} = E$, and
(4) $\frac{\partial P}{\partial t} = -v\frac{\partial P}{\partial x} \approx -v(P_0/\delta)$.

Therefore, $E = \Gamma\frac{\partial P}{\partial t} = -\Gamma v(P_0/\delta)$, or $v = \frac{3}{2}\frac{E}{P_0}\frac{\delta}{\Gamma}$, exactly the same as Equation (14.125).

When we consider the steady polarization induction $P = P_0 + p = P_0 + p_0 e^{j(\omega t + \Phi)}$ (Φ: phase lag), according to the input AC electric field $E = E_0 e^{j\omega t}$. From the following equation,

$$\mu\frac{\partial^2 p}{\partial t^2} + \Gamma\frac{\partial p}{\partial t} + \alpha(P_0 + p) + \beta(P_0 + p)^3 = \mu\frac{\partial^2 p}{\partial t^2} + \Gamma\frac{\partial p}{\partial t} + \left(\alpha + 3\beta {P_0}^2\right)p = E, \tag{14.127}$$

we obtain

$$\varepsilon\cdot\varepsilon_0 = \frac{\partial P}{\partial E} = \frac{\partial p}{\partial E} = \frac{p_0}{E_0} = \frac{e^{-j\Phi}}{-\omega^2\mu + j\omega\Gamma - 2\alpha}. \quad (14.128)$$

If we adopt the following notations:

$$\omega_0^2 = -2\alpha/\mu, \quad (14.129)$$

$$2\zeta\omega_0 = \Gamma/\mu, \quad (14.130)$$

the permittivity and the dielectric loss tanΦ can be obtained as

$$|\varepsilon\cdot\varepsilon_0| = \frac{1}{\sqrt{(-2\alpha - \mu\omega^2)^2 + (2\mu\zeta\omega_0\omega)^2}}, \quad (14.131)$$

$$\tan\Phi = \frac{2\mu\zeta\omega_0\omega}{-2\alpha - \mu\omega^2}. \quad (14.132)$$

For a low frequency, $\varepsilon\cdot\varepsilon_0$ approaches to $1/(-2\alpha)$ and tanΦ are expressed as $\Gamma\omega/(-2\alpha)$. In conclusion, the dielectric loss is expressed in proportion to the domain wall viscous damping factor Γ and the measuring frequency ω in the above single domain-wall model. The damping factor Γ is originated from various factors, such as impurity doping (i.e., "hard" and "soft" PZT's) and crystallographic dislocations. How to further analyze the origin of the damping factor Γ is remained to the reference book by Sidorkin [9]. It is also worth noting that dielectric loss tanΦ will enhance significantly with increasing the temperature to the Curie point ($-2\alpha \to 0$). Both permittivity and the dissipation factor tanΦ are expected to exhibit the maximum around the Curie temperature range, that is already a well-known fact in various ferroelectrics experimentally.

14.3. Nonlinear Elastic Performances in the Crystal Lattice

14.3.1. Phonon Mode in Harmonic and Anharmonic Crystals

We discussed primarily the harmonic lattice vibration in Chapter 11, and the heat conduction in Chapter 12. This Section 14.3 introduced the importance of the lattice anharmonicity (i.e., lattice spring nonlinearity) to generate thermal expansion, electrostriction, and isothermal compressibility of the crystal under equilibrium status; that is, from static viewpoint. In the following Section 14.4, we introduce the anharmonic lattice vibration in crystals and discuss the relationship with the thermal conductivity from the phonon interaction (i.e., collision) viewpoint. The discussion in these sections is highly indebted to "Solid State Physics" authored by Ashcroft and Mermin [12], and by Kittel [13]. The phenomena dominated by the lattice anharmonicity are categorized into "equilibrium" and "transport" properties, described in the following.

Equilibrium Properties

We can find many equilibrium properties in crystals observable at any temperature, to which we need to adopt "anharmonic" terms in the ionic interaction energy to explain consistently. As we already learned, "thermal expansion" and "electrostriction" are the important ones. In a rigorously harmonic crystal, the equilibrium crystal size/volume would not depend on temperature (i.e., no thermal dilatation!). The existence of anharmonic terms is also the key to explain the elastic constant dependence on temperature and stress, as well as the difference between the adiabatic and isothermal elastic constants. Subsection Adiabatic Elastic Compliance in Chapter 2 derived the relationship: $s_{adia}^{E,S} = s_{iso}^{E,T}\left(1 - k^{PT^2}\right)$, where $k^{PT^2} = \frac{\alpha_L{}^2}{\left(\frac{C_p}{T}\right)s^E}$. The reader will learn how to handle the anharmonicity in the lattice vibration mathematically in the following part of this section.

Transport Properties

Two lattice vibration modes do not interact in a pure harmonic crystal; a single wave does not decay or change form with time. The wave will spread in the whole crystal, and no localization is expected. Thus, rigorously harmonic crystals should exhibit an "infinite thermal conductivity" as explained in Chapter 11. However, the thermal conductivity of a normal insulating material (that is, electron transfer contribution is neglected) is still limited by various factors: (1) even in a "crystallographically perfect" crystal, the lattice vibration anharmonicity generates the resistance of phonon transfer in the crystal, (2) crystal imperfection, such as impurity doping, ionic vacancies, and dislocations. These two important factors on the transport property are described in Section 14.4. Let me remind you of the "particle–wave duality" idea again here: heat transfer requires localized phonons, which interact with each other (i.e., so-called "phonon collision"), leading to the resistivity to transfer thermal energy. Wave or phonon coupling/interaction, and the wave localization principle is the key to understand the heat conductivity mechanisms.

14.3.2. Nonlinearity in Crystal Potential

If the effective elastic energy potential for the crystal atoms possesses nonlinearity or anharmonicity, "thermal expansion", "electrostriction", and "isothermal compressibility" come out under equilibrium status. According to our previous paper [14], we introduce the derivation process of these effects.

The potential energy U in a crystal is determined by a "relative distance" of atoms; that is, for instance, in NaCl crystal, supposing that Na position is $\boldsymbol{R}'$ and Cl position is $\boldsymbol{R}$ in the physical coordinate, the potential is defined by $\boldsymbol{r} = \boldsymbol{R} - \boldsymbol{R}'$. Due to the crystal lattice periodicity, we take additional considerations. We shall here use the theory of cohesive forces in ionic crystals, proposed by Born [15]. In the interests of simplicity, we derive various formulae for a two-ion rock-salt structure. We start from the potential function involving an inverse power type of repulsive quantum-mechanical energy and the Coulombic energy, illustrated in Figure 14.21:

$$U = -\frac{Mq^2}{r} + \frac{Nb}{r^n}, \tag{14.133}$$

where M is the Madelung constant for Coulombic energy, instead of merely the nearest neighbor's interaction. This is to take all crystal lattice periodic atoms into account. (Refer to Example Problem 14.5 on how to obtain the Madelung constant.)

On the other hand, N in the second term is the coordination number, and b a potential constant for the quantum mechanical energy. We assume relatively large numbers 9–11 for quantum mechanical repulsive potential $1/r^n$. Expanding the potential function around the equilibrium position ($r_0^{n-1} = nNb/Mq^2$ from the condition $\frac{\partial U}{\partial r} = 0$), we obtain the form as a function of Δr (=$r - r_0$):

$$\Delta U = U(r) - U(r_0) = f(\Delta r)^2 - g(\Delta r)^3, \tag{14.134}$$

where $f = (n-1)Mq^2/2r_0^3$ and $g = (n+4)(n-1)Mq^2/6r_0^4$. It is essential to realize the curvature difference in the positive and negative region of Δr, as seen from Figure 14.21; that is, the lattice spring is softer for extension than for contraction. For keeping the positive value of g, the negative sign was adopted in front of g in Equation (11.134).

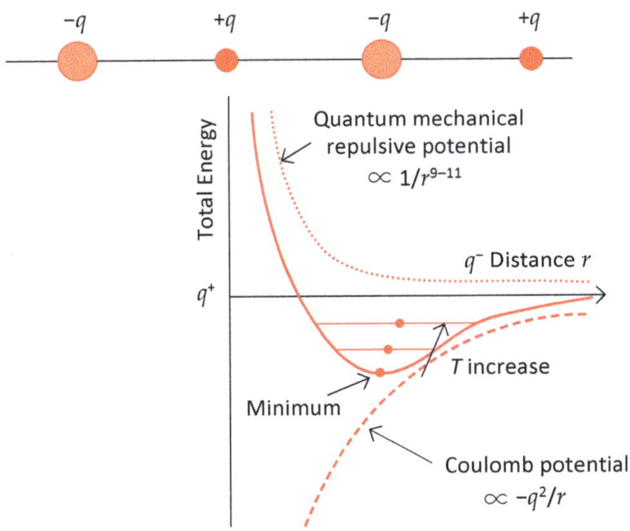

Figure 14.21. 1D ionic crystal model by Born for a two-ion rock-salt structure. Source: Figure by author.

14.3.3. Thermal Expansion and Electrostriction

The ionic displacement Δr is supposed to be generated under a small electric field (E) applied and under a finite temperature (T). Using the Boltzmann distribution for Gibbs energy $\Delta V_{\pm} = \Delta U \pm qE\Delta r$ under, the average equilibrium separation at an elevated temperature under an applied electric field E is approximated as follows:

$$\begin{aligned} < \Delta r_{\pm} > &\sim \int_{-\infty}^{\infty} \Delta r \exp\left(-\frac{\Delta V_{\pm}}{k_B T}\right) d\,\Delta r \Big/ \int_{-\infty}^{\infty} \exp\left(-\frac{\Delta V_{\pm}}{k_B T}\right) d\Delta r \\ &\sim \frac{3gk_B}{4f^2} T \pm \frac{q}{2f} E + \frac{3gq^2}{4f^3} E^2, \end{aligned} \tag{14.135}$$

where subscripts $\pm$ denote the position shifts for ion pairs (Na^{+1} and Cl^{-1}) in terms of the electric field, respectively (i.e., opposite direction due to the charge difference $+q$ and $-q$). Refer to Example Problem 14.4 for the derivation process.

Knowing the crystal unit cell size is given by $(2r_0)$, the strain is therefore given by the summation of the + and − shifts:

$$\frac{<\Delta r_+> + <\Delta r_->}{2r_0} = \frac{3gk_B}{4f^2r_0}T + \frac{3gq^2}{4f^3r_0}E^2, \tag{14.136}$$

where the first term represents thermal expansion and the second term, electrostriction (no piezoelectricity is expected in this cubic symmetry). Note that the second term in Equation (14.135) $\pm\frac{q}{2f}E$ corresponding to the absolute position shifts of Na^{+1} and Cl^{-1}, which is in the same direction (i.e., just the translation), does not contribute to the crystal lattice strain! Figure 14.21 visualizes the $-q$ ion average position drift (with respect to $+q$ position) with elevating temperature. Due to the softer lattice spring performance for extension, thermal expansion (i.e., positive strain) is observed. The reader can understand that both thermal expansion and electrostrictive coefficients originate from "g", which is an anharmonic term $g(\Delta r)^3$ in Equation (14.134), and that neither thermal expansion nor electrostriction occur when the crystal is purely harmonic (that is, only $f(\Delta r)^2$ term in Equation (14.134)). Knowing the polarization P, obtained from the harmonic term and given by,

$$P = \frac{q<\Delta r>}{2r_0^3} = \frac{q^2}{4fr_0^3}E, \tag{14.137}$$

the thermal expansion coefficient α_L and electrostrictive Q coefficient (defined by $(\Delta r/r) = QP^2$) can be describe with atomic parameters in the Born model as:

$$\alpha_L = \frac{3gk_B}{4f^2r_0} = \frac{(n+4)k_B}{2n(n-1)Nb}r_0^n \tag{14.138}$$

$$Q = (\frac{3gq^2}{4f^3r_0})/(\frac{q^2}{4fr_0^3})^2 = \frac{4(n+4)M}{nNb}r_0^{n+3} \tag{14.139}$$

Here, k_B and M are Boltzmann and Madelung constants, respectively.

14.3.4. Isothermal Compressibility

Using the "First Law" of thermodynamics of $dU = -pdV$ (p: hydrostatic pressure, V: volume), the isothermal compressibility χ_T becomes:

$$\frac{1}{\chi_T} = -V\left(\frac{\partial p}{\partial V}\right)_T = V\left(\frac{\partial^2 U}{\partial V^2}\right)_T. \tag{14.140}$$

Changing the variable from V to r and developing the result leads to the equation

$$\chi_T = \frac{18r_0^4}{(n-1)Mq^2} = \frac{18}{n(n-1)Nb}r_0^{n+3}. \tag{14.141}$$

Comparing Equations (14.139) and (14.141), we obtain the relationship $\chi_T \propto Q$. The compressibility and electrostrictive coefficient are induced strain originated from the same crystal lattice anharmonic potential against the force and electric field; we can say that elastically soft crystals also exhibit soft electrostrictively!

Example Problem 14.4

Considering the following anharmonic atomic potential energy in a diatomic ionic crystal ($+q$ and $-q$);

$$\Delta U = f(\Delta r)^2 - g(\Delta r)^3, \quad \text{(P14.4.1)}$$

where Δr ($=r - r_0$), which is the distance modulation from the equilibrium position r_0, calculate the average atomic position shifts $< \Delta r_\pm >$ for a + and − ions, when an electric field E is applied. $\Delta V_\pm = \Delta U \pm qE\Delta r$ can be adopted for the Boltzmann distribution function as

$$< \Delta r_\pm > \sim \int_{-\infty}^{\infty} \Delta r \exp\left(-\frac{\Delta V_\pm}{k_B T}\right) d\,\Delta r \Big/ \int_{-\infty}^{\infty} \exp\left(-\frac{\Delta V_\pm}{k_B T}\right) d\Delta r. \quad \text{(P14.4.2)}$$

Solution

The potential $\Delta V_\pm$ is expressed as

$$\Delta V_\pm = f(\Delta r)^2 - g(\Delta r)^3 \pm qE\Delta r. \quad \text{(P14.4.3)}$$

Taking into account, g, $qE \ll f$,

$$\begin{aligned}
\exp\left(-\tfrac{\Delta V_\pm}{k_B T}\right) &= \exp\left(-\tfrac{f(\Delta r)^2}{k_B T}\right)\exp\left(-\tfrac{-g(\Delta r)^3 \pm qE\Delta r}{k_B T}\right) \\
&= \exp\left(-\tfrac{f(\Delta r)^2}{k_B T}\right)\left[1 + \tfrac{g}{k_B T}(\Delta r)^3 \mp \tfrac{qE}{k_B T}\Delta r\right] \\
= \exp\left(-\tfrac{f(\Delta r)^2}{k_B T}\right)&\left[1 + \tfrac{g}{k_B T}(\Delta r)^3 + \cdots\right]\left[1 \mp \tfrac{qE}{k_B T}\Delta r + \tfrac{1}{2}\left(\tfrac{qE}{k_B T}\right)^2(\Delta r)^2\right] \\
&= \exp\left(-\tfrac{f(\Delta r)^2}{k_B T}\right)\left[1 + \tfrac{g}{k_B T}(\Delta r)^3 \mp \tfrac{qE}{k_B T}\Delta r \mp \tfrac{gqE}{(k_B T)^2}(\Delta r)^4 \right. \\
&\quad \left. + \tfrac{1}{2}\left(\tfrac{qE}{k_B T}\right)^2(\Delta r)^2 + \tfrac{1}{2}\left(\tfrac{g}{k_B T}\right)\left(\tfrac{qE}{k_B T}\right)^2(\Delta r)^5\right]
\end{aligned} \quad \text{(P14.4.4)}$$

As the odd-power of $(\Delta r)^n$ will disappear in the integration from $-\infty$ to ∞, we neglect the even-power of $(\Delta r)^n$ (including "1") in Equation (P14.4.4), then

$$< \Delta r_\pm > \sim \frac{\int_{-\infty}^{\infty} \Delta r \exp\left(-\frac{f(\Delta r)^2}{k_B T}\right)\left[\frac{g}{k_B T}(\Delta r)^3 \mp \frac{qE}{k_B T}\Delta r + \frac{1}{2}\left(\frac{g}{k_B T}\right)\left(\frac{qE}{k_B T}\right)^2(\Delta r)^5\right] d\,\Delta r}{\int_{-\infty}^{\infty} \exp\left(-\frac{f(\Delta r)^2}{k_B T}\right) d\,\Delta r}, \quad \text{(P14.4.5)}$$

where we neglect g, qE terms in the denominator calculation. Now, we use well-known integral equations relating to the $\exp(-ax^2)$:

$$\int_0^\infty x^n \exp\left(-ax^2\right)dx = \frac{\Gamma\left[\frac{n+1}{2}\right]}{2a^{\frac{n+1}{2}}}. \quad \text{(P14.4.6)}$$

Here, $\Gamma\left(\frac{1}{2}\right) = \sqrt{\pi}$, $\Gamma\left(\frac{3}{2}\right) = \frac{1}{2}\sqrt{\pi}$, $\Gamma\left(\frac{5}{2}\right) = \frac{1\cdot 3}{2^2}\sqrt{\pi}$, $\Gamma\left(\frac{7}{2}\right) = \frac{1\cdot 3\cdot 5}{2^3}\sqrt{\pi}$, $\Gamma\left(\frac{9}{2}\right) = \frac{1\cdot 3\cdot 5\cdot 7}{2^4}\sqrt{\pi}, \cdots$

The denominator is equal to $\int_{-\infty}^{\infty} \exp\left(-\frac{f(\Delta r)^2}{k_B T}\right)d\Delta r = \sqrt{\frac{\pi k_B T}{f}}$, while the numerator 1st, 2nd and 3rd terms are calculated [note the factor "2" for the integration $\int_{-\infty}^{\infty} x^n \exp(-ax^2)dx$] as:

$$\int_{-\infty}^{\infty} \frac{g}{k_B T}(\Delta r)^4 \exp\left(-\frac{f(\Delta r)^2}{k_B T}\right)d\,\Delta r = \frac{g}{k_B T}\,\Gamma\left(\tfrac{5}{2}\right)\left(\tfrac{k_B T}{f}\right)^{5/2},$$

$$\mp\int_{-\infty}^{\infty} \frac{qE}{k_B T}(\Delta r)^2 \exp\left(-\frac{f(\Delta r)^2}{k_B T}\right)d\,\Delta r = \frac{qE}{k_B T}\,\Gamma\left(\tfrac{3}{2}\right)\left(\tfrac{k_B T}{f}\right)^{3/2},$$

$$\int_{-\infty}^{\infty} \frac{1}{2}\left(\frac{g}{k_B T}\right)\left(\frac{qE}{k_B T}\right)^2 (\Delta r)^6 \exp\left(-\frac{f(\Delta r)^2}{k_B T}\right)d\,\Delta r = \frac{1}{2}\left(\frac{g}{k_B T}\right)\left(\frac{qE}{k_B T}\right)^2 \Gamma\left(\tfrac{7}{2}\right)\left(\tfrac{k_B T}{f}\right)^{7/2}.$$

Finally, we obtain our targeted equation:

$$< \Delta r_{\pm} > \sim \frac{3gk_B}{4f^2}T \pm \frac{q}{2f}E + \frac{3gq^2}{4f^3}E^2, \quad \text{(P14.4.7)}$$

Example Problem 14.5

To understand the reason why the ferroelectricity will disappear with decreasing particle size, we can consider the energy fluctuation for a nano-size ferroelectric particle as follows: Consider a one-dimensional finite chain of two kinds of ions +q and −q, arranged alternately with a distance of a (see Figure 14.22), as you challenged in Chapter Problem 1.1. A nano-size crystal grows gradually, starting from a single positive ion, and adding a pair of negative or positive ions, thus keeping a crystal size $2na$ ($n = 1, 2, 3, \ldots$). With increasing crystal size, the crystal Coulomb energy will be changed as:

$$U_1 = \left(\frac{2}{4\pi\varepsilon_0\varepsilon}\right)\left[-\left(\frac{q^2}{a}\right)\right],$$

$$U_2 = \left(\frac{2}{4\pi\varepsilon_0\varepsilon}\right)\left[-\left(\frac{q^2}{a}\right) + \left(\frac{q^2}{2a}\right)\right],$$

$$U_2 = \left(\frac{2}{4\pi\varepsilon_0\varepsilon}\right)\left[-\left(\frac{q^2}{a}\right) + \left(\frac{q^2}{2a}\right) - \left(\frac{q^2}{3a}\right)\right],$$

$$\cdots\cdots\cdots\cdots$$

For the infinite (large) crystal, we can calculate the "Madelung Constant" when the saturated energy is expressed by $U = \left(\frac{M}{4\pi\varepsilon_0\varepsilon}\right)\left[-\left(\frac{q^2}{a}\right)\right]$, with the relation: $ln(1 + x)$

$= x - x^2/2 + x^3/3 - x^4/4 + \cdots = 2log2 = 1.386$ is called "Madelung constant" for one-dimensional chain.

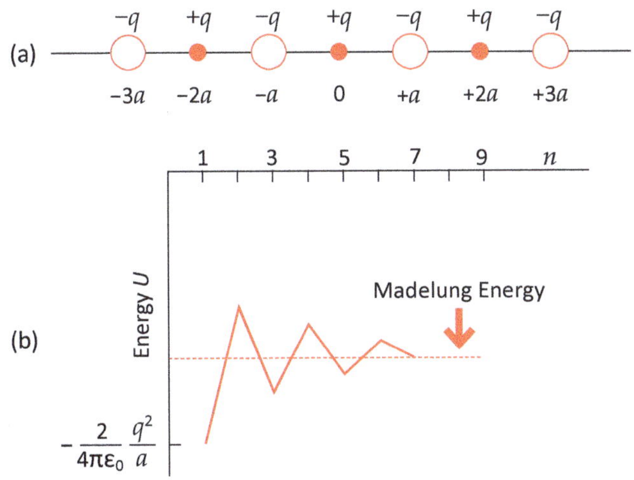

Figure 14.22. Madelung energy calculation in 1D diatomic ionic lattice chain. (**a**) 1D lattice chain; (**b**) coulombic energy change. Source: Figure by author.

Now, the problem assigned to the reader is on a 2D array. A two-dimensional array of positive and negative ions forms a square pattern, with alternative charges at each adjacent position, as shown in Figure 14.23.

(a) Calculate the Madelung constant, which is larger than the Madelung constant for the 1D chain ($2\,ln2 = 1.386$).

(b) By increasing the crystal size layer by layer, how many layers are required to stabilize the energy fluctuation less than $\pm 0.1\%$ around the Madelung energy?

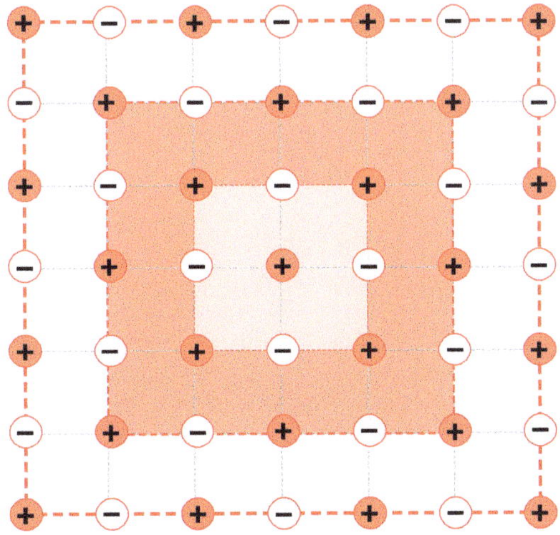

Figure 14.23. Madelung energy calculation in 2D ionic lattice square pattern. Source: Figure by author.

Solution

We select an area with boundaries "through" the outermost ions, that is, toned layers in Figure 14.23. We will use the fraction on these ions that is shared by this area, i.e., one-half of the edge ions and one-fourth of the corner ions in the 2D pattern.

First Layer:

− ions at the distance a: four with 1/2
+ ions at $\sqrt{2}a$: four with 1/4
$-2/1 + 1/\sqrt{2} = -1.2929$

Second Layer:

− ions at the distance a: four with 1/2
+ ions at $\sqrt{2}a$: four with 3/4
+ ions at $2a$: four with 1/2
− ions at $\sqrt{5}a$: eight with 1/2
+ ions at $2\sqrt{2}a$: four with 1/4
$-2/1 + 3/\sqrt{2} + 2/2 - 4/\sqrt{5} + 1/(2\sqrt{2}) = -0.3140$

Third Layer:

$2/2 - 4/\sqrt{5} + 3/(2\sqrt{2}) - 2/3 + 4/\sqrt{10} - 4/\sqrt{13} + 1/(3\sqrt{2}) = -0.0036$

The fourth square layer is small enough.

(a) Madelung Constant 1) +2) +3) $\simeq -1.610(5)$ [This is larger than that for the 1-D chain (2ln2 = 1.386)].

(b) Since (-0.0036)/(-1.610) = 0.2%, to keep the energy fluctuation below 0.1%, $n = 4$ is required. The crystal size $8a \times 8a$ is required. Note that the 2-D crystal exhibits a much stable structure than the 1-D crystal; that is, smaller crystal size may provide ferroelectricity with the crystal dimensionality.

14.4. Lattice Vibration and Thermal Conductivity

Section 14.4.1 describes the "mode coupling" possibility even in harmonic lattice vibrations in crystal imperfections, started from simple small number lattice chains to large number atomic models. Section 14.4.2 handles the phonon interaction and collision processes. Finally, a thermal conductance model is introduced in Section 14.4.3.

14.4.1. Phonon Mode Coupling in Crystal Imperfections

This section introduces how the imperfection in a crystal affects the lattice vibrations in practice. Though this may not directly induce the thermal transfer, the reader can understand how the lattice vibration modes are localized and couple each other even in "harmonic lattice" vibrations. We start from simple 3-mass–4-spring models in order to describe the vibration eigen modes variation with slight "mass" or "spring constant" changes. The discussion is extended to large number atom crystals in the latter part.

Imperfect Lattice Vibration—Mass Modulation

Let us consider the modulated lattice vibration in a crystal imperfection. Figure 14.24a illustrates a 1D "atom–spring" connection model with "harmonic springs". Only three atoms are taken into account in our further discussion from the mathematical simplicity. Considering harmonic oscillation, that is, $\frac{\partial^2 x_n}{\partial t^2} = -\omega^2 x_n$, we construct the Newton dynamic equations for three masses (refer to Equation (11.1) in Chapter 11):

$$\begin{cases} -m_1\omega^2 x_1 + (k_1 x_1 + k_2(x_1 - x_2)) = f_1 \\ -m_2\omega^2 x_2 + (k_2(x_2 - x_1) + k_3(x_2 - x_3)) = f_2 \\ -m_3\omega^2 x_3 + (k_3(x_3 - x_2) + k_4 x_3) = f_3 \end{cases} \tag{14.142}$$

or

$$\begin{pmatrix} k_1 + k_2 & -k_2 & 0 \\ -k_2 & k_2 + k_3 & -k_3 \\ 0 & -k_3 & k_3 + k_4 \end{pmatrix} \begin{pmatrix} x_1 \\ x_2 \\ x_3 \end{pmatrix} - \omega^2 \begin{pmatrix} m_1 & 0 & 0 \\ 0 & m_2 & 0 \\ 0 & 0 & m_3 \end{pmatrix} \begin{pmatrix} x_1 \\ x_2 \\ x_3 \end{pmatrix} = \begin{pmatrix} f_1 \\ f_2 \\ f_3 \end{pmatrix}. \tag{14.143}$$

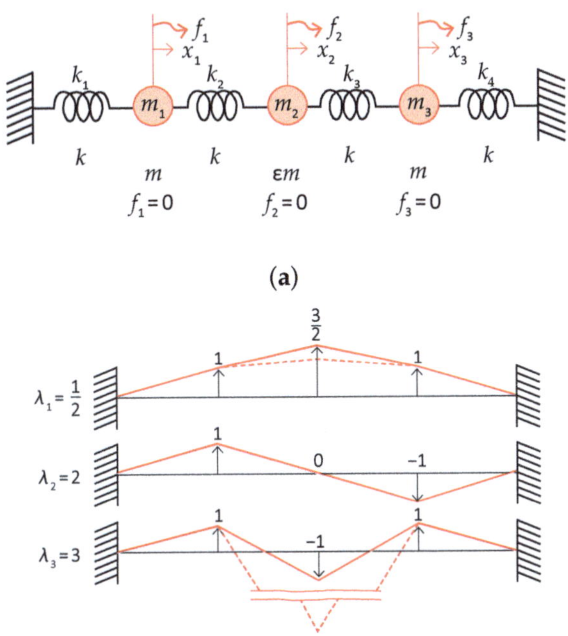

(b)

Figure 14.24. (**a**) 3 mass–4 spring model. m_2 has a different mass. (**b**) Eigen functions for three λ_1, λ_2, and λ_3, which correspond to a half-wave, one-wave, and 1.5-wave mode, respectively. Source: Figure by author.

We adopt first the mass modulation case: (1) all springs are the same with spring constant k, (2) masses are the same with m, except for one center mass with εm (ε is the normalized mass with respect to m), and (3) no force is applied for calculating eigen function under free oscillation. The reader can recognize that m_2 center mass may be an "impurity" atom. Under this specified case, Equation (14.143) can be transformed into:

$$\begin{pmatrix} 2k & -k & 0 \\ -k & 2k & -k \\ 0 & -k & 2k \end{pmatrix} \begin{pmatrix} x_1 \\ x_2 \\ x_3 \end{pmatrix} - \omega^2 \begin{pmatrix} m & 0 & 0 \\ 0 & \varepsilon m & 0 \\ 0 & 0 & m \end{pmatrix} \begin{pmatrix} x_1 \\ x_2 \\ x_3 \end{pmatrix} = \begin{pmatrix} 0 \\ 0 \\ 0 \end{pmatrix}. \tag{14.144}$$

Then,

$$\begin{gathered} \begin{pmatrix} 2 & -1 & 0 \\ -1 & 2 & -1 \\ 0 & -1 & 2 \end{pmatrix} \begin{pmatrix} x_1 \\ x_2 \\ x_3 \end{pmatrix} - \frac{m\omega^2}{k} \begin{pmatrix} 1 & 0 & 0 \\ 0 & \varepsilon & 0 \\ 0 & 0 & 1 \end{pmatrix} \begin{pmatrix} x_1 \\ x_2 \\ x_3 \end{pmatrix} = \\ \begin{pmatrix} 2-\lambda & -1 & 0 \\ -1 & 2-\varepsilon\lambda & -1 \\ 0 & -1 & 2-\lambda \end{pmatrix} \begin{pmatrix} x_1 \\ x_2 \\ x_3 \end{pmatrix} = \begin{pmatrix} 0 \\ 0 \\ 0 \end{pmatrix}. \end{gathered} \tag{14.145}$$

Here, we used a new notation for normalizing the "eigen frequency square":

$$\lambda = \frac{m\omega^2}{k} = \left(\frac{\omega}{\omega_0}\right)^2, \tag{14.146}$$

where $\omega_0 = \sqrt{k/m}$, which is the resonance frequency of the "one-mass–one spring" system.

Eigen Frequency

The eigen frequency square λ (or frequencies ω) can be obtained by taking the determinant of Equation (14.136) equal to "zero".

$$\begin{aligned} \begin{vmatrix} 2-\lambda & -1 & 0 \\ -1 & 2-\varepsilon\lambda & -1 \\ 0 & -1 & 2-\lambda \end{vmatrix} &= (2-\lambda)^2(2-\varepsilon\lambda) - 2(2-\lambda) \\ &= (2-\lambda)\left[\varepsilon\lambda^2 - 2(\varepsilon+1)\lambda + 2\right] = 0. \end{aligned} \tag{14.147}$$

We can now obtain three roots for λ, which are eigen values:

$$\lambda_1 = [(\varepsilon+1) - \sqrt{\varepsilon^2+1}]/\varepsilon; \lambda_2 = 2; \text{and } \lambda_3 = [(\varepsilon+1) + \sqrt{\varepsilon^2+1}]/\varepsilon. \tag{14.148}$$

The subscripts, "1", "2", and "3" are put from low to high frequencies. Eigen values are tabulated for typical ε values below:

ε	λ_1	λ_2	λ_3
4/3	$1/2 = 0.5$	2	3
1	$2 - \sqrt{2} = 0.59$	2	$2 + \sqrt{2} = 3.14$
1/3	$4 - \sqrt{10} = 0.84$	2	$4 + \sqrt{10} = 7.16$

The reader can understand that the middle λ_2 is not affected by the center mass modulation, but λ_1 and λ_3 are modulated: in comparison with the values for $\varepsilon = 1$, $(2 \pm \sqrt{2})$, the heavier mass provides smaller values (i.e., lower frequencies), while the lighter mass exhibits larger values. In particular, by reducing the impurity mass, the

λ_3 frequency increases significantly in comparison with that $(2+\sqrt{2})$ in the uniform lattice chain.

Eigen Function

Let us calculate the "eigen mode function" in the case of $\varepsilon = 4/3$, which corresponds to a heavier doping mass. Eigen mode for $\lambda_1 = 1/2$ can be obtained from Equation (14.145) as:

$$\begin{pmatrix} 2-\frac{1}{2} & -1 & 0 \\ -1 & 2-\frac{4}{3}\cdot\frac{1}{2} & -1 \\ 0 & -1 & 2-\frac{1}{2} \end{pmatrix} \begin{pmatrix} \psi_{11} \\ \psi_{21} \\ \psi_{31} \end{pmatrix} = 0. \quad (14.149)$$

Thus, $\psi_{11} = 1$, $\psi_{21} = 3/2$, and $\psi_{31} = 1$. Similarly for $\lambda_2 = 2$, $\psi_{12} = 1$, $\psi_{22} = 0$, and $\psi_{32} = -1$; for $\lambda_3 = 3$, $\psi_{13} = 1$, $\psi_{23} = -1$, and $\psi_{33} = 1$. The results on the eigen mode functions are illustrated in Figure 14.24b (Solid lines). Note that the amplitudes of each eigen mode functions are plotted by adjusting $\psi_{11} = \psi_{12} = \psi_{13} = 1$ [unit], which should be normalized later in the practical numerical calculation process. Note also that the eigen mode functions ψ_{11}, ψ_{21}, and ψ_{31} are the motion amplitude when oscillated at a particular eigen frequency, λ_1, λ_2, or λ_3, not the actual displacement of the mass, x_1, x_2, or x_3, directly under external force. The mass displacement under external force applied should be calculated by combining these three eigen modes in a suitable ratio (refer to Subsection Phonon—Phonon Interaction, Collision). Eigen functions for three, λ_1, λ_2, and λ_3, correspond roughly to a half-wave (all mass displacements are in the same sign), one-wave (the mass displacements are symmetrical with the node at the center mass), and 1.5-wave mode (three masses show up-down successive amplitudes), respectively. As the mass-modulated center mass is at the node (no motion) in the λ_2 mode, the mass modulation (i.e., ε change) does not affect the eigen frequency $\lambda_2 = 2$.

We calculate next the eigen function in the case of $\varepsilon = 1/3$, which corresponds to a lighter doping mass. Eigen mode for $\lambda_1 = (4-\sqrt{10})$ can be obtained from Equation (14.145) as:

$$\begin{pmatrix} 2-(4-\sqrt{10}) & -1 & 0 \\ -1 & 2-\frac{1}{3}\cdot(4-\sqrt{10}) & -1 \\ 0 & -1 & 2-(4-\sqrt{10}) \end{pmatrix} \begin{pmatrix} \psi_{11} \\ \psi_{21} \\ \psi_{31} \end{pmatrix} = 0. \quad (14.150)$$

Thus, $\psi_{11} = 1$, $\psi_{21} = \left(\sqrt{10}-2\right) = 1.16$, and $\psi_{31} = 1$. Similarly for $\lambda_2 = 2$, $\psi_{12} = 1$, $\psi_{22} = 0$, and $\psi_{32} = -1$; for $\lambda_3 = 3$, $\psi_{13} = 1$, $\psi_{23} = -\left(2+\sqrt{10}\right) = -5.16$, and $\psi_{33} = 1$. The results are also superposed in Figure 14.24b in the dashed lines. Eigen functions for three, λ_1, λ_2, and λ_3, correspond to a half-wave, one-wave, and 1.5-wave mode, respectively, the same as the previous results. The difference can be found only in the nearest neighbors of the center mass m_2. Due to a light mass of m_2, the amplitude at λ_1 is suppressed, while that at λ_3 is significantly amplified (overscale in this figure). Note again that the λ_2 mode does not change at all, because the m_2 is situated at the node. It is not difficult to estimate $\lambda_1 = \left[(\varepsilon+1) - \sqrt{\varepsilon^2+1}\right]/\varepsilon$; $\lambda_2 = 2$; and $\lambda_3 = \left[(\varepsilon+1) + \sqrt{\varepsilon^2+1}\right]/\varepsilon$ for $\varepsilon \to 0$ limit. $\lambda_1 \to 1$; $\lambda_2 = 2$; and $\lambda_3 \to \infty$. In conclusion, the mass change itself without changing the coupling (spring) strength, three eigen frequencies are not merged, but keeping the three modes separately without making so-called "mode coupling". Most importantly, light-weight impurity doping enhances the vibration amplitude of that atom locally at the highest eigen frequency, λ_3, indicating the phonon localization (see Subsection Localized Impurity Lattice Vibration).

Lattice Mode Coupling—Spring Constant Modulation

Next, we adopt the "spring constant modulation" case: (1) all masses are the same with m with no mass at the center (i.e., two mass model), (2) springs are the same with spring constant k, except for two center springs with εk (ε is the normalized spring constant with respect to k), and (3) free oscillation (no force is applied) in order to calculate the eigen mode functions. Refer to Figure 14.25a. The missing center mass and modification of the adjacent springs may indicate a model of an "atomic vacancy" or discontinuity of the oscillation mode. Under the above specified case, Equation (14.143) can now be transformed into:

$$\begin{pmatrix} k+\varepsilon k & -\varepsilon k & 0 \\ -\varepsilon k & 2\varepsilon k & -\varepsilon k \\ 0 & -\varepsilon k & \varepsilon k + k \end{pmatrix}\begin{pmatrix} x_1 \\ x_2 \\ x_3 \end{pmatrix} - \omega^2 \begin{pmatrix} m & 0 & 0 \\ 0 & 0 & 0 \\ 0 & 0 & m \end{pmatrix}\begin{pmatrix} x_1 \\ x_2 \\ x_3 \end{pmatrix} = \begin{pmatrix} 0 \\ 0 \\ 0 \end{pmatrix}. \quad (14.151)$$

Then

$$\begin{aligned} &\begin{pmatrix} 1+\varepsilon & -\varepsilon & 0 \\ -\varepsilon & 2\varepsilon & -\varepsilon \\ 0 & -\varepsilon & 1+\varepsilon \end{pmatrix}\begin{pmatrix} x_1 \\ x_2 \\ x_3 \end{pmatrix} - \frac{m\omega^2}{k}\begin{pmatrix} 1 & 0 & 0 \\ 0 & 0 & 0 \\ 0 & 0 & 1 \end{pmatrix}\begin{pmatrix} x_1 \\ x_2 \\ x_3 \end{pmatrix} \\ &= \begin{pmatrix} 1+\varepsilon-\lambda & -\varepsilon & 0 \\ -\varepsilon & 2\varepsilon & -\varepsilon \\ 0 & -\varepsilon & 1+\varepsilon-\lambda \end{pmatrix}\begin{pmatrix} x_1 \\ x_2 \\ x_3 \end{pmatrix} = \begin{pmatrix} 0 \\ 0 \\ 0 \end{pmatrix}. \end{aligned} \quad (14.152)$$

Here, we used the notation Equation (14.146) again: $\lambda = \frac{m\omega^2}{k}$.

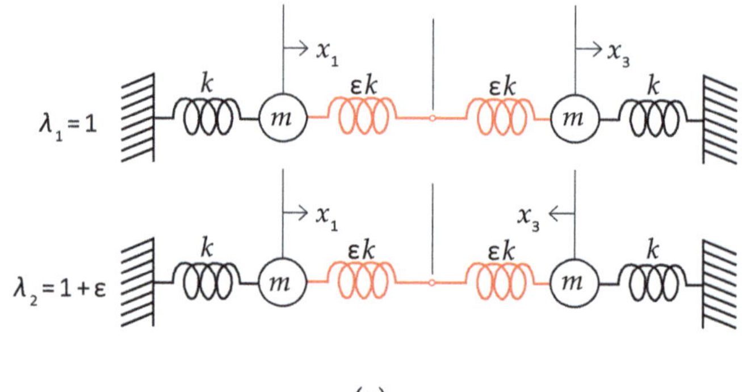

(a)

Figure 14.25. *Cont.*

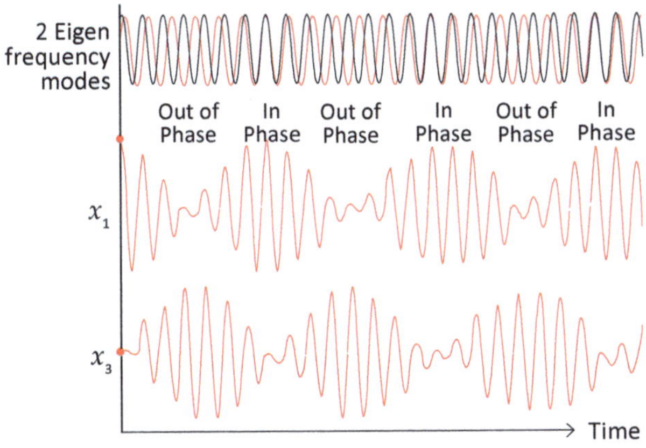

(b)

Figure 14.25. (**a**) A 2 mass–4 spring model. $m_2 = 0$ and center springs are weak. (**b**) Two eigen functions for λ_1 and λ_2 as a function of time (top); and mass vibration beat of displacement x_1 and x_3. Source: Figure by author.

Eigen Frequency

The eigen frequencies λ or ω under free condition can be obtained by taking the determinant of Equation (14.152) equal to "zero".

$$\begin{vmatrix} 1+\varepsilon-\lambda & -\varepsilon & 0 \\ -\varepsilon & 2\varepsilon & -\varepsilon \\ 0 & -\varepsilon & 1+\varepsilon-\lambda \end{vmatrix} = 2\varepsilon(1+\varepsilon-\lambda)^2 - 2\varepsilon^2(1+\varepsilon-\lambda) \\ = 2\varepsilon(1-\lambda)(1+\varepsilon-\lambda) = 0. \quad (14.153)$$

We can now obtain two roots for λ, which are eigen frequencies:

$$\lambda_1 = 1; \text{ and } \lambda_2 = (1+\varepsilon). \quad (14.154)$$

Note that because m_2 was set to be zero, only two eigen frequencies and modes appear in this case. You can verify that when $\varepsilon = 1$, the solution is the same as the mass zero ($\varepsilon = 0$) status in the previous section. For the reader's reference; when we put $m_2 = m$, very low frequency $\lambda_3 = 2\varepsilon$ comes out (primarily m_2 and εk vibration), in addition to the solutions of $\lambda_1 = (1+\varepsilon)$; and $\lambda_2 = \left(1+\varepsilon+\frac{9}{4}\varepsilon^2\right)$.

Eigen Function

Let us calculate the eigen function in the case of small ε (low spring constant, or weak coupling between m_1 and m_3). Eigen function for $\lambda_1 = 1$ can be obtained from Equation (14.152) as:

$$\begin{pmatrix} 1+\varepsilon-1 & -\varepsilon & 0 \\ -\varepsilon & 2\varepsilon & -\varepsilon \\ 0 & -\varepsilon & 1+\varepsilon-1 \end{pmatrix} \begin{pmatrix} \psi_{11} \\ \psi_{21} \\ \psi_{31} \end{pmatrix} = 0. \quad (14.155)$$

Thus, $\psi_{11} = 1$, $\psi_{21} = 0$, and $\psi_{31} = 1$. Similarly for $\lambda_2 = (1+\varepsilon)$,

$$\begin{pmatrix} 1+\varepsilon-(1+\varepsilon) & -\varepsilon & 0 \\ -\varepsilon & 2\varepsilon & -\varepsilon \\ 0 & -\varepsilon & 1+\varepsilon-(1+\varepsilon) \end{pmatrix} \begin{pmatrix} \psi_{11} \\ \psi_{21} \\ \psi_{31} \end{pmatrix} = 0, \tag{14.156}$$

$\psi_{12} = 1$, $\psi_{22} = 0$, and $\psi_{32} = -1$. The results are illustrated in Figure 14.25a. Note that the eigen functions for two λ_1 and λ_2 correspond to in-phase (all mass displacements are in the same sign), and out-of-phase (the mass displacements are symmetrical with the node at the center mass), respectively. In conclusion, the spring constant changes two eigen frequencies significantly, and reducing the center part coupling makes λ_1 and λ_2 be merged. Thus, so-called "mode coupling" is expected, which is further discussed in Subsection Mode Coupling Effect.

Normalized Mode Functions

The mass motion in physical coordinates can be obtained by the conversion from the "*eigen mode coordinate*". This subsection describes the conversion process in practice. The mass–spring combination shown in Figure 14.26a is analyzed by the dynamic equations, by coupling the adjacent masses with springs (in physical coordinates), where each individual mass cannot be analyzed independently from the adjacent couplings. On the other hand, the meaning of eigen frequency and its corresponding eigen mode are visually shown in Figure 14.26b. The 3 mass–4 spring model in Figure 14.24a has three eigen frequencies, λ_1, λ_2 and λ_3, and three corresponding eigen mode functions. The three eigen mode functions based on the effective mass and spring constant are independent of each other (no interaction in-between), which is called an "orthogonal relationship", and each mode at that eigen frequency does not depend on time; in contrast, the actual mass motion x_1, x_2, and x_3 are a mixed mode of the above three eigen mode functions, and time dependent in general according to the external force.

Let us start from the dynamic equations based on the eigen mode coordinate, for instance, in the 3 mass–4 spring model:

$$\begin{cases} \ddot{Z}_1 + \lambda_1 Z_1 = g_1 \\ \ddot{Z}_2 + \lambda_2 Z_2 = g_2, \\ \ddot{Z}_3 + \lambda_3 Z_3 = g_3 \end{cases} \tag{14.157}$$

where Z_n and g_n are the displacement and force in the eigen mode coordinate, and Z_1, Z_2 and Z_3 are mutually independent. Note that the effective mass in the eigen mode coordinate in Equation (14.157) becomes all unity, because of the eigen function normalization in terms of the mass, as we repeat again later:

$$m_1^* = m_2^* = m_3^* = 1. \tag{14.158}$$

We denote the three eigen functions as:

$$\begin{cases} (\psi_1) = \begin{pmatrix} \psi_{11} \\ \psi_{21} \\ \psi_{31} \end{pmatrix} \\ (\psi_2) = \begin{pmatrix} \psi_{12} \\ \psi_{22} \\ \psi_{32} \end{pmatrix} \\ (\psi_3) = \begin{pmatrix} \psi_{13} \\ \psi_{23} \\ \psi_{33} \end{pmatrix} \end{cases}. \tag{14.159}$$

Here, the first suffix i of ψ_{ij} (matrix "row") corresponds to the mass number m_i, and the second suffix j (matrix "column") corresponds to the eigen value λ_j. The total eigen function is defined by

$$[\psi] = [(\psi_1), (\psi_2), (\psi_3)] = \begin{pmatrix} \psi_{11} & \psi_{12} & \psi_{13} \\ \psi_{21} & \psi_{22} & \psi_{23} \\ \psi_{31} & \psi_{32} & \psi_{33} \end{pmatrix}. \tag{14.160}$$

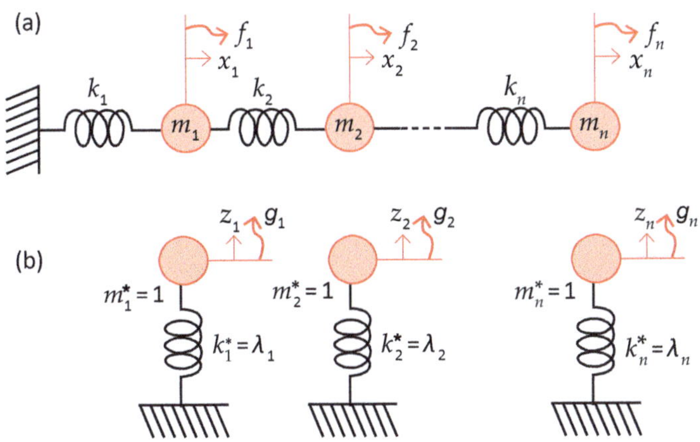

Figure 14.26. Normalized mode function derivation process: relation between (**a**) physical mass–spring coordinate, and (**b**) eigen mode coordinate. Note each eigen mode is isolated. Source: Figure by author.

The necessary equation to transform the forces between physical and eigen mode coordinates is:

$$\begin{pmatrix} g_1 \\ g_2 \\ g_3 \end{pmatrix} = [\psi]^t \begin{pmatrix} f_1 \\ f_2 \\ f_3 \end{pmatrix} = \begin{pmatrix} \psi_{11} & \psi_{21} & \psi_{31} \\ \psi_{12} & \psi_{22} & \psi_{32} \\ \psi_{13} & \psi_{23} & \psi_{33} \end{pmatrix} \begin{pmatrix} f_1 \\ f_2 \\ f_3 \end{pmatrix}. \tag{14.161}$$

In order to obtain the force vector $(g_1\ g_2\ g_3)$ in the eigen mode coordinate, we transform the force vector $(f_1\ f_2\ f_3)$ in the physical coordinate by multiplying $[\psi]^t$. Since the eigen mode function $[\psi]$ is defined by assembling each eigen mode function (ψ_n) in a column, to get all contributions of f_1, f_2, and f_3 to λ_n mode, we should use the "transposed matrix" $[\psi]^t$.

Example Numerical Values

A calculation example is taken from the 3 mass–4 spring model explained in the previous subsection, in particular mass modulation $\varepsilon = 4/3$ (i.e., heavier mass model). The numerical values used are summarized below:

m_1	m_2	m_3	k_1	k_2	k_3	k_4		
3	4	3	1	1	1	1		
λ_1	λ_2	λ_3	f_1	f_2	f_3			
1/6	2/3	1	1	0	0			
ψ_{11}	ψ_{21}	ψ_{31}	ψ_{12}	ψ_{22}	ψ_{32}	ψ_{13}	ψ_{23}	ψ_{33}
1	3/2	1	1	0	−1	1	−1	1

In order to simplify the calculation, $m_1 = 3$ (3 times more than the calculation in Subsection Phonon—Quantization, Energy, Momentum, Velocity) was taken rather than general mass m. Accordingly, $\lambda_1 = 1/6$, $\lambda_2 = 2/3$, and $\lambda_3 = 1$ (1/3 of the previously calculated). Recall the eigen value $\lambda_1 = \omega_1^2$ (because of $m_1^* = 1$); that is, the eigen value is not directly proportional to the frequency, but the square of the angular eigen frequency.

Normalization

Since the eigen mode functions in the table are not normalized, each mode is normalized in terms of the mass matrix [M]:

$$(\psi_1)^t[M](\psi_1) = \begin{pmatrix} 1 & \frac{3}{2} & 1 \end{pmatrix} \begin{bmatrix} 3 & 0 & 0 \\ 0 & 4 & 0 \\ 0 & 0 & 3 \end{bmatrix} \begin{pmatrix} 1 \\ \frac{3}{2} \\ 1 \end{pmatrix} = 3 + 9 + 3 = 15. \tag{14.162}$$

Thus, the new (ψ_1) is expressed by:

$$(\psi_1) = \frac{1}{\sqrt{15}} \begin{pmatrix} 1 \\ \frac{3}{2} \\ 1 \end{pmatrix} = \begin{pmatrix} \frac{1}{\sqrt{15}} \\ \frac{3}{2\sqrt{15}} \\ \frac{1}{\sqrt{15}} \end{pmatrix}. \tag{14.163}$$

Normalizing also for (ψ_2) and (ψ_3), the total $[\psi] = [(\psi_1), (\psi_2), (\psi_3)]$ is obtained:

$$[\psi] = [(\psi_1), (\psi_2), (\psi_3)] = \begin{pmatrix} \frac{1}{\sqrt{15}} & \frac{1}{\sqrt{6}} & \frac{1}{\sqrt{10}} \\ \frac{3}{2\sqrt{15}} & 0 & -\frac{1}{\sqrt{10}} \\ \frac{1}{\sqrt{15}} & -\frac{1}{\sqrt{6}} & \frac{1}{\sqrt{10}} \end{pmatrix} = \begin{pmatrix} 0.26 & 0.41 & 0.32 \\ 0.39 & 0 & -0.32 \\ 0.26 & -0.41 & 0.32 \end{pmatrix}. \tag{14.164}$$

Due to this eigen function normalization in terms of the mass, the effective mass in the eigen mode coordinate becomes all unity, $m_1^* = m_2^* = m_3^* = 1$, as mentioned already in Equation (14.158).

Time Dependence of Z_n

We now apply $f_1 = 1$ on m_1, and $f_2 = f_3 = 0$. From Equation (14.160), we can obtain $(g_1\ g_1\ g_1)$

$$\begin{pmatrix} g_1 \\ g_2 \\ g_3 \end{pmatrix} = [\psi]^t \begin{pmatrix} f_1 \\ f_2 \\ f_3 \end{pmatrix} = \begin{pmatrix} \frac{1}{\sqrt{15}} & \frac{3}{2\sqrt{15}} & \frac{1}{\sqrt{15}} \\ \frac{1}{\sqrt{6}} & 0 & -\frac{1}{\sqrt{6}} \\ \frac{1}{\sqrt{10}} & -\frac{1}{\sqrt{10}} & \frac{1}{\sqrt{10}} \end{pmatrix} \begin{pmatrix} 1 \\ 0 \\ 0 \end{pmatrix} = \begin{pmatrix} \frac{1}{\sqrt{15}} \\ \frac{1}{\sqrt{6}} \\ \frac{1}{\sqrt{10}} \end{pmatrix}. \tag{14.165}$$

Thus, Equation (14.157) is transformed (the effective masses are all unity) into

$$\begin{cases} \ddot{Z}_1 + \frac{1}{6} Z_1 = \frac{1}{\sqrt{15}} \\ \ddot{Z}_2 + \frac{2}{3} Z_2 = \frac{1}{\sqrt{6}} \\ \ddot{Z}_3 + Z_3 = \frac{1}{\sqrt{10}} \end{cases}. \tag{14.166}$$

Since the above three equations are independent of each other, we now obtain the time dependence of Z_n merely by sin and cos functions:

$$\begin{cases} Z_1(t) = \frac{1}{\frac{1}{\sqrt{6}}} \times \frac{1}{\frac{1}{\sqrt{15}}} \int_0^t \sin \frac{1}{\sqrt{6}}(t-\tau) d\tau = 6\sqrt{15}(1 - \cos \frac{1}{\sqrt{6}} t) \\ Z_2(t) = \frac{1}{\sqrt{\frac{2}{3}}} \times \frac{1}{\frac{1}{\sqrt{6}}} \int_0^t \sin \sqrt{\frac{2}{3}}(t-\tau) d\tau = \frac{3}{2}\sqrt{6}(1 - \cos \sqrt{\frac{2}{3}} t) \\ Z_3(t) = \frac{1}{\sqrt{1}} \times \frac{1}{\frac{1}{\sqrt{10}}} \int_0^t \sin (t-\tau) d\tau = \sqrt{10}(1 - \cos t) \end{cases}. \tag{14.167}$$

Response Function of $x_n(t)$

Finally, we obtain each mass displacement x_n as a function of time, which is related as:

$$[x] = [\psi][Z]. \tag{14.168}$$

Thus,

$$[x] = \begin{pmatrix} x_1(t) \\ x_2(t) \\ x_3(t) \end{pmatrix} = \begin{pmatrix} \frac{1}{\sqrt{15}} \\ \frac{3}{2\sqrt{15}} \\ \frac{1}{\sqrt{15}} \end{pmatrix} \times Z_1(t) + \begin{pmatrix} \frac{1}{\sqrt{6}} \\ 0 \\ -\frac{1}{\sqrt{6}} \end{pmatrix} \times Z_2(t) + \begin{pmatrix} \frac{1}{\sqrt{10}} \\ -\frac{1}{\sqrt{10}} \\ \frac{1}{\sqrt{10}} \end{pmatrix} \times Z_3(t)$$

$$= \begin{pmatrix} \frac{1}{\sqrt{15}} \\ \frac{3}{2\sqrt{15}} \\ \frac{1}{\sqrt{15}} \end{pmatrix} \times 6\sqrt{15}(1 - \cos \frac{1}{\sqrt{6}} t) + \begin{pmatrix} \frac{1}{\sqrt{6}} \\ 0 \\ -\frac{1}{\sqrt{6}} \end{pmatrix} \times \frac{3}{2}\sqrt{6}(1 - \cos \sqrt{\frac{2}{3}} t)$$

$$+ \begin{pmatrix} \frac{1}{\sqrt{10}} \\ -\frac{1}{\sqrt{10}} \\ \frac{1}{\sqrt{10}} \end{pmatrix} \times \sqrt{10}(1 - \cos t).$$

Finally, we obtain each individual mass point movement as a function time:

$$\begin{cases} x_1(t) = \frac{17}{2} - 6\cos\frac{1}{\sqrt{6}}t - \frac{3}{2}\cos\sqrt{\frac{2}{3}}t - \cos t \\ x_2(t) = 8 - 9\cos\frac{1}{\sqrt{6}}t \qquad\qquad\qquad + \cos t\,. \\ x_3(t) = \frac{11}{2} - 6\cos\frac{1}{\sqrt{6}}t + \frac{3}{2}\cos\sqrt{\frac{2}{3}}t - \cos t \end{cases} \tag{14.169}$$

Even though only m_1 is excited by a step-wise force, all moss positions $q_n(t)$ oscillate under a mixed mode of all three eigen mode functions, starting from $x_1(0) = x_2(0) = x_3(0) = 0$. We can also recognize that the lowest eigen frequency mode [i.e., $\cos\frac{1}{\sqrt{6}}t$] contributes the largest for all three positions.

Mode Coupling Effect

We reconsider the spring constant modulation case already discussed in Subsection Lattice Mode Coupling—Spring Constant Modulation: (1) all masses are the same with m with no mass at the center (i.e., two mass model), and (2) springs are the same with spring constant k, except for two center springs with εk (ε is the normalized spring constant with respect to k). Refer to Figure 14.25a. We consider here "free oscillation" (no external force) started from the initial conditions at $t = 0$:

$x_1 = x_0,\ \dot{x}_1 = 0;\ x_3 = 0,\ \dot{x}_2 = 0.$

Under the above specified case, Equation (14.143) can now be transformed into:

$$\begin{pmatrix} k+\varepsilon k & -\varepsilon k & 0 \\ -\varepsilon k & 2\varepsilon k & -\varepsilon k \\ 0 & -\varepsilon k & \varepsilon k + k \end{pmatrix} \begin{pmatrix} x_1 \\ x_2 \\ x_3 \end{pmatrix} - \omega^2 \begin{pmatrix} m & 0 & 0 \\ 0 & 0 & 0 \\ 0 & 0 & m \end{pmatrix} \begin{pmatrix} x_1 \\ x_2 \\ x_3 \end{pmatrix} = \begin{pmatrix} 0 \\ 0 \\ 0 \end{pmatrix}.$$

Then, using the notation Equation (14.146) again: $\lambda = \frac{m\omega^2}{k}$, the above equation is transformed into

$$\begin{pmatrix} 1+\varepsilon-\lambda & -\varepsilon & 0 \\ -\varepsilon & 2\varepsilon & -\varepsilon \\ 0 & -\varepsilon & 1+\varepsilon-\lambda \end{pmatrix} \begin{pmatrix} x_1 \\ x_2 \\ x_3 \end{pmatrix} = \begin{pmatrix} 0 \\ 0 \\ 0 \end{pmatrix}.$$

We obtained two roots for λ, which are eigen values:

$\lambda_1 = 1;$ and $\lambda_2 = (1+\varepsilon).$

If we convert the above eigen values into the eigen frequencies, using $\lambda = \frac{m\omega^2}{k}$, we obtain:

$$\omega_1 = \sqrt{k/m} = \omega_0,\ \text{and}\ \omega_2 = \sqrt{k/m}\sqrt{(1+\varepsilon)} \approx \omega_0(1+\frac{\varepsilon}{2}). \tag{14.170}$$

The eigen function in the case of small ε (low spring constant, or weak coupling between m_1 and m_3). Eigen function for $\lambda_1 = 1$ can be obtained from Equation (14.152) as:

$$\begin{pmatrix} 1+\varepsilon-1 & -\varepsilon & 0 \\ -\varepsilon & 2\varepsilon & -\varepsilon \\ 0 & -\varepsilon & 1+\varepsilon-1 \end{pmatrix} \begin{pmatrix} \psi_{11} \\ \psi_{21} \\ \psi_{31} \end{pmatrix} = 0,$$

leading to $\psi_{11} = 1$, $\psi_{21} = 0$, and $\psi_{31} = 1$. Similarly for $\lambda_2 = (1+\varepsilon)$,

$$\begin{pmatrix} 1+\varepsilon-(1+\varepsilon) & -\varepsilon & 0 \\ -\varepsilon & 2\varepsilon & -\varepsilon \\ 0 & -\varepsilon & 1+\varepsilon-(1+\varepsilon) \end{pmatrix}\begin{pmatrix} \psi_{11} \\ \psi_{21} \\ \psi_{31} \end{pmatrix} = 0,$$

$\psi_{12} = 1$, $\psi_{22} = 0$, and $\psi_{32} = -1$. The results were visualized in Figure 14.25a. The eigen mode functions for two, λ_1 and λ_2, corresponding to in-phase (all mass displacements are in the same sign) and out-of-phase (the mass displacements are symmetrical with the node at the center mass), respectively.

Using the same derivation process of eigen mode functions and mass displacement functions in the previous subsections, it is not difficult to derive mass motion as a function of time:

$$\begin{cases} x_1(t) = \frac{1}{2}x_0(\cos\omega_1 t + \cos\omega_2 t) \\ x_2(t) = \frac{1}{2}x_0(\cos\omega_1 t - \cos\omega_2 t) \end{cases}. \tag{14.171}$$

Figure 14.25b Top shows two eigen functions for ω_1 and ω_2 as a function of time. You can notice that there are two sinusoidal oscillations with multiple overlapping (in-phase) and out-of-phase parts periodically. Now the solution of the mass positions consists of a linear superposition of both eigen mode functions $\cos\omega_1 t$ and $\cos\omega_2 t$ in-phase and out-of-phase. To clarify the nature of the solutions of Equation (14.171), we transform them by using elementary trigonometric relations, and the approximation, $\omega_2 - \omega_1 = \frac{\varepsilon}{2}\omega_0$ and $\omega_2 + \omega_1 = 2\omega_0$:

$$\begin{cases} x_1(t) = x_0(\cos\omega_0 t \cdot \cos\frac{1}{4}\varepsilon\omega_0 t) \\ x_2(t) = x_0(\sin\omega_0 t \cdot \sin\frac{1}{4}\varepsilon\omega_0 t) \end{cases}. \tag{14.172}$$

Therefore, $x_1(t)$ is essentially a simple harmonic oscillation with frequency ω_0, starting from the "maximum" amplitude x_0. This ω_0 is the resonance frequency of one mass m and one spring k connection system; that is, $\omega_0 = \sqrt{k/m}$. On the contrary, the $\cos\frac{1}{4}\varepsilon\omega_0 t$ term itself varies in a simple harmonic matter, though much more slowly on account of the smallness of ε. This second term generates an amplitude envelope of the fast sinusoidal variation of $\cos\omega_0 t$, as shown in Figure 14.25b Center. In-phase part exhibits the maximum amplitude, while out-of-phase part shows the minimum (almost zero) amplitude. In particular, the amplitude decays slowly to zero at a time $t = 2\pi/\varepsilon\omega_0$. On the other hand, $x_2(t)$ is also essentially a simple harmonic oscillation with frequency ω_0, started from "zero" with 90° phase delay from $x_1(t)$. The oscillations of x_2 built up after the $x_1(t)$ vibration from zero to the maximum x_0 (Figure 14.25b Bottom). As time continues, the pattern reverses, so that one complete to-and-fro transfer of energy takes place in a time $4\pi/\varepsilon\omega_0$, during which each individual oscillator will have executed $2/\varepsilon$ cycles of period $2\pi/\omega_0$. Exchange of lattice vibration energy between the weakly coupled spring oscillators indicates the "phonon mode coupling" and "phonon energy transfer".

Localized Impurity Lattice Vibration

We extend to consider now an infinite monatomic (mass M) lattice chain connected by the same spring constant K, except for the origin impurity atom mass $m = M(1-\varepsilon)$ [16]. The dynamic equation of this lattice chain model (similar to Section 11.1.1) is described under the "periodic boundary" condition by

$$-M\omega^2(1-\varepsilon\delta_{n0})u_n = -K(2u_n - u_{n-1} - u_{n+1}) \quad [-\infty < n < \infty]. \tag{14.173}$$

In a perfect lattice chain ($\varepsilon = 0$), the lattice vibration frequency exists

$$0 \le \omega \le \omega_L \equiv 2\sqrt{K/M}. \tag{14.174}$$

Is there a possibility to exhibit an additional eigen vibration mode in the range $\omega > \omega_L$ because of the impurity? Equation (14.174) leads to the following "difference equation" except for $n = 0$ [refer to Equation (11.5)]:

$$u_{n+1} - \left(2 - \frac{M\omega^2}{K}\right)u_n + u_{n-1} = 0 \quad [n \neq 0]. \tag{14.175}$$

In the range $\omega > \omega_L$, we get the relation $2 - \frac{M\omega^2}{K} < -2$, so that we can take parameter change as

$$2 - \frac{M\omega^2}{K} = -2\cosh\kappa \quad [\kappa > 0]. \tag{14.176}$$

Thus, we can find a possible solution: $u_n \alpha (-1)^n \exp(\pm\kappa n)$. Under the boundary condition that $n \to \pm\infty$ needs to remain a realistic solution satisfying $|u_n| < \infty$, the solution should be only in the form of

$$u_n \propto (-1)^n \exp(-\kappa|n|) \quad [-\infty < n < \infty]. \tag{14.177}$$

Now, the parameter κ can be determined from the dynamic equation, Equation (14.173), for $n = 0$, which should satisfy Equation (14.177):

$$2(1+\cosh\kappa)(1-\varepsilon) = 2[1+\exp(-\kappa)]. \tag{14.178}$$

We obtain the required conditions as follows:

$$\begin{cases} \exp(-\kappa) = (1-\varepsilon)/(1+\varepsilon) \\ \omega^2 = \omega_L^2/(1-\varepsilon^2) \end{cases}. \tag{14.179}$$

In order to realize the range $\omega > \omega_L$, $\varepsilon > 0$ is required. In conclusion, as long as one impurity atom with mass m "lighter than the other lattice mass M", we can expect an impurity vibration mode with a frequency a little higher than the normal spectrum top ω_L. As derived from Equation (14.177), this mode should decay exponentially with increasing $|n|$ from the position $n = 0$. That is, this mode is "localized" around the origin position.

Ishii showed the computer simulation results on a 1D chain lattice model with $N = 50$ and a couple of impurity atoms with $m = 0.33M$, which is shown in Figure 14.27 [16]. The "frequency square spectral density" $G(\omega^2)$ defined as

$$G(\omega^2) = \frac{g(\omega)}{2\omega}$$
$$\left[\text{in a normal nonatomic lattice chain, this is equal to } \frac{1}{\pi\omega\sqrt{\omega_L{}^2 - \omega^2}}\right] \tag{14.180}$$

is shown in Figure 14.27a, where many spiky peaks can be observed above the normal top frequency ω_L. As we discussed in Equation (14.177), the impurity vibration modes should be localized, which is also demonstrated in the computer simulation in Figure 14.27b. Mode number is arranged from low to high frequency sequence (50 modes in total equal to $N = 50$). In comparison with the low n states, which distribute rather uniformly in a whole crystal, the higher number states (which correspond to the sharp and spiky spectrum density modes) are clearly localized some particular position in a crystal and vibration decays rather sharply with the distance. This argument is consistent with the conclusion from a simple 3-mass–4-spring model with one mass lighter than other lattice masses shown in Figure 14.24b.

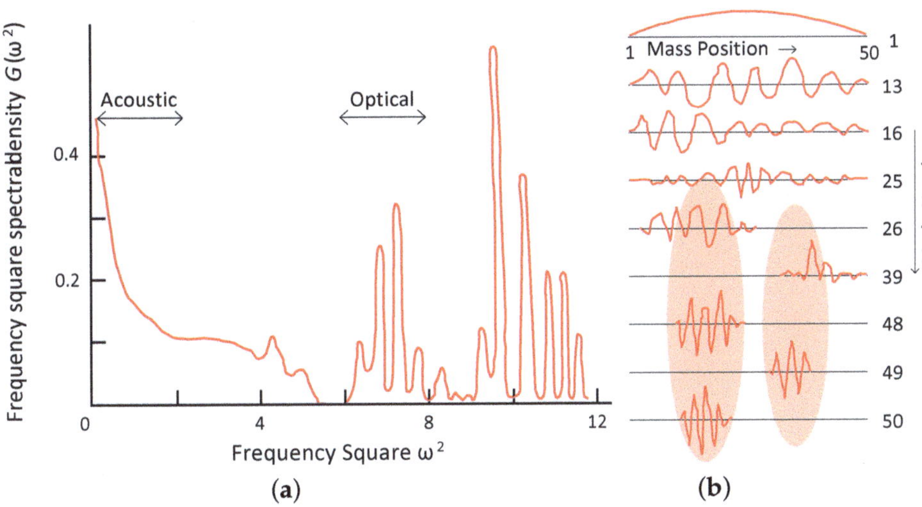

Figure 14.27. (**a**) Frequency square spectral density, and (**b**) eigen modes in a 1D lattice chain with some light-weight impurity doping. Phonon localization is realized with the impurity doping. Source: Figure by author, adapted from [16].

14.4.2. Phonon Collision Process

Light is an electromagnetic wave which follows Maxwell wave propagation equations. On the other hand, light is a particle, a so-called "photon" based on Planck constant: $h = 6.626 \times 10^{-34}$ [J·s] or $\hbar = 1.054 \times 10^{-34}$ [J·s]. Photon energy and momentum are defined by $E = \hbar\omega$ and $p = \hbar k$, respectively. Note that though the photon does not have mass, the momentum can be defined. Similarly, the lattice vibration is a mechanical wave, while at the same time it is a sort of particle called a "phonon".

Phonon—Quantization, Energy, Momentum, Velocity

(a) Quantization of Energy

The lattice vibration energy can be quantized. This energy quantum is called a "phonon". Each eigen vibration mode in a crystal lattice corresponds to one phonon. Thermal vibrations in a crystal are thermally excited phonons. The energy of a vibration mode of angular frequency ω is expressed on the basis of the Planck constant $\hbar$:

$$E = (n + \frac{1}{2})\hbar\omega. \tag{14.181}$$

when the mode is excited to quantum number n; that is, when the mode is occupied by n phonons. The term $(\frac{1}{2})\hbar\omega$ is the zero point energy of the mode, which is the lowest quantum energy of the frequency ω mode. We can translate this energy into the vibration wave energy as follows.

Consider the mode $u = u_0 \cos Kx \cos \omega t$ (standing wave), where u is the displacement of a volume element ρdV from the equilibrium position in a crystal. The energy of the oscillator is given by the sum of kinetic and potential energy, when averaged in terms of time, a half and a half ratio; that is, $\frac{1}{2}(n + \frac{1}{2})\hbar\omega$ for each. Since the kinetic energy of a unit volume particle is expressed by $\frac{1}{2}\rho(\frac{\partial u}{\partial t})^2$ (ρ: mass density), we can evaluate the time average kinetic energy as

$$\frac{1}{2}\rho V \overline{(\omega u)^2} = \frac{1}{2}\rho V \omega^2 u_0^2 \overline{\cos^2 \omega t} = \frac{1}{4}\rho V \omega^2 u_0^2. \tag{14.182}$$

Thus,

$$u_0^2 = 2\left(n + \frac{1}{2}\right)\hbar/\rho V\omega. \tag{14.183}$$

This relates the crystal displacement in a given frequency vibration mode to quantum mechanics Planck constant $\hbar$ and phonon occupancy n of the modes.

(b) Phonon momentum

A phonon of wave vector k interacts with particles such as phonons and electrons as if it had a momentum of $\hbar k$, the same formula as photons. The phonons on the crystal lattice do not carry actual physical momentum because a phonon coordinate involves relative coordinates (that is, $\boldsymbol{r} = \boldsymbol{R} - \boldsymbol{R'}$) of the atoms. Considering a 1D lattice chain with periodic mass M, and the vibration amplitude of the mass as u_α, the physical momentum of a whole crystal can be expressed by

$$p = M\frac{d}{dt}\sum_\alpha u_\alpha \quad [\alpha = 1, 2, \cdots, N]. \tag{14.184}$$

When the crystal carries a phonon k, which is expressed by $u_\alpha = u_0 e^{j\alpha ka}$ (except for $k = 0$. This is obtained from the "periodic boundary condition", referring to Chapter 11), Equation (14.184) is transformed into

$$p = M\frac{d}{dt}\sum_\alpha u_0 e^{j\alpha ka} = Mu_0\frac{d}{dt}(1 - e^{jNka})/(1 - e^{jka}). \tag{14.185}$$

Due to the "periodic boundary condition", the last atom's displacement $u_0 e^{jNka}$ should be equal to the first atom's displacement:

$$u_0 e^{jNka} = u_0. \tag{14.186}$$

This leads the conclusion, $p = M\frac{d}{dt}\sum_\alpha u_0 e^{j\alpha ka} = 0$. The only exception mode $k = 0$, since this is just a uniform translation of the whole crystal, no phonon momentum can be carried.

A phonon behaves as if its momentum were $\hbar k$ for most applications, which is called the "crystal momentum". For example, this "phonon momentum" is used to explain the incident X-ray "photon" and the scattered "photon" relation.

(c) Phonon velocity

We have mentioned the mass velocity ($\frac{\partial u}{\partial t}$) based on the mass vibration displacement in the previous subsection. The total summed velocity becomes zero from Equation (14.185), while the averaged velocity of each mass is obtained from Equation (14.183),

$$\omega u_0 = \sqrt{2\left(n + \frac{1}{2}\right)\hbar/\rho V}. \tag{14.187}$$

However, these are not a phonon velocity. The velocity of a wave packet (localized or isolated phonon) is the "group velocity" or "sound velocity", defined as

$$v_g = d\omega/dk \text{ or in 3D } \boldsymbol{v}_g = grad_{\boldsymbol{k}}\, \omega(\boldsymbol{k}), \tag{14.188}$$

which is obvious from the general wave function

$$u = u_0 e^{j(kx \pm \omega t)}. \tag{14.189}$$

The group velocity is the velocity of energy transmission in the crystal. For instance, the 1D monatomic lattice chain model in Chapter 11 gives the relation of the eigen frequency to the wave vector through Equation (11.14):

$$\omega_\alpha = 2\sqrt{\frac{K}{M}}\sin\frac{\alpha\pi}{2N} = 2\sqrt{\frac{K}{M}}\sin\frac{k_\alpha a}{2}. \tag{14.190}$$

Taking the first derivative of ω in terms of k,

$$v_g = \frac{d\omega}{dk} = a\sqrt{\frac{K}{M}}\cos\frac{ka}{2} \approx a\sqrt{\frac{K}{M}}[1 - \frac{1}{2}\left(\frac{ka}{2}\right)^2]. \tag{14.191}$$

For small k region, v_g is constant, and the formula $\omega = v_g k$ can be applied; while for the k region close to $k = \pi/a$ (i.e., Brillouin zone boundary), since $\cos\frac{ka}{2} \approx 0$, v_g approaches zero.

(d) Wave Equation vs. Diffusion Equation

The wave equation of a rod material is described by

$$\frac{\partial^2 u}{\partial t^2} = v^2 \frac{\partial^2 u}{\partial x^2}, \tag{14.192}$$

where u is the displacement of a small volume ρdV, x is the rod length coordinate, and v is the sound velocity, given by $1/\sqrt{\rho s_{11}}$ (ρ: mass density, s_{11}: elastic compliance along x-direction). We can verify that the solution includes a rather general function like $u(x,t) = f(x - vt)$. From practical first and second derivatives in terms of time t and the coordinate x (we use a new parameter, $X = (x - vt)$),

$$\frac{\partial u}{\partial x} = \frac{\partial f}{\partial X}\frac{\partial X}{\partial x} = \frac{\partial f}{\partial X} \rightarrow \frac{\partial^2 u}{\partial x^2} = \frac{\partial^2 f}{\partial X^2}; \text{ while } \frac{\partial u}{\partial t} = \frac{\partial f}{\partial X}\frac{\partial X}{\partial t} = -v\frac{\partial f}{\partial X} \rightarrow \frac{\partial^2 u}{\partial t^2} = v^2\frac{\partial^2 f}{\partial X^2}.$$

Thus, we can derive the original equation $\frac{\partial^2 u}{\partial t^2} = v^2 \frac{\partial^2 u}{\partial x^2}$; that is, $f(x - vt)$ is a solution!

Suppose that the following Gaussian distribution of the initial displacement (this is a model of the local pinching condition):

$$u(x,t) = \exp\left[-\frac{(x \pm vt)^2}{a^2}\right]. \tag{14.193}$$

At the initial $t = 0$, a single peak Gaussian distribution is the starting shape. As long as this formula is a kind of $f(x - vt)$, it is obvious to verify that this Gaussian distribution will satisfy the wave equation. With time-lapse, keeping the curve shape, but the wave is split into two waves, rightward and leftward with the velocity v (this is called the "group velocity" or "sound velocity"). Figure 14.28a shows this situation, which is analogous to a "wave packet" (or a "localized phonon") traveling in a crystal. Note, however, that the phonon velocity v is constant only for an acoustic mode (i.e., low frequency and wavevector range, $\omega = vk$). With approaching the Brillouin zone boundary, v is significantly decreased.

We learned the diffusion equation in Chapter 12:

$$\frac{\partial T}{\partial t} = \alpha_T \frac{\partial^2 T}{\partial x^2}, \tag{14.194}$$

where α_T is the "thermal diffusivity". In order to emphasize the difference between the "diffusion equation" Equation (14.194) and the "wave equation" Equation (14.192), we will take again a Gaussian distribution for the localized heat source:

$$T = T_0 \exp\left(-\frac{x^2}{a^2}\right) \quad \text{at } t = 0. \tag{14.195}$$

Recall the solving process by using the Laplace transform explained in Subsection Laplace Transform Approach in Chapter 12. Taking $\tilde{T}$ as the Laplace transform of $T(x,t)$ (i.e., $\Theta = L[\theta(x,t)]$), we have

$$\left(\frac{\partial^2 \tilde{T}}{\partial x^2}\right) = \frac{s}{\alpha_T}\tilde{T}. \tag{14.196}$$

We may assume the solution form as

$$\tilde{T} = Ae^{\sqrt{\frac{s}{\alpha_T}}x} + Be^{-\sqrt{\frac{s}{\alpha_T}}x}. \tag{14.197}$$

Knowing the inverse Laplace transform, $L^{-1}\left[e^{-a\sqrt{s}}\right] = \frac{a}{2\sqrt{\pi t^3}}e^{-a^2/4t}$ and $a = \mp\frac{x}{\sqrt{\alpha_T}}$, and using the initial Equation (14.195), the solution can be obtained as

$$T(x,t) = \frac{T_0}{\sqrt{(1+\frac{4\alpha_T t}{a^2})}}exp[-\frac{x^2}{(a^2+4t\alpha_T)}]. \tag{14.198}$$

Figure 14.28b shows the local temperature diffusion process in a crystal, following Equation (14.198). The solution clearly evolves from the wave equation result in Figure 14.28a. The heat simply spreads out on a time scale of order a^2/α_T, which will be small if α_T is large; that is, the crystal has a good thermal diffusivity or thermal conductivity. This diffusing speed rate is evaluated by the phonon mean-free path length and collision rate, as discussed in Section 14.4.3.

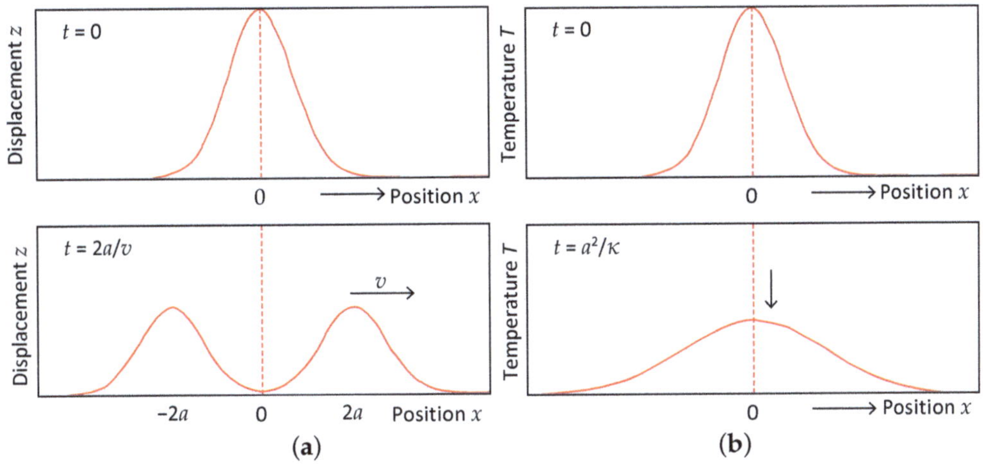

Figure 14.28. (**a**) Wave packet traveling in a crystal, following the wave equation. (**b**) Local temperature diffusion process in a crystal, following the diffusion equation. Source: Figure by author.

Brillouin Zone

Let us review the 1D monatomic and diatomic lattice chain model discussed in Chapter 11, recited in Figure 14.29a Top, which resulted in the eigen frequency $\omega(k)$ vs. wavevector k dispersion curve shown in Figure 14.29b Top, where the k range is only from $-\pi/a$ to π/a. Why is this narrow k range sufficient?

The lattice vibration wave is illustrated in Figure 14.30, where the component atoms are vibrating in an atomic potential well (equivalent to the harmonic spring connection) represented by a sinusoidal thin sold line. When we describe the "traveling wave" as

$$u = u_0 \exp j(kx \pm \omega t), \tag{14.199}$$

the velocity is given by

$$v_g = \frac{d\omega}{dk}. \tag{14.200}$$

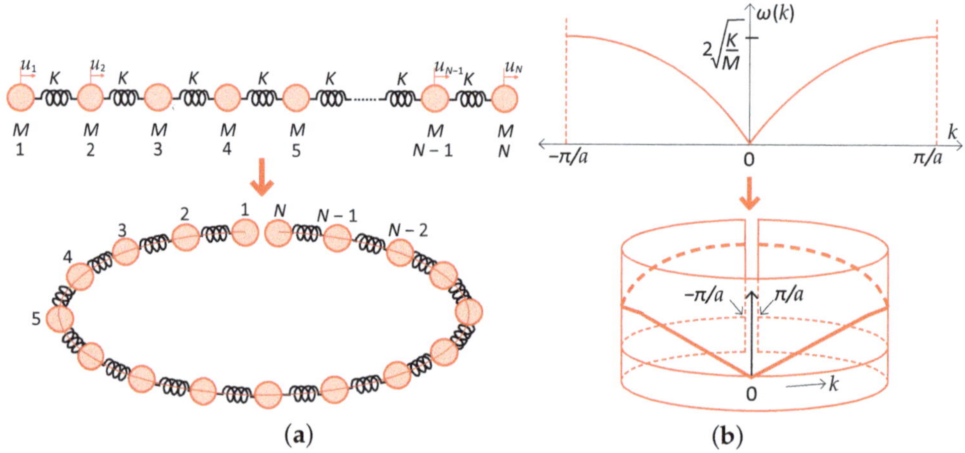

Figure 14.29. (**a**) One-dimensional monatomic lattice chain model (Top) and under the periodic boundary condition (ring) (Bottom). (**b**) Eigen frequency $\omega(k)$ vs. wavevector k dispersion curve (Top) and its folding picture. Source: Figure by author.

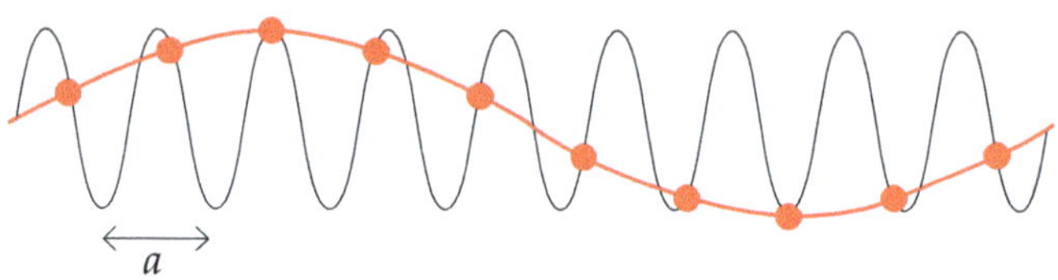

Figure 14.30. Lattice traveling wave shown by thick solid line, the component atoms of which are vibrating in an atomic potential well represented by sinusoidal thin sold line. Source: Figure by author.

Introducing the atomic distance "a", and denoting the atomic displacement of the n-th atom as u_0, the ratio of the displacements of two successive atoms is given by

$$u_{n+1}/u_n = \exp j(ka). \tag{14.201}$$

Supposing $u_1 = u_0 \exp j(ka)$, we obtain $u_N = u_0 \exp j(Nka)$. If we adopt the "periodic boundary condition", that is, as shown in Figure 14.29a Bottom, two ends of the 1D lattice chain are topologically connected as a "ring", and the N-th atom should be exactly the same as the hypothetical *0*-th atom:

$$u_N = u_0 \exp j(Nka) \equiv u_0. \tag{14.202a}$$

Accordingly, we obtain

$$\exp j(Nka) = 1 \rightarrow Nka = 2\alpha\pi(\alpha = 0, \pm 1, \pm 2, \cdots). \tag{14.202b}$$

Though the wavevector k can be changed from $-\infty$ to ∞, as long as we take a minimum 2π interval, all waves $\exp j(nka)$ will behave exactly the same in a periodic fashion. As shown in Figure 14.29b Bottom, we can consider the ω vs. k dispersion curve on a "cylindrical space". Normally, k from $(-\pi/a)$ to (π/a) range is sufficient, which is called the "first Brillouin zone". Since the zone ends $(-\pi/a)$ and (π/a) are equivalent (or connected on the cylindrical space), the larger k wave corresponds to the second-round position on the cylinder space, which is called "second Brillouin zone". The need for the second Brillouin zone is introduced in the next section on the phonon collision process.

If we reconsider the sound velocity in this view, the group velocity is given by $v_g = \frac{d\omega}{dk}$. For $k = 0$, all atomic displacement $u_n = u_0$ (constant). Since this corresponds to just a simple translation, group velocity is obviously zero. For the zone boundary $k = \pm\pi/a$, the displacement $u_n = u_0 \exp j(nka) = (-1)^n u_0$. This expression is not a "traveling wave", but a "standing wave", that is, the group velocity is obviously zero. This can also be verified as follows: since $\omega = 2\sqrt{\frac{K}{M}}\sin\frac{ka}{2}$, $v_g = \frac{d\omega}{dk} = a\sqrt{\frac{K}{M}}\cos\frac{ka}{2} = 0$ (Note $ka = \pm\pi$). The traveling wave property is maintained during the interval $-\pi/a < k < \pi/a$.

Phonon—Phonon Interaction, Collisio

(a) Crystal Anharmonicity and Wave Packet

Thermal energy can be stored in the lattice vibration normal phonon modes as a vibration amplitude. However, in a perfectly harmonic crystal, the phonon states are stationary, wide-spread in the crystal uniformly with a monotone frequency as a wave (that is, NOT an isolated wave packet or particle-like phonon). This situation comes from the "uncertainty principle" single frequency ω "phonon" particle will not identify its position. Since phonon vibration is not disturbed by dopants, for example, we can say the thermal resistance is zero, or "thermal conductivity is infinite", leading to completely uniform temperature distribution in a crystal. However, when the atomic energy potential includes nonlinear term, "cubic" anharmonic term introduced in Equation (14.134) or "quartic" term, the resonance frequency should include at least $2\omega_0$ or $3\omega_0$, higher order harmonic modes. According to the uncertainty of the resonance frequency from the definite $\omega = \omega_0$ to $\Delta\omega = |\omega - \omega_0|$, the phonon distribution changes from infinitely wide-spread state in a crystal to a sort of packet status (i.e., localized existence). Figure 14.31 demonstrates a phonon wave packet generation from the anharmonic lattice vibration. We assume the normal phonon eigenfunctions as

$$u_\alpha(t) \alpha \sin k_\alpha a \cdot \cos \omega_\alpha t. \tag{14.203}$$

Taking into account the frequency square spectral density, $\frac{g(\omega)}{2\omega}$, as the summation weight, and the low frequency acoustic mode dispersion relation $k_\alpha \propto \omega_\alpha$ (i.e., Debye model), we calculate the sum of $u_n(t)$'s, which exist in $\Delta\omega$

$$\sum_{\alpha=1}^{n} u_\alpha(t) \propto \sum_{\alpha=1}^{n} \frac{\sin \omega_\alpha a \cos \omega_\alpha t}{\omega_\alpha}. \tag{14.204}$$

Individual wave forms (time dependence) $u_\alpha(t)$ are illustrated for ω_α= 1, 2, 3 and 0.2 in Figure 14.31, for the reader's reference. Here, we took the atomic distance a = 1 as a normalized unit. One, two, and three sinusoidal eigen wave forms and a rather flat long-wavelength shape (ω_α= 0.2) are shown. When we sum up wave forms up to $\omega_\alpha = 3$, the top wave packet can be obtained. Note that if we add ω_α up to ∞ ideally, the wave shape should theoretically be a square pulse inserted in Figure 14.31. Once multiple phonons are generated synchronously via the anharmonic potential interactions, the phonon energy localization is expected (not uniformly distributed as a separated harmonic vibration), leading to the concept of wave-to-particle transition (i.e., the reason of the terminology introduction of "phonon" from the elastic lattice vibration wave). Recall the discussion in Subsection Localized Impurity Lattice Vibration, where the impurity vibration modes (even under "harmonic" potential) can be localized, as demonstrated in the computer simulation in Figure 14.27b. If we rephase the above argument in a reverse way, by having an excess of phonons with similar directed group velocities (i.e., by touching a heat source on the solid crystal), the anharmonic part of the ionic interaction plays the wave packet into creation, destruction or scattering of various frequency phonons, which corresponds to "thermal resistivity" (i.e., inverse of thermal conductivity).

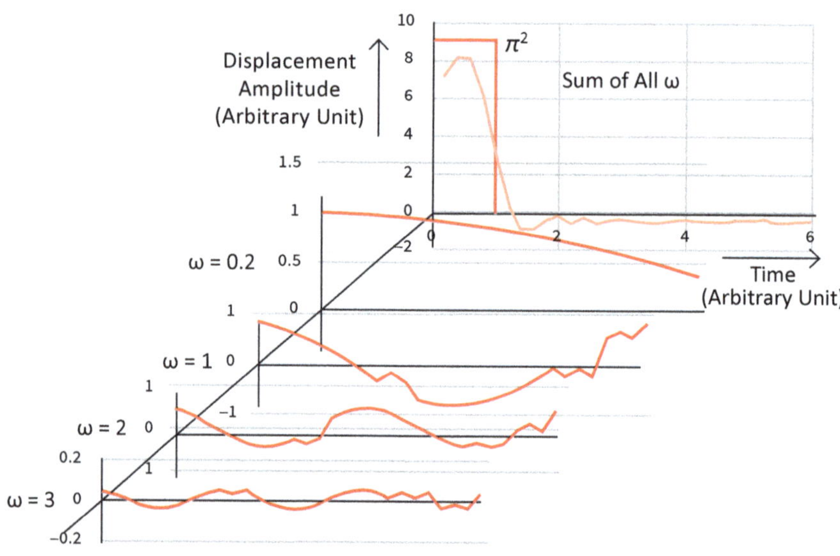

Figure 14.31. Phonon wave packet generation from the anharmonic lattice vibration. Source: Figure by author.

(b) Phonon Mean Free Path

Once isolated phonon modes are existing in a crystal, we now consider the isolated phonon (as a particle) transfer in the crystal lattice. The phonon "mean free path l" is defined as the average transfer distance of one phonon until its scattering by (1) geometrical boundary (like a crystal surface), (2) lattice imperfection (such as impurity, crystal deficit (vacancy, dislocation, etc.), and (3) other phonons. If the crystal lattice force is rigorously harmonic, there is no mechanism for collisions between different phonons (i.e., infinite mean free path in a crystallo-graphically perfect crystal). With anharmonic lattice interactions, there is a coupling between different phonons, which limits the value of the mean free path. Since the theory of the anharmonic coupling on thermal resistivity is beyond this book's objective, we briefly explain the empirical laws and three-phonon collision process in the section.

The mean free path length seems to be proportional to $1/T$ at high temperature. Since the total number of excited phonons is proportional to T, the collision probability of a given phonon would be proportional to the number of phonons, leading to $l \propto 1/T$. The thermal resistivity/conductivity is defined during the phonon transfer process, that is, heat transfer from a high temperature to a low temperature to finalize the equilibrium status. Note that the phonon collisions with a static imperfection or a crystal boundary will not establish thermal equilibrium, because such collisions do not change the energy of individual phonons: the frequency of the incident phonon and that of the scattered phonon is the same. Realizing the frequency modulation from the incident phonon and the scattered phonon is essential to establish the phonon energy change (Recall the phonon energy is given by proportional to ω, $E = (n + \frac{1}{2})\hbar\omega$).

(b) Three-phonon collision process

We consider three-phonon collision process. One phonon k_1 collides with another phonon k_2, then k_3 is the scattered phonon, expressed as:

$$\mathbf{k}_1 + \mathbf{k}_2 = \mathbf{k}_3. \tag{14.205}$$

The total momentum of the phonons does not change by such a collision (Figure 14.32a). Since the momentum (defined by "$\hbar k$") change can be calculated as:

$$J = \sum_k n_k \hbar k, \tag{14.206}$$

where n_k is the phonon density (number of phonons with wavevector k), then in the equilibrium status, the process in Equation (14.205) (i.e., $\mathbf{k}_3 - \mathbf{k}_1 - \mathbf{k}_2 = 0$) establish $J = 0$; that is, no total momentum remains, or no heat flow is expected. This process is called "normal collision process".

However, if we generate hot phonons on one end of the crystal rod by attaching a heat source, the hot phonons down a rod with keeping $\mathbf{J} \neq 0$. How can we explain it? Rudolf Peierls (German and British, 1907–1996) contributed the important three-phonon process for the thermal conductivity theory, so-called "Umklapp" (German meaning "flipping over") collision process, expressed as:

$$\mathbf{k}_1 + \mathbf{k}_2 = \mathbf{k}_3 + \mathbf{G}, \tag{14.207}$$

where $\mathbf{G}$ is a reciprocal lattice vector (wavevector) with x, y, and z component magnitude of integer number times of $2\pi/a$, as illustrated in Figure 14.32b. When $\mathbf{k}_1$ and $\mathbf{k}_2$ are both positive, $\mathbf{k}_3$ should also be positive direction in the normal process, while in the Umklapp process, according to the negative $\mathbf{G}$, positive $\mathbf{k}_1$ and $\mathbf{k}_2$ can generates negative $\mathbf{k}_3$ [$= \mathbf{k}_1 + \mathbf{k}_2 - \mathbf{G}$]. The "negative" $\mathbf{k}_3$, that is, the backward phonon scattering is the key to explain the thermal "resistance". This reciprocal lattice vector addition can be understood from the cylindrical map of the dispersion curve

(Figure 14.29b); $\boldsymbol{G}$ adding corresponds to the second round (or the second Brillouin zone) position ($k_3' = k_1 + k_2$), which is equivalent to the first Brillouin zone position ($k_3 = k_1 + k_2 - G$). At temperatures higher than the "Debye temperature" θ_D (Recall Subsection Debye Approximation in Chapter 11), all phonons are excited because $k_B T > \hbar\omega_L$. Thus, a substantial portion of all phonon collisions are U-process.

The energy of phonons k_1 and k_2 suitable for Umklapp to occur is of the order of $\left(\frac{1}{2}\right)k_B T$, because the magnitudes of the phonons k_1 and k_2 must be longer than $\left(\frac{1}{2}\right)G$ (otherwise, addition will not reach out of the first Brillouin zone). The Umklapp process should conserve energy just as for the normal process, because the second-round rotation on the dispersion curve cylinder should be equivalent to the first Brillouin zone performance. However, because of a little low temperature, the number of suitable phonons of the high energy $\left(\frac{1}{2}\right)k_B\theta_D$ required may vary roughly in proportion to $e^{-\theta_D/2T}$, according to the Boltzmann factor. In summary, the phonon mean free path seems to be the mean free path for Umklapp collisions between phonons and for all collisions between phonons.

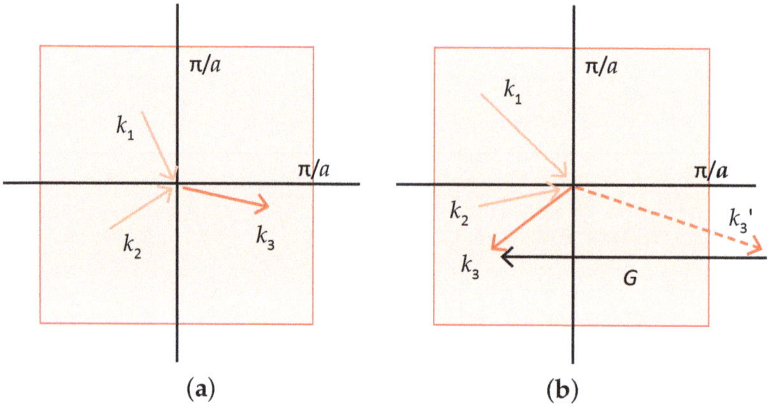

Figure 14.32. (**a**) Normal $k_1 + k_2 = k_3$, and (**b**) Umklapp $k_1 + k_2 = k_3 + G$ phonon collision processes in a 2D square lattice model. Source: Figure by author.

14.4.3. Thermal Conductance Model

First, the sound velocity of the longitudinal wave (p-wave) is faster than the transverse waves (s-waves) in dielectric solid. Thus, thermal conductivity seems to be determined primarily by the speed of longitudinal phonons. Second, phonons in the acoustical branch dominate the phonon heat conduction as they have greater energy dispersion and a greater distribution of phonon velocities. Additional "optical modes" can also be caused by the presence of charge or mass at lattice points. Though it is implied that the sound velocity of the optical modes is low, and their contribution to the lattice thermal conduction is small in general [17], the optical mode contribution seems to also be important in ferroelectric materials such as PZTs, because of their low-frequency "soft-phonon" modes, which are highly interacted with the electric field.

Phenomenological Expression of Thermal Conductivity

Let us review the phenomenological treatment in Chapter 12. The thermal conductivity λ is defined by

$$q_x = -\lambda\left(\frac{\partial T}{\partial x}\right)dt \text{ or } dq = \lambda\left(\frac{\partial^2 T}{\partial x^2}\right)dxdt, \quad (14.208)$$

where q_x is the heat flux (or heat flow), that is, quantity of heat passing through a cross section of crystal rod per unit area per unit time. The unit of q should be [J/m^2/s = W/m^2]. We introduce heat capacitance C_p, the required heat quantity for increasing 1 °C per unit volume,

$$dq = C_p dTdV = C_p dTdx \quad [dV = Sdx, \text{ where } S = 1 \text{ (unit area) here}]. \quad (14.209)$$

From Equations (14.208) and (14.209), we obtain

$$C_p d\theta dx = \lambda\left(\frac{\partial^2 T}{\partial x^2}\right)dxdt \rightarrow \left(\frac{\partial T}{\partial t}\right) = \frac{\lambda}{C_p}\left(\frac{\partial^2 T}{\partial x^2}\right). \quad (14.210)$$

Quantum Phonon Expression

When the phonon number $\overline{n}$ deviates from the equilibrium value $\overline{n}_0$, thermal current q_x arises as expressed by

$$q_x = \frac{1}{V}\sum \hbar\omega(\overline{n} - \overline{n}_0)v_x, \quad (14.211)$$

where $\hbar$ is the "reduced Planck constant" ($= h/2\pi$), and v_x is the energy transport velocity (i.e., group velocity) of the phonon. There are two mechanisms to cause time variation of $\overline{n}$ in a particular thin slice segmented region in a disk sample: (1) The number of phonons that diffuse into and diffuse out between the considering region and neighboring regions, and (2) phonon decay inside the same region into other phonons. A special form of the Boltzmann equation provides

$$\frac{d\overline{n}}{dt} = \left(\frac{\partial \overline{n}}{\partial t}\right)_{diff.} + \left(\frac{\partial \overline{n}}{\partial t}\right)_{decay}. \quad (14.212)$$

Time variation in the latter term is described with a relaxation time (τ) approximation [14]. Assuming the spirit of "Drude model", the phonon collision occurs in a distance $l = v_x\tau$ (v_x: energy transport velocity) in terms of the relaxation time τ. Though the microscopic origin is not clear, this relaxation time concept has already been integrated in Chapter 5.

$$\left(\frac{\partial \overline{n}}{\partial t}\right)_{decay} = -(\overline{n} - \overline{n}_0)/\tau. \quad (14.213)$$

When we consider a "steady-state" condition such as a case that temperature T_1 and T_2 is maintained on both sides on a crystal plate for transferring the thermal energy steadily, we may assure $\frac{d\bar{n}}{dt} = 0$; that is, the local thermal equilibrium (i.e., dynamic equilibrium) is assumed, leading to the equation

$$\left(\frac{\partial \bar{n}}{\partial t}\right)_{diff} = -\left(\frac{\partial \bar{n}}{\partial t}\right)_{decay} = -v_x \frac{\partial \bar{n}_0}{\partial T}\frac{\partial T}{\partial x}. \quad (14.214)$$

Using the relaxation time approximation for the Boltzmann equation and assuming steady-state conditions, the phonon thermal conductivity λ can be determined:

$$\lambda = C_p {v_x}^2 \tau. \quad (14.215)$$

An alternative derivation process is as follows: Knowing the temperature difference between the ends of a mean free path "l" of the phonon

$$\Delta T = \frac{dT}{dx} l = \frac{dT}{dx} v_x \tau. \quad (14.216)$$

The net heat flux (Equation (14.211)) is therefore described as

$$q_x = -C_p \langle {v_x}^2 \rangle \tau \frac{dT}{dx}. \quad (14.217)$$

The averaging the velocity relation between one direction and three directions: $\langle {v_x}^2 \rangle = \frac{1}{3}\langle v^2 \rangle$ provides the final formula:

$$\lambda = \frac{1}{3} C_p v^2 \tau = \frac{1}{3} C_p v l. \quad (14.218)$$

E- and *D*-Constant Thermal Conductivity

Finally, we consider the empirically obtained formula of "secondary electrothermal coupling factor k_{33}^{λ}" in Chapter 12, which is expressed by:

$$\lambda_{33}^{D} = \lambda_{33}^{E}\left(1 - {k_{33}^{\lambda}}^2\right). \quad (14.219)$$

The reader still remembers a significant difference of the thermal conductivity according to the electric constraint condition, that is, *E*-constant (short circuit) or *D*-constant (open circuit). The experimental result on a Hard PZT (APC 841) gives $\lambda^{D}{}_{33} = 0.61\ \lambda^{E}{}_{33}$, and ${k_{33}^{\lambda}}^2 = \frac{T{p'}^2}{\lambda_{33}^{E}\varepsilon_0 \varepsilon^X} = 0.39$.

If we believe the thermal conductivity expression Equation (14.218), we need to find out the origin: is it due to significant electric constraint dependence of (a) heat capacitance C_p, (b) sound velocity v, or (c) the relaxation time τ? We discuss these three factors below.

(a) Heat Capacitance C_p

Subsection Specific Heat Capacity—Scalar Parameter gives

$$C_p^D = C_p^E\left(1 - {k^{ET}}^2\right), \quad (14.220)$$

where the primary "electrothermal coupling factor" k^{ET} is given by

$$k^{ET^2} = \frac{p^2}{\left(\frac{\rho c_p^E}{T}\right)\varepsilon_0 \varepsilon^X}. \quad (14.221)$$

Since $k^{ET^2} = 0.11 \times 10^{-6}$ in a Hard PZT (very small!), we can neglect this contribution.

(b) Sound Velocity v

The sound velocity is given by $v = 1/\sqrt{\rho s_{33}}$, then the elastic compliance follows

$$s_{33}^D = s_{33}^E\left(1 - {k_t}^2\right). \quad (14.222)$$

where k_t is the thickness electromechanical coupling factor. D-constant boundary condition decreases the elastic compliance (i.e., elastically hardening), leading the enhancement of the sound velocity. This tendency gives an opposite argument to explain the thermal conductivity relation $\lambda_{33}^D = \lambda_{33}^E\ (1 - {k_{33}^{\lambda}}^2)$.

(c) Relaxation Time τ

In conclusion, the significant difference between λ_{33}^D and λ_{33}^E needs to be explained by the difference of the relaxation time τ according to the electric boundary condition. That is, the internal "depolarization field" in an open-circuit crystal may decrease the relaxation time τ significantly. If we assume the "internal electric field" accelerates: (1) the number of phonons that diffuse in and out between the considering and neighboring regions, and (2) phonon decay inside the same region into other phonons, the relaxation time decrease can be explained.

Chapter Essentials

1. Large Swings of the Pendulum—Nonlinear Dynamic Equation:
   $\frac{\partial^2\theta}{\partial t^2} = -\left(\frac{g}{L}\right)\cdot\sin\theta = -\omega^2\sin\theta$,
   $T_{\theta_0} = 4\sqrt{\frac{L}{g}}\int_0^{\pi/2}\frac{d\phi}{\sqrt{1-k^2\sin^2\phi}} = 4\sqrt{\frac{L}{g}}\cdot K(k)$ where "complete elliptic integral of the first kind" is $K(k) = \int_0^{\pi/2}\frac{d\phi}{\sqrt{1-k^2\sin^2\phi}}$.
2. Coulomb (Friction) Damping:
   $m\ddot{u} + cu = \pm F$,
   $u = a\cos(\omega t) + \frac{A}{\omega^2}(1-\cos(\omega t))$ for $0 < t < T$; $u(T) = -a + \frac{2A}{\omega^2}$,
   $u = a\cos(\omega t) + \frac{A}{\omega^2}(1-\cos(\omega t)) - \frac{2A}{\omega^2}(1-\cos(\omega(t-T)))$ for $T < t < 2T$, $u(2T) = a - \frac{4A}{\omega^2}$
   ………
   Resonance frequency: $\omega = \sqrt{c/m}$, and "linearly decay" of amplitude with time by $\frac{2A}{\omega^2}$.
3. Admittance Frequency Spectrum Distortion Phenomena:
   $L_A\frac{d^2I_1}{dt^2} + (R_{A1} + R_{A2}{I_1}^2)\frac{dI_1}{dt} + \frac{I_1}{C_1} + \frac{{I_1}^3}{C_2} = \omega V$,

* Resistivity (loss factor) nonlinearity - Q_m decrease;
*Capacitance (elastic compliance) nonlinearity—Spectrum distortion and frequency hysteresis.

4. Two-Spring–Mass Buckling Model—Mechanical Bistability:
$F = kR(\alpha^2\theta - \theta^3)$.
5. Ginzburg–Landau Functional—Domain Wall Structure:
$F(P(x),T) = \int dx[\frac{\alpha}{2}P(x)^2 + \frac{\beta}{4}P(x)^4 + \frac{\kappa}{2}(\nabla P(x))^2]$.
Domain wall structure:
$P(x) = P_0\tanh(\frac{x}{\delta})$, $\delta = \frac{1}{P_0}\sqrt{\frac{2\kappa}{\beta}} = \sqrt{\frac{2\kappa}{-\alpha}}$.
Domain wall energy:
$\gamma_0 = -\frac{2}{3}\alpha P_0^2\delta = \frac{4}{3}P_0^2(\frac{\kappa}{\delta})$.
6. Dynamic domain wall motion is analyzed by:
$\mu\frac{\partial^2 P}{\partial t^2} + \Gamma\frac{\partial P}{\partial t} - \kappa\frac{\partial^2 P}{\partial x^2} + \alpha P + \beta P^3 = E$,
where Γ is the dissipation factor and E is the applied external electric field E.
Permittivity and dielectric loss $\tan\Phi$ can be obtained as
$|\varepsilon\varepsilon_0| = \frac{1}{\sqrt{(-2\alpha-\mu\omega^2)^2+(2\mu\zeta\omega_0\omega)^2}}$,
$\tan\Phi = \frac{2\mu\zeta\omega_0\omega}{-2\alpha-\mu\omega^2}$.
Here, $\omega_0^2 = -2\alpha/\mu$, and $2\zeta\omega_0 = \Gamma/\mu$. For a low frequency,
$\varepsilon\varepsilon_0 \approx 1/(-2\alpha)$,
$\tan\Phi \approx \Gamma\omega/(-2\alpha)$.
7. Nonlinearity in Crystal Potential:
$\Delta U = U(r) - U(r_0) = f(\Delta r)^2 - g(\Delta r)^3$
Thermal expansion and electrostriction are originated from anharmonic term g:
Strain $x = \frac{<\Delta r_+>+<\Delta r_->}{2r_0} = \frac{3gk_B}{4f^2r_0}T + \frac{3gq^2}{4f^3r_0}E^2$.
8. Impurity on the Lattice Vibration:
Impurity doping with a light-weight mass introduces localized wave packets (i.e., isolated phonons) in high frequency range in a simple 3-mass–4-spring model and a large lattice mass–spring model.
9. Anharmonicity in the lattice potential introduces higher-order harmonic high frequency wave modes, which generates wave packets (i.e., isolated phonons).
10. Phonon energy is described by
$E = (n + \frac{1}{2})\hbar\omega$,
which follows the Boltzmann distribution.
11. Phonon momentum is described by
$p = \hbar k$.
Two phonon collision processes: (a) Normal $\boldsymbol{k}_1 + \boldsymbol{k}_2 = \boldsymbol{k}_3$, and (b) Umklapp $\boldsymbol{k}_1 + \boldsymbol{k}_2 = \boldsymbol{k}_3 + \boldsymbol{G}$.
12. Thermal conductivity—Phonon interaction viewpoint:
$\lambda = \frac{1}{3}C_p v^2\tau = \frac{1}{3}C_p vl$ (C_p: heat capacitance, v: sound velocity, τ: phonon relaxation time)

In pyroelectrics, the depolarization field may reduce the relaxation time τ significantly.

Check Point

1. (T/F) We demonstrate large swings of a pendulum with a mass and solid rod under free vibration started from a rest position (angle θ). By increasing the cant angle θ, close to the upside-down position, the cycle period T decreases because the acceleration force is increased. True or false?
2. (T/F) We consider a mass–spring oscillator under free vibration with Coulomb (friction) damping condition, started from a spring largely extended position. The vibration amplitude decays exponentially with time lapse. True or false?
3. We consider a LCR circuit with nonlinear performance in terms of current for all L, C, and R components. Which component's nonlinearity contributes significantly on the admittance spectrum shape skew and hysteresis?
4. (T/F) The solution of the nonlinear differential equation $\kappa(\frac{d^2P}{dx^2}) = \alpha P + \beta P^3$ (boundary condition: $P(-\infty) = -P_0$, $P(+\infty) = P_0$) includes $P(x) = P_0 \tanh(\frac{x}{\delta})$, where $\delta = \frac{1}{P_0}\sqrt{\frac{2\kappa}{\beta}} = \sqrt{\frac{2\kappa}{-\alpha}}$. True or false?
5. (T/F) One-atom 1D lattice chain model with N atoms connected by the same lattice "harmonic" springs results in N eigen wave modes with all sinusoidal waves. True or false?
6. (T/F) The thermal expansion or electrostriction cannot be observed in a rigorously harmonic atomic potential crystal. True or false?
7. (T/F) The isolated phonon can be generated by the light-weight mass atom doping in a crystal, even though the lattice potential is rigorously harmonic. True or false?
8. (T/F) The isolated phonon can be generated by the anharmonicity of the lattice potential. True or false?
9. There are two phonon collision processes: (a) Normal: $\mathbf{k}_1 + \mathbf{k}_2 = \mathbf{k}_3$, and (b) Umklapp: $\mathbf{k}_1 + \mathbf{k}_2 = \mathbf{k}_3 + \mathbf{G}$. Which process contributes to the "thermal resistance"?
10. (T/F) Thermal conductivity is expressed as $\lambda = \frac{1}{3} C_p v \tau$, where C_p: heat capacitance, v: sound velocity, τ: phonon relaxation time. True or false?

Chapter Problems

14.1 Analyze the mechanical bistability function in a bent plate, as illustrated in Figure 14.33 below. Suppose the compressive force T on a total length l plate generates two stable positions a and $-a$ along the perpendicular directions at the center points.

Hint

Necessary parameters for the "stressed rod" analysis:

- Area: A, Bending rigidity: EI (E: flexural modulus (Pa), I: second moment of area (m)), Critical stress: $T_C = \pi^2 EI/l^2$,
- Perpendicular displacement (stable point): $y_0(x) = a\sin\frac{\pi}{l}x$,
- Distributed load on the rod: $q\sin\frac{\pi}{l}x$,

- Perpendicular displacement: $y(x) = a_1 \sin \frac{\pi}{l} x$,
- Normalized force: $\alpha = T/T_C$; $a_1 = \frac{u}{\alpha-1} a$,
- Normalized center displacement: $\xi = \frac{a_1}{a} = \frac{u}{\alpha-1}$,
- Normalized load: $u = \frac{l^4}{\pi^4} \frac{q}{EIa}$,
- Normalized moment of inertia: $m = \frac{4I}{Aa^2}$,

From the following two relations,

$$\begin{cases} \text{Original rod length} = \int_0^l \sqrt{1+\left(\frac{dy_0}{dx}\right)^2} dx + \frac{T_C l}{EA} \\ \text{Loaded rod length} = \int_0^l \sqrt{1+\left(\frac{dy}{dx}\right)^2} dx + \frac{Tl}{EA} \end{cases}.$$

we obtain

$$1 = \frac{u^2}{(\alpha-1)^2} + (\alpha-1)m$$

Then, we finally obtain the following nonlinear equation:

$$\xi - \xi^3 = mu.$$

We can use Figure 14.33 for further discussion.

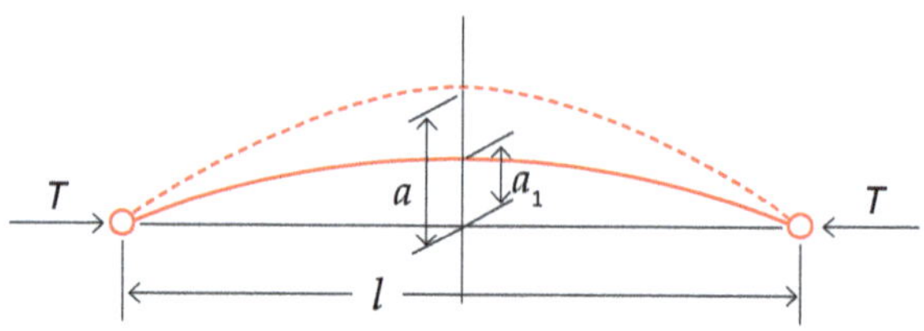

Figure 14.33. Mechanical bistability in a bent plate. Source: Figure by author.

14.2 We consider the minimization of the time-independent Ginzburg–Landau functional with respect of P,

$$F(P(x),T) = \int_{-\infty}^{\infty} [\tfrac{\alpha}{2} P(x)^2 + \tfrac{\beta}{4} P(x)^4 + \tfrac{\kappa}{2} (\tfrac{dP}{dx})^2] dx.$$

By changing the polarization P by δP, we calculate the free energy change

$$F(P+\delta P) = \int_{-\infty}^{\infty} [f(P+\delta P) + \tfrac{\kappa}{2}(\tfrac{d(P+\delta P)}{dx})^2] dx$$

$$= \int [f(P) + \tfrac{\kappa}{2}(\tfrac{dP}{dx})^2] dx + \int [f'(P)\delta P + \kappa(\tfrac{dP}{dx})\tfrac{d(\delta P)}{dx}] dx + \cdots$$

$$= F(P) + \delta F + \delta^2 F + \cdots$$

From the first derivation $\delta F = 0$, we can derive

$$\kappa(\tfrac{d^2P}{dx^2}) = \alpha P + \beta P^3.$$

The sign of the second variation $\delta^2 F$ makes it possible to evaluate the stability (maximum or minimum) of the corresponding solution. Calculate $\delta^2 F$ practically, then discuss the system stability from the sign of $\delta^2 F$.

<u>Hint</u>

$$\delta^2 F = \int [\tfrac{f''(P)}{2!}(\delta P)^2 + \tfrac{\kappa}{2}[\tfrac{d(\delta P)}{dx}]^2] dx + \cdots = \int \delta P [\tfrac{\kappa}{2}\tfrac{d^2}{dx^2} + \tfrac{1}{2}\tfrac{d^2 f}{dP^2}] \delta P dx$$

Thus, you need to solve the dynamic equation in a potential field $V(x) = \frac{1}{2}\frac{d^2 f}{dP^2} = \frac{1}{2}(\alpha + 3\beta P(x)^2)$. Verify maximum $V(x) = -\alpha > 0$ away from the boundary, and $\delta^2 F > 0$. Thus, we can conclude that $\delta F = 0$ point corresponds to the minimum point.

14.3 In Section 14.2.1, we adopted the second-order transition case, from the static domain wall structure equation:

$\kappa(\frac{d^2P}{dx^2}) = \alpha P + \beta P^3$.

When we expand the discussion to the first-order transition,

$f(P) = (1/2)\alpha P^2 + (1/4)\beta P^4 + (1/6)\gamma P^6$,

discuss the differences from the second-order type in terms of the domain wall structure formula and the domain wall energy (Figure 14.34).

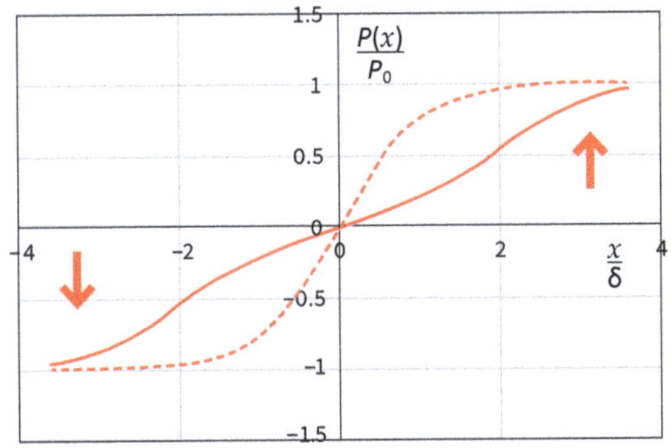

Figure 14.34. Polarization distribution profile of the domain wall for the case of the first-order transition. Source: [3] ©Uchino, K. *High-Power Piezoelectrics and Loss Mechanisms*. CRC Press, 2020; p. 316. Reproduced by permission of Taylor & Francis Group.

Hint

We start from the equation given by $\kappa\left(\frac{d^2P}{dx^2}\right) = \alpha P + \beta P^3 + \gamma P^5$, where $\beta < 0$, $\gamma > 0$. Away from the domain boundary, the spontaneous polarization is now given by $P_0 = \frac{\beta}{\gamma}(\sqrt{1 - \frac{\alpha\gamma}{\beta^2}} - 1)$.

Then, similar handling to Equation (9.48), we obtain the following equation:

$\frac{\kappa}{2}(\frac{dP}{dx})^2 = f[P(x)] - f[P_0] = [P_0^2 - P^2]^2[\frac{\gamma}{6}P^2 + \frac{\beta}{4} + \frac{\gamma}{3}P_0^2]$.

We can obtain the following formulae:

$P(x) = P_0 \frac{\sinh(\frac{x}{\delta})}{\sqrt{\cosh^2(\frac{x}{\delta}) + \varepsilon}}$,

$\delta = \sqrt{\frac{\kappa}{\gamma P_0^4 + \frac{\beta}{2}P_0^2}}$,

$\varepsilon = \frac{2\gamma P_0^2}{4\gamma P_0^2 + 3\beta}$.

Refer to the inserted figure. Note the presence of a metastable (or flat) state at $P = 0$ as an intermediate state in the first-order transition case, in comparison with a simple $\tanh(x/\delta)$ curve. The domain wall energy density can be calculated as follows:

$$\gamma_0 = \int_{-\infty}^{\infty} \left[f[P(x)] - f[P_0] + \frac{\kappa}{2}\left(\frac{dP}{dx}\right)^2 \right] dx = 2\int_{-\infty}^{\infty} [f[P(x)] - f[P_0]] dx$$
$$= 2\int_{-\infty}^{\infty} \left[P_0^2 - P^2\right]^2 \left[\frac{\gamma}{6}P^2 + \frac{\beta}{4} + \frac{\gamma}{3}P_0^2\right] dx = \frac{\alpha P_0^2}{\delta}(1+\varepsilon)^2 \int_{-\infty}^{\infty} \frac{\cosh^2 t}{\varepsilon + \cosh^2 t} dt = K P_0^2\left(\frac{\kappa}{\delta}\right)$$
$[K = \int_{-\infty}^{\infty} \frac{\cosh^2 t}{\varepsilon+\cosh^2 t} dt$ is a numerical factor].

References

1. Pipes, L.A. *Applied Mathematics for Engineers and Physicists*, 2nd ed.; McGraw-Hill Book Company: New York, NY, USA, 1958.
2. Acheson, D. *From Calculus to Chaos: An Introduction to Dynamics*; Oxford University Press: Oxford, UK, 1997.
3. Uchino, K. *High-Power Piezoelectrics and Loss Mechanisms*; CRC Press: Boca Raton, FL, USA, 2020.
4. Uchino, K. *Micromechatronics*, 2nd ed.; CRC Press: Boca Raton, FL, USA, 2019.
5. Tuncdemir, S.; Ural, S.O.; Koc, B.; Uchino, K. Design of Translation Rotary Ultrasonic Motor with Slanted Piezoelectric Ceramics. *Jpn. J. Appl. Phys.* **2011**, *50*, 027301. [CrossRef]
6. Uchino, K. Pulse Drive and Inertial Motors of Piezoelectrics. In Proceedings of the 6th Conference Noise and Vibration Emerging Methods, Ibiza, Spain, 7–9 May 2018.
7. Uchino, K.; Negishi, H.; Hirose, T. Drive Voltage Dependence of Electromechanical Resonance in PLZT Piezoelectric Ceramics. *Japan. J. Appl. Phys.* **1989**, *28* (Suppl. 28-2), 47–49. [CrossRef]
8. Sato, R.; Taniguchi, T.; Ohba, M. *Characteristics of a Piezoelectric Bimorph in Use of an Actuator and the Application to a Piezoelectric Relay*; No. 70; Omron Technics, Omron Group: Kyoto, Japan, 1983; p. 52.
9. Sidorkin, A.S. *Domain Structure in Ferroelectrics and Related Materials*; Visa Books Private Ltd.: New Delhi, India, 2017.
10. Chenskii, E.V. Domain size in a ferroelectric crystal. *Phys. Solid State* **1973**, *14*, 1940.
11. Bishop, A.R.; Domani, E.; Krumhansl, J.A. Quantum correction to domain walls in a model (1D) ferroelectric. *Phys. Rev. B* **1976**, *14*, 2966. [CrossRef]
12. Ashcroft, N.W.; Mermin, N.D. *Solid State Physics*; W. B. Saunders Co.: Orlando, FL, USA, 1976.
13. Kittel, C. Solid State Physics. In *Solid State Physics*, 5th ed.; John Wiley & Sons, Inc.: New York, NY, USA, 1976.
14. Uchino, K.; Cross, L.E. Electrostriction and its Interrelation with Other Anharmonic Properties of Materials. *Japan. J. Appl. Phys.* **1980**, *19*, L171–L173. [CrossRef]
15. Born, M.; Göppert-Mayer, M. *Handbuch der Physik*; Springer: Berlin, Germany, 1933; Volume 24, p. 623.
16. Ishii, K. Vibration and Eigenvalue Problem. *Mod. Math.* **1972**, *5*, 24–32.
17. Pichanusakorn, P.; Bandaru, P. Nanostructured thermoelectrics. *Mater. Sci. Eng. R Rep.* **2009**, *67*, 19–63. [CrossRef]

Appendix A. Answers to "Check Point"

Chapter 1

1) Dipole reorientation
2) Lorentz factor
3) False (frequency should be THz for permittivity)
4) 50%
5) False ($1/n^2$ should be expanded)
6) True
7) False (200 °C higher)
8) False
9) PVDF, polyvinylidene difluoride
10) Lead zirconate titanate

Chapter 2

1) True
2) True
3) $k^2 = \frac{h^2}{c^D \kappa_0 \kappa^x}$
4) False ($s^D = s^E(1-k^2)$)
5) $\varepsilon^x = \varepsilon^X(1-k^2)$
6) True
7) Thermal expansion
8) Pyroelectric effect
9) False (P_S decreases)
10) $|k_{33}|$ (recall $k^2 = \frac{d^2}{s^E \varepsilon_0 \varepsilon^x X}$)

Chapter 3

1) False (another diagonal compressive stress is required)
2) 6 (symmetric matrix)
3) 18
4) 36
5) $\varepsilon_{11}, \varepsilon_{33}$
6) d_{33}, d_{31}, and d_{15}
7) s_{11} and s_{12}
8) $E = \frac{1}{s_{11}}$, $\sigma = -s_{12}/s_{11}$
9) $\lambda = c_{12},\ \mu = c_{66} = \frac{1}{2}(c_{11} - c_{12})$
10) False (around x-axis $\begin{pmatrix} 1 & 0 & 0 \\ 0 & \cos\theta & \sin\theta \\ 0 & -\sin\theta & \cos\theta \end{pmatrix}$)
11) (c) ($(x,y,z) \rightarrow (-x,y,z)$)

Chapter 4

1) By changing P to $-P$, the energy should be the same, $G_1(P) = G_1(-P)$.
2) False (d shows maximum just below T_C)
3) False (higher)
4) $d = 2\varepsilon_0 \varepsilon_r P_S Q$
5) False ($\propto \sqrt{T_C - T}$)
6) True
7) False (-2 times steeper)
8) False (all maximum)
9) False (temperature sensitive as with ε^2)
10) True

Chapter 5

1) True
2) True
3) False (inversely proportional)
4) True
5) True
6) False (circle center is below $\varepsilon'' = 0$ axis)
7) True
8) True
9) $\frac{\varepsilon_S}{2} + j0$
10) ω_0 (maximum $\varepsilon'' = \frac{\varepsilon_S}{2}$)

Chapter 6

1) False (linear decrease)
2) Viscous damping
3) 1
4) 1/s
5) False (it is $\sin(at)/a$)
6) True
7) False ($Q_m = 1/2\zeta$)
8) True
9) False (−40 dB/decade)
10) False (counterclockwise)
11) $\tan\delta' = (1/2\pi)(w_e/U_e)$
12) False (combination ($2\tan\theta' - \tan\delta'$))
13) True ($\varepsilon^x = \varepsilon^x(1-k^2)$)
14) False ($s^D = s^E(1-k^2)$)
15) $\frac{1}{1-k^2}\begin{bmatrix} 1 & k^2 & -2k^2 \\ k^2 & 1 & -2k^2 \\ 1 & 1 & -1-k^2 \end{bmatrix}$ ("invertible")

Chapter 7

1) False (both are mechanical resonance)
2) 2
3) False (admittance maximum)
4) 0° (resistive)
5) Quadrantal frequencies
6) False (antiresonance mode is a half-wavelength)
7) True
8) $Q_M = 1/\tan\phi'$
9) $Q_M = 1/\tan\phi$
10) False (resonance is more uniform)
11) $Q_A < Q_B$
12) False (short circuit and open circuit correspond to resonance and antiresonance)
13) False (at the resonance frequency)
14) False (theoretically different)
15) False ($Q_A < Q_B$)
16) False (antiresonance is better)
17) Between resonance and antiresonance frequencies
18) False ($E = -\left(\frac{P_S}{\varepsilon_0}\right)$)
19) True
20) True

Chapter 8

1) $1/s$
2) $u(t) = 0$ for $0 < t < a$; $u(t) = m(t-a)$ for $a \leq t$
3) False (exactly to the resonance period)
4) 100%
5) True
6) False (Short-condition is softer)
7) True
8) True
9) $Q_m = (1/2)\omega_0\tau$
10) True

Chapter 9

1) True
2) True
3) False ($\varepsilon^x = \varepsilon^X(1-k^2)$)
4) False ($s^D = s^E(1-k^2)$)
5) $Q = \sqrt{L/C}/R$
6) $-C_d$
7) $\Phi = \frac{2wd_{31}}{s_{11}^E}$
8) True
9) $Q_M = 1/\tan\phi_{11}{}'$
10) $Q_A < Q_B$

Chapter 10

1) False ($Z = \sqrt{\rho c}$; elastic stiffness)
2) $Z = \sqrt{\rho/s} = 20.3 \times 10^6 =$ 20.3 Mrayls
3) False (impedance matching)
4) Rayl
5) $v_p = \sqrt{c/\rho}$
6) Matching layer
7) True
8) 0.5 kJ
9) $1/(2 \times 3.14 \times 100 \times 10^{-9}) = 1.59$ MΩ
10) DC–DC converter
11) Buck converter
12) Diode
13) True
14) False (2500 times; current 50 times)
15) $s_{eff}^E = s^E\left[1 - \left(\frac{S}{t}\right)\frac{j\omega d^2}{s^E j\omega C}\right] = s^E\left[1-k^2\right] = s^D$
16) $s_{eff}^E = s^E\left[1 - \left(\frac{S}{t}\right)\frac{d^2}{s^E \cdot 2C}\right] = s^E\left(1 - \frac{1}{2}k^2\right)$

Chapter 11

1) True
2) False (degeneracy is for the periodic boundary condition)
3) True
4) (2), in the opposite directions
5) $\gamma = 1$
6) True
7) True
8) First: thermal expansion; second: electrostriction
9) True
10) Partially true (impurities and crystal deficiencies also cause the thermal resistance)

Chapter 12

1) True
2) False (time derivative should be the first derivative $\left(\frac{\partial\theta}{\partial t}\right) = \alpha_T\left(\frac{\partial^2\theta}{\partial x^2}\right)$)
3) True
4) True
5) $c_p = C_p/\rho$ (specific heat capacity is defined per unit mass)
6) False (heat flux and temperature gradient are both vectors; thus, λ should be a tensor)
7) False (since it is not an equilibrium condition, it cannot be written as a potential)
8) Lars Onsager (1903–1976)
9) $c_p^D = c_p^E\left(1 - k^{ET^2}\right)$
10) Dielectric loss $\tan\delta'$
11) Elastic loss $\tan\phi'$
12) False (maximum temperature rise can be observed at its nodes)

Chapter 13

1) True
2) Decrease (because the PLZT is elongated along the 3-axis due to electrostriction)
3) 50%
4) False (expansion is based on $1/n_{ij}^2(E)$, not on $1/n_{ij}(E)$)
5) False (lower refractive index gives higher light speed)
6) Extraordinary ray (lower refractive index gives higher light speed)
7) 9/65/35
8) Blue (because λ is the shortest)
9) False (high n layer on the top for waveguide)
10) PLZT ($V_{z,\lambda/2} = d\sqrt{\frac{\lambda_0}{Ln_0{}^3(R_{11}-R_{12})}}$; L can be reduced for a larger $(R_{11} - R_{12})$ material)

Chapter 14

1) False (T increases significantly, because the pendulum almost stops at the upside-down position)
2) False (the amplitude decays linearly with time)
3) C (capacitance nonlinearity)
4) True
5) True
6) True
7) True
8) True
9) "Umklapp" process
10) False ($\lambda = \frac{1}{3}C_p v^2\tau = \frac{1}{3}C_p vl$, where C_p is the heat capacitance, v is the sound velocity, τ is the phonon relaxation time, and l is the mean free path length)

MDPI
St. Alban-Anlage 66
4052 Basel
Switzerland
www.mdpi.com

MDPI Books Editorial Office
E-mail: books@mdpi.com
www.mdpi.com/books

www.ingramcontent.com/pod-product-compliance
Lightning Source LLC
Chambersburg PA
CBHW060408220926
51850CB00003B/7